ENGLISH HISTORICAL DOCUMENTS

General Editor
DAVID C. DOUGLAS
M.A., F.B.A.

ENGLISH HISTORICAL DOCUMENTS

General Editor: DAVID C. DOUGLAS, M.A., F.B.A.

*The following is a complete list of volumes in preparation; those marked * are already published.*

GENERAL PREFACE

ENGLISH HISTORICAL DOCUMENTS is a work designed to meet a present need. Its purpose is to make generally accessible a wide selection of the fundamental sources of English history.

During the past half-century there has been an immense accumulation of historical material, but only a fraction of this has been made readily available to the majority of those who teach or who study history. The transcendent importance of the original authorities is recognized, but direct approach to them remains difficult, and even some of the basic texts (which are frequently quoted) are hard to consult. A gulf has thus opened between the work of the specialist scholar and those students, both at schools and universities, who best can profit by his labours. Historical studies tend too often today to consist of a commentary on documents which are not included in the available books; and, in the absence of any representative and accessible collection of the sources, the formation of opinion proceeds without that direct study of the evidence which alone can give validity to historical judgment. Correspondingly, the reading public, outside schools and universities, has no adequate means of checking, by reference to the evidence itself, tendentious or partial interpretations of the past.

The editors of these volumes consider that this situation now calls for a remedy. They have striven to supply one by providing what they hope can be regarded as an authoritative work of primary reference.

An enterprise of this nature could only be effective if planned on a large scale. In scope and content, therefore, these volumes differ materially from the conventional 'source-books' which usually contain only a restricted number of selected extracts. Here, within much wider limits, each editor has sought to produce a comprehensive *corpus* of evidence relating generally to the period with which he deals. His aim, in each case, has been to present the material with scholarly accuracy, and without bias. Editorial comment has thus been directed in the main towards making the evidence intelligible, and not to drawing conclusions from it. Full account has been taken of modern textual criticism to compile a reliable collection of authentic testimony, but the reader has in general been left to pass his own judgment upon this, and to appraise for himself the value of current historical verdicts. For this reason, everything in this work has been presented in such a manner as to be comprehensible by readers of English, and critical bibliographies have been added to assist further investigation.

The decision to display the texts (where necessary) in an English translation was thus dictated by the general purpose of this work. A translated text can, of course, never be a complete substitute for the original. But those who, today, can utilize a document in Anglo-Saxon, Latin or Old French are few, and are decreasing in number. This is certainly to be regretted. Nevertheless, there seems no adequate reason why the majority of those interested in English history should be arbitrarily deprived of the opportunity to consult the basic sources of their study. In this work therefore, there is nothing that cannot be used by those who can only read English. At the same time, in every case where a translation appears, a reference is given to the place where the text in its original language may be found. In like manner, spelling and punctuation have been adapted to modern usage in all texts prior to 1714. After that date, all documents are in their original form.

The editors of these volumes are fully aware of the magnitude of the undertaking to which they have addressed themselves. They are conscious of the hazards of selecting from the inexhaustible store of historical material. They realize also the difficulties involved in editing so large a mass of very varied texts in accordance with the exigent demands of modern scholarship. They believe, however, that the essential prerequisite for the healthy development of English historical studies is wider acquaintance with the original authorities for English history. And they are content that their work should be judged by the degree to which they have succeeded in promoting this object.

DAVID DOUGLAS

VOLUME VIII

ENGLISH HISTORICAL DOCUMENTS
1660–1714

ENGLISH
HISTORICAL DOCUMENTS

1660–1714

Edited by

ANDREW BROWNING

M.A., D.Litt.

Professor of History in the University of Glasgow

1953

EYRE & SPOTTISWOODE

15 Bedford Street, London, W.C.2

This book is printed in Great Britain
for Eyre & Spottiswoode (Publishers) Ltd.,
15 Bedford Street, London, W.C.1,
by Jarrold & Sons Ltd.,
Norwich

ACKNOWLEDGEMENTS

TO the many friends whose advice and suggestions have contributed so much to the compilation of this volume (even when practical considerations have led to the modification of these suggestions almost out of recognition) the editor offers his most sincere thanks. In particular he wishes to record his gratitude to the general editor of the series, Professor David C. Douglas, whose encouragement has been unfailing; to Dr. George S. Pryde, who has given unwearied assistance in connexion with the section on Scotland; and to Mr. C. Douglas Chandaman, who has not merely made many valuable suggestions in connexion with the section on Finance but has also read the proofs of the entire volume with meticulous care.

Permission to print documents and passages still under copyright has been most generously accorded. For this permission grateful acknowledgements are due to the Controller of H.M. Stationery Office, the many publications of which have been placed under heavy contribution; the executors of the late Basil Lubbock (*Barlow's Journal*, ed. Basil Lubbock); the executors of the late J. Pepys Cockerell (*Private Correspondence and Miscellaneous Papers of Samuel Pepys, 1679–1703*, ed. J. R. Tanner); the Royal Historical Society (*The Lauderdale Papers*, ed. Osmund Airy; *Iter Bellicosum, Adam Wheeler his Account of 1685*, ed. Henry Elliot Malden); the Cambridge Antiquarian Society (*Cambridge under Queen Anne*, ed. J. E. B. Mayor); the Navy Records Society (*Life of Sir John Leake*, ed. G. A. R. Callender; *Samuel Pepys's Naval Minutes*, ed. J. R. Tanner; *Byng Papers*, ed. W. C. B. Tunstall); the Hakluyt Society (*Bombay in the Days of Queen Anne*, ed. S. T. Sheppard); The Clarendon Press (*The Life of Edward, Earl of Clarendon*; *Burnet's History of My Own Time*, ed. Osmund Airy; *A Supplement to Burnet's History of My Own Time*, ed. H. C. Foxcroft; *The Journal of John Stevens*, ed. Robert H. Murray); the Cambridge University Press (*Economic Writings of Sir William Petty*, ed. C. H. Hull); Basil Blackwell (*Patriarcha . . . and Other Political Works of Sir Robert Filmer*, ed. Peter Laslett; *Oxford in 1710*, ed. W. H. and W. J. C. Quarrell); Constable and Company, Ltd. (*The Petty Papers*, ed. Marquis of Lansdowne); The Cresset Press Limited (*The Journeys of Celia Fiennes*, ed. Christopher Morris); Longmans, Green & Co., Limited (*English Historical Review*); and Jackson, Son & Co., Ltd. (*Scottish Historical Review*).

University of Glasgow,
April 1953

ANDREW BROWNING

NOTE ON DATES

In this volume all dates mentioned in the text, whether of events at home or of events abroad, are given according to the Old Style of reckoning which was still used in England; but the year is taken as beginning on 1 January, not on 25 March. Dates mentioned in documents are given as they appear in these documents, but where confusion may thus be caused a note is appended. Fuller information on this rather troublesome matter may be found in Appendix I.

CONTENTS

PAGE

E. COMPOSITION OF THE HOUSES

(a) House of Lords

(b) House of Commons

F. DISPUTES BETWEEN THE HOUSES

G. DEVELOPMENT OF PARTIES

Part III. PUBLIC FINANCE

G. ORIGIN AND GROWTH OF THE NATIONAL DEBT

PART IV. THE CHURCH

A. TOLERATION AND PERSECUTION

(a) Royal attempts at comprehension and toleration, 1660–1662

(b) Clarendon Code, 1661–1670

(c) First Indulgence, 1672–1673

(d) Parliamentary persecution, 1673–1681

(e) Second Indulgence, 1687–1688

Part V. LOCAL GOVERNMENT AND SOCIAL LIFE

B. GOVERNORS AND GOVERNED

C. TRANSPORT, COMMUNICATIONS, AND WEATHER VAGARIES

D. SCIENCE, EDUCATION, SCEPTICISM, AND SUPERSTITION

E. PLAGUE AND FIRE

F. SPORT, TRAGEDY, AND CRIME

G. CONTEMPORARY STATISTICS

Part VI. TRADE AND PLANTATIONS

A. GENERAL ORGANIZATION

B. EAST INDIES

C. WEST INDIES

D. WEST AFRICA

E. NORTH AMERICA

F. MEDITERRANEAN OUTPOSTS

PART VII. SCOTLAND

A. END OF THE ENGLISH OCCUPATION

B. RECONSTRUCTION IN CHURCH AND STATE

C. PERSECUTION AND INDULGENCE

D. INSURRECTION

Part VIII. IRELAND

H. PARLIAMENT AND THE PENAL LAWS

PART IX. ARMED FORCES

A. THE MILITIA

B. THE ARMY

(a) Origin, discipline, and recruitment

(b) Engagements on land

PART XI. SOVEREIGNS, POLITICIANS, AND SOME OTHER MEN

B. STATESMEN AND POLITICIANS

C. SOLDIERS, CLERGYMEN, AND CIVIL OFFICIALS

(a) George Monck, duke of Albemarle

(b) Hugh Mackay

(c) Patrick Sarsfield

(d) Samuel Pepys

(e) John Evelyn

(f) Slingsby Bethel

(g) Titus Oates

(h) Gilbert Burnet, bishop of Salisbury

(i) Henry Sacheverell

(j) John Churchill, duke of Marlborough

APPENDICES

INDEX

TABLES, MAPS, AND DIAGRAMS

GENEALOGICAL TABLES

MAPS

DIAGRAMS

INTRODUCTION

INTRODUCTION

A RESTORATION, it has been well said, is always a revolution. In human affairs it is never possible to set back the clock, and re-establish a political or social system which has once been effectively displaced. The usurping system may indeed be swept away, but even the most sincere efforts to re-create its predecessor can result only in the evolution of a third system, which may well prove entirely different from them both.

In this lies the tragedy of the later Stuart period. By 1660 the peoples of the British Isles had become heartily tired of revolutions, anxious for the establishment of a settled and orderly system once more, and convinced that the best prospect of achieving this result lay in a return to something like the position before the outbreak of the civil wars. Yet in practice the restoration which they so ardently desired was to prove as elusive as a will-o'-the-wisp. Much in the old system was now so completely out of date that it could not possibly be re-established. Moreover, the controversies which had originally led to the civil wars were not dead, but only dormant, and there was no real agreement how far the restoration, even in theory, should go.

Thus the later Stuart period, far from being a period of peace and order, proved to be one of the most unsettled periods in British history. It began with what was substantially one revolution, and ended with what came near to being another. Its central feature has long been recognized as *the* Revolution in British history. Throughout its course the threat of revolution was always lurking in the background, only too often grimly apparent in the foreground, and held in check by little more than a widespread conviction, based on sad experience, that violent methods were to be avoided. Charles II was haunted by the fear that he might have to set out again on his travels. James II actually went. William III threatened to go. Only Anne endured to the end of her unrestful reign without thought of a breach between herself and her people, to die worn out before she was fifty years of age.

Nor was it only in the political sphere that unsettlement prevailed. The glorious confidence in their religious mission which had inspired so many on both sides in the civil wars had vanished long before the Restoration. The once powerful Puritan party, split into antagonistic factions, had lost faith in its own ideals and sunk into disrepute. The Church, emerging victorious from its time of trial, found it hard to distinguish between the religious and the political aspects of its success. With the decay of religion had gone a decline in moral standards and in ideas of good behaviour. All accepted codes, in fact, had been

3

shaken, and the later Stuart world hardly knew by what lights to guide its conduct.

Underlying everything else was a strong undercurrent of economic unrest. Prices had long been rising, and though the process had by this time virtually ceased, the necessary readjustment on a new level had not yet taken place. All classes complained that their expenditure had increased, but shut their eyes to the fact that their income had usually done so too. War and revolutionary ideas between them had shattered the social fabric. Large numbers of men had abandoned the occupations to which they had been brought up, and either could not or would not return to them. Land in very considerable amounts had changed owners. The stable England of the earlier part of the seventeenth century had vanished, and a long process of reconstruction, not just some magic 'restoration', was to prove necessary before stability could again be attained.

It was one of the misfortunes of the people of later Stuart times that in their long and painful struggle back to sanity they were very badly led. The common assumption that dishonesty and cleverness are inseparably connected has secured for many Restoration statesmen a wholly undeserved reputation for ability. In actual fact most of them were singularly inexpert practitioners of the baser arts of politics, who contrived to do their country the maximum amount of harm while doing themselves remarkably little good. But at the critical moment of the Restoration the less reputable politicians were in the background, and England had the immense advantage of being guided for a brief period by the two ablest men in the country, the newly restored monarch himself and his chief minister, Lord Chancellor Sir Edward Hyde, soon to be created earl of Clarendon.

Charles was at his best in the early years of his reign. He interfered little in affairs, behaved with great dignity in a difficult situation, and by his immense personal charm helped to soothe the susceptibilities of the innumerable representatives of all parties who felt they were being neglected or ill used. As son and heir of the 'Royal Martyr' he had it in his power to exercise a greater influence than anyone else on the general tone of the settlement, and he used that influence almost entirely for good. Without seeming in any way neglectful of his father's memory he yet threw his weight on the side of moderation, and it was largely due to him that so little blood was shed on the scaffold, and that the Act of Indemnity and Oblivion, granting an amnesty for nearly all offences of the previous eighteen years, was eventually passed. The Cavalier gibe, that the Act meant indemnity for enemies and oblivion for friends, did not move him. He fully realized that a statesman seeking to unite a divided people must not think in terms of enemies and friends.

Clarendon was the ideal adviser for Charles in the circumstances of the moment. Honest, resolute and indefatigable, he had once himself been an opponent of Charles I, and had enough sympathy with both sides in the original quarrel to be able to act as mediator between them. The land settlement embodied in the Act of Indemnity and Oblivion, which required the restoration of all land confiscated by the Government, but recognized all sales by legitimate owners, even when effected under practical duress, was the offspring of his practised legal mind, and, however inequitable, caused less upheaval and discontent than any other solution of the problem would have done. The Church settlement was in general accordance with his ideas, though the name 'Clarendon Code', given to the series of statutes recognizing the supremacy of the Anglican communion and depressing its rivals, conveys an exaggerated impression of the length to which he wished to go. Most important of all, the constitutional settlement, with its insistence on the supremacy of the law, and its conception of king and Parliament as substantially equal powers working harmoniously together, was due primarily to him. His enemies among the discontented Cavaliers later declared that he had deliberately frustrated every attempt to provide the king with a sufficient revenue to make him independent, and though there seems to be no real foundation for the charge, it is not altogether out of keeping with his general policy. To Clarendon and, under his guidance, to Charles, restoration meant a return to the position obtaining in the spring of 1642, and for that conception of restoration there was almost certainly more support in the country at large than there would have been for any other.

Unfortunately neither Charles nor Clarendon appreciated the fact that the admirable principles which they supported in England could with equal advantage be observed in Scotland and Ireland, and that it might be worth their while, in the interests of all three kingdoms, to do what they could to promote a similar moderation and readiness to compromise there. As a result the restoration in Scotland was encouraged to go much too far, while the restoration in Ireland was prevented from going nearly far enough, in each case because that was the course which seemed most in consonance with the immediate interests of England. Despite the lessons plainly embodied in the events of the previous twenty years, English statesmen still failed to realize that the three kingdoms of the British Isles were inseparably connected together, and that the interests of one could not be promoted by ignoring the interests of the others. Their selfish and short-sighted policy in this particular was to be one of the main causes of the very unrest which all were so anxious to bring to an end.

Clarendon's real weakness, however, was not so much selfishness or lack of foresight as an inability to appreciate the age in which he was now living. Of a naturally conservative temper, enhanced by his profession and by advancing years, he was still dominated by the ideas and ideals of the reign of Charles I.

At first this was an actual qualification for his task as leader of the nation, for it was towards some of these ideas and ideals that the English people were vaguely groping. But once the immediately necessary work of restoration had been accomplished, and the age of Charles I had been revived as far as that seemed possible or desirable, his conservative outlook became a serious handicap, for it prevented him from sympathizing with the new aspirations by which the nation was being moved, and even from establishing good relations with the men of the post-war generation who were beginning to come forward. As early as 1662 he felt that his power was slipping from him, and though for a time he was buoyed up by premature attempts on the part of his enemies to drive him from office, and it was not until 1667 that he was dismissed by the king and impeached by an angry Parliament, he had long before his fall been gradually giving place to a group of men very different in character and antecedents from himself.

Among the characteristic evils of restorations is the almost inevitable rise to prominence of two types of men whose influence on events is apt to be wholly mischievous. Most conspicuous among these is the *émigré*, the politician driven into exile by the preceding convulsions, who has lost touch, during his period of residence abroad, with his native land, and yet on his return fails to appreciate either that fact or its implications. Of this type was Henry Bennet, appointed Secretary of State in 1662 and later created earl of Arlington. For some years Charles's agent in Spain, he had imitated the formal manners of the grandees there with such success as to earn for himself the nickname of 'The Spaniard'. He also married a Dutch wife, and embraced Catholicism at least so far as to have little genuine sympathy with the English Church. His strength lay in a knowledge of foreign languages and an understanding of foreign affairs rare among Englishmen of the day, in great personal influence with Charles, and in a capacity for enlisting the services, though not for retaining the loyalty, of capable subordinates such as Sir Thomas Clifford and Sir Joseph Williamson.

Scarcely less characteristic of restorations is the disillusioned politician, who, having seen all sorts of principles tried and found wanting in the preceding period, has ceased to believe in any principles whatever. Of this type were George Villiers, duke of Buckingham, and Anthony Ashley Cooper, created Lord Ashley and later earl of Shaftesbury. Both were too much in love with foreign models, French in the case of Buckingham and Dutch in the case of Ashley, to be genuinely English; but neither was un-English in the sense in which that term could be applied to Arlington. Buckingham was still capable of erratic flashes of enthusiasm for any cause that happened to catch his fancy; but Ashley prided himself rather on being superior to such weaknesses, and on his skill in turning the enthusiasms of others to his own advantage. Their strength lay in a remarkable capacity for enlisting popular support, though

Buckingham, when in favour, had also an influence with the king which few could rival.

Under the guidance of these men and their associates Charles and Charles's policy rapidly deteriorated. Within two or three years of his accession the task of acquiring a genuine understanding of the unfamiliar people among whom his lot was now cast, and of finding solutions for their innumerable perplexing problems, had proved more than the king could face. Unlike Clarendon, his new advisers, themselves none too well acquainted with normal English institutions, saw little need for any such understanding on his part, and were much more inclined to distract his attention with visionary projects or sordid pleasures than to urge upon him the dull and ungrateful task of government along orthodox lines. His marriage to the Catholic Catherine of Braganza, his sale of Dunkirk to the French, his issue of a declaration of indulgence in 1662, even his entrance into war with the United Netherlands in 1664, were all of them steps which a genuine English king with genuinely English advisers would at least have hesitated to take.

Nevertheless the blame for all these steps was laid upon Clarendon, and together with the mismanagement apparent in the Dutch War did much to bring about his fall. Popular opinion singled out Sir William Coventry as the only man among the Chancellor's opponents with the ability, the public spirit and the intimate knowledge of England necessary to enable him to take the place of first minister; but Coventry either could not or would not make himself personally acceptable at Charles's court, and the king was thus left exposed to the rival influences of Arlington, supported by Clifford, on the one side, and Buckingham, sometimes supported by Ashley, on the other. Arlington and Buckingham, however, were both inspired by curiously discordant motives. At home Arlington was associated with the Catholics; yet abroad he favoured the Dutch. At home Buckingham inclined towards the dissenters, and had allies even among the republicans; yet abroad he was influenced mainly by a great admiration for the king of France. Confusion inevitably followed. For two years after Clarendon's fall Arlington and Buckingham, alternately or in occasional association with each other, held the chief power in the State, and as neither very well knew what he was aiming at beyond the retention of his position the policy of the government became subject to the most astonishing variations.

Even worse was the situation which arose when Charles realized the opportunity afforded by the rivalries of his ministers, and began deliberately to play upon these rivalries with the object of securing unquestioned control for himself. The French system of government had always had a great attraction for him, and in France he could see his cousin, Louis XIV, pursuing that very policy with conspicuous success. What Charles did not sufficiently grasp was that such a policy, if it were to be genuinely effective, would require much greater industry and a much steadier application to business than he was capable of displaying. By pitting his ministers against each other he did not secure control for himself, but merely ensured that nobody should be in control at all. With a few brief intervals that was to remain substantially the situation for the rest of his reign.

Out of this confusion was born the Secret Treaty of Dover. It may be questioned whether anyone in England who took part in the negotiation of that treaty was really clear what purpose he expected the treaty to serve, and certainly no two were in complete agreement on the point; but they could all find some features of which they approved in it. The main developments for which it provided were a joint attack by English and French on the United Netherlands, in which England should take charge of naval operations, with some assistance from a French squadron, and France should take charge of land operations, with some assistance from an English expeditionary force; a considerable subsidy to be paid by France to England so long as the war should last; division of the spoils on agreed lines; a formal declaration by Charles that he was a Catholic; and an additional subsidy from France, as well as a body of French troops to assist him in maintaining his authority, after the declaration was made. On 22 May 1670 the treaty was signed by Arlington, Clifford and two of Charles's less important Catholic supporters, Lord Arundell of Wardour and Sir Richard Bellings. On 21 December 1670 a sham treaty, identical with the first except in its omission of all mention of Charles's declaration of Catholicism, was signed by Clifford, Arlington, Buckingham and Ashley, together with the statesman to whom Charles had entrusted the destinies of Scotland, John Maitland, earl and later duke of Lauderdale. On 2 February 1672 the sham treaty was redrawn and signed again by the same men.

The purely fortuitous circumstance that the initials of these five men's names can be arranged to form the word 'Cabal' did much at the time, and has done more since, to draw attention to their association with each other. But that association was purely temporary, and had no solid foundation whatever. Far from being joint supporters of a common policy they were bitter rivals, who were supporting two different policies, and were doing even that largely because of the fear entertained by each that if he refused the others would agree, and so outdistance him in their race for the royal favour. Once the five names were appended to the false treaty they had indeed this to bind them together, that they were all threatened by the same danger if Parliament should come to hear of what they had done. Yet even this was a cause of division as much as of union, for each hoped to be able to shuffle out of the responsibility by throwing it on the others.

Had the policy succeeded all might have been well, at least as far as they were concerned; but it had scarcely been begun when it became obvious that it was going to break down. The attack on the Dutch was, from the English point of view, a failure. The declaration of indulgence, which was Charles's first step in the direction of Catholicism, roused great indignation not merely among churchmen but also among supporters of the constitution, who disliked this extravagant exercise of the royal authority. The stop of the Exchequer, by which he secured the funds necessary for his policy, was bitterly resented in commercial circles, and by making it difficult to borrow practically compelled him to summon Parliament, which immediately attacked the declaration of indulgence. By the spring of 1673 the situation looked ominous indeed.

It says much for Charles's native sagacity that he recognized almost at once how completely he had gone astray, cancelled his declaration after only a brief struggle, and less than a year later made peace with the Dutch. Meanwhile the Test Act, which had been Parliament's reply to the declaration, had practically compelled the duke of York and Clifford to resign their offices; Shaftesbury had read the signs of the times and considered it advisable to join the opposition; and Buckingham and Arlington, after vainly endeavouring to blame each other for all that had been done, had sunk into the background. By the spring of 1674 the Cabal was no more than an evil memory.

Nevertheless the spectre of the Secret Treaty of Dover was to haunt Charles for the rest of his life. His people were never able to make out precisely what work of darkness had been attempted during the years 1672 and 1673; but they guessed much, suspected more, and regarded the king thereafter with a distrust none the less profound because they shrank from admitting it even to themselves. Had Charles at any time in the following four years made a bold and sincere declaration in favour of a national policy he might even then have recovered the national confidence; but such a declaration would have had to be unequivocally anti-French, and Charles was in no position to make a real stand against the French monarch. In the Secret Treaty, Louis possessed what was virtually a guarantee of moderately good behaviour on Charles's part, for though he had no desire to ruin Charles, who was the most accommodating ruler of England he was at all likely to find, he could in the last resort reveal the treaty to the English people and so produce an irreconcilable antagonism between them and their sovereign. Charles frequently declared that having joined with Louis in a war against the Dutch he could not in honour so far reverse his policy as to join with the Dutch in a war against Louis. The truth is that he was restrained, but not so much by honour as by fear of possible disclosures. From 1674 onwards, in fact, Charles was in the unfortunate position of being virtually blackmailed by the French king.

In this lies the explanation of Danby's singularly unfruitful ministry. Appointed Lord High Treasurer on Clifford's resignation in June 1673, with the idea that he might assist in restoring the credit of the Cabal, Sir Thomas Osborne, later created earl of Danby, soon showed a capacity for dealing with the vital problem of finance which entitled him to repudiate all connexion with the Cabal and inaugurate a policy of his own. The importance of his rise to prominence lay in the fact that he was a typical representative of the land-owning class whom the Restoration had again placed at the head of affairs, and also of the younger generation of Englishmen whose outlook was not dominated either by the traditions of Charles I's reign or by the jealousies and misconceptions engendered by the civil wars and the period of exile. In him England as it was now constituted might hope at last to find a reliable spokesman, and through his agency it might anticipate the genuine settlement which had hitherto proved so elusive.

In substance Danby's policy was a return to that of Clarendon, involving a Restoration going back no further than 1642, a frank acceptance of all that had been accomplished by that date, and an admission even of some of the results of the period that had followed. But in all matters of detail he was very much a man of his own time. His outlook was less lofty than that of Clarendon, and more in keeping with that of his contemporaries. The firm alliance of Church and State which was his fundamental aim, as it had been Clarendon's, he conceived of as having a political rather than a religious basis, and as being directed not so much against dissenters as against opponents of the monarchy. The growing commercial interest, upon which Clarendon had looked with some doubt, was in his view to be encouraged, and not retained in any undue subordination to the older landed interest. The enemies against whom he considered it necessary to take precautions were the Catholics rather than the Protestant nonconformists at home, and the French rather than the Dutch abroad. In all probability his policy came as near being a national policy as was practicable at the time. Unfortunately both for him and for the people of England it was almost impossible that it should succeed.

The main trouble was that few could believe it was seriously intended. Danby had risen to eminence as a follower of the duke of Buckingham, and so was himself the object of some suspicion. King Charles had completely forfeited the confidence originally reposed in him, and was known to incline to a policy very different from that professed by Danby. Worst of all, the duke of York, who exercised over Charles the influence often enjoyed by a determined though stupid man over an intelligent but less resolute associate, had made it increasingly apparent that he was not only a Catholic but a bigoted Catholic, who could scarcely be expected, under any circumstances, to give genuine approval

to Danby's schemes. The fatal weakness in Danby's position was that to maintain himself at court he had to enlist the duke's support, and yet so long as the
duke was one of his supporters there was little prospect that his own Anglican,
anti-Catholic and anti-French policy would be accepted at its face value.

So far as domestic affairs were concerned Danby was not unsuccessful. His
scheme of a non-resisting test, by which all in official positions were to be
required to swear that they would not attempt any alteration in Church or
State, failed, it is true, to secure acceptance; but it is at least doubtful whether
he was much interested in the actual test, or put it forward with any more
serious object than that of making a formal repudiation of the policy of the
Cabal. On the whole, his royalist and Anglican outlook was approved by
Parliament and the country at large, and even his efforts to marshal a party in
its favour, though his methods were widely condemned, met with a considerable measure of success. Of finance he had early proved himself a master, and
had he required to provide only for normal peace expenditure at home he could
almost certainly have made the government solvent, and dispelled the belief in
extravagance and waste at court which had done so much to discredit the
existing system.

Very different was the position in foreign affairs, for the attack on the
Dutch, from which Charles had derived so little profit, had proved much more
beneficial to Louis XIV; and although the emperor, the king of Spain and other
princes had taken the field against the French it seemed only too probable that
Louis might overrun the entire Netherlands and impose his will on the rest of
Europe. Even the English, accustomed as they were to disregard events abroad,
could not ignore this prospect of French dominance, the more so as Louis had
associated his rule with a peculiarly aggressive and persecuting form of Catholicism, which was driving French Protestants in increasing numbers to seek
refuge in neighbouring states. Throughout England there arose an insistent
demand that something should be done to check the progress of France, and no
government that failed to take appropriate action had any chance of retaining
the support of the country at large.

Danby himself was quite willing to strike in on behalf of the Dutch, and in
the late autumn of 1677 scored one of his greatest triumphs, when he not only
brought about the marriage of James's elder daughter Mary to the Dutch
stadtholder, William of Orange, but prevailed with Charles to join William in
an effort to force terms of peace on Louis. Before embarking on actual war,
however, he insisted on the need for adequate supplies from Parliament, while
Parliament, before granting supplies, insisted equally strongly on a guarantee
that war was actually intended. On this rock of suspicion and mistrust the whole
project of war in aid of the Dutch showed every sign of suffering shipwreck, to

the secret relief of the English king, whose object was not so much to wage war on France as to extort subsidies from the French king in return for remaining neutral. Inevitably his attitude, viewed with suspicion from the very beginning, was represented in an even more sinister light than the facts justified; the whole policy of the government was discredited; and Danby, who had largely inspired that policy, was widely accused of having encouraged the very developments he had done his utmost to prevent.

Such was the situation when, like a bolt from the blue, Titus Oates appeared upon the scene with his account of a vast Jesuit conspiracy aiming at the assassination of the king, the elevation of the duke of York to the throne, and the forcible reconversion of England to Catholicism. There was little that was genuinely original in Oates's narrative. Many plots, real and imaginary, of Catholics on one side and of nonconformists and republicans on the other, had already been foisted on the long-suffering citizens of England, and much of what Oates had to say was borrowed directly from these earlier revelations. But Oates's account came at a time when the public were feeling peculiarly uneasy in any case; in spite of patent absurdities it contained just enough truth to make it credible; and it had the strange fortune to be seized upon at once by all parties as a weapon which they might use for their own advantage. Danby and the courtiers believed they might employ it to produce a wave of enthusiasm in favour of Charles and the monarchy. The duke of York and his followers believed they might employ it to demonstrate the general falsity of the charges made against the Catholics, and so discredit their enemies. Shaftesbury and the opposition, after a momentary hesitation, realized that it was a weapon forged to their hands, and proceeded to turn it against the Catholics and the government. Under their inspiration a wave of excitement swept the country; some thirty-five individuals, most of them innocent of any real crime, were executed for complicity in the plot; and Parliament showed itself ready to adopt almost any measures which might safeguard the country from the imaginary dangers threatening it.

One of the earliest results of the popular frenzy was the impeachment and imprisonment of Danby, whose reluctant participation in the last of Charles's subsidy intrigues with France was revealed to Parliament by the English ambassador through whom it had been conducted. Yet it was Danby's estimate of the general situation which eventually proved correct, for the ultimate effect of the revelations made by Titus Oates was largely to rehabilitate Charles in the eyes of his subjects. Fear that the king was working underground to promote the interests of Catholicism was superseded by a firm conviction that the Catholics were working underground to secure the destruction of the king. Had Charles seized the opportunity to pose as a national Protestant sovereign, and set himself at the head of the anti-Catholic frenzy that developed every-where, he might indeed have made himself easy and secure for life, and possibly have established a permanent settlement of the country, though on a much more advanced basis than either Clarendon or Danby would have contemplated. But such a course of action was impossible for him, partly because he himself had no faith in Oates's revelations, but much more because it would have meant abandoning his brother James, in whose interests the Catholic conspiracy was believed to have been engineered. Charles had little affection and less respect for James, whose obstinate adherence to his newly acquired belief in Catholi-cism he regarded, not altogether with justice, as the principal cause of his own troubles; but he had a surprising veneration for the royal title and dignity, and fully realized that any abandonment of the cause of the heir was almost bound to involve, sooner or later, an abandonment of the cause of the Crown.

It is significant of Charles's limitations as a statesman that the only occasions on which he was genuinely successful were occasions on which the policy called for was one of masterly inactivity. At the crisis of the Restoration he had greatly enhanced his own prestige, and also improved the chances of a peaceful settlement, by an attitude of dignified non-interference in the rivalries of parties, and a calm acceptance of whatever was required by the law and by Parliament. Now, at the crisis of the Popish Plot, he pursued the same course. He did nothing to disprove Oates's revelations, false though he knew many of his statements to be. He made no serious attempt to save Danby, despite the fact that the policy of that minister had had his full approval. He offered every conceivable concession in connexion with the duke of York, short of accepting his complete exclusion from the throne. At every stage he took his stand on the law or admitted custom of the country, and left it to his opponents to ruin themselves by trying to find any other acceptable solution of the problem confronting them.

A more astute or more honest man than Shaftesbury would not have fallen into the trap thus laid for him. But Shaftesbury had his own ends to serve, and was too confident of his own cleverness to believe that he could be outwitted by a monarch who had shown such a lack of capacity for pursuing any active policy with success. Since the dissolution of the Cabal towards the close of 1673 he had been rapidly working his way to the front as one of the leaders of the opposition; but his notorious untrustworthiness and love for extreme courses had hitherto prevented him from securing any very large following, and the majority of the discontented had retained their allegiance to other and more moderate men. Now in the heated atmosphere engendered by the Plot he saw his opportunity of outbidding all his rivals for popular support, by advocating a more advanced policy than they could bring themselves to countenance, and so uniting the whole opposition under his standard. In three successive Parliaments he secured the introduction of bills designed to exclude the duke of York altogether from the throne, and even threatened, if necessary, to force the bills through by means of mob violence.

Unfortunately for himself, while he was successful in gaining a large measure of support for the proposed exclusion of James, he was completely unsuccessful in devising any generally acceptable alternative. A republic, in view of the memories still entertained of the Commonwealth, was not to be thought of; yet another future sovereign was hard to find. The surviving children of James were both daughters, both under age, the elder abroad and the younger as yet unmarried. William of Orange, next heir in his own right and also husband of the elder daughter, was a foreigner, not very well known in England, and not in the least likely to prove a mere tool in the hands of Shaftesbury or anyone else. Other possible candidates for the throne were either Catholics, too young, or too remotely connected with the occupant to be as yet seriously considered. As a result Shaftesbury determined to advance the claims of the eldest son whom Charles II had acknowledged, James, duke of Monmouth, a young man of great personal charm but weak character, who, in spite of many stories circulated about the marriage of his mother to Charles, was generally recognized to be illegitimate.

In thus putting forward a supposititious heir Shaftesbury was guilty of the same indefensible tactics as James himself was to have laid to his charge eight years later, and substantially the same result followed. Reverence for the royal line was much too strong to allow of such a fraud being countenanced, and as the passions aroused by the Plot slowly waned, the supporters of exclusion gradually lost confidence in the justice, or even practicability, of their own aims. With the unexpected dissolution of the last Exclusion Parliament in the early spring of 1681, Shaftesbury's following simply disintegrated, and towards the close of the following year Shaftesbury himself was forced to seek refuge on the Continent, where he died a few weeks later. Within five months of his death his associates in England had been denounced as engaged in a conspiracy to seize the king and duke of York as they passed by the Rye House on their road home from Newmarket, and the most active and dangerous among them had been arrested.

It is doubtful whether there was much more reality about the Rye House conspiracy than there was about the Popish Plot. In both cases there was a great deal of vague talk about ends to be secured, accompanied by a certain amount of actual planning for action on illegal or treasonable lines; but in neither case was anything actually attempted, or even, perhaps, very seriously contemplated. The instruments by means of which so much had been made of the earlier conspiracy, however, were equally available for use in connexion with the later, and the Court did not hesitate to employ them in order to secure the execution, exile or imprisonment of its opponents. By the close of 1683 open opposition to Charles in England had ceased to exist.

A more energetic or revengeful man might have seized the opportunity afforded by so striking a victory to carry the war far into the enemies' territory; but Charles made no attempt to introduce a reign of terror. By legal process, it is true, he secured control of the borough corporations, and with them their representation in the House of Commons; but he refrained from summoning the packed Parliament which these proceedings seemed to foreshadow. By pressure on the judges he obtained the release of Danby from the Tower; but he did not readmit him to his counsels. By dubious expedients he practically restored the duke of York to office; but he did not allow him to monopolize the government. The failure of the Rye House conspiracy was not followed by any increase in the standing army or attempt to raise money by illegal means. There is evidence, indeed, that having got rid of the most extravagant among his opponents, and induced the remainder to see reason, Charles was meditating a settlement which would commend itself to all moderate men. But if so, his scheme died with him. In the early days of February 1685 he was carried off by a sudden illness, and his brother, in spite of all the efforts that had been made to exclude him, quietly ascended the throne.

The success of Charles, followed so quickly by his death, sealed the fate of the Stuart dynasty. James was by no means a complete fool. During Charles's reign he had shown himself well aware of the danger to which he had exposed himself by his open profession of Catholicism, and ready to adopt any reasonable expedient for mitigating that danger. But he was a man who tended to be dominated by a few simple ideas, and among his earliest convictions, based upon the unhappy experience of his own father, was the need for firmness in a ruler. By weakness and instability, he was thoroughly convinced, Charles I had forfeited his life and Charles II had come near to forfeiting his throne. During his closing years, however, the latter monarch had adopted a more determined attitude, and success had immediately followed. All that was necessary, James concluded, was that he in turn should prove resolute, and the monarchy would soon be elevated to what he considered its rightful place in England.

If confirmation was required for this diagnosis of the situation it was soon forthcoming. The supporters of James, or Tories, as they were now coming to be called, were only too anxious to interpret his actions in the most favourable light, if for no other reason than a desire to justify their own attitude at the time of the Exclusion Bill. Their opponents, the Whigs, were momentarily too depressed to offer much criticism. Except where religion was concerned James had much more real sympathy than Charles with the national outlook, and his attitude on some points, notably his early refusal to continue Charles's slavish subordination to France, greatly commended him to the majority of his subjects. As a result all went well for some months. Parliament willingly voted supplies far in excess of those enjoyed by Charles. The earl of Argyll when he raised the standard of rebellion in Scotland, and Monmouth when he followed his example in the south-west of England, received only local support, and were easily suppressed. Everything conspired to emphasize the security of the king's position, and to convince James that only the half-hearted and irresolute measures of his predecessors had stood in the way of a genuine recovery from the depths to which monarchy and the Catholic religion had fallen. Where Clarendon had carried the Restoration to 1642, and Charles had scarcely imagined that it could be carried beyond 1625 or 1603, James began to contemplate carrying it to 1558.

Had he proceeded with reasonable caution and tact it is at least possible that he might have achieved a considerable measure of success. The Restoration, and even the Reformation, in England were not so far distant as to make a modification of their character quite impracticable. But caution and tact were both foreign to James's nature, and in addition he was becoming increasingly influenced by practical considerations which called for haste. He was fifty-two years of age, and had just been reminded by the death of his brother, who was only three years his senior, that his remaining time on earth was not likely to be long. His immediate heirs were his two daughters, who were both Protestants and both now married to Protestants. Obviously if anything was to be done it had to be done at once. Of this fact James was daily reminded by the small circle of Catholic clergy and laymen on whose advice he chiefly relied, a strange collection of adventurers, whose policy was regarded with disfavour by responsible Catholic opinion both at home and abroad, but who wished to make the most they could for themselves and their religion out of the opportunity afforded by the support of the kings of England and France.

Quite suddenly, in consequence, as the year 1685 drew to a close, James cast all caution aside, and began to press forward, in the most reckless fashion, with all the measures which he had contemplated as likely to strengthen the royal authority or advance the interests of the Catholic Church. Parliament having failed to support him as far as he had hoped, new methods were devised for bringing pressure to bear on constituencies and on individual members. The repeal of the Test Act having been refused, a decision in favour of the dispensing power was obtained from the law courts, the Act was virtually ignored, and Catholics in considerable numbers were introduced not merely into civil, but also into military, and even into ecclesiastical office. The universities, on which depended the whole intellectual life of the nation, were attacked, and several of their colleges were transformed into Catholic seminaries. The army, already greatly increased in order to deal with Monmouth's rebellion, was still further developed, and the practice was begun of stationing a large part of it, during the summer months, in the neighbourhood of London, with a view to over-awing the city.

Meanwhile James endeavoured to disarm criticism by professing a firm belief in the virtues of toleration, and not merely issued a very comprehensive declaration of indulgence, but required the clergy to make themselves in some sense a party to his action by reading it from the pulpit. His subjects in England, however, gravely doubted the sincerity of his professions, and were confirmed in their growing mistrust of his policy by reports of contemporary developments in Scotland and Ireland. In both these kingdoms the later Stuart monarchs, largely on the advice of English statesmen, had based their authority on an alliance with the Protestant episcopalian minority against their religious opponents. The straits to which the Scottish Presbyterians were thus reduced had roused the misgivings even of the English Parliament as early as 1674, and the development of James's Catholic policy, threatening the Scottish episcopalians as well, made the situation still more ominous. The power which Englishmen themselves had assisted the king to secure in Scotland might now, it appeared, be used against the religion and liberties of England. But the warning which made the deepest impression came from Ireland. There the king practically repudiated the alliance with the Protestant minority, handed over the administration to the Catholic majority, and encouraged the remodelling of the army on Catholic lines. So great was the alarm that Protestants in increasing numbers began to leave the country.

Nevertheless, so long as it appeared improbable that James's policy would last longer than his life, English public opinion was opposed to the adoption of active measures against him. Meetings of dissatisfied politicians were indeed held; communication was established with William and Mary, the nearest heirs to the throne, and a formal statement of their attitude to the developing crisis was eagerly sought; but all this was with a view to the future rather than to the immediate present. Even the prosecution of the seven bishops who protested against the obligation to read the declaration of indulgence from the pulpit, although it roused much indignation, would not alone have inspired resistance. What brought matters to a head was the fear that James's system might prove permanent, originated as early as the close of 1687 by the announcement that the queen was with child. With singular lack of tact the Catholic adventurers who surrounded the throne hailed the expected birth as a miracle vouchsafed in aid of the true religion, and declared their conviction that the child would be a boy, who would take precedence of his half-sisters in the succession. The natural reply of the disappointed Protestants was that the whole affair was a fraud, and that the child, if any should be produced, would not be the offspring of the king and queen at all. On 10 June 1688 the unfortunate child was born, to become known to history as the Old Pretender. Three weeks later, on the very day the seven bishops were acquitted, a formal invitation was dispatched to William of Orange requesting him to come over with an army to aid his supporters in England.

The precise purpose of this invitation was probably more than its seven signatories could themselves have explained; nor are modern analogies of popular movements against governments of much value in casting light on its significance. Even the opponents of Charles I had disclaimed the name of rebels, and had sought to justify their attitude by using the king's own authority to restrain his person. The opponents of James, with the warning of the civil wars before them, were still less inclined to enter into actual rebellion. Not merely was rebellion contrary to the political principles which they had ostentatiously espoused, but it had been shown to be destructive of the whole social system on which their own position depended. The kingly office, in their eyes, was not so much a public trust, from which a man might be dismissed for incompetence or misconduct, as a private estate, of which he could not be deprived without a serious threat to the titles of all other property owners. On the other hand, they conceived of themselves as having a direct personal interest in that estate. As principal tenants they believed they had a right to see that it was administered properly and without waste, and to invite the heir, whose interest was even greater than theirs, to lead them in an effort to restrain any undesirable activities on the part of the owner. What exact form the restraint might most fittingly assume it was for events to determine.

To William, however, with his eyes fixed upon the conflict between France and the chief powers of Europe then on the point of breaking out, the position was much simpler. The Catholic policy pursued by James, and the growing estrangement between him and his subjects, indicated that the old dependence of the English monarch on France would soon have to be renewed, and in a more slavish form than ever. At all costs such a development must be prevented, and the alliance of England secured for the coalition already forming to resist French domination. Without hesitation, accordingly, William accepted the summons to England, and prepared to cross over with the force which he had for some time been gathering together.

As a military operation the expedition on which he thus embarked was hazardous in the extreme. Working from a base which his departure would leave dangerously insecure, he proposed to cross the North Sea under convoy of a fleet not markedly superior in strength to the fleet which he might expect to encounter, and then land in England with an army less than one-third the size of the force awaiting him there. The common criticism that James was foolishly complacent regarding William's enterprise is strangely misplaced. Only the direst necessity, or complete confidence that no resistance was to be anticipated, could have justified such an enterprise at all.

It is not surprising, therefore, that contemporaries saw the direct intervention of Providence in the remarkable series of events which enabled it to succeed –the persistence of the 'Protestant wind', which immobilized the English fleet in the Thames, while it carried the Dutch westwards down the Channel, instead of northwards towards the Humber, where they were expected; the opportune change in the direction of the wind, which checked the English pursuit at the same time as it carried the Dutch safely into Tor Bay; the singular failure of the king to force an engagement on the invaders as they advanced on London; and his still more surprising decision to abandon his army, retire to his capital, dispatch his wife and infant son to France, and then set out to follow them. But these events did much more than secure the success of the invasion; they practically handed over control of the entire insurrectionary movement to William of Orange. In the neighbourhood of York and Nottingham the leading English conspirators were eagerly awaiting a signal for the native rising to which they conceived of William as merely an assistant; but without the shelter of his covering force they dared not move, and by the time they ventured to do so their opportunity of exercising any real influence on events had passed. Even the peers in London, who made a praiseworthy attempt, on the flight of James, to set up a provisional government of their own, found their lack of any force capable of maintaining order to be an insuperable handicap, and were further disheartened by James himself, who, on being brought back from his flight, strongly disapproved of their proceedings. To William alone, and to the disciplined army which he commanded, could the country look for protection from the anarchy and civil war which were their overmastering fear, and especially after James had embarked on a second and more successful attempt to escape to France. Little hesitation was therefore felt in inviting the prince to provide for the meeting of a Parliament or Convention, and in the interval before it could assemble to assume the executive government himself.

While the temporary settlement thus effected was not in any way decisive of the final settlement, it strongly suggested what that settlement was likely to be. Immediately upon the meeting of the Convention in January 1689 differences of opinion began to appear; but these differences were not so much over what should be done as over the best way of doing it. That James could not be allowed to return to England as the real ruler of the country was generally admitted. That William was the only available substitute was sufficiently obvious. But many, out of consideration for the fallen monarch, and more out of regard for monarchy itself, were anxious that the change from James to William should be effected as unostentatiously as possible, and with the smallest shock to existing institutions that ingenuity could contrive. Hence the proposal, strongly supported in the Lords, that James should be allowed to retain the title of king, while the exercise of the royal authority should be entrusted to William as regent; and the contention, less widely accepted, that James having abdicated by his flight, and the prince of Wales being supposititious, Mary was already queen, and should immediately be proclaimed, with William as prince consort. It may be questioned whether either of these schemes would have stood the test of experience; but William effectively negatived them both by declaring that he would be neither regent nor prince consort, and the inevitable decision was then reached that William and Mary should be recognized as joint sovereigns, with the regal power vested in William. At the same time a state-ment of grievances and appropriate remedies was hastily drawn up, embodied in a Declaration of Rights, presented, along with the crown, to the new sovereigns, and formally accepted by them.

The settlement thus effected was not so much a fresh departure as a revision, in the light of experience, of the settlement reached at the Restoration. The unquestioning acceptance of indefeasible hereditary monarchy at that time, and the failure to impose any conditions on the restored monarch, were recognized to have been mistakes, which had tempted Charles II, and still more his brother James, to carry the Restoration much further than the nation desired. A reaction in the opposite direction might now have been anticipated; but this was happily avoided, and a more generally acceptable interpretation of the Restoration adopted. Hereditary monarchy was still retained as a main principle of the constitution, but with a tacit proviso that in extreme cases the strict rules of hereditary succession might have to be modified. The imposition of conditions or restrictions on the monarch was accepted as a normal thing, though those embodied in the Declaration of Rights were as mild and conservative, and in some cases as vague, as could well have been devised. All really controversial problems were left to be dealt with after mature deliberation at a later date.

In the very moderation of this settlement lay its chief title to permanence, and the better prospect which it created for the future of England was still further improved by the fact that it was accompanied by a much more equitable solution than had been previously adopted of the problems of Scotland. In that kingdom news of the English Revolution had released a mass of pent-up discontent which had swept the prevailing system out of existence; and without a blow having been struck in favour of James the crown was offered to, and accepted by, William and Mary. Unmindful of their earlier mistake, the majority of Englishmen would still have liked to force Scotland to conform to the English model, and prevent her from exercising that very right of self-determination which they were claiming so vigorously for themselves. But the king was no longer, as in 1660, on their side. As between the aspirations of England and Scotland, William saw little to choose; and both he and the more statesmanlike among his supporters in England fully realized that the general situation was much too threatening to allow of any unnecessary conflict between the two nations. With remarkably little opposition, in consequence, the Scots were able to secure the establishment of the Presbyterian Church which was the principal object of the great majority among them, and the recognition of their Parliament as virtually independent of royal control. It has often been pointed out that the institution of two independent Parliaments in countries united under one monarch made either complete separation or parliamentary union almost inevitable. It has not been so frequently realized that by reducing the ill-feeling between the two countries it made union at least possible.

Nevertheless the new ruler was to have an uneasy and harassing reign. The faulty leadership which had been one of the afflictions of the peoples of the British Isles since the death of Cromwell was not improved by the Revolution. Selfish rivalries over the titles, offices and other rewards distributed among its supporters, faint-hearted doubts as to the permanence of the changes it effected, conscientious scruples regarding the moral or legal justification for the whole movement, all combined to produce a degree of uncertainty regarding the future which had the most deplorable results. Many politicians felt constrained to insure against all eventualities by maintaining some connexion with every candidate who might put forward a claim to the throne. Others changed from side to side as the course of events suggested would be most profitable to themselves. Few indeed proved capable of fixing on one settled course of action, pursuing it themselves, and recommending it effectively to the nation at large as the policy to be adopted.

Nor was William himself capable of giving acceptable guidance. Unlike Charles, or even James, he was sadly lacking in those qualities which make for popularity. Imperious, taciturn, reserved, impatient of the ceremonies and display which give to monarchy much of its attraction, with an ill-concealed contempt for many of the worthless men who surrounded his throne, he gave much needless offence, for which his constant ill-health was regarded as a very insufficient excuse. Not merely was he a foreigner, but he gave his chief confidence to foreigners, and let it be seen that he believed himself to have good reason for doing so. The natural result was widespread criticism and misrepresentation of his own actions, against which he was largely defenceless. His services to England, great though they were admitted to be, were declared to have been inspired by purely selfish considerations. Many asserted that his sole object in coming to England had been to gain the crown. Others attributed to him a sinister design to subordinate the interests of England to those of the United Netherlands.

Yet the differences between him and his new subjects, fundamental though they appeared to be, were in reality not so much differences of aim as differences of emphasis. There was general agreement that the power of the French king on the Continent must be reduced, and that the return of James to England, with its accompanying threat of Catholicism and despotic government, must be averted. There was also a general realization that these two objects were very closely interconnected. But while the king thought mainly in terms of the first, the people, and even most of the ministers, were intent only on the second. From this simple difference in outlook arose much of the misunderstanding which was to cause so much trouble between William and his Parliaments.

Even on the crucial problem of English participation in the European war there might have been serious divergence of opinion, had circumstances not arisen which temporarily merged the two aspects of the main problem into one. Within three months of his flight from England, James reappeared, supported by French officers, arms and money, in Ireland, where he proposed to establish himself firmly as king with a view to using it as a base for the recovery of England and Scotland. On no point was English public opinion more sensitive than on developments in Ireland, and James's action was immediately followed not merely by an insistent demand for the reconquest of that country but also by whole-hearted support of William's declaration of war on France. In this an apparent contradiction was involved, for any entanglement in Ireland was bound to reduce England's capacity for intervention in Europe; and William for that very reason proved extremely reluctant to take the Irish problem seriously. On the outcome of the Irish struggle, however, it was soon apparent that the ultimate fate of England and of Europe largely depended, and once that fact had been grasped no hesitation was shown in devoting the greater part of the resources of England to the reduction of the country. By the autumn of 1691 it had been more completely subdued than ever before in its history.

On its subjugation followed a settlement freeing England from embarrassment on the side of Ireland even more effectually than it had already been freed from embarrassment on the side of Scotland, though by entirely different means. Instead of more consideration being shown for the native Irish than in 1660, no consideration at all was shown for them, and they were handed over to the mercies of the English settlers whom they had endeavoured to dispossess, subject always to the supervision, in its own interests, of the English Parliament. The result in the end was to be disaster for all concerned, but for the moment the stern repression of the native Irish at least solved the Irish problem. Not until the reign of George III was Ireland again to prove a serious menace to England.

Meanwhile the contest in Europe had to some extent been neglected, and it was with a firm determination to infuse new vigour into it that William returned to the Continent in the spring of 1691. Unfortunately the state of military science at the time, coupled with conditions in the Low Countries, which formed the main theatre of operations, rendered the prospect of any striking results exceedingly remote. Under the inspiration of two great engineers, the French Vauban and the Dutch Cohorn, the art of fortification had been developed to a level which gave the defence a tremendous advantage over the attack. In the Netherlands effective communication was by means of an intricate system of waterways, blocked at every strategic point by fortresses which the artillery of the time could reduce, if at all, only by a methodical and lengthy process. Military operations, in consequence, generally took the form of long-drawn-out sieges, which frequently produced no result whatever. Manœuvres in the field were apt to be equally unspectacular and inconclusive, consisting of endless marches and countermarches, designed to secure the advantages of position without which no commander would venture to attack; and as transport was entirely horse-drawn even these could not begin until spring had produced a sufficient supply of fodder, or continue long after the growth had ceased. The object of all commanders was not so much to secure victory as to avoid defeat, and above all to refrain from hazarding excessive losses among the professional soldiery, who took so long to train and were so expensive to equip.

A continental war waged under such conditions was little calculated to rouse enthusiasm in a people who had no real interest in continental affairs, and no previous experience of the scale of expenditure which a genuine European war was bound to involve. Even the stimulus of occasional success was lacking, for William was more skilful as a politician than as a soldier, and more renowned for a capacity for recovering from defeats than for any ability to win victories. Suddenly called upon in his earliest manhood to rescue the Dutch republic from the depths to which it had been reduced by the joint attack of Louis XIV and Charles II, he had received no systematic instruction in military affairs, and had had to learn by painful experience from his own mistakes. His strategic conceptions were often excellent, but his tactical performance generally faulty, mainly owing to an inadequate grasp of the necessary detail. Of the great French generals of the seventeenth century only Luxemburg remained; but until his death at the beginning of 1695 Luxemburg was more than a match for William.

To Englishmen in general the defeats at Steinkirk and Landen, together with the loss of fortress after fortress, seemed a poor return for the vast sums, as they considered them, lavished on the war. The preservation of the Revolution settlement which William's campaigns, however inglorious, ensured, was taken for granted, and scarcely placed to his credit at all.

A feature of William's reign, in consequence, was a gradual development of the conviction, always latent in the English outlook, that active intervention on the Continent was to be deprecated, and that English participation in any European war should be confined to operations at sea. Even in that sphere William at first was by no means strikingly successful. Under the direction of Colbert the naval power of France had been developed until it surpassed that of England and the United Netherlands combined; and the war was little more than a year old when the allies suffered a defeat off Beachy Head which threw England itself open to invasion. It is true that the decision reached in that battle was decisively reversed two years later off La Hogue; but even after that the allies proved quite unable to make any effective descents on the French coast or protect their own commerce against the depredations of French privateers. In the very year after La Hogue the greatest catastrophe of the war took place, when the vast Smyrna fleet of several hundred English and Dutch merchant vessels was trapped by the French off Lagos, and almost wholly scattered, captured or destroyed.

Nevertheless it was at sea that William's greatest success was eventually achieved. Almost alone in England he grasped the importance of reviving Cromwell's control of the Mediterranean, with a view to sustaining the dwindling war effort of his ally Spain, and not merely dispatched the main fleet through the strait of Gibraltar to destroy the French naval power in that sea but later instructed it to winter, if necessary, at Cadiz. By this bold stroke he relieved the city of Barcelona, then in imminent danger of capture by a French army, shut up the French fleet in Toulon harbour, where it proved too large for the resources of the port and rapidly declined in efficiency, and brought the French campaign in Spain to a practical standstill. Had his subjects in England understood the motives of his undertaking and realized the extent of his success they would have been confirmed in their belief in the efficacy of sea power; but to the great majority among them it was merely an added grievance that the fleet had been sent so far away, and on the discovery of a plot to assassinate William, to be followed by a French invasion, they insisted on its recall. Little more than a year later the war was brought to an end by the treaty of Ryswick, leaving the vague belief that England's sphere was on the sea, unenlightened by any understanding of how sea power might be employed, to exercise a somewhat unfortunate effect during the ensuing peace.

That treaty, with its guarantee of the succession as determined by Parliament, was warmly welcomed by the English people, who conceived of it as removing all genuine cause of hostility to France, putting an immediate end to the heavy financial drain caused by the war, and enabling attention to be devoted to the domestic affairs in which their real interest lay. Unfortunately this produced a more serious cleavage than before between king and people, for William had never been interested in English domestic affairs or understood much about them. Not merely was his mind full of other matters which he considered infinitely more important, but for many years he had been accustomed to spend at least half his time outside of England campaigning on the Continent.

One of his main objects since his accession, in consequence, had been to find an English statesman capable of guiding his footsteps through the labyrinth of English politics, who would relieve him of most of the burden of purely English affairs. The first to whom he turned was George Savile, marquis of Halifax, the 'Trimmer' of Charles II's reign, whose attitude to English parties and party rivalries had much in common with his own. But Halifax soon proved to be much better at indicating what policy should be pursued than at giving effect to any policy at all, and was allowed to resign early in 1690. More helpful was his successor, Halifax's life-long rival the earl of Danby, now marquis of Carmarthen, a past-master in the art of manipulating parties, and a politician of unquestioned ability, who served William well for four years. But Carmarthen proved to be too much influenced by personal and party motives, and after 1694 declined in importance. Finally William made at once his best and his worst choice when he turned to Robert Spencer, earl of Sunderland, probably the ablest, though almost certainly the most unscrupulous, man at his disposal. But Sunderland had been associated with too many of the worst actions of James II, and proved too timorous to face the hostility in which his renewed elevation threatened to involve him. At the very close of 1697, when the conclusion of peace had made guidance in domestic affairs more necessary than ever for William, he resigned in a fit of panic the post of Lord Chamberlain to which he had only recently been appointed.

One man to whom William conspicuously refrained from turning was John Churchill, earl and later duke of Marlborough. It is just possible that in professional jealousy may be found the fundamental reason for his omission, for both men were soldiers, and William, though unquestionably the less skilful, had yet for political reasons to retain the supreme command. More probably, however, the root cause of their estrangement lay in the part played by Churchill in bringing over James's army to the side of the Dutch invader. William had not hesitated to profit by Churchill's behaviour; but his strict military outlook made it difficult for him to conquer a certain aversion to a general who had betrayed his own commander-in-chief. Whatever the precise reasons for the initial breach between the two men its effects were sufficiently disastrous. Apart from the increase of title granted to him, William signally failed to give Marlborough the recognition which he not unjustly considered his due, whether for his part in the Revolution or for his considerable military services immediately afterwards. Marlborough retaliated by inducing Princess Anne, with whom he had great influence through his wife, to advance claims which seriously embarrassed William and greatly offended Queen Mary; by coming forward himself as the spokesman and representative of the large body of Englishmen who resented the favour shown by William to the Dutch; and by entering into treasonable, though probably harmless, correspondence with France. William thereupon dismissed Marlborough from all his offices, and refused to employ him at all. The death of Mary in 1694 was followed by a reconciliation between William and Anne, and by somewhat improved relations between William and Marlborough; but it was not till the end of the reign that Marlborough was fully restored to favour. From the resignation of Sunderland until then William had no English minister on whom he felt he could safely rely.

Nor were his relations with English parties any happier than his relations with English statesmen. All parties and factions, in England, in the Netherlands or elsewhere, were obnoxious to him, as obstacles in the way of that union to curb the power of France which it was his life's task to create. But the English parties, with their furious quarrels over what seemed to him the merest trivialities, and their persistent resurrection of wrongs and injuries done long before his time, were peculiarly exasperating. The one thing they appeared to have in common was a love of irresponsible obstruction, and even for that their reasons were different. The Tories, as it has been epigrammatically put, opposed the king because the king was William; the Whigs opposed William because William was king. The only passion which could occasionally draw them together was hostility to all foreign influences in England, and of these influences William was apt to be regarded as the very fountain and embodiment.

In the difficult period which immediately followed his accession the party to which William could most naturally look for support was the Whig party, which claimed, not altogether justly, to have placed the crown upon his head. But the Whigs were only too well aware of the services they had rendered, and inclined to presume upon them. They failed to realize the bad impression they had made by their previous support of Monmouth, the suspicion aroused by the known republicanism of some of their number, and the desperate anxiety of William for a general amnesty, a settlement of the revenue, and an energetic prosecution of the war. Revenge for past injuries was their principal object, and William's chief function in their eyes was to assist them to secure that revenge. William, however, had no intention of being merely king of the Whigs. Early in 1690, accordingly, when the lengths to which they were prepared to go were shown by an attempted proscription of all who had taken part in the attack on the town charters under Charles and James, his patience gave way, and he turned to the Tories. Changes in the very mixed ministry on which he had hitherto relied were accompanied by a dissolution of the Whig Convention, and without much difficulty a Tory Parliament was secured in its place.

King and Tories had not a little in common. The Tory party was the party of prerogative, and William was no more inclined to consent to any diminution of his prerogative than his predecessors of the House of Stuart. The Tories had been mainly responsible for his marriage with Mary, which had been instrumental in bringing the crown within his grasp. The Tory leaders were more experienced administrators than the Whigs, and were better acquainted with the art of parliamentary management, the use of which William was reluctantly coming to regard as essential to his success. For some time, in consequence, so long as Catholicism remained unsubdued in Ireland and the French still threatened at sea, all went moderately well under Tory auspices. But the Tories were inclined to be dominated by the High Churchmen among them, who viewed with doubt William's title to the throne, introduced needless divisions by their quarrels with nonconformists and latitudinarians, and were on bad terms with England's Protestant allies abroad. Further, they were not wholehearted in the prosecution of the war, the burden of which fell largely on the Tory landowners, while any benefits to be derived from it seemed destined for the Whig merchants. Towards the close of 1693, accordingly, as the crisis of the war drew near, William again reversed his policy, and under the influence of Sunderland and the five statesmen known as the Whig Junto gradually built up a ministry which was almost exclusively Whig. As on the previous occasion, the change of ministers was confirmed at the ensuing general election, a Whig House of Commons being returned in 1695.

In truth William's only hope lay in the moderate men of both parties, and his dislike of being dominated by either thus combined with purely practical considerations to impel him in the direction of mixed ministries, inclining now one way and now the other. Such a middle course, however, inevitably exposed him to attack from both sides; and as the reign progressed circumstances arose which made the attacks increasingly violent. The death in 1694 of Queen Mary, who was much more popular, and possessed much the better hereditary title to the throne, greatly weakened his position with the Tories, many of whom began to look forward to the accession of Anne. The conclusion of the war by the treaty of Ryswick had somewhat the same effect on his position with the Whigs, who resumed their old attitude of hostility towards the occupant of the throne. Unless in exceptional circumstances the function of Parliament, as they conceived it, was to criticize rather than to help.

This was the more unfortunate inasmuch as the situation in Europe, as it appeared to William, was still extremely threatening. Charles II of Spain, whose death had long been anticipated, was obviously drawing towards his end, and the succession to his vast dominions was already in dispute between the Bavarian electoral prince, the Austrian Archduke Charles, and the French Philip of Anjou. William's primary object was to preserve the peace by means of an equitable adjustment of all claims reached before Charles died; and to that end he concluded with Louis of France two successive partition treaties, the first assigning the bulk of the Spanish inheritance to the electoral prince, with compensation to the other claimants, and the second, drawn up on the death of the electoral prince, similarly assigning the bulk of the inheritance to the archduke, with compensation to his sole remaining rival. Failing a satisfactory settlement, William sought to provide against all eventualities by perpetuating the alliance of the powers recently engaged against France, and by keeping the armed forces of England and the United Netherlands at the highest possible level of strength and efficiency. But the irresponsible Whig Parliament elected in 1698, and still more its Tory successor, were completely uninterested in the Spanish succession, shut their eyes to the possibility of a coming conflict, denounced the partition treaties as having been concluded without parliamentary sanction, and sought both to curtail expenditure and provide against possible despotic tendencies on the part of the ruler by reducing the armed forces to a mere shadow of what they had been during the war.

The darkest hour for William came towards the close of 1700, when the king of Spain at length died, leaving his entire dominions by will to the French claimant, with reversion, in the event of the legacy not being accepted, to the Austrian claimant. The sole object of the Spanish monarch in making this peculiar arrangement was to ensure that whoever got his dominions they should be preserved intact; but the effect of his action was almost to compel Louis XIV to repudiate the partition treaty which he had concluded with William, for if the will were accepted the French claimant would gain the entire Spanish dominions, whereas if the will were rejected France would most probably lose even the compensation it had been promised by the treaty. With little hesitation Philip, supported by Louis, accepted the will, and William found himself powerless to do anything in retaliation beyond denouncing the breach of faith involved. So low had his prestige fallen, and so great was the general disinclination for another war, that both the English and the Dutch showed themselves quite willing to recognize Philip as king of Spain so long as the principle was observed that the crowns of France and Spain should never be united.

The very ease, however, with which this success was achieved tempted Louis to go too far. With typical indifference to all interests but his own, he not merely safeguarded Philip's title to the French succession but proceeded to treat the Spanish dominions as if they belonged to France. In the early months of 1701 French troops occupied the Spanish possessions in Italy and the Netherlands, expelling the Dutch from the fortresses they garrisoned in the latter territory. Steps were taken towards reorganizing the trade of the Spanish Empire with a view to excluding the merchants of the Maritime Powers. Finally, on the death of James II in the autumn of the same year, Louis committed his crowning folly by recognizing his son, the Old Pretender, as king of England.

On the Continent it was William's task to consolidate a second Grand Alliance against the aggressive power of France; but in England he had little to do but stand aside and let events take their course. Without inducement from him the Whigs, both government supporters and opposition, rallied to the cause he had so long had at heart. Somewhat more reluctantly the bulk of the Tories followed. To facilitate the latter development William had come to an understanding with the most skilful parliamentary manager among them, Robert Harley. To provide for future eventualities he had cast personal resentment aside, taken Marlborough into partnership in all his recent work, introduced him to the courts and councils of Europe, and practically nominated him as the man who was to carry on his task when he was gone. Having securely laid the foundations of success he then performed his last great service for his cause by opportunely dying, when he had virtually nothing more to contribute to its advancement, and might by his continued existence have perpetuated those misunderstandings and resentments which had proved so disastrous before.

Meanwhile the Revolution settlement, vaguely outlined in the Bill of Rights, had slowly, and with considerable misgiving on William's part, been completed. The position of Parliament in the constitution had been more precisely defined. The power of the purse had been so employed as to secure for the views of the House of Commons real influence on the administration of the country, and the expression of these views had been facilitated by the development of an effective party organization. The standing army, still an object of intense jealousy, had been brought indirectly under parliamentary control. Religious toleration had been partially established; the oppressive treason law had been amended; and a considerable degree of freedom had been accorded to the Press. Finally, by the Act of Settlement of 1701, additional remedial provisions, suggested by the experience of William's own reign, had been laid down, and the succession itself, inadequately defined by the Bill of Rights as passing from

William and Mary to Anne and her children, and then to any children of William by a second wife, had been further entailed on the Electress Sophia of Hanover and her heirs.

It is significant that these measures were by no means exclusively the work of one party. Some were Whig in origin, some Tory, and behind them there was a very considerable amount of general agreement. Englishmen were at length beginning to feel that the development of their country was on the right lines, that the successive extravagances of 1661, 1679 and 1687 were things of the past, and that the promised land of stability and orderly government was slowly coming into view. All that was necessary to complete the process, it was widely believed, was a native sovereign to occupy the throne.

It was thus in an atmosphere of general reconciliation, and of national union in face of a common danger, that Queen Anne succeeded William, and her accession itself served to improve the situation. Anne indeed had in many ways an easier task than any of her immediate predecessors. Born and brought up in England, the daughter of an indubitably English mother and a more or less English father, she had never left her native country except for a few brief visits to Scotland and the Continent, and was more genuinely English than any sovereign since Elizabeth. On the other hand, she had neither the clear vision of William, the determination of James, nor the sagacity of Charles, and, as a woman, was bound to be dependent in practical affairs on some man, who must, if he were to be permanently successful as her adviser, be free from strong party ties. Fortune, which had denied to her husband every qualification for the post except honesty of purpose and freedom from partisanship, had indeed supplied her with a military and political genius in the duke of Marlborough; but although Marlborough was not himself a partisan his wife most definitely was, and it was unfortunately with the wife rather than with the husband that Anne's association lay.

Unfortunately also the duchess of Marlborough's party was not the party towards which Anne naturally inclined. Anne had as little desire as William to be the mere head of a faction, and throughout her reign strove with considerable success to be a real queen of all her people. But unlike William she had a genuine understanding of what English parties stood for, and could not but realize that the High Church principles in which she believed so firmly were safe only in Tory hands. It was on this that the extreme Tories were counting when they assumed that her accession meant the beginning of a golden age for themselves, and made a bold attempt to monopolize office under the new government. But their over-confidence no less than their obvious lack of interest in the continental war soon proved their undoing. Anne's first great service to her country was to approve the formal declaration of war for which William had made all arrangements, and to give her confidence to the moderate Tories led by Marlborough and his ally, the new Lord Treasurer Godolphin. Once the war was fairly begun the successes of that brilliant combination were soon to put an end to extreme Tory hopes, at least for a time.

The general conditions under which the War of the Spanish Succession was fought were substantially the same as those which had obtained in the wars of William III; but the soldier-statesman who had now come to the front was fully capable of mastering these conditions. No war, Marlborough recognized, can really be won simply by avoiding defeat; and in the case of the allies a genuine victory was essential, for the contest began with Louis XIV in virtual possession of all the territory which was in dispute. On the other hand, the French, who might have achieved victory of a kind by merely sitting still, were extremely reluctant to do so, partly because they had a confident belief in their own superiority, partly because they had formed, and retained for some years, a low opinion of Marlborough's capacity, and partly because France, after the efforts it had already made, was scarcely in a condition to face a prolonged struggle.

It was this last factor which was to dominate the situation. The alliance of the French with the Bavarians, their preliminary operations in 1703 and their advance on Vienna in 1704, were the main features in a well-conceived attempt on their part to end the war at a blow by striking directly at the keystone of the allied arch; and the attempt was defeated only by Marlborough's equally well-conceived march to the Danube, followed by his victories at the Schellenberg and Blenheim. The campaign of 1706 arose out of a determined French effort to take the offensive, which enabled Marlborough to meet and defeat Marshal Villeroi at the battle of Ramillies, and clear the French out of practically the whole of the Spanish Netherlands, at the same time as the imperial forces, by their victory at Turin, were driving them out of Italy. Similarly the campaign of 1708 originated in a French endeavour, with the assistance of Belgian sympathizers, to recover the ground they had lost, which gave Marlborough the opportunity of crushing Marshal Vendôme and the duke of Burgundy at Oudenarde. All three campaigns involved field operations in the grand manner, capable of producing really decisive results. Blenheim virtually deprived the French of all hope of victory in the war. Ramillies confronted them with the imminent prospect of defeat. Oudenarde brought them practically to their knees.

In England the effect of these victories, and more particularly of the second, was immense. Domestic controversies, already relegated to the background, were momentarily stilled, and all, or nearly all, united in enthusiastic support of the war. Even the ancient antagonism between England and Scotland was in some degree mitigated. The negotiations for the parliamentary union of the two countries, then pursuing their halting course, were facilitated by the provision of a more inspiring theme to occupy the public attention, and by a feeling aroused in Scotland no less than in England, that if union must come it was at least coming on a basis of success in which both countries had taken an honourable part.

Unfortunately enthusiasm for the war soon showed signs of going much too far. In forming his Grand Alliance against France the object of William III had been, not to wrest the Spanish inheritance from the French claimant, but merely to secure adequate compensation for the Austrian archduke and safeguards for the commercial interests of the Maritime Powers. Now under the influence of scarcely anticipated success these limited objectives began to appear wholly insufficient, and an increasing demand was raised, both in England and abroad, for 'no peace without Spain'.

The effect of this demand on the conduct of the war was almost wholly mischievous. Marlborough's successes were no mere chance victories, as his English enemies, and some even of his French opponents, were wont to declare. They were the natural outcome of his broad strategic outlook, acquired by early service with the great Turenne, his uncanny instinct for reading his opponent's mind, immense attention to the details on which the success of all military movements depends, unwearying care for the comfort and welfare of his troops, the use of the latest tactical devices, and an almost unexampled presence of mind on the field of battle, where commanders-in-chief still personally directed, and sometimes took part in, operations. But even Marlborough's capacity for victory was limited. He could not exercise control in four widely separated theatres of war, and the only companion in arms in whom he had real confidence, or who had shown any genuine ability to cope with even the less skilful among the French marshals, was the imperialist commander, Prince Eugene.

In truth Marlborough was hard put to it to exercise effective control in any theatre of war at all. By virtue of Queen Anne's commission he had undisputed command over all troops in English pay; but these never constituted more than about a third of his main army. As regards the forces of the United Netherlands his authority was shared by the Dutch field deputies who accompanied the armies in their campaigns, and disputed by many of the Dutch generals, who, especially in the early stages of the war, were bitterly jealous of the superior position accorded to him. Over the German contingents who completed his motley array he had no real authority at all, and in dealing with their commanders he had to solve all sorts of problems of precedence, rank and dignity, which bulked much more largely in their eyes than the successful prosecution of the war. Only by exercise of the most monumental patience, by constant cajolery, conciliation and even bribery, could he assemble the allied army together and direct its movements towards any intelligible end.

In this lies the explanation of the curious alternations of success and comparative failure in his campaigns, and the regular spacing of his greatest victories at intervals of two years. After a year of failure, due to their own dilatoriness and intransigence, Marlborough's associates tended to give him a free hand. After a year of success, due to his better control of the situation, they tended to resume their obstructive practices. Of any capacity for seeing the war as a whole they were sublimely innocent. Each consulted only his own selfish interests, and grasped the conditions only of his own sphere of operations.

Spain, however, was not the special concern of anyone on the allied side. It was remote from all the other theatres of war, in the Netherlands, on the Rhine and in Italy; it was more readily accessible from France than from any of the leading allied countries; and it was peculiarly difficult to operate in, partly owing to the rugged nature of the land and partly owing to the stubborn character of the people. The fatal mistake made by nearly all the allies was to assume that the defeat of the French would enable them to settle the Spanish question as they pleased. It scarcely occurred to them that they might also have to defeat the Spaniards.

For this error there was some excuse, for in the early stages of the war the Spaniards might have been content with either candidate for the throne, and to the very end they remained divided in opinion. Catalonia, ever a law to itself, adopted the cause of the Archduke Charles. Aragon and Valencia somewhat hesitatingly followed the same course. But the heart of the country, centring on Castile, after an initial period of doubt, decided in favour of Philip, and this attitude the allies found it impossible to shake. The French might be unpopular; but the heretic English, Dutch and Germans soon proved even more so. Philip V might be a weakling; but at least he was from the very beginning, in Spain, an obvious rallying point for Spanish national sentiment, whereas his rival, Charles III, was slow to present himself, and when he did so appeared rather in the character of a foreigner supported by foreign arms.

From the very outbreak of hostilities Marlborough fully appreciated the peculiar conditions of the Spanish conflict, and more especially the importance of sea power in connexion with it. Following the policy inaugurated by William III he laid the greatest stress on the need for an effective control of the Mediterranean; supported the alliance with Portugal which provided England with a secure base at Lisbon; inspired the attempts, unfortunately unsuccessful, which were made to seize Cadiz and Toulon; and was largely responsible for the capture and retention of Gibraltar and Port Mahon. But he could not himself direct operations so far distant from Flanders, and in his absence all was left

3

to depend on the erratic brilliance of the earl of Peterborough, and on the more reliable but somewhat pedestrian talent of the earl of Galway, and of James, later Earl Stanhope. Twice the allied forces succeeded in occupying Madrid, only to find it impossible to maintain themselves there in the midst of a hostile population; and towards the close of 1710 allied hopes were irretrievably shattered by the defeat and surrender of Stanhope at Brihuega. From first to last, in spite of the most remarkable vicissitudes of fortune, the Spanish campaigns were little more than failures, serving only to absorb an ever-increasing proportion of the allied war effort which might have been more profitably expended in the Netherlands.

That Marlborough in these circumstances persistently lent his countenance to the demand for 'no peace without Spain' is one of the most surprising features of his career; but his judgment, though always acute, was by no means infallible. Almost alone among the great captains of history, he had been denied any real chance of showing what he could accomplish until he was comparatively advanced in years. Too young for high command in the reign of Charles, he was handicapped by his religion under James, and out of favour under William. By the time his opportunity came, with the accession of Anne, he was over fifty years of age, and when he won the battle of Oudenarde he was nearly sixty. The passing of the years had not appreciably weakened his perceptions or diminished his skill, but it had greatly accentuated the strain imposed upon him by the endless and complicated negotiations in which he had always to take a leading part, the interminable winter journeys throughout Europe by means of which alone he could maintain good relations among the allies, and the summer campaigns and engagements which kept him for hours on end in the saddle, personally superintending operations. It is scarcely to be wondered at if his spirit sometimes faltered, and if on this and other problems he too readily complied with the views of his energetic wife and his Whig associates.

Almost inevitably such compliance involved allowing the war itself to become a matter of party rivalry, and in permitting this to happen Marlborough made his fatal mistake. After the dismissal of the High Tories in the early years of the reign the conduct of the war had been entrusted, with the full approval of ruler and people, to what would now be called a coalition government, resting primarily on three very moderate Tories–Marlborough himself in the field, Godolphin in the Lords and at the Treasury, and Harley in the Commons. The enthusiasm roused by Marlborough's victories, however, had led to the return of definitely Whig Parliaments in 1705 and 1708, mainly because the Whigs were more whole-heartedly in favour of the war, and this in turn led to a constantly increasing demand, which Marlborough would have done well to check, for the appointment of more Whigs to ministerial posts. In 1706 the first serious step towards the formation of a Whig ministry was taken; in 1708 Harley, who advocated reliance on non-party ministries even in time of peace, was dismissed from office; by 1709 the ministry had become almost exclusively Whig.

To the changes involved Queen Anne had given her assent only with the greatest reluctance; and their cumulative effect was to alienate her not merely from the Whig leaders, who thus threatened to dominate the government, but also from her old friend the duchess of Marlborough, who had been instrumental in forcing the transformation upon her, and even from Godolphin and the duke of Marlborough, who had at least lent it their countenance. To an increasing extent Mrs. Masham, a distant relative of the Harleys, took the place of the duchess in the royal favour, thus rousing Lady Marlborough to a pitch of uncontrolled jealousy which still further alienated the queen. More ominous for the future was the slow growth of a popular suspicion, inspired largely by war weariness, that the war was not really a national but merely a Whig war, designed to serve the interests of one party, and to keep one small group of men, if not indeed one man, in the position of power to which they had attained. As early as May 1709 Marlborough was contemplating a request that his post of captain-general should be granted to him for life; and in the autumn of the same year he greatly impaired his reputation throughout the country by making an insistent, though unsuccessful, demand to that effect. The charge made against him, that he was seeking to become another Cromwell, was without real justification, but it was none the less damaging on that account.

The crisis of affairs was reached in the early months of 1709, when the French, weakened by repeated defeats, and reduced to the lowest depths of economic distress by a winter of unprecedented severity, showed themselves willing to accept almost any terms of peace. Britain and her allies, however, insisted that Philip V must be required to surrender the throne of Spain to Charles III, and as they had been unable to compel him to do so themselves virtually demanded that Louis XIV should perform the task for them. This was as much beyond Louis's power as it was beyond theirs, and no course therefore remained open to the French monarch but to issue a despairing appeal for support to his own people and to continue the war. The result was the gradual development of a conviction in England that however necessary Marlborough and the Whigs might be for the prosecution of the war they were a grave obstacle to the conclusion of a peace, and would have to be removed.

Two events abroad helped to increase the general dissatisfaction. One was Marlborough's success in the autumn of 1709 at Malplaquet, the most costly of all his victories, which demonstrated the power of resistance still possessed by France, and the serious nature of the burden assumed by the allies in refusing to come to terms with her ruler. The other was the death of the Emperor Joseph in the spring of 1711, followed by the recognition of Charles III as ruler of all the Austrian dominions, which made him as great a danger on the throne of Spain as ever Philip V was likely to be. But the dominant feature in the situation was a comparatively insignificant development at home, the ill-advised impeachment of Dr. Henry Sacheverell for his ostentatiously public criticism of the Revolution and the whole ensuing settlement. Although he had achieved notoriety as an advocate of High Church doctrines long before 1709, Sacheverell had not the capacity to be the real leader of any party; but for the position of figurehead of a movement inspired from other sources and manipulated by abler men he had every necessary qualification. Before his trial had even begun the mere mention of his name was enough to rouse the wildest enthusiasm, under cover of which Harley and all who were discontented with the Whig supremacy could unite to carry through the changes in leadership and policy which they had at heart.

The main difficulty lay in bringing about the necessary transformation without prematurely alienating Britain's allies abroad or shattering public confidence at home. To that end Harley, Henry St. John and their associates made the most of the personal rivalries and jealousies which separated the Whigs from each other and from Marlborough and Godolphin, encouraging the queen to dismiss them one by one; while at the same time they entered into secret negotiations with France for a peace, and yet professed to the allies their readiness to continue the war. The objects of their policy were not unsound. The Whig ministry had long outstayed its welcome, and its gradual dissolution during the summer of 1710 was ratified by the return of a strongly Tory Parliament in the autumn of the same year. Peace was undoubtedly overdue, and the terms eventually laid down, though specially favourable to Britain, were not in general unreasonable, leaving France free to develop along her own lines without being able any longer to threaten the liberties of Europe. The methods employed, on the other hand, were discreditable in the extreme. At home they involved a campaign of the vilest calumny against Marlborough, whose hold over the affections of his soldiers was not reflected in any similar hold over the affections of the civil population, and who could do little to defend himself. Abroad they involved the maintenance of an army in the field under secret orders not to fight, and the base betrayal not merely of the interests but even of the military plans of Dutch, Hanoverians, Catalans and other allies.

In political circles the settlement left much bitterness behind; but elsewhere it was welcomed with almost unmixed relief. The ferocity of party warfare under Anne is apt to convey an entirely wrong impression of the general situation. Except in moments of crisis such as the Sacheverell trial the ordinary citizen was little affected. By the close of William's reign the main problems of English domestic politics had been virtually solved, and Marlborough's victories on the Continent ensured that the decisions reached should not be subject to any interference from without. As a result the country under Anne was at last settling down on a basis which all, or nearly all, could accept. It is significant that little remedial legislation was passed, or even advocated, during the entire reign, and much of that little proved ephemeral. Even the outstanding controversies of the moment were losing their appeal. Few but the most bigoted any longer believed that the Church was in danger, except from its own intemperate supporters. Still fewer believed that the Protestant succession was in danger, except from the extravagances of the political parties, who in their fury against each other seemed capable of anything. But party cries which had so long served their purpose were not lightly to be abandoned, and the parties thus became committed to maintaining a conflict which at bottom was largely fictitious. The situation had indeed greatly changed since the days of Charles and James. Far from genuine hopes and fears inspiring the parties it was now the parties that inspired the hopes and fears.

Nevertheless the position was one of grave danger, for the extremists on both sides had gone too far to draw back. Especially the Tories by their trafficking with France and their conduct of the peace negotiations had compromised themselves so seriously with the elector of Hanover, the Protestant heir and one of the stoutest supporters of the war, that they were almost compelled in self-defence to become Jacobites. Had the Pretender shown any disposition to temporize concerning his religion in a way which would have removed the apprehensions of sound Churchmen, he might have secured a considerable measure of support; but to his credit he refused to do so, and thus left the extreme Tories unwilling to advocate his claims, and yet hopelessly divided between those who despaired of coming to terms with Hanover and those who believed that a reconciliation was at least possible.

Of the latter group the leader was still Harley, now earl of Oxford, who hoped, by means of the tortuous diplomacy in which he so frequently lost his way, to combine the more reasonable among the extreme Tories with the moderates who were his natural supporters, and obtain a settlement of the succession problem which would guarantee satisfactory terms for all. Of the former group the leader was St. John, now Viscount Bolingbroke, alienated from Oxford by the indeterminate policy which his colleague was pursuing, and resolved on something more decisive. Both were in communication with the Pretender, but Oxford with a view to insuring against all possible eventualities, Bolingbroke in a vain effort to find some solution of the religious problem which would enable him to place the Pretender on the throne.

In the closing stages of Anne's reign, indeed, the bad leadership which had been one of the features of the whole period of the later Stuarts reached the very lowest depths. The Whigs had shown real capacity for conducting the war, but none for concluding a peace. The Tories had reversed the process, concluding by dubious methods a not unsatisfactory peace while grossly mismanaging the war. Now the ineffectiveness of those who had long held the balance was to become apparent. Anne herself, prematurely old, in failing health and bewildered by the complexities of a situation which might well have puzzled a stronger brain than hers, had developed into a mere bundle of negations. She would not settle the succession problem one way by allowing any member of the House of Hanover to come to England so long as she was alive, nor would she settle it the other way by showing any countenance to the Pretender so long as he remained a Catholic; she would not support Oxford any longer, and yet she could not trust Bolingbroke. Oxford, also in poor health, was finding his natural irresolution and confusion of mind developing like a creeping paralysis, and was indulging too freely in drink. Bolingbroke, as energetic as ever but without any real plan of operations, was endeavouring to find relief in yet more violent activity, leading he knew not whither.

Out of such a situation any result might have emerged. The Tories were in undisputed control, but they were so uncertain as to the best policy to pursue, and so divided by personal animosities among themselves, that they were scarcely in a position to take any decisive action either collectively or singly. On 27 July, Bolingbroke at length induced the queen to dismiss Oxford, and began to fill the ministry with his own creatures, with a view to getting affairs entirely into his own hands. On 1 August, Queen Anne, who had been badly shaken by the final dissensions among her ministers, performed her last service for her country by dying, like William III, at the most opportune moment. Bolingbroke was quite unprepared, and knew neither what to do nor how to do it. The Whigs and the Hanoverian Tories, on the other hand, were fully determined to enforce the law of the succession as it stood, and had nothing to fear from Harley and his following, who were willing to co-operate with them. Almost without challenge, in consequence, and with general, if not very enthusiastic, approval throughout the country, George I was accepted as king, and England, after its half-century of turmoil, passed on into the comparative quietude of the early Hanoverian period.

BIBLIOGRAPHY

The standard guide to the authorities is the *Bibliography of British History, Stuart Period, 1603–1714*, edited by Godfrey Davies, and issued under the direction of the Royal Historical Society and the American Historical Association (Oxford, 1928); but this has already in some measure been superseded by Clyde Leclare Grose, *A Select Bibliography of British History, 1660–1760* (Chicago, 1939), which has in turn been amplified and brought up to date by the same writer's "Studies of 1931–40 on British History 1660–1760", in *Journal of Modern History*, XII (1940), pp. 515–534. For the closing years of the period exceptionally full guidance is provided by William Thomas Morgan and Chloe Siner Morgan, *A Bibliography of British History, 1700–1715, with Special Reference to the Reign of Queen Anne* (5 vols., Bloomington, 1934–1942). Most useful as a short introduction to the authorities is E. R. Adair, *The Sources for the History of the Council in the Sixteenth and Seventeenth Centuries* (London, 1924), one of the many valuable volumes in the "Helps for Students of History" series, much wider in its scope than its title might suggest. Of guides to the most recent publications *Writings on British History*, compiled by Alexander Taylor Milne for the Royal Historical Society, is the most complete; but the six volumes which have appeared (London, 1937–1952) deal only with the publications of the six years 1934–1939. Until the series can be brought up to date, therefore, recourse must be had to the *Annual Bulletin of Historical Literature*, published by the Historical Association, and to the lists of articles printed each year in the July number of *The English Historical Review*.

The State Papers preserved in the Public Record Office are extremely valuable, and have not received nearly as much attention as they deserve, especially in view of the extent to which they have been printed, summarized, or otherwise made readily available to historians. With the exception of two short intervals, from 1685 to 1689 and from 1704 to 1714, the *Calendar of State Papers Domestic* is complete for the later Stuart period (41 vols., 1860–1947); and for the greater part of the reign of Charles II, as well as for much of the reign of William III, it has been particularly fully and ably edited. The State Papers Foreign have not been calendared at all; but considerable selections from them have been printed by unofficial agencies or by individual historians, and are mentioned later in their appropriate place (pp. 847–848). Of the records of the Privy Council only those concerned with its colonial activities have been printed, and these are accordingly referred to in the sections on 'The Monarchy' (p. 52) and 'Plantations' (p. 530), as are the Treasury Papers and Treasury Books in the section on 'Public Finance' (p. 277).

Almost as important as the State Papers are the dispatches of the ambassadors and other representatives whom nearly every Court in Europe found it advisable at this time to maintain in England, and whose main function it was to keep their superiors at home in touch with developments there. Extensive selections from the dispatches of the French representatives are to be found in J. J. Jusserand, *A French Ambassador at the Court of Charles the Second* (London, 1892); Sir John Dalrymple, *Memoirs of Great Britain and Ireland* (3 vols., Edinburgh, 1771–1788); Marquise Campana de Cavelli, *Les derniers Stuarts à Saint-Germain en Laye* (2 vols., Paris, 1871); François A. M. A. Mignet, *Négociations relatives à la Succession d'Espagne sous Louis XIV* (4 vols., Paris, 1835–1842); Charles James Fox, *A History of the Early Part of the Reign of James the Second* (London, 1808); and *Letters of William III and Louis XIV and of their Ministers*, edited by Paul Grimblot (2 vols., London, 1848). Dispatches from representatives of several Italian states are included in the *Calendar of State Papers and Manuscripts relating to English Affairs existing in the*

Archives and Collections of Venice and in other Libraries of Northern Italy, edited by Allen B. Hinds, which has been carried as far as 1675 (vols. XXXII–XXXVIII, 1931–1947). Others are printed, along with a selection from the dispatches of the Austrian representative, in Campana de Cavelli, *Les derniers Stuarts*. Among German states Brandenburg was specially interested in English affairs, and two most important collections of dispatches from its representatives are printed in *Briefe aus England über die Zeit von 1674 bis 1678 in Gesandtschafts-Berichten des Ministers Otto von Schwerin*, edited by Leopold von Orlich (Berlin, 1837); and in Leopold von Ranke, *A History of England principally in the Seventeenth Century* (6 vols., Oxford, 1675), VI, pp. 144–274. Denmark also was interested, and the dispatches of one of its representatives are printed in *The First Triple Alliance: the Letters of Christopher Lindenov, Danish Envoy to London, 1668–1672*, translated and edited by Waldemar Westergaard (New Haven, 1947).

General collections of correspondence are numerous and valuable. Sir John Dalrymple's *Memoirs*, already referred to (p. 39), contains an immense accumulation of the most varied character, to which a useful guide and index is provided by Michael Jolliffe, "The Documents in Dalrymple's *Memoirs of Great Britain and Ireland*", in *Bulletin of the Institute of Historical Research*, XX (1946), pp. 119–130. Scarcely less important are *State Papers and Correspondence illustrative of the Social and Political State of Europe from the Revolution to the Accession of the House of Hanover*, edited by John M. Kemble (London, 1857), which throws light on developments at home as well as abroad; *Miscellaneous State Papers from 1501 to 1726*, edited by Philip Yorke, earl of Hardwicke, vol. II (London, 1778), which is of value mainly for the reigns of William and Anne; and *Original Papers containing the Secret History of Great Britain from the Restoration to the Accession of the House of Hanover*, edited by James Macpherson (2 vols., London, 1775). Much criticism has been directed against the last of these collections, and the documents in it should be used with some caution. The chief articles dealing with the subject are J. F. Chance, "Corrections to James Macpherson's *Original Papers*", in *English Historical Review*, XIII (1898), pp. 533–549; Arthur Parnell, "James Macpherson and the Nairne Papers", *ibid.*, XII (1897), pp. 254–284; Godfrey Davies, "Macpherson and the Nairne Papers", *ibid.*, XXXV (1920), pp. 367–376; and the appendix, "On the Autobiographical Memoirs of King James II of England", in Ranke's *History of England*, VI, pp. 29–45.

Among the publications of the Historical Manuscripts Commission the most valuable are *Calendar of the Manuscripts of the Marquess of Ormonde, New Series*, vols. III–VIII (1904–1920), especially vol. IV, which includes "Letters of Sir Robert Southwell to James, first duke of Ormond, 1677–1686", keeping Ormonde informed, during his absence in Ireland, of the course of events in England; *The Manuscripts of the Duke of Portland*, vols. II–X (1893–1931), which are concerned mainly with the fortunes of the Harley family; "The Manuscripts of the Earl of Lindsey", in *Fourteenth Report, Appendix*, IX (1895), pp. 367–457, and *Supplementary Report on the Manuscripts of the late Earl of Lindsey, 1660–1702* (1942), both dealing with a section of the papers of the earl of Danby; *The Manuscripts of the Earl of Dartmouth*, vols. I and III (1887 and 1896), containing a large number of letters written by the duke of York when in exile under Charles II, as well as material for the history of the Revolution and of Tangier; *Report on the Manuscripts of the late Reginald Rawdon Hastings*, vol. II (1930); *The Manuscripts of the Duke of Rutland*, vol. II (1889); *The Manuscripts of Lord Kenyon* (1894), relating chiefly to Lancashire; *The Manuscripts of F. J. Savile Foljambe* (1897), containing a further collection of the letters of James II; and *The Manuscripts of Sir William Fitzherbert* (1893), consisting largely of papers connected with the Popish Plot.

The Camden Society, now amalgamated with the Royal Historical Society, has published *Savile Correspondence*, edited by William Durrant Cooper (1858), a series of letters to and from Henry Savile, younger brother of the marquis of Halifax, between the years 1661 and 1687;

Letters of Humphrey Prideaux to John Ellis, 1674–1722, edited by Edward Maunde Thompson (1875), of value mainly for the picture it draws of Oxford life, and later of local conditions in Norfolk; and *Correspondence of the Family of Hatton, 1601–1704*, by the same editor (2 vols., 1878), a particularly varied collection belonging almost entirely to the later Stuart period. Other collections are *The Ellis Correspondence*, edited by George Agar Ellis (2 vols., London, 1829), a miscellaneous selection from the letters addressed during the years 1686–1688 to the same John Ellis as corresponded with Humphrey Prideaux; *Letters of Rachel, Lady Russell*, edited by Lord John Russell (2 vols., London, 1853); *Letters of Philip, second Earl of Chesterfield* (London, 1835), containing both Chesterfield's own letters and many of the replies; and *The Wentworth Papers, 1705–39*, edited by James J. Cartwright (London, 1883).

Owing to the strict censorship of the Press maintained in accordance with the Licensing Act of 1662 the newspapers of the later Stuart period are singularly uninformative. At the time of the Restoration and during the Popish Plot scare, when restrictions were in abeyance, many ephemeral publications sprang into existence, and after 1695, when the Licensing Act expired, more reputable journals began to be established both in London and in the provinces. The first daily newspaper, *The Daily Courant*, came into existence in March 1702, and the reign of Anne was marked by a great development of the periodical Press. But throughout the greater part of the later Stuart period the only newspaper in existence was *The London Gazette*, established in November 1665 as *The Oxford Gazette* and renamed in February 1666, which gave a purely official version of events at home and abroad. Much more valuable to the historian than the newspapers, in consequence, are contemporary newsletters, which can be found scattered through almost all collections of correspondence, and of which several lengthy series have been published. Outstanding among these published collections are *The Manuscripts of S. H. le Fleming*, calendared under the direction of the Historical Manuscripts Commission (London, 1890), which covers roughly the years 1660–1701; *Catalogue of the Collection of Autograph Letters and Historical Documents formed by Alfred Morrison: Second Series: the Bulstrode Papers, 1667–75* (1897), consisting of letters written to Sir Richard Bulstrode while resident at Brussels; *Letters addressed from London to Sir Joseph Williamson while Plenipotentiary at the Congress of Cologne in the years 1673 and 1674*, edited by W. D. Christie for the Camden Society (2 vols., 1874), which should be read in conjunction with other letters of the same series printed in the *Calendar of State Papers Domestic*, and the corrections to the earlier selection there indicated; and *The Portledge Papers*, edited by Russell J. Kerr and Ida Coffin Duncan (London, 1928), a series covering the years 1687–1697.

The pamphlet literature of the period is extensive, and often of great value to the historian. Much of the best of it has been gathered together in general collections, whether contemporary, as *State Tracts, being a Collection of several Treatises relating to the Government*, privately printed in the Reign of Charles II (London, 1689), *State Tracts, being a further Collection of several choice Treatises relating to the Government from the year 1660 to 1689* (London, 1692), *A Collection of Papers relating to the present Juncture of Affairs in England* (12 parts, London, 1688–1689), and *A Collection of State Tracts published on Occasion of the late Revolution in 1688 and during the Reign of King William III* (3 vols., London, 1705–1707); or put together at a later date, as *The Harleian Miscellany or a Collection of scarce, curious and entertaining Pamphlets and Tracts found in the late Earl of Oxford's Library* (8 vols., London, 1744–1746; 12 vols., London, 1808–1811; 10 vols., London, 1808–1813), *Collection of scarce and valuable Tracts selected from public as well as private Libraries, particularly that of the late Lord Somers* (16 vols., London, 1748–1752; 13 vols., London, 1809–1815), *Stuart Tracts, 1603–1693*, edited by C. H. Firth (Westminster, 1903), and *Later Stuart Tracts*, edited by George A. Aitken (Westminster, 1903). The pamphlets of some of the more prolific writers have also been gathered together, those of the marquis of Halifax in H. C. Foxcroft,

The Life and Letters of Sir George Savile, first Marquis of Halifax (2 vols., London, 1898), and in *The Complete Works of George Savile, first Marquess of Halifax*, edited by Walter Raleigh (Oxford, 1912); those of Sir William Temple in *The Works of Sir William Temple*, edited by Jonathan Swift (2 vols., London, 1720); those of Swift himself in *The Prose Works of Jonathan Swift*, edited by Temple Scott (12 vols., London, 1897–1908); and those of Defoe in *A True Collection of the Writings of the Author of the True Born Englishman* (2 vols., London, 1703–1705; 20 vols., Oxford, 1840).

Ballads and satires are also of considerable value. The most useful general collections are *Poems on Affairs of State* (5th edition, 4 vols., London, 1703–1707); *Political Ballads of the Seventeenth and Eighteenth Centuries*, edited by W. Walker Wilkins (2 vols., London, 1860); *The Roxburghe Ballads*, edited by W. Chappell and J. W. Ebsworth (9 vols., Hertford, 1871–1897); *The Bagford Ballads, illustrating the Last Years of the Stuarts*, edited by J. W. Ebsworth (2 vols., Hertford, 1878); *Naval Songs and Ballads*, edited by C. H. Firth for the Navy Records Society (1908); *Broadside Ballads of the Restoration Period*, edited by F. Burlington Fawcett (London, 1930); and *The Pepys Ballads*, edited by Hyder Edward Rollins (8 vols., Cambridge, Mass., 1929–1932). Among satirists Marvell and Dryden stand supreme. Their works should be studied in *The Poems and Letters of Andrew Marvell*, edited by H. M. Margoliouth, vol. I, *Poems* (Oxford, 1927), and in *The Poetical Works of John Dryden*, edited by W. D. Christie (London, 1904).

An immense amount of information of the most miscellaneous character is contained in *Angliae Notitia, or the Present State of England*, first produced by Edward Chamberlayne in 1669, and continued after his death by his son John. Although not appearing regularly each year this was substantially an annual publication, comparable in character to a modern almanac or year-book. After 1707 its title was changed to *Magnae Britanniae Notitia*, and it became increasingly subject to competition from a rival publication, which, beginning in 1691 as *The New State of England*, by Guy Miege, changed its title in 1707 to *The Present State of Great Britain*, and in 1711 to *The Present State of Great Britain and Ireland*. A useful index to the earlier series is provided by Muriel M. S. Arnett, "List of Office-Holders in *Angliae Notitia*", in *Bulletin of the Institute of Historical Research*, xv (1937), pp. 24–30; and a similar index to the later series by Michael Jolliffe, "List of Office-Holders in Guy Miege's *New State of England* and *Present State of Great Britain*", ibid., xvii (1940), pp. 130–138.

It is one of the attractions of later Stuart times that some of the best contemporary histories, memoirs and diaries have become literary classics, and are both easy to procure and entertaining to read. Outstanding among these is Gilbert Burnet, *History of My Own Time*, which covers practically the whole period, and is indispensable for an understanding of it. The best edition is that by Osmund Airy, but only two volumes of this, carrying the narrative as far as 1685, have been published (Oxford, 1897 and 1900). The best complete edition is that by M. J. Routh (6 vols., Oxford, 1833). The surviving fragments of Burnet's earlier memoirs, on which his *History* was based, are printed, together with other valuable material, in H. C. Foxcroft, *A Supplement to Burnet's History of My Own Time* (Oxford, 1902). Burnet's account has been criticized, as incomplete, inaccurate and prejudiced, in T. Salmon, *An Impartial Examination of Bishop Burnet's History of his Own Times* (2 vols., London, 1724); in B. Higgons, *Historical and Critical Remarks on Bishop Burnet's History of his Own Time* (London, 1725); and in the writings of more modern historians. Much of the criticism is well founded, for Burnet was seldom as fully informed as he supposed, always wrote in haste, and was incurably careless. But his ideals at least were high, his pursuit of them earnest, and, in spite of many failures, his success in achieving them not inconsiderable. The best assessments of the value of his work are by Leopold von Ranke in his *History of England*, vi, pp. 45–87, and by C. H. Firth in his essay on "Burnet as a Historian", printed originally as an introduction to T. E. S. Clarke and H. C. Foxcroft,

A Life of Gilbert Burnet, Bishop of Salisbury (Cambridge, 1907), and reprinted in Sir Charles Firth, *Essays Historical and Literary* (Oxford, 1938), pp. 174–209.

Among memoirs and diaries three are of special importance, both in themselves and as supplementing each other to a remarkable degree. Easily the most famous of these, the *Diary of Samuel Pepys*, covers only the years 1660–1669, and is the work of a laborious civil servant who wrote chiefly for his own gratification. Its value lies in the light it throws on the Court, on the administration of the navy, on life in London and its neighbourhood, and on the character and mentality of Pepys himself. It has passed through many editions, the best and most complete of which, by Henry B. Wheatley (10 vols., London, 1893–1899), is now to be superseded by one still more exact. Somewhat wider in its appeal is the *Diary of John Evelyn*, for Evelyn was a cultured gentleman and a man of leisure, who continued to record his thoughts and experiences from before the Restoration till shortly before his death in 1706, and was as much at home in the world of science and art as in that of politics. It also has appeared in many editions; but even the two best, by Henry B. Wheatley (4 vols., London, 1879), and by Austin Dobson (3 vols., London, 1906), are incomplete and unsatisfactory, and a new edition is in course of preparation. Very different from both of these is the *Memoirs of Sir John Reresby*, which nominally covers the period from the Restoration to 1689, but is reasonably full only from about 1678 onwards. Reresby was a country squire, who wrote for the edification of his descendants, and was interested mainly in the army and in local Yorkshire politics. The only complete edition of his *Memoirs* is that by Andrew Browning (Glasgow, 1936).

Burnet's great predecessor as a historian of his own time, the earl of Clarendon, belongs to the early rather than to the later Stuart period, but *The Life of Edward, Earl of Clarendon, being a Continuation of the History of the Great Rebellion from the Restoration to his Banishment in 1667* (2 vols., Oxford, 1857), is of the first importance for the opening years of the reign of Charles II. Much information about the central core of the same reign may be found in the surviving fragments of Sir William Temple's memoirs, printed in *The Works of Sir William Temple*, edited by Jonathan Swift (2 vols., London, 1720); and in *Diary of the Times of Charles the Second*, by Henry Sidney, edited with illustrative letters by R. W. Blencowe (2 vols., London, 1843). The reaction which marked the closing years of Charles and the reign of James is illustrated in *The Lives of the Norths*, by Roger North, edited by Augustus Jessopp (3 vols., London, 1890), consisting of Roger's own autobiography and his lives of his brothers, Francis, Dudley and John. *The Autobiography of Sir John Bramston*, edited by Lord Braybrooke for the Camden Society (1845), is of value primarily for the reign of James II and the Revolution, but continues as far as 1699. Important for the same period are *The Diary of Thomas Cartwright*, 1686–1687, edited by Joseph Hunter for the Camden Society (1843); and *The Correspondence of Henry Hyde, Earl of Clarendon, and of his Brother, Laurence Hyde, Earl of Rochester, with the Diary of Lord Clarendon from 1687 to 1690*, edited by Samuel Weller Singer (2 vols., London, 1828).

The *Memoirs of Thomas Bruce, Earl of Ailesbury*, edited by W. E. Buckley for the Roxburghe Club (2 vols., 1890), is a work of a most exasperating kind. Written in the extreme old age of its author, it owes almost as much to his imagination as to his memory, and yet in so far as it can be trusted is of real importance for the period 1678–1714. It should be used with the greatest caution, and only after reference to Lady Burghclere's criticisms in the *Quarterly Review*, CCIII (1905), pp. 548–571. Even more imaginative in character is the *Memoirs of Count Grammont*, by Count Anthony Hamilton, edited by Gordon Goodwin (2 vols., London, 1903), which provides a vivid picture of the English Court in the early years of Charles II's reign, but makes no pretence of factual accuracy.

In a category by itself stands *The Life of James the Second, collected out of Memoirs writ of his own Hand*, edited by J. S. Clarke (2 vols., London, 1816). The anonymous author or compiler of this tantalizing work has been identified as a certain William Dicconson, who had at his disposal James's own memoirs, letters and papers, and wrote about the year 1707. Unfortunately the original material which he was allowed to use was destroyed during the course of the French Revolution, and it is now a matter of guesswork how much of it was embodied in the *Life* he wrote. In so far as the *Life* is based on James's papers it is of the first importance; in so far as it is derived from Dicconson alone it is of little or none; and there is no reliable test by means of which the gold can be distinguished from the dross. With the *Life* should be compared the extracts from James's memoirs printed in Macpherson's *Original Papers*, already mentioned (p. 40).

Other contemporary or semi-contemporary narratives are more impersonal and pedestrian in character. Narcissus Luttrell, *A Brief Historical Relation of State Affairs from September 1678 to April 1714* (6 vols., Oxford, 1857), is based mainly on newspapers and newsletters, and though not always accurate is of value for establishing events and dates. Somewhat similar in character, though connected with Oxford rather than with London, is *The Life and Times of Anthony Wood, 1632–1695, described by Himself,* collected from his diaries and other papers by Andrew Clark (5 vols., Oxford, 1891–1900). *The History of England, by Mr. Rapin de Thoyras*, continued from the Revolution to the Accession of King George II by N. Tindal (5 vols., London, 1743–1745), is based on much research, and is specially valuable for the Revolution, in which Rapin, a Huguenot exile from France, himself took part. The third volume of *A Complete History of England from the Earliest Time to the Death of King William III* (London, 1706; enlarged edition 1719) was bitterly denounced by the Tories during the lifetime of its author, White Kennett; but in spite of pronounced Whig views it is a work of considerable merit. A. Boyer, *The History of the Reign of Queen Anne digested into Annals* (11 vols., London, 1703–1713), is to a large extent the basis of the same writer's *History of the Life and Reign of Queen Anne* (London, 1722). Although marked by a strong Whig bias, both are valuable compilations, specially useful for the history of Parliament. An illuminating survey of other histories written in the early eighteenth century is provided by C. H. Firth, "The Development of the Study of Seventeenth-Century History", in *Transactions of the Royal Historical Society, Third Series*, VII (1913), pp. 25–48.

Nothing has yet been done to deprive T. B. Macaulay, *The History of England from the Accession of James II*, of the position it has enjoyed for a century as the classic general history of the period. Its failings in the shape of partisanship, over-emphasis, and neglect of certain aspects of history, are sufficiently obvious, and have been unsparingly indicated by the small men who love to disparage the great; but its striking merits, historical no less than literary, bid fair to rank it among the immortals. Many excellent editions are available, the best being that by Charles Harding Firth, in six volumes with nearly a thousand carefully selected illustrations (London, 1913–1915). There are some useful notes in T. F. Henderson's edition (5 vols., Oxford, 1931), and much valuable criticism and appreciation in Sir Charles Firth, *A Commentary on Macaulay's History of England* (London, 1938). Macaulay's second chapter, on England from 1660 to 1685, is little more than a sketch; but the gap thus left at the beginning of his narrative has been filled by David Ogg, *England in the Reign of Charles II* (2 vols., Oxford, 1934). Macaulay's death occurred before he had carried his published work beyond 1697, and the chapters formed out of the material he left behind continue, in somewhat fragmentary fashion, only as far as 1702; but the gap thus created at the end has been similarly filled by George Macaulay Trevelyan, *England under Queen Anne* (3 vols., London, 1930–1934). These three writers together provide a consecutive and large-scale survey of the affairs of England, Scotland and Ireland for the whole of the later Stuart period.

The elucidation of that period also owes much to foreign scholars. Ranke's *History of*

England is primarily of use for foreign affairs, but also gives an unbiased survey of the activities of parties, and contains a large number of valuable documents. Onno Klopp, *Der Fall des Hauses Stuart und die Succession des Hauses Hannover, 1660–1714* (14 vols., Vienna, 1875–1888), is based mainly on the Austrian dispatches, as François A. J. Mazure, *Histoire de la Révolution de 1688 en Angleterre* (3 vols., Paris, 1825), is on the French dispatches. Wolfgang Michael, *England under George I: the Beginnings of the Hanoverian Dynasty* (London, 1936), has some valuable introductory chapters on the reign of Queen Anne.

Other works dealing with only part of the period are John Lingard, *A History of England to 1688* (10 vols., London, 1849–1851), which presents the moderate English Catholic point of view; Sir James Mackintosh, *History of the Revolution in England in 1688* (London, 1834), the documents collected for which, partly printed in the appendix and all now preserved in the British Museum, were extensively used by Macaulay; and Earl Stanhope, *History of England, comprising the Reign of Queen Anne until the Peace of Utrecht, 1701–1713* (London, 1870), written to fill in the gap between the close of Macaulay's *History* and the beginning of Stanhope's own work on the eighteenth century. John Pollock, *The Popish Plot* (London, 1903), covers a very restricted field, but one full of controversies and unsolved problems. The same period is tackled from a slightly different angle in Francis S. Ronalds, *The Attempted Whig Revolution of 1678–1681* (Urbana, Ill., 1937).

Of single-volume histories the most recent, and in many ways the best, is G. N. Clark, *The Later Stuarts, 1660–1714* (Oxford, 1934), which, however, suffers somewhat from trying to cover too many different aspects of history in too few pages. For a fuller account of political events recourse should be had to the relevant volumes of *The Political History of England*, edited by W. Hunt and R. L. Poole, vol. VII, 1660–1702, by Richard Lodge (London, 1910), being particularly clear and well balanced, and more impartial than vol. VIII, 1702–1760, by I. S. Leadam (London, 1909). George Macaulay Trevelyan, *England under the Stuarts* (London, 1904), is a brilliant but too brief sketch. The essays in *The Cambridge Modern History*, vol. v, *The Age of Louis XIV* (Cambridge, 1908), are uneven, though some are of the highest value.

Genealogical tables of the royal family and of many of the leading houses in Britain are to be found in H. B. George, *Genealogical Tables illustrative of Modern History*, edited by J. R. H. Weaver (1930), and in *The Cambridge Modern History*, vol. XIII (1911); lists of bishops and officers of state in *Handbook of British Chronology*, edited by F. M. Powicke for the Royal Historical Society (London, 1939), and in *A Political Index to the Histories of Great Britain and Ireland*, by Robert Beatson (3rd edition, 3 vols., London, 1806); useful maps in *The Cambridge Modern History Atlas* (1912), R. L. Poole, *Historical Atlas of Modern Europe* (Oxford, 1896–1902), Ramsay Muir and George Philip, *Philips' Atlas of Ancient, Mediaeval and Modern History* (London, 1938), and William R. Shepherd, *Historical Atlas* (New York, 1929). The best single map illustrating the Stuart period is *A Map of Seventeenth-Century England, with Description, Chronological Tables, and a Map of London circa 1660*, published by the Ordnance Survey Office (Southampton, 1930).

Part I
THE MONARCHY

THE MONARCHY

Introduction

THE Restoration of 1660 was, in appearance at least, primarily a restoration of the monarchy. Not merely was Charles II invited back to the throne of his ancestors, but he was permitted to ascend that throne without having subscribed to any conditions or given any guarantees beyond the vague and conditional promises embodied in the declaration he had voluntarily issued from Breda.[1] The proclamation in which Parliament announced the kingdom's acknowledgement of his title recognized that he had legally been king since the death of his father;[2] and his actual landing at Dover on 25 May was the signal for a tremendous outburst of popular enthusiasm, which continued to manifest itself throughout his leisurely progress towards London, and culminated, after his entry into the city on 29 May, his thirtieth birthday,[3] in an Act of Parliament making that day a day of thanksgiving for ever.[4] The non-monarchical governments of the preceding eleven years and the more prominent among their supporters became the object of widespread execration, which was not restrained even by a decent reverence for the dead.[5]

Nevertheless the restored monarchy was far from being the monarchy of Elizabeth, James I or Charles I. Nothing could erase from men's minds the recollection that a king had been executed because a considerable section of his subjects disapproved of his proceedings, and that the country had conducted its affairs fairly successfully for eleven years thereafter without a king at all. It is true that the monarch now had a basis of political theory on which to found his claims, for the divine right doctrines which had appealed only to a small circle of extremists under the early Stuarts had come, in the prevailing wave of reaction against the ideas of the Commonwealth, to be more widely accepted. The revival of the practice of touching for the king's evil was symptomatic of a real change in popular feeling.[6] Considerable influence was already being exercised by the theories of Sir Robert Filmer, whose greatest work, *Patriarcha, or the Natural Power of Kings asserted against the Unnatural Liberty of the People*, written before 1642 though published posthumously in 1680, was soon to be recognized as embodying the orthodox creed of the absolutists.[7] But the average Englishman who professed a belief in that creed was more inclined to regard it as a weapon with which to confound his adversaries than as a faith by which to guide his own conduct, and in time of trial was apt to have his outlook determined by traditional ideas which were little favourable to absolutism.

Thus the Restoration was not marked by any serious attempt to re-establish the royal authority as it had been before the outbreak of the controversies leading to the civil wars. As a matter of course it was assumed that all legislation since the separation of king and Parliament early in 1642 was invalid, and the Acts and Ordinances not only of the Commonwealth Parliaments but also of the later sessions of the Long Parliament were thus swept away. But the earlier legislation of the Long Parliament,

[1] No. 1. [2] No. 2. [3] No. 3. [4] No. 4.
[5] No. 5. [6] No. 9. [7] No. 10.

to which Charles I, under whatever pressure, had given his assent, and which had done so much to reduce his power, was in substance retained; and not merely individual restrictions but also the principle of restriction itself were thus made permanent. Four important statutes were passed, imposing heavy penalties on all who traduced the king or publicly maintained doctrines subversive of the restored order,[1] defining the right to petition in such a way as to prevent it from being used to exert undue influence over the government,[2] formally recognizing the king as the sole head of the armed forces of the nation,[3] and providing machinery to enable him to exercise his undoubted prerogative of controlling the Press.[4] But beyond that Parliament was not prepared to go until the rise of the Jacobite danger after the Revolution made it fearful for the safety of William III.[5]

In substance this meant that any power of legislating or levying taxation which the king had previously enjoyed was permanently denied him; and under these conditions the control of the executive which he admittedly possessed was bound to prove largely illusory. Imposing lists could easily be drawn up of the powers which he still could exercise;[6] but the mere fact that it was considered worth while to draw up such lists shows that the royal prerogative was definitely on the defensive. Far from being able to increase his authority the king was hard put to it to retain what power he had, and in his efforts to do so was reduced to a policy of obstruction and evasion which contrasts strangely with the more forthright methods of the early Stuarts. By using his dispensing or suspending power as extensively as possible he could in effect nullify any legislation which he found obnoxious. By exercising his control over the judges, and through them over juries, he could, within limits, obtain whatever interpretation of the law and whatever verdicts he desired. By employing various devices against the use of which provision had not yet been made he could on occasion imprison at pleasure, and so bring pressure to bear on individuals.

All these methods of maintaining the royal authority were regarded with great disfavour in the country, but it was over the extended use of the first of them that the chief conflict between king and Parliament took place. Charles II had recourse to the dispensing and suspending powers mainly in ecclesiastical affairs, where he considered that his position as supreme governor of the Church gave him special claims; but his attempt in 1662 to secure parliamentary recognition for his right to grant exemption from the Act of Uniformity[7] had to be quietly abandoned, and ten years later his much more determined effort to establish toleration on his own authority[8] met with such opposition in Parliament that he found it necessary to make a formal withdrawal.[9] James, on the other hand, boldly laid claim to the dispensing power in all spheres, and when Parliament remonstrated[10] secured an emphatic decision in his favour from the law courts;[11] but his declarations of indulgence,[12] although received with much ostensible and some real gratitude,[13] inspired also the strongest opposition, which was greatly increased when he sought to make the Church a party to its own destruction by requiring the clergy to read the declaration publicly from the pulpit.[14] Seven bishops signed a petition against the duty thus imposed on them;[15] and the prosecution of these men for seditious libel so far united the nation in their support that the judges hesitated to declare the petition a libel,[16] and the jury returned a verdict of not guilty.

[1] No. 6. [2] No. 7. [3] No. 302. [4] No. 8.
[5] No. 12. [6] No. 11. [7] Nos. 135, 137. [8] No. 140.
[9] No. 13. [10] No. 14. [11] No. 15. [12] Nos. 146, 149.
[13] Nos. 147, 148. [14] No. 16. [15] No. 17. [16] No. 18.

Little more than a year later the dispensing and suspending powers were both declared illegal by the Bill of Rights.[1]

To the practice of bringing pressure to bear on juries Parliament took exception at a very early stage,[2] and shortly afterwards the case of Edward Bushell[3] gave rise to a famous judgment in which the practice was explicitly condemned.[4] Not until 1696, however, did a long-overdue Act reforming the procedure in treason trials deprive the king of his right to nominate the jury before whom a peer could be tried when Parliament was not sitting,[5] and not until the passing of the Act of Settlement was the independence of the judges fully established.[6]

Even more troublesome was the royal power of imprisoning, for in the midst of the recurring crises which marked the later Stuart period it was felt that this power should not too readily be restricted. At the height of the Popish Plot frenzy the famous Habeas Corpus Act was forced through Parliament, improving the machinery for preventing illegal detention;[7] but even this was accomplished only by a trick,[8] and although most strenuous methods were at times adopted for enforcing the Act,[9] it had to be temporarily suspended on several occasions during the reign of William III.[10]

So long, however, as the course pursued by the later Stuarts was kept within the bounds of reason, the horror inspired by the fate of Charles I ensured that they personally should not be called to account, and their problem, if they sought to evade control, became therefore one of protecting their agents. For this purpose secrecy seemed the best method. The regular channel through which the royal authority was supposed to be exercised was still the Privy Council; but the decay of that body had been rendered inevitable when the need for conciliating all shades of opinion at the Restoration had led to the admission to it of so many members as to make it quite unwieldy.[11] All the later Stuarts had to work through committees of the Privy Council, and found in this fact an excellent excuse for entrusting their most secret projects to a small inner ring of advisers whose identity was often unknown.[12] As early as 1679 Charles II deemed it expedient to remodel the Privy Council with a view to meeting the criticism which this development provoked;[13] but the scheme was abandoned as soon as it had served its immediate purpose, and the project then fell into the hands of the opposition, some of whom at the time of the Revolution proposed to establish what was virtually a supreme council of state,[14] and others of whom at the close of William's reign endeavoured to regulate the Privy Council in such a way as to restore it to its former place in the constitution.[15] Not merely did most of the ministers sincerely believe that it was their duty to carry out the king's commands,[16] but their salaries were so high, and their actual gains so much higher,[17] that they were reluctant to risk the loss of office which failure to obey might cause. Protests against their extravagant gains were not infrequent;[18] but little result followed, and the main problem of the executive had to be left in the end for the Hanoverians to solve.

In other circumstances the ill-feeling roused by these many controversies might have led to a movement against monarchy itself; but in England under the later Stuarts the memory of conditions under the Commonwealth was still strong, and republican ideas were entertained only by a very small section of the population. The

[1] No. 40. [2] No. 19. [3] No. 20. [4] No. 21. [5] No. 22.
[6] No. 43. [7] No. 23. [8] No. 24. [9] No. 26. [10] No. 25.
[11] No. 27. [12] No. 28. [13] No. 29. [14] No. 30. [15] No. 43.
[16] No. 75. [17] No. 31. [18] No. 32.

particular form taken by discontent was in consequence a tendency rather to tamper with the succession to the throne. At the root of the succession problem lay the simple fact that the House of Stuart was dying out. In 1660 there had appeared little likelihood of any such development. Charles was then a man in the prime of life, bound shortly to marry. He had two younger brothers, James and Henry; two sisters, Mary and Henrietta; a young nephew, William of Orange; and an aunt, Elizabeth of Bohemia, who was herself the mother of a numerous progeny.[1] The early years of his reign, however, proved tragic years for his family. Henry, Mary and Elizabeth were all carried off by small-pox within eighteen months of each other. Henrietta died in June 1670, poisoned, it was generally believed, by her jealous husband, Philip, duke of Orleans. Moreover, it was becoming increasingly apparent that Charles could hardly hope for any children by the wife he had married, and that James's two daughters, Mary and Anne, might be the only members of his family to survive childhood.

The real basis of the succession problem, however, was the unpopular policy that the Stuarts were pursuing, and in particular the growing tendency among them to embrace Catholicism. Charles's own inclination in that direction, although not un-suspected, was never taken very seriously, and it came as a shock to many when he eventually died a Catholic.[2] But James openly professed Catholicism, and rejected all efforts made to bring him back to the national Church; Henrietta's two young daughters were brought up as Catholics; and the majority of Elizabeth's children inclined the same way. Thus the only successors to Charles in whom his Protestant subjects could have any real confidence were James's daughters, Mary and Anne; their cousin, William of Orange; and Elizabeth's youngest daughter, Sophia.

At an early stage in the reign of Charles it was proposed to secure a satisfactory adjustment of the succession, either by obtaining a divorce for Charles, which would enable him to remarry and have legitimate issue, or by declaring that one of his illegitimate children, preferably James, duke of Monmouth, was in fact legitimate; but the real origin of the problem came with the rise of the Popish Plot scare,[3] which by bringing forward the immediate prospect of the substitution of James for Charles made the question a vital and practical issue. The reply of the malcontents was the introduction into Parliament of three Exclusion Bills, excluding James altogether from the succession,[4] and when these failed to secure acceptance[5] the formation of the Rye House conspiracy, which aimed at the seizure and deposition, if not at the assassina-tion, of both Charles and James.[6] After the death of Charles had placed James on the throne[7] this conspiracy found its natural sequel in the attempt of Monmouth to establish his own title by force of arms,[8] and a few years later in the invitation to William of Orange to come to England and exercise some controlling influence over James.[9]

At the Revolution which followed every effort was made to preserve the principle of strict hereditary monarchy, but with only superficial success. James was in effect deposed, and William and Mary were placed on the throne instead[10] under conditions designed to make a repetition of James's misgovernment impossible.[11] Although determined by a Whig Parliament which was much influenced by the ideas of John Locke,[12] this settlement was shortly afterwards confirmed by a Tory Parliament which

[1] Table 1.   [2] No. 37.   [3] Nos. 33, 34.   [4] No. 35.
[5] Map 3.   [6] No. 36.   [7] No. 37.   [8] No. 38.
[9] No. 39.   [10] Table 1.   [11] No. 40.   [12] No. 56.

would have repudiated such ideas,[1] and might well have proved adequate had it not been for the continued failure of the Stuart line to produce heirs. The exclusion of James and his direct descendants[2] could scarcely prove of much value unless William, Mary or Anne had descendants, and of that there seemed to be little prospect. On the death of Mary various possible brides were suggested for William;[3] and on the death of Anne's husband, Prince George of Denmark, she in turn was desired by Parliament to consider the thought of a second marriage.[4] But the final settlement was a result partly of the death of Anne's last surviving child, William, duke of Gloucester, which led to the entailing of the crown, under further conditions, on Sophia and her descendants,[5] to the exclusion both of the Orleans line[6] and of the Palatine line;[7] and partly of the death of James II himself,[8] which by bringing into prominence the danger still threatening from James's son, the Old Pretender, led to the adoption of strenuous measures to ensure that the settlement should actually be carried out.[9] It was largely in virtue of these measures that on the death of Anne,[10] George I succeeded peacefully to the throne.

[1] No. 41.   [2] Table 2.   [3] No. 42.   [4] No. 65.   [5] Table 3.
[6] Table 4.   [7] Table 5.   [8] No. 44.   [9] No. 45.   [10] No. 46.

BIBLIOGRAPHY

An extremely useful guide to royal activities of one type is *Bibliotheca Lindesiana, a Bibliography of Royal Proclamations of the Tudor and Stuart Sovereigns and Others published under Authority, 1485–1714*, vol. I, *England and Wales*, vol. II, *Scotland and Ireland*, edited by R. R. Steele (Oxford, 1910). Royal letters are collected in *The Letters, Speeches and Declarations of King Charles II*, edited by Arthur Bryant (London, 1935), and *The Letters and Diplomatic Instructions of Queen Anne*, edited by Beatrice Curtis Brown (London, 1935).

The monarchy in general is best studied in the standard works on constitutional and legal history, to which a useful introductory guide has been provided by the Historical Association in Helen M. Cam and A. S. Turberville, *A Short Bibliography of English Constitutional History* (London, 1929). Henry Hallam, *The Constitutional History of England from the Accession of Henry VII to the Death of George II* (8th edition, 3 vols., London, 1855), although biased in its conclusions and sadly out of date, is still valuable. F. W. Maitland, *The Constitutional History of England* (Cambridge, 1908), although deplorably brief, and written as long ago as 1887, is too brilliant a sketch to be ignored. T. P. Taswell-Langmead, *English Constitutional History*, should be used only in the tenth edition by T. F. T. Plucknett (London, 1947). D. L. Keir, *The Constitutional History of Modern Britain, 1485–1937* (4th edition, London, 1950), is solid and reliable, but devotes only one lengthy chapter to the later Stuarts. Sir William R. Anson, *The Law and Custom of the Constitution*, vol. II, *The Crown* (4th edition, by A. Berriedale Keith, Oxford, 1935), though concerned mainly with the present position, discusses at some length its historical foundations. Wider in its scope than any of the foregoing is Sir William Holdsworth, *A History of English Law*, vol. VI of which (London, 1929) provides an admirable survey of the constitutional history of the later Stuarts. The best text-books concerned primarily with the period are J. R. Tanner, *English Constitutional Conflicts of the Seventeenth Century, 1603–1689* (Cambridge, 1928); Sir John A. R. Marriott, *The Crisis of English Liberty* (Oxford, 1930); I. Deane Jones, *The English Revolution, an Introduction to English History, 1603–1714* (London, 1931); and Mark A. Thomson, *A Constitutional History of England, 1642 to 1801* (London, 1938).

On the subject of the Privy Council, the chief instrument of the monarchy in the exercise of its executive power, much has recently been written. The introductions to the *Acts of the Privy Council of England, Colonial Series*, vols. I and II (edited by W. L. Grant and James Munro, 1908–1910), contain a valuable discussion of the committee system as it developed under the later Stuarts, while the addendum to vol. V of the same series (1912) gives useful lists, taken from the official register, of the members of the Council. An immense amount of ill-digested information has been gathered together in Edward Raymond Turner, *The Privy Council of England in the Seventeenth and Eighteenth Centuries, 1603–1784* (2 vols., Baltimore, 1927–1928), and the same writer's *The Cabinet Council of England in the Seventeenth and Eighteenth Centuries, 1622–1784* (2 vols., Baltimore, 1930–1932); but for the elucidation of that and other information it is necessary to consult a series of articles which are by no means agreed as to their conclusions. Among these are Edward I. Carlyle, "Clarendon and the Privy Council, 1660–67", in *English Historical Review*, XXVII (1912), pp. 251–273; H. W. V. Temperley, "Inner and Outer Cabinet and Privy Council between 1679 and 1783", *ibid.*, pp. 682–699, "Documents illustrative of the Powers of the Privy Council in the Seventeenth Century", *ibid.*, XXVIII (1913), pp. 127–131, and "Inner and Outer Cabinets in the Eighteenth Century", *ibid.*, XXXI (1916), pp. 291–296; Sir William Anson, "The Cabinet in the Seventeenth and Eighteenth Centuries", *ibid.*, XXIX (1914), pp. 56–78; and Godfrey Davies, "Council and Cabinet, 1679–88", *ibid.*, XXXVII (1922), pp. 47–66.

Of other organs of the central government there are valuable studies in Florence M. Greir Evans, *The Principal Secretary of State, a Survey of the Office from 1558 to 1680* (Manchester, 1923), and the same writer's "Emoluments of the Principal Secretaries of State in the Seventeenth

54

Century", in *English Historical Review*, XXXV (1920), pp. 513–528; Mark A. Thomson, *The Secretaries of State, 1681–1782* (Oxford, 1932); Doris M. Gill, "The Treasury, 1660–1714", in *English Historical Review*, XLVI (1931), pp. 600–622, and the same writer's "The Relationship between the Treasury and the Excise and Customs Commissioners, 1660–1714", in *Cambridge Historical Journal*, IV (1932), pp. 94–99.

E. F. Churchill, "The Dispensing Power and the Defence of the Realm", in *Law Quarterly Review*, XXXVII (1921), pp. 412–441, "The Dispensing Power of the Crown in Ecclesiastical Affairs", *ibid.*, XXXVIII (1922), pp. 297–316, 420–434, and "Dispensations under the Tudors and Stuarts", in *English Historical Review*, XXXIV (1919), pp. 409–415, are specially valuable for the subject with which they deal. Clarence C. Crawford, "The Writ of Habeas Corpus", in *American Law Review*, XLII (1908), pp. 481–499, and the same writer's "The Suspension of the Habeas Corpus Act and the Revolution of 1689", in *English Historical Review*, XXX (1915), pp. 613–630, illustrate the problem of the liberty of the subject. Samuel Rezneck, "The Statute of 1696, a Pioneer Measure in the Reform of Judicial Procedure in England", in *Journal of Modern History*, II (1930), pp. 5–26, brings out the true significance of one of the less familiar among the remedial measures which followed the Revolution.

There are useful introductions to the development of political theory in G. P. Gooch, *Political Thought in England from Bacon to Halifax* (London, 1914); H. J. Laski, *Political Thought in England from Locke to Bentham* (London, 1920); G. P. Gooch, *English Democratic Ideas in the Seventeenth Century* (2nd edition, with notes by H. J. Laski, Cambridge, 1927); W. A. Dunning, *A History of Political Theories from Luther to Montesquieu* (New York, 1905); and *The Social and Political Ideas of some English Thinkers of the Augustan Age, 1650–1750*, a series of lectures by different authorities edited by F. J. C. Hearnshaw (London, 1928). J. Neville Figgis, *The Theory of the Divine Right of Kings* (2nd edition, Cambridge, 1914), is the standard work on the subject with which it deals; and Filmer's writings can best be studied in *Patriarcha and Other Political Works of Sir Robert Filmer*, edited by Peter Laslett (Oxford, 1949).

A. RESTORATION OF THE MONARCHY

1. Declaration of Breda, 1660

(*Journals of the House of Lords*, XI, pp. 7–8)

CHARLES R.

Charles, by the grace of God, king of England, Scotland, France and Ireland, Defender of the Faith, &c., to all our loving subjects, of what degree or quality soever, greeting.

If the general distraction and confusion which is spread over the whole kingdom doth not awaken all men to a desire and longing that those wounds which have so many years together been kept bleeding may be bound up, all we can say will be to no purpose. However, after this long silence we have thought it our duty to declare how much we desire to contribute thereunto, and that as we can never give over the hope in good time to obtain the possession of that right which God and nature hath made our due, so we do make it our daily suit to the Divine Providence that he will, in compassion to us and our subjects after so long misery and sufferings, remit and put us into a quiet and peaceable possession of that our right, with as little blood and damage to our people as is possible. Nor do we desire more to enjoy what is ours than that all our subjects may enjoy what by law is theirs, by a full and entire administration of justice throughout the land, and by extending our mercy where it is wanted and deserved.

And to the end that the fear of punishment may not engage any, conscious to themselves of what is past, to a perseverance in guilt for the future, by opposing the quiet and happiness of their country in the restoration both of king, peers and people to their just, ancient and fundamental rights, we do by these presents declare that we do grant a free and general pardon, which we are ready upon demand to pass under our great seal of England, to all our subjects, of what degree or quality soever, who within forty days after the publishing hereof shall lay hold upon this our grace and favour, and shall by any public act declare their doing so, and that they return to the loyalty and obedience of good subjects (excepting only such persons as shall hereafter be excepted by Parliament). Those only excepted, let all our loving subjects, how faulty soever, rely upon the word of a king, solemnly given by this present declaration, that no crime whatsoever committed against us or our royal father before the publication of this shall ever rise in judgment or be brought in question against any of them, to the least endamagement of them, either in their lives, liberties or estates, or (as far forth as lies in our power) so much as to the prejudice of their reputations by any reproach or term of distinction from the rest of our best subjects; we desiring and ordaining that henceforward all notes of discord, separation and difference of parties be utterly abolished among all our subjects, whom we invite and conjure to a perfect union among themselves, under our protection, for the re-settlement of our just rights and theirs in a free Parliament, by which, upon the word of a king, we will be advised.

And because the passion and uncharitableness of the times have produced several opinions in religion, by which men are engaged in parties and animosities against each other, which, when they shall hereafter unite in a freedom of conversation, will be composed or better understood, we do declare a liberty to tender consciences, and that no man shall be disquieted or called in question for differences of opinion in matter of religion which do not disturb the peace of the kingdom; and that we shall be ready to consent to such an Act of Parliament as upon mature deliberation shall be offered to us for the full granting that indulgence.

And because, in the continued distractions of so many years and so many and great revolutions, many grants and purchases of estates have been made to and by many officers, soldiers and others, who are now possessed of the same and who may be liable to actions at law upon several titles, we are likewise willing that all such differences, and all things relating to such grants, sales and purchases, shall be determined in Parliament, which can best provide for the just satisfaction of all men who are concerned.

And we do further declare that we will be ready to consent to any Act or Acts of Parliament to the purposes aforesaid, and for the full satisfaction of all arrears due to the officers and soldiers of the army under the command of General Monck, and that they shall be received into our service upon as good pay and conditions as they now enjoy.

Given under our sign manual and privy signet,
at our court at Breda,
this 4/14 day of April 1660,
in the twelfth year of our reign.

2. Proclamation of Charles II, 1660

(Journals of the House of Lords, XI, p. 19)

A PROCLAMATION OF BOTH HOUSES OF PARLIAMENT
FOR PROCLAIMING OF
HIS MAJESTY KING OF ENGLAND, SCOTLAND, FRANCE AND IRELAND
DEFENDER OF THE FAITH, &C.

Although it can no way be doubted but that his Majesty's right and title to his crowns and kingdoms is and was every way completed by the death of his most royal father of glorious memory, without the ceremony or solemnity of a proclamation, yet since proclamations in such cases have been always used, to the end that all good subjects might upon this occasion testify their duty and respects, and since the armed violence and other the calamities of these many years last past have hitherto deprived us of any such opportunity wherein we might express our loyalty and allegiance to his Majesty, we, therefore, the Lords and Commons now assembled in Parliament, together with the lord mayor, aldermen and commons of the city of London and other freemen of this kingdom now present, do, according to our duty and allegiance, heartily, joyfully and unanimously acknowledge and proclaim that immediately upon the decease of our late Sovereign Lord King Charles the imperial crown of the realm of England, and of all the kingdoms, dominions and rights belonging to the same, did by inheritance, birthright and lawful and undoubted succession descend and come to his most excellent Majesty Charles the Second, as being lineally, justly and lawfully next heir of the blood royal of this realm, and that by the goodness and providence of Almighty God he is of England, Scotland, France and Ireland the most potent, mighty and undoubted king, Defender of the Faith, &c. And thereunto we most humbly and faithfully do submit and oblige ourselves, our heirs and posterities for ever.

Dated the 8th day of May 1660.

3. Anonymous pamphlet on the return of the king, 1660
(*Stuart Tracts*, ed. C. H. Firth, pp. 425–430)

ENGLAND'S JOY

OR A RELATION OF THE MOST REMARKABLE PASSAGES FROM
HIS MAJESTY'S ARRIVAL AT DOVER TO HIS ENTRANCE AT WHITEHALL

Being come aboard one of the fairest of those ships which attended at Helvoetsluys for wafting him over from the Hague in Holland, and therein having taken leave of his sister the Princess Royal, he set sail for England on Wednesday evening, May 23rd, 1660; and having during his abode at sea given new names to that whole navy, consisting of twenty-six goodly vessels, he arrived at Dover on the Friday following about two o'clock in the afternoon. Ready on the shore to receive him stood the Lord General Monck, as also the earl of Winchilsea, constable of Dover Castle, with divers persons of quality on the one hand, and the mayor of Dover accompanied by his brethren of that corporation on the other, with a rich canopy. As soon as he had set foot on the shore the Lord General, presenting himself before him on his knee and kissing his royal hand, was embraced by his Majesty, and received divers gracious expressions of the great sense he had of his loyalty and in being so instrumental in his restoration. There also did the corporation of Dover and the earl of Winchilsea do their duties to him in like sort, all the people making joyful shouts, the great guns from the ships and castle telling aloud the happy news of this his entrance upon English ground.

From thence, taking coach immediately with his royal brothers, the dukes of York and Gloucester, he passed to Barham Down, a great plain lying betwixt Dover and Canterbury, where were drawn up divers gallant troops of horse, consisting of the nobility, knights and gentlemen of note clad in very rich apparel, commanded by the duke of Buckingham, earls of Oxford, Derby, Northampton, Winchilsea, Lichfield, and the Lord Viscount Mordaunt; as also the several foot regiments of the Kentish men. Being entered the Down on horseback, where multitudes of the country people stood making loud shouts, he rode to the head of each troop, they being placed on his left hand three deep, who, bowing to him, kissed the hilts of their swords and then flourished them above their heads, with no less acclamations, the trumpets in the meantime also echoing the like to them.

In the suburb at Canterbury stood the mayor and aldermen of that ancient city, who received him with loud music and presented him with a cup of gold of two hundred and fifty pounds value; whence, after a speech made to him by the recorder, he passed to the Lord Campden's house, the mayor carrying the sword before him. . . . From Canterbury he came on Monday to Rochester, where the people had hung up, over the midst of the streets as he rode, many beautiful garlands curiously made up with costly scarves and ribbons, decked with spoons and bodkins of silver and small plate of several sorts, and some with gold chains in like sort as at Canterbury, each striving to outdo the other in all expressions of joy.

On Tuesday, May the 29th (which happily fell out to be the anniversary of his Majesty's birthday), he set forth from Rochester in his coach, but afterwards took horse on the farther side of Blackheath, on which spacious plain he found divers great and eminent troops of horse in a most splendid and glorious equipage, and a kind of rural triumph expressed by the country swains in a morrice dance with the old music of tabor and pipe, which was performed with all agility and cheerfulness imaginable. . . . From thence passing on he came into Saint George's Fields in Southwark, where the lord mayor and aldermen of London in their scarlet, with the recorder and other city council, waited for him in a large tent hung with tapestry, in which they had placed a chair of state with a rich canopy over it. When he came thither the lord mayor presented him with the city sword and the recorder made a speech to him, which being done he alighted and went into the tent, where a noble banquet was prepared for him. . . .

In this magnificent fashion his Majesty entered the borough of Southwark about half past three o'clock in the afternoon, and within an hour after the city of London at the bridge, where he found the windows and streets exceedingly thronged with people to behold him, and the wall adorned with hangings and carpets of tapestry and other costly stuff, and in many places sets of loud music, all the conduits as he passed running claret wine, and the several Companies in their liveries with the ensigns belonging to them, as also the trained bands of the city standing along the streets as he passed, welcoming him with loyal acclamations; and within the rails where Charing Cross formerly was, a stand of six hundred pikes consisting of knights and gentlemen as had been officers in the armies of his late Majesty of blessed memory, the truly noble and valiant Sir John Stawell, knight of the honourable order of the bath (a person famous for his eminent actings and sufferings), being in the head of them.

From which place, the citizens in velvet coats and gold chains being drawn up on each hand, and divers companies of foot soldiers, his Majesty passed betwixt them and entered Whitehall at seven o'clock, the people making loud shouts, and the horse and foot several volleys of shots, at this his happy arrival; where the House of Lords and Commons of Parliament received him, and kissed his royal hand. At the same time likewise the reverend bishops of Ely, Salisbury, Rochester and Chichester in their episcopal habits, with divers of the long oppressed orthodox clergy, met in that royal chapel of King Henry the Seventh of Westminster, and there also sang *Te Deum*, &c., in praise and thanks to Almighty God for this his unspeakable mercy, in the deliverance of his Majesty from many dangers, and so happily restoring him to rule these kingdoms according to his just and undoubted right.

4. Act for a perpetual thanksgiving, 1660
(*Statutes of the Realm*, v, p. 237)

AN ACT FOR A PERPETUAL ANNIVERSARY THANKSGIVING
ON THE NINE AND TWENTIETH DAY OF MAY

(*12 Car. II, cap. 14*)

Forasmuch as Almighty God, the King of Kings and sole Disposer of all earthly crowns and kingdoms, hath by his all-swaying providence and power miraculously demonstrated in the view of all the world his transcendent mercy, love and graciousness towards his most excellent Majesty Charles the Second, by his especial grace of England, Scotland, France and Ireland king, Defender of the true Faith, and all his Majesty's loyal subjects of this his kingdom of England and the dominions thereunto annexed, by his Majesty's late most wonderful, glorious, peaceable and joyful restoration to the actual possession and exercise of his undoubted hereditary, sovereign and regal authority over them (after sundry years' forced extermination into foreign parts by the most traitorous conspiracies and armed power of usurping tyrants and execrable perfidious traitors), and that without the least opposition or effusion of blood through the unanimous, cordial, loyal votes of the Lords and Commons in this present Parliament assembled, and passionate desires of all other his Majesty's subjects, which inexpressible blessing (by God's own most wonderful dispensation) was completed on the twenty-ninth day of May last past, being the most memorable birthday not only of his Majesty both as a man and prince, but likewise as an actual king . . . be it therefore enacted by the king's most excellent Majesty, the Lords and Commons in this present Parliament assembled, and by the authority of the same, that all and singular ministers of God's word and sacraments, in every church, chapel and other usual place of divine service and public prayer which now are or hereafter shall be within this realm of England and the respective dominions thereof, and their successors, shall in all succeeding ages annually celebrate the twenty-ninth day of May by rendering their hearty public praises and thanksgivings unto Almighty God for all the forementioned extraordinary mercies, blessings and deliverances received and mighty acts done thereon, and declare the same to all the people there assembled and the generations yet to come, that so they may for ever praise the Lord for the same, whose name alone is excellent, and his glory above the earth and heavens.

II. And be it further enacted that all and every person and persons inhabiting within this kingdom and the dominions thereunto belonging shall upon the said day annually resort with diligence and devotion to some usual church, chapel or place where such public thanksgivings and praises to God's most Divine Majesty shall be rendered, and there orderly and devoutly abide during the said public thanksgivings, prayers, preaching, singing of psalms and other service of God there to be used and ministered.

III. And to the end that all persons may be put in mind of their duty thereon, and be the better prepared to discharge the same with that piety and devotion as becomes them, be it further enacted that every minister shall give notice to his parishioners publicly in the church at morning prayer the Lord's Day next before every such twenty-ninth day of May for the due observation of the said day, and shall then likewise publicly and distinctly read this present Act to the people.

5. Order of the Lords and Commons for the exhumation of Oliver Cromwell, 1660

(Journals of the House of Lords, XI, p. 205)

Ordered by the Lords and Commons assembled in Parliament, that the carcasses of Oliver Cromwell, Henry Ireton, John Bradshaw, Thomas Pride, whether buried in Westminster Abbey or elsewhere, be with all expedition taken up, and drawn upon a hurdle to Tyburn, and there hanged up in their coffins for some time, and after that buried under the said gallows; and that James Norfolk, esquire, sergeant-at-arms attending the House of Commons, do take care that this order be put in effectual execution by the common executioner for the county of Middlesex and all such others to whom it shall respectively appertain, who are required in their several places to conform to and observe this order with effect; and the sheriff of Middlesex is to give his assistance herein as there shall be occasion. And the dean of Westminster is desired to give directions to his officers of the Abbey to be assistant in the execution of this order.

B. ROYAL PREROGATIVE

6. Act for the preservation of the king, 1661

(Statutes of the Realm, v, pp. 304–306)

AN ACT FOR SAFETY AND PRESERVATION OF
HIS MAJESTY'S PERSON AND GOVERNMENT
AGAINST TREASONABLE AND SEDITIOUS PRACTICES AND ATTEMPTS

(13 Car. II, stat. I, cap. 1)

The Lords and Commons assembled in Parliament, deeply weighing and considering the miseries and calamities of wellnigh twenty years before your Majesty's happy return, and withal reflecting upon the causes and occasions of so great and deplorable confusions, do in all humility and thankfulness acknowledge your Majesty's incomparable grace and goodness to your people in your free and general pardon, indemnity and oblivion,[1] by which your Majesty hath been pleased to deliver your subjects not only from the punishment but also from the reproach of their former miscarriages, which unexampled piety and clemency of your Majesty hath inflamed the hearts of us your subjects with an ardent desire to express all possible zeal and duty in the care and preservation of your Majesty's person, in whose honour and happiness consists the good and welfare of your people, and in preventing (as much as may be) all treasonable and seditious practices and attempts for the time to come; and because the growth and increase of the late troubles and disorders did in a very great measure proceed from a multitude of seditious sermons, pamphlets and speeches daily preached, printed and published with a transcendent boldness, defaming the person and government of your Majesty and your royal father, . . . and (above all) from a wilful mistake of the supreme and lawful authority, whilst men were forward to cry up and maintain those orders and ordinances, oaths and covenants, to be acts legal and warrantable, which in themselves had not the least colour of law or justice to support them, . . . we therefore, the Lords and Commons in Parliament assembled, having duly considered the premises, and remembering that in the thirteenth year of the reign of Queen Elizabeth of ever blessed memory a right good and profitable law was made for preservation of her Majesty's person,[2] do most humbly beseech your most excellent Majesty that it may be enacted, and be it enacted . . . that if any person or persons whatsoever after the four and twentieth day of June in the year of our Lord one thousand six hundred sixty and one, during the natural life of our most gracious sovereign lord the king (whom Almighty God preserve and bless with a long and prosperous reign), shall within the realm or without compass, imagine, invent, devise or intend death or destruction, or any bodily harm tending to death or destruction, maim or wounding, imprisonment or restraint of the person of the same our sovereign lord the king, or to deprive or depose him from the style, honour or kingly name of the imperial crown of this realm or of any other his Majesty's dominions or countries, or to levy war

[1] No. 53.   [2] 13 Eliz., cap. 1.

63

against his Majesty within this realm or without, or to move or stir any foreigner or strangers with force to invade this realm or any other his Majesty's dominions or countries being under his Majesty's obeisance, and such compassings, imaginations, inventions, devices or intentions or any of them shall express, utter or declare by any printing, writing, preaching or malicious and advised speaking, being legally convicted thereof upon the oaths of two lawful and credible witnesses upon trial, or otherwise convicted or attainted by due course of law, then every such person and persons so as aforesaid offending shall be deemed, declared and adjudged to be traitors, and shall suffer pains of death, and also lose and forfeit as in cases of high treason.

II. And be it further enacted . . . that if any person or persons at any time after the four and twentieth day of June in the year of our Lord one thousand six hundred sixty and one during his Majesty's life shall maliciously and advisedly publish or affirm the king to be an heretic or a papist, or that he endeavours to introduce popery, or shall maliciously and advisedly by writing, printing, preaching or other speaking express, publish, utter or declare any words, sentences or other thing or things to incite or stir up the people to hatred or dislike of the person of his Majesty or the established government, then every such person and persons, being thereof legally convicted, shall be disabled to have or enjoy, and is hereby disabled and made incapable of having, holding, enjoying or exercising, any place, office or promotion, ecclesiastical, civil or military, or any other employment in Church or State other than that of his peerage, and shall likewise be liable to such further and other punishments as by the common laws or statutes of this realm may be inflicted in such cases.

III. And to the end that no man hereafter may be misled into any seditious or unquiet demeanour out of an opinion that the Parliament begun and held at Westminster upon the third day of November in the year of our Lord one thousand six hundred and forty is yet in being, which is undoubtedly dissolved and determined, and so is hereby declared and adjudged to be fully dissolved and determined, or out of an opinion that there lies any obligation upon him from any oath, covenant or engagement whatsoever to endeavour a change of government either in Church or State, or out of an opinion that both Houses of Parliament or either of them have a legislative power without the king, all which assertions have been seditiously maintained in some pamphlets lately printed, and are daily promoted by the active enemies of our peace and happiness, be it therefore further enacted . . . that if any person or persons at any time after the four and twentieth day of June in the year of our Lord one thousand six hundred sixty and one shall maliciously and advisedly, by writing, printing, preaching or other speaking, express, publish, utter, declare or affirm that the Parliament begun at Westminster upon the third day of November in the year of our Lord one thousand six hundred and forty is not yet dissolved or is not determined, or that it ought to be in being or hath yet any continuance or existence, or that there lies any obligation upon him or any other person from any oath, covenant or engagement whatsoever to endeavour a change of government either in Church or State, or that both Houses of Parliament or either House of Parliament have or hath a legislative power without the king, or any other words to the same effect, that then every such person and persons so as aforesaid offending shall incur the danger and penalty of a premunire mentioned in a statute made in the sixteenth year of the reign of King Richard the Second; and it is hereby also declared, that the oath usually called the Solemn League and Covenant was in itself an unlawful oath, and imposed upon the subjects of this realm against the fundamental laws and liberties of this kingdom, and that all orders and ordinances, or pretended orders and ordinances, of both or either Houses of Parliament for imposing of oaths, covenants or engagements, levying of taxes or raising of forces and arms, to which the royal assent either in person or by commission was not expressly had or given, were in their first creation and making, and still are and so shall be taken to be, null and void to all intents and purposes whatsoever. Provided nevertheless that all and every person and persons, bodies politic and corporate, who have been or shall at any time hereafter be questioned for anything acted or done by colour of any the orders or ordinances hereinbefore mentioned and declared to be null and void, and are indemnified by an Act intituled, *An Act of free and general pardon, indemnity and oblivion*,[1] made in the twelfth year of his Majesty's reign that now is, or shall be indemnified by any Act of Parliament, shall and may make such use of the said orders and ordinances for their indemnity according to the true intent and meaning of the said Act, and no other, as he or they might have done if this Act had not been made, anything in this Act contained to the contrary notwithstanding. . . .

V. Provided always, and be it enacted, that no person or persons shall be indicted, arraigned, condemned, convicted or attainted for any of the treasons or offences aforesaid, unless the same offender or offenders be thereof accused by the testimony and deposition of two lawful and credible witnesses upon oath, which witnesses at the time of the said offender or offenders' arraignment shall be brought in person before him or them face to face, and shall openly avow and maintain upon oath what they have to say against him or them concerning the treason or offences contained in the said indictment, unless the party or parties arraigned shall willingly without violence confess the same.

VI. Provided likewise, and be it enacted, that this Act or anything therein contained shall not extend to deprive either of the Houses of Parliament or any of their members of their just ancient freedom and privilege of debating any matters or business which shall be propounded or debated in either of the said Houses, or at any conferences or committees of both or either of the said Houses of Parliament, or touching the repeal or alteration of any old or preparing any new laws or the redressing of any public grievance, but that the said members of either of the said Houses, and the assistants of the House of Peers and every of them, shall have the same freedom of speech and all other privileges whatsoever as they had before the making of this Act, anything in this Act to the contrary thereof in any wise notwithstanding.

VII. Provided always, and be it ordained and enacted, that no peer of this realm shall be tried for any offence against this Act but by his peers, and further that every peer who shall be convicted of any offence against this Act after such conviction be disabled during his life to sit in Parliament, unless his Majesty shall graciously be pleased to pardon him. . . .

[1] No. 53.

7. Act against tumultuous petitioning, 1661

(Statutes of the Realm, v, p. 308)

AN ACT AGAINST TUMULTS AND DISORDERS
UPON PRETENCE OF PREPARING OR PRESENTING
PUBLIC PETITIONS OR OTHER ADDRESSES TO HIS MAJESTY
OR THE PARLIAMENT

(13 Car. II, stat. I, cap. 5)

Whereas it hath been found by sad experience that tumultuous and other disorderly soliciting and procuring of hands by private persons to petitions, complaints, remonstrances and declarations and other addresses to the king, or to both or either Houses of Parliament, for alteration of matters established by law, redress of pretended grievances in Church or State, or other public concernments, have been made use of to serve the ends of factious and seditious persons gotten into power, to the violation of the public peace, and have been a great means of the late unhappy wars, confusions and calamities in this nation; for preventing the like mischief for the future, be it enacted . . . that no person or persons whatsoever shall from and after the first of August one thousand six hundred sixty and one solicit, labour or procure the getting of hands or other consent of any persons above the number of twenty or more to any petition, complaint, remonstrance, declaration or other address to the king or both or either Houses of Parliament for alteration of matters established by law in Church or State, unless the matter thereof have been first consented unto and ordered by three or more justices of that county, or by the major part of the grand jury of the county or division of the county, where the same matter shall arise, at their public assizes or general quarter-sessions, or if arising in London by the lord mayor, aldermen and commons in common council assembled; and that no person or persons whatsoever shall repair to his Majesty or both or either of the Houses of Parliament upon pretence of presenting or delivering any petition, complaint, remonstrance or declaration or other addresses accompanied with excessive number of people, nor at any one time with above the number of ten persons, upon pain of incurring a penalty not exceeding the sum of one hundred pounds in money and three months imprisonment without bail or mainprize for every offence, which offence to be prosecuted at the Court of King's Bench or at the assizes or general quarter-sessions within six months after the offence committed, and proved by two or more credible witnesses.

II. Provided always, that this Act or anything therein contained shall not be construed to extend to debar or hinder any person or persons not exceeding the number of ten aforesaid to present any public or private grievance or complaint to any member or members of Parliament after his election and during the continuance of the Parliament, or to the king's Majesty, for any remedy to be thereupon had, nor to extend to any address whatsoever to his Majesty by all or any the members of both or either Houses of Parliament during the sitting of Parliament, but that they may enjoy their freedom of access to his Majesty as heretofore hath been used.

8. Licensing Act, 1662

(Statutes of the Realm, v, pp. 428-433)

AN ACT FOR PREVENTING THE FREQUENT ABUSES
IN PRINTING SEDITIOUS, TREASONABLE AND UNLICENSED BOOKS AND PAMPHLETS,
AND FOR REGULATING OF PRINTING AND PRINTING-PRESSES

(14 Car. II, cap. 33)

Whereas the well-government and regulating of printers and printing-presses is matter of public care and of great concernment, especially considering that by the general licentiousness of the late times many evil-disposed persons have been encouraged to print and sell heretical, schismatical, blasphemous, seditious and treasonable books, pamphlets and papers, and still do continue such their unlawful and exorbitant practice, to the high dishonour of Almighty God, the endangering the peace of these kingdoms, and raising a disaffection to his most excellent Majesty and his government, for prevention whereof no surer means can be advised than by reducing and limiting the number of printing-presses, and by ordering and settling the said art or mystery of printing by Act of Parliament in manner as hereinafter is expressed; the king's most excellent Majesty, by and with the consent and advice of the Lords Spiritual and Temporal and Commons in this present Parliament assembled, doth therefore ordain and enact, and be it ordained and enacted by the authority aforesaid, that no person or persons whatsoever shall presume to print or cause to be printed, either within this realm of England or any other his Majesty's dominions, or in the parts beyond the seas, any heretical, seditious, schismatical or offensive books or pamphlets, wherein any doctrine or opinion shall be asserted or maintained which is contrary to the Christian faith or the doctrine or discipline of the Church of England, or which shall or may tend or be to the scandal of religion, or the Church, or the government or governors of the Church, State or commonwealth, or of any corporation or particular person or persons whatsoever, nor shall import, publish, sell or disperse any such book or books or pamphlets, nor shall cause or procure any such to be published or put to sale, or to be bound, stitched or sewed together.

II. And be it further ordained and enacted . . . that no private person or persons whatsoever shall at any time hereafter print or cause to be printed any book or pamphlet whatsoever, unless the same book and pamphlet, together with all and every the titles, epistles, prefaces, proems, preambles, introductions, tables, dedications and other matters and things thereunto annexed, be first entered in the book of the register of the Company of Stationers of London, except Acts of Parliament, proclamations, and such other books and papers as shall be appointed to be printed by virtue of any warrant under the king's Majesty's sign manual, or under the hand of one or both of his Majesty's Principal Secretaries of State, and unless the same book and pamphlet, and also all and every the said titles, epistles, prefaces, proems, preambles, introductions, tables, dedications and other matters and things whatsoever thereunto annexed, or therewith to be imprinted, shall be first lawfully licensed and authorized to be printed by such person and persons only as shall be constituted and appointed to license the same according to the direction and true meaning of this present Act hereinafter expressed, and by no other, that is to say, that all books concerning the common laws of this realm shall be printed by the special allowance of the Lord Chancellor or Lord Keeper of the Great Seal of England for the time being, the Lords Chief Justices and Lord Chief Baron for the time being, or one or more of them, or by their or one or more of their appointments; and that all books of history concerning the state of this realm, or other books concerning any affairs of state, shall be licensed by the Principal Secretaries of State for the time being or one of them, or by their or one of their appointments; and that all books to be imprinted concerning heraldry, titles of honour and arms, or otherwise concerning the office of Earl Marshal, shall be licensed by the Earl Marshal for the time being or by his appointment, or in case there shall not then be an Earl Marshal shall be licensed by the three kings of arms, Garter, Clarencieux and Norroy, or any two of them, whereof Garter, principal king of arms, to be one; and that all other books to be imprinted or reprinted, whether of divinity, physic, philosophy or whatsoever other science or art, shall be first licensed and allowed by the lord archbishop of Canterbury and lord bishop of London for the time being, or one of them, or by their or one of their appointments, or by either one of the chancellors or vice-chancellors of either of the universities of this realm for the time being; provided always that the said chancellors or vice-chancellors of either of the said universities shall only license such books as are to be imprinted or reprinted within the limits of the said universities respectively, but not in London or elsewhere, not meddling either with books of the common laws or matters of state or government, nor any book or books the right of printing whereof doth solely and properly belong to any particular person or persons, without his or their consent first obtained in that behalf. . . .

X. And be it further enacted . . . that for the time to come no man shall be admitted to be a master printer until they who are now actually master printers shall be by death or otherwise reduced to the number of twenty, and from thenceforth the number of twenty master printers shall be continued, and no more, besides the king's printers and the printers allowed for the universities, to have the use and exercise of printing of books at one time, and but four master founders of letters for printing, the which said master printers and four master founders of letters for printing shall be nominated, appointed and allowed by the lord archbishop of Canterbury and lord bishop of London for the time being; . . . and every person and persons which shall hereafter be allowed or permitted to have the use of a printing-press or printing-house, upon or before such his allowance obtained, shall become bound with sureties to his Majesty in the Court of King's Bench, or before some one or more of the justices of assize or the justices of the peace at their several quarter-sessions, in the sum of three hundred pounds, not to print or suffer to be printed in his house or press any book or books whatsoever but such as shall from time to time be lawfully licensed. . . .

XIV. And for the better discovering of printing in corners without licence, be it further enacted . . . that one or more of the messengers of his Majesty's Chamber, by warrant under his Majesty's sign manual or under the hand of one or both of his Majesty's Principal Secretaries of State, or the master and wardens of the said Company of Stationers or any one of them, shall have power and authority with a constable to take unto them such assistance as they shall think needful, and at what time they shall think fit, to search all houses and shops where they shall know, or upon some probable reason suspect, any books or papers to be printed, bound or stitched, especially printing-houses, booksellers' shops and warehouses, and bookbinders' houses and shops, and to view there what is imprinting, binding or stitching, and to examine whether the same be licensed, and to demand a sight of the said licence, and if the said book so imprinting, binding or stitching shall not be licensed then to seize upon so much thereof as shall be found imprinted, together with the several offenders, and to bring them before one or more justices of the peace, who are hereby authorized and required to commit such offenders to prison, there to remain until they shall be tried and acquitted, or convicted and punished for the said offences; and in case the said searchers shall upon their said search find any book or books or part of books unlicensed, which they shall suspect to contain matters therein contrary to the doctrine or discipline of the Church of England, or against the state and government, then upon such suspicion to seize upon such book or books or part of book or books, and to bring the same unto the said lord archbishop of Canterbury and lord bishop of London for the time being or one of them, or to the Secretaries of State or one of them respectively, who shall take such further course for the suppressing thereof as to them or any of them shall seem fit. . . .

XVI. And be it further enacted . . . that every printer shall reserve three printed copies of the best and largest paper of every book new printed, or reprinted by him with additions, and shall before any public vending of the said book bring them to the master of the Company of Stationers and deliver them to him, one whereof shall be delivered to the Keeper of his Majesty's Library, and the other two to be sent to the vice-chancellors of the two universities respectively, for the use of the public libraries of the said universities. . . .

XXIII. Provided also, that neither this Act nor anything therein contained shall extend to restrain the keeping and using of a printing-press in the city of York, so as all books of divinity there printed be first licensed by the archbishop of York for the time being or such person or persons whom he shall appoint, and all other books whatsoever there printed be first licensed by such persons respectively to whom the licensing thereof doth or shall appertain by the rules hereinbefore mentioned, and so as no bibles be there printed, nor any other book whereof the original copy is or shall be belonging to the Company of Stationers in London or any member thereof, and so as the archbishop or lord mayor of York for the time being do execute within the said city (which they are hereby empowered to do) all the powers and rules in this Act concerning searchers for unlicensed books, and impose and levy the said penalties in the like cases, anything in this Act to the contrary notwithstanding.

XXIV. Provided, that this Act shall continue and be in force for two years, to commence from the tenth of June one thousand six hundred sixty and two, and no longer.

9. Count Lorenzo Magalotti's description of the ceremony of touching for the king's evil, 1669

(Travels of Cosmo, Grand Duke of Tuscany, pp. 214–216)

As it was now near noon his Highness took leave, and returned by the way of New-market. Before entering the town he alighted from his carriage, and went on foot with his attendants to the king's residence, where he was introduced into his Majesty's chamber, who was waiting there till everything necessary was prepared for the ceremony which he is accustomed to perform publicly every Friday, that of touching for the king's evil, according to the ancient usage of the first Catholic kings of England, which was handed down to their successors, continued after the apostasy, and preserved to the time of the present king.

When his Majesty was informed that all was ready he went from his chamber into a room adjoining, where was placed on a table a cushion, on which lay the prayer-book appointed by the Anglican ritual for the use of his Majesty. As soon as he appeared, and at a signal given by him, the two assistant ministers, dressed in their surplices, began the prayers with a great appearance of devotion, his Highness stand-ing, while they were read, in another room; from which, when the service was finished, he passed into the room in which those who were afflicted with the king's evil were assembled, for the purpose of observing the ceremony, from the side of the door which led into the room. A carpet was spread upon the floor, and upon it was a seat, on which the king seated himself; and certain invocations in the English language, taken from the prayer-book, having been read by one of the ministers, his Majesty began the ceremony of touching the patients in the part affected. These were conducted into the king's presence one at a time, and as they knelt before him he touched them with both his hands, after which, without interfering with the others who came after them, each returned to his former situation.

This being over, the minister, kneeling with all the bystanders, the king alone remaining seated, repeated some other prayers, after which, all rising, the diseased came again in the same order as before to his Majesty, who put round their necks a ribbon of an azure colour, from which was suspended a medallion of gold stamped with his own image, in shape and weight resembling an Hungarian sequin. The whole ceremony being ended, the king returned to his chamber, and his Highness to his quarters, and dined as usual.

10. Sir Robert Filmer's justification of the prerogative, 1680

(Patriarcha, ed. 1949, chaps. I, III, V, XXII and XXVI)

Within the last hundred years many of the schoolmen and other divines have published and maintained an opinion that mankind is naturally endowed and born with freedom from all subjection, and at liberty to choose what form of govern-ment it please, and that the power which any one man hath over others was at the first by human right bestowed according to the discretion of the multitude. This tenet was first hatched in the schools for good divinity, and hath been fostered by succeeding papists. The divines of the reformed churches have entertained it, and the common people everywhere tenderly embrace it as being most plausible to flesh and blood, for that it prodigally distributes a portion of liberty to the meanest of the multitude, who magnify liberty as if the height of human felicity were only to be found in it, never remembering that the desire of liberty was the cause of the fall of Adam. But howsoever this opinion hath of late obtained great reputation, yet it is not to be found in the ancient fathers and doctors of the primitive church; it contradicts the doctrine and history of the Holy Scriptures, the constant practice of all ancient monarchies, and the very principles of the law of nature. It is hard to say whether it be more erroneous in divinity or dangerous in policy.

Upon the grounds of this doctrine both Jesuits and some zealous favourers of the Geneva discipline have built a perilous conclusion, which is that the people or multitude have power to punish or deprive the prince if he transgress the laws of the kingdom. . . . This desperate assertion, whereby kings are made subject to the censures and deprivations of their subjects, follows (as the authors of it conceive) as a necessary consequence of that former position of the supposed natural equality and freedom of mankind, and liberty to choose what form of government it please. . . . The rebellious consequence which follows this prime article of the natural freedom of mankind may be my sufficient warrant for a modest examination of the original truth of it. Much hath been said, and by many, for the affirmative. Equity requires that an ear be reserved a little for the negative. . . .

I come now to examine that argument which is used by Bellarmine, and is the one and only argument I can find produced by any author for the proof of the natural liberty of the people. It is thus framed. That God hath given or ordained power is evident by Scripture; but God hath given it to no particular man, because by nature all men are equal: therefore he hath given power to the people or multitude. To answer this reason, drawn from the equality of mankind by nature, I will first use the help of Bellarmine himself, whose words are these, "If many men had been created out of the earth, all they ought to have been princes over their posterity." In these words we have an evident confession that creation made man prince of his posterity. And indeed not only Adam but the succeeding patriarchs had by right of fatherhood royal authority over their children. . . . For as Adam was lord of his children, so his children under him had a command over their own children, but still with subordination to the first parent, who is lord paramount over his children's children to all generations, as being the grandfather of his people.

I see not then how the children of Adam, or of any man else, can be free from subjection to their parents. And this subordination of children is the fountain of all regal authority by the ordination of God himself. From whence it follows that civil power not only in general is by divine institution, but even the assigning of it specifically to the eldest parent; which quite takes away that new and common distinction which refers only power universal or absolute to God, but power respective in regard of the special form of government to the choice of the people. Nor leaves it any place for such imaginary pactions between kings and their people as many dream of.

This lordship which Adam by creation had over the whole world, and by right descending from him the patriarchs did enjoy, was as large and ample as the absolutest dominion of any monarch which hath been since the creation. . . .

It may seem absurd to maintain that kings now are the fathers of their people, since experience shows the contrary. It is true all kings be not the natural parents of their subjects; yet they all either are, or are to be reputed, as the next heirs of those progenitors who were at first the natural parents of the whole people, and in their right succeed to the exercise of supreme jurisdiction. And such heirs are not only lords of their own children, but also of their brethren and all others that were subject to their fathers. . . . As long as the first fathers of families lived, the name of patriarchs did aptly belong unto them. But after a few descents, when the true fatherhood itself was extinct, and only the right of the father descended to the true heir, then the title of prince or king was more significant to express the power of him who succeeds only to the right of that fatherhood which his ancestors did naturally enjoy. By this means it comes to pass that many a child, by succeeding a king, hath the right of a father over many a grey-headed multitude. . . .

Hitherto I have endeavoured to show the natural institution of regal authority, and to free it from subjection to an arbitrary election of the people. It is necessary also to inquire whether human laws have a superiority over princes, because those that maintain the acquisition of royal jurisdiction from the people do subject the exercise of it to human positive laws. But in this also they err. For as kingly power is by the law of God, so it hath no inferior law to limit it. The father of a family governs by no other law than by his own will, not by the laws or wills of his sons or servants. There is no nation that allows children any action or remedy for being unjustly governed. And yet for all this every father is bound by the law of nature to do his best for the preservation of his family.

But much more is a king always tied by the same law of nature to keep this general ground, that the safety of his kingdom be his chief law. He must remember that the profit of every man in particular, and of all together in general, is not always one and the same, that the public is to be preferred before the private, and that the force of laws must not be so great as natural equity itself. Which cannot fully be comprised in any laws, but is to be left to the religious arbitrament of those who know how to manage the affairs of state, and wisely to balance the particular profit with the counterpoise of the public, according to the infinite variety of times, places, persons.

A proof unanswerable for the superiority of princes above laws is this, that there were kings long before there were any laws. For a long time the word of the king was the only law. . . .

There can be no laws without a supreme power to command or make them. In all aristocracies the nobles are above the laws, and in all democracies the people. By the like reason in a monarchy the king must of necessity be above the laws. There can be no sovereign majesty in him that is under them. That which giveth the very being to a king is the power to give laws. Without this power he is but an equivocal king. . . .

11. Sir William Petty's enumeration of the royal powers, 1685

(*Economic Writings*, ed. C. H. Hull, II, pp. 630–632)

THE POWERS OF THE KING OF ENGLAND
10 December 1685

1. The king has a prerogative which lawyers must expound.

2. The king makes peers in Parliament, who are perpetual legislators, as also the last and highest judicature of England and Ireland, and have great privileges and immunities for themselves and servants.

3. The king is the fountain of honour, titles and precedencies, and of all the powers which the Lord Marshal and heralds exercise.

4. The king makes bishops, and they priests and deacons and clerks of the convocation, and has also all the power which the Pope had formerly. Bishops make chancellors and other officers of the spiritual courts, have power to excommunicate, &c.

5. The king makes the chancellors of the universities, makes heads and fellows in several colleges, and is also visitor in some cases.

6. The king has the power of coinage, and can give the name, matter, fineness, character and shape to all species of money, and can cry money up and down by his proclamation, which some extend to this, viz., that if A. lend B. 100*l.* weighing 29 pounds of sterling silver, if the king by his proclamation declare that one ounce of silver shall be afterwards called one hundred pounds, that then, B. paying to A. the said ounce of silver, the debt is answered.

7. The king makes sheriffs, and they juries upon life and estate, limb and liberty, as also jailers, bailiffs and executioners of all sorts.

8. The king makes a Chancellor, or chief judge in equity, who stops proceedings in other courts of law, &c. The Chancellor makes justices of the peace, and they high and petty constables and sessions of peace, &c.

9. The king makes judges *durante beneplacito*. They set fines and punish at their own discretion in several cases. They govern proceedings at law, declare and interpret the law, reprieve, &c.; and the king can suspend the law, pardon or prosecute.

10. The king can give charters for boroughs to Parliament; appoint electors and judges of elections; prorogue, adjourn and dissolve Parliaments from time to time and from place to place; disapprove the Speaker, &c.

11. The king appoints his lieutenants to command the grand standing militia, can press any man to serve his allies beyond seas as soldiers, can equip and appoint what number of ships and seamen he pleases, and their wages, and *pari ratione* a mercenary army to serve at land, as also guards for his person of several sorts.

12. The king has some revenue by common law and prerogative, and can by his judges interpret statutes concerning the branches and the collection thereof.

13. The king has great power over forests and mines, colonies, monopolies.

14. The king can do no wrong, and his coming to the Crown clears him from all punishments, &c., due before, and obedience to him after coronation excuses from[1]

[1] Unfinished.

15. The king, by ceasing or forbearing to administer the several powers above named, can do what harm he pleases to his subjects.

12. Act for the security of the Crown, 1696
(*Statutes of the Realm*, VII, pp. 114–117)
AN ACT FOR THE BETTER SECURITY OF HIS MAJESTY'S ROYAL PERSON AND GOVERNMENT
(7 & 8 Gul. III, cap. 27)

Whereas the welfare and safety of this kingdom and the reformed religion do next under God entirely depend upon the preservation of your Majesty's royal person and government, which by the merciful providence of God of late have been delivered from the bloody and barbarous attempts of traitors and other your Majesty's enemies, who there is just reason to believe have been in great measure encouraged to undertake and prosecute such their wicked designs, partly by your Majesty's great and undeserved clemency towards them, and partly by the want of a sufficient provision in the law for the securing offices and places of trust to such as are well affected to your Majesty's government, and for the repressing and punishing such as are known to be disaffected to the same; for remedy whereof, may it please your Majesty that it may be enacted, and be it enacted . . . that from and after the first day of May one thousand six hundred ninety-six all and every person and persons who shall refuse to take the oaths mentioned and appointed to be taken in an Act of Parliament made in the first year of the reign of his present Majesty and the late queen of blessed memory, intituled, *An Act for the abrogating of the oaths of supremacy and allegiance and appointing other oaths*,[1] or either of them, when tendered to him or them by any persons lawfully authorized to administer or tender the same, or shall refuse or neglect to appear when lawfully summoned in order to have the said oaths tendered to him or them, shall until he or they have duly taken the said oaths be liable to incur, forfeit, pay and suffer all and every the penalties, forfeitures, sums of money, disabilities and incapacities which by the laws and statutes of this realm now in force or any of them are inflicted upon popish recusants duly convict of recusancy. . . .

II. And be it further enacted . . . that if any person or persons shall from and after the said first day of May maliciously by writing, printing, preaching, teaching or advised speaking, utter, publish or declare that his present Majesty is not the lawful and rightful king of these realms, or that the late King James or the pretended prince of Wales hath any right or title to the crown of these realms, or that any other person or persons hath or have any right or title to the same otherwise than according to an Act of Parliament made in the first year of the reign of his present Majesty and the late queen, intituled, *An Act declaring the rights and liberties of the subject and settling the succession of the crown*,[2] such person or persons, being thereof lawfully convicted, shall incur the danger and penalty of premunire mentioned in the Statute of Premunire made in the sixteenth year of the reign of King Richard the Second.

[1] I Gul. & Mar., cap. 8.   [2] No. 40.

III. And whereas for the better preservation of his Majesty's royal person and government against the aforesaid wicked and traitorous designs, upon a full discovery thereof, great numbers of his Majesty's good subjects have entered into and subscribed an association in the words following, viz.:

Whereas there has been a horrid and detestable conspiracy formed and carried on by papists and other wicked and traitorous persons for assassinating his Majesty's royal person in order to encourage an invasion from France to subvert our religion, laws and liberty, we whose names are hereunto subscribed do heartily, sincerely and solemnly profess, testify and declare that his present Majesty King William is rightful and lawful king of these realms, and we do mutually promise and engage to stand by and assist each other to the utmost of our power in the support and defence of his Majesty's most sacred person and government against the late King James and all his adherents; and in case his Majesty come to any violent or untimely death (which God forbid) we do hereby further freely and unanimously oblige ourselves to unite, associate and stand by each other in revenging the same upon his enemies and their adherents, and in supporting and defending the succession of the crown according to an Act made in the first year of the reign of King William and Queen Mary, intituled, *An Act declaring the rights and liberties of the subject and settling the succession of the crown.*

Be it therefore declared and enacted . . . that the said association so entered into and subscribed, and every part thereof, was, is and shall stand, remain and be good and lawful to all intents, constructions and purposes whatsoever according to the true meaning, intent and purport of the same.

IV. And be it further enacted . . . that the commissioners appointed by an Act of this present Parliament for the taking, examining and stating the public accounts, and all and every person or persons that shall bear any office or offices, civil or military, or shall receive any pay, salary, fee or wages by reason of any patent or grant from his Majesty, or shall have command or place of trust from or under his Majesty or from any of his Majesty's predecessors, or by his or their authority, or by authority derived from him or them within the realm of England, dominion of Wales or town of Berwick-upon-Tweed, or in his Majesty's navy or in the several islands of Jersey and Guernsey, or shall be of the Household or in the service or employment of his Majesty or of his Royal Highness Prince George or her Royal Highness the Princess Anne of Denmark, . . . shall . . . subscribe the aforesaid association. . . .

XV. And be it enacted . . . that from and after the determination of this present Parliament every person that shall hereafter be chosen a member of the House of Commons, when he takes the oath and subscribes the declaration according to an Act made in the first year of King William and Queen Mary, shall also at the same time subscribe the association in this Act prescribed; and that every person refusing so to do shall be adjudged, and is hereby declared to be, incapable and disabled in law to all intents and purposes whatsoever to sit in the said House of Commons or give any voice therein during that Parliament; and that in such case a new writ or writs shall issue out of the High Court of Chancery by warrant or warrants from the Speaker of the House of Commons for the time being, and by order of the said House, for the election of a new member or members to serve in the House of Commons in the place or places of such member or members so disabled, to all intents and purposes as if such member or members were naturally dead. . . .

XVIII. And be it further enacted . . . that no person who shall refuse to take the oaths directed by an Act made in the first year of the reign of his present Majesty and the late Queen Mary, intituled, *An Act for abrogating of the oaths of supremacy and allegiance and appointing other oaths*, or being Quakers shall refuse to subscribe the declaration of fidelity directed by one other Act of Parliament made in the said first year of the reign of his present Majesty and the late queen, intituled, *An Act for exempting their Majesties' Protestant subjects dissenting from the Church of England from the penalties of certain laws*,[1] which oaths and subscription respectively the sheriff or chief officer taking the poll at any election of members to serve in Parliament at the request of any one of the candidates are hereby empowered and required to administer, shall be admitted to give any vote for the election of any knight of the shire, citizen, burgess or baron of the cinque ports to serve in Parliament.

XIX. And be it further enacted . . . that it shall and may be lawful to detain in custody without bail or mainprize any person who is, or shall before the last day of Trinity Term one thousand six hundred ninety-six be, committed upon information upon oath against him for high treason, until the first day of December one thousand six hundred ninety-six, unless such person should be sooner bailed by order of Council signed by six of his Majesty's Privy Council, any law or statute to the contrary notwithstanding.

XX. And for the better securing of the succession of the crown in such manner as in and by an Act made in the first year of the reign of King William and Queen Mary, intituled, *An Act declaring the rights and liberties of the subject and settling the succession of the crown*, is provided, limited and appointed, be it further enacted . . . that no commission, either civil or military, shall cease, determine or be void by reason of the death or demise of his present Majesty or of any of his heirs or successors, kings or queens of this realm, but that every such commission shall be, continue and remain in full force and virtue for the space of six months next after any such death or demise, unless in the meantime superseded, determined or made void by the next and immediate successor to whom the imperial crown of this realm according to the Act of settlement hereinbefore mentioned is limited and appointed to go, remain or descend.

[1] No. 151.

C. LIMITATION OF THE PREROGATIVE

(a) DISPENSING AND SUSPENDING POWERS

13. Speech of Charles II in support of his declaration of indulgence, the Commons' addresses on the subject, and the king's replies, 1673

(Journals of the House of Commons, IX, pp. 246–266)

(i) 5 February 1673

MY LORDS AND GENTLEMEN,

I am glad to see you here this day. I would have called you together sooner, but that I am willing to ease you and the country till there were an absolute necessity.

Since you were last here I have been forced to a most important, necessary and expensive war, and I make no doubt but you will give me suitable and effectual assistance to go through with it. I refer you to my declaration for the causes, and indeed the necessity, of this war, and shall now only tell you that I might have digested the indignities to my own person rather than have brought it to this extremity, if the interest as well as the honour of the whole kingdom had not been at stake. And if I had omitted this conjuncture perhaps I had not again ever met with the like advantage.

You will find that the last supply you gave me did not answer expectation for the ends you gave it, the payment of our debts. Therefore I must in the next place recommend them again to your special care.

Some few days before I declared the war I put forth my declaration for indulgence to dissenters,[1] and have hitherto found a good effect of it by securing peace at home when I had war abroad. There is one part of it that hath been subject to misconstruction, which is that concerning the papists, as if more liberty were granted them than to the other recusants, when it is plain there is less, for the others have public places allowed them, and I never intended that they should have any, but only have the freedom of their religion in their own houses, without any concern of others. And I could not grant them less than this when I had extended so much more grace to others, most of them having been loyal and in the service of me and of the king my father. And in the whole course of this indulgence I do not intend that it shall any way prejudice the Church; but I will support its rights and it in its full power. Having said this, I shall take it very, very ill to receive contradiction in what I have done. And I will deal plainly with you: I am resolved to stick to my declaration.

There is one jealousy more that is maliciously spread abroad, and yet so weak and frivolous that I once thought it not of moment enough to mention, but it may have gotten some ground with some well-minded people; and that is that the forces I have raised in this war were designed to control law and property. I wish I had had more forces the last summer. The want of them then convinces me I must raise more against this next spring, and I do not doubt but you will consider the charge of them in your supplies.

[1] No. 140.

77

I will conclude with this assurance to you, that I will preserve the true reformed Protestant religion and the Church as it is now established in this kingdom, and that no man's property or liberty shall ever be invaded.

(ii) 14 February 1673

MOST GRACIOUS SOVEREIGN,

We, your Majesty's most loyal and faithful subjects, the Commons assembled in Parliament, do in the first place, as in all duty bound, return your Majesty our most humble and hearty thanks for the many gracious promises and assurances which your Majesty hath several times during this present Parliament given to us, that your Majesty would secure and maintain unto us the true reformed Protestant religion, our liberties and properties, which most gracious assurances your Majesty hath out of your great goodness been pleased to renew unto us more particularly at the opening of this present session of Parliament.

And further we crave leave humbly to represent that we have, with all duty and expedition, taken into our consideration several parts of your Majesty's last speech to us, and withal the declaration therein mentioned for indulgence to dissenters, dated the fifteenth of March last; and we find ourselves bound in duty to inform your Majesty that penal statutes in matters ecclesiastical cannot be suspended but by Act of Parliament.

We therefore, the knights, citizens and burgesses of your Majesty's House of Commons, do most humbly beseech your Majesty that the said laws may have their free course until it shall be otherwise provided for by Act of Parliament, and that your Majesty would graciously be pleased to give such directions herein that no apprehensions or jealousies may remain in the hearts of your Majesty's good and faithful subjects.

(iii) 24 February 1673

CHARLES R.

His Majesty hath received an address from you; and he hath seriously considered of it, and returneth you this answer:

That he is very much troubled that that declaration, which he put out for ends so necessary to the quiet of his kingdom, and especially in that conjuncture, should have proved the cause of disquiet in his House of Commons, and give occasion to the questioning of his power in ecclesiastics, which he finds not done in the reigns of any of his ancestors. He is sure he never had thoughts of using it otherwise than as it hath been intrusted in him, to the peace and establishment of the Church of England and the ease of all his subjects in general. Neither doth he pretend to the right of suspending any laws wherein the properties, rights or liberties of any of his subjects are concerned, nor to alter anything in the established doctrine or discipline of the Church of England. But his only design in this was to take off the penalties the statutes inflict upon dissenters, and which he believes, when well considered of, you yourselves would not wish executed according to the rigour and letter of the law.

Neither hath he done this with any thought of avoiding or precluding the advice of his Parliament; and if any bill shall be offered him which shall appear more proper to attain the aforesaid ends, and secure the peace of the Church and kingdom, when tendered in due manner to him, he will show how readily he will concur in all ways that shall appear good for the kingdom.

Given at the Court at Whitehall,
the 24th of February 1672/3.

(iv) 26 February 1673

MOST GRACIOUS SOVEREIGN,

We, your Majesty's most humble and loyal subjects, the knights, citizens and burgesses in this present Parliament assembled, do render to your sacred Majesty our most dutiful thanks for that, to our unspeakable comfort, your Majesty hath been pleased so often to reiterate unto us those gracious promises and assurances of maintaining the religion now established, and the liberties and properties of your people. And we do not in the least measure doubt but that your Majesty had the same gracious intentions in giving satisfaction to your subjects by your answer to our last petition and address. Yet upon a serious consideration thereof we find that the said answer is not sufficient to clear the apprehensions that may justly remain in the minds of your people, by your Majesty's having claimed a power to suspend penal statutes in matters ecclesiastical, and which your Majesty does still seem to assert in the said answer to be intrusted in the Crown, and never questioned in the reigns of any your ancestors; wherein we humbly conceive your Majesty hath been very much misinformed, since no such power was ever claimed or exercised by any of your Majesty's predecessors, and if it should be admitted might tend to the interrupting of the free course of the laws, and altering the legislative power, which hath always been acknowledged to reside in your Majesty and your two Houses of Parliament.

We do therefore with an unanimous consent become again most humble suitors unto your sacred Majesty, that you would be pleased to give us a full and satisfactory answer to our said petition and address, and that your Majesty would take such effectual order that the proceedings in this matter may not for the future be drawn into consequence or example.

(v) 3 March 1673[1]

MOST GRACIOUS SOVEREIGN,

We, your Majesty's most loyal subjects, the Lords Spiritual and Temporal and Commons in this present Parliament assembled, being very sensible of the great dangers and mischiefs that may arise within this your Majesty's realm by the increase of popish recusants amongst us; and considering the great resort of priests and Jesuits into this kingdom, who daily endeavour to seduce your Majesty's subjects from their religion and allegiance, and how desirous your loyal subjects are that no popish recusants be admitted into employments of trust and profit, and especially into military commands over the forces now in your Majesty's service; and having a tender regard

---

[1] This address was adopted by the Commons on 3 March, approved by the Lords with some amendments on 7 March, and presented to the king by both Houses the same day.

to the preservation of your Majesty's person and the peace and tranquillity of this kingdom, do in all humility desire that your Majesty would be pleased to issue out your royal proclamation to command all priests and Jesuits (other than such as, not being natural-born subjects to your Majesty, are obliged to attend upon your royal consort the queen) to depart within thirty days out of this your Majesty's kingdom: and that if any priest or Jesuit shall happen to be taken in England after the expiration of the said time, that the laws be put in due execution against them; and that your Majesty would please in the said proclamation to command all judges, justices of the peace, mayors, bailiffs and other officers to put the said laws in execution accordingly.

That your Majesty would likewise be pleased that the Lord Chancellor of England shall, on or before the five and twentieth day of March instant, issue out commissions of *dedimus potestatem* to the judge advocate and commissaries of the musters and such other persons as he shall think fit (not being officers commanding soldiers) to tender the oaths of allegiance and supremacy to all officers and soldiers now in your Majesty's service and pay; and that such as refuse the said oaths may be immediately disbanded, and not allowed or continued in any pay or pension: and that the Chancellor shall require due returns to be made thereof within some convenient time after the issuing out of the said commissions.

That the said commissaries of the musters be commanded and enjoined by your Majesty's warrant, upon the penalty of losing their places, not to permit any officer to be mustered in the service and pay of your Majesty until he shall have taken the oaths of allegiance and supremacy and received the sacrament of the Lord's Supper according to the laws and usage of the Church of England; and that every soldier serving at land shall take the said oaths before his first muster, and receive the sacrament in such manner before his second muster.

And this we present, in all dutifulness, to your Majesty's princely wisdom and consideration, as the best means for the satisfying and composing the minds of your loyal subjects, humbly desiring your Majesty graciously to accept of this our petition, as proceeding from hearts and affections entirely devoted to your Majesty's service, and to give it your royal approbation.

(vi) 8 March 1673

MY LORDS AND GENTLEMEN,

Yesterday you presented me an address as the best means for the satisfying and composing the minds of my subjects; to which I freely and readily agreed, and shall take care to see it performed accordingly. I hope, on the other side, you gentlemen of the House of Commons will do your part, for I must put you in mind it is near five weeks since I demanded a supply, and what you voted unanimously upon it did both give life to my affairs at home and disheartened my enemies abroad. But the seeming delay it hath met with since has made them take new courage, and they are now preparing for this next summer a greater fleet (as they say) than ever they had yet, so that if the supply be not speedily dispatched it will be altogether ineffectual, and the safety, honour and interest of England must of necessity be exposed. Pray lay this to heart, and let not the fears and jealousies of some draw an inevitable ruin upon us all.

MY LORDS AND GENTLEMEN,

If there be any scruple remain yet with you concerning the suspension of penal laws,[1] I here faithfully promise you that what hath been done in that particular shall not for the future be drawn into consequence or example. And as I daily expect from you a bill for my supply, so I assure you I shall as willingly receive and pass any other you shall offer me that may tend to the giving you satisfaction in all your just grievances.

14. Speech of James II in support of the standing army and the Catholic officers, and the address of the Commons in reply, 1685

(*Journals of the House of Commons*, IX, pp. 756, 758)

(i) 9 November 1685

MY LORDS AND GENTLEMEN,

After the storm that seemed to be coming upon us when we parted last, I am glad to meet you all again in so great peace and quietness. God Almighty be praised, by whose blessing that rebellion was suppressed. But when we reflect what an inconsiderable number of men began it, and how long they carried it on without any opposition, I hope everybody will be convinced that the militia, which hath hitherto been so much depended on, is not sufficient for such occasions, and that there is nothing but a good force of well-disciplined troops in constant pay that can defend us from such as, either at home or abroad, are disposed to disturb us. And in truth, my concern for the peace and quiet of my subjects, as well as for the safety of the government, made me think it necessary to increase the number to the proportion I have done. This I owed as well to the honour as the security of the nation, whose reputation was so infinitely exposed to all our neighbours, by having so evidently lain open to this late wretched attempt, that it is not to be repaired without keeping such a body of men on foot that none may ever have the thought again of finding us so miserably unprovided.

It is for the support of this great charge, which is now more than double to what it was, that I ask your assistance in giving me a supply answerable to the expense it brings along with it. And I cannot doubt but what I have begun, so much for the honour and defence of the government, will be continued by you with all the cheerfulness that is requisite for a work of so great importance.

Let no man take exception that there are some officers in the army not qualified, according to the late Tests, for their employments. The gentlemen, I must tell you, are most of them well known to me, and having formerly served with me in several occasions, and always approved the loyalty of their principles by their practice, I think fit now to be employed under me. And I will deal plainly with you, that after having had the benefit of their service in such time of need and danger, I will neither expose them to disgrace, nor myself to want of them, if there should be another rebellion to make them necessary for me.

---

[1] The king had cancelled his declaration of indulgence on the previous evening.

I am afraid some men may be so wicked to hope and expect that a difference may happen between you and me upon this occasion. But when you consider what advantages have arisen to us in a few months by the good understanding we have hitherto had; what wonderful effects it hath already produced in the change of the whole scene of affairs abroad, so much more to the honour of this nation and the figure it ought to make in the world; and that nothing can hinder a further progress in this way, to all our satisfactions, but fears and jealousies amongst ourselves, I will not apprehend that such a misfortune can befall us as a division, or but a coldness, between me and you, nor that anything can shake you in your steadiness and loyalty to me who, by God's blessing, will ever make you returns of all kindness and protection, with a resolution to venture even my own life in the defence of the true interest of this kingdom.

(ii) 16 November 1685

Most gracious Sovereign,

We, your Majesty's most loyal and faithful subjects, the Commons in Parliament assembled, do in the first place, as in duty bound, return your Majesty our most humble and hearty thanks for your great care and conduct in the suppression of the late rebellion, which threatened the overthrow of this government both in Church and State and the utter extirpation of our religion by law established, which is most dear unto us, and which your Majesty has been graciously pleased to give us repeated assurances you will always defend and support, which with all grateful hearts we shall ever acknowledge.

We further crave leave to acquaint your Majesty that we have with all duty and readiness taken into our consideration your Majesty's gracious speech to us. And as to that part of it relating to the officers in the army not qualified for their employments according to an Act of Parliament made in the twenty-fifth year of the reign of your Majesty's royal brother of blessed memory, entituled, *An Act for preventing dangers which may happen from popish recusants*,[1] we do out of our bounden duty humbly represent unto your Majesty that those officers cannot by law be capable of their employments, and that the incapacities they bring upon themselves thereby can no ways be taken off but by an Act of Parliament.

Therefore out of that great deference and duty we owe unto your Majesty, who has been graciously pleased to take notice of their services to you, we are preparing a bill to pass both Houses for your royal assent, to indemnify them from the penalties they have now incurred. And because the continuance of them in their employments may be taken to be a dispensing with that law without Act of Parliament (the consequence of which is of the greatest concern to the rights of all your Majesty's dutiful and loyal subjects, and to all the laws made for security of their religion), we therefore, the knights, citizens and burgesses of your Majesty's House of Commons, do most humbly beseech your Majesty that you would be graciously pleased to give such directions therein that no apprehensions or jealousies may remain in the hearts of your Majesty's good and faithful subjects.

[1] No. 143.

15. Chief Justice Herbert in the case *Godden* v. *Hales,* 1686
(State Trials, XI, pp. 1195–1199)

This is a case of great consequence, but of as little difficulty as ever any case was that raised so great an expectation, for if the king cannot dispense with this statute he cannot dispense with any penal law whatsoever. . . . There is no law whatsoever but may be dispensed with by the supreme lawgiver, as the laws of God may be dispensed with by God himself, as it appears by God's command to Abraham to offer up his son Isaac. So likewise the law of man may be dispensed with by the legislator, for a law may be either too wide or too narrow, and there may be many cases which may be out of the conveniencies which did induce the law to be made; for it is impossible for the wisest law-maker to foresee all the cases that may be or are to be remedied, and therefore there must be a power somewhere able to dispense with these laws. . . .

My brother Powell said he was inclined to be of the same opinion, but he would rather have some more time to consider of it; but he has since sent by my brother Holloway to let us know that he does concur with us. To these eleven judges there is one dissenter, brother Street, who yet continues his opinion that the king cannot dispense in this case; but that is the opinion of one single judge against the opinion of eleven. We were satisfied in our judgments before, and having the concurrence of eleven out of twelve we think we may very well declare the opinion of the court to be that the king may dispense in this case; and the judges go upon these grounds:

i. That the kings of England are sovereign princes.

ii. That the laws of England are the king's laws.

iii. That therefore it is an inseparable prerogative in the kings of England to dispense with penal laws in particular cases and upon particular necessary reasons.

iv. That of those reasons and those necessities the king himself is sole judge. And then, which is consequent upon all,

v. That this is not a trust invested in or granted to the king by the people, but the ancient remains of the sovereign power and prerogative of the kings of England, which never yet was taken from them, nor can be.

16. Order in Council requiring James II's declaration of indulgence to be read in churches, 1688
(London Gazette, 3–7 May 1688)

AT THE COURT AT WHITEHALL, THE 4TH OF MAY 1688

It is this day ordered by his Majesty in Council, that his Majesty's late gracious declaration, bearing date the 27th of April last,[1] be read at the usual time of divine service, upon the 20th and 27th of this month, in all churches and chapels within the cities of London and Westminster and ten miles thereabout, and upon the 3rd and 10th of June next in all other churches and chapels throughout this kingdom. And it is hereby further ordered, that the right reverend the bishops cause the said declaration to be sent and distributed throughout their several and respective dioceses to be read accordingly.

[1] No. 149.

17. Petition of the Seven Bishops, 1688

(Collectanea Curiosa, ed. John Gutch, I, pp. 336–337)

TO THE KING'S MOST EXCELLENT MAJESTY,

The humble petition of William, archbishop of Canterbury, and of divers of the suffragan bishops of that province now present with him, in behalf of themselves and others of their absent brethren, and of the clergy of their respective dioceses,

Humbly sheweth,

That the great averseness they find in themselves to the distributing and publishing in all their churches your Majesty's late declaration for liberty of conscience proceedeth neither from any want of duty and obedience to your Majesty, our holy mother, the Church of England, being both in her principles and constant practice unquestionably loyal, and having to her great honour been more than once publicly acknowledged to be so by your gracious Majesty, nor yet from any want of due tenderness to dissenters, in relation to whom they are willing to come to such a temper as shall be thought fit when that matter shall be considered and settled in Parliament and Convocation, but among many other considerations from this especially, because that declaration is founded upon such a dispensing power as hath often been declared illegal in Parliament, and particularly in the years 1662, 1672, and in the beginning of your Majesty's reign, and is a matter of so great moment and consequence to the whole nation, both in Church and State, that your petitioners cannot in prudence, honour or conscience so far make themselves parties to it as the distribution of it all over the nation, and the solemn publication of it once and again even in God's house and in the time of his divine service, must amount to in common and reasonable construction.

Your petitioners therefore most humbly and earnestly beseech your Majesty that you will be graciously pleased not to insist upon their distributing and reading your Majesty's said declaration.

And your petitioners shall ever pray, &c.

William Canterbury

William St. Asaph	Thomas Bath and Wells	
Francis Ely	Thomas Peterborough	
John Chichester	Jonathan Bristol	
Henry London[1]	William Norwich	Robert Gloucester
Seth Salisbury	Peter Winchester	Thomas Exeter

18. Summing up of Chief Justice Wright and opinion of Justice Holloway in the Seven Bishops' Case, 1688

(State Trials, XII, pp. 422–426)

(i) Wright

Gentlemen, thus stands the case. It is an information against my lords the bishops, his grace my lord of Canterbury and the other six noble lords; and it is for preferring, composing, making and publishing, and causing to be published, a seditious libel. The way that the information goes is special, and it sets forth that the king was

---
[1] The last six names were added separately at later dates.

graciously pleased, by his royal power and prerogative, to set forth a declaration of indulgence for liberty of conscience in the third year of his reign; and afterwards, upon the 27th of April in the fourth year, he comes and makes another declaration; and afterwards in May orders in Council that this declaration should be published by my lords the bishops in their several dioceses; and after this was done my lords the bishops come and present a petition to the king, in which were contained the words which you have seen. . . .

Gentlemen, upon the point of the publication I have summed up all the evidence to you; and if you believe that the petition which these lords presented to the king was this petition, truly, I think, that is a publication sufficient. If you do not believe it was this petition, then my lords the bishops are not guilty of what is laid to their charge in this information, and consequently there needs no inquiry whether they are guilty of a libel. But if you do believe that this was the petition they presented to the king, then we must come to inquire whether this be a libel.

Now, gentlemen, anything that shall disturb the government, or make mischief and a stir among the people, is certainly within the case of *Libellis Famosis*; and I must in short give you my opinion, I do take it to be a libel. Now this being a point of law, if my brothers have anything to say to it I suppose they will deliver their opinions.

(ii) Holloway

Look you, gentlemen, it is not usual for any person to say anything after the Chief Justice has summed up the evidence. It is not according to the course of the Court. But this is a case of an extraordinary nature, and there being a point of law in it, it is very fit everybody should deliver their own opinion. The question is, whether this petition of my lords the bishops be a libel or no. Gentlemen, the end and intention of every action is to be considered; and likewise in this case we are to consider the nature of the offence that these noble persons are charged with. It is for delivering a petition, which, according as they have made their defence, was with all the humility and decency that could be; so that if there was no ill intent, and they were not (as it is not nor can be pretended they were) men of evil lives or the like, to deliver a petition cannot be a fault, it being the right of every subject to petition. If you are satisfied there was an ill intention of sedition or the like, you ought to find them guilty. But if there be nothing in the case that you find, but only that they did deliver a petition to save themselves harmless, and to free themselves from blame, by shewing the reason of their disobedience to the king's command, which they apprehended to be a grievance to them, and which they could not in conscience give obedience to, I cannot think it is a libel. It is left to you, gentlemen, but that is my opinion.

(b) CONTROL OF JUDGES AND JURIES

19. Resolutions of the Commons on the punishment of juries, 13 December 1667

(Journals of the House of Commons, IX, p. 37)

The House then proceeded to the hearing of the Lord Chief Justice Keeling as to his defence to the matters charged against him.

Resolved, &c. That a chair be brought into the House for his lordship to rest upon.

The Lord Chief Justice Keeling, being called in, made his defence to the matters charged against him . . .

Resolved, &c. That the precedents and practice of fining or imprisoning jurors is illegal.

Resolved, &c. That this House proceed no further upon the matter against the Lord Chief Justice Keeling.

Ordered. That the Lord St. John have leave to bring in a bill for declaring the fining and imprisoning of jurors illegal.

20. Newsletter account of the case of Edward Bushell, 1670–1671
(British Museum Additional MSS. 36916, ff. 191, 233)

10 September 1670. Since my last of the 1st instant we have little news but what the sessions at the Old Bailey hath afforded, where there were several Quakers indicted for tumultuously assembling in the streets on Sundays and there preaching to the people. At first the court fined every one of them twenty nobles for not pulling off their hats. Then young Penn, Sir William Penn's son, and Captain Mead were the first that were tried, who being men of parts held the court hard to it, there being never a judge, only Sir John Howell the recorder, who committed several errors there.

The first was his summing up the evidence to the jury when he had sent the prisoners from the bar, where they ought then to have been; but there being some of the jury they would not agree, upon which they were locked up all Saturday night, and the court adjourned till Sunday morning and then sat for two hours. But then the jury was not agreed on such a verdict as the court would accept, upon which they were locked up again till Monday morning, to which time the court adjourned; and then the jury brought them in both not guilty, for which the recorder fined them forty marks a man, and imprisonment till they paid it. He said in open court that we should never be at quiet till it was with us as it is in the Church of Rome, where they have the Inquisition, by which they are free from those disturbances we are troubled with. He said other things as extravagant, which make a good noise in the city.

Upon discharge of that jury another were summoned, who found the rest of the Quakers guilty as they stood indicted. Some lawyers say that the court ought not to have sat on Sunday, and therefore what they did then and since is void.

18 November 1671. The last week the Lord Chief Justice Vaughan, by the appointment of all the judges, delivered in the Court of Common Pleas their opinion in the case of the jurymen that were committed by Sir Samuel Sterling and the recorder for not giving a verdict according to the directions of the court, that their commitment was not legal, and that juries ought not to be punished for giving their verdicts according to their consciences, which is business of great concernment and much talked of.

21. Judgment of Chief Justice Vaughan in Bushell's Case, 1671
(State Trials, VI, pp. 1002–1019)

In the present case it is returned that the prisoner, being a juryman among others charged at the sessions court of the Old Bailey to try the issue between the king and

Penn and Mead upon an indictment for assembling unlawfully and tumultuously, did *contra plenam et manifestam evidentiam*, openly given in court, acquit the prisoners indicted, in contempt of the king, &c.

The court hath no knowledge by this return whether the evidence given were full and manifest, or doubtful, lame and dark, or indeed evidence at all material to the issue, because it is not returned what evidence in particular, and as it was delivered, was given. For it is not possible to judge of that rightly which is not exposed to a man's judgment. But here the evidence given to the jury is not exposed at all to this court, but the judgment of the court of sessions upon that evidence is only exposed to us, who tell us it was full and manifest. But our judgment ought to be grounded upon our own inferences and understandings, and not upon theirs. . . .

Another fault in the return is that the jurors are not said to have acquitted the persons indicted against full and manifest evidence corruptly, and knowing the said evidence to be full and manifest against the persons indicted, for how manifest soever the evidence was, if it were not manifest to them, and that they believed it such, it was not a finable fault, nor deserving imprisonment, upon which difference the law of punishing jurors for false verdicts principally depends. . . .

I would know whether anything be more common than for two men, students, barristers or judges, to deduce contrary and opposite conclusions out of the same case in law. And is there any difference that two men should infer distinct conclusions from the same testimony? Is anything more known than that the same author, and place in that author, is forcibly urged to maintain contrary conclusions, and the decision hard which is in the right? Is anything more frequent in the controversies of religion than to press the same text for opposite tenets? How then comes it to pass that two persons may not apprehend, with reason and honesty, what a witness, or many, say, to prove in the understanding of one plainly one thing, but in the apprehension of the other clearly the contrary thing? Must therefore one of these merit fine and imprisonment because he doth that which he cannot otherwise do, preserving his oath and integrity? And this often is the case of the judge and jury.

I conclude, therefore, that this return, charging the prisoners to have acquitted Penn and Mead against full and manifest evidence first, and next without saying that they did know and believe that evidence to be full and manifest against the indicted persons, is no cause of fine or imprisonment.

And, by the way, I must here note that the verdict of a jury and evidence of a witness are very different things in the truth and falsehood of them. A witness swears but to what he hath heard or seen, generally or more largely to what hath fallen under his senses. But a juryman swears to what he can infer and conclude from the testimony of such witnesses, by the act and force of his understanding, to be the fact inquired after, which differs nothing in the reason, though much in the punishment, from what a judge, out of various cases considered by him, infers to be the law in the question before him. . . .

We come now to the next part of the return, viz., that the jury acquitted those indicted against the direction of the court in matter of law, openly given and declared to them in court.

The words, that the jury did acquit against the direction of the court in matter of law, literally taken and *de plano*, are insignificant and not intelligible, for no issue can be joined of matter in law, no jury can be charged with the trial of matter in law barely, no evidence ever was or can be given to a jury of what is law or not; nor no such oath can be given to, or taken by, a jury to try matter in law; nor no attaint can lie for such a false oath. . . .

If the meaning of these words, finding against the direction of the court in matter of law, be, that if the judge, having heard the evidence given in court (for he knows no other), shall tell the jury, upon this evidence, the law is for the plaintiff or for the defendant, and you are under the pain of fine and imprisonment to find accordingly, then the jury ought of duty so to do, every man sees that the jury is but a troublesome delay, great charge, and of no use in determining right and wrong; and therefore the trials by them may be better abolished than continued, which were a strange new-found conclusion after a trial so celebrated for many hundreds of years. For if the judge, from the evidence, shall by his own judgment first resolve upon any trial what the fact is, and so knowing the fact, shall then resolve what the law is, and order the jury penally to find accordingly, what either necessary or convenient use can be fancied of juries, or to continue trials by them at all? . . .

Without a fact agreed it is as impossible for a judge, or any other, to know the law relating to that fact, or direct concerning it, as to know an accident that hath no subject. Hence it follows that the judge can never direct what the law is in any matter controverted without first knowing the fact, and then it follows that without his previous knowledge of the fact the jury cannot go against his direction in law, for he could not direct. But the judge, *qua* judge, cannot know the fact possibly but from the evidence which the jury have; but (as will appear) he can never know what evidence the jury have, and consequently he cannot know the matter of fact, nor punish the jury for going against their evidence, when he cannot know what their evidence is.

It is true, if the jury were to have no other evidence for the fact but what is deposed in court, the judge might know their evidence, and the fact from it, equally as they, and so direct what the law were in the case, though even then the judge and jury might honestly differ in the result from the evidence, as well as two judges may, which often happens. But the evidence which the jury have of the fact is much other than that, for,

1. Being returned of the vicinage whence the cause of action ariseth, the law supposeth them thence to have sufficient knowledge to try the matter in issue (and so they must) though no evidence were given on either side in court; but to this evidence the judge is a stranger.

2. They may have evidence from their own personal knowledge, by which they may be assured, and sometimes are, that what is deposed in court is absolutely false; but to this the judge is a stranger, and he knows no more of the fact than he hath learned in court, and perhaps by false depositions, and consequently knows nothing.

3. The jury may know the witnesses to be stigmatized and infamous, which may be unknown to the parties, and consequently to the court.

4. In many cases the jury are to have view necessarily, in many by consent, for their better information. To this evidence likewise the judge is a stranger.

5. If they do follow his direction they may be attainted, and the judgment reversed, for doing that which if they had not done they should have been fined and imprisoned by the judge, which is unreasonable.

6. If they do not follow his direction, and be therefore fined, yet they may be attainted, and so doubly punished by distinct judicatures for the same offence, which the common law admits not. . . .

7. To what end is the jury to be returned out of the vicinage whence the cause of action ariseth; to what end must hundredors be of the jury, whom the law supposeth to have nearer knowledge of the fact than those of the vicinage in general; to what end are they challenged so scrupulously to array and pole; to what end must they have such a certain freehold, and be *probi et legales homines*, and not of affinity with the parties concerned; to what end must they have in many cases the view, for their exacter information chiefly; to what end must they undergo the heavy punishment of the villainous judgment, if after all this they implicitly must give a verdict by the dictates and authority of another man, under pain of fines and imprisonment, when sworn to do it according to the best of their own knowledge?

8. A man cannot see by another's eye, nor hear by another's ear. No more can a man conclude or infer the thing to be resolved by another's understanding or reasoning. And though the verdict be right the jury give, yet they, being not assured it is so from their own understanding, are forsworn, at least *in foro conscientiae*.

9. It is absurd a jury should be fined by the judge for going against their evidence, when he who fineth knows not what it is. . . . And it is as absurd to fine a jury for finding against their evidence when the judge knows but part of it, for the better and greater part of the evidence may be wholly unknown to him. . . .

The legal verdict of the jury to be recorded is finding for the plaintiff or defendant. What they answer, if asked, to questions concerning some particular fact is not of their verdict essentially, nor are they bound to agree in such particulars. If they all agree to find their issue for the plaintiff or defendant they may differ in the motives wherefore, as well as judges, in giving judgment for the plaintiff or defendant, may differ in the reasons wherefore they give that judgment, which is very ordinary.

22. Trials for Treason Act, 1696

(*Statutes of the Realm*, VII, pp. 6–7)

AN ACT FOR REGULATING OF TRIALS IN CASES OF TREASON AND MISPRISION OF TREASON

(*7 & 8 Gul. III, cap. 3*)

Whereas nothing is more just and reasonable than that persons prosecuted for high treason and misprision of treason, whereby the liberties, lives, honour, estates, blood and posterity of the subjects may be lost and destroyed, should be justly and equally tried, and that persons accused as offenders therein should not be debarred of all just and equal means for defence of their innocencies in such cases ; in order thereunto, and for the better regulation of trials of persons prosecuted for high treason and misprision of such treason, be it enacted . . . that from and after the five and twentieth day of March in the year of our Lord one thousand six hundred ninety-six all and every person and persons whatsoever that shall be accused and indicted for high treason, whereby any corruption of blood may or shall be made to any such offender or offenders or to any the heir or heirs of any such offender or offenders, or for misprision of such treason, shall have a true copy of the whole indictment, but not the names of the witnesses, delivered unto them or any of them five days at the least before he or they shall be tried for the same, whereby to enable them and any of them respectively to advise with counsel thereupon to plead and make their defence, . . . and that every such person so accused and indicted, arraigned or tried for any such treason as aforesaid, or for misprision of such treason, from and after the said time shall be received and admitted to make his and their full defence by counsel learned in the law, and to make any proof that he or they can produce by lawful witness or witnesses who shall then be upon oath for his and their just defence in that behalf; and in case any person or persons so accused or indicted shall desire counsel, the court before whom such person or persons shall be tried, or some judge of that court, shall and is hereby authorized and required, immediately upon his or their request, to assign to such person and persons such and so many counsel not exceeding two as the person or persons shall desire, to whom such counsel shall have free access at all seasonable hours, any law or usage to the contrary notwithstanding.

II. And be it further enacted, that from and after the said five and twentieth day of March . . . no person or persons whatsoever shall be indicted, tried or attainted of high treason whereby any corruption of blood may or shall be made to any such offender or offenders or to any the heir or heirs of any such offender or offenders, or of misprision of such treason, but by and upon the oaths and testimony of two lawful witnesses, either both of them to the same overt act, or one of them to one and another of them to another overt act of the same treason, unless the party indicted and arraigned or tried shall willingly without violence in open court confess the same, or shall stand mute or refuse to plead, or in cases of high treason shall peremptorily challenge above the number of thirty-five of the jury, any law, statute or usage to the contrary notwithstanding. . . .

IV. And be it further enacted . . . that if two or more distinct treasons of diverse heads or kinds shall be alleged in one bill of indictment, one witness produced to prove one of the said treasons and another witness produced to prove another of the said treasons shall not be deemed or taken to be two witnesses to the same treason within the meaning of this Act.

V. And to the intent that the terror and dread of such criminal accusations may in some reasonable time be removed, be it further enacted . . . that from and after the said five and twentieth day of March . . . no person or persons whatsoever shall be indicted, tried or prosecuted for any such treason as aforesaid, or for misprision of such treason, that shall be committed or done within the kingdom of England, dominion of Wales or town of Berwick-upon-Tweed after the said five and twentieth day of March . . . unless the same indictment be found by a grand jury within three years next after the treason or offence done and committed; and that no person or persons shall be prosecuted for any such treason, or misprision of such treason, committed or done, or to be committed or done, within the kingdom of England, dominion of Wales or town of Berwick-upon-Tweed before the said five and twentieth day of March, unless he or they shall be indicted thereof within three years after the said five and twentieth day of March.

VI. Always provided and excepted that if any person or persons whatsoever shall be guilty of designing, endeavouring or attempting any assassination on the body of the king by poison or otherwise, such person or persons may be prosecuted at any time notwithstanding the aforesaid limitation.

VII. And that all and every person and persons who shall be accused, indicted or tried for such treason as aforesaid, or for misprision of such treason, after the said five and twentieth day of March . . . shall have copies of the panel of the jurors who are to try them, duly returned by the sheriff and delivered unto them and every of them so accused and indicted respectively, two days at the least before he or they shall be tried for the same; and that all persons so accused and indicted for any such treason as aforesaid shall have the like process of the court where they shall be tried to compel their witnesses to appear for them at any such trial or trials as is usually granted to compel witnesses to appear against them. . . .

X. And whereas by the good laws of this kingdom in cases of trials of commoners for their lives a jury of twelve freeholders must all agree in one opinion before they can bring a verdict either for acquittal or condemnation of the prisoner, and whereas upon the trials of peers or peeresses a major vote is sufficient either to acquit or condemn, be it further enacted . . . that upon the trial of any peer or peeress either for treason or misprision all the peers who have a right to sit and vote in Parliament shall be duly summoned twenty days at least before every such trial to appear at every such trial, and that every peer so summoned and appearing at such trial shall vote in the trial of such peer or peeress so to be tried, every such peer first taking the oaths mentioned in an Act of Parliament made in the first year of the reign of King William and Queen Mary, entituled, *An Act for abrogating the oaths of supremacy and allegiance and appointing other oaths,*[1] and also every such peer subscribing and audibly repeating the declaration mentioned in *An Act for the more effectual preserving the king's person and government by disabling papists from sitting in either House of Parliament,*[2] and made in the thirtieth year of the reign of the late King Charles the Second.

XI. Provided always, that neither this Act nor anything therein contained shall any ways extend to or be construed to extend to any impeachment or other proceedings in Parliament in any kind whatsoever.

XII. Provided also, that this Act nor anything therein contained shall any ways extend to any indictment of high treason, nor to any proceedings thereupon, for counterfeiting his Majesty's coin, his great seal or privy seal, his sign manual or privy signet.

[1] 1 Gul. & Mar., cap. 8.   [2] No. 144.

(c) POWER OF IMPRISONING

23. Habeas Corpus Act, 1679

(Statutes of the Realm, v, pp. 935–938)

AN ACT FOR THE BETTER SECURING THE LIBERTY OF THE SUBJECT
AND FOR PREVENTION OF IMPRISONMENTS BEYOND THE SEAS

(31 Car. II, cap. 2)

Whereas great delays have been used by sheriffs, gaolers and other officers to whose custody any of the king's subjects have been committed for criminal or supposed criminal matters, in making returns of writs of Habeas Corpus to them directed, by standing out an Alias and Pluries Habeas Corpus and sometimes more, and by other shifts to avoid their yielding obedience to such writs, contrary to their duty and the known laws of the land, whereby many of the king's subjects have been and hereafter may be long detained in prison, in such cases where by law they are bailable, to their great charge and vexation; for the prevention whereof and the more speedy relief of all persons imprisoned for any such criminal or supposed criminal matters, be it enacted . . . that whensoever any person or persons shall bring any Habeas Corpus directed unto any sheriff or sheriffs, gaoler, minister or other person whatsoever, for any person in his or their custody, and the said writ shall be served upon the said officer or left at the gaol or prison with any of the under-officers, under-keepers or deputy of the said officers or keepers, that the said officer or officers, his or their under-officers, under-keepers or deputies, shall within three days after the service thereof as aforesaid (unless the commitment aforesaid were for treason or felony plainly and specially expressed in the warrant of commitment), upon payment or tender of the charges of bringing the said prisoner, to be ascertained by the judge or court that awarded the same and endorsed upon the said writ, not exceeding twelve pence per mile, and upon security given by his own bond to pay the charges of carrying back the prisoner if he shall be remanded by the court or judge to which he shall be brought according to the true intent of this present Act, and that he will not make any escape by the way, make return of such writ, and bring or cause to be brought the body of the party so committed or restrained unto or before the Lord Chancellor or Lord Keeper of the Great Seal of England for the time being, or the judges or barons of the said court from whence the said writ shall issue, or unto and before such other person or persons before whom the said writ is made returnable according to the command thereof, and shall then likewise certify the true causes of his detainer or imprisonment, unless the commitment of the said party be in any place beyond the distance of twenty miles from the place or places where such court or person is or shall be residing, and if beyond the distance of twenty miles and not above one hundred miles, then within the space of ten days, and if beyond the distance of one hundred miles then within the space of twenty days after such delivery aforesaid and not longer.

II. And to the intent that no sheriff, gaoler or other officer may pretend ignorance of the import of any such writ, be it enacted . . . that all such writs shall be marked in this manner, *Per statutum tricesimo primo Caroli Secundi Regis*, and shall be signed by the person that awards the same; and if any person or persons shall be or stand committed or detained as aforesaid for any crime, unless for treason or felony plainly expressed in the warrant of commitment, in the vacation time and out of term, it shall and may be lawful to and for the person or persons so committed or detained (other than persons convict or in execution by legal process), or anyone on his or their behalf, to appeal or complain to the Lord Chancellor or Lord Keeper or any one of his Majesty's justices, either of the one bench or of the other, or the barons of the Exchequer of the degree of the coif; and the said Lord Chancellor, Lord Keeper, justices or barons or any of them, upon view of the copy or copies of the warrant or warrants of commitment and detainer, or otherwise upon oath made that such copy or copies were denied to be given by such person or persons in whose custody the prisoner or prisoners is or are detained, are hereby authorized and required, upon request made in writing by such person or persons, or any on his, her or their behalf, attested and subscribed by two witnesses who were present at the delivery of the same, to award and grant an Habeas Corpus under the seal of such court whereof he shall then be one of the judges, to be directed to the officer or officers in whose custody the party so committed or detained shall be, returnable *immediate* before the said Lord Chancellor or Lord Keeper, or such justice, baron or any other justice or baron of the degree of the coif of any of the said courts; and upon service thereof as aforesaid the officer or officers, his or their under-officer or under-officers, under-keeper or under-keepers or their deputy, in whose custody the party is so committed or detained, shall within the times respectively before limited bring such prisoner or prisoners before the said Lord Chancellor or Lord Keeper, or such justices, barons or one of them before whom the said writ is made returnable, and in case of his absence before any other of them, with the return of such writ and the true causes of the commitment and detainer: and thereupon within two days after the party shall be brought before them the said Lord Chancellor or Lord Keeper, or such justice or baron before whom the prisoner shall be brought as aforesaid, shall discharge the said prisoner from his imprisonment, taking his or their recognizance with one or more surety or sureties in any sum according to their discretions, having regard to the quality of the prisoner and nature of the offence, for his or their appearance in the Court of King's Bench the term following, or at the next assizes, sessions, or general gaol delivery of and for such county, city or place where the commitment was, or where the offence was committed, or in such other court where the said offence is properly cognizable, as the case shall require, and then shall certify the said writ with the return thereof and the said recognizance or recognizances into the said court where such appearance is to be made, unless it shall appear unto the said Lord Chancellor or Lord Keeper, or justice or justices, or baron or barons, that the party so committed is detained upon a legal process, order or warrant out of some court that hath jurisdiction of criminal matters, or by some warrant signed and sealed with the hand and seal of any of the said justices or barons, or some justice or justices of the peace, for such matters or offences for the which by the law the prisoner is not bailable. . . .

IV. And be it further enacted . . . that if any officer or officers, his or their under-officer or under-officers, under-keeper or under-keepers or deputy, shall neglect or refuse to make the returns aforesaid, or to bring the body or bodies of the prisoner or prisoners according to the command of the said writ within the respective times aforesaid, or upon demand made by the prisoner or person in his behalf shall refuse to deliver, or within the space of six hours after demand shall not deliver, to the person so demanding a true copy of the warrant or warrants of commitment and detainer of such prisoner, which he and they are hereby required to deliver accordingly, all and every the head gaolers and keepers of such prisons, and such other person in whose custody the prisoner shall be detained, shall for the first offence forfeit to the prisoner or party grieved the sum of one hundred pounds; and for the second offence the sum of two hundred pounds, and shall and is hereby made incapable to hold or execute his said office. . . .

V. And for the prevention of unjust vexation by reiterated commitments for the same offence, be it enacted . . . that no person or persons which shall be delivered or set at large upon any Habeas Corpus shall at any time hereafter be again imprisoned or committed for the same offence by any person or persons whatsoever, other than by the legal order and process of such court wherein he or they shall be bound by recognizance to appear, or other court having jurisdiction of the cause; and if any other person or persons shall knowingly contrary to this Act recommit or imprison, or knowingly procure or cause to be recommitted or imprisoned for the same offence or pretended offence any person or persons delivered or set at large as aforesaid, or be knowingly aiding or assisting therein, then he or they shall forfeit to the prisoner or party grieved the sum of five hundred pounds. . . .

VI. Provided always, and be it further enacted, that if any person or persons shall be committed for high treason or felony plainly and specially expressed in the warrant of commitment, upon his prayer or petition in open court the first week of the term or first day of the sessions of oyer and terminer or general gaol delivery to be brought to his trial, shall not be indicted some time in the next term, sessions of oyer and terminer or general gaol delivery after such commitment, it shall and may be lawful to and for the judges of the Court of King's Bench and justices of oyer and terminer or general gaol delivery, and they are hereby required, upon motion to them made in open court the last day of the term, sessions or gaol delivery either by the prisoner or anyone in his behalf, to set at liberty the prisoner upon bail, unless it appear to the judges and justices upon oath made that the witnesses for the king could not be produced the same term, sessions or general gaol delivery; and if any person or persons committed as aforesaid, upon his prayer or petition in open court the first week of the term or first day of the sessions of oyer and terminer or general gaol delivery to be brought to his trial, shall not be indicted and tried the second term, sessions of oyer and terminer or general gaol delivery after his commitment, or upon his trial shall be acquitted, he shall be discharged from his imprisonment.

VII. Provided always, that nothing in this Act shall extend to discharge out of prison any person charged in debt or other action, or with process in any civil cause, but that after he shall be discharged of his imprisonment for such his criminal offence he shall be kept in custody according to law for such other suit. . . .

IX. Provided also, and be it further enacted . . . that it shall and may be lawful to and for any prisoner and prisoners as aforesaid to move and obtain his or their Habeas Corpus as well out of the High Court of Chancery or Court of Exchequer as out of the Courts of King's Bench or Common Pleas or either of them; and if the said Lord Chancellor or Lord Keeper or any judge or judges, baron or barons for the time being of the degree of the coif of any of the courts aforesaid in the vacation time, upon view of the copy or copies of the warrant or warrants of commitment or detainer, or upon oath made that such copy or copies were denied as aforesaid, shall deny any writ of Habeas Corpus by this Act required to be granted being moved for as aforesaid, they shall severally forfeit to the prisoner or party grieved the sum of five hundred pounds. . . .

X. And be it enacted and declared . . . that an Habeas Corpus according to the true intent and meaning of this Act may be directed and run into any county palatine, the cinque ports or other privileged places within the kingdom of England, dominion of Wales or town of Berwick-upon-Tweed, and the islands of Jersey or Guernsey, any law or usage to the contrary notwithstanding.

XI. And for preventing illegal imprisonments in prisons beyond the seas, be it further enacted . . . that no subject of this realm that now is or hereafter shall be an inhabitant or resiant of this kingdom of England, dominion of Wales or town of Berwick-upon-Tweed shall or may be sent prisoner into Scotland, Ireland, Jersey, Guernsey, Tangier or into any parts, garrisons, islands or places beyond the seas which are or at any time hereafter shall be within or without the dominions of his Majesty, his heirs or successors; and that every such imprisonment is hereby enacted and adjudged to be illegal. . . .

XII. Provided always, that nothing in this Act shall extend to give benefit to any person who shall by contract in writing agree with any merchant or owner of any plantation, or other person whatsoever, to be transported to any parts beyond seas, and receive earnest upon such agreement, although that afterwards such person shall renounce such contract. . . .

XV. Provided also, that if any person or persons at any time resiant in this realm shall have committed any capital offence in Scotland or Ireland, or any of the islands or foreign plantations of the king, his heirs or successors, where he or she ought to be tried for such offence, such person or persons may be sent to such place, there to receive such trial in such manner as the same might have been used before the making of this Act, anything herein contained to the contrary notwithstanding. . . .

XX. And because many times persons charged with petty treason or felony, or as accessories thereunto, are committed upon suspicion only, whereupon they are bailable or not according as the circumstances making out that suspicion are more or less weighty, which are best known to the justices of peace that committed the persons and have the examinations before them, or to other justices of the peace in the county; be it therefore enacted, that where any person shall appear to be committed by any judge or justice of the peace, and charged as accessory before the fact to any petty treason or felony, or upon suspicion thereof, or with suspicion of petty treason or felony, which petty treason or felony shall be plainly and specially expressed in the warrant of commitment, that such person shall not be removed or bailed by virtue of this Act, or in any other manner than they might have been before the making of this Act.

24. Gilbert Burnet's account of the passing of the Habeas Corpus Act, 1679
(Supplement to Burnet's History of My Own Time, pp. 351-352)

And since I am now upon this point (which is the chief fence of the liberty of England) I will tell a very odd account of the way in which the Act for the Habeas Corpus was carried. It was vehemently pressed by the country party, but as vehemently opposed by the Court, as that which would be a great diminution of the prerogative; so the much greater part of the House of Lords opposed it. When it came to the final vote the House divided upon it, and there being always two named to be the tellers of the House, one of either side, the Lords Norris (now earl of Abingdon) and Grey were the men. Grey, believing that his side, which was for the bill, had lost it, leaped from twenty-four to thirty-five, and so told ten wrong, which the other not perceiving the report was made for the bill. So by this artifice, though it was indeed cast out by the Lords, it was passed, and the royal assent was given to it in the year 1679.

25. Act suspending the Habeas Corpus Act, 1689
(Statutes of the Realm, VI, p. 24)

AN ACT FOR EMPOWERING HIS MAJESTY TO APPREHEND
AND DETAIN SUCH PERSONS AS HE SHALL FIND
JUST CAUSE TO SUSPECT ARE CONSPIRING
AGAINST THE GOVERNMENT

(1 Gul. & Mar., cap. 2)

For the securing the peace of the kingdom in this time of imminent danger against the attempts and traitorous conspiracies of evil-disposed persons, be it enacted . . . that every person or persons that shall be committed by warrant of their Majesties' most honourable Privy Council, signed by six of the said Privy Council at least, for suspicion of high treason, may be detained in safe custody till the seventeenth day of April in the year of our Lord one thousand six hundred eighty and nine, without bail or mainprize; and that no judge or other person shall bail or try any such person or persons so committed without order from their said Majesties' Privy Council, signed by six of the said Privy Council at least, till the said seventeenth day of April, any law or statute to the contrary notwithstanding.

II. Provided always, that from and after the said seventeenth day of April the said persons so committed shall have the benefit and advantage of an Act made in the one and thirtieth year of King Charles the Second, entituled, *An Act for the better securing the liberty of the subject and for prevention of imprisonment beyond the seas*,[1] and also of all other laws and statutes any way relating to or providing for the liberty of the subjects of this realm;

[1] No. 23.

III. And that this present Act shall continue until the said seventeenth day of April and no longer.

IV. Provided always, and be it enacted, that nothing in this Act shall be construed to extend to the ancient rights and privileges of Parliament, or to the imprisonment or detaining of any member of either House of Parliament, until the matter of which he stands suspected be first communicated to the House of which he is a member, and the consent of the said House obtained for his commitment or detaining.

26. Narcissus Luttrell's account of the enforcement of the Habeas Corpus Act, 1693

(Brief Historical Relation of State Affairs, III, p. 26)

January, 1693. A bricklayer being pressed by Captain Cook and carried to the Tower, some of his friends brought a Habeas Corpus directed to the captain who had him in custody, which he not obeying, the Lord Chief Justice granted a special warrant ordering the sheriffs to assist his tip-staves, and if occasion to raise the posse, to take the captain; which will be a trial of skill between the civil and military power.

5

D. ORGANS OF THE CENTRAL GOVERNMENT

27. Earl of Clarendon's account of appointments made at the Restoration, 1660

(*Life of Edward Earl of Clarendon*, ed. 1857, I, pp. 311–315)

The king had upon great deliberation whilst he was beyond the seas, after his return appeared in view, firmly resolved to reform those excesses which were known to be in great offices, especially in those of his household, whilst the places were vacant, and to reform all extravagant expenses there; and first himself to gratify those who had followed and served him, in settling them in such inferior offices and places as custom had put in the disposal of the great officers, when they should become vacant after their admission. And of this kind he had made many promises, and given many warrants under his sign manual to persons who to his own knowledge had merited those obligations. But most of those predeterminations, and many other resolutions of that kind, vanished and expired in the jollity of the return, and new inclinations and affections seemed to be more seasonable.

The General, who was the sole pillar of the king's confidence, had by the Parliament been invested (before the king's return) in all the offices and commands which Cromwell had enjoyed. He was Lieutenant of Ireland, and general of all the armies and forces raised, or to be raised, in the three kingdoms; and it was not fit that he should be degraded from either upon his Majesty's arrival. Therefore all diligence was used in dispatching grants of all those commands to him under the great seal of England. And that he might be obliged to be always near his Majesty's person, he was presently sworn gentleman of the bedchamber, and might choose what office he liked best in the Court. . . . He made choice to be Master of the Horse, and was immediately gratified with it; and thereby all those poor gentlemen, who had promises and warrants for several places depending upon that great officer, were disappointed, and offered the king's sign manual to no purpose for their admission. . . . And hereby not only many honest men, who had several ways served the king, and spent the fortunes they had been masters of, were denied the recompenses the king had designed to them, but such men who had been most notorious in the malice against the Crown from the beginning of the rebellion, or had been employed in all the active offices to affront and oppress his party, were for money preferred and admitted into those offices, and became the king's servants, very much against his will, and with his manifest regret on the behalf of the honest men who had been so unworthily rejected. . . .

The settling this great officer in the stables made it necessary to appoint a Lord Steward of the Household, who was a necessary officer for the Parliament, being by the statute appointed to swear all the members of the House of Commons; and to this charge the marquis of Ormonde had been long designed, and was then sworn. And they had both their tables erected according to the old models, and all those excesses which the irregular precedents of former times had introduced, and which the king had so solemnly resolved to reform before it could be said to trench upon the rights of particular persons. . . .

That he might give a lively instance of his grace to those who had been of the party which had been faulty, according to his declaration from Breda, he made of his own free inclination and choice the earl of Manchester (who was looked upon as one of the principal heads of the presbyterian party) Lord Chamberlain of his house; who, continuing still to perform all good offices to his old friends, complied very punctually with all the obligations and duties which his place required, never failed being at chapel and at all the king's devotions with all imaginable decency, and by his extraordinary civilities and behaviour towards all men did not only appear the fittest person the king could have chosen for that office in that time, but rendered himself so acceptable to all degrees of men that none but such who were implacable towards all who had ever disserved the king were sorry to see him so promoted. . . . With his the two other white staves were disposed of to those to whom they were designed, when the king was prince of Wales, by his father; and all other inferior officers were made, who were to take care of the expenses of the house, and were a great part of it. . . .

The king had in his purpose, long before his return, to make the earl of Southampton (who was the most valued and esteemed of all the nobility, and generally thought worthy of any honour or office) Lord High Treasurer of England. But he desired first to see some revenue settled by the Parliament, and that part of the old which had been sold and dispersed by extravagant grants and sales reduced into the old channel, and regularly to be received and paid, and the Customs to be put in such order (which were not yet granted, and only continued by orders as illegal as the late times had been accustomed to, and to the authority whereof he had no mind to administer), before he was willing to receive the staff. And so the office of the Treasury was by commission executed by several lords of the Council, whereof the Chancellor, as well by the dignity of his place as by his still being Chancellor of the Exchequer, was one, and so engaged in the putting the Customs likewise into commissioners' hands, and settling all the other branches of the revenue in such manner as was thought most reasonable, in all debates whereof his Majesty himself was still present and approved the conclusion.

But after a month or two spent in this method, in the crowd of so much business of several natures, the king found so little expedition that he thought it best to determine that commission, and so gave the staff to the earl of Southampton and made him Treasurer. And the Chancellor at the same time surrendering his office of Chancellor of the Exchequer into the king's hands, his Majesty, upon the humble desire of the earl, conferred that office upon Sir Anthony Ashley Cooper, who had married his niece, and whose parts well enough qualified him for the discharge thereof, though some other qualities of his, as well known, brought no advantage to his Majesty by that promotion. And from this time the Chancellor would never intermeddle in the business of the Exchequer, nor admit any applications to him in it. However the friendship was so great between the Treasurer and him, and so notorious from an ancient date and from a joint confidence in each other in the service of the last king, that neither of them concluded any matter of importance without consulting with the other.

And so the Treasurer, marquis of Ormonde, the General, with the two Secretaries of State, were of that secret committee with the Chancellor, which under the notion of foreign affairs were appointed by the king to consult all his affairs before they came to a public debate; and in which there could not be a more united concurrence of judgments and affections.

28. Sir William Temple's description of the Cabal, 1670–1674
(Works, ed. 1740, I, p. 378)

Thus happily ended our part of a war so fatal to the rest of Christendom in the consequences of it, which no man perhaps now alive will see the end of, and had been begun and carried on, as far as it would go, under the ministry of five men who were usually called the Cabal, a word unluckily falling out of the five first letters of their names, that is Clifford, Arlington, Buckingham, Ashley and Lauderdale. But though the counsels and conduct of these men had begun the war with two unusual strains to the honour of the Crown, in the attack of the Smyrna fleet and stopping the bank, yet it must be allowed them to have succeeded well in the honours they proposed to themselves, Clifford having gained by it the place of High Treasurer and title of a baron, Ashley the Chancellor's place and an earldom, Arlington an earldom with the Garter, and Lauderdale a dukedom with the Garter. The duke of Buckingham, being already possessed of all the honours the Crown could give of that kind, contented himself to make no better a bargain in this matter than he used to do in all others that concerned him, and so pretended no further than commands in the army. And thus, instead of making so great a king as they pretended by this Dutch war and French alliance, they had the honour of making only four great subjects.

29. Declaration remodelling the Privy Council, 1679
(State Tracts of the Reign of Charles II, II, pp. 99–101)

HIS MAJESTY'S DECLARATION
FOR THE DISSOLUTION OF HIS LATE PRIVY COUNCIL
AND FOR CONSTITUTING A NEW ONE,
MADE IN THE COUNCIL CHAMBER AT WHITEHALL,
APRIL THE TWENTIETH, 1679

My Lords,

His Majesty hath called you together at this time to communicate unto you a resolution he hath taken in a matter of great importance to his Crown and government, and which he hopes will prove of the greatest satisfaction and advantage to his kingdoms in all affairs hereafter both at home and abroad. And therefore he doubts not of your approbation, however you may seem concerned in it.

In the first place his Majesty gives you all thanks for your service to him here and for all the good advices you have given him, which might have been more frequent if the great number of this Council had not made it unfit for the secrecy and dispatch that are necessary in many great affairs. This forced him to use a smaller number of you in a Foreign Committee, and sometimes the advices of some few among them (upon such occasions) for many years past. He is sorry for the ill success he has found in this course, and sensible of the ill posture of affairs from that, and some unhappy accidents, which have raised great jealousies and dissatisfactions among his good subjects, and thereby left the Crown and government in a condition too weak for those dangers we have reason to fear both at home and abroad.

These his Majesty hopes may be yet prevented by a course of wise and steady counsels for the future, and these kingdoms grow again to make such a figure as they have formerly done in the world, and as they may always do if our union and conduct were equal to our force. To this end he hath resolved to lay aside the use he may have hitherto made of any single ministry or private advices or Foreign Committees for the general direction of his affairs, and to constitute such a Privy Council as may not only by its number be fit for the consultation and digestion of all business both domestic and foreign, but also by the choice of them out of the several parts this state is composed of may be the best informed in the true constitutions of it, and thereby the most able to counsel him in all the affairs and interests of this Crown and nation. And by the constant advice of such a Council his Majesty is resolved hereafter to govern his kingdoms, together with the frequent use of his Great Council of Parliament, which he takes to be the true ancient constitution of this state and government.

Now, for the greater dignity of this Council, his Majesty resolves their constant number shall be limited to that of thirty. And for their greater authority there shall be fifteen of his chief officers who shall be Privy Councillors by their places. And for the other fifteen he will choose ten out of the several ranks of the nobility and five commoners of the realm, whose known abilities, interest and esteem in the nation shall render them without all suspicion of either mistaking or betraying the true interests of the kingdom, and consequently of advising him ill.

In the first place therefore, and to take care of the Church, his Majesty will have the archbishop of Canterbury and bishop of London for the time being; and to inform him well in what concerns the laws, the Lord Chancellor and one of the Lord Chief Justices; for the navy and stores (wherein consists the chief strength and safety of the kingdom), the Admiral and Master of the Ordnance; for the Treasury, the Treasurer and Chancellor of the Exchequer (or whenever any of these charges are in commission then the First Commissioner to serve here in their room). The rest of the fifteen shall be the Lord Privy Seal, the Master of the Horse, Lord Steward and Lord Chamberlain of his Household, the Groom of the Stole and the two Secretaries of State. And these shall be all the offices of his kingdom to which the dignity of Privy Councillor shall be annexed. The others his Majesty has resolved, and hopes he has not chosen ill. His Majesty intends besides to have such princes of his blood as he shall at any time call to this board, being here in Court; a President of the Council whenever he shall find it necessary, and the Secretary of Scotland when any such shall be here. But these, being uncertain, he reckons not of the constant number of thirty which shall never be exceeded.

To make way for this new Council his Majesty hath now resolved to dissolve this old one, and does hereby dissolve it, and from this time excuses your further attendance here, but with his repeated thanks for your service hitherto, and with the assurance of his satisfaction in you so far that he should not have parted with you but to make way for this new constitution, which he takes to be, as to the number and choice, the most proper and necessary for the uses he intends them. And as most of you have offices in his service, and all of you particular shares in his favour and good opinion, so he desires you would continue to exercise and deserve them with the same diligence and good affections that you have hitherto done, and with confidence of his Majesty's kindness to you, and of those testimonies you shall receive of it upon other occasions.

Therefore, upon the present dissolution of this Council, his Majesty appoints and commands all those officers he hath named to attend him here to-morrow at nine in the morning as his Privy Council, together with those other persons he designs to make up the number, and to each of whom he has already signed particular letters to that purpose; and commands the Lord Chancellor to see them issued out accordingly, which is the form he intends to use, and that hereafter they shall be signed in Council, so that nothing may be done unadvisedly in the choice of any person to a charge of so great dignity and importance to the kingdom.

Names of the Lords of his Majesty's most honourable Privy Council

His Highness Prince Rupert
William, lord archbishop of Canterbury
Heneage, Lord Finch, Lord Chancellor of England
Anthony, earl of Shaftesbury, Lord President of the Council
Arthur, earl of Anglesey, Lord Privy Seal
Christopher, duke of Albemarle
James, duke of Monmouth, Master of the Horse
Henry, duke of Newcastle
John, duke of Lauderdale, Secretary of State for Scotland
James, duke of Ormonde, Lord Steward of the Household
Charles, lord marquis of Winchester
Henry, lord marquis of Worcester
Henry, earl of Arlington, Lord Chamberlain of the Household
James, earl of Salisbury
John, earl of Bridgewater
Robert, earl of Sunderland, one of his Majesty's Principal Secretaries of State
Arthur, earl of Essex, First Lord Commissioner of the Treasury
John, earl of Bath, Groom of the Stole
Thomas, Lord Viscount Fauconberg
George, Lord Viscount Halifax
Henry, lord bishop of London
John, Lord Robartes
Denzil, Lord Holles
William, Lord Russell
William, Lord Cavendish

Henry Coventry, esq., one of his Majesty's Principal Secretaries of State
Sir Francis North, knt., Lord Chief Justice of the Common Pleas
Sir Henry Capel, knight of the bath, First Commissioner of the Admiralty
Sir John Ernly, knt., Chancellor of the Exchequer
Sir Thomas Chicheley, knt., Master of the Ordnance
Sir William Temple, bart.
Edward Seymour, esq.
Henry Powle, esq.

30. Anonymous proposal for a council of state, 1689

(*Somers Tracts*, ed. 1809–1815, X, p. 197)

NOW IS THE TIME: A SCHEME FOR A COMMONWEALTH

The thing that offers itself in this great conjuncture is to have a grand committee of Lords and Commons (forty at least from each House) to be as a privy council, or council of state, or governing senate. It were to be wished that twenty of each forty might be for life, and the other twenty biennial, ten going off every year; or half might be changed annually. Each senator or counsellor to have for his salary maintenance one thousand pounds a year. This would be such an advancement to the nobility and gentry as England never saw. And the charge is a trifle. There is more spent in some monarchies upon hawks, hounds and whores.

The Prince to preside in this council or senate (or such person as he shall appoint in his stead), and to have ten votes at least. He must also be general and admiral, and must have such further powers, and such a maintenance or revenue as his infinite merits require; but withal such as are consistent with the government he designs for us. The Prince's maintenance should equal or exceed that of all the senators put together.

All that are of this council, and all that hope to be (that is all the considerable men of the nation), will by this means be firm to the Prince. And so will those others who have the great privilege of choosing them, whereby they may have confidence in their administration. And this one thing will give the Prince so strong an interest that he need fear no pretension that can be against him. It will be better than a standing army, the necessity whereof nothing can prevent but such a standing council.

The Parliament to be chosen triennially, and to meet annually.

It is believed that such a constitution as this would effectually secure us (according to the Prince's good intentions) from popery and tyranny. And the Prince will be the glorious author of the Britannic liberty as his grandfather was of the Belgic. The Genoese to this day adore the memory of Andrea Doria, who chose rather to make them a free state than to be their prince. Barely to change our master would but revive the feuds of York and Lancaster, and involve us in the like calamities.

These things to continue but during the life of the king, and not to prejudice a Protestant successor.

31. Duties and salaries of State and Household officials, 1691

(Angliae Notitia, ed. 1692, pp. 98–141)

Next to the king and princes of the blood are reckoned the great officers of the crown, whereof there are nine, viz., the Lord High Steward of England, the Lord High Chancellor, the Lord High Treasurer, the Lord President of the king's Council, the Lord Privy Seal, the Lord Great Chamberlain, the Lord High Constable, the Earl Marshal and the Lord High Admiral.

The first great officer of the crown, according to the account of our ancestors, was the Lord High Steward of England, or Viceroy. . . . He was anciently the highest officer under the king, and his power so exorbitant that it was thought fit not longer to trust it in the hands of any subject. . . . The last that had a state of inheritance in this high office was Henry of Bolingbroke . . . afterwards king of England, since which time they have been made only *pro hac vice*, to officiate either at a coronation . . . or else for the arraignment of some peer of the realm. . . . During his stewardship he bears a white staff in his hand, and the trial being over openly breaks it; and so his office ends.

Next the Lord High Chancellor. . . . His office is to keep the king's great seal, to judge not according to the common law, as other civil courts do, but to moderate the rigour of the law, and to judge according to equity, conscience or reason; to bestow all ecclesiastical benefices in the king's gift under 20*l.* yearly in the king's books. And for this and other causes he was ever, till of late years, a clergyman. . . . The salary from the king was 848*l.* per annum, and when the Star Chamber was up, 200*l.* per annum more for his attendance there . . .

The third great officer of the crown is the Lord High Treasurer of England, who receives this high office by delivery of a white staff to him by the king, and holds it *durante beneplacito regis*. . . . He is a lord by his office, under whose charge and government is all the king's revenue kept in the Exchequer. He hath also the check of all the officers any way employed in collecting imposts, customs, tributes or other revenues belonging to the crown. He hath the gift of all customers, comptrollers and searchers in all the ports of England. . . . The ancient annual salary of the Lord High Treasurer of England was in all 383*l.* 7*s.* 8*d.*, but the late salary was 8,000*l.* per annum.

The fourth great officer . . . is the Lord President of the king's Privy Council, an officer as ancient as King John's time. . . . His office is to attend upon the king, to propose business at Council table, and then to report to the king the several transactions there. It hath been always granted by letters under the great seal *durante beneplacito*. . . .

The fifth, the Lord Privy Seal, who is a lord by his office, under whose hands pass all charters and grants of the king, and pardons signed by the king, before they come to the great seal of England; also divers other matters of less concernment, as for the payment of money, &c., which do not pass the great seal. . . . His salary was 1,500*l.* per annum. . . .

The sixth great officer of the crown is the Lord Great Chamberlain of England, an officer of great antiquity, to whom belongs livery and lodging in the king's court and certain fees. . . . Moreover to this great officer belongs the care of providing all things in the House of Lords in time of Parliament, and to that end he hath an apartment near the Lords' House. . . . This honour . . . is at present enjoyed by Robert, earl of Lindsey.

The seventh great officer is the Lord High Constable of England, . . . whose power and jurisdiction was anciently so great that it was thought too great for any subject. . . . But since, upon occasion of coronations . . . and at solemn trials by combat . . . there is created *pro illa vice* a Lord High Constable. His power and jurisdiction is the same with the Earl Marshal, with whom he sits judge in the Marshal's Court, and takes place of the Earl Marshal.

The eighth great officer of the crown is the Earl Marshal of England. . . . He is an earl, some say, by his office, whereby he taketh, as the Constable doth, cognizance of all matters of war and arms. . . . Anciently he had several courts under him, but hath now only the Marshalsea, where he may sit in judgment against criminals offending within the verge of the king's court. . . .

The ninth and last great officer of the crown is the Lord High Admiral of England, whose trust and honour is so great that this office hath usually been given either to some of the king's younger sons, near kinsman, or to some one of the highest and chiefest of all the nobility. . . . To the Lord High Admiral of England is by the king intrusted the management of all maritime affairs, as well in respect of jurisdiction as protection. He is that high officer or magistrate to whom is committed the government of the king's navy, with power of decision in all cases maritime, as well civil as criminal; of all things done upon or beyond the sea in any part of the world; all things done upon the sea-coasts in all ports and havens, and upon all rivers below the first bridge next towards the sea. . . .

The court of the king of England is a monarchy within a monarchy, consisting of ecclesiastical, civil and military persons and government.

For the ecclesiastical government of the king's court there is first a dean of the king's chapel, who is usually some grave, learned prelate chosen by the king, and who as dean acknowledgeth no superior but the king; for as the king's palace is exempt from all inferior temporal jurisdiction so is his chapel from all spiritual. . . . By the dean are chosen all other officers of the chapel. . . . The present dean of the chapel is Dr. Henry Compton, bishop of London, whose fee is 200*l.* yearly, and a table. . . .

For the civil government of the king's court the chief officer is . . . the Lord Steward of the king's Household. . . . He hath authority over all officers and servants of the king's house except those of his Majesty's chapel, chamber and stable. He by his office, without any commission, judgeth of all discords, as treasons, murders, felonies, bloodsheds committed in the court or within the verge, which is every way within twelve miles of the chief tunnel of the court. Only London by charter is exempted. . . . To the Lord Steward belongs at the beginning of Parliaments to attend the king's person, and to minister the oaths of allegiance and supremacy to all the several members of the House of Commons, and at the end of Parliaments to adjust the parliamentary expenses, &c. The Lord Steward is a white staff officer, for he in the king's presence carrieth a white staff, and at other times, going abroad, it is carried by a footman bareheaded. This white staff is taken for a commission. At the death of the king, over the hearse made for the king's body, he breaketh this staff, and thereby dischargeth all the officers, whom the succeeding king, out of his mere grace, doth re-establish so many in the same offices as his Majesty shall think fit. This eminent employment is now enjoyed by the earl of Devonshire, whose fee is 1,200*l.*

The next officer is the Lord Chamberlain, who hath the oversight of all officers belonging to the king's chamber, except the precinct of the king's bedchamber, which is wholly under the Groom of the Stole; and all above stairs, who are all sworn by him. . . . He hath also the oversight of the officers of the Wardrobe. . . . Moreover he hath the oversight of the sergeants-at-arms, of all physicians, apothecaries, chirurgeons, barbers, &c. To him also belongeth the oversight of the chaplains, though himself be a layman. . . . The fee of the Lord Chamberlain of the king's House is 100*l.* yearly, and sixteen dishes each meal, with all the appurtenances. This office is now in the hands of the earl of Dorset. . . .

The third great officer of the king's court is the Master of the Horse. . . . This great officer hath now the ordering and disposal of all the king's stables. . . .

Under these three principal officers of his Majesty's Household are almost all the other officers and servants. First, under the Lord Steward, in the Counting House, are the Treasurer of the Household, Comptroller, Cofferer, Master of the Household, two Clerks of the Greencloth, two Clerks Comptrollers, two yeomen, the Cofferer's clerks or clerks of the assignment, two grooms, two messengers.

It is called the Counting House because the accounts for all expenses of the king's Household are there taken daily by the Lord Steward, the Treasurer, Comptroller, the Cofferer, the Master of the Household, the two Clerks of the Greencloth and the two Clerks Comptrollers. . . . In the Counting House is the Greencloth, which is a court of justice continually sitting in the king's house, composed of the persons last mentioned, whereof the three first are usually of the king's Privy Council. To this court, being the first and most ancient court of England, is committed the charge and oversight of the king's court royal for matters of justice and government, with authority for maintaining the peace within twelve miles' distance wheresoever the court shall be, and within the king's house the power of correcting all the servants therein that shall any way offend. . . .

A list of his Majesty's Household officers and servants
attending in the several offices below stairs,
under the command of William, earl of Devonshire, Lord Steward

Board of Greencloth

	Wages			Board-wages		
William, earl of Devonshire, Lord Steward	100	00	00	1,360	00	00
Francis, Viscount Newport, Treasurer and Cofferer of the Household	223	14	08	1,092	02	06
Thomas Wharton, esquire, Comptroller	107	17	06	1,092	02	06
Thomas Felton, esquire, Master of the Household	66	13	04	433	06	08

	Wages			Board-wages		
Sir William Forrester, knight, Clerk of the Green-cloth	44	06	08	455	13	04
Sir James Forbes, knight, Clerk of the Green-cloth	44	06	08	455	13	04
Peter Isaac, esquire, Clerk Comptroller	44	06	08	455	13	04
Thomas Vivian, esquire, Clerk Comptroller[1]	44	06	08	455	13	04

*A list of his Majesty's officers and servants in
ordinary above stairs*

Lord Chamberlain, the Right Honourable Charles, earl of Dorset and Middlesex, whose salary is 100*l.*, board-wages 1,100*l.* per annum.

Vice-Chamberlain, Sir John Lowther, baronet, whose salary is 66*l.* 13*s.* 4*d.*, board-wages 492*l.* 15*s.* . . . .

Gentlemen of the Bedchamber are nine, whereof the first is Groom of the Stole, that is . . . groom or servant of the long robe or vestment, he having the office and honour to present and put on his Majesty's first garment or shirt every morning, and to order the things of the bedchamber. The Gentlemen of the Bedchamber consist usually of the prime nobility of England, whose office in general is, each one in his turn, to wait one week in every nine weeks in the king's bedchamber, there to lie by the king on a pallet bed all night, and in the absence of the Groom of the Stole to supply his place. . . . Each, 1,000*l.* per annum.[2]

*A list of his Majesty's officers and servants
under the Master of the Horse*

Master of the Horse, Henry of Nassau, lord of Auverquerque, whose salary is 1,200*l.* per annum.

Avener and clerk marshal, Anthony Rowe, esquire, whose salary is 260*l.* per annum.

Equerries, . . . the salary to each 256*l.* per annum.

Pages of honour, . . . salary to each 156*l.* per annum.[3] . . .

Upon the king are also attending in his court the Lords of the Privy Council, Secretaries of State, the reverend judges, the learned College of Civilians, the king's Counsel at Law, the King's Serjeants at law, the Masters of Requests. . . .

32. Speech of Sir Charles Sedley in the Commons on the extravagance of the Civil List, 1691

(Somers Tracts, ed. 1809–1815, x, pp. 331–332)

We have provided for the navy, we have provided for the army, and now at the latter end of a session here is a new reckoning brought us; we must provide likewise for the civil list. Truly, Mr. Speaker, it is a sad reflection that some men should wallow in wealth and places, whilst others pay away in taxes the fourth part of

---

[1] The names of nearly a hundred lesser officials follow, with their salaries.

[2] Lesser officials are also given.   [3] Other subordinates of the Master of the Horse follow.

their yearly revenue for the support of the same government. We are not upon equal terms for his Majesty's service. The courtiers and great officers charge as it were in armour; they feel not the taxes by reason of their places; while the country gentlemen are shot through and through with them.

The king is pleased to lay his wants before us, and I am confident expects our advice upon it. We ought therefore to tell him what pensions are too great, what places may be extinguished during this time of war and public calamities. His Majesty is encompassed with, and sees nothing but, plenty, great tables, coaches and six horses and all things suitable, and therefore cannot imagine the want and misery of the rest of his subjects. He is a wise and virtuous prince; but he is but a young king, encompassed and hemmed in among a company of crafty old courtiers (to say no more of them), with places some of 3,000, some of 6,000, and some 11,000. I am told the commissioners of the treasury have 3,000*l*. a year apiece.

Certainly such pensions, whatever they may have been formerly, are much too great in the present want and calamities that reign everywhere else, and it is a general scandal that a government so sick at heart as ours should look so well in the face. We must save the king money wherever we can, for I am afraid our work is too big for our purses if things be not managed with all the thrift imaginable. When the people of England see that all is saved that can be saved, that there are no exorbitant pensions nor unnecessary salaries, that all is applied to the use for which it was given, we shall give and they will cheerfully pay whatever his Majesty can want to secure the Protestant religion, to keep out the king of France, aye, and King James too, whom, by the way, I have not heard named this session, whether out of fear, respect or discretion I cannot tell. I conclude, Mr. Speaker, let us save the king what we can, and then let us proceed to give him what we are able.

E. DETERMINATION OF THE SUCCESSION

33. Anonymous account of the Popish Plot, 1678
(Historical Manuscripts Commission, *Kenyon MSS.*, pp. 105-109)
31 October, 1678

Since my last, wherein I discovered to you the first account of this horrible plot, great hath been the diligence both of the Council and Parliament in bringing the same to light, wherein their endeavours have been so happy that they are now arrived to the bottom of it, and it lies now before both Houses in its own monstrous shape, it being no less than the murder of the king, the subversion of our religion, laws and properties, the introducing of popery and a tyrannical arbitrary government by an army, our common and statute laws to be abolished and annihilated, and a mixture of military and civil law introduced, where council of war should supply this place of our courts of justice, and the rank for the jury, with many such differences too tedious to express here. But I hope by this timely and miraculous discovery we may be able to destroy this cockatrice in the egg, which will yet certainly devour us if he be hatched.

The manner of proceedings have been thus. One Mr. Oates being a minister in Sussex, by reason of some lawsuits with persons which were too powerful for him he was forced to quit his parish, and, coming into London, fell into acquaintance with Mr. Tonge, a minister who hath been many years a diligent inquirer into the practices and principles of the Jesuits, and had published several books against them. This man, finding Oates by reason of poverty inclined to travel to seek a livelihood amongst the papists abroad, endeavoured to divert him by giving him full information of their wicked principles and practices. Whereupon Oates resolves to try the truth, and promised, if he found it to be as Tonge informed, he would renounce that religion and return again to the Protestant Church.

Oates thereupon, some years since, goes and enters himself a novice in the college of the Jesuits in St. Omer, where, behaving himself with great zeal, diligence, and demonstrating his abilities, he was soon taken notice of and thought a fit instument to convey the intelligence and correspondency of this hellish plot to most of the courts in Christendom. In acting whereof, by opening letters and packets intrusted with him and thereby gaining some light, he so insinuated himself wherever he came that in time he came to the depth and counsels of the design. Whereby, about April last, understanding the execution of this horrid villainy to be at hand, and that commissions were signed by the Pope for all bishops and other clergy, for the officers of state and of their armies, he began to fear it would be executed before he should find means to discover it.

And being ready to lay hold of all opportunities to come for England to do it, it fell out that a book called *The Jesuits' Morals*, which Tonge had translated, came to their hands, for which upon consultation it was agreed Tonge should be killed; but a fit person was wanting to do it. Whereupon Oates offered to undertake it, and had a note given him to receive £50 here when it was done; and in the meantime he was directed to one Ireland, a priest in the Savoy, to accommodate him with lodging and necessaries. Whereupon Oates prepares for the journey, the college loads him with packets and commissions for all sorts of conspirators, which he brings over and with his own hand delivers; but in the interim underhand resorts to Tonge and acquaints him with the whole design, of which having drawn a short relation he desires Tonge to give it privately to the king, and offer to make it good, if his Majesty would conceal the thing and appoint a council to sit and hear it.

Tonge, not being willing to undertake it alone, took one Kirkby, a merchant, and went to the king upon the 13th of August, where they acquainted him with the substance of it; but the papers being several sheets, and the king not caring for trouble, gave leave to acquaint and employ the Treasurer to manage it. They were unwilling to consent, but the king saying he dare trust his life and crown in his hands they could not refuse. All this while Oates was concealed. The matter thus settled, Tonge several times presses the Treasurer, but nothing done in six weeks, though the 2nd of September, whereon the king was to be murdered, was past. Whereon Tonge, doubting some future trouble in case Oates should be killed or recant, causes Oates to draw an exact narrative containing fifteen or sixteen sheets, and to swear it before Sir Edmund Berry Godfrey, who perused and took notes out of it, and, according to his custom keeping fair with both sides, he acquaints the Treasurer, Coleman and some others with the business, and finding Coleman so deep in the plot there was no possibility of avoiding of it he advises Coleman to impeach, which it is said he did, and swore something before Godfrey which he entered in a pocket-book; and that also he discovered to the Treasurer, and he to the duke of York.

I say no more; but Godfrey was chid and the matter fit to be concealed, and Godfrey was murdered soon after, being, as appeared plainly, strangled, and after carried and laid in a ditch near Primrose Hill, and his own sword run through him, nothing missing but his band and pocket-book wherein were his notes concerning this affair. His murder raised a great spirit in the people, which could not be outfaced by the party and their adherents that murdered him, though there wanted neither diligence nor impudence in that party in all places to make it appear he murdered himself. To-morrow he is to be buried from the hall of Bridewell, where I believe thousands will appear to attend his corpse to St. Martin's.

But to return to the plot. Godfrey, having taken the information, was forced to bring it to Council about the end of September 1678, where Oates appeared and made it good beyond all scruple, and thereupon Coleman, one Langhorne a counsellor, and nine Jesuits were committed and their houses and lodgings searched, but the matter done so publicly and divers days given before the warrants issued, so that they generally had notice enough to remove what they had a mind should not be seen, and yet such papers and letters were found both in Coleman's and Langhorne's studies that give a full relation of the most horrid massacre and slaughter that ever was heard, which have been since sorted and produced both before the Council and Parliament. Since the sitting of the Parliament, Oates hath been every day examined before them, speaking five or six hours at a time, giving particular demonstration of the whole affair, wherein he hath clearly proved the manner and design of the fire of London,

Southwark, and many other fires, with the intended massacre in the fire of London, the design of raising the Blackheath army, with the reasons and occasions of the several Dutch wars in order to this design, the raising of the present army and the general peace to ensue for the completing the work, the raising and maintaining privately 20,000 men at this time, with the general and all other officers, all which are now in readiness to join with the army, the greatest part whereof they thought themselves sure of; and in Ireland they had likewise a general and army ready, and Scotland the same.

The manner to put it in execution was thus. One Conyers, a Jesuit, with four Irish ruffians, undertook to murder the king at Windsor, 21 September last, and thereupon a great cry was to be made that the fanatics had murdered the king, an alarm presently thereupon to be given to the whole army, being then about 16,000 quartered in and near London, whereof two regiments of 4,000 men, consisting all of Irish, Scots and French papists, were about a month before brought out of France and quartered about Barnet, Enfield, St. Albans, Ware, &c., were immediately to march to London to assist the proclaiming the duke of York, and under that pretence to fall upon and to massacre and slaughter the people under the notion of fanatics who had murdered the king, and then to have assisted the papists all over the kingdom to do the like. The duke of York was to take the crown by gift from the Pope, and lest any opposition should be made the French were to be ready with an army and fleet to seize upon our fleet, burn and destroy such as opposed and take the rest, and then the whole nation to be shared among this crew, viz., the ancient Church lands amongst the clergy, the murdered Protestants' lands amongst the great officers, both civil and military, and the plunder of cities and towns amongst the soldiers and rabble of Irish and French papists. This is the substance of what is collected from the several informations, proofs and papers which have been seized and made out.

Things thus appearing, the Commons locked themselves up for many hours, sent for Chief Justice Scroggs to them, who issued out at one time forty or fifty warrants against noblemen and others. The high constables were sent for also into the House, and the warrants there delivered to them, and the House kept still shut to prevent intelligence; and that night and next day six lords and divers persons of less quality were seized and committed to the Tower, King's Bench, Newgate, Gatehouse and other prisons. The particulars you may perceive in a list annexed hereunto.

Divers letters of Coleman's dated 1674 and 1675 (for all of later date are removed) have been read in both Houses, and some letters of the duke's in his custody of the like date, whereby the king is in a most abusive manner characterized as a person not fit to govern or be trusted, and the Parliament, both Lords and Commons, described as a company of beggarly, sottish, corrupt, mean people, and to be disposed of for slender sums of money to give up religion, law, property, kingdom and what not; with great importunity to the Pope, French, &c., to furnish money for effecting speedily the aforesaid glorious design, and multitude of such stuff, which would make every Englishman's heart ache to hear or think those in whose power we are should deserve such characters.

Things thus standing, some intimation was brought to the lord mayor and aldermen on Saturday last that on Sunday in sermon time some attempt would be made upon the city, whereupon they ordered strong double watches to be set of house-keepers in person, and the lights to be renewed at 12 o'clock at night, the gates to be shut all Sunday and the watches to continue till relieved at night, which was per-formed. And Doctor Stillingfleet having been attempted by a fellow in a gentile habit, who brought a counterfeit letter as from the bishop of London to desire him to come to him in the evening, and brought a coach to carry him, intending to have served him as Sir Edmund Godfrey was, but was prevented; partly an extra-ordinary business would not permit him to go out, and partly jealousy, which made the doctor answer him if he could go he would make use of his own coach, which made the fellow vanish, and the doctor, waiting on the bishop the next day, found the letter and pretence wholly counterfeit. Thereupon on Sunday about forty persons a guard waited on the doctor to church and home.

On Sunday a committee of lords, viz., Winchester, Shaftesbury, the Treasurer, Halifax and Cornbury, being appointed by the Lords, went to Coleman to Newgate and examined him, who had been long a close prisoner and knew nothing of Godfrey's death, and upon his examination, finding persons of several interests, could not tell what to say, but to the main point referred himself to his examination taken by Sir Edmund Godfrey, which troubled some there, who began to hint that Godfrey was dead; but Shaftesbury managed it so wisely that he turned it off, and in the conclusion he confessed the letters, and that he had acted nothing in the business but by the duke's order, with the privity and advice of the Lord Arundell of Wardour, and seemed very desirous to have leave to speak with the king, and being demanded the reason, to know how far he might name the duke in the business, which was the next day reported to the Lords.

Whereupon high debates were tending to the impeachment of the duke, but the duke's party was so great and avoided the blow at that time. Whereupon the Com-mons ordered a committee to go to Newgate to examine Coleman; but when they came his note was changed. He would own nothing of the duke, but said what he had done was for religion sake. And the Lords refusing to send down the report to the Commons, and Coleman having turned his tale, things stand at present, and it is now doubted the matter will not be thoroughly canvassed, and, some money being well placed, we shall be contented with the hanging three or four inconsiderable fellows and some law against popery, which will keep our throats from being cut a month at least.

Sir, I fear I have been too tedious; but understanding from some friends you were much in the dark in this business made me enlarge. On Monday last the king sent for the lord mayor and aldermen, and thanked them for their care and loyalty, and desired them to raise their trained bands and keep guard for their better security, so that yesterday a regiment was upon the guard and to be relieved and so continue till further order. Whitehall is close shut up and no passage to it but through the wicket at the great gate, and a strict examination of all that are suffered to pass in or out.

34. John Dryden on the Plot

(Absalom and Achitophel, ll. 108-117)

From hence began that Plot, the nation's curse,
Bad in itself, but represented worse,
Raised in extremes, and in extremes decried,
With oaths affirmed, with dying vows denied,
Not weighed or winnowed by the multitude,
But swallowed in the mass, unchewed and crude.
Some truth there was, but dashed and brewed with lies
To please the fools and puzzle all the wise.
Succeeding times did equal folly call
Believing nothing or believing all.

35. Exclusion Bill, 1680

(Manuscripts of the House of Lords, 1678-1688, pp. 195-197)

AN ACT FOR SECURING OF THE PROTESTANT RELIGION
BY DISABLING JAMES, DUKE OF YORK,   •
TO INHERIT THE IMPERIAL CROWN OF ENGLAND AND IRELAND
AND THE DOMINIONS AND TERRITORIES THEREUNTO BELONGING

Whereas James, duke of York, is notoriously known to have been perverted from the Protestant to the popish religion, whereby not only great encouragement hath been given to the popish party to enter into and carry on most devilish and horrid plots and conspiracies for the destruction of his Majesty's sacred person and government, and for the extirpation of the true Protestant religion, but also, if the said duke should succeed to the imperial crown of this realm, nothing is more manifest than that a total change of religion within these kingdoms would ensue, for the prevention whereof be it therefore enacted . . . that the said James, duke of York, shall be and is by authority of this present Parliament excluded and made for ever incapable to inherit, possess or enjoy the imperial crown of this realm and of the kingdom of Ireland and the dominions and territories to them or either of them belonging, or to have, exercise or enjoy any dominion, power, jurisdiction or authority within the same kingdoms, dominions or any of them.

And be it further enacted . . . that if the said James, duke of York, shall at any time hereafter challenge, claim or attempt to possess or enjoy, or shall take upon him to use or exercise any dominion, power, authority or jurisdiction within the said kingdoms, dominions or any of them as king or chief magistrate of the same, that then he the said James, duke of York, for every such offence shall be deemed and adjudged guilty of high treason, and shall suffer the pains, penalties and forfeitures as in cases of high treason.

And further, that if any person or persons whatsoever shall assist, aid, maintain, abet or willingly adhere unto the said James, duke of York, in such his challenge, claim or attempt, or shall of themselves attempt or endeavour to put or bring the said James, duke of York, into the possession or exercise of any regal power, jurisdiction or authority within the kingdoms or dominions aforesaid, or shall by writing or preaching advisedly publish, maintain or declare that he hath any right, title or authority to exercise the office of king or chief magistrate of the kingdoms and dominions aforesaid, that then every such person shall be deemed and adjudged guilty of high treason, and shall suffer and undergo the pains, penalties and forfeitures aforesaid.

And be it further enacted . . . that if the said James, duke of York, shall at any time from and after the fifth day of November in the year of our Lord God one thousand six hundred and eighty return or come into or within any of the kingdoms or dominions aforesaid, that then he, the said James, duke of York, shall be deemed and adjudged guilty of high treason, and shall suffer the pains, penalties and forfeitures as in cases of high treason; and further, that if any person or persons whatsoever shall be aiding or assisting unto such return of the said James, duke of York, that then every such person shall be deemed and adjudged guilty of high treason, and shall suffer as in cases of high treason.

And be it further enacted . . . that the said James, duke of York, or any other person being guilty of any of the treasons aforesaid, shall not be capable of or receive benefit by any pardon otherwise than by Act of Parliament. . . .

And be it further enacted and declared, and it is hereby enacted and declared, that it shall and may be lawful to and for all magistrates, officers and other subjects whatsoever of the kingdoms and dominions aforesaid, and they are hereby enjoined and required, to apprehend and secure the said James, duke of York, and every other person offending in any of the premises, and with him or them in case of resistance to fight, and him or them by force to subdue, for all which actings and for so doing they are and shall be by virtue of this Act saved harmless and indemnified.

Provided, and be it hereby declared, that nothing in this Act contained shall be construed, deemed or adjudged to disable any person from inheriting or enjoying the imperial crown of the realms and dominions aforesaid (other than the said James, duke of York), but that in case the said James, duke of York, shall survive his now Majesty and the heirs of his Majesty's body, the said imperial crown shall descend to and be enjoyed by such person and persons successively during the lifetime of the said James, duke of York, as should have inherited and enjoyed the same in case the said James, duke of York, were naturally dead, anything in this Act contained to the contrary notwithstanding.

And be it enacted . . . that during the life of the said James, duke of York, this Act shall be given in charge at every assizes and general sessions of the peace within the kingdoms, dominions and territories aforesaid, and also shall be openly read in every cathedral, collegiate church, parish church and chapel within the aforesaid kingdoms, dominions and territories by the several and respective parsons, vicars, curates and readers thereof, who are hereby required, immediately after divine service in the forenoon, to read the same twice in every year, that is to say on the five and twentieth day of December and upon Easter Day, during the life of the said James, duke of York.

36. Letter from the duke of Ormonde to the earl of Arran on the Rye House Plot, 1683

(Historical Manuscripts Commission, *Ormonde MSS.*, N.S., VII, pp. 51–52)

St. James's Square,
22 June 1683

The king has appointed a Council to be held at Hampton Court to-morrow in the morning, and will hold another in the afternoon. The principal occasion is the discovery of a damnable conspiracy for killing the king and the duke as they came from Newmarket to London this last spring; and, though I am as slow as any man in my belief of such discoveries and attempts, yet I believe it highly probable that the thing would have been attempted, if the fire which burned a great part of Newmarket had not driven the king from thence eight or ten days sooner than he intended and prefixed for his stay there. The discoverer is a substantial citizen, zealously factious and active on the Whig party, and so bold that it was he that arrested the lord mayor when nobody else could be found hardy enough to undertake it. He says it was remorse of conscience and horror of so bloody a fact, and for prevention of the like villainy, that moved him to repent and discover, and we are charitably to believe him, though the fear of some of the conspirators being beforehand with him might have some share in his conversion.

The manner of effecting the execrable fact and the means of the actors' escape was thus laid. There is one Rumbold, heretofore an officer of Cromwell's, blind of an eye, who has a house near a gate in the road where toll is paid for permission to pass by a gravelled causeway over a large meadow. In this house and in the garden and yards belonging to it, which were hid from passengers' view by high ditches, trees and weeds, twelve of the actors were so planted, four of them were to shoot blunderbusses into the king's coach, three or four to let fly at the coachman and postillion, and the rest at the guards that ride behind the coach, which must come close by the ditch, and make some little stop at the gate; and the guards are not above six when the king makes but a day's journey from Newmarket to London. But to have time enough to do their work they had contrived to have a cart stand cross the causeway, which should seem to do so by the unskilfulness of the carters, who were to be disguised conspirators, or by the awkwardness of the horses. They were to have somewhere thereabouts about thirty horse more. With these and by their knowledge of by-ways they were to get to London, where they had prepared for a rising; and if they had not it is not to be doubted but that upon their effecting of such a design there would have been one.

The substance of all this is confessed by one that is apprehended, accused by the informer. The rest of those named by him are fled upon apprehension of being discovered, but how they came to have that apprehension is not clearly known. Besides those that were sought for many more have quit their houses and abscond. We are yet upon the track, but it is hoped every day will show us more light, and who were principal in the contrivance. This is what my memory serves me to write, and therefore I will not answer for exactness in all particulars; but I am fully satisfied that there was a formed design to commit the treason, and I believe all men that are not given over to incredulity, or resolved to be rebels, will be convinced.

37. Report of the French ambassador to Louis XIV on the death of Charles II, 1685

(Sir John Dalrymple, *Memoirs of Great Britain and Ireland*, App., 1, pp. 94–98)

18 February[1] 1685

The letter I do myself the honour to write to your Majesty to-day is only to give you an exact account of what happened, of most importance, at the death of the king of England. His illness, which began on Monday morning the 12th of February,[2] had divers changes the following days. Sometimes he was thought out of danger, and then something happened that made it judged his disorder was mortal. In fine, on Thursday, 15th February,[3] about noon, I was informed from a good quarter that there were no hopes, and that the physicians believed he could not hold out the night.

I went immediately to Whitehall. The duke of York had given orders to the officers who guarded the door of the ante-chamber to let me pass at any hour. He was continually in the king his brother's room. From time to time he came out to give orders upon what was passing in the town. The report was more than once spread that the king was dead. As soon as I arrived the duke of York said to me, "The physicians think the king in extreme danger; I desire you to assure your master that he shall always have in me a faithful and grateful servant." I was five hours in the king's ante-chamber. The duke of York made me come into the bedchamber several times, and spoke to me of what was passing without doors, and of the assurances given him from every quarter that all was very quiet in the town, and that he should be proclaimed king the moment the king his brother was dead.

I went out for some time to go to the duchess of Portsmouth's apartment. I found her overwhelmed with grief, the physicians having taken all hopes from her. However, instead of speaking to me of her affliction and the loss she was on the point of sustaining, she went into a small closet and said to me, "Monsieur the ambassador, I am going to tell you the greatest secret in the world, and my head would be in danger if it was known. The king of England at the bottom of his heart is a Catholic; but he is surrounded with Protestant bishops, and nobody tells him his condition nor speaks to him of God. I cannot with decency enter the room, besides that the queen is almost constantly there. The duke of York thinks of his own affairs, and has too many of them to take the care he ought of the king's conscience. Go and tell him I have conjured you to warn him to think of what can be done to save the king's soul. He commands the room, and can turn out whom he will. Lose no time, for if it is deferred ever so little it will be too late."

I returned instantly to find the duke of York, and begged him to make a pretence of going to the queen, who had left the king's room, and who, having fainted, was

---

[1] 8/18 February.   [2] 2/12 February.   [3] 5/15 February.

just blooded. The room communicated with both apartments. I followed him to the queen's and told him what the duchess of Portsmouth said to me. He recovered himself as from a deep lethargy and said, "You are in the right; there is no time to lose. I will hazard all rather than not do my duty on this occasion." An hour after, he returned under the same pretence of going to the queen, and told me he had spoken to the king his brother, and found him resolved not to take the sacrament which the Protestant bishops had pressed him to receive; that this had surprised them much, but that one or other of them would remain always in the room, if he did not find a pretence to make everybody leave it, in order that he might have an opportunity of speaking to the king his brother with freedom, and disposing him to make a formal renunciation of heresy and confess himself to a Catholic priest.

We thought of various expedients. The duke of York proposed that I should ask leave to speak to the king his brother, to tell him something in secret from your Majesty, and that everybody should go out. I offered to do so, but represented to him that besides the great rumour it would make, there was no likelihood of my being allowed to remain in private with the king of England and himself long enough for what we had to do. The duke of York then bethought himself of sending for the queen, as if it had been to take her last farewell, and ask pardon of the king if she had ever in anything disobeyed him, who was on his part to return the same ceremony to her. At last the duke of York resolved to speak to the king his brother in presence of the company, yet so as no person might hear what he said to him, because this would remove all suspicion, and it would be believed that he spoke to him only of affairs of state, and of what he wished to be done after his death.

Thus without any further precaution the duke of York stooped down to the king his brother's ear, after having ordered that no one should approach. I was in the room, and more than twenty persons at the door, which was open. What the duke of York said was not heard; but the king of England said from time to time very loud, "Yes, with all my heart." He sometimes made the duke of York repeat what he said, because he did not easily hear him. This lasted near a quarter of an hour. The duke of York again went out as if he had gone to the queen, and said to me, "The king has consented that I should bring a priest to him; but I dare not bring any of the duchess's; they are too well known. Send and find one quickly."

I told him I would do it with all my heart, but I believed too much time would be lost, and that I had just seen all the queen's priests in a closet near the chamber. He said, "You are right." At the same time he perceived the count of Castel Melhor, who with warmth embraced the proposal made him, and undertook to speak to the queen. He came back in an instant and said, "Should I hazard my head in this, I would do it with pleasure; but I do not know one of the queen's priests who understands or speaks English." On this we resolved to send to the Venetian resident for an English priest; but as the time pressed, the count of Castel Melhor went where the queen's priests were, and found amongst them one Huddleston, a Scotsman, who saved the king of England after the battle of Worcester, and who by Act of Parliament had been excepted from all the laws made against the Catholics and against the priests. They put a wig and gown on him to disguise him, and the count of Castel

Melhor conducted him to the door of an apartment that joined by a small step to the king's chamber.

The duke of York, to whom I had given notice that all was ready, sent Chiffinch to receive and bring in Mr. Huddleston. Soon after he said aloud, "The king wills that everybody should retire, except the earls of Bath and Feversham." The first was lord of the bedchamber, and the other was in waiting. The physicians went into a closet, the door of which was immediately shut, and Chiffinch brought Mr. Huddleston in. The duke of York in presenting him said, "Sire, here is a man who saved your life, and is now come to save your soul." The king answered, "He is welcome." He afterwards confessed himself with great sentiments of devotion and repentance.

The count of Castel Melhor had taken care to have Huddleston instructed by a Portuguese monk of the barefooted Carmelites in what he had to say to the king on such an occasion, for of himself he was no great doctor; but the duke of York told me he acquitted himself very well in his function, and that he made the king formally promise to declare himself openly a Catholic if he recovered his health. He then received absolution, the communion and even the extreme unction. All this lasted about three-quarters of an hour. In the ante-chamber every one looked at another, but nobody said anything but by their eyes and in whispers. The presence of Lord Bath and Lord Feversham, who are Protestants, has satisfied the bishops a little; but the queen's women and the other priests saw so much going and coming that I do not think the secret can be long kept.

After the king of England received the communion his disorder became a little better. It is certain he spoke more intelligibly, and had more strength. We hoped that God was willing to work a miracle by restoring him; but the physicians judged his illness was not abated, and that he could not outlive the night. He nevertheless appeared much more easy, and spoke with more feeling and understanding than he had done from ten at night to eight in the morning. He often spoke quite aloud to the duke of York in terms full of tenderness and friendship. He twice recommended to him the duchess of Portsmouth and the duke of Richmond. He recommended to him also all his other children. He made no mention of the duke of Monmouth, good or bad. He often expressed his confidence in the mercy of God. The bishop of Bath and Wells, who was his chaplain, read some prayers and spoke to him of God. The king showed by his head that he heard him. The bishop was not officious in saying anything particular to him, or proposing that he should make a profession of his faith. He was apprehensive of a refusal, but feared still more, as I believe, to irritate the duke of York.

The king of England was perfectly sensible the whole night, and spoke upon all things with great calmness. At six o'clock in the morning he asked what hour it was, and said, "Open the curtains, that I may once more see day." He suffered great pain, and at seven o'clock they bled him in hopes that it might lessen his pain. At half an hour after eight he began to speak with great difficulty; at ten his senses were quite gone; and he died at noon without any struggle or convulsion. The new king retired to his apartment, was unanimously acknowledged, and then proclaimed.

38. Proclamation of the duke of Monmouth on taking the title of king, 1685

(Historical Manuscripts Commission, *Bath MSS.*, II, pp. 170–171)

JAMES R.

Whereas upon our first landing at Lyme in our county of Dorset on Thursday the 11th day of this instant month of June, we did publish a declaration in the name of ourself, by the name of James, duke of Monmouth, and the noblemen, gentlemen and others now in arms for defence and vindication of the Protestant religion, and of the laws, rights and privileges of England, from the invasion made upon them, and for delivering the kingdom from the usurpation and tyranny of James, duke of York; wherein amongst other things therein contained we did declare that out of the love we bear to the English nation, whose welfare and settlement we did infinitely prefer to whatever might concern ourselves, we would not at present insist upon our title, but leave the determination thereof to the authority of a Parliament legally chosen and acting with freedom; since which it hath pleased Almighty God to succeed and prosper us hitherto in a very eminent manner, and also disposed the hearts of our loving subjects that from all parts of the country they flock in unanimously for the defence of our person and of the righteous cause we are engaged in; by which we have been enabled to march from Lyme aforesaid unto our good town of Taunton to the terror and amazement of all our enemies round about us: and whereas as well during our said march as since our coming to Taunton aforesaid all our loving subjects have with warm and repeated solicitations importuned us to exert and take upon us our sovereign and royal authority of king as well as of the power of a general, that we might thereby be enabled to make use of the laws and statutes of the realm in conjunction with our arms for their safety and preservation; and have likewise earnestly implored us for their own sakes not to defer the execution of our kingly office to so late a period as is mentioned in the said declaration, for that it will in all probability render the progress of our arms more slow, and thereby give our enemies a longer season to harass and impoverish our kingdom: we could not but with great reluctancy incline to consent to anything that might seem to be a departure from our said declaration, and thereby raise any diffidence amongst the sober and virtuous, or give occasion to wicked and malicious men to arraign the sincerity of our intentions; but as the said clause in the said declaration was inserted under this prospect, to convince the world that we postponed all things to the safety and welfare of our people, and that we consulted not so much our own interest as their prosperity, being so convinced both from the circumstances of affairs and from united advice of all our loving people's petitions that it was absolutely necessary for their protection and defence that we should immediately insist upon our title to the crowns of England, Scotland, France and Ireland, and the dominions and territories thereunto belonging, as son and heir apparent to Charles the Second, king of England, our royal father lately deceased: we have therefore suffered ourselves to be prevailed upon, and have complied with the earnest importunities and necessities of our people, giving way to our being proclaimed king on the 20th day of this instant June at our town of Taunton aforesaid; which we hereby solemnly declare we have consented unto out of tenderness and for the interest of all our loving subjects, and not upon any motives arising from ourself.

And we do further declare and faithfully promise upon the word of a king that we will inviolably keep and perform all and every the articles, sentences and clauses specified and comprised in our said declaration for the good of our kingdom and benefit of all our loyal subjects; and that we will in our first Parliament pass into laws all methods therein contained for the relief, ease and safety of our people.

Given at our camp at Taunton,

the 21st day of June,

in the first year of our reign.

39. Letter of invitation to William of Orange, 1688

(Sir John Dalrymple, *Memoirs of Great Britain and Ireland*, App., I, pp. 228–231)

30 June 1688

We have great satisfaction to find by 35 [Russell], and since by Monsieur Zuylestein, that your Highness is so ready and willing to give us such assistances as they have related to us. We have great reason to believe we shall be every day in a worse condition than we are, and less able to defend ourselves, and therefore we do earnestly wish we might be so happy as to find a remedy before it be too late for us to contribute to our own deliverance. But although these be our wishes, yet we will by no means put your Highness into any expectations which may misguide your own councils in this matter; so that the best advice we can give is to inform your Highness truly both of the state of things here at this time and of the difficulties which appear to us.

As to the first, the people are so generally dissatisfied with the present conduct of the government in relation to their religion, liberties and properties (all which have been greatly invaded), and they are in such expectation of their prospects being daily worse, that your Highness may be assured there are nineteen parts of twenty of the people throughout the kingdom who are desirous of a change, and who, we believe, would willingly contribute to it, if they had such a protection to countenance their rising as would secure them from being destroyed before they could get to be in a posture able to defend themselves. It is no less certain that much the greatest part of the nobility and gentry are as much dissatisfied, although it be not safe to speak to many of them beforehand; and there is no doubt but that some of the most considerable of them would venture themselves with your Highness at your first landing, whose interests would be able to draw great numbers to them whenever they could protect them and the raising and drawing men together. And if such a strength could be landed as were able to defend itself and them till they could be got together into some order, we make no question but that strength would quickly be increased to a number double to the army here, although their army should all remain firm to them; whereas we do upon very good grounds believe that their army then would be very much divided among themselves, many of the officers being so discontented that they continue in their service only for a subsistence (besides that some of their minds are known already), and very many of the common soldiers do daily shew such an aversion to the popish religion that there is the greatest probability imaginable of great numbers of deserters which would come from them should there be such an occasion; and amongst the seamen it is almost certain there is not one in ten who would do them any service in such a war.

Besides all this, we do much doubt whether this present state of things will not yet be much changed to the worse before another year, by a great alteration which will probably be made both in the officers and soldiers of the army, and by such other changes as are not only to be expected from a packed Parliament, but what the meeting of any Parliament (in our present circumstances) may produce against those who will be looked upon as principal obstructers of their proceedings there, it being taken for granted that if things cannot then be carried to their wishes in a parliamentary way other measures will be put in execution by more violent means; and although such proceedings will then heighten the discontents, yet such courses will probably be taken at that time as will prevent all possible means of relieving ourselves.

These considerations make us of opinion that this is a season in which we may more probably contribute to our own safeties than hereafter (although we must own to your Highness there are some judgments differing from ours in this particular), insomuch that if the circumstances stand so with your Highness that you believe you can get here time enough, in a condition to give assistances this year sufficient for a relief under these circumstances which have been now represented, we who subscribe this will not fail to attend your Highness upon your landing and to do all that lies in our power to prepare others to be in as much readiness as such an action is capable of, where there is so much danger in communicating an affair of such a nature till it be near the time of its being made public. But, as we have already told your Highness, we must also lay our difficulties before your Highness, which are chiefly, that we know not what alarm your preparations for this expedition may give, or what notice it will be necessary for you to give the States beforehand, by either of which means their intelligence or suspicions here may be such as may cause us to be secured before your landing. And we must presume to inform your Highness that your compliment upon the birth of the child (which not one in a thousand here believes to be the queen's) hath done you some injury, the false imposing of that upon the princess and the nation being not only an infinite exasperation of people's minds here, but being certainly one of the chief causes upon which the declaration of your entering the kingdom in a hostile manner must be founded on your part, although many other reasons are to be given on ours.

If upon a due consideration of all these circumstances your Highness shall think fit to adventure upon the attempt, or at least to make such preparations for it as are necessary (which we wish you may), there must be no more time lost in letting us know your resolution concerning it, and in what time we may depend that all the preparations will be ready, as also whether your Highness does believe the preparations can be so managed as not to give them warning here, both to make them increase their force and to secure those they shall suspect would join with you. We need not say anything about ammunition, artillery, mortar pieces, spare arms, &c., because if you think fit to put anything in execution you will provide enough of these kinds, and will take care to bring some good engineers with you; and we have desired Mr. H[erbert] to consult you about all such matters, to whom we have communicated our thoughts in many particulars too tedious to have been written, and about which no certain resolutions can be taken till we have heard again from your Highness.

25. Shrewsbury.   31. Bishop of London.
24. Devonshire.   35. Russell.
27. Danby.   33. Sidney.
29. Lumley.

40. Bill of Rights, 1689

(*Statutes of the Realm*, VI, pp. 142–145)

AN ACT DECLARING THE RIGHTS AND LIBERTIES OF THE SUBJECT AND SETTLING THE SUCCESSION OF THE CROWN

(*1 Gul. & Mar. sess. 2, cap. 2*)

Whereas the Lords Spiritual and Temporal and Commons assembled at Westminster, lawfully, fully and freely representing all the estates of the people of this realm, did upon the thirteenth day of February in the year of our Lord one thousand six hundred eighty-eight[1] present unto their Majesties, then called and known by the names and style of William and Mary, prince and princess of Orange, being present in their proper persons, a certain declaration in writing made by the said Lords and Commons in the words following, viz.:

Whereas the late King James the Second, by the assistance of divers evil counsellors, judges and ministers employed by him, did endeavour to subvert and extirpate the Protestant religion and the laws and liberties of this kingdom;

By assuming and exercising a power of dispensing with and suspending of laws and the execution of laws without consent of Parliament;

By committing and prosecuting divers worthy prelates for humbly petitioning to be excused from concurring to the said assumed power;

By issuing and causing to be executed a commission under the great seal for erecting a court called the Court of Commissioners for Ecclesiastical Causes;

By levying money for and to the use of the Crown by pretence of prerogative for other time and in other manner than the same was granted by Parliament;

By raising and keeping a standing army within this kingdom in time of peace without consent of Parliament, and quartering soldiers contrary to law;

By causing several good subjects being Protestants to be disarmed at the same time when papists were both armed and employed contrary to law;

By violating the freedom of election of members to serve in Parliament;

By prosecutions in the Court of King's Bench for matters and causes cognizable only in Parliament, and by divers other arbitrary and illegal courses;

And whereas of late years partial corrupt and unqualified persons have been returned and served on juries in trials, and particularly divers jurors in trials for high treason which were not freeholders;

[1] 1688/9.

And excessive bail hath been required of persons committed in criminal cases to elude the benefit of the laws made for the liberty of the subjects;

And excessive fines have been imposed;

And illegal and cruel punishments inflicted;

And several grants and promises made of fines and forfeitures before any conviction or judgment against the persons upon whom the same were to be levied;

All which are utterly and directly contrary to the known laws and statutes and freedom of this realm;

And whereas the said late King James the Second having abdicated the government and the throne being thereby vacant, his Highness the prince of Orange (whom it hath pleased Almighty God to make the glorious instrument of delivering this kingdom from popery and arbitrary power) did (by the advice of the Lords Spiritual and Temporal and divers principal persons of the Commons) cause letters to be written to the Lords Spiritual and Temporal being Protestants, and other letters to the several counties, cities, universities, boroughs and cinque ports, for the choosing of such persons to represent them as were of right to be sent to Parliament, to meet and sit at Westminster upon the two and twentieth day of January in this year one thousand six hundred eighty and eight,[1] in order to such an establishment as that their religion, laws and liberties might not again be in danger of being subverted, upon which letters elections having been accordingly made;

And thereupon the said Lords Spiritual and Temporal and Commons, pursuant to their respective letters and elections, being now assembled in a full and free representative of this nation, taking into their most serious consideration the best means for attaining the ends aforesaid, do in the first place (as their ancestors in like case have usually done) for the vindicating and asserting their ancient rights and liberties declare

That the pretended power of suspending of laws or the execution of laws by regal authority without consent of Parliament is illegal;

That the pretended power of dispensing with laws or the execution of laws by regal authority, as it hath been assumed and exercised of late, is illegal;

That the commission for erecting the late Court of Commissioners for Ecclesiastical Causes, and all other commissions and courts of like nature, are illegal and pernicious;

That levying money for or to the use of the Crown by pretence of prerogative, without grant of Parliament, for longer time, or in other manner than the same is or shall be granted, is illegal;

That it is the right of the subjects to petition the king, and all commitments and prosecutions for such petitioning are illegal;

That the raising or keeping a standing army within the kingdom in time of peace, unless it be with consent of Parliament, is against law;

That the subjects which are Protestants may have arms for their defence suitable to their conditions and as allowed by law;

That election of members of Parliament ought to be free;

[1] 1688/9.

That the freedom of speech and debates or proceedings in Parliament ought not to be impeached or questioned in any court or place out of Parliament;

That excessive bail ought not to be required, nor excessive fines imposed, nor cruel and unusual punishments inflicted;

That jurors ought to be duly impanelled and returned, and jurors which pass upon men in trials for high treason ought to be freeholders;

That all grants and promises of fines and forfeitures of particular persons before conviction are illegal and void;

And that for redress of all grievances, and for the amending, strengthening and preserving of the laws, Parliaments ought to be held frequently.

And they do claim, demand and insist upon all and singular the premises as their undoubted rights and liberties, and that no declarations, judgments, doings or proceedings to the prejudice of the people in any of the said premises ought in any wise to be drawn hereafter into consequence or example; to which demand of their rights they are particularly encouraged by the declaration of his Highness the prince of Orange as being the only means for obtaining a full redress and remedy therein. Having therefore an entire confidence that his said Highness the prince of Orange will perfect the deliverance so far advanced by him, and will still preserve them from the violation of their rights which they have here asserted, and from all other attempts upon their religion, rights and liberties, the said Lords Spiritual and Temporal and Commons assembled at Westminster do resolve that William and Mary, prince and princess of Orange, be and be declared king and queen of England, France and Ireland and the dominions thereunto belonging, to hold the crown and royal dignity of the said kingdoms and dominions to them, the said prince and princess, during their lives and the life of the survivor of them, and that the sole and full exercise of the regal power be only in and executed by the said prince of Orange in the names of the said prince and princess during their joint lives, and after their deceases the said crown and royal dignity of the said kingdoms and dominions to be to the heirs of the body of the said princess, and for default of such issue to the Princess Anne of Denmark and the heirs of her body, and for default of such issue to the heirs of the body of the said prince of Orange. And the Lords Spiritual and Temporal and Commons do pray the said prince and princess to accept the same accordingly.

And that the oaths hereafter mentioned be taken by all persons of whom the oaths of allegiance and supremacy might be required by law, instead of them; and that the said oaths of allegiance and supremacy be abrogated.

I, A.B., do sincerely promise and swear that I will be faithful and bear true allegiance to their Majesties King William and Queen Mary. So help me God.

I, A.B., do swear that I do from my heart abhor, detest and abjure as impious and heretical this damnable doctrine and position, that princes excommunicated or deprived by the Pope or any authority of the see of Rome may be deposed or murdered by their subjects or any other whatsoever. And I do declare that no foreign prince, person, prelate, state or potentate hath or ought to have any jurisdiction, power, superiority, pre-eminence or authority, ecclesiastical or spiritual, within this realm. So help me God.

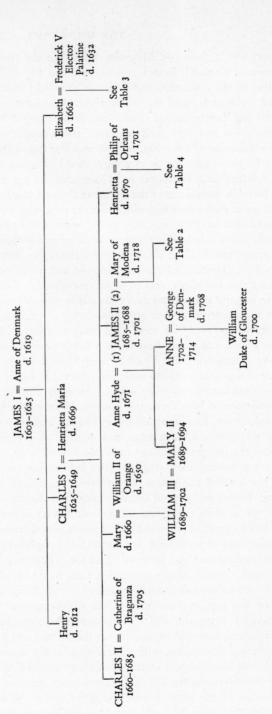

TABLE 1

*The English Succession
as determined by the Bill of Rights*

Upon which their said Majesties did accept the crown and royal dignity of the kingdoms of England, France and Ireland, and the dominions thereunto belonging, according to the resolution and desire of the said Lords and Commons contained in the said declaration. And thereupon their Majesties were pleased that the said Lords Spiritual and Temporal and Commons, being the two Houses of Parliament, should continue to sit, and with their Majesties' royal concurrence make effectual provision for the settlement of the religion, laws and liberties of this kingdom, so that the same for the future might not be in danger again of being subverted, to which the said Lords Spiritual and Temporal and Commons did agree, and proceed to act accordingly. Now in pursuance of the premises the said Lords Spiritual and Temporal and Commons in Parliament assembled, for the ratifying, confirming and establishing the said declaration and the articles, clauses, matters and things therein contained by the force of a law made in due form by authority of Parliament, do pray that it may be declared and enacted that all and singular the rights and liberties asserted and claimed in the said declaration are the true, ancient and indubitable rights and liberties of the people of this kingdom, and so shall be esteemed, allowed, adjudged, deemed and taken to be; and that all and every the particulars aforesaid shall be firmly and strictly holden and observed as they are expressed in the said declaration, and all officers and ministers whatsoever shall serve their Majesties and their successors according to the same in all times to come. And the said Lords Spiritual and Temporal and Commons, seriously considering how it hath pleased Almighty God in his marvellous providence and merciful goodness to this nation to provide and preserve their said Majesties' royal persons most happily to reign over us upon the throne of their ancestors, for which they render unto him from the bottom of their hearts their humblest thanks and praises, do truly, firmly, assuredly and in the sincerity of their hearts think, and do hereby recognize, acknowledge and declare, that King James the Second having abdicated the government, and their Majesties having accepted the crown and royal dignity as aforesaid, their said Majesties did become, were, are and of right ought to be by the laws of this realm our sovereign liege lord and lady, king and queen of England, France and Ireland and the dominions thereunto belonging, in and to whose princely persons the royal state, crown and dignity of the said realms with all honours, styles, titles, regalities, prerogatives, powers, jurisdictions and authorities to the same belonging and appertaining are most fully, rightfully and entirely invested and incorporated, united and annexed. And for preventing all questions and divisions in this realm by reason of any pretended titles to the crown, and for preserving a certainty in the succession thereof, in and upon which the unity, peace, tranquillity and safety of this nation doth under God wholly consist and depend, the said Lords Spiritual and Temporal and Commons do beseech their Majesties that it may be enacted, established and declared, that the crown and regal government of the said kingdoms and dominions, with all and singular the premises thereunto belonging and appertaining, shall be and continue to their said Majesties and the survivor of them during their lives and the life of the survivor of them, and that the entire, perfect and full exercise of the regal power and government be only in and executed by his Majesty in the names of both their Majesties during their joint lives; and after their deceases the said crown and premises shall be and remain to the heirs of the body of her Majesty, and for default of such issue to her Royal Highness the Princess Anne of Denmark and the heirs of her body, and for default of such issue to the heirs of the body of his said Majesty; and thereunto the said Lords Spiritual and Temporal and Commons do in the name of all the people aforesaid most humbly and faithfully submit themselves, their heirs and posterities for ever, and do faithfully promise that they will stand to, maintain and defend their said Majesties, and also the limitation and succession of the crown herein specified and contained, to the utmost of their

TABLE 2

The English Succession showing heirs excluded by the Bill of Rights

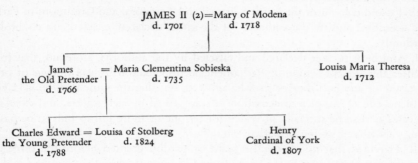

powers with their lives and estates against all persons whatsoever that shall attempt anything to the contrary. And whereas it hath been found by experience that it is inconsistent with the safety and welfare of this Protestant kingdom to be governed by a popish prince, or by any king or queen marrying a papist, the said Lords Spiritual and Temporal and Commons do further pray that it may be enacted, that all and every person and persons that is, are or shall be reconciled to or shall hold communion with the see or Church of Rome, or shall profess the popish religion, or shall marry a papist, shall be excluded and be for ever incapable to inherit, possess or enjoy the crown and government of this realm and Ireland and the dominions thereunto belonging or any part of the same, or to have, use or exercise any regal power, authority or jurisdiction within the same; and in all and every such case or cases the people of these realms shall be and are hereby absolved of their allegiance; and the said crown and government shall from time to time descend to and be enjoyed by such person or persons being Protestants as should have inherited and enjoyed the same in case the said person or persons so reconciled, holding communion or professing or marrying as aforesaid were naturally dead; and that every king and queen of this realm who at any time hereafter shall come to and succeed in the imperial crown of this kingdom shall on the first day of the meeting of the first Parliament next after his or her coming to the crown, sitting in his or her throne in the House of Peers in the presence of the Lords and Commons therein assembled, or at his or her coronation before such person or persons who shall administer the coronation oath to him or her at the time of his or her taking the said oath (which shall first happen), make, subscribe and audibly repeat the declaration mentioned in the statute made in the thirtieth year of the reign of King Charles the Second entituled, *An Act for the more effectual preserving the king's person and government by disabling papists from sitting in either House of Parliament.*[1] But if it shall happen that such king or queen upon his or her succession to the crown of this realm shall be under the age of twelve years, then every such king or queen shall make, subscribe and audibly repeat the said declaration at his or her coronation or the first day of the meeting of the first Parliament as aforesaid which shall first happen after such king or queen shall have attained the said age of twelve years. All which their Majesties are contented and pleased shall be declared, enacted and established by authority of this present Parliament, and shall stand, remain and be the law of this realm for ever; and the same are by their said Majesties, by and with the advice and consent of the Lords Spiritual and Temporal and Commons in Parliament assembled and by the authority of the same, declared, enacted and established accordingly.

II. And be it further declared and enacted by the authority aforesaid, that from and after this present session of Parliament no dispensation by *non obstante* of or to any statute or any part thereof shall be allowed, but that the same shall be held void and of no effect, except a dispensation be allowed of in such statute, and except in such cases as shall be specially provided for by one or more bill or bills to be passed during this present session of Parliament.

III. Provided that no charter or grant or pardon granted before the three and twentieth day of October in the year of our Lord one thousand six hundred eighty-nine shall be any ways impeached or invalidated by this Act, but that the same shall be and remain of the same force and effect in law and no other than as if this Act had never been made.

41. Act of Recognition, 1690

(*Statutes of the Realm*, VI, p. 156)

AN ACT FOR RECOGNIZING KING WILLIAM AND QUEEN MARY,
AND FOR AVOIDING ALL QUESTIONS TOUCHING THE ACTS
MADE IN THE PARLIAMENT ASSEMBLED AT WESTMINSTER
THE THIRTEENTH DAY OF FEBRUARY
ONE THOUSAND SIX HUNDRED EIGHTY-EIGHT[2]

(*2 Gul. & Mar., sess. 1, cap. 1*)

We, your Majesties' most humble and loyal subjects, the Lords Spiritual and Temporal and Commons in this present Parliament assembled, do beseech your most excellent Majesties that it may be published and declared in this high court of Parliament, and enacted by authority of the same, that we do recognize and acknowledge your Majesties were, are and of right ought to be by the laws of this realm our sovereign liege lord and lady, king and queen of England, France and Ireland and the dominions thereunto belonging, in and to whose princely persons the royal state,

[1] No. 144.   [2] 1688/9.

crown and dignity of the said realms, with all honours, styles, titles, regalities, preroga-tives, powers, jurisdictions and authorities to the same belonging and appertaining, are most fully, rightfully and entirely invested and incorporated, united and annexed. And for the avoiding of all disputes and questions concerning the being and authority of the late Parliament assembled at Westminster the thirteenth day of February one thousand six hundred eighty-eight,[1] we do most humbly beseech your Majesties that it may be enacted, and be it enacted by the king and queen's most excellent Majesties, by and with the advice and consent of the Lords Spiritual and Temporal and Commons in this present Parliament assembled and by authority of the same, that all and singular the Acts made and enacted in the said Parliament were and are laws and statutes of this kingdom, and as such ought to be reputed, taken and obeyed by all the people of this kingdom.

42. Report on possible brides for William III, 1696
(*Correspondentie van Willem III en Bentinck*, part i, II, pp. 80-81)
LIST OF PRINCESSES, ROYAL, ELECTORAL AND OF OTHER MOST DISTINGUISHED HOUSES,
OF MARRIAGEABLE AGE AND OF THE PROTESTANT RELIGION,
LUTHERAN OR REFORMED

The princess royal of Sweden, fifteen years of age. She is very tiny, and a Lutheran. The princess royal of Denmark, eighteen years of age, tall, of excellent disposi-tion, well-bred and graced with the best qualities of her sex. She is a Lutheran, like the king her father; but the queen her mother, who is Reformed, has inspired her with the same opinions.

The princess electoral of Brandenburg, fourteen years of age, very well-bred, of a sweet-tempered disposition, extremely devout, and of the Protestant religion.

The princess of Hesse-Cassel, sixteen years of age, well endowed both in mind and body, of moderate height, of a gentle and kindly disposition and of the Reformed religion.

The princess of Saxe-Eisenach, twenty-five years of age, with a striking appearance and charming temper; Lutheran.

The princess of Holstein-Gottorp, twenty years of age, of excellent reputation; Lutheran.

43. Act of Settlement, 1701
(*Statutes of the Realm*, VII, pp. 636-638)
AN ACT FOR THE FURTHER LIMITATION OF THE CROWN
AND BETTER SECURING THE RIGHTS AND LIBERTIES OF THE SUBJECT
(12 & 13 Gul. III, cap. 2)

Whereas in the first year of the reign of your Majesty and of our late most gracious Sovereign Lady Queen Mary (of blessed memory) an Act of Parliament was made, entituled, *An Act for declaring the rights and liberties of the subject and for settling the succession of the crown*,[2] wherein it was (amongst other things) enacted, established and

---

[1] 1688/9.   [2] No. 40.

declared, that the crown and regal government of the kingdoms of England, France and Ireland and the dominions thereunto belonging should be and continue to your Majesty and the said late queen during the joint lives of your Majesty and the said queen and to the survivor, and that after the decease of your Majesty and of the said queen the said crown and regal government should be and remain to the heirs of the body of the said late queen, and for default of such issue to her Royal Highness the Princess Anne of Denmark and the heirs of her body, and for default of such issue to the heirs of the body of your Majesty; and it was thereby further enacted, that all and every person and persons that then were or afterwards should be reconciled to or shall hold communion with the see or Church of Rome, or should profess the popish religion or marry a papist, should be excluded, and are by that Act made forever incapable to inherit, possess or enjoy the crown and government of this realm and Ireland and the dominions thereunto belonging or any part of the same, or to have, use or exercise any regal power, authority or jurisdiction within the same, and in all and every such case and cases the people of these realms shall be and are thereby absolved of their allegiance; and that the said crown and government shall from time to time descend to and be enjoyed by such person or persons being Protestants as should have inherited and enjoyed the same in case the said person or persons so reconciled, holding communion, professing or marrying as aforesaid were naturally dead; after the making of which statute and the settlement therein contained your Majesty's good subjects, who were restored to the full and free possession and enjoyment of their religion, rights and liberties by the providence of God giving success to your Majesty's just undertakings and unwearied endeavours for that purpose, had no greater temporal felicity to hope or wish for than to see a royal progeny descending from your Majesty, to whom (under God) they owe their tranquillity, and whose ancestors have for many years been principal assertors of the reformed religion and the liberties of Europe, and from our said most gracious sovereign lady, whose memory will always be precious to the subjects of these realms; and it having since pleased Almighty God to take away our said sovereign lady and also the most hopeful Prince William, duke of Gloucester (the only surviving issue of her Royal Highness the Princess Anne of Denmark), to the unspeakable grief and sorrow of your Majesty and your said good subjects, who under such losses being sensibly put in mind that it standeth wholly in the pleasure of Almighty God to prolong the lives of your Majesty and of her Royal Highness, and to grant to your Majesty or to her Royal Highness such issue as may be inheritable to the crown and regal government aforesaid by the respective limitations in the said recited Act contained, do constantly implore the divine mercy for those blessings, and your Majesty's said subjects having daily experience of your royal care and concern for the present and future welfare of these kingdoms, and particularly recommending from your throne a further provision to be made for the succession of the crown in the Protestant line for the happiness of the nation and the security of our religion, and it being absolutely necessary for the safety, peace and quiet of this realm to obviate all doubts and contentions in the same by reason of any pretended titles to the crown, and to maintain a certainty in the succession thereof to which your subjects may safely have recourse for their protection in

TABLE 3

The English Succession
as determined by the Act of Settlement

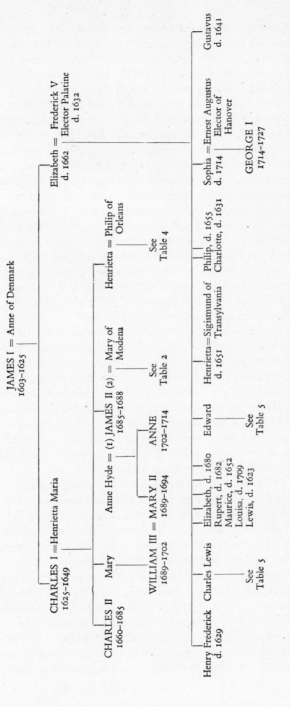

JAMES I = Anne of Denmark
1603–1625

CHARLES I = Henrietta Maria
1625–1649

Elizabeth = Frederick V
d. 1662   Elector Palatine
              d. 1632

CHARLES II
1660–1685

Mary

Anne Hyde = (1) JAMES II (2) = Mary of Modena
                  1685–1688

Henrietta = Philip of Orleans

See Table 4

WILLIAM III = MARY II
1689–1702   1689–1694

ANNE
1702–1714

See Table 2

Henrietta = Sigismund of
d. 1651   Transylvania

Philip, d. 1655
Charlotte, d. 1631

Sophia = Ernest Augustus
d. 1714   Elector of Hanover

Gustavus
d. 1641

GEORGE I
1714–1727

Henry Frederick
d. 1629

Charles Lewis

See Table 5

Elizabeth, d. 1680
Rupert, d. 1682
Maurice, d. 1652
Louisa, d. 1709
Lewis, d. 1623

Edward

See Table 5

case the limitations in the said recited Act should determine: therefore for a further provision of the succession of the crown in the Protestant line, we your Majesty's most dutiful and loyal subjects the Lords Spiritual and Temporal and Commons in this present Parliament assembled do beseech your Majesty that it may be enacted and declared, and be it enacted and declared by the king's most excellent Majesty, by and with the advice and consent of the Lords Spiritual and Temporal and Commons in this present Parliament assembled and by the authority of the same, that the most excellent Princess Sophia, electress and duchess dowager of Hanover, daughter of the most excellent Princess Elizabeth, late queen of Bohemia, daughter of our late Sovereign Lord King James the First of happy memory, be and is hereby declared to be the next in succession in the Protestant line to the imperial crown and dignity of the said realms of England, France and Ireland, with the dominions and territories thereunto belonging, after his Majesty and the Princess Anne of Denmark and in default of issue of the said Princess Anne and of his Majesty respectively, and that from and after the deceases of his said Majesty our now sovereign lord, and of her Royal Highness the Princess Anne of Denmark, and for default of issue of the said Princess Anne and of his Majesty respectively, the crown and regal government of the said kingdoms of England, France and Ireland and of the dominions thereunto belonging, with the royal state and dignity of the said realms, and all honours, styles, titles, regalities, prerogatives, powers, jurisdictions and authorities to the same belonging and appertaining, shall be, remain and continue to the said most excellent Princess Sophia and the heirs of her body being Protestants; and thereunto the said Lords Spiritual and Temporal and Commons shall and will in the name of all the people of this realm most humbly and faithfully submit themselves, their heirs and posterities, and do faithfully promise that after the deceases of his Majesty and her Royal Highness, and the failure of the heirs of their respective bodies, to stand to, maintain and defend the said Princess Sophia and the heirs of her body being Protestants, according to the limitation and succession of the crown in this Act specified and contained, to the utmost of their powers with their lives and estates against all persons whatsoever that shall attempt anything to the contrary.

II. Provided always, and it is hereby enacted, that all and every person and persons who shall or may take or inherit the said crown by virtue of the limitation of this present Act, and is, are or shall be reconciled to, or shall hold communion with, the see or Church of Rome, or shall profess the popish religion or shall marry a papist, shall be subject to such incapacities as in such case or cases are by the said recited Act provided, enacted and established; and that every king and queen of this realm who shall come to and succeed in the imperial crown of this kingdom by virtue of this Act shall have the coronation oath administered to him, her or them at their respective coronations, according to the Act of Parliament made in the first year of the reign of his Majesty and the said late Queen Mary, entituled, *An Act for establishing the coronation oath*,[1] and shall make, subscribe and repeat the declaration in the Act first above recited, mentioned or referred to in the manner and form thereby prescribed.

III. And whereas it is requisite and necessary that some further provision be made

---

[1] 1 Gul. & Mar., cap. 6.

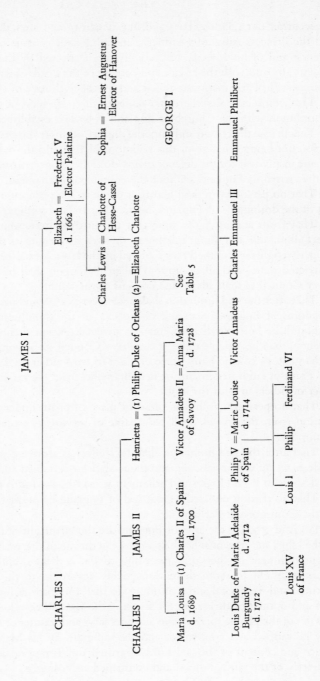

TABLE 4

The English Succession

showing heirs excluded by the Act of Settlement – Orleans line

for securing our religion, laws and liberties from and after the death of his Majesty and the Princess Anne of Denmark, and in default of issue of the body of the said princess and of his Majesty respectively, be it enacted by the king's most excellent Majesty, by and with the advice and consent of the Lords Spiritual and Temporal and Commons in Parliament assembled and by the authority of the same;

That whosoever shall hereafter come to the possession of this crown shall join in communion with the Church of England as by law established.

That in case the crown and imperial dignity of this realm shall hereafter come to any person not being a native of this kingdom of England this nation be not obliged to engage in any war for the defence of any dominions or territories which do not belong to the crown of England without the consent of Parliament.

That no person who shall hereafter come to the possession of this crown shall go out of the dominions of England, Scotland or Ireland without consent of Parliament.

That from and after the time that the further limitation by this Act shall take effect all matters and things relating to the well governing of this kingdom which are properly cognizable in the Privy Council by the laws and customs of this realm shall be transacted there, and all resolutions taken thereupon shall be signed by such of the Privy Council as shall advise and consent to the same.

That after the said limitation shall take effect as aforesaid no person born out of the kingdoms of England, Scotland or Ireland, or the dominions thereunto belonging (although he be naturalized or made a denizen, except such as are born of English parents), shall be capable to be of the Privy Council, or a member of either House of Parliament, or to enjoy any office or place of trust either civil or military, or to have any grant of lands, tenements or hereditaments from the crown to himself or to any other or others in trust for him.

That no person who has an office or place of profit under the king, or receives a pension from the crown, shall be capable of serving as a member of the House of Commons.[1]

That after the said limitation shall take effect as aforesaid judges' commissions be made *quam diu se bene gesserint*, and their salaries ascertained and established, but upon the address of both Houses of Parliament it may be lawful to remove them.

That no pardon under the great seal of England be pleadable to an impeachment by the Commons in Parliament.

IV. And whereas the laws of England are the birthright of the people thereof, and all the kings and queens who shall ascend the throne of this realm ought to administer the government of the same according to the said laws, and all their officers and ministers ought to serve them respectively according to the same, the said Lords Spiritual and Temporal and Commons do therefore further humbly pray that all the laws and statutes of this realm for securing the established religion and the rights and liberties of the people thereof, and all other laws and statutes of the same now in force, may be ratified and confirmed, and the same are by his Majesty, by and with the advice and consent of the said Lords Spiritual and Temporal and Commons, and by authority of the same, ratified and confirmed accordingly.

[1] See No. 45.

TABLE 5

The English Succession

showing heirs excluded by the Act of Settlement–Palatine line

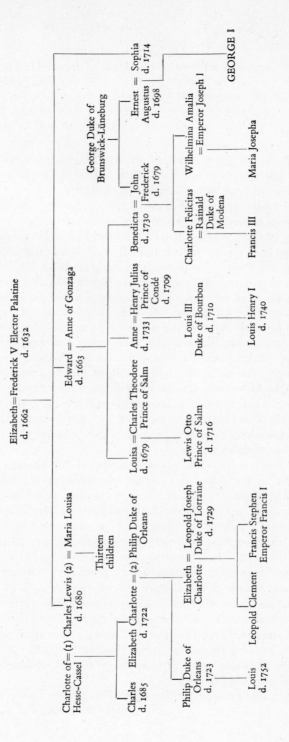

44. Anonymous account of the death of James II, 1701
(*Somers Tracts*, ed. 1809–1815, XI, pp. 339–342)

AN EXACT ACCOUNT OF THE SICKNESS AND DEATH OF THE LATE KING JAMES II,

AS ALSO OF THE PROCEEDINGS AT ST. GERMAINS THEREUPON, 1701,

IN A LETTER FROM AN ENGLISH GENTLEMAN IN FRANCE TO HIS FRIEND IN LONDON

SIR,

I doubt not but you have heard of the indisposition, and since of the death, of the king. Therefore it is no news to you. However I cannot omit giving you a short particular of both, which take as followeth, viz.

On Friday, the second of this instant September,[1] his Majesty, being at chapel on his knees, fainted away, which some of his servants perceiving supported him from falling, put him into his chair, and carried him to his lodgings, where after an hour's time he came pretty well to himself again, ate heartily, continued so, sleeping and dozing, till Sunday (by intervals speaking to those about him), when, about half an hour past two in the afternoon, on a sudden he was taken so ill that he could not speak; by reason of an imposthumation breaking within him, and nature endeavouring to discharge it, he was almost suffocated. This occasioned the report that he was dead, which presently flew to Paris and consequently all over Europe; but by bleeding and other proper remedies a considerable quantity of that corrupt matter passed both ways, Sunday, Monday and Tuesday, but none on Wednesday or Thursday. He slept well that night; on Friday was better, only he had an intermitting fever which left him that night. He continued so till about eleven o'clock Sunday night, when the physicians observed a lethargy in him, and fearing he might die in that condition they applied the blistering plaster betwixt his shoulders with good effect. Yet, a disposition to doze and sleep continuing in him, they applied those plasters to his ankles, afterwards to his head, but without success.

In this condition his Majesty continued till Monday night, when everybody thought he was departing; but the physicians giving him somewhat inwardly he presently began to discharge both ways, then rested till near five next morning. Awaking, he spoke to the curate of the parish (who watched by him) to give him the sacrament, which he accordingly did: at which time he forgave several persons by name, all his enemies, and everyone that had wronged him; prayed Father Saunders and all the rest about him to declare it to the world; called for all his servants and exhorted them to be constant to their principles; thanked them for their fidelity to him; sent for the prince and princess, charged them to be constant in their religion and that no hopes of crowns or sceptres should make them do a thing unworthy their birth, and above all to be obedient to the queen; gave them his blessing; desired that all his servants might continue on the same foot they now were, and that all his subjects would acknowledge his son for their lawful king and sovereign. So from that time the physicians resolved to apply no further remedies, but leave his Majesty to the will of Almighty God.

The king of France came to see his Majesty, but he was speechless. Whereupon he

[1] 22 August/2 September.

went to comfort the queen and sent for the prince of Wales; told them, maugre all the difficulties he had met with in his great council, yet, having the unanimous consent of the Dauphin and all the rest of the princes of the blood, he resolved to acknowledge and declare the prince his Majesty's lawful heir and successor to the imperial crown of England, &c.; and that he should be so acknowledged by France, Spain and Portugal, and that he would by his ambassadors proclaim him as such in all the courts of Europe. After some time the king came to himself again, and being told of this declaration sent for the prince next day; told him he had not seen him since the king of France had been there; charged him, during his minority, exactly to observe the king of France's counsel and direction in all things; and said he had sent my Lord Middleton to Marly to give the king of France thanks for the same.

The king of France, hearing his Majesty was somewhat better, came to St. Germains to see him; and when he was entered the lodgings said he was not only come to see the king but also on an affair of great weight; whereupon all persons were withdrawing; but he called them all in again, caused all the doors to be opened, that everybody might enter that belonged to the king, and then commanded that as soon as the king should be dead the prince of Wales should be proclaimed king of Great Britain with his ordinary titles, declaring he would also cause the same to be done at Versailles, and (by his ambassadors) in all the courts of Europe; that his body should be removed from the queen's apartment to his own (and gave order to the captain of the guards to attend his corpse accordingly); and told all that belonged to the king they should continue on the same foot they were at present till he could do no more for them. While the king of France was making this speech the whole Court was in tears; but when he had done they clapt their hands for joy, which caused that great monarch to weep.

The king desired to be buried privately at St. Germains, dying there in exile; but the king of France told him that was the only thing in the world he could not grant him, for he would lay him where he would have the honour to lie by him himself. And on Friday the 17th instant,[1] about three in the afternoon, the king died, the day he always fasted in memory of our blessed Saviour's passion, the day he ever desired to die on, and the ninth hour, according to the Jewish account, when our Saviour was crucified. His death was edifying to men, and no doubt precious to God. As soon as he was departed the great master of the ceremonies of France (by the king's order) proclaimed the prince of Wales king of Great Britain and all the dominions thereunto belonging with the usual ceremony. The queen is appointed regent. My Lord Middleton gave up the great seal. All the lords have taken the oath of fidelity, the servants have kissed his Majesty's hand, and everything stands as it did in the late king's days.

And now I cannot omit telling you two remarkable passages. The one is that when the king first fainted in the chapel, when he first fell ill, it was on Good Friday, on singing the anthem, the two first verses of the last chapter of the Lamentations, "Remember, O Lord, what is come upon us: consider, and behold our reproach. Our inheritance is turned to strangers, our houses to aliens." Which was so touching,

---

[1] Friday, 5/16 September.

and made such an impression on his Majesty, that he never perfectly recovered it, although he went to the waters of Bourbon. The other is, the king of France, upon his Majesty's sickness, called his great council, which consisted of twenty-three persons. All but seven were against proclaiming the prince so soon. The Dauphin, being the last that was to speak, rose up in some heat, and said it would be a great piece of cowardice, and unworthy the crown of France, to abandon a prince of their own blood, especially one that was so dear to them as the son of King James; that for his part he was resolved not only to hazard his life but all that was dear to him for his restoration. The king of France said, "I am of Monseigneur's opinion"; and so said all the princes of the blood.

45. Regency Act, 1707

(Statutes of the Realm, VIII, pp. 738–743)

AN ACT FOR THE SECURITY OF HER MAJESTY'S PERSON AND GOVERNMENT
AND OF THE SUCCESSION TO THE CROWN OF GREAT BRITAIN
IN THE PROTESTANT LINE

(6 Annae, cap. 41)

Whereas by the happy union of England and Scotland it is become necessary to make divers alterations in relation to an Act passed in the Parliament of England in the fourth year of the reign of her present Majesty (whom God long preserve), entituled, *An Act for the better security of her Majesty's person and government and of the succession to the crown of England in the Protestant line,*[1] and to extend the provisions of the said Act throughout the whole United Kingdom, for the better security of our most gracious sovereign's person and government, and of the succession to the crown of Great Britain in the Protestant line as it is now by the laws and statutes of this realm settled, limited and appointed; be it therefore enacted . . . that if any person or persons shall maliciously, advisedly and directly, by writing or printing, maintain and affirm that our sovereign lady the queen that now is, is not the lawful and rightful queen of these realms, or that the pretended prince of Wales, who now styles himself king of Great Britain, or king of England by the name of James the Third, or king of Scotland by the name of James the Eighth, hath any right or title to the crown of these realms, or that any other person or persons hath or have any right or title to the same otherwise than according to an Act of Parliament made in England in the first year of the reign of their late Majesties King William and Queen Mary of ever blessed and glorious memory, entituled, *An Act declaring the rights and liberties of the subject and settling the succession of the crown,*[2] and one other Act made in England in the twelfth year of the reign of his said late Majesty King William the Third, entituled, *An Act for the further limitation of the crown and better securing the rights and liberties of the subject,*[3] and the Acts lately made in England and Scotland mutually for the union of the two kingdoms, or that the kings or queens of this realm, with and by the authority of Parliament, are not able to make laws and statutes of sufficient force and validity to

---

[1] 6 Annae, cap. II.   [2] No. 40.   [3] No. 43.

limit and bind the crown and the descent, limitation, inheritance and government thereof, every such person or persons shall be guilty of high treason, and being thereof lawfully convicted shall be adjudged traitors, and shall suffer pains of death and all losses and forfeitures as in cases of high treason. . . .

IV. And be it further enacted . . . that this present Parliament or any other Parliament which shall hereafter be summoned and called by her Majesty Queen Anne, her heirs or successors, shall not be determined or dissolved by the death or demise of her said Majesty, her heirs or successors, but such Parliament shall and is hereby enacted to continue, and is hereby empowered and required, if sitting at the time of such demise, immediately to proceed to act, notwithstanding such death or demise, for and during the term of six months and no longer, unless the same be sooner prorogued or dissolved by such person to whom the crown of this realm of Great Britain shall come, remain and be, according to the Acts for limiting and settling the succession and for the union above-mentioned.[1] . . .

V. And be it further enacted . . . that if there be a Parliament in being at the time of the death of her Majesty, her heirs or successors, but the same happens to be separated by adjournment or prorogation, such Parliament shall immediately after such demise meet, convene and sit, and shall act, notwithstanding such death or demise, for and during the time of six months and no longer, unless the same shall be sooner prorogued or dissolved as aforesaid.

VI. And be it further enacted . . . that in case there is no Parliament in being at the time of such demise that hath met and sat, then the last preceding Parliament shall immediately convene and sit at Westminster, and be a Parliament to continue as aforesaid to all intents and purposes as if the same Parliament had never been dissolved, but subject to be prorogued and dissolved as aforesaid.

VII. Provided always, and it is hereby declared, that nothing in this Act contained shall extend or be construed to extend to alter or abridge the power of the queen, her heirs or successors, to prorogue or dissolve Parliaments, nor to repeal or make void one Act of Parliament made in England in the sixth year of the reign of their said late Majesties King William and Queen Mary, entituled, *An Act for the frequent meeting and calling of Parliaments*,[2] but that the said Act shall continue in force in everything that is not contrary to or inconsistent with the direction of this Act; and the said *Act for the frequent meeting and calling of Parliaments* is hereby declared and enacted to extend to the Parliament of Great Britain as fully and effectually to all intents, constructions and purposes as if the same were herein and hereby particularly recited and enacted.

VIII. And be it further enacted . . . that the Privy Council of her Majesty, her heirs or successors, for the kingdom of Great Britain shall not be determined or dissolved by the death or demise of her Majesty, her heirs or successors, but such Privy Council shall continue and act as such by the space of six months next after such demise, unless sooner determined by the next successor to whom the imperial crown of this realm is limited and appointed to go, remain and descend; nor shall the office or place of Lord Chancellor or Lord Keeper of the Great Seal of Great Britain, or of Lord High

---

[1] See No. 52.   [2] No. 51.

Treasurer of Great Britain, Lord President of the Council for Great Britain, Lord Privy Seal of Great Britain, Lord High Admiral of Great Britain, or of any of the great officers of the queen or king's household for the time being; nor shall any office, place or employment, civil or military, within the kingdoms of Great Britain or Ireland, dominion of Wales, town of Berwick-upon-Tweed, isles of Jersey, Guernsey, Alderney and Sark, or any of her Majesty's plantations become void by reason of the demise or death of her present Majesty, her heirs or successors, queens or kings of this realm; but the said Lord Chancellor or Lord Keeper of the Great Seal of Great Britain, the Lord High Treasurer of Great Britain, the Lord President of the Council, the Lord Privy Seal, the Lord High Admiral of Great Britain, the great officers of the household and every other person and persons in any of the offices, places and employments aforesaid shall continue in their respective offices, places and employments for the space of six months next after such death or demise, unless sooner removed and discharged by the next in succession as aforesaid. . . .

X. And be it further enacted . . . that whensoever her Majesty (whom God long preserve) shall happen to demise and depart this life without issue of her body, the Privy Council for Great Britain in being at the time of such demise of her Majesty shall with all convenient speed cause the next Protestant successor entitled to the crown of Great Britain by virtue of the Acts before mentioned to be openly and solemnly proclaimed in Great Britain and Ireland, in such manner and form as the preceding kings and queens respectively have been usually proclaimed after the demise of their respective predecessors, and that all and every member and members of the said Privy Council wilfully neglecting or refusing to cause such proclamation to be made shall be guilty of high treason, and being thereof lawfully convicted shall be adjudged traitors, and shall suffer pains of death and all losses and forfeitures as in cases of high treason. . . .

XI. And because it may happen that the next Protestant successor may at the time of such demise of her Majesty be out of the realm of Great Britain in parts beyond the seas, be it therefore enacted . . . that for the continuing of the administration of the government in the name of such Protestant successor until her or his arrival in Great Britain the seven officers hereinafter named who shall be in the possession of their offices at the time of such demise of her Majesty, that is to say the archbishop of Canterbury at that time being, the Lord Chancellor or Lord Keeper of the Great Seal of Great Britain at that time being, the Lord High Treasurer of Great Britain at that time being, the Lord President of the Council for Great Britain at that time being, the Lord Privy Seal of Great Britain at that time being, the Lord High Admiral of Great Britain at that time being and the Lord Chief Justice of the Queen's Bench at that time being, shall be, and are by virtue of this Act constituted and appointed Lords Justices of Great Britain, and are and shall be by virtue of this Act empowered in the name of such successor, and in her and his stead, to use, exercise and execute all powers, authorities, matters and acts of government and administration of government in as full and ample manner as such next successor could use or execute the same if she or he were present in person within this kingdom of Great Britain, until such successor shall arrive or otherwise determine their authority.

XII. Nevertheless be it further enacted . . . that such person who by the limitations aforesaid is or shall be next to succeed to the crown of this realm in case of her Majesty's demise without issue shall and is hereby empowered, at any time during her Majesty's life, by three instruments under her or his hand and seal, revocable or to be altered at her and his will and pleasure, to nominate and appoint such and so many persons, being natural-born subjects of this realm of Great Britain, as she or he shall think fit to be added to the seven officers before named to be Lords Justices as aforesaid, who shall be empowered by authority of this Act to act with them as Lords Justices of Great Britain as fully and in the same manner as if they had been herein particularly named; which said Lords Justices or the major part of them which shall assemble, so as such major part be not fewer than five, shall and may use and exercise all the powers and authorities before-mentioned as fully and effectually to all intents and purposes as if all of them had been assembled together and consenting. . . .

XXIII. Provided always, that if any of the aforesaid seven officers other than the office of Lord High Treasurer of Great Britain shall be in commission at the time of such demise of her Majesty, that then the first commissioner of such respective commission shall be one of the said Lords Justices of Great Britain, and use, exercise and execute all powers, authorities, matters and acts of government by this Act vested in the said Lords Justices of Great Britain according to the directions and provisions of this Act, in as full and ample manner as if such office or offices were in the hands of a single person; provided that if there be no Lord High Treasurer of Great Britain, and the office of Treasurer of the Exchequer shall be in commission, then the first in that commission shall be one of the Lords Justices of Great Britain.

XXIV. And be it further enacted . . . that no person who shall have in his own name, or in the name of any person or persons in trust for him or for his benefit, any new office or place of profit whatsoever under the crown, which at any time since the five and twentieth day of October in the year of our Lord one thousand seven hundred and five have been created or erected, or hereafter shall be created or erected, nor any person who shall be commissioner or sub-commissioner of prizes, secretary or receiver of the prizes, nor any comptroller of the accompts of the army, nor any commissioner of transports, nor any commissioner of the sick and wounded, nor any agent for any regiment, nor any commissioner for any wine licences, nor any governor or deputy-governor of any of the plantations, nor any commissioners of the navy employed in any of the out-ports, nor any person having any pension from the crown during pleasure, shall be capable of being elected, or of sitting or voting, as a member of the House of Commons in any Parliament which shall be hereafter summoned and holden.

XXV. Provided always, that if any person, being chosen a member of the House of Commons, shall accept of any office of profit from the crown during such time as he shall continue a member, his election shall be and is hereby declared to be void, and a new writ shall issue for a new election as if such person so accepting was naturally dead. Provided, nevertheless, that such person shall be capable of being again elected as if his place had not become void as aforesaid. . . .

XXVII. Provided also, that nothing herein contained shall extend or be construed to extend to any member of the House of Commons, being an officer in her Majesty's navy or army, who shall receive any new or other commission in the navy or army respectively. . . .

XXIX. And be it further enacted and declared, that every person disabled to be elected or to sit or vote in the House of Commons of any Parliament of England shall be disabled to be elected or to sit or vote in the House of Commons of any Parliament of Great Britain. . . .

46.   John Arbuthnot on the death of Anne, 1714
(Works of Jonathan Swift, ed. Walter Scott, XVI, p. 222)

I thank you for your kind letter, which is very comfortable upon such a melancholy occasion. My dear mistress's days were numbered even in my imagination, and could not exceed such certain limits; but of that small number a great deal was cut off by the last troublesome scene of this contention among her servants. I believe sleep was never more welcome to a weary traveller than death was to her.

Part II
PARLIAMENT

PARLIAMENT

Introduction

THE restoration of Parliament, though less striking, was more thorough and complete, and was to prove of more permanent importance than that of the monarchy. For thirteen years Parliament had been held in subordination by the army, and subjected to every species of indignity. Its leaders had been arrested, its members expelled, its upper House abolished, and its whole constitution altered. But at no time had it been denied that there should be a Parliament, or that government should be based upon it; and towards the close of the Commonwealth period such Parliaments as had been permitted to exist had been inclining more and more to assume their old form and character. Thus as the power of the army waned Parliament almost automatically resumed its place as an essential factor in the government, and with enhanced prestige due to the obvious fact that it had proved indispensable. Even the Lords, hesitatingly but of their own accord, reassembled; and it was Parliament that recalled the king, not the king who restored Parliament.

A natural consequence of the altered balance of power which this implied was the tacit assumption, made at the Restoration, that the king no longer enjoyed his former complete control over Parliament for its summons, sitting and dissolution. The very first Act to which Charles was required to give his assent, indeed, was one declaring that the Convention to which he owed his recall was a true Parliament, though it had been elected and had assembled without any authority from him;[1] and both that Act and the later Act recognizing the restored monarchy[2] laid it down that the Long Parliament of the reign of Charles I was dissolved, although no dissolution had been pronounced, or statute declaring a dissolution accepted, by any king. Finally in 1664 the Triennial Act of the Long Parliament was in substance re-enacted, though the cumbersome machinery provided in the earlier Act with a view to ensuring that Parliament should actually meet every three years was omitted from the new measure.[3]

In accordance with this Act, Parliament met throughout the greater part of Charles II's reign with commendable frequency,[4] and the main grievance of its champions came to be the wholly unexpected one, not that it was held in abeyance, but that the same Parliament was kept in being much too long. In the spring of 1677, when the Cavalier Parliament had been in existence for nearly sixteen years, the duke of Buckingham raised this grievance in the House of Lords, arguing that by two Acts of the reign of Edward III a meeting of Parliament was required at least once every year, and that therefore a recent prorogation for the unprecedented space of fifteen months must be regarded as equivalent to a dissolution, putting an end to that Parliament altogether.[5] But the only result was that the Lords themselves committed Buckingham and his supporters to the Tower for their reflections on Parliament, and refused to release them until they had made a full submission.

The main problem of the summons and duration of Parliament, however, still remained to be solved, and came prominently to the front in both its aspects when Charles towards the close of his reign dispensed with Parliament for more than three years, and James (though in rather unusual circumstances) pursued the same course.

---

[1] No. 47. [2] No. 6. [3] No. 48. [4] Diagram 1. [5] No. 49.

Following the precedent of 1660, the Convention of 1689, which conferred the crown upon William and Mary, required the assent of William to a formal statute by which it declared itself to be a true Parliament, although it had been summoned by William before he was king.[1] The Bill of Rights rather feebly declared that "Parliaments ought to be held frequently".[2] But the real solution of the problem, so far as the law was concerned, came with the Triennial Act of 1694, which provided not merely that there must be a meeting of Parliament every three years but also that no Parliament could legally remain in existence for longer than three years.[3] Thereafter the only serious difficulty concerned the position of Parliament on the demise of the sovereign, for in its new position of importance the old rule, that in such an event it was automatically dissolved, was bound to produce grave inconveniences. This difficulty was met by an Act of 1696, which laid it down that on the death of the sovereign the existing Parliament, or, if there was no Parliament in being, the previous Parliament, should meet and continue to function, unless dissolved, for the space of six months.[4] Ten years later, after the union between England and Scotland, these provisions were confirmed for the Parliament of Great Britain.[5]

Meanwhile the problem had been settled much more satisfactorily in practice than it had in law. So great was the need of William and Anne for money with which to conduct their wars on the Continent, and so essential the annual authorization of the standing army,[6] that Parliament had in fact to be summoned each year. So necessary also was William's presence on the Continent during the summer that meetings for the greater part of his reign were scarcely practicable except during the winter. Immediately after the Revolution, in consequence, it became the custom that Parliament should assemble every autumn and sit until the spring of the following year,[7] and this custom has persisted in essentials ever since.

This regular and frequent meeting of Parliament, by giving rise to a class of politicians who devoted their main energies to the conduct of affairs, greatly increased its effective strength, as did also its success in securing full recognition of such necessary privileges as freedom of speech,[8] and the right of the Commons to elect their own Speaker.[9] One of the most striking powers which any legislative body can exercise is that of exempting from penalty actions which when they were performed were illegal, and this power the Parliaments of the later Stuarts were called upon to exercise again and again—in 1660 for the benefit of those who had acted during the civil wars and under the Commonwealth,[10] in 1689 for the benefit of those who had assisted the Revolution, and repeatedly thereafter for the benefit of those who had found it necessary to take irregular action in dealing with threatened invasion or rebellion. Under the inspiration to some extent of the theories of John Locke,[11] who would certainly have refused to countenance their worst extravagances, the Commons began indeed to claim an almost irresponsible position. Their treatment of the gentlemen of Kent, who ventured to present a petition criticizing their attitude in foreign affairs, roused widespread dissatisfaction.[12] Their assertion of an exclusive right not merely to determine disputed elections but also to decide who had the right to vote had to be checked by the law courts and the House of Lords.[13]

In all this, however, there was nothing essentially new, and the real advance made by Parliament was rather in the associated spheres of finance and administration.

[1] No. 50.   [2] No. 40.   [3] No. 51.   [4] No. 52.   [5] No. 45.
[6] No. 311.   [7] Diagram 1.   [8] No. 54.   [9] No. 55.   [10] No. 53.
[11] No. 56.   [12] No. 57.   [13] No. 58.

Having at last secured recognition of its sole authority over the raising of supplies, it now proceeded tentatively to assume some control over the disposal of them. Beginning in 1665, it adopted with increasing frequency the practice of appropriating particular taxes to particular purposes.[1] In 1667, after a long controversy with the crown, it appointed by statute a commission for auditing certain accounts,[2] which had many successors. On the solid foundation thus secured it then proceeded to erect a power of criticizing and advising, if not actually directing, the executive, mainly by means of formal addresses to the sovereign. These addresses dealt with the most diverse subjects—foreign policy,[3] the trustworthiness of individual ministers,[4] the use of the royal veto on legislation,[5] even the possible remarriage of Queen Anne[6]—and, as is shown by the increasingly conciliatory and evasive character of the replies, became more and more influential as time passed.

On the other hand, the king was not without means of bringing pressure to bear on Parliament. Charles II adopted the practice of regular attendance on the House of Lords in order that he might influence their debates.[7] When faced with a strong opposition in Parliament he did not disdain to appeal over their heads to his people.[8] Both Charles and James made extensive use of legal processes to secure the forfeiture of charters of towns, with the object of bringing the towns, and with them their representatives in Parliament, more under their own control.[9] James owed his success with the Parliament of 1685 largely to practices of this nature,[10] and two years later endeavoured to secure a still more favourable Parliament by personal interviews with existing members, and by bringing pressure to bear on all lords lieutenants, deputy lieutenants, justices of the peace and others who might be able to influence elections.[11]

To all appearance the last word was bound to lie with Parliament, for it had in its hands the much-dreaded weapon of impeachment, backed if necessary by attainder or bill of pains and penalties. The later Stuart period was indeed the golden age of impeachments. Danby was the object of impeachment three times, Clarendon twice, and most prominent statesmen at least once. The impeachment was sometimes designed, as in the case of Clarendon,[12] to prevent a fallen statesman from recovering his authority; sometimes, as in the case of Danby,[13] to drive a powerful statesman from office; and sometimes, as in the case of Sacheverell,[14] merely to discredit an individual who had made himself obnoxious to the House of Commons. But in every case it suffered, as a weapon of parliamentary control, from the fact that it had to prove not merely incompetence or even ill intentions but actual breaches of the law. Clarendon, with his mind dwelling in a vanished age, could thus defend himself by maintaining that he had not broken any law;[15] and Danby, with a better appreciation of the real point now at issue, by arguing that what he had done was not merely legal but specially authorized by the king in a sphere in which the royal power was supreme, and therefore, as most people would still have admitted, beyond the competence of Parliament to criticize.[16] Where impeachment for any reason failed, Parliament could have recourse to Acts of banishment[17] or of attainder,[18] which being legislative measures did not require the same proof of guilt; but the result as a rule was to raise dissension between the Lords, who, as befitted their character, endeavoured to maintain a judicial attitude, and the Commons, who were inspired almost entirely by political

[1] No. 59. [2] No. 60. [3] Nos. 61, 64. [4] No. 62.
[5] No. 63. [6] No. 65. [7] No. 66. [8] No. 67.
[9] No. 68. [10] No. 69. [11] No. 70. [12] No. 71.
[13] No. 74. [14] No. 78. [15] No. 72. [16] No. 75.
[17] No. 73. [18] No. 77.

motives. Although so alarming and so frequently employed, in fact, impeachment and attainder were generally recognized to be largely ineffective, and just as likely to recoil on their promoters as to injure anyone else.[1]

Strangely enough the composition of Parliament led to little serious controversy. Almost as a matter of course the bishops, who had been excluded from the House of Lords by one of the last statutes to which Charles I had given his assent, were reinstated;[2] and though their presence among the peers, a solid body of supporters for each monarch in turn, was regarded with considerable disfavour, criticism rarely took a more serious form than an attempt to restrict their competence. Charles, James, William and Anne were all allowed without protest to increase the size of the House and maintain their influence in it by extensive creations of new peers. Even Anne's unprecedented action in creating a batch of twelve peers to facilitate the acceptance of the treaty of Utrecht[3] roused little more than a party opposition. The most serious trouble, in fact, arose over a comparatively minor point, the resolution adopted by the Lords, in defiance of both law and common sense, that a Scottish peer given a British title did not thereby become entitled to be a member of their body.[4]

Similarly in the Commons the enfranchising of the borough of Newark by royal charter was criticized as an unwarrantable exercise of an out-of-date prerogative, and the enfranchising of the county and city of Durham by statute[5] met with a good deal of opposition. But the general framework of the House of Commons, which was thus completed, and which was to remain unchanged, so far as England was concerned, until 1821, was accepted almost without question. It was widely recognized that representation bore little relation either to population or to wealth.[6] Elaborate tables were drawn up, on a none too accurate basis,[7] comparing the various counties with each other.[8] Treatises were written setting forth the principles on which Parliament should be founded.[9] But the subject remained almost purely academic. Under the Commonwealth there had been an extensive redistribution of seats, and in spite of the most obvious inequalities[10] redistribution was therefore out of favour. More concern, indeed, was expressed about the transformation of the English Parliament into the Parliament of Great Britain,[11] which was not at all popular; about the desirability of a property qualification for members of the Commons, which was at last imposed,[12] though without much effect; and about the poor attendance in both Houses, which had long been a cause of worry to statesmen. Under the later Stuarts, however, there was a considerable improvement on this last point, the average attendance of Lords Temporal and members of the Commons rising sharply,[13] although that of the Lords Spiritual appreciably declined.[14]

Had the two Houses of Parliament proved unable to work harmoniously together any real growth in the power of Parliament would have been impossible; but the clashes between them, although they attracted much attention, were not frequent or exceptionally bitter. The Lords were jealous of the increased prestige acquired by the Commons during the civil wars and interregnum, and disliked the solid foundation on which that prestige continued to rest–the claim of the Commons to the exclusive right of initiating financial measures,[15] and even of amending such measures.[16] Most emphatically of all they objected to the practice adopted by the Commons under

[1] No. 76.   [2] No. 79.   [3] No. 81.   [4] No. 80.
[5] No. 82.   [6] No. 84.   [7] Nos. 199, 200.   [8] No. 85.
[9] No. 83.   [10] Map 2.   [11] Nos. 86, 270.   [12] No. 87.
[13] Appendix III.   [14] Diagram 2.   [15] No. 88.   [16] No. 90.

William and Anne of forcing through measures of any kind on which they felt strongly by 'tacking' them to bills of supply;[1] and in their opposition to this practice, although they had to give way several times, they were eventually successful. The Commons on their part were jealous of the judicial powers and privileges enjoyed by the Lords, which could be used even against members of their own body, and were able to defeat the attempt of the Lords to act as a court of first instance in civil cases, though not their more reasonable claim to hear appeals from courts of equity.[2] But quarrels over these and other issues rarely prevented Lords and Commons from acting together in more important matters.

For this underlying harmony much was due to the gradual growth of political parties, which ensured that in each House there should always be some members who were prepared to see the point of view of the other. With so much power now in its hands Parliament had inevitably to develop an elementary organization in order to exercise it in a responsible manner. Clarendon at an early stage realized the need for a body of supporters in the House of Commons if the policy of the government was to have any real prospect of being accepted, and was responsible for the formation of a rudimentary Court party there.[3] Arlington carried the process much further,[4] and Danby further still.[5] The existence of a Court party then led to the development of a Country or opposition party,[6] which received much encouragement from France,[7] and was provided with an effective organization, a headquarters, and even something of the nature of standardized instructions[8] by Shaftesbury. The real test of Shaftesbury's organization came with the Exclusion Bill contest, when he contrived to enlist an astonishing volume of support from the districts in which his influence was supreme;[9] and the successors of the two parties formed at this time are to be found in the groups supporting and opposing William's title to the throne at the Revolution.[10] Thereafter Whigs and Tories, as they had come to be called, remained a permanent feature of political life, though the Court generally tried to maintain its own organization independent of both,[11] and the inclination of individuals to adopt different attitudes in Church and State produced a most confusing situation, especially under Anne.[12]

[1] Nos. 91, 276. [2] No. 89. [3] No. 92. [4] No. 93.
[5] No. 94. [6] No. 95. [7] No. 96. [8] No. 97.
[9] Map 3. [10] Map 4. [11] No. 98. [12] No. 99.

BIBLIOGRAPHY

The formal record of the proceedings of the two Houses is to be found in *Journals of the House of Lords*, vols. XI–XIX; *Journals of the House of Commons*, vols. VIII–XVII; and the *Votes of the House of Commons*, regularly printed after 1680 by authority of the Speaker. All public Acts which received the royal assent are printed in *Statutes of the Realm*, vols. V–IX (London, 1819–1822). Many of the bills which failed to secure acceptance, as well as an immense mass of documents connected with the work of the Lords, are among the *Manuscripts of the House of Lords*, calendared as far as 1693 by the Historical Manuscripts Commission (7 vols., 1879–1895), and from that date to 1712 by the House itself (9 vols., 1900–1949). All protests with reasons (though not those without reasons) are given in *A Complete Collection of the Protests of the Lords*, edited by James E. Thorold Rogers, vol. I (Oxford, 1875). The composition of the House of Commons is indicated in the official *Return of the Names of every Member returned to serve in each Parliament* (2 vols., 1878), which, however, requires correction on a number of points.

During the reigns of the later Stuarts the right of each House to prohibit any publication of its proceedings was still jealously guarded, and as neither House published, or even kept, an adequate record of its own there is a lamentable dearth of detailed information about parliamentary activities. Many members, however, were in the habit of making notes of proceedings for their own satisfaction, while others made a practice of transmitting accounts to their friends or constituents; and of these rather scrappy notes and accounts a considerable number have survived. Outstanding among those which have been printed is *Debates of the House of Commons from the year 1667 to the year 1694, collected by Anchitell Grey* (10 vols., London, 1763). On a smaller scale, but also of value, are *The Diary of John Milward, Member of Parliament for Derbyshire, September 1666 to May 1668*, edited by Caroline Robbins (Cambridge, 1938), and *The Parliamentary Diary of Sir Edward Dering, 1670–1673*, edited by Basil Duke Henning (New Haven, 1940). *Proceedings and Debates of the British Parliaments respecting North America*, edited by Leo F. Stock, vols. I–III (Washington, 1924–1930), is of value for other than purely American developments. Exceptionally detailed and illuminating are the letters written by Andrew Marvell, member for Hull till his death in 1678, of which the most complete and accurate collection is to be found in *The Poems and Letters of Andrew Marvell*, edited by H. M. Margoliouth vol. II, *Letters* (Oxford, 1927).

An official history of Parliament has long been under consideration, and some progress with it has already been made; but a considerable time must inevitably elapse before it can reach the seventeenth century, and meanwhile reliance has to be placed on the very unsatisfactory and out-of-date *Parliamentary History of England*, edited by William Cobbett, vols. IV–VI of which (London, 1808–1810) cover the years 1660–1714; on the scattered sources of information on which this compilation is itself based; and on a number of individual books and articles. Of outstanding importance are "The House of Lords under Charles II", in *English Historical Review*, XLIV (1929), pp. 400–417, XLV (1930), pp. 58–77; *The House of Lords in the Reign of William III* (Oxford, 1913); and *The House of Lords in the Eighteenth Century* (Oxford, 1927), all by A. S. Turberville, and all general studies illustrating the important part still played by the Lords, both in the political and in the social world. E. S. de Beer, "The House of Lords in the Parliament of 1680", in *Bulletin of the Institute of Historical Research*, XX (1943), pp. 22–37, is an interesting examination of the activities of the Lords in one particular session. There are no general studies of the Commons, but much miscellaneous information may be derived from Edward and Annie G. Porritt, *The Unreformed House of Commons: Parliamentary Representation before 1832* (2 vols., Cambridge, 1903 and 1909).

Individual Parliaments and individual elections have received a good deal of attention, the most important studies being Louise Fargo Brown, "The Religious Factors in the Convention Parliament", in *English Historical Review*, XXII (1907), pp. 51–63; Caroline Robbins, "The Oxford Session of the Long Parliament of Charles II, 9–31 October, 1665", in *Bulletin of the*

Institute of Historical Research, XXI (1948), pp. 214–224; E. Lipson, "The Elections to the Exclusion Parliaments, 1679–1681", in *English Historical Review*, XXVIII (1913), pp. 59–85; M. Dorothy George, "Elections and Electioneering, 1679–81", ibid., XLV (1930), pp. 552–578; R. H. George, "Parliamentary Elections and Electioneering in 1685", in *Transactions of the Royal Historical Society, Fourth Series*, XIX (1936), pp. 167–195; J. H. Plumb, "The Elections to the Convention Parliament of 1689", in *Cambridge Historical Journal*, V (1937), pp. 235–254; N. Sykes, "The Cathedral Chapter of Exeter and the General Election of 1705", in *English Historical Review*, XLV (1930), pp. 260–272; William Thomas Morgan, "An Eighteenth-Century Election in England, 1710", in *Political Science Quarterly*, XXXVII (1922), pp. 585–604; and Mary Ransome, "The Press in the General Election of 1710", in *Cambridge Historical Journal*, VI (1939), pp. 209–221. Eric G. Forrester, *Northamptonshire County Elections and Electioneering, 1695–1832* (Oxford, 1941), and Philip Styles, "The Corporation of Bewdley under the later Stuarts", in *University of Birmingham Historical Journal*, I (1947), pp. 92–133, are valuable studies of particular constituencies. Mary Ransome, "The Parliamentary Career of Sir Humphry Mackworth", ibid., I (1948), pp. 232–254, is a similar study of an individual.

Much has been done to trace the development and illustrate the activities of political parties in both Houses of Parliament, but more particularly in the House of Commons, where their influence was always greater. In this connexion the outstanding work is Keith Feiling, *A History of the Tory Party, 1640–1714* (Oxford, 1924), which has not only superseded earlier studies such as G. Wingrove Cooke, *The History of Party*, vol. I, *1666–1714* (London, 1836), and C. B. Roylance Kent, *The early History of the Tories, 1660–1702* (London, 1908), but has gone far towards establishing a new interpretation of the later Stuart period. William Thomas Morgan, *English Political Parties and Leaders in the Reign of Queen Anne, 1702–1710* (New Haven, 1920), is the fruit of much research, and has been continued in the same writer's "The Ministerial Revolution of 1710 in England", in *Political Science Quarterly*, XXXVI (1921), pp. 184–210. With it should be associated Felix Salomon, *Geschichte des letzten Ministeriums Königin Annas von England, 1710–14* (Gotha, 1894).

The bulk of recent work on party development, however, has taken the form of articles designed to solve particular problems connected with it. Among these articles the most important are Wilbur Cortez Abbott, "The Long Parliament of Charles II", in *English Historical Review*, XXI (1906), pp. 21–56, 254–285; and the same writer's "The Origin of English Political Parties", in *American Historical Review*, XXIV (1919), pp. 578–602; E. S. de Beer, "Members of the Court Party in the House of Commons, 1670–1678", in *Bulletin of the Institute of Historical Research*, XI (1934), pp. 1–23; and Andrew Browning, "Parties and Party Organization in the Reign of Charles II", in *Transactions of the Royal Historical Society, Fourth Series*, XXX (1948), pp. 21–36. R. R. Walcott, "Division Lists of the House of Commons, 1689–1715", in *Bulletin of the Institute of Historical Research*, XIV (1936), pp. 25–36, catalogues all known printed lists of divisions, and itself prints one for the Parliament of 1705. It has been supplemented in E. S. de Beer, "Division Lists of 1688–1715: some Addenda", ibid., XIX (1942), pp. 65–66; and since the compilation of both of these there has appeared Andrew Browning and Doreen J. Milne, "An Exclusion Bill Division List", ibid., XXIII (1950), pp. 205–225.

Two useful articles on the relations of Parliament and the executive are R. M. Lees, "Constitutional Importance of the Commissioners for Wool, 1689: an Administrative Experiment of the Reign of William III", in *Economica*, XL (1933), pp. 147–168, 264–274; and the same writer's "Parliament and the Proposal for a Council of Trade, 1695–6", in *English Historical Review*, LIV (1939), pp. 38–66. On attempts of the government to interfere with the freedom of borough elections the most illuminating studies are J. H. Sacret, "The Restoration Government and Municipal Corporations", in *English Historical Review*, XLV (1930), pp. 232–259; Robert H. George, "The Charters granted to English Parliamentary Corporations in 1688", ibid., LV (1940), pp. 47–56; and the same writer's "Note on the Bill of Rights: Municipal Liberties and Freedom of Parliamentary Elections", in *American Historical Review*, XLII (1937), pp. 670–679. The attitude of the Crown to parliamentary bills is the subject of Charles E. Fryer, "The Royal Veto under Charles II", in *English Historical Review*, XXXII (1917), pp. 103–111.

A. SUMMONS AND DURATION

47. Act legalizing the Convention, 1660

(*Statutes of the Realm*, v, p. 179)

AN ACT FOR REMOVING AND PREVENTING
ALL QUESTIONS AND DISPUTES
CONCERNING THE ASSEMBLING AND SITTING OF THIS PRESENT PARLIAMENT

(*12 Car. II, cap. 1*)

For the preventing all doubts and scruples concerning the assembling, sitting and proceeding of this present Parliament, be it declared and enacted, and it is declared and enacted by the king our sovereign lord, and by the Lords and Commons in Parliament assembled and by authority of the same, that the Parliament begun and holden at Westminster the third day of November in the sixteenth year of the reign of the late King Charles of blessed memory is fully dissolved and determined; and that the Lords and Commons now sitting at Westminster in this present Parliament are the two Houses of Parliament, and so shall be and are hereby declared, enacted and adjudged to be to all intents, constructions and purposes whatsoever, notwithstanding any want of the king's Majesty's writ or writs of summons, or any defect or alteration of or in any writ or writs of summons, or any other defect or default whatsoever; as if this Parliament had been summoned by writ or writs in his Majesty's name according to the usual form, and as if his Majesty had been present in person at the assembling and commencement of this present Parliament. Provided always that this present Parliament may be dissolved by his Majesty after the usual manner, as if the same had been summoned by writ or writs in his Majesty's name.

II. Provided also, and it is hereby enacted, that his Majesty's royal assent to this bill shall not determine this present session of Parliament.

48. Triennial Act, 1664

(*Statutes of the Realm*, v, p. 513)

AN ACT FOR THE ASSEMBLING AND HOLDING OF PARLIAMENTS
ONCE IN THREE YEARS AT THE LEAST,
AND FOR THE REPEAL OF AN ACT ENTITULED
*AN ACT FOR THE PREVENTING OF INCONVENIENCIES HAPPENING BY THE LONG
INTERMISSION OF PARLIAMENTS*[1]

(*16 Car. II, cap. 1*)

Whereas the Act made in the Parliament begun at Westminster the third day of November in the sixteenth year of the reign of our late Sovereign Lord King Charles of blessed memory, entituled, *An Act for the preventing of inconveniencies happening by the long intermission of Parliaments*,[1] is in derogation of his Majesty's just rights and

[1] 16 Car. I, cap. 1.

prerogative inherent to the imperial crown of this realm for the calling and assembling of Parliaments, and may be an occasion of manifold mischiefs and inconveniencies and much endanger the peace and safety of his Majesty and all his liege people of this realm, be it therefore enacted . . . that the said Act . . . and all and every the articles, clauses and things therein contained is, shall be and are hereby wholly repealed, annulled and utterly made void, and are hereby declared to be null and void to all intents and purposes whatsoever, as if the said Act had never been had or made, anything in the said Act contained to the contrary in any wise notwithstanding.

II. And because by the ancient laws and statutes of this realm made in the reign of King Edward the Third Parliaments are to be held very often, your Majesty's humble and loyal subjects the Lords Spiritual and Temporal and the Commons in this present Parliament assembled most humbly do beseech your most excellent Majesty that it may be declared and enacted, and be it declared and enacted . . . that hereafter the sitting and holding of Parliaments shall not be intermitted or discontinued above three years at the most, but that within three years from and after the determination of this present Parliament, and so from time to time within three years after the determination of any other Parliament or Parliaments, or if there be occasion more often, your Majesty, your heirs and successors do issue out your writs for calling, assembling and holding of another Parliament, to the end there may be a frequent calling, assembling and holding of Parliaments once in three years at the least.

49. Speech of the duke of Buckingham declaring the Cavalier Parliament to be dissolved, 1677

(*Parliamentary History*, IV, pp. 815–823)

15 February 1677

My Lords, I have often troubled your lordships with my discourse in this House, but I confess I never did it with more trouble to myself than I do at this time. . . . The question, in my opinion, which now lies before your lordships is not what we are to do, but whether at this time we can do anything as a Parliament, it being very clear to me that the Parliament is dissolved; and if in this opinion I have the misfortune to be mistaken I have another misfortune joined to it, for I desire to maintain the argument with all the judges and lawyers in England, and leave it afterwards to your lordships to decide whether I am in the right or no. This, my Lords, I speak, not out of arrogance, but in my own justification, because if I were not thoroughly convinced that what I have now to urge is grounded upon the fundamental laws of England, and that the not pressing it at this time might prove to be of a most dangerous consequence both to his Majesty and the whole nation, I should have been loth to start a notion which perhaps may not be very agreeable to some people. And yet, my Lords, when I consider where I am, whom I now speak to, and what was spoken in this place about the time of the prorogation, I can hardly believe what I have to say will be distasteful to your lordships.

I remember very well how your lordships were then displeased with the House of

Commons, and I remember too as well what reasons they gave to you to be so. It is not so long since but that I suppose your lordships may call to mind that, after several odd passages between us, your lordships were so incensed that a motion was made here for an address to his Majesty about the dissolution of this Parliament; and though it failed of being carried in the affirmative by two or three voices, yet this in the debate was remarkable, that it prevailed with much the major part of your lordships that were here present, and was only overpowered by the proxies of those lords who never heard the arguments. What change there has been since, either in their behaviour or in the state of our affairs, that should make your lordships change your opinion, I have not yet heard; and therefore if I can make it appear (as I presume I shall) that by law the Parliament is dissolved, I presume your lordships ought not to be offended at me for it.

I have often wondered how it should come to pass that this House of Commons, in which there are so many honest and so many worthy gentlemen, should yet be less respectful to your lordships, as certainly they have been, than any House of Commons that were ever chosen in England; and yet if the matter be a little inquired into the reason of it will plainly appear. For, my Lords, the very nature of the House of Commons is changed. They do not think now that they are an assembly that are to return to their own homes and become private men again (as by the laws of the land and the ancient constitution of Parliaments they ought to be), but they look upon themselves as a standing senate, and as a number of men picked out to be legislators for the rest of their lives. And if that be the case, my Lords, they have reason to believe themselves our equals. But, my Lords, it is a dangerous thing to try new experiments in a government. . . . For all governments are artificial things, and every part of them has a dependence one upon another; and with them, as with clocks and watches, if you should put great wheels in the place of little ones, and little ones in the place of great ones, all the movements would stand still; so that we cannot alter any one part of a government without prejudicing the motions of the whole. . . .

But it is not my business to find fault, and therefore, if your lordships will give me leave, I shall go on to show you why, in my opinion, we are at this time no Parliament. The ground of this opinion of mine is taken from the ancient and unquestionable statutes of this realm; and give me leave to tell your lordships by the way that statutes are not like women, for they are not one jot the worse for being old. The first statute that I shall take notice of is that in the 4th of Edw. III, cap. 14, thus set down in the printed book: item, "It is accorded that a Parliament shall be holden every year once, and more often, if need be." Now though these words are as plain as a pikestaff, and no man living, that is not a scholar, could possibly mistake the meaning of them, yet the grammarians of those days did make a shift to explain that the words "if need be" did relate as well to the words "every year once" as to the words "more often", and so by this grammatical whimsy of theirs have made this statute to signify just nothing at all. For this reason, my Lords, in the 36th of the same king's reign a new Act of Parliament was made, in which those unfortunate words "if need be" are left out, and that Act of Parliament is thus printed, relating to Magna Carta and other statutes made for the public good; item, "For maintenance of these articles and statutes, and the redress of divers mischiefs and grievances which daily happen, a Parliament shall be holden every year, as at other time was ordained by another statute." Here now, my Lords, there is not left the least colour or shadow for mistake, for it is plainly declared that the kings of England must call a Parliament once within a year; and the reasons why they are bound to do so are as plainly set down, namely, "for the maintenance of Magna Carta and other statutes of the same importance, and for preventing the mischiefs and grievances which daily happen".

The question then remaineth whether these statutes have been since repealed by any other statutes or no. The only statutes I ever heard mentioned for that are the two Triennial Bills, the one made in the last king's[1] and the other in this king's reign.[2] The Triennial Bill in the last king's reign was made for the confirmation of the two above-mentioned statutes of Edw. III, for Parliaments having been omitted to be called every year according to those statutes, a statute was made in the last king's reign to this purpose, that if the king should fail of calling a Parliament according to the statutes of Edw. III then the third year the people should meet of themselves, without any writs at all, and choose their Parliament-men. This way of the people's choosing their Parliament of themselves being thought disrespectful to the king, a statute was made in this last Parliament, which repealed the Triennial Bill; and after the repealing clause (which took notice only of the Triennial Bill made in the last king's reign) there was in this statute a paragraph to this purpose, that because, by the ancient statutes of the realm made in the reign of Edw. III, Parliaments are to be held very often, it should be enacted that within three years after the determination of that present Parliament Parliaments should not be discontinued above three years at most, and be holden oftener if need required. There have been several half kind of arguments drawn out of these Triennial Bills against the statutes of Edw. III, which I confess I could never remember, nor indeed those that urged them to me ever durst own, for they always laid their faults upon somebody else, like ugly, foolish children, whom, because of their deformity and want of wit, the parents are ashamed of, and so turn them out on the parish.

But, my Lords, let the arguments be what they will, I have this short answer to all that can be wrested out of these Triennial Bills, that the first Triennial Bill was repealed before the matter now disputed of was in question, and the last Triennial Bill will not be in force till the question be decided, that is till the Parliament is dissolved. The whole matter, my Lords, is reduced to this short dilemma. Either the kings of England are bound by the Acts above mentioned of Edw. III, or else the whole government of England by Parliaments and by the laws above is absolutely at an end. For if the kings of England have power by an order of theirs to invalidate an Act made for the maintenance of Magna Carta, they have also power by an order of theirs to invalidate Magna Carta itself. And if they have power by an order of theirs to invalidate the statute *De tallagio non concedendo*, then they may not only, without the help of a Parliament, raise money when they please, but also take away any man's estate when they please, and deprive everyone of his liberty or life as they please.

This, my Lords, I think is a power that no judge or lawyer will pretend the kings

---

[1] 16 Car. I, cap. I.   [2] No. 48.

of England to have; and yet this power must be allowed them or else we that are met here this day cannot act as a Parliament, for we are now met by virtue of the last prorogation, and that prorogation is an order of the king's point-blank contrary to the two Acts of Edw. III. For the Acts say that a Parliament shall be holden once within a year, and the prorogation saith a Parliament shall not be held within a year, but some months after, and this (I conceive) is a plain contradiction, and consequently that the prorogation is void. Now if we cannot act as a Parliament by virtue of the last prorogation, I beseech your lordships by virtue of what else can we act. Shall we act by virtue of the king's proclamation? Pray, my Lords, how so? Is a proclamation of more force than a prorogation? Or if a thing that hath been ordered the first time be not valid, doth the ordering it the second time make it good in law? I have heard, indeed, that two negatives make an affirmative; but I never heard before that two nothings ever made anything.

Well, but how then are we met? Is it by our own adjournment? I suppose nobody has the confidence to say that. Which way then is it? Do we meet by accident? That, I think, may be granted; but an accidental meeting can no more make a Parliament than accidental clapping a crown upon a man's head can make a king. There is a great deal of ceremony required to give a matter of that moment a legal sanction. The laws have reposed so great a trust and so great a power in the hands of a Parliament that every circumstance relating to the manner of their electing, meeting and proceeding is looked after with the nicest circumspection imaginable. For this reason the king's writs about the summons of Parliament are to be issued out verbatim, according to the form prescribed by the law, or else that Parliament is void and null. For the same reason if a Parliament summoned by the king's writ do not meet the very same day that it is summoned to meet upon, that Parliament is void and null. And by the same reason if Parliaments be not legally adjourned *de die in diem*, those Parliaments must be also void and null. . . .

It is plain, then, in my opinion, that we are no more a Parliament, and I humbly conceive your lordships ought to give God thanks for it, since it has thus pleased Him, by His providence, to take you out of a condition wherein you must have been entirely useless to his Majesty, to yourselves and the whole nation. For, I do beseech your lordships, if nothing of this I have urged were true, what honourable excuse could we find for our acting again with the House of Commons, except we could pretend such an exquisite art of forgetfulness as to avoid calling to mind all that passed between us the last session, and unless we could have also a faculty of teaching the same art to the whole nation. What opinion could they have of us, if it should happen that the very same men who were so earnest the last session for having the House of Commons dissolved, when there was no question of their lawful sitting, should be now willing to join with them again, when without question they are dissolved? Nothing can be more dangerous to a king or a people than that the laws should be made by an assembly of which there can be a doubt whether they have a power to make laws or no; and it would be in us inexcusable if we should overlook this danger, since there is for it so easy a remedy, which the law requires and which all the nation longs for.

The calling a new Parliament it is that only can put his Majesty into a possibility of receiving supplies; that can secure your lordships the honour of sitting in this House like peers and your being serviceable to your king and country; and that can restore to all the people of England their undoubted rights of choosing men frequently to represent their grievances in Parliament. . . . My motion, therefore, to your lordships shall be, that we humbly address ourselves to his Majesty, and beg of him, for his own sake as well as for the people's sake, to give us speedily a new Parliament, that so we may unanimously, before it is too late, use our utmost endeavours for his Majesty's service, and for the safety, the welfare, and the glory of the English nation.

50. Act legalizing the Convention, 1689

(*Statutes of the Realm*, VI, pp. 23–24)

AN ACT FOR REMOVING AND PREVENTING
ALL QUESTIONS AND DISPUTES
CONCERNING THE ASSEMBLING AND SITTING OF THIS PRESENT PARLIAMENT

(*1 Gul. & Mar., cap. 1*)

For preventing all doubts and scruples which may in any wise arise concerning the meeting, sitting and proceeding of this present Parliament, be it declared and enacted . . . that the Lords Spiritual and Temporal and Commons convened at Westminster the two and twentieth day of January in the year of our Lord one thousand six hundred eighty-eight,[1] and there sitting on the thirteenth day of February following, are the two Houses of Parliament, and so shall be and are hereby declared, enacted and adjudged to be, to all intents, constructions and purposes whatsoever, notwithstanding any want of writ or writs of summons or any other defect of form or default whatsoever, as if they had been summoned according to the usual form; and that this present Act and all other Acts to which the royal assent shall at any time be given before the next prorogation after the said thirteenth of February shall be understood, taken and adjudged in law to begin and commence upon the said thirteenth of February, on which day their said Majesties, at the request and by the advice of the Lords and Commons, did accept the crown and royal dignity of king and queen of England, France and Ireland, and the dominions and territories thereto belonging.

II. And be it further enacted . . . that the Act made in the thirtieth year of King Charles the Second entituled, *An Act for the more effectual preserving the king's person and government by disabling of papists from sitting in either House of Parliament*,[2] and all other Acts of Parliament, as to so much of the said Act or Acts only as concerns the taking the oaths of supremacy and allegiance or either of them in the said Act or Acts respectively mentioned by any member or members of either House of Parliament with relation to their sitting and voting in Parliament, shall be and are hereby repealed to all intents and purposes, anything in the said recited Act or Acts to the contrary notwithstanding.

III. And be it further enacted, that the taking the oaths hereinafter mentioned, and the making, subscribing and repeating the declaration in the said Act of the thirtieth

---

[1] 1688/9.   [2] No. 144.

year of King Charles the Second mentioned, by every member of either House of this present Parliament from and after the first day of March next ensuing, in such manner as the taking the said oaths of allegiance and supremacy and the making, subscribing and repeating the said declaration in the said last mentioned Act are required, shall be good and effectual to all intents and purposes as if the said oaths of allegiance and supremacy had been taken and the said declaration had been made, subscribed and repeated in such manner and at such time as by the said Act or Acts or any of them they are required; and that in all future Parliaments the oaths hereinafter mentioned, and the declaration in the said Act made in the thirtieth year of King Charles the Second mentioned, shall be taken, made, subscribed and repeated by every member of either House of Parliament within the time and in the same manner and form and under the penalties and disabilities as the said oaths of allegiance and supremacy and the said declaration by the said Act of the thirtieth year of King Charles the Second are limited, ordained and appointed to be taken, made, subscribed and repeated, and not at any other time or in any other manner, to enable them to sit and vote in Parliament, anything in the said Act or Acts or any of them to the contrary notwithstanding.

IV. And it is hereby further enacted and declared . . . that the oaths above appointed by this Act to be taken in the stead and place of the oaths of allegiance and supremacy shall be in the words following and no other :

I, A.B., do sincerely promise and swear that I will be faithful and bear true allegiance to their Majesties King William and Queen Mary. So help me God.

I, A.B., do swear that I do from my heart abhor, detest and abjure as impious and heretical that damnable doctrine and position, that princes excommunicated or deprived by the Pope or any authority of the see of Rome may be deposed or murthered by their subjects or any other whatsoever, and I do declare that no foreign prince, person, prelate, state or potentate hath or ought to have any power, jurisdiction, superiority, pre-eminence or authority, ecclesiastical or spiritual, within this realm. So help me God.

V. Provided always, and be it declared, that this present Parliament may be dissolved after the usual manner as if the same had been summoned and called by writ.

51. Triennial Act, 1694

(*Statutes of the Realm*, VI, p. 510)

AN ACT FOR THE FREQUENT MEETING AND CALLING OF PARLIAMENTS

(6 & 7 Gul. & Mar., cap. 2)

Whereas by the ancient laws and statutes of this kingdom frequent Parliaments ought to be held, and whereas frequent and new Parliaments tend very much to the happy union and good agreement of the king and people, we, your Majesties' most loyal and obedient subjects the Lords Spiritual and Temporal and Commons in this present Parliament assembled, do most humbly beseech your most excellent Majesties that it may be declared and enacted in this present Parliament, and it is hereby declared and enacted . . . that from henceforth a Parliament shall be holden once in three years at the least.

II. And be it further enacted . . . that within three years at the farthest from and after the dissolution of this present Parliament, and so from time to time for ever hereafter within three years at the farthest from and after the determination of every other Parliament, legal writs under the great seal shall be issued by directions of your Majesties, your heirs and successors for calling, assembling and holding another new Parliament.

III. And be it further enacted . . . that from henceforth no Parliament whatsoever that shall at any time hereafter be called, assembled or held shall have any continuance longer than for three years only at the farthest, to be accounted from the day on which by the writs of summons the said Parliament shall be appointed to meet.

IV. And be it further enacted . . . that this present Parliament shall cease and determine on the first day of November which shall be in the year of our Lord one thousand six hundred ninety-six, unless their Majesties shall think fit to dissolve it sooner.

52. Act for the continued sitting of Parliament, 1696
(*Statutes of the Realm*, VII, p. 84)

AN ACT FOR THE CONTINUING,
MEETING AND SITTING OF A PARLIAMENT
IN CASE OF THE DEATH OR DEMISE OF HIS MAJESTY,
HIS HEIRS AND SUCCESSORS[1]

(*7 & 8 Gul. III, cap. 15*)

Whereas this kingdom of England may be exposed to great dangers by the invasion of foreigners, or by the traitorous conspiracies of wicked and ill-disposed persons, whenever it shall please God to afflict these realms by the death of our gracious sovereign King William (whom God long preserve), or by the death of any of his heirs and successors, before a Parliament can be summoned and called by the next heir and successor to the crown; for prevention whereof be it enacted . . . that this present Parliament, or any other Parliament which shall hereafter be summoned and called by his Majesty King William, his heirs and successors, shall not determine or be dissolved by the death or demise of his said Majesty, his heirs and successors, but such Parliament shall and is hereby enacted to continue, and is hereby empowered and required immediately to meet, convene and sit, and to act, notwithstanding such death or demise, for and during the time of six months and no longer, unless the same shall be sooner prorogued or dissolved by such person who shall be next heir to the crown of this realm of England in succession, according to an Act of Parliament made in the first year of the reign of King William and Queen Mary, entituled, *An Act declaring the rights and liberties of the subject and settling the succession of the crown*;[2] and if the said Parliament shall be so prorogued then it shall meet and sit on and upon the day unto which it shall be prorogued, and continue for the residue of the said time of six months, unless sooner prorogued or dissolved as aforesaid.

[1] See No. 45.   [2] No. 40.

II. And it is hereby further enacted . . . that in case there shall be no Parliament in being at the time of the death or demise of his Majesty, or any of his heirs and successors, then the last preceding Parliament shall immediately convene and sit, and is hereby empowered and required to act as aforesaid to all intents and purposes as if the said Parliament had never been dissolved.

III. Provided always, and it is hereby declared, that nothing in this Act contained shall extend or be construed to extend to alter or abridge the power of the king, his heirs and successors, to prorogue or dissolve Parliaments, nor to repeal or make void one Act of Parliament made in the sixth and seventh years of the reign of his present Majesty King William, entituled, *An Act for the frequent meeting and calling of Parliaments*,[1] but that the said Act shall continue in force in everything that is not contrary to or inconsistent with the direction of this Act.

[1] No. 51.

7

I. Parliament of England

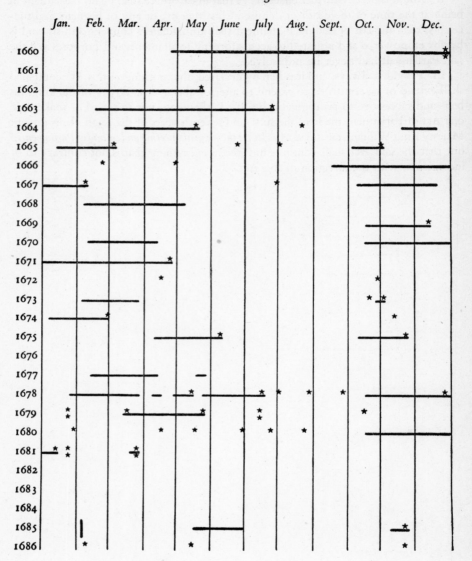

Diagram 1

SESSIONS OF PARLIAMENT

Periods during which Parliament was continuously in session are indicated by a heavy black line. Short and formal adjournments are ignored. Prorogations are indicated by a single asterisk, dissolutions by two asterisks, and the death of a sovereign by a heavy vertical line.

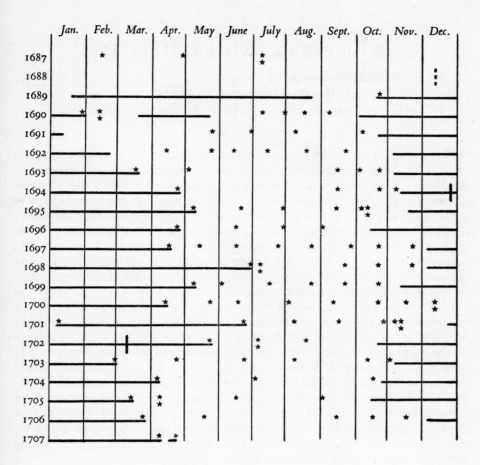

II. Parliament of Great Britain

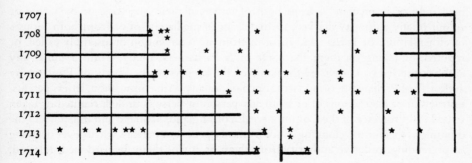

B. POWERS AND PRIVILEGES

53. Act of indemnity and oblivion, 1660
(*Statutes of the Realm*, v, pp. 226–234)

AN ACT OF FREE AND GENERAL PARDON, INDEMNITY AND OBLIVION

(*12 Car. II, cap. 11*)

The king's most excellent Majesty, taking into his gracious and serious consideration the long and great troubles, discords and wars that have for many years past been in this kingdom, and that divers of his subjects are by occasion thereof and otherwise fallen into, and be obnoxious to, great pains and penalties, out of a hearty and pious desire to put an end to all suits and controversies that by occasion of the late distractions have arisen and may arise between all his subjects, and to the intent that no crime whatsoever committed against his Majesty or his royal father shall hereafter rise in judgment or be brought in question against any of them to the least endamagement of them, either in their lives, liberties, estates, or to the prejudice of their reputations, by any reproach or term of distinction, and to bury all seeds of future discords and remembrance of the former as well in his own breast as in the breasts of his subjects one towards another, and in performance of his royal and gracious word signified by his letters to the several Houses of Parliament now assembled, and his declarations in that behalf published, is pleased that it may be enacted, and be it enacted by the king's most excellent Majesty, with the advice and consent of the Lords and Commons in this present Parliament assembled, first, that all and all manner of treasons, misprisions of treasons, murthers, felonies, offences, crimes, contempts and misdemeanours, counselled, commanded, acted or done since the first day of January in the year of our Lord one thousand six hundred thirty-seven,[1] by any person or persons before the twenty-fourth day of June in the year of our Lord one thousand six hundred and sixty, other than the persons hereafter by name excepted in such manner as they are hereafter excepted, by virtue or colour of any command, power, authority, commission, warrant or instructions from his late Majesty King Charles, or his Majesty that now is, or from any other person or persons deriving or pretending to derive authority, mediately or immediately, from both or either of their Majesties, or by virtue or colour of any authority derived, mediately or immediately, of or from both Houses or either House of Parliament, or of or from any convention or assembly called, or reputed, or taking on them the name of, a Parliament, or by, from or under any authority styled or known by the name of the keepers of the liberty of England by author ty of Parliament, or by virtue or colour of any writ, commission, letters patents, instruction or instructions of or from any person or persons tituled, reputed or taken to be Lord Protector of the Commonwealth of England, Scotland and Ireland, and the dominions thereunto belonging . . . or from any person or persons whatsoever deriving or pretending to derive authority from them or any of them, be pardoned, released, indemnified, discharged and put in utter oblivion.

[1] 1637/8.

II. And that all and every the person and persons acting, advising, assisting, abetting and counselling the same, they, their heirs, executors and administrators (except as before is excepted) be and are hereby pardoned, released, acquitted, indemnified and discharged from the same. . . .

54. Resolutions of the Lords and Commons affirming the privilege of freedom of speech, 1667

(Journals of the House of Lords, XII, p. 166)

Resolved, &c.

That the Act of Parliament 4 Hen. VIII, commonly entituled *An Act concerning Richard Strode*, is a general law, extending to indemnify all and every the members of both Houses of Parliament, in all Parliaments, for and touching any bills, speaking, reasoning or declaring of any matter or matters in and concerning the Parliament to be communed and treated of; and is a declaratory law of the ancient and necessary rights and privileges of Parliament.

Resolved, &c.

That the judgment given 5 Car. against Sir John Eliot, Denzil Holles and Benjamin Valentine, esquires, in the King's Bench, was an illegal judgment, and against the freedom and privilege of Parliament.

55. Letters from Edward Cooke to the duke of Ormonde on the election of a Speaker by the Commons, 1679

(Historical Manuscripts Commission, *Ormonde MSS.*, N. S., IV, pp. 345–360)

[Saturday] 8 March 1679. We are now got into our new Parliament almost. . . . On Thursday morning they met, and by your grace's commission were sworn in the inner Court of Wards. Before noon the king summoned them up to the Lords' bar where he entertained them with the inclosed gracious speech, and the Chancellor with this eloquent one. . . As soon as they were returned within their walls Colonel Birch anticipated Sir John Ernly, who was to propose Sir Thomas Meres for Speaker, and nominates the old Speaker with a blunt, subtle harangue on the experience they had of him, whose hypocritical denial and excuses served turn to give encouragement to Sir Thomas Lee and some other members to force his willing body into that desirable chair, and so adjourned till two in the afternoon yesterday.

The king's hour of three being come, the Black Rod fetched them up to present their Speaker, who saith he was the night before with the king, to acquaint him with the proceedings of the House and to know his Majesty's pleasure, who owned great satisfaction in the choice the Commons had made. And accordingly, with a remarkable confidence (nay, beyond his own usual proportion), he delivered a short account to the king, that in pursuance of his Majesty's commands the Commons had met to choose their Speaker, and that he was the result of that choice, and that if he pleased to approve of it he would serve both them and him as well as he could, omitting the usual form of pleading his infirmities to argue his being excused, which was much wondered at. But the Chancellor, having liberally magnified his great parts and multiplied his signal services, closed with a "but that his Majesty, designing him for other parts of his service, excused him from that, and commanded them to make a new choice by eleven this morning".

This great surprise to most so warmed them, and they the rest, that as soon as they returned to the House debates grew high; but to nip them in the bud the House adjourned till this morning, ordering precedents to be searched whether ever any Speaker had been so refused. Besides the offence many took at Mr. Seymour's haughty behaviour (as they called it), most were dissatisfied that he closed so roughly with these words, that if the king would approve of the choice he would serve them and him, not styling them so much as the Commons nor him so much as the king, and postponing him to them, which, though charity might have allowed to be a mistake in another, yet seeing it came from so florid a speaker, and was so all of a piece with the rest of his deportment, was ill enough taken from him. Yet this unexpected refusal of him in the morning, who was so well received by the king but the night before (as he himself affirms and most believe, though for some reasons I am yet none of those), hath occasioned many satirical reflections on a friend of mine.

This morning when they met they found their task too hard for so sudden a dispatch, and therefore sent this inclosed address by my Lord Russell, accompanied with my Lord Cavendish, Sir Robert Carr and Sir Henry Capel, for longer time. The king used them so obligingly that they boasted of it to the House, lengthened their time till Tuesday, and did insinuate into them that the best expedient would be to decline both Seymour and Meres, and pitch upon some third person, which it is thought will be Powle, if a third person be admitted of. . . .

15 March 1679. As for parliamentary affairs, when on Monday morning the Commons met (for the Lords did not sit that day) they renewed their debate of the election of their Speaker, and talked themselves into a confident belief that it was an undoubted privilege of theirs to elect their own Speaker and only formal for the king to approve; and thereupon that day ended in the delegating a committee to draw up not an address but a representation of their right to this choice, which I here inclose, and which on Tuesday the 11th was presented by my Lord Russell, Lord Cavendish (both which are grown sufficiently moderate, and the latter the darling of his father), Sir Robert Carr, Sir Henry Capel, Mr. Powle, Sir John Ernly and one more. The king no sooner heard it read to him by Mr. Powle but he gave this short extempore answer, "You do but lose time. Return to the House and do as I have directed."

This surprising answer, when reported to the House, kindled some heats, which at present were raked up by an adjournment of the debate till Wednesday morning, which was early resumed; and they soon resolved on a new address (which I also here inclose), whose contents need no paraphrase, the burden of which being to beseech his Majesty's review of their former representation, in which the king gratified them, deferring his answer till next morning. In the meantime, reflecting on the difficulty that the new Commons were brought into by the subtlety of the old ones, he was most graciously pleased thus to extricate them—Thursday morning the king in his robes summons the House to the Lords' bar, where by the mouth of the Lord Chancellor he prorogued them till Saturday morning (this morning). It was a prorogation that all things begun and unfinished might be annihilated, and but for a day, that no time beyond what was absolutely necessary might be lost, fitting a plaster so exactly to the sore that when they next meet they might without galling their own privileges proceed to the election of a new Speaker. . . .

This morning his Majesty in his robes summoned the Commons by the Black Rod to the Lords' bar, where in a short speech his Majesty advised them not to lose time, because they had much to do; hinted the reason of the prorogation; and referred them to the Chancellor, who in a few words also reminded them of the great opportunities they had to do national good, of the king's readiness to concur with them, referred them to the steps he had made already, particularly in this very prorogation, mentioned the great preparations our neighbours were making, referred to his former speech, and concluded with hastening them to choose their Speaker, who (to avoid loss of any more time) the king would expect should be presented to him on Monday morning at ten o'clock. The Commons, as soon as they were returned and crowded into the House, which will not hold them all, there scarce being a member wanting and for several places yet four sit on double returns, my Lord Russell broke the ice, took notice of the difficulties they had hitherto been involved in, the proper expedient the king had contrived to extricate them out of them, and that now he conceived their proper work was to choose their Speaker, and proposed one Serjeant Gregory as a proper person for that employment, who had been marked out at court without any exceptions being made against him. My Lord Cavendish seconded it, but Mr. Sacheverell stood up, owned his adherence to the former choice, and that since he foresaw he would be singular in that opinion craved leave to withdraw. Immediately (to confirm his belief of his own singularity) each corner of the House echoed, "Go, go", and my Lord Cavendish confirming Lord Russell's choice they two forced Serjeant Gregory to the chair, interrupting his just pleading his own insufficiency, who craved their leave, since they would not excuse him themselves, that he might beseech his Majesty to dispense with him. He being pressed to the chair, the House was immediately adjourned until Monday morning. This day's proceedings hath much bettered our hopes and prospects of future happiness, moderation being like to be most in fashion. . . .

18 March 1679. Yesterday . . . the Commons . . . presented their Speaker. The king, &c., being all robed, he acted his part to the life (Serjeant Gregory by name), in deed and word pleading his own insufficiency, ill becoming what he said, and yet not becoming that employment. Much to seek how and what to say; but what he said was that the Commons, notwithstanding all he could say against himself, had chosen him, and if his Majesty could not relieve him he would serve (not them and him, as Seymour said) his Majesty and the government as best he could. The eloquent Chancellor (who needed no such foil) told him the king understood him too well, and especially coming with such credentials (the Commons' choice), to release him, and that his Majesty preferred innocency and integrity before greater accomplishments without it, and confirmed the choice.

He then as well as he could expressed his resolution to serve his Majesty in that and all things, and proceeded according to custom (though not with customary confidence or eloquence) to petition for those three essentials, liberty of speech, liberty of persons from arrest, and of access to the king's ear, all which the Chancellor, by the king's order, granted most graciously, and concluded with this expression, "As for yourself, Mr. Speaker, you may be sure that he whom the king hath created by his power he will preserve by his goodness." At which it is reported my Lord Shaftesbury afterwards took offence, taking notice of the great care that ought to be of avoiding all exasperating and offensive expressions, and that some had fallen from the woolsack, both before and now, which might bear so ill constructions that he wished they might not be entered in their journals; and that my Lord Chancellor should reply he would consent that no more should be entered than that such a day the Commons offered a Speaker and the king refused him, and that such a day the Commons offered him their Speaker and he approved him. Thus ruggedly all things begin.

56. John Locke on Parliament, 1690

(*Second Treatise of Civil Government*, ed. 1764, pars. 95–97, 134, 143–144, 149, 151)

Men being, as has been said, by nature all free, equal and independent, no one can be put out of this estate, and subjected to the political power of another, without his own consent. The only way whereby anyone divests himself of his natural liberty and puts on the bonds of civil society is by agreeing with other men to join and unite into a community for their comfortable, safe and peaceable living one amongst another, in a secure enjoyment of their properties and a greater security against any that are not of it. This any number of men may do, because it injures not the freedom of the rest. They are left as they were in the liberty of the state of nature. When any number of men have so consented to make one community or government, they are thereby presently incorporated, and make one body politic, wherein the majority have a right to act and conclude the rest.

For when any number of men have, by the consent of every individual, made a community, they have thereby made that community one body, with a power to act as one body, which is only by the will and determination of the majority. For that which acts any community being only the consent of the individuals of it, and it being necessary to that which is one body to move one way, it is necessary the body should move that way whither the greater force carries it, which is the consent of the majority; or else it is impossible it should act or continue one body, one community, which the consent of every individual that united into it agreed that it should. And so every one is bound by that consent to be concluded by the majority. And therefore we see that in assemblies empowered to act by positive laws, where no number is set by that positive law which empowers them, the act of the majority passes for the act of the whole, and of course determines, as having by the law of nature and reason the power of the whole.

And thus every man, by consenting with others to make one body politic under one government, puts himself under an obligation to every one of that society to submit to the determination of the majority and to be concluded by it; or else this original compact, whereby he with others incorporates into one society, would signify nothing, and be no compact, if he be left free and under no other ties than he was in before in the state of nature. . . .

The great end of men's entering into society being the enjoyment of their properties in peace and safety, and the great instrument and means of that being the laws established in that society, the first and fundamental positive law of all commonwealths is the establishing of the legislative power, as the first and fundamental natural law, which is to govern even the legislative itself, is the preservation of the society and (as far as will consist with the public good) of every person in it. This legislative is not only the supreme power of the commonwealth but sacred and unalterable in the hands where the community have once placed it; nor can any edict of any body else, in what form soever conceived or by what power soever backed, have the force and obligation of a law, which has not its sanction from that legislative which the public has chosen and appointed. For without this the law could not have that which is absolutely necessary to its being a law, the consent of the society over whom nobody can have a power to make laws but by their own consent and by authority received from them; and therefore all the obedience which by the most solemn ties anyone can be obliged to pay ultimately terminates in this supreme power, and is directed by those laws which it enacts. . . .

The legislative power is that which has a right to direct how the force of the commonwealth shall be employed for preserving the community and the members of it. But because those laws which are constantly to be executed, and whose force is always to continue, may be made in a little time, therefore there is no need that the legislative should be always in being, not having always business to do. And because it may be too great a temptation to human frailty, apt to grasp at power, for the same persons who have the power of making laws to have also in their hands the power to execute them, whereby they may exempt themselves from obedience to the laws they make, and suit the law, both in its making and execution, to their own private advantage, and thereby come to have a distinct interest from the rest of the community, contrary to the end of society and government; therefore in well ordered commonwealths, where the good of the whole is so considered as it ought, the legislative power is put into the hands of divers persons who, duly assembled, have by themselves or jointly with others a power to make laws, which when they have done, being separated again, they are themselves subject to the laws they have made, which is a new and near tie upon them to take care that they make them for the public good.

But because the laws that are at once and in a short time made have a constant and lasting force, and need a perpetual execution or an attendance thereunto, therefore it is necessary there should be a power always in being which should see to the execution of the laws that are made and remain in force; and thus the legislative and executive power come often to be separated. . . .

Though in a constituted commonwealth, standing upon its own basis and acting according to its own nature, that is acting for the preservation of the community, there can be but one supreme power, which is the legislative, to which all the rest are and must be subordinate, yet the legislative being only a fiduciary power to act for certain ends, there remains still in the people a supreme power to remove or alter the legislative when they find the legislative act contrary to the trust reposed in them; for all power given with trust for the attaining an end being limited by that end, whenever that end is manifestly neglected or opposed the trust must necessarily be forfeited, and the power devolve into the hands of those that gave it, who may place it anew where they shall think best for their safety and security. And thus the community perpetually retains a supreme power of saving themselves from the attempts and designs of any body, even of their legislators, whenever they shall be so foolish or so wicked as to lay and carry on designs against the liberties and properties of the subject; . . . and thus the community may be said in this respect to be always the supreme power, but not as considered under any form of government, because this power of the people can never take place till the government be dissolved. . . .

In some commonwealths where the legislative is not always in being, and the executive is vested in a single person who has also a share in the legislative, there that single person in a very tolerable sense may also be called supreme; not that he has in himself all the supreme power, which is that of law-making, but because he has in him the supreme execution from whom all inferior magistrates derive all their several subordinate powers, or at least the greatest part of them. Having also no legislative superior to him, there being no law to be made without his consent, which cannot be expected should ever subject him to the other part of the legislative, he is properly enough in this sense supreme. But yet it is to be observed that though oaths of allegiance and fealty are taken to him, it is not to him as supreme legislator but as supreme executor of the law, made by a joint power of him with others, allegiance being nothing but an obedience according to law, which when he violates he has no right to obedience, nor can claim it otherwise than as the public person vested with the power of the law, and so is to be considered as the image, phantom or representative of the commonwealth, acted by the will of the society declared in its laws; and thus he has no will, no power, but that of the law. But when he quits this representation, this public will, and acts by his own private will, he degrades himself, and is but a single private person without power and without will, that has any right to obedience, the members owing no obedience but to the public will of the society.

57. Anonymous satire on the treatment of the Kentish petitioners by the Commons, 1701

(Somers Tracts, ed. 1809–1815, XI, pp. 253–254)

Some book-learned fools pretend to find a flaw
In our late senate votes for want of law,
And insolently say the men of Kent
Were rudely handled by the Parliament.
Knowledge of things would teach them every hour
That law is but an heathen word for power.

Might, right, force, justice, equity,
Are terms synonymous, and must agree;
For who shall e'er the argument confute,
Where power prevails, and no man dare dispute?
    Nature has left this tincture in the blood,
That all men would be tyrants if they could,
Not kings alone, not ecclesiastic pride,
But Parliaments, and all mankind beside.
All men, like Phaeton, would command the reins,
'Tis only want of power that restrains.
    Then why should we think strange the Parliament
The people's late petitions should resent?
'Tis fatal to tyrannic power when they
Who should be ruined grumble to obey;
And tyrants never can complete their reign
So long as injured subjects dare complain.
If they do not their first address withstand,
What now they supplicate, they'll soon command;
By first suppressing early discontent
They aimed the consequences to prevent,
For well they knew that should the nation try
To ask once more, they durst not twice deny.
    England has this one fate peculiar to her,
Never to want a party to undo her.
The Court, the King, the Church, the Parliament,
Alternately pursue the same intent,
Under the specious term of liberty
The passive injured people to betray.
And it has always been the people's fate
To see their own mistakes when 'twas too late;
Senseless of danger, sleepy and secure,
Till their distempers grew too strong to cure,
Till they're embraced by the approaching grave,
And none but Jove and miracles can save.
    In vain bold heroes venture to redeem
A people willinger to sink than swim.
If there's a Brutus in the nation found,
That dares patrician usurpation wound,
He's sure to find an ignominious grave,
And perish by the people he would save.
    Such are by virtue signalized in vain;
We'll own the merit, but abuse the men.
Marius saved Rome, and was by Rome despised,
And many a Russell we have sacrificed.

Then who for English freedom would appear,
Where lives of patriots are never dear,
And streams of generous blood flow unregarded there?
    Posterity will be ashamed to own
The actions we their ancestors have done,
When they for ancient precedents inquire,
And to the journals of this age retire,
To see one tyrant banished from his home
To set five hundred traitors in his room.
They'll blush to find the head beneath the tail,
And representing treachery prevail.
They'll be amazed to see there was but five
Whose courage could their liberty survive,
While we that durst illegal power dethrone
Should basely be enslaved by tyrants of our own.

58. Judgment of Chief Justice Holt in the case *Ashby* v. *White*, 1704
(*English Reports*, XC, pp. 1188–1189)

The case is truly stated, and the only question is whether or not, if a burgess of a borough, that has an undoubted right to give his vote for the choosing a burgess of Parliament for that borough, is refused giving his vote, [he] has any remedy in the king's courts for this wrong against the wrongdoer. All my brothers agree that he has no remedy; but I differ from them, for I think the action well maintainable that the plaintiff had a right to vote, and that, in consequence thereof, the law gives him a remedy if he is obstructed, and this action is the proper remedy. By the common law of England every commoner hath a right not to be subjected to laws made without their consent; and because it cannot be given by every individual man in person, by reason of number and confusion, therefore that power is lodged in their representatives, elected by them for that purpose, who are either knights, citizens or burgesses; and the grievance here is that the party, not being allowed his vote, is not represented. The election of knights of shires is by freeholders, and a freeholder has a right to vote by reason of his freehold, and it is a real right . . .

This is a noble franchise and right, which entitles the subject in a share of the government and legislature. And here, the plaintiff having this right, it is apparent that the officer did exclude him from the enjoyment of it, wherein none will say he has done well, but wrong to the plaintiff. And it is not at all material whether the candidate that he would have voted for were chosen, or likely to be; for the plaintiff's right is the same, and, being hindered of that, he has injury done him for which he ought to have remedy. It is a vain thing to imagine there should be right without a remedy, for want of right and want of remedy are convertibles. If a statute gives a right, the common law will give remedy to maintain it; and wherever there is injury it imports a damage. . . .

Although this matter relates to the Parliament, yet it is an injury precedaneous to the Parliament; and where parliamentary matters come before us as incident to a cause of action concerning the property of the subject, which we in duty must determine, though the incident matter be parliamentary we must not be deterred, but are bound by our oaths to determine it. The law consists, not in particular instances, but in the reason that rules them; and if, where a man is injured in one sort of right, he has a good action, why shall he not have it in another? And though the House of Commons have right to decide elections, yet they cannot judge of the charter originally, but secondarily in the determination of the election; and therefore, where an election does not come in debate, as it doth not in this case, they have nothing to do. And we are to exert and vindicate the queen's jurisdiction, and not to be frighted because it may come in question in Parliament. And I know nothing to hinder us from judging of matters depending on charter or prescription.

C. RELATIONS WITH THE EXECUTIVE

(a) PARLIAMENTARY PRESSURE ON THE SOVEREIGN

59. Supply and appropriation Act, 1665
(*Statutes of the Realm*, v, pp. 570–574)

AN ACT FOR GRANTING THE SUM
OF TWELVE HUNDRED AND FIFTY THOUSAND POUNDS
TO THE KING'S MAJESTY FOR HIS PRESENT FURTHER SUPPLY

(*17 Car. II, cap. 1*)

V. And to the intent that all moneys to be lent to your Majesty, and moneys that shall be due upon such contracts for wares and goods which shall be delivered for this service, may be well and sufficiently secured out of the moneys arising and payable by this Act, be it further enacted . . . that there be provided and kept in his Majesty's Exchequer, to wit, in the office of the Auditor of the Receipt, one book or register, in which book or register all moneys that shall be paid into the Exchequer by this Act shall be entered and registered apart and distinct from . . . all other moneys or branches of your Majesty's revenue whatsoever; and that also there be one other book or register provided or kept in the said office of all orders and warrants to be made by the Lord Treasurer and Under-Treasurer, or by the Commissioners of the Treasury for the time being, for payment of all and every sum and sums of money to all persons for moneys lent, wares or goods bought, or other payments directed by his Majesty relating to the service of this war, and that no moneys leviable by this Act be issued out of the Exchequer during this war but by such order or warrant, mentioning that the moneys payable by such order or warrant are for the service of your Majesty in the said war respectively.

VI. That also there be the like book or register provided and kept by the said Auditor of all moneys paid out or issued by virtue of such orders and warrants.

VII. That it shall be lawful for any person or persons willing to lend any money, or to furnish any wares, victuals, necessaries or goods on the credit of this Act, at the usual times when the Exchequer is open, to have access unto and view and peruse all or any of the said books for their information of the state of those moneys and all engagements upon them, for their better encouragement to lend any moneys or furnish any goods as aforesaid, and. . . that all and every person and persons who shall lend any moneys to your Majesty, and pay the same into the Receipt of the Exchequer, shall immediately have a tally of loan struck for the same, and an order for his repayment bearing the same date with his tally, in which order shall be also a warrant contained for payment of interest for forbearance after the rate of six per cent per annum for his consideration, to be paid every six months until the repayment of his principal; and that all person and persons who shall furnish your Majesty, your officers of the navy or ordnance, with any wares, goods, victuals or other necessaries for the service aforesaid shall upon certificate of the commissioners and officers of the navy, or of the master or commissioners and officers of the ordnance or some of them, without delay forthwith have made out to them warrants or orders for the payment of the moneys due or payable unto them, which certificates the said officers of your navy, commissioners and officers of the ordnance, shall make without fee, charge or delay; and that all orders for the repayment of money lent shall be registered in course according to the date of the tallies respectively; and that all orders signed by the Lord Treasurer and Under-Treasurer of the Exchequer for payment of money for goods, wares, victuals and other necessaries furnished to your Majesty, your officers, master or commissioners aforesaid shall be registered in course according to the time of bringing to the office of the Auditor of Receipt the certificates above-mentioned; and that all orders so signed for payments directed by his Majesty shall be entered in course according to their respective dates, and none of the sorts of orders above-mentioned, either for loans of money, supplies of wares, goods, victuals or necessaries, or by special direction, shall have preference one before another, but shall all be entered in their course according to the dates of the tallies, the time of bringing the certificates, and the dates of the orders for payments directed by his Majesty, as they are in point of time respectively before each other; and that all and every person and persons shall be paid in course according as their orders shall stand entered in the said register-book, be it orders for payments directed by his Majesty, or for moneys lent, or for wares, commodities or other necessaries furnished as aforesaid. . . .

X. And be it further enacted by the authority aforesaid, that every person or persons to whom any money shall be due by virtue of this Act after warrant or order entered for payment thereof, his executors, administrators or assigns, by endorsement of his order or warrant, may assign and transfer his interest and benefit of such warrant to any other, which being notified, and an entry and memorial thereof also made in the said registry for warrants (which the officers shall on request without fees or charge accordingly make), shall entitle such assignee, his executors, administrators and assigns, to the benefit thereof and payment thereon; and such assignee may in like manner assign again, and so *toties quoties*, and afterwards it shall not be in the power of such person or persons who have made such assignments to make void, release or discharge the same, or the moneys thereby due or any part thereof.

XI. And in case any person or persons be willing to advance the tax they them-selves are to pay, or the tax of any tithing, hundred, parish, division or county, for six months or more unto the receiver-general of that place or county, the said receiver-general is hereby authorized to receive the same, and to make deduction of so much for interest after the rate of six per cent per annum as the advance amounts unto, and the receiver's acquittance shall be a sufficient discharge for the same, which money so advanced shall be accounted for and paid into the Exchequer by itself quarterly.

60. Act constituting a commission of audit, 1667

(Statutes of the Realm, v, pp. 624–627)

AN ACT FOR TAKING THE ACCOMPTS
OF THE SEVERAL SUMS OF MONEY THEREIN MENTIONED

(19 & 20 Car. II, cap. 1)

Whereas many and great aids and provisions have been given, raised and assigned for the necessary defence of your Majesty and your kingdoms in the late great and important wars, to the end that both your Majesty and this whole kingdom may be satisfied and truly informed whether all the same moneys and provisions have been faithfully issued out and expended in and about the preparing and setting forth of your royal navy and other the management and carrying on the said war, and with such care, fidelity and good husbandry as the nature of such services would admit of, according to your Majesty's own gracious and princely desires and the earnest expectations of your most loyal subjects, than which nothing can encourage them more cheerfully to undergo the like burthens in time to come for the necessary defence of your Majesty and your realms, may it therefore please your most excellent Majesty that it may be enacted, and be it enacted . . . that William Lord Brereton, baron of Leighlin in the kingdom of Ireland; William Pierrepont, esquire; Sir George Savile, baronet; Giles Dunster, esquire; Sir James Langham, knight; Henry Osborne, esquire; Sir William Turner, alderman of the city of London; George Thompson, esquire; and John Gregory, esquire, or any five or more of them, shall be commissioners for the taking of the accompts of the sum of twenty-four hundred three score and seventeen thousand and five hundred pounds granted by a late Act of this present Parliament entituled, *An Act for granting of a royal aid to the king's Majesty of twenty-four hundred three score and seventeen thousand and five hundred pounds to be raised, levied and paid in the space of three years;*[1] and of twelve hundred and fifty thousand pounds granted by another late Act of this present Parliament entituled, *An Act for granting the sum of twelve hundred and fifty thousand pounds to the king's Majesty for his present further supply;*[2] and of two hundred and ten thousand pounds granted for three months at the rate of three score and ten thousand pounds per mensem by another Act entituled, *An Act for ordering the forces in the several counties of this kingdom;*[3] and also for taking the accompts of all such moneys as have been raised or charged by a late Act of this present Parliament entituled, *An Act for raising moneys by a poll and otherwise towards the maintenance of this present war,*[4] and by another Act of this present Parliament entituled, *An explanatory Act for raising moneys by a poll and otherwise towards the maintenance of this present war;*[5] and of the sum of twelve hundred fifty-six thousand three hundred forty-seven pounds thirteen shillings granted by another late Act of this present Parliament entituled, *An Act for granting the sum of twelve hundred fifty-six thousand three hundred forty-seven pounds thirteen shillings to the king's Majesty towards the maintenance of the present war;*[6] and of all such moneys as have arisen by the Customs granted to his Majesty by an Act of this present Parliament[7]

[1] No. 115.   [2] 17 Car. II, cap. 1.   [3] No. 303.   [4] 18 Car. II, cap. 1.
[5] 18 & 19 Car. II, cap. 6.   [6] 18 & 19 Car. II, cap. 13.   [7] No. 103.

and have been applied to the service of the war; and of such prizes as have been taken during the said late war for his Majesty's use; and of all other moneys, provisions and things whatsoever which have been raised or assigned for or towards the fitting, furnishing or setting out to sea any of the navies or ships employed in the said late war, or for or touching the management or maintenance thereof: and to that end the said commissioners or any five or more of them are hereby authorized and required to call before them all treasurers, receivers, paymasters, principal officers and commissioners of the navy and ordnance respectively, victuallers, pursers, muster-masters and clerks of the cheque, accountants and all officers and keepers of his Majesty's stores and provisions for war as well for land as sea, and all other persons whatsoever employed in the management of the said war, or requisite for the discovery of any frauds relating thereunto, to make perfect and true accounts of all such of the moneys as have come to any of their hands respectively, and to bring in and deliver the same to the said commissioners or any five or more of them without delay, . . . whereby it may appear what moneys they have received and how the same have been disbursed, and what ammunition, provisions and stores of any kind which were in his Majesty's storehouses or yards or elsewhere have been employed in the said war after the first day of September one thousand six hundred sixty-four; . . . and to examine all such merchants and tradesmen, and their books, receipts and acquittances, and all such seamen and others as shall be thought fit to be heard, touching any frauds, oppressions or exactions practised or used by any person or persons intrusted or employed in or about the payment or receipt of any of the said moneys, or the buying or providing of any of the said provisions, wares or materials, or the custody, ordering or disposing of the same; . . . and to inquire and find out what moneys have been or ought to have been set apart for the Chest from the four and twentieth day of June one thousand six hundred and sixty, and how the same have been paid or disposed of, . . . and whether any sums of money, and how much, arising by the Customs and subsidy of tonnage and poundage ever since the first of September one thousand six hundred sixty-four hath been issued and allowed for and towards the maintenance of the said war; and also to inquire and find out the numbers and values of all the prize ships and goods which have been taken for his Majesty's use during the said war, and their several bills of lading, and how the same ships and goods or any of them have been appraised, valued, sold, embezzled or otherwise disposed of; . . . and also to inquire by whose means, counsel or procurement it came to pass that the ships, seamen, mariners and others were generally discharged by tickets and not paid with money. . . .

VII. This Act, as to the powers of taking and examining of accounts and administering of oaths, to endure for the space of three years from the end of this present session of Parliament next ensuing and no longer.

VIII. Provided always, . . . whereas several seamen after service done to his Majesty expected to receive their wages, and instead thereof had tickets delivered them for their money due to them for their service or otherwise, upon pretence that there was a want of money to pay them, to the great discouragement of the said seamen; and whereas for a present supply of themselves and their families they have been necessitated to sell the said tickets for less than the sum of money mentioned in them, which tickets have been sold from man to man, be it therefore, and it is hereby, enacted . . . that the said commissioners shall be and are hereby empowered to compel each buyer of such tickets, or such who purchased from them, to restore to the several persons from whom they purchased them all or as much of the said money as they shall think fit (upon the computation of interest or any other consideration), which remains to make up the full account or sum contained in, and which was due upon, the said tickets, and such person or persons that have so bought tickets, and shall refuse by order of the said commissioners to repay to any person or persons such sum or sums of money as they shall adjudge him to pay, preserving to each party the full principal and interest at least, then in such a case and upon all such refusals, it shall and may be lawful, and the said commissioners are hereby empowered, to send to any gaol or gaols all such persons so refusing, until they shall obey the order or orders of the said commissioners.

61. Address of the Commons in favour of alliances against France, and the king's reply, 1677

(*Journals of the House of Commons*, IX, pp. 425–426)

(i) 25 May 1677

MAY IT PLEASE YOUR MOST EXCELLENT MAJESTY,

Your Majesty's most loyal and dutiful subjects, the Commons in Parliament assembled, having taken into their serious consideration your Majesty's gracious speech, do beseech your Majesty to believe it is a great affliction to them to find themselves obliged at present to decline the granting your Majesty the supply your Majesty is pleased to demand, conceiving it is not agreeable to the usage of Parliament to grant supplies for maintenance of wars and alliances before they are signified in Parliament; which the two wars against the States of the United Provinces since your Majesty's happy restoration, and the league made with them in January 1668 for preservation of the Spanish Netherlands, sufficiently prove, without troubling your Majesty with instances of greater antiquity. From which usage if we should depart, the precedent might be of dangerous consequence in future times, though your Majesty's goodness gives us great security during your Majesty's reign, which we beseech God long to continue.

This consideration prompted us, in our last address to your Majesty before our late recess, humbly to mention to your Majesty our hopes that before our meeting again your Majesty's alliances might be so fixed as that your Majesty might be graciously pleased to impart them to us in Parliament, that so our earnest desires of supplying your Majesty for prosecuting those great ends we had humbly laid before your Majesty might meet with no impediment or obstruction, being highly sensible of the necessity of supporting as well as making the alliances humbly desired in our former addresses, and which we still conceive so important to the safety of your Majesty and your kingdoms that we cannot, without unfaithfulness to your Majesty and those we represent, omit upon all occasions humbly to beseech your Majesty, as we now do, to enter into a league, offensive and defensive, with the States General of the United Provinces, against the growth and power of the French king, and for the preservation of the Spanish Netherlands, and to make such other alliances with such other of the confederates as your Majesty shall think fit and useful to that end. In doing which, that no time may be lost, we humbly offer to your Majesty these reasons for the expediting it:

I. That if the entering into such alliances should draw on a war with the French king, it would be least detrimental to your Majesty's subjects at this time of the year, they having now fewest effects within the dominions of that king.

II. That though we have great reason to believe the power of the French king to be dangerous to your Majesty and your kingdoms when he shall be at more leisure to molest us, yet we conceive the many enemies he hath to deal with at present, together with the situation of your Majesty's kingdoms, the unanimity of your people in this cause, the care your Majesty hath been pleased to take of your ordinary guard for the sea, together with the credit provided by the late Act entituled, *An Act for an additional Excise for three years*,[1] make the entering into and declaring alliances very safe, until we may in a regular way give your Majesty such further supplies as may enable your Majesty to support your alliances and defend your kingdoms.

III. Because of the great danger and charge which must necessarily fall upon your Majesty's kingdoms, if, through want of that timely encouragement and assistance which your Majesty's joining with the States of the United Provinces and other the confederates would give them, the said States, or any other considerable part of the confederates, should this next winter or sooner make a peace or truce with the French king (the prevention whereof hitherto must be acknowledged to be a singular effect of God's goodness to us); which if it should happen, your Majesty would afterwards be necessitated with fewer, perhaps with no alliances or assistances, to withstand the power of the French king, which hath so long and so successfully contended with so many and potent adversaries, and, whilst he continues his overbalancing greatness, must always be dangerous to his neighbours, since he would be able to oppress any one confederate before the rest could get together and be in so good a posture of offending him as they now are, being jointly engaged in a war. And if he should be so successful as to make a peace, or disunite the present confederation against him, it is much to be feared whether it would be possible ever to reunite it. At least it would be a work of so much time and difficulty as would leave your Majesty's kingdoms exposed to much misery and danger.

Having thus discharged our duty, in laying before your Majesty the dangers threatening your Majesty and your kingdoms, and the only remedy we can think of for preventing it and securing and quieting the minds of your Majesty's people, with some few of those reasons which have moved us to this and our former addresses on this subject, we most humbly beseech your Majesty to take this matter into your most serious consideration, and to take such resolutions as may not leave it in the power of any neighbouring prince to rob your people of that happiness which they enjoy under your Majesty's gracious government, beseeching your Majesty to rest confident and

[1] 29 Car. II, cap. 2.

assured that when your Majesty shall be pleased to declare such alliances in Parliament we shall hold ourselves obliged, not only by our promises and assurances given and now with great unanimity renewed in a full House, but by the zeal and desires of those whom we represent, and by the interest of all our safeties, most cheerfully to give your Majesty such speedy supplies and assistances as may fully and plentifully answer the occasions, and by God's blessing preserve your Majesty's honour and the safety of your people.

All which is most humbly submitted to your Majesty's great wisdom.

(ii) 28 May 1677

GENTLEMEN,

Could I have been silent I would rather have chosen to be so than to call to mind things so unfit for you to meddle with as are contained in some part of your address, wherein you have intrenched upon so undoubted a right of the Crown that I am confident it will appear in no age (when the sword was not drawn) that the prerogative of making peace and war hath been so dangerously invaded. You do not content yourselves with desiring me to enter into such leagues as may be for the safety of the kingdom, but you tell me what sort of leagues they must be, and with whom; and as your address is worded it is more liable to be understood to be by your leave than your request that I should make such other alliances as I please with other of the confederates. Should I suffer this fundamental power of making peace and war to be so far invaded (though but once) as to have the manner and circumstances of leagues prescribed to me by Parliament, it is plain that no prince or state would any longer believe that the sovereignty of England rests in the Crown; nor could I think myself to signify any more to foreign princes than the empty sound of a king. Wherefore you may rest assured that no condition shall make me depart from, or lessen, so essential a part of the monarchy; and I am willing to believe so well of this House of Commons that I am confident these ill consequences are not intended by you.

These are, in short, the reasons why I can by no means approve of your address. And yet, though you have declined to grant me that supply which is so necessary to the ends of it, I do again declare to you that, as I have done all that lay in my power since your last meeting, so I will still apply myself by all means I can to let the world see my care both for the security and satisfaction of my people, although it may not be with those advantages to them which by your assistance I might have procured.

62. Address of the Commons for the removal of the earl of Halifax, and the king's reply, 1680

(Journals of the House of Commons, IX, pp. 660, 663)

(i) 22 November 1680

MOST GRACIOUS SOVEREIGN,

We, your Majesty's most dutiful and loyal subjects, the Commons in this present Parliament assembled, being deeply sensible of the manifold dangers and mischiefs which have been occasioned to this your kingdom by the dissolution of the last

Parliament, and by the frequent prorogations of this present Parliament, whereby the papists have been greatly encouraged to carry on their hellish and damnable conspiracies against your royal person and government and the Protestant religion now established amongst us, and have had many opportunities to contrive false and malicious plots against the lives and honours of several of your loyal Protestant subjects; and having just reason to believe that the said dissolution was promoted by the evil and pernicious counsels of George, earl of Halifax, do therefore most humbly pray your Majesty, for the taking away of occasions of distrust and jealousy between your Majesty and us your loyal Commons, and that we may with greater cheerfulness proceed to perfect those matters now before us, which tend to the safety and honour of your sacred person and government, and to the preservation of the true Protestant religion both to ourselves and to our posterity, that you would be graciously pleased to remove the said George, earl of Halifax, from your presence and counsels for ever.

(ii) 26 November 1680

CHARLES R.

His Majesty, having received the address of this House relating to the earl of Halifax, hath thought fit to return this answer:

That he conceives the said address to be liable to several exceptions; but, having a great desire to preserve all possible good understanding with this House, he chooses to decline to enter into particulars, to avoid all occasions of dispute. He therefore thinks fit to tell them that he doth not find the grounds in the address of this House to be sufficient to induce him to remove the earl of Halifax; but he answers them at the same time that whenever this House shall, in a due and regular course, prove any crime either against the said earl of Halifax or any other person, who either now is or shall hereafter be in his Council, he will leave him or them to their own legal defence without interposing to protect them.

63. Representation of the Commons on the king's rejection of the Place Bill, and the king's reply, 1694

(Journals of the House of Commons, XI, pp. 72, 74)

(i) 27 January 1694

MAY IT PLEASE YOUR MOST EXCELLENT MAJESTY,

We, your Majesty's most dutiful and loyal subjects, the Commons in Parliament assembled, think ourselves bound, in duty to your Majesty, humbly to represent that the usage in Parliament in all times hath been that what bills have been agreed by both Houses, for the redress of grievances or other public good, have, when tendered to the Throne, obtained the royal assent; and that there are very few instances in former reigns where such assent in such cases hath not been given, and those attended with great inconveniences to the Crown of England, especially where the same hath been withheld by insinuations of particular persons, without the advice of the Privy Council, thereby creating great dissatisfaction and jealousies in the minds of your people.

Your Commons therefore, out of their sincere desire of the welfare of your Majesty and your government, and that you may always reign in prosperity and happiness in the affection of your subjects, cannot without grief of heart reflect that since your Majesty's accession to the Crown several public bills, made by advice of both Houses of Parliament, have not obtained the royal assent, and in particular one bill, entituled, *An Act touching free and impartial proceedings in Parliament*, which was made to redress a grievance and take off a scandal relating to the proceedings of your Commons in Parliament, after they had freely voted great supplies for the public occasions; which they can impute to no other cause than the insinuations of particular persons, who take upon them, for their own particular ends, to advise your Majesty contrary to the advice of Parliament; and therefore cannot but look on such as enemies to your Majesty and your kingdom.

Upon these considerations we humbly beseech your Majesty to believe that none can have so great a concern and interest in the prosperity and happiness of your Majesty and your government as your two Houses of Parliament, and do therefore humbly pray that for the future your Majesty would graciously be pleased to hearken to the advice of your Parliament, and not to the secret advices of particular persons who may have private interests of their own, separate from the true interest of your Majesty and your people.

(ii) 31 January 1694

GENTLEMEN,

I am very sensible of the good affections you have expressed to me upon many occasions, and of the zeal you have shown for our common interest. I shall make use of this opportunity to tell you that no prince ever had a higher esteem for the constitution of the English government than myself, and that I shall ever have a great regard to the advice of Parliaments. I am persuaded that nothing can so much conduce to the happiness and welfare of this kingdom as an entire confidence between the king and people, which I shall by all means endeavour to preserve. And I assure you I shall look upon such persons to be my enemies who shall advise anything that may lessen it.

64. Joint address of Lords and Commons against any peace leaving Spain under the House of Bourbon, and the queen's reply, 1707

(*Journals of the House of Lords*, XVIII, pp. 400–403)

(i) 22 December 1707

We, your Majesty's most dutiful and obedient subjects, the Lords Spiritual and Temporal and Commons in Parliament assembled, having been always fully persuaded that nothing could restore a just balance of power in Europe but the reducing the whole Spanish monarchy to the obedience of the House of Austria, and having seen several great parts of that monarchy, by the blessing of God upon the victorious arms of your Majesty and your allies, already in the possession of that House, do think it not only seasonable but necessary at this juncture humbly to offer this our unanimous opinion to your Majesty, that no peace can be honourable or safe for your Majesty or your allies if Spain, the West Indies, or any part of the Spanish monarchy, be suffered to remain under the power of the House of Bourbon.

When we consider what efforts this kingdom has continued to make from the beginning of the war, we cannot but think a much greater impression might have been made upon the enemy before this time if some of your allies, who seem principally concerned and have reaped the most immediate advantage, had seconded your Majesty with like vigour, whereby France might have been equally pressed on all sides. We are obliged to return our humble thanks to your Majesty for the care you have taken, and the instances you have used with his Imperial Majesty, for sending a considerable force to the relief of Spain under the command of Prince Eugene, as being certainly the most likely method to restore the affairs of the confederacy in that country. But the frequent disappointments we have observed on the part of the Emperor and Empire, to the great prejudice of the common cause, makes us think it our duty, in order that the war may be brought to a speedy and happy conclusion, to beseech your Majesty to make the most pressing instances to the Emperor, that he would with all expedition send powerful succours to his brother the king of Spain under the conduct of that great and successful general, that he would timely and effectually make good what has been concerted for his putting twenty thousand men under the command of the duke of Savoy, and would also make use of his utmost power and interest for strengthening the army upon the Rhine, which is now happily put under the command of that wise and valiant prince the elector of Hanover.

We believe no part of this can be refused, upon your Majesty's earnest interposition, who have done such great things for the House of Austria; and this being complied with we may reasonably hope, by God's assistance, the next will prove a happy and glorious campaign.

(ii) 7 January 1708

My Lords and Gentlemen,

I am fully of your opinion that no peace can be honourable or safe for us or for our allies till the entire monarchy of Spain be restored to the House of Austria, and very well pleased to find that the measures I have concerted for the succour of the king of Spain are so well approved by both Houses of Parliament. I shall continue my most pressing instances with the Emperor for the hastening of further succours, and that they may be commanded by Prince Eugene, as also upon all other particulars mentioned in your address.

---

65. **Joint address of Lords and Commons desiring the queen not to decline the thought of a second marriage, and the queen's reply, 1709**

(*Journals of the House of Lords*, XVIII, pp. 620–623)

(i) 27 January 1709

Most gracious Sovereign,

We, your Majesty's most loyal and dutiful subjects, the Lords Spiritual and Temporal and Commons in Parliament assembled, being truly and deeply sensible of the many and great blessings we have enjoyed during the whole course of your Majesty's most glorious reign, do most humbly conceive we should be inexcusably wanting to ourselves and the whole kingdom if we should neglect to use our most zealous endeavours that those blessings may be derived down to future ages; and therefore, with hearts full of the most profound respect and duty to your royal person, we most humbly beseech your Majesty graciously to consider the universal desires and most humble supplications of your faithful subjects, that your Majesty would not so far indulge your just grief as to decline the thoughts of a second marriage. This would be an unspeakable joy to your people, who would join their most fervent prayers to Almighty God to bless your Majesty with royal issue, all of them concurring in this opinion, that no greater happiness can be desired for your kingdoms than that they and their children may long continue under the gentle and gracious government of your Majesty and your posterity.

(ii) 29 January 1709

The frequent marks of duty and affection to my person and government which I receive from both Houses of Parliament must needs be very acceptable to me. The provision I have made for the Protestant succession will always be a proof how much I have at my heart the future happiness of the kingdom. The subject of this address is of such a nature that I am persuaded you do not expect a particular answer.

(b) ROYAL PRESSURE ON PARLIAMENT

66. Resolution of the Lords welcoming the presence of the king, 1670

(*Journals of the House of Lords*, XII, pp. 318, 322)

21 March 1670. The House was adjourned into a committee to proceed in the debate of the bill to prevent and suppress seditious conventicles. And the committee being in debate of a clause of the said bill, his Majesty coming unexpectedly into the House, the House was resumed.

Then his Majesty said to the Lords that he is come to renew a custom of his predecessors, long discontinued, to be present at debates, but not to interrupt the freedom thereof; and therefore desired the Lords to sit down, and put on their hats, and proceed in their business. Upon which, the Lords taking their places and putting on their hats, the House was again adjourned into a committee during pleasure, and the debate was proceeded in.

24 March 1670. Ordered, that the humble thanks of this House be presented to his Majesty for his gracious presence in this House, lately renewed, according to the custom of his royal predecessors, though the same had been discontinued for many years past.

67. Declaration of Charles II to his people, 1681
(*Memoirs relating to the Earl of Danby*, App., pp. 99–106)

HIS MAJESTY'S DECLARATION TO ALL HIS LOVING SUBJECTS,
TOUCHING THE CAUSES AND REASONS THAT MOVED HIM
TO DISSOLVE THE TWO LAST PARLIAMENTS

It was with exceeding great trouble that we were brought to the dissolving of the two last Parliaments without more benefit to our people by the calling of them, but having done our part in giving so many opportunities of providing for their good it cannot be justly imputed to us that the success hath not answered our expectation. We cannot at this time but take notice of the particular causes of our dissatisfaction, which at the beginning of the last Parliament we did recommend to their care to avoid, and expected we should have had no new cause to remember them.

We opened the last Parliament which was held at Westminster with as gracious expressions of our readiness to satisfy the desires of our good subjects, and to secure them against all their just fears, as the weighty consideration either of preserving the established religion and the liberty and property of our subjects at home, or of supporting our neighbours and allies abroad, could fill our heart with, or possibly require from us. And we do solemnly declare that we did intend, as far as would have consisted with the very being of the government, to have complied with anything that could have been proposed to us to accomplish those ends.

We asked of them the supporting the alliances we had made for the preservation of the general peace in Christendom. We recommended to them the further examination of the Plot. We desired their advice and assistance concerning the preservation of Tangier. We offered to concur in any remedies that could be proposed for the security of the Protestant religion that might consist with preserving the succession of the crown in its due and legal course of descent. To all which we met with most unsuitable returns from the House of Commons–addresses in the nature of remonstrances rather than of answers; arbitrary orders for taking our subjects into custody for matters that had no relation to privileges of Parliament; strange illegal votes declaring divers eminent persons to be enemies to the king and kingdom, without any order or process of law, any hearing of their defence, or any proof so much as offered against them.

Besides these proceedings they voted as followeth on the 7th of January last:

Resolved, that whosoever shall lend or cause to be lent by way of advance any money upon the branches of the king's revenue arising by Customs, Excise or Hearth Money shall be adjudged to hinder the sitting of Parliaments, and shall be responsible for the same in Parliament.

Resolved, that whosoever shall buy any tally of anticipation upon any part of the king's revenue, or whosoever shall pay any such tally hereafter to be struck, shall be adjudged to hinder the sitting of Parliaments, and shall be responsible for the same in Parliament.

Which votes, instead of giving us assistance to support our allies, or enable us to preserve Tangier, tended rather to disable us from contributing towards either by our own revenue or credit, not only exposing us to all dangers that might happen either at home or abroad, but endeavouring to deprive us of the possibility of supporting the government itself, and to reduce us to a more helpless condition than the meanest of our subjects.

And on the 10th of the same month they passed another vote, in these words:

Resolved, that it is the opinion of this House that the prosecution of Protestant dissenters upon the penal laws is at this time grievous to the subject, a weakening of the Protestant interest, an encouragement to popery and dangerous to the peace of the kingdom.

By which vote, without any regard to the laws established, they assumed to themselves a power of suspending Acts of Parliament, whereas our judges and ministers of justice neither can nor ought, in reverence to the votes of either or both the Houses, break the oaths they have taken for the due and impartial execution of our laws, which by experience have been found to be the best support both of the Protestant interest and of the peace of the kingdom.

These were some of the unwarrantable proceedings of that House of Commons which were the occasion of our parting with that Parliament, which we had no sooner dissolved but we caused another to be forthwith assembled at Oxford, at the opening of which we thought it necessary to give them warning of the errors of the former, in hopes to have prevented the like miscarriages. And we required of them to make the laws of the land their rule, as we did and do resolve they shall be ours. We further added that what we had formerly and so often declared concerning the succession, we could not depart from it; but to remove all reasonable fears that might arise from the possibility of a popish successor's coming to the crown, if means could be found that in such a case the administration of the government might remain in Protestant hands, we were ready to hearken to any expedient by which the religion established might be preserved and the monarchy not destroyed.

But contrary to our offers and expectation we saw that no expedient would be entertained but that of a total exclusion, which we had so often declared was a point that in our own royal judgment so nearly concerned us, both in honour, justice and conscience, that we could never consent to it. In short we cannot, after the sad experience we have had of the late civil wars, that murdered our father of blessed memory and ruined the monarchy, consent to a law that shall establish another most unnatural war, or at least make it necessary to maintain a standing force for the preserving the government and the peace of the kingdom. And we have reason to believe, by what passed in the last Parliament at Westminster, that if we could have been brought to give our consent to a bill of exclusion the intent was not to rest there but to pass further, and to attempt some other great and important changes even in present.

The business of Fitzharris, who was impeached by the House of Commons of high treason and by the House of Lords referred to the ordinary course of law, was on the sudden carried on to that extremity by the votes which the Commons passed on the 26th of March last that there was no possibility left of a reconciliation. The votes were these:

Saturday, 26th March, afternoon. ·

Resolved, that it is the undoubted right of the Commons in Parliament assembled to impeach before the Lords in Parliament any peer or commoner, for treason or any other crime or misdemeanour, and that the refusal of the Lords to proceed in Parliament upon such impeachment is a denial of justice and a violation of the constitution of Parliaments.

Resolved, that in the case of Edward Fitzharris, who by the Commons hath been impeached of high treason before the Lords, with a declaration that in convenient time they would bring up the articles against him, for the Lords to resolve that the said Fitzharris should be proceeded with according to the course of common law and not by way of impeachment at this time is a denial of justice, and a violation of the constitution of Parliaments, and an obstruction to the further discovery of the Popish Plot, and of great danger to his Majesty's person and the Protestant religion.

Resolved, that for any inferior court to proceed against Edward Fitzharris, or any other person lying under an impeachment in Parliament, for the same crimes for which he or they stand impeached is a high breach of the privilege of Parliament.

It was a matter extremely sensible to us to find an impeachment made use of to delay a trial that we had directed against a professed papist, charged with treasons against us of an extraordinary nature; and certainly the House of Peers did themselves right in refusing to give countenance to such a proceeding. But when either of the Houses are so far transported as to vote the proceedings of the other to be a denial of justice, a violation of the constitution of Parliaments, of danger to our person and the Protestant religion, without conferences first had to examine upon what grounds such proceedings were made and how far they might be justified, this puts the two Houses out of capacity of transacting business together, and consequently is the greatest violation of the constitution of Parliaments. This was the case; and every day's continuance being like to produce new instances of further heat and anger between the two Houses, to the disappointment of all public ends for which they were called, we found it necessary to put an end to this Parliament likewise.

But notwithstanding all this let not the restless malice of ill men who are labouring to poison our people, some out of fondness of their old beloved commonwealth principles and some out of anger at their being disappointed in the particular designs they had for the accomplishment of their own ambition and greatness, persuade any of our good subjects that we intend to lay aside the use of Parliaments; for we do still declare that no irregularities in Parliaments shall ever make us out of love with Parliaments, which we look upon as the best method for healing the distempers of the kingdom, and the only means to preserve the monarchy in that due credit and respect which it ought to have both at home and abroad. And for this cause we are resolved, by the blessing of God, to have frequent Parliaments, and both in and out of Parliament to use our utmost endeavours to extirpate popery, and to redress all the grievances of our good subjects, and in all things to govern according to the laws of the kingdom.

And we hope that a little time will so far open the eyes of all our good subjects that our next meeting in Parliament shall perfect all that settlement and peace which shall be found wanting either in Church or State; to which as we shall contribute our utmost endeavours, so we assure ourselves that we shall be assisted therein by the loyalty and good affections of all those who consider the rise and progress of the late troubles and confusions, and desire to preserve their country from a relapse; and who cannot but remember that religion, liberty and property were all lost and gone when the monarchy was shaken off, and could never be revived till that was restored.

Given at our court at Whitehall,
the 8th day of April 1681.

68. Petition of the city of London to Charles II in defence of their charter, and the king's reply, 1683

(*State Trials*, VIII, pp. 1273–1283)

(i) Petition, presented 18 June 1683

TO THE KING'S MOST EXCELLENT MAJESTY,

The humble petition of the lord mayor, aldermen and commons of the city of London, in common council assembled, sheweth,

That your petitioners are heartily and most unfeignedly sorry for the misgovernment of this your city of late years, whereby the citizens have fallen under your Majesty's displeasure, which occasioned a *quo warranto* to be brought against them; upon which judgment hath been pronounced for the seizure of their liberties and franchises into your Majesty's hands; that your petitioners are deeply sensible of, and thankfully acknowledge, the great favour of this opportunity of application to your royal grace, vouchsafed them by means of your Majesty's not requiring judgment to be immediately entered thereupon; and now, considering this our distressed condition, we humbly cast ourselves at your royal feet, imploring your princely compassion and grace to be extended to this your ancient city, most humbly begging your Majesty's pardon for all our offences.

And we do, in the name of ourselves and all the citizens, humbly tender, and pray your Majesty to accept, the most solemn promises and assurances of constant loyalty and obedience to your Majesty, your heirs and successors, and of our regular and dutiful administration of your government of this city for the future; wherein we submit ourselves to your Majesty's good pleasure, and humbly beg your Majesty's commands and directions, which we will with all humility and thankfulness obey.

And your petitioners shall ever pray.

(ii) Reply, delivered by the Lord Keeper, Sir Francis North

My Lord Mayor, I am by the king's command to tell you, that he hath considered the humble petition of the city of London, where so many of the present magistrates and other eminent citizens are of undoubted loyalty and affection to his service; that for their sakes his Majesty will show the city all the favour they can reasonably desire.

It was very long before his Majesty took resolutions to question their charter. It was not the seditious discourses of the coffee-houses, the treasonable pamphlets and libels daily published and dispersed thence into all parts of the kingdom, the outrageous tumults in the streets, nor the affronts to his courts of justice could provoke him to it. His Majesty had patience until disorders were grown to that height that nothing less seemed to be designed than a ruin to the government both of Church and State, for the factious party were not content with the practice of these insolencies, but endeavoured to have them publicly countenanced by the magistrates; and for that end, in all elections, they stickled to choose the most disaffected into offices of the greatest trust in the government, and carried themselves with that heat and violence that it was a terror to all sober and discreet citizens. And the city was so unhappily divided into parties that there was no likelihood it could return to good order so long as the factious retained any hopes of procuring the election of magistrates of their own party for their impunity.

It was high time to put a stop to this growing evil. This made it necessary for his Majesty to inquire into their abuse of franchises, that it might be in his power to make a regulation sufficient to restore the city to its former good government. It was not for punishment, but merely for the good of the city, that he took this course. And now the king hath obtained judgment in a *quo warranto* it is not his intention to prejudice them either in their properties or customs. Nay, lest the entering a judgment upon record might have consequences fatal to them, his Majesty was so tender of them that he caused Mr. Attorney to forbear the same at present, that the city might have some time to consider their own condition.

My Lord, I must needs say the city hath not been well advised to defer their application to his Majesty thus long, even till the court hath pronounced judgment. It had been done with a much better grace if it had been more early. His Majesty's affection to the city is too great to reject their suit for that cause; but for that reason you will have the less time to deliberate upon the particulars the king doth require of you. And indeed there will be little need of deliberation, for his Majesty hath resolved to make the alterations as few and as easy as may be consistent with the good government of the city and peace of the kingdom. They are these:

His Majesty requires your submission to these regulations:

That no lord mayor, sheriff, recorder, common serjeant, town-clerk or coroner of the city of London, or steward of the borough of Southwark, shall be capable of, or be admitted to, the exercise of their respective offices before his Majesty shall have approved them under his sign manual.

That if his Majesty shall disapprove the choice of any person to be lord mayor, and signify the same under his sign manual to the lord mayor, or in default of a lord mayor to the recorder or senior alderman, the citizens shall within one week proceed to a new choice. And if his Majesty shall in like manner disapprove the second choice, his Majesty may, if he so please, nominate a person to be lord mayor for the ensuing year.

If his Majesty shall in like manner disapprove the persons chosen to be sheriffs, or either of them, his Majesty may appoint persons to be sheriffs for the ensuing year by his commission, if he so please.

Nevertheless the elections of these officers may be according to the ancient usage of the city, with these restrictions:

The lord mayor and court of aldermen may, with leave of his Majesty, displace any alderman, recorder, common serjeant, town-clerk, coroner of the said city, and steward of the said borough.

Upon the election of any alderman, if any of the persons that shall be presented to the court of aldermen by the ward shall be judged unfit, upon such declaration by the said court, the ward shall proceed to the choice of other persons in the room of such or so many of them as are so disapproved; and if the said court shall disapprove such second choice they may appoint any others in their room.

The justices of the peace to be by the king's commission, which his Majesty will grant according to the usual method, unless upon extraordinary occasions, when his Majesty shall think it necessary for his service.

These matters are to be settled in such a manner as shall be approved by his Majesty's Attorney and Solicitor-General and counsel learned in the law.

My Lord Mayor, These regulations being made, his Majesty will not only pardon this prosecution but confirm your charter in such manner as may be consistent with them. The city ought to look upon this as a great condescension on his Majesty's part, it being in the nature of a reservation of a small part of what is already in his power by the judgment, and of those things which will conduce as much to their own good and quiet as to his service. If the city should look upon it with another eye, and neglect a speedy compliance, yet his Majesty hath done his part, and demonstrated his affection to the city, by giving them this opportunity. And if there shall be any heavy consequence of this judgment, which it will behove you well to consider, the fault will lie at their doors in whose power it now is to bring this affair to a happy conclusion.

My Lord Mayor, The term draws towards an end, and midsummer day is at hand, when some of the officers use to be chosen, whereof his Majesty will reserve the approbation. Therefore it is his Majesty's pleasure that you return to the city and consult the common council, that he may speedily know your resolutions thereupon, and accordingly give his directions. That you may see the king is in earnest, and the matter is not capable of delay, I am commanded to let you know he hath given order to his Attorney-General to enter up judgment on Saturday next unless you prevent it by your compliance in all these particulars.

69. Gilbert Burnet on the methods employed by the Court to influence the elections of 1685

(*History of His Own Time*, ed. 1833, III, pp. 16–18)

At the same time a Parliament was summoned, and all arts were used to manage elections so that the king should have a Parliament to his mind. Complaints came up from all the parts of England of the injustice and violence used in elections, beyond what had ever been practised in former times. And this was so universal over the whole nation that no corner of it was neglected. In the new charters that had been granted the election of the members was taken out of the hands of the inhabitants and restrained to the corporation-men, all those being left out who were not acceptable at court. In some boroughs they could not find a number of men to be depended on, so the neighbouring gentlemen were made the corporation-men; and in some of these, persons of other counties, not so much as known in the borough, were named. This was practised in the most avowed manner in Cornwall by the earl of Bath, who to secure himself the groom of the stole's place, which he held all King Charles's time, put the officers of the guards' names in almost all the charters of that county, which sending up forty-four members, they were for most part so chosen that the king was sure of their votes on all occasions.

These methods were so successful over England that when the elections were all returned the king said there were not above forty members but such as he himself wished for. They were neither men of parts nor estates; so there was no hope left, either of working on their understandings, or of making them see their interest in not giving the king all at once. Most of them were furious and violent, and seemed resolved to recommend themselves to the king by putting everything in his power, and by ruining all those who had been for the exclusion. Some few had designed to give the king the revenue only from three years to three years. The earl of Rochester told me that was what he looked for, though the post he was in made it not so proper for him to move in it. But there was no prospect of any strength in opposing anything that the king should ask of them.

This gave all thinking men a melancholy prospect. England now seemed lost, unless some happy accident should save it. All people saw the way for packing a Parliament now laid open. A new set of charters and corporation-men, if those now named should not continue to be still as compliant as they were at present, was a certain remedy, to which recourse might be easily had. The boroughs of England saw their privileges now wrested out of their hands, and that their elections, which had made them so considerable before, were hereafter to be made as the Court should direct; so that from henceforth little regard would be had to them, and the usual practices in courting, or rather in corrupting, them would be no longer pursued.

Thus all people were alarmed, but few durst speak out or complain openly. Only the duke of Monmouth's agents made great use of this to inflame their party. It was said, here was a Parliament to meet that was not the choice and representative of the nation, and therefore was no Parliament. So they upon this possessed all people with dreadful apprehensions, that a blow was now given to the constitution which could not be remedied but by an insurrection. It was resolved to bring up petitions against some elections that were so indecently managed that it seemed scarce possible to excuse them; but these were to be judged by a majority of men who knew their own elections to be so faulty that to secure themselves they would justify the rest, and fair dealing was not to be expected from those who were so deeply engaged in the like injustice.

70. James II's instructions to the duke of Beaufort, 1687
(Historical Manuscripts Commission, *Twelfth Report*, IX, pp. 89–91)
(i) Letter dated Whitehall, 12 February 1687

I forgot when you went out of town to give you directions to speak with such Parliament-men as you shall see in the country about what I intend to endeavour to have done when they shall meet next, which is to have the two tests and penal laws repealed, that my Catholic subjects may be in the same condition the rest of my subjects are. Therefore pray take pains with such as make difficulty to promise to comply with my so reasonable desires, and get as many of them as you can to promise you positively that they will do it, so that against you come back hither you may be able to give me a true account; and send to such as are anything near you to come to you that you may speak with them about it.

As for the Herefordshire men that are in town, I have spoken with all of them, and they have fully satisfied me. I hear Sir John Morgan is in the country. Be sure to send for him and speak with him, for if he will not comply (of which I do not doubt) he shall be no longer in my pay. Speak also to as many as you can of the Welsh members, and take great care to get none but such as you can be sure of to be chosen in the vacancies which are where you have to do. I have a very good prospect of being able to carry it in both Houses, but no pains must be spared to gain people, which is all I have now to say.

(ii) Memorandum in Beaufort's handwriting, 26 October 1687

This paper was delivered me by his Majesty with his own hand on Wednesday, the 26th of October 1687, at his Cabinet Council in Lord Sunderland's office, Lord Chancellor, Lord President, Lord Middleton, Lord Dartmouth and Lord Godolphin sitting with him, and Mr. Bridgeman, one of the clerks, standing by, and is the same with that delivered to the duke of Norfolk, earl of Bath, Lord Preston and Lord Waldegrave, who were called in and received theirs the same sitting.

The king's endorsed instructions, 26 October, 1687

That the lord lieutenant of the counties of Gloucester, Hereford, Monmouth, North Wales, South Wales, and of the city of Bristol, do call before him all the deputy lieutenants and justices of peace within his lieutenancy, either jointly or separately as he shall think best, and ask him one by one the following questions:

1. If in case he shall be chosen knight of the shire, or burgess of a town, when the king shall think fit to call a Parliament, whether he will be for taking off the penal laws and the tests.

2. Whether he will assist and contribute to the election of such members as shall be for taking off the penal laws and tests.

3. Whether he will support the king's declaration for liberty of conscience by living friendly with those of all persuasions, as subjects of the same prince and good Christians ought to do.

As he shall ask these questions of all deputy lieutenants and justices of the peace, so he shall particularly write down what every one answers, whether he consents, refuseth or is doubtful; that he likewise do bring the king as good an account as he can of all the several corporations within his lieutenancy, what persons of such as are willing to comply with these measures have credit enough of their own to be chosen Parliament-men, or may be chosen if assisted by their friends; and lastly what Catholics and what dissenters are fit to be added to the list of deputy lieutenants or to the commission of the peace throughout the said lieutenancy.

D. IMPEACHMENTS AND ATTAINDERS

71. Articles of impeachment against the earl of Clarendon, 1667
(*Journals of the House of Commons*, IX, p. 16)

I. That the earl of Clarendon hath designed a standing army to be raised, and to govern the kingdom thereby; advised the king to dissolve this present Parliament, to lay aside all thoughts of Parliaments for the future, to govern by a military power, and to maintain the same by free quarter and contribution.

II. That he hath in the hearing of many of his Majesty's subjects falsely and seditiously said that the king was in his heart a papist, popishly affected, or words to that effect.

III. That he hath received great sums of money for passing the Canary patent and other illegal patents, and granted illegal injunctions to stop proceedings at law against them and other illegal patents formerly granted.

IV. That he hath advised and procured divers of his Majesty's subjects to be imprisoned, against law, in remote islands, garrisons and other places, thereby to prevent them from the benefit of the law, and to introduce precedents for imprisoning any other of his Majesty's subjects in like manner.

V. That he hath corruptly sold several offices, contrary to law.

VI. That he procured his Majesty's Customs to be farmed at under-rates, knowing the same, and great pretended debts to be paid by his Majesty, to the payment of which his Majesty was not in strictness bound, and hath received great sums of money for procuring the same.

VII. That he received great sums of money from the Company of Vintners, or some of them, or their agents, for enhancing the prices of wines, and for freeing of them from the payments of legal penalties which they had incurred.

VIII. That he hath in short time gained to himself a greater estate than can be imagined to be lawfully gained in so short a time, and contrary to his oath hath procured several grants under the great seal from his Majesty to himself and his relations of several of his Majesty's lands, hereditaments and leases, to the disprofit of his Majesty.

IX. That he introduced an arbitrary government in his Majesty's plantations, and hath caused such as complained thereof before his Majesty and Council to be long imprisoned for so doing.

X. That he did reject and frustrate a proposal and undertaking approved by his Majesty, for the preservation of Nevis and St. Christopher's and reducing the French plantations to his Majesty's obedience, after the commissions were drawn up for that purpose, which was the occasion of our great losses and damages in those parts.

XI. That he advised and effected the sale of Dunkirk to the French king, being part of his Majesty's dominions, together with the ammunition, artillery and all sorts of stores there, and for no greater value than the said ammunition, artillery and stores were worth.

8

XII. That the said earl did unduly cause his Majesty's letters patents under the great seal to one Dr. Crowther to be altered, and the enrolment thereof to be unduly razed.

XIII. That he hath in an arbitrary way examined and drawn into question divers of his Majesty's subjects concerning their lands, tenements, goods and chattels and properties, determined thereof at the Council table, and stopped proceedings at law by order of the Council table, and threatened some that pleaded the statutes of 17 Car. I.

XIV. That he hath caused *quo warrantos* to be issued out against most of the corporations of England immediately after their charters were confirmed by Act of Parliament, to the intent he might receive great sums of money from them for renewing their charters, which when they complied withal he caused the said *quo warrantos* to be discharged, or prosecution thereupon to cease.

XV. That he procured the bills of settlement for Ireland, and received great sums of money for the same, in most corrupt and unlawful manner.

XVI. That he hath deluded and betrayed his Majesty and the nation in foreign treaties and negotiations relating to the late war, and discovered and betrayed his secret counsels to his enemies.

XVII. That he was a principal author of the fatal counsel of dividing the fleet about June 1666.

72. Earl of Clarendon's apology, 1667
(*Journals of the House of Lords*, XII, pp. 154–156)

To the Right Honourable the Lords Spiritual and Temporal in Parliament assembled, the humble petition and address of Edward, earl of Clarendon.

MAY IT PLEASE YOUR LORDSHIPS,

I cannot express the insupportable trouble and grief of mind I sustain, under the apprehension of being misrepresented to your Lordships, and when I hear how much of your Lordships' time hath been spent upon the mention of me, as it is attended with more public consequences, and of the differences in opinion which have already or may probably arise between your Lordships and the honourable House of Commons, whereby the great and weighty affairs of the kingdom may be obstructed in a time of so general a dissatisfaction. I am very unfortunate to find myself to suffer so much under two very disadvantageous reflections, which are in no degree applicable to me:

The first, from the greatness of my estate and fortune, collected and made in so few years, which if it be proportionable to what is reported may very reasonably cause my integrity to be suspected.

The second, that I have been the sole manager and chief minister in all the transactions of state since the king's return into England to August last, and therefore that all miscarriages and misfortunes ought to be imputed to me and to my counsels.

Concerning my estate, your Lordships will not believe that after malice and envy hath been so inquisitive and so sharp-sighted I will offer anything to your Lordships but what is exactly true. And I do assure your Lordships, in the first place, that excepting from the king's bounty I have never received or taken one penny but what was generally understood to be the just and lawful perquisites of my office by the constant practice of the best times, which I did in my own judgment conceive to be that of my Lord Coventry and my Lord Ellesmere, the practice of which I constantly observed, although the office in both their times was lawfully worth double to what it was to me and I believe now is; that all the courtesies and favours which I have been able to obtain from the king for other persons, in Church or State or in Westminster Hall, have never been worth me five pounds, so that your Lordships may be confident I am as innocent from corruption as from any disloyal thought, which, after near thirty years service of the Crown in some difficulties and distresses, I did never suspect would have been objected to me in my age. And I do assure your Lordships, and shall make it very manifest, that the several sums of money and some parcels of land which his Majesty hath bountifully bestowed upon me since his return into England are worth more than all I have amounts to, so far I am from advancing my estate by any indirect means. And though this bounty of his Majesty hath very far exceeded my merit or my expectation, yet some others have been as fortunate at least in the same bounty who had as small pretences to it, and have no great reason to envy my condition.

Concerning the other imputation, of the credit and power of being chief minister and so causing all to be done that I had a mind to, I have no more to say than that I had the good fortune to serve a master of a very great judgment and understanding, and to be always joined with persons of great ability and experience, without whose advice and concurrence never anything hath been done. Before his Majesty's coming into England he was constantly attended by the then marquis of Ormonde, the late Lord Colepeper and Mr. Secretary Nicholas, who were equally trusted with myself, and without whose joint advice and concurrence, when they were all present (as some of them always were), I never gave any counsel. As soon as it pleased God to bring his Majesty into England he established his Privy Council, and shortly out of them a number of honourable persons of great reputation, who for the most part are still alive, as a Committee for Foreign Affairs and consideration of such things as in the nature of them required much secrecy, and with these persons he vouchsafed to join me; and I am confident this committee never transacted anything of moment, his Majesty being always present, without presenting the same first to the Council Board; and I must appeal to them concerning my carriage, and whether we were not all of one mind in all matters of importance.

For more than two years I never knew any difference in the Councils, or that there were any complaints in the kingdom, which I wholly impute to his Majesty's great wisdom and the entire concurrence of his counsellors, without the vanity of assuming anything to myself; and therefore I hope I shall not be singly charged with anything that hath since fallen out amiss. But from the time that Mr. Secretary Nicholas was removed from his place there were great alterations; and whosoever knows anything of the Court or Councils knows well how much my credit hath since that time been diminished, though his Majesty graciously vouchsafed still to hear my advice in most of his affairs. Nor hath there been from that time to this above one or two persons brought to the Council, or preferred to any considerable office in the Court, who have been of my intimate acquaintance or suspected to have any kindness for me, and most of them notoriously known to have been very long my enemies, and of different judgments and principles from me both in Church and State, and who have taken all opportunities to lessen my credit with the king and with all other persons, by misrepresenting and misreporting all that I said or did. . . .

In my humble opinion the great misfortunes of the kingdom have proceeded from the war, to which it is notoriously known that I was always most averse, and may without vanity say I did not only foresee but did declare the mischiefs we should run into by entering into a war before any alliances made with the neighbour princes. . . . As I did from my soul abhor the entering into this war, so I never presumed to give any advice or counsel for the way of managing it, but by opposing many propositions which seemed to the late Lord Treasurer and myself to be unreasonable, as the payment of the seamen by tickets, and many other particulars which added to the expense.

My enemies took all occasions to inveigh against me, and, making friendship with others out of the Council, of more licentious principles and who knew well enough how much I disliked and complained of the liberty they took to themselves of reviling all councils and counsellors, and turning all things serious and sacred into ridicule, they took all ways imaginable to render me ingrateful to all sorts of men (whom I shall be compelled to name in my defence), persuading those who miscarried in any of their designs that it was the Chancellor's doing, whereof I never knew anything. However they could not withdraw the king's favour from me, who was still pleased to use my service with others; nor was there ever anything done but upon the joint advice of at least the major part of those who were consulted with. And as his Majesty commanded my service in the late treaties, so I never gave the least advice in private, nor wrote one letter to any person in either of those negotiations but upon the advice of the Council and after it was read in Council, or at least by the king himself and some other. And if I prepared any instructions or memorials, it was by the king's command and the request of the Secretaries, who desired my assistance; nor was it any wish of my own that any ambassador should give me an account of the transactions, but to the Secretaries, with whom I was always ready to advise.

Nor am I conscious to myself of having ever given advice that hath proved mischievous or inconvenient to his Majesty; and I have been so far from being the sole manager of affairs that I have not in the whole last year been above twice with his Majesty in any room alone, and very seldom in the two or three years preceding. And since the Parliament at Oxford it hath been very visible that my credit hath been very little, and that very few things have been hearkened to which have been proposed by me, but contradicted *eo nomine* because proposed by me.

I most humbly beseech your Lordships to remember the office and trust I had for seven years, in which in discharge of my duty I was obliged to stop and obstruct many men's pretences, and to refuse to set the seal to many pardons and other grants which would have been profitable to those who procured them, and many whereof, upon my representation to his Majesty, were for ever stopped, which naturally have raised many enemies to me. And my frequent concurring, upon the desires of the late Lord Treasurer, with whom I had the honour to have a long and fast friendship to his death, in representing several excesses and exorbitancies, the yearly issues so far exceeding the revenue, provoked many persons concerned, of great power and credit, to do me all the ill offices they could. And yet I may faithfully say that I never meddled with any part of the revenue, or the administration of it, but when I was desired by the late Lord Treasurer to give him my assistance and advice (having had the honour formerly to serve the Crown as Chancellor of the Exchequer), which was for the most part in his Majesty's presence. . . . Nor have I in my life, upon all the treaties or otherwise, received the value of one shilling from all the kings and princes in the world (except the books of the Louvre print sent me by the Chancellor of France by that king's direction) but from my own master, to whose entire service and to the good and welfare of my country no man's heart was ever more devoted.

This being my present condition I do most humbly beseech your Lordships to retain a favourable opinion of me, and to believe me to be innocent from those foul aspersions until the contrary shall be proved, which, I am sure, can never be by any men worthy to be believed. And since the distempers of the time and the differences between the two Houses in the present debate, with the power and malice of my enemies (who give out that they shall prevail with his Majesty to prorogue or dissolve his Parliament in displeasure, and threaten to expose me to the rage and fury of the people), may make me be looked upon as the cause which obstructs the king's service and the unity and peace of the kingdom, I most humbly beseech your Lordships that I may not forfeit your Lordships' favour and protection by withdrawing myself from so powerful a persecution, in hope that I may be able by such withdrawing hereafter to appear and make my defence, when his Majesty's justice (to which I shall always submit) may not be obstructed or controlled by the power and malice of those who have sworn my destruction.

73. Act banishing the earl of Clarendon, 1667
(*Statutes of the Realm*, v, p. 628)

AN ACT FOR BANISHING AND DISENABLING
THE EARL OF CLARENDON

(*19 & 20 Car. II, cap. 2*)

Whereas Edward, earl of Clarendon, having been impeached by the Commons assembled in Parliament of treason and other misdemeanours, hath knowingly withdrawn himself and is fled, whereby justice cannot be done upon him according to his demerit, be it enacted . . . that the said Edward, earl of Clarendon, shall and do suffer perpetual exile, and be for ever banished this realm and all other his Majesty's dominions, and shall be for ever disabled from having, holding or enjoying any office or place of public trust or any other employment whatsoever.

II. And be it further enacted . . . that it shall be, and be taken to be, treason for the said earl at any time to return into or be found in England or any other his Majesty's dominions after the first day of February according to the accompt of England one thousand six hundred sixty-seven,[1] and that in case the said earl shall at any time

[1] 1667/8.

return into or be found in England or any other his Majesty's dominions after the said first day of February that the said earl shall suffer the pains and penalties of treason, and be made incapable of any pardon from the king's Majesty, his heirs and successors but by Act of Parliament; and that all correspondency with the said earl, except it be of his children or such persons as shall be licensed by the king in Council concerning his estate and domestic affairs only after the said first day of February, shall be, and be taken to be, of the same nature as correspondency with a traitor, and the offender therein shall suffer such pains and penalties as by the laws of this realm are to be inflicted upon such persons as keep correspondence with traitors. . . .

III. Provided always, that if the said earl of Clarendon shall on or before the said first day of February next render himself unto one of his Majesty's principal Secretaries of State, or to the Lieutenant of the Tower of London for the time being, in order to his trial which shall be in Parliament, that then and in such case all and every the penalties and disabilities by this Act imposed upon the said earl of Clarendon shall be utterly void and of no effect, anything hereinbefore contained to the contrary notwithstanding.

74. Articles of impeachment against the earl of Danby, 1678
(*Journals of the House of Commons*, IX, p. 561)

ARTICLES OF IMPEACHMENT OF HIGH TREASON, AND OTHER HIGH CRIMES,
MISDEMEANOURS AND OFFENCES, AGAINST THOMAS, EARL OF DANBY,
LORD HIGH TREASURER OF ENGLAND

I. That he hath traitorously encroached to himself regal power, by treating in matters of peace and war with foreign princes and ambassadors, and giving instructions to his Majesty's ambassadors abroad, without communicating the same to the Secretaries of State and the rest of his Majesty's Council, and against the express declaration of his Majesty and his Parliament, thereby intending to defeat and overthrow the provisions which had been deliberately made by his Majesty and his Parliament for the safety and preservation of his Majesty's kingdoms and dominions.

II. That he hath traitorously endeavoured to subvert the ancient and well-established form of government in this kingdom, and instead thereof to introduce an arbitrary and tyrannical way of government; and the better to effect this his purpose he did design the raising of an army upon pretence of a war against the French king, and then to continue the same as a standing army within this kingdom; and an army being so raised, and no war ensuing, an Act of Parliament having passed to pay off and disband the same, and a great sum of money being granted for that end, he did continue this army contrary to the said Act, and misemployed the said money, given for disbanding, to the continuance thereof; and issued out of his Majesty's revenue divers great sums of money for the said purpose, and wilfully neglected to take security from the Paymaster of the Army as the said Act required, whereby the said law is eluded and the army is yet continued, to the great danger and unnecessary charge of his Majesty and the whole kingdom.

III. That he, traitorously intending and designing to alienate the hearts and affections of his Majesty's good subjects from his royal person and government, and to hinder the meeting of Parliaments, and to deprive his sacred Majesty of their safe and wholesome counsels, and thereby to alter the constitution of the government of this kingdom, did propose and negotiate a peace for the French king upon terms disadvantageous to the interest of his Majesty and his kingdoms, for the doing whereof he did endeavour to procure a great sum of money from the French king, for enabling of him to carry on and maintain his said traitorous designs and purposes to the hazard of his Majesty's person and government.

IV. That he is popishly affected, and hath traitorously concealed, after he had notice, the late horrid and bloody plot and conspiracy contrived by the papists against his Majesty's person and government, and hath suppressed the evidence and reproachfully discountenanced the king's witnesses in the discovery of it, in favour of popery, immediately tending to the destruction of the king's sacred person and the subversion of the Protestant religion.

V. That he hath wasted the king's treasure by issuing out of his Majesty's Exchequer and several branches of his revenue, for unnecessary pensions and secret services, to the value of two hundred thirty-one thousand six hundred and two pounds within two years, and that he hath wholly diverted out of the known method and government of the Exchequer one whole branch of his Majesty's revenue to private uses, without any account to be made of it to his Majesty in the Exchequer, contrary to the express Act of Parliament which granted the same; and he hath removed two of his Majesty's commissioners of that part of the revenue for refusing to consent to such his unwarrantable actings therein and to advance money upon that branch of the revenue for private uses.

VI. That he hath by indirect means procured from his Majesty for himself divers considerable gifts and grants of inheritance of the ancient revenue of the crown, even contrary to Acts of Parliament.

75. Earl of Danby's speech to the Lords in his own defence, 1678
(Memoirs relating to the Earl of Danby, App., pp. 40–48)

MY LORDS,

I hope you will not enter upon any other business before you have given that liberty to me, which is the privilege of every peer, to be heard upon any accusation that is brought against him, though of far less moment than what hath been newly read against myself.

I confess I should have heard this charge with horror if the matter of it had been true, but I thank God I know my innocency to be so great that it protects me from all sorts of fear, but that of lying under so black a character as may be believed by those that cannot hear my defence, though I have the confidence to think that it is not truly believed in the hearts of the greatest part of those that have been informed against me. I must needs confess that I thought myself the last man in this kingdom that should ever have been in danger of being accused for treason, because I know no man that abhors it more, and that would pursue it more vigorously than myself against any that should be guilty of it. Nay, to such a degree is my detestation of that crime that were I sure the dearest child I have were guilty of it I would willingly be his executioner.

My Lords, I know this is not the time for me to enter regularly upon my defence, because I know your Lordships will first order me a copy of my charge and appoint me a time for my vindication, when I doubt not but to do it to the full satisfaction of your Lordships and all the world. In the meantime I will only beg leave to observe to your Lordships that those articles in this charge which can seem to have anything of treason in them have their answer so obvious that there is very little in them which may not be answered by many others as well as myself, and some of them by every man in the kingdom.

The first, which is the assuming regal power, I confess I do not understand, having never in my life done anything of great moment, either at home or relating to foreign matters, for which I have not always had his Majesty's command. And although I am far from having been the most cautious man in taking care of my own security (which perhaps my great innocence hath been the cause of), yet I have not been so wanting of common prudence as in the most material things not to have had his Majesty's orders and directions under his own hand, and particularly for the letters now made use of against me.

The second, I think, doth scarce need my giving any answer to, it being obvious that the army was no more raised by me than by every lord in this House; and whoever is in that station which I hold must certainly be a fool to desire anything which creates a want of money, especially so great an one as the charge of an army must necessarily and immediately produce. And for one part of the article, concerning the Paymaster of the Army, it is in fact otherwise, for security from the Paymaster has been taken in the sum of four hundred thousand pounds.

The third is of the same nature with the first, and comes from the same foundation, which is what a gentleman[1] hath thought fit to produce to the House of Commons. I will not now censure his action. I think it will do enough for itself. I will only say that although I take it for one of the greatest misfortunes which can befall a man to lie under such a charge of the House of Commons, yet I would much sooner choose to be under that unhappiness than under his circumstances.

The fourth article is not only false in every part of it, but it is not possible to believe it true without my being the greatest fool on earth, as well as the blackest villain. For were I capable of such a wickedness, yet the more wicked any man is the more he is carried to his own interest; and is it possible anything under heaven can agree less with my interest than the destruction of this king? Can I possibly hope to be better than I am? And is it not apparent that there is not one man living whose happiness depends so much as mine upon the preservation of his person?

My Lords, I know there is not a man in the world that can in his heart think me guilty of that part of the article, if I should say nothing to it. But besides, I was so far from concealing this hellish plot that it is notoriously known his Majesty sent me the first notice of it, together with forty-three heads of the information, before I knew

[1] Ralph Montagu.

a syllable of it from anybody else. And it hath been owned at the bar of the House of Commons by him from whom only I had the intelligence that he had all the encouragement and dispatch from me that I could give him. Besides, when it was disclosed to the Council Board, he told some of the Clerks of the Council (as he had done me divers times before) that it would have been much better, and more would have been discovered, if it had been longer kept private. Besides this, I had the fortune to be particularly instrumental in seizing Mr. Coleman's papers, without which care there had not one of them appeared, and consequently the best and most material evidence which is yet of the plot had been wholly wanting. And certainly this is the first time that any man was accused to be the concealer of that plot whereof he hath been a principal means of procuring the discovery.

For that part of the article that says I am popishly affected, I thank God that the contrary is so known to all the world that even some of those that voted against me did own their knowledge of the falsity of that allegation; and I hope I have through my whole life given so good testimony of my religion, both in my own family and by my services to the Church (whenever it hath lain in my power), that I shall not need much vindication in that particular. And I hope your Lordships will forgive me my weakness in telling you that I have a younger son in the House of Commons whom I shall love the better as long as I live for moving to have that part of the article to stand against me, that by that pattern it might appear with what sort of zeal the whole hath been carried to my prejudice.

The fifth article will, upon examination, appear to be as ill grounded as any of the rest; and I am sorry I am able to give one reason, which is that I have known no treasure in my time to waste, having entered upon an empty treasury and never seen one farthing given to his Majesty (in almost six years) that hath not been appropriated to particular uses, and strictly so applied by me, as the Acts have directed. And there hath not been one of those aids which, instead of giving the king money, hath not cost him more out of his own purse to the same uses, as doth appear by the larger dimensions of the new ships, and so in other things; insomuch that I take upon me the vanity to say that by the payments I have made to the navy and seamen beyond former times, the paying off the greatest part of the debt which was stopped in the Exchequer before my time, by my own punctuality in the course of payments, and by other things which I am able to shew, I doubt not but to appear meritorious instead of being criminal upon that article.

As to the sixth article, which mentions my great gettings, I cannot deny but that I serve a master whose goodness and bounty hath been a great deal more to me than I have deserved, and to whom I can never pay gratitude enough by all the services of my life. But when the particulars of those gettings shall appear it will be found very contrary to what is suggested abroad, and that in near six years time in this great place I have not got half that which many others have got in lesser places in half that time. And from the examination of this, which I desire may be seen, there will arise matter to accuse my prudence in not having done for my family what justly I might, but nothing to arraign either my honour, my conscience or my faithful service to the Crown.

My Lords, if my obedience to the king shall not be my crime, I think nothing else will stick upon me from these articles, for my own heart flatters me to believe that I have done nothing but as a true Protestant and a faithful servant both to my king and country. Nay, I am as confident as that now I speak, that had I either been a papist or friend to the French, I had not been now accused, for I have reason to believe that the principal informer of the House of Commons hath been assisted by French advice to this accusation; and if the gentleman were as just to produce all he knows for me as he hath been malicious to shew what may be liable to misconstruction against me, or rather against the king (as indeed it is), no man could vindicate me more than himself, under whose hand I have to shew how great an enemy to France I am thought, how much I might have had to have been otherwise, and what he himself might have had for getting me to take it.

But I do not wonder this gentleman will do me no right, when he does not think fit to do it to his Majesty (upon whom chiefly this matter must reflect), although he knows, as will appear under his hand, that the greatest invitations to his Majesty for having money from France have been made by himself; that if his Majesty would have been tempted for money he might have sold towns for as much as if they had been his own, and the money have been conveyed as privately as he pleased; that his Majesty might have made matches with France, if he would have consented to give them towns; and yet that the king hath always scorned to yield the meanest village that was not agreed to by the Spaniard and Hollander. That gentleman hath often pretended how much his own interest in France was diminished, only by being thought my friend. And besides divers other instances I have under his hand to shew the malice of the French Court against me, I sent two of his letters to the House of Commons, which shew how Monsieur Ruvigny was sent hither on purpose to ruin me, which I am well assured at this time they would rather see than of any one man in England.

Besides what that gentleman could say of this kind (if he pleased), I hope his Majesty will give me leave (in my defence) to say in his presence, and in the hearing of divers lords with whom I have the honour to sit in the Committee of Foreign Affairs, that which were it not true his Majesty must think me the impudentest and worst of men to affirm before him, that ever since I had the honour to serve his Majesty to this day I have delivered it as my constant opinion that France was the worst interest his Majesty could embrace, and that they were the nation in the world from whom I did believe he ought to apprehend the greatest danger, and who have both his person and government under the last degree of contempt, for which reason alone (were there no other) I would never advise his Majesty to trust to their friendship.

My Lords, it is my greatest happiness that your Lordships are my judges, whose wisdom and justice are so great that you will both discern the truth of the evidence when it shall come before you, and in the meantime distinguish truly what the crimes are (if they could be proved) and not what they are called. For this reason this House hath wisely provided to have the special matter before them, to the end they may be satisfied whether the charge have its right denomination, for otherwise it were to no purpose to desire special matter, unless it were to see whether the special matter alleged be what it is called. As for example, if a man were accused of having traitorously passed the river in a pair of oars, this is special matter, and styled treason by inserting the word 'traitorously'; yet your Lordships would not therefore proceed as taking it for treason. So in this case I beg, for all your Lordships' sakes as well as my own, that you will please to use that caution which will be necessary for all your Lordships' safety and seats in this House. For I beseech your Lordships to consider whither such a precedent may go hereafter. What the House of Commons may do in such a case there is no question but his Majesty may do the same by his attorney; and what either of them may do against one lord they may do against more (and we have seen it done in our days against all the bishops at once). Were it not very precariously, then, that your Lordships hold your seats here, when by either of these ways as many of your Lordships as for a time it might be convenient to remove should be at the mercy of having a thing called treason whether it be so or no.

Truly, my Lords, I have reason to believe that in the House of Commons the matter of my charge (if proved) was not thought to amount to treason, either by statute or common law; and I hope your Lordships have too sad an example in your memory ever to assist the making of treason by accumulation. I should therefore not only wrong my own innocence but the right of the peers, to submit to answer matters of misdemeanour as a criminal in treason.

My Lords, I wonder not at the malicious prosecution of those who would have me taken for what they truly are. For I am well assured that neither the French take me to be of their interest nor the papists to be of their religion. But I am troubled to fall under so severe a censure of the House of Commons, although I cannot blame them, but my accusers who have so wrongfully informed them.

My Lords, I will conclude with this comfort, that I do not in the least apprehend the matter of my charge under the security of your Lordships' justice, and will therefore trouble your Lordships no longer at this time but only to pray your directions whether I am to withdraw, which I shall readily obey.

76. Speech on Danby's impeachment attributed to the earl of Carnarvon, 1678

(*Parliamentary History*, IV, p. 1073)

My Lords, I understand but little of Latin, but a good deal of English, and not a little of the English history, from which I have learnt the mischiefs of such kind of prosecutions as these, and the ill fate of the prosecutors. I could bring many instances, and those very ancient; but, my Lords, I shall go no farther back than the latter end of Queen Elizabeth's reign, at which time the earl of Essex was run down by Sir Walter Ralegh. My Lord Bacon, he ran down Sir Walter Ralegh, and your Lordships know what became of my Lord Bacon. The duke of Buckingham, he ran down my Lord Bacon, and your Lordships know what happened to the duke of Buckingham. Sir Thomas Wentworth, afterwards earl of Strafford, ran down the duke of Buckingham, and you all know what became of him. Sir Harry Vane, he ran down the earl of

Strafford, and your Lordships know what became of Sir Harry Vane. Chancellor Hyde, he ran down Sir Harry Vane, and your Lordships know what became of the Chancellor. Sir Thomas Osborne, now earl of Danby, ran down Chancellor Hyde, but what will become of the earl of Danby your Lordships best can tell. But let me see that man that dare run the earl of Danby down, and we shall soon see what will become of him.

77. Act attainting Sir John Fenwick, 1697
(*Statutes of the Realm*, VII, p. 165)

AN ACT TO ATTAINT SIR JOHN FENWICK, BARONET, OF HIGH TREASON

(*8 & 9 Gul. III, cap. 4*)

Whereas Sir John Fenwick, baronet, was upon the oaths of George Porter, esquire, and Cardell Goodman, gentleman, at the sessions of oyer and terminer held for the city of London on the eight and twentieth day of May one thousand six hundred ninety-six, indicted of high treason in compassing and imagining the death and destruction of his Majesty, and adhering to his Majesty's enemies by consulting and agreeing with several persons (whereof some have been already attainted, and others not yet brought to their trial for the said treasons) at several meetings to send Robert Charnock, since attainted and executed for high treason in conspiring to assassinate his Majesty's sacred person (whom God long preserve), to the late King James in France to incite and encourage the French king to invade this kingdom with an armed force by promising to join with and assist him with men and arms upon such invasion, of which treasons the said Sir John Fenwick is guilty; and whereas the said Sir John Fenwick did obtain his Majesty's favour to have his trial delayed from time to time upon his repeated promises of making an ingenious and full confession of his knowledge of any design or conspiracy against his Majesty's person or government, and of the persons therein concerned; and whereas he has so far abused his Majesty's great mercy and indulgence therein, that instead of making such confession he hath contrived and framed false and scandalous papers as his informations, reflecting on the fidelity of several noble peers, divers members of the House of Commons and others only by hearsay, and contriving thereby to undermine the government and create jealousies between the king and his subjects, and to stifle the real conspiracy; and whereas Cardell Goodman, one of the witnesses against the said Sir John Fenwick to prove the said treason, lately and since the several times appointed for the trial of the said Sir John Fenwick, at one of which times the said Sir John Fenwick had been accordingly tried had it not been for the expectation of the said discoveries so often promised by him, is withdrawn, so that the said Cardell Goodman cannot be had to give evidence upon any trial, be it enacted . . . that the said Sir John Fenwick be and is hereby convicted and attainted of high treason, and shall suffer the pains of death and incur all forfeitures as a person attainted of high treason.

78. Articles of impeachment against Henry Sacheverell, 1710

(*Journals of the House of Commons*, XVI, pp. 257–258)

ARTICLES EXHIBITED BY THE KNIGHTS, CITIZENS,
AND BURGESSES IN PARLIAMENT ASSEMBLED, IN THE NAME OF
THEMSELVES AND OF ALL THE COMMONS OF GREAT BRITAIN,
AGAINST HENRY SACHEVERELL, DOCTOR IN DIVINITY,
IN MAINTENANCE OF THEIR IMPEACHMENT AGAINST HIM
FOR HIGH CRIMES AND MISDEMEANOURS

Whereas his late Majesty King William the Third, then prince of Orange, did with an armed force undertake a glorious enterprise for delivering this kingdom from popery and arbitrary power, and divers subjects of this realm, well affected to their country, joined with and assisted his late Majesty in the said enterprise, and it having pleased Almighty God to crown the same with success, the late happy revolution did take effect and was established: and whereas the said glorious enterprise is approved by several Acts of Parliament, and amongst others by an Act made in the first year of the reign of King William and Queen Mary, entituled, *An Act declaring the rights and liberties of the subject and settling the succession of the crown*,[1] and also by one other Act made in the same year, entituled, *An Act for preventing vexatious suits against such as acted in order to the bringing in their Majesties or for their service*,[2] and also by one other Act made in the same year, entituled, *An Act for appropriating certain duties for paying the States General of the United Provinces their charges for his Majesty's expedition into this kingdom and for other uses*;[3] and the actings of the said well affected subjects in aid and pursuance of the said enterprise are also declared to have been necessary, and that the same ought to be justified: and whereas the happy and blessed consequences of the said revolution are the enjoyment of the light of God's true religion established among us, and of the laws and liberties of the kingdom; the uniting her Majesty's Protestant subjects in interest and affection by a legal indulgence or toleration granted to dissenters; the preservation of her Majesty's sacred person; the many and continual benefits arising from her Majesty's wise and glorious administration; and the prospect of happiness to future ages by the settlement of the succession of the crown in the Protestant line, and the union of the two kingdoms: and whereas the Lords Spiritual and Temporal and Commons in Parliament assembled did by their address of the seventeenth of December, in the year of our Lord 1705, lay before her Majesty the following vote or resolution, viz., that the Church of England as by law established, which was rescued from the extremest danger by King William the Third of glorious memory, is now by God's blessing, under the happy reign of her Majesty, in a most safe and flourishing condition, and that whoever goes about to suggest and insinuate that the Church is in danger under her Majesty's administration is an enemy to the queen, the Church and the kingdom; and by their said address did humbly beseech her Majesty to take effectual measures for making the said vote or resolution public, and also for punishing the authors and spreaders of such seditious and scandalous

---

[1] No. 40.   [2] 1 Gul. & Mar., sess. 2, cap. 8.   [3] 1 Gul. & Mar., cap. 28.

reports; and on the 20th day of the same December her Majesty was pleased to issue her royal proclamation accordingly: yet nevertheless the said Henry Sacheverell preached a sermon at the assizes held at Derby, August the 15th in the year of our Lord 1709, and afterwards published the same in print, with a dedication thereof; and the said Henry Sacheverell also preached a sermon at the cathedral church of Saint Paul before the lord mayor, aldermen and citizens of London, on the fifth day of November last, being the anniversary thanksgiving to Almighty God for the deliverance from the gunpowder treason, and for beginning the late happy revolution by giving his late Majesty a safe arrival here, and for completing the same by making all opposition fall before him till he became our king and governor; which said sermon he, the said Henry Sacheverell, afterwards likewise published in print, with a dedication thereof to Sir Samuel Garrard, baronet, lord mayor of the city of London, and with a wicked, malicious and seditious intention to undermine and subvert her Majesty's government and the Protestant succession as by law established, to defame her Majesty's administration, to asperse the memory of his late Majesty, to traduce and condemn the late happy revolution, to contradict and arraign the resolutions of both Houses of Parliament, to create jealousies and divisions among her Majesty's subjects, and to incite them to sedition and rebellion.

First. He, the said Henry Sacheverell, in his said sermon preached at Saint Paul's, doth suggest and maintain that the necessary means used to bring about the said happy revolution were odious and unjustifiable, that his late Majesty in his declaration disclaimed the least imputation of resistance, and that to impute resistance to the said revolution is to cast black and odious colours upon his late Majesty and the said revolution.

Secondly. He, the said Henry Sacheverell, in his said sermon preached at Saint Paul's, doth suggest and maintain that the aforesaid toleration granted by law is unreasonable, and the allowance of it unwarrantable; and asserts that he is a false brother with relation to God, religion or the Church who defends toleration and liberty of conscience. . . .

Thirdly. He, the said Henry Sacheverell, in his said sermon preached at Saint Paul's, doth falsely and seditiously suggest and assert that the Church of England is in a condition of great peril and adversity under her Majesty's administration, and in order to arraign and blacken the said vote or resolution of both Houses of Parliament, approved by her Majesty as aforesaid, he, in opposition thereto, doth suggest the Church to be in danger, and as a parallel mentions a vote that the person of King Charles the First was voted to be out of danger at the same time that his murderers were conspiring his death, thereby wickedly and maliciously insinuating that the members of both Houses who passed the said vote were then conspiring the ruin of the Church.

Fourthly. He, the said Henry Sacheverell, in his said sermons and books, doth falsely and maliciously suggest that her Majesty's administration, both in ecclesiastical and civil affairs, tends to the destruction of the constitution, and that there are men of characters and stations in Church and State who are false brethren, and do themselves weaken, undermine and betray, and do encourage and put it in the power of others,

who are professed enemies, to overturn and destroy, the constitution and establishment; . . . and that his said malicious and seditious suggestions may make the stronger
impression upon the minds of her Majesty's subjects, he, the said Henry Sacheverell,
doth wickedly wrest and pervert divers texts and passages of Holy Scripture.

All which crimes and misdemeanours the Commons are ready to prove, not only
by the general scope of the same sermons or books, but likewise by several clauses,
sentences and expressions in the said sermons or books contained; and that he, the
said Henry Sacheverell, by preaching the sermons and publishing the books aforesaid,
did abuse his holy function, and hath most grievously offended against the peace of
her Majesty, her crown and dignity, the rights and liberties of the subject, the laws
and statutes of this kingdom, and the prosperity and good government of the same.
And the said Commons by protestation, saving to themselves the liberty of exhibiting
at any time hereafter any other article or impeachment against the said Henry
Sacheverell, and also of replying to his answers or any of them, and of offering proofs
of all the premises or any of them, or of any other article or impeachment that shall be
exhibited by them, as the case, according to the course of Parliament, shall require, do
pray that he, the said Henry Sacheverell, may be put to answer to all and every the
premises, and that such proceeding, examination, trial, judgment and exemplary
punishment may be thereupon had and executed as is agreeable to law and justice.

E. COMPOSITION OF THE HOUSES

(a) HOUSE OF LORDS

79. Act restoring the temporal authority of ecclesiastical persons, 1661

(Statutes of the Realm, v, p. 306)

AN ACT FOR REPEAL OF AN ACT OF PARLIAMENT ENTITULED,
*AN ACT FOR DISENABLING ALL PERSONS IN HOLY ORDERS TO EXERCISE
ANY TEMPORAL JURISDICTION OR AUTHORITY*

(13 Car. II, stat. I, cap. 2)

Whereas at the Parliament begun at Westminster the third day of November in the sixteenth year of the reign of our late Sovereign Lord King Charles of blessed memory since deceased, an Act of Parliament was made entituled, *An Act for disenabling all persons in Holy Orders to exercise any temporal jurisdiction or authority*,[1] which Act hath made several alterations prejudicial to the constitution and ancient rights of Parliament and contrary to the laws of this land, and is by experience found otherwise inconvenient, be it enacted . . . that the said Act . . . and every clause, matter and thing therein contained, shall be and is hereby from henceforth repealed, annulled and made void to all intents and purposes whatsoever.

80. Protest against the decision of the Lords not to allow the duke of Hamilton to take his seat, 1711

(J. E. T. Rogers, Protests of the Lords, I, pp. 208–209)

20 December 1711

1st. Because, as we apprehend, by this resolution the prerogative of the Crown in granting patents of honour, with all privileges depending thereon, to the peers of Great Britain who were peers of Scotland at the time of the union, as well as the right of the duke of Brandon to sit and vote in Parliament, are taken away; and this prerogative of the Crown and right of the duke depending upon the construction of an Act of Parliament, though counsel, by order of the House, were heard at the bar, and all the judges were ordered to attend at the same time, yet the opinion of the judges was not permitted to be asked touching the construction of the said Act of Parliament.

2ndly. Because the prerogative of the Crown, as we conceive, in granting patents of honour, with the privileges depending thereon, ought not, on the construction of any Act of Parliament, to be taken away, unless there be plain and express words to that purpose in the said Act; and we conceive there are no such plain and express words for that purpose in the Act of Union.

3rdly. Because by this resolution all the peers of Great Britain who were peers of Scotland at the time of the union are supposed to be incapable of receiving any patent of honour from the Crown, by virtue whereof they may be entitled to the privileges

[1] 17 Car. I, cap. 27.

of sitting and voting in Parliament and sitting on the trial of peers; which, we conceive, is repugnant to the fourth article of the Act of Union, which declares the privileges and advantages which do or may belong to the subjects of either kingdom, except where it is otherwise expressly agreed in those articles, in which, we apprehend, there is no such provision.

4thly. Because the duke of Queensberry, in all respects in the same case as the duke of Hamilton, was introduced, sat and voted in this House in matters of the highest importance, in two several Parliaments as duke of Dover, by virtue of a patent passed since the union; and in consequence of such sitting and voting his vote in the election of peers of Scotland was rejected, and as a further consequence thereof the marquis of Lothian was removed from his seat in this House, which he had an undeniable title to if the duke of Queensberry's patent as duke of Dover had not given him a title to sit and vote in this House.

5thly. Because by this resolution the peers of Scotland are reduced to a worse condition in some respects than the meanest or most criminal of subjects.

6thly. Because we conceive this resolution may be construed to be a violation of the treaty between the two nations.

81. Gilbert Burnet's account of the special creation of twelve peers, 1712
(*History of His Own Time*, ed. 1833, VI, pp. 93–96)

A few days after this the queen wrote him[1] a letter complaining of the ill treatment she received from him, and discharged him of all his employments. This was thought very extraordinary after such long and eminent services. Such accidents, when they happen, show the instability of all human things. This was indeed so little expected that those who looked for precedents could find none since the disgrace of Belisarius in Justinian's time. The only thing pretended to excuse it was his being considered as the head of those who opposed the peace, on which the Court seemed to set their hearts.

But they, finding the majority of the House of Lords could not be brought to favour their designs, resolved to make an experiment that none of our princes had ventured on in former times. A resolution was taken up very suddenly of making twelve peers all at once. Three of these were called up by writ, being eldest sons of peers, and nine more were created by patent. Sir Miles Wharton, to whom it was offered, refused it. He thought it looked like the serving a turn, and that whereas peers were wont to be made for services they had done he would be made for services to be done by him. So he excused himself, and the favourite's husband, Mr. Masham, was put in his room. And whereas formerly Jeffreys had the vanity to be made a peer while he was Chief Justice, which had not been practised for some ages, yet the precedent set by him was followed, and Trevor, Chief Justice of the Common Pleas, was now advanced to be a peer. This was looked upon as an undoubted part of the prerogative, so there was no ground in law to oppose the receiving the new lords into the House; nor was it possible to raise in the ancient peers a sense of the indignity that

[1] Duke of Marlborough.

was now put upon their House, since the Court did by this openly declare that they were to be kept in absolute submission and obedience.

When the second of January[1] came they were all introduced into the House of Lords without any opposition; and when that was over, the Lord Keeper delivered a message from the queen commanding them to adjourn forthwith to the fourteenth, for by that time her Majesty would lay matters of great importance before the two Houses. Upon this a great debate arose. It was said that the queen could not send a message to any one House to adjourn, when the like message was not sent to both Houses. The pleasure of the prince in convening, dissolving, proroguing or ordering the adjournment of Parliaments was always directed to both Houses, but never to any one House without the same intimation was made at the same time to the other. The consequence of this, if allowed, might be the ordering one House to adjourn while the other was left to sit still, and this might end in a total disjointing of the constitution. The vote was carried for adjourning by the weight of the twelve new peers. It is true the odds in the books is thirteen, but that was because one of the peers, who had a proxy, without reflecting on it, went away when the proxies were called for.

(b) HOUSE OF COMMONS

82. Act enfranchising Durham, 1673
(*Statutes of the Realm*, v, p. 795)

AN ACT TO ENABLE THE COUNTY PALATINE OF DURHAM
TO SEND KNIGHTS AND BURGESSES
TO SERVE IN PARLIAMENT

(*25 Car. II, cap. 9*)

Whereas the inhabitants of the county palatine of Durham have not hitherto had the liberty and privilege of electing and sending any knights and burgesses to the high court of Parliament, although the inhabitants of the said county palatine are liable to all payments, rates and subsidies granted by Parliament equally with the inhabitants of other counties, cities and boroughs in this kingdom who have their knights and burgesses in the Parliament, ... wherefore may it please your Majesty that it may be enacted, and be it enacted ... that from time to time and at all times from and after the end of this present session of Parliament the said county palatine of Durham may have two knights for the same county, and the city of Durham two citizens to be burgesses for the same city, for ever hereafter to serve in the high court of Parliament, to be elected and chosen by virtue of your Majesty's writ to be awarded by the Lord Chancellor or Lord Keeper of the Great Seal of England for the time being in that behalf to the lord bishop of Durham or his temporal chancellor of the said county of Durham, and a precept to be thereupon grounded and made by the lord bishop of Durham or his temporal chancellor for the time being to the sheriff of the said county for the time being, and the same election from time to time be made in manner and

[1] 1711/12.

form following, that is to say, the elections of the knights to serve for the said county palatine from time to time hereafter to be made by the greater number of freeholders of the said county palatine of Durham which from time to time shall be present at such elections, accordingly as is used in other counties in this your Majesty's kingdom, and that the election of the said burgesses from time to time to serve in the high court of Parliament for the city of Durham to be made from time to time by the major part of the mayor, aldermen and freemen of the said city of Durham which from time to time shall be present at such elections, which said knights and burgesses and every of them so elected and chosen shall be returned by the said sheriff into the chancery of England in due form and upon the like pains as be ordained for the sheriff or sheriffs of any other county of this kingdom to make his or their returns in the like cases. . . .

83. Earl of Shaftesbury's observations on elections, c. 1680
(Somers Tracts, ed. 1809–1815, VIII, pp. 396–403)

SOME OBSERVATIONS
CONCERNING THE REGULATING OF ELECTIONS FOR PARLIAMENT,
FOUND AMONG THE EARL OF SHAFTESBURY'S PAPERS
AFTER HIS DEATH,
AND NOW RECOMMENDED TO THE CONSIDERATION
OF THIS PRESENT PARLIAMENT, 1689

The Parliament of England is that supreme and absolute power which gives life and motion to the English government. It directs and actuates all its various procedures, is the parent of our peace, defender of our faith and foundation of our properties; and as the constitution of this great spring and *primum mobile* of affairs is in strength and beauty, so will also all acts and performances which are derived from it bear a suitable proportion and similitude. . . . It is from the fruit of this great council that we must expect our nutriment, and from its branches our protection. I hope therefore it may not seem over-officious if, with the skilful gardener, I do open and expose the roots of this great tree of the commonwealth, with an intent that every branch and fibre may with the greater ease and conveniency be so trimmed and laid that no defects or redundancies may continue, but that every individual of this great body may happily conspire to produce that peace and tranquillity in the nation which may be expected from their councils and a well-constituted government.

It seems then reasonable to believe that the privilege of sending representatives to Parliament (though grounded upon a natural and fundamental right in the people) was at first immediately derived from the king, for that, where histories and records begin to transmit memorials to succeeding ages, we find him sending his writs directed to such persons, towns or vills, which he thought most considerable within the kingdom, by virtue of which writs elections were accordingly made and representatives returned to Parliament. That the king's prerogative does still extend to grant this franchise to such other towns or villages as he shall think fit I cannot affirm, because some learned in the law assure us it cannot legally be done but by Act of Parliament.

But others are again of a contrary opinion, as was adjudged in the case of Dungannon and Newark. It is certain that parliamentary matters were never settled otherwise than by Act of Parliament, as appears by several statutes in such cases made; and we also find the privilege of sending members to Parliament given to several places by Act of Parliament, which had been unnecessary could the king alone have granted it by any other method. It is, moreover, a thing of very dangerous consequence to have such a power lodged in the king alone, for then he might thereby enfranchise what number of vills he pleases, and by the same power place the election of their representatives in a select number, such as he should always have the power to direct and appoint, which would be in effect to choose his own Parliament, and thereby to make or repeal what laws he pleases. Wherefore I conceive this point ought now to be settled so as for the future to obviate all such inconveniences which might otherwise ensue.

Another thing which also requires the care of this great council is to limit and restrain the exorbitancies of a *quo warranto*, so that the electing boroughs may have their privileges and immunities secured from the judgment of a corrupt judge, who derives his being and holds his judicial breath only *ad voluntatem domini*. If this grievance be not obviated by some good law, a king may as well destroy all the old boroughs as erect new ones, to the inevitable overthrow of our laws and government.

In the next place, I conceive it may become the prudence of this Parliament (from which we may expect the foundations of our happiness will be so laid as to become impregnable against all the future assaults of an invading tyranny) to look into the constitutions and customs of such boroughs which have right to elect, and which in several particulars seem to require a touch of the supreme authority to set them right. The first inconvenience they labour under is the variety of their respective titles, some claiming to elect by prescription, others by grant; some again by a select number, others by the populacy; some by the magistrate and burgesses, others by the magistrate, burgesses and freemen, others again by the magistrate, burgesses, freemen and commonalty; and some also in respect of their ancient borough houses only, the rest of the town, which is the much more considerable part, being excluded. The grievance which grows from this difference of title in several boroughs is often ambiguity and uncertainty of title in the same borough, for sometimes the select number contends with the community, one borough house with another, &c. And from hence it is that we have usually so many petitioners in each Parliament, the magistrate not knowing which of right ought to be returned. Nor can a committee of elections ever settle their respective titles by a final determinative judgment, for we find it often giving an opinion upon one and the same title, and in the same borough, differently, as favour and power can make the stronger interest. All this may be remedied by an Act, which should give one and the same new title to all the electing boroughs in England and Wales, by which alone they should all for the future claim to send members to Parliament. . . .

The design of choosing the members of Parliament by the people was that no laws should be made, no moneys raised, nor any course pursued by those who sit at the helm, but with the steerage and direction of the people by their representatives. Now by all the laws and rules of representation no town, city or body of people can be represented without a vote in the choice of their representative. That the Parliament, as now constituted, is no equal representative of the people is notorious, in that several boroughs so inconsiderable that they contain not above three or four houses send each of them two representatives to Parliament, whilst others which contain an hundred times their number of houses, people, trade and wealth have no representative at all in the management of public affairs. So also the county of Cornwall sends no less than forty-three members to Parliament, whilst the city and whole county of Chester sends but four, and the twelve counties of Wales but twenty-four amongst them all.

From this inequality of representation it follows that Acts are often made which redound to the prejudice of the whole body of the people, merely to advance the gain and advantage of some particular places, as was that which prohibited the importation of Irish cattle, being carried principally by the supernumerary votes of some counties which have more electing boroughs than upon a just and equal dividend do fall to their share; and these being generally of a dry and barren soil are thereby chiefly adapted to the breeding of cattle, which benefit would have been diminished by an inlet of beasts from Ireland. This inconvenience may be easily removed by depriving towns of less note of this franchise, and bestowing it upon others of greater consideration in the same or in other counties which most want it, as do those of Cambridge, Bedford, Hertford, Huntingdon, &c.

Where the electing right is committed to a select number, I think it were desirable that the electors should be chosen annually, and not be tenants for life in their electorate. This would in a great degree prevent pre-engagements and corruption, which often happens where a power by long continuance in one person is apt to stagnate and putrify. The great number of electors in popular boroughs, and in choosing knights of the shire, requires to be regulated and limited, and the power of election to be fixed in the optimacy only. My reasons for this are that amongst the electing crowd the majority is generally of a mean and abject fortune in the world, and thereby subject not only to disorders and quarrels, but to be misguided also by their ignorance and total want of that discerning faculty which electors in such weighty concerns ought to have. They are, moreover, under the temptation of being corrupted and seduced by the inveiglements of a little money or a pot of ale, whilst those whose circumstances are more enlarged have their thoughts so likewise, being thereby raised beyond such low allurements, and rendered more careful how, and into whose hands, they dispose of this great trust, the breach whereof might at once rob and deprive them of that their substance, which has been the acquisition, perhaps, of some ages.

It was for those and several other reasons mentioned in the preamble that by the statute of 8 Hen. VI, cap. 7, it was enacted that no knight of the shire should be chosen by any who had not a freehold of the clear yearly value of 40s. per annum, which was then as much in value as 40l. per annum is now, or has been since the finding out of the American treasure and the enlargement of our trade. And I think it but reasonable that as the value of money falls, so the wealth of the electors should rise, and that electing votes in the county should again be limited to such only who now have lands and tenements to that value which 40s. per annum bore in those times when this Act was made. . . .

As the persons electing ought to be men of substance, so in a proportioned degree ought also the members elected. It is not safe to make over the estates of the people in trust to men who have none of their own, lest their domestic indigencies, in conjunction with a foreign temptation, should warp them to a contrary interest, which in former Parliaments we have sometimes felt to our sorrow. Wealth and substance will also give a lustre and reputation to our great council, and a security to the people, for their estates are then pawned and so many pledges for their good behaviour, becoming thereby equal sharers themselves in the benefit or disadvantage which shall result from their own acts and counsels.

Thus a good estate may be a good security to engage faith and honesty, but he who sits at the helm of government ought not only to be a graduate in fortune but in prudence and experience also. To me it seems extremely irregular to see the unfledged youth make his first advances into the world in the quality of a burgess for Parliament, chosen upon no other account but because it was his fortune, by his father's early death, to become the landlord of a neighbouring borough, or is perhaps its best customer, deriving from thence the necessaries of a numerous family. Forty years (whereof twenty-five are generally spent in childhood and vanity) seem to be few enough to entitle anyone to the grandeur and gravity of an English senator; and why so many who seem by their greenness to be as yet but a novelty to the world should be admitted to a place in this great council, whilst those of greater age, wisdom and experience must be excluded, I do not understand.

By the 1 Hen. V, cap. 1, it is enacted that every knight of the shire should be chosen out of such who are resident in the county, and every citizen and burgess from amongst the citizens and burgesses of the cities and boroughs electing. How far this Act ought to be observed will be worth consideration, for a confinement in this case seems to be an abridgement of a free choice, and it often happens that men of the greatest knowledge and experience in the affairs of the kingdom have their abode principally in the metropolis, especially such of the long robe, who by their profession are obliged to it. But the non-observance of this Act on the other side has been often the occasion that courtiers have bolted into country boroughs, and by the strength of their purse and liberal baits have so seduced these poor rural animals as to obtain an election from them, though to the ruin and overthrow of their own laws and liberties. The choosing of such men to serve in Parliament might probably be obviated by an Act prohibiting the expense of any money, by treats or otherwise, in order to be elected, it being only to these indirect methods that such persons usually owe their success.

But when all is done it will be found difficult (though with the greatest art) to bring an old, irregular structure into a convenient uniformity, otherwise than by razing it to the ground and erecting a new pile by some better contrived design. . . . A true and perfect model to build by is what I dare not pretend to give, yet that which follows may afford some hints and assistance to a better fancy and judgment.

In respect, then, that every individual person in the nation has a natural right to vote in this great council, but, this being impracticable, they are forced to do it by proxy, that is by devolving this right upon certain common representatives indifferently chosen for certain select numbers and communities of men, in which the whole body of the people is or ought to be comprehended; and whereas every paterfamilias or housekeeper is a natural prince, and is invested with an absolute power over his family, and has by necessary consequence the votes of all his family, man, woman and child, included in his; let then the sheriff's precepts be directed to every parish within his county, which, the next Sunday following the receipt thereof, may be publicly read after the forenoon sermon in church, thereby giving notice to all the housekeepers in the parish to meet at a convenient place and certain hour the day following, in order to choose an elector for the county. Let also the churchwardens of each parish prepare a list of eight or ten of the most eminent persons for wealth, gravity and wisdom in their parish, this list to be brought the next day to the place of election, to this purpose, that every housekeeper do, by a dot with a pen, adjoined to the person's name whom he inclines to elect, declare his choice, and that by the plurality of dots the elector be returned by the churchwardens to the sheriff.

This done in each parish, let the sheriff prepare a list in the same manner of the names of all the gentry in the county who are each worth in lands and movables at least 10,000*l.*, all debts paid, and not under forty years of age; which being in readiness, let all the representatives of parishes, chosen as aforesaid, repair to the county town the very next day after the parish election is over, and there proceed to elect out of the sheriff's list seven, nine or eleven members to serve in Parliament, or so many as upon a just dividend shall be thought expedient to complete the number of members which are to act in this great council. Before the electors proceed to choose for the county it might probably be convenient to administer an oath to this purpose, that their vote is no way pre-engaged, and that they will choose, without favour or affection, such members as in their conscience they do believe most fit to serve in Parliament; and that to the members elected, upon their admission to the House, this oath, together with the others in use, be administered, viz., that they are worth 10,000*l.*, all their debts paid, and that directly or indirectly they did not expend any money or gratuity whatsoever in order to their election; and that they neither have nor will receive any gratuity whatsoever upon the account of their vote in Parliament; but that they will, in all matters that shall come before them, act uprightly according to their conscience and understanding, without any private design, favour or affection to any.

That to prevent the inconveniences of fear and favour in electing the method be such that none may know on whom the electors' votes were conferred, and it may be thus performed. Suppose a room with two opposite doors, and a table in the middle on which the list shall be spread. All the electors being at one door, let them go in one by one, each writing down his dots and going out of the room at the other door before another comes in; or if this may prove tedious, it is only placing more tables in the room, with every one a list on it, and so many may then be admitted in at once as there are lists, which will make greater dispatch, and yet no discovery, in that every list is upon a separate table.

To prevent also all fraud and indirect practice, it will be convenient that the officers concerned in the elections, both in parishes and in the county, be upon their oaths. It is also fit that a limited allowance be made for the expense of the day, which is to be in parishes at the parish charge, and in the county town at the charge of the county. If any controversy arise about elections, either in the parishes or counties (which in this method can scarcely be supposed), it may be decided by the votes of the remaining persons upon the list, who pretend to no election. If several persons happen to have an equal number of votes it shall be determined by lot. If any person from any part of England shall send his name to any particular county, to be inserted in their list as a person qualified to serve in Parliament, it may be done, but none to stand candidate in more than one list at a time, lest he should be chosen in both counties and so occasion the trouble of a new election. That the same list of candidates shall continue till the dissolution of the Parliament, if it sits not above three years, and upon the intermediate death or removal of any of the members for the county then he who had the next majority of votes upon the list to succeed in his place, without further trouble or charge of election.

By this method the Parliament will be a perfect representative of the whole body of the people, and also of every numerical person in the kingdom. Here can be no partial (and consequently prejudicial) Acts made by separate interests and factions. None will sit in this great council but men of gravity, wisdom, integrity and substance. No pensionary members; no unfair elections; no foul returns; no petitioners kept in attendance till a dissolution; no *quo warrantos* to destroy the natural, fundamental rights of the people; no room for corruption, bribery and debauchery, either in the electors or the members elected; no patrimonies wasted in the extravagancies of an election; no bankrupts shrouding themselves under the shelter of a parliamentary privilege; no unruly rabbles, tumults, factions and disorders in election amongst the commonalty; no heats and animosities amongst the gentry, often caused by their violent competitions; but all will be managed with that evenness, justice and temper, that nothing can more effectually conduce to the securing of our liberties and properties, the grandeur of our government, and the honour of our nation, than such an establishment.

84. Sir William Petty's criticisms of the distribution of seats, c. 1685
(Petty Papers, ed. Marquis of Lansdowne, I, pp. 7–8)

OF THE HOUSE OF COMMONS

1. This House consists of 513 members, viz., of 91 chosen by freeholders and 422 by 211 corporations.

2. These 513 members have from £500,000 to £800,000 estate, and are men of good estimation with the people.

3. There are about 160,000 freeholders and not 40,000 members of corporations in England, in all under 200,000; whereas there are above 800,000 others who have no vote at all.

4. The elections in 52 shires and 211 corporations are governed by less than 2,000 active men.

5. The 160,000 freeholders who choose but 91 members are worth about 160 millions, supposing the lands of England to be worth 8 millions per annum and 20 years purchase; whereas the 40,000 choose 422 members, and are not worth 20 millions.

6. There be 10 of the 211 corporations which send but 22 members (viz., London, Westminster, Southwark, York, Newcastle, Exeter, Bristol, Canterbury, Coventry, Chester), which are worth double to the other 201 corporations which send 400 members.

7. The county of Cornwall sends ten times as many members as Cheshire.

8. The number of members bears no kind of proportion to the tax assessed and subsidy lately set upon each county.

9. In some places a set and small number choose; in others an uncertain number of freemen; in others the proprietors of lands within the corporation, &c.

There is nothing more odious and grievous in the dispensation of authorities, or in the levying of taxes, than inequality.

85. Anonymous pamphlet claiming greater representation for London, 1702
(*Somers Tracts*, ed. 1809–1815, XII, pp. 399–416)

The representative of the commons of England at this day consists of 513 persons, under the distinguishment of knights, citizens and burgesses, the barons of the cinque ports being comprehended under the latter head; and the several districts of the kingdom whence these deputies (as in France, Poland, Holland and elsewhere such are and have been called) are sent be obviously as followeth. The 40 shires of England find 80 knights, and the 12 shires of Wales 12, in all 92 knights, elected by the freeholders of the several counties. The cities, boroughs and ports of England are 204, which all send 409 deputies, and the 12 in Wales 12, together making 421, who with the 92 knights make up the roll of that august assembly. Among the boroughs of England Bewdley, Banbury, Abingdon, Monmouth and Higham Ferrers send each but one; London, Oxford and Cambridge, every one four; and the rest all two apiece; in most of which places privileged to elect every housekeeper contributing to the church and poor (as a freeman of England) has a vote, but in some that right of the electors is restrained, and in others enlarged profusely. . . .

For my part, I do not allow myself to debate the alteration of anything hitherto established; but as a sincere lover of his country I think it better becomes to justify and applaud all the parts of that constitution under which we have lived so long the happiest people under heaven. Therefore if any object that the west carries an unreasonable overbalance in this representative, I answer (granting the supposition) there is even a felicity in that error, for those counties have the best of our ports, they are our immediate frontier towards France, and so the dominion of the Channel is their sole barrier; they lie in the line of navigation; the riches of our mines and most important manufactures are on that side. If others object that the landholders are not proportionably represented to the inhabitants of boroughs, I say the practice in the most of the said boroughs, being (for some ages past) to return gentlemen of considerable estates in land, has in some sort transmitted their right to the same interest. And hereby it is we are built on a firm foundation, there being no such caution of good behaviour to the public as a valuable concern in it. . . .

In pursuance of the intended method I am to lay down a scale or standard by which to examine the several proportions of the body represented, in the choice whereof (having no precedent) I hope to be the more easily excused if the rule by which other things are tried be itself not perfect. . . . The method of taxation called a royal aid, which is become more frequent with us of some years past than any other, is what I have fixed upon. . . . The particular Act I have taken of that sort is that which by an assessment of two shillings per pound on all revenues did raise in the year 1700 the sum of 989,965*l*. 19*s*. 6½*d*. from the whole kingdom, by the several proportions hereunder specified, as in the Act more at large appears; which said sum, being subdivided by 513 (the number of the kingdom's representatives), does produce 1930*l*. to be the standard by which every county may be known whether it be over- or underrepresented in Parliament, and by what degrees it is so. Not that I argue the body ought to be represented by such shares without distinction, but, craving leave only to state matter of fact in the form following, I hope not to frame thence any malignant inference, or unworthy of a gentleman.

Of the aforesaid tax	*l.*	*s.*	*d.*	*Sends members*	*Its proportion*
Bedfordshire paid	14,277	7	5¾	4	7½
Berkshire paid	20,527	0	4	9	10½
Buckinghamshire paid	23,830	8	9	14	12¼
Cambridgeshire paid	16,413	1	6	6	8½
Cheshire paid	14,299	12	11¾	4	7½
Cornwall paid	15,987	13	0	44	8¼
Cumberland paid	· 1,856	19	1¼	6	1
Derbyshire paid	12,046	19	10¾	4	6¼
Devonshire paid	41,291	11	8	26	21½
Dorsetshire paid	16,558	3	9¼	20	8½
Durham paid	5,298	17	2¾	4	2¾
Essex paid	45,503	10	10	8	23
Gloucestershire paid	23,761	6	5	8	12
Herefordshire paid	10,204	13	4	8	5½
Hertfordshire paid	21,486	12	8	6	11
Huntingdonshire paid	7,748	12	6	4	4
Kent paid	41,721	14	2	18	21½
Lancashire paid	10,494	17	3¼	14	5½
Leicestershire paid	17,435	19	6¾	4	9
Lincolnshire paid	36,113	5	2	12	19
Middlesex paid	153,877	1	5¼	8	79¼
Monmouth paid	4,906	3	2¾	3	2½

Of the aforesaid tax	l.	s.	d.	Sends members	Its proportion
Norfolk paid	42,330	6	2	12	22
Northamptonshire paid	24,053	13	4½	9	12½
Northumberland paid	7,274	8	8	8	3¾
Nottinghamshire paid	13,638	5	4¾	8	7
Oxfordshire paid	19,591	13	1½	9	10
Rutlandshire paid	2,762	11	11¼	2	2½
Shropshire paid	14,530	9	6¾	12	7½
Somersetshire paid	36,236	11	9	18	19
Southamptonshire paid	27,594	3	0¼	26	14½
Staffordshire paid	13,560	11	7	10	7
Suffolk paid	36,909	12	7	16	19
Surrey paid	33,507	6	9¼	14	17¼
Sussex paid	30,410	0	6½	28	16
Warwickshire paid	16,932	5	4	6	10½
Westmorland paid	1,522	11	10¾	4	0¾
Wiltshire paid	25,836	3	11½	34	13½
Worcestershire paid	16,848	9	3½	9	8¾
Yorkshire paid	45,816	5	8	30	23¾
Wales entire paid	21,968	16	8	24	11½
	989,965	19	6½	513	513

To demonstrate that there is no parallel in the kingdom to the case of Middlesex I have no more to do than to state some proportions in the recited appropriations on the several counties, as followeth:

Of the counties most over-represented	sends	for	Of the counties most under-represented	sends	for
Cumberland	6	1	Middlesex	8	79¼
Westmorland	4	0¾	Essex	8	23
Cornwall	44	8¼	Leicester	4	9
Wiltshire	34	13½	Cheshire	4	7½
Dorset	20	8½	Bedford	4	7½
Lancaster	14	5½	Norfolk	12	22
Those of Wales	24	11½	Hertfordshire	6	11
Northumberland	8	4	Warwick	6	10
Sussex	28	15¾	Lincoln	12	19

As to the first class of this table, the over-represented, I am no ways concerned to reflect upon it, and have drawn it only for illustration of the case in hand. . . . Touching the second part of this table, the under-represented, the most distinguished are three; Leicester, which has about one half of its proportion; Essex, which has about one third;

and Middlesex one tenth; so that the case of the latter is undoubtedly without any parallel. Wherefore if a way of redress may be proposed for her, which can never be drawn into consequence or applicable to any other, and which is at the same time beneficial to the kingdom in general, I hope not to deserve ill from any in offering such a one. But before I descend to the said proposal one thing more ought to be premised, that the county of Middlesex, because of its entire dependence on her two great cities, is to be considered as their suburbs; and therefore I shall not offer anything on behalf of the freehold election (that being conceived not disproportioned to other counties in general), but what I have to say is in behalf of London and Westminster, abstractedly taken.

Considering the promise to make no use of my standard of proportions which will not hold good by any other whatsoever, and that henceforth I am restrained to speak of London and Westminster, it follows to show that the other cities of the kingdom will have as little reason to emulate any favour paid to these as the counties in competition with Middlesex could pretend. In the Act recited the quota of London was 61,667*l.* 1*s.* 3½*d.*; that of Westminster was 31,729*l.* 0*s.* ¾*d.*; whereas Norwich paid 5,259*l.* 5*s.* 11½*d.*; Bristol 3,695*l.* 15*s.* 4*d.*; York 2,319*l.* 14*s.* 0*d.*; Oxford 1,867*l.* 4*s.* 10*d.*; Cambridge 1,423*l.* 1*s.* 6½*d.* We see then that the advantage of argument rises higher by this comparison than the former one of counties; wherefore, having thought fit to mention it, I do willingly abridge myself of it lest any ill construction should arise.

By the standard used the proportion of Middlesex would be to have 79 members of Parliament; but since it is certain the rights of particular places ought to be waived if inconsistent with the welfare of the community, and the inequality of other counties (warranted by prescription) will not justify any pretensions to approach the like, I suppose myself to have abundantly expressed the native English jealousy for the untainted honour of our constitution, and to have obviated all perverse constructions, when I offer on behalf of Middlesex but a quarter part, by this standard, of her proportion, viz., that London might find twelve and Westminster six citizens for our Parliament, which with the knights would be in all twenty for Middlesex. . . .

But because no one shall suspect that this inequality is due solely to a false standard or balance used, I am content the quota proposed be examined by two other scales which an ingenious author has furnished us with. He says the number of living souls in the kingdom is computed at five millions and a half, whereof within the bills of mortality are five hundred and thirty thousand. He says the latest books of hearth-money reckon a million and three hundred thousand houses in the kingdom (the lowest cottages included), whereof the accurate survey of London and Westminster (about the same time taken) reports therein near one hundred thousand; so that Middlesex, rising higher than both those proportions, may well be estimated one tenth part of the whole kingdom, by which account her members in Parliament would be fifty-one. . . .

Wherefore taking it for granted that Middlesex justly bears two parts in thirteen of all subsidies levied in the kingdom, then can it be unreasonable she should have two in fifty-one of the representative, which is the sum of our proposal when allowed.

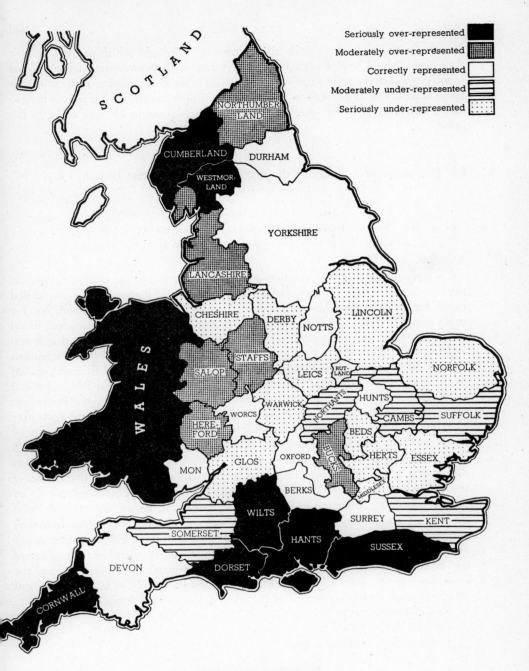

Seriously over-represented ▪

Moderately over-represented ▨

Correctly represented ▢

Moderately under-represented ▤

Seriously under-represented ⊡

2. ENGLAND AND WALES

SHOWING INEQUALITIES IN PARLIAMENTARY REPRESENTATION

(*See Appendix IV*)

Or what sufficient reason can be given that some boroughs which pay but 20*l*. for their quota should be represented equally in estates with Westminster, which pays as often 31,729*l*. to the support of the government? Not that a degree in the representative is pleadable in proportion to the degree of such payments; but only where so vast a difference is in the one, there some distinction ought likewise to be in the other. . . .

86. Proclamation summoning the first Parliament of Great Britain, 1707
(*London Gazette*, 5–9 June 1707)

A PROCLAMATION DECLARING HER MAJESTY'S PLEASURE
FOR HOLDING THE FIRST PARLIAMENT OF GREAT BRITAIN,
AND APPOINTING THE TIME AND PLACE OF MEETING THEREOF

ANNE R.

Whereas in pursuance of the two-and-twentieth article of the treaty of union, as the same hath been ratified and confirmed by two Acts of Parliament, the one passed in the Parliament of England and the other in the Parliament of Scotland, we, for many weighty reasons, have thought fit to declare by our royal proclamation, issued under our great seal of England on the twenty-ninth day of April last, that it was expedient that the Lords of Parliament of England, and Commons of the Parliament of England which then stood prorogued to the thirtieth day of April aforesaid, should be members of the respective Houses of the first Parliament of Great Britain for and on the part of England; and whereas in pursuance of an Act passed in the Parliament of Scotland for settling the manner of electing the sixteen peers and forty-five members to represent Scotland in the Parliament of Great Britain (which Act is by the two-and-twentieth article aforesaid declared to be as valid as if the same had been part of and engrossed in the said treaty) sixteen peers and forty-five commissioners for shires and burghs have been chosen to be the members of the respective Houses of the said first Parliament of Great Britain for and on the part of Scotland; we do by this our royal proclamation under the great seal of Great Britain, with the advice of our Privy Council, declare and publish our will and pleasure to be, and do hereby appoint, that our first Parliament of Great Britain shall meet and be holden at our city of Westminster on Thursday the twenty-third day of October next, whereof the Lords Spiritual and Temporal, and the knights, citizens and burgesses, and the commissioners for shires and burghs of our said first Parliament of Great Britain, and all others whom it may concern, are hereby required to take notice.

Given at our court at St. James's,
the fifth day of June 1707,
in the sixth year of our reign.

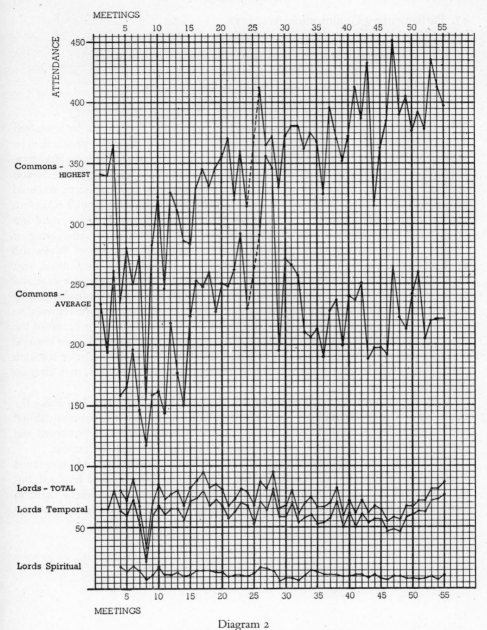

Diagram 2

ATTENDANCE OF LORDS AND COMMONERS AT EACH MEETING OF PARLIAMENT

(*See Appendix III*)

87. Parliamentary Qualification Act, 1711

(*Statutes of the Realm*, IX, pp. 365–366)

AN ACT FOR SECURING THE FREEDOM OF PARLIAMENTS
BY THE FARTHER QUALIFYING THE MEMBERS
TO SIT IN THE HOUSE OF COMMONS

(*9 Annae, cap. 5*)

For the better preserving the constitution and freedom of Parliament, be it enacted ... that from and after the determination of this present Parliament no person shall be capable to sit or vote as a member of the House of Commons for any county, city, borough or cinque port within that part of Great Britain called England, the dominion of Wales and town of Berwick-upon-Tweed, who shall not have an estate, freehold or copyhold, for his own life or for some greater estate either in law or equity to and for his own use and benefit, of or in lands, tenements or hereditaments, over and above what will satisfy and clear all encumbrances that may affect the same, lying or being within that part of Great Britain called England, the dominion of Wales and town of Berwick-upon-Tweed, of the respective annual value hereafter limited, viz., the annual value of six hundred pounds above reprises for every knight of a shire and the annual value of three hundred pounds above reprises for every citizen, burgess or baron of the cinque ports; and that if any person who shall be elected or returned to serve in any Parliament as a knight of a shire or as a citizen, burgess or baron of the cinque ports shall not at the time of such election and return be seized of or entitled to such an estate in lands, tenements or hereditaments as for such knight or for such citizen, burgess or baron respectively is hereinbefore required or limited, such election and return shall be void.

II. Provided always, that nothing in this Act contained shall extend to make the eldest son or heir apparent of any peer or lord of Parliament, or of any person qualified by this Act to serve as knight of a shire, incapable of being elected and returned and sitting and voting as a member of the House of Commons in any Parliament.

III. Provided always, that nothing in this Act contained shall extend or be construed to extend to either of the universities in that part of Great Britain called England, but that they and each of them may elect and return members to represent them in Parliament as heretofore they have done, anything herein contained to the contrary notwithstanding. . . .

F. DISPUTES BETWEEN THE HOUSES

88. Protest in the House of Lords against the failure of the House to insist on its right of initiating financial measures, 1662

(Journals of the House of Lords, XI, p. 469)

19 May 1662

Whereas a bill, entituled, *An Act for enlarging and amending the common highways,*[1] came from the House of Commons, unto which the Lords added two several provisos, laying a charge for the repair of two bridges, which provisos were rejected by the House of Commons upon this ground, given to the Lords at several conferences by some members of the House of Commons, viz., that the Lords have no power to begin any bill, or add any clause to any bill, that in any kind charged money, either for repairing or paving of highways, mending of bridges or other public use; which we conceived to be against the privilege of this House and many precedents, as a statute made in the fourth and fifth of Philip and Mary for assessing all persons therein mentioned for horse-arms and foot-arms, and another Act in the time of Queen Elizabeth for repair of Dover Pier, and one other Act in the fifth year of the said queen for relief of the poor, and other Acts; all which began in the House of Peers, and were assented to by the Commons, and by the royal assent passed into laws: and whereas the House of Peers did after the said conference pass this vote in the affirmative, viz., to agree with the House of Commons in leaving out the two provisos, asserting their privileges at a conference: and whereas before the putting the said vote we whose names are hereunto subscribed desired liberty of our dissent unto the said vote, we do for the reasons abovesaid, and to assert so much as in us lies so important and ancient a privilege of the House of Peers, enter our dissent and protestation against this vote.

89. Resolutions of the Commons on the judicial powers of the Lords, 1668 and 1675

(John Hatsell, *Precedents of Proceedings in the House of Commons,* ed. 1818, III, pp. 372–373, 376–377; *Journals of the House of Commons,* IX, pp. 330, 342–343, 380–381)

(i) 2 May 1668

Resolved,

1. That the Lords' taking cognizance of, and their proceeding upon, the matter set forth and contained in the petition of Thomas Skinner, merchant, against the Governor and Company of Merchants of London trading to the East Indies concerning the taking away the petitioner's ship and goods and assaulting his person, and their lordships' overruling the plea of the said Governor and Company (the said cause coming before that House originally only upon the complaint of the said Skinner), being a common plea, is not agreeable to the laws of the land and tending to deprive the subject of his right, ease and benefit due to him by the said laws.

---

[1] 14 Car. II, cap. 6.

2. That the Lords' taking cognizance of the right and title of the island in the petition mentioned, and giving damages thereupon against the said Governor and Company, is not warranted by the laws of this kingdom.

3. That Thomas Skinner, merchant, in commencing and prosecuting a suit by petition in the House of Lords against the Company of Merchants trading to the East Indies, wherein several members of this House are parties concerned with the said Company in their particular interests and estates, and in procuring judgment therein, with direction to be served upon the Governor, being a member of this House, or upon the deputy-governor of the said Company of Merchants, is a breach of the privilege of this House.

(ii) 9 May 1668

Resolved, &c., that whosoever shall be aiding or assisting in putting the order or sentence of the House of Lords, in the case of Thomas Skinner against the East India Company, in execution shall be deemed a betrayer of the rights and liberties of the Commons of England and an infringer of the privileges of this House.

(iii) 5 May 1675

Resolved, &c., that a message be sent to the Lords to acquaint them, that this House hath received information that there is a petition of appeal depending before them at the suit of Thomas Sherley, esquire, against Sir John Fagg, a member of this House, to which petition he is by order of the House of Lords directed to answer on Friday next, and to desire the Lords to have regard to the privileges of this House.

(iv) 20 May 1675

Sir Thomas Lee reports from the committee appointed to draw up reasons to be offered at the conference to be had with the Lords upon the privileges of this House, which were . . . severally agreed to, which are as followeth, viz.,

1. That by the laws and usage of Parliament privilege of Parliament belongs to every member of the House of Commons in all cases except treason, felony and breach of the peace, which hath often been declared in Parliament without any exception of appeals before the Lords.

2. That the reason of that privilege is that the members of the House of Commons may freely attend the public affairs in that House without disturbance or interruption, which doth extend as well to appeals before the House of Peers as to proceedings in other courts.

3. That by the constant course and usage of Parliament no member of the House of Commons can attend the House of Lords without the especial leave of that House first obtained, much less be summoned or compelled so to do.

4. If the Lords shall proceed to hear and determine any appeal where the party neither can nor ought to attend, such proceedings would be contrary to the rules of justice.

5. That the not determining of an appeal against a member of the House of

Commons is not a failure of justice, but only a suspension of proceedings in a particular case during the continuance of that Parliament, which is but temporary.

6. That in case it were a failure of justice it is not to be remedied by the House of
Lords alone, but it may be by Act of Parliament.

(v) 19 November 1675

Whereas this House hath been informed of several appeals depending in the House
of Lords from courts of equity, to the great violation of the rights and liberties of the
Commons of England, it is this day resolved and declared, that whosoever shall
solicit, plead or prosecute any appeal against any commoner of England from any
court of equity before the House of Lords shall be deemed and taken a betrayer of the
rights and liberties of the Commons of England, and shall be proceeded against
accordingly.

90. Resolutions of the Commons on money bills, 1671 and 1678
(*Journals of the House of Commons*, IX, pp. 235, 509)

(i) 13 April 1671

Resolved, &c., *nemine contradicente*, that in all aids given to the king by the
Commons the rate or tax ought not to be altered by the Lords.

(ii) 3 July 1678

Resolved, &c., that all aids and supplies, and aids to his Majesty in Parliament, are
the sole gift of the Commons; and all bills for the granting of any such aids and
supplies ought to begin with the Commons; and that it is the undoubted and sole
right of the Commons to direct, limit and appoint in such bills the ends, purposes,
considerations, conditions, limitations and qualifications of such grants, which ought
not to be changed or altered by the House of Lords.

91. Protests and resolutions of the Lords against tacking, 1692
(*Journals of the House of Lords*, XV, p. 90)

23 February 1692

Then the House went into consideration, and proceeded on the bill entituled, *An
Act for raising money by a poll payable quarterly for one year for the carrying on a
vigorous war against France*.[1]

The earl of Mulgrave reported from the lords committees appointed to consider
of expedients for the preservation of the privileges of this House, in reference to the
poll bill, some proceedings agreed on by them therein.

And after consideration thereof the House was adjourned during pleasure, and
put into a committee upon the said bill.

[1] 3 Gul. & Mar., cap. 6.

And after some time spent in the said committee the House was resumed.

And the Lord Godolphin reported, that the committee had gone through the bill without any amendment, and that the committee think fit there should be some entry made in the books upon occasion of passing the last clause in the bill.

Then, *hodie tertia vice lecta est billa*, entituled, *An Act for raising money by a poll payable quarterly for one year for the carrying on a vigorous war against France*.

The question was put, whether this bill shall pass?

It was resolved in the affirmative. . . .

Leave having been asked and given for any lord to dissent if the question was carried in the affirmative, these lords do dissent, for the reasons following:

Because the substance of the proviso added at the end of the bill, for the taking the accompts of the public moneys, hath been in a bill by itself this present session of Parliament, which, having not passed through the two Houses by reason of their disagreement upon some amendments offered by the Lords to the said bill, ought not, by the known and constant methods of proceedings, to be brought in again in the same session; and consequently we conceive the tacking of the said proviso to this poll bill is unparliamentary, highly prejudicial to the privileges of the Peers, and may be of dangerous consequence to the prerogative of the Crown. . . .[1]

Then the question was put, whether there shall be an entry made in the book upon occasion of the passing the last clause in the bill entituled, *An Act for raising money by a poll payable quarterly for one year for the carrying on a vigorous war against France*?

It was resolved in the affirmative. . . .

Then this was agreed to be entered, as followeth:

The Lords in Parliament, being extremely sensible of that imminent danger to which not only this nation but a great part of Christendom might be exposed if either the necessary supply of money or his Majesty's voyage beyond sea in this extraordinary conjuncture should receive any delay, have agreed to the bill entituled, *An Act for raising money by a poll payable quarterly for one year for the carrying on a vigorous war against France*, without any amendments, and out of zeal to the public good have purposely avoided to take notice of the irregularities relating to the clause for taking the accompts. But to prevent any ill consequences from such a precedent for the future they have thought fit to declare solemnly, and to enter upon their books for a record to all posterity, that they will not hereafter admit, upon any occasion whatsoever, of a proceeding so contrary to the rules and methods of Parliament.

Leave having been asked and given for any lord to dissent if the question was carried in the affirmative, these lords do dissent, for the reasons following:

Because we conceive that an entry on the Journal of this House, to excuse the complying at this time in a thing so unparliamentary as the matter now in question is, upon the account of the present necessity or danger, how pressing or imminent soever, will be of no force to prevent the doing the same when the like necessity or danger may be pretended; but the consenting once to such unprecedented proceedings may always be made use of as one argument more for the agreeing to them for the future.[2]

---

[1] Seven signatures follow.　　　　　　　　[2] The same seven signatures follow.

G. DEVELOPMENT OF PARTIES

92. Earl of Clarendon's account of his own organization, *c.* 1663

(Life of Edward Earl of Clarendon, ed. 1857, I, pp. 308, 609–621)

[1660] That the king might be the more vacant to those thoughts and divertisements which pleased him best, he appointed the Chancellor and some others to have frequent consultations with such members of the Parliament who were most able and willing to serve him, and to concert all the ways and means by which the transactions in the Houses might be carried with the more expedition and attended with the best success. These daily conferences proved very beneficial to his Majesty's service, the members of both Houses being very willing to receive advice and direction and to pursue what they were directed, and all things were done there in good order and succeeded well. . . .

[1663] To this time the king had been content to refer the conduct of his affairs in the Parliament to the Chancellor and the Treasurer, who had every day conference with some select persons of the House of Commons who had always served the king and upon that account had great interest in that assembly, and in regard of the experience they had and their good parts were hearkened to with reverence; and with those they consulted in what method to proceed in disposing the House sometimes to propose, sometimes to consent to, what should be most necessary for the public, and by them to assign parts to other men whom they found disposed and willing to concur in what was to be desired; and all this without any noise, or bringing many together to design, which ever was and ever will be ingrateful to Parliaments, and however it may succeed for a little time will in the end be attended with prejudice.

But there were two persons now introduced to act upon that stage who disdained to receive orders or to have any method prescribed to them, who took upon them to judge of other men's defects and thought their own abilities beyond exception.

The one was Sir Harry Bennet, who had procured himself to be sent agent or envoy into Spain as soon as the king came from Brussels, being a man very well known to the king and for his pleasant and agreeable humour acceptable to him. . . . Shortly after his arrival, though not so soon as he thought his high merit deserved, his Majesty conferred the only place then void (and that had been long promised to a noble person who had behaved himself very well towards his Majesty and his blessed father) upon him, which was the office of Privy Purse; received him into great familiarity, and into the nightly meeting, in which he filled a principal place to all intents and purposes. The king very much desired to have him elected a member in the House of Commons, and commanded the Chancellor to use his credit to obtain it upon the first opportunity; and in obedience to that command he did procure him to be chosen about the time we are now speaking of, when the Parliament assembled in February.

The other person was Mr. William Coventry, the youngest son of a very wise father, the Lord Coventry, who had been Lord Keeper of the Great Seal of England for many years with an universal reputation. . . . He had sat a member in the House of Commons from the beginning of the Parliament, with very much reputation of an able man. He spoke pertinently, and was always very acceptable and well heard, and was one of those with whom they who were trusted by the king in conducting his affairs in the lower House consulted very frequently, but not so much, nor relied equally upon his advice, as upon some few others who had much more experience, which he thought was of use only to ignorant and dull men, and that men of sagacity could see and determine at a little light, and ought rather to persuade and engage men to do that which they judged fit than consider what themselves were inclined to do; and so did not think himself to be enough valued and relied upon, and only to be made use of to the celebrating the designs and contrivance of other men, without being signal in the managery, which he aspired to be.

Nor did any man envy him the province, if he could indeed have governed it, and that others who had more useful talents would have been ruled by him. However, being a man who naturally loved faction and contradiction, he often made experiments how far he could prevail in the House by declining the method that was prescribed, and proposing somewhat to the House that was either beside or contrary to it, and which the others would not oppose, believing in regard of his relation that he had received newer directions. And then if it succeeded well (as sometimes it did) he had argument enough to censure and inveigh against the Chancellor for having taken so ill measures of the temper and affections of the House, for he did not dissemble in his private conversation (though his outward carriage was very fair) that he had no kindness for him, which in gratitude he ought to have had. . . .

When those two persons, Sir Harry Bennet and Mr. Coventry (between whom there had been as great a league of friendship as can be between two very proud men equally ill-natured), came now to sit together in the House of Commons, though the former of them knew no more of the constitution and laws of England than he did of China, nor had in truth a care or tenderness for Church or State, but believed France was the best pattern in the world, they thought they should have the greatest wrong imaginable if they did not entirely govern it, and if the king took his measures of what should be done there from anybody but themselves. They made friendships with some young men, who spake confidently and often, and upon some occasions seemed to have credit in the House. And upon a little conversation with those men, who being country gentlemen of ordinary condition and mean fortunes were desirous to have interest in such a person as Sir Harry Bennet, who was believed to have great credit with the king, he believed he understood the House and what was to be done there as well as any man in England.

He recommended those men to the king as persons of sublime parts, worthy of his Majesty's caressing; that he would undertake to fix them to his service, and when they were his own he might carry what he would in the House of Commons. The men had parts indeed and good affections, and often had resorted to the Chancellor, received advice from him, and thought themselves beholden to him, being at that time entirely governed by Sir Hugh Pollard, who was himself still advised by the

Chancellor (with whom he had a long and fast friendship) how he should direct his friends, having indeed a greater party in the House of Commons willing to be disposed of by him than any man that ever sat there in my time. But now these gentlemen had got a better patron. The new courtier had raised their value, and talked in another dialect to them, of recompenses and rewards, than they had heard formerly. He carried them to the king, and told his Majesty in their own hearing what men of parts they were, what services they had done for him, and how much greater they could do; and his Majesty received and conferred with them very graciously, and dismissed them with promises which made them rich already.

The two friends before mentioned agreed so well between themselves that whether they spoke together or apart to the king they said always the same things, gave the same information, and took care that both their masters might have the same opinions and judgments. They magnified the affections of the House of Commons, which were so great and united that they would do whatsoever his Majesty would require; that there were many worthy and able men of whose wisdom the House was so well persuaded that they commonly consented to whatsoever they proposed; and that these men complained that they had no directions given to them which way they might best serve the king; they knew not what he desired, which when they should do, it would quickly appear how much they were at the king's disposal, and all things which now depended long would be hereafter dispatched in half the time.

The king wondered very much that his friends in the House were no better informed, of which he had never heard any complaint before, and wished them to speak with the Chancellor, for neither of these men were yet arrived at the confidence to insinuate in the least degree any ill-will or prejudice to him, though they were not united in any one thing more than the desire of his ruin and the resolution to compass it by all the ill arts and devices they could use; but till it should be more seasonable they dissembled to both their masters to have a high esteem of him, having not yet credit enough with either to do him harm. They said they would very willingly repair to him and be directed by him, but they desired that his Majesty himself would first speak to him (because it would not so well become them) to call those persons whom they had recommended to him to meet together with the rest with whom he used to advise, which the persons they named they were sure would be very glad of, having all of them a great esteem of the Chancellor and being well known to him; as indeed they were, and most of them obliged by him.

The king willingly undertook it; and being shortly after attended by the Chancellor his Majesty told him all that the other two had said to him, and did not forget to let him know the great goodwill they had both professed towards him. He asked him what he thought of such and such men, and particularly named Mr. Clifford and Mr. Churchill and some other men of better quality and much more interest, who, he said, took it ill that they were not particularly informed what the king desired and which way they might best serve him; and bade him that at the next meeting of the rest these men might likewise have notice to be present, together with Sir Harry Bennet and Mr. William Coventry, for Harry Coventry (who was a much wiser man than his brother, and had a much better reputation with wise men) was constantly in those councils.

The Chancellor told him that great and notorious meetings and cabals in Parliament had been always odious in Parliament, and though they might produce some success in one or two particulars till they were discovered they had always ended unluckily, until they were introduced in the late ill times by so great a combination that they could not receive any discountenance; yet that they who compassed all their wicked designs by those cabals were so jealous that they might be overmatched by the like practices that when they discovered any three or four of those who were used to concur with them to have any private meetings they accused them to conspire against the Parliament. That when his Majesty returned, and all the world was full of joy and delight to serve him, and persons were willing and importunate to receive direction how they might do it in that Convention, care had been taken, without any noise or bringing any prejudice upon those who were willing to be instruments towards the procuring what was desirable and to prevent what would be ingrateful, that little notice might be taken of them, which had good success.

That since this Parliament the Lord Treasurer and he had by his Majesty's direction made choice of some persons eminent for their affection to the Crown, of great experience and known abilities, to confer with for the better preparing and conducting what was to be done in the House of Commons. But the number of them was not so great as to give any umbrage; nor did they meet oftener together with them than upon accidents and contingencies was absolutely necessary, but appointed those few who had a mutual confidence in each other, and every one of which had an influence upon others and advised them what to do, to meet by themselves, either at the Lord Bridgeman's or Mr. Attorney's chambers, who still gave notice to the other two of what was necessary, and received advice. That there were very few of any notable consideration who did not frequently repair to both of them, either to dine with them or to perform some office of civility, with every one of whom they conferred, and said what was necessary to inform and oblige them what was fit for them to do.

That two of those who were named by his Majesty, Mr. Clifford and Mr. Churchill, were honest gentlemen and received the advice they were to follow from Sir Hugh Pollard, who had in truth a very particular influence upon all the Cornish and Devonshire men. And that his Majesty might know that he had not been well informed that the others named by him took it unkindly that they did not know his pleasure, who were leading men, as indeed they were, he assured his Majesty that there was not one of those who was not particularly consulted with and advertised by some person who was chosen by every one of them for that purpose, and that they would by no means resort to any meeting, fearing to undergo the odious name of undertakers, which in all Parliaments hath been a brand. But as they had never opposed anything that related to his service, so upon any private insinuation they had been ready to propose anything, which would not have been so acceptable from any who had been known to have relation to his service or to depend on those who had.

He besought his Majesty to consider whether anything had hitherto, in near three years, fallen out amiss or short of what he had expected in the wary administration that had been in that affair, and did not conceal his own fears that putting it into a more open and wider channel, his Majesty's own too public speaking with the members of Parliament and believing what every man who was present told him passed in debates, and who for want of comprehension as well as memory committed many mistakes in their relations, would be attended with some inconveniences not easy to be remedied. The king was not dissatisfied with the discourse, but seemed to approve it. However he would have Sir Harry Bennet, Mr. Clifford and Churchill called to the next meeting, and because they were to be introduced into company they had not used to converse with that it should be at the Chancellor's chamber, who should let the rest know the good opinion his Majesty had of those who were added to the number.

By this means and with these circumstances this alteration was made in the conduct of the king's service in the Parliament, upon which many other alterations followed by degrees, though not at once. Yet presently it appeared that this introduction of new confidants was not acceptable to those who thought they had very well discharged their trust. Sir Harry Bennet was utterly unknown to them, a man unversed in any business, who never had nor ever was like to speak in the House, except in his ear who sat next him to the disadvantage of some who had spoken, and had not the faculties to get himself beloved, and was thought by all men to be a Roman Catholic, for which they had not any other reason but from his indifference in all things which concerned the Church.

When they met first at the Chancellor's chamber, as the king had directed, they conferred freely together with little difference of opinion, though it appeared that they who had used to be together before did not use the same freedom as formerly in delivering their particular judgments, not having confidence enough in the new-comers, who in their private meetings afterwards took more upon them, rather to direct than to advise, so that the others grew unsatisfied in their conversation. And though the meetings continued at one of the places before mentioned, some always discontinued their attendance, so that by degrees there were less resolutions taken than had been formerly. Nor was there so cheerful a concurrence or so speedy a dispatch of the business depending in the House as had been.

93. Anonymous pamphlet attacking the earl of Arlington's organization, 1669
(State Papers Domestic, Charles II, 266, No. 152)

THE ALARM[1]

Like the dumb man who found his tongue when he saw an arm lifted to kill his father, so I, who never meddled with anything beyond my private concernments, being an enemy to knowing, much more to writing, state matters, cannot yet forbear

[1] Endorsed by Joseph Williamson, "A libel scattered in Westminster Hall, 20 October 1669, at the meeting of Parliament."

when I see my country in danger by the united villainy of so many that conspire against it. When I see it is become the office of men in power to lay snares for our liberties, and the practice of men in trust to betray them; when all the industry which should be used to maintain the government is applied to alter it; when I see the end is resolved, and that they differ only in the means, the only question remaining being whether it is by deceit or violence that we are to be enslaved, I can no longer suppress those English thoughts that boil within me, my heart swelleth with a just anger against men who would raise their fortunes out of the ruins of their country, and, having accidentally some knowledge of the steps by which we are to be destroyed, I could not let that guilt lie upon me as not to impart my fears and the grounds of them to some of those few English gentlemen the corruption of this age hath left us. . . .

Know then, my dear countrymen, that the present counsels go upon these foundations: first, if possible, to gain this Parliament to such a compliance that they shall be liberal of their money and sparing in their grievances, supply the king without looking back upon ill conduct or falling heavy upon the authors of it. If this fail, it must be dissolved and a new one chosen; and if that should not answer what is expected from it, force is to be set up as the last and surest expedient. Towards the first these arts are used, viz., the threatening those members who, either out of vanity or interest, are loath to part with their authority, that the king will infallibly dissolve them upon their non-compliance, intimating they have no way of securing themselves to be magistrates for life but by adhering to the Court, which will be a mutual support to them. To the well-meaning and disinterested men it is pressed, of what ill consequence it may be to ravel into things past, which they miscall flying in the king's face; that his Majesty, being sensible of what hath been amiss, is now disposed to take new measures such as shall be agreeable to his people; that all things conspire to make us the happiest nation in the world, if the king hath the concurrence of the Parliament in such things as he expecteth from them; but if the peevishness and faction of some, the ill-timed zeal of others, shall destroy these fair hopes by insisting on such things to the king as tend to his diminution, and by wounding him through the sides of his ministers, if, instead of supplying the king's wants, and putting him in a condition to support himself and protect us, they shall misspend their time in grievances and complaints, they will turn his heart from them, and drive him into a necessity of following those counsels which in his nature he is averse to, by which they will lay the groundwork of such confusions as perhaps in our time we may not see the way out of. . . .

But there is another sort of men harder to be treated with, men of a more refined understanding, and so exact in the calculation of men's parts that they will judge them to a farthing, their measure being according as a man gets more or less by them. . . . They love the king to such a degree that they worship his image; but then it must be upon his coin; their idolatry goeth no further. . . . This goeth hard with an empty Exchequer, but what will not an able minister, that is afraid too, do to soften these angry men? If a little money will turn these mastiffs into spaniels is it not well bestowed? Therefore these gentlemen must be represented to the king as wellmeriting men that have not had due recompense. He must be told these are the heroes of the House, the rest but a dull herd wholly at their dispose; that every one of these hath a legion of members in his belly so that in purchasing them he buyeth the whole House; that though his Majesty soweth in tears he shall reap in joy, since every shilling so bestowed shall produce a thousand in a subsidy. These arguments prevailing, money that is wanting to pay wages is found to corrupt a Parliament.

The great instruments of this distribution are, first, my Lord Arlington, who, besides promises of this or that place, telleth out ready money to these hirelings who engage to betray their country for it. You may imagine his lordship desireth the king may be put into a condition not to want Parliaments. He knoweth they are saucy things and make bold to inquire both into the faults and the abilities of men in power, and he hath just wit enough to be sensible he cannot bear the scrutiny. The poor man is but the sign of a Secretary, can do nothing that belongeth to his place but receive the profits of it, and, to do him right, he loveth business no better than business loveth him; but he hath not yet got ten thousand pound a year, and till then he will not leave the box, though he cannot drive. . . .

The next in this negotiation is his man Clifford, who you may be sure layeth about him. Here is one hath a great mind to be a minister, perhaps because his father was one. He playeth at no small game, nor catcheth at small profits, by which he would seem to neglect his fortune, but it is that he may make it all at once. He sets up to be generous, by being free of the king's wine at his table and of his money in the Treasury; but do not mistake the man, he hath too much ambition and too little money to be content. He would be at the top, and thinketh of it at this very hour; and if things succeed as he hath laid them you will see him throw off my Lord Arlington's livery and set up for himself. But in order to this the great work of cheating the Parliament must be carried on, in which he neither spareth his own pains nor the king's money. . . .

Shall I forget my Lord Ashley? Good God! what a knave is here? This is knavery bound up in little, the very abridgement of villainy. The world calleth him an ingenious man; I suppose it is because he is not hanged, a thing he deserveth at least once a day. To speak truth, he hath some good nature, for he pitieth an honest man, and wonders at his mistake. He is said to understand the king's revenue. No wonder, for he hath a share in every farm. . . . His business at this time is to go of errands to Parliament men to convince them by his own experience how wise a thing it is to be a knave.

What shall we say of Sir Thomas Littleton, that angry man against the Court till he was silenced by a good place. He is now at last content everything should be let alone. He is grown very discreet and mighty tender of discomposing things now he hath got what he grumbled for. You will find him of opinion that the king's ministers ought to be sacred, that his Majesty must be supplied, with the rest of those dutiful maxims that are natural to men who hope to get by them. . . .

This is the game now playing. These men go up and down cheapening all we have, and if care be not taken we shall have no other security from being sold but that there is not money enough to buy us. These gentlemen are indeed very zealous to get the king supplied, but we must not mistake them so as to think it is for his sake. They only do as a gamester I knew, who solicited and took great pains to procure money for a country gentleman, not out of kindness but with the prospect of playing with him for it and cheating him. But to the point. If these arts succeed, here is a Parliament to be kept like a led horse that at last will kick us out of our liberties. But if these designs do not take, then here is a great deal of money ill laid out. My gentleman must cast about how to get it back again. The natural expedient to men that are uneasy is to change. If these cards are unkind they will take another pack. Upon this logic the king must dissolve the Parliament. If you ask why, it is for not betraying their trust. Mark the contrivance. It hath perhaps been a grievance that it hath continued so long, and now it will be so cunningly ordered that the nation will dislike the breaking them. But let that pass. Our great men are resolved to try in this case, and let them do so. They will find nothing will do but their last remedy, and that is an army. Well, this will be plain dealing, worth a hundred of all their small tricks to pick our pockets. This will be brave open robbery.

In the meantime it is a pious design to persuade a good king to be a tyrant, and to endeavour to make a free people slaves; an honourable contrivance to make a prince destroy the liberties of a people that called him in; a deep advice to bid him throw away the title he hath to govern by law, to take up that of force, to which every man hath an equal right that can attain to it. When this is to be done Sir Thomas Clifford will be no small man; a great part of the military model of government will be left to him. In his nature he loveth absolute power, and therefore whispereth it to the king, a plausible text to princes; and to make it more so he persuadeth it is easy to be compassed. By this he recommends himself to favour and insinuateth himself into power, gets to be trusted with the secret and the contrivance. In short he is one that needeth a civil war, and therefore sure to promote a standing army. . . .

Were the consequence of preserving these men in their greatness anything else than the ruin of the nation men might be persuaded to lament and acquiesce, but in this case it is become part of our allegiance to take care the king may not be undone. We need not fear but he will forgive the importunity of a people that loveth him, or that he will take it ill if, in this exigency, we wrestle with him for a blessing. Gentlemen, this is the critical time of saving England. Yet a little more sleep, a little more slumber, and want cometh upon us like an armed man. Let these weeds take a little deeper root, and they may perhaps grow out of the reach of a Parliament. Pluck them up, therefore, before they grow too big. Show the nation a Parliament can do something else as well as give away their money. Relieve the king from his wants, but at the same time rescue him from his ministers. Acquit yourselves of the duty you owe him, but remember you owe something too to those that chose you. Farewell.

94. Anonymous libel on the earl of Danby's organization, 1677

(Parliamentary History, iv, App., pp. xxii–xxxiv)

A SEASONABLE ARGUMENT
TO PERSUADE ALL THE GRAND JURIES IN ENGLAND TO PETITION
FOR A NEW PARLIAMENT,
OR
A LIST OF THE PRINCIPAL LABOURERS
IN THE GREAT DESIGN OF POPERY AND ARBITRARY POWER,
WHO HAVE BETRAYED THEIR COUNTRY TO THE CONSPIRATORS AND
BARGAINED WITH THEM TO MAINTAIN A STANDING ARMY IN ENGLAND
UNDER THE COMMAND OF THE BIGOTED POPISH DUKE, WHO
BY THE ASSISTANCE OF THE LORD LAUDERDALE'S SCOTCH ARMY,
THE FORCES IN IRELAND, AND THOSE IN FRANCE, HOPES
TO BRING ALL BACK TO ROME

BEDFORDSHIRE

[County] Sir Humphrey Winch, baronet, hath from the Court 500*l.* per annum salary, and was of the Council of Trade and Plantations.

BERKSHIRE

Windsor Sir Thomas Higgons, knight, hath a pension of 500*l.* per annum, and hath had 4,000*l.* in gifts: married to the earl of Bath's sister.

Sir Francis Winnington, knight, Solicitor-General to the king, which place is worth 1,500*l.* per annum.

Reading Sir Thomas Dolman has 200*l.* per annum pension, and was assisted by the Court in the cheating will, whereby he got [John] Quarles his estate, valued at 1,600*l.*: now Clerk of the Council, which is worth 500*l.* per annum, and is promised to be Secretary of State.

Richard Aldworth, esquire, Auditor in the Exchequer, which is worth 400*l.* per annum; he is also the archbishop's secretary, and has got by boons at several times 3,000*l.*

Wallingford Sir John Bennet, knight of the bath, has got of the poor, indigent Cavalier's money 26,000*l.*, and other ways near 40,000*l.* more.

BUCKINGHAMSHIRE

[*Buckingham Borough*] Sir Richard Temple, Commissioner of the Customs, which is worth 1,200*l.* per annum.

Sir William Smith, as honest as Sir Richard Temple.

Chipping Wycombe Sir Robert Sawyer, a lawyer of as ill reputation as his father, has had for his attendance this session 1,000*l.*, and is promised (as he insinuates) to be Attorney-General and Speaker of the House of Commons.

Amersham Sir William Drake, baronet, under the command of his father-in-law, the Chief Baron Montague, who enjoys 1,500*l.* per annum during the king's pleasure.

CAMBRIDGESHIRE

[*County*]
Sir Thomas Hatton, a man of no estate but his pension.

Sir Thomas Chicheley, Master of the Ordnance, and has had 2,000*l.* given him, and the reversion of his place to his son.

University
Sir Charles Wheeler, a foot captain who once promised himself to be Master of the Rolls; now Governor of Nevis.

Cambridge
Borough
William Lord Alington; in debt very much, a Court pensioner and in hopes of a white staff; a cully.

CHESHIRE

[*County*]
Thomas Cholmondeley, promised a great place at Court, but not only deceived but laughed at, poor gentleman.

Chester
Robert Werden, esquire, a betrayer of the Old Cavaliers (with [Sir Richard] Willis) and of Sir George Booth; the duke of York's creature, and gentleman of his bedchamber.

CORNWALL

[*County*]
Sir Jonathan Trelawny, baronet; one that is known to have sworn himself into 4,000*l.* at least, in his account of the Prize Office; Controller to the duke, and has got in gratuities to the value of 10,000*l.*, beside what he is promised for being an informer.

Sir John Coriton, baronet, a Commissioner of the Prizes, and besides a patentee for setting up lights upon the sea-coast.

Launceston
Sir Charles Harbord, Surveyor-General, has got 100,000*l.* of the king and kingdom. He was formerly a solicitor of Staples Inn, till his lewdness and poverty brought him to Court.

Liskeard
Bernard Grenville, esquire, a bedchamber man, has got in boons at several times 20,000*l.*

Helston
Sidney Godolphin, esquire, a bedchamber man.

Sir William Godolphin, baronet, had 1,200*l.* per annum out of the fee farm rents, and governor of Scilly Island.

Truro
John Arundell, esquire; his father, from a small fortune, raised to be a lord, and hath now 2,000*l.* per annum pension out of the Excise, and hath got in boons 20,000*l.*

Camelford
Sir William Godolphin, knight, under-secretary to the Lord Arlington, now ambassador in Spain, and lately turned papist, hath got in boons 30,000*l.*

West Looe
John Trelawny, esquire, cup-bearer to the king, captain to a troop of horse in Ireland, and 200*l.* per annum pension.

John Trelawny, esquire, own son to honest Sir Jonathan Trelawny.

East Looe
Charles Osborne, the Treasurer's brother, has an office in the Customs.

Henry Seymour, esquire, of the bedchamber, has the Hanaper Office, is Controller of the Customs at London, and has got 40,000*l.* in Duchy leases, and other boons.

Bossiney Robert Robartes, esquire. Victuals and protections in Whitehall out of privilege time, and 50*l.* a session.

Michael Francis, Lord Hawley, captain of his Majesty's troop, a gentleman of the bedchamber to the duke, and Court buffoon, has got in boons 20,000*l.*

St. Mawes Arthur Spry, a Commissioner of the Prizes, 400*l.* per annum pension, has raised his estate from 100 per annum to 800 by being a member.

Sir Joseph Tredenham, the son of an attorney, and by marrying the Speaker's sister has got a considerable pension.

Callington Sir Cyril Wyche, Secretary to the Lieutenancy in Ireland, brother-in-law to the two earls of Bath and St. Albans.

[CUMBERLAND]

Carlisle Sir Philip Howard, captain of the horse guards, got in patents and boons 4,000*l.*

Sir Christopher Musgrave, knight, captain of a foot company, 200*l.* per annum pension, and to succeed his father in the government of Carlisle.

DEVONSHIRE

[County] Sir Coplestone Bampfield, baronet, much addicted to tippling, presented to the king by his pretended wife, Betty Roberts, in Pall Mall.

Exeter Sir James Smith, knight, major of the king's regiment, has received 10,000*l.* in boons; kinsman to the duke of Albemarle.

Thomas Walker, esquire, a Commissioner of the Prizes, where he feathered his nest to some purpose; received 500*l.* this session, besides preferring his brother to be Collector of the Customs of Exeter.

Totnes Sir Edward Seymour, baronet, the Speaker's father and an indigent pensioner.

Sir Thomas Berry, knight, a pensioner of 200*l.* per annum, got for him by the Lord Clifford, his brother-in-law.

Plymouth Sir Gilbert Talbot, knight, Master of the Jewel Office.

Plympton Earle Sir Nicholas Slanning, knight of the bath, Sir George Carteret's son-in-law, the king's carver, 2,000*l.* in boons, and governor of Pendennis in reversion.

Honiton Sir Courteney Pole, first mover of the Chimney Money, for which he had ——

Sir Peter Prideaux, knight, the lord of Bath's brother-in-law. Constant Court dinners, and 300*l.* per annum pension.

Beeralston Sir John Maynard, knight, the King's Serjeant-at-Law.

Tiverton Sir Henry Ford, once Secretary for Ireland. A pension of 300*l.* per annum, which is almost all he has to subsist on.

DORSETSHIRE

Corfe Castle   Lord Latimer, son to the Lord Treasurer.

Lyme Regis   Sir John Shaw, once a vintner's boy, got of the Crown, out of the Customs and by other ways, 60,000*l.*

Weymouth   Sir Winston Churchill was a Commissioner of the Court of Claims in Ireland, now one of the Clerks of the Green Cloth. He preferred his own daughter to the duke of York, and has got in boons 10,000*l.* He has published in print that the king may raise money without his Parliament.

Bridport   George Bowerman, esquire, once an under-clerk in the Six Clerks Office, now Master of the Ballast Office (a place no less oppressive than illegal), worth 1,500*l.* per annum.

Wareham   George Pitt, quondam servant to the duke of York, but turned out, and was promised to have the money it cost him, 2,500*l.*

DURHAM

[County]   John Tempest, esquire, a papist, a pensioner and a Court dinner man, has got a customer's place at Hull for his son.

ESSEX

Harwich   Thomas King, esquire, a pensioner for 50*l.* a session, &c., meat and drink, and now and then a suit of clothes.

GLOUCESTER

[County]   Sir Baynham Throckmorton; a grant of Kingswood Forest, and 200*l.* per annum.

Maldon[1]   Sir Richard Wiseman; a 1,000*l.* per annum pension, and keeper of one of the Treasurer's public parliamentary tables.

    Sir William Wiseman; at Sir Richard's devotion.

HAMPSHIRE

Winchester   Sir Robert Holmes, first an Irish livery-boy, then a highwayman, now bashaw of the Isle of Wight, got in boons and by rapine 100,000*l.* The cursed beginner of the two Dutch wars.

    Laurence Hyde the elder; a pension of 200*l.* per annum, and a constant Court dinner man.

Southampton   Sir Richard Ford, knight, joint contriver of the two Dutch wars, for which he had 10,000*l.*, and yet is scarce able to live.

    Thomas Knollys, esquire, the Treasurer's kinsman: 400*l.* per annum pension.

Portsmouth   Sir George Carteret, baronet, a vice-chamberlain, once Treasurer of Ireland, and the Navy, in which two places he cheated the Crown of 40,000*l.*, as upon account was made apparent. He has wisely conveyed great part of his estate beyond sea; therefore deservedly made a Privy Councillor.

Petersfield   Thomas Neale, esquire, now turned brewer since he has consumed

---

[1] Really in Essex.

a rich wife's fortune and his own estate. He has a promise his son shall marry Moll Davis's daughter, and to be made a viscount and maintained if his brew-house fail. Formerly called Golden Neale, now Brazen Groom Porter.

Stockbridge

Sir Robert Howard, Auditor of the Receipt of the Exchequer, worth 3,000*l.* per annum. Many great places and boons he has had; but his whore Uphill spends all, and now refuses to marry him.

Robert Phelips, esquire, bedchamber man, got in gifts 20,000*l.*

Newton in the
Isle of
Wight

Sir John Holmes, Sir Robert's brother, a cowardly, baffled sea-captain, twice poxed, and once whipped with a dog-whip, as many gentlemen can testify; chosen in the night, without the head-officer of the town and but one burgess; yet voted well-elected this last session.

[Andover]

Sir Kingsmill Lucy, baronet, has had 1,000*l.* and a promise of a Court place.

HEREFORD

[County]

Thomas Price, esquire; 500*l.* given him, and 300*l.* per annum pension, and protection in Whitehall during prorogations.

Hereford City

Herbert Westfaling, esquire; 500*l.* in money, and an office in the Custom House worth 150*l.* per annum.

Weobley

Sir John Barneby, knight; 500*l.* given him.

Sir Thomas Williams, once a poor quack chemist, now the king's chemist, has got at least 40,000*l.* by making provocatives for lechery; and yet at this time all his land is under extent, and his protection only keeps him out of prison.

HERTFORDSHIRE

[County]

Sir Richard Franklin; a pension of 400*l.* per annum.

HUNTINGDON

*Huntingdon
Borough*

Sir John Cotton, a madman who cut his own throat, and now cuts his country's by his vote.

Sir Lionel Walden, 8,000*l.* in the king's debt, a Blackheath captain and a papist, at present has a company of foot, and 1,000*l.* given him.

KENT

[County]

Sir Thomas Peyton; the coal farm, worth 2,000*l.* per annum; has had many boons, and yet has spent all and his own estate to boot. This is Peyton the informer.

Canterbury

Sir Edward Master, knight, a great wittol, &c.

Thomas Hardres, serjeant-at-law, promised to be a judge.

Rochester

Sir Francis Clerke, a Commissioner of the Prizes, and a constant receiver of all public money, and a constant diner at Court tables.

Maidstone

Thomas Harlackenden, esquire, whose only livelihood is in his pension.

Sir Robert Barnham also.

Queenborough   James Herbert, esquire, is but fifteen years old, but son-in-law to the Treasurer, and therefore of age to dispose of the people's money.

LANCASHIRE

[County]   Sir Roger Bradshaigh, a papist, has a lease from the Crown.

Lancaster   Richard Kirby, esquire, one of a very small estate, a captain of guards and a Commissioner for the Hackney Coaches, has had 500*l.* in boons.

Richard Harrison, esquire; a small pension proportionable to his understanding.

Preston   Edward Rigby, esquire, serjeant-at-law, promised to be a Welsh judge.

Sir John Otway, Solicitor of the Duchy, and rewarded with a considerable boon in the fee farm rents.

Newton   Richard, Lord Gorges; a pension of 500*l.* per annum.

Clitheroe   Sir John Heath, Attorney to the Duchy, a great drinker and a suspected papist.

Sir Thomas Stringer, a dancing-master's son, got 30,000*l* under the duke of Albemarle.

Wigan   Charles, earl of Ancram, a poor Scot; 500*l.* per annum pension.

Sir Jeffrey Shakerley, Governor of Chester; a pension of 500*l.* per annum.

LEICESTERSHIRE

[County]   George Faunt, esquire; 500*l.* out of the last tax, and is a constant receiver of all taxes.

Leicester Borough   Sir William Hartopp, a pensioner of 200*l.* per annum, and promised to be Clerk of the Kitchen, threatens to sue his town for his wages because he hears they will choose him no more.

LINCOLNSHIRE

[County]   Sir Robert Carr, baronet; 20,000*l.* in boons; Chancellor of the Duchy; two wives living at this time, one Arlington's sister.

Great Grimsby   William Broxolme, esquire, an indigent papist, has had 5,000*l.* given him.

Stamford   Peregrine Bertie, esquire, the Treasurer's brother-in-law, has a pension and a troop of horse.

MIDDLESEX

[County]   Sir Lancelot Lake, much in debt, has a promise that his elder brother's son shall not be naturalized; a notorious cuckold.

Sir Thomas Allen, whose understanding is as great as his honesty; a close embracer of rogues; had a boon of 1,000*l.*

Westminster   Sir Philip Warwick, once secretary to Archbishop Laud; before that a poor singing boy; got artificially from the Treasurer Southampton and the king 40,000*l.*; now Clerk of the Signet; never lies more than when he professes to speak the sincerity of his heart.

Sir Richard Everard; 500*l.*, and that being near spent must have more, or seek a new way to get bread.

NORFOLK

[*Norwich*] Christopher Jay, esquire, a prisoner in the King's Bench, an old decrepit lecher, has 50*l.* a session.

Francis Cory, esquire, no better than Jay.

King's Lynn Robert Coke, esquire, the Treasurer's son-in-law, who by his privilege protects himself from the payment of the money, viz., 8,000*l.*, that was spent at his election.

Robert Wright, esquire; Pepys his pensioner, and has 40*s.* a day allowed him by the seamen as their counsel, but uses them as he does the nation, viz., betrays them.

Great Yarmouth Sir William Doyley got 7,000*l.* out of the Dutch prisoners' allowance, and starved many of them to death; a pension of 500*l.* per annum. His son is a teller in the Exchequer.

Thetford Sir Allen Apsley, the king's falconer, worth 1,200*l.* per annum; the duke's treasurer, worth ——; got by boons and other acts 60,000*l.*; a red-letter man, if of any religion.

Sir Joseph Williamson, once a poor foot-boy, then a servitor, now Principal Secretary of State and pensioner to the French king.

Castle Rising Samuel Pepys, esquire, once a taylor, then serving-man to the Lord Sandwich, now Secretary to the Admiralty, got by passes and other illegal ways 40,000*l.*

NORTHAMPTON

Northampton Henry, Lord O'Brien, by his wife's interest has got of Secretary
Borough Williamson 1,500*l.* and the reversion of Cobham Park and other estates that were in the Crown, worth 13,000*l.* per annum. His son married the Treasurer's daughter.

Higham Ferrers Sir Louis Palmer, a great trader in protections, and sells cheap. His father was Attorney-General.

Brackley Robert Spencer, esquire, a bedchamber man to the king, and in debt over ears.

NORTHUMBERLAND

[*County*] Sir John Fenwick, a captain under the duke of Monmouth and promised a place at Court, had 2,000*l.* given him for his election.

Sir Ralph Delavall had 2,000*l.* given him, and has a pension of 500*l.* per annum.

Newcastle Sir Francis Anderson, a pensioner to the Treasurer.

Morpeth Sir George Downing, a poor child bred up on charity, like Judas betrayed his master. What then can his country expect? He drew and advised the oath of renouncing the king's family, and took it first himself. For his honesty, fidelity, &c., rewarded by his Majesty with 80,000*l.* at least, and is Commissioner of the Customs; the House bell to call the Courtiers to vote at six o'clock at night; an Exchequer teller.

Berwick-on-Tweed   Daniel Collingwood, esquire, a Court janizary; a pension of 300*l.* per annum; governor of Holy Island.

Viscount Dunblane, fifteen years old, the Treasurer's son, bribed the mayor falsely to return him.

NOTTINGHAMSHIRE

[County]   Sir Francis Leeke, baronet, governor of the Blockhouse at Gravesend; a foot company and 500*l.* in money.

East Retford   Sir Edward Dering, baronet, Commissioner of the Court of Claims in Ireland; the Chancellor's brother-in-law; promised to be Secretary of State after Coventry; now Commissioner of the Customs in London, worth 1,200*l.* per annum.

OXFORDSHIRE

University   Laurence Hyde, Master of the Robes to the king, has had in boons 20,000*l.*

New Woodstock   Thomas Howard, esquire, the lord of Suffolk's brother; 400*l.* per annum pension.

RUTLAND

[County]   Edward Noel, esquire, Lord Lieutenant of Hampshire, Lord Warden of the New Forest; and other great favours promised him, which he need not doubt of, being the Treasurer's nephew.

SHROPSHIRE

[County]   Sir Francis Lawley, a pensioner, one of the horses in Madame Fontelet's coach.

Ludlow   Somerset Fox, a pensioner of 300*l.* per annum.

Sir Job Charlton, serjeant-at-law, Chief Justice of Chester, a dull Welsh judge; 500*l.* per annum for his Speaker's place.

Much Wenlock   George Weld, esquire, a Commissioner of the Excise in Ireland; 2,000*l.* in money; a declared enemy to his country.

Bishops Castle   Edmund Waring, esquire, a Commissioner of the Excise; a pension to keep him out of prison; Sir Job Charlton's brother-in-law.

William Oakeley, esquire, brother-in-law to Charlton and Waring, has a small pension.

SOMERSETSHIRE

Bath   Sir William Bassett, Henry Seymour's son-in-law; 1,000*l.* given him by Clifford. He has a promise of a place in the Law Act. Always drunk when he can get money.

Wells   Maurice, Lord Fitzhardinge, one of that family which had from the Crown in boons and places 200,000*l.*, beside the unnatural honour given to the younger brother for pimping, which came afterwards to the father and so to this lord. He is colonel of horse in Ireland.

Taunton   Sir William Portman, in hopes to be a lord, much priest-ridden.

Bridgwater	Sir Edmund Wyndham, Knight Marshal; in boons 5,000*l*. His wife was the king's nurse.
Minehead	Thomas Wyndham, esquire, bedchamber man to the king, as also equerry. He married a Court ——.

STAFFORDSHIRE

[County]	Randolph Egerton, esquire, a captain in the guards, has had in boons 1,000*l*.
Lichfield	Richard Dyott, esquire, a sea-captain, kinsman to Sir Robert Carr; 400*l*. per annum pension.
[*Stafford Borough*]	Walter Chetwynd; courted, treated and complimented out of his vote.
Newcastle-under-Lyme	[William] Leveson Gower, esquire, son-in-law to the earl of Bath, had a great estate fall to him by chance; but honesty and wit never came by accident.

SUFFOLK

[County]	Sir Henry Felton, a pensioner, and his son a bedchamber man.
Dunwich	Sir John Pettus; a pension of 300*l*. per annum. All his estate is under extent.
	William Wood, esquire, master of the king's dock, his shipwright, and a violent man for taxes.
Sudbury	Sir Robert Cordell, a poor gentleman that has almost spent all.
Leominster[1]	Major [Humphrey] Cornwall; a pension of 200*l*. per annum, and a captain in the army.
Eye	Sir George Reeve, though possessed of a great estate yet content with a small pension, and promises that he shall be paid a great sum of money he had in the bankers' hands; of no religion.
	Robert Reeve, his son. No less than the Treasurer's table is sufficient to feed his monstrous carcase.
Bury St. Edmunds	Sir John Duncombe, a pensioner of 2,000*l*. per annum; in boons 20,000*l*.
	William Duncombe, his son.

SURREY

[County]	Sir Adam Browne, baronet, the Treasurer's cousin-german and the duke of York's vassal.
Southwark	Sir Thomas Bludworth, a mercenary alderman of London, not to be forgotten for his pissing out the fire.
Bletchingley	Sir William Hayward, a commissioner in the sale of the fee farm rents, by which he got 2,000*l*.; a privy chamber man, and a grant of 2,000*l*. in money.
	Sir Edward Bysshe, King at Arms; 100*l*. a session, yet very poor.
Reigate	Sir John Werden, the duke of York's secretary, a favourer of popery.

---

[1] In Herefordshire.

Guildford   Thomas Dalmahoy, esquire, a Scotch serving-man, a creature of Lauderdale's, chosen by the duke of York, who was in pension at his election and voted for him.

SUSSEX

[County]   Sir William Morley, knight of the bath, a constant Court dinner man.

Chicheste   Richard May, esquire, a lawyer, recorder of Chichester, a pensioner, and promised to be heir to Baptist May if he votes.

Horsham   Sir John Covert, baronet; wheedled with promises; much in debt.

Midhurst   Baptist May, esquire, Privy Purse; 1,000*l.* per annum allowance; got besides in boons for secret service 40,000*l.* This is he that said 500*l.* per annum was enough for a country gentleman, to drink ale, eat beef, and to stink with, &c.

Lewes   Sir John Stapley, an indigent.

Sir Thomas Woodcock, deputy governor of Windsor Castle; a foot company; 200*l.* per annum pension. He set up a deed to gain his niece's estate, which was found to be forged by a jury at the King's Bench bar, and now stands upon his privilege to prevent a decree in Chancery to have it cancelled.

Steyning   Henry Goring, esquire; 200*l* per annum pension and Court dinners.

Bramber   Percy Goring, esquire; 200*l.* per annum pension.

New Shoreham   Henry Goring, esquire; 500*l.*, and promised a pension.

East Grinstead   Edward Sackville, esquire, lieutenant to the Yeomen of the Guard.

Arundel   Roger, earl of Orrery, President of Munster, and a regiment of horse in Ireland.

Francis, Viscount Longford, formerly Treasurer of Ireland, which he sold for 14,000*l.*, now a pensioner of 500*l.* per annum.

WARWICKSHIRE

[County]   Sir Robert Holt, baronet; 1,000*l.* given him, and protection from his creditors; brought out of gaol this last session, when outlawed after judgment.

Sir Henry Puckering, alias Newton, paymaster to the popish standing army, and allowance for keeping a table every session.

Warwick   Sir Francis Compton, knight, captain of a troop of horse.

WESTMORLAND

[County]   Sir Philip Musgrave, baronet; a regiment of foot; governor of Carlisle; given him in fee farm rents 6,000*l.*

Appleby   Thomas Tufton, esquire, bedchamber man to the duke of York.

WILTSHIRE

Salisbury   Sir Stephen Fox, from a poor foot-boy, and then singing boy, has got in places by the Court 150,000*l.*; Clerk of the Green Cloth.

Wilton   Sir John Birkenhead, a poor ale-house keeper's son, got, by lying, to be one of the Masters of the Request and Faculty Office, and in boons 3,000*l.*

Hindon   Edward Seymour, who had for four years 2,000*l.* pension to betray the country party, for which he then appeared; but, since he hath shown himself barefaced, and is Treasurer of the Navy and Speaker, one of the Commissioners of the Admiralty, and of the popish cabal, received 6,000*l.* per annum.

Robert Hyde, esquire, had sold his vote before he came into the House, and had 1,000*l.* for this last (his first) session.

Westbury   Thomas Wanklin, esquire, once a poor serving-man, now one of the Commissioners of the Excise in Ireland, and 50*l.* a session; kept an inn at Kingston three years, now keeps a tavern in Essex Buildings in the Strand.

Devizes   George Johnson, esquire, a lawyer and a Welsh judge, the Treasurer's solicitor, and an impudent ——; has the reversion of the Master of the Rolls, but some say that is only in trust for Baron Bertie.

Chippenham   Francis Gwyn, esquire, one of the Commissioners of the Excise in Ireland, had 500*l.* given him.

Malmesbury   Philip Howard, esquire, of the duke's bedchamber: 300*l.* per annum pension.

Sir Thomas Estcourt, reversioner of the Judge of the Marshalsea, his father's own son, converted to the Church of Rome by his young, handsome mother-in-law, with whom he is very inward.

Cricklade   Sir John Ernly, a Commissioner of the Navy and Chancellor of the Exchequer, always votes as directed.

Great Bedwin   Henry Clerke, an indigent Commissioner of the Prizes, and a place in the Customs House at Bristol worth 200*l.* per annum.

Daniel Finch, esquire, the Chancellor's son.

Ludgershall   William Ashburnham, esquire, got by the Court 50,000*l.*; Cofferer.

George Legge, esquire, supposed to be a papist, of the duke's bedchamber, and governor of Portsmouth; in boons 40,000*l.*

Old Sarum   Sir Edward Nicholas, knight, got by the Court 10,000*l.*

Marlborough   Sir John Elwes, knight, very poor, but a place in Ireland of 300*l.* per annum; a Court admirer.

WORCESTERSHIRE

[County]   Samuel Sandys, senior, esquire; a boon given him in the Excise which he sold for 13,500*l.*

Worcester City   Thomas Street, esquire, a Welsh judge, promised other preferments, had 500*l.* given him.

Droitwich   Samuel Sandys, junior, esquire, son of ——; 13,500*l.*

Henry Coventry, Secretary of State, the breaker of the Triple League, as he himself affirmed when he went to Sweden.

Evesham   Sir John Hanmer, a prodigal gentleman of the horse to the Master of the Horse, Commissioner of the Excise in Ireland, and a troop of horse in Ireland; 2,000*l.* given him in money.

YORKSHIRE

[County]　　　Conyers Darcy, esquire, assisted by the Court in stealing the Lord Lexington's sister from her guardian for his son.

Sir Thomas Slingsby, governor of Scarborough Castle, never gave his country one vote, who voted all for him when chosen knight of the shire.

Knaresborough　　　Valiant Sir John Talbot, a foot company, a company of dragoons, a Commissioner of the Prizes, of the Excise, and for the sale of fee farm rents; 800*l.* per annum out of the Wiltshire Excise, the reversion of the Jewel Office.

Ripon　　　Sir John Nicholas, knight of the bath, Clerk of the Council, got by the Court 40,000*l.*

Sir Edmund Jennings, made high sheriff of Yorkshire (against a vote of Parliament), which is worth 1,000*l.*; promised a pension and place at Court.

Hedon　　　Henry Guy, esquire, groom of the bedchamber.

Aldborough　　　Sir Solomon Swale, baronet, one whose word will not pass for 3*d.* where he is known, got by the Court 600*l.*; an old papist if not priest, but his bald pate excuses his tonsure; a forger of wills.

Sir John Reresby, the Treasurer's creature, sold himself and country to him.

Thirsk　　　Sir William Wentworth, Sir Allen Apsley's son-in-law, much in debt; his wife has a place under the duchess of York, he a pension of 500*l.* per annum; in boons 3,000*l.*

Northallerton　　　Sir Gilbert Gerard, a soldier of fortune. He has got by the Court, and the late bishop of Durham (whose daughter he married), 30,000*l.*, but at present it is most spent; but he hopes his friend the Treasurer will repair all breaches.

Pontefract　　　Sir William Lowther, Commissioner of the Customs, a man whose honesty and integrity oftener fails him than his wit.

CINQUE PORTS

Hastings　　　Sir Denny Ashburnham married Mr. John Ashburnham's daughter; got in places 10,000*l.*

Rye　　　Sir John Robinson, baronet, Lieutenant of the Tower, got in places and gifts, by his wife's interest and other ways, 40,000*l.*; sheriff of London at the execution of Dr. Hewit, and a notorious R—— in the late times

Hythe　　　John Hervey, esquire, the queen's Treasurer, that told the king he had been voting against his conscience to save his Majesty.

Sir Leoline Jenkins, son of a taylor, judge of the Admiralty, was in hopes to be archbishop of Canterbury; employed in four embassies, and whose indefatigable industry in promoting a peace for France has been our ——. He affirmed in the House of Commons that upon necessity the king might raise money without Act of Parliament.

Dover	George Montague, esquire, Abbot Montague's brother, Master of St. Catherine's Hospital; in gifts 3,000*l*.
Sandwich	John Strode, governor of Dover, Commissioner of the Prizes, got by several indirect ways from the king and kingdom 10,000*l*.

WALES

Beaumaris	John Robinson, esquire; 400*l*. per annum pension.
Brecon Borough	Sir Herbert Price, baronet, Master of the Household, got in boons 10,000*l*.
Cardiganshire[1]	Sir Charles Cotterell, Master of the Ceremonies, got in gifts 11,000*l*.
Carmarthen Borough	John, Lord Vaughan, governor of Jamaica; 1,000*l*. per annum pension.
[*Carnarvon County*]	Robert, Lord Bulkeley, the Chancellor's brother-in-law, by whose means he is guardian to Sir William Williams, worth 1,000*l*. per annum to him.
Denbighshire	John Wynne, esquire; 400*l*. given him in money.
Flintshire	Sir Thomas Hanmer, baronet, 500*l*. per annum pension.
Flint Borough	Roger Whitley, esquire, Knight Harbinger, farmer of the Post Office, by which he has got a vast estate.
Merioneth[2]	Andrew Newport, esquire; 400*l*. per annum pension; a squire of the body.

The publisher begs pardon of those gentlemen here named, if he has, for want of better information, undervalued the price and merit of their voices, which he shall be ready upon their advertisement to amend; but more particularly he must beg the excuse of many more gentlemen, no less deserving, whom he hath omitted, not out of any malice, or for want of good will, but of timely notice. But in general the House was, if they please to remember, this last session by three of their own members told that there were among them several papists, fifty outlaws, and pensioners without number; so that upon examination they may arrive at a better knowledge amongst themselves, and do one another more right, than we (howsoever well affected) can possibly do without doors.

95. Gilbert Burnet's account of the opposition, c. 1677

(*History of My Own Time*, ed. Airy, II, pp. 89–93)

In opposition to these[3] a great party was formed, who declared more heartily for the Protestant religion and for the interest of England. The duke of Buckingham and the earl of Shaftesbury opened many of their eyes, and let them know the designs of

---

[1] Really Cardigan Borough.   [2] Really Montgomery County.   [3] The Court party.

the Court; and indeed they were then so visible that there was enough seen without such secret intelligence to convince the most incredulous.

Sir William Coventry had the greatest credit of any man in the House. He never meddled personally with any minister. He had a perfect understanding of affairs. So he laid open the errors of government with the more authority because he mixed no passion or private resentments with it. His brother the Secretary usually answered him with much life in a repartee, but not with the weight and force with which he spoke.

Colonel Birch was a man of a peculiar character. He had been a carrier at first, and retained still, even to an affectation, the clownishness of his education. He got up in the progress of the wars to be a colonel, and to be concerned in the Excise; and in the Restoration he was found to be so useful in managing the Excise that he was put in a good post. He was the roughest and boldest speaker in the House, and talked in the language and phrases of a carrier, but with a beauty and eloquence that was always acceptable. I heard Coventry say he was the best speaker to carry a popular assembly before him that he had ever known. He spoke always with much life and heat, but judgment was not his talent.

Waller was the delight of the House, and even at eighty he said the liveliest things of any among them. He was only concerned to say that which should make him be applauded, but he never laid the business of the House to heart, being a vain and empty, though a witty, man. He deserves a character, as being one of the great refiners both of our language and poetry, and he was for near sixty years one of the best of all our writers.

The two men of quality that were the most considered were the Lord Russell and the Lord Cavendish. Russell was a man of great candour, and of a general reputation; universally beloved and trusted; of a generous and obliging temper. He had given such proofs of an undaunted courage, and of an unshaken firmness, that I never knew any man who had so entire a credit in the nation as he had. He quickly got out of some of the disorders into which the Court had drawn him, and ever after that his life was unblemished in all respects. He had from his first education an inclination to favour the nonconformists, and wished the laws could have been made easier to them, or they more pliant to the law. He was a slow man, and of little discourse; but he had a true judgment, when he considered things at his own leisure. His understanding was not defective; but his virtues were so eminent that they would have more than balanced real defects if any had been found in the other.

Cavendish, now duke of Devonshire, was a libertine both in principle and practice. He went off from the Court at first upon resentments for some disappointments there. He was an ambitious and revengeful man; but he had the courage of a hero, with a much greater proportion both of wit and knowledge than is usual in men of his birth. He had a softness in his exterior deportment, to which there was nothing within that was answerable.

Littleton and Powle were the men that laid the matters of the House with the greatest dexterity and care. Powle was very learned in precedents and parliament journals, which goes a great way in their debates; and when he had leisure to prepare himself he was a clear and strong speaker. Littleton was the ablest and vehementest arguer of them all. He commonly lay quiet till the end of a debate; and he often ended it speaking with a strain of conviction and authority that was not easily resisted. I lived the very next door to him for several years, and we spent a great deal of our time every day together. He told me all their management; and commonly, when he was to put his whole strength to argue any point, he used to talk it over with me, and to set me to object all that I could against him. He lived wholly in London; so matters were most in his hands during the intervals of Parliament, and by his means it was that I arrived at such a knowledge of their intrigues. He was a wise and worthy man, who had studied much modern history and the present state and interests of Europe.

Sir Thomas Lee was a man that valued himself upon artifice and cunning, in which he was a great master, without being out of countenance when it was discovered. Vaughan, the Chief Justice's son, was a man of great integrity, had much Welsh pride, and did great service. These were the chief men that preserved the nation from a very deceitful and practising Court, and from a corrupt House of Commons; and by their skill and firmness they, from a small number who began the opposition, grew at last to be the majority.

96. Report of the French ambassador to Louis XIV on his parliamentary associates in England, 1679

(Sir John Dalrymple, *Memoirs of Great Britain and Ireland*, App., pp. 260–264, 315–316)

14 December[1] 1679

SIRE,

Conformable to the orders your Majesty has given me, I have re-entered into a correspondence with the persons in Parliament who I thought might be useful to your service hereafter. I had always kept measures with them to make use of them in time of need. I shall at present give your Majesty the detail, as you order by your last dispatch.

I have at all times taken great care to manage Lord Holles, and I believe I have kept him in very favourable sentiments for your Majesty's interests. He is the man of all England for whom the different cabals have the most consideration. He is respected in general by all parties, but principally by the Presbyterians. Nothing did me so much service with him as the offer I made him on your Majesty's part of a box with your picture set with diamonds. He made great acknowledgments for this mark of your Majesty's esteem; but he has not accepted the present, and I have it still. I have pressed him many times to take it. He has always excused himself, and told me that he should serve your Majesty with less scruple and more usefully if he did not accept it, and that he could not resolve to take it without the permission of the king of Great Britain, being at present of his Council. I opposed with very good reasons the proposal he made to me of telling his Britannic Majesty that your Majesty would make him a present, under the very improbable pretence of his not having received one at the expiration of his embassy to France. In the meantime I can assure your

---

[1] 4/14 December.

Majesty that in the affair of the High Treasurer and the disbanding of the army no person was more useful to your Majesty than Lord Holles.

Although he does not often go to Parliament he is consulted by many people, and his advice has great weight. He is very moderate upon the subject of the duke of York, and declares he cannot consent to his exclusion; but at the same time he is of opinion that the power of a Catholic king of England should be limited. He is apprehensive the Court will always adhere to the design of governing more absolutely than the laws of England admit, and he knows that your Majesty alone can facilitate the success of such a design. Upon this account he wishes that the nation may not be stirred up against France, and believes it would be a great imprudence to give any cause of discontent to a prince so powerful, and who can so easily hurt them.

I sometimes see Lord Holles, but, not to give suspicion by too frequent visits, we have correspondence together by Sir John Baber. He is a man who has great credit with Lord Holles, and who is greatly considered amongst the Presbyterians. He has been very useful to me on many occasions, and it is through him I have been informed in time of what passes in the different cabals. I have had, through the same person, a strict connexion with Sir Thomas Littleton, who is one of the most considerable in the House of Commons, and whose opinions have always been the most followed. I have also kept a particular correspondence with Mr. Powle. He was put into the Council when the persons who opposed the Court were put there. He has so conducted himself since that time that he will always be useful when the Parliament shall meet. He is a man fit to fill one of the first posts in England. He is very eloquent and very able. Our first correspondence came through Mr. Montagu's means, but I have since kept it by my own, and very secretly.

Mr. Harbord is another of those whom I have made use of, and who bore an active part in the affair of the Treasurer and the disbanding the troops; but it would be difficult to employ him at present. He has considerable credit amongst people in the country. He would be more fit if a minister was to be attacked than he will be to speak in Parliament against an alliance which the Court would make and the other party hinder.

These four have touched what was promised them when the disbanding the troops should be finished and the High Treasurer removed from affairs. I send a memorial apart, by which your Majesty will see what has been given for this, and some other expenses laid out by your orders.

Mr. Sidney has been of great use to me on many occasions. He is a man who was in the first wars, and who is naturally an enemy to the Court. He has for some time been suspected of being gained by Lord Sunderland; but he always appeared to me to have the same sentiments, and not to have changed maxims. He has a great deal of credit amongst the Independents, and is also intimate with those who are the most opposite to the Court in Parliament. He was elected for this present one. I gave him only what your Majesty permitted me. He would willingly have had more, and if a new gratification was given him it would be easy to engage him entirely. However, he is very favourably disposed to what your Majesty may desire, and is not willing that England and the States General should make a league. He is upon bad terms with his brother, who is in Holland, and laughs at the Court's making use of him as a negotiator. I believe he is a man who would be very useful if the affairs of England should be brought to extremities.

Since the time that an alliance has been spoken of between the States General and England, I have taken a great deal of care to nourish the diffidence which some of the most considerable persons in Parliament have of the prince of Orange. They are apprehensive that his union with the Court will render the government more firm and give it more authority; but to say the truth, as it appears to me, I do not believe it would be possible to prevent the Parliament from approving a league made with the States General to guarantee the peace. All that could be done afterwards (if it should happen) would be to hinder the Parliament from giving considerable sums. I therefore do not think I ought to propose to your Majesty the making any new expense at present, the success of which might be very doubtful. It will be always time enough to give and promise new rewards to those whose services may be wished for, when it is seen if the Parliament is to be assembled.

If your Majesty thinks I ought again to press Lord Holles to accept the box of diamonds, I may by means of Lady Holles make him accept it. I do not presume she will be so difficult as he has been. I shall also wait your Majesty's orders for offering anything to the others of whom I have made mention, but shall not make use of the permission you may give unless on occasions which I shall think essential to your service.

I ought to give your Majesty an account of what regards Mr. Montagu separate from the others, being engaged as he is in your Majesty's interests by particular considerations. I have had trouble enough to defend myself for these six months against his solicitations for the payment of the sum which was promised him for the ruin of the High Treasurer. He alleges that the condition is fulfilled on his part. I have always endeavoured to make him understand that it was an affair not entirely finished, and that being fully assured of what had been promised to him he ought not to make himself uneasy whether the payment be made a little sooner or later. . . . Your Majesty will remember, if you please, that Mr. Montagu spoke to me in the month of January last, to try if you would favour the duke of Monmouth's pretensions. It was the principal motive of his journey to France when he was seized at Dover. Mr. Montagu knew well afterwards, by the reservedness with which I spoke to him upon that affair, that your Majesty was not disposed to support so unjust a design, and which then appeared very chimerical. However, upon other affairs we have always had a good correspondence, and have preserved the greatest union.

He has often spoken to me of getting Lord Shaftesbury into your Majesty's interests, and alleges that it would not be impossible if a considerable sum were employed. I do not know if your Majesty will judge it useful to your service to endeavour at it at present. It would be a very proper means to stir up new embarrassments to the king of England, and Lord Shaftesbury would be still more bold if he found himself secretly supported by your Majesty. But it will be difficult to turn him from his engagements against the duke of York, and to prevent his bestirring himself for the elevation of the duke of Monmouth, or for that of the prince of Orange; for his designs are difficult enough to penetrate, and perhaps his principal end is to endeavour the establishment of a republic, of which he would aim at being chief.

If your Majesty will give me leave to say what I think ought to be done at present with regard to Mr. Montagu, I think you might command me to give him positive assurances of the payment of what was promised him, and that a certain time be named on which this payment shall be actually made. If after this your Majesty will, by his means and those of Lady Harvey his sister, gain any members of Parliament, I can answer that two persons cannot be found more proper to traverse all the designs of the Court. It was by an intrigue of Lady Harvey that I caused to be continued at Brussels a certain person named Bulstrode, who, as Monsieur de Louvois at that time informed me, was useful to your Majesty's service. It has been my principal application with those whom I have at present mentioned to take away from them the least suspicion that your Majesty will enter into a treaty with the king of England. I have, however, taken care not to use positive words upon this, especially to my Lord Holles. I have only told him in general that your Majesty will never enter into any engagement with his Britannic Majesty which might be prejudicial to the liberties and privileges of the English.

I will say nothing to your Majesty upon the subject of the duke of Buckingham, because he is not here at present, and your Majesty knows of yourself of what use he may be to your service. I do not doubt but he is dissatisfied with the refusal I gave him this summer of the twenty thousand crowns which he wanted the power of disposing of. I would rather let him think that I made this saving of myself than let him know that I did it by order. As I saw he had a design of going to France, and doubt not he has been there, I imagine, when he appears here, I shall find him disposed to serve your Majesty when occasions shall present. It does not appear to me he has great credit in Parliament, but he may be useful with regard to the populace and in times of troubles. It is not the most regular minds which always strike the most considerable strokes. . . .

State of the money employed by M. de Barillon,
ambassador from Louis XIV in England,
since 22 December[1] 1678

By the memorial which I sent to Court on 22 December 1678 I had remaining in bills of exchange and ready money the sum of 21,915*l.* 16*s.* 7*d.* sterling, which makes in French money 292,211*l.*

Since the said 22 December to this day, the 14 December 1679, I have given, to wit:

To the duke of Buckingham, 1,000 guineas, which makes 1,087*l.* 10*s.* sterling.

To Mr. Sidney, 500 guineas, which makes 543*l.* 15*s.* sterling.

For the support of Sir Richard Bulstrode in his employment at Brussels, 400 guineas, which makes 435*l.* sterling.

To Sir John Baber, 500 guineas, which makes 543*l.* 15*s.* sterling.

[1] 12/22 December.

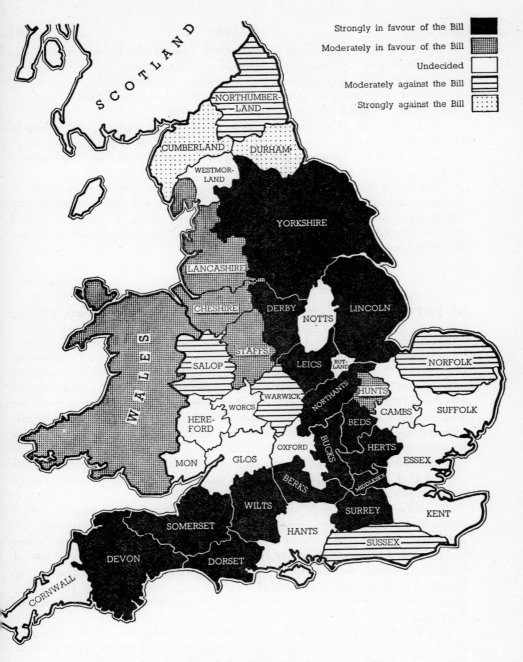

Strongly in favour of the Bill
Moderately in favour of the Bill
Undecided
Moderately against the Bill
Strongly against the Bill

3. ENGLAND AND WALES

SHOWING DISTRIBUTION OF SUPPORTERS AND OPPONENTS OF THE FIRST EXCLUSION BILL IN THE
HOUSE OF COMMONS

To Sir Thomas Littleton, 500 guineas, which makes 543*l.* 15*s.* sterling.

To Mr. Powle, 500 guineas, which makes 543*l.* 15*s.* sterling.

To Mr. Harbord, 500 guineas, which makes 543*l.* 15*s.* sterling.

Total of the expense made to this day, 14 December 1679, 4,241*l.* 5*s.* sterling, which makes in French money 56,550*l.*

On 22 December 1678 I had remaining 21,915*l.* 16*s.* 7*d.* sterling, which makes in French money 292,211*l.*

Since the said 22 December I have given 4,241*l.* 5*s.*, which makes in French money 56,550*l.*

Thus I have remaining, this 14 December 1679, only the sum of 17,674*l.* 11*s.* 7*d.* sterling, which makes in French money 235,661*l.*, of which sum I have in ready money 2,674*l.* 11*s.* 7*d.* sterling, which makes in French money 35,661*l.* The remainder, which is 15,000*l.* sterling, or 200,000*l.* French money, is in bills of exchange which have not been negotiated.

97. Earl of Shaftesbury's instructions to his supporters in Parliament, 1681

(W. D. Christie, *Life of Shaftesbury*, II, pp. cxi–cxii)

GENTLEMEN,

We have chosen you two our knights to represent this county at the Parliament to be holden at Oxford the twenty-first of March next, and we do give you sufficient power to act on our behalf in all things that shall be found by joint advice with the members of Parliament chosen for other places to be for our public good and welfare, which we must leave to your integrities and prudence. Only there are some particulars so manifestly and indisputably necessary that we cannot omit to give you our instructions and directions beforehand in them.

First. We all expect that you should to the last insist for a bill to exclude the duke of York by name, and all other popish successors, from coming to the imperial crown of this realm.

Secondly. That you insist upon an adjustment to be made betwixt the king's prerogative of calling, proroguing and dissolving Parliaments and the rights of the people to have annual Parliaments to dispatch and provide for those important affairs and business that can nowhere else be taken care of; for without the certainty of Parliaments meeting in due distance of time from each other, and their sitting so long as shall be necessary for the dispatch of the affairs of the nation, it is not possible but that our laws, liberties, lives and estates should become in a short time at the will of the prince.

Thirdly. We expect you should restore us to that liberty we and our forefathers have enjoyed until these last forty years, of being free from guards and mercenary soldiers, it being the inseparable right of a free nation that they themselves, and no separate number of paid or hired men, should have the guard of their own prince, government and laws.

Lastly. Although we mention these three particulars as most necessary to us, yet

10

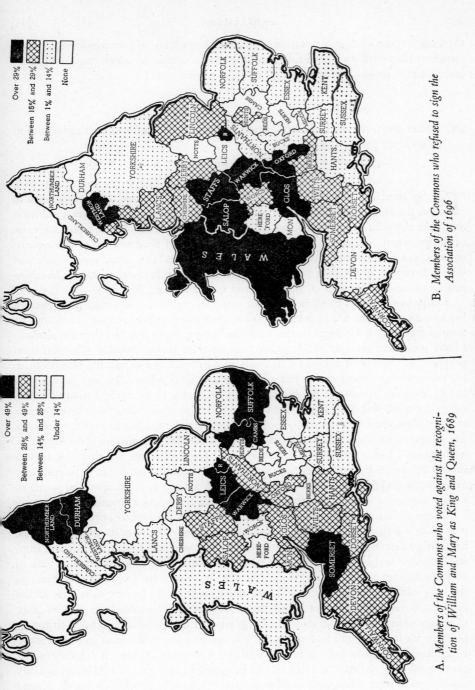

A. *Members of the Commons who voted against the recognition of William and Mary as King and Queen, 1689*

Over 49%
Between 26% and 49%
Between 14% and 25%
Under 14%

B. *Members of the Commons who refused to sign the Association of 1696*

Over 29%
Between 15% and 29%
Between 1% and 14%
None

4. ENGLAND AND WALES

SHOWING DISTRIBUTION OF 'JACOBITES' OR EXTREME TORIES

there are several others of great importance which we leave to your wisdoms, assuring ourselves that until you have fully provided for a complete security against popery and arbitrary power you will not give any of our money.

98. Letter from the earl of Sunderland to the earl of Portland on the formation of a Court party, 1693

(Correspondentie van Willem III en Bentinck, part i, ii, pp. 38–40)

London, 20 June 1693, O.S.

The Speaker, Mr. Guy and I have done a great deal in order to persuade men to serve the king, and I think with good success. They have acted with great industry, diligence and skill. Most of those we named to you being fixed, I have talked to many of the principal, and doubt not but they will do well. I need not tell you the particulars of what will suffice such as are to have money, but I can assure you it will come within compass. But I must be particular concerning such as are to have something besides money, as the earls of Mulgrave and Bath and Lord Brandon.

I hope you will not think that because some are right set others may be neglected, for two or three bad angry men will spoil what many others cannot mend, and be assured that there is sufficient matter ready and preparing to disorder the next sessions. I have spoken to the earl of Mulgrave, and have let him know that what has been proposed for him is all agreed to, but only that he must not expect the title till there is a promotion, which he takes just as if the whole were refused. He says he valued it chiefly because he thought he should have it alone, for to be made a marquis when others are made dukes, he had rather be as he is; and so looks upon the whole business at an end. I desired him not to do so, for I would represent what he said. I write only the substance of what passed. At last with great difficulty he promised to engage in nothing till I had an answer to the letter I said I would write, but that that answer should determine him positively one way or other, and that he would look upon any delay or uncertainty as a denial, for he says if such a thing as this in question comes so hard it must be a very foolish thing of him to think of being a courtier.

I hope the king will agree to the whole, and not put him off to a promotion, for if he does he is lost, and you know it is then to no purpose to manage the House of Lords, for though a great deal more is necessary all the rest will be insignificant without him, and I think if he behaves himself well it will be more to the king's advantage than to his to make him a marquis, and declare he does so because he is satisfied with him. As the king's affairs stand, nothing will give more credit to the government after all the boldness or rather deadness of it, and the dissatisfaction which has been showed, than to engage men of estates and understanding, who are interested and cautious, to appear publicly for it; and I will be bold to say, if it can be done to this man and some more I shall name, when the king returns, it will give a new life to business, which must be given some way or other. If a title should be granted to the earl of Mulgrave, nobody can except against it but such as have the same sort of pretensions, who all depend upon the king and may very well stay, and will be the more desirous of such favours.

Concerning the earl of Bath I do propose that the king will pass by Lord Lansdowne's fault, make amends to John Grenville for what was taken from him, and then tell the earl of Bath how he expects to be served by him and his family. I hope the king will promise my Lord Brandon a regiment of horse at the end of these sessions, my lord of Oxford's when it falls, and to make him a major-general. I could say a great deal in his behalf to show all this to be reasonable, and particularly the chief part, his being a major-general; but I will say only this, that without excepting any man none can do more good or hurt than he, and if the king takes him into his service he will be well served by him.

The earl of Stamford and other lords must have money. I would be glad more of that House might be gained; but the means are difficult, and therefore I will mention nothing of it till the king returns, though I have important things to offer. I desire you will lay this before the king, and I hope you will make all easy concerning Mulgrave, Bath and Brandon, for what is proposed for every one of them is necessary to gain them, and it is necessary to gain every one of them. To make the king's business go on, nothing must be neglected or thought superfluous. Pray, my Lord, let me know the king's mind as soon as you can, particularly in relation to the three lords. The Speaker and his friend are positively of my opinion.

Mr. Smith's nephew must not be forgot. Sir Robert Howard is in very ill humour. He thinks himself extremely ill used, but may soon be set right, and I hope will be. Since I came hither Sir William Trumbull has been with me to excuse his not going into Ireland. The reasons are unfit for a letter. They relate to the ministers, and particularly to Lord Rochester. After many complaints of them he professed all the duty possible for the king; and before he left me he desired me to write to your lordship to recommend him to the bishop of Canterbury to be judge of the Prerogative Court in the place of Sir Richard Raynes, who is dying. I told him I did not believe my credit could do a thing of that kind, but I thought his might, and therefore if he would give me his request in writing I would send it to you, which I now inclose. I believe he is the fittest man in England for the employment, and that he is entirely for this government. If you will recommend him, pray let me know it.

I cannot end this letter without conjuring you to persuade the king not to stay a moment longer abroad than is necessary. If people write you truth you will hear so much of the discontent, or rather rage, people are in concerning the fleets, the admirals and the ministers, that it is to no purpose to mention anything of it. I have made use of my friend's ciphers for letters and for names. It is so long since I have writ anything of this kind I am afraid you will hardly read this letter. I am for ever yours.

99. Paul de Rapin-Thoyras on Whigs and Tories under Anne
(*Historical Dissertation upon Whig and Tory*, pp. 21–108)

Then[1] it was that two parties began to be formed in the kingdom, one whereof was for the king and the other for the Parliament. . . . The king's friends were at first called Cavaliers, which name was afterwards changed into that of Tories. Those of

[1] Early in 1642.

the Parliament, who were then called Roundheads, afterwards received the name of Whigs.

The origin of these two names of Whig and Tory was this. At that time the denomination of Tory was applied to certain robbers or banditti in Ireland, who lurked upon the mountains or in the islands which form the vast bogs of that country. They are now called rapparees. As the king's enemies accused him of favouring the Irish rebellion, which broke out at the same time, they gave his friends the name of Tories. On the other hand the latter, to be even with their adversaries, who were strictly united with the Scots, nicknamed them Whigs, who were in Scotland the same sort of banditti as the Tories in Ireland. It appears by this that these two names are as ancient as the beginning of the troubles, though they did not come into fashion till many years afterwards. . . . These are the two parties that began to divide England in the time of Charles I, and which divide it still. The papists immediately ranged themselves on the side of the king, who was not so much their enemy as the Parliament was; and they have ever since remained united with the Tory party. . . .

The king's party consisted of two sorts of men, one whereof had chiefly in view the political interest of the king and Crown, and the other that of the Church of England. But they were all united in this point, that they found their reciprocal advantage in the king's prosperity, without which they could never hope to succeed in their designs. For this reason they were looked upon as only one party, under the name either of Cavaliers or Royalists. This mixture of two different views in the same party has continued to this day, and is not one of the least causes of the confusion of ideas which arises upon the word Tory. To distinguish one from the other as clearly as I can I shall call the former Political or State Cavaliers, and the latter Ecclesiastical or Church Cavaliers.

Each of these two parties was again subdivided into two others. For among the Political Cavaliers were men who, persisting in the maxims of the duke of Buckingham, Archbishop Laud and the earl of Strafford, wished to see the king absolute and in a condition to destroy the privileges of Parliament. These may be called the Arbitrary; but they were few in number, and very unable to support the king in his adversity, though in his prosperity they had made a great noise in the kingdom. The other branch of Political Cavaliers consisted of those whom I shall call Moderate. These indeed wished to see the royal power vested with its proper rights, but not with any prerogatives contrary to the ancient constitution of the government. The other Cavaliers, that I have called Ecclesiastical, were also divided into two branches, whereof one consisted of Rigid Churchmen, that is of people that would not give up the least tittle of the practice of the Church of England. Those of the other branch were less scrupulous and less obstinate, and may be called the Mitigate.

In opposition to the Cavaliers or Royalists, who followed the king's party, the Roundheads or Parliamentarians were divided into two chief branches, namely the Political and Ecclesiastical. The principal aim of the former was to maintain the rights of the people, and of the latter to advance presbytery. Each of these two branches was also subdivided into two others, one whereof consisted of Republicans, whose aim was to sap the very foundations of the regal power, and to turn England into a republic. The other comprehended the Moderate men, who only sought to put it out of the king's power to abuse his prerogative, but were still for leaving him in possession of his just rights. Thus much for the Political or State Roundheads or Parliamentarians. As for the Ecclesiastical ones, they also formed two branches, whereof the first consisted of Rigid Presbyterians, whose view was the destruction of the hierarchy, and the other of Moderate Presbyterians, who would have been satisfied with much less, and perhaps with a bare toleration. . . .

Under a king of so much wisdom and prudence as William III it was almost impossible for the difference of principles to have occasioned any disorders, if the Ecclesiastical Tories could have been contented with seeing their Church uppermost. But the Rigids of that party could not be easy while they saw the Presbyterians enjoy an entire liberty of conscience, exercise their religion in public and possess places notwithstanding the Act of Conformity which had been made in King Charles the Second's reign. They could not help suspecting that the intention of the Whigs was to undermine the Church of England by degrees, and that the king concurred with them in this design. What had been done during the Long Parliament made them fear the same attacks now. But the truth is the Arbitrary Tories, having lost King James, their head and defender, insinuated these fears and suspicions into the Ecclesiastical ones, in order to animate them against King William. . . . From hence proceeded the reports that ran among the people that the Church was in danger. This convinced the Whigs that the Arbitrary Tories had not thrown up their projects, and that if ever they got into power again they would be sure to make use of the pretence of religion to ruin them, as King James had done before. Thus the animosity between the two parties was kept up in spite of all King William could do to hinder it.

The dispute now seemed to be upon the account of religion only, neither the Arbitrary Tories nor the Republican Whigs having an opportunity of pushing their principles. This has given occasion to many people to form a false idea of the differences that reign between the two parties, and to imagine that they consist solely in their diversity of sentiments with relation to the government of the Church. But this is certainly a mistake. When a fair opportunity offers, the Arbitrary Tories show plainly that the safety of the Church of England is not the only motive of their actions; and it is likely the Republican Whigs would remember their old maxims if the times favoured them. . . .

When Queen Anne succeeded to the throne the mediocrity of her understanding made it easy to judge that her ministry would have much more share in the government than herself. Again, her education made people fear she would throw herself into the hands of the Arbitrary Tories and of the Rigids, of which her uncle, the earl of Rochester, was looked upon as the leader.

That lord was equally dreaded both by the Moderate Tories and the Whigs, as a dangerous man, and one that would carry matters to the highest extremities. . . . It is exceedingly probable that he would have been set at the helm by the queen, his niece; but they say the apprehensions the Moderate Tories were in of seeing him in so elevated a post prevailed upon them to resolve to unite with the Whigs in order to prevent it. . . . The Lord Godolphin, the Lord Marlborough and some other heads of the Moderate Tories were those that joined the Whig party, which they strengthened more by their prudence than by their number or credit. Ever since that time the Moderate Tories and the Moderate Whigs have been but one and the same party.

It would be unnecessary to relate in this place with how much glory, both to England in general and the queen in particular, this new ministry directed the affairs of the public. . . . During their administration the Arbitrary Tories and the Rigid Ecclesiastics were totally excluded from civil employments and ecclesiastical dignities; and if they had kept in till the queen's death those two branches of the Tory party would undoubtedly have been greatly lessened both in number and credit.

Yet the queen could not without some impatience endure to see herself as it were constrained to follow the advice of those whom she had a right to command, and who, if we may believe the public reports, did not allow her to be directed by her own judgment or inclinations. The Arbitrary Tories, getting a hint of this, or perhaps having by some means instilled these sentiments into her, plied her daily with arguments that might foment her chagrin, which they did by the assistance of a certain lady that was much in her confidence. They succeeded so well in this contrivance that, having completely persuaded her she was a slave, they inspired her with a resolution of setting herself free. This intrigue was managed with so much art and secrecy that the ministry found themselves outed before they could take the proper measures to prevent their ruin. Of a sudden the Arbitrary and Rigid Tories were put in their places. The Parliament, in which the Whigs had a great majority of voices, was dissolved, and the queen called another, wherein the new ministry took care to have such members elected as were wholly devoted to their party. Everybody that is in the least acquainted with England must know how much influence the court has in elections. Besides, they added vast numbers to their faction by fomenting jealousies with respect to religion, and by persuading the people that the Church had been in woeful peril during the administration of the last ministry, and that it would always be so whenever the Whigs were at the helm. It was by these suggestions that they revived the fury of the Ecclesiastical Tories, and egged them on to commit such violences upon the Presbyterians as ought never to be suffered in a well-regulated state. . . .

Hitherto things went swimmingly for the new ministry; but they full well knew that the chimerical terrors they had spread among the people could not live long, though for the present they did them admirable service. Besides, even though they had been sure to keep up this disposition in the people, yet the queen might die soon, enjoying but an indifferent state of health. In this case they had too much reason to fear that all they had been doing would be overturned at once by the elector of Hanover, who was obliged for his succession chiefly to the Whigs. . . . Their party was too weak to subsist by its own strength, if they should have the king against them, as experience had often convinced them during the reign of King William and the beginning of the queen's. They concluded therefore (at least if we may judge by their actions) that their safest way would be to settle the Pretender upon the throne, that they might never want a protector when the queen was gone. . . .

After having gone through this short history of the rise and progress of the two parties of Whig and Tory, the reader, I believe, will not be displeased to see a more particular account of their views, interests, strength and characters. . . .

The Political or State Tories are divided, as I said before, into two branches, whereof the one we may call the Arbitrary Tories. They are commonly called in England by the name of High-Flyers. . . . These are for making the king absolute in England as he is in France and some other countries, and his will they think ought to pass for a law. . . . We may easily judge that in such a country as England this party cannot be very numerous; and yet it is by no means despicable, for three reasons. First, because the heads of this party are men of high quality, and generally favourites, or ministers of state, or others that possess the greatest posts at court and the most eminent dignities in the Church. As these are not likely to submit to the leading of any but themselves, they generally by means of their high stations make themselves the chiefs and masters of all the Tory party. . . .

In the second place this particular branch of the Tories is considerable upon this account, that when they are in the ministry they get the Tory clergy to make the pulpits ring with the doctrine of passive obedience, which is of no small use to them in bringing the people to their side. They persuade the parsons that all they intend is to ruin the Presbyterians, and with this insinuation draw them in to preach up a dogma which in its consequences is equally prejudicial to all the subjects. Instances of this were seen in the reigns of Charles II, James II, and the latter end of Queen Anne.

Lastly, the Arbitrary Tories become very powerful when they have a king on their side, as they have often had; and then it is that the liberty of the nation is in danger. We have had proofs of this in the reigns of James II, Charles I, Richard II, Edward II and Henry III, for the party of Arbitrary Tories is more ancient than is generally imagined.

The second branch of the Political or State Tories consists of those I have before called Moderate. These are for not depriving the king of any of his prerogatives, but they would by no means sacrifice to him the privileges of the subject. These are true Englishmen; they have the real good of their country at heart, and are resolved to maintain the constitution of the government in the same condition it was transmitted down to them from their ancestors. They have often saved the State, and will save it again, whenever they see it in danger, either from the Arbitrary Tories or the Republican Whigs, by making a noble stand against all such as would break in upon the constitution. It would be injustice to these to confound them with the former under the same name of Tories.

As there are two branches of the State Tories, so there are also two of State Whigs, namely the Republican and the Moderate Whigs. The Republican Whigs are a remnant of the party of the Long Parliament, which undertook to change the government into a republic. These do now make so pitiful a figure that they only serve to fortify the party of the other Whigs, with whom they commonly join. . . .

The second branch of the State Whigs is made up of the Moderate Whigs, who are very near of the same principles with the Moderate Tories, and who ought to be looked upon as true Englishmen, that are for preserving the government upon its ancient foundations. In this they would be entirely like the Moderate Tories if there were not this difference, that the Moderate Tories incline more to the side of the king, and the Moderate Whigs to the side of the Parliament. . . . These latter make a jest of the doctrine of passive obedience when the consequences of it are pushed too far. They aver that the king's power is limited to certain prerogatives, which he cannot without injustice exceed; and therefore they are persuaded that whenever he is guilty of any usurpation on that side the people have a right to resist his enterprises. It is an easy inference from hence that they do not believe the king may dispense with the laws. . . .

It must be remembered that hitherto I have spoken of the Whigs and Tories only in reference to the government and not to religion. I would by no means confound two things that ought to be carefully distinguished. All the Churchmen are not Tories, when a point of government is in dispute; nor are all the Presbyterians Whigs, as several imagine. There are several Presbyterians who are in this case of the principles of the Moderate Tories, and who would be no less unwilling to see the king despoiled of his prerogatives than to see the subjects deprived of their rights. So there are also a great number of Churchmen, and many bishops, who are Whigs, nay very good Whigs, if we consider them only with relation to the government and in opposition to the Arbitrary Tories. This shows how necessary it is to make a distinction between the Political or State Whigs and Tories and the Ecclesiastical Whigs and Tories. . . .

After King Charles II was restored to the throne the different branches of the two parties began to be distinguished. . . . Some among the Presbyterians intimated that they would willingly relax somewhat of the stiffness of their principles, and many Churchmen were of opinion that in favour of peace some condescension might be shown the Presbyterians. These moderate men therefore of both parties were those that formed the two branches of Mitigated Whigs and Tories. But the majority of both parties stuck firm to their principles with inconceivable stubbornness. Among the Churchmen there were a vast many who would not for the world recede one single tittle from the practice of their Church; and among the Presbyterians there were those that were as much shocked at the sight of a minister officiating in a surplice as they could be at an heretical sermon, and who looked upon all the ceremonies the Church of England had retained as downright idolatry and superstition. This was what gave birth to the two parties of Rigid Churchmen and Presbyterians which remain at this day. The hierarchy is the chief article upon which they are divided. Both sorts are comprised under the denomination of Whig and Tory, because the Rigid Churchmen join the Tories and the Rigid Presbyterians the Whigs. . . .

After having given as clear an account as I was able of the two parties we must next examine their several motives and interests. If we will believe what each of them says of himself, nothing can be more just, more equitable, more reasonable than the principles they act upon. They are guided wholly by the glory of God, the honour of the king, the good of the public, the benefit of the nation. For my part, if I am allowed to give my opinion, private interest is the first mover of their actions. Ever since the two parties have been formed every man has laboured assiduously to get the better of his antagonists, because from that superiority flow places, honours and dignities, which the reigning party distribute to their own members, exclusive of the contrary faction. This induced King William to say that if he had good places enough to bestow he should soon unite the two parties. . . .

But when I say that interest is their chief motive I would not be thought to exclude several other motives besides, which may affect as well the heads as the members of each party. Some believe their principles really tend to the good of the kingdom; others act out of a religious motive; some through revenge, a spirit of party, and for the honour of obtaining the victory. There are an infinite number of other motives, of which it would be unnecessary to give a particular account, because such a detail would lead us into the examination of the conduct of private persons. . . . We had better examine into the strength of the two parties and their several interests. . . . I shall begin with the Tories.

It is at first very hard to believe that in such a country as England, where the subject enjoys so many fine privileges of which other nations are now deprived, there should be a set of people that long to see the king invested with an unlimited power. . . . Yet it is but too certain that there has always been such a party in England, and that it is still subsisting, though it is disowned by most of those that are engaged in it. . . . The great art of that party consists in pulling the Church into the scrape, by seeming wonderful zealous for all her rights. By this means they mingle themselves with the Ecclesiastical Tories (whose number is very great), avoid alarming the Moderate Tories, and lastly lie snug till they have drawn in all the party to serve their private ends. But with all their caution and artifice they have the ill luck never to be able to get to the end of their race. After having made themselves the heads of the whole Tory party, and after having led the Moderate and the Ecclesiastical part of them to one certain point by secret turnings and windings, they are at last obliged to take some particular steps which discover their whole plot. Then they lose great numbers of their friends, who not only leave them in the lurch but even join with the Whig party. A proof of this was seen in King James the Second's time, who found himself of a sudden deserted by all the world at the very time when he thought he had just attained the height of his wishes. If in the last year of Queen Anne the Arbitrary Tories, who governed in her name, had proceeded to revoke the Act of Succession (as they intended), it is exceedingly probable they would have met with the same mortification; and I do not at all doubt but the like revolution will always happen upon the like occasion. . . .

The party or branch of Moderate Tories is vastly more numerous than that of Arbitrary Tories. Whatever advantage these latter may have by the quality of their leaders, the others are still the more powerful, because they maintain a good cause—I mean the conservation of the king's just prerogatives. This is an interest which is properly the interest of the whole English nation, which must never expect to be happy under any other government besides that which has been so many ages established in their country. This branch of Moderate Tories does also become more considerable every time any attempt is made to extend or contract the royal power. If it is to contract it, they are joined by all the Whigs; if to extend it, they have the assistance of all the other Tories.

Yet it sometimes happens that the situation of affairs produces an alteration as well in the principles as in the interests of that party. When the king favours the Tories in general (that is to say when he gives them the places and employments), nothing can loosen the Moderate ones from his interest. But if he leans to the other side they have not the same affection for him. Then if they perceive that the Whigs by way of prevention of future usurpations, which is pretty common with them, go about to lessen some part of the royal prerogative, they do not much scruple to join them; but their intent in this is only to let the king know their strength. This artifice they often put in practice during the reign of King William, who often changed his ministries. In general the interest of the Moderate Tories is to oppose the attempts the Whigs might make against the king's authority, because by this they keep up their credit at court and among the people. But at the same time they ought to be very cautious that under the specious colour of being of the same name and party the Arbitrary Tories do not lead them further than they intend to go.

As for the Ecclesiastical or Church Tories, we may easily judge that their party takes in almost the whole kingdom, since that branch is composed of all the members of the Church of England; so that when religion is the point in dispute between the Whigs and Tories the former are by no means able to cope with their adversaries. From hence it proceeds that the Ecclesiastical Tories are never afraid of showing their spleen against the Presbyterian Whigs, because their number gives them a great superiority. The case is not the same with the Presbyterian Whigs, who, even in the time of their greatest prosperity, dare not show the least inclination of attacking the Church of England. They did it once, during the Long Parliament; and the Tories will never forget their having done so. They fancy the Whig party to be an enemy always ready to sap the foundations of their Church, and from what they have done once draw inferences of what they would do again if it lay in their power. This is what makes them so ready to swallow the suspicions that are from time to time scattered among them, that the Church is in danger. . . .

It is true that among the Ecclesiastical Tories there are many who see through the trick by which the whole party is engaged in a ferment, which turns to the account only of a few. Of this number are those I have called the Mitigate, among whom are some that are possessed of the highest dignities in the Church; but they are not the strongest. The Rigids are much more numerous. This last branch is made up of almost all the inferior clergy, of some few bishops, of the two universities and particularly of Oxford; and these bodies are attended by an infinite number of laymen. Of these Rigids consists High Church, that is a Church without the least mixture of Presbytery. These men are so bigoted to the minutest ceremony in the Church of England that they would not give up the most insignificant point, by which obstinacy they show that they are not so much acted by a zeal for religion as by a rancorous party spirit. . . .

The papists are also reckoned a branch of the Tories, because they are attached to that party. As they can never hope to make their religion national but by means of an absolute king, it is not surprising that they should herd with the Arbitrary Tories. Indeed this would be no great support to the Tories if they were no more than the papists that are in England, who have neither employments nor votes in elections; but this admission of the papists ties to the Tory interest some foreign powers that may be very useful to them upon certain occasions. . . .

After having shown the views, strength and interests of the Tory party we must now proceed to the four opposite branches of the Whigs. As for the Republicans, they are very few in number, and go downwards more and more every day. There is not the least likelihood of their ever having such another opportunity as they had during the troubles in the time of King Charles I.

I have already said that the chief difference between the Moderate Whigs and the Moderate Tories consists in that these latter incline more to the prerogatives of the king and the former to the privileges of the subject; but notwithstanding this they easily unite when the nation is in danger. If the Moderate Whigs had not so many Presbyterians among them it might be hoped that the two branches of Moderate Tories and Moderate Whigs would always remain united, as they seemed to be after the death of King William. When I say the one inclines more to the king and the other more to the people I do not relate what they say of themselves but what is really true. The two parties on the contrary aver that their sole intention is to maintain the government in the condition wherein it has been settled for several ages; so that to hear them one would think they never formed but one and the same party. . . .

We come now to the Whigs I before called Ecclesiastical. These are all Presbyterians, and are only a wing of the main body of the Whigs, which consists of the Church of England. Yet even these Presbyterians may be divided into two branches. The first is of Rigid Presbyterians, who absolutely reject not only the hierarchy of the Church but also all the ceremonies that are practised in the Church of England. Their number is pretty considerable in England; but what adds greater weight to them is that all Scotland is for them. . . . It is very easy to conceive that the interest of the Rigid Presbyterians is not that the affairs of the Church should remain upon the foot they now stand, since it can be only by some great revolution that their religion must become national. Accordingly they are looked upon as dangerous people, and are never set at the head of the Whig party, which they would conduct very scurvily.

Lastly, there is another branch of the Ecclesiastical Whigs, which comprehends the Mitigate Presbyterians, and also all the other nonconformists, as Quakers, Anabaptists, &c., who find more support among the Whigs than among the Tories, though at the bottom their junction is of no great service to the party. The Mitigate Presbyterians, who are much less scrupulous, less fiery, less obstinate than the Rigid ones, can with a safe conscience go to Church, and even take the sacrament there, if it is their interest so to do. . . .

We are now to give a yet more complete idea of the two parties of Whig and Tory by drawing both their characters.

The Tories in general are supercilious and haughty. They treat the Whigs with the utmost contempt, and even with rigour, whenever they are uppermost. As the Tory party consists mostly of episcopalians, who are the body of the nation, they look upon themselves to be the reigning party, and cannot bear the equality, much less the superiority, of their adversaries. I cannot better compare the behaviour of the Tories towards the Whigs than to that of the papists towards the Protestants in those countries where the Roman Catholics are the most numerous and have the support of the government. It is with great regret that the Tories allow the Presbyterians even liberty of conscience. . . . The last years of Queen Anne will afford most flagrant instances of that party's fury.

They have also another character: it is that they are prodigious hot, and drive on like madmen. They have often destroyed their own designs by that fault. When they are in the ministry they push on their schemes with inconceivable rapidity. Very remarkable proofs of what I advance may be seen in the reign of Charles II, James II and the late queen. Yet it must be owned that this rapidity is not always to be ascribed to the heat of their passion, but that sometimes it is grounded upon policy. As the Arbitrary Tories, who are generally at the head of the party, do often enter into projects of changing the constitution, they are obliged to make a quick use of the opportunities that offer, because those opportunities are of a nature not to last long. . . .

Another character of the Tories is that they change their principles according as their party is uppermost or undermost. When they have a king on their side they cry up might and main the doctrine of passive obedience, and affirm that the subjects must obey their king without daring to examine the legality of his commands, because at that time they would fain persuade the Whigs to suffer themselves to be oppressed without resistance. But when the government is in the hands of the contrary party, then they hush that doctrine or quite bury it in oblivion. . . . But they have a distinction always ready to answer this objection between a king *de jure* and a king *de facto*, and they aver it is to the king *de jure* that they owe their obedience; and he that favours them is always sure to be king *de jure*, whether he is actually upon the throne or has only some vain pretensions to it.

Let us now proceed to the character of the Whigs. Those of that party that are of the number of the Rigid Presbyterians are a stubborn, heady people, that perhaps would be no less fiery and passionate than the Tories if they were at the helm. But as these have not had the direction of the party ever since the Long Parliament it is not upon them that we are to form the general character of the Whigs, whereas that of the Tories must be drawn from the Arbitrary Tories and the Rigids, who are their heads and leaders.

Those that are at the head of the Whig party are much more moderate than the heads of the Tories. Besides, they commonly act upon fixed principles, from which they never vary, except when they are obliged to do something for the Presbyterians to keep them tight. Far from going about to carry things with a high hand, as the Tories do, they make to their point by slow steps, without passion and without violence. Their greatest trouble is to repress the warmth of some among them who, if they had their will, would put all into confusion. . . .

The Whigs are accused of being very greedy of riches and honours, and of not giving suitable rewards to their adherents, which often makes their friends drop off and forsake them. I have nothing to say to this point, not being sufficiently informed of the particular affairs of the party. . . .

As for the Ecclesiastical Whigs, who are no other than the Presbyterians, all that can be said relating to them is that they are greatly prejudiced against episcopacy and all the rest of the hierarchy of the Church. The question is whether this prejudice is well grounded, or whether, even if it is, that is a reasonable cause of separation. As for my particular, I look upon this dispute to be of but little importance. For this reason I cannot approve of the rigidity of the Presbyterians in a country where the Reformation is established after the manner it is in England, since there is no difference between the two Churches in matters of faith and in essentials. . . .

It may be positively affirmed it is not the interest of the kingdom that one of the parties should become so superior as to meet with no contradiction. If it were the Arbitrary Tories they would bring England under a despotic government; if the Moderate Tories, their inclination to the prerogatives of the Crown will at length enable the sovereign to undertake what he pleases, and to shake off the troublesome yoke of Parliaments; if the papists, England will quickly lose her religion and liberty. On the other hand, if the Republican Whigs regain the advantage they have lost, there will be no longer talk of the kingdom but of the republic of England, as in the time of Cromwell. Lastly, if the Moderate Whigs might carry matters how they pleased, they would take so many precautions against the increase of the royal power that they would perhaps reduce the king to the condition of a doge of Venice.

As for the extremes of the two parties in point of religion, it is certain that if ever the Presbyterians have it in their power to act without opposition they will not be satisfied till they have totally destroyed hierarchy and, in general, the whole Church of England. But again, if the Rigid Episcopalians had no counterpoise to their power, nothing less is to be expected than an open persecution of Presbyterians; and we know not whether they would allow them so much as a bare liberty of conscience.

It is certain the true good and advantage of the kingdom is not to be found in any of the views which the heads of the two parties seem to have an eye to. The only method that can in time restore peace and tranquillity is to let the government remain upon its ancient foundations, and the Church in the condition wherein the Reformation placed it. . . . If this method is not observed it will always be safer for the State that the division should continue as it is at present than that one of the parties should enjoy a superiority, which would be more fatal to the public than the equality their discord keeps them in. Nothing, I think, can put an end to this kind of intestine war but the prudence of a just and equitable king, moderate in his desires, of few passions, a lover of the Protestant religion, and who makes it his whole study to procure the good and happiness of his subjects. This we may justly hope for from the prince that now fills the throne.

Part III
PUBLIC FINANCE

PUBLIC FINANCE

Introduction

IN the sphere of finance no real restoration was either possible or desired. For two centuries before the return of Charles the financial system inherited from the Middle Ages, with its fixed revenue from crown lands and feudal dues, and its restricted expenditure of a correspondingly stable type, had been steadily breaking down. Increased activity on the part of the central government had led to a rapid rise in expenditure at the same time as an influx of the precious metals from the New World, by raising the general level of prices, had produced a heavy fall in the real revenue. By the time of Elizabeth it had become abundantly clear, not merely that the sovereign could no longer hope, in medieval fashion, to "live of his own", but also that the traditional methods of raising revenue were antiquated, burdensome, and unlikely to provide a good foundation on which to build anew.

Thus under the early Stuarts the medieval system was already tottering to its fall when it was shattered beyond repair by the outbreak of the Civil War. Money in large amounts had to be raised at once, and was raised by the most up-to-date and effective methods – Excise duties, increased Customs duties, and a new tax on land and other property which came to be known as the assessment. The Commonwealth governments, when the civil wars came to an end, accepted the principle that the basis of taxation had changed, sold the crown lands, abolished feudalism, and relied for their regular revenue almost entirely on the new taxes. To reverse their work would have meant running counter to a natural development which the recent troubles had not produced but only hastened.

Unfortunately the times were singularly unpropitious for a satisfactory and permanent reconstruction a long new lines. As a result of eighteen years of civil disturbance and foreign adventure the country was not merely disorganized but financially exhausted. The Commonwealth governments, like most revolutionary governments, had been living far beyond their resources, and at the moment of the Restoration were on the verge of bankruptcy. A statement drawn up early in 1660[1] shows debts totalling roughly £2,000,000, as well as an estimated deficit for that year of nearly £1,100,000. In addition the restored monarch was himself heavily in debt to those who had contributed towards his maintenance during the period of his exile, while there were also large debts coming down from the reign of Charles I, representing partly the borrowings of that monarch,[2] and partly those of the Long Parliament before the expulsion of its more moderate members by Colonel Pride.[3] The total burden of indebtedness under which Charles II began his reign cannot have been appreciably less than £3,000,000, and may well have been considerably more.

Thus the financial settlement reached by the Restoration Parliaments was bound to be unsatisfactory. By means of repeated assessments, and a poll tax graded according to rank,[4] they contrived to raise supplies sufficient to discharge the bulk of the heavy arrears due to the army and some part of those due to the navy,[5] thus making possible

[1] No. 100.   [2] No. 102.   [3] No. 101.   [4] No. 113.   [5] No. 124.

273

a process of disbandment which freed them from a political danger and from a crushing financial burden. But the remaining debts of the crown were left untouched; the expedients adopted for bridging the gap between the abandonment of one system of finance and the establishment of another, including as they did even the authorization of the last benevolence in English history,[1] were ill-chosen; and the provision made for normal expenditure was hopelessly inadequate.

Almost as a matter of course the idea that the king should "live of his own" in the strict medieval sense was for ever abandoned; but in place of this hereditary "king's own" it was in effect proposed to substitute a parliamentary "king's own" of £1,200,000 a year, which it was hoped might serve much the same purpose. Part of this sum was to be provided by such of the old hereditary revenues as could be recovered,[2] with the exception of the feudal dues, which it was determined at an early stage to abolish in return for a hereditary land tax;[3] but the bulk of it had inevitably to be raised by the more efficient taxes now in favour.

Of these the Customs duties were granted to the restored monarch for life by a statute, generally known as the Great Statute,[4] which was destined to be kept in force by repeated renewals for the remainder of the Stuart period. The Excise was divided into two equal portions, one of which, contrary to the original decision in favour of a land tax, was assigned to the crown in perpetuity as compensation for the loss of the feudal dues,[5] while the other was granted to the reigning monarch for life. By placing their main reliance on these two taxes the Restoration Parliaments implicitly sanctioned a change which had long been impending from direct to indirect taxation as the normal method of raising revenue in time of peace; but at first, owing to the exhausted state of the country, the returns both to Customs and to Excise were very disappointing, and it was found necessary to supplement them with a new direct tax, levied on houses and generally known as the Hearth Tax,[6] which was granted to the crown in perpetuity, and was to form a third main item in the royal revenue.

Even with this addition, however, the ordinary revenue for the greater part of Charles II's reign fell woefully short of its supposed level, and successive ministers found it impossible by any retrenchment of expenses to make ends meet.[7] To discharge the inevitable deficits and provide for abnormal expenditure due to war they had to rely on special grants, which were voted with reluctance, and also invariably fell short of their estimated yield. Of these special grants the most frequently employed and the most productive was a continuation of the Commonwealth assessment, based at first on the same apportionment of the total sum to be raised as had prevailed immediately before the Restoration, and later on a modification of that apportionment which was to remain in use until it in turn was revised in the reign of William III.[8] Immense though they seemed to contemporaries, however, these special grants were never adequate for their purpose, and sheer lack of money was largely responsible for two of the most discreditable features of Charles's reign – his partial repudiation of his debts,[9] and his practice of subordinating the foreign policy of England to that of France in return for subsidies from the French king.[10]

The lessons to be learnt from the financial difficulties of Charles were not lost upon James. From the moment of his accession that monarch adopted a high-handed attitude, continuing to collect the revenues which had legally expired with the death

---

[1] No. 114.   [2] No. 120.   [3] No. 108.   [4] No. 103.   [5] No. 107.
[6] No. 109.   [7] No. 120.   [8] No. 115.   [9] No. 128.   [10] No. 338.

of his predecessor,[1] and pressing Parliament most strongly for additional supplies for himself. Half a century earlier the levying of unauthorized Customs and Excise duties would have inspired the bitterest opposition; but the practical inconvenience involved in the temporary cessation of such important taxes as these had now become was so obvious and so serious that James's action was condoned by Parliament, and the loyal enthusiasm inspired by the coronation and by Monmouth's landing led not merely to the reimposition of existing taxes but also to the grant of others on a very considerable scale. No new principle was involved, for the additional taxes practically all took the form of increased Customs duties; but their general effect was to place James in a much better financial position than any other Stuart sovereign. Had he not seen fit, in the interests of his general policy, to raise his army to four times the size it had reached under Charles, his income would indeed have greatly exceeded his expenditure.[2]

Thus William succeeded to what was in his eyes a most unfortunate financial inheritance, an inheritance which he himself considerably impaired by his voluntary surrender of the extremely unpopular Hearth Tax.[3] Parliament was resolved not to repeat its mistake of making the crown too independent, especially as regards funds which might be used for the support of the armed forces. It therefore readjusted its conception of the "king's own" so as to embrace only the funds requisite for the civil expenditure of the government, voted the king the parliamentary Excise for life, and assigned a sum of £600,000 from this and the purely hereditary revenues of the crown towards the payment of this Civil List; but the Customs duties, which were primarily intended for the upkeep of the army and navy, it granted only for a period of years at a time.[4] Later in the reign the Civil List was increased to £700,000,[5] but even so it fell short of William's requirements, while the peace establishment of army and navy proved utterly inadequate during the war with France which occupied much the greater part of his reign. Thus William was even more at the mercy of Parliament than Charles had been, and in order to support what seemed to contemporaries a vast expenditure[6] he had to obtain from it not merely the annual assessments or land taxes from which the bulk of his revenue was actually drawn, but also a remarkable array of ill-devised and not very productive taxes,[7] the main purpose of which was to provide the funds on the strength of which it might be possible to borrow.

It is this practice of borrowing which forms the dominant feature in the financial history of Anne's reign. Under Anne the burden of the war with France became even heavier than under William;[8] but no new expedients in the way of taxation were devised to meet the growing charge. The only tax specially associated with the reign, in fact, the stamp tax on newspapers,[9] was designed to serve a political rather than a financial purpose. Borrowing, however, became so customary as to evoke relatively little comment, and to lead even to the reluctant acceptance of the idea of a national debt as a semi-permanent institution.

Previous to the Restoration there had been nothing comparable to the national debt of modern times. Revenue and expenditure had never been so nicely adjusted that the one came in at precisely the right time to meet the other, and monarchs in all ages had thus been compelled to borrow, especially when expenditure was suddenly increased by the outbreak of war. But the debts they incurred were temporary in character, and with due allowance for the slowness of early financial operations may

---

[1] No. 104.   [2] No. 121.   [3] No. 110.
[4] No. 105.   [5] No. 106.   [6] No. 122.
[7] Nos. 111, 116, 117.   [8] No. 123.   [9] No. 119.

be compared to the day to day borrowing or floating debt of later times. Further, they were royal debts, for which only the king's personal credit was pledged. Parliament and the nation had no direct responsibility for or connexion with them.

The initial cause of the change lay in the heavy debts with which Charles II found himself burdened even after Parliament had ostensibly dealt with the problem of arrears due to the Commonwealth forces,[1] debts of which no representation on his part[2] ever induced Parliament to effect a proper settlement. From the very beginning of his reign he was forced to live on borrowed money, deferring payments as long as possible, farming the main branches of the revenue to financiers who could provide large sums in advance, and on the outbreak of war with the Dutch accepting Parliament's provision for loans on the incoming taxes, these loans to be repaid with interest, in the order in which they had been made, as the money reached the Exchequer.[3] Distrust of the whole financial situation grew so serious that at the crisis of the Dutch war it was found necessary to issue a proclamation declaring such payments in course out of the Exchequer to be inviolable;[4] and for some years the payments were duly made.[5] Yet in 1672, by the operation known as the stop of the Exchequer,[6] Charles put an end to a large section of them, took his revenues into his own hands,[7] and offered in return only to recognize the sums due as a debt on which interest at the rate of 6 per cent would be paid.

As presented to the public the expedient to which Charles had recourse was a purely temporary one, for he professed to believe that Parliament would shortly make provision for the payment of the debt; but Parliament conspicuously failed to do so, and the real effect of the stop of the Exchequer was thus to create a permanent debt, as was substantially recognized five years later when it was funded, the interest being charged on the hereditary Excise.[8] So great, however, was the unfunded debt, the claims of which were more pressing,[9] and so inadequate the revenue, that before the close of Charles's reign the government had begun to default on the interest, thereby giving rise to a long controversy as to whether the king could legally alienate in perpetuity revenues fixed in him and his successors, and what was the proper remedy in case of his undertaking not being carried out. Not until the close of William's reign was the matter settled, when Parliament gave legislative sanction to the payment of the interest, though in a modified form little satisfactory to the creditors.[10]

Meanwhile the French wars had inevitably led to the contracting of other debts for the repayment of which Parliament had made itself responsible. From the Revolution till the close of Anne's reign, in fact, the national debt was steadily, and in the eyes of contemporaries rapidly, increasing. Even the peace of Ryswick did little more than call a brief halt in the process. By 1714 the total debt had risen to more than £36,000,000,[11] and the interest on it to approximately £3,000,000.

[1] Nos. 100–102, 124.   [2] No. 125.   [3] No. 59.
[4] No. 126.   [5] No. 127.   [6] No. 128.
[7] No. 129.   [8] No. 130.   [9] No. 131.
[10] No. 132.   [11] No. 133; diagram 3.

BIBLIOGRAPHY

The principal sources of information for the financial history of the later Stuarts are the very disappointing *Calendar of Treasury Papers*, edited by Joseph Redington, only the first four volumes of which (1868–1879) deal with the period, and the magnificent *Calendar of Treasury Books*, edited by William A. Shaw, which has already devoted twenty volumes (1904–1952), some of them in several parts, to the years 1660–1706, and four more (1949–1952) to the years 1708–1711. Unfortunately Shaw did not live long enough to write a considered survey of his own work, and the introductions to his various volumes, although of great value, are insufficiently co-ordinated, needlessly repetitive, and disfigured by prejudices which further reflection might have led him to modify. More dispassionate in tone, and still useful as an introduction to Stuart finance, is his earliest investigation of the subject, "The Beginnings of the National Debt", in *Historical Essays by Members of the Owens College*, edited by T. F. Tout and James Tait (Manchester, 1907), pp. 391–422. For the years immediately succeeding the Revolution there is much valuable information, largely set forth in tabular form, in the official *Return of the whole Amount of the National Debt of Great Britain and Ireland from 1691* (1857), and *Accounts of the Net Public Income and Expenditure of Great Britain in each financial Year from 1688 to 1801* (1869).

The standard work on taxation is Stephen Dowell, *A History of Taxation and Taxes in England from the earliest Times to the present Day* (4 vols., London, 1884–1885), but this is very inadequate for the period and badly out of date. William Kennedy, *English Taxation, 1640–1799, an Essay on Policy and Opinion* (London, 1913), is concerned with the effects rather than with the details of taxation. Edward Hughes, *Studies in Administration and Finance, 1558–1825, with special reference to the history of Salt Taxation in England* (Manchester, 1934), is admirable for the rather specialized subjects with which it deals. There is a useful account of the position under Queen Anne in I. S. Leadam, "The Finance of Lord Treasurer Godolphin", in *Transactions of the Royal Historical Society*, Third Series, IV (1910), pp. 21–32; and information on more technical matters in Sir John Craig, *Newton at the Mint* (Cambridge, 1946).

On the Customs duties the standard treatise is Hubert Hall, *A History of the Custom Revenue in England from the Earliest Times to 1827* (2 vols., London, 1885), and more recent studies H. Atton and H. H. Holland, *The King's Customs* (London, 1908), and Elizabeth E. Hoon, *Organization of the English Customs System, 1696–1786* (New York, 1938). Other sources of revenue are dealt with in Lydia M. Marshall, "The Levying of the Hearth Tax, 1662–1688", in *English Historical Review*, LI (1936), pp. 628–646; and Edward Hughes, "The English Stamp Duties, 1664–1764", *ibid.*, LVI (1941), pp. 234–264.

The goldsmith bankers and the early years of the Bank of England form the main subject of R. D. Richards, *The Early History of Banking in England* (London, 1929), which should be read in conjunction with Dorothy K. Clark, "Edward Backwell as a Royal Agent", in *Economic History Review*, IX (1938), pp. 45–55, the same writer's "A Restoration Goldsmith Banking House", in *Essays in Modern English History in Honor of Wilbur Cortez Abbott* (Cambridge, Mass., 1941), and Clyde L. Grose, "The Dunkirk Money, 1662", in *Journal of Modern History*, V (1933), pp. 1–18. J. E. Thorold Rogers, *The First Nine Years of the Bank of England, an Enquiry into a Weekly Record of the Price of Bank Stock, 1694–1703* (Oxford, 1887), covers somewhat the same ground. A. Andréades, *History of the Bank of England, 1640–1903* (London, 1924), devotes only half a dozen chapters to the seventeenth century. Useful articles are A. V. Judges, "The Origins of English Banking", in *History*, XVI (1931), pp. 138–145; Andrew Browning, "The Stop of the Exchequer", *ibid.*, XIV (1930), pp. 333–337; R. D. Richards, "Stop of the Exchequer", in *Economic History*, II (1933), pp. 45–62, and the same writer's "The Lottery in the History of English Government Finance", in *Economic Journal*, III (1934), pp. 57–76. E. L. Hargreaves, *The National Debt* (London, 1930), contains a bibliography of contemporary works.

A. INDEBTEDNESS OF THE GOVERNMENT AT THE RESTORATION

100. Estimate of debts inherited from the Commonwealth, 1660

(*Calendar of Treasury Books*, VII, pp. 1632–1643)

A BRIEF VIEW OF THE PUBLIC REVENUE OF ENGLAND, SCOTLAND AND IRELAND
RESPECTIVELY FOR THE YEAR ENSUING 1660,
WITH THE CHARGE AND EXPENSE OF THE SAME
ACCORDING TO THE PRESENT RECEIPTS AND PAYMENTS,
TOGETHER WITH THE STATE OF THE PUBLIC DEBTS OF THE NATIONS
AS APPEARS TO THE COMMITTEE OF THE REVENUE AS FOLLOWETH:

The income of England

By assessments of 70,000*l.* by the month for six months ending the 24th of June 1660	420,000	0	0
By Customs of subsidies in the port of London and the outports	302,622	16	10½
By Excise of goods imported into the port of London and the outports, and of all inland commodities and of beer and ale, &c.	370,505	3	4
By Receivers General, arising chiefly out of papists' and delinquents' estates	54,087	5	9
By probate of wills	5,561	1	2
By postage of letters	14,000	0	0
By fines for alienations	3,772	13	4
By the Hanaper Office	3,772	10	4
By the sea coal in farm	1,838	12	6
By Wine Licences	967	15	0
By Post Fines in farm	3,000	0	0
By fines and amerciaments in the Pipe	840	6	8
By the profits of sheriffs of counties and cities	498	13	4
By the profits of seizures and extents	840	0	0
By the bailiffs of liberties	50	0	0
By the rent of the Alnage	997	1	11
By the issues of jurors	1,000	0	0
By minute rents, &c.	1,044	12	11
By the Forest of Dean	nil		
By the Mint	nil		
By Tenths and First Fruits	nil		
The whole annual income of England is	1,185,398	13	1½

The income of Scotland

By assessments of 12,000l. a month for six months ending the 24th of June 1660	72,000	0	0
By property and constant rent payable into the Exchequer	5,324	18	5½
By casualties and uncertain rent received by sheriffs and accomptable into the Exchequer	576	3	5
By compositions of signatures in the Exchequer	929	6	0
By Customs inward and outward	6,705	4	10
By the Excise of goods imported	8,011	0	6
By the Excise of foreign salt	1,124	9	5
By the Excise of inland salt	550	0	0
By the Excise of beer, ale and aquavitae	47,444	13	4
By the forfeiture of goods uncustomed and unexcised	595	10	11½
By the interest of moneys set apart for judges' salaries	391	5	0

The whole annual income of Scotland is	143,652	11	11

The income of Ireland

By assessments of 18,000l. a month for six months ending the 24th of June 1660	108,000	0	0
By Customs and Excise in farm	70,000	0	0
By rent of land, houses, etc.	20,679	0	0
By the rent of impropriations	7,611	0	0
By sheriff's accompts, the Hanaper accompt, with fines and amerciaments	1,500	0	0

The whole annual income of Ireland is	207,790	0	0
The whole annual income of England, Scotland and Ireland is	1,536,841	5	0½

The issues or expenses of England

In pay of the army in England from the 16th of January last, consisting of 9 regiments of horse, 14 regiments and 8 companies of foot, with General Officers, train of artillery, life guard, garrisons and contingencies, 49,084l. 2s. 8d. per month	638,093	14	8

In part of the pay of the army in Scotland
out of the assessments of England, 11,400*l.*
per month   148,200   0   0
In part of the pay of the army in Ireland out
of the assessments of England, 8,000*l.*
per month   104,000   0   0
In pay of the Forces at Jamaica, 4,153*l.* 2*s.* 0*d.*
per month   53,990   6   0
In pay of the Forces in Flanders, 5,951*l.* 5*s.* 0*d.*
per month   77,366   5   0
                                         ————————

The whole pay of the Land Forces is yearly   1,021,650   5   8

In pay of the navy and fleets at sea from the
1st of February last, as well for a summer
as winter guard, as follows:
In the charge of setting forth so many ships
this summer as may employ 20,000 men
for 8 months at 4*l.* per man per month
for a medium   640,000   0   0
In the charge of setting to sea so many ships
as may employ 5,250 men for 6 months
winter service at 4*l.* per man per month
by a medium   126,000   0   0
In the ordinary charge of the Yards for a
whole year   50,000   0   0
In the supply of the stores, the magazines
being much exhausted, by estimate   100,000   0   0
                                         ————————

The whole charge of the navy for this year is   916,000   0   0

In interest paid for 268,047*l.* 19*s.* 6*d.* charged
by Acts and Ordinances of Parliament on
the Excise for a year   20,490   17   2
In repairs of the State's houses yearly   5,650   0   0
In allowances to public ministers employed
abroad for public contingencies, by esti-
mate   20,000   0   0
For liberates in the Court of Exchequer and
Receipt, and for a defalcation upon sea
coal   582   16   0¾
In allowances, fees and salaries paid out of
the Exchequer   6,027   8   10

In pensions and annuities paid out of the Exchequer	5,389	10	8
In salaries to judges in England and Wales and 500*l.* pension paid to the earl of Nottingham out of the Exchequer	16,286	13	4
In salaries, fees and charges incident and extraordinary in managing of the office of Excise	37,226	10	10
In the like for managing the Customs	42,714	3	5
In salaries to the clerks, messengers and door-keeper attending the Committee for the Army	660	0	0
In salaries to the agents in the several counties for bringing in the Monthly Assessments	880	0	0
Paid for the rent of the house wherein the Committee for the Army sits	40	0	0
In contingent charges of the Office for books, ink, paper, wax, post of letters and Acts for Assessments to the agents and for fire and candle, etc.	69	0	9
In salaries to the Receivers General, collectors and Commissioners' clerks for collecting, etc., of the said assessments	13,900	8	4
In salaries to the Treasurers at War, their deputies and clerks	2,400	0	0
In salaries to the Committee of Appeals and their attendant, by estimate	2,000	0	0
In the like to judges and other officers employed in the probate of wills	2,584	10	0
In the like paid and allowed to the Clerk of the Hanaper for extraordinary charges	3,873	6	11
In the like fees and allowances to the officers of the Alienation Office	1,044	17	0
In fees to the officers of the Mint with their diet and incident charges	1,154	19	5
In officers' salaries, rent and other charges for the office of Wine Licences, by estimate	600	0	0
In fees and allowances to the auditors and receivers of the revenue	4,287	10	7
In allowances in the Pipe upon sheriff's accompts by warrants from the Commissioners of the Treasury and the judgment of the Court of Exchequer for several necessary occasions	5,541	14	10

In pensions and allowances to maimed
soldiers, their widows and children at Ely
House, etc., by estimate   30,000   0   0

The whole sum is   223,404   8   1¾
The whole issues of England for a year are   2,161,054   13   9¾

The issues of Scotland for a year

In pay of the army in Scotland, consisting of
5 regiments of horse, 11 regiments and
1 company of foot, 4 companies of
dragoons, with the General Officers, train
of artillery, garrisons and contingencies
at 26,551*l*. 14*s*. 2*d*. per month   345,172   4   2
In salaries to the Council and their officers   9,410   11   0
In the contingent charges of the Council   350   0   0
In salaries to the Court of Exchequer   1,833   4   2
In the contingent charges of the Exchequer   80   10   2½
In salaries to the Courts of Justice   4,246   4   0
In contingent charges of the Courts of Justice   485   12   0
In salaries to the Commissioners of the Cus-
toms and Excise   4,177   9   6
In the contingent charges of the said Com-
missioners   771   9   4
In salaries to the Court of Admiralty with
their officers and contingencies   539   16   10
In charges of an hospital   587   10   6
In fire and candle to soldiers for guards   5,297   19   4
In pensions and other temporary contingen-
cies   8,915   15   9

The whole issues for Scotland for a year are   381,868   6   9½

The issues of Ireland for a year

In the pay of the army in Ireland, consisting
of 6 regiments and 2 troops of horse, 11
regiments and 10 companies of foot, 1
regiment of dragoons, a life guard of
horse, a foot guard, with the General
Officers and the charge of an hospital and
reparations of garrisons, 23,967*l*. 17*s*. 4*d*.
per month   311,582   5   4
In allowances to the Council and the Clerks
of the Council and their clerks and atten-
dants   7,600   0   0

In allowances to the Lord Chancellor and the officers of the Chancery	2,258	0	0
In allowances to the Lord Chief Justice of the Upper Bench and Judges and Clerks of the Crown	1,167	10	0
In allowances to the Lord Chief Justice of the Common Pleas, two judges and pro-thonotaries	1,007	10	0
In allowances to the Chancellor, Chief Baron and two barons of the Exchequer, with other officers and payments by liberate	1,991	15	0
In pay and allowances to the justices of assize in five circuits	1,000	0	0
In pay to the Lord President of Connaught and two Provost Marshals of Leinster and Munster	1,887	0	0
In pay to the overseers of the hospital of Dublin, nine muster masters, five commissaries of stores, to the overseers of the State's houses, with an allowance to the Provost and Fellows of Trinity College	1,807	8	4
In pay of eight Receivers of the Revenue	165	0	0
In pay to 28 comptrollers and searchers of the Customs	1,150	0	0
In pensions to maimed soldiers, widows and orphans of soldiers	3,000	0	0
In allowances and contingencies, extraordinary gratuities and other casual expenses	8,000	0	0

The whole issues of Ireland for a year	342,616	8	8

The annual income of England is	1,185,398	13	$1\frac{1}{2}$
The annual issues and expenses of England are	2,161,054	19	$9\frac{3}{4}$

The balance is	975,656	6	$8\frac{1}{4}$

The annual income of Scotland is	143,652	11	11
The annual issues and expenses of Scotland are	381,868	6	9

The balance is	238,215	14	10

The annual income of Ireland is	207,790	0	0
The annual issues and expenses of Ireland are	342,616	8	8

The balance is		134,826	8	8

The annual incomes of England, Scotland
and Ireland are   1,536,841   5   0½
The annual issues and expenses of England,
Scotland and Ireland are   2,885,539 15   2¾

Out of which deducting the monthly sums
of 11,400*l*. paid [out of the English
revenue] to the army in Scotland and
8,000*l*. monthly [similarly] paid to the
army in Ireland before mentioned, which
in a year comes to 252,200*l*.; so the
balance of the three kingdoms is   1,096,498   10   2¼

The state of the debt owing by the Commonwealth

To the navy unto the 1st of February last, as
appears by certificate from the officers of
the navy and treasurer of the navy   690,112   0   0
To the army in England to the 16th of
January last, as is certified by the Committee of the Army   281,364 15 10
To the army in Scotland, as is certified by the
deputy paymaster   162,785   0   0
To the army in Ireland to the 15th of
January last, as is certified by the Council
of Officers and signed by Colonel Bridges 310,000   0   0
To the Forces in Jamaica to
the 1st of February
1657/8   68,697   0   5½
And from that day to the
20th of April last   41,531   5   4
And from that date to the
1st of February last   31,186 12   0

As appears by several certificates from the
paymaster for those Forces   141,415   3   3
As for the debt due to the Forces in Flanders,
we have no certain accompt, nor of what
Forces are there in service and pay, nor
when taken on; but according to the
establishment delivered last year at

5,951*l*. 5*s*. 0*d*. per month the pay due to
those Forces from the 1st day of August
1658 (in which month we find moneys
first issued to them) unto the 12th of
March instant comes to 124,976*l*. 5*s*. 0*d*.,
of which we find as yet no more paid
them than 54,889*l*. 11*s*. 3*d*., according to
which accompt the debt remaining (besides what may be due before August
1658) is ·   70,086   13   9

To several persons for several sums of money
charged upon the Exchequer, in all
amounting to   79,734   6   11½

To several persons for moneys charged by
Acts and Ordinances of Parliament upon
the Excise, as by the accompt of the
Commissioners of Excise appears   264,547   14   6

And by several Acts of Parliament to particular persons charged on the Excise and
Exchequer, by estimate   40,000   0   0

To Mr. Embree, Surveyor General, for the
State's houses, etc.; to divers others for
materials, workmanship in the repair
of Westminster Hall, etc., Whitehall,
St. James's, Hampton Court, Windsor,
Somerset House, Greenwich and in
repairing and building several Guards
[Houses] for horse and foot from 1656,
November 30, to 1659, October 15, as
appears by an abstract of an accompt
thereof under the hand of Mr. Barrington
one of the Auditors of Imprests   11,676   10   5

The whole sum is   2,051,722   4   8½

Besides which the issues and expenses of
England, Scotland and Ireland before
mentioned exceed the income this year
the sum of   1,095,708   10   9

which is a growing debt, and will be due
before the end of the year.

And so the whole debt of the three nations is
at present and will be by the end of the
year   3,147,430   14   10¼

101. Statement of debts inherited from the Long Parliament, 1660

(Journals of the House of Commons, VIII, pp. 237–243)

A report was presented to the House on the 18th day of December 1660, by Colonel Birch, which is here entered, and is as followeth:

At the committee to whom the bill for Excise was referred . . .

Ordered, that Colonel Birch do report to the House all the debts charged upon the Excise by the Lords and Commons before the seventh day of December 1648, and yet unsatisfied, except such as were payable to any of the persons excepted in the Act of Oblivion, in order to be inserted into the bill of Foreign and Inland Excise. . . .

The total of moneys charged upon the Receipt of the Excise by the ordinances and orders aforesaid, the sum of £319,968 8s. 6½d.

102. Statement of debts inherited from Charles I, 1660

(Journals of the House of Commons, VIII, p. 244)

At the committee for public debts
September 3rd, 1660

O rdered, that it be reported to the House as the opinion of this committee, that the debts hereafter mentioned are such as the Parliament is bound in honour to take care of, which now stand charged as underwritten.

There is charged upon his Majesty's Exchequer, as appears by a certificate returned by order of the Lord Treasurer, which is secured by his Majesty's lands, and was charged thereupon by his late Majesty during the late troubles, the sum of   65,000 0 0

There is likewise charged there, and tallies struck for the same, for money lent to his late Majesty by divers of the nobility and gentry, as appears certified by the Lord Treasurer, the sum of   50,000 0 0

There was charged by the Lords and Commons, the 22 of April 1646, upon his Majesty's revenue, for the yearly support of the queen of Bohemia, his Majesty's aunt, 10,000l. per annum, whereof there remains in arrear, for the time it was continued, and upon former ordinances   50,000 0 0

There is charged upon his Majesty's Exchequer, for wares and commodities about the years 1641 and 1642, for which privy seals were given, as appears by the before-mentioned certificates of the Lord Treasurers   60,000 0 0

There is due to the old farmers of the Customs, for money paid by direction of the Lords and Commons in the year 1642, and likewise to his Majesty in the same year in ready money, for which they had tallies struck upon their receipt of the Customs by way of anticipation   253,000 0 0

Due to the Princess Royal for her portion, for which his present Majesty is engaged	40,000	0	0
Due from his Majesty to the late Tin Farmers, certified as aforesaid	11,600	0	0
	529,600	0	0

Memorandum. The aforementioned debts were all charged by his late Majesty, and for which his present Majesty is engaged in honour to see satisfied, and are humbly offered to the Parliament by this committee as debts which in honour they are bound to take care of.

Memorandum. That no part of the debts of his present Majesty, either in England or elsewhere, are brought into this account.

B. CUSTOMS

103. The Great Statute, 1660

(*Statutes of the Realm*, v, pp. 181–205)

A SUBSIDY GRANTED TO THE KING
OF TONNAGE AND POUNDAGE AND OTHER SUMS OF MONEY
PAYABLE UPON MERCHANDISE EXPORTED AND IMPORTED

(*12 Car. II, cap. 4*)

The Commons assembled in Parliament, reposing trust and confidence in your Majesty in and for the guarding and defending of the seas against all persons intending, or that shall intend, the disturbance of your said Commons in the intercourse of trade and the invading of this your realm, for the better defraying the necessary expenses thereof, which cannot otherwise be effected without great charge to your Majesty, do, by and with the advice and consent of the Lords in this your present Parliament assembled and by the authority of the same, to the intent aforesaid give and grant unto you, our supreme liege lord and sovereign, one subsidy called tonnage, that is to say of every ton of wine of the growth of France or of any the dominions of the French king or crown of France that shall come into the port of London and the members thereof by way of merchandise by your natural born subjects the sum of four pounds and ten shillings of current English money and so after that rate, and by strangers and aliens six pounds of the like money; and of every ton of the like wine which shall be brought into all and every the other ports and places of this kingdom and the dominions thereof by way of merchandise by your natural born subjects the sum of three pounds, and by aliens four pounds and ten shillings; and of every but or pipe of muscadels, malmseys, cuts, tents, alicants, bastards, sacks, canaries, malagoes, madeiroes and other wines whatsoever commonly called sweet wines of the growth of the Levant, Spain, Portugal or any of them, or of any the islands or dominions to them or any of them belonging, or elsewhere, that shall come or be brought into the port of London by your natural born subjects the sum of forty-five shillings of current English money and so after that rate, and by strangers and aliens three pounds of like money; and of every but and pipe of the like wine which shall come or be brought into all, every or any the other ports and places of this kingdom and dominions thereof by way of merchandise by your natural born subjects the sum of thirty shillings, and by strangers forty-five shillings; and of every awm of Rhenish wine, or wine of the growth of Germany, that shall be brought into this your realm and the dominions thereof by your natural born subjects the sum of twenty shillings of current English money, and by strangers and aliens twenty and five shillings, which several rates are the same which are expressed in a certain book of rates hereinafter mentioned and referred unto: and also one other subsidy called poundage, that is to say of all manner of goods and merchandise of every merchant, natural born subject, denizen and alien, to be carried out of this realm or any your Majesty's dominions to the same belonging, or to be brought into the same by way of merchandise, of the value of every twenty shillings of the same goods and merchandise according to the several and particular rates and values of the same goods and merchandises as the same are particularly and respectively rated and valued in the said book of rates hereinafter mentioned and referred unto, twelve pence and so after that rate; and of every twenty shillings value of any the native commodities of this realm, or manufactures wrought of any such native commodities, to be carried out of this realm by every or any merchant alien, according to the value thereof in the said book expressed, twelve pence over and above the twelve pence aforesaid, except and foreprised out of this grant of subsidy of poundage all manner of woollen cloths made or wrought, or to be made or wrought, within this realm of England commonly called Old Draperies, and all wines before limited to pay subsidy of tonnage, and all manner of fish English taken and brought by English bottoms into this realm, and all manner of fresh fish and bestial that shall come into this your realm, and all other goods and merchandises which in the said book of rates are mentioned to be Custom-free.

II. And further we your said Commons, by the advice, assent and authority aforesaid, do give and grant unto you, our said liege lord and sovereign, for the causes aforesaid one other subsidy, that is to say of and for every short woollen cloth to be exported by your natural born subjects of this your realm and the dominions thereof called broad-cloth, not exceeding twenty-eight yards in length and threescore and four pounds in weight, the sum of three shillings and four pence of current English money, and of every cloth of greater length and weight proportionably according to the same rate, and of every other short cloth of Old Drapery of lesser length and weight, accounting so many pieces to a short cloth as are limited and appointed thereunto by the said book of rates, to be likewise exported by your said natural born subjects, the like sum of three shillings four pence and so after that rate, and by strangers and aliens six shillings and eight pence for every short cloth accounted as aforesaid, which several rates are accordingly expressed in the said book of rates hereinafter mentioned and referred unto; to have, hold, take, enjoy and perceive the subsidies aforesaid . . . from the four and twentieth day of June inclusively in the twelfth year of your Majesty's reign for and during your Majesty's life, which God long preserve. . . .

V. Provided always, that it shall and may be lawful to all and every your subjects at his and their will and pleasure to convey and transport out of this realm in ships and other vessels of any the subjects of this realm all and every kind of herrings and other sea fish to be taken on the sea by any the subjects aforesaid from or out of any port or harbour of this realm to any place out of your Majesty's dominions without paying any Custom, subsidy or poundage moneys. . . .

VI. And because no rates can be imposed upon merchandise imported or exported by subjects or aliens but by common consent in Parliament, be it further enacted and declared by the authority aforesaid, that the rates intended by this present Act shall be the rates mentioned and expressed in one book of rates, intituled, . . .[1] and subscribed

[1] As on p. 291.

with the hand of Sir Harbottle Grimston, baronet, Speaker of the House of Commons, which said book of rates composed and agreed on by your Majesty's said Commons, and also every article, rule and clause therein contained, shall be and remain during your Majesty's life as effectual to all intents and purposes as if the same were included particularly in the body of this present Act. . . .

XI. And be it further enacted . . . that it shall and may be lawful, immediately after the passing of this Act, for any person or persons to ship, carry out and transport by way of merchandise these several sorts of goods following, that is to say gunpowder, when the same doth not exceed the price of five pounds the barrel, and wheat, rye, peas, beans, barley, malt and oats, beef, pork, bacon, butter, cheese, candles, when the same do not exceed in price at the ports from whence they are laden and at the time of their lading these prices following, that is to say, wheat, the quarter, forty shillings; rye, beans and peas, the quarter, twenty-four shillings; barley and malt, the quarter, twenty shillings; oats, the quarter, sixteen shillings; beef, the barrel, five pounds; pork, the barrel, six pounds ten shillings; bacon, the pound, six pence; butter, the barrel, four pounds ten shillings; cheese, the hundred, one pound ten shillings; candles, the dozen pound, five shillings, paying the respective rates appointed by this Act and no more, any former law, statute, prohibition or custom to the contrary in any wise notwithstanding. . . .

XII. And be it further enacted . . . that over and above the rates hereinbefore mentioned there shall be paid unto your Majesty of every ton of wine of the growth of France, Germany, Portugal or Madeira brought into the port of London or elsewhere the sum of three pounds current English money within the space of nine months after the importing; and of every ton of all other wines brought in as aforesaid the sum of four pounds of like current money within the space of nine months after the importing thereof, for the payment of which duties accordingly the importer shall give good security; and if any of the said wines for which the additional duty in this clause mentioned is paid, or secured at the importation, be exported within twelve months after their importation, then the aforesaid additional duty in this clause mentioned shall be returned, or the security discharged, as to so much as shall be so exported; and if at the importation the importer shall pay for the same ready money he shall be allowed after the rate of ten per cent for a year. . . .

The Rates of Merchandises,
that is to say the subsidy of tonnage, the subsidy of poundage and the
subsidy of woollen cloths or Old Drapery, as they are rated and agreed on by the
Commons House of Parliament, set down and expressed in this book, to be paid
according to the tenor of the Act of Tonnage and Poundage, from the four and
twentieth day of June inclusively, in the twelfth year of his
Majesty's reign, during his Majesty's life.[1]

---

[1] Some thousands of items are listed in alphabetical order, of which only a very small selection is here printed.

[Rates inward]

A

	l.	*s.*	*d.*
Alum, the hundredweight, containing 112 pounds	2	0	0
Apples ⎰ the bushel			4
the barrel, containing 3 bushels		1	0
called pippins or rennets, the barrel, containing 3 bushels		3	0
Aqua vitae ⎰ the barrel	2	13	4
the hogshead	4	0	0

B

	l.	*s.*	*d.*
Bacon ⎰ of Ireland, the flitch		5	0
of Westphalia and Hamburg or the like, the hundredweight, containing 112 pounds	1	6	8
Bandoleers, the hundred, containing five score		16	8
Beef ⎰ of Ireland or Scotland, the barrel	1	0	0
or pork of Ireland or Scotland, per ton	6	0	0
Bow staves, the hundred, containing six score staves	4	0	0
Bridles, the dozen	1	0	0
Butter ⎰ the barrel	1	0	0
of Ireland, the hundredweight, containing 112 pounds		10	0

C

	l.	*s.*	*d.*
Cables, tarred or untarred, the hundredweight, containing 112 pounds		13	4
Calicoes, fine or coarse, the piece		10	0
Cheese, the hundredweight, containing 112 pounds		6	8
Cloth. All manner of woollen cloth imported, per yard	8	10	0
Coals of Scotland, the ton		6	8
Corn — Wheat — Wheat imported not exceeding the price of 5s. 6d. the bushel at the place of importation, by the bushel		5	0
When it shall exceed that rate, by the quarter		6	8
Rye — Imported not exceeding the price of 4s. 6d. the bushel at the place of importation, by the bushel		3	4
When it shall exceed that rate, by the quarter		5	0
Beans / Barley / Malt — Imported not exceeding the price of 3s. 6d. the bushel at the place of importation, by the bushel		3	4
When it shall exceed that rate, by the quarter		5	0
Coverlets of Scotland, the piece		15	0
Cushions of Scotland, the dozen		10	0

E

	l.	*s.*	*d.*
Eggs, the hundred, containing six score		1	8
Elephants' teeth, the hundredweight, containing 112 pounds	4	0	0

F

	l.	s.	d.
Flannel, the yard		1	8
Frieze, of Ireland, the yard			9

H

Handkerchiefs, the dozen	3	0	0
Hats { of beaver wool or hair, the hat	10	0	0
of Bruges, the dozen	10	0	0
Dutch felts or hats made of wool, the piece	1	0	0
Spanish or Portugal felts, the dozen	5	0	0
of silk, French making, the dozen	3	0	0
of Venice, the dozen	3	0	0
of wool or worsted, trimmed, the dozen	3	0	0
Honey { the barrel	2	0	0
the ton	12	0	0
Hops, the hundredweight, containing 112 pounds	15	0	0
Horses or mares, the horse or mare	10	0	0

L

Lead ore, the ton	4	0	0
Linseed, the bushel		5	0

M

Maps, printed, the ream	4	0	0
Masts { for ships, small, the mast		3	4
middle, the mast		10	0
great, the mast	1	0	0
Meal of wheat or rye, the last, containing 12 barrels	3	0	0
Metheglin, the hogshead	2	0	0

N

Napkins, French making, the dozen		12	0
Neats tongues { Tongues of Russia, the piece			2
the barrel		10	0
the dozen		2	6
Neckerchiefs, of Flanders making, the dozen	6	0	0

O

Oats, the quarter, containing eight bushels		4	0
Onions { the barrel		3	4
the hundred bunches		16	8
seed, the hundredweight, containing 112 pounds	4	0	0
Oranges and lemons, the thousand	1	0	0

P

		l.	*s.*	*d.*
Paper { Blue paper, the ream			10	0
Brown paper, the bundle			3	0
Demy paper, the ream			12	0
Ordinary printing and copy paper, the ream			4	6
Royal paper, the ream		1	0	0
Parchment { the dozen, containing 12 sheets			7	0
the roll, containing 6 dozen		2	2	0
Planks of Ireland, the hundred foot, containing five score			12	6
Pork { the side			5	0
the ton		6	0	0
Potatoes, the hundredweight, containing 112 pounds			16	8

R

Ribbon of silk of all sorts, the pound	4	0	0
Rice, the hundredweight, containing 112 pounds	1	6	8

S

Sheep imported from Ireland to England by the score	5	0	0
Sword blades { of Venice, Turkey, or fine blades, the dozen	1	10	0
coarse, of Flanders making, the dozen	1	0	0

V

Valances of Scotland, the piece		8	0
Vinegar, the ton	5	0	0

W

Wine lees, the ton	4	0	0

Y

Yarn { Cable yarn, the hundredweight, containing 112 pounds		13	4
Cotton yarn, the pound		1	0
Sail yarn, the pound			6
Scotch yarn, the pound		1	0

[Rates outward]

A

Alum, English, the hundredweight, containing 112 pounds	1	0	0
Apples, the bushel		1	0
Apples called pippins, the bushel		1	0
Aqua vitae, the hogshead	2	0	0

		l.	*s.*	*d.*
B				
Bacon, the flitch			10	0
Bandoleers, the hundred collars			10	0
Beef, the barrel		3	0	0
Bridles, the dozen			1	8
Butter, good or bad, the barrel		3	0	0

		l.	*s.*	*d.*
C				
Cheese, the hundredweight, containing 112 pounds		1	0	0
Coals	Sea coals, the chalder, Newcastle measure, exported by English in English-built bottoms	8	0	0
	Sea coals, the chalder, London measure, exported by English in English-built bottoms	5	0	0
Corn	Barley, the quarter, containing 8 bushels		10	0
	Malt, the quarter		10	0
	Beans, the quarter		10	0
	Oats, the quarter		6	8
	Pease, the quarter		10	0
	Wheat, the quarter	1	0	0
	Rye, the quarter		10	0
	Buckwheat, the quarter		10	0

		l.	*s.*	*d.*
F				
Flannel, the yard				4
Friezes, the yard				6
Fustians of English making of all sorts to go out free				

		l.	*s.*	*d.*
H				
Hake fish, the hundred, containing six score			3	4
Hats	Beavers and demicastors of English making, the dozen	2	0	0
	Felts and all other hats, the dozen		10	0
Hops, the hundredweight, at 112 pounds		1	10	0
Horses	Stone horses, the piece	66	13	4
	Geldings or nags, the piece	20	0	0
	Geldings or nags to the English plantations	10	0	0
	Mares, the mare	126	13	4

		l.	*s.*	*d.*
L				
Linseed, the quarter, containing 8 bushel		3	0	0

		l.	*s.*	*d.*
M				
Maps and sea charts of all sorts, the hundredweight, containing 112 pounds			5	0

O

		l.	s.	d.
Oatmeal { the bushel			3	4
{ the barrel, containing 3 bushels			10	0
Oysters, the small barrel, in pickle			1	4
Oxen, the ox		6	13	4

P

	l.	s.	d.
Parchment, the roll		13	4
Pork, the barrel	4	0	0

S

	l.	s.	d.
Sprats, the cade, containing a thousand		1	8

V

	l.	s.	d.
Velours, the double piece, containing 15 yards	1	0	0
Vinegar of wine, the ton	2	6	8

W

	l.	s.	d.
Watches of all sorts, the piece		10	0
Worsted { narrow, English, the piece		15	0
{ broad, English, the piece	1	0	0
Wine lees, the butt	1	0	0

Y

	l.	s.	d.
Yarn called grogram yarn, the pound		4	0

Tonnage

	l.	s.	d.
Beer { For every ton of beer to be exported in shipping English-built, in money		2	0
{ For every ton of beer exported in any other shipping, in money		6	0

104. Proclamation continuing the Customs, 1685

(*London Gazette*, 9–12 February 1685)

A PROCLAMATION FOR CONTINUING THE COLLECTION
OF THE CUSTOMS AND SUBSIDIES
OF TONNAGE AND POUNDAGE

JAMES R.

We have upon mature consideration thought fit to call a Parliament, speedily to be assembled, in which we make no doubt but care will be taken for settling a sufficient revenue on the Crown for the support of the government; the necessities of which in maintenance of the navy for defence of our kingdom, and the advantages of trade, requiring that the Customs and subsidies of tonnage and poundage, and other sums of money payable upon merchandises exported and imported, be continued to be collected as in the time of our dearest brother lately deceased, we do therefore by and with the advice of our Privy Council require, and our will and pleasure is, that the said duties be collected accordingly by all and singular the officers and collectors within all and every our ports in any of our dominions, not doubting of a ready compliance herein from all our loving subjects.

Given at our court at Whitehall,
the ninth day of February,
in the first year of our reign.

105. Act imposing Customs duties, 1690

(*Statutes of the Realm*, VI, pp. 166–169)

AN ACT FOR GRANTING TO THEIR MAJESTIES
A SUBSIDY OF TONNAGE AND POUNDAGE AND OTHER SUMS OF MONEY
PAYABLE UPON MERCHANDISES EXPORTED AND IMPORTED

(*2 Gul. & Mar., cap. 4*)

The Commons assembled in Parliament, reposing trust and confidence in your Majesties for the guarding and defending of the seas against all persons who shall attempt to invade this your realm, or to disturb your subjects in their trade and commerce, towards the defraying the necessary charge thereof, and also for the better enabling your Majesties to prosecute the present war against the French king, and for the reducing of Ireland with speed and vigour, have cheerfully and unanimously given and granted, and do hereby give and grant unto your Majesties the subsidy of tonnage and poundage and other sums of money given and granted unto his late Majesty King Charles the Second for his life by an Act of Parliament made in the twelfth year of his reign, entituled, *A subsidy granted to the king of tonnage and poundage and other sums of money payable upon merchandise exported and imported,*[1] according to the rates in the said Act mentioned and rules and orders thereunto annexed (other than such concerning which it is otherwise provided or ordained by any Act made in the last Parliament); and do most humbly beseech your Majesties that it may be enacted, and be it enacted . . . that the aforesaid subsidy of tonnage and poundage and other sums of money payable upon merchandise be levied, collected and paid unto their Majesties for the term of four years, to commence and be computed from the four and twentieth day of December in the year of our Lord one thousand six hundred and ninety, and that the aforesaid Act . . . shall be of full force and effect to all intents and purposes during the said term of four years. . . .

IV. And whereas their Majesties are contented and pleased that the subsidy of tonnage and poundage and other the duties aforesaid should be made a fund of credit, in confidence that their good subjects will in due time make provision for taking off the anticipation thereof, be it enacted . . . that it shall and may be lawful to and for any person or persons, natives or foreigners, bodies politic or corporate, to advance and

[1] No. 103.

lend to their Majesties in the Receipt of their Exchequer upon the credit of this Act any sum or sums of money not exceeding the sum of five hundred thousand pounds in the whole, and to have and receive for the forbearance of all such moneys as shall be lent before the tenth day of June one thousand six hundred and ninety interest not exceeding the rate of eight pounds per cent per annum, and for what shall be lent after the said tenth day of June interest not exceeding seven pounds per cent per annum. . . .

106. Civil List Act, 1698

(*Statutes of the Realm*, VII, pp. 382–385)

AN ACT FOR GRANTING TO HIS MAJESTY
A FURTHER SUBSIDY OF TONNAGE AND POUNDAGE
TOWARDS RAISING THE YEARLY SUM
OF SEVEN HUNDRED THOUSAND POUNDS,
FOR THE SERVICE OF HIS MAJESTY'S HOUSEHOLD
AND OTHER USES THEREIN MENTIONED, DURING HIS MAJESTY'S LIFE

(*9 Gul. III, cap. 23*)

We, your Majesty's most dutiful and loyal subjects, the Commons of England in Parliament assembled, being deeply sensible of the great blessings which by the goodness of Almighty God we and all other the subjects of your Majesty's realms and dominions, in the free exercise of the true Christian religion (the most valuable benefit which can be bestowed upon any nation or people), as also in our liberties and properties, do fully enjoy under your Majesty's most auspicious government, and being desirous to make a grateful acknowledgment of your Majesty's unparalleled grace and favour to us your Commons, and particularly for the great and successful undertakings and achievements whereby your Majesty hath been the happy instrument of securing the aforesaid blessings to us and our posterities, have therefore freely and unanimously resolved to increase your Majesty's revenue during your Majesty's reign (which God long continue), and do give and grant unto your most excellent Majesty the further rates, duties and sums of money hereinafter mentioned, and do humbly beseech your Majesty that it may be enacted, and be it enacted . . . that over and above all subsidies of tonnage and poundage, and over and above all additional duties . . . for or upon any wines, goods or merchandises whatsoever imported or to be imported, there shall be raised, levied, collected, paid and satisfied unto his Majesty one other subsidy called tonnage for and upon all wines which from and after the last day of January which shall be in the year of our Lord one thousand six hundred ninety-nine,[1] at any time or times during his Majesty's life, shall be imported or brought into the kingdom of England, dominion of Wales or town of Berwick-upon-Tweed, that is to say, of every ton of wine of the growth of France or of any the dominions of the French king or crown of France that shall come into the port

---

[1] 1699/1700.

of London and the members thereof by way of merchandise by his Majesty's natural born subjects, the sum of four pounds and ten shillings of current English money and so after that rate. . . .[1]

XI. And whereas it is intended that the yearly sum of seven hundred thousand pounds shall be supplied to his Majesty for the service of his Household and family, and for other his necessary expenses and occasions, out of the hereditary rates and duties of Excise upon beer, ale and other liquors which were granted to the Crown in the twelfth year of the reign of King Charles the Second;[2] and out of the rates and duties of Excise of beer, ale and other liquors payable for the term of his Majesty's life by an Act of Parliament made and passed in the second year of the reign of his Majesty and the late queen of blessed memory, . . . and out of the revenue of the general letter office, or Post Office, . . . and out of the small branches of his Majesty's revenue hereinafter mentioned and expressed, that is to say, the First Fruits and Tenths of the clergy, the fines for writs of covenant and writs of entry payable in the Alienation Office, the post fines, the revenue of the wine licenses, the moneys arising by sheriffs' proffers and compositions in the Exchequer and by the seizures of uncustomed and prohibited goods, the revenue of the duchy of Cornwall and any other revenue arising by the rents of lands in England or Wales or for fines of leases of the same or any of them, and the duty of four and a half per cent in specie arising in Barbados and the Leeward Islands in America; and out of the moneys which from and after the commencement of this Act shall arise by the further subsidies and duties hereby granted; be it therefore further enacted . . . that if the said great and small branches and revenues hereinbefore mentioned . . . shall produce in clear money more than the yearly sum of seven hundred thousand pounds, to be reckoned from the five and twentieth day of December which shall be in the year of our Lord one thousand six hundred ninety-nine, that then the overplus of such produce (being more than the said yearly sum of seven hundred thousand pounds) shall not be issued, disposed, made use of or applied to any use or purpose or upon any pretext whatsoever without the authority of Parliament. . . .

[1] The provisions continue as in the first paragraph of the Great Statute of Customs of 1660 (No. 103).
[2] As in No. 107.

C. EXCISE

107. Act abolishing feudal tenures and imposing hereditary Excise, 1660

(Statutes of the Realm, v, pp. 259–266)

AN ACT TAKING AWAY THE COURT OF WARDS AND LIVERIES,
AND TENURES *IN CAPITE* AND BY KNIGHTS SERVICE AND PURVEYANCE,
AND FOR SETTLING A REVENUE UPON HIS MAJESTY
IN LIEU THEREOF

(12 Car. II, cap. 24)

Whereas it hath been found by former experience that the Courts of Wards and Liveries and tenures by knights service either of the king or others, or by knights service *in capite* or socage *in capite* of the king, and the consequents upon the same, have been much more burthensome, grievous and prejudicial to the kingdom than they have been beneficial to the king; and whereas since the intermission of the said Court, which hath been from the four and twentieth day of February which was in the year of our Lord one thousand six hundred forty and five,[1] many persons have by will and otherwise made disposal of their lands held by knights service, whereupon divers questions might possibly arise unless some seasonable remedy be taken to prevent the same; be it therefore enacted . . . that the Court of Wards and Liveries, and all wardships, liveries, primer seisins and ousterlemains, values and forfeitures of marriages by reason of any tenure of the king's Majesty or of any other by knights service, and all mean rates and all other gifts, grants, charges incident or arising for or by reason of wardships, liveries, primer seisins or ousterlemains, be taken away and discharged . . . from the said twenty-fourth day of February one thousand six hundred forty-five;[1] . . . and that all fines for alienation, seizures and pardons for alienations, tenure by homage, and all charges incident or arising for or by reason of wardship, livery, primer seisin or ousterlemain or tenure by knights service, escuage, and also *aid pur fille marier et pur fair fitz chivalier*, and all other charges incident thereunto, be likewise taken away and discharged from the said twenty-fourth day of February; . . . and that all tenures by knights service of the king or of any other person, and by knights service *in capite*, and by socage *in capite* of the king, and the fruits and consequents thereof, happened or which shall or may hereafter happen or arise thereupon or thereby, be taken away and discharged; . . . and all tenures of any honours, manors, lands, tenements or hereditaments of any estate of inheritance at the common law held either of the king or of any other person or persons, bodies politic or corporate, are hereby enacted to be turned into free and common socage to all intents and purposes from the said twenty-fourth day of February one thousand six hundred forty-five. . . .[1]

II. And that the same shall for ever hereafter stand and be discharged of all tenure by homage, escuage, voyages royal and charges for the same, wardships incident to

---

[1] 1645/6.

tenure by knights service, and values and forfeitures of marriage and all other charges incident to tenure by knights service, and of and from *aid pur fille marier et aid pur fair fitz chivalier*, any law, statute, custom or usage to the contrary in any wise notwithstanding; and that all conveyances and devises of any manors, lands, tenements and hereditaments made since the said twenty-fourth of February shall be expounded to be of such effect as if the same manors, lands, tenements and hereditaments had been then held and continued to be holden in free and common socage only, any law, statute, custom or usage to the contrary hereof any wise notwithstanding.

III. And be it further ordained and enacted . . . that one Act made in the reign of King Henry the Eighth intituled, *An Act for the establishment of the Court of the King's Wards*,[1] and also one Act of Parliament made in the three and thirtieth year of the reign of the said King Henry the Eighth concerning the officers of the Court of Wards and Liveries,[2] and every clause, article and matter in the said Acts contained, shall from henceforth be repealed and utterly void.

IV. And be it further enacted . . . that all tenures hereafter to be created by the king's Majesty, his heirs or successors, upon any gifts or grants of any manors, lands, tenements or hereditaments of any estate of inheritance at the common law, shall be in free and common socage. . . .

VII. Provided also and be it further enacted, that this Act or anything therein contained shall not take away, or be construed to take away, tenures in frankalmoign, or to subject them to any greater or other services than they now are, nor to alter or change any tenure by copy of court roll or any services incident thereunto, nor to take away the honorary services of grand serjeanty other than of wardship, marriage and value of forfeiture of marriage, escuage, voyages royal, and other charges incident to tenure by knights service and other than *aid pur fair fitz chivalier* and *aid pur fille marier*.

VIII. And be it further enacted . . . that where any person hath or shall have any child or children under the age of twenty-one years and not married at the time of his death, that it shall and may be lawful to and for the father of such child or children, whether born at the time of the decease of the father or at that time *in ventre sa mère*, or whether such father be within the age of twenty-one years or of full age, by his deed executed in his lifetime or by his last will and testament in writing in the presence of two or more credible witnesses, . . . to dispose of the custody and tuition of such child or children for and during such time as he or they shall respectively remain under the age of twenty-one years or any lesser time, to any person or persons in possession or remainder other than popish recusants; and that such disposition of the custody of such child or children made since the twenty-fourth of February one thousand six hundred forty-five,[3] or hereafter to be made, shall be good and effectual against all and every person or persons claiming the custody or tuition of such child or children as guardian in socage or otherwise. . . .

XI. And whereas by like experience it hath been found that though divers good, strict and wholesome laws have been made in the times of sundry his Majesty's most noble progenitors, some extending so far as to life, for redress of the grievances and oppressions committed by the persons employed for making provisions for the king's

---

[1] 32 Hen. VIII, cap. 46.   [2] 33 Hen. VIII, cap. 22.   [3] 1645/6.

household, carriages and other purveyance for his Majesty and his occasions, yet divers oppressions have been still continued, and several counties have submitted themselves to sundry rates and taxes and compositions to redeem themselves from such vexations and oppressions; and forasmuch as the Lords and Commons assembled in Parliament do find that the said remedies are not fully effectual, and that no other remedy will be so effectual and just as to take away the occasion thereof, especially if satisfaction and recompense shall be therefor made to his Majesty, his heirs and successors, which is hereby provided to his Majesty's good liking and content, his Majesty is therefore graciously pleased that it may be enacted . . . that from henceforth no sum or sums of money or other thing shall be taken, raised, taxed, rated, imposed, paid or levied for or in regard of any provision, carriages or purveyance for his Majesty, his heirs or successors; and that henceforth no person or persons by any warrant, commission or authority under the great seal or otherwise, by colour of buying or making provision or purveyance for his Majesty or any queen of England for the time being, or of any the children of any king or queen of England for the time being or that shall be, or for his, their or any of their household, shall take any timber, fuel, cattle, corn, grain, malt, hay, straw, victual, cart, carriage or other thing whatsoever of any the subjects of his Majesty, his heirs or successors, without the free and full consent of the owner or owners thereof had and obtained without menace or enforcement, nor shall summon, warn, take, use, or require any of the said subjects to furnish or find, any horses, oxen or other cattle, carts, ploughs, wains or other carriages for the use of his Majesty, his heirs or successors, or of any queen of England or of any child or children of any the kings or queens of England for the time being, for the carrying the goods of his Majesty, his heirs or successors or the said queens or children or any of them without such full and free consent as aforesaid, any law, statute, custom or usage to the contrary notwithstanding.

XII. And be it further enacted, that no pre-emption shall be allowed or claimed in the behalf of his Majesty or of any his heirs or successors, or of any the queens of England, or of any the children of the royal family for the time being, in market or out of market, but that it be for ever hereafter free to all and every of the subjects of his Majesty to sell, dispose or employ his said goods to any other person or persons as him listeth. . . .

XIV. And now to the intent and purpose that his Majesty, his heirs and successors, may receive a full and ample recompense and satisfaction, as well for the profits of the said Court of Wards and the tenures, wardships, liveries, primer seisins, ousterlemains and other the premises and perquisites incident thereunto, and for all arrears any way due for the same, as also for all and all manner of purveyance and provisions hereinbefore mentioned and intended to be taken away and abolished, and all sums of money due or pretended to be due or payable for and in respect of any compositions for the same, be it therefore enacted . . that there shall be paid unto the king's Majesty, his heirs and successors, for ever hereafter in recompense as aforesaid, the several rates, impositions, duties and charge hereinafter expressed, and in manner and form following, that is to say:

For every barrel of beer or ale above six shillings the barrel brewed by the common brewer or any other person or persons who doth or shall sell or tap out beer or ale publicly or privately, to be paid by the common brewer or by such other person or persons respectively, and so proportionably for a greater or lesser quantity, one shilling three pence.

For every barrel of six shillings beer or ale or under, brewed by the common brewer[1] . . . three pence.

For all cider and perry made and sold by retail upon every hogshead to be paid by the retailer thereof, and so proportionably for a greater or lesser measure, one shilling three pence.

For all metheglin or mead sold, whether by retail or otherwise, to be paid by the maker thereof, upon every gallon, one halfpenny.

For every barrel of beer commonly called vinegar beer brewed by any common brewer or in any common brew house, six pence.

For every gallon of strong water or aqua vitae made and sold, to be paid by the maker thereof, one penny.

For every barrel of beer or ale imported from beyond the seas, three shillings.

For every tun of cider or perry imported from beyond the seas, and so proportionably for a greater or lesser quantity, five shillings.

For every gallon of spirits made of any kind of wine or cider imported, two pence.

For every gallon of strong water perfectly made imported from beyond the seas, four pence.

For every gallon of coffee made and sold, to be paid by the maker, four pence.

For every gallon of chocolate, sherbet and tea made and sold, to be paid by the maker thereof, eight pence. . . .

XXVII. And it is further ordained and enacted by the authority aforesaid, that the Lord Treasurer or Commissioners of the Treasury for the time being, or such other person or persons as his Majesty, his heirs and successors shall appoint, shall have power, and are hereby authorized and empowered, from time to time to treat, contract, conclude and agree with any person or persons for or concerning the farming of all or any the rates, duties and charges in this Act mentioned upon beer, ale, perry, cider, or other the liquors aforesaid, in any the respective counties, cities or places of this realm or dominions thereof, as may be for the greatest benefit and advantage of the said receipt, so as the same exceed not the term of three years. . . .

XXIX. Provided always, to the end the aforesaid duty may be paid with most ease to the people, it is hereby further enacted, that the Lord Treasurer, Commissioners of the Treasury or other persons aforesaid shall not within six months after the commencement of this Act treat, conclude or agree with any person or persons touching the farming of this duty upon beer and ale in any the respective counties or places of this realm or dominions thereof other than with such person or persons as by the justices of peace of the said counties or places, or the major part of them at their public quarter-sessions, shall be nominated and appointed in that behalf, which person or persons is to have the first refusal of any such farm respectively, and may take the same, anything in this Act to the contrary thereof in any wise notwithstanding;

---

[1] As above.

provided that the said duty shall not be let to any other person or persons than to the person or persons recommended by the justices under the rate that it shall be tendered to and refused by such person or persons so recommended. . . .

XXXIII. And for the better managing, collecting, securing, levying and recovering of all and every the said rates and charges of Excise hereby imposed and set upon all or any the commodities before mentioned, to the end the same may be paid and disposed of according to the intent of this present Act, be it further enacted . . . that one principal head office shall be erected and continued in the city of London or within ten miles thereof from time to time as long as his Majesty shall think fit for this duty, unto which all other offices for the same within England and Wales and the town and port of Berwick shall be subordinate and accountable, which said office shall be managed by such officers as shall be appointed by the king's Majesty as aforesaid, who, or any two of them, are hereby appointed and constituted commissioners and governors for the management of his Majesty's receipt of the Excise, and to sit in some convenient place in the city of London or within ten miles thereof from time to time as long as his Majesty shall think fit for the ends aforesaid. . . .

XXXVI. And it is further enacted, that all parts of the cities of London and Westminster, with the borough of Southwark and the several suburbs thereof and parishes within the weekly bills of mortality, shall be under the immediate care, inspection and management of the said head office, and such and so many subordinate commissioners and sub-commissioners and other officers and ministers for the execution of the premises shall be from time to time nominated and appointed by his Majesty, his heirs and successors, in all and every other the counties, cities, towns and places within this kingdom of England, dominion of Wales and port of Berwick, as from time to time his Majesty, his heirs and successors, shall think fit. . . .

108. Incidence of feudal burdens cancelled by statute, 1660

(*Journals of the House of Commons*, VIII, pp. 178–179)

8 November 1660

AN APPORTIONMENT OF ONE HUNDRED THOUSAND POUNDS PER ANNUM,

TO BE SETTLED ON HIS MAJESTY

IN COMPENSATION FOR THE COURT OF WARDS

County	*Apportionment of compensation*		*Excise farm of 1662*[1]	
	£	*Percentage of total*	£	*Percentage of total*
Bedford	1,400	1·4	1,700	·62
Berkshire	1,700	1·7	2,700	·98

[1] For purposes of comparison with the proposed compensation, which was worked out on what was believed to be an equitable basis, the figures of the first Excise farm (*Calendar of Treasury Books*, I, pp. 424–439) are given in parallel column, and the percentage of the total sum to be raised is indicated in each case. For later Excise farms, see No. 196.

County	Apportionment of compensation		Excise farm of 1662	
	£	Percentage of total	£	Percentage of total
Buckingham	1,900	1·9	2,100	·76
Cambridge	1,800	1·8	4,500	1·64
Cheshire	1,400	1·4	2,600	·95
Cornwall	2,400	2·4	2,000	·73
Cumberland	400	·4	900	·33
Derby	1,400	1·4	2,150	·78
Devon	5,000	5·0	8,600	3·13
Dorset	2,000	2·0	2,600	·95
Durham	700	·7	3,600	1·31
Essex	4,800	4·8	8,000	2·91
Gloucester	2,500	2·5	3,700	1·35
Hampshire	3,000	3·0	2,800	1·02
Hereford	1,600	1·6	1,600	·58
Hertford	1,800	1·8	4,300	1·56
Huntingdon	900	·9	1,400	·51
Kent	4,800	4·8	13,000	4·73
Lancashire	1,600	1·6	3,800	1·38
Leicester	1,800	1·8	3,000	1·09
Lincoln	4,000	4·0	7,500	2·73
Middlesex	3,000 ⎫			
London City	4,000 ⎬ 8·8		118,000	42·91
Surrey	1,800 ⎭			
Norfolk	4,800	4·8	13,000	4·73
Northampton	2,500	2·5	3,000	1·09
Northumberland	700	·7	1,100	·40
Nottingham	1,400	1·4	2,600	·95
Oxford	1,700	1·7	3,800	1·38
Rutland	380	·38	1,000	·36
Shropshire	1,900	1·9	2,800	1·02
Somerset	4,000	4·0	4,400	1·60
Bristol City	250	·25	3,400	1·24
Stafford	1,400	1·4	2,600	·95
Suffolk	4,800	4·8	6,500	2·36
Sussex	2,600	2·6	3,600	1·31
Warwick	1,800	1·8	2,600	·95
Westmorland	300	·3	900	·33
Wiltshire	2,700	2·7	2,500	·91
Worcester	1,800	1·8	2,600	·95

County	Apportionment of compensation		Excise farm of 1662	
	£	Percentage of total	£	Percentage of total
Yorkshire,				
West Riding	2,520 ⎫			
North Riding	1,930 ⎬	5·8	13,500	4·91
East Riding	1,350 ⎭			
Anglesey	260 ⎫			
Carnarvon	260			
Denbigh	450			
Flint	260 ⎬	2·0	2,000	·73
Merioneth	220			
Montgomery	550 ⎭			
Cardigan	350 ⎫			
Carmarthen	450			
Glamorgan	700 ⎬	2·0	1,500	·55
Pembroke	500			
Brecknock	450 ⎫			
Monmouth	800 ⎬	1·49	1,500	·55
Radnor	240 ⎭			
	100,020		275,450	

D. HOUSE TAXES

109. Act imposing Hearth Tax, 1662

(*Statutes of the Realm*, v, pp. 390–393)

AN ACT FOR ESTABLISHING AN ADDITIONAL REVENUE
UPON HIS MAJESTY, HIS HEIRS AND SUCCESSORS,
FOR THE BETTER SUPPORT
OF HIS AND THEIR CROWN AND DIGNITY

(*14 Car. II, cap. 10*)

Forasmuch as nothing conduceth more to the peace and prosperity of a nation, and the protection of every single person therein, than that the public revenue thereof may be in some measure proportioned to the public charges and expenses, we therefore, your Majesty's most loyal and obedient subjects the Commons assembled in Parliament, having duly considered the premises, do give and grant unto your most excellent Majesty, your heirs and successors, the rates and duties hereinafter mentioned, and do most humbly beseech your Majesty that it may be enacted, and be it enacted . . . that from and after the five and twentieth day of March in the year of our Lord God one thousand six hundred sixty and two every dwelling and other house and edifice, and all lodgings and chambers in the Inns of Court, Inns of Chancery, colleges and other societies that are or hereafter shall be erected within the kingdom of England, dominion of Wales and town of Berwick-upon-Tweed (other than such as in this Act are hereafter excepted and declared), shall be chargeable, and by this present Act be and are charged, with the annual payment to the king's Majesty, his heirs and successors, for every fire-hearth and stove within every such house, edifice, chambers and lodgings as aforesaid, the sum of two shillings by the year, to be paid yearly and every year at the Feast of St. Michael the Archangel[1] and the Feast of the Annunciation of the blessed Virgin St. Mary,[2] by even and equal portions, the first payment thereof to be paid upon the Feast day of St. Michael the Archangel which shall be in the year of our Lord one thousand six hundred sixty and two. . . .

XVI. Provided always, that no person who by reason of his poverty or the smallness of his estate is exempted from the usual taxes, payments and contributions towards the Church and poor shall be charged or chargeable with any the duties by this Act imposed, anything hereinbefore to the contrary notwithstanding.

XVII. Provided always, and be it hereby enacted, that if the churchwardens and overseers of the poor of the parish, together with the minister of the same, or any two of them (whereof the minister to be one), shall in writing under their hands yearly certify their belief that the house wherein any person doth inhabit is not of greater value than twenty shillings per annum upon the full improved rent, and that neither the person so inhabiting nor any other using the same messuage hath, useth or

---

[1] 29 September.   [2] 25 March.

occupieth any lands or tenements of their own or others of the yearly value of twenty shillings per annum, nor hath any lands, tenements, goods or chattels of the value of ten pounds in their own possession or in the possession of any other in trust for them, that then . . . the said house is hereby for that year discharged of and from all the duties by this Act imposed, anything herein to the contrary notwithstanding. . . .

XIX. Provided that this Act or anything herein contained shall not extend to charge any blowing house and stamp furnace or kiln, or any private oven within any of the houses hereby charged, nor any hearth or stove within the site of any hospital or alms-house for the relief of poor people whose endowment and revenue doth not exceed in true value the sum of one hundred pounds by the year. . . .

110. Act abolishing Hearth Tax, 1689

(*Statutes of the Realm*, VI, pp. 61–62)

AN ACT FOR THE TAKING AWAY THE REVENUE
ARISING BY HEARTH MONEY

(*1 Gul. & Mar., cap. 10*)

Whereas his Majesty, having been informed that the revenue of Hearth Money was grievous to the people, was pleased by his gracious message sent to the Commons assembled in Parliament to signify his pleasure either to agree to a regulation of it or to the taking it wholly away, as should be thought most convenient by the said Commons; and whereas upon mature deliberation the said Commons do find that the said revenue cannot be so regulated but that it will occasion many difficulties and questions, and that it is in itself not only a great oppression to the poorer sort but a badge of slavery upon the whole people, exposing every man's house to be entered into and searched at pleasure by persons unknown to him; we, your Majesty's most dutiful and loyal subjects the Commons, being filled with a most humble and grateful sense of your Majesty's unparalleled grace and favour to your people, not only by restoring their rights and liberties, which have been invaded contrary to law, but in desiring to make them happy and at ease by taking away such burthens as by law were fixed upon them, by which your Majesty will erect a lasting monument of your goodness in every house in the kingdom, do most humbly beseech your Majesty that the said revenue of Hearth Money may be wholly taken away and abolished; and be it enacted . . . that an Act made in the Parliament begun at Westminster the eighth day of May in the thirteenth year of the reign of his late Majesty King Charles the Second, entituled, *An Act for the establishing an additional revenue upon his Majesty, his heirs and successors, for the better support of his and their crown and dignity*;[1] and another Act made in the second session of the said Parliament in the fifteenth year of his said late Majesty's reign, entituled, *An additional Act for the better ordering and collecting the revenue arising by Hearth Money*;[2] and another Act made in the sixteenth year of the reign of his said late Majesty, entituled, *An Act for collecting the duty arising by*

[1] No. 109.   [2] 15 Car. II, cap. 13.

Hearth Money by the officers to be appointed by his Majesty,[1] and all and every the articles, clauses and things in the said several Acts contained, shall be and are hereby wholly repealed, annulled and utterly made void. . . .

II. Provided always, and be it declared and enacted, that nothing in this Act contained shall be taken or construed to hinder or prejudice the collecting, levying, answering or paying the said revenue arising by Hearth Money which shall grow due on the five and twentieth day of March in the year of our Lord one thousand six hundred eighty-nine, and all arrears of the said duty which now are due and payable by the said Acts. . . .

III. Act imposing Window Tax, 1696

(*Statutes of the Realm,* VII, pp. 86–94)

AN ACT FOR GRANTING TO HIS MAJESTY
SEVERAL RATES OR DUTIES UPON HOUSES
FOR MAKING GOOD THE DEFICIENCY OF THE CLIPPED MONEY

(*7 & 8 Gul. III, cap. 18*)

We, your Majesty's most dutiful and loyal subjects, the Commons in Parliament assembled, being deeply sensible of the great mischiefs occasioned and brought upon your Majesty's subjects by the clipping of the current coin of this kingdom, and that it is necessary in order to prevent the like evils for the future that such clipped money should be recoined, and in regard such of your Majesty's good subjects in whose hands such clipped money shall happen to be must sustain great loss and damage by reason of the deficiency thereof upon the recoining, unless some recompense be provided to make good such defect to the several owners and proprietors thereof, have therefore cheerfully and unanimously given and granted to your Majesty as a supply and aid for and towards the making good the deficiency of such clipped money the rates, duties, impositions and sums of money hereinafter mentioned; and we most humbly beseech your Majesty that it may be enacted, and be it enacted . . . that from and after the five and twentieth day of March in the year of our Lord one thousand six hundred ninety-six, for and during the term of seven years to commence and be accounted from the said five and twentieth day of March and no longer, there shall be charged, raised, levied and paid unto his Majesty, his heirs and successors, for and upon every dwelling-house inhabited that now are or hereafter shall be erected within the kingdom of England, dominion of Wales and town of Berwick-upon-Tweed (other than and except cottages) the annual or yearly sums of money hereinafter mentioned, that is to say, every such dwelling-house inhabited . . . the yearly sum of two shillings; and for every such dwelling-house inhabited having ten windows or more and under the number of twenty, the sum of four shillings yearly over and above the said yearly sum of two shillings; and for every such dwelling-house inhabited having twenty windows or more, the yearly sum of eight shillings over and above the said yearly

[1] 16 Car. II, cap. 3.

sum of two shillings; which said sums of money shall be paid yearly and every year during the said term of seven years upon the nine and twentieth day of September and the five and twentieth day of March by even and equal portions, the first payment thereof to be made upon the nine and twentieth day of September which shall be in the year of our Lord one thousand six hundred ninety-six.

II. And be it further enacted, that the payments and duties hereby granted shall be charged only upon the inhabitants or occupiers for the time being of such dwelling-house, his executors or administrators, and not on the landlord who let or demised the same, his heirs, executors, administrators or assigns. . . .

XXVIII. Provided always, and be it further enacted and declared, that such dwelling-houses only where the occupier or occupiers thereof, by reason of his, her or their poverty or the smallness of their estates, is or are exempted from the usual taxes, payments and contributions towards the Church and poor, shall be construed or understood to be excepted out of this Act or discharged of the duty hereby granted as cottages and no other, anything herein contained to the contrary notwithstanding. . . .

XXX. Provided always, and it is hereby enacted by the authority aforesaid, that from and after the four and twentieth day of June one thousand six hundred ninety and six, it shall and may be lawful to and for any person or persons, natives or foreigners, bodies politic or corporate, to advance and lend unto his Majesty upon the security of this Act, any sum or sums of money not exceeding the sum of twelve hundred thousand pounds, and to have and receive for the forbearance of six hundred thousand pounds thereof which shall be first lent interest not exceeding the rate of seven pounds for every one hundred pounds, and for the remainder of the said twelve hundred thousand pounds interest not exceeding eight pounds for every one hundred pounds for one whole year; and moreover that no money so lent upon the security of this Act shall be rated or assessed by virtue of any Act of Parliament whatsoever. . . .

XXXV. And whereas in and by an Act of this present Parliament entituled, *An Act for remedying the ill state of the coin of the kingdom*,[1] it is provided and enacted that the clipped moneys therein mentioned, which were or at any time or times within the time therein expressed should be brought or paid into the Receipt of Exchequer, should be melted and recoined; . . . and that true accounts should be kept in the said Receipt of Exchequer, . . . to the end the differences between the sums in tale of the said clipped moneys and the sums in tale of the said new moneys proceeding therefrom from time to time might be plainly known and manifested, and to the end the deficiencies which would thereby be occasioned . . . might be ascertained, in order to the making them good at the public charge as by the said Act more at large appeareth; it is hereby further enacted . . . that all the moneys which shall be raised by virtue of this present Act of Parliament by loans to be made as aforesaid, and all the moneys which shall be raised and paid into the Exchequer of or for the rates, duties and impositions hereby granted, other than and except so much of the said rates, duties or impositions as is hereinbefore appointed to be applied to the repayment and satisfaction of the said loans and the interest thereof, or for payment of salaries or other

[1] No. 206.

allowances in and by this Act otherwise specially directed, shall be appropriated and applied, and the same are hereby appropriated, for or towards the supplying and making good the deficiencies of the said clipped moneys. . . .

112. Incidence of Hearth and Window Taxes, 1689 and 1708

(G. Chalmers, *Estimate of the Comparative Strength of Great Britain*, ed. 1804, p. 216)

A COMPARATIVE VIEW OF THE NUMBER OF HOUSES
IN EACH COUNTY OF ENGLAND AND WALES
AS THEY APPEARED IN THE HEARTH BOOKS OF LADY DAY 1690,
AND AS THEY WERE MADE UP AT THE TAX OFFICE IN 1708

Counties	No. of houses 1690	No. of houses charged 1708
Bedfordshire	12,170	5,479
Berks	16,996	7,558
Bucks	18,688	8,604
Cambridge	18,629	7,220
Chester	25,592	11,656
Cornwall	26,613	9,052
Cumberland	15,279	2,509
Derby	24,944	8,260
Devon	56,202	16,686
Dorset	17,859	4,133
Durham	53,345	6,298
Essex	40,545	16,250
Gloucester	34,476	13,285
Hereford	16,744	6,913
Hertford	17,488	7,447
Huntingdon	8,713	3,992
Kent	46,674	21,871
Lancashire	46,961	22,588
Leicester	20,448	8,584
Lincoln	45,019	17,571
London, &c.	111,215	47,031
Norfolk	56,579	12,097
Northampton	26,904	9,218
Northumberland	included in Durham	6,787
Nottingham	17,818	7,755
Oxford	19,627	8,502

Counties	No. of houses 1690	No. of houses charged 1708
Rutland	3,661	1,498
Salop	27,471	11,452
Somerset	45,900	19,043
Southampton, &c.	28,557	14,331
Stafford	26,278	10,812
Suffolk	47,537	15,301
Surrey, &c.	40,610	14,071
Sussex	23,451	9,429
Warwick	22,400	9,461
Westmorland	6,691	1,904
Wilts	27,418	11,373
Worcester	24,440	9,178
York	121,052	44,779
Anglesey		1,040
Brecon		3,370
Cardigan		2,042
Carmarthen		3,985
Carnarvon		1,583
Denbigh		4,753
Flint	79,221	2,653
Glamorgan		5,020
Merioneth		1,900
Monmouth		3,289
Montgomery		4,047
Pembroke		2,764
Radnor		2,092
	1,319,215	508,516

E. MISCELLANEOUS GRANTS AND ASSESSMENTS

113. Act imposing poll tax, 1660

(Statutes of the Realm, v, pp. 207–225)

AN ACT FOR THE SPEEDY PROVISION OF MONEY
FOR DISBANDING AND PAYING OFF THE FORCES OF THIS KINGDOM
BOTH BY LAND AND SEA

(12 Car. II, cap. 9)

Whereas the present raising of great sums of money for the speedy disbanding of the forces both by land and sea is a matter of vast consequence and urgent necessity, so that not only the happiness and peace of his Majesty's kingdoms but also the well-being and prosperity of them depends upon it, which said sums of money cannot be so suddenly raised as the pressing occasions do require without some extraordinary means used, to the which all his Majesty's subjects in this visible exigence of the kingdom will heartily and cheerfully submit, seeing it is to free themselves from so great a burthen and daily increasing charge, may it therefore please your most excellent Majesty that it may be enacted, and be it enacted . . . that all and every person and persons who at the time of the execution of this Act shall be of the several ranks and degrees hereafter mentioned shall to the purpose aforesaid contribute and pay the several sums of money hereafter in this Act set down and appointed, that is to say, every person of the degree of a duke of England, Scotland or Ireland inhabiting and residing within this kingdom shall pay the sum of one hundred pounds; every person of the degree of a marquis . . . the sum of fourscore pounds; every person of the degree of an earl . . . the sum of threescore pounds; every person of the degree of a viscount . . . the sum of fifty pounds; every person of the degree of a baron . . . the sum of forty pounds; every eldest son of a duke of any of the said three kingdoms and inhabiting or residing within this kingdom, being of the age of one and twenty years, the sum of threescore pounds; every eldest son of a marquis . . . the sum of fifty pounds; the eldest son of an earl . . . the sum of forty pounds; every eldest son of a viscount . . . the sum of thirty-five pounds; every eldest son of a baron . . . thirty pounds; every person of the degree of a baronet of any of the said three kingdoms or of Nova Scotia, and inhabiting or residing within this kingdom, the sum of thirty pounds; every person that is a knight of the order of the bath . . . the sum of thirty pounds; every person who is a knight bachelor . . . the sum of twenty pounds; every serjeant-at-law the sum of twenty pounds; every person of the degree of an esquire, or so reputed, inhabiting and residing within this kingdom and above the age of one and twenty years, the sum of ten pounds. Every widow respectively, according to her husband's degree, shall pay the third part rated by this Act upon that degree of which the husband of such widow was in his lifetime.

II. And be it further enacted . . . that all and every person and persons of the several ranks and degrees hereafter in this Act mentioned shall . . . pay the several sums of money . . . appointed, that is to say, every parson or vicar being possessed of a parsonage or vicarage or other estate of the clear yearly value of one hundred pounds the sum of forty shillings; every doctor in the civil or canon laws, and every advocate, the sum of five pounds; every person who is a judge or commissioner in the Courts of Admiralty or of the Probate of Wills the sum of twenty pounds; every person who hath practised as a proctor in either of the courts aforesaid the sum of five pounds; every doctor of physic the sum of ten pounds.

III. And be it further enacted . . . that all and every person and persons of the several degrees and qualities hereafter mentioned shall . . . pay the several sums of money . . . set down in this Act, that is to say, the lord mayor of the city of London shall pay the sum of forty pounds; every such person who either is now sheriff or alderman of the said city of London, or hath fined for sheriff or alderman of London, the sum of twenty pounds; every person who hath been or now is deputy to any alderman within the said city ten pounds; the town clerk of London twenty pounds; every person who is of the common council of the said city the sum of five pounds; every person who hath been or now is master of any of the twelve first companies of the said city, or hath fined for master of any of the said twelve companies, the sum of ten pounds; every person who hath been or now is warden of any of the said twelve first companies of the said city, or hath fined for warden of any of the said companies, six pounds thirteen shillings and four pence; every person who is of the livery of any of the said twelve first companies the sum of five pounds; every person who is of the yeomanry of either of the said twelve first companies three pounds; every person who is or hath been master of either of the companies of Dyers, Brewers, Leather Sellers, Girdlers, Stationers, Woodmongers, Upholsterers, Apothecaries, Pewterers, Tallow-Chandlers, Armourers or Saddlers, the sum of six pounds; every person who hath been warden of either of the said companies five pounds; every person who is of the livery of any of the said companies three pounds; every person who is of the yeomanry of the said companies one pound; every person who hath been or is master of any of the companies of Barber Chirurgeons, White Bakers, Wax Chandlers, Cutlers, Butchers, Carpenters, Painters, Cordwainers, Coopers, Scriveners, Brown Bakers, Turners or Innholders, the sum of three pounds; every person who is or hath been warden of any of the said companies two pounds; every person who is of the livery of any of the said companies one pound; every person who is or hath been master of either of the companies of Founders, Curriers, Masons, Bricklayers, Joiners, Plasterers, Weavers, Fruiterers, Marblers, Embroiderers, Poulterers, Cooks or Plumbers, the sum of one pound; every person who is or hath been warden of any of the said companies fifteen shillings; every person that is of the livery of the said companies ten shillings; every person who is or hath been of the livery of either of the companies of Bowyers, Fleshers, Blacksmiths, Bottlemakers, Woolpackers, Farriers, Paviors, Loriners, Glaziers, Clerks or Watermen, five shillings; every person who is a freeman of any company within the city of London the sum of one shilling; every person that keepeth one or more hackney-coaches shall pay for every hackney-coach and pair of horses that he so keepeth the sum of ten shillings; every person who is a merchant stranger, if he be of the degree of a knight, the sum of forty pounds, if below that degree and he be a merchant trading to sea the sum of ten pounds, if trading within the land the sum of five pounds; every person being an alien born, and using or exercising any trade, mystery or manual occupation within any of the cities or corporations of this kingdom, being a housekeeper, the sum of ten shillings; every person who is an English merchant inhabiting and residing in or about the said city of London, and not free of the said city, the sum of ten pounds; every English factor residing within the said city the sum of forty shillings; every person who is or hath been an alderman in any city within this kingdom, if he be below the degree of a knight or esquire, the sum of five pounds.

IV. And be it further enacted . . . that all and every such person and persons who is possessed of any of the several offices or places hereafter mentioned in their own rights shall pay the several sums hereafter set down, that is to say, the prothonotary of the Court of King's Bench the sum of one hundred pounds; the Clerk of the Crown of the Court of King's Bench aforesaid twenty pounds; the custos brevium of the said court forty pounds; the marshal of the King's Bench fifty pounds; the Master of the Rolls threescore pounds; the Clerk of the Crown in the Court of Chancery forty pounds; the clerk of the rules in the King's Bench ten pounds; the Warden of the Fleet fifty pounds; the Clerk of the Hanaper forty pounds; . . .[1] every person in any office or place under his Majesty (except his Majesty's household servants in ordinary) who receiveth the yearly fee of ten pounds, the sum of ten pounds; the Lieutenant of the Tower of London fifty pounds; every person that can dispend in lands, leases, money, stock or otherwise of his or her own proper estate one hundred pounds per annum, the sum of forty shillings, and so proportionably for a greater or lesser estate, provided it extend not to persons under five pounds yearly; every person, being a single person and above the age of sixteen years, the sum of twelve pence; and every other person, of what estate or degree soever he or she be, within his Majesty's kingdom of England and dominion of Wales, not rated before in this present Act nor receiving alms, and being above sixteen years of age, shall pay six pence. . . .

VIII. And it is further enacted . . . that if any person or persons of what degree, rank or quality soever, inhabiting or residing within the city of London or within fifteen miles distant from the said city, shall before the time limited by this Act pay unto Sir Richard Browne, baronet, Sir John Langham, baronet, Sir William Wheeler, knight, Sir William Vincent, knight, Thomas Rich, esquire, and the chamberlain of the city of London for the time being (who are hereby constituted and appointed treasurers for the receiving and issuing of all and singular the sums of money by this Act intended to be raised), or unto any two of them, and shall receive from the said treasurers or any two of them a certificate or acquittance acknowledging the receipt of such sums, the said parties severally shall thereby be discharged of, for or concerning the said sums, and all such payments shall be taken as an acceptable service to his Majesty and the kingdom.

IX. And it is further enacted . . . that if any person or persons shall lend the sum of one hundred pounds or any greater sum to and for the use and purposes in this

---

[1] A large number of other officials follow, who are individually assessed.

present Act mentioned and declared, such person shall do very good and acceptable service to the kingdom.

X. And be it further enacted, that any person or persons that shall so lend and advance such sum or sums of money as aforesaid for this present occasion, and shall before the first day of August one thousand six hundred and sixty ensuing pay and deliver the same to such person or persons as are authorized by this present Act to receive the moneys charged hereby upon the respective inhabitants of the city of London, shall be secured by this Act for the repayment of the said moneys at such time and place as by the lenders of the said moneys shall be required and agreed upon, and also of the interest and damage sustained by the forbearance thereof after the rate of six pounds per cent for a year and until such time as they shall respectively have received again the said sums so lent and advanced. . . .

XVI. Provided likewise, that no person or persons of what degree or quality soever shall be doubly charged by this Act, but that every person shall pay the greatest proportion he or she is charged withal by this Act.

XVII. And be it further enacted by the authority aforesaid, that all and every the sum and sums of money to be levied and raised by virtue of this present Act shall (by the treasurers in and by this Act appointed) be employed and disposed for and towards the paying of the arrears, disbanding and discharging the respective forces of this kingdom by land and sea who were in pay the tenth day of June one thousand six hundred and sixty, and to no other use or purpose whatsoever, and that an accompt of all the said moneys shall be given by the said treasurers to this or the next or any other succeeding Parliament, or to such person or persons as shall by this or any other succeeding Parliament be thereunto appointed. . . .

114. Act for a benevolence, 1661

(*Statutes of the Realm*, v, p. 307)

AN ACT FOR A FREE AND VOLUNTARY PRESENT
TO HIS MAJESTY

(*13 Car. II, stat. I, cap. 4*)

We, your Majesty's most loyal and obedient subjects the Lords and Commons in Parliament assembled, taking into consideration your Majesty's great and important occasions for a speedy supply of moneys, which can no ways be so readily raised as by a free and voluntary present to your Majesty from those who are able and willing to aid your Majesty in this sudden exigency, as a testimony of their affections to your Majesty and in ease of the poorer sort of your subjects, do therefore beseech your Majesty that it may be enacted, and be it enacted . . . that your Majesty may issue out such and so many several commissions under your Majesty's great seal of England into the several counties, cities, towns corporate and all other places in England and Wales and town of Berwick-upon-Tweed, directed to such persons as your Majesty shall think fit, for the receiving of such subscriptions as your Majesty's good subjects shall voluntarily offer for supply of your Majesty's pressing occasions, and likewise to issue such other commissions to such other persons as your Majesty shall think fit for collecting and receiving the moneys so subscribed, the acquittance of which respective receivers or of any one of them are immediately to be made and given without any fee upon payment made, and shall be an absolute discharge for the sum so subscribed. . . .

III. Provided always that no person not being a peer of this realm shall in such offer or present to your Majesty exceed the sum of two hundred pounds, nor any peer of this realm the sum of four hundred pounds.

IV. Provided also that no commissions to be issued out by virtue of this Act shall be of force or continue as to the receiving of any moneys or subscriptions for moneys after the feast of St. John the Baptist[1] which shall be in the year of our Lord one thousand six hundred sixty and two.

V. And be it hereby declared that no commissions or aids of this nature can be issued out or levied but by authority of Parliament, and that this Act and the supply hereby granted shall not be drawn into example for the time to come.

115. Act granting a Royal Aid, 1665

(*Statutes of the Realm*, v, pp. 525–552)

AN ACT FOR GRANTING A ROYAL AID UNTO THE KING'S MAJESTY
OF TWENTY-FOUR HUNDRED THREESCORE AND SEVENTEEN THOUSAND AND FIVE
HUNDRED POUNDS, TO BE RAISED, LEVIED AND PAID
IN THE SPACE OF THREE YEARS

(*16 & 17 Car. II, cap. 1*)

We, your Majesty's most dutiful and loyal subjects the Commons assembled in Parliament, taking into consideration the great and apparent dangers which now threaten this kingdom, and that for prevention thereof your Majesty hath found yourself obliged to equip and set out to sea a royal navy for the preservation of your Majesty's ancient and undoubted sovereignty and dominion in the seas and the trade of your Majesty's subjects; . . . and being deeply sensible of that extraordinary charge and expense with which your Majesty's present engagement ought to be supported, and of those inconveniences which must needs befall the nation if we should be wanting to ourselves in this so weighty and important occasion, . . . do humbly beseech your Majesty that it may be enacted, and be it enacted . . . that for the righting of your Majesty and your Majesty's subjects against the Dutch the sum of twenty-four hundred threescore and seventeen thousand and five hundred pounds shall be raised, levied and paid unto your Majesty within the space of three years in manner following, that is to say, the sum of threescore and eight thousand eight hundred and nineteen pounds and nine shillings by the month, for thirty-six months beginning from the five and twentieth day of December one thousand six hundred sixty-four, shall be assessed, taxed, collected, levied and paid by twelve quarterly payments in the several counties, cities, boroughs, towns and places within England and Wales and the town

[1] 24 June.

of Berwick-upon-Tweed, according to the several rules and proportions and in such manner as is hereafter expressed, that is to say, for every month of the said thirty-six months.

	1661[1]			1665			1707[1]		
	l.	*s.*	*d.*	*l.*	*s.*	*d.*	*l.*	*s.*	*d.*
Bedfordshire	933	6	8	896	17	9	27,862	3	10½
Bedford							692	11	1
Berkshire	1,088	17	10	1,132	6	7	40,075	10	8
New Windsor							978	10	0
Buckinghamshire	1,283	6	8	1,315	6	5	46,449	19	2½
Buckingham							613	0	5½
Wycombe							358	17	6
Cambridgeshire	1,102	10	0	1,020	0	0	21,960	14	3½
Isle of Ely	367	10	0	349	17	11	8,008	5	7½
University and town							2,846	3	1
Cheshire	770	0	0	801	5	6	27,014	18	10½
Chester	85	11	2				1,584	7	0
Cornwall	1,633	6	8	1,540	18	3	31,975	6	0
Cumberland	108	0	0	168	6	1	3,713	18	2½
Derbyshire	933	6	8	862	8	4	24,093	19	9½
Devon	3,003	15	6	3,229	19	2	77,875	2	10½
Exeter	107	6	8	116	7	4	4,708	0	5½
Dorset	1,311	10	6	1,344	10	5	32,759	18	6½
Poole	10	14	0	10	19	8	328	2	0
Durham	153	14	4	323	16	9	10,597	14	5½
Essex	3,500	0	0	3,098	8	10	85,816	10	5
Maldon							584	18	0
Colchester							2,845	6	3
Harwich							403	13	0
Gloucestershire	1,626	6	8	1,808	10	3	46,116	10	2
Gloucester	162	11	2	39	8	0	1,396	4	8
Herefordshire	1,166	13	4	1,131	13	4	19,311	13	8
Hereford							763	17	4
Leominster							333	15	8
Hertfordshire	1,400	0	0	1,345	16	3	41,808	13	4
St. Albans							774	2	0
Huntingdonshire	622	4	6	633	14	2	15,064	12	4
Huntingdon							432	12	8

[1] For purposes of comparison with the Royal Aid, figures are here printed in parallel columns for the similar taxes imposed immediately after the Restoration and immediately after the parliamentary union between England and Scotland. The tax imposed in 1661 was a tax of £70,000 a month apportioned in accordance with a scheme which had been adopted under the Commonwealth; that of 1665 a tax of £68,819 9s. 0d. a month apportioned in accordance with a modification of the Commonwealth scheme; and that of 1707 (No. 118) a tax of £1,995,882 0s. 5½d. a year apportioned in accordance with a new valuation made in 1692. No other apportionment of the property or land tax was adopted under the later Stuarts, but the total sum exacted varied considerably.

	1661			1665			1707		
	l.	*s.*	*d.*	*l.*	*s.*	*d.*	*l.*	*s.*	*d.*
Kent	3,655	11	2	3,326	18	8	75,610	7	8
Canterbury							1,762	5	8
Dover							1,923	13	9
Folkestone							144	19	0
Fordwich							77	8	0
Faversham							519	10	3
Tenterden							1,032	6	0
Sandwich							991	16	6
New Romney							249	17	0
Lydd							769	19	6
Hythe							236	14	0
Lancashire	933	6	8	1,006	13	6	20,989	14	6$\frac{1}{2}$
Leicestershire	1,088	17	8	1,084	14	3	34,112	1	7$\frac{1}{2}$
Leicester							639	12	0
Lincolnshire	2,722	4	10	2,575	2	0	72,167	15	0
London	4,666	13	4	5,091	11	4	123,334	2	7
Middlesex	1,788	17	10	2,240	10	0	108,558	1	7
Serjeants Inn, Fleet Street							65	4	0
Serjeants Inn, Chancery Lane							31	4	0
Inner Temple							400	0	0
Middle Temple							272	16	0
Lincoln's Inn							341	7	6
Gray's Inn							252	13	4
Whitehall and St. James's							30,754	6	3
Westminster							63,092	1	5
Monmouthshire	466	13	4	390	0	0	9,812	6	5$\frac{1}{2}$
Norfolk	3,624	8	10	3,370	12	0	71,204	19	4
Norwich	186	13	4	180	0	0	8,518	11	11
Great Yarmouth							2,820	3	1
Kings Lynn							1,814	14	0
Thetford							· 239	0	0
Northamptonshire	1,400	0	0	1,413	18	2	47,172	18	10
Northampton							830	7	10
Northumberland	179	19	10	372	15	8	11,822	18	0
Newcastle	35	11	8				2,580	16	4
Berwick	5	16	8				145	3	0
Nottinghamshire	903	4	4	873	8	0	25,662	0	2
Nottingham	30	2	4				1,614	10	7$\frac{1}{2}$
Oxfordshire	1,127	15	6	1,135	10	8	35,421	11	11

	1661			1665			1707		
	l.	*s.*	*d.*	*l.*	*s.*	*d.*	*l.*	*s.*	*d.*
University							111	17	2
Oxford							3,613	16	6
Rutland	272	4	6	240	8	11	5,525	3	10½
Shropshire	1,322	4	4	1,203	14	2	28,834	17	1½
Ludlow							226	2	0
Somerset	2,722	4	6	2,771	10	8	63,790	4	4
Bristol	171	2	2	199	8	4	7,391	10	8
Bath							443	6	0
Wells							481	17	6
Bridgwater							366	5	0
Southamptonshire	2,022	4	4	2,189	8	8	48,119	19	11½
Southampton							794	10	1
Isle of Wight							6,273	16	0
Staffordshire	919	6	8	852	11	8	26,700	3	10
Lichfield	14	0	0	13	0	0	420	19	4
Suffolk	3,655	11	2	3,298	10	8	68,332	2	6
Ipswich							2,061	3	6
Bury St. Edmunds							2,106	3	0
Dunwich							40	3	6
Eye							502	0	0
Sudbury							506	8	8
Thetford							79	4	0
Surrey	1,565	5	6	1,597	0	2	66,692	14	6½
Southwark	184	14	6						
Sussex	1,905	11	2	1,821	7	9	58,100	16	7
Hastings							378	6	0
Seaford							141	18	0
Pevensey							1,088	10	0
Rye							473	18	0
Winchelsea							405	0	0
Warwickshire	1,244	8	10	1,192	8	9	37,400	15	11
Coventry							2,463	14	9
Westmorland	73	19	4	116	0	0	3,045	3	9½
Wiltshire	1,944	8	10	1,966	17	7	49,736	11	5
New Sarum							1,935	16	6
Worcestershire	1,182	4	4	1,053	19	0	31,422	7	3
Worcester	62	4	6	55	9	6	2,239	9	8
Yorkshire	3,043	8	10	3,469	5	2			
York							4,639	8	0
Kingston-upon-Hull	67	13	4				2,053	2	4
West Riding							39,362	1	1
North Riding							26,376	3	8

	1661			1665			1707		
	l.	s.	d.	l.	s.	d.	l.	s.	d.
East Riding							19,127	2	11
Anglesey	135	14	4	125	13	8	1,633	7	11
Brecknock	361	13	4	282	10	5½	2,873	18	4
Brecon							177	19	8
Cardiganshire	213	10	0	105	15	9½	1,372	16	2
Carmarthenshire	352	6	8	272	6	8	4,140	3	11½
Carmarthen							229	18	8
Carnarvonshire	202	4	4	146	12	2	2,337	6	7
Denbighshire	272	4	6	223	10	7	6,800	0	0
Flintshire	135	14	6	118	17	4	2,314	17	0
Glamorganshire	458	17	8	378	17	10	7,906	9	10
Merionethshire	124	8	10	100	16	1	2,432	15	10
Montgomeryshire	295	11	0	276	12	2	5,852	18	4
Pembrokeshire	406	0	0	326	10	0	2,997	17	8½
Haverfordwest	14	11	8	15	3	5	174	17	4
Radnorshire	254	6	8	174	6	8	2,692	6	0

II. And be it further enacted . . . that all and every the persons hereafter named shall be commissioners of and for the several and respective counties, cities, boroughs, towns and places hereafter named, that is to say,. . .[1]

III. And be it further enacted and declared, that the several commissioners aforesaid shall meet together at the most usual and common place of meeting within each of the said counties, cities, boroughs, towns and places respectively, on or before the tenth day of March now next ensuing;[2] and the said commissioners or so many of them as shall be present at the said first general meeting, or the major part of them, are hereby authorized and required to put this present Act in execution according to the best of their judgments and discretions, and shall then if they see cause subdivide and distribute themselves so into lesser numbers as two or more of the said commissioners may be appointed for the service of each hundred or other division, and as may best conduce to the carrying on of his Majesty's service hereby required. . . .

V. And be it enacted . . . that the commissioners within the several divisions or hundreds, or any two or more of them, are hereby authorized and required to cause the said several proportions charged on the respective divisions and on every parish and place therein for the said three years assessment to be equally assessed and taxed, and to appoint two or more assessors in each parish or place for the perfecting thereof, who are hereby required with all care and diligence to assess the same equally by a pound rate upon all lands, tenements, hereditaments, annuities, rents, parks, warrens, goods, chattels, stock, merchandise, offices (other than judicial and military offices, and offices relating to the navy under the command of the Lord High Admiral, and offices within his Majesty's household), tolls, profits and all other estates, both real and personal, within the limits, circuits and bounds of their respective parishes and places. . . .

[1] The names of the commissioners follow.   [2] 1665.

XIII. And the several and respective tenants or tenant of all houses and lands which shall be rated by virtue of this Act are hereby required and authorized to pay such sum or sums of money as shall be rated upon such house or lands, and to deduct out of the rent so much of the said rates as in respect of the said rents of every such house and lands the landlord should or ought to pay and bear; and the said landlords, both mediate and immediate, according to their respective interests, are hereby required to allow such deductions and payments upon receipt of the residue of the rents. . . .

116. Tonnage Act, 1694

(Statutes of the Realm, VI, pp. 483–495)

AN ACT FOR GRANTING TO THEIR MAJESTIES
SEVERAL RATES AND DUTIES UPON TONNAGE OF SHIPS AND VESSELS,
AND UPON BEER, ALE AND OTHER LIQUORS,
FOR SECURING CERTAIN RECOMPENSES AND ADVANTAGES IN THE SAID ACT
MENTIONED TO SUCH PERSONS AS SHALL VOLUNTARILY ADVANCE
THE SUM OF FIFTEEN HUNDRED THOUSAND POUNDS
TOWARDS THE CARRYING ON THE WAR AGAINST FRANCE

(5 & 6 Gul. & Mar., cap. 20)

We, your Majesties' most dutiful and loyal subjects the Commons assembled in Parliament, for the further supply of your Majesties' extraordinary occasions for and towards the necessary defence of your realms, do humbly present your Majesties with the further gift of the impositions, rates and duties hereinafter mentioned, and do beseech your Majesties that it may be enacted, and be it enacted . . . that for and during the term of four years commencing from the first day of June in the year of our Lord one thousand six hundred ninety and four there shall be throughout the kingdom of England, dominion of Wales and town of Berwick-upon-Tweed raised, levied, collected and paid unto and for the use of their Majesties, their heirs and successors, for and upon the tonnage of all ships and vessels wherein at any time or times, and for every time, during the said term of four years there shall be imported any goods or merchandises into this kingdom of England, dominion of Wales or town of Berwick-upon-Tweed from any the parts, places or countries hereafter mentioned, or wherein during the said term there shall be carried coastwise from any port, member or creek in the kingdom of England, dominion of Wales or town of Berwick-upon-Tweed unto any other port, creek or member within the same kingdom, dominion, port or town, the several and respective rates, impositions, duties and sums of money hereinafter mentioned, that is to say, for every ton of the burthen or contents of any ship or vessel importing goods, wares or merchandises from[1]

East Indies or any parts south or east of the Cape of Good Hope	30s.
Italy or Turkey	15s.
Portugal or Spain	10s.
Plantations, lands or places in the West Indies	10s.
Holland, United Provinces, Netherlands or Flanders	3s.
Norway, Hamburg, Baltic Sea, eastland countries or ports or places north of Holland	5s.

[1] The duties are not given in tabulated form in the Act.

Ireland or Scotland	2s.
Any port or place in the Mediterranean not otherwise charged in the Act	15s.
Guinea or Africa outside the Straits	20s.
Hudson's Bay	20s.
Canaries, Madeira or western islands	10s.
Greenland, Muscovy or Russia	10s.
Coasting trade in England, Wales or Berwick	6d.

IX. And whereas by an Act of Parliament made in the second year of their Majesties' reign, entituled, *An Act for granting to their Majesties several additional duties upon beer, ale and other liquors for four years from the time that an Act for doubling the duty of Excise upon beer, ale and other liquors during the space of one year doth expire*,[1] it was enacted, that from and after the seventeenth day of November in the year of our Lord one thousand six hundred ninety and one there should be throughout their Majesties' kingdom of England, dominion of Wales and town of Berwick-upon-Tweed raised, levied, collected and paid unto their Majesties, their heirs and successors, during the space and term of four years and no longer, for beer, ale, cider and other liquors therein mentioned by way of Excise, over and above all other duties, charges and impositions by any former Act or Acts which should be then unexpired set and imposed, in such manner as therein is mentioned, which rates and duties aforesaid by Act of Parliament made in the third and fourth years of their now Majesties' reign are continued until the seventeenth day of May one thousand six hundred and ninety-seven, be it further enacted, that for the further encouragement of such persons who shall voluntarily contribute towards the raising and paying into their Majesties' Exchequer any sum or sums not exceeding in the whole the sum of fifteen hundred thousand pounds upon the several terms and recompenses hereinafter mentioned, that from and after the seventeenth day of May which shall be in the year of our Lord one thousand six hundred ninety and seven there shall be throughout their Majesties' kingdom of England, dominion of Wales and town of Berwick-upon-Tweed raised, levied, collected and paid unto their Majesties, their heirs and successors, for beer, ale, cider and other liquors hereinafter expressed, by way of Excise over and above all duties, charges and impositions by any former Act or Acts then unexpired set and imposed, one moiety or half part of the several rates and duties of Excise granted by the said last mentioned Act, in manner and form following, that is to say, . . .[2]

XVIII. And be it further enacted . . . that it shall and may be lawful to and for their Majesties, by commission under the great seal of England, to authorize and appoint any number of persons to take and receive all such voluntary subscriptions as shall be made on or before the first day of August which shall be in the year of our Lord one thousand six hundred ninety-four, by any person or persons, natives or foreigners, bodies politic or corporate, for and towards the raising and paying into the Receipt of the Exchequer the said sum of twelve hundred thousand pounds, part of the sum of fifteen hundred thousand pounds. . . .

XIX. And be it further enacted, that it shall and may be lawful to and for their

---

[1] 2 Gul. & Mar., sess. 2, cap. 10.   [2] The duties follow.

Majesties by letters patents under the great seal of England to limit, direct and appoint how and in what manner and proportions, and under what rules and directions, the said sum of twelve hundred thousand pounds, part of the said sum of fifteen hundred thousand pounds, and the said yearly sum of one hundred thousand pounds, part of the said yearly sum of one hundred and forty thousand pounds, and every or any part or proportion thereof, may be assignable or transferable, assigned or transferred, to such person or persons only as shall freely and voluntarily accept of the same and not otherwise, and to incorporate all and every such subscribers and contributors, their heirs, successors or assigns, to be one body corporate and politic by the name of the Governor and Company of the Bank of England, and by the same name of the Governor and Company of the Bank of England to have perpetual succession and a common seal. . . .

XXVI. And to the intent that their Majesties' subjects may not be oppressed by the said corporation by their monopolizing or engrossing any sort of goods, wares or merchandises, be it further declared and enacted . . . that the said corporation to be made and created by this Act shall not at any time during the continuance thereof deal or trade . . . with any of the stock-moneys or effects of or any wise belonging to the said corporation in the buying or selling of any goods, wares or merchandises whatsoever. . . .

XXVII. Provided that nothing herein contained shall any ways be construed to hinder the said corporation from dealing in bills of exchange, or in buying or selling bullion, gold or silver, or in selling any goods, wares or merchandise whatsoever which shall really and bona fide be left or deposited with the said corporation for money lent and advanced thereon, and which shall not be redeemed at the time agreed on or within three months after, or from selling such goods as shall or may be the produce of lands purchased by the said corporation.

XXVIII. Provided always, and be it enacted . . . that all and every bill or bills obligatory and of credit under the seal of the said corporation made or given to any person or persons shall and may by endorsement thereon under the hand of such person or persons be assignable and assigned to any person or persons who shall voluntarily accept the same, and so by such assignee *toties quoties* by endorsement thereupon. . . .

XXIX. Provided always, and it is hereby further enacted, that if the governor, deputy-governor, the directors, managers, assistants or other members of the said corporation so to be established shall upon the account of the said corporation at any time or times purchase any lands or revenues belonging to the Crown, or advance or lend to their Majesties, their heirs or successors, any sum or sums of money by way of loan or anticipation on any part or parts, branch or branches, fund or funds of the revenues now granted or belonging, or hereafter to be granted or belonging, to their Majesties, their heirs or successors, other than such fund or funds, part or parts, branch or branches of the said revenues only on which a credit of loan is or shall be granted by Parliament, that then the said governor, deputy-governor, directors, managers or assistants or other members of the said corporation who shall consent, agree to or approve of the advancing or lending to their Majesties, their heirs or successors, such sum or sums of money as aforesaid, and each and every of them so agreeing, consenting or approving, and being thereof lawfully convicted, shall for every such offence forfeit treble the value of every such sum or sums of money so lent. . . .

XXXIV. And be it further enacted, that any moneys payable to any person or persons upon or by virtue of this Act shall not be charged or chargeable with any rates, duties or impositions whatsoever. . . .

117. Act imposing tax on births, deaths and marriages, and on bachelors and widowers, 1695

(*Statutes of the Realm*, VI, pp. 568–583)

AN ACT FOR GRANTING TO HIS MAJESTY
CERTAIN RATES AND DUTIES UPON MARRIAGES, BIRTHS AND BURIALS,
AND UPON BACHELORS AND WIDOWERS, FOR THE TERM OF FIVE YEARS,
FOR CARRYING ON THE WAR AGAINST FRANCE WITH VIGOUR

(6 & 7 Gul. & Mar., cap. 6)

We, your Majesty's most dutiful and loyal subjects the Commons in Parliament assembled, from a deep sense of the many great occasions which engage your Majesty in many extraordinary expenses for the necessary defence of your realms and the prosecution of a war against France with vigour, have cheerfully and unanimously given and granted unto your Majesty as an additional supply and aid the rates, duties, impositions and sums of money hereinafter mentioned; and we most humbly beseech your Majesty that it may be enacted, and be it enacted . . . that from and after the first day of May in the year of our Lord one thousand six hundred ninety and five, for and during the term of five years to commence and be accounted from the said first day of May and no longer, there shall be raised, levied and paid to his Majesty, his heirs and successors (over and above all other duties whatsoever), for and upon the burial of all persons who shall be buried within the said term of five years at any place within the kingdom of England, dominion of Wales and town of Berwick-upon-Tweed, the several and respective duties and sums of money hereinafter mentioned, that is to say, . . .[1]

(*a*) *Burials, births and marriages*

	Burials			Births		Marriages		
	Wife or widow	Eldest son	Other child	Eldest son	Other child	The party	Eldest son	Younger son
Duke or archbishop	£50	£30	£25	£30	£25	£50	£30	£25
Marquis	40	25	20	25	20	40	25	20
Earl	30	20	15	20	15	30	20	15

[1] Similar provision follows for taxes on births, on marriages, on bachelors over the age of twenty-five and on widowers without children, the effect being here shown in tabular form on the model of the tables in S. Dowell, *A History of Taxation*, II, pp. 409–410.

(a) Burials, births and marriages

	Burials			Births		Marriages		
	Wife or widow	Eldest son	Other child	Eldest son	Other child	The party	Eldest son	Younger son
Viscount	£25	£17½	£13⅓	£17½	£13⅓	£25	£17½	£13⅓
Baron or bishop	20	15	12	15	12	20	15	12
Baronet or knight of the bath	15	5	1	5	1	15	5	1
Knight bachelor or dean	10	5	1	5	1	10	5	1
King's serjeant at law	20	1	1	1	1	20	1	1
Serjeant at law	15	1	1	1	1	15	1	1
Esquire	5	1	1	1	1	5	1	1
Gentleman	1	1	1	1	1	1	1	1
Doctor of Divinity, Law or Physic	5	1	1	1	1	5	1	1
Persons of £50 per annum or £600 personal estate	1	0½	0½	0½	0½	1	0½	0½
All persons, including the above		4s.			2s.		2s. 6d.	

(b) Bachelors and widowers

	The party	Eldest son	Younger son
Duke or archbishop	£12½	£7½	£6¼
Marquis	10	6¼	5
Earl	7½	5	3¾
Viscount	6¼	4⅜	3⅓
Baron or bishop	5	3¾	3
Baronet or knight of the bath	3¾	1¼	1¼
Knight bachelor	2½	1¼	0¼
King's serjeant at law	5	0¼	0¼
Serjeant at law	3¾	0¼	0¼
Esquire	1¼	0¼	0¼
Gentleman	0¼	0¼	0¼
Doctor of Divinity, Law or Physic	1¼	0¼	0¼
Persons of £50 per annum or £600 personal estate	0¼	0⅛	0⅛
All persons, including the above, except those in receipt of alms	1s.	1s.	1s.

XX. And be it further enacted, for the better levying and collecting the duties granted by this Act, that all persons in Holy Orders, deans, parsons, deacons, vicars, curates and their or any of their substitutes, do within their respective parishes, precincts and places take an exact and true account, and keep a register in writing, of all and every person or persons married, buried, christened or born in his or their respective parishes or precincts, or in such common burying-places as their respective parishioners are usually buried in, to which book or register the collectors for the respective parishes and places and all other persons concerned shall have free access to view the same at all seasonable times without any fee or reward. . . .

XXI. And be it further enacted . . . that the parents of every child which shall be born at any time within the said term of five years, or one of them, shall within five days after such birth give notice to the collectors, or one of them, of the parish or place where such child was born, and of the Christian name of such child and the day of its birth. . . .

XLVIII. And whereas the fellows, students, scholars and exhibitioners of the foundations or endowments of any college or hall in the two universities are by the statutes in their respective colleges and halls to be displaced from their places and maintenance therein if they shall marry, be it enacted . . . that the rates and taxes by this Act imposed or to be imposed on bachelors shall not extend to such fellows, students or scholars of houses or scholars having exhibitions in any such colleges or halls, anything herein contained to the contrary notwithstanding. . . .

LI. And be it enacted . . . that it shall and may be lawful to and for any person or persons, natives or foreigners, bodies politic or corporate, to advance and lend to his Majesty into the Receipt of his Exchequer upon the credit of this Act any sum or sums of money not exceeding the sum of six hundred and fifty thousand pounds in the whole, and to have and receive for the forbearance of all such moneys as shall be lent interest not exceeding the rate of eight pounds per cent per annum. . . .

118. Act imposing land tax in Great Britain, 1707

(*Statutes of the Realm*, VIII, pp. 637–726)

AN ACT FOR GRANTING AN AID TO HER MAJESTY
TO BE RAISED BY A LAND TAX IN GREAT BRITAIN
FOR THE SERVICE OF THE YEAR ONE THOUSAND SEVEN HUNDRED AND EIGHT

(*6 Annae, cap. 35*)

M ost gracious Sovereign, we, your Majesty's most dutiful and loyal subjects, the Commons of Great Britain in Parliament assembled, finding it necessary for the preservation and good of this whole united kingdom to furnish such ample supplies of money as may sufficiently enable your Majesty to carry on and finish the present war with success, have cheerfully and unanimously given and granted, and by this present Act (towards the raising of such supplies) do give and grant, unto your Majesty the several and respective rates and assessments hereafter mentioned; and we do humbly beseech your Majesty that it may be enacted, and be it enacted . . . that the sum of two millions forty-three thousand eight hundred thirty-six pounds sixteen shillings and fivepence halfpenny shall be raised, levied and paid unto her Majesty within the kingdom of Great Britain by such proportions and in such manner and form as are hereafter in this Act expressed.

II. And it is hereby declared and enacted . . . that the sum of one million nine hundred ninety-five thousand eight hundred eighty-two pounds and fivepence half-penny . . . shall be raised, levied and paid unto her Majesty within the space of one year from the five and twentieth day of March one thousand seven hundred and eight, and shall be assessed and taxed in the several counties, cities, boroughs, towns and places of England, Wales and Berwick-upon-Tweed according to the proportions and in the manner following, that is to say. . . .[1]

XCVIII. And be it enacted . . . that the sum of forty-seven thousand nine hundred fifty-four pounds sixteen shillings, residue of the said sum of two millions forty-three thousand eight hundred thirty-six pounds sixteen shillings and fivepence halfpenny by this Act granted, shall be raised and levied in that part of Great Britain called Scotland by an eight months cess of five thousand nine hundred ninety-four pounds seven shillings of lawful money of Great Britain for every month, the said cess to be raised out of the land rent of Scotland according to the monthly proportions within the respective shires, stewartries, cities and boroughs hereinafter expressed, that is to say. . . .[2]

119. Stamp Act, 1711

(*Statutes of the Realm*, IX, pp. 595–639)

AN ACT FOR LAYING SEVERAL DUTIES UPON ALL SOAP AND PAPER
MADE IN GREAT BRITAIN OR IMPORTED INTO THE SAME, .
AND UPON SEVERAL KINDS OF STAMPED VELLUM, PARCHMENT AND PAPER,
AND UPON CERTAIN PRINTED PAPERS, PAMPHLETS AND ADVERTISEMENTS,
FOR RAISING THE SUM OF EIGHTEEN HUNDRED THOUSAND POUNDS
BY WAY OF A LOTTERY TOWARDS HER MAJESTY'S SUPPLY . . .

(*10 Annae, cap. 18*)

CXIII. And be it enacted . . . that there shall be raised, levied, collected and paid, to and for the use of her Majesty, her heirs and successors, for and upon all books and papers commonly called pamphlets, and for and upon all newspapers or papers containing public news, intelligence or occurrences, which shall at time or times within or during the term last mentioned be printed in Great Britain to be dispersed and made public, and for and upon such advertisements as are hereinafter mentioned, the respective duties following, that is to say:

For every such pamphlet or paper contained in half a sheet or any lesser piece of paper so printed, the sum of one halfpenny sterling.

For every such pamphlet or paper, being larger than half a sheet and not exceeding

---

[1] The apportionment of the English part of the tax is shown in No. 115.
[2] The apportionment of the Scottish part of the tax is shown in No. 262.

one whole sheet, so printed, a duty after the rate of one penny sterling for every printed copy thereof.

And for every such pamphlet or paper, being larger than one whole sheet and not exceeding six sheets in octavo or in a lesser page, or not exceeding twelve sheets in quarto or twenty sheets in folio, so printed, a duty after the rate of two shillings sterling for every sheet of any kind of paper which shall be contained in one printed copy thereof.

And for every advertisement to be contained in *The London Gazette* or any other printed paper, such paper being dispersed or made public weekly or oftener, the sum of twelve pence sterling. . . .

F. REVENUE AND EXPENDITURE

120. Estimates made during the reign of Charles II

(i) Revenue, 4 September 1660

(Journals of the House of Commons, VIII, p. 150)

Sir Heneage Finch reports from the committee to whom it was referred to consider of a revenue to be settled on the king's Majesty, and the state of the late king's revenue, an estimate of the present revenue of his Majesty, and several resolves of the said committee, that is to say:

That according to the best information the committee could receive from the officers heretofore employed about the revenue, the total of the revenue which came unto his late Majesty amounted, from the year 1637 to the year 1641 inclusive, *communibus annis*, unto eight hundred ninety-five thousand eight hundred and nineteen pounds five shillings, whereof two hundred and ten thousand four hundred ninety-three pounds seventeen shillings and fourpence did arise by payments, partly not warranted by law, partly expired; and that the expenses of his said late Majesty's government did amount, *communibus annis*, to about two hundred thousand pounds a year above the receipt; in which computation the incomes arising by ship-money are not comprehended; and that by estimate the present revenue of his now Majesty may be computed at eight hundred and nineteen thousand three hundred ninety-eight pounds or thereabouts, that is to say:

By the Customs	400,000*l.*
the composition for the Court of Wards	100,000*l.*
the revenue of farms and rents	263,598*l.*
the Office of Postage	21,500*l.*
the proceeds of Dean Forest	4,000*l.*
the imposition on sea coal exported	8,000*l.*
Wine Licences and other additions	22,300*l.*
	819,398*l.*

Of which sum forty-five thousand six hundred ninety-eight pounds eighteen shillings and sevenpence, part of the said two hundred sixty-three thousand five hundred ninety-eight pounds for farms and rents, is casual, and for the most part lost, viz., for the Mint, alum, transportation of gold, New Year's gifts, and installed debts.

He also reports some resolves of the said committee, viz. . . .

That the said committee think fit that the revenue for the constant yearly support of his Majesty be a revenue of twelve hundred thousand pounds a year. . .

Resolved, that the present king's Majesty's revenue shall be made up twelve hundred thousand pounds a year.

(ii) Revenue, 4 June 1663

(Journals of the House of Commons, VIII, p. 498)

Sir Charles Harbord reports from the committee appointed to inspect the several branches of his Majesty's revenue, that the committee had carefully inspected and examined the several branches of the revenue, and had commanded him to return a report of the present values of the several branches of the revenue; which he opened in his place, and after delivered in his report in writing at the Clerk's table, which was as followeth:

	Present yearly values			Future full values		
	l.	s.	d.	l.	s.	d.
The Customs let to farm for five years from Michaelmas 1662 at 390,000l. per annum, the king paying the patent fees to the officers and making such defalcations as are agreed by the grant	390,000	0	0	400,000	0	0
The revenue in lands and rents in charge in the Exchequer and Duchies of Lancaster and Cornwall, including the queen's jointure, being well managed, may be computed at, per annum, besides forests, parks and chases unimproved	100,000	0	0	100,000	0	0
Dean Forest, Sir John Winter being satisfied, and 14,000 acres enclosed and improved, may raise a constant revenue of, per annum	–	–	–	5,000	0	0
Excise of beer, ale, &c., now worth	274,950	0	0	274,950	0	0
Hearths and stoves, as now certified	170,603	12	0	170,603	12	0
First Fruits and Tenths, communibus annis	18,800	0	0	18,800	0	0
The coinage and pre-emption of tin, now valued at, per annum	12,000	0	0	12,000	0	0
The Post Office in lease for about four years to come, at, per annum	21,500	0	0	26,000	0	0
Wine Licences, as now settled, may raise a revenue of	20,000	0	0	20,000	0	0
Alienation Office produceth, communibus annis, a revenue of 3,600l., whereof 1,546l. 12s. is paid into and accounted for by the Hanaper, and so remains de claro, per annum	2,053	8	0	3,600	0	0
	1,009,907	0	0	1,030,953	12	0
The profits of the seals of the King's Bench and Common Pleas, in lease at the rent of 1,653l. 14s. paid into the Hanaper yearly; but are estimated to be worth, communibus annis, above the said rent, 1,500l.	1,653	14	0	3,153	14	0
The profits of the sixpenny writs in Chancery, in lease at 1,000l. per annum and paid into the Hanaper yearly, but estimated to be worth, communibus annis, above the said rent and charges of execution, 375l.	1,000	0	0	1,375	0	0

	Present yearly values l. s. d.			Future full values l. s. d.		
Hanaper Office receives 1,546l. 12s. out of the Alienation Office, and 1,653l. 14s. for the farm of the seals of the King's Bench and Common Pleas, and 1,000l. per annum for the farm of the sixpenny writs in Chancery, and all other profits of the Great Seal there paid, computed to be, *communibus annis*, 1,500l.; but all is now spent in this Office, *ut per comput. inde*	-	-	-	1,500	0	0
Post Fines, in lease at the rent of	2,275	6	0	3,000	0	0
Issues of jurors, in lease at the rent of	1,000	0	0	1,660	0	0
Green Wax, in lease at the rent of	577	5	5	1,068	0	0
Green Wax of the Duchy of Lancaster	-	-	-	200	0	0
Aulnage, in lease at the rent of	997	1	11	3,000	0	0
Newcastle coals at 12d. per chaldron for the inland vent only, in lease at	1,836	12	6	8,000	0	0
Ballast of ships, estimated to be worth, *communibus annis*, claimed and enjoyed by the Trinity House without any rent	-	-	-	1,000	0	0
	9,339	19	10	23,956	14	0
Faculties included in the Hanaper	400	0	0	400	0	0
Licence of exportation of white cloth, in lease at the rent of	100	0	0	800	0	0
Prizage and butlerage of wines, in lease at	500	0	0	2,000	0	0
Traitors' estates, besides those that were granted to the heirs, and the impropriations given to the Church, estimated at 8,000l. per annum, whereupon there is above 27,000l. debt and many encumbrances and jointures; and so computed to be worth *de claro*	5,000	0	0	5,000	0	0
Recusants' estates, as they were before the troubles. There are now no convictions	-	-	-	18,600	0	0
	6,000	0	0	26,800	0	0
Total	1,025,246	19	10	1,081,710	6	0

(iii) *Scheme of retrenchment, 1668*
(*Calendar of Treasury Books*, VII, pp. 1651–1652)

Revenue	l.	Expenditure	l.	s.	d.
Customs	400,000	The navy ordinary	200,000	0	0
Excise	340,000	The army and garrisons	182,000	0	0
Chimney money	170,000	The city of Tangier	55,500	0	0

Revenue		Expenditure			
	l.		*l.*	*s.*	*d.*
The smaller branches of the revenue	120,000	His Majesty's household	90,000	0	0
		Buildings and repairs	8,000	0	0
		His Majesty's privy purse	12,000	0	0
		Intelligence	4,000	0	0
		The treasury of the chamber	20,000	0	0
		The great wardrobe	16,000	0	0
		The band of gentlemen pensioners	3,000	0	0
		The robes	5,000	0	0
		The jewel house	2,000	0	0
		The office of the ordnance, ordinary and extraordinary	30,000	0	0
		The queen consort	23,000	0	0
		The queen mother	40,000	0	0
		Ambassadors, agents, &c.	20,000	0	0
		Foreign ambassadors	10,000	0	0
		The twelve judges	12,000	0	0
		The courts of Ludlow and masters of Chancery and requests	2,500	0	0
		Angel gold for healing	1,200	0	0
		The master of the horse for purchase of horses	2,000	0	0
		The master of the stud horses	500	0	0
		Creation money to the nobility	1,500	0	0
		Lord Privy Seal's diet	1,400	0	0
		Liberates of the Exchequer	1,500	0	0
		Dormant privy seals	300	0	0
		Chief officers of the falconry (besides an allowance of keeping two cast of hawks)	1,000	0	0
		Harriers	700	0	0
		Tents	500	0	0
		The Tower expenses	768	0	0
		Gamekeepers and keepers of forests	107	15	10
			746,475	15	10
		Interest paid yearly	150,000	0	0
		Deductions upon farms and for other accidents and contingencies	100,000	0	0
1,030,000		Total	996,475	15	10

Remains, 33,524*l.* 4*s.* 2*d.*

(iv) Revenue, c. 1675

(British Museum, Additional MSS. 28042, f. 50)

Customs	£650,000
Excise	550,000
Chimney Money	151,000
Law Duty	19,500
Tenths, &c.	16,000
Alienations	4,000
Small branches	20,000
	1,410,500

(v) Scheme of retrenchment, 1676

(*Calendar of State Papers Domestic*, 1675–1676, p. 324; *Calendar of Treasury Books*, v, 117)

	Before retrenchment	After
Navy	£340,000	£300,000
Ordnance	60,000	40,000
Forces and garrisons	212,000	212,000
Tangier	57,200	57,200
Household	107,000	52,247
Privy purse	38,000	36,000
Works	14,000	10,000
Treasurer of the chamber	30,000	20,000
Band of gentlemen pensioners	6,000	3,000
Stables, horses and studs	11,500	10,000
Great wardrobe	22,000	16,000
Jewel house	5,000	4,000
Ambassadors, envoys and for presents	50,000	40,000
Robes	5,000	4,000
Management of the { Customs		50,000
Excise	10,000	10,000
Wine Licences		2,000
Law Duty		1,500
Salaries and fees payable at the Exchequer	81,839	49,000
Post Office defalcations	5,000	4,000
Interest of moneys to the goldsmiths	70,000 ⎫	
Interest of other money to be daily borrowed	30,000 ⎭	100,000
Liberates at the Exchequer	2,000	1,500
Tents and toils	2,000	1,500
Tower expenses	768	768
Casual disbursements not proper to be under any head	15,000	10,000
Healing medals	2,000	2,000
Secretaries for intelligence	5,000	5,000

	Before retrenchment	After
Annual payments to the queen and his Royal Highness	36,209 ⎫	110,000
Pensions of grace	145,257 ⎬	
Secret service		20,000
New Year's gifts		3,600
	─────────	─────────
	1,362,770[1]	1,175,315

121. Statements for the reign of James II presented to the House of Commons, 1689

(*Journals of the House of Commons*, x, pp. 37–38, 55)

(*i*) *A computation of the several branches of the revenue*

	l.	s.	d.
The Old Customs made, in the year 1685,	532,143	9	6½
in the year 1686,	595,688	7	10½
in the year 1687,	630,700	15	0½
in the year 1688,	551,497	18	11¾

	l.	s.	d.			
The medium of the four years is	577,507	12	10¼ ⎫			
The duties, late in the Wood Farm, Coal Farm and Salt Farm, and the grant of the French tonnage, all newly expired	19,500	0	0 ⎬ 609,126	17	2¼
The four and half per cent rent of the Logwood Farm, and seizures of uncustomed and prohibited goods	12,119	4	4 ⎭			
The Excise made, in the year 1685	567,064	12	7½			
in the year 1686	581,664	4	8¼			
in the year 1687	623,891	1	7½			
in the year 1688	636,358	12	8½			
The medium of the four years is				610,486	10	9[2]
The Hearth Money, per annum, about				200,000	0	0
The Post Office, per annum, about				55,000	0	0
The small branches, per annum, about				26,350	15	5½
				───────		
				1,500,964	3	4¾

The New Impositions
granted in the late King James the Second's time

	l.	s.	d.
Wine and vinegar, for eight years, produced from Michaelmas 1687 to Michaelmas 1688	172,901	10	8¾
Remained to come, four years, half, from Christmas last, ending the 24th of June 1693.			
Tobacco and sugar, for the same time, produced in the same year	148,861	8	0
French linen, brandy, silks, &c., for five years, produced in the said year	93,710	8	1½
Remained to come, one year, half, the first of January last.			

Memorandum. These two last branches are charged with the loan of 84,888*l.* 6*s.* 9*d.* with interest, which is to be paid in the course of the register as it comes in.

[1] Really 1,362,773.   [2] Really £602,244 12*s.* 11*d.*

(ii) An Abstract of the Expenses of the late King James the Second by actual payments in money for three years from Lady Day 1685 to Lady Day 1688, viz.

In the several years ended at	*Lady Day 1686*			*Lady Day 1687*			*Lady Day 1688*			*Mediums*		
To the navy	367,130	13	6	444,805	4	10	440,452	0	3	417,462	12	$10\frac{1}{3}$
Ordnance	70,300	0	0	86,904	11	$2\frac{1}{2}$	93,275	16	7	83,493	9	$3\frac{1}{6}$
Forces	547,124	7	9	664,259	6	10	621,265	9	$9\frac{1}{2}$	610,883	1	$5\frac{1}{2}$
Household	52,600	0	0	66,156	15	$8\frac{3}{4}$	79,261	10	10	66,006	2	$2\frac{1}{4}$
Treasurer of the Chamber	23,272	17	5	26,527	2	7	35,529	15	8	28,443	5	$2\frac{2}{3}$
Wardrobe	10,000	0	0	14,600	0	0	20,775	11	$10\frac{1}{2}$	15,125	3	$11\frac{1}{2}$
Robes	1,780	4	3	3,750	0	0	2,500	0	0	2,676	14	9
Works	28,429	19	8	25,285	0	0	20,276	18	2	24,663	19	$3\frac{1}{3}$
Foreign ministers	37,435	7	2	32,447	18	8	28,089	2	11	32,657	9	7
Stables	4,200	0	0	12,090	7	8	16,846	11	$5\frac{1}{4}$	11,045	13	$0\frac{2}{5}$
Sundry fees and salaries paid at the Exchequer and elsewhere	43,479	9	$7\frac{1}{4}$	50,863	6	$5\frac{1}{2}$	65,144	1	$8\frac{1}{4}$	56,495	12	7
Pensions and annuities	117,443	18	$4\frac{1}{2}$	158,910	2	$3\frac{3}{4}$	163,757	11	1	146,703	17	$3\frac{1}{12}$
Band of Pensioners	3,000	0	0	9,000	0	0	6,000	0	0	6,000	0	0
Bounties, in gross sums, paid at the Exchequer	44,886	0	6	14,913	11	$6\frac{1}{2}$	23,242	0	0	27,680	10	$8\frac{1}{6}$
Secret Services, per Mr. Guy	93,890	16	$6\frac{1}{2}$	85,941	13	3	90,072	14	$10\frac{3}{4}$	89,968	8	$2\frac{3}{4}$
per Secretary of State	5,000	0	0	8,950	0	0	4,250	0	0	6,066	13	4
per Sir Stephen Fox	10,000	0	0	9,600	0	0	8,400	0	0	9,333	6	8
Privy Purse	25,950	0	0	27,300	0	0	26,000	0	0	26,416	13	4
Mint paid out of coinage												
Jewels and plate	21,087	0	0	10,400	0	0	15,733	18	2	15,740	6	$0\frac{2}{3}$
Impost bills	96	12	0	96	12	0	96	12	0	96	12	0

In the several years ended at	Lady Day 1686	Lady Day 1687	Lady Day 1688	Mediums
Contingencies not reducible to the foregoing heads	15,961 15 3	30,043 15 5¼	21,204 8 3	22,403 6 3¾

| | 1,523,069 2 0¼ | 1,792,845 8 6¼ | 1,782,174 3 7¼ | 1,699,363 2 9[1] |

Memorandum, the principal and interest to the bankers and their assigns, and the interest of moneys borrowed.

Notes referring to the estimate of the expense of the Crown

Navy. In the last four years of King Charles the Second the charge of the navy was never less than 400,000*l.* per annum.

Household. In King Charles the Second's time computed at 107,000*l.*

Ordnance. The ordnance was always paid 1,000*l.* the week and 2,000*l.* the quarter, which is per annum 60,000*l.* And this ordinary was never less. What was more, as in the medium, was paid by peculiar warrants.

Forces. In the last six years of King Charles the Second the expense of the forces amounted to about 300,000*l.* per annum.

Treasurer of the Chamber. The annual expense in King Charles the Second's time was computed at 30,000*l.*

Robes. King Charles the Second, when all heads were retrenched, continued the robes at the expense of 5,000*l.* per annum.

Pensions and annuities. By the medium, it appears, one year's payment, 146,703*l.* 17*s.* 3*d.*

In these years was 50,000*l.* paid to the queen consort every year.

To the queen dowager, 18,200*l.* yearly.

To the prince and princess of Denmark yearly 32,000*l.*; but their expenses have exceeded this about 8,000*l.* a year, which has been paid out of bounty in gross.

Privy purse. In King Charles the Second's time the privy purse was computed at 30,000*l.* per annum.

Impost bills. In King Charles the Second's time was 3,600*l.* per annum.

Contingencies, &c. As clerkships, repairing the highways, lawsuits, liberates in the Exchequer and other casualties.

The charge of the Crown, by the medium presented, is yearly	1,699,363	2 9
In King Charles the Second's time the charge of the forces was about	300,000	0 0
	1,399,363	2 9

Charges upon the revenue

Mr. Thomas Fox, for the security of his place of Receiver of the Customs, by tally	20,000	0 0
Mr. Duncombe, for the same, on the Excise	20,000	0 0
The city, on the Excise	185,525	0 0

[1] Really £1,699,362 18*s.* 0¾*d.*

To Mr. Hornby, on the Excise	5,000	0	0
To Mr. Hall, on the Hearth Money	47,000	0	0
	277,525	0	0

There is in arrear to the army and navy about	300,000	0	0
There is also a yearly charge of 79,566*l.* 14*s.* 2*d.* for perpetual interest to the goldsmiths and their assigns, which is now in arrear, at Lady Day next, for six years	477,400	5	0

122. Statement for the reign of William III
(*Somers Tracts*, ed. 1809–1815, XII, p. 382)

A GENERAL ABSTRACT

OF THE RECEIPTS AND ISSUES OF THE PUBLIC REVENUE, TAXES AND LOANS, DURING THE REIGN OF HIS LATE MAJESTY KING WILLIAM, THAT IS TO SAY FROM THE 5TH OF NOVEMBER 1688, FROM WHICH TIME THE PARLIAMENT APPOINTED THE SAID ACCOUNTS SHOULD COMMENCE, TO THE 25TH OF MARCH 1702, BEING THE FIRST DETERMINATION OF THE ACCOUNTS AFTER THE DEMISE OF HIS SAID LATE MAJESTY, WHICH HAPPENED ON THE 8TH OF MARCH PRECEDING

Customs   *Receipts*

Customs besides drawbacks, damages, salaries, &c.	4,285,697	1	6
Ditto from Christmas 1699 to the 1st of August 1706	934,923	8	0½
Impositions on linen, silk, &c., that ended 1st July 1690	143,880	9	6½
Ditto on tobacco and sugar	1,374,232	17	8¼
Ditto on wines and vinegar	1,750,388	15	7
Ditto on East India goods, &c., from Christmas 1690	1,801,906	2	9¾
Additional imposition on merchandises, and commenced 1st March 1692/3 to the 1st March 1696, thence to the 1st August 1706	501,120	2	0¾
New duty on coffee and tea, &c., and ditto continued for paying interest of Irish transports	105,203	11	3½
Additional duty on brandy from the 1st March 1693/4	22,691	7	0¼
Tonnage duty from 1st June 1694 and ending 17th May 1696	175,335	16	6
Duty on coals taken off 17th May 1696	22,004	19	3
Duty on glass and earthenware as relating to the Coal Act	7,750	0	0
25 per cent French goods	161,349	9	2
New duty on coals for 5 years from 15th May 1698	465,857	6	1
5s. per ton French ships, granted 12 Car. II	1,908	7	2
22s. per pound East India silks	19,140	5	5
Plantation duty, granted 25 Car. II	4,708	16	2
Arrears of additional impositions on wine entered in 1689	1,900	0	0
New subsidy of tonnage and poundage for two years and three quarters	464,297	8	9½
Additional tonnage and poundage from January 1699 for his Majesty's life	634,548	11	7½
Cinders 5s. per chaldron	1,221	0	3½
15 per cent on India wrought silks and muslins, granted 11 & 12 William	116,767	18	6
	13,296,833	14	6

Excise   *Receipts*

Hereditary and temporary Excise net	5,918,887	17	4¾
Low wines from 24th December 1690	166,392	17	6
Double Excise from 17th November 1690 to ditto 1691	612,291	3	3½
Additional Excise of 9d. per barrel from Michaelmas 1689, appropriated	339,610	15	9¼
Additional Excise, viz., 9d. per barrel, determined 24th July 1692, and double 9d., commenced 17th November 1691, ended 17th May	1,732,497	15	3
Complements of Excise, 24d. per barrel to 24th July 1692, and 30d. per barrel thence to the 17th November 1692	381,080	5	9¾
Excise for 99 years in the Million Fund Act, from 25th January 1692/3	1,229,727	17	5¾
Imposition on salt from 25th March 1694, 12d. per bushel, granted 7 William, joined with whale fins, Scots linen, &c., granted 9 & 10 William for 8 years from 10th July 1698	436,724	3	0¾
9d. Excise continued from 17th May 1697 for Million Lottery tickets, thence for 16 years	644,396	14	6
9d. Excise, made hereditary from 17th May 1697 for the Bank and annuities for 1, 2 and 3 lives in lieu of 5/7ths and 3/7ths tonnage	618,532	5	6¾
Duty on malt from 20th April 1697	922,983	10	3¼
Additional duty on salt of 8d. from 25th March 1697 to 25th December 1699	103,191	16	3½
20d. per bushel salt from 1st July 1698 (for the East India Company) and 8d. from 25th December 1699	276,474	12	6
Duty on leather	208,102	16	9
Whale fins, Scots linen and arrears of glass-ware, &c.	46,420	15	10
Low wines joined with coffee and 15 per cent muslins by an Act 12 and 13 William	12,012	13	2
	13,649,328	0	5¾

Hearth Money, Letter Money, &c.

Hearth Money, besides charges of getting in	221,763	18	0¼
Letter Money, besides charges of management	871,054	17	11½
Small branches and casualties	915,778	11	8½
	2,308,597	7	8¼

Land Taxes

Present aid or six months' tax for 1689	4,914	7	3½
First aid for 12d. in the pound for 1689	496,108	6	1
2s. aid for 1690	1,015,732	2	7
Additional 12d. for 1690	507,866	0	8½
First twelve months' aid for 1691	1,613,747	9	1
Second ditto for 1692	1,613,874	13	5
First 4s. aid for 1693	1,922,712	19	4½
Second ditto for 1694	1,913,488	16	4¼
Third ditto for 1695	1,860,039	10	2
Fourth ditto for 1696	1,736,248	1	10¾
3s. aid for 1697	1,244,789	4	0
Additional 12d. for 1697	418,646	10	11
Second 3s. aid for 1,484,015l. 1s. 11¾d. over and above 229,696l. 4s. 10d. transferred to pay annuities to the Bank, &c., for 1698	1,188,021	18	1

Land Taxes (*contd.*)   *Receipts*

Third 3s. aid for the same sum for 1699	1,431,771	6	8½
Second 2s. aid for 989,965l. 19s. 6d. for 1700	951,066	6	5
1/3rd and 2/3rds of fourth 3s. aid	859,051	15	2½
	19,174,059	8	3½

Polls

First poll for 1689	288,438	2	1½
Review of the first poll, and an additional poll for 1690	23,059	7	1
Second poll for 1690	239,958	7	11½
First quarterly poll for 1692	579,178	11	2½
Review of ditto for 1693	6,388	4	0
Second quarterly poll for 1694	486,321	2	2½
Capitation for 1697	612,912	16	9
Third quarterly poll for 1698	321,397	16	3½
	2,557,649	7	7½

Promiscuous taxes

Smugglers' fines to Michaelmas 1698	19,500	0	0
Exchequer bills issued by virtue of an Act for establishing a land bank anno 1695 (158,589l. being repaid as *per contra*)	159,173	1	0
Joint stock charged by Act of Parliament, 1692, two quarterly payments	43,219	0	0
First Million Act in 1693, annuities by 9d. Excise for 99 years	1,000,000	0	0
Fines and rent on hackney coaches for 1694	41,150	0	0
Paper and parchment duties for 1694, continued to 28th of June 1698	205,566	1	2¾
New duties on ditto for two years from the 1st of March 1698	17,813	8	9½
Million lottery or contributions on salt for 1694	934,512	17	7
On the Tonnage Act by the Bank of England for 1694	1,200,000	0	0
On annuities for 1694 for 1, 2 and 3 lives for 300,000l.	300,000	0	0
Duties on marriages, births, burials, &c., commencing 1st May 1695 and ending 1st May 1700	258,094	1	10½
Subscriptions to the National Land Bank	1,775	0	0
Duties on houses or windows	53,466	10	0½
Money or plate at 6s. an ounce for Malt Lottery tickets	17,615	13	1
Additional duty on stamped paper, made perpetual with salt, for the East India Company	153,487	11	5½
Subscriptions of 2,000,000l. for East India trade	1,882,413	9	0½
Parchment and paper stamped duties continued from 1698 to 1st August 1706	152,098	16	10
Purchasing of reversionary annuities by several Acts of Parliament passed in several years	581,750	15	0
Duties on glass and earthenware	15,732	1	7
Licences to hawkers and pedlars	26,513	15	1
Duties on marriages, births, &c., continued from 1st May 1700 to 1st August 1700	17,423	16	2½
	7,531,305	18	11¾

Divers receipts   *Receipts*

Letter money overpaid in 1696	102	16	5
Surcharged on the Commissioners of Excise in 1697	89,695	13	$6\frac{1}{4}$
Coinage money from 1698 inclusive, in the other years placed with small branches	42,658	10	1
Tellers' malt benefits in 1698	1,715	0	0
Imprest repaid in 1696 and 1699	162,036	4	$2\frac{1}{2}$
Accompts of new money from the Mint in years 1697, 1698 and 1699, in aid of 2,599,797*l.* 14*s.* 10*d. per contra*, deficient at Michaelmas 1696	184,656	17	$11\frac{1}{2}$
Poll, anno 1697	50	0	0

480,915 2 $2\frac{1}{4}$

General total   58,698,688 19 8

of the general account of money borrowed and repaid within the time of this account in several years, the money borrowed exceeding the money repaid in those years respectively the sum of 13,348,680*l.* 5*s.* $10\frac{1}{4}d.$ though in other years the money repaid exceeded the money borrowed in those years respectively the sum of 3,341,903*l.* 8*s.* $8\frac{3}{4}d.$ as *per contra*, which reduceth the net money more than repaid during the whole time of this account to 10,006,776*l.* 17*s.* $1\frac{1}{2}d.$ 13,348,680 5 $10\frac{1}{4}$

72,047,369 5 $6\frac{1}{4}$

That remained on the 5th of November 1688 in the Exchequer, in the hands of the several Receivers   80,138 18 $0\frac{1}{4}$

Error $\frac{1}{4}$

72,127,508 3 $6\frac{3}{4}$

Navy   *Issues*

To Anthony, Lord Viscount Falkland, late Treasurer of the Navy, for the navy and victualling	198,068	0	1	
To the earl of Orford, late Treasurer of the Navy, on the same account	16,940,521	9	$10\frac{1}{4}$	19,822,141 4 $6\frac{1}{2}$
To the Right Hon. Sir Thomas Littleton, Treasurer of the Navy, on the same account	2,683,551	14	7	

Army

For the service of Ireland

Mr. Harbord	1,073,228	12	$7\frac{1}{2}$	
Mr. Henly	4,560	0	$7\frac{1}{2}$	3,851,655 1 $0\frac{1}{4}$
Mr. Fox and Lord Coningsby	2,773,866	7	$9\frac{1}{4}$	
To the earl of Ranelagh for the forces under his pay	18,164,951	14	$0\frac{1}{2}$	22,017,706 15 $0\frac{3}{4}$
To Colonel Hill, governor of the Leeward Islands, for his own soldiers and arrears	1,100	0	0	

Ordnance

To the Treasurer of the Ordnance for sea and land service   3,008,535 16 10

44,848,383 16 $5\frac{1}{4}$

Issues

Civil List

To the Cofferer of the Household				1,300,130	2	2¾
Treasurer of the Chambers	484,763	16	1½			
Ditto for the charges of the late queen's coffins	328	16	0	485,092	12	1½
Great Wardrobe	319,876	8	2¾			
Ditto for the late queen's mourning	42,844	4	5	362,720	12	7¾
Robes	57,128	2	2½			
Ditto to Lord Sidney upon account for clothes furnished King Charles II when he was Master of that office	5,120	0	3	62,248	2	5½
Paymaster of the Works	474,050	15	1½			
Ditto on account of the late queen's funeral	4,000	0	0			
Mr. Roberts, Paymaster of the Works at Windsor, on account for works there over and above what has been paid thereunto out of the revenues of the honour and castle of Windsor	5,000	0	0	483,050	15	1½

Gardens
Upon account of making his Majesty's gardens, over and above the gardeners' salaries payable by the Treasurer of the Chamber until 1695	115,097	12	7½			
On the contract for 4,800*l.* per annum commencing from 1695	16,800	0	0	133,797	12	7½
On the new allowance of 2,600*l.* per annum which commenced from Christmas 1700	1,900	0	0			

Stables for buying horses, and for liveries and extraordinaries	235,965	15	3½	698,719	2	6
Foreign ministers for ordinaries and extraordinaries	462,753	7	2½			
Fees and salaries				858,056	16	9
Pensions and annuities				686,189	17	7
Queen Dowager				178,031	15	4
Late queen's Treasurer				506,386	10	0¼
Ditto for French Protestants				75,000	0	0
Prince and princess of Denmark				638,921	15	7½
Duke of Gloucester, on 1,500*l.* per annum				37,500	0	0
Band of Gentlemen Pensioners				69,000	0	0

Secret Service
Secretaries of the Treasury	616,323	7	2			
Secretaries of State	76,963	19	6	775,387	6	8
Particular persons, by his Majesty's warrants under his royal sign manual	82,100	0	0			

Privy Purse	483,555	0	0			
Ditto for purchasing fee farm rents { To the earl of Portland	24,571	5	4	541,726	5	4
{ To the Lord Somers *et al.*	33,600	0	0			
Jewels				66,006	0	0
Plate				102,843	13	8
Bounties paid at the Exchequer to several persons by his Majesty's particular warrants in that behalf				226,823	19	1

Civil List (*contd.*)   *Issues*

Monsieur Fleury for goods taken from the French at Bourbon Fort, Hudson's Bay, and given to the Hudson's Bay Company, which by the treaty of Ryswick were to be restored			1,086	18	0

Subscriber of 2,000,000*l*. for the East India trade an allowance of 1*l*. per cent 20,000 0 0

The receivers of 2,000,000*l*. in reward, and for charges in passing their accounts 16,000 0 0

To Mr. Stratford, in part of 20,000*l*. in cloth sent to Sweden 12,000 0 0

Earl of Ranelagh for Lord Fairfax	600	0	0		
Bounty to officers' widows	1,670	0	0		
To French officers	730	0	0	3,633	3	0
For liveries for Lumley's trumpeters	393	3	0		
For Court drums and fifes, salary	240	0	0		

Contingents of divers natures, viz., Law charges, Liberates of the Exchequer, riding charges to messengers of the Court and Receipt of Exchequer, rewards and extraordinary charges to receivers of taxes and to several others on sundry occasions, surplusages of accounts, printers' bills, sundry works and repairs by the Surveyors of the Woods, the private roads and other particular offices, his Majesty's subscription of 10,000*l*. to the Bank of England, a like sum to the new East India Company, as also 3,000*l*. for carrying on the trade, bounties for apprehending highwaymen, traitors and libellers, money paid for purchasing land to be laid into his Majesty's park at Windsor, and very many other accidental payments 534,809 1 10¾

Divers Issues 8,880,506 2 9

States General, pursuant to an Act of Parliament, anno 1689 .... 600,000 0 0

Servants of King Charles II by ditto Act 60,000 0 0

To the Mint out of the Coinage Duty, &c., which includes several payments relating to the recoinage in general 259,584 17 7¼

Redemption of captives 1,000 0 0

Privy Purse of the late King James at the Exchequer 200 0 0

Principal money lent *tempore Jacobi II* 138,412 19 9

To several for money advanced in the west in 1688 .... 4,000 0 0

Interest money paid to several out of the revenues, taxes and loans, and for divers other causes 5,216,530 2 4¼

Interest to the Bank of England 875,880 16 9¼

Annuities { On survivorship, and 14 per cent on the Million Act, &c. 1,079,809 2 9¼

On the tonnage for one, two and three lives for 300,000*l*. 287,059 14 11¾

On Lottery for a Million paid in for 16 years annuity 1,049,776 15 5¼

To the Malt Lottery Office, in part of 1,200,000*l*. principal and interest 760,142 6 0

To the Treasurer of the Excise, to satisfy tallies of Excise and Post Office 467,000 0 0

To the English East India Company and General Society trading thither on 160,000*l*. per annum 429,962 3 11½

To the trustees for circulating Exchequer Bills, for premiums, salaries, &c., besides 43,435*l*. inclusive, in account of interest 1697 .... 254,119 3 7½

Principal money repaid, more than borrowed, for several years 3,341,903 8 8¾

Divers Issues (*contd.*)   *Issues*

To receivers of taxes in reward for extraordinaries	5,446	9	8½
To Peter Hume, gentleman, to be applied as his Majesty should direct	5,200	0	0
New money, in part of 122,584*l.* 2*s.* 1*d.* old money recoined, paid the army and navy	84,963	8	8¼
To the Commissioners of Excise in new money, the proceeds of old money received from them	56,988	11	5
Clipt money delivered to be recoined more than it produced to Michaelmas 1696, in aid whereof there was returned from the Mint in after years more than was sent thither in those years as *per contra* 184,656*l.* 17*s.* 11¼*d.*, which reduceth the general deficiency of the recoinage to 2,415,140*l.* 16*s.* 10¼*d.*, the deficiency in the year 1696 amounting to	2,599,797	14	10
To the four Tellers of the Exchequer in Exchequer Bills, to be delivered to such persons as brought money for them in 1695	158,589	0	0
Imprest money repaid to the Treasurer of the Navy, being old money new coined	4,422	3	7¼
New money to the earl of Ranelagh, the proceed of 13,000*l.* in old hammered money	6,497	9	0¾
To several, for a reward of 6*s.* an ounce for wrought plate brought in to be coined	3,846	17	8¾
To the Treasurer of Greenwich Hospital, pursuant to the address of Parliament	19,500	0	0
To the Commissioners for Forfeited Estates in Ireland	3,133	15	0
To the Commissioners for stating and determining Accounts, for incidents, &c.	3,500	0	0
To the Tellers of the Exchequer for a loss on 89,196½ guineas received at 22*s.* and issued at 21*s.* 6*d.*	2,229	18	3
Interest of the Bankers' debt	466	7	7

	17,779,243	1	11

General total	71,508,133	1	1¼
That remained a balance at the foot of the half year's account ending at Lady Day 1702	619,159	13	6½

	72,127,292	14	7¾
Add that remained at Michaelmas 1699 more than was carried forward to the account of 1700, occasioned by several sums then remaining in the hands of several receivers, for which they afterwards accounted with the Auditors of the Imprest	1,326	7	7¾
Deduct that was carried to account from Michaelmas 1701 more than the balance at Michaelmas 1701, occasioned by so much less applied out of the second and third aid, anno 1699, to pay arrears on annuities for one, two and three lives, and was afterwards applied to the cancelling of Exchequer Bills instead of those annuities	1,110	12	8¾

	72,127,508	3	6¾

123. Votes of supply under Anne

(N. Tindal's Continuation of Rapin's *History of England*, ed. 1743–1747, V, 179–196)

(i) Session 1702–1703

For 40,000 men for sea service	£2,080,000
For the ordinary of the navy	129,314
For 40,000 land forces	833,826
For 10,000 additional forces	178,180
Ordnance for land service	70,973
For guards and garrisons	350,000
Subsidies to the allies	51,843
	3,694,136

(ii) Session 1704–1705

For 40,000 men for sea service	£2,080,000
For the ordinary of the navy	100,000
For ordnance stores for sea service	40,000
For building a wharf and storehouse at Portsmouth	10,000
For 40,000 land forces	885,193
For 10,000 additional forces	177,511
For 10,000 men to serve in Portugal	222,379
Subsidies to the allies	370,119
Subsidy to the duke of Savoy	40,000
Recruit horses lost at Schellenberg and Blenheim	6,725
Ditto for foreign troops in English pay	24,665
For an additional regiment on the Portuguese establishment	5,135
For surgeons for the hospital in Portugal	244
Expenses in the Portugal service last year	68,546
Ordnance for land service	120,000
Transport service	60,000
For 5,000 troops of augmentation, their levy	11,844
Ditto, their pay	87,125
For guards and garrisons	357,000
For circulating Exchequer bills	4,000
	4,670,486

(iii) Session 1706–1707

For 40,000 men for sea service	£2,080,000
Ordinary of the navy	120,000
Guards and garrisons	357,000
For 40,000 men for land service	893,706

For 10,000 additional forces, and proportion for 3,000 Palatines	211,762
Interest debentures	49,000
Wharf and storehouse at Portsmouth	10,000
Ordnance for land service	120,000
Transport service	144,000
For circulating Exchequer bills	3,500
The queen's proportion of subsidies to the king of Denmark	37,500
Ditto of 13,000 men in the Portugal service	150,000
Ditto of subsidies to the duke of Savoy	160,000
Ditto of 8,000 men sent to the duke of Savoy	50,000
Subsidies to the landgrave of Hesse-Cassel	5,952
Ditto to the elector of Trier	5,952
Ditto to the Elector Palatine	4,761
For 20,562 men to serve in Spain and Portugal	445,350
For 8,833 additional forces for the same service	186,296
To the duke of Savoy, expended in the defence of Turin	50,000
Loan to the Emperor last year	47,500
Levy, &c., for the forces under Earl Rivers	63,661
Pay of general officers in Portugal	3,014
The queen's proportion for 3,000 Palatines last year	26,692
Agio bread and forage for the Prussians	37,012
Ditto last year	19,755
Levy-money for horses killed in Flanders	35,753
For horses dead, English, Danish and Hanoverian, 1705, 1706	36,701
For prosecuting King Charles's successes in Spain	50,000
Garrison at Gibraltar	3,520
Additional subsidies to Hesse-Cassel	20,000
Expenses on the Hessian troops last year	11,780
	5,540,167

(iv) Session 1709–1710

For 40,000 men for sea service	£2,080,000
Ordinary of the navy	120,000
For 40,000 land forces	901,992
For 10,000 additional forces	177,511
The queen's proportion of 3,000 Palatines	34,251
Ditto of 4,000 Saxons	43,251
Ditto of Bothmer's regiment	9,269
Augmentation of troops in Flanders	220,000
Subsidies of the allies	567,845
Guards and garrisons	543,775

Ordnance for land service	130,000
Forces in Spain and Portugal	1,126,035
Extraordinary expenses in the war	234,974
Interest of debentures	49,357
Transport service	144,000
For circulating Exchequer bills	2,000
	6,384,260

(v) Session 1711–1712

For 40,000 men for sea service	£2,080,000
Ordinary of the navy	180,000
Recoinage in Scotland, and deficiency in coinage	4,615
Interest of South Sea stock	535,332
For 40,000 land forces	886,223
For 10,000 additional forces	177,511
For 15,178 troops of augmentation	260,993
Forces in Spain to Lady Day	225,385
Ditto, the other three quarters	250,000
Forces in Portugal	196,452
Ordnance for land service	111,983
For the fortifications of Edinburgh Castle	2,500
Ditto Fort William	1,620
Ditto Dumbarton Castle	308
For the church at Rotterdam	2,500
For guards and garrisons	499,730
Transport service	80,000
Deficiencies last year	589,839
Extraordinary charges of the war	243,020
Subsidies to the allies	328,956
	6,656,967

G. ORIGIN AND GROWTH OF THE NATIONAL DEBT

124. Interim account of the disbanding of the army presented to the House of Commons, 1660

(Journals of the House of Commons, VIII, pp. 176–177)

6 November 1660

Sir William Doyley reports from the committee for disbanding the army what progress hath been made in that service, declaring what forces they have paid off, what sums have been paid to every particular garrison, regiment, troop and company, and for discharging of ships; as also what forces are not paid off, with an estimate what money will be necessary to pay off the land forces to the sixth of November instant, and the ships to the seventeenth of September last; and what money, both certain and casual, the Parliament hath consigned to those uses, with a balance between the charge and the money consigned; the substance whereof is as followeth, viz.:

Disbanded in England

Twenty-two garrisons	20,023	18	7				
General Officers with the train	1,642	13	6				
Fifteen regiments of foot	117,966	0	6	217,986	3	9
Four regiments of horse	55,353	11	2				
Six ships paid off	23,000	0	0				

Disbanded in Scotland

The General Officers and train	797	11	$3\frac{1}{4}$				
Edinburgh garrison	206	4	0				
Two regiments of foot	20,149	8	8	32,416	14	$8\frac{1}{4}$
One regiment of horse	11,263	10	9				
Sum total issued and paid				250,402	18	$5\frac{1}{4}$

Forces to be disbanded in England

Eleven garrisons	13,877	4	0				
Three regiments of foot	39,308	13	0				
Nine regiments of horse, with the Life Guard of horse	168,416	8	10	359,734	15	10
Nineteen ships, by estimate	138,132	10	0				

Forces to be disbanded in Scotland or paid off

Garrisons	3,118	0	2				
Four regiments of foot	48,685	19	0				
Major-General Morgan's troop	3,636	8	10	75,681	14	6
Lord Falkland's regiment of horse	20,241	6	6				
Total				435,416	10	4

Besides divers sums falling under several heads in the said report specified.

Moneys appointed by Parliament to pay off the forces by land and sea

Assignations on the three months' assessments commencing

24 June 1660	23,000	0	0				
And	40,000	0	0				
By the Poll Bill, estimated at	210,000	0	0	}	413,000	0	0
Two months' assessments	140,000	0	0				

So there wants, to answer the sum paid and the charge of the forces to be
  disbanded, amounting together to 685,819*l.* 8*s.* 9¼*d.*, the sum of 272,819 8 9¼
Besides the said other sums from casual and uncertain charges, estimated at 150,000 0 0

And so the money to be provided on the clear balance is 422,819 8 9¼

The total of the monthly charge by land and sea in England and Scotland,
  undisbanded, is by the said report computed at 32,653 12 0
He also reports an account of the moneys received into the treasury of the
  Chamber of London at Guildhall, upon the account of the Poll Bill,
  amounting to 73,185 4 0
Received upon the loan 24,445 0 0

                                         In toto 97,630 4 0
Of which paid by the book 86,376 15 4
Resting in cash, to balance 11,253 8 8

125. Speech of Charles II to the Commons on the financial situation, 1663

(Journals of the House of Commons, VIII, pp. 500–501)

12 June 1663

MR. SPEAKER, AND YOU GENTLEMEN OF THE HOUSE OF COMMONS,

  I have sent for you this day to communicate with you, as good friends ought to do, when they discover the least jealousy growing which may lessen their confidence in each other. . . .

  You cannot take it amiss (you shall use as much freedom with me when you please) that I tell you there hath not appeared that warmth in you of late in the consideration of my revenue as I expected, as well from some of your messages as from my own confidence in your care and kindness. It hath been said to myself that it is usual for Parliaments to give the Crown extraordinary supplies upon emergent occasions, but not to improve the constant revenue of the Crown. I wish (and so do you) that nothing had been lately done in and by Parliaments but what was usual. But if ill Parliaments contrive the ruin and disinherison of the Crown, God forbid but good Parliaments should repair it, how unusual soever it is. If you yourselves had not in an extraordinary manner improved my revenue, the government could not have been supported; and if it be not yet improved in the proportion you have designed, I cannot doubt but you will proceed in it with your old alacrity.

  I am very well contented that you proceed in your inspection. I know it will be to my advantage, and that you will neither find my receipts so great nor my expenses so exorbitant as you imagine. And for an evidence of the last I will give you presently an account of the issues of the twelve hundred thousand pounds you so liberally gave me, not one penny whereof was disposed but upon full deliberation with myself and by my own order, and I think you will all say for the public service. But, Gentlemen, this inquisition cannot be finished in the short time we can now conveniently stay together; and yet if you do not provide before we part for the better paying and collecting what you have already given me, you can hardly presume what it will amount to; and if you do not support even what you have already given me by some addition, you will quickly see lawful ways found out to lessen the revenue more than you imagine. And therefore I cannot but expect that your wisdom will seasonably and speedily provide a remedy for that growing mischief.

Believe me, Gentlemen, the most disaffected subjects in England are not more unwilling to pay any tax or imposition you lay upon them than I am to receive it. God knows I do not long more for any blessing in this world than that I may live to call a Parliament, and not ask or receive any money from them. I will do all I can to see that happy day. I know the vast burdens the kingdom hath borne these last twenty years and more, that it is exceedingly impoverished. But, alas, what will that which is left do them good if the government cannot be supported, if I am not able to defray the charge that is necessary for their peace and security. I must deal plainly with you, and I do but discharge my conscience in that plainness. If you do not, besides the improving my revenue in the manner I have recommended to you, give me some present supply of money to enable me to struggle with those difficulties I am pressed with, I shall have a very melancholic summer, and shall much apprehend the public quiet. . . .

I assure you I have so great occasion of money here, which my revenue cannot supply me with, that I every day omit the doing somewhat that is very necessary for the public benefit. These, sure, are just motives to persuade you to give me a supply as have ever moved a House of Commons; and therefore I conjure you to go cheerfully about it, and let me not be disappointed in my confidence of your affections. . . .

126. Proclamation declaring the inviolability of the Exchequer, 1667

(*London Gazette*, 17–20 June 1667)

Whitehall, June 18

This day, his Majesty having understood that divers of his good and loyal subjects, goldsmiths and others, who have advanced great sums of money for the public service, which are sufficiently secured to them upon several branches of his Majesty's revenue and other moneys arising by several late Acts of Parliament, have, upon occasion taken from the late attempt of the Dutch fleet and the false reports spread thereof, been pressed in an unusual manner with many sudden demands by their creditors for present payment, through fears and apprehensions, which may weaken the credit of his Majesty's said subjects, bring an undervalue on his Majesty's said securities, and in consequence endanger the public safety in this present conjuncture, his Majesty has therefore thought fit (as well for satisfying the minds of his good subjects, whose fears so transported them to call for their moneys in such a manner, as to allay such jealousies and misapprehensions as may be taken up by those concerned in the said securities) to declare that, as the course of payments in the Exchequer hath hitherto been punctual and according to due order even in this time of disturbance and interruption of payments amongst his subjects, so his Majesty's steadfast resolution is for preferring inviolably to all his good subjects who have lent or advanced any moneys for his service as aforesaid all and every the securities and assignments any ways made by his Majesty for and towards the repayment and satisfaction of the said several sums of money, and that his Majesty will not upon any occasion whatsoever permit or suffer any alteration, anticipation or interruption to be made of his said subjects' securities, but that they shall from time to time receive the moneys so secured unto them in the same course and method as they were charged and ought to be satisfied.

Which resolution his Majesty will likewise hold firm and sacred in all future assignments and securities to be by his Majesty granted upon any other advance of money by any of his subjects upon any future occasion for his service, his Majesty not doubting, upon the publishing this his royal word and declaration of his sincere intention, but that all reasonable persons will rest satisfied that their fears were causeless and their respective interests in no danger at all, and that no evil can happen unto them on this occasion, since the securities by his Majesty to them given being inviolable his Majesty doubts not but that his said subjects will satisfy every person both their principal and interest as they have formerly done with untainted reputation. And of this his declaration his Majesty straitly charges and commands his High Chancellor of England, the Lords Commissioners of his Treasury, the Chancellor and Under-Treasurer of his Exchequer, and all other his officers and ministers whatsoever whom it doth or may concern, to take notice and duly to observe the same as they will be answerable to his Majesty at their utmost perils.

127. Intimation of money available for repayment in course, 1667

(London Gazette, 29 July–1 August 1667)

Advertisement

The Officers of the Receipt of his Majesty's Exchequer, in pursuance of the payments upon orders registered on the Act for 1,250,000*l.*, are ready to make payment of the 358th order in course, and so do proceed according to the direction of the said Act as fast as the money comes in.

They think fit also to give notice that money hath been kept in bank in the Exchequer for the payment of the 135th and 153th order ever since they came in course to be paid. And likewise money is ready for the payment of the orders hereafter mentioned, viz., the 336, 338, 339, 343, 350, 351, 352, 353, 354, 355, 356, 357 and 358, all the preceding orders having been already paid.

Also upon the Act for Poll Money the said officers are come to the payment of the two and fiftieth order in course.

128. Proclamation announcing the stop of the Exchequer, 1672

(London Gazette, 4–8 January 1672)

On Tuesday the 2nd instant his Majesty, being present in Council, was pleased to declare that seeing all the princes and states his neighbours were making great preparations for war, both by sea and land, his Majesty, for the safety of his government and people, looked upon himself as obliged to make such preparations as might be proportionable for the protection both of the one and the other, and to that end had already given orders for the fitting and preparing a very considerable fleet to be ready against the spring; that by this inevitable necessity, his Majesty considering the great charges that must attend such preparations, and after his serious debates and best considerations not finding any possibility to defray such unusual expenses by the usual ways and means of borrowing moneys, by reason his revenues were so anticipated and engaged, he was necessitated (contrary to his own inclinations), upon these emergencies and for the public safety at the present, to cause a stop to be made of the payment of any moneys now being or to be brought into his Exchequer, for the space of one whole year ending the last day of December next, unto any person or persons whatsoever by virtue of any warrant, securities or orders, whether registered or not registered therein, and payable within that time, excepting only such payments as shall grow due upon orders on the subsidy, according to the Act of Parliament, and orders and securities upon the fee farm rents, both which are to be proceeded upon as if such a stop had never been made.

And that his Majesty's pleasure and declaration might be speedily and effectually put in execution, his Majesty did order Sir Heneage Finch, knight and baronet, his Attorney General, forthwith to prepare a bill for his royal signature, and so to pass the great seal, thereby requiring and commanding the Lords Commissioners of his Treasury immediately to order and direct all and every the officers of his Majesty's Exchequer to postpone all warrants and orders, whether registered or not registered, and other securities and payments whatsoever (except as before excepted) until the last day of December next; and that in the meantime the Lords Commissioners of his Treasury be required and authorized to cause payment to be made of the interest that is or shall grow due, at the rate of six pounds per cent, unto every person that shall have money due to him or them upon such warrants, orders or securities so postponed and deferred, and that the payment of such interest may be justly made the Lords Commissioners of his Treasury are to be authorized and required to cause the debt of every particular person, and the said interest thereof, to be truly stated.

And the Lords of his Majesty's Treasury being further to be ordered to employ and dispose of all the said moneys so stopped and detained, for the preparing, setting forth and payment of his Majesty's fleet, and other public services in order to the preservation and safety of his Majesty's government and defence of his people, as his Majesty shall from time to time order and direct, his Majesty, as far as in him lies, to take away all apprehensions or terror that might possess any of his subjects' spirits, declaring that no person whatsoever shall be defrauded of anything that is justly due to him, nor shall this restraint which his Majesty had been compelled (not being able for the present to find any other expedient) to lay upon such moneys as are or shall be paid into his Exchequer continue longer than the aforesaid last day of December, and that then no new warrants, orders or securities shall intervene to break the course of such payments.

And his Majesty was further graciously pleased to declare that nothing could have urged his Majesty to an act of this nature but such a conjuncture of affairs when all the neighbouring princes and states were making such threatening preparations that his government could not be safe without appearing in the same posture.

129. Letter from Richard Langhorne to Lord Hatton on the stop of the Exchequer, 1672

(British Museum, Additional Manuscripts, 29553, f. 358)

Epiphany[1] 1672

. . . I could almost wish your lordship here for one day to see the strange amazement and consternation which is amongst our moneyed men upon this occasion, viz., it being resolved that we must immediately set forth a fleet of 22 sail of good ships (to fetch something from France), and prepare for 60 sail of our best ships to be ready early in the spring. His Majesty sent to the bankers in Lombard Street to advance a considerable sum of present moneys. This they refused. Upon this refusal his Majesty by advice of his Council (where it suffered a long debate) resolved to shut up his Exchequer and make stop of all private moneys, by which means all the moneys charged upon the Exchequer and daily issued to the bankers and private persons is stopped and applied to the public use, and all private payments for the present stayed; just as in the case of a private man who, having mortgaged his estate and put the mortgagee into possession, upon a disappointment of a further advance from his mortgagee, is enforced to enter upon his mortgagee by the agreement of his tenants, and make use of his rents to buy bread until he can be otherwise supplied. Upon this stop of the Exchequer the bankers can pay no moneys to their creditors, which are all the moneyed men and all the merchants of London. Bills of exchange from foreign parts accepted here cannot be paid, so it is believed this week will return bills into foreign parts protested to the value of 50,000*l.*, and the next week more, and so onwards. But there is no remedy; the public must be served.

In truth the consternation as to this particular is greater than in Chatham business. And though it is probable at the long run no man shall lose, yet I believe it certain that the trade of bankers is totally destroyed by this accident, for no man will ever hereafter run the like hazards when he shall consider upon what contingency he puts moneys into goldsmiths' hands. But withal I think it is as certain that moneys will run more in specie about the kingdom, and securities upon land, as also the price of land, will be more valuable than of late years since the trade of bankers was in vogue. . . .

[1] 6 January

130. Settlement of the bankers' debt created by the stop of the Exchequer, 1677

(Calendar of Treasury Books, III, p. xlviii)

	Sum due			Interest		
	l.	*s.*	*d.*	*l.*	*s.*	*d.*
Sir Robert Viner	416,724	13	1½	25,003	9	4
Edward Backwell	295,994	16	6	17,759	13	8
Joseph Hornby of London, goldsmith	22,548	5	6	1,352	17	10
Gilbert Whitehall of London, goldsmith	248,866	3	5	14,931	19	4
George Snell of London, goldsmith	10,894	14	5	653	13	6
Bernard Turner of London, goldsmith	16,275	9	8	976	10	6
Jeremiah Snow	59,780	18	8	3,586	17	0
John Lindsey of London, goldsmith	85,832	17	2	5,149	17	4
Robert Welsted	11,307	12	1	678	9	0
Thomas Rowe	17,615	17	8	1,056	19	0
John Portman	76,760	18	2	4,605	13	0
Isaac Collier	1,784	6	4	107	1	1
John Thruston, esq.	5,208	8	0	312	10	0
Isaac Legouch	5,370	3	8	322	4	0
Robert Ryves of London, goldsmith	16,368	4	4	982	1	8
Sir Edmund Turner, a late Customs farmer	4,592	11	8	275	11	8
Dr. Edward Chamberlain	706	1	9¾	42	7	0
George Toriano, merchant	129	14	8	7	15	4
Sir John Shaw	9,355	10	4¼	561	6	6
Francis Millington	1,285	7	2½	77	2	6
Henry Johnson, esq.	1,388	11	0¼	83	5	9
Robert Wynne	567	7	0	34	0	0
Richard Lant	1,844	0	7	110	12	0
Isaac Alvarez, or Sampson Bickford, assignee of the said Alvarez	1,580	13	4	94	16	0
William Gomeldon	2,157	16	5	129	10	0

131. Estimate of unfunded debt, 1679

(Calendar of Treasury Books, VII, p. 1661)

TOTAL OF THE [CURRENT AND UNFUNDED] DEBT

31 March 1679

Debt by tallies on the three great branches of the revenue [viz., Customs, Excise and Hearth Money]	1,090,757*l.*
Debt by money advanced on the farm of Excise and Hearth Money	400,000
Debt to offices, &c., for which no funds are yet assigned	1,229,437
	2,720,194

There will come in from Sir John James and partners 101,000*l.* of orders on the [eighteen months'] tax, when their accounts shall be stated and their demands cleared.

It is alleged that the tallies do clear the old troops to midsummer, by computation 55,000*l.*

There is tin deposited in Mr. Kent's hands to the value of 30,000*l.*

132. Legislative settlement with the bankers, 1701

(Statutes of the Realm, VII, pp. 723–727)

AN ACT FOR APPROPRIATING THREE THOUSAND SEVEN HUNDRED POUNDS WEEKLY
OUT OF CERTAIN BRANCHES OF EXCISE FOR PUBLIC USES
AND FOR MAKING A PROVISION FOR THE SERVICE OF
HIS MAJESTY'S HOUSEHOLD AND FAMILY AND OTHER HIS NECESSARY OCCASIONS

(12 & 13 Gul. III, cap. 12)

XXIV. Provided always, and be it further enacted . . . that in lieu and discharge of certain perpetual annual payments, and of all arrears thereof, granted by his late Majesty King Charles the Second by letters patent out of the said hereditary revenue of Excise in satisfaction of certain principal sums mentioned in the said letters patent to be then due from his said late Majesty to the respective patentees therein named, the said hereditary revenue of Excise shall from and after the twenty-sixth day of December one thousand seven hundred and five be and stand charged and chargeable for ever with the payment of annual sums after the rate of three pounds per cent per annum for the principal sums mentioned in the said respective letters patent, to be issued and paid out of the said revenue by quarterly payments out of the Receipt of his Majesty's Exchequer by the officers of the same unto the respective owners and proprietors of such annual sums, and to their heirs and assigns for ever, . . . the said annual payments after the rate of three pounds per cent to be subject nevertheless to be redeemed upon payment of a moiety of the principal sums mentioned in the said respective letters patent.

133. Total funded and unfunded debt, 1691–1714

(Accounts of the net Public Income and Expenditure of Great Britain, II, p. 298)

Funded and unfunded debt at the close of each
financial year

1691	3,130,000*l.*	1696	11,579,178*l.*
1692	3,310,547	1697	14,522,925
1693	5,902,839	1698	15,445,416
1694	6,734,297	1699	13,799,355
1695	8,436,846	1700	12,607,080

1701	12,552,486*l.*	1708	15,518,406*l.*
1702	12,767,225	1709	18,933,339
1703	12,325,779	1710	21,335,645
1704	12,363,474	1711	22,398,425
1705	12,135,351	1712	34,922,688
1706	12,388,030	1713	34,699,847
1707	15,244,299	1714	36,175,460

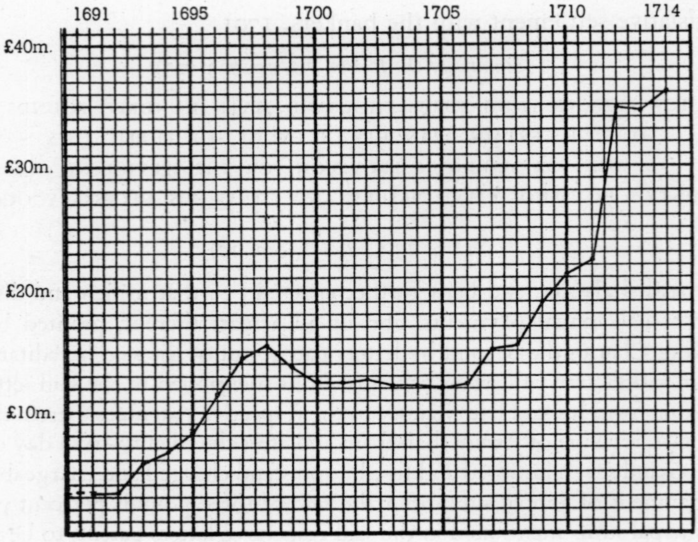

Diagram 3

GROWTH OF THE NATIONAL DEBT, 1691–1714

Part IV
THE CHURCH

THE CHURCH

Introduction

OF all institutions in England that which gained most by the Restoration was the Church. In its case, indeed, something more than a restoration was effected, for the position accorded to it after 1660 was loftier and more secure than any it had previously enjoyed. The extravagances of its opponents when in power, and the state of religious anarchy for which they were largely responsible, had silenced all but the most extreme among its critics, and produced a tremendous wave of enthusiasm in its favour. Puritanism, so powerful a movement under the early Stuarts, sank after 1660 into disrepute. Especially among the upper classes the majority of Puritan families readily conformed to a Church which they had proposed to purify but had never intended to leave. The remainder cut themselves free, and either became definitely Presbyterian or threw in their lot with the Independents.

Of this restored Church the restored monarch was accepted without question as the supreme governor. No fresh recognition of his authority was required, for the Long Parliament had been too disunited in its attitude to the Church to make any substantial changes in ecclesiastical affairs before 1642, and all legislation since that date was disregarded. Charles thus succeeded to all the ecclesiastical prerogatives of his ancestors, except that he was debarred by statute from setting up any court similar in character to the Court of High Commission. In this way was established an alliance between Church and Crown which was to be a factor of immense importance under the later Stuarts. Erastianism, so strenuously denounced by many of the Puritans, was accepted as a principle. The Church gloried in its submission to the king, and endeavoured by every means within its power to exalt his authority. The king on his part was expected to use that authority to maintain the rights and privileges of the Church.

The weak point in this alliance lay in the unwillingness of some of the monarchs to observe their side of the bargain. Of all the later Stuarts only Mary and Anne were faithful children of the Church, and even in ecclesiastical affairs Mary was much under the influence of her Calvinistic husband. Thus for the greater part of the period an underlying conflict of interests prevailed, the monarch seeking to ease the lot of his co-religionists, or achieve some less creditable object, by establishing a measure of toleration, the Church endeavouring to strengthen its position against the two obvious sources of danger, the Roman Catholics on the one hand and the advanced Protestants on the other.

The divergence of interests became apparent immediately after the Restoration, when Charles, with the ostensible object of implementing the promise of "liberty to tender consciences" contained in the Declaration of Breda,[1] and the real object, more probably, of asserting his own authority in ecclesiastical matters, put forward a scheme of comprehension in the Worcester House Declaration of 1660,[2] and then advocated a measure of toleration in a further declaration of 1662.[3] The reply of the Church

---

[1] No. 1. [2] No. 134. [3] No. 135.

party was the so-called Clarendon Code,[1] a series of four statutes, which not merely defined the position of the Church but imposed heavy disabilities, both religious and political, on all who failed to conform to it. Of these four statutes the Conventicle Act, passed originally in 1664 as a temporary and experimental measure, had to be renewed in a harsher form in 1670;[2] and this was done with the consent, if not at the instigation, of Charles himself. Yet immediately afterwards the king took advantage of the discontent which it aroused to make a further effort at toleration in what is usually called the first Declaration of Indulgence,[3] in virtue of which a large number of licences for nonconformist worship were issued.[4] The reply of the Church party was not merely a parliamentary protest which led to the withdrawal of the declaration,[5] but also the two Test Acts, one excluding all nonconformists and recusants from office,[6] and the other excluding them from Parliament.[7] So bright for a time appeared the prospects of the Church that even his normal tendency to support the Court could not restrain the archbishop of Canterbury from pressing for the complete extirpation of Catholicism.[8]

There Charles had the wisdom to let the matter rest; but James had no sooner ascended the throne than he began to devise means for improving the position of those who refused to conform to the Church, and to that end issued in 1687 a second Declaration of Indulgence,[9] representing a considerable advance on that of Charles. This in substance was an attempt to secure the support of Catholics and Protestant nonconformists for the Crown in a joint effort to reduce the pretensions of the Anglicans, and at first the feeling of relief among the persecuted minority was so great that addresses of thanks for the indulgence were presented in considerable numbers.[10] A year later James sought to deepen the impression he had made by repeating his declaration in more emphatic terms,[11] and by issuing an order in Council requiring it to be read in all churches at the time of divine service.[12] But few nonconformists could regard with real favour a toleration which was shared with Catholics and dependent entirely on a strained exercise of the royal prerogative. When given time for reflection, in consequence, they preferred to accept the overtures now made to them by the indignant Anglicans, and join the alliance in the general interests of Protestantism and political liberty on which the Revolution was based. As a reward they were given, after that event, the so-called Toleration Act of 1689, which in actual fact did no more than exempt certain carefully defined classes of Dissenters from certain specific penalties designed to prevent the exercise of their faith.[13]

The Toleration Act thus mitigated the religious, but not the political disabilities of the Dissenters, and one of the grievances of the extreme Churchmen thereafter came to be the practice adopted by many Protestant nonconformists of conforming just sufficiently to qualify themselves for office, while at the same time, in their religious observances, taking advantage of the concessions intended for those who did not conform. So long as William remained upon the throne this caused little trouble; but immediately upon the accession of Anne efforts were made by Parliament to check the practice, culminating in the Occasional Conformity Act of 1711.[14] Two years later was passed the Schism Act, the object of which was to take out of the hands of the Dissenters the education of their own children.[15] Thus it was on a note of renewed persecution that the later Stuart period came to an end.

[1] Nos. 136–139.	[2] No. 139.	[3] No. 140.
[4] Nos. 141, 142.	[5] No. 13.	[6] No. 143.
[7] No. 144.	[8] No. 145.	[9] No. 146.
[10] Nos. 147, 148.	[11] No. 149.	[12] No. 16.
[13] No. 151.	[14] No. 154.	[15] No. 155.

Meanwhile the established Church and other religious organizations had settled down to live more or less peaceably together. Of the distribution of the dissenting congregations a rough idea may be obtained from the licences for their services issued in accordance with the Declaration of Indulgence of 1672, which show that their main strength lay in the south-west and in the home counties.[1] Of the relative numbers of Anglicans, Protestant nonconformists and Catholics a more exact estimate is provided by the religious census of 1676, authorized by Archbishop Sheldon of Canterbury at the instigation of the earl of Danby, and supervised by Bishop Compton of London.[2] There is little doubt that the returns made to Compton's inquiries somewhat exaggerate the predominance of the Anglicans,[3] but otherwise the picture they draw is probably accurate enough, and suggests much the same distribution as the licences of 1672.[4]

In spite of its numerical preponderance over its rivals, however, the established Church was not in an altogether healthy condition. Its services, though viewed with modified approval by Catholic visitors from the Continent,[5] were still distasteful to many of its newly acquired adherents. Its victory over Puritanism had been achieved at the expense of a subservience to political authority little in keeping with a high level of spiritual life. Its virtual renunciation of its traditional privilege of taxing its own clergy, commendable enough in itself, had yet the result of depriving Convocation of one of its few essential functions, and so of making the summons of the Parliament of the Church practically unnecessary.[6] Worst of all, its financial organization had grave defects. The stipends of many of the lower clergy were so small as to preclude all possibility that the Church would attract a sufficient number of worthy recruits to its service, while even among the higher clergy disparities existed so great as seriously to impair its unity.[7] Much was done to remedy the worst of these evils by the institution of Queen Anne's bounty;[8] but the consequent reforms did not become genuinely effective until the reign of George II, and even then much still remained to be done.

Thus the nonconformist bodies were given an opportunity of recovering somewhat from the low level to which they had sunk after the Restoration. Their complete and obviously permanent failure to impress their ideas on the whole of England did much to remedy the disunion which had been their chief weakness. In particular the Presbyterians, the largest and wealthiest body among them, finding there was no hope of making themselves supreme, developed a much greater readiness to throw in their lot with the Independents, the next largest body, from whom, apart from questions of organization, they differed very little.[9] Where they were strong, in consequence, the nonconformists prospered greatly, in some districts being better provided with the material necessities of religious observance than the established Church itself.[10]

[1] Map 6.   [2] No. 156.   [3] Nos. 157, 158.
[4] Map 5.   [5] No. 160.   [6] No. 159.
[7] No. 161.   [8] Nos. 162, 163.   [9] No. 164.
[10] No. 165.

BIBLIOGRAPHY

An elementary but useful guide to the authorities is *A Bibliography of Church History*, compiled for the Historical Association by J. P. Whitney (London, 1923). More specialized are Claude Jenkins, *Ecclesiastical Records* (London, 1920), one of the volumes in the "Helps for Students of History" series; Henry M. Dexter, *The Congregationalism of the Last Three Hundred Years as seen in its Literature* (London, 1880); William T. Whitley, *A Baptist Bibliography, being a Register of the Chief Materials for Baptist History, whether in Manuscript or in Print* (2 vols., London, 1916 and 1922); Joseph Smith, *A Descriptive Catalogue of Friends' Books, or Books written by Members of the Society of Friends, commonly called Quakers* (2 vols., London, with Supplement, 1893), and the same writer's *Bibliotheca anti-Quakeriana, or a Catalogue of Books adverse to the Society of Friends, together with the Answers* (London, 1873); John H. Pollen, *Sources for the History of Roman Catholics in England, Ireland and Scotland, 1533–1795* (London, 1921); and Joseph Jacobs and Lucien Wolf, *Bibliotheca Anglo-Judaica, a Bibliographical Guide to Anglo-Jewish History* (London, 1888).

Among the mass of contemporary materials should be specially noted *Original Records of Early Nonconformity under Persecution and Indulgence*, edited by G. Lyon Turner (3 vols., London, 1911–1914); *Reliquiae Baxterianae, or Mr. Richard Baxter's Narrative of the Most Memorable Passages of His Life and Times*, edited by Matthew Sylvester (London, 1696); Edmund Calamy, *Abridgement of Mr. Baxter's History of His Life and Times, with a Particular Account of the Ministers ejected after the Restoration* (2 vols., London, 1727), and the same writer's *An Historical Account of My Own Life, with some Reflections on the Times I Have Lived In, 1671–1731*, edited by John Towill Rutt (2 vols., London, 1829); *A Journal or Historical Account of the Life of George Fox*, edited by Norman Penney (2 vols., Cambridge, 1911); *The Rev. Oliver Heywood, 1630–1702, His Autobiography, Diaries, Anecdote and Event Books*, edited by J. Horsfall Turner (4 vols., Brighouse, 1882–1885); and *Letters of John Pinney, 1679–1699*, edited by Geoffrey F. Nuttall (Oxford, 1939). *Collectanea Curiosa*, edited by John Gutch (2 vols., Oxford, 1781), consists of a very miscellaneous selection from the papers of Archbishop Sancroft; and *Magdalen College and King James II, 1686–88*, edited by J. R. Bloxam for the Oxford Historical Society (1886), includes virtually all the documents bearing on the controversy with which it deals. *The Household Account Book of Sarah Fell of Swarthmoor Hall, 1673–78*, edited by Norman Penney (Cambridge, 1920), is of value for Quaker no less than for social history.

There is no good general history of the Christian Church in England, but a moderately impartial though sadly out-of-date account may be found in John Stoughton, *History of Religion in England from the Opening of the Long Parliament* (6 vols., London, 1881). The most useful works dealing with the Establishment are the *History of the English Church*, edited by William R. W. Stephens and William Hunt, vol. VI of which, by William H. Hutton (London, 1903), covers the years 1625–1714; C. J. Abbey and J. H. Overton, *The English Church in the Eighteenth Century* (2 vols., London, 1878); J. H. Overton, *Life in the English Church, 1660–1714* (London, 1885); and on the legal side Felix Makower, *The Constitutional History and Constitution of the Church of England* (London, 1895). The best accounts of the nonjurors are Thomas Lathbury, *A History of the Nonjurors, their Controversies and Writings* (London, 1845); J. H. Overton, *The Nonjurors, Their Lives, Principles and Writings* (London, 1902); and Lucy M. Hawkins, *Allegiance in Church and State, the Problem of the Nonjurors in the English Revolution* (London, 1928).

For the nonconformists in general Daniel Neal, *The History of the Puritans or Protestant Nonconformists from the Reformation to the Revolution*, edited by Joshua Toulmin (5 vols., Bath, 1793–1797), is still of value. There is also a good though uninspired survey in C. E. Whiting, *Studies in English Puritanism, 1660–88* (London, 1931); and an interesting discussion of one particular problem in A. C. Dudley, "Nonconformity under the Clarendon Code", in *American*

Historical Review, XVIII (1913), pp. 65–78. Of the Presbyterians the best account is A. H. Drysdale, *History of the Presbyterians in England, Their Rise, Decline and Revival* (London, 1889); of the Congregationalists, R. W. Dale, *History of English Congregationalism*, edited by Sir. A. W. W. Dale (London, 1907); of the Baptists, William J. Whitley, *A History of British Baptists* (London, 1932); and of the Quakers, W. C. Braithwaite, *The Second Period of Quakerism, 1660–1725* (London, 1919). Two careful studies of the position of nonconformists after the grant of a measure of toleration are Frank Bate, *The Declaration of Indulgence, 1672, a Study in the Rise of Organised Dissent* (London, 1908), and Alexander Gordon, *Freedom after Ejection, a Review (1690–92) of Presbyterian and Congregational Nonconformity in England and Wales* (Manchester, 1917). Richard B. Schlatter, *The Social Ideas of Religious Leaders, 1660–1688* (Oxford, 1940), shows how much the churches had in common on some points.

Two important articles are Norman Sykes, "Queen Anne and the Episcopate", in *English Historical Review*, L (1935), pp. 433–464; and Ethyn Williams Kirby, "The Quakers' Efforts to Secure Civil and Religious Liberty, 1660–96", in *Journal of Modern History*, VII (1935), pp. 401–421. The best short introduction to the whole problem of toleration as conceived in the seventeenth century is H. M. Gwatkin, "Religious Toleration in England", in *The Cambridge Modern History*, V (1908), pp. 324–337. More substantial, but covering a much wider field than the seventeenth century, is the same writer's *Church and State in England to the Death of Queen Anne* (London, 1917). D. Nobbs, "Philip Nye on Church and State", in *Cambridge Historical Journal*, V (1935), pp. 41–59; A. A. Seaton, *The Theory of Toleration under the Later Stuarts* (Cambridge, 1911); and H. F. Russell-Smith, *The Theory of Religious Liberty in the Reigns of Charles II and James II* (Cambridge, 1911), all deal with the same fundamental problem of the age.

A. TOLERATION AND PERSECUTION

(a) ROYAL ATTEMPTS AT COMPREHENSION AND TOLERATION, 1660–1662

134. Worcester House Declaration, 1660

(*Journals of the House of Lords*, XI, pp. 179–182.)

HIS MAJESTY'S DECLARATION
TO ALL HIS LOVING SUBJECTS
OF HIS KINGDOM OF ENGLAND AND DOMINION OF WALES
CONCERNING ECCLESIASTICAL AFFAIRS

CHARLES R.

How much the peace of the State is concerned in the peace of the Church, and how difficult a thing it is to preserve order and government in civil whilst there is no order or government in ecclesiastical affairs, is evident to the world; and this little part of the world, our own dominions, hath had so late experience of it that we may very well acquiesce in the conclusion without enlarging ourself in discourse upon it. . . .

In our letter to the Speaker of the House of Commons from Breda we declared how much we desired the advancement and propagation of the Protestant religion; that neither the unkindness of those of the same faith towards us, nor the civilities and obligations from those of a contrary profession (of both which we have had abundant evidence), could in the least degree startle us or make us swerve from it; and that nothing can be proposed to manifest our zeal and affection for it to which we will not readily consent. And we said then that we did hope in due time ourself to propose somewhat for the propagation of it that will satisfy the world that we have always made it both our care and our study, and have enough observed what is most like to bring disadvantage to it. And the truth is we do think ourself the more competent to propose, and with God's assistance to determine, many things now in difference, from the time we have spent and the experience we have had in most of the reformed churches abroad, in France, in the Low Countries and in Germany, where we have had frequent conferences with the most learned men, who have unanimously lamented the great reproach the Protestant religion undergoes from the distempers and too notorious schisms in matters of religion in England. . . .

When we were in Holland we were attended by many grave and learned ministers from hence, who were looked upon as the most able and principal assertors of the Presbyterian opinions, with whom we had as much conference as the multitude of affairs which were then upon us would permit us to have, and to our great satisfaction and comfort found them persons full of affection to us, of zeal for the peace of the Church and State, and neither enemies (as they have been given out to be) to episcopacy or liturgy, but modestly to desire such alterations in either as without shaking foundations might best allay the present distempers. . . . For the better doing whereof we did intend, upon our first arrival in this kingdom, to call a synod of divines, as the most proper expedient to provide a proper remedy for all those differences and dissatisfactions which had or should arise in matters of religion. . . .

Whilst we continued in this temper of mind and resolution, and have so far complied with the persuasion of particular persons and the distemper of the time as to be contented with the exercise of our religion in our own chapel, according to the constant practice and laws established, without enjoining that practice and the observation of those laws in the churches of the kingdom, . . . we have found ourself not so candidly dealt with as we have deserved, and that there are unquiet and restless spirits who, without abating any of their own distemper in recompense of the moderation they find in us, continue their bitterness against the Church, and endeavour to raise jealousies of us and to lessen our reputation by their reproaches, as if we were not true to the professions we have made. And in order thereunto they have very unseasonably caused to be printed, published and dispersed throughout the kingdom a declaration heretofore printed in our name during the time of our being in Scotland, of which we shall say no more than that the circumstances by which we were enforced to sign that declaration are enough known to the world, and that the worthiest and greatest part of that nation did even then detest and abhor the ill usage of us in that particular, when the same tyranny was exercised there by the power of a few ill men which at that time had spread itself over this kingdom. . . .

This over-passionate and turbulent way of proceeding, and the impatience we find in many for some speedy determination in these matters, whereby the minds of men may be composed and the peace of the Church established, hath prevailed with us to invert the method we had proposed to ourself, and even in order to the better calling and composing of a synod (which the present jealousies will hardly agree upon), by the assistance of God's blessed Spirit, which we daily invoke and supplicate, to give some determination ourself to the matters in difference, until such a synod may be called as may without passion or prejudice give us such further assistance towards a perfect union of affections, as well as submission to authority, as is necessary. . . .

We must for the honour of all those of either persuasion with whom we have conferred declare that the professions and desires of all for the advancement of piety and true godliness are the same, their professions of zeal for the peace of the Church the same, of affection and duty to us the same; they all approve episcopacy; they all approve a set form of liturgy; and they all disapprove and dislike the sin of sacrilege and the alienation of the revenue of the Church. And if upon these excellent foundations, in submission to which there is such a harmony of affections, any superstructures should be raised, to the shaking those foundations and to the contracting and lessening the blessed gift of charity which is a vital part of Christian religion, we shall think ourselves very unfortunate, and even suspect that we are defective in that administration of government with which God hath entrusted us.

We need not profess the high affection and esteem we have for the Church of England as it is established by law, the reverence to which hath supported us, with God's blessing, against many temptations. Nor do we think that reverence in the least degree diminished by our condescensions not peremptorily to insist on some particulars of ceremony which, however introduced by the piety and devotion and order of former times, may not be so agreeable to the present. . . . And we hope this charitable compliance of ours will dispose the minds of all men to a cheerful submission to that authority the preservation whereof is so necessary for the unity and peace of the Church, and that they will acknowledge the support of the episcopal authority to be the best support of religion by being the best means to contain the minds of men within the rules of government. And they who would restrain the exercise of that holy function within the rules which were observed in the primitive times must remember and consider that, the ecclesiastical power being in those blessed times always subordinate and subject to the civil, it was likewise proportioned to such an extent of jurisdiction as was most agreeable to that. And as the sanctity and simplicity and resignation of that age did then refer many things to the bishops which the policy of succeeding ages would not admit, at least did otherwise provide for, so it can be no reproach to primitive episcopacy if, where there have been great alterations in the civil government from what was then, there have been likewise some difference and alteration in the ecclesiastical, the essence and foundation being still preserved. . . . And therefore we have not the least doubt but that the present bishops will think the present concessions now made by us to allay the present distempers very just and reasonable, and will very cheerfully conform themselves thereunto.

I. We do in the first place declare our purpose and resolution is and shall be to promote the power of godliness, to encourage the exercises of religion, both public and private, and to take care that the Lord's Day be applied to holy exercises, without unnecessary divertisements; and that insufficient, negligent and scandalous ministers be not permitted in the Church; and that as the present bishops are known to be men of great and exemplary piety in their lives, which they have manifested in their notorious and unexampled sufferings during these late distempers, and of great and known sufficiency of learning, so we shall take special care, by the assistance of God, to prefer no man to that office and charge but men of learning, virtue and piety, who may be themselves the best examples to those who are to be governed by them. And we shall expect, and provide the best we can, that the bishops be frequent preachers, and that they do very often preach themselves in some church of their diocese, except they be hindered by sickness or other bodily infirmities, or some other justifiable occasion, which shall not be thought justifiable if it be frequent.

II. Because the dioceses, especially some of them, are thought to be of too large extent, we will appoint such a number of suffragan bishops in every diocese as shall be sufficient for the due performance of their work.

III. No bishop shall ordain, or exercise any part of jurisdiction which appertains to the censures of the Church, without the advice and assistance of the presbyters; and no chancellors, commissaries or officials as such shall exercise any act of spiritual jurisdiction in these cases, viz., excommunication, absolution, or wherein any of the ministry are concerned with reference to their pastoral charge. . . . As to excommunication our will and pleasure is that no chancellor, commissary or official shall decree any sentence of excommunication or absolution, or be judges, in those things wherein any of the ministry are concerned, as is aforesaid. Nor shall the archdeacon exercise any jurisdiction without the advice and assistance of six ministers of his archdeaconry, whereof three to be nominated by the bishop and three by the election of the major part of the presbyters within the archdeaconry.

IV. To the end that the deans and chapters may be the better fitted to afford counsel and assistance to the bishops, both in ordination and the other offices mentioned before, we will take care that those preferments be given to the most learned and pious presbyters of the diocese, and moreover that an equal number (to those of the chapter) of the most learned, pious and discreet presbyters of the same diocese, annually chosen by the major vote of all the presbyters of that diocese present at such elections, shall be always advising and assisting, together with those of the chapter, in all ordinations, and in every part of jurisdiction which appertains to the censures of the Church, and at all other solemn and important actions in the exercise of the ecclesiastical jurisdiction, wherein any of the ministry are concerned; provided that at all such meetings the number of the ministers so elected and those present of the chapter shall be equal, and not exceed one the other, and that to make the numbers equal the juniors of the exceeding number be withdrawn, that the most ancient may take place. Nor shall any suffragan bishop ordain, or exercise the forementioned offices and acts of spiritual jurisdiction, but with the advice and assistance of a sufficient number of the most judicious and pious presbyters annually chosen as aforesaid within his precincts. And our will is that the great work of ordination be constantly and solemnly performed by the bishop and his aforesaid presbytery at the four set times and seasons appointed by the Church for that purpose.

V. We will take care that confirmation be rightly and solemnly performed, by the information and with the consent of the minister of the place, who shall admit none to the Lord's Supper till they have made a credible profession of their faith, and promised obedience to the will of God, according as is expressed in the considerations of the rubric before the catechism; and that all possible diligence be used for the instruction and reformation of scandalous offenders, whom the minister shall not suffer to partake of the Lord's Table until they have openly declared themselves to have truly repented and amended their former naughty lives. . . . But besides the suffragans and their presbytery every rural dean (those deans, as heretofore, to be nominated by the bishop of the diocese), together with three or four ministers of that deanery chosen by the major part of all the ministers within the same, shall meet once in every month to receive such complaints as shall be presented to them by the ministers or churchwardens of the respective parishes, and also to compose all such differences betwixt party and party as shall be referred unto them by way of arbitration, and to convince offenders, and reform all such things as they find amiss, by their pastoral reproofs and admonitions. . . . Moreover the rural dean and his assistants are in their respective divisions to see that the children and younger sort be carefully instructed by the respective ministers of every parish in the grounds of Christian religion, and be able to give a good account of their faith and knowledge, and also of their Christian conversation conformable thereunto, before they be confirmed by the bishop or admitted to the sacrament of the Lord's Supper.

VI. No bishop shall exercise any arbitrary power, or do or impose anything upon the clergy or the people but what is according to the known law of the land.

VII. We are very glad to find that all with whom we have conferred do in their judgments approve a liturgy, or set form of public worship, to be lawful, which in our judgment, for the preservation of unity and uniformity, we conceive to be very necessary; and though we do esteem the liturgy of the Church of England, contained in the *Book of Common Prayer* and by law established, to be the best we have seen (and we believe that we have seen all that are extant and used in this part of the world, and well know what reverence most of the reformed churches, or at least the most learned men in those churches, have for it), yet, since we find some exceptions made against several things therein, we will appoint an equal number of learned divines of both persuasions to review the same and to make such alterations as shall be thought most necessary, and some additional forms (in the scripture phrase, as near as may be) suited unto the nature of the several parts of worship; and that it be left to the minister's choice to use one or other at his discretion. . . .

VIII. Lastly, concerning ceremonies, which have administered so much matter of difference and contention, and which have been introduced by the wisdom and authority of the Church for edification and the improvement of piety, we shall say no more but that we have the more esteem of all and reverence for many of them by having been present in many of those churches where they are most abolished or discountenanced; and it cannot be doubted but that, as the universal Church cannot introduce one ceremony in the worship of God that is contrary to God's Word expressed in the Scripture, so every national Church, with the approbation and consent of the sovereign power, may and hath always introduced such particular ceremonies as in that conjuncture of time are thought most proper for edification and the necessary improvement of piety and devotion in the people, though the necessary practice thereof cannot be deduced from Scripture; and that which before was and in itself is indifferent ceases to be indifferent after it is once established by law. And therefore our present consideration and work is to gratify the private consciences of those who are grieved with the use of some ceremonies by indulging to and dispensing with their omitting those ceremonies, not utterly to abolish any which are established by law (if any are practised contrary to law the same shall cease), which would be unjust and of ill example, and to impose upon the conscience of some for the satisfaction of the conscience of others, which is otherwise provided for.

As it could not be reasonable that men should expect that we should ourself decline, or enjoin others to do so, to receive the blessed sacrament upon our knees, which in our conscience is the most humble, most devout and most agreeable posture for that holy duty, because some other men, upon reasons best, if not only, known to themselves, choose rather to do it sitting or standing, we shall leave all decisions and determinations of that kind, if they shall be thought necessary for a perfect and entire unity and uniformity throughout the nation, to the advice of a national synod, . . . provided that none shall be denied the sacrament of the Lord's Supper though they do not use the gesture of kneeling in the act of receiving.

In the meantime, out of compassion and compliance towards those who would forbear the cross in baptism, we are content that no man shall be compelled to use the same, or suffer for not doing it. . . .

No man shall be compelled to bow at the name of Jesus, or suffer in any degree for not doing it; without reproaching those who out of their devotion continue that ancient ceremony of the Church.

For the use of the surplice, we are contented that all men be left to their liberty to do as they shall think fit, without suffering in the least degree for wearing or not wearing it; provided that this liberty do not extend to our own chapel, cathedral or collegiate churches, or to any college in either of our universities. . . .

And because some men, otherwise pious and learned, say they cannot conform unto the subscription required by the canon, nor take the oath of canonical obedience, we are content, and it is our will and pleasure (so they take the oaths of allegiance and supremacy), that they shall receive ordination, institution and induction, and shall be permitted to exercise their function, and to enjoy the profits of their livings, without the said subscription or oath of canonical obedience; and moreover that no person in the universities shall for the want of such subscription be hindered in the taking of their degrees; lastly, that none be judged to forfeit his presentation or benefice, or be deprived of it, upon the statute of the 13th of Queen Elizabeth, chapter the 12th, so he read and declare his assent to all the articles of religion, which only concern the confession of the true Christian faith, and the doctrine of the sacraments comprised in the book of articles in the said statute mentioned. . . .

To conclude, and in this place to explain what we mentioned before and said in our letter to the House of Commons from Breda, that we hoped in due time ourself to propose somewhat for the propagation of the Protestant religion, . . . we do conjure all our loving subjects to acquiesce in and submit to this our declaration concerning those differences, which have so much disquieted the nation at home, and given such offence to the Protestant churches abroad, and brought such reproach upon the Protestant religion in general from the enemies thereof. . . . And we hope and expect that all men will henceforward forbear to vent any such doctrine in the pulpit, or to endeavour to work in such manner upon the affections of the people, as may dispose them to an ill opinion of us and the government, and to disturb the peace of the kingdom, which if all men will in their several vocations endeavour to preserve with the same affection and zeal we ourself will do, all our good subjects will, by God's blessing upon us, enjoy as great a measure of felicity as this nation hath ever done, and which we shall constantly labour to procure for them as the greatest blessing God can bestow upon us in this world.

Given at our court at Whitehall,
this twenty-fifth day of October 1660.

135. Declaration in favour of toleration, 1662

(E. Cardwell, *Documentary Annals of the Reformed Church of England*, II, pp. 260–269)

HIS MAJESTY'S DECLARATION
TO ALL HIS LOVING SUBJECTS

CHARLES R.

As it hath pleased Almighty God so wonderfully to restore us to the throne of our ancestors, and our subjects to happy peace and tranquillity, without the least blood shed by the military sword, so, having still earnestly wished that both might be secured and maintained with the least effusion possible of the same by the sword of justice, as desiring much rather to cure the ill intentions of the disaffected by our clemency than to punish the effects by rigour of law, we cannot but express our great grief and trouble that the unpardonable as well as incurable malignity of some should have carried them anew to such traitorous practices against our person and government as have necessitated us to make fresh examples by the death of any more of our subjects. But as the publicness of their trial in the ordinary course of law hath by their conviction sufficiently satisfied the world of the enormity of their crimes, so we have thought fit, at the same time that we are forced to punish, to endeavour as much as in us lieth the preventing all occasions of the like for the future by this declaration, wherein our principal aim is to apply proper antidotes to all those venomous insinuations by which (as we are certainly informed) some of our subjects of inveterate and unalterable ill principles do daily endeavour to poison the affections of our good people by misleading their understandings, and that principally by four sorts of most false and malicious scandals, which we do look upon as the grounds of those traitorous attempts.

The first, by suggesting unto them that having attained our ends in re-establishing our regal authority, and gaining the power into our own hands by a specious condescension to a general Act of Indemnity,[1] we intend nothing less than the observation of it, but on the contrary by degrees to subject the persons and estates of all such who stood in need of that law to future revenge, and to give them up to the spoil of those who had lost their fortunes in our service.

Secondly, that upon pretence of plots and practices against us we intend to introduce a military way of government in this kingdom.

Thirdly, that having made use of such solemn promises from Breda, and in several declarations since, of ease and liberty to tender consciences, instead of performing any part of them we have added straiter fetters than ever, and new rocks of scandal to the scrupulous, by the Act of Uniformity.[2]

Fourthly and lastly, we find it as artificially as maliciously divulged throughout the whole kingdom that at the same time we deny a fitting liberty to those other sects of our subjects whose consciences will not allow them to conform to the religion established by law, we are highly indulgent to papists, not only in exempting them from the penalties of the law but even to such a degree of countenance and encouragement as may even endanger the Protestant religion.

[1] No. 53.   [2] No. 137.

Upon occasion of all which wicked and malicious suggestions, . . . we think that in our fatherly care to prevent any misleading of those who are so dear to us we owe unto them and to ourselves this publication of our steadfast resolutions in all these particulars.

As to the first point, concerning the Act of Indemnity, certainly there can be no greater evidence that the passing it proceeded from the clemency of our nature, as well as from the present conjuncture of that Parliament wherein it was first framed, than that we have been pleased to make it our especial care to have it confirmed by a new Act in this, a Parliament composed of members so full of affections to our person, and of zeal for the public good, as we could never have cause to apprehend their exacting from us a confirmation of anything that had been extorted or had at present been judged by us prejudicial to either; and therefore as we not only consented unto but most earnestly desired the passing that Act at first and confirming it since, as being no less conformable to our nature than conducible to a happy settlement, so we do hereby most solemnly renew unto all our subjects concerned in it this engagement on the word of a king, that it shall never be in the power of any person or interest whatsoever to make us decline from the religious observance of it. . . .

Which most sincere profession of ours may suffice also to expose the wickedness and falsehood of the other malice, concerning the design of introducing a way of government by military power. It is true that we should not think we discharged rightly what we owe to the public peace and to the freedom and security of Parliaments, as well as to the safety of our person, if, whilst we daily discover such multitudes of distempered minds and such dangerous practices issuing from them, we should from want of sufficient guards put it in the power of those rebellious spirits to undertake probably at any time what they have at several times so madly attempted for the ruin and destruction of us all. Of which, certainly, besides the present occasion of new precaution as well as new severity, we suppose all our good subjects need not a livelier nor more moving instance than what their memories can furnish them with from the desperate undertaking of Venner and his crew,[1] which (as mad as it was) we leave to all the world to judge of how dangerous a consequence it might have been, without that little strength remaining of those forces which (to give our people a testimony of our founding all our security rather in their affections than in any military power) we had so frankly disbanded, and which afterwards, by advice of our Council, merely upon motives of the public safety, we consented to increase to that moderate proportion which was indeed absolutely necessary. . . .

As for the third, concerning the non-performance of our promises, we remember well the very words of those from Breda, viz., We do declare a liberty to tender consciences, . . .[2] we remember well the confirmations we have made of them since upon several occasions in Parliament; and as all these things are still fresh in our memory so are we still firm in the resolution of performing them to the full. But it must not be wondered at, since that Parliament to which those promises were made in relation to an Act never thought fit to offer us any to that purpose, and being so zealous as we are (and by the grace of God shall ever be) for the maintenance of the true Protestant

---

[1] No. 308.　　　　　　　　　　　　　　[2] As in No. 1.

religion, finding it so shaken (not to say overthrown) as we did, we should give its establishment the precedency before matters of indulgence to dissenters from it. But that once done (as we hope it is sufficiently by the Bill of Uniformity), we are glad to lay hold on this occasion to renew unto all our subjects concerned in those promises of indulgence by a true tenderness of conscience this assurance, that as in the first place we have been zealous to settle the uniformity of the Church of England in discipline, ceremony and government, and shall ever constantly maintain it, so as for what concerns the penalties upon those who (living peaceable) do not conform thereunto through scruple and tenderness of misguided conscience, but modestly and without scandal perform their devotions in their own way, we shall make it our special care so far forth as in us lies, without invading the freedom of Parliament, to incline their wisdom at this next approaching sessions to concur with us in the making some such Act for that purpose as may enable us to exercise with a more universal satisfaction that power of dispensing which we conceive to be inherent in us. . . .

In the last place, as to that most pernicious and injurious scandal, so artificially spread and fomented, of our favour to papists; as it is but a repetition of the same detestable arts by which all the late calamities have been brought upon this kingdom in the time of our royal father of blessed memory (who, though the most pious and zealous Protestant that ever reigned in this nation, could never wash off the stains cast upon him by that malice, but by his martyrdom), we conceive all our subjects should be sufficiently prepared against that poison by memory of those disasters, especially since nothing is more evident than that the wicked authors of this scandal are such as seek to involve all good Protestants under the odious name of papists, or popishly affected. Yet we cannot but say upon this occasion that our education and course of life in the true Protestant religion has been such, and our constancy in the profession of it so eminent in our most desperate condition abroad among Roman Catholic princes, whenas the appearance of receding from it had been the likeliest way, in all human forecast, to have procured us the most powerful assistances of our re-establishment, that should any of our subjects give but the least admission of that scandal unto their beliefs we should look upon it as the most unpardonable offence that they can be guilty of towards us.

It is true that as we shall always according to justice retain, so we think it may become us to avow to the world, a due sense we have of the greatest part of our Roman Catholic subjects of this kingdom having deserved well from our royal father of blessed memory, and from us, and even from the Protestant religion itself, in adhering to us with their lives and fortunes for the maintenance of our crown in the religion established, against those who, under the name of zealous Protestants, employed both fire and sword to overthrow them both. We shall with as much freedom profess unto the world that it is not in our intention to exclude our Roman Catholic subjects who have so demeaned themselves from all share in the benefit of such an Act as in pursuance of our promises the wisdom of our Parliament shall think fit to offer unto us for the ease of tender consciences. . . . But at the same time that we declare . . . our gracious intentions already expressed to such of our Roman Catholic subjects as shall live peaceably, modestly and without scandal, we would have them all know that if for doing what their duties and loyalties obliged them to, or from our acknowledgment of their well-deserving, they shall have the presumption to hope for a toleration of their profession, . . . or to obtain the least remission in the strictness of those laws which either are or shall be made to hinder the spreading of their doctrine to the prejudice of the true Protestant religion, . . . they shall quickly find we know as well to be severe when wisdom requires, as indulgent when charity and sense of merit challenge it from us.

With this we have thought fit to arm our good subjects' minds against the practices of our ill ones, by a true knowledge of our own, of which now rightly persuaded we make no question but that whosoever they be from whom they can derive the spreading or fomenting of any of those wicked suggestions, they will look upon them with detestation as the most dangerous enemies of our crown and of the peace and happiness of the nation; and that what we have here published will happily prepare them all to a cheerful expectation of the approaching sessions of Parliament....

In order to which, although it be foreign to the main scope of this our declaration, which is principally to prevent the mischiefs aimed at by the scandals therein mentioned, . . . yet we cannot forbear hinting here unto our good subjects four particulars wherein we think to give them the most important marks of our care. First, in punishing by severe laws that licentiousness and impiety which since the dissolution of government we find to our great grief hath overspread the nation. Secondly, as well by sumptuary laws as by our own example of frugality to restrain the excess in men's expenses which is grown so general and so exorbitant, beyond all bounds either of their qualities or fortunes. Thirdly, so to perfect what we have already industriously begun in the retrenching of all our own ordinary and extraordinary charges in navy, garrisons, household and all their dependants as to bring them within the compass of our settled revenue, that thereby our subjects may have little cause to apprehend our frequent pressing them for new assistants. And lastly, so to improve the good consequences of these three particulars to the advancement of trade that all our subjects finding (as well as other nations envying) the advantage this hath of them in that prime foundation of plenty, they may all with minds happily composed by our clemency and indulgence (instead of taking up thoughts of deserting their professions or transplanting) apply themselves comfortably and with redoubled industry to their several vocations, in such manner as the private interest of every one in particular may encourage him to contribute cheerfully to the general prosperity.

Given at our court at Whitehall,
this twenty-sixth day of December,
in the fourteenth year of our reign.

(b) CLARENDON CODE, 1661–1670

136. Corporation Act, 1661
(*Statutes of the Realm*, v, pp. 321–323)

AN ACT

FOR THE WELL GOVERNING AND REGULATING OF CORPORATIONS

(*13 Car. II, stat. II, cap. 1*)

Whereas questions are likely to arise concerning the validity of elections of magistrates and other officers and members in corporations, as well in respect of removing some as placing others during the late troubles, contrary to the true intent and meaning of their charters and liberties, and to the end that the succession in such corporations may be most probably perpetuated in the hands of persons well affected to his Majesty and the established government, it being too well known that, notwithstanding all his Majesty's endeavours and unparalleled indulgence in pardoning all that is past, nevertheless many evil spirits are still working; wherefore for prevention of the like mischief for the time to come, and for preservation of the public peace both in Church and State, be it enacted . . . that commissions shall before the twentieth day of February next[1] be issued forth under the great seal of England unto such persons as his Majesty shall appoint for the executing of the powers and authorities hereinafter expressed, and that all and every the persons to be named commissioners in the said commissions respectively shall by virtue of this Act be commissioners respectively for and within the several cities, corporations and boroughs, and cinque ports and their members and other port towns within the kingdom of England, dominion of Wales and town of Berwick-upon-Tweed, for which they shall be respectively nominated and appointed.

II. And be it further enacted . . . that no charter of any corporation, cities, towns, boroughs, cinque ports and their members and other port towns in England or Wales or town of Berwick-upon-Tweed, shall at any time hereafter be avoided for or by reason of any act or thing done or omitted to be done before the first day of this present Parliament.

III. And be it further enacted . . . that all persons who upon the four and twentieth day of December one thousand six hundred sixty and one shall be mayors, aldermen, recorders, bailiffs, town clerks, common council men and other persons then bearing any office or offices of magistracy, or places or trusts or other employment relating to or concerning the government of the said respective cities, corporations and boroughs, and cinque ports and their members and other port towns, shall, at any time before the five and twentieth day of March one thousand six hundred sixty and three, when they shall be thereunto required by the said respective commissioners or any three or more of them, take the oaths of allegiance and supremacy and this oath following:

I, A.B., do declare and believe that it is not lawful upon any pretence whatsoever

[1] 1662.

to take arms against the king, and that I do abhor that traitorous position of taking arms by his authority against his person, or against those that are commissioned by him. So help me God.

And also at the same time shall publicly subscribe before the said commissioners or any three of them this following declaration:

I, A.B., do declare that I hold that there lies no obligation upon me or any other person from the oath commonly called the Solemn League and Covenant, and that the same was in itself an unlawful oath, and imposed upon the subjects of this realm against the known laws and liberties of the kingdom.

IV. And that all such of the said mayors and other the persons aforesaid, by whom the said oaths are to be taken and declaration subscribed as aforesaid, who shall refuse to take and subscribe the same within the time and in manner aforesaid, shall from and immediately after such refusal be by authority of this Act *ipso facto* removed and displaced of and from the said offices and places respectively. . . .

V. And nevertheless be it further enacted . . . that the said commissioners or any five or more of them shall have full power by virtue of this Act, by order and warrant under their hands and seals, to displace or remove any of the persons aforesaid from the said respective offices and places or trusts aforesaid, if the said commissioners or the major part of them then present shall deem it expedient for the public safety, although such persons shall have taken and subscribed, or be willing to take and subscribe, the said oaths and declaration.

VI. And be it also enacted, that the said respective commissioners or any five or more of them as aforesaid shall have power to restore such person or persons as have been illegally or unduly removed into the places out of which he or they were removed, and also to put and place into the offices and places which by any of the ways aforesaid shall be void respectively some other person or persons then being, or which have been, members or inhabitants of the said respective cities, corporations and boroughs, and cinque ports and their members and other port towns, who shall before the said respective commissioners or any three or more of them take the said oaths of allegiance and supremacy and the said other oath, and subscribe the declaration hereinbefore particularly mentioned. . . .

IX. Provided also, and be it enacted . . . that from and after the expiration of the said commissions no person or persons shall forever hereafter be placed, elected or chosen in or to any the offices or places aforesaid that shall not have within one year next before such election or choice taken the sacrament of the Lord's Supper according to the rites of the Church of England, and that every such person and persons so placed, elected or chosen shall likewise take the aforesaid three oaths and subscribe the said declaration at the same time when the oath for the due execution of the said places and offices respectively shall be administered; and in default hereof every such placing, election and choice is hereby enacted and declared to be void. . . .

XI. Provided also, and be it hereby enacted, that the powers granted to the commissioners by virtue of this Act shall continue and be in force until the five and twentieth of March one thousand six hundred sixty-three and no longer. . . .

137. Act of Uniformity, 1662

(Statutes of the Realm, v, pp. 364–370)*

AN ACT FOR THE UNIFORMITY OF PUBLIC PRAYERS,
AND ADMINISTRATION OF SACRAMENTS, AND OTHER RITES AND CEREMONIES;
AND FOR ESTABLISHING THE FORM OF MAKING,
ORDAINING AND CONSECRATING BISHOPS, PRIESTS AND DEACONS
IN THE CHURCH OF ENGLAND

(14 Car. II, cap. 4)

Whereas in the first year of the late Queen Elizabeth there was one uniform order of common service and prayer, and of the administration of sacraments, rites and ceremonies in the Church of England (agreeable to the Word of God and usage of the primitive church), compiled by the reverend bishops and clergy, set forth in one book entituled, *The Book of Common Prayer and administration of sacraments and other rites and ceremonies in the Church of England*, and enjoined to be used by Act of Parliament holden in the said first year of the said late queen entituled, *An Act for the uniformity of common prayer and service in the Church and administration of the sacraments*;[1] . . . and yet, this notwithstanding, a great number of people in divers parts of this realm, following their own sensuality, and living without knowledge and due fear of God, do wilfully and schismatically abstain and refuse to come to their parish churches and other public places where common prayer, administration of the sacraments and preaching of the Word of God is used upon the Sundays and other days ordained and appointed to be kept and observed as holy days; and whereas by the great and scandalous neglect of ministers in using the said order or liturgy so set forth and enjoined as aforesaid great mischiefs and inconveniences during the times of the late unhappy troubles have arisen and grown, and many people have been led into factions and schisms, to the great decay and scandal of the reformed religion of the Church of England, and to the hazard of many souls; for prevention whereof in time to come, for settling the peace of the Church, and for allaying the present distempers which the indisposition of the time hath contracted, the king's Majesty, according to his declaration of the five and twentieth of October one thousand six hundred and sixty,[2] granted his commission under the great seal of England to several bishops and other divines to review the *Book of Common Prayer* and to prepare such alterations and additions as they thought fit to offer; and afterwards the convocations of both the provinces of Canterbury and York being by his Majesty called and assembled and now sitting, his Majesty hath been pleased to authorize and require the presidents of the said convocations and other the bishops and clergy of the same to review the said *Book of Common Prayer* and the book of the form and manner of the making and consecrating of bishops, priests and deacons, and that after mature consideration they should make such additions and alterations in the said books respectively as to them should seem meet and convenient, and should exhibit and present the same to his Majesty in writing for his further allowance or confirmation; since which time, upon full and mature deliberation, they the said presidents, bishops and clergy of both

---

[1] 1 Eliz., cap. 2.   [2] No. 134.

provinces have accordingly reviewed the said books, and have made some alterations which they think fit to be inserted to the same, and some additional prayers to the said *Book of Common Prayer* to be used upon proper and emergent occasions, and have exhibited and presented the same unto his Majesty in writing in one book entituled, *The Book of Common Prayer and administration of the sacraments and other rites and ceremonies of the church according to the use of the Church of England, together with the psalter or psalms of David, pointed as they are to be sung or said in churches, and the form and manner of making, ordaining and consecrating of bishops, priests and deacons*; all which his Majesty, having duly considered, hath fully approved and allowed the same, and recommended to this present Parliament. . . .

Now in regard that nothing conduceth more to the settling of the peace of this nation (which is desired of all good men), nor to the honour of our religion and the propagation thereof, than an universal agreement in the public worship of Almighty God, . . . be it enacted . . . that all and singular ministers in any cathedral, collegiate or parish church or chapel or other place of public worship within this realm of England, dominion of Wales and town of Berwick-upon-Tweed shall be bound to say and use the morning prayer, evening prayer, celebration and administration of both the sacraments and all other the public and common prayer in such order and form as is mentioned in the said book annexed and joined to this present Act, and entituled, *The Book of Common Prayer and administration of the sacraments* . . . ,[1] and that the morning and evening prayers therein contained shall upon every Lord's Day, and upon all other days and occasions and at the times therein appointed, be openly and solemnly read by all and every minister or curate in every church, chapel or other place of public worship within this realm of England and places aforesaid.

II. And to the end that uniformity in the public worship of God (which is so much desired) may be speedily effected, be it further enacted . . . that every parson, vicar or other minister whatsoever, who now hath and enjoyeth any ecclesiastical benefice or promotion within this realm of England or places aforesaid, shall in the church, chapel or place of public worship belonging to his said benefice or promotion, upon some Lord's Day before the Feast of Saint Bartholomew[2] which shall be in the year of our Lord God one thousand six hundred sixty and two, openly, publicly and solemnly read the morning and evening prayer appointed to be read by and according to the said *Book of Common Prayer* at the times thereby appointed, and after such reading thereof shall openly and publicly before the congregation there assembled declare his unfeigned assent and consent to the use of all things in the said book contained and prescribed, in these words and no other:

I, A.B., do declare my unfeigned assent and consent to all and every thing contained and prescribed in and by the book entituled, *The Book of Common Prayer and administration of the sacraments and other rites and ceremonies of the church according to the use of the Church of England, together with the psalter or psalms of David, pointed as they are to be sung or said in churches, and the form or manner of making, ordaining and consecrating of bishops, priests and deacons.*

III. And that all and every such person who shall (without some lawful

---

[1] As above.　　　　　　　　　　[2] 24 August.

impediment to be allowed and approved of by the ordinary of the place) neglect or refuse to do the same within the time aforesaid (or in case of such impediment within one month after such impediment removed) shall *ipso facto* be deprived of all his spiritual promotions. . . .

IV. And be it further enacted . . . that every person who shall hereafter be presented or collated or put into any ecclesiastical benefice or promotion within this realm of England and places aforesaid shall in the church, chapel or place of public worship belonging to his said benefice or promotion, within two months next after that he shall be in the actual possession of the said ecclesiastical benefice or promotion, upon some Lord's Day openly, publicly and solemnly read the morning and evening prayers appointed. . . .[1]

V. And be it further enacted . . . that in all places where the proper incumbent of any parsonage or vicarage or benefice with cure doth reside on his living and keep a curate, the incumbent himself in person (not having some lawful impediment to be allowed by the ordinary of the place) shall once at the least in every month openly and publicly read the common prayers and service in and by the said book prescribed, and (if there be occasion) administer each of the sacraments and other rites of the Church, in the parish church or chapel of or belonging to the same parsonage, vicarage or benefice in such order, manner and form as in and by the said book is appointed, upon pain to forfeit the sum of five pounds to the use of the poor of the parish for every offence. . . .

VI. And be it further enacted . . . that every dean, canon and prebendary of every cathedral or collegiate church, and all masters and other heads, fellows, chaplains and tutors of or in any college, hall, house of learning or hospital, and every public professor and reader in either of the universities and in every college elsewhere, and every parson, vicar, curate, lecturer and every other person in Holy Orders, and every schoolmaster keeping any public or private school, and every person instructing or teaching any youth in any house or private family as a tutor or schoolmaster, who upon the first day of May which shall be in the year of our Lord God one thousand six hundred sixty-two, or at any time thereafter, shall be incumbent or have possession of any deanery, canonry, prebend, mastership, headship, fellowship, professor's place or reader's place, parsonage, vicarage, or any other ecclesiastical dignity or promotion, or of any curate's place, lecture or school, or shall instruct or teach any youth as tutor or schoolmaster, shall before the Feast Day of Saint Bartholomew which shall be in the year of our Lord one thousand six hundred sixty-two, or at or before his or their respective admission to be incumbent or have possession aforesaid, subscribe the declaration or acknowledgment following, *scilicet*,

I, A.B., do declare that it is not lawful upon any pretence whatsoever to take arms against the king, and that I do abhor that traitorous position of taking arms by his authority against his person or against those that are commissioned by him, and that I will conform to the liturgy of the Church of England as it is now by law established; and I do declare that I do hold there lies no obligation upon me or on any other person from the oath commonly called the Solemn League and Covenant to endeavour

---

[1] Continued as in the two preceding sections.

any change or alteration of government either in Church or State, and that the same was in itself an unlawful oath, and imposed upon the subjects of this realm against the known laws and liberties of this kingdom.

VII. And if any schoolmaster or other person instructing or teaching youth in any private house or family as a tutor or schoolmaster shall instruct or teach any youth as a tutor or schoolmaster before licence obtained from his respective archbishop, bishop or ordinary of the diocese according to the laws and statutes of this realm (for which he shall pay twelve pence only), and before such subscription and acknowledgment made as aforesaid, then every such schoolmaster and other instructing and teaching as aforesaid shall for the first offence suffer three months imprisonment without bail or mainprize, and for every second and other such offence shall suffer three months imprisonment without bail or mainprize and also forfeit to his Majesty the sum of five pounds; and after such subscription made every such parson, vicar, curate and lecturer shall procure a certificate under the hand and seal of the respective archbishop, bishop or ordinary of the diocese (who are hereby enjoined and required upon demand to make and deliver the same), and shall publicly and openly read the same, together with the declaration or acknowledgment aforesaid, upon some Lord's Day within three months then next following in his parish church, where he is to officiate, in the presence of the congregation there assembled in the time of divine service, upon pain that every person failing therein shall lose such parsonage, vicarage or benefice, curate s place or lecturer's place respectively, and shall be utterly disabled and *ipso facto* deprived of the same. . . .

VIII. Provided always, that from and after the twenty-fifth day of March which shall be in the year of our Lord God one thousand six hundred eighty-two there shall be omitted in the said declaration or acknowledgment so to be subscribed and read these words following, *scilicet*,

And I do declare that I do hold there lies no obligation on me or any other person from the oath commonly called the Solemn League and Covenant to endeavour any change or alteration of government either in Church or State, and that the same was in itself an unlawful oath, and imposed upon the subjects of this realm against the known laws and liberties of this kingdom,

So as none of the persons aforesaid shall from thenceforth be at all obliged to subscribe or read that part of the said declaration or acknowledgment.

IX. Provided always, and be it enacted, that from and after the Feast of Saint Bartholomew which shall be in the year of our Lord one thousand six hundred sixty and two no person who now is incumbent and in possession of any parsonage, vicarage or benefice, and who is not already in Holy Orders by episcopal ordination, or shall not before the said Feast Day of Saint Bartholomew be ordained priest or deacon according to the form of episcopal ordination, shall have, hold or enjoy the said parsonage, vicarage, benefice with cure or other ecclesiastical promotion within this kingdom of England or the dominion of Wales or town of Berwick-upon-Tweed, but shall be utterly disabled and *ipso facto* deprived of the same, and all his ecclesiastical promotions shall be void as if he was naturally dead.

X. And be it further enacted . . . that no person whatsoever shall thenceforth be capable to be admitted to any parsonage, vicarage, benefice or other ecclesiastical promotion or dignity whatsoever, nor shall presume to consecrate and administer the Holy Sacrament of the Lord's Supper, before such time as he shall be ordained priest according to the form and manner in and by the said book prescribed, unless he have formerly been made priest by episcopal ordination, upon pain to forfeit for every offence the sum of one hundred pounds, one moiety thereof to the king's Majesty, the other moiety thereof to be equally divided between the poor of the parish where the offence shall be committed and such person or persons as shall sue for the same, .. and to be disabled from taking or being admitted into the order of priest by the space of one whole year then next following.

XI. Provided that the penalties in this Act shall not extend to the foreigners or aliens of the foreign reformed churches allowed, or to be allowed, by the king's Majesty, his heirs and successors in England. . . .

XIII. And be it further enacted . . . that no form or order of common prayers, administration of sacraments, rites or ceremonies, shall be openly used in any church, chapel or other public place of or in any college or hall in either of the universities, the colleges of Westminster, Winchester or Eton or any of them, other than what is prescribed and appointed to be used in and by the said book; and that the present governor or head of every college and hall in the said universities and of the said colleges of Westminster, Winchester and Eton, within one month after the Feast of Saint Bartholomew which shall be in the year of our Lord one thousand six hundred sixty and two, and every governor or head of any of the said colleges or halls hereafter to be elected or appointed within one month next after his election or collation and admission into the same government or headship, shall openly and publicly in the church, chapel or other public place of the same college or hall, and in the presence of the fellows and scholars of the same or the greater part of them then resident, subscribe unto the Nine and Thirty Articles of religion mentioned in the statute made in the thirteenth year of the reign of the late Queen Elizabeth,[1] and unto the said book, and declare his unfeigned assent and consent unto and approbation of the said articles and of the same book, and to the use of all the prayers, rites and ceremonies, forms and orders in the said book prescribed and contained according to the form aforesaid; and that all such governors or heads of the said colleges and halls or any of them as are or shall be in Holy Orders shall once at least in every quarter of the year (not having a lawful impediment) openly and publicly read the morning prayer and service in and by the said book appointed to be read in the church, chapel or other public place of the same college or hall, upon pain to lose and be suspended of and from all the benefits and profits belonging to the same government or headship by the space of six months by the visitor or visitors of the same college or hall; and if any governor or head of any college or hall suspended for not subscribing unto the said articles and book, or for not reading of the morning prayer and service as aforesaid, shall not, at or before the end of six months next after such suspension, subscribe unto the said articles and book and declare his consent thereunto as aforesaid, or read the morning prayer and service as aforesaid, then such government or headship shall be *ipso facto* void.

[1] 13 Eliz., cap. 12.

XIV. Provided always, that it shall and may be lawful to use the morning and evening prayer and all other prayers and service prescribed in and by the said book in the chapels or other public places of the respective colleges and halls in both the universities, in the colleges of Westminster, Winchester and Eton, and in the convocations of the clergies of either province in Latin, anything in this Act contained to the contrary notwithstanding. . . .

XXII. Provided also, and be it enacted . . . that a true printed copy of the said book entituled, *The Book of Common Prayer* . . . , shall at the costs and charges of the parishioners of every parish church and chapelry, cathedral church, college and hall, be attained and gotten before the Feast Day of Saint Bartholomew in the year of our Lord one thousand six hundred sixty and two, upon pain of forfeiture of three pounds by the month for so long time as they shall then after be unprovided thereof by every parish or chapelry, cathedral church, college and hall making default therein.

XXIII. Provided always, and be it enacted . . . , that the bishops of Hereford, Saint David's, Asaph, Bangor, and Llandaff and their successors shall take such order among themselves for the souls' health of the flocks committed to their charge within Wales that the book hereunto annexed be truly and exactly translated into the British or Welsh tongue, and that the same so translated, and being by them or any three of them at the least viewed, perused and allowed, be imprinted to such number at least so that one of the said books so translated and imprinted may be had for every cathedral, collegiate and parish church and chapel of ease in the said respective dioceses and places in Wales where the Welsh is commonly spoken or used before the first day of May one thousand six hundred sixty-five; and that from and after the imprinting and publishing of the said book so translated the whole divine service shall be used and said by the ministers and curates throughout all Wales within the said dioceses where the Welsh tongue is commonly used in the British or Welsh tongue; . . . and one other *Book of Common Prayer* in the English tongue shall be bought and had in every church throughout Wales in which the *Book of Common Prayer* in Welsh is to be had by force of this Act before the first day of May one thousand six hundred sixty and four, and the same book to remain in such convenient places within the said churches that such as understand them may resort at all convenient times to read and peruse the same, and also such as do not understand the said language may by conferring both tongues together the sooner attain to the knowledge of the English tongue, anything in this Act to the contrary notwithstanding. . . .

138. Five Mile Act, 1665

(*Statutes of the Realm*, v, p. 575)

AN ACT FOR RESTRAINING NONCONFORMISTS
FROM INHABITING IN CORPORATIONS

(7 *Car. II, cap. 2*)

Whereas divers parsons, vicars, curates, lecturers and other persons in Holy Orders have not declared their unfeigned assent and consent to the use of all things contained and prescribed in the *Book of Common Prayer and administration of the sacraments and other rites and ceremonies of the church according to the use of the Church of England,* or have not subscribed the declaration or acknowledgment contained in a certain Act of Parliament made in the fourteenth year of his Majesty's reign and intituled, *An Act for the uniformity of public prayers and administration of sacraments and other rites and ceremonies, and for the establishing the form of making, ordaining and consecrating of bishops, priests and deacons in the Church of England,*[1] according to the said Act or any other subsequent Act; and whereas they or some of them, and divers other person and persons not ordained according to the form of the Church of England, and as have since the Act of Oblivion[2] taken upon them to preach in unlawful assemblies, conventicles or meetings under colour or pretence of exercise of religion, contrary to the laws and statutes of this kingdom, have settled themselves in divers corporations in England, sometimes three or more of them in a place, thereby taking an opportunity to distil the poisonous principles of schism and rebellion into the hearts of his Majesty's subjects, to the great danger of the Church and kingdom: be it therefore enacted ... that the said parsons, vicars, curates, lecturers and other persons in Holy Orders, or pretended Holy Orders, or pretending to Holy Orders, and all stipendiaries and other persons who have been possessed of any ecclesiastical or spiritual promotion, and every of them, who have not declared their unfeigned assent and consent as aforesaid, and subscribed the declaration aforesaid, and shall not take and subscribe the oath following:

I, A.B., do swear that it is not lawful upon any pretence whatsoever to take arms against the king, and that I do abhor that traitorous position of taking arms by his authority against his person, or against those that are commissionated by him, in pursuance of such commissions, and that I will not at any time endeavour any alteration of government either in Church or State.

II. And all such person and persons as shall take upon them to preach in any unlawful assembly, conventicle or meeting under colour or pretence of any exercise of religion, contrary to the laws and statutes of this kingdom, shall not at any time from and after the four and twentieth day of March which shall be in this present year of our Lord God one thousand six hundred sixty and five,[3] unless only in passing upon the road, come or be within five miles of any city, or town corporate, or borough that sends burgesses to the Parliament, within his Majesty's kingdom of England, principality of Wales or of the town of Berwick-upon-Tweed, or within five miles of any parish, town or place wherein he or they have since the Act of Oblivion been parson, vicar, curate, stipendiary or lecturer, or taken upon them to preach in any unlawful assembly, conventicle or meeting under colour or pretence of any exercise of religion, contrary to the laws and statutes of this kingdom, before he or they have taken and subscribed the oath aforesaid before the justices of peace at their quarter-sessions to be holden for the county, riding or division next unto the said corporation, city or borough, parish, place or town in open court (which said oath the said justices are hereby empowered there to administer), upon forfeiture for every such offence the sum of forty pounds of lawful English money, the one third part thereof to his Majesty and his successors, the other third part to the use of the

[1] No. 137.   [2] No. 53.   [3] 1665/6.

poor of the parish where the offence shall be committed, and the other third part thereof to such person or persons as shall or will sue for the same. . . .

III. Provided always, and be it further enacted . . . that it shall not be lawful for any person or persons restrained from coming to any city, town corporate, borough, parish, town or place as aforesaid, or for any other person or persons as shall not first take and subscribe the said oath, and as shall not frequent divine service established by the laws of this kingdom, and carry him or herself reverently, decently and orderly there, to teach any public or private school, or take any boarders or tablers that are taught or instructed by him or herself or any other, upon pain for every such offence to forfeit the sum of forty pounds, to be recovered and distributed as aforesaid.

IV. Provided also, and be it further enacted . . . that it shall be lawful for any two justices of the peace of the respective county, upon oath to them of any offence against this Act, which oath they are hereby empowered to administer, to commit the offender for six months without bail or mainprize, unless upon or before such commitment he shall before the said justices of the peace swear and subscribe the aforesaid oath and declaration. . . .

139. Conventicle Act, 1670

(*Statutes of the Realm*, v, 648-651)

AN ACT

TO PREVENT AND SUPPRESS SEDITIOUS CONVENTICLES

(*22 Car. II, cap. 1*)

For providing further and more speedy remedies against the growing and dangerous practices of seditious sectaries and other disloyal persons, who under pretence of tender consciences have or may at their meetings contrive insurrections (as late experience hath shown), be it enacted . . . that if any person of the age of sixteen years or upwards, being a subject of this realm, at any time after the tenth day of May next,[1] shall be present at any assembly, conventicle or meeting under colour or pretence of any exercise of religion in other manner than according to the liturgy and practice of the Church of England in any place within the kingdom of England, dominion of Wales or town of Berwick-upon-Tweed, at which conventicle, meeting or assembly there shall be five persons or more assembled together over and besides those of the same household, if it be in a house where there is a family inhabiting, or if it be in a house, field or place where there is no family inhabiting then where any five persons or more are so assembled as aforesaid, it shall and may be lawful to and for any one or more justices of the peace of the county, limit, division, corporation or liberty wherein the offence aforesaid shall be committed, or for the chief magistrate of the place where such offence aforesaid shall be committed, and he and they are hereby required and enjoined upon proof to him or them respectively made of such offence, either by confession of the party or oath of two witnesses (which oath the said justice and justices of the peace and chief magistrate respectively are hereby empowered and required to administer), or by notorious evidence and circumstance

[1] 1670.

of the fact, to make a record of every such offence under his or their hands and seals respectively, which record so made as aforesaid shall to all intents and purposes be in law taken and adjudged to be a full and perfect conviction of every such offender for such offence; and thereupon the said justice, justices and chief magistrate respectively shall impose on every such offender so convict as aforesaid a fine of five shillings for such first offence, which record and conviction shall be certified by the said justice, justices or chief magistrate at the next quarter-sessions of the peace for the county or place where the offence was committed.

II. And be it further enacted   . . that if such offender so convicted as aforesaid shall at any time again commit the like offence or offences contrary to this Act, and be thereof in manner aforesaid convicted, then such offender so convict of such like offence or offences shall for every such offence incur the penalty of ten shillings, which fine and fines for the first and every other offence shall be levied by distress and sale of the offender's goods and chattels, or in case of the poverty of such offender upon the goods and chattels of any other person or persons who shall be then convicted in manner aforesaid of the like offence at the same conventicle, at the discretion of the said justice, justices or chief magistrate respectively, so as the sum to be levied on any one person in case of the poverty of other offenders amount not in the whole to above the sum of ten pounds upon occasion of any one meeting as aforesaid. . . .

III. And be it further enacted . . that every person who shall take upon him to preach or teach in any such meeting, assembly or conventicle, and shall thereof be convicted as aforesaid, shall forfeit for every such first offence the sum of twenty pounds, to be levied in manner aforesaid upon his goods and chattels, and if the said preacher or teacher so convicted be a stranger, and his name and habitation not known, or is fled and cannot be found, or in the judgment of the justice, justices or chief magistrate before whom he shall be convicted shall be thought unable to pay the same, the said justice, justices or chief magistrate respectively are hereby empowered and required to levy the same by warrant as aforesaid upon the goods and chattels of any such persons who shall be present at the same conventicle, . . . and if such offender so convicted as aforesaid shall at any time again commit the like offence or offences contrary to this Act, and be thereof convicted in manner aforesaid, then such offender so convicted of such like offence or offences shall for every such offence incur the penalty of forty pounds, to be levied and disposed as aforesaid.

IV. And be it further enacted . . . that every person who shall wittingly and willingly suffer any such conventicle, meeting or unlawful assembly aforesaid to be held in his or her house, outhouse, barn, yard or backside, and be convicted thereof in manner aforesaid, shall forfeit the sum of twenty pounds to be levied in manner aforesaid upon his or her goods and chattels, or in case of his or her poverty or inability as aforesaid upon the goods and chattels of such persons who shall be convicted in manner aforesaid of being present at the same conventicle, and the money so levied to be disposed of in manner aforesaid.

V. Provided always, and be it enacted . . . that no person shall by any clause of this Act be liable to pay above ten pounds for any one meeting in regard of the poverty of any other person or persons. . . .

14

VIII. And be it further enacted ... that the justice, justices of the peace and chief magistrate respectively, or the respective constables, headboroughs and tithing-men by warrant from the said justice, justices or chief magistrate respectively, shall and may with what aid, force and assistance they shall think fit for the better execution of this Act, after refusal or denial to enter, break open and enter into any house or other place where they shall be informed any such conventicle as aforesaid is or shall be held, as well within liberties as without, and take into their custody the persons there unlawfully assembled, to the intent they may be proceeded against according to this Act; and that the lieutenants or deputy lieutenants or any commissionated officer of the militia or other of his Majesty's forces with such troops or companies of horse and foot, and also the sheriffs and other magistrates and ministers of justice, ... with such other assistance as they shall think meet or can get in readiness with the soonest, on certificate made to them respectively under the hand and seal of any one justice of the peace or chief magistrate of his particular information or knowledge of such unlawful meeting or conventicle held or to be held in their respective counties or places, and that he with such assistance as he can get together is not able to suppress and dissolve the same, shall and may and are hereby required and enjoined to repair unto the place where they are so held or to be held, and by the best means they can to dissolve, dissipate or prevent all such unlawful meetings, and take into their custody such and so many of the said persons so unlawfully assembled as they shall think fit, to the intent they may be proceeded against according to this Act. . . .

X. And be it further enacted ... that if any constable, headborough, tithing-man, churchwarden or overseer of the poor, who shall know or be credibly informed of any such meetings or conventicles held within his precincts, parish or limits, and shall not give information thereof to some justice of the peace or the chief magistrate and endeavour the conviction of the parties according to his duty, ... and be thereof convicted in manner aforesaid, he shall forfeit for every such offence the sum of five pounds, to be levied upon his goods and chattels and disposed in manner aforesaid; and that if any justice of the peace or chief magistrate shall wilfully and wittingly omit the performance of his duty in the execution of this Act he shall forfeit the sum of one hundred pounds, the one moiety to the use of his Majesty, the other moiety to the use of the informer. . . .

XII. And be it further enacted ... that this Act and all clauses therein contained shall be construed most largely and beneficially for the suppressing of conventicles, and for the justification and encouragement of all persons to be employed in the execution thereof. . . .

XIII. Provided also, that no person shall be punished for any offence against this Act unless such offender be prosecuted for the same within three months after the offence committed. . . .

(c) FIRST INDULGENCE, 1672–1673

140. Declaration of Indulgence, 1672
(E. Cardwell, *Documentary Annals of the Reformed Church of England*, II, pp. 282–286)

HIS MAJESTY'S DECLARATION TO ALL HIS LOVING SUBJECTS

CHARLES R.

Our care and endeavours for the preservation of the rights and interests of the Church have been sufficiently manifested to the world by the whole course of our government since our happy restoration, and by the many and frequent ways of coercion that we have used for reducing all erring or dissenting persons, and for composing the unhappy differences in matters of religion which we found among our subjects upon our return. But it being evident by the sad experience of twelve years that there is very little fruit of all those forcible courses, we think ourself obliged to make use of that supreme power in ecclesiastical matters which is not only inherent in us but hath been declared and recognized to be so by several statutes and Acts of Parliament. And therefore we do now accordingly issue this our declaration, as well for the quieting the minds of our good subjects in these points, for inviting strangers in this conjuncture to come and live under us, and for the better encouragement of all to a cheerful following of their trade and callings, from whence we hope by the blessing of God to have many good and happy advantages to our government, as also for preventing for the future the danger that might otherwise arise from private meetings and seditious conventicles.

And in the first place, we declare our express resolution, meaning and intention to be that the Church of England be preserved and remain entire in its doctrine, discipline and government as now it stands established by law; and that this be taken to be, as it is, the basis, rule and standard of the general and public worship of God, and that the orthodox conformable clergy do receive and enjoy the revenues belonging thereunto; and that no person, though of a different opinion and persuasion, shall be exempt from paying his tithes or other dues whatsoever. And further we declare that no person shall be capable of holding any benefice, living or ecclesiastical dignity or preferment of any kind in this our kingdom of England who is not exactly conformable.

We do in the next place declare our will and pleasure to be that the execution of all and all manner of penal laws in matters ecclesiastical, against whatsoever sort of nonconformists or recusants, be immediately suspended, and they are hereby suspended; and all judges, judges of assize and gaol delivery, sheriffs, justices of the peace, mayors, bailiffs and other officers whatsoever, whether ecclesiastical or civil, are to take notice of it, and pay due obedience thereunto.

And that there may be no pretence for any of our subjects to continue their illegal meetings and conventicles, we do declare that we shall from time to time allow a sufficient number of places, as they shall be desired, in all parts of this our kingdom for the use of such as do not conform to the Church of England, to meet and assemble in in order to their public worship and devotion, which places shall be open and free to all persons. But to prevent such disorders and inconveniencies as may happen by this our indulgence, if not duly regulated, and that they may be the better protected by the civil magistrate, our express will and pleasure is that none of our subjects do presume to meet in any place until such place be allowed and the teacher of that congregation be approved by us.

And lest any should apprehend that this restriction should make our said allowance and approbation difficult to be obtained, we do further declare that this our indulgence, as to the allowance of the public places of worship and approbation of the teachers, shall extend to all sorts of nonconformists and recusants except the recusants of the Roman Catholic religion, to whom we shall in no wise allow public places of worship, but only indulge them their share in the common exemption from the execution of the penal laws, and the exercise of their worship in their private houses only.

And if after this our clemency and indulgence any of our subjects shall presume to abuse this liberty, and shall preach seditiously, or to the derogation of the doctrine, discipline or government of the established Church, or shall meet in places not allowed by us, we do hereby give them warning, and declare we will proceed against them with all imaginable severity. And we will let them see we can be as severe to punish such offenders, when so justly provoked, as we are indulgent to truly tender consciences.

Given at our court at Whitehall,
this 15th day of March,
in the four and twentieth year of our reign.

141. Petition for a licence from certain of the inhabitants of Manchester, 1672
(State Papers Domestic, Charles II, 320, f. 117)

To the king's most excellent Majesty,

The humble address and petition of several inhabitants of the town of Manchester in the county palatine of Lancaster, in the name of themselves and sundry others of the same town,

Humbly showeth,

That your Majesty's gracious declaration of the 15th of March last past, wherein your Majesty's indulgence to us is so fully manifested, is with all humble thankfulness acknowledged by us. And professing our loyalty to your sacred Majesty with all sincerity, and resolving by the grace of God to use the liberty so given us with that moderation and peaceableness that your Majesty may not have cause to repent the favour afforded to us therein, we are humble petitioners to your sacred Majesty that in pursuance thereof your Majesty would be graciously pleased to allow and license Mr. Henry Newcome, Master in Arts (being of the Presbyterian persuasion), our former minister in this place, to exercise his ministerial function amongst us; and that the house of the said Mr. Newcome hired for that purpose, situate in Manchester, may be the place allowed for their meeting.

For which royal favour to the said Mr. Newcome and us, your Majesty's most humble petitioners shall ever pray, &c.[1]

[1] Fourteen signatures follow.

142. Licence for nonconformist worship to Oliver Heywood, 1672
(*Autobiography, Diaries and Event Books*, ii, p. 17)

CHARLES R.

Charles, by the Grace of God King of England, Scotland, France and Ireland, Defender of the Faith, &c., to all mayors, bailiffs, constables and other our officers and ministers, civil and military, whom it may concern, Greeting. In pursuance of our declaration of the 15th of March 1671/2, we do hereby permit and license Oliver Heywood, of the Presbyterian persuasion, to be a teacher of the congregation allowed by us in a room or rooms in the house of John Butterworth in the parish of Halifax in the county of York, for the use of such as do not conform to the Church of England who are of the persuasion commonly called Presbyterian; with further license and permission to him, the said Oliver Heywood, to teach in any other place licensed and allowed by us according to our said declaration.

Given at our Court at Whitehall, the 25th day of July,
in the 24th year of our reign, 1672.

By his Majesty's command,
Arlington.

(*d*) PARLIAMENTARY PERSECUTION, 1673–1681

143. First Test Act, 1673
(*Statutes of the Realm*, v, pp. 782–785)

AN ACT FOR PREVENTING DANGERS
WHICH MAY HAPPEN FROM POPISH RECUSANTS

(*25 Car. II, cap. 2*)

For preventing dangers which may happen from popish recusants, and quieting the minds of his Majesty's good subjects, be it enacted . . that all and every person or persons, as well peers as commoners, that shall bear any office or offices, civil or military, or shall receive any pay, salary, fee or wages by reason of any patent or grant from his Majesty, or shall have command or place of trust from or under his Majesty, or from any of his Majesty's predecessors, or by his or their authority or by authority derived from him or them within the realm of England, dominion of Wales or town of Berwick-upon-Tweed, or in his Majesty's navy or in the several islands of Jersey and Guernsey, or shall be of the household or in the service or employment of his Majesty or of his Royal Highness the duke of York, who shall inhabit, reside or be within the city of London or Westminster, or within thirty miles distant from the same, on the first day of Easter term that shall be in the year of our Lord one thousand six hundred seventy-three or at any time during the said term, all and every the said person and persons shall personally appear before the end of the said term, or of Trinity term next following, in his Majesty's High Court of Chancery, or in his Majesty's Court of King's Bench, and there in public and open court between the hours of nine of the clock and twelve in the forenoon take the several oaths of supremacy and allegiance (which oath of allegiance is contained in the statute made in the third year of King James)[1] by law established; . . . and that all and every of the said respective persons and officers not having taken the said oaths in the said respective courts aforesaid shall on or before the first day of August one thousand six hundred seventy-three, at the quarter-sessions for that county or place where he or they shall be, inhabit or reside on the twentieth day of May, take the said oaths in open court between the said hours of nine and twelve of the clock in the forenoon; and the said respective officers aforesaid shall also receive the sacrament of the Lord's Supper according to the usage of the Church of England at or before the first day of August in the year of our Lord one thousand six hundred and seventy-three in some parish church upon some Lord's Day, commonly called Sunday, immediately after divine service and sermon.

II. And be it further enacted . . . that all and every person or persons that shall be admitted, entered, placed or taken into any office or offices . . .[2] after the first day of Easter term aforesaid, and shall inhabit, be or reside when he or they is or are so admitted or placed within the cities of London or Westminster or within thirty miles of the same, shall take the said oaths aforesaid in the said respective court or courts aforesaid in the next term after such his or their admittance or admittances into the office or offices, employment or employments aforesaid, between the hours aforesaid and no other; . . . and that all and every such person or persons to be admitted after the said first day of Easter term as aforesaid not having taken the said oaths in the said courts aforesaid shall, at the quarter-sessions for that county or place where he or they shall reside next after such his admittance or admittances into any of the said respective offices or employments aforesaid, take the said several and respective oaths as aforesaid; and all and every such person and persons so to be admitted as aforesaid shall also receive the sacrament of the Lord's Supper according to the usage of the Church of England within three months after his or their admittances in or receiving their said authority and employment, in some public church upon some Lord's Day, commonly called Sunday, immediately after divine service and sermon. . . .

III. And be it further enacted . . . that all and every the person or persons aforesaid that do or shall neglect or refuse to take the said oaths and sacrament in the said courts and places and at the respective times aforesaid shall be *ipso facto* adjudged incapable and disabled in law to all intents and purposes whatsoever to have, occupy or enjoy the said office or offices, employment or employments, . . . and every such office and place, employment and employments shall be void, and is hereby adjudged void.

IV. And be it further enacted, that all and every such person or persons that shall neglect or refuse to take the said oaths or the sacrament as aforesaid within the times and in the places aforesaid and in the manner aforesaid, and yet after such neglect and refusal shall execute any of the said offices or employments after the said times expired wherein he or they ought to have taken the same, and being thereupon lawfully convicted, . . . every such person and persons shall be disabled from thenceforth to sue, or use any action, bill, plaint or information in course of law, or to prosecute any suit

---

[1] 3. Jac. I, cap. 4.   [2] As in the preceding section.

in any court of equity, or to be guardian of any child or executor or administrator of any person, or capable of any legacy or deed of gift or to bear any office within this realm of England, dominion of Wales or town of Berwick-upon-Tweed, and shall forfeit the sum of five hundred pounds, to be recovered by him or them that shall sue for the same. . . .

VIII. And be it further enacted . . . that at the same time when the persons concerned in this Act shall take the aforesaid oaths of supremacy and allegiance they shall likewise make and subscribe this declaration following, under the same penalties and forfeitures as by this Act is appointed:

I, A.B., do declare that I do believe that there is not any transubstantiation in the sacrament of the Lord's Supper, or in the elements of bread and wine, at or after the consecration thereof by any person whatsoever.

XIII. Provided also, that nothing in this Act contained shall extend to make any forfeiture, disability or incapacity in, by or upon any non-commission officer or officers in his Majesty's navy, if such officer or officers shall only subscribe the declaration therein required in manner as the same is directed. . . .

XV. Provided also, that this Act or anything therein contained shall not extend to the office of any high constable, petty constable, tithing-man, headborough, overseer of the poor, churchwardens, surveyor of the highways or any like inferior civil office, or to any office of forester or keeper of any park, chase, warren or game, or of bailiff of any manor or lands, or to any like private offices, or to any person or persons having only any the before mentioned or any the like offices.

144. Second Test Act, 1678

(Statutes of the Realm, v, 894–896)

AN ACT FOR THE MORE EFFECTUAL PRESERVING THE KING'S PERSON AND GOVERNMENT BY DISABLING PAPISTS FROM SITTING IN EITHER HOUSE OF PARLIAMENT

(30 Car. II, stat. 2, cap. 1)

Forasmuch as divers good laws have been made for preventing the increase and danger of popery in this kingdom, which have not had the desired effects by reason of the free access which popish recusants have had to his Majesty's court, and by reason of the liberty which of late some of the recusants have had and taken to sit and vote in Parliament; wherefore, and for the safety of his Majesty's royal person and government, be it enacted . . . that from and after the first day of December which shall be in the year of our Lord God one thousand six hundred seventy and eight no person that now is or hereafter shall be a peer of this realm, or member of the House of Peers, shall vote or make his proxy in the House of Peers, or sit there during any debate in the said House of Peers, nor any person that now is or hereafter shall be a member of the House of Commons shall vote in the House of Commons, or sit there during any debate in the said House of Commons after their Speaker is chosen, until such peer or member shall from time to time respectively and in manner following first take the several oaths of allegiance and supremacy, and make, subscribe and audibly repeat this declaration following:

I, A.B., do solemnly and sincerely in the presence of God profess, testify and declare that I do believe that in the sacrament of the Lord's Supper there is not any transubstantiation of the elements of bread and wine into the body and blood of Christ at or after the consecration thereof by any person whatsoever; and that the invocation or adoration of the Virgin Mary or any other saint and the sacrifice of the mass, as they are now used in the Church of Rome, are superstitious and idolatrous. And I do solemnly in the presence of God profess, testify and declare that I do make this declaration and every part thereof in the plain and ordinary sense of the words read unto me, as they are commonly understood by English Protestants, without any evasion, equivocation or mental reservation whatsoever, and without any dispensation already granted me for this purpose by the Pope or any other authority or person whatsoever, or without any hope of any such dispensation from any person or authority whatsoever, or without thinking that I am or can be acquitted before God or man or absolved of this declaration or any part thereof, although the Pope or any other person or persons or power whatsoever should dispense with or annul the same, or declare that it was null and void from the beginning.

Which said oaths and declaration shall be in this and every succeeding Parliament solemnly and publicly made and subscribed betwixt the hours of nine in the morning and four in the afternoon by every such peer and member of the House of Peers at the table in the middle of the said House before he take his place in the said House of Peers, and whilst a full House of Peers is there with their Speaker in his place, and by every such member of the House of Commons at the table in the middle of the said House, and whilst a full House of Commons is there duly sitting with their Speaker in his chair, and that the same be done in either House in such like order or method as each House is called over by respectively.

II. And be it further enacted, that from and after the said first day of December every peer of this realm and member of the House of Peers, and every peer of the kingdom of Scotland or of the kingdom of Ireland, being of the age of one and twenty years or upwards, . . . and every member of the said House of Commons, not having as aforesaid taken the said oaths and made and subscribed the said declaration, and every person now or hereafter convicted of popish recusancy, who hereafter shall at any time after the said first day of December come advisedly into or remain in the presence of the king's Majesty or queen's Majesty, or shall come into the court or house where they or any of them reside, as well during the reign of his present Majesty (whose life God long preserve) as during the reigns of any his royal successors kings or queens of England, shall incur and suffer all the pains, penalties, forfeitures and disabilities in this Act mentioned or contained, unless such peer, member or person so convicted do respectively in the next term after such his coming or remaining take the said oaths and make and subscribe the said declaration in his Majesty's High Court of Chancery between the hours of nine and twelve in the forenoon.

III. And be it further enacted . . . that if any person that now is or hereafter shall be a peer of this realm, or member of the House of Peers or member of the House of

Commons, shall presume to do anything contrary to this Act, or shall offend in any of the cases aforesaid, that then every such peer and member so offending shall from thenceforth be deemed and adjudged a popish recusant convict to all intents and purposes whatsoever, and shall forfeit and suffer as a popish recusant convict, and shall be disabled to hold or execute any office or place of profit or trust, civil or military, in any of his Majesty's realms of England or Ireland, dominion of Wales or town of Berwick-upon-Tweed, or in any of his Majesty's islands or foreign plantations to the said realms belonging, and shall be disabled from thenceforth to sit or vote in either House of Parliament, or make a proxy in the House of Peers, or to sue or use any action, bill, plaint or information in course of law, or to prosecute any suit in any court of equity, or to be guardian of any child or executor or administrator of any person, or capable of any legacy or deed of gift; and shall forfeit for every wilful offence against this Act the sum of five hundred pounds, to be recovered and received by him or them that shall sue for the same. . . .

IV. And be it further enacted . . . that from the said first day of December it shall and may be lawful to and for the House of Peers and House of Commons or either of them respectively, as often as they or either of them shall see occasion, either in this present Parliament or any other hereafter to be holden, to order and cause all or any of the members of their respective Houses of Parliament openly in their respective Houses of Parliament to take the said oaths, and to make and subscribe the said declaration, at such times and in such manner as they shall appoint. And if any peer shall, contrary to such order made by their said House, wilfully presume to sit therein without taking the said oaths and subscribing the said declaration according to the said order, every such peer or member of the House of Peers so presuming to sit shall be adjudged, and is hereby declared, to be incapable and disabled in law to all intents and purposes whatsoever to sit in the said House of Peers and give any voice therein, either by proxy or otherwise howsoever, during that Parliament. And if any member or members of the House of Commons shall, contrary to such order made by their House, wilfully presume to sit therein without taking the said oaths and making and subscribing the said declaration, every such member or members of the House of Commons so presuming to sit shall be adjudged, and is hereby declared, to be incapable and disabled in law to all intents and purposes whatsoever to sit in the said House of Commons or give any voice therein during that Parliament.

V. And be it enacted, that in every case where any member or members of the House of Commons shall by virtue of this Act be disabled to sit or vote in the House of Commons, then and in every such case, without any further conviction or other proceeding against such member or members, the place or places for which they or any of them were elected is hereby declared void, and a new writ or writs shall issue out of the High Court of Chancery by warrant or warrants from the Speaker of the House of Commons for the time being, and by order of the said House, for the election of a new member or members to serve in the House of Commons in the place or places of such member or members so disabled, to all intents and purposes as if such member or members were naturally dead.

VI. And be it further enacted . . . that from and after the first day of December one thousand six hundred seventy and eight every person then being, and who after that time shall be, a sworn servant to the king's or queen's Majesty, not having before that time duly taken the oaths and made and subscribed the declaration contained in an Act entituled, *An Act for preventing dangers which may happen from popish recusants*,[1] shall take the said oaths and make and subscribe the declaration before expressed in his Majesty's High Court of Chancery in the manner aforesaid, either in the next term after the said first day of December or in the next term after any such person shall be so sworn a servant, or in case of lawful impediment by sickness proved upon oath and allowed to be such under the hand of the Lord Chancellor or Lord Keeper for the time being then in the next term after such impediment removed; and if any such person shall refuse or neglect to do the same, and yet after such refusal or neglect shall advisedly come into or remain in the presence of the king's or queen's Majesty, or shall come into the court or house where they or any of them reside, as well during the reign of his present Majesty as during the reigns of his and their royal successors kings or queens of England and every of them, every such person shall be disabled to hold any place as such sworn servant, and shall incur and suffer all the pains, penalties, forfeitures and disabilities in this Act mentioned or contained.

VII. Provided that nothing in this Act shall relate to or have any effect upon any person being a natural-born subject of the king of Portugal who now is or hereafter shall be a sworn servant to the queen's Majesty, not exceeding nine in number at any one time, nor to such women servants as her Majesty shall under her hand and seal from time to time for that purpose be pleased to nominate, the said women servants so nominated not exceeding the number of nine at any one time. . . .

XI. Provided always, that nothing in this Act contained shall extend to his Royal Highness the duke of York.

145. Letter from Archbishop Sancroft to Bishop Compton of London on the prosecution of papists, 1681

(E. Cardwell, *Documentary Annals of the Reformed Church of England*, II, pp. 296–298)

RIGHT REVEREND LORD AND BROTHER,

His Majesty having yesternight in Council (to the great satisfaction and joy of us all) declared his royal will and pleasure that all papists and popish recusants throughout the realm be forthwith vigorously prosecuted, and the laws of the land made against them effectually put in execution, to the end that by such wholesome severity (so seasonable and necessary at this time) they may by God's blessing upon his Majesty's pious intentions, and the endeavours of his good subjects in pursuance of the same, be either reduced into the bosom of the Church or driven out of the kingdom, I could not but immediately reflect how highly it concerns, and how well it may beseem, me and my brethren, and all that are intrusted with the manage of any jurisdiction under us, to contribute all we can, and particularly what the laws of the land and the canons of the Church require of us, for the promoting and accomplishing (if it may be) so good a design, which tends so manifestly to the glory of God, the honour of his

[1] No. 143.

Majesty's government, the prosperity and flourishing estate of that excellent religion by the peculiar blessing of heaven established among us, and the quiet and tranquillity of the whole realm.

I have therefore thought fit at present (till other and further methods may be debated and resolved on) to require all the bishops within this province and every of them, and I do hereby require them, that those three canons against popish recusants agreed upon in the synod begun at London A.D. 1603, namely the lxvth, lxvith, and the cxivth be by them, and all that hold or exercise any jurisdiction under them, forthwith exactly observed and effectually put in ure, considering how acceptable a service it will be to Almighty God to assist his Majesty's pious purpose herein, and on the other side how severe a punishment the last canon of the three appoints to those who shall neglect their duty herein, which will (I doubt not) without partiality or connivance be inflicted on them.

My Lord, my request to your lordship is that you will not only take notice of all this yourself, but cause a copy hereof, by you attested, to be transmitted to every bishop of this province in the name of

Your affectionate brother,
William Canterbury

April 9, 1681.

(e) SECOND INDULGENCE, 1687–1688

146. Declaration of Indulgence, 1687

(E. Cardwell, Documentary Annals of the Reformed Church of England, II, pp. 308–312)

HIS MAJESTY'S GRACIOUS DECLARATION
TO ALL HIS LOVING SUBJECTS
FOR LIBERTY OF CONSCIENCE

JAMES R.

It having pleased Almighty God not only to bring us to the imperial crown of these kingdoms through the greatest difficulties, but to preserve us by a more than ordinary providence upon the throne of our royal ancestors, there is nothing now that we so earnestly desire as to establish our government on such a foundation as may make our subjects happy, and unite them to us by inclination as well as duty; which we think can be done by no means so effectually as by granting to them the free exercise of their religion for the time to come, and add that to the perfect enjoyment of their property, which has never been in any case invaded by us since our coming to the crown; which, being the two things men value most, shall ever be preserved in these kingdoms during our reign over them as the truest methods of their peace and our glory.

We cannot but heartily wish, as it will easily be believed, that all the people of our dominions were members of the Catholic Church. Yet we humbly thank Almighty God it is, and hath of long time been, our constant sense and opinion (which upon divers occasions we have declared) that conscience ought not to be constrained, nor people forced in matters of mere religion; it has ever been directly contrary to our inclination, as we think it is to the interest of government, which it destroys by spoiling trade, depopulating countries and discouraging strangers; and finally, that it never obtained the end for which it was employed. And in this we are the more confirmed by the reflections we have made upon the conduct of the four last reigns; for after all the frequent and pressing endeavours that were used in each of them to reduce this kingdom to an exact conformity in religion it is visible the success has not answered the design, and that the difficulty is invincible.

We therefore, out of our princely care and affection unto all our loving subjects, that they may live at ease and quiet, and for the increase of trade and encouragement of strangers, have thought fit by virtue of our royal prerogative to issue forth this our declaration of indulgence, making no doubt of the concurrence of our two Houses of Parliament when we shall think it convenient for them to meet.

In the first place we do declare that we will protect and maintain our archbishops, bishops and clergy, and all other our subjects of the Church of England in the free exercise of their religion as by law established, and in the quiet and full enjoyment of all their possessions, without any molestation or disturbance whatsoever.

We do likewise declare that it is our royal will and pleasure that from henceforth the execution of all and all manner of penal laws in matters ecclesiastical, for not coming to Church, or not receiving the sacrament, or for any other nonconformity to the religion established, or for or by reason of the exercise of religion in any manner whatsoever, be immediately suspended; and the further execution of the said penal laws and every of them is hereby suspended.

And to the end that by the liberty hereby granted the peace and security of our government in the practice thereof may not be endangered, we have thought fit, and do hereby straitly charge and command all our loving subjects, that as we do freely give them leave to meet and serve God after their own way and manner, be it in private houses or places purposely hired or built for that use, so that they take especial care that nothing be preached or taught amongst them which may any ways tend to alienate the hearts of our people from us or our government; and that their meetings and assemblies be peaceably, openly and publicly held, and all persons freely admitted to them; and that they do signify and make known to some one or more of the next justices of the peace what place or places they set apart for those uses.

And that all our subjects may enjoy such their religious assemblies with greater assurance and protection, we have thought it requisite, and do hereby command, that no disturbance of any kind be made or given unto them, under pain of our displeasure and to be further proceeded against with the utmost severity.

And forasmuch as we are desirous to have the benefit of the service of all our loving subjects, which by the law of nature is inseparably annexed to and inherent in our royal person, and that none of our subjects may for the future be under any discouragement or disability (who are otherwise well inclined and fit to serve us) by reason of some oaths or tests that have been usually administered on such occasions, we do hereby further declare that it is our royal will and pleasure that the oaths commonly called the oaths of supremacy and allegiance, and also the several tests and declarations mentioned in the Acts of Parliament made in the 25th and 30th years of the reign of our late royal brother King Charles the Second,[1] shall not at any time hereafter be required to be taken, declared or subscribed by any person or persons whatsoever, who is or shall be employed in any office or place of trust, either civil or military, under us or in our government. And we do further declare it to be our pleasure and intention from time to time hereafter to grant our royal dispensations under our great seal to all our loving subjects so to be employed, who shall not take the said oaths, or subscribe or declare the said tests or declarations, in the above-mentioned Acts and every of them.

And to the end that all our loving subjects may receive and enjoy the full benefit and advantage of our gracious indulgence hereby intended, and may be acquitted and discharged from all pains, penalties, forfeitures and disabilities by them or any of them incurred or forfeited, or which they shall or may at any time hereafter be liable to, for or by reason of their nonconformity or the exercise of their religion, and from all suits, troubles or disturbances for the same, we do hereby give our free and ample pardon unto all nonconformists, recusants and other our loving subjects for all crimes and things by them committed or done contrary to the penal laws formerly made relating to religion and the profession or exercise thereof, hereby declaring that this our royal pardon and indemnity shall be as good and effectual to all intents and purposes as if every individual person had been therein particularly named, or had particular pardons under our great seal, which we do likewise declare shall from time to time be granted unto any person or persons desiring the same, willing and requiring our judges, justices and other officers to take notice of and obey our royal will and pleasure hereinbefore declared.

And although the freedom and assurance we have hereby given in relation to religion and property might be sufficient to remove from the minds of our loving subjects all fears and jealousies in relation to either, yet we have thought fit further to declare that we will maintain them in all their properties and possessions, as well of church and abbey lands as in any other their lands and properties whatsoever.

Given at our court at Whitehall,
the fourth day of April 1687,
in the third year of our reign.

147. Address of thanks from the Presbyterians of London, 1687
(London Gazette, 28 April–2 May 1687)

TO THE KING'S MOST EXCELLENT MAJESTY,
The humble address of several ministers of the gospel in and about the city of London, commonly called Presbyterians.

May it please your Majesty,
We, your most obedient subjects, who among many others do rejoice in the fruit of your royal bounty, do hereby most humbly and heartily make our grateful acknowledgment to Almighty God, who hath thus inclined your royal mind, and to

[1] Nos. 143, 144.

yourself, Dread Sovereign, whose princely pity now rescues us from our long sufferings, and by the same royal act restores God to the empire over conscience, and publisheth to the world your Christian judgment that conscience may not be forced, and your resolution that such force shall not be attempted in your kingdoms during your reign, which God grant may be long over us. We likewise return your Majesty most unfeigned thanks for your tender care of our rights and properties, and for declaring your further inclination to engage your two Houses of Parliament in a concurrence with you in so excellent a work, which we pray and hope God will incline them to for His glory, your Majesty's joy and honour, and for the welfare of all your Majesty's loyal subjects, that we, with others your Majesty's subjects, in a just security under your protection, may with a constant emulation strive to be most forward and faithful in our allegiance to your person and crown.

Be pleased, Dread Sovereign, graciously to accept this humble acknowledgment and unfeigned thanks of your Majesty's most obedient subjects, who do and shall, as in duty bound, ever pray, &c.

148. Address of thanks from the city of Gloucester, 1687
(London Gazette, 23–27 June 1687)

To the king's most excellent Majesty,

The humble address of the mayor, several of the aldermen, common council-men, gentlemen and burgesses, whose names are subscribed hereto, in behalf of themselves and several hundreds of the freemen of your Majesty's ancient city of Gloucester.

May it please your Majesty,

We, your Majesty's most loyal and obedient subjects, considering your passage to the royal throne has been through many unparalleled difficulties both by sea and land, we cannot but conclude the Almighty has preserved you for His own honour and glory, and to us the best of kings and the best of governments. And being convinced of what your Majesty observes, that since it hath not been in the power of human policies to reunite us in one judgment in matters of religion, your Majesty hath taken the wisest and most Christian expedient to supply that by publishing your declaration for liberty of conscience, whereby you have put an end to the groans and lamentations of many thousands of our innocent and industrious fellow subjects, strengthened the foundations of your monarchy, and given new life and vigour to your people and trade. And this, Great Sir, next to God's providence, we own proceeds from your royal wisdom and goodness, in assuming that undoubted and necessary power of dispensing with penal statutes about religion which we assert to be an inherent prerogative of your imperial crown.

At present, Dread Sovereign, the most effectual evidence we can give of our thankfulness for this blessing is to acknowledge our great joy and satisfaction to see all your people quiet at their devotions and comfortable in their several trades and employments. And we do assure you, whenever there shall be occasion to elect members of Parliament for this your city, we will endeavour to send you such as shall not only confirm by their votes the whole scope of your royal declaration, but comply with whatever else may tend to the honour of God, the peace and safety of your royal person and government, and the prosperity of your people.

And we shall always pray for your Majesty's long life and happy reign over us.

149. Declaration of Indulgence, 1688
(E. Cardwell, *Documentary Annals of the Reformed Church of England*, II, pp. 313–315)

THE KING'S DECLARATION FOR LIBERTY OF CONSCIENCE

JAMES R.

Our conduct has been such in all times as ought to have persuaded the world that we are firm and constant to our resolutions. Yet that easy people may not be abused by the malice of crafty, wicked men, we think fit to declare that our intentions are not changed since the 4th of April 1687, when we issued out our declaration for liberty of conscience in the following terms. . . .[1]

Ever since we granted this indulgence we have made it our principal care to see it preserved without distinction, as we are encouraged to do daily by multitudes of addresses, and many other assurances we receive from our subjects of all persuasions, as testimonies of their satisfaction and duty; the effects of which we doubt not but the next Parliament will plainly show, and that it will not be in vain that we have resolved to use our utmost endeavours to establish liberty of conscience on such just and equal foundation as will render it unalterable, and secure to all people the free exercise of their religion for ever, by which future ages may reap the benefit of what is so undoubtedly for the general good of the whole kingdom. It is such a security we desire, without the burden and constraint of oaths and tests, which have been un-happily made by some governments but could never support any; nor should men be advanced by such means to offices and employments, which ought to be the reward of services, fidelity and merit.

We must conclude that not only good Christians will join in this but whoever is concerned for the increase of the wealth and power of the nation. It would perhaps prejudice some of our neighbours, who might lose part of those vast advantages they now enjoy, if liberty of conscience were settled in these kingdoms, which are, above all others, most capable of improvements, and of commanding the trade of the world. In pursuance of this great work we have been forced to make many changes both of civil and military officers throughout our dominions, not thinking any ought to be employed in our service who will not contribute towards establishing the peace and greatness of their country, which we most earnestly desire, as unbiassed men may see by the whole conduct of our government, and by the condition of our fleet and of our armies, which with good management shall be constantly the same, and greater if the safety or honour of the nation require it.

We recommend these considerations to all our subjects, and that they will reflect on their present ease and happiness, how for above three years that it hath pleased God to permit us to reign over these kingdoms we have not appeared to be that prince our enemies would have made the world afraid of; our chief aim having been not to be

---

[1] The declaration of 1687 (No. 146) follows.

the oppressor but the father of our people, of which we can give no better evidence than by conjuring them to lay aside all private animosities as well as groundless jealousies, and to choose such members of Parliament as may do their parts to finish what we have begun for the advantage of the monarchy over which Almighty God has placed us, being resolved to call a Parliament that shall meet in November next at furthest.

Given at our court at Whitehall,
the 27th day of April 1688,
in the fourth year of our reign.

(f) PARLIAMENTARY TOLERATION, 1678–1700

150. Act concerning heresy, 1678

(*Statutes of the Realm*, v, p. 850)

AN ACT FOR TAKING AWAY THE WRIT
DE HERETICO COMBURENDO

(*29 Car. II, cap. 9*)

Be it enacted . . . that the writ commonly called *breve de heretico comburendo*, with all process and proceedings thereupon in order to the executing such writ, or following or depending thereupon, and all punishment by death in pursuance of any ecclesiastical censures, be from henceforth utterly taken away and abolished, any law, statute, canon, constitution, custom or usage to the contrary heretofore or now in force in any wise notwithstanding.

II. Provided always, that nothing in this Act shall extend or be construed to take away or abridge the jurisdiction of Protestant archbishops or bishops or any other judges of any ecclesiastical courts in cases of atheism, blasphemy, heresy or schism and other damnable doctrines and opinions, but that they may proceed to punish the same according to his Majesty's ecclesiastical laws by excommunication, deprivation, degradation and other ecclesiastical censures not extending to death, in such sort and no other as they might have done before the making of this Act, anything in this law contained to the contrary in any wise notwithstanding.

151. Toleration Act, 1689

(*Statutes of the Realm*, VI, pp. 74–76)

AN ACT FOR EXEMPTING THEIR MAJESTIES' PROTESTANT SUBJECTS
DISSENTING FROM THE CHURCH OF ENGLAND
FROM THE PENALTIES OF CERTAIN LAWS

(*1 Gul. & Mar., cap. 18*)

Forasmuch as some ease to scrupulous consciences in the exercise of religion may be an effectual means to unite their Majesties' Protestant subjects in interest and affection, be it enacted . . . that neither the statute made in the three and twentieth year of the reign of the late Queen Elizabeth entitled, *An Act to retain the queen's Majesty's subjects in their due obedience,*[1] nor the statute made in the twenty-ninth year of the said queen entitled, *An Act for the more speedy and due execution of certain branches of the statute made in the three and twentieth year of the queen's Majesty's reign,*[2] viz., the aforesaid Act, nor that branch or clause of a statute made in the first year of the reign of the said queen entitled, *An Act for the uniformity of common prayer and service in the Church and administration of the sacraments,*[3] whereby all persons having no lawful or reasonable excuse to be absent are required to resort to their parish church or chapel or some usual place where the common prayer shall be used, upon pain of punishment by the censures of the Church and also upon pain that every person so offending shall forfeit for every such offence twelve pence, nor the statute made in the third year of the reign of the late King James the First entitled, *An Act for the better discovering and repressing popish recusants,*[4] nor that other statute made in the same year entitled, *An Act to prevent and avoid dangers which may grow by popish recusants,*[5] nor any other law or statute of this realm made against papists or popish recusants, except the statute made in the five and twentieth year of King Charles the Second entitled, *An Act for preventing dangers which may happen from popish recusants,*[6] and except also the statute made in the thirtieth year of the said King Charles the Second entitled, *An Act for the more effectual preserving the king's person and government by disabling papists from sitting in either House of Parliament,*[7] shall be construed to extend to any person or persons dissenting from the Church of England that shall take the oaths mentioned in a statute made this present Parliament entitled, *An Act for removing and preventing all questions and disputes concerning the assembling and sitting of this present Parliament,*[8] and shall make and subscribe the declaration mentioned in a statute made in the thirtieth year of the reign of King Charles the Second entitled, *An Act to prevent papists from sitting in either House of Parliament,*[9] which oaths and declaration the justices of peace at the general sessions of the peace to be held for the county or place where such person shall live are hereby required to tender and administer to such persons as shall offer themselves to take, make and subscribe the same, and thereof to keep a register. . . .

III. And be it further enacted . . . that all and every person and persons that shall as aforesaid take the said oaths, and make and subscribe the declaration aforesaid, shall not be liable to any pains, penalties or forfeitures mentioned in an Act made in the five and thirtieth year of the reign of the late Queen Elizabeth entitled, *An Act to retain the queen's Majesty's subjects in their due obedience,*[10] nor in an Act made in the two and twentieth year of the reign of the late King Charles the Second entitled, *An Act to prevent and suppress seditious conventicles;*[11] nor shall any of the said persons be prosecuted in any ecclesiastical court for or by reason of their nonconforming to the Church of England.

IV. Provided always, and be it enacted . . . that if any assembly of persons dissenting from the Church of England shall be had in any place for religious worship with the doors locked, barred or bolted during any time of such meeting together, all and every

[1] 23 Eliz., cap. 1.
[2] 29 Eliz., cap. 6.
[3] 1 Eliz., cap. 2.
[4] 3 Jac. I, cap. 4.
[5] 3 Jac. I, cap. 5.
[6] No. 143.
[7] No. 144.
[8] No. 50.
[9] No. 144.
[10] 35 Eliz., cap. 1.
[11] No. 139.

person or persons that shall come to and be at such meeting shall not receive any benefit from this law, but be liable to all the pains and penalties of all the aforesaid laws recited in this Act for such their meeting, notwithstanding his taking the oaths and his making and subscribing the declaration aforesaid; provided always, that nothing herein contained shall be construed to exempt any of the persons aforesaid from paying of tithes or other parochial duties, or any other duties to the church or minister, nor from any prosecution in any ecclesiastical court or elsewhere for the same. . . .

VI. And be it further enacted . . . that no person dissenting from the Church of England in Holy Orders or pretended Holy Orders or pretending to Holy Orders, nor any preacher or teacher of any congregation of dissenting Protestants, that shall make and subscribe the declaration aforesaid, and take the said oaths at the general or quarter-sessions of the peace to be held for the county, town, parts or division where such person lives (which court is hereby empowered to administer the same), and shall also declare his approbation of and subscribe the articles of religion mentioned in the statute made in the thirteenth year of the reign of the late Queen Elizabeth,[1] except the thirty-fourth, thirty-fifth and thirty-sixth, and these words of the twentieth article, viz., "the Church hath power to decree rites or ceremonies, and authority in controversies of faith, and yet", shall be liable to any of the pains or penalties mentioned in an Act made in the seventeenth year of the reign of King Charles the Second entitled, *An Act for restraining nonconformists from inhabiting in corporations,*[2] nor the penalties mentioned in the aforesaid Act made in the two and twentieth year of his said late Majesty's reign, for or by reason of such persons preaching at any meeting for the exercise of religion, nor to the penalty of one hundred pounds mentioned in an Act made in the thirteenth and fourteenth of King Charles the Second entitled, *An Act for the uniformity of public prayers and administration of sacraments and other rites and ceremonies, and for establishing the form of making, ordaining and consecrating of bishops, priests and deacons in the Church of England,*[3] for officiating in any congregation for the exercise of religion permitted and allowed by this Act; . . . provided that such person shall not at any time preach in any place but with the doors not locked, barred or bolted as aforesaid.

VII. And whereas some dissenting Protestants scruple the baptizing of infants, be it enacted . . . that every person in pretended Holy Orders, or pretending to Holy Orders, or preacher or teacher, that shall subscribe the aforesaid articles of religion except before excepted, and also except part of the seven and twentieth article touching infant baptism, and shall take the said oaths and make and subscribe the declaration aforesaid in manner aforesaid, every such person shall enjoy all the privileges, benefits and advantages which any other dissenting minister as aforesaid might have or enjoy by virtue of this Act. . . .

X. And whereas there are certain other persons, dissenters from the Church of England, who scruple the taking of any oath, be it enacted . . . that every such person shall make and subscribe the aforesaid declaration and also this declaration of fidelity following, viz.,

---

[1] 13 Eliz., cap. 12.   [2] No. 138.   [3] No. 137.

I, A.B., do sincerely promise and solemnly declare before God and the world that I will be true and faithful to King William and Queen Mary, and I do solemnly profess and declare that I do from my heart abhor, detest and renounce as impious and heretical that damnable doctrine and position that princes excommunicated or deprived by the Pope or any authority of the see of Rome may be deposed or murthered by their subjects or any other whatsoever, and I do declare that no foreign prince, person, prelate, state or potentate hath or ought to have any power, juris-diction, superiority, pre-eminence or authority, ecclesiastical or spiritual, within this realm.

And shall subscribe a profession of their Christian belief in these words,

I, A.B., profess faith in God the Father, and in Jesus Christ his Eternal Son, the true God, and in the Holy Spirit, one God blessed for evermore, and do acknowledge the Holy Scriptures of the Old and New Testament to be given by divine inspiration.

And every such person that shall make and subscribe the two declarations and profession aforesaid, being thereunto required, shall be exempted from all the pains and penalties of all and every the aforementioned statutes made against popish recusants or Protestant nonconformists, and also from the penalties of an Act made in the fifth year of the reign of the late Queen Elizabeth entitled, *An Act for the assurance of the queen's royal power over all estates and subjects within her dominions,*[1] for or by reason of such persons not taking or refusing to take the oath mentioned in the said Act, and also from the penalties of an Act made in the thirteenth and fourteenth years of the reign of King Charles the Second entitled, *An Act for preventing mischiefs that may arise by certain persons called Quakers refusing to take lawful oaths,*[2] and enjoy all other the benefits, privileges and advantages under the like limitations, provisos and condi-tions which any other dissenters shall or ought to enjoy by virtue of this Act. . . .

XIII. Provided always, and it is the true intent and meaning of this Act, that all the laws made and provided for the frequenting of divine service on the Lord's Day, commonly called Sunday, shall be still in force and executed against all persons that offend against the said laws, except such persons come to some congregation or assembly of religious worship allowed or permitted by this Act.

XIV. Provided always, and be it further enacted . . . that neither this Act nor any clause, article or thing herein contained shall extend or be construed to extend to give any ease, benefit or advantage to any papist or popish recusant whatsoever, or any person that shall deny in his preaching or writing the doctrine of the Blessed Trinity as it is declared in the aforesaid articles of religion. . . .

XVI. Provided always, that no congregation or assembly for religious worship shall be permitted or allowed by this Act until the place of such meeting shall be certified to the bishop of the diocese, or to the archdeacon of that archdeaconry, or to the justices of the peace at the general or quarter-sessions of the peace for the county, city or place in which such meeting shall be held, and registered in the said bishop's or archdeacon's court respectively, or recorded at the said general or quarter-sessions. . . .

---

[1] 5 Eliz., cap. 1.   [2] 14 Car. II, cap. 1.

152. Act in relief of Quakers, 1696

(Statutes of the Realm, VII, p. 152)

AN ACT THAT THE SOLEMN AFFIRMATION AND DECLARATION
OF THE PEOPLE CALLED QUAKERS SHALL BE ACCEPTED
INSTEAD OF AN OATH IN THE USUAL FORM

(7 & 8 Gul. III, cap. 34)

Whereas divers dissenters commonly called Quakers, refusing to take an oath in courts of justice and other places, are frequently imprisoned and their estates sequestered by process of contempt issuing out of such courts, to the ruin of themselves and families, for remedy thereof, be it enacted . . . that from and after the fourth day of May which shall be in the year of our Lord one thousand six hundred ninety-six every Quaker within this kingdom of England, dominion of Wales or town of Berwick-upon-Tweed who shall be required upon any lawful occasion to take an oath in any case where by law an oath is required shall instead of the usual form be permitted to make his or her solemn affirmation or declaration in these words following, viz.,

I, A.B., do declare in the presence of Almighty God, the witness of the truth of what I say,

which said solemn affirmation or declaration shall be adjudged and taken, and is hereby enacted and declared, to be of the same force and effect to all intents and purposes in all courts of justice and other places where by law an oath is required. . . .

II. And be it further enacted . . . that if any Quaker making such solemn affirmation or declaration shall be lawfully convicted wilfully, falsely and corruptly to have affirmed or declared any matter or thing which, if the same had been in the usual form, would have amounted to wilful and corrupt perjury, every such Quaker so offending shall incur the same penalties and forfeitures as by the laws and statutes of this realm are enacted against persons convicted of wilful and corrupt perjury. . . .

V. Provided, and be it enacted, that no Quaker or reputed Quaker shall by virtue of this Act be qualified or permitted to give evidence in any criminal causes, or serve on any juries, or bear any office or place of profit in the government, anything in this Act contained to the contrary in any wise notwithstanding. . . .

(g) RENEWED PARLIAMENTARY PERSECUTION, 1700-1714

153. Act against Popery, 1700

(Statutes of the Realm, VII, pp. 586-587)

AN ACT FOR THE FURTHER PREVENTING
THE GROWTH OF POPERY

(11 Gul. III, cap. 4)

Whereas there has been of late a much greater resort into this kingdom than formerly of popish bishops, priests and Jesuits, and they do very openly and in insolent manner affront the laws and daily endeavour to pervert his Majesty's natural-born subjects, which has been occasioned by neglect of the due execution of the laws already in force; for preventing the further growth of popery and of such treasonable and execrable designs and conspiracies against his Majesty's person and government and the established religion as have lately, as well as frequently heretofore, been brought to light and happily defeated by the wonderful providence of God, be it enacted . . . that from and after the five and twentieth day of March one thousand and seven hundred all and every person and persons who shall apprehend and take one or more popish bishop, priest or Jesuit, and prosecute him or them so apprehended and taken until he or they be convicted of saying mass or of exercising any other part of the office or function of a popish bishop or priest within these realms, shall have and receive from the sheriff or sheriffs of the county where such conviction shall be made (without paying any fee for the same) for every such offender so convicted the sum of one hundred pounds within four months after such conviction. . . .

III. And for a further remedy against the growth of popery, over and beyond the good laws already made, be it further enacted . . . that if any popish bishop, priest or Jesuit whatsoever shall say mass, or exercise any other part of the office or function of a popish bishop or priest within these realms or the dominions thereunto belonging, or if any papist or person making profession of the popish religion shall keep school or take upon themselves the education or government or boarding of youth in any place within this realm or the dominions thereto belonging, and such person or persons being thereof lawfully convicted, that then every such person shall on such conviction be adjudged to perpetual imprisonment in such place or places within this kingdom as the king by advice of his Privy Council shall appoint.

IV. And be it also further enacted . . . that from and after the nine and twentieth day of September which shall be in the year of our Lord one thousand seven hundred, if any person educated in the popish religion or professing the same shall not within six months after he or she shall attain the age of eighteen years take the oaths of allegiance and supremacy, and also subscribe the declaration set down and expressed in an Act of Parliament made in the thirtieth year of the reign of the late King Charles the Second intituled, *An Act for the more effectual preserving the king's person and government by disabling papists from sitting in either House of Parliament*,[1] to be by him or her made, repeated and subscribed in the Courts of Chancery or King's Bench or quarter-sessions of the county where such person shall reside, every such person shall in respect of him or herself only, and not to or in respect of any of his or her heirs or posterity, be disabled and made incapable to inherit or take by descent, devise or limitation in possession, reversion or remainder, any lands, tenements or hereditaments within this kingdom of England, dominion of Wales or town of Berwick-upon-Tweed; and that during the life of such person, or until he or she do take the said oaths and make, repeat and subscribe the said declaration in manner as aforesaid, the next of his or her kindred which shall be a Protestant shall have and enjoy the said lands, tenements and hereditaments; . . . and that from and after the tenth day of April which shall be in the year of our Lord one thousand seven hundred every papist or person making profession of the popish religion shall be disabled, and is hereby made incapable, to purchase either in his or her own name, or in the name of any other

[1] No. 144.

person or persons to his or her use or in trust for him or her, any manors, lands, profits out of lands, tenements, rents, terms or hereditaments within the kingdom of England, dominion of Wales and town of Berwick-upon-Tweed. . . .

VI. And whereas by an Act made in the third year of King James the First intituled, *An Act to prevent and avoid dangers which may grow by popish recusants,*[1] whosoever shall be convicted of sending or causing to be sent any child or any other person under their government into parts beyond the seas out of the king's obedience, to the intent that such child or person so sent should be educated in the Romish religion contrary to the said Act, is to forfeit one hundred pounds, one half to the king's Majesty and the other half to him that shall sue for the same, for the greater encouragement and reward of those who shall discover such offenders be it enacted . . . that the said sum of one hundred pounds shall be to the sole use and benefit of him or her who shall discover and convict any person so offending. . . .

VII. And to the end that the Protestant children of popish parents may not in the lifetimes of such their parents for want of fitting maintenance be necessitated in compliance with their parents to embrace the popish religion contrary to their own inclinations, be it enacted . . . that from and after the said five and twentieth day of March one thousand seven hundred, if any such parent in order to the compelling such his or her Protestant child to change his or her religion shall refuse to allow such child a fitting maintenance suitable to the degree and ability of such parent and to the age and education of such child, then upon complaint thereof made to the Lord High Chancellor of England, or Lord Keeper of the Great Seal, or Commissioners for the Great Seal for the time being, it shall be lawful for the said Lord Chancellor, Lord Keeper or Commissioners to make such order therein as shall be agreeable to the intent of this Act.

154. Occasional Conformity Act, 1711

(*Statutes of the Realm,* IX, pp. 551–553)

AN ACT FOR PRESERVING THE PROTESTANT RELIGION
BY BETTER SECURING THE CHURCH OF ENGLAND AS BY LAW ESTABLISHED,
AND FOR CONFIRMING THE TOLERATION GRANTED TO
PROTESTANT DISSENTERS BY AN ACT INTITULED,
*AN ACT FOR EXEMPTING THEIR MAJESTIES' PROTESTANT SUBJECTS
DISSENTING FROM THE CHURCH OF ENGLAND FROM THE PENALTIES OF
CERTAIN LAWS*[2]
AND FOR SUPPLYING THE DEFECTS THEREOF,
AND FOR THE FURTHER SECURING THE PROTESTANT SUCCESSION
BY REQUIRING THE PRACTISERS OF THE LAW IN NORTH BRITAIN
TO TAKE THE OATHS AND SUBSCRIBE THE DECLARATION THEREIN MENTIONED

(*10 Annae, cap. 6*)

Whereas an Act was made in the thirteenth year of the reign of the late King Charles the Second intituled, *An Act for the well governing and regulating of corporations,*[3] and another Act was made in the five and twentieth year of the reign of the said

---

[1] 3 Jac. I, cap. 5.   [2] No. 151.   [3] No. 136.

late King Charles the Second intituled, *An Act for the preventing dangers which may happen from popish recusants*,[1] both which Acts were made for the security of the Church of England as by law established, now for the better securing the said Church, and quieting the minds of her Majesty's Protestant subjects dissenting from the Church of England, and rendering them secure in the exercise of their religious worship, as also for the further strengthening of the provision already made for the security of the succession to the crown in the House of Hanover, be it enacted . . . that if any person or persons after the five and twentieth day of March which shall be in the year of our Lord one thousand seven hundred and twelve, either peers or commoners, who have or shall have any office or offices, civil or military, or receive any pay, salary, fee or wages by reason of any patent or grant from or under her Majesty or any of her Majesty's predecessors or of her heirs or successors, or shall have any command or place of trust from or under her Majesty, her heirs or successors, or from any of her Majesty's predecessors, or by her or their authority or by authority derived from her or them, within that part of Great Britain called England, the dominion of Wales or town of Berwick-upon-Tweed, or in the navy, or in the several islands of Jersey or Guernsey, or shall be admitted into any service or employment in the household or family of her Majesty, her heirs or successors, or if any mayor, alderman, recorder, bailiff, town clerk, common council-man or other person bearing any office of magistracy or place or trust or other employment relating to or concerning the government of any the respective cities, corporations, boroughs, cinque ports and their members or other port towns within that part of Great Britain called England, the dominion of Wales, town of Berwick, or either of the isles aforesaid, who by the said recited Acts or either of them were or are obliged to receive the sacrament of the Lord's Supper according to the rites and usage of the Church of England as aforesaid, shall at any time after their admission into their respective offices or employments, or after having such patent or grant, command or place of trust as aforesaid, during his or their continuance in such office or offices, employment or employments, or having such patent or grant, command or place of trust or any profit or advantage from the same, knowingly or willingly resort to or be present at any conventicle, assembly or meeting within England, Wales, Berwick-upon-Tweed or the isles aforesaid for the exercise of religion in other manner than according to the liturgy and practice of the Church of England in any place within that part of Great Britain called England, dominion of Wales and town of Berwick-upon-Tweed or the isles aforesaid, at which conventicle, assembly or meeting there shall be ten persons or more assembled together over and besides those of the same household, if it be in any house where there is a family inhabiting, or if it be in an house or place where there is no family inhabiting then where any such ten persons are so assembled as aforesaid, or shall knowingly and willingly be present at any such meeting in such house or place as aforesaid, although the liturgy be there used, where her Majesty (whom God long preserve) and the Princess Sophia, or such others as shall from time to time be lawfully appointed to be prayed for, shall not there be prayed for in express words according to the liturgy of the Church of England, except where such particular offices of the liturgy are used

[1] No. 143.

wherein there are no express directions to pray for her Majesty and the royal family, shall forfeit forty pounds, to be recovered by him or them that shall sue for the same. . . .

II. And be it further enacted, that every person convicted in any action to be brought as aforesaid, or upon any information, presentment or indictment in any of her Majesty's courts at Westminster, or at the assizes, shall be disabled from thenceforth to hold such office or offices, employment or employments, or to receive any profit or advantage by reason of them or of any grant as aforesaid, and shall be adjudged incapable to bear any office or employment whatsoever within that part of Great Britain called England, the dominion of Wales or the town of Berwick-upon-Tweed or the isles of Jersey or Guernsey.

III. Provided always, and be it further enacted . . . that if any person or persons who shall have been convicted as aforesaid . . . shall after such conviction conform to the Church of England for the space of one year without having been present at any conventicle, assembly or meeting as aforesaid, and receive the sacrament of the Lord's Supper according to the rites and usage of the Church of England at least three times in the year, every such person or persons shall be capable of the grant of any the offices or employments aforesaid. . . .

VII. And it is hereby further enacted and declared . . . that the toleration granted to Protestant dissenters by the Act made in the first year of the reign of King William and Queen Mary intituled, *An Act for exempting their Majesties' Protestant subjects dissenting from the Church of England from the penalties of certain laws*,[1] shall be and is hereby ratified and confirmed, and that the same Act shall at all times be inviolably observed for the exempting of such Protestant dissenters as are thereby intended from the pains and penalties therein mentioned. . . .

X. And be it further enacted . . . that on or before the fifteenth day of June next all advocates, writers to the signet, notaries public and other members of the College of Justice within that part of her Majesty's kingdom of Great Britain called Scotland shall be and are hereby obliged to take and subscribe the oath appointed by the Act of the sixth year of her Majesty's reign intituled, *An Act for the better security of her Majesty's person and government*,[2] before the Lords of Session of the aforesaid part of her Majesty's kingdom, except such of the said persons who have already taken the same; and if any of the persons aforesaid do or shall neglect or refuse to take and subscribe the said oath as aforesaid, such person shall be *ipso facto* adjudged incapable and disabled in law to have, enjoy or exercise in any manner his said employment or practice.

XI. And be it further enacted . . . that in all time coming no person or persons shall be admitted to the employment of advocate, writer to the signet, notary public or any office belonging to the said College of Justice until he or they have taken and subscribed the aforesaid oath in manner as is above directed.

[1] No. 151. [2] No. 45.

155. Schism Act, 1714

(Statutes of the Realm, IX, pp. 915–917)

AN ACT TO PREVENT THE GROWTH OF SCHISM,
AND FOR THE FURTHER SECURITY OF THE CHURCHES OF ENGLAND
AND IRELAND AS BY LAW ESTABLISHED

(13 Annae, cap. 7)

Whereas by an Act of Parliament made in the thirteenth and fourteenth years of his late Majesty King Charles the Second intituled, *An Act for the uniformity of public prayers and administration of sacraments and other rites and ceremonies, and for establishing the form of making, ordaining and consecrating bishops, priests and deacons in the Church of England*,[1] it is amongst other things enacted that every schoolmaster keeping any public or private school, and every person instructing or teaching any youth in any house or private family as a tutor or schoolmaster, should subscribe before his or their respective archbishop, bishop or ordinary of the diocese a declaration or acknowledgment, in which amongst other things was contained as follows, viz., "I, A.B., do declare that I will conform to the liturgy of the Church of England as it is now by law established"; . . . and whereas notwithstanding the said Act sundry papists and other persons dissenting from the Church of England have taken upon them to instruct and teach youth as tutors or schoolmasters, and have for such purpose openly set up schools and seminaries, whereby if due and speedy remedy be not had great danger might ensue to this Church and State; for the making of the said recited Act more effectual and preventing the danger aforesaid, be it enacted . . . that every person or persons who shall from and after the first day of August next ensuing[2] keep any public or private school or seminary, or teach and instruct any youth as tutor or schoolmaster within that part of Great Britain called England, the dominion of Wales or town of Berwick-upon-Tweed, before such person or persons shall have subscribed so much of the said declaration and acknowledgment as is before recited, and shall have had and obtained a licence from the respective archbishop, bishop or ordinary of the place under his seal of office . . ., and shall be thereof lawfully convicted, . . . shall and may be committed to the common gaol of such county, riding, city or town corporate as aforesaid, there to remain without bail or mainprize for the space of three months to commence from the time that such person or persons shall be received into the said gaol.

II. Provided always, and be it hereby enacted, that no licence shall be granted by any archbishop, bishop or ordinary, unless the person or persons who shall sue for the same shall produce a certificate of his or their having received the sacrament according to the usage of the Church of England in some parish church within the space of one year next before the grant of such licence, under the hand of the minister and one of the churchwardens of the said parish, nor until such person or persons shall have taken and subscribed the oaths of allegiance and supremacy and abjuration as appointed by law, and shall have made and subscribed the declaration against transubstantiation contained in the Act made in the twenty-fifth year of the reign of King Charles the

---

[1] No. 137.   [2] 1714.

Second intituled, *An Act for preventing dangers which may happen from popish recusants,*[1] before the said archbishop, bishop or ordinary. . . .

III. And be it further enacted . . . that any person who shall have obtained a licence and subscribed the declarations and taken and subscribed the oaths as above appointed, and shall at any time after, during the time of his or their keeping any public or private school or seminary or instructing any youth as tutor or schoolmaster, knowingly or willingly resort to or be present at any conventicle, assembly or meeting within England, Wales or town of Berwick-upon-Tweed for the exercise of religion in any other manner than according to the liturgy and practice of the Church of England, or shall knowingly and willingly be present at any meeting or assembly for the exercise of religion, although the liturgy be there used, where her Majesty (whom God long preserve) and the elector of Brunswick or such others as shall from time to time be lawfully appointed to be prayed for shall not there be prayed for in express words according to the liturgy of the Church of England, except where such particular offices of the liturgy are used wherein there are no express directions to pray for her Majesty and the royal family, shall be liable to the penalties in this Act, and shall from thenceforth be incapable of keeping any public or private school or seminary, or instructing any youth as tutor or schoolmaster. . . .

VIII. Provided always, that this Act or anything therein contained shall not extend or be construed to extend to any tutor teaching or instructing youth in any college or hall within either of the universities of that part of Great Britain called England, nor to any tutor who shall be employed by any nobleman or noblewoman to teach his or her own children, grandchildren or great-grandchildren only in his or her family, provided such tutor so teaching in any nobleman or noblewoman's family do in every respect qualify himself according to this Act except only in that of taking a licence from the bishop. . . .

XII. Provided always, that this Act shall not extend or be construed to extend to any person who as a tutor or schoolmaster shall instruct youth in reading, writing, arithmetic or any part of mathematical learning only, so far as such mathematical learning relates to navigation or any mechanical art only, and so as such reading, writing, arithmetic or mathematical learning shall be taught in the English tongue only.

XIII. And whereas by an Act of Parliament made in Ireland . . .[2] it is enacted concerning schoolmasters and other persons instructing youth in private families in Ireland as in and by the above recited Act is enacted concerning schoolmasters and others instructing youth in private families in that part of Great Britain called England; and whereas it is reasonable that where the law is the same the remedy and means for enforcing the execution of the law should be the same; be it therefore enacted . . . that all and every the remedies, provisions and clauses in and by this Act given, made and enacted shall extend and be deemed, construed and adjudged to extend to Ireland in as full and effectual manner as if Ireland had been expressly named and mentioned in all and every the clauses in this Act.

[1] No. 143.   [2] Irish Act of Uniformity, 1666.

B. THE ESTABLISHMENT AND ITS RIVALS

(a) ECCLESIASTICAL CENSUS, 1676

156. Letter from Archbishop Sheldon to Bishop Compton of London authorizing the census, 1676

(D. Wilkins, *Concilia*, IV, p. 598)

RIGHT REVEREND AND MY VERY GOOD LORD,

I have thought fit, for some reasons me thereunto especially moving, to pray and require your lordship (and by you the rest of my brethren the bishops) that forthwith upon receipt hereof you send letters both to your archdeacons and commissaries within your respective dioceses, willing and straitly charging them that, as well by conference with the ministers as churchwardens of each parish within their jurisdiction, or such others as may best give them the most punctual satisfaction, they particularly inform themselves as to the several points and queries hereafter mentioned; and that, having gained the most certain information therein that they are able, they presently after their next visitation of Easter ended transmit their account thereupon in writing unto their several diocesans, and they unto your lordship, to be communicated to me with your first conveniency. And to the end that they may be the more circumspect and sudden in the performance of this business, I think it not unnecessary that there be some advertisement intimated unto them that the matters inquired of may nearly concern them in the exercise of their jurisdictions. So not doubting of your lordship's care in the premises, &c.

The inquiries are these that follow: ·

First. What number of persons, or at least families, are by common account and estimation inhabiting within each parish subject unto them?

Secondly. What number of popish recusants, or such as are suspected for recusancy, are there among such the inhabitants aforesaid?

Thirdly. What number of other dissenters are resident in such parishes, which either obstinately refuse or wholly absent themselves from the communion of the Church of England at such times as by law they are required?

It cannot be unknown unto your lordship and the rest of my brethren the bishops by what artifices and insinuations the established doctrine and discipline of the Church of England hath been both heretofore and now lately impugned; and amongst other specious pretences the consideration of the number of dissenters hath been an argument much insisted upon, as if their party were either too formidable to be suppressed, or that the combination of the several factions being infinite it were but lost labour to reinforce the censure and execution of the laws provided against them. For manifestation of which groundless and untrue assertion, and other important reasons me thereunto moving, I have thought fit at this time to pray and require your lordship. . . . And so soon as I shall receive satisfaction as to the particulars I shall be able from the fact itself to unmask and lay open the prejudices and misapprehensions wherewith some unwary persons are abused by the designs of our adversaries.

I shall, I hope, justify the diligence, zeal and integrity of both myself and brethren in the management of the charge committed to our care. And lastly, having done this, I do not doubt but the pretended increase of schism and superstition will no longer be imputed to our easiness or inadvertency; and the just number of dissenters being known their suppression will be a work very practicable, if they be not emboldened by the countenance of other authority than ourselves.

157. Letter from Bishop Morley of Winchester to the earl of Danby on the results of the census, 1676

(Historical Manuscripts Commission, *Eleventh Report*, VII, p. 14)

MY LORD,

I remember your lordship was pleased to think it fit an inquiry should be made in all the several dioceses of this kingdom by their respective bishops, what proportion or disproportion of number there is betwixt papists and not papists, as likewise betwixt other nonconformists and conformists, in order (as your lordship was then pleased to tell me) to the obviating or answering of an objection the king seemed to have against his declaring his resolution to suppress conventicles, namely, his Majesty's having been informed that the number of those that were to be suppressed did very much exceed the number of those that were to suppress them, and consequently, as the effecting of it would be impossible, so the attempting of it would be dangerous, especially if it should (as probably it would) unite the papists and all other the several sects of nonconformists together against us.

I have, therefore, for his Majesty's and your lordship's satisfaction, presumed to send you the inclosed abstract of the account I have received from my archdeacons of Hampshire and Surrey, and which they, in their late visitation of their several provinces, received from the several ministers and churchwardens of the several respective deaneries and parishes in the aforesaid counties, whereby your lordship may see that the odds of number is very much more for us than the king was informed it was against us, at least if the returns from other dioceses be answerable to this of mine, as generally I verily believe they will be. And then I hope, the king and the laws and the chief ministers of state, together with so considerable an advantage of number, being on our side, there will appear to be neither danger in attempting, nor any great difficulty in effecting, this great work, which is absolutely necessary for the securing of the legally established government of the Church, and consequently as absolutely necessary for the securing of the legally established government in the State also. And therefore I doubt not but all wise statesmen, as well as all orthodox churchmen, will be for the effectual prosecution of it. At least I think so, and think so the rather because your lordship seemed to me to be of the same opinion.

Your lordship's very humble servant,
George Winchester

Farnham Castle, 10 June 1676

Of the number of papists set down in the inclosed abstract there are but few above an hundred in Surrey. All the rest are in Hampshire, as appears by the book I have sent to my lord of London (and which I presume he will show unto your lordship), containing a particular account of the several sorts that were to be numbered, from the ministers and churchwardens of all the several parishes in the whole diocese. The persons numbered in the account are all of both sexes from sixteen years old upwards, that being the age at which men and women are required by the canon to receive the communion.

158. Figures disclosed by the census

(Calendar of State Papers Domestic, 1693, pp. 448-450)

THE NUMBER OF FREEHOLDERS IN ENGLAND, CONFORMISTS, NONCONFORMISTS AND PAPISTS

	Conformists	*Nonconformists*	*Papists*
Province of Canterbury	2,123,362	93,151	11,878
Province of York	353,892	15,525	1,978
	2,477,254	108,676	13,856

According to which account the proportion of

Conformists to nonconformists is $22\frac{4}{5}$

Conformists to papists is $178\frac{10}{13}$ ⎫

Conformists and nonconformists together to papists is $186\frac{2}{3}$ ⎬ to one

⎭

Papists in the several provinces above the age of 16

Canterbury	142	Coventry and Lichfield	1,949
London	2,069	Hereford	714
Winchester	968	Gloucester	124
Rochester	64	Bristol	199
Norwich	671	Peterborough	163
Lincoln	1,244	Oxford	358
Ely	14	St. Davids	217
Chichester	385	Llandaff	551
Salisbury	548	Bangor	19
Exeter	298	St. Asaph	275
Bath and Wells	176		
Worcester	719		11,867

	Conformists	*Non-conformists*	$\%$[1]	*Papists*	$\%$[1]
Canterbury	59,596	6,287	9·52	143	·22
London	263,385	20,893	7·30	2,069	·72
Winchester	150,937	7,904	4·95	968	·61

[1] Percentage of the total. These columns are not part of the original document.

	Conformists	Non-conformists	%	Papists	%
Rochester	27,886	1,752	5·90	64	·22
Norwich	168,760	7,934	4·47	671	·32
Lincoln	215,077	10,001	4·42	1,244	·55
Ely	30,917	1,416	4·38	14	·04
Chichester	49,164	2,452	4·72	385	·75
Salisbury	103,671	4,075	3·76	548	·51
Exeter	207,570	5,406	2·54	298	·14
Bath and Wells	145,464	5,856	3·87	176	·12
Worcester	37,489	1,325	3·35	719	1·82
Coventry and Lichfield	155,720	5,042	3·10	1,949	1·20
Hereford	65,942	1,076	1·59	714	1·05
Gloucester	64,734	2,363	3·52	128	·19
Bristol	66,200	2,200	3·21	199	·29
Peterborough	91,444	2,031	2·17	167	·18
Oxford	38,812	1,122	2·79	358	·89
St. David's	68,242	2,368	3·34	217	·31
Llandaff	39,248	719	1·77	551	1·36
Bangor	28,016	247	·87	19	·07
St. Asaph	45,088	635	1·38	275	·58
	2,123,362	93,104		11,876	

There are in the province of Canterbury 23,740 papists. Half of these are under the age of 16 years, viz., 11,870. A seventh part of these are of age [60] and above. Taking out of the said number of papists the two last sums, which make in all 15,261, there remain then 8,479, of which one half are women. There remain therefore in the province of Canterbury fit to bear arms 4,239 papists.

The province of York has only a sixth part of the people as that of Canterbury has, viz., 3,956, whereof half are under the age of 16, viz., 1,978, and a seventh part above 60, viz., 565, and of the aforesaid sixth part one half are women. The total therefore of papists in the province of York fit to bear arms is 701; joining which to the total of the papists in the province of Canterbury fit to bear arms makes the total of the papists throughout all England fit to bear arms to be 4,940.

There being everywhere as many under the age of 16 as above it, the total of the papists in the whole province is 23,740.

An account of the province of Canterbury

In taking these accounts we find these things observable:

1. That many left the Church upon the late indulgence who before did frequent it.

2. Sending for the present inquiries has caused many to frequent the Church.

3. That they are Walloons chiefly that make up the number of dissenters in Canterbury, Sandwich and Dover.

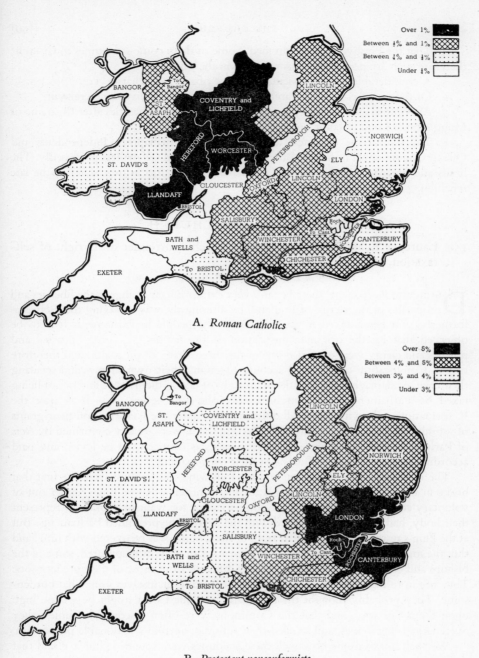

Over 1%

Between ½% and 1%

Between ¼% and ½%

Under ¼%

A. *Roman Catholics*

Over 5%

Between 4% and 5%

Between 3% and 4%

Under 3%

B. *Protestant nonconformists*

5. PROVINCE OF CANTERBURY

SHOWING THE PERCENTAGE OF ROMAN CATHOLICS AND PROTESTANT
NONCONFORMISTS IN THE TOTAL POPULATION OF EACH DIOCESE, 1676

4. That the Presbyterians are divided. Some of them come sometimes to Church; therefore such are not wholly dissenters upon the third inquiry.

5. A considerable part of dissenters are not of any sect whatsoever.

6. Of those that come to Church very many do not receive the sacrament.

7. At Ashford and at other places we find a new sort of heretics after the name of Muggleton, a London tailor, in number 30.

8. The rest of the dissenters are Presbyterians, Anabaptists, Independents and Quakers, about equal numbers; only two or three called self-willers professedly. The heads and preachers of the several factions are such as had a great share in the late rebellion.

(b) ANGLICAN CHURCH

159. Laurence Echard's account of the Church's surrender of its right of self-taxation, 1665

(*History of England*, ed. 1718, III, pp. 129–130)

During this Parliament[1] there began a very extraordinary change in the liberties and properties of the clergy of England, by altering the way of taxing themselves as formerly, and being taxed in common with the people in Parliament. It is to be observed that by the original constitution of the nation the Lords Spiritual and prelates and clergy were esteemed one of the three estates of the realm, and therefore met in Convocation on the civil account of giving their own money and securing their own secular rights and liberties. This right of taxing themselves, and of not being taxed by Parliaments, had been inviolably observed before as well as after the Reformation, only with this small difference, that after the Reformation their grants of subsidy, for the more certainty of collecting them, were usually confirmed by Acts of Parliament. And yet they gave benevolences as formerly, to be levied and paid according to rules and constitutions of their own making.

The rebellion in the late reign, and the following usurpations, were the first that broke in upon this peculiar privilege, for the ministers of those times, either out of voluntary compliance, affectation of popularity, or for want of proxies to represent their body, had their benefices taxed with the laity in the pretended Parliaments. But at the king's restoration this ancient right of the Church was recovered with him; and thus the matter continued for the first four years. But now, as it appeared, some of the bishops and clergy fell into sentiments very different from those of their predecessors. They began to think this customary method of taxing themselves somewhat burdensome. They probably thought the expectations of the Court might be set too high upon them this way, and that the Commons were often discontented unless they overcharged themselves, and swelled their subsidies beyond a reasonable proportion.

We shall not examine how well these jealousies were founded; but it is said that the apprehension of these and other inconveniences brought Archbishop Sheldon and some other leading prelates into a concert with Chancellor Clarendon, Treasurer Southampton and some others of the ministry. And now at a consultation it was

[1] Session 1664–1665.

concluded that the clergy should silently waive the ancient custom of taxing their own body, and suffer themselves to be included in the money bills prepared by the House of Commons. And to encourage their assent to this cession two of their four subsidies they had granted last year were to be remitted; and over and above they had the promise of a clause for saving their ancient rights.

This being complied withal, the security was accordingly given, and a very clear comprehensive proviso inserted in the *Act for granting a Royal Aid unto the king's Majesty*,[1] which ought not to be forgot. It stands thus: "Provided always, and be it enacted by the authority aforesaid, that all spiritual promotions, and all lands, possessions or revenues annexed to, and all goods and chattels growing or renewed upon, the same or elsewhere, appertaining to the owners of the said spiritual promotions or any of them, which are or shall be charged or made contributing to this Act towards the payment aforesaid, during the time therein appointed (which was to be raised, levied and paid in the space of three years), shall be absolutely freed and discharged from the two last of the four subsidies granted by the clergy to his Majesty, his heirs and successors, by an Act made in the former session of this present Parliament, entituled, *An Act for confirming of four subsidies granted by the clergy*,[2] any clause or thing in the said Act to the contrary notwithstanding. Provided always, that nothing herein contained shall be drawn into example to the prejudice of the ancient rights belonging unto the Lords Spiritual and Temporal or clergy of this realm, or unto either of the said universities, or unto any colleges, schools, alms-houses, hospitals or cinque ports."

Notwithstanding this saving proviso, which has expressly secured all rights, the clergy seemed to have acquiesced for the future, and never after reassumed their great claim; and from this time, during the whole reign, the Convocation met principally for form's sake. The parochial clergy, however, gained one privilege which they had not before, which was their voting for members of the House of Commons; but whether they were gainers or losers in the whole has been a matter of some dispute. Yet we think a little consideration may determine whether the gaining of the latter privilege be a full compensation for the waiving, if not the losing, the former.

160. Count Lorenzo Magalotti's description of an English cathedral service, 1669
(*Travels of Cosmo, Grand Duke of Tuscany*, pp. 129–131)

On the 7th [April 1669] his Highness went to the cathedral church [of Exeter] at the hour of prayer, about nine o'clock, and stood a considerable time in conversation with Signor Castiglini and Sergeant-Major Andrews in the body of the church, observing with much curiosity the place set apart for the offices of religion, which are performed according to the Anglican liturgy by the clergy assisted by the bishop, who is at present Dr. Anthony Sparrow, lately elected to this see, which was vacated by the translation of Dr. Seth Ward to that of Salisbury. The bishop was seated in a marble tabernacle, on the Epistle-side, on a seat covered with red cloth, dressed in the habit which was used by the Catholic bishops of the kingdom before the apostasy, namely, a

---

[1] No. 115.   [2] 15 Car. II, cap. 10.

surplice over a black vest and a mantle of the same colour. On his head he wore a small cap, similar to that of the Roman pontiffs, without any other ornament; and before him, on the edge of the tabernacle, over which was extended a large canopy of red cloth, was placed a cushion, and on that the book. And under the tabernacle, on a level with the floor of the church, in an inclosure of wood, stood the wife of the bishop, and his children, no less than nine in number.

In the prebendal stalls sat, according to their rank, the dignitaries and canons in their canonical habits, i.e., a surplice and a mantle of black silk, differing in shape from that of the bishop, as being narrower both before and behind. These, in conjunction with other regular choristers, sang the psalms in the English language, in a chant similar to the Gregorian, making their pauses to the sound of the organ, which has been erected lately on the wall separating the choir from the rest of the church, and is of a most exquisite tone. In reciting the prayers ordained by their ritual they all fell on their knees, the choir making alternate responses; and after a chapter from Scripture and from one of the epistles of St. Paul had been read a minister went to the altar in his surplice, and turning round to the people read distinctly, standing, the Commandments of the Decalogue; and at each commandment the choir answered in their own language, with a musical cadence, "Lord, have mercy upon us".

When this was over a hymn was first given out by a singer under the pulpit, and then sung by the whole choir; and this being ended the preacher, in his surplice, immediately began his sermon, leaning on a cushion placed in the middle of the pulpit, which is opposite to the bishop's seat, who is obliged to attend at the prescribed times, both at morning prayers and at vespers, and at all the other offices.

161. Ecclesiastical Revenues, 1680

(A Book of the Valuations of all the Ecclesiastical Preferments in England and Wales, 1680)

(a) Bishops

	l.	s.	d.
Canterbury	4,233	18	8
York	1,000	0	0
Bangor	131	16	4
Bath and Wells	527	14	2
Bristol	383	8	4
Carlisle	531	4	11
Chester	420	1	8
Chichester	677	1	3
Durham	2,821	1	5
Ely	2,134	18	5
Exeter	1,566	14	6
Gloucester	315	7	2
Hereford	768	10	10
Lichfield and Coventry	703	5	2
Lincoln	830	18	1

	l.	s.	d.
Llandaff	154	14	1
London	1,117	8	4
Norwich	499	8	7
Oxford	354	16	4
Peterborough	414	19	11
Rochester	358	3	8
St. Asaph	187	11	6
St. David's	457	1	10
Salisbury	1,367	11	8
Winchester	3,885	3	3
Worcester	1,049	17	3

(b) Lower clergy[1]
County of Devon

Deanery of Exeter	158	0	0
Precentorship in the cathedral church of Exeter	99	13	4
Chancellorship there	59	0	0
Treasurership there	32	17	3
Archdeaconry of Exeter	60	15	8
Archdeaconry of Cornwall	50	6	3
Archdeaconry of Totnes	36	19	3
Archdeaconry of Barnstaple	48	19	8
Subdeanery of the said church	22	10	0
In the cathedral church of Exeter there are			
24 prebends, each of which amounts to	4	0	0
Prebend of Carswill is worth per annum	2	13	4

Deanery of Honiton

Rectory of Honiton	40	4	2
Rectory of Gittisham	21	8	10
Vicarage of Seaton	17	3	6
Vicarage of Axmouth	23	19	2
Rectory of St. Pancras	2	10	10
Rectory of Uplyme	20	8	11
Rectory of Combpyne	8	11	7
Rectory of Musbury	19	11	7
Rectory of Southleigh	11	8	8

County of Hertford

Rectory of North Berkhampstead	21	1	2
Rectory of Berkhampstead	20	0	0

[1] A selection.

	l.	s.	d.
Rectory of Tring	77	13	4
Rectory of Flamstead	41	6	8
Vicarage of Great Gaddesden	10	1	10
Rectory of Little Gaddesden	11	12	8
Rectory of Aldbury	20	8	6
Rectory of Shenley	16	8	0
Rectory of Puttenham	10	1	0
Vicarage of Kensworth	9	13	4
Vicarage of Aldenham	24	0	0
Vicarage of North Mimms	10	0	0
Vicarage of Hemel Hempstead	16	1	10
Rectory of Wheathampstead with the chapel of Harpenden	42	1	10
Vicarage of Kings Langley	8	0	0

County of York

Deanery of the metropolitan church of York	308	10	7
Precentorship in the said church	89	10	8
Prebend of Ulleskelf	24	11	8
Archdeaconry of York	90	3	0
Chancellorship of York	85	6	8
Treasurership there	233	6	8
Subdeanery there	50	4	0
Archdeaconry of the East Riding	62	14	2
Archdeaconry of Cleveland	26	0	8
Archdeaconry of Nottingham	61	0	8

Deanery of Pontefract

Rectory of Ackworth	22	1	0
Rectory of Crofton	10	0	1
Rectory of Methley	25	8	11
Rectory of Castleford	20	13	1
Rectory of Emley	14	0	6
Vicarage of Halifax	84	14	6
Vicarage of Normanton	7	0	0
Vicarage of Adlingfleet	9	12	10
Vicarage of Featherstone	5	8	6
Vicarage of Almondbury	20	7	11

162. Queen Anne's Bounty Act, 1704

(Statutes of the Realm, VIII, pp. 303-304)

AN ACT FOR THE MAKING MORE EFFECTUAL HER MAJESTY'S GRACIOUS INTENTIONS
FOR THE AUGMENTATION OF THE MAINTENANCE OF THE POOR CLERGY,
BY ENABLING HER MAJESTY TO GRANT IN PERPETUITY
THE REVENUES OF THE FIRST-FRUITS AND TENTHS,
AND ALSO FOR ENABLING ANY OTHER PERSONS
TO MAKE GRANTS FOR THE SAME PURPOSE

(2 & 3 Annae, cap. 20)

Whereas at a Parliament holden in the six and twentieth year of the reign of King Henry the Eighth the first-fruits, revenues and profits for one year upon every nomination or appointment to any dignity, benefice, office or promotion spiritual within this realm, or elsewhere within the said king's dominions, and also a perpetual yearly rent or pension amounting to the value of the tenth part of all the revenues and profits belonging to any dignity, benefice or promotion spiritual whatsoever within any diocese of this realm or in Wales, were granted to the said King Henry the Eighth, his heirs and successors; . . . and whereas a sufficient settled provision for the clergy in many parts of this realm have never yet been made, by reason whereof divers mean and stipendiary preachers are in many places entertained to serve the cures and officiate there, who, depending for their necessary maintenance upon the good-will and liking of their hearers, have been and are thereby under temptation of too much complying, and suiting their doctrines and teaching to the humours rather than the good of their hearers, which hath been a great occasion of faction and schism and contempt of the ministry; and forasmuch as your Majesty, taking into your princely and serious consideration the mean and insufficient maintenance belonging to the clergy in divers parts of this your kingdom, has been most graciously pleased . . . not only to remit the arrears of your tenths due from your poor clergy, but also to declare unto your most dutiful and loyal Commons your royal pleasure and pious desire that the whole revenue arising from the first-fruits and tenths of the clergy might be settled for a perpetual augmentation of the maintenance of the said clergy in places where the same is not already sufficiently provided for, we, your Majesty's most dutiful and loyal subjects, the Commons of England in Parliament assembled . . . do most humbly beseech your Majesty that it may be enacted, and be it enacted . . . that it shall and may be lawful for the queen's most excellent Majesty, by her letters patents under the great seal of England, to incorporate such persons as her Majesty shall therein nominate or appoint to be one body politic and corporate, to have a common seal and perpetual succession, and also at her Majesty's will and pleasure, by the same or any other letters patents, to grant, limit or settle to or upon the said corporation and their successors for ever all the revenue of first-fruits and yearly perpetual tenths of all dignities, offices, benefices and promotions spiritual whatsoever, to be applied and disposed of to and for the augmentation of the maintenance of such parsons, vicars, curates and ministers officiating in any church or chapel within the kingdom of England, dominion of Wales and town of Berwick-upon-Tweed, where the liturgy and rites of the Church of England as now by law established are or shall be used and observed, . . . the statute made in the first year of her said Majesty's reign entituled, *An Act for the better support of her Majesty's household and of the honour and dignity of the Crown*,[1] or any other law to the contrary in any wise notwithstanding. . . .

IV. And for the encouragement of such well disposed persons as shall by her Majesty's royal example be moved to contribute to so pious and charitable a purpose, and that such their charity may be rightly applied, be it enacted . . . that all and every person and persons having in his or their own right any estate or interest in possession, reversion or contingency of or in any lands, tenements or hereditaments, or any property of or in any goods or chattels, shall have full power . . . to give and grant to and vest in the said corporation and their successors all such his, her or their estate, interest or property in such lands, tenements and hereditaments, goods and chattels, or any part or parts thereof, for and towards the augmentation of the maintenance of such ministers as aforesaid, officiating in such church or chapel where the liturgy and rites of the said Church are or shall be so used or observed as aforesaid, and having no settled competent provision belonging to the same. . . .

163. Address of thanks for the queen's bounty from the clergy of the diocese of Canterbury, 1704

(London Gazette, 18–22 May 1704)

To THE QUEEN'S MOST EXCELLENT MAJESTY,

The humble address of the archbishop, dean and chapter, and parochial clergy of Canterbury.

May it please your most sacred Majesty.

The extraordinary compassion and encouragement which your Majesty hath been pleased to extend to the poorer clergy in this kingdom, by applying your royal bounty of first-fruits and tenths to their more comfortable subsistence, justly obliges the whole order to be particular in their most humble and thankful acknowledgments, since all have indeed their share in it, for even they who do not actually receive this charity have yet the truly Christian satisfaction of seeing their brethren and fellow-servants put in a more easy and decent condition of living, and somewhat of that contempt taken off which reflected on the rest from their low circumstances. We may all be entirely assured of your Majesty's favour to our body, since you have been so graciously pleased to make its meanest members the object of your pious care and beneficence, which do not, like private charities, give relief alone, but bring honour also with them from the fountain whence they flow.

Your Majesty so liberally upon all occasions imparting to your subjects the blessings you receive from God, they must be not only ungrateful to so truly nursing a mother but enemies to themselves, who do not heartily join in all the prayers made for your Majesty's long and happy reign, and who do not contribute their utmost

---

[1] 1 Annae, cap. 1.

endeavours to render it such by leading quiet, peaceable and honest lives under you. Thus we in particular shall always pray ourselves, and thus both by our doctrine and example shall by God's assistance teach your Majesty's subjects in our respective cures always to pray and practise.

May it please Almighty God to reward and to perpetuate the noble fruits of your Majesty's piety and great goodness by all possible blessings upon your own royal person and government, and by continuing to preserve our most holy religion in the Church of England, and the Protestant succession as established by law.

(c) NONCONFORMIST ORGANIZATIONS

164. Gilbert Burnet on the rise and development of dissent, 1662–1689

(*History of His Own Time*, ed. 1833, I, pp. 349–350; III, pp. 161–162; IV, pp. 14–22)

(i) 1662

There was a great debate in Council, a little before St. Bartholomew's day, whether the Act of Uniformity should be punctually executed or not. Some moved to have the execution of it delayed to the next session of Parliament. Others were for executing it in the main, but to connive at some eminent men, and to put curates into their churches to read and officiate according to the common prayer, but to leave them to preach on till they should die out. The earl of Manchester laid all these things before the king with much zeal but with no great force. Sheldon, on the other hand, pressed the execution of the law. England was accustomed to obey laws; so while they stood on that ground they were safe, and needed fear none of the dangers that seemed to be threatened. He also undertook to fill all the vacant pulpits that should be forsaken in London better and more to the satisfaction of the people than they had been before; and he seemed to apprehend that a very small number would fall under the deprivation, and that the gross of the party would conform.

On the other hand those who led the party took great pains to have them all stick together. They infused it into them that if great numbers stood out, that would show their strength and produce new laws in their favour, whereas they would be despised if, after so much noise made, the greater part of them should conform. So it was thought that many went out in the crowd to keep their friends company. Many of these were distinguished by their abilities and zeal. They cast themselves upon the providence of God and the charity of their friends, which had a fair appearance, as of men that were ready to suffer persecution for their consciences. This begot esteem and raised compassion, whereas the old clergy, now much enriched, were as much despised. But the young clergy that came from the universities did good service.

(ii) 1687

The dissenters were divided into four main bodies, the Presbyterians, the Independents, the Anabaptists and the Quakers. The two former had not the visible distinction of different rites; and their depressed condition made, that the dispute about the constitution and subordination of churches, which had broken them when power was in their hands, was now out of doors: and they were looked on as one body, and were above three parts in four of all the dissenters. The main difference between these was that the Presbyterians seemed reconcilable to the Church, for they loved episcopal ordination and a liturgy, and upon some amendments seemed disposed to come into the Church; and they liked the civil government and limited monarchy. But as the Independents were for a commonwealth in the state, so they put all the power of the Church in the people, and thought that their choice was an ordination; nor did they approve of set forms of worship. Both were enemies to this high prerogative that the king was assuming, and were very averse to popery. They generally were of a mind as to the accepting the king's favour, but were not inclined to take in the papists into a full toleration. Much less could they be prevailed on to concur in taking off the tests.

The Anabaptists were generally men of virtue and of an universal charity; and as they were far from being in any treating terms with the Church of England, so nothing but an universal toleration could make them capable of favour or employments. The Quakers had set up such a visible distinction in the matter of the hat, and saying "thou" and "thee", that they had all as it were a badge fixed on them; so they were easily known.

(iii) 1689

I happened to come into the House of Lords when two great debates were managed with much heat in it. The one was about the toleration and comprehension, and the other was about the imposing the oaths on the clergy. And I was engaged at my first coming there to bear a large share in both.

That which was long insisted on in the House of Lords was that, instead of the clause positively enacting that the clergy should be obliged to take the oaths, the king might be empowered to tender them; and then the refusal was to be punished according to the clause as it stood in the Act. It was thought such a power would oblige them to their good behaviour, and be an effectual restraint upon them. They would be kept quiet at least by it, whereas if they came under deprivation, or the apprehensions of it, that would make them desperate, and set them on to undermine the government. It was said that the clergy, by the offices of the Church, did solemnly own their allegiance to God in the sight of all their people; that no oath could lay deeper engagements on them than those acts of religious worship did; and if they should either pass over those offices, or perform them otherwise than as the law required, there was a clear method, pursuant to the Act of Uniformity, to proceed severely against them. It was also said that in many different changes of government oaths had not proved so effectual a security as was imagined. Distinctions were found out, and senses were put on words, by which they were interpreted so as to signify but little when a government came to need strength from them. And it ill became those who had formerly complained of these impositions to urge this with so much vehemence.

On the other hand it was urged that no man ought to be trusted by a government, chiefly in so sacred a concern, who would not give security to it, especially since the oath was brought to such low and general terms. The expedient that was proposed

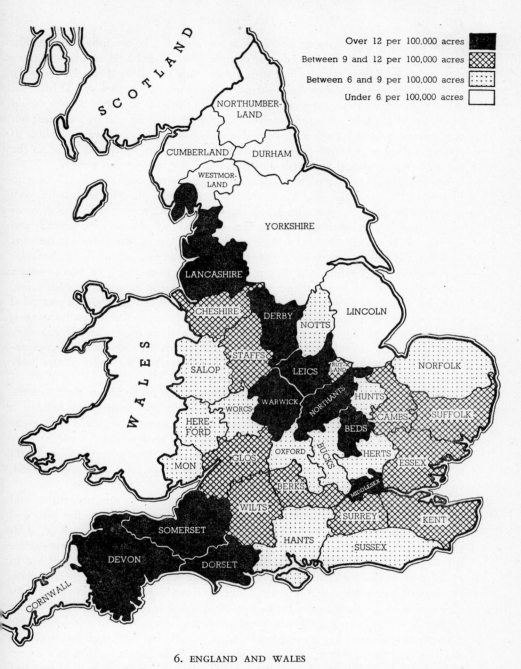

Over 12 per 100,000 acres

Between 9 and 12 per 100,000 acres

Between 6 and 9 per 100,000 acres

Under 6 per 100,000 acres

SCOTLAND

NORTHUMBER-
LAND

CUMBERLAND   DURHAM

WESTMOR-
LAND

YORKSHIRE

LANCASHIRE

CHESHIRE   DERBY   LINCOLN

NOTTS

WALES

STAFFS

SALOP   LEICS   RUT-   NORFOLK
                   LAND

WARWICK   NORTHANTS   HUNTS

WORCS   SUFFOLK
                    CAMBS

HERE-
FORD   BEDS

GLOS   OXFORD   HERTS
                  BUCKS
MON   ESSEX

BERKS   MIDDLESEX

WILTS   SURREY   KENT

SOMERSET   HANTS   SUSSEX

DEVON   DORSET

CORNWALL

6. ENGLAND AND WALES

WING DISTRIBUTION OF PROTESTANT NONCONFORMISTS AS INDICATED BY THE LICENCES FOR
SONS AND PLACES ISSUED IN ACCORDANCE WITH THE PROVISIONS OF THE DECLARATION OF
INDULGENCE OF 1672

would put a hardship upon the king, which was always to be carefully avoided. The day prefixed was at the distance of some months, so that men had time sufficient given them to study the point; and if in that time they could not satisfy themselves as to the lawfulness of acknowledging the government it was not fit that they should continue in the highest posts of the Church. An exception of twelve was proposed, who should be subject to the law, upon refusing the oaths, when required to it by the king; but that was rejected, and all the mitigation that was obtained was a power to the king to reserve a third part of the profits of any twelve benefices he should name to the incumbents who should be deprived by virtue of this Act. And so it passed. . . .

As for the Act of Comprehension, some progress was made in it. . . . Those who had moved for this bill, and afterwards brought it into the House, acted a very disingenuous part, for while they studied to recommend themselves by this show of moderation they set on their friends to oppose it; and such as were very sincerely and cordially for it were represented as the enemies of the Church, who intended to subvert it. When the bill was sent down to the House of Commons it was let lie on the table; and instead of proceeding in it they made an address to the king for summoning a convocation of the clergy to attend, according to custom, on the session of Parliament. The party that was now beginning to be formed against the government pretended great zeal for the Church, and declared their apprehensions that it was in danger, which was imputed by many to the earl of Nottingham's management. These, as they went heavily into the toleration, so they were much offended with the bill of comprehension, as containing matters relating to the Church in which the representative body of the clergy had not been so much as advised with.

Nor was this bill supported by those who seemed most favourable to the dissenters. They set it up for a maxim that it was fit to keep up a strong faction both in Church and State, and they thought it was not agreeable to that to suffer so great a body as the Presbyterians to be made more easy, or more inclinable to unite to the Church. They also thought that the toleration would be best maintained when great numbers should need it and be concerned to preserve it. So this good design being zealously opposed, and but faintly promoted, it fell to the ground.

The clergy began now to show an implacable hatred to the nonconformists, and seemed to wish for an occasion to renew old severities against them. But wise and good men did very much applaud the quieting the nation by the toleration. . . . This bill gave the king great content. He in his own opinion always thought that conscience was God's province, and that it ought not to be imposed on; and his experience in Holland made him look on toleration as one of the wisest measures of government. He was much troubled to see so much ill humour spreading among the clergy, and by their means over a great part of the nation. He was so true to his principle herein that he restrained the heat of some who were proposing severe Acts against papists. He made them apprehend the advantage which that would give the French, to alienate all the papists of Europe from us, who from thence might hope to set on foot a new Catholic league, and make the war a quarrel of religion, which might have very bad effects. Nor could he pretend to protect the Protestants in many places of Germany and in Hungary unless he could cover the papists in England from all severities on the account of their religion. This was so carefully infused into many, and so well understood by them, that the papists have enjoyed the real effects of the toleration though they were not comprehended within the statute that enacted it.

165. Nonconformists in the suburbs of London and Westminster, 1711

(*Journals of the House of Commons*, XVI, pp. 582–583)

The said committee, having also taken into consideration the instructions from the House, to consider what churches are wanting within the cities of London and Westminster and suburbs thereof, and also to consider of the scheme laid before the House by the lower house of Convocation (referred likewise to this committee), do find:

That the computations in the said scheme have been carefully made.

That within the parishes mentioned in the said scheme there are but 28 churches, and chapels, or tabernacles, 18.

That there are within these parishes meeting-houses for Presbyterians, 26; Anabaptists, 23; for Quakers, 14; for Independents, 12, in all 75, and also 13 French congregations.

That there are, by computation, within the said parishes 80,159 families, and in those families about 513,000 souls.

That allowing the 18 chapels, or tabernacles, to be capable of receiving as many persons as 8 churches do, and supposing the present number of churches upon that allowance to be 36, and 4,750 souls to belong to each of those 36 churches, they will in the whole contain but 171,000 souls, which is only a third part of the said 513,000 souls; so that there will be about 342,000 (being two thirds of the whole number of souls) for whom no churches are as yet provided.

That upon the foot of this computation 72 new churches would be requisite for the reception of those two thirds, if all of them were of the communion of the Church of England; but the committee do compute that the number of French Protestants and dissenters within the said parishes mentioned in the said scheme do amount to about 101,500, which being deducted out of 342,000 there will remain 240,500 of the communion of the Church of England for whom no churches are provided.

Whereupon the committee came to the following resolution:

Resolved, that it is the opinion of this committee that in the several parishes in and about the suburbs of the cities of London and Westminster 50 new churches are necessary to be erected for the reception of all such as are of the communion of the Church of England, computing 4,750 souls to each church.

Part V

LOCAL GOVERNMENT AND SOCIAL LIFE

LOCAL GOVERNMENT AND SOCIAL LIFE

Introduction

ENGLAND in the later Stuart period bore little resemblance to England of the twentieth century. Not only was the industrialization of the country merely beginning, and even the development of its commerce still in an early stage, but the whole outlook of its inhabitants, as befitted a community mainly agricultural in character, was vastly different. Far from being national or international, it was intensely local and provincial. Every village, every town, every county had a genuine life of its own, which meant infinitely more to those who took part in it than the life of England as a whole. Many men ran their entire course from the cradle to the grave without straying as much as ten miles from the place where they were born, and even for the well-to-do the county town was apt to be the most distant centre of common intercourse.

By this provincialism the natural diversity of England, sufficiently marked in any case, was enhanced to a degree which made any general description of the country impossible. The south-west,[1] the south-east,[2] the north,[3] the midlands[4] and Wales,[5] all had their own characteristics, lovingly set forth by visitors, some foreign but more English, who saw much to praise and little to condemn; and within each of these areas in turn the greatest variety prevailed. The pride which seventeenth-century Englishmen manifested in their native land was largely based on abysmal ignorance of conditions elsewhere; but it had also a solid foundation in the fact that England within its own borders contained nearly everything then necessary for the maintenance of a prosperous community.

An almost inevitable accompaniment of the variety of local conditions was a high degree of local self-government. To some extent this was democratic in character. Most of the drudgery of administration was performed by the petty constables, churchwardens, overseers of the poor and other unpaid officials who, if not elected by, were at least drawn from, the general body of the people. But the prevailing tone of the administration, and still more of society, was aristocratic;[6] and the tendency was for it to become more so. The real rulers of the countryside, and even of the small towns, were the gentry, who provided the justices of the peace, the deputy-lieutenants and the officers for the militia. On them still fell the duty, imposed by Elizabeth's Statute of Artificers, of determining scales of wages;[7] and they could also fix prices,[8] though their regulations, especially as regards prices, were so frequently ignored as to give a somewhat unreliable indication of the wages and prices actually paid.[9] They supervised the administration of the poor law, and it was largely in their supposed interests that the ill-advised law of settlement was adopted, practically confining

[1] No. 166.   [2] No. 167.   [3] No. 168.
[4] No. 169.   [5] No. 170; map 7.   [6] No. 173.
[7] No. 174.   [8] No. 175.   [9] Diagram 4.

labourers to their native parish.[1] In their interests also was the restriction of the right to take game to those with a sufficient property qualification;[2] while a serious though rather ineffectual attempt was even made to strengthen their local pre-eminence by confining to them the privilege of being elected to the House of Commons.[3]

At the root of the prevailing provincialism lay the difficulty of communication. Roads were rendered impassable by dust in summer and by mud in winter. Bridges were few, with the result that travellers were much at the mercy of flooded rivers The postal system, as yet in the early stages of its development, was inefficient and expensive.[4] Highwaymen abounded,[5] especially towards the close of the period, when their numbers were augmented by discharged (or even undischarged) soldiers, and by real or pretended Jacobites. Moreover, the weather, which governed human activities much more in the seventeenth than it does in the twentieth century, tended towards extremes. Later Stuart England suffered from three visitations which were long remembered, and which did much more than interrupt communications—the great storm of 1703, and the great frosts of 1683–1684[6] and 1708–1709.[7] The storm came near to deciding the War of the Spanish Succession at its very outset, for only excellent seamanship enabled the English navy and the English merchant marine to avoid absolutely crippling losses.[8] The frost of 1708–1709 did much to bring the same war to a conclusion by the additional hardships it imposed on all the principal combatants.

Nevertheless England was by no means entirely without a common life. In London it had a single undisputed centre of trade, of industry, of government and even of culture. The universities were active, but failed to satisfy the standards of foreign visitors,[9] who were more impressed by the newly founded Royal Society, and the interest taken by the Court in its enthusiastic, if somewhat ill-directed, pursuit of scientific knowledge.[1] For those who made no claim to social or political eminence the main centres of intercourse and for the exchange of ideas were the coffee-houses, which, however, the government regarded as hotbeds of sedition and endeavoured to suppress.[11] On every side a spirit of inquiry was developing which was to bear good fruit in the eighteenth century. Traditional conceptions were being re-examined.[12] The belief in witchcraft which had long hung like a cloud over the country was slowly fading away.[13]

Beneath its veil of culture, however, the later Stuart period was in many respects a barbarous age, and one in which life everywhere remained precarious in the extreme. Medical science had scarcely even begun to develop, and had as yet failed to discover any method of combating the plague, which devastated London and other towns in 1665;[14] small-pox, which was always present; or even the perfectly ordinary diseases to which the majority of deaths in normal times were due. Families were extremely large, but the death-rate among children so heavy as to keep the population almost steady at about five-and-a-half million.[15] Fires were of deplorably frequent occurrence, and were apt to prove extremely destructive of life and property, for houses were built largely of wood, much too close together, and with little regard for means of exit in time of emergency; while the fire-fighting organization and equipment were

[1] No. 171.   [2] No. 172.   [3] No. 87.
[4] No. 176.   [5] No. 178.   [6] No. 177.
[7] No. 180.   [8] No. 179.   [9] No. 185.
[10] No. 181.   [11] No. 182.   [12] No. 183.
[13] No. 184.   [14] Nos. 186, 187.   [15] No. 198.

of the most primitive character. The Great Fire of London[1] has been allowed to bulk too largely among such disasters. Other fires, in London and elsewhere,[2] were in their limited sphere scarcely less destructive.

As might be expected in such a society there was much that was rough and degrading. Duels were of everyday occurrence, and occasioned by the most trivial causes.[3] Organized games had not yet been developed, and sport was as a rule of the most brutal description.[4] Owing to the lack of any proper police force, crime was rampant,[5] and the details of it often revolting.[6] Suicides were peculiarly frequent, carried through with the greatest determination, and inspired often by nothing more than a general weariness of life.[7]

Towards a better situation, however, the way was already being indicated by a small band of enthusiasts who were devoting themselves to a study of the actual state of the nation and of the means by which it might be improved. The difficulties in the way of these pioneer statisticians and social reformers were, it is true, immense. Even the government had no accurate knowledge of such vital facts as the population of the country, the occupations and incomes of its inhabitants, and the extent of its shipping. One of the first suggestions put forward by the reformers was a proposal for an elementary census,[8] but there was no serious chance that this would be adopted. The extraordinary method employed by the astronomer Edmund Halley for estimating the area of the various counties of England[9] is only typical of the expedients to which the statisticians were reduced in their search for basic facts.

Nevertheless they were not entirely without a foundation on which to build, a foundation provided mainly by the revenue returns in the hands of the government. The Excise farms[10] supplied them with estimates of taxable wealth made by rival groups of experienced financiers. The proposed assessment of the compensation for the feudal dues,[11] and the various assessments for the property tax,[12] supplied similar estimates, based on Commonwealth figures, and influenced, no doubt, by political considerations, made by Parliament. Returns to poll and other taxes[13] threw light on population, and returns to hearth or window taxes on numbers of houses.[14] The Church also had its figures to contribute,[15] and the statisticians could rely on their own observation and that of other travellers through the country.[16] On this highly dubious basis they erected, by careful sifting and examination, a remarkable superstructure of conclusions,[17] constituting the best that could be achieved at the time. Many of their conclusions were really little better than guesswork, but at least they involved a beginning of the scientific method of approach to economic and social problems, and a beginning made along the right lines.

[1] No. 188.	[2] No. 189.	[3] No. 190.
[4] Nos. 191, 192.	[5] No. 193.	[6] No. 194.
[7] No. 195.	[8] No. 197.	[9] No. 199.
[10] No. 196.	[11] No. 108.	[12] Nos. 115, 118.
[13] Nos. 113, 117, 201.	[14] No. 112.	[15] No. 158.
[16] Nos. 166–170.	[17] Nos. 198, 200.	

BIBLIOGRAPHY

The sources of local and social history are inevitably so scattered, and the literature on the subject so vast and of so varied a quality, that it is virtually impossible to compile a complete or satisfactory account of either. The best guide to the authorities is Arthur L. Humphreys, *A Handbook to County Bibliography, being a Bibliography of Bibliographies relating to the Counties and Towns of Great Britain and Ireland* (London, 1917); but of more immediate practical value are likely to prove J. C. Hearnshaw, *Municipal Records* (London, 1918), and four of the pamphlets published by the Historical Association—*Parish History and Records*, by A. Hamilton Thompson (London, 1926); *A Short Bibliography of Local History*, by the same writer (London, 1928); *Local History Handlist, a Short Bibliography and List of Sources for the Study of Local History and Antiquities*, prepared by the Local History Committee of the Association (London, 1947); and *County Records*, by F. G. Emmison and Irvine Gray (London, 1948).

The last half-century has witnessed the publication of a vast mass of local records, much of it of the greatest value; but this is of service primarily for the history of individual counties and boroughs, and is almost beyond the capacity of the student of general history to handle. Fortunately the later Stuart period is rich in contemporary descriptions of the land and the people, written some by Englishmen and some by foreigners; and round these the information derived from more scattered sources can be gathered. Of the English accounts the best known was first edited, under the title *Through England on a Side-Saddle*, by Emily W. Griffiths (London, 1888), but has been re-edited in a much more complete and accurate form as *The Journeys of Celia Fiennes*, by Christopher Morris (London, 1947). Although dull and badly written, it is full of careful observations made on long journeys lasting intermittently from 1685 to 1703. More readable, but less convincing, are the travel journals of Thomas Baskerville, which are still largely in manuscript, but from which considerable extracts have been printed in *The Manuscripts of the Duke of Portland*, II, pp. 263–314. Somewhat different in character is the *Tour* of Daniel Defoe. Although in form an account of certain specific journeys, it is in reality the fruit of the experience gained in many more journeys extending over a wide period, chiefly during the reign of Anne. The best edition is *A Tour through the Whole Island of Great Britain, divided into Circuits or Journies, giving a Particular and Diverting Account of whatever is Curious and Worth Observation*, edited by G. D. H. Cole (2 vols., London, 1927). It should be read in conjunction with the large number of Defoe's letters printed in *The Manuscripts of the Duke of Portland*, vol. IV.

Among foreign accounts the most illuminating are *Travels of Cosmo the Third, Grand Duke of Tuscany, through England, 1669*, by Count Lorenzo Magalotti (London, 1821), which, however, deals only with a small part of the country during a period of a few months; *Le Voyageur d'Europe*, by A. Jouvin de Rochefort (6 vols., Paris, 1672), the sections of which dealing with England, Scotland and Ireland have been translated and frequently printed; *A Voyage to England, containing Many Things relating to the State of Learning, Religion and Other Curiosities*, by Samuel de Sorbière (London, 1709); *Memoirs and Observations in his Travels over England, with some Account of Scotland and Ireland*, by H. Misson de Valbourg (London, 1719); *Letters describing the Character and Customs of the English and French Nations*, by B. L. Muralt (London, 1726); and *Merkwürdige Reisen durch Niedersachsen, Holland und England*, by Zacharias Conrad von Uffenbach (3 vols., Ulm, 1753), of which the part on Cambridge has been translated, edited and published as *Cambridge under Queen Anne*, by John E. B. Mayor (Cambridge, 1911); the part on Oxford as *Oxford in 1710*, by W. H. and W. J. C. Quarrell (Oxford, 1928); and the part on London as *London in 1710*, by W. H. Quarrell and Margaret Mare (London, 1934).

The Account Book of a Kentish Estate, 1616–1704, edited by E. C. Lodge (Oxford, 1927), is of importance mainly as a record of prices and conditions of labour. Similar in character are *Chirk Castle Accounts, 1666–1753*, edited by W. M. Myddelton (Horncastle, 1931); "Extracts from the

434

Journal and Account Book of Timothy Burrell, 1683–1714", edited by R. W. Blencowe, in *Sussex Archaeological Collections*, III (1850), pp. 117–172; and "The Account Book of James Wilding, Undergraduate of Merton College, 1682–88", edited by E. Gordon Duff, in *Oxford Historical Society Collectanea*, I (1885), pp. 249–268.

Of great value as material for social history are collections of family letters. Among these should be noted *Memoirs of the Verney Family from the Letters at Claydon House*, by Frances P., Lady Verney, and Margaret M., Lady Verney (4 vols., London, 1892–1899), *Verney Letters of the Eighteenth Century from the MSS. at Claydon House*, edited by Margaret Maria, Lady Verney (2 vols., London, 1930), and the all too brief calendar of "The Manuscripts of Sir Harry Verney at Claydon House", printed in the *Seventh Report of the Royal Commission on Historical Manuscripts* (1879), pp. 433–509; *The House of Lyme from its Foundation to the End of the Eighteenth Century*, and *Lyme Letters, 1660–1760*, both edited by Lady Newton (London, 1917 and 1925); *The Oxinden and Peyton Letters, 1642–1670*, edited by Dorothy Gardiner (London, 1937); *Conway Letters, the Correspondence of Anne, Viscountess Conway, Henry More and their Friends, 1642–1684*, edited by Marjorie Hope Nicolson (London, 1930); *The Flemings in Oxford, being Documents selected from the Rydal Papers in Illustration of the Lives and Ways of Oxford Men, 1650–1700*, edited by John Richard Magrath for the Oxford Historical Society (3 vols., 1904–1924); and *Letters of the Sitwells and Sacheverells, illustrating Country Life and Public Events in the Seventeenth and Eighteenth Centuries*, by Sir George Sitwell (2 vols., Scarborough, 1900–1901). *Postman's Horn, an Anthology of the Letters of Latter Seventeenth-Century England*, by Arthur Bryant (London, 1946), is an artificial selection, and therefore at once more and less interesting than a natural accumulation of letters. More restricted in its scope is *The Diary of Robert Hooke, 1672–1680*, edited by Henry W. Robinson and Walter Adams (London, 1935), which is important mainly for the light it throws on the history of science and architecture.

The whole field of local government is covered by the standard work on the subject – Sidney and Beatrice Webb, *English Local Government from the Revolution to the Municipal Corporations Act* (9 vols., London, 1906–1929). Useful works dealing with a more restricted sphere are E. G. Dowdell, *A Hundred Years of Quarter Sessions: the Government of Middlesex from 1660 to 1760* (Cambridge, 1932); A. H. A. Hamilton, *Quarter Sessions from Queen Elizabeth to Queen Anne* (London, 1878), which is mainly concerned with Devon; and Eleanor Trotter, *Seventeenth-Century Life in the Country Parish, with Special Reference to Local Government* (Cambridge, 1919), which is based on the quarter-sessions records of the North Riding of Yorkshire. With these may be associated Max Beloff, *Public Order and Popular Disturbances, 1660–1714* (Oxford, 1938), an inquiry into the character and meaning of the movements that the local authorities were often expected to handle.

The standard general authority on local history is the monumental *Victoria History of the Counties of England*, edited by William Page and others, of which more than a hundred volumes have appeared (Westminster, 1900–1951). It deals with the natural, political, ecclesiastical, social and economic history of each county separately, in as many volumes as the importance of the county requires, and is still in progress.

The most pretentious and comprehensive introduction to the social history of the period is *Social England, a Record of the Progress of the People in Religion, Laws, Learning, Arts, Industry, Commerce, Science, Literature and Manners*, vol. IV (1603–1714), edited by H. D. Traill (London, 1903). The essays in this co-operative work, however, are of unequal merit, are too brief, and in many cases are badly out of date. The best practical introduction, in consequence, is to be found in the appropriate sections of the standard general histories. Macaulay's famous third chapter, depicting the state of England at the accession of James II, is not only an admirable piece of work in itself but has inspired a critical examination by Sir Charles Firth, printed originally in *History*, XVII (1932), pp. 201–219, and reprinted with little alteration in Firth's *Commentary on Macaulay's History*, pp. 112–141. David Ogg and G. M. Trevelyan, in their histories of England under Charles II and Queen Anne (*supra*, p. 44), have both followed Macaulay's example and written introductory surveys of the country and the people.

The best single-volume account of social development is George Macaulay Trevelyan, *English Social History* (London, 1944), now appearing in an illustrated edition; but the amount of space assigned in this to the later Stuart period is necessarily very limited. More directly helpful are Mary Coate, *Social Life in Stuart England* (London, 1924), a series of essays on different aspects of society; Gladys Scott Thomson, *Life in a Noble Household, 1641–1700* (London, 1937), based upon the household papers of the first duke of Bedford, and the same writer's *The Russells in Bloomsbury* (London, 1940); Arthur Bryant, *The England of Charles II* (London, 1934), an admirable sketch; and John Ashton, *Social Life in the Reign of Queen Anne* (London, 1883), which is particularly full and complete, and prints many extracts from its sources.

Joan Parkes, *Travel in England in the Seventeenth Century* (Oxford, 1925), is the best survey of the subject with which it deals. A particular form of transport is studied in T. S. Willan, *River Navigation in England, 1600–1750* (Oxford, 1936), and the same writer's *The English Coasting Trade, 1600–1750* (Manchester, 1938). Joseph C. Hemmeon, *The History of the British Post Office* (Cambridge, Mass., 1912), is an admirable account of the whole postal system. Less satisfactory, but of more immediate value for the period of the later Stuarts, is J. Wilson Hyde, *The Early History of the Post in Grant and Farm* (London, 1894), which goes no further than 1685. H. C. Darby, *The Draining of the Fens* (Cambridge, 1940), is concerned largely with the seventeenth century. The very considerable part taken by women in industry is fully illustrated in Alice Clark, *The Working Life of Women in the Seventeenth Century* (London, 1919).

The most valuable contemporary accounts of the plague are Nathaniel Hodges, *Loimologia, or an Historical Account of the Plague in London in 1665* (London, 1720), the work of a physician who continued practising in the capital right through the course of the pestilence; and Daniel Defoe, *A Journal of the Plague Year* (London, 1722), which is fiction, but based largely on fact. Walter George Bell, *The Great Plague in London in 1665* (London, 1924), is the only serious modern examination of the event, based on much research and admirably written. It should be read in conjunction with William Kelly, "Visitations of the Plague at Leicester", in *Transactions of the Royal Historical Society*, VI (1877), pp. 395–447, which emphasizes the fact that London was not the only city to be scourged. Two associated and equally valuable works by W. G. Bell are *The Great Fire of London in 1666* (London, 1920), of which there is an excellent appreciation and criticism in E. Jeffries Davis, "The Great Fire of London", in *History*, VIII (1923), pp. 40–44; and *The Rebuilding of London after the Great Fire* (London, 1940), of which there is also a good appreciation by A. H. Thomas in *History*, XXV (1940), pp. 97–112, and which should be studied in conjunction with John Evelyn, *London Revived*, edited by E. S. de Beer (Oxford, 1938).

Thomas Birch, *The History of the Royal Society of London for improving of Natural Knowledge* (4 vols., London, 1756–1757), deals with its subject only as far as 1687, after which recourse must be had to C. R. Weld, *A History of the Royal Society, with Memoirs of the Presidents* (2 vols., London, 1848). There is some interesting supplementary information in Dorothy Stimson, "Dr. Wilkins and the Royal Society", in *Journal of Modern History*, III (1931), pp. 539–563; Charles C. Gillispie, "Physick and Philosophy, a Study of the Influence of the College of Physicians of London upon the Foundation of the Royal Society", *ibid.*, XXIX (1947), pp. 210–225; and E. S. de Beer, "The Earliest Fellows of the Royal Society", in *Bulletin of the Institute of Historical Research*, XV (1937), pp. 79–93.

A. LAND AND PEOPLE

166. Count Lorenzo Magalotti on the south-west, c. 1669

(Travels of Cosmo, Grand Duke of Tuscany, pp. 115–163)

Finding ourselves close to land, in order that we might not overshoot the point of Plymouth in the night, we began to tack backwards and forwards, and continued in this manner till four o'clock of the morning of the 1st of April,[1] when the wind got round to the north, being thus directly in the teeth of those who attempted to enter the harbour. Yet thanks to the goodness of the ship, and the great exertions and industry of the pilot, they so gained upon the wind in five or six tacks that they succeeded in coming to an anchor before two o'clock in the afternoon. . . .

Plymouth in the last century was a poor village, inhabited by fishermen. It is now so increased in buildings and population that it may be reckoned among the best cities of England, having between twelve and fifteen thousand inhabitants. This great advantage it derives from the capaciousness and convenience of a large bay, which, extending itself inland between two promontories, not only admits ships to a tranquil and secure sheltering place, but conveys them with the tide, which is here very powerful, into two other bays still farther inland, being the spacious channels of two rivers, which empty themselves into the sea, one to the west and the other to the east of the farthest point of the larger bay. The first, which is the Tamar, is navigable for six miles by the largest men-of-war which the king possesses, and for ten by merchant ships of all kinds; and as its windings form frequent bays, surrounded by mountains, it affords them perfectly secure places of retreat. Vessels could formerly get three or four miles up the other river, but as the channel is narrower, and the cutting down of the roads for the purpose of reducing the land to a state of cultivation has loosened the earth from the neighbouring mountains, this, coming down with the rain, has so filled up the bottom that little more than a mile is practicable for the larger frigates. . . .

The life of the city is navigation. The inhabitants export lead and tin in greater quantities than any other article, and with these they go to the Canaries and to the western islands. To Barbados, in the new world, and in every part of Europe, they act as carriers, conveying merchandise from place to place at an immense profit to themselves. Hence it is that in Plymouth only women and boys are to be seen, the greater part of the men living at sea; and hence also the town is exceedingly well supplied, all the necessaries of life being found there, and everything exempt from duty except wine, which, as it is not produced in this island, is necessarily imported from foreign countries. . . . In the neighbourhood are very rich veins of marble of different colours, some of which are black veined with white, and take a most beautiful polish. At a little distance some mines of tin have been opened, . . . which yield eighty per cent, besides a considerable quantity of gold and silver. Not far from these they have discovered

---

[1] 22 March/1 April 1669. Count Magalotti uses the new style throughout.

another of loadstone, which, although very far from rich, shows that the earth has a great disposition to the production of minerals. The sea produces oysters in great abundance and of excellent quality, and the rivers a great quantity of salmon. . . .

On the 5th of the same month . . . they took their departure. . . . They passed through the small village of Horrabridge, consisting of a few houses thatched with straw, and after travelling some distance arrived at Okehampton to sleep. . . . The whole of the country was hilly, with some rather abrupt mountains. Some parts were desert, and others tolerably fertile, cultivated with wheat and oats, the fields being surrounded with hedges and dry walls. Okehampton is a place of little account, situated on the small river Okement. The houses are built of earth and stone and thatched with straw, and its whole consequence is derived from the abundance of cheese produced in the adjacent country, which is famous for cows; and this is sold in considerable quantities to the dealers who come hither every week in great numbers.

On the 6th after dinner they departed, and arrived in the evening at Exeter, going by the direct road till they passed Crediton, . . . a village with a considerable population, all of whom are occupied in the wool manufactory. The country was uneven, but more fertile and better inhabited than that passed over the preceding day. Everywhere were seen fields surrounded with rows of trees, meadows of the most beautiful verdure, gentlemen's seats, and small collections of houses. . . .

Exeter, the capital of the county of Devon, is a small city, situated on the river Exe, about ten miles from the sea. The river there empties itself into a large bay, up which the largest vessels, even those of three hundred tons burden, can pass safely as far as Topsham, a village three miles from Exeter, whence merchandise is conveyed in smaller boats quite up to the city. The advantage of this commerce is very great, about thirty thousand persons being continually employed in the county in making baize and different sorts of light cloth. It is sold to all parts, being sent to the West Indies, Spain, France and Italy, but the greater part goes into the Levant. The very best cloth is also made, both for home consumption and for exportation, but the trade in this is not considerable in comparison with the other. There is not a cottage in all the county, nor in that of Somerset, where white lace is not made in great quantities, so that not only the whole kingdom is supplied with it, but it is exported in very great abundance. The population of the city is from twenty to twenty-five thousand souls, amongst which, according to the custom of the kingdom, there is no nobility except such as come from time to time from their country houses, which are their constant residence, to look after their affairs. . . .

On the 8th his Highness . . . got into his coach and departed for Axminster, where he arrived at an early hour. The road was through an uneven country, divided into fields under the plough and spacious meadows for feeding cows, in which this district abounds. At first we suffered a good deal of inconvenience, because they had to travel a road full of water, and muddy though not deep. We passed through Honiton, a small but populous village situated in a valley, and having ascended a hill from which we could see the sea we arrived at Axminster. . . . Axminster is a collection of two hundred houses, many of which are made of mud and thatched with straw. It contains nothing considerable except the parish church, which has a tower in which are bells so well tuned that their sound is exceedingly harmonious and agreeable. The trade of the inhabitants consists in the manufactory of woollen cloth.

On the 9th, having travelled twelve miles through a country more cultivated, pleasanter and more fertile than on the preceding day, we arrived at Hinton St. George, a villa of my Lord John Paulet, so called from a village of that name from which he takes the title of baron. . . . The villa of my Lord Paulet is an ancient, irregular building, faced on the outside with a sort of porous stone. The house, therefore, is of a noble appearance, good and spacious. Nor are gardens wanting, both for utility and pleasure. One of them contains every kind both of culinary vegetables and fruit that grows in this climate. In the other there is a parterre very different from the common style of English gardens. These are usually walks of sand, made perfectly level by rolling them with a stone cylinder through the axis of which a lever of iron is passed, whose ends, being brought forward and united together in form of a triangle, serve to move it backwards or forwards; and between the walks are smooth grass plots covered with the greenest turf, without any other ornament. This of my Lord Paulet is a meadow divided into several compartments of brick-work, which are filled with flowers.

Round the house is the park, three miles in circumference, surrounded by a thick row of trees. . . . In this park are six hundred deer, to which the mixture of plain, of hill, of coppice-wood and meadow-land, together with two plentiful springs of water which are within the same enclosure, afford a most suitable abode. The deer are of two sorts, black and red. The latter, though smaller, fatten sooner than the others. They begin to hunt them early in June, and continue it for six weeks. They hunt only the fattest, driving them with dogs into a corner of the park. They kill about one hundred annually. In winter, when the pasture fails, they give them hay and leaves of trees. . . . Near the house is a wood for pheasants, with its walks cut with the greatest exactness, which greatly enhances its pleasantness. . . .

Three leagues from Axminster you leave Devonshire, and crossing a small tongue of the county of Dorset enter that of Somerset, in which is Hinton St. George. From Hinton St. George we went to dine, on the 10th, at Dorchester, passing through the villages of Crewkerne, South Perrott, Maiden Newton and Frampton. Having passed Crewkerne, which is about three miles from Hinton St. George, they re-entered the county of Dorset, of which Dorchester is the capital. . . . Dorchester is a simple town, standing on an inclined plane. . . . It contains altogether only from ten to twelve thousand inhabitants, so that the county of which it is the capital would deserve a better. The foundation of the soil may be said to be entirely of flint-stone, but so covered with earth that perhaps more beautiful pasture cannot be found in all England. The cattle are in consequence innumerable, and from them the gentry of the county derive the chief part of their revenues. The whole of the country is uneven, but open; and the meadows are not so naked but that coppice-wood is frequently to be seen, particularly in the valleys, which, being almost all of them watered by frequent and copious pools, or rather by small rivulets, produce very green pasture, perpetually covered with cattle. On this account the dwellings seem more thinly scattered than in the counties of Devon and Somerset. In proof of the prodigious quantity of cattle it is said that in a circuit of three miles round Dorchester they reckon above forty thousand head of oxen and sheep. . . .

Early on the morning of the 11th his Highness departed from Dorchester, convoyed by a great many horse-soldiers belonging to the militia of the county, to secure him from robbers, from which this district is not free. The country is uneven, the greater part pasture-land with a prodigious number of sheep, and the rest under the plough. . . . Twelve miles from Dorchester we came to Blandford, a little town of four thousand souls situated in a small valley watered by the river Stour. . . . The whole of this day's journey was thirty miles, and at the distance of about six miles from Salisbury we entered the county of Wilts, of which that city is the capital. . . . Salisbury . . . is built at the foot of the hills, in order to protect it from the winds, on the rivers Avon and Nadder. These, being diverted from their natural course, run in several channels through the city, traversing the streets, and form several islands, which are made into gardens and rendered fruitful by industry and the vicinity of the water. The church and the square, in which is the town-house, bear away the palm amongst the most remarkable things which it contains, the other buildings being, both in point of materials and structure, like those of the other cities of England. It is a well-frequented place, and abounds with everything, both from its trade and from the convenience of its situation. It is estimated to contain above sixteen thousand inhabitants.

Intending to sleep that night at Basingstoke, his Highness departed for that place, and travelling through an open and desolate country took refreshment at the small village of Sutton. Then continuing his journey through a country chiefly devoted to pasture, and in some parts woody, he discovered, two miles from Basingstoke, a troop of horse consisting of fifty-four men, excellently mounted, of the royal regiment of my lord Aubrey de Vere, earl of Oxford, commanded by his lieutenant. They came by the king's orders to attend upon and be at the disposal of his Highness, as was intimated to him by the commander. . . . His Highness, having arrived early at Basingstoke, walked on foot through the town, which is wretched, both in regard to the buildings, the greater part of which are of wood, and the total absence of trade. . . .

On the morning of the 14th, which was Palm Sunday, his Highness attended at the benediction, and after he had privately heard mass with his suite everything was arranged for his departure for Egham. . . . We travelled fourteen miles through a country nearly level and entirely open, appropriated to pasturage, as is all the rest of the territory of Hampshire through which we passed, and dined at Okested, a small village. In the evening we reached Egham. This also is rather a village than a town. . . .

On the 15th, having heard mass, his Highness . . . went to see the villa of my Lord Henry Percy, earl of Northumberland, called Sion. . . . Thence resuming our journey through the same sort of country as that which we had lately travelled, level, open, and full of villages and houses, we arrived at Brentford, which is half a mile from the villa, and eleven from Egham. . . . After dinner his Highness wished all his retinue to proceed to London, retaining only the noblemen and a few others. . . . In this manner his Highness entered London, having passed over the whole tract of seven

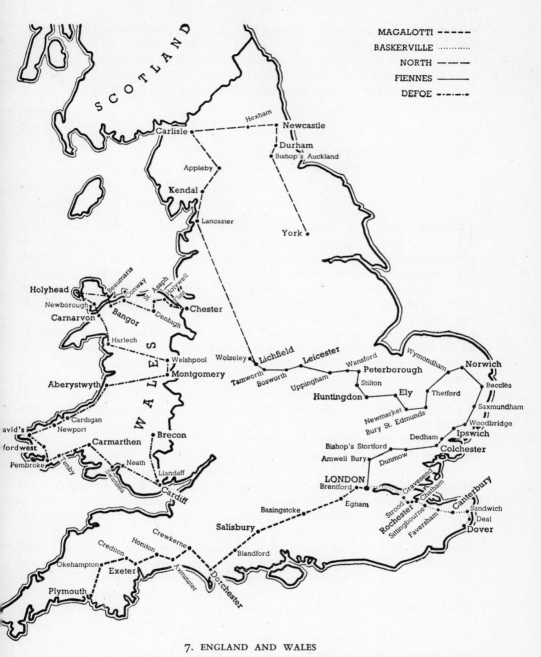

7. ENGLAND AND WALES

SHOWING THE ROUTES FOLLOWED BY COUNT MAGALOTTI, THOMAS BASKERVILLE, SIR FRANCIS
NORTH, CELIA FIENNES AND DANIEL DEFOE

miles, which, after leaving Brentford, is truly delicious from the abundance of well-built villas and country-houses which are seen in every direction. Without the city a numerous crowd of people were assembled on foot, in carriages and on horse-back to see him pass. Before the gate of St. James's Palace the usual guard were on parade. About two hours before sunset his Highness alighted at the house of my Lord Henry Jermyn, earl of St. Albans.

167. Thomas Baskerville on the south-east, *c.* 1670

(Historical Manuscripts Commission, *Portland MSS.*, II, pp. 276–281)

AN ACCOUNT OF SOME REMARKABLE THINGS
IN A JOURNEY BETWEEN LONDON AND DOVER

Between London and Gravesend by water is accounted sixty miles, and by land twenty. The usual passage by water for people, not to mention ships, is either in tilt-boats or wherries. The tilt-boat passengers in 1661 gave 8*d.* apiece for their pass; but such as go in wherries, as they can agree. But the number of persons which they carry in either of these boats are stinted by law, though commonly they do transgress it for love of gain, when they get from the stairs. In four hours' time, having the tide with them, they usually go between town and town.

Gravesend is as it were the door to London by water, for here all ships must give an account of their lading before they have leave to go forward on their journey to sea. The town and river of Gravesend is guarded with two castles, though at present but one, that on the Essex side, is made use of; and unto this all wherries or other boats going by this castle must give an account of their business, where they are going. It has its subsistence by travellers both by sea and land that go to and from the metropolitan city. . . .

From hence to Rochester is seven miles. In the way you shall meet two inns before you come to Gad's Hill, a dangerous place for robbing. Being past it a mile or more as you descend the hill, the pleasant situation of Rochester is discovered in the bottom. This city is made up of three towns, viz., Strood on the west, Rochester and Chatham on the eastern side of the river. It hath, as a man may say, four props to support it, viz., the road from France to London, the navigable river, the cathedral and its dependants, and the residence of great part of the royal navy when they are unrigged. It hath, to unite Strood and Rochester, a stately bridge of stone. Through eleven high and large arches proud Neptune charges the sweet purling stream of Medway, making it recoil ten miles towards its fountain, two miles beyond Maidstone, a great town in Kent, for so far the industrious seamen can navigate their enriching vessels by the help of tides. There was on this bridge before the bars of iron were set up many robberies committed in dark nights, those desperate villains sometimes adding murder to their theft, throwing such persons whom they had despoiled of their goods over the bridge into the water.

This cathedral church is the worst built and most ruinated of any I have seen in England. . . . The choir is handsomely repaired since our late happy change, and the rest will be with what expedition is possible. The organ by good fortune was preserved in a tavern in Greenwich, and is now erected in its proper place. . . .

In the river along by Chatham I told thirty stout ships then riding within the command of the castle of the western side of the river, except the *Royal Sovereign*, which lay at Gillingham, two miles lower. In the late engagement, before the restoration of our king, between the Dutch and us, she was at sea, though they told me 700 men are but enough to man her. She carries between 80 and an 100 guns. The gun rooms (for she hath three decks and two gun rooms, one under another) are about sixty paces long. Her stern and quarters are curiously carved and painted, with imagery work in poetical fancies, and richly overlaid with gold. In the lanthorn, that erected in the midst of the stern, I stood upright, it being capacious enough to receive the properest man in England standing upright. The king's cabin is richly painted and gilded, and so is the great cabin, which hath outlets into two galleries on the quarters. Sixty men are constantly kept in pay to keep her clean and wait on strangers, here being built for the more commodious going aboard her a bridge or way from the bank side to the lowest ebb of water. For her defence, and to examine those that pass up and down the river, a little lower do constantly ride two ships, whose names were the *Bramble* and *Truelove*; and these ships are the utmost constant guards on this river. But since the restoration of the king, some two or three years after, the Dutch came up the river and took away the *Royal Charles*, and had burnt the rest of the fleet had they not been speedily sunk. The king hath now built on the isle a little below the town of Queenborough a strong and noble fort for the security of these parts. . . .

But to return, for the reparation and rigging of the navy here the king hath his carpenters' yard, the fairest of any I have yet seen. In one of the docks lay the *Prince*, little inferior to the *Sovereign* for bigness. The king's pay to the carpenters is 2s. a day, and leave to carry away chips in their arms at breakfast, dinner-time, and the ending of their day's work, which is at 6 o'clock, at which time they likewise begin in the morning all the summer-time. Close by this yard is erected a house for spinning and making of cables, 440 of my paces long, and as long again without doors. . . .

From Rochester to Rainham, four miles; then to Newington, three; Sittingbourne, the next stage for post-horses, three miles more. In the way thither and beyond grow plenty of chestnut trees. You cannot march the streets of this town on foot in your way but they will be earnestly calling after you to ride their horses; but could I get off as freely as come on I should say the invitation were more acceptable. Four miles further on the road lies Green Street; three miles further than that Ospringe. . . .

This street standing on the road belongeth to the town of Faversham, distant a quarter of a mile lower on the left hand, being spacious and full of inhabitants, enriched by a creek of the sea on which hoys come to the town. It being now about the 25th of August they have a fair which does last for two days, to which the Londoners and clothiers of the adjacent country bring much cheese and cloth to supply the necessities of these parts. Hence you may go while the fair lasteth every day by water to London, and at other times twice a week in hoys.

Two miles from this town lies Boughton. On the top of Boughton Hill is displayed to you one of the fairest prospects in England. Westward you shall discover a spacious plain, and the meanders of the famous rivers Thames and Medway fertilizing it; north-east the river's mouth and azure ocean; south-east, four miles forward in a bottom, the tower of Canterbury's cathedral and the hills beyond it; southward an enclosed country fruitful in cornfields and orchards. From the top of this hill is a fine gravelly way leisurely descending through the midst of pleasant woods, made sociable by several booths where the good-wives stand ready to invite you taste a cup of their good liquor.

At the bottom stands a village called Harbledown leading almost into Canterbury, which on this side is watered with a sweet river, that admits boats some two miles below the town to bring commodities, from thence carted to the city. Before the invention of guns this was a strong place, being circled with a formidable wall and deep dike, and at the southern end a castle much consumed by mouldering time. Within the walls there is a court-house erected, where they keep sessions for the county. Sixteen churches the town and its suburbs may boast of, the chief being Christ Church, the seat of the metropolitan of that province. . . .

In the body of this church I told, from the west door to the iron partition where they go up into the choir, sixty-eight paces. Within these grates there is an ascent of stairs to the choir, walled on both sides breast high, and under them a vaulted passage. From the top of these stairs Thomas à Becket, archbishop of Canterbury, after he was stabbed, was thrown over into the north aisle, and buried in a little chapel by it. But from thence his bones were removed and dug up, and buried in the east end of the church behind the high altar, the pavement over them being richly inlaid with precious stones of various colours, on which stood his shrine, so much resorted to in popish times, where were offered gifts of great value. . . .

Two miles from Canterbury in the road lies Bridge, a small thoroughfare town, thirteen miles from Dover. Being got up the hill you shall march on pleasant downs in sight of Sir Anthony Aucher's house in the parish of Bishopsbourne. . . .

Sandwich was formerly more frequented by seamen when the haven and river were not so choked by sand. Nevertheless hoys and some small ships do come up to the town in the river that comes from Canterbury, which with the trade of malting, constantly employing some vessels towards London, keeps this place from decay. . . .

Four miles southerly on the beach of the sea stands New Deal, lately built on gained ground from the sea, whose dominion formerly did extend to Old Deal, two miles further into the land, to which this new town is parish. That part of the sea which washeth this shore is called the Downs, here being so many little downs of sand blown up by the wind. On this place is the usual rendezvous of such of the king's navy that come out of the rivers when they go forth on some expedition, and also for ships of many others as they trade to and fro, this intercourse of shipping being the only reason that induces men to build in this place. But when foreigners cast anchor here they must pay something towards the maintaining of lights, constantly kept burning in the night in this place to give warning to ships of the dangerous places.

For land defence and security of the road here are three castles, Sandown on the north side of the town, Walmer on the south side, and Deal Castle close by the town. At sea hereabouts, or riding in the road, are for the most part some men-of-war, because England hath not any road lying more commodious to command the sovereignty of the narrow seas than this. No fleet can pass by them in clear weather without being seen of them, the land of France being, between Deal and Dover, in sight of such as walk on the shore.

Seven miles distant from Deal lies Dover, the chief of the cinque ports, being nearest to France. In the way you shall meet with two parishes, viz., Walmer and Ringwold, both furnished with guns; besides this, to satiate the stranger's prying eyes, a sweet prospect over the curled ocean and her floating inhabitants into the fertile kingdom of France, till in a spacious plain half a mile on this side you are invited to behold the imperious towers of Dover Castle, triple walled, standing on a mount, cut off from the other part of the hill by deep bottoms or coombs. On this side of the hill, in the bottom under the command of this stately fort, lies the town of Dover. The descent to it very steep, it lies in streets stretching this way and that way, as the level betwixt the white cliffy rocks and sea will permit, and a good part on the sands, here being a pier made by art in the town for the safeguard of shipping, where they discharge their lading, close by standing a handsome warehouse for the reception of such goods as are brought here. . . .

And now to speak a little in general of Kent. It is one of the best-cultivated counties of any in England, and great part of my way that I went being through delicious orchards of cherries, pears and apples, and great hop gardens. In husbandry affairs they are very neat, binding up all sorts of grain in sheaves. They give the best wages to labourers of any in England, in harvest giving four and five shillings for an acre of wheat, and 2s. a day meat and drink, which doth invite many stout workmen hither from the neighbouring country to get in their harvest, so that you shall find, especially on Sundays, the roads full of troops of workmen with their scythes and sickles, going to the adjacent town to refresh themselves with good liquor and victuals, but many of them poor men paying dearly for coming hither, marching off with Kentish agues, which many times consume all they have got before they go home again. The most dangerous places for taking this disease are the Isles of Sheppey, Thanet, and the adjacent levels near the river and sea, for in these isles the waters are not so wholesome as in other parts, or more especially to those not bred with it.

Some, peradventure, may ask why the inhabitants of this country cannot do their own work as well as in other places. In answer to this question I shall give them two reasons. The first and main one is their near neighbourhood to the sea, which invites many of their ablest men to that employment. The second is the neatness they use, which requires the more hands to accomplish it.

For carriage all the country in general do use waggons, not so high in the beds as our carts, on which doubtless they can draw a greater burden with more facility than we can with our carts on two wheels, with a like company of horses.

The most part of Kent is employed either to tillage, orchards or woods, except Romney Marsh, which is great place of grazing, to which the drovers and butchers go twice a week, where they are met by the owners of the grounds and have markets to buy and sell as their occasion requires. . . . Maidstone, the usual place where the Kentish assizes are kept, is watered with the Medway on the west, extending some houses by the help of a bridge to the other side of the river. It is populous, round-formed, and built on declining ground, refreshed in the main street with two sweet conduits of water; and for the shelter of market people are three common houses. . . . Her chief manufacture is the making of thread and buttons, the grounds hereabouts yielding flax for the purpose, but not so much as they use; which husbandry was brought from Flanders hither.

From hence to Gravesend is fifteen miles, to which they have two ways, that by Rochester the fairest and best for horsemen, that on the west side the river the nearest and most pleasant for footmen, leading along the banks of the Medway for three miles lower through Aylesford, a sweet country town. . . . From hence your way leads on foot through Cobham Park, a place which will feast the spectator's eyes with delightful objects, fair lawns bedecked with flourishing groves of yew, oak, teal and hawthorn trees, under which the nimble deer and coneys do sport the time away. This park, or rather paradise, I may call it, belongs to the duke of Richmond and Lennox, in which he hath at the upper end a fair palace surrounded with stately groves of elm and walnuts, and such tall sycamore trees that had I not seen them I could not have imagined a sycamore could have attained to such height and bigness. . . . From hence it is four miles to Gravesend.

168. Roger North on the north, c. 1676
(*Lives of the Norths*, ed. 1826, I, pp. 277–297)

But now to return to his lordship,[1] and his circuiteering. He took an opportunity one summer to turn by the north, which begins at York and concludes at Lancaster; but in winter it is usual to omit the counties of Durham, Northumberland, Cumberland and Westmorland. His lordship was curious to visit the coal-mines in Lumley Park, which are the greatest in the north and produce the best coal, and, being exported at Sunderland, are distinguished as of that place. These collieries had but one drain of water drawn by two engines, one of three stories, the other of two. All the pits, for two or three miles together, were drained into those drains. The engines are placed in the lowest places, that there may be the less way for the water to rise, and if there be a running stream to work the engines it is happy. Coal lies under the stone, and they are twelve months in sinking a pit. . . . When they are by the side of a hill they drain by a level carried a mile under ground and cut through rock to the value of £5,000 or £6,000, and where there is no rock it is supported with timber.

In the way towards the north his lordship visited the Lord Rutland at Belvoir Castle, where the prospect is much as that is from Windsor, but hath this advantage, that the subjacent country is most of it chase ground, and that is so detrimental that the people offered £1,500 per annum rent charge of inheritance to be released; but that is kept against an exigence in the family (if any should happen), and so to preserve a better estate. There was little of curiosity to be observed in the city of York, besides the metropolitan church, which is a stately one indeed, only disgraced by a wooden roof framed archwise, but manifestly seen. . . . At Durham the bishop entertained,

[1] Chief Justice Sir Francis North.

who is a sort of sovereign, or count palatine, there, but much shrunk below the ancient authority and dignity. All process of law is original, without dependence on London. The cathedral church shows the most of gothic antiquity of any in England, and the marks of old ruin are to be seen by the different orders of the supports. Those which are very large and round, with semicircular arches, are the most antique. The bishop carried his lordship to his ancient seat called Auckland, which is to Durham as Croydon to Lambeth; and the entertainment was in all points, while his lordship stayed in that palatinate, as I may term it, truly great and generous. And thence the road lay to Newcastle over a very delightful plain, having Lumley Castle in view on the left hand most part of the way.

His lordship's entertainment at Newcastle was very agreeable, because it went most upon the trades of the place, as coal-mines, salt-works and the like, with the wonders that belonged to them; and the magistrates were solicitous to give him all the diversion they could. . . . Some of the aldermen related strange histories of their coal-works, and one was by Sir William Blackett, who cut into a hill in order to drain the water, and conquered all difficulties of stone and the like till he came to clay, and that was too hard for him, for no means of timber or walls would resist, but all was crowded together; and this was by the weight of the hill bearing upon a clay that yielded. In this work he lost £20,000. Another thing that is remarkable is their way-leaves, for when men have pieces of ground between the colliery and the river they sell leave to lead coals over their ground, and so dear that the owner of a rood of ground will expect £20 per annum for this leave. The manner of the carriage is by laying rails of timber from the colliery down to the river, exactly straight and parallel; and bulky carts are made with four rowlets fitting these rails, whereby the carriage is so easy that one horse will draw down four or five chaldron of coals, and is an immense benefit to the coal merchants. . . .

From Tynemouth his lordship, by invitation, went to dine at Seaton Delavall. Sir Ralph Delavall entertained us exceeding well, and not so much with eating and drinking, which appertains properly to the brute and not to the man, but with very ingenious discourse, and showing us many curiosities, of which he himself was author, in that place. The chief remarkable there was a little port, which that gentle-man, with great contrivance and after many disappointments, made for securing small craft that carried out his salt and coal; and he had been encouraged in it by King Charles the Second, who made him collector and surveyor of his own port, and no officer to intermeddle there. It stands at the mouth of a rill (as it is called) of water, which, running from the hills, had excavated a great hollow in the fall as it ran. The ground at the sea is a hard, impenetrable, flat rock; and for cover of the vessels, which else in the rage must be dashed to pieces, Sir Ralph had built, or rather often rebuilt, a pier of stone, that fended off the surge to the north-east, and at high water gave entrance near a little promontory of the shore turning in by the north; and at low water the vessels lay dry upon the rock. This had been built of square stone with and without cement; but all was heaved away with the surge, and for a great while nothing could be found strong enough to hold against the lifting and sucking of the water. At length Sir Ralph, at an immense cost, bound every joint of the stone, not only laterally but upright, with dovetails of heart of oak let into the stone; and that held effectually, for if the stones were lifted up they fell in their places again. This little harbour was apt to silt up with the sea sand, for remedying of which he used the back water of his rill, and that kept the channel always open. And for that end he had an easy and sure device, which was sluice gates built across the channel of the rill, which during tide of flood were shut, and so the water gathered to a great head above till low water, and then the sluices opened let the gathered water come down all at once, which scoured away the sand that every tide lodged upon the rock, and washed it as clean as a marble table. . . .

The county of Northumberland hath been exceedingly infested with thieving of cattle, which is the remains of the Border trade, since the union with Scotland, after the way used in time of peace before. For as in Italy the murderer, running into the next territory, was safe, so here they stole on either side, and the other under a different jurisdiction was an asylum. This was so great a mischief that all the considerable farmhouses (the houses of gentlemen were castles of course) were built of stone in the manner of a square tower with an overhanging battlement, and underneath the cattle were lodged every night. In the upper room the family lodged, and when the alarm came they went up to the top, and with hot water and stones from the battlement fought in defence of their cattle. The advantage of the union was so great to these countries that the Lord Grey of Werke's estate, which before was not above £1,000 per annum, hath since risen to £7,000 or £8,000, which is at least a sixfold improvement. After the union, to prevent this thieving trade, the Crown sent commissioners of oyer and terminer directed to an equal number of English and Scotch, extending to certain limits on each side of the Border, and being continued it is therefore called the Border commission; and these meet in their sessions and hang up at another rate than the assizes, for we were told that at one sessions they hanged eighteen for not reading *sicut clerici*.

This hath made a considerable reform; but yet there is need of an officer they call a country keeper, who hath a salary from the country, and is bound to make good all the stolen cattle unless found out and restored. When his lordship was there one Mr. Widdrington was keeper, with £500 per annum salary. The country is yet very sharp upon thieves, and a violent suspicion there is next to conviction. When his lordship held the assizes at Newcastle there was one Mungo Noble (supposed to be a great thief) brought to trial before his lordship upon four several indictments, and his lordship was so much a south-country judge as not to think any of them well proved. One was for stealing a horse of a person unknown; and the evidence amounted to no more than that a horse was seen feeding upon the heath near his shiel (which is a cottage made in open places of turf and flag), and none could tell who was the owner of it. In short the man escaped, much to the regret of divers gentlemen who thought he deserved to be hanged; and that was enough. While the judge at the trial discoursed of the evidence and its defects, a Scotch gentleman upon the bench who was a Border commissioner made a long neck towards the judge, and, "My laird," said he, "send him to huzz and yees neer see him mere." This country was then much troubled with bedlamers. One was tried before his lordship for killing another of his own trade, whom he surprised asleep and with his great staff knocked on the head, and then bragged that he had given him "a sark full of sere benes", that is a shirt full of sore bones. He would not plead to the country, because there were horse-copers amongst them, till the press was ready; and then he pleaded and was at last hanged. They were a great nuisance in the country, frighting the people in their houses and taking what they listed, so that a small matter with the countrymen would do such a fellow's business.

From Newcastle his lordship's route lay to Carlisle. The Northumberland sheriff gave us all arms, that is a dagger, knife, penknife and fork, altogether. And because the hideous road along by the Tyne, for the many and sharp turnings and perpetual precipices, was for a coach, not sustained by main force, impassable, his lordship was forced to take horse, and to ride most part of the way to Hexham. . . . Here his lordship saw the true image of a Border country. The tenants of the several manors are bound to guard the judges through their precinct, and out of it they would not go, no, not an inch, to save the souls of them. They were a comical sort of people, riding upon negs, as they call their small horses, with long beards, cloaks, and long broad-swords with basket hilts, hanging in broad belts, that their legs and swords almost touched the ground. And every one in his turn, with his short cloak and other equipage, came up cheek by jowl and talked with my lord judge. His lordship was very well pleased with their discourse, for they were great antiquarians in their own bounds. . . .

The rest of the country to Carlisle was more pleasant and direct, and bating hunger and thirst, which will not be quenched by anything to be fastened upon there but what the bounty of the skies affords, was passed over with content. At Carlisle nothing extraordinary occurred but good ale and small beer, which was supplied to their lordships from the prebends' houses; and they boasted of brewing it at home, but being asked with what malt they made answer that it was south-country malt. . . . In Cumberland the people had joined in a sort of confederacy to undermine the estates of the gentry by pretending a tenant-right, which there is a customary estate not unlike our copyholds; and the verdict was sure for the tenants' right whatever the case was. The gentlemen, finding that all was going, resolved to put a stop to it by serving on common juries. I could not but wonder to see pantaloons and shoulder-knots crowding among the common clowns, but this account was a satisfaction.

From hence we went, through a plain but stony road, in the view of hideous mountains called Furness Hills, to Appleby in Westmorland. There is little of a shire town to be found there, being but as it were a village; only there is the castle, an ancient fortified seat of the earl of Thanet's. . . . The earl of Thanet is the hereditary sheriff of that county, the only one of that quality in England, and had ordered a sumptuous entertainment to be given by one Mr. Gambetes, his steward, to the judges. . . .

There was a high feud that had been carried on in this country with a world of heat, between the Musgraves and their friends on the one side and the Lowthers, Fletchers and divers other gentlemen on the other. And if one may borrow a distinction of much later date, I may say the former were Tory and the other Whig. It is certain that the Musgraves were envied by their neighbours, for they were courtiers,

16

and having been Cavaliers, and also very serviceable in Parliament (it seems that some so early knew how to value their services there), were favoured, having the government of Carlisle a sort of frontier, and also were farmers at easy rates of a duty upon cattle out of Scotland, which duty some said, as they had ordered the matter, was gained from the Parliament on purpose to be granted to them whose project it was. The difference formed itself upon the division of the country (if I may borrow the words) into Cisalpine and Transalpine regions, and the question was in which of these the general sessions should be held, each side holding stiffly to his own convenience: and sometimes they had the general quarter-sessions at both places, which was very absurd. And this dispute had its purlieus fraught with general and original slanders raised on either side against the other, which ran so high that the whole country ran into the faction. Good people were scandalized, and the king himself importuned and troubled about it; and his Majesty was pleased to recommend the matter to his lordship to compose in his circuit if he could.

At his arrival at Appleby he appointed the gentlemen to attend him, which they did. The Musgraves spoke for themselves; the other side had a counsel, but left little to him, but Sir John Lowther, since Lord Lonsdale, managed most on that side. His lordship gave neither a victory over the other (which in the north is much desired), but proposed an expedient which was then new, though of later years much in use in divers counties. And it is expressed in a memorandum his lordship took in an almanac, viz., "There being a controversy concerning holding the quarter-sessions at two places in Westmorland, Mr. Baron Bertie and myself, upon conference with all the justices, delivered our opinions that there could be but one general quarter-sessions in one county for one quarter, and that if conveniency required attendance at other places it must be by way of adjournment; and we proposed that way, to which they readily agreed. And we advised that at the close of every sessions order should go for summoning the next, which should be done by writ under the seal of the court; and we directed the form of a precept, 1676." And thus the mighty difference was composed, and all the business of the sessions hath proceeded accordingly ever since. . . .

His lordship's next remove was to Lancaster, but he lodged at Kendal by the way. That is a scattered town in an inclosed country, very stony and dirty; and we could not without a chagrin observe the common people walk barefoot, and the children leaping as if they had hoofs and those shod with iron; but it is almost the same all over the north. This town, so situated and out of the way, is yet celebrated for much woollen manufacture sent from thence to most parts of England. . . . From hence to Lancaster is a very rugged journey, and upon the tops of some hills one would not give a groat for all the land he could see, it being nothing but hard and impenetrable rock, white as snow; but in the valleys there was fertility enough. This county (as that of Durham) is palatine, but more august and regular; and all the proceedings commencing and ending there afforded more law business than other counties that deal only by *nisi prius*; which made his stay longer. . . .

In the return homewards from Lancaster his lordship took all the advantage he could of seeing great towns and places of note. He stayed some days with Sir Roger

Bradshaigh, whose lordship is famous for yielding the cannel (or candle) coal. It is so termed, as I guess, because the manufacturers in that country use no candle, but work by the light of their coal fire. The property of it is to burn and flame till it is all consumed, without leaving any cinder. It is lighted by a candle like amber, and the grate stands not against the back of a large chimney, as common coal grates, but in the middle, where ballads are pasted round, and the folk sit about it working or merry-making. His lordship saw the pits where vast piles of that coal were raised, and it is pity the place wants water-carriage, else London would be in the better part served with it. . . .

His lordship pitched next at the city of Lichfield, and as his use was took the advantage of spending his Sunday there. . . . This cathedral church was beaten to pieces in the late wars, but by the zeal and diligence of Bishop Hacket was rebuilt as entirely as if it had never been injured, and chiefly with the money he raised by barefaced begging. No gentleman lodged, or scarce baited, in the city, to whom he did not pay his respects by way of visit, which ended in plausible entreaties for some assistance towards rescuing his distressed church from ruin. And that he brought about so effectually, and adorned his choir so completely and politely, as I have not seen a more laudable and well-composed structure for the purpose in the country anywhere. . . .

169. Celia Fiennes on East Anglia and the Midlands, c. 1698
(*Journeys of Celia Fiennes*, ed. C. Morris, pp. 142–165)

From London to Amwell Bury, which is in Hertfordshire, nineteen miles, where I stayed a day or two. Thence to Bishops Stortford in Essex, thirteen miles. Thence to Dunmow, eight long miles through several little villages. It is very deep way especially after rains. This is a little market-town. They are altogether taken up about the spinning and preparing for the baize. All along between that and Colchester you pass but half a mile ere one comes to two or three houses all along the road. It is from Dunmow to Colchester twenty-two miles, and mostly clay deep way.

Colchester is a large town in the compass of ground. Formerly there were sixteen churches, though now much of it is ruinated. . . . There is a large street which runs a great length down to the bridge, near a mile long. About the middle of it runs another broad street and near its length, in which is the market-cross and town-hall, and a long building like stalls on purpose to lay their baize when exposed to sale. Great quantities are made here and sent in bales to London, that is forty-four miles distant. The whole town is employed in spinning, weaving, washing, drying and dressing their baize, in which they seem very industrious. . . .

The town looks like a thriving place by the substantial houses, well-pitched streets, which are broad enough for two coaches to go abreast, besides a pitched walk on either side by the houses, secured by stumps of wood, and is convenient for three to walk together. Their buildings are of timber, of loam and laths and much tiling. The fashion of the country runs much in long roofs and great cantilevers and peaks. Out of these great streets run many little streets, but not very narrow. Mostly old buildings, except a few houses built by some Quakers, that are brick and of the London mode. The town did extend itself to the sea, but now its ruins set it three miles off. The low grounds all about the town are used for the whitening their baize for which this town is remarkable, and also for exceeding good oysters; but it is a dear place, and to gratify my curiosity to eat them on the place I paid dear. It is a town full of dissenters. Two meetings very full, besides Anabaptists and Quakers. Formerly the famous Mr. Stockton was minister there till he died.

From Colchester to Ipswich is eighteen miles, and thence to Dedham nine miles, the way pretty good except four or five miles they call the Severals, a sort of deep moor ground and woody. At this place I passed over a wooden bridge, pretty large with timber rails, of which make they build their bridges in these parts. And now I go into Suffolk, which is not so rich land as that part of Essex I passed through, which was meadows and grounds with great burdens of grass and corn.

So I went to Ipswich, nine miles more. This is a very clean town, and much bigger than Colchester is now. Ipswich has twelve churches; their streets of a good size, well pitched with small stones; a good market-cross railed in. I was there on Saturday, which is their market day, and saw they sold their butter by the pint, twenty ounces for sixpence, and often for fivepence or fourpence. They make it up in a mould just in the shape of a pint pot, and so sell it. Their market-cross has good carving, the figure of Justice carved and gilt. There is but three or four good houses in the town. The rest is much like the Colchester buildings, but it seems more shattered. And indeed the town looks a little disregarded, and by inquiry found it to be through pride and sloth, for though the sea would bear a ship of 300 ton up quite to the quay, and the ships of the first rate can ride within two miles of the town, yet they make no advantage thereof by any sort of manufacture, which they might do as well as Colchester and Norwich, so that the ships that bring their coals go light away. Neither do they address themselves to victual or provide for ships. They have a little dock where formerly they built ships of two or three hundred ton; but now little or nothing is minded save a little fishing for the supply of the town. . . .

Thence I went to Woodbridge, seven miles; mostly lanes, enclosed countries. This is a little market-town, but has a great meeting for the dissenters. Thence to Wickham, five miles more. But these are all very long miles. Thence to Saxmundham, eight miles more. This is a pretty big market-town. The ways are pretty deep; mostly lanes, very little commons. . . . So to Blyford, eight miles, where is the remains of the walls of an abbey, and there is still a very fine church. . . .

I rode in sight of St. George's Channel in the way from Colchester and Ipswich, and so to Norwich. Sometimes it was in view, then lost again. To Beccles is eight miles more, which in all was thirty-six miles from Ipswich, but exceeding long miles. They do own they are forty-one measured miles. This is a little market-town, but it is the third biggest town in the county of Suffolk – Ipswich, Bury St. Edmunds and this. Here was a good big meeting-place; at least 400 hearers; and they have a very good minister, one Mr. Killinghall. He is but a young man, but seemed very serious. I was there the Lord's Day. Sir Robert Rich is a great supporter of them, and contributed to the building the meeting-place, which is very neat. . . .

At the town's end one passes over the river Waveney on a wooden bridge railed with timber, and so you enter into Norfolk. It is a low flat ground all hereabout, so that the least rains they are overflowed by the river and lie under water, as they did when I was there; so that the road lay under water, which is very unsafe for strangers to pass, by reason of the holes and quicksands and loose bottom. The ordinary people both in Suffolk and Norfolk knit much and spin, some with the rock and fuseau as the French does, others at their wheels out in the street and lanes as one passes. It is from this town to Norwich twelve miles, and it is ten to Yarmouth, where they build some small ships, and is a harbour for them, and where they victual them. Also Harwich about twelve or fourteen miles also. But the miles are here as long again as about London, and pretty deep way, especially after rains. These miles are much longer than most miles in Yorkshire.

Norwich opens to view a mile distance by the help of a hill whereon is a little village. . . . Thence I went to Wymondham, a little market-town, five miles, mostly on a causey, the country being low and moorish; and the road on the causey was in many places full of holes, though it is secured by a bar at which passengers pay a penny a horse in order to the mending the way, for all about is not to be rode on unless it is a very dry summer. Thence we went mostly through lanes, where you meet the ordinary people knitting four or five in a company under the hedges, to Attleborough, five miles more, which is such another little market-town. Then over an open down like Salisbury Plain, four miles more, to a little village, still finding the country full of spinners and knitters. Thence to Thetford, six miles more, which was formerly a large place, but now much decayed, and the ruins only shew its dimensions. . . . Here I lay, which is still in Norfolk.

Next day I went to Euston Hall, which was the Lord Arlington's, and by his only daughter's marriage with the duke of Grafton is his son's by her. It is two miles from Thetford. . . . At the back gate I crossed over the river Waveney, which is the division of the two counties, and entered Suffolk, and passed over perfect downs champion country just like Salisbury Plain; and the winds have a pretty power here, and blow strongly in the winter, not well to be endured.

So to Bury St. Edmunds, eight miles; but as has been often observed before the miles are very long. I passed by two or three little villages, and about two miles off there is the town of Bury St. Edmunds, which appears standing on a great hill. The towers and buildings look so compact and well together with the trees and gardens thick about it the prospect was wonderfully pleasant. . . .

Thence I went to Admiral Russell's, who is now Lord Orford, a long ten miles, and losing my way made it twelve miles. It is pretty good way. I passed by a village or two, and in a mile of Lord Orford's house I enter Cambridgeshire. It stands three miles from Newmarket. . . . From thence I went eight miles to Ely, which were as long as the twelve I came from Bury St. Edmunds, the ways being very deep. It is mostly lanes and low moorish ground. For four miles together I passed over a low ground on each side defended by the fen dikes, which are deep ditches with drains. The fens are full of water and mud. These also encompass their grounds; each man's part ten or a dozen acres apiece or more; so these dikes are the fences. On each side they plant willows, so there is two rows of trees runs round the ground, which looks very finely to see a flat of many miles so planted; but it must be ill to live there.

All this while Ely Minster is in one's view at a mile distant you would think; but go, it is a long four miles. A mile distant from the town is a little hamlet, from which I descended from a steep hill, and so cross a bridge over water which enters into the Island of Ely; and so you pass a flat on a gravel causey, which way the bishop is at the charge to repair, else there would be no passing in the summer. This is secured by some dikes which surround more grounds as the former, full of rows of trees, willows round them, which makes Ely look finely through those trees, and that stands very high. In the winter this causey is overflowed, and they have no way but boats to pass in. . . . That bridge was over the river Linn, which comes from Norfolk and does almost encompass the Island of Ely, which is twenty miles in bigness, in which are several little towns, as Wisbech and many others.

There is another river that joins with the Linn, which composes this land into an island. At this bridge is a gate, but by reason of the great rains the roads were full of water even quite to the town, which you ascend a very steep hill into; but the dirtiest place I ever saw. Not a bit of pitching in the streets, so it is a perfect quagmire, the whole city. Only just about the palace and churches the streets are well enough for breadth; but for want of pitching it seems only a harbour to breed and nest vermin in, of which there is plenty enough, so that though my chamber was near twenty steps up I had frogs and slow-worms and snails in my room, but suppose it was brought up with the faggots. But it cannot but be infested with all such things, being altogether moorish, fenny ground which lies low. It is true, were the least care taken to pitch their streets, it would make it look more properly an habitation for human beings, and not a cage or nest of unclean creatures. It must needs be very unhealthy, though the natives say much to the contrary, which proceeds from custom and use. . . .

From this city I passed over those higher grounds, on which was some good corn, but mostly is for grass for their cattle. You see many pretty little towns, four or five in view together two or three miles distant. I went to Sutton, one of them, six miles off the city. This was a little market-town. Thence on the fen banks, on the top of which I rode at least two miles with the fens on both sides, which now were mostly under water, a vast tract of such grounds which are divided by the dikes without trees as those I observed before. And these high banks are made to drain and fence out the water from the lower grounds, and so from one bank to another, which are once in many acres of land 100, so that at length it does bear off the water. But in the winter it returns, so as they are forced to watch, and be always in repairing those banks; and considering the vast allowance yearly for draining those fens, at least £3,000 per annum, I wonder they have not perfectly run off the water, and so barricaded it as not to so it often overflows it again, as it does in many places. But they are all a lazy sort of people, and are afraid to do too much. . . . This brought me to the Hermitage, a long eight miles in all from Ely town, and here I repassed the river Linn on a wooden bridge, and so went out of the Island of Ely, which was in Cambridgeshire, and entered into Huntingdonshire.

There was another bridge over a deep place of the river, under which the boats and barges went, and this bridge was in the water. . . . But I rather chose to ride round and ferry over in a boat (twopence a horse) to a little town. This river runs along by St. Ives, which was an old monastery and a rich one. From this ferry it is eight miles to Huntingdon town. . . .

From Huntingdon town I went to Stilton, nine miles more, and thence I went to the city of Peterborough in Lincolnshire, which was five long miles, the ways deep and full of sloughs. It stands very high, and to be seen at a great distance, the towers of the Minster being all in view. One would think it but a quarter of a mile when you have a mile or two still to it. The whole city looks very well and handsomely built, but mostly timber work. You pass over a long stone bridge. The streets are very clean and neat, well pitched and broad as one shall see anywhere. There is a very spacious market-place, a good cross and town hall on the top. The cathedral is a magnificent building standing in the midst on advanced ground, all stone, the walls very neatly wrought. . . . Here is a palace for the bishop of stone building very neat, and the doctors' houses all in a space called the College, very neat but nothing curious. The river Linn washes the town almost round it. Looks like a very industrious, thriving town. Spinning and knitting amongst the ordinary people. . . .

There was no gates to Peterborough town, and as I passed the road I saw upon the walls of the ordinary people's houses, and walls of their out-houses, the cow dung plastered up to dry in cakes, which they use for firing. It is a very offensive fuel, but the country people use little else in these parts. Wansford is five miles from Peterborough, where I passed over the bridge which entered me into Northamptonshire, the town being part in that shire which is towards London, the other in Lincolnshire, which a mile or two farther joins with Rutlandshire at Stamford, which town stands in the three counties. . . .

Thence I went to Duddington, five miles, and passed over a very good stone bridge. Here we are near the quarries of stone, and all the houses and walls are built of stone as in Gloucestershire. This river and bridge entered me into Leicestershire, which is a very rich country, red land, good corn of all sorts and grass, both fields and inclosures. You see a great way upon their hills, the bottoms full of inclosures, woods, and different sort of manuring and herbage, amongst which are placed many little towns, which gives great pleasure of the travellers to view. The miles are long, but hitherto pretty hard good way to Uppingham, five miles more, which is a neat market-town. Saturday is their market, which is very good, affording great quantities of corn, leather, yarn and cattle; such a concourse of people that my landlord told me used to have a hundred horse set up at his inn, and there were many public houses here. You see very large, fine sheep, and very good land; but very deep, bad roads from hence to Leicester, . . . being full of sloughs, clay deep way, that I was near eleven hours going but twenty-five miles (as they reckon it) between Wansford and Leicester town. . . .

Leicester town stands on the side of a little rising ground, though at a distance from the adjacent hills it looks low; but it is a good prospect. . . . St. Martin's Church, which is one of the biggest (there is none very big, and none fine); but here I saw Heyrick's tomb, who was mayor of the town, and was married to one wife fifty-two years, in all which time he buried neither man, woman nor child, though most times he had twenty in his family. His age was seventy-nine, and his widow ninety-seven at her death. She saw 142 of her posterity together. They have a water house, and a water-mill to turn the water into the pipes to serve the town, as it is in London. It comes but once a day, so they save the water in deep leaden tubs or cisterns for their use. There are wells in some streets to draw water by a hand wheel for the common use of the town. . . .

This country, as I said, was all rich deep land, and they plough their land all with ploughs without wheels, as they do in Oxfordshire and other deep lands. From thence I passed to Bosworth, eight miles . . . and so into Warwickshire over a bridge. . . . Thence three miles more to Tamworth, a neat town built of brick and mostly new. In sight at its approach it looked like Lichfield, but not a quarter so big a market-town. It stands half in Warwickshire and half in Staffordshire. And so to Lichfield over a large stone bridge that crosses the Tamworth river that gives name to the town. To Lichfield is five miles more, all very good way, mostly gravel. I went it in an hour. . . . They have in this town a custom at Whitsuntide, the Monday and Tuesday, called the Green Bower Feast, by which they hold their charter. The bailiff and sheriff assist at the ceremony of dressing up babies with garlands of flowers and greens, and carry it in procession through all the streets, and then assemble themselves at the market-place, and so go on in a solemn procession through the great street to a hill beyond the town, where is a large bower made with greens, in which they have their feast. Many lesser bowers they make about for the conveniency of the whole company, and for selling fruit, sweetmeats and gingerbread, which is a chief entertainment. Thence I went to Wolseley, seven miles farther, to Sir Charles Wolseley, where I stayed six weeks.

170. Daniel Defoe on Wales, c. 1710
(*A Tour through Great Britain*, ed. 1724–1727, II, letters III–IV, pp. 78–102)

We now entered South Wales. The provinces which bear the name of South Wales are these–Glamorgan, Brecknock, Radnor, Carmarthen, Pembroke and Cardigan. . . . Brecknockshire is a mere inland county, as Radnor is. The English jestingly (and I think not very improperly) call it Breakneckshire. It is mountainous to an extremity except on the side of Radnor, where it is something more low and level. It is well watered by the Wye and the Usk. . . . Upon the latter stands the town of Brecknock, the capital of the county. . . .

Though this county be so mountainous, provisions are exceeding plentiful and also very good all over the county. Nor are these mountains useless even to the city of London, as I have noted of other counties, for from hence they send yearly great herds of black cattle to England, and which are known to fill our fairs and markets, even that of Smithfield itself. The yellow mountains of Radnorshire are the same, and their product of cattle is the same. . . . There is a kind of desert on that side, which is scarce habitable or passable, so we made it our north boundary for this part of our journey, and turned away to Glamorganshire.

Entering this shire from Radnor and Brecknock we were saluted with Monuch-denny Hill on our left and the Black Mountain on the right, and all a ridge of horrid rocks and precipices between, over which, if we had not had trusty guides, we should never have found our way. . . . But after a day and a night conversing thus with rocks and mountains our guide brought us down into a most agreeable vale opening to the south, and a pleasant river running through it called the Taff, and following the course of this river we came in the evening to the ancient city of Llandaff and Cardiff, standing almost together. Llandaff is the seat of the episcopal see, and a city; but Cardiff, which is lower on the river, is the port and town of trade, and has a very good harbour opening into the Severn sea about four miles below the town. . . .

The south part of this country is a pleasant and agreeable place, and is very populous. It is also a very good, fertile and rich soil; and the low grounds are so well covered with grass, and stocked with cattle, that they supply the city of Bristol with butter in very great quantities, salted and barrelled up, just as Suffolk does the city of London. The chief seaport is Swansea, a very considerable town for trade, and has a very good harbour. Here is also a very great trade for coals and culm, which they export to all the ports of Somerset, Devon and Cornwall, and also to Ireland itself; so that one sometimes sees a hundred sail of ships at a time loading coals here. . . .

Having thus touched at what is most curious on this coast we passed through the land of Gower, and going still west we came to Carmarthen. . . . This is an ancient but not a decayed town, pleasantly situated on the river Towy, which is navigable up to the town for vessels of a moderate burthen. The town indeed is well built and populous, and the country round it is the most fruitful of any part of all Wales, considering that it continues to be so for a great way, namely, through all the middle of the county and a great way into the next. Nor is this county so mountainous and wild as the rest of this part of Wales, but it abounds in corn and in fine flourishing meadows, as good as most are in Britain, and in which are fed a very great number of good cattle. . . . We found the people of this county more civilized and more courteous than in the more mountainous parts, where the disposition of the inhabitants seems to be rough like the country; but here, as they seem to converse with the rest of the world by their commerce, so they are more conversable than their neighbours.

The next county west is Pembrokeshire, which is the most extreme part of Wales on this side, in a rich, fertile and plentiful country, lying on the sea-coast, where it has the benefit of Milford Haven, one of the greatest and best inlets of water in Britain. . . . Before we quitted the coast we saw Tenby, the most agreeable town on all the sea-coast of South Wales except Pembroke, being a very good road for shipping, and well frequented. Here is a great fishery for herring in its season, a great colliery, or rather export of coals; and they also drive a very considerable trade to Ireland.

From hence the land, bearing far into the sea, makes a promontory called St. Gowans Head or Point; but as we found nothing of moment was to be seen there we crossed over the isthmus to Pembroke, which stands on the east shore of the great Haven of Milford. This is the largest and richest, and at this time the most flourishing, town of all South Wales. Here are a great many English merchants, and some of them men of good business; and they told us there were near 200 sail of ships belonged to

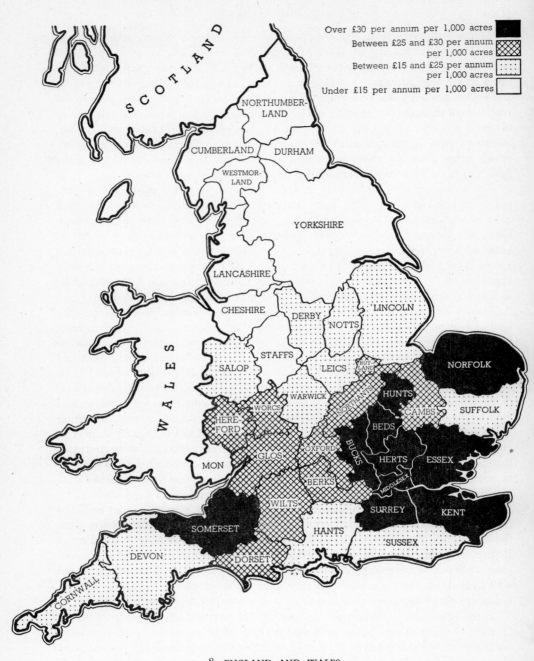

8. ENGLAND AND WALES

SHOWING DISTRIBUTION OF WEALTH AS INDICATED BY THE APPORTIONMENT OF THE ROYAL AID
OF 1665

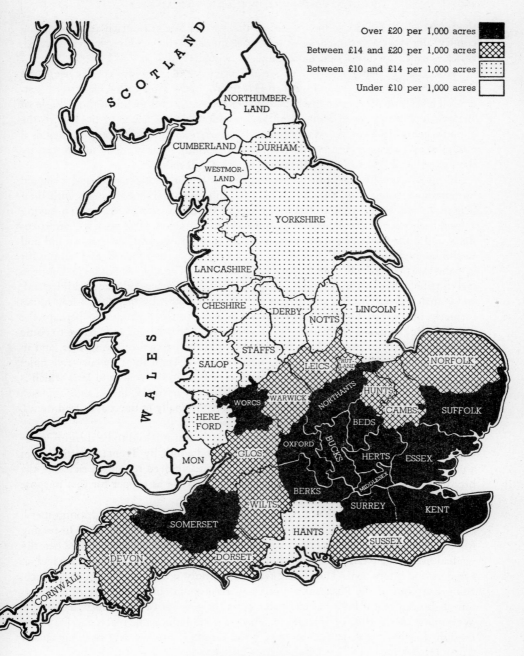

Over £20 per 1,000 acres

Between £14 and £20 per 1,000 acres

Between £10 and £14 per 1,000 acres

Under £10 per 1,000 acres

SCOTLAND

NORTHUMBER-LAND

CUMBERLAND DURHAM

WESTMOR-LAND

YORKSHIRE

LANCASHIRE

CHESHIRE DERBY NOTTS LINCOLN

WALES

SALOP STAFFS LEICS RUT-LAND NORFOLK

WORCS WARWICK NORTHANTS HUNTS CAMBS SUFFOLK

HERE-FORD BEDS

MON GLOS OXFORD BUCKS HERTS ESSEX

MIDDLESEX

BERKS SURREY KENT

WILTS SOMERSET HANTS SUSSEX

DEVON DORSET

CORNWALL

9. ENGLAND AND WALES

HOWING DISTRIBUTION OF WEALTH AS INDICATED BY THE RETURNS TO THE POLL TAX OF 1692 the town, small and great. In a word, all this part of Wales is a rich and flourishing county; but especially this part is so very pleasant and fertile, and is so well cultivated, that it is called by distinction Little England beyond Wales. . . .

From hence, being resolved to see the utmost extent of the county west, we ferried over the haven . . . and went to Haverford, or by some called Haverfordwest. . . . . Haverford is a better town than we expected to find in this remote angle of Britain. It is strong, well built, clean and populous. From hence to St. Davids the country begins to look like Wales again, dry, barren and mountainous. St. Davids is not a bishop's see only, but was formerly an archbishop's, which, they tell us, was by the Pope transferred to Dol in Brittany, where it still remains. . . .

From hence we turned north, keeping the sea in our west prospect and a rugged mountainous country on the east, where the hills even darkened the air with their height. As we went on we passed by Newport, on the river Nevern, a town having a good harbour, and consequently a good trade with Ireland. Here we left Pembrokeshire, and after about twenty-two miles came to the town of Cardigan, an old and well-inhabited town on the river Teiffi. It is a very noble river indeed, and famous for its plenty of the best and largest salmon in Britain. . . . The town is not large, has been well fortified; but that part is now wholly neglected. It has a good trade with Ireland, and is enriched very much, as is all this part of the country, by the famous lead mines formerly discovered by Sir Carbery Pryse, which are the greatest and perhaps the richest in England, and particularly as they require so little labour and charge to come at the ore, which in many places lies within a fathom or two of the surface, and in some even bare to the very top. Going north from the Teiffi about twenty-five miles we came to Aberystwyth. . . . This town is enriched by the coals and lead which is found in its neighbourhood, and is a populous, but a very dirty, black, smoky place; and we fancied the people looked as if they lived continually in the coal or lead mines. However, they are rich, and the place is very populous.

The whole county of Cardigan is so full of cattle that it is said to be the nursery or breeding-place for the whole kingdom of England south by Trent; but this is not a proof of its fertility, for though the feeding of cattle indeed requires a rich soil, the breeding them does not, the mountains and moors being as proper for that purpose as richer land.

Now we entered North Wales, . . . which contains the counties of Montgomery, Merioneth, Carnarvon, Denbigh and Flint shires, and the isle of Anglesey. In passing Montgomeryshire we were so tired with rocks and mountains that we wished heartily we had kept close to the sea-shore; but it not much mended the matter if we had, as I understood afterwards. The river Severn is the only beauty of this county, which, rising I say out of the Plynlimon mountain, receives instantly so many other rivers into its bosom that it becomes navigable before it gets out of the county, namely, at Welshpool, on the edge of Shropshire. This is a good fashionable place, and has many English dwelling in it, and some very good families; but we saw nothing farther worth remarking.

The vales and meadows upon the bank of the Severn are the best of this county. I had almost said the only good part of it. Some are of opinion that the very water of the Severn, like that of Nile, impregnates the valleys, and when it overflows leaves a virtue behind it particularly to itself. . . . This county is noted for an excellent breed of Welsh horses, which, though not very large, are exceeding valuable, and much esteemed all over England. All the north and west part of the county is mountainous and stony. . . .

Merionethshire lies west from Montgomeryshire. . . . The principal river is the Dovey, which rises among the unpassable mountains which range along the centre of this part of Wales, and which we call unpassable for that even the people themselves called them so. We looked at them indeed with astonishment, for their rugged tops and the immense height of them. . . . There is but few large towns in all this part, nor is it very populous. Indeed much of it is scarce habitable; but it is said there are more sheep in it than in all the rest of Wales. . . . The mountainous country spoken of runs away north through this county and almost the next (I mean Carnarvonshire), where Snowdon Hill is a monstrous height. . . .

That side of the country of Carnarvon which borders on the sea is not so mountainous, and is both more fertile and more populous. The principal town in this part is Carnarvon. . . . It is a small but strong town, clean and well built, and considering the place the people are very courteous and obliging to strangers. It is seated on the firth or inlet called Menai, parting the isle of Anglesey, or Mona, from the mainland. And here is a ferry over to the island called Abermenai Ferry, and from thence a direct road to Holyhead, where we went for no purpose but to have another view of Ireland, though we were disappointed, the weather being bad and stormy. . . .

There is nothing of note to be seen in the isle of Anglesey but the town and castle of Beaumaris. . . . As we went to Holyhead by the south part of the island from Newborough, and came back through the middle to Beaumaris, we saw the whole extent of it, and indeed it is a much pleasanter country than any part of North Wales that we had yet seen, and particularly is very fruitful for corn and cattle. Here we crossed the *fretum* or strait of Menai again, and came to Bangor, . . . a town noted for its antiquity, its being a bishop's see, and an old, mean looking, and almost despicable cathedral church. . . . From Bangor we went north (keeping the sea on our left hand) to Conway. This is the poorest but pleasantest town in all this county for the bigness of it. It is seated on the bank of a fine river, which is not only pleasant and beautiful, but is a noble harbour for ships, had they any occasion for them there. The stream is deep and safe, and the river broad as the Thames at Deptford. It only wants a trade suitable to so good a port, for it infinitely outdoes Chester or Liverpool itself. . . .

We have but little remarkable in the road from Conway to Holywell but crags and rocks all along the north shore of Denbigh till we came to Denbigh town. This is the county town, and is a large, populous place, which carries something in its countenance of its neighbourhood to England; but that which was most surprising, after such a tiresome and fatiguing journey over the inhospitable mountains of Merioneth and Carnarvonshire, was that descending now from the hills we came into a most pleasant, fruitful, populous and delicious vale, full of villages and towns, the fields shining with corn just ready for the reapers, the meadows green and flowery, and a fine river with a mild and gentle stream running through it. Nor is it a small or casual intermission, but we had a prospect of the country open before us for above twenty miles in length and from five to seven miles in breadth, all smiling with the same kind of complexion, which made us think ourselves in England again all of a sudden.

In this pleasant vale, turning north from Denbigh and following the stream of the river, we came to St. Asaph, a small city with a cathedral, being a bishopric of tolerable good value, though the church is old. . . . From hence we come to Holywell. The stories of this well of St. Winifred are that the pious virgin being ravished and murthered, this healing water sprang out of her body when buried. . . . The Romanists indeed believe it, as it is evident from their thronging hither to receive the healing sanative virtue of the water, which they do not hope for as it is a medicinal water but as it is a miraculous water. . . . There is a little town near the well, which may indeed be said to have risen from the confluence of the people hither, for almost all the houses are either public houses or let into lodgings. And the priests that attend here, and are very numerous, appear in disguise. Sometimes they are physicians, sometimes surgeons, sometimes gentlemen, and sometimes patients, or anything as occasion presents. Nobody takes notice of them as to their profession, though they know them well enough, no, not the Roman Catholics themselves; but in private they have their proper oratories in certain places, whither the votaries resort. . . .

From hence we passed by Flint Castle, a known place but of no significance, and then in a few hours we crossed the river Dee, and arrived at the city of West Chester. . .

The only support we had in this heavy journey was that we generally found their provisions very good and cheap, and very good accommodations in the inns, and that the Welsh gentlemen are very civil, hospitable and kind, the people very obliging and conversable, and especially to strangers; but when we let them know we travelled merely in curiosity to view the country, and be able to speak well of them to strangers, their civility was heightened to such a degree that nothing could be more friendly, willing to tell us everything that belonged to their country, and to show us everything that we desired to see.

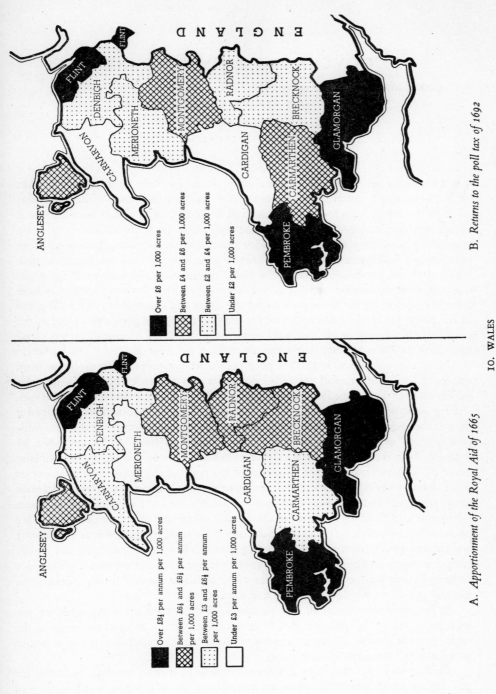

A. *Apportionment of the Royal Aid of 1665*

B. *Returns to the poll tax of 1692*

10. WALES

SHOWING DISTRIBUTION OF WEALTH AS INDICATED BY PROPERTY AND POLL TAXES

B. GOVERNORS AND GOVERNED

171. Poor Law Amendment Act, 1662

(*Statutes of the Realm*, v, pp. 401–405)

AN ACT FOR THE BETTER RELIEF
OF THE POOR OF THIS KINGDOM

(*14 Car. II, cap. 12*)

Whereas the necessity, number and continual increase of the poor, not only within the cities of London and Westminster, with the liberties of each of them, but also through the whole kingdom of England and dominion of Wales, is very great and exceeding burthensome, being occasioned by reason of some defects in the law concerning the settling of the poor, and for want of a due provision of the regulations of relief and employment in such parishes or places where they are legally settled, which doth enforce many to turn incorrigible rogues and others to perish for want, together with the neglect of the faithful execution of such laws and statutes as have formerly been made for the apprehending of rogues and vagabonds and for the good of the poor; for remedy whereof, and for the preventing the perishing of any of the poor, whether young or old, for want of such supplies as are necessary, may it please your most excellent Majesty that it may be enacted, and be it enacted . . . that whereas by reason of some defects in the law poor people are not restrained from going from one parish to another, and therefore do endeavour to settle themselves in those parishes where there is the best stock, the largest commons or wastes to build cottages, and the most woods for them to burn and destroy, and when they have consumed it then to another parish, and at last become rogues and vagabonds, to the great discouragement of parishes to provide stocks where it is liable to be devoured by strangers, be it therefore enacted . . . that it shall and may be lawful, upon complaint made by the churchwardens or overseers of the poor of any parish to any justice of peace within forty days after any such person or persons coming so to settle as aforesaid in any tenement under the yearly value of ten pounds, for any two justices of the peace, whereof one to be of the quorum, of the division where any person or persons that are likely to be chargeable to the parish shall come to inhabit, by their warrant to remove and convey such person or persons to such parish where he or they were last legally settled, either as a native, householder, sojourner, apprentice or servant, for the space of forty days at the least, unless he or they give sufficient security for the discharge of the said parish, to be allowed by the said justices.

II. Provided always that all such persons who think themselves aggrieved by any such judgment of the said two justices may appeal to the justices of the peace of the said county at their next quarter-sessions, who are hereby required to do them justice according to the merits of their cause.

III. Provided also, that (this Act notwithstanding) it shall and may be lawful for any person or persons to go into any county, parish or place to work in time of harvest, or at any time to work at any other work, so that he or they carry with him or them a certificate from the minister of the parish and one of the churchwardens and one of the overseers for the poor for the said year, that he or they have a dwelling-house or place in which he or they inhabit, and hath left wife and children or some of them there (or otherwise as the condition of the person shall require), and is declared an inhabitant or inhabitants there; and in such case if the person or persons shall not return to the place aforesaid when his or their work is finished, or shall fall sick or impotent whilst he or they are in the said work, it shall not be accounted a settlement in the cases abovesaid, but that it shall and may be lawful for two justices of the peace to convey the said person or persons to the place of his or their habitation as aforesaid under the pains and penalties in this Act prescribed. . . .

IV. And for the further redress of the mischiefs intended to be hereby remedied, be it enacted . . . that from thenceforth there be and shall be one or more corporation or corporations, workhouse or workhouses within the cities of London and West-minster, and within the boroughs, towns and places of the county of Middlesex and Surrey, situate, lying and being within the parishes mentioned in the weekly bills of mortality. . . .

VI. And it is further enacted . . . that it shall and may be lawful to and for the said president and governors of the said corporations for the time being or any two of them, or to or for any person authorized and appointed by them or any two of them, from time to time to apprehend or cause to be apprehended any rogues, vagrants, sturdy beggars or idle or disorderly persons within the said cities and liberties, places, divisions and precincts, and to cause them to be kept and set to work in the several and respective corporations or workhouses; and it shall and may be lawful for the major part of the justices of peace in their quarter-sessions to signify unto his Majesty's Privy Council the names of such rogues, vagabonds, idle and disorderly persons and sturdy beggars as they shall think fit to be transported to the English plantations, and upon the approbation of his Majesty's Privy Council to the said justices of peace signified which persons shall be transported it shall and may be lawful for any two or more of the justices of the peace them to transport, or cause to be transported, from time to time during the space of three years next ensuing the end of this present session of Parliament to any of the English plantations beyond the seas, there to be disposed in the usual way of servants for a term not exceeding seven years. . . .

XVI. And whereas for want of some encouragement to such person or persons as shall apprehend rogues, vagabonds and sturdy beggars, the statutes made in the nine and thirtieth year of Queen Elizabeth and first year of King James,[1] in which statutes the constable, headborough or tithing-man of every parish that shall not apprehend such rogues, vagabonds and sturdy beggars which shall pass through or be found in their said parish unapprehended, such constable headborough or tithing-man shall forfeit as in the said statutes is expressed, are not duly executed, be it therefore enacted . . . that it shall and may be lawful to and for any justice of peace to whom any rogue, vagabond or sturdy beggar so apprehended shall be brought, to reward any person or persons that shall apprehend any rogue, vagabond or sturdy beggar by granting

[1] 39 Eliz., cap. 4, and 1 Jac. I, cap. 7.

unto such person or persons an order or warrant under his hand and seal to the constable, headborough or tithing-man of such parish where such rogue, vagabond or sturdy beggar passed through unapprehended, requiring him to pay such person or persons the sum of two shillings for every rogue, vagabond or sturdy beggar which shall be so apprehended. . . .

172. Game Act, 1671

(*Statutes of the Realm*, v, pp. 745–746)

AN ACT FOR THE BETTER PRESERVATION OF THE GAME,
AND FOR SECURING WARRENS NOT INCLOSED,
AND THE SEVERAL FISHINGS OF THIS REALM

(*22 & 23 Car. II, cap. 25*)

Whereas divers disorderly persons, laying aside their lawful trades and employments, do betake themselves to the stealing, taking and killing of conies, hares, pheasants, partridges and other game intended to be preserved by former laws, with guns, dogs, trammels, lowbells, hays and other nets, snares, hare-pipes and other engines, to the great damage of this realm and prejudice of noblemen, gentlemen and lords of manors and others, owners of warrens, for remedy thereof be it enacted . . . that all lords of manors or other royalties not under the degree of an esquire may from henceforth, by writing under their hands and seals, authorize one or more gamekeeper or gamekeepers within their respective manors or royalties, who being thereunto so authorized may take and seize all such guns, bows, greyhounds, setting-dogs, lurchers or other dogs to kill hares or conies, ferrets, trammels, lowbells, hays or other nets, hare-pipes, snares or other engines for the taking and killing of conies, hares, pheasants, partridges or other game as within the precincts of such respective manors shall be used by any person or persons who by this Act are prohibited to keep or use the same; and moreover that the said gamekeeper or gamekeepers or any other person or persons (being thereunto authorized by warrant under the hand and seal of any justice of the peace of the same county, division or place) may in the daytime search the houses, outhouses or other places of any such person or persons by this Act prohibited to keep or use the same, as upon good ground shall be suspected to have or keep in his or their custody any guns, bows, greyhounds, setting-dogs, ferrets, cony-dogs or other dogs to destroy hares or conies, hays, trammels or other nets, lowbells, hare-pipes, snares or other engines aforesaid, and the same and every or any of them to seize, detain and keep, to and for the use of the lord of the manor or royalty where the same shall be so found or taken, or otherwise to cut in pieces or destroy as things by this Act prohibited to be kept by persons of their degree.

II. And it is hereby enacted and declared, that all and every person and persons, not having lands and tenements or some other estate of inheritance in his own or his wife's right of the clear yearly value of one hundred pounds per annum, or for term of life or having lease or leases of ninety-nine years or for any longer term of the clear yearly value of one hundred and fifty pounds, other than the son and heir apparent of an esquire, or other person of higher degree, and the owners and keepers of forests, parks, chases or warrens, being stocked with deer or conies, for their necessary use in respect of the said forests, parks, chases or warrens, are hereby declared to be persons by the laws of this realm not allowed to have or keep for themselves or any other person or persons any guns, bows, greyhounds, setting-dogs, ferrets, cony-dogs, lurchers, hays, nets, lowbells, hare-pipes, gins, snares or other engines aforesaid, but shall be and are hereby prohibited to have, keep or use the same. . . .

VIII. Provided always, and be it further enacted . . ., that if any person or persons shall find him or themselves aggrieved by any judgment which shall happen to be given by any justice of the peace by virtue of this Act, it shall and may be lawful for such person or persons so aggrieved to appeal unto the justices of peace in their general quarter-sessions which shall happen to be held next after such judgment given, who, or the greater number of them, are hereby authorized and empowered to give such relief, and make such order therein, as shall be agreeable to the tenor of this Act; and such judgment, order or determination as by the said justices shall be made upon the said appeal shall be final to all intents and purposes whatsoever, if no title to any land, royalty or fishery be therein concerned. . . .

173. Edward Chamberlayne in praise of the nobility and gentry, 1674
(Angliae Notitia, 8th ed., 1, pp. 40–44)

As some years before the late troubles no people of any kingdom in the world enjoyed more freedom from slavery and taxes, so generally none were freer from evil tempers and humours, none more devoutly religious, willingly obedient to the laws, truly loyal to the king, lovingly hospitable to neighbours, ambitiously civil to strangers or more liberally charitable to the needy. No kingdom could show a more valiant, prudent nobility, a more learned, pious clergy, or a more contented, loyal commonalty. The men were generally honest, the wives and women chaste and modest, parents loving, children obedient, husbands kind, masters gentle and servants faithful. In a word, the English were then according to their native tempers, the best neighbours, best friends, best subjects and the best Christians in the world. Good nature was a thing so peculiar to the English nation, and so appropriated by Almighty God to them (as a great person observed), that it cannot well be translated into any other language, or practised by any other people.

Amongst these excellent tempers, amongst this goodly wheat, whilst men slept the enemy came and sowed tares. There sprang up of later years a sort of people sour, sullen, suspicious, querulous, censorious, peevish, envious, reserved, narrow-hearted, close-fisted, self-conceited, ignorant, stiff-necked, children of Belial (according to the genuine signification of the word), ever prone to despise dominion, to speak evil of dignities, to gainsay order, rule and authority; who have accounted it their honour to contend with kings and governors, and to disquiet the peace of kingdoms; whom no deserts, no clemency could ever oblige, neither oaths nor promises bind; breathing nothing but sedition and calumnies against the established government, aspiring without measure, railing without reason and making their own wild fancies the square and rule of their consciences; hating, despising or disrespecting the nobility, gentry and superior clergy, &c.

These, lurking in all quarters of England, had at length with their pestilential breath infected some of the worse-natured and worse-nurtured gentry, divers of the inferior clergy, most of the tradesmen and very many of the peasantry, and prevailed so far as not only to spoil the best governed state and ruin the purest and most flourishing Church in Christendom, but also to corrupt the minds, the humours and very natures of so many English, that notwithstanding the late happy Restoration of the king and bishops, the incessant joint endeavours and studies of all our governors to reduce this people to their pristine happiness, yet no man now living can reasonably hope to see in his time the like blessed days again. . . .

The nobility and chief gentry of England have been even by strangers compared to the finest flower, but the lower sort of common people to the coarsest bran. The innate good-nature, joined with the liberal education and converse with strangers in foreign countries, render those exceeding civil; whereas the wealth, insolence and pride of these, and the rare converse with strangers, have rendered them so distasteful, not only to the few strangers who frequent England but even to their own gentry, that they could sometimes wish that either the country were less plentiful, or that the impositions were heavier. For by reason of the great abundance of flesh and fish, corn, leather, wool, &c., which the soil of its own bounty with little labour doth produce, the peasants, at their ease and almost forgetting labour, grow rich, and hereby so proud, insolent and careless that they neither give that humble respect and awful reverence which in other kingdoms is usually given to nobility, gentry and clergy, nor are they so industrious or so skilful in manufactures as some of our neighbour nations; so that in England it is no paradox to affirm that as too much indigence in the inferior sort of people doth depress the spirits and dull the minds of them so too plentiful and wanton a fortune causeth in them a laziness and less industry, that state commonly enjoying most peace and order and happiness where either the moderate barrenness of the country, or want of ground or multitude of imposts (as in Holland), do necessitate the common people to be industrious in their callings, and so to mind their own as not to disturb the State and Church affairs. Moreover of the English, especially of the peasantry, it hath been formerly and unhappily observed that then it is happiest with them when they are somewhat pressed and in a complaining condition.

174. Wage assessments

(i) Worcestershire, 1663

(Historical Manuscripts Commission, *Various Collections*, I, p. 323)

	l.	s.	d.
A bailie of husbandry by the year	4	0	0
A chief hind by the year	3	6	8
An ordinary husbandman	2	10	0

	l.	s.	d.
A labourer by the day, without meat and drink, from the feast of All Saints until Candlemas	0	0	7
and with meat and drink	0	0	3
after Candlemas until harvest, without meat and drink	0	0	8
and with meat and drink	0	0	4
A mower by the day, without meat and drink	0	1	0
and with meat and drink	0	0	6
A reaper the like as a mower			
A woman reaper, without meat and drink	0	0	8
and with meat and drink	0	0	4
Sawyers by the hundred, without meat and drink	0	2	4
with meat and drink	0	1	2
A thatcher by the day, without meat	0	1	0
and with meat and drink	0	0	6
A carpenter by the day, without meat and drink	0	1	0
and with meat and drink	0	0	6
A mason, the like wages as a carpenter			
A labourer with a carpenter or a mason by the day, without meat and drink	0	0	10
A maid-servant by the year	1	10	0
A dairy-maid or chief maid-servant by the year	2	0	0

(ii) Somerset, 1666–1685

(*Quarter Sessions Records for the County of Somerset*, IV, pp. 13, 99, 224; Historical Manuscripts Commission, *Seventh Report*, pp. 698–699)

	1666			1671			1677			1685		
	l.	s.	d.	l.	s.	d.	l.	s.	d.	l.	s.	d.
Men servants per annum	4	0	0	4	0	0	4	0	0	4	10	0
Maid-servants per annum	2	0	0	2	0	0	2	0	0	2	10	0
Mowers per diem, finding themselves		1	4		1	4		1	2		1	2
at meat and drink			8			8			7			7
Men making hay, finding themselves		1	0			10			10			10
at meat and drink			6			6			6			6
Women making hay, finding themselves												7
at meat and drink												4
Men at corn harvest, finding themselves		1	4		1	4					1	2
at meat and drink			8			8						8
Women at corn harvest, finding themselves			10			10			7			
at meat and drink			6			6			5			

	1666			1671			1677			1685		
	l.	s.	d.	l.	s.	d.	l.	s.	d.	l.	s.	d.
Masons, carpenters and tilers from 15 March to 15 September, finding themselves		1	4		1	4		1	2		1	2
at meat and drink			8			6			7			7
The same from 15 September to 15 March, finding themselves		1	2					1	0		1	0
at meat and drink			7									7
Threshers and ditchers from 15 March to 15 September, finding themselves		1	0		1	0			10		1	0
at meat and drink			6			6			5			5
The same from 15 September to 15 March, finding themselves			10			10			8			8
at meat and drink			5			5			4			4
Mowing an acre of grass, finding themselves		1	2					1	2		1	2
Making an acre of grass to hay		1	6		1	2		1	6		1	6
Mowing an acre of barley			10						10		1	1
Cutting and binding an acre of wheat		3	0		3	0		3	0		3	0
Mowing an acre of oats						10						
Cutting and binding an acre of beans					2	0		2	0		2	0
Drawing an acre of hemp								4	6		4	6
Spinners, 16 ounces the pound, for pinions									3			3
our own country wool									4			4
Spanish wool									10			10
worsted wool									10			10

175. Extracts from account books of Sir Harbottle and Sir Samuel Grimston, 1683–1700

(Historical Manuscripts Commission, *Verulam Manuscripts*, pp. 209–216)

1683

			l.	s.	d.
Jan.	1.	For a dozen of flambeaus		16	0
		Mr. Barker, for drawing my master's tooth		10	0
	22.	Paid Miss Betty Grimston's French master for a quarter and a half	4	10	0
		Mr. Howard, for tuning her harpsicals		5	0
		Paid the page's master for a month's teaching		15	0
	29.	Silk to make Miss Mary a coat	1	12	0
Feb.	5.	For a looking-glass for Miss Elizabeth Grimston	1	10	0
	12.	A pair of spurs for the page			6
		For Miss Grimston and Miss Mary seeing a play		8	0

1683

			l.	s.	d.
Feb.	26.	For the page's coat		17	0
		For a music book for the page		1	0
		For cutting both the children's hair		10	0
Mar.	5.	A pound of sweetmeats		4	0
		Three pounds of sausages		1	6
		Writing-master for both the children	3	13	0
	26.	Cutting the page's hair			6
Apr.	9.	The huntsman's board-wages, ten weeks and a half	2	2	0
	31.	Paid for the page's waistcoat, silk		13	0
		The page's hat		8	6
		For gloves for him		2	6
May	7.	A shoulder-knot and hat-band for the page		4	8
		Lace on the page's hat		5	0
June	18.	Paid Miss Grimston's singing-master for a month	2	0	0
	25.	Dr. Lower for corsets to Miss Mary	6	9	0
July	2.	A dancing-book for the page		2	6
	9.	The page's stockings, with green tops		7	0
	17.	For a bathing tub	1	5	0
Oct.	1.	A velvet saddle for my master	3	7	6
	18.	Paid the huntsman for making his suit		10	0
	22.	For a portmanteau trunk		11	0
Dec.	16.	For a French grammar		2	6
		Aesop's *Fables*		4	0

1684

			l.	s.	d.
Jan.	21.	Pair of shoes for the page		3	8
		A sword for him		5	0
		A belt for him		3	0
	28.	A fiddler on Miss Grimston's birthday		5	0
Feb.	4.	A music book for the page		2	6
		For eleven tunes for the page			10
	25.	Mr. Isaac, for teaching the two ladies to dance, three months	12	0	0
		Paid the writing-master for both the ladies	4	5	6
May	25.	Mr. Presgrave, for setting Mary's arm		10	0
Nov.	3.	Two quilted caps for the page		2	4
Dec.	8.	Paid for the page's peruke		16	0
	22.	Paid the tailor for six livery suits, making and all materials	12	0	0
	29.	For two pots to make tea, with brass and copper	1	0	0

1685

			l.	s.	d.
Jan.	5.	Cleaning and blacking the page's sword		1	0
		A pair of ear-rings for Miss Mary Grimston		9	0

1693

			l.	*s.*	*d.*
Oct.	27.	Given my master for his pocket as he went a-hunting	1	0	0
Nov.	3.	Given Mr. Smith towards building a poor man's house London:		10	0
Nov.	21.	For a hat for my master		13	0
		A velvet cap		10	0
	24.	Sir Thomas Stamp, for half a year's rent for the house at Soho, taxes deducted	92	9	10
Dec.	11.	One quire of large paper for accounts			8
		Six quires of small paper for letters		1	3
	16	For a hunting saddle		18	0
	21.	Paid Harding for the *Historical Dictionary*	2	0	0

1694

Jan.	3.	Given one that brought my master a copy of verses		5	0
		Paid the train soldier for Soho House, finding himself arms and powder, three days		9	0
		The muster-master's pay			6
Apr.	4.	Two pair of leather spectacles		5	0
		Fourteen gallons of sack	3	17	0
	21.	To Sir Godfrey Kneller for the picture	22	0	0
June	23.	The first payment of the poll tax for my master and lady	3	2	0
Sept.	20.	Paid the mole-catcher for half a year's catching moles in the park and pony-yards		8	0

1695

		Paid Mr. Page on account of the election expenses at St. Albans	324	17	8
May	7.	Paid the coach maker for one year's keeping the coaches	30	0	0
	30.	Paid to Sir Michael Cole for wine	28	15	0
		Smith, the tailor, for six liveries	19	0	0

1696

Jan.	12.	For a peruke for my master	6	0	0
Mar.	24.	For six dozen of Welsh ale	1	4	0
Apr.	2.	For a Suffolk cheese		4	6
		Two pounds of coffee of Mr. Meure		12	0
		One pound of tobacco		2	0
July	8.	Saffron for a maid who had the jaundice			2
Oct.	12.	Dr. Cotesworth's fees, five days	5	5	0
Nov.	10.	Two pair of cotton stockings for my master		7	0
	19.	Paid Mr. Parker, at the Globe Tavern in Fleet Street, for a hogshead of white wine	16	0	0
		and charges		4	0

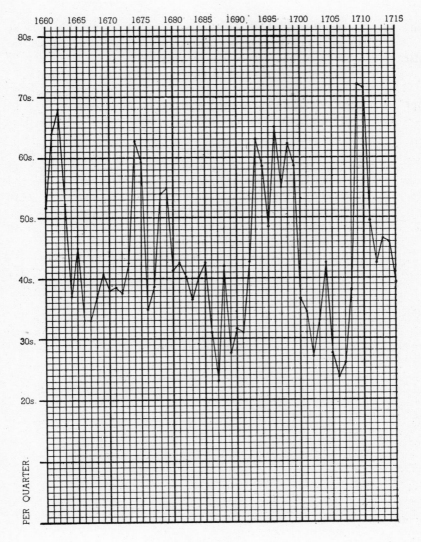

Diagram 4

WHEAT PRICES, 1660–1715
(R. E. Prothero, *English Farming Past and Present*, p. 440)

1696

			l.	s.	d.
Dec. 27.	Four pounds of hair powder			2	0
	Six ounces of snuff			6	0
31.	Paid for two hogsheads of red wine		30	0	0

1697

Jan. 29.	To Mr. Russell, the coffin maker		35	0	0
	For a ream of paper before the tax			7	6
Mar. 30.	A new door-glass to my master's chariot		1	4	0
	Paid for 57 *Gazettes* had to Gorhambury in 1696. and for 84 *Post Boys*			7	0
Apr. 2.	A pair of cinnamon-coloured stockings for my master			7	0
16.	Two pairs of shoes for my master			10	0

1700

Set of six new harness for the coach		12	0	0
The tailor's bill for making the liveries and greatcoat for the coachman and postilion, and a coat for my master		10	12	0
To the draper, Mr. Crosfield, his bill of cloth for the liveries aforesaid and a coat for my master		19	0	0
Paid on the casual account from the 25th of March, 1700, to the 17th of October, 1700, being the day of my master's death		414	14	0

C. TRANSPORT, COMMUNICATIONS AND WEATHER VAGARIES

176. Post Office Act, 1660

(*Statutes of the Realm*, v, pp. 297–301)

AN ACT

FOR ERECTING AND ESTABLISHING A POST OFFICE

(12 Car. II, cap. 35)

Whereas for the maintenance of mutual correspondencies and prevention of many inconveniencies happening by private posts several public post offices have been heretofore erected for carrying and recarrying of letters by posts to and from all parts and places within England, Scotland and Ireland and several parts beyond the seas, the well-ordering whereof is a matter of general concernment and of great advantage as well for preservation of trade and commerce as otherwise, to the end therefore that the same may be managed so that speedy and safe dispatches may be had, which is most likely to be effected by erecting one general post office for that purpose, be it therefore enacted . . . that there be from henceforth one general letter office erected and established in some convenient place within the city of London, from whence all letters and packets whatsoever may be with speed and expedition sent unto any part of the kingdoms of England, Scotland and Ireland or any other of his Majesty's dominions, or unto any kingdom or country beyond the seas, at which said office all returns and answers may be likewise received, and that one master of the said general letter office shall be from time to time appointed by the king's Majesty, his heirs and successors, to be made or constituted by letters patents under the great seal of England by the name and style of his Majesty's Postmaster General, which said master of the said office and his deputy and deputies by him thereunto sufficiently authorized, and his and their servants and agents and no other person or persons whatsoever, shall from time to time have the receiving, taking up, ordering, dispatching, sending post or with speed and delivering of all letters and packets whatsoever which shall from time to time be sent to and from all and every the parts and places of England, Scotland and Ireland and other his Majesty's dominions, and to and from all and every the kingdoms and countries beyond the seas where he shall settle or cause to be settled posts or running messengers for that purpose, except such letters as shall be sent by coaches, common known carriers of goods by carts, waggons or pack-horses, . . . and except letters of merchants and masters which shall be sent by any masters of any ships, barques or other vessel of merchandise, . . . and also except letters to be sent by any private friend or friends in their ways of journey or travel, or by any messenger or messengers sent on purpose for or concerning the private affairs of any person or persons, and also except messengers who carry and recarry commissions or the return thereof, affidavits, writs, process or proceedings or the returns thereof issuing out of any court.

II. And be it further enacted . . . that such Postmaster General for the time being as shall from time to time be made and constituted by his Majesty, his heirs and successors, and the respective deputies or substitutes of such Postmaster General, and no other person or persons whatsoever, shall prepare and provide horses and furniture to let to hire unto all through posts and persons riding in post, by commission or without, to and from all and every the parts and places of England, Scotland and Ireland, where any post roads are or shall be settled and established.

III. And be it further enacted . . . that it shall and may be lawful to and for such Postmaster General . . . and his deputy or deputies . . . to demand, have, receive and take for the portage and conveyance of all such letters which he shall so convey, carry or send post as aforesaid, and for the providing and furnishing horses for through posts or persons riding in post as aforesaid, according to the several rates and sums of lawful English money hereafter mentioned, and not to exceed the same, that is to say,

For the port of every letter not exceeding one sheet to or from any place not exceeding fourscore English miles distant from the place where such letter shall be received, two pence. . . .

And for the port of every letter not exceeding one sheet above the distance of fourscore English miles from the place where the same shall be received, three pence.

And for the like port of a letter not exceeding two sheets, six pence, and proportionably to the same rates for the like port of all packets of letters. . . .

And for the port of every letter not exceeding one sheet from London unto the town of Berwick, or from thence to the city of London, three pence of English money. . . .

And for the port of every letter not exceeding one sheet from England unto the city of Dublin in Ireland, or from the city of Dublin in Ireland unto England, six pence of English money. . . .

And for all and every the letters, packets and parcels of goods that shall be carried or conveyed to or from any of his Majesty's said dominions to or from any other parts or places beyond the seas, according to the several and respective rates that now are and have been taken for letters, packets and parcels so conveyed, being rated either by the letter or by the ounce weight, that is to say. . . .[1]

V. And it shall and may be lawful to and for such Postmaster General and his deputy and deputies to ask, demand, take and receive of every person that he or they shall furnish and provide with horses, furniture and guide to ride post in any of the post roads as aforesaid, three pence of English money for each horse's hire or postage for every English mile, and four pence for the guide for every stage. . . .

XII. Provided also, and be it enacted . . . that no person or persons shall be capable of having, using or exercising the office of Postmaster General, or any other employment relating to the said office, unless he or they shall first take the oaths of allegiance and supremacy. . . .

---

[1] Rates follow for continental towns as far east as Danzig, Constantinople and Aleppo.

177. John Evelyn's account of the great frost of 1683–1684

(*Diary*, ed. 1879, II, pp. 425–429)

27 December 1683. I went to visit Sir John Chardin, a French gentleman who had travelled three times by land into Persia, and had made many curious researches in his travels, of which he was now setting forth a relation. It being in England this year one of the severest frosts that had happened of many years, he told me the cold in Persia was much greater, the ice of an incredible thickness. . . .

1 January 1684. The weather continuing intolerably severe, streets of booths were set up upon the Thames. The air was so very cold and thick, as of many years there had not been the like. . . .

6 January. The river quite frozen.

9 January. I went across the Thames on the ice, now become so thick as to bear not only streets of booths, in which they roasted meat, and had divers shops of wares quite across as in a town, but coaches, carts and horses passed over. So I went from Westminster stairs to Lambeth, and dined with the archbishop. . . . After dinner and discourse with his grace till evening prayers Sir George Wheeler and I walked over the ice from Lambeth stairs to the horse ferry. . . .

16 January. The Thames was filled with people and tents selling all sorts of wares as in the city.

24 January. The frost continuing more and more severe, the Thames before London was still planted with booths in formal streets, all sorts of trades and shops furnished and full of commodities, even to a printing press, where the people and ladies took a fancy to have their names printed, and the day and year set down when printed on the Thames. This humour took so universally that it was estimated the printer gained £5 a day for printing a line only at sixpence a name, besides what he got by ballads, &c. Coaches plied from Westminster to the Temple, and from several other stairs to and fro, as in the streets; sleds, sliding with skates, a bull-baiting, horse and coach races, puppet-plays and interludes, cooks, tippling and other lewd places, so that it seemed to be a bacchanalian triumph or carnival on the water, whilst it was a severe judgment on the land, the trees not only splitting as if lightning-struck, but men and cattle perishing in divers places, and the very seas so locked up with ice that no vessels could stir out or come in; the fowls, fish and birds and all our exotic plants and greens universally perishing. Many parks of deer were destroyed, and all sorts of fuel so dear that there were great contributions to preserve the poor alive.

Nor was this severe weather much less intense in most parts of Europe, even as far as Spain and the most southern tracts. London, by reason of the excessive coldness of the air hindering the ascent of the smoke, was so filled with the fuliginous steam of the sea-coal that hardly could one see across the streets; and this, filling the lungs with its gross particles, exceedingly obstructed the breast, so as one could scarcely breathe. Here was no water to be had from the pipes and engines, nor could the brewers and divers other tradesmen work, and every moment was full of disastrous accidents.

4 February. I went to Sayes Court to see how the frost had dealt with my garden, where I found many of the greens and rare plants utterly destroyed, the oranges and

myrtles very sick, the rosemary and laurels dead to all appearance, but the cypress likely to endure it.

5 February. It began to thaw, but froze again. My coach crossed from Lambeth to the horse ferry at Millbank, Westminster. The booths were almost all taken down, but there was first a map or landscape cut in copper representing all the manner of the camp, and the several actions, sports and pastimes thereon, in memory of so signal a frost. . . .

8 February. The weather was set in to an absolute thaw and rain, but the Thames still frozen.

10 February. After eight weeks missing the foreign posts there came abundance of intelligence from abroad.

178. Act for suppressing highwaymen, 1693

(*Statutes of the Realm*, VI, pp. 390–391)

AN ACT
FOR ENCOURAGING THE APPREHENDING OF HIGHWAYMEN

(4 Gul. & Mar., cap. 8)

Whereas the highways and roads within the kingdom of England and dominion of Wales have been of late time more infested with thieves and robbers than formerly, for want of due and sufficient encouragement given and means used for the discovery and apprehension of such offenders, whereby so many murders and robberies have been committed that it is become dangerous in many parts of the nation for travellers to pass on their lawful occasions, to the great dishonour of the laws of this realm and the government thereof; for remedy whereof be it enacted . . . that from and after the five and twentieth day of March one thousand six hundred ninety and three all and every person and persons who shall apprehend and take one or more such thieves or robbers, and prosecute him or them so apprehended and taken until he or they be convicted of any robbery committed in or upon any highway, passage, field or open place, shall have and receive from the sheriff or sheriffs of the county where such robbery and conviction shall be made and done, without paying any fee for the same, for every such offender so convicted the sum of forty pounds within one month after such conviction. . . .

V. And be it further enacted, that if any person or persons being out of prison shall from and after the said five and twentieth day of March commit any robbery, and afterwards discover two or more person or persons who already hath or hereafter shall commit any robbery, so as two or more of the person or persons discovered shall be convicted of such robbery, any such discoverer shall himself have, and is hereby entitled to, the gracious pardon of their Majesties, their heirs and successors, for all robberies which he or they shall have committed at any time or times before such discovery made, which pardon shall be likewise a good bar to any appeal brought for any such robbery.

179. List of naval vessels lost in the Great Storm, 1703

(N. Tindal's Continuation of Rapin's *History of England*, ed. 1743–1747, III, p. 625)

Vanguard. A second-rate; 640 men; 90 guns. Lost in Chatham harbour; no men nor guns aboard.

Northumberland, Captain Greenway. A third-rate, 446 men, 70 guns. Lost on the Goodwin Sands, no men saved.

Stirling Castle, Captain Johnson. A third-rate; 446 men; 70 guns. Lost on the Goodwin Sands, 63 men saved, with the captain, three lieutenants and chaplain.

Restoration, Captain Emms. A third-rate; 446 men; 70 guns. Lost on the Goodwin Sands; no men saved.

Resolution, Captain Lisle. A third-rate; 446 men; 70 guns. Lost on the coast of Sussex; all the men saved.

Mary, Rear-Admiral Beaumont, Captain Edward Hopson. A fourth-rate; 346 men; 64 guns. Lost on the Goodwin Sands; captain and purser ashore, and but one man more saved.

York, Captain Smith. A fourth-rate; 332 men, 60 guns. Lost at Harwich, all the men saved but four.

Newcastle, Captain Carter. A fourth-rate, 274 men; 54 guns. Lost at Spithead; the carpenter and 23 men more saved.

Reserve, Captain Anderson. A fourth-rate; 226 men; 48 guns. Lost at Yarmouth; the captain, surgeon and 21 more saved.

Lichfield prize, Captain Chamberlain. A fifth-rate; 155 men; 32 guns. Lost on the coast of Sussex; all the men saved.

Arundel, Captain Deering. A fifth-rate; 145 men; 32 guns. Lost at Bristol; all the men saved.

Mortar bomb-ship, Captain Raymond. A sixth-rate; 65 men; 12 guns. Lost on the Goodwin Sands; all the men drowned.

Suffolk hospital, Captain Watkins. A sixth-rate; 80 men; 10 guns. Lost at Bristol; all the men saved.

Eagle advice-boat, Captain Bostock. A sixth-rate; 54 men; 10 guns. Lost on the coast of Sussex; all the men saved.

Vesuvius fire-ship, Captain Paddon. A sixth-rate; 45 men; 8 guns. Lost at Spithead; all the men saved.

Canterbury store-ship, Captain Blake. A sixth-rate; 40 men; 8 guns. Lost at Bristol; 13 men saved.

180. Narcissus Luttrell's account of the winter of 1708–1709

(*Brief Historical Relation of State Affairs*, VI, pp. 393–416)

SATURDAY, 8th January 1709. On 26th of December last it began to freeze, and so continued with snow every day more or less till about Thursday, the 6th instant, when the snow ceased, which was then very deep; but it lay on the ground without the least thaw, and continued freezing till the 9th in the evening, when there was a very great fog, when the weather began to give and the snow to melt. It was very sharp, and the Thames was frozen over in several places, and people walked upon the same.

Tuesday, 25th January. The frost that began on 26th of the preceding month continued for above a fortnight with great violence here in England and in foreign parts, where several were frozen to death in many countries and there were very great snows. But about the 11th or 12th of this month the weather broke, and the snow melted very gently, but in two or three days after, before the snow was quite gone, it began to freeze again, and froze very hard after, and a good deal of snow fell again; and this very day it snowed all day, and there was a very high wind, which blew the snow upon the ground up in the air like a whirlwind.

Saturday, 29th January. Yesterday the weather began to give and the snow to melt, so that it was a very gentle thaw, and continued the same all this day.

Tuesday, 15th February. The frost which began yesterday was sevennight continues still very severe, so that the Thames in some places was frozen over.

Saturday, 19th February. The frost which began the 6th of this month, and was very great, began yesterday to abate, and in the afternoon the weather began to give, and this day continued very gently without any rain.

Thursday, 3rd March. The 26th of last month it began to freeze again very sharp, and since, it snowed pretty much, and the weather hath continued very cold since, freezing hard in the night and thawing in the day, until this evening, when it did not seem to freeze.

Thursday, 10th March. There were letters by the last foreign post which advised that within the island of Paris some thousands of men, women and children have been lately starved to death with hunger and cold.

D. SCIENCE, EDUCATION, SCEPTICISM AND SUPERSTITION

181. Count Lorenzo Magalotti on the Royal Society, 1669

(*Travels of Cosmo, Grand Duke of Tuscany*, pp. 185–189)

On the morning of the 25th[1] his Highness . . . went in his carriage, with his usual retinue, to Arundel House, in the interior of Gresham College, given by Henry Howard of Norfolk for the sittings of the academy or Royal Society, which meets every Thursday after dinner to take cognizance of matters of natural philosophy, and for the study and examination of chemical, mechanical and mathematical subjects.

This Royal Academy took its origin from some philosophers of London, and was restored in the reign of King Charles II, who (besides his own inclination) in order to encourage the genius of men of quality (who, at the time that there was no court in this kingdom, applied themselves diligently to such studies) established and confirmed it, making himself in fact its founder by granting it the most ample privileges, which are recorded in a book ratified by the king, the duke of York and Prince Rupert. This institution is governed by a council, consisting of twenty members elected out of the whole body of the society, the head of which is the president, at present the earl of Brouncker,[2] who, sitting on a seat in the middle of the table of the assembly, has a large silver mace with the royal arms lying before him, with which it is customary for the mace-bearer or the porter of the academy to walk before him. Persons of every nation and religion and profession are admitted among the academicians, and they are under no other obligation than to swear to the observance of the statutes, and to attend the meetings as often as is in their power (especially those for the election of officers), to promote its interests, and not to do anything to its prejudice.

At their meetings no precedence or distinction of place is observed, except by the president and secretary. The first is in the middle of the table, and the latter at the head of it, on his left hand, the other academicians taking their seats indifferently on benches of wood with backs to them arranged in two rows. And if anyone enters unexpectedly after the meeting has begun everyone remains seated, nor is his salutation returned except by the president alone, who acknowledges it by an inclination of the head, that he may not interrupt the person who is speaking on the subject or experiment proposed by the secretary. They observe the ceremony of speaking to the president uncovered, waiting from him for permission to be covered, and explaining their sentiments in few words relative to the subject under discussion; and to avoid confusion and disorder one does not begin before the other has ended his speech. Neither are opposite opinions maintained with obstinacy, but with temper, the language of civility and moderation being always adopted amongst them, which renders them so much the more praiseworthy as they are a society composed of persons of different nations. . . .

The cabinet, which is under the care of Dr. Robert Hooke, a man of genius and

[1] 15/25 April 1669.   [2] William, second Viscount Brouncker, the first president of the Society.

of much esteem in experimental matters, was founded by Daniel Colwall, now treasurer of the academy, and is full of the greatest rarities, brought from the most distant parts, such as quadrupeds, birds, fishes, serpents, insects, shells, feathers, seeds, minerals, and many petrifactions, mummies and gums. And every day, in order to enrich it still more, the academicians contribute everything of value which comes into their hands, so that in time it will be the most beautiful, the largest, and the most curious in respect of natural productions that is anywhere to be found. Amongst these curiosities the most remarkable are an ostrich whose young were always born alive, an herb which grew in the stomach of a thrush, and the skin of a moor, tanned, with the beard and hair white. But more worthy of observation than all the rest is a clock whose movements are derived from the vicinity of a loadstone; and it is so adjusted as to discover the distance of countries at sea by the longitude. Towards this the planets or satellites of Jupiter are of great service, by the observation of whose eclipses (these succeeding one another almost every day) they are studying to find out a method of forming astronomical tables in order to discover the true meridians of the earth, for the different meridians will be shown by the different hours at which they will happen, when observed at different places, beginning from the east and proceeding westward.

The academy has a library (given also by my Lord Henry Howard, and continually increasing in the number of its books) for the convenience of the academicians, and particularly of the two professors, who are to live in the said college (as soon as the fund from which their stipend is to be paid can be arranged) in the apartments preparing for that purpose, distinct from the halls and chambers appropriated to the meeting and to the council. And it is to be their duty to refer to the society all subjects on which their opinion shall be required, and to collect the philosophical and mechanical experiments from the authors who shall be discussed, in order to facilitate the discovery of truth.

182. Proclamation suppressing coffee-houses, 1675

(London Gazette, 27–30 December 1675)

CHARLES R.

Whereas it is most apparent that the multitude of coffee-houses of late years set up and kept within this kingdom, the dominion of Wales and the town of Berwick-upon-Tweed, and the great resort of idle and disaffected persons to them, have produced very evil and dangerous effects, as well for that many tradesmen and others do therein misspend much of their time, which might and probably would otherwise be employed in and about their lawful callings and affairs, but also for that in such houses, and by occasion of the meetings of such persons therein, divers false, malicious and scandalous reports are devised and spread abroad, to the defamation of his Majesty's government and to the disturbance of the peace and quiet of the realm, his Majesty hath thought it fit and necessary that the said coffee-houses be for the future put down and suppressed, and doth (with the advice of his Privy Council) by this his royal proclamation strictly charge and command all manner of persons that they or any of them do not presume, from and after the 10th day of January next ensuing, to keep any public coffee-house, or to utter or sell by retail in his, her or their house or houses (to be spent or consumed within the same) any coffee, chocolate, sherbet or tea, as they will answer the contrary at their utmost perils.

And for the better accomplishment of this his Majesty's royal pleasure his Majesty doth hereby will and require the justices of peace within their several counties, and the chief magistrates in all cities and towns corporate, that they do at the next respective general sessions of the peace to be holden within their several and respective counties, divisions and precincts, recall and make void all licences at any time heretofore granted for the selling or retailing of any coffee, chocolate, sherbet or tea ; and that they or any of them do not for the future make or grant any such licence or licences to any person or persons whatsoever.

And his Majesty doth further hereby declare, that if any person or persons shall take upon them, him or her, after his, her or their licence or licences recalled, or otherwise without licence, to sell by retail (as aforesaid) any of the liquors aforesaid, that then the person or persons so offending shall not only be proceeded against upon the statute made in the fifteenth year of his Majesty's reign (which gives the forfeiture of five pounds for every month wherein he, she or they shall offend therein)[1] but shall (in case they persevere to offend) receive the severest punishments that may by law be inflicted.

Given at our court at Whitehall,
this twenty-ninth day of December 1675,
in the seven and twentieth year of our reign.

183. Samuel Pepys's reflections on the building of the Ark, c. 1684
(Naval Minutes, ed. J. R. Tanner, pp. 205–207)

Noah's Ark must needs be made of some extraordinary timber and plank, that could remain good after having been an hundred years in building, whereas our thirty new ships are some of them rotten within less than five. Moreover Mr. Shere computes from its dimensions that six months would have sufficed to have built what Moses assigns an hundred years for. And enquire also how carpenters and caulkers came to be found if she was the first ship ; what account could be given of all that ado for the preserving of one little family that would of course have the curiosity of coming to see this great work ; and lastly how they all agreed (contrary to all human practice in like cases of distresses, and particularly that of the *Gloucester* and the burning of London within my own observation) to see this means of safety enjoyed by so few persons and oxen and asses, suffering the universality of mankind to perish without contention for a share in it.

Mr. Shere also notes that every country yet known has something particular in the shape of their ships and vessels, and those even the most barbarous ; whereas it seems reasonable that they should have some sort of uniformity did they all derive the same from the same example of the Ark. But so far are they from the Ark that no one

[1] 15 Car. II, cap. 14.

nation builds like it, but every one totally different from it and better than it; and with this, further observes that there is none of these differences of builts that can be said to be wholly accidental, but upon examination will be found strictly adapted to some peculiar circumstances requiring the same rather than any other, with respect to some particularity relating either to the winds, depths, currents, heats or colds, trades and uses, kinds, strength, lastingness or other quality of the materials, their floods, tides, length and nature of voyages or some other, with this only distinction, that as by time and practice some nations do become more knowing in naval architecture their form of built provides for the answering more of these accidents, and as they are less knowing the less perfect is their building in reference thereto; and consequently where they remain most ignorant and barbarous at this day their vessels appear most simple, and yet therein the most excellent, forasmuch as they (namely those of Greenland and India) are found using the most perfect figure of a body that is allowed in the world to be the most apt to pass through the water, namely long and narrow, and so are the canoes; Sir William Petty yielding to me that every degree of our departure from that shape is a lessening of our advantage therein as to sailing for the sake of some other necessary circumstances of convenience to be provided for, inconsistent with that figure, circumstances, I mean, relating to some or other more or less of those before enumerated, and which seem of all others to be least answered in the form described by Moses of the Ark, even beneath that of the Indian canoes saving for its content.

184. Roger North's account of Sir Francis North's attitude to the popular belief in witchcraft

(Lives of the Norths, ed. 1826, I, pp. 266–271)*

In trials of some criminals, whose cases proved very obscure or doubtful, as to such, especially if they were capital, he was infinitely scrutinous, but never more puzzled than when a popular cry was at the heels of a business, for then he had his jury to deal with, and if he did not tread upon eggs they would conclude sinistrously and be apt to find against his opinion. And for this reason he dreaded the trying of a witch. It is seldom that a poor old wretch is brought to trial upon that account, but there is at the heels of her a popular rage that does little less than demand her to be put to death; and if a judge is so clear and open as to declare against that impious vulgar opinion that the devil himself has power to torment and kill innocent children, or that he is pleased to divert himself with the good people's cheese, butter, pigs and geese, and the like errors of the ignorant and foolish rabble, the countrymen (the triers) cry, this judge hath no religion, for he doth not believe witches; and so, to show they have some, hang the poor wretches. All which tendency to mistake requires a very prudent and moderate carriage in a judge, whereby to convince, rather by detecting of the fraud than by denying authoritatively such power to be given to old women.

His lordship was somewhat more thoughtful upon this subject, because that in the year in which Mr. Justice Raymond was his co-judge in that circuit two old women were hurried out of the country to be tried at Exeter for witchcraft, and the city rang with tales of their preternatural exploits, as the current of such tattle useth to overflow. Nay, they went so far as to say that the judges' horses were at a stand and could not draw the coach up the Castle Lane, all which the common sort firmly believed. It fell out that Raymond sat on the crown side there, which freed his lordship of the care of such trials; but he had really a concern upon him at what happened, which was that his brother Raymond's passive behaviour should let those poor women die. The cases were so far clear, viz., that the old women confessed and owned in court that they were witches. These were two miserable old creatures, that one may say, as to sense or understanding, were scarce alive, but were overwhelmed with melancholy and waking dreams, and so stupid as no one could suppose they knew either the construction or consequence of what they said. All the rest of the evidence was trifling. I, sitting in the court the next day, took up the file of informations taken by the justices, which were laid out upon the table, and against one of the old women read thus, "This informant saith he saw a cat leap in at her (the old woman's) window when it was twilight, and this informant farther saith that he verily believeth the said cat to be the devil, and more saith not." The judge made no nice distinctions, as how possible it was for old women in a sort of melancholy madness, by often thinking in pain and want of spirits, to contract an opinion of themselves that was false; and that their confession ought not to be taken against themselves without a plain evidence that it was rational and sensible, no more than that of a lunatic or distracted person. But he left the point upon the evidence fairly (as they call it) to the jury, and they convicted them both, as I remember; but one most certainly was hanged.

The first circuit his lordship went westward Mr. Justice Rainsford, who had gone former circuits there, went with him; and he said that the year before a witch was brought to Salisbury and tried before him. Sir James Long came to his chamber and made a heavy complaint of this witch, and said that if she escaped his estate would not be worth anything, for all the people would go away. It happened that the witch was acquitted, and the knight continued extremely concerned; therefore the judge, to save the poor gentleman's estate, ordered the woman to be kept in gaol, and that the town should allow her 2s. 6d. per week, for which he was very thankful. The very next assizes he came to the judge to desire his lordship would let her come back to the town. And why? They could keep her for 1s. 6d. there, and in the gaol she cost them a shilling more.

His lordship had not the good fortune of escaping all business of that kind, for at Taunton Dean he was forced to try an old man for a wizard; and for the curiosity of observing the state of a male witch or wizard I attended in the court, and sat near where the poor man stood. The evidence against him was the having bewitched a girl of about thirteen years old; for she had strange and unaccountable fits, and used to cry out upon him, and spit out of her mouth straight pins; and whenever the man was brought near her she fell in her fits, and spit forth straight pins. His lordship wondered at the straight pins, which could not be so well couched in the mouth as crooked ones, for such only used to be spit out by the people bewitched. He examined the witnesses very tenderly and carefully, and so as none could collect what his opinion was, for he was fearful of the jurymen's precipitancy if he gave them any offence. When the poor man was told he must answer for himself, he entered upon a defence as orderly and well expressed as I ever heard spoke by any man, counsel or other; and if the attorney-general had been his advocate I am sure he would not have done it more sensibly. The sum of it was malice, threatening, and circumstances of imposture in the girl, to which matters he called his witnesses, and they were heard.

After this was done the judge was not satisfied to direct the jury before the imposture was fully declared, but studied and beat the bush awhile, asking sometimes one and then another, questions as he thought proper. At length he turned to the justice of peace that committed the man and took the first examinations, and, "Sir," said he, "pray will you ingenuously declare your thoughts, if you have any, touching these straight pins which the girl spit, for you saw her in her fit?" Then, "My Lord," said he, "I did not know that I might concern myself in this evidence, having taken the examination and committed the man. But since your lordship demands it, I must needs say I think the girl, doubling herself in her fit as being convulsed, bent her head down close to her stomacher and with her mouth took pins out of the edge of that, and then righting herself a little spit them into some by-standers' hands." This cast an universal satisfaction upon the minds of the whole audience, and the man was acquitted. As the judge went down stairs, out of the court, a hideous old woman cried, "God bless your lordship." "What's the matter, good woman?" said the judge. "My Lord," said she, "forty years ago they would have hanged me for a witch, and they could not; and now they would have hanged my poor son."

185. Zacharias Conrad von Uffenbach on the universities, 1710

(a) Cambridge

(*Cambridge under Queen Anne*, ed. J. E. B. Mayor, pp. 123–198)

On Sunday, 27 July[1] 1710, we set out at 8 a.m. from Littlebury, and reached Cambridge before 12, a distance of ten English miles. . . .

On Monday morning, 28 July, it rained very hard till noon, when we took a little stroll to view the town, which, however, excepting the colleges, is no better than a village, or, if I must compare it to a town, is like Höchst. So too the inns, of which there are two, are very ill-appointed and expensive. We had a recommendation from Baron Nimtsch to a widow, Mrs. Lemons, who gave us indeed a friendly entertainment, though the board and lodging were none of the best.

In the afternoon our hostess sent for an Italian, Ferrari, to speak to us, as he spoke some French, and to serve as our guide. He was very polite, and offered to show us everything. . . . He led us from one college to another, and told us the state of this university, which is certainly very bad. We were amazed that no courses of lectures at all are delivered, and only in winter three or four lectures are given by the professors to the bare walls, for no one comes in. On the other hand the scholars or students have some of them a professor or old fellow of a college, whom they call tutor, who instructs them, the noblemen and other men of fortune, called fellow-commoners, admitting the poor, who serve them as servants, to attend with them. In summer,

---

[1] 16/27 July. Dates throughout are new style.

however, scarcely anything is done, both students and professors being either in the country or in London. . . .

On the 29th of July we visited with Dr. Ferrari first Trinity College, the finest of all the colleges here. It is a double and right royal structure, with two square courts. We saw first the chapel, in the first court to the right, very handsome, well-lighted, long, but somewhat narrow. The altar is of wood, very massive and well made. Behind it we noticed four very fine pictures painted on the wall with water colours, representing Christ, St. John, Mary the Mother and Mary Magdalene. There is nothing else there worthy of notice. Dr. Ferrari next showed us the hall, or room in which the fellows and scholars dine. This is very large, but ugly, smoky, and smelling so strong of bread and meat that it would be impossible for me to eat a morsel in it. On both sides there are placed long, narrow tables, and wooden benches.

Afterwards we went into the second court, to the library, which is a large building, exceedingly handsome, and set apart for the purpose. It could not be handsomer or more convenient for a library. It is very light, long and well-lighted, and also highly decorated, for not only is the floor inlaid with white and black marble but also the cases are all of oak, with excellent and very artistic carvings. It is very neat, made like little closets—an excellent device, because in the first place you can stow away many more books, on both sides and on the walls, and in the next place it is good for those who study there, as they are not put out by seeing others facing them. At the top and bottom of the room there are locked closets, four, that is, in all, with doors of open work. Here the manuscripts are kept. The other closets have no doors. The arrangement of the printed books is not at all good, as it is not according to subjects, or, as it is also called, according to faculties, but according to benefactors, as they have been bequeathed. This is probably done in order to allure others by such good examples. So too the donor's arms are suspended over each. . . .

Afterwards we saw two other colleges from the outside, and Clare Hall pleased us especially on account of the fine new buildings behind. . . . It has also the finest walks or alleys. In the afternoon we went first to St. John's College. We saw first of all the library, in a tolerably large room. The books are more tidy than we have found them elsewhere in England. . . . Afterwards we went behind the college over the new bridge across the little river Cam, from which Cambridge may derive its name. . . . On the other side of the bridge is a garden belonging to the college, in which are fine alleys and a bowling-green. We did not, however, stay long in the garden, but as we heard the bell ring for sermon went to King's Chapel, the finest here. It is certainly an incomparably elegant building of stone, especially as regards the quantity of carved work about it. . . . We heard the sermon, and admired exceedingly the goodness of the organ, for it is small, and yet of a deep and extremely pleasant tone. . . .

On the 30th of July in the afternoon we wished to look through the manuscripts in Trinity College. . . . From thence we went to the Greek's Coffee-House, so called because the host is a born Greek. There we read all the journals and other news which may be seen there. . . . In this coffee-house, particularly in the morning and after 3 o'clock in the afternoon, you meet the chief professors and doctors, who read the papers over a cup of coffee and a pipe of tobacco and converse on all subjects, and thus you can make their acquaintance; for here they are universally far more polite than scholars in London and elsewhere, and are also delighted to see strangers, fewer of whom come hither than to Oxford. When we had spent an hour here Dr. Ferrari came for us, and took us to the Music Club in Christ's College. This music meeting is held generally every week. There are no professional musicians there, but simply bachelors, masters and doctors of music, who perform. It is surprising, as they make such ado about music, and even create professors and doctors of music, that still this nation achieves scarcely anything in it. . . .

In the morning of 31 July we saw Gonville and Caius College. It is a passable building. . . . We could not see what we most wished to see, the library, because the keeper of the keys, or librarian, was out of town. We were shown the room, which is not at all large, and also assured that there was no great number. But as I boasted of the manuscripts, the list of which I had read in the *Catalogus Manuscriptorum Angliae*, a master of arts, one of those present, said that he happened to have the key for them, for they were deposited in another place. I was overjoyed at it, but still more confounded when he brought us into a miserable garret under the roof, which could have been very little or not at all visited, for the top step was buried in pigeons' dung, and the manuscripts lay thick with dust on the floor and elsewhere about the room, in such disorder that although there was a written catalogue of them there I could find nothing at all. . . .

In the afternoon we visited Dr. Bentley, who is Master of Trinity College, and has built himself an excellent house, or wing, to live in, so that he is as well lodged as the queen at St. James's, or better. The rooms are very large and of extraordinary height, the floors curiously inlaid with all kinds of wood, the panels in every room very fine (as now in England tapestry is no longer in fashion, but all is panelled at great cost), the window panes of extraordinary size, and the windows themselves very large and high. He has been greatly reproached for this building, since he endeavoured arbitrarily and without consent of the other fellows to eject a fellow, who as *Doctor Juris* occupied the rooms of a *Doctor Medicinae*. Many controversial pamphlets have appeared upon the subject, filled with personalities, which do no honour to the otherwise famous and very learned Dr. Bentley, but rather serve to degrade him and to scandalize many honest folk. And so indeed I heard many complain of his extreme arrogance, though he tries to be very polite towards strangers, and for an Englishman speaks good and tolerably intelligible Latin. . . .

On 7 August we were in Peterhouse, which, though the oldest college, is yet new and well built. The library is in a poor room of moderate size. The manuscripts stand partly over the door and at the very top of the cases, and were so buried in dust that the librarian was forced to send for a towel for me to wear as a pinafore, that I might not dirty myself too much. . . .

On 9 August, Sunday afternoon, we went again to Trinity College for the sermon, and also heard fine music, especially on the organ. The English excel specially herein, whereas on all other instruments they are mean performers; though they also make much ado of their chimes, and aim at an artistic and agreeable style of ringing; but we could not fancy the clatter, rather were much annoyed to hear it so often, for the scholars or young students mount the towers and ring when they please, often for hours together. . . .

On 10 August we were in Bennet or Corpus Christi College. It is an old and poor building, indeed one of the ugliest colleges, lying entirely among the houses, so that one cannot see it and must approach it by a mean entrance. But this college has the choicest manuscripts of all, which can only be seen with great difficulty; for as it is a legacy, which, if a single codex is lost, passes to another college, there are three keys to it, kept by three different persons, whom it is very difficult to bring together. . . .

On the whole I must further report of Cambridge that the place itself is not at all large, and about as mean as a village, or as Höchst near Frankfurt; and were it not for the many fine colleges here it would be one of the sorriest places in the world. Nor is the entertainment good. One must dine every day pretty nearly alike, as on mutton, etc. . . .

Accordingly, as we found nothing more to do here, we set off on Thursday morning, 14 August. . . .

(b) Oxford

(*Oxford in 1710*, ed. W. H. and W. J. C. Quarrell, pp. 1–61)

On 16 August,[1] Saturday, we drove to Bicester, seven miles, a very wretched place, like almost all the towns with the exception of London, although they are so attractively painted in the English books of description. When we again drove off in the early afternoon we had ten English miles to go to reach Oxford, which we might have done in good time had not one of the front wheels broken half-way there, and . . . we . . . had to go the whole way on foot, leaving the lightened carriage to follow as it could. . . . . At last, after 8 o'clock in the evening, we entered Oxford, ten English miles. . . .

In the afternoon of 17 August we wandered about to see the town generally, and found it rather better than Cambridge, though were it not for the more important colleges the place would be not unlike a large village. As among other places we passed the Physic Garden or *Hortus Medicus* we entered to have a look at it. It is opposite Magdalen College, not very large, and fairly well laid out, but it is ill-kept, and everything in the flower-beds appeared wild and over-grown. The large yews provide the chief ornament; I have nowhere met with finer or better-trained specimens than here. . . .

On 18 August, Monday morning, our first care was to view the world-famed public library of this University, or the Bodleian, as it is commonly called after its founder, and to make ourselves known to the librarian. We asked him to let us have a pass, for unless this is in order no book may be touched, and one sees nothing except what the assistant librarians choose to show for an honorarium, only too often all sorts of rubbish little likely to please anyone who is in search of something more profound. But as it costs about eight shillings and some trouble to gain an entrance,

[1] 5/16 August 1710.

most strangers content themselves with a casual inspection. Every moment brings fresh spectators of this description, and, surprisingly enough, amongst them peasants and womenfolk, who gaze at the library as a cow might gaze at a new gate, with such a noise and trampling of feet that others are much disturbed. So that we might not proceed likewise, we begged the chief librarian, Dr. Hudson, to procure us a pass, which he readily gave. We supposed that this happened out of courtesy, but learned later it was rather from cupidity, and in anticipation of getting large donations out of us. . . .

On the morning of 19 August we went to see Queen's College. When the new building is finished this will be a truly regal edifice. The library is unusual, and certainly fine; but that of Trinity College, Cambridge, far excels it in size, magnificence and grace. The books are not so numerous, and the number of manuscripts, which mostly consist of modern works in the English language, is still less. . . .

As they seemed to have nothing else to show us here, we went to New College, a large, fine, regular edifice. At the back it has a very mediocre garden, consisting of three walks and four flower-borders. . . . We wished to see the library, and discovered it in two wretched little rooms, one above the other. As the librarian was not to be found, and we had no guide with us, we did not care to stay, though we should not have found anything if we had. . . .

As it was still early we inspected the Sheldonian Theatre, and were soon through with it. We had imagined it much larger and quite different. It is a graceful, pretty building, as may be seen in all the books, which are stated to be published *ex Theatro Sheldoniano*, really by the University Press. In the theatre (or rather under it) very few books are printed, as it is thought this might damage the building. The far-famed printing-office, therefore, is housed in a small edifice not far from the theatre, until another printing-office can be built. The whole building is nothing really but one large hall, in which conferring of degrees and solemn functions take place. All around are seats ranged one above the other right to the top. For this reason, probably, it is called the theatre, as it resembles one in this particular. . . .

In the afternoon we went to the Bodleian Library, where we were instructed to take the oath; but the Proctor, as he is called (really *Procurator Academiae*), who was to receive it was not there, for an Englishman, owing to a general lack of courtesy, is seldom up to time. Just as we were about to go, a Dr. Hartmann of Königsberg (son of the well-known Hartmann who wrote *De Succino*) came into the library with some other strangers who had dined with us, with the intention of making a rapid survey of the place, and of having things shown to them in the way I have already referred to. They asked us to accompany them, possibly so that we might contribute something to the crown that the sub-librarian must have. We allowed ourselves to be persuaded, just to see what miserable stuff is shown to people like these, and how little profit they would derive from it. We ran through the three corridors together without moving a single book, and the sub-librarian Crab (an arch-ignoramus who, were it not that this was his living, would have preferred sitting in a tavern to being in the library) merely remarked that there were theological books here. In the lowest corridor he pointed out, or indicated with his finger, where the manuscripts were, without reaching down a single one or taking us up to them, for which in any case the short time he allowed the strangers would not have been long enough. . . .

On 20 August in the morning we went with the sub-librarian Crab to the *Procurator Universitatis*, Mr. Williams of Exeter College, of which he is a fellow, to take the oath *pro admissione ad Bibliothecam Universitatis*. . . . After we had each of us paid eight shillings, . . . we were given permission to go into the library every day from 8 to 11 in the morning and from 2 to 5 in the afternoon with the exception of Saturday, when the library closes at 4 o'clock. . . .

On 23 August we wished to go to the Ashmolean Museum; but it was market day, and all sorts of country-folk, men and women, were up there. . . . Accordingly we inspected Trinity College. This college consists of two courts, of which the first is very poor except the chapel, the second is somewhat newer and better. At the side of the second court is a great garden, in which, however, there are neither trees nor shrubs, nothing but grass plots and several small yews, which are not unpleasant. But the chapel of this college is incomparably beautiful, and is built in the Italian style without a ceiling. Inside it is decorated all over with genuine cedarwood, so that when one enters the chapel it not only presents an incomparable appearance, but also gives off a thoroughly agreeable and excellent perfume. This need not cause surprise, since cedarwood is neither rare nor costly here, for it grows luxuriantly in Ireland and is shipped over at a trifling expense. The altar is especially beautiful and graceful, with carved foliage and fine ornamentation. . . .

We spent the morning of 27 August in the Bodleian Library. In the afternoon we inspected Corpus Christi College. . . . The library of this college is neither large nor unusual as far as space is concerned, but the books are numerous and good, and a large room is to be built on as soon as possible. The chapel is small but neat, and has a beautiful large entrance door of cedarwood like that in Trinity College. Behind is a fairly large new and handsome building. . . . Passing through the new building to the back, one comes straight into a very beautiful long avenue which does not belong to this college but to Christ Church College. We walked along this avenue to the last-mentioned college to hear prayers, as it was just 4 o'clock. The chapel of this college, like all the rest of it, is on a great scale, and, unlike the others, is built like a real church in the form of a cross, of which the chapel proper takes half of the largest portion, and is separated from the remainder by a wooden screen. As it was too large for the services and number of fellows, the whole church was not necessary.

The great window in the chapel is quite unusually well painted – I mean the one in the real chapel, where prayers are read. . . . The painting in this window represents with incomparable art the birth of Christ in life size; and the light and shade caused by the brightness of the Nativity Star in the heavens are particularly admirable. Though, when we were examining it, it was nearly evening and therefore already somewhat dusk, and also a dull day with no sunshine, yet the glory of the colouring, more particularly in the clouds, was extraordinarily beautiful, so that this new work is really far preferable to the old painting on glass which is so much praised and counted amongst the lost arts. The painting in the other windows of the church is fine also, but not by the same hand and rather resembling the old style. . . .

Near the church is a great building in which the library is housed, but which we could not see on this occasion. It was too late, and also just meal time, for in the colleges they dine very early in the evening. We saw the hall or dining-room, which is fearfully large and high, but otherwise poor and ugly in appearance. It also reeks so strongly of bread and meat that one cannot remain in it, and I should find it impossible to dine and live there. The disgust was increased (for the table was already set) when we looked at the coarse and dirty and loathsome table-cloths, square wooden plates, and the wooden bowls into which the bones are thrown. This odious custom obtains in all the colleges. The fellows of the colleges as well as the students or scholars must dine here, but the most important have their meals brought to their rooms at an incredibly high cost. . . .

The morning of 30 August we devoted again to the treasures in the Bodleian, and in the afternoon we inspected Christ Church library. This is a fairly large, fine building on the ground floor, with a considerable proportion of good books in good condition. The library door is made in a special way, so that it closes behind one of itself. The people belonging to the college who were with us knew nothing of any manuscripts. We had soon finished here, and as it was still early we went to a book-shop and bought some books, mostly in English, such as are not to be had either in Holland or in Germany. Books are so dear in England that it would be the greatest folly to purchase Latin books, which in Holland can be had for a third of what one must pay here, for the poorest duodecimo volume costs eighteen pence or two shillings (over half a reichsthaler). The best point is that in the book-sellers' shops here one buys neatly bound volumes, and never even sees unbound books; and all are in neat calf leather, such as English books are renowned for. Not only can one use the books immediately, but one can also inspect them beforehand in the shops, though for the most part the English are not so minute. Indeed Herr Karger assured me on his word of honour that he had seen an Englishman purchase a yard or ell of books as they stood, because that was the exact amount blank in his bookshelf at home. . . .

The 31 August was Sunday. In the afternoon we went to Magdalen College to attend the service, and also to take the opportunity of seeing the notorious Dr. Sacheverell (who, as already mentioned, is a fellow of this college), because we had been assured that he would be present, and had seen him the previous day riding by our house on his way home from the country. He travels everywhere in this district, stirring up the people, who hold him in such honour that they flock to him in hundreds, especially the women; and then his journal is printed every week in London like the newspapers, and sold at a high price. We saw him very well during the whole of the service, and could not help being surprised that such an upstanding and pleasant looking man should ever have commenced so foul a business. . . .

On 25 September . . . after lunch we saw the library in All Souls College, *Collegium Omnium Animarum*. This is a small, poor room with an inconsiderable number of books. But as a Colonel Codrington has bequeathed ten thousand pounds sterling (an amazing sum of money, which could have been turned to better purpose than making a palace for these worthless fellows, as they for the most part are)—as, I say, he has left this sum for the rebuilding of the college, and added to it his fine collection of books worth three thousand pounds, a new library is to be built. This Codrington is reported to have been a very clever man, for when King William came to Oxford for the first time and was to be received in the Sheldonian Theatre, the Orator of the University was taken ill the same day, and amongst all the members of the University (the scandal of it!) no one could be found who could really make a speech. So Codrington dressed himself up as a professor, and in the name of the University delivered a brilliant address in Latin, which greatly pleased the king, who did not recognize him. . . .

E. PLAGUE AND FIRE

186. Nathaniel Hodges's account of the Great Plague, 1665

(Loimologia, or an Historical Account of the Plague in London in 1665, pp. 1–28)

The Plague which we are now to give an account of discovered the beginnings of its future cruelties about the close of the year 1664, for at that season two or three persons died suddenly in one family at Westminster, attended with like symptoms that manifestly declared their origin. Hereupon some timorous neighbours, under apprehensions of a contagion, removed into the city of London, who unfortunately carried along with them the pestilential taint, whereby that disease, which was before in its infancy in a family or two, suddenly got strength and spread abroad its fatal poisons; and merely for want of confining the persons first seized with it the whole city was in a little time irrecoverably infected. . . .

It is to be taken notice that a very hard frost set in on December, which continued three months and seemed greatly to deaden the contagion, and very few died during that season; . . . but upon the frost breaking, the contagion got ground, and gradually got out of its confinements, like a flame that for some time seems smothered, and suddenly breaks out with aggravated fury.

As soon as the magistracy, to whom belonged the public care, saw how the contagion daily increased and had now extended itself to several parishes, an order was immediately issued out to shut up all the infected houses, that neither relations nor acquaintance might unwarily receive it from them, and to keep the infected from carrying it about with them. . . . In order whereunto it is to be observed that a law was made for marking the houses of infected persons with a red cross, having with it this subscription, *Lord have mercy upon us*; and that a guard should there continually attend, both to hand to the sick the necessaries of food and medicine and to restrain them from coming abroad until forty days after their recovery. But although the lord mayor and all inferior officers readily and effectually put these orders in execution, yet it was to no purpose, for the Plague more and more increased, and the consternation of those who were thus separated from all society, unless with the infected, was inexpressible; and the dismal apprehensions it laid them under made them but an easier prey to the devouring enemy. And this seclusion was on this account much the more intolerable, that if a fresh person was seized in the same house but a day before another had finished the quarantine it was to be performed over again, which occasioned such tedious confinements of sick and well together that sometimes caused the loss of the whole.

But what greatly contributed to the loss of people thus shut up was the wicked practices of nurses, for they are not to be mentioned but in the most bitter terms. These wretches, out of greediness to plunder the dead, would strangle their patients and charge it to the distemper in their throats. Others would secretly convey the pestilential taint from sores of the infected to those who were well. And nothing indeed deterred these abandoned miscreants from prosecuting their avaricious purposes by all the methods their wickedness could invent, who, although they were without witnesses to accuse them, yet it is not doubted but divine vengeance will overtake such wicked barbarities with due punishment. Nay, some were remarkably struck from heaven in the perpetration of their crimes, and one particularly amongst many, as she was leaving the house of a family, all dead, loaded with her robberies, fell down dead under her burden in the streets. . . .

But to return. The infection had long doubtfully reigned, and continued through May and June with more or less severity, sometimes raging in one part, and then in another, as in a running sort of fight. As often as the number of funerals decreased great hopes were conceived of its disappearance. Then on a sudden again their increase threw all into dejection, as if the whole city was soon to be unpeopled, which uncertainty gave advantage to the distemper, because persons were more remiss in their provisions against it during such fluctuation. It must not, however, be omitted with what precipitation the trembling inhabitants left the city, and how they flocked in such crowds out of town as if London had quite gone out of itself, like the hurry of a sudden conflagration, all doors and passages are thronged for escape. Yet after the chief of the people were fled, and thereby the nourishment of this cruel enemy had been in a great measure taken away, yet it raged still. And although it seemed once to slay as Parthians in their flight it soon returned with redoubled fury, and killed not by slow paces but almost immediately upon seizure; not unlike what is often seen in battle, when after some skirmishes of wings and separate parties the main bodies come to engage. . . .

Thus therefore in the space of one week were eight thousand persons cut off, and when things came to extremity all helps were called in. So it began now to be solely the magistrates' business how to put a stop to this cruel devastation and save some part of the city at last from the grave. First then therefore were appointed a monthly fast for public prayers to deprecate the anger of heaven. Nor proved it in vain, or were their supplications altogether fruitless, for if we have any regard to the temperature of the season the whole summer was refreshed with moderate breezes, sufficient to prevent the air's stagnation and corruption and to carry off the pestilential steams. The heat was likewise too mild to encourage such corruption and fermentation as helps to taint the animal fluids and pervert them from their natural state.

The government, however, to the duty of public prayers neglected not to add what assistances might be had from medicine, to which purpose his Majesty, with the divine helps, called in also all that was human, and by his royal authority commanded the College of Physicians of London jointly to write somewhat in English that might be a general directory in this calamitous exigence. Nor was it satisfactory to that honoured society to discharge their regards for the public with that only, but some were chose out of their number and appointed particularly to attend the infected on all occasions. Two also out of the court of aldermen were required to see this hazardous task executed, so that, encouraged with all proper means, this province was cheerfully undertaken, and all possible caution was used fully to answer the intention. . . . But all our care and pains were eluded, for the disease, like the Hydra's heads, was no sooner extinguished in one family but it broke out in many more with aggravations, so that in a little time we found our task too great, and despaired of putting an entire stop to the infection. . . .

After, then, all endeavours to restrain the contagion proved of no effect, we applied ourselves altogether to the care of the diseased, and in the prosecution of which, it may be affirmed without boasting, no hazards to ourselves were avoided. But it is incredible to think how the Plague raged amongst the common people, insomuch that it came by some to be called the poor's Plague. Yet although the more opulent had left the town, and that it was almost left uninhabited, the commonalty that were left felt little of want, for their necessities were relieved with a profusion of good things from the wealthy, and their poverty was supported with plenty. . . .

In the months of August and September the contagion changed its former slow and languid pace, and having as it were got master of all made a most terrible slaughter, so that three, four or five thousand died in a week, and once eight thousand. . . . In some houses carcases lay waiting for burial, and in others persons in their last agonies. In one room might be heard dying groans, in another the ravings of a delirium, and not far off relations and friends bewailing both their loss and the dismal prospect of their own sudden departure. Death was the sure midwife to all children, and infants passed immediately from the womb to the grave. Who would not burst with grief to see the stock for a future generation hang upon the breasts of a dead mother, or the marriage bed changed the first night into a sepulchre, and the unhappy pair meet with death in their first embraces. Some of the infected run about staggering like drunken men, and fall and expire in the streets; while others lie half-dead and comatose, but never to be waked but by the last trumpet. Some lie vomiting as if they had drunk poison, and others fall dead in the market while they are buying necessaries for the support of life. . . . The divine was taken in the very exercise of his priestly office, to be enrolled amongst the saints above; and some physicians, as before intimated, could not find assistance in their own antidotes, but died in the administration of them to others. And although the soldiery retreated from the field of death, and encamped out of the city, the contagion followed and vanquished them. Many in their old age, others in their prime, sunk under its cruelties. Of the female sex most died, and hardly any children escaped; and it was not uncommon to see an inheritance pass successively to three or four heirs in as many days. The number of sextons were not sufficient to bury the dead; the bells seemed hoarse with continual tolling, until at last they quite ceased. The burying places would not hold the dead, but they were thrown into large pits dug in waste grounds, in heaps, thirty or forty together; and it often happened that those who attended the funerals of their friends one evening were carried the next to their own long home. . . .

About the beginning of September the disease was at the height, in the course of which month more than twelve thousand died in a week. But at length, that nothing might go untried to divert the contagion, it was ordered by the governors who were left to superintend those calamitous affairs (for the Court was then removed to Oxford) to burn fires in the streets for three days together. Yet while this was in debate the physicians concerned were diffident of the success, as the air in itself was un-infected, and therefore rendered such a showy and expensive a project superfluous and of no effect; and these conjectures we supported by the authority of antiquity and Hippocrates himself. Notwithstanding which the fires were kindled in all the streets. But alas, the controversy was soon decided, for before the three days were quite expired the heavens both mourned so many funerals, and wept for the fatal mistake, so as to extinguish even the fires with their showers. I shall not determine any other person's conjecture in this case, whether these fires may more properly be deemed the ominous forerunners of the ensuing conflagration, or the ensuing funerals. But whether it was from the suffocating qualities of the fuel, or the wet constitution of air that immediately followed, the most fatal night ensued, wherein more than four thousand expired. . . .

Nor in this account are we to neglect that the contagion spread its cruelties into the neighbouring countries, for the citizens which crowded in multitudes into the adjacent towns carried the infection along with them, where it raged with equal fury; so that the Plague, which at first crept from one street to another, now reigned over whole counties, leaving hardly any place free from its insults. And the towns upon the Thames were more severely handled, not perhaps from a great moisture in the air from thence, but from the tainted goods rather that were carried upon it. Moreover some cities and towns of the most advantageous situation for a wholesome air did notwithstanding feel the common ruin. . . .

But the worst part of the year being now over, and the height of the disease, the Plague by leisurely degrees declined, as it had gradually made its first advances. And before the number infected decreased its malignity began to relax, insomuch that few died, and those chiefly such as were ill managed. Hereupon that dread which had been upon the minds of the people wore off, and the sick cheerfully used all the means directed for their recovery; and even the nurses grew either more cautious or more faithful, insomuch that after some time a dawn of health appeared. . . .

About the close of the year, that is on the beginning of November, people grew more healthful, and such a different face was put upon the public that although the funerals were yet frequent, yet many who had made most haste in retiring made the most to return, and came into the city without fear, insomuch that in December they crowded back as thick as they fled. The houses which before were full of the dead were now again inhabited by the living, and the shops which had been most part of the year shut up were again opened, and the people again cheerfully went about their wonted affairs of trade and employ. And even what is almost beyond belief, those citizens who before were afraid even of their friends and relations would without fear venture into the houses and rooms where infected persons had but a little before breathed their last. . . . They had the courage now to marry again, and betake to the means of repairing the past mortality; and even women before deemed barren were said to prove prolific, so that although the contagion had carried off, as some computed, about one hundred thousand, after a few months their loss was hardly discernible.

187. Letter from Samuel Pepys to Lady Carteret on the Plague, 1665
(*Diary and Correspondence of Samuel Pepys*, ed. Braybrooke, VI, pp. 102–103)

Woolwich, 4 September 1665

The absence of the court and emptiness of the city takes away all occasion of news, save only such melancholy stories as would rather sadden than find your ladyship any divertisement in the hearing, I having stayed in the city till above 7,400 died in one week, and of them above 6,000 of the Plague, and little noise heard day or night but tolling of bells; till I could walk Lombard Street and not meet twenty persons from one end to the other, and not fifty upon the Exchange; till whole families, ten and twelve together, have been swept away; till my very physician, Dr. Burnet, who undertook to secure me against any infection, having survived the month of his own house being shut up, died himself of the Plague; till the nights, though much lengthened, are grown too short to conceal the burials of those that died the day before, people being thereby constrained to borrow daylight for that service; lastly, till I could find neither meat nor drink safe, the butcheries being everywhere visited, my brewer's house shut up, and my baker, with his whole family, dead of the Plague. . . .

Greenwich begins apace to be sickly; but we are, by the command of the king, taking all the care we can to prevent its growth; and meeting to that purpose yesterday after sermon with the town officers, many doleful informations were brought us, and among others this, which I shall trouble your ladyship with the telling. Complaint was brought us against one in the town for receiving into his house a child newly brought from an infected house in London. Upon inquiry we found that it was the child of a very able citizen in Gracechurch Street, who, having lost already all the rest of his children, and himself and wife being shut up and in despair of escaping, implored only the liberty of using the means for the saving of this only babe, which with difficulty was allowed, and they suffered to deliver it, stripped naked, out at a window into the arms of a friend, who, shifting into fresh clothes, conveyed it thus to Greenwich, where, upon this information from Alderman Hooker, we suffer it to remain. This I tell your ladyship as one instance of the miserable straits our poor neighbours are reduced to.

188. John Evelyn's account of the Great Fire of London, 1666
(*Diary*, ed. 1879, II, pp. 200–207)

2nd September. This fatal night about ten began the deplorable fire near Fish Street in London.

3rd. I had public prayers at home. The fire continuing, after dinner I took coach with my wife and son, and went to the bank side in Southwark, where we beheld that dismal spectacle, the whole city in dreadful flames near the water side; all the houses from the bridge, all Thames Street and upwards towards Cheapside, down to the Three Cranes, were now consumed; and so returned exceeding astonished what would become of the rest.

The fire having continued all this night (if I may call that night which was light as day for ten miles round about, after a dreadful manner), when conspiring with a fierce eastern wind in a very dry season, I went on foot to the same place, and saw the whole south part of the city burning from Cheapside to the Thames, and all along Cornhill (for it likewise kindled back against the wind as well as forward), Tower Street, Fenchurch Street, Gracechurch Street, and so along to Bainard's Castle, and was now taking hold of St. Paul's Church, to which the scaffolds contributed exceedingly. The conflagration was so universal, and the people so astonished, that from the beginning, I know not by what despondency or fate, they hardly stirred to quench it, so that there was nothing heard or seen but crying out and lamentation, running about like distracted creatures without at all attempting to save even their goods, such a strange consternation there was upon them; so as it burned both in breadth and length the churches, public halls, Exchange, hospitals, monuments and ornaments, leaping after a prodigious manner from house to house and street to street, at great distances one from the other, for the heat with a long set of fair and warm weather had even ignited the air, and prepared the materials to conceive the fire, which devoured after an incredible manner houses, furniture and everything.

Here we saw the Thames covered with goods floating, all the barges and boats laden with what some had time and courage to save, as on the other the carts, &c., carrying out to the fields, which for many miles were strewed with movables of all sorts, and tents erecting to shelter both people and what goods they could get away. ... All the sky was of a fiery aspect, like the top of a burning oven, and the light seen above forty miles round about for many nights. God grant mine eyes may never behold the like, who now saw above 10,000 houses all in one flame. The noise and cracking and thunder of the impetuous flames, the shrieking of women and children, the hurry of people, the fall of towers, houses and churches, was like an hideous storm, and the air all about so hot and inflamed that at the last one was not able to approach it, so that they were forced to stand still and let the flames burn on, which they did for near two miles in length and one in breadth. The clouds also of smoke were dismal, and reached upon computation near fifty miles in length. Thus I left it this afternoon burning, a resemblance of Sodom or the Last Day. It forcibly called to my mind that passage–*Non enim hic habemus stabilem civitatem*–the ruins resembling the picture of Troy. London was, but is no more. Thus I returned.

4th. The burning still rages, and it was now gotten as far as the Inner Temple; all Fleet Street, the Old Bailey, Ludgate Hill, Warwick Lane, Newgate, Paul's Chain, Watling Street now flaming, and most of it reduced to ashes. The stones of Paul's flew like granados, the melting lead running down the streets in a stream, and the very pavements glowing with fiery redness, so as no horse nor man was able to tread on them; and the demolition had stopped all the passages, so that no help could be applied, the eastern wind still more impetuously driving the flames forward. Nothing but the almighty power of God was able to stop them, for vain was the help of man.

5th. It crossed towards Whitehall; but oh, the confusion there was then at that Court. It pleased his Majesty to command me among the rest to look after the quenching of Fetter Lane end, to preserve if possible that part of Holborn, whilst the rest of the gentlemen took their several posts, some at one part, some at another (for now they began to bestir themselves, and not till now, who hitherto had stood as men intoxicated, with their hands across), and began to consider that nothing was likely to put a stop but the blowing up of so many houses as might make a wider gap than any had yet been made by the ordinary method of pulling them down with engines. This some stout seamen proposed early enough to have saved near the whole city; but this some tenacious and avaricious men, aldermen, &c., would not permit, because their houses must have been of the first. . . .

It now pleased God by abating the wind, and by the industry of the people, when almost all was lost, infusing a new spirit into them, that the fury of it began sensibly to abate about noon, so as it came no farther than the Temple westward, nor than the entrance of Smithfield north; but continued all this day and night so impetuous toward Cripplegate and the Tower as made us all despair. It also brake out again in the Temple; but the courage of the multitude persisting, and many houses being blown up, such gaps and desolations were soon made as, with the former three days' consumption, the back fire did not so vehemently urge upon the rest as formerly. There was yet no standing near the burning and glowing ruins by near a furlong's space.

The coal and wood wharves and magazines of oil, rosin, &c., did infinite mischief, so as the invective which a little before I had dedicated to his Majesty and published, giving warning what might probably be the issue of suffering those shops to be in the city, was looked on as a prophecy.

The poor inhabitants were dispersed about St. George's Fields and Moorfields, as far as Highgate and several miles in circle, some under tents, some under miserable huts and hovels, many without a rag or any necessary utensils, bed or board, who from delicateness, riches and easy accommodations in stately and well-furnished houses were now reduced to extremest misery and poverty. . . .

7th. I went this morning on foot from Whitehall as far as London Bridge, through the late Fleet Street, Ludgate Hill, by St. Paul's, Cheapside, Exchange, Bishopsgate, Aldersgate, and out to Moorfields, thence through Cornhill, &c., with extraordinary difficulty, clambering over heaps of yet smoking rubbish, and frequently mistaking where I was, the ground under my feet so hot that it even burnt the soles of my shoes. In the meantime his Majesty got to the Tower by water, to demolish the houses about the graff, which, being built entirely about it, had they taken fire and attacked the White Tower where the magazine of powder lay, would undoubtedly not only have beaten down and destroyed all the bridge, but sunk and torn the vessels in the river, and rendered the demolition beyond all expression for several miles about the country.

At my return I was infinitely concerned to find that goodly church, St. Paul's, now a sad ruin, and that beautiful portico (for structure comparable to any in Europe, as not long before repaired by the late king) now rent in pieces, flakes of vast stone split asunder, and nothing remaining entire but the inscription in the architrave, showing by whom it was built, which had not one letter of it defaced. It was astonishing to see what immense stones the heat had in a manner calcined, so that all the ornaments, columns, friezes, capitals and projectures of massy Portland stone flew off, even to the very roof, where a sheet of lead covering a great space (no less than six acres by measure) was totally melted. The ruins of the vaulted roof falling broke into St. Faith's, which being filled with the magazines of books belonging to the Stationers and carried thither for safety, they were all consumed, burning for a week following. . . . Thus lay in ashes that most venerable church, one of the most ancient pieces of early piety in the Christian world, besides near 100 more; the lead, iron work, bells, plate, &c., melted; the exquisitely wrought Mercers' Chapel, the sumptuous Exchange, the august fabric of Christ Church, all the rest of the Companies' Halls, splendid buildings, arches, entries, all in dust; the fountains dried up and ruined, whilst the very waters remained boiling; the voragos of subterranean cellars, wells and dungeons, formerly warehouses, still burning in stench and dark clouds of smoke, so that in five or six miles traversing about I did not see one load of timber unconsumed, nor many stones but what were calcined white as snow.

The people who now walked about the ruins appeared like men in some dismal desert, or rather in some great city laid waste by a cruel enemy; to which was added the stench that came from some poor creatures' bodies, beds, and other combustible goods. Sir Thomas Gresham's statue, though fallen from its niche in the Royal Exchange, remained entire, when all those of the kings since the Conquest were broken to pieces. Also the standard in Cornhill and Queen Elizabeth's effigies, with some arms on Ludgate, continued with but little detriment, whilst the vast iron chains of the city streets, hinges, bars and gates of prisons were many of them melted and reduced to cinders by the vehement heat. Nor was I yet able to pass through any of the narrower streets, but kept the widest; the ground and air, smoke and fiery vapour, continued so intense that my hair was almost singed, and my feet insufferably surbated. . . .

I then went towards Islington and Highgate, where one might have seen 200,000 people of all ranks and degrees dispersed and lying along by their heaps of what they could save from the fire, deploring their loss, and though ready to perish for hunger and destitution, yet not asking one penny for relief, which to me appeared a stranger sight than any I had yet beheld. His Majesty and Council indeed took all imaginable care for their relief by proclamation for the country to come in and refresh them with provisions. In the midst of all this calamity and confusion there was, I know not how, an alarm begun that the French and Dutch, with whom we were now in hostility, were not only landed but even entering the city. There was in truth some days before great suspicion of those two nations joining; and now, that they had been the occasion of firing the town. This report did so terrify, that on a sudden there was such an uproar and tumult that they ran from their goods, and taking what weapons they could come at they could not be stopped from falling on some of those nations whom they casually met, without sense or reason. The clamour and peril grew so excessive that it made the whole Court amazed, and they did with infinite pains and great difficulty reduce and appease the people, sending troops of soldiers and guards to cause them to retire into the fields again, where they were watched all this night. I left them pretty quiet, and came home sufficiently weary and broken.

189. Narcissus Luttrell's notices of other fires, 1679–1699

(Brief Historical Relation of State Affairs, I, pp. 7–8, 238, 253; IV, pp. 327–329, 527)

The 26th [January 1679], about eleven at night, broke out a fire in the chamber of one Mr. Thornbury, in Pump Court, in the Middle Temple. It burnt very furiously, and consumed, in the Middle Temple, Pump Court, Elm Tree Court, Vine Court, Middle Temple Lane and part of Brick Court. It burnt down also, in the Inner Temple, the cloisters and greatest part of Hare Court. The library was blown up. The Thames being frozen there was great scarcity of water, it being so bitter a frost the water hung in icicles at the eaves of the houses. The engines played away many barrels of beer to stop the fire; but the chief way of stopping the fire was by blowing up houses, in doing which many were hurt, and particularly the earl of Feversham, whose skull was almost broken; but he is now in some hopes of recovery. This fire lasted till the next day at noon, and it is suspected was begun by treachery. . . .

On Sunday, the 19th of November [1682], about ten at night, broke out a dismal fire at Wapping. It burnt all that night, and the next day till about seven in the evening, in which time it consumed near 1,000 houses. There being a great wind it burnt most furiously, notwithstanding the playing of several engines and the blowing up divers houses. The duke of Albemarle and Lord Craven, with the lord mayor and sheriffs and others, were there to give the necessary orders for the quenching thereof. It burnt down to Wapping dock, where a small vessel or two was consumed, and a very stately merchant ship, which has been on the stocks for this two years, narrowly escaped. There were many persons blown up and killed. Some say forty or fifty; others more. Divers of the houses were insured. Particularly one Sir William Warren had near 500*l.* per annum insured, so that it will be the less prejudicial to the owners. . . .

On the 22nd instant [March 1683], at night, between nine and ten, a fire happened at the town of Newmarket, which began in a stable by the carelessness of a groom taking tobacco. The wind being high it burnt so furiously that it consumed above half the town, being quite one side thereof; but his Majesty's house received no damage. However, it proved a great loss, several persons being burnt, and divers fine coaches and horses. . . .

Just now [4 January 1698] a great fire broke out at Colonel Stanley's lodgings in Whitehall, adjoining to the earl of Portland's, which is also on fire, and still burns very violently. . . . The fire at Whitehall began the 4th instant about five in the afternoon, and continued till about seven the next morning. It is said to begin by the carelessness of a servant putting charcoal ashes into a closet. The Lord Portland and the earl of Essex's lodgings were saved, but the king's, queen's, earl of Montagu's, duke of Devonshire's, the Protestant and popish chapels, the guard chamber, duke of Shrewsbury's office, Mr. Chancellor Montagu's, Lord Chancellor's and archbishop's lodgings, the Treasury and Council Chambers and the long gallery leading to the Gatehouse were all burnt. The Banqueting House is standing; and in the afternoon his Majesty took a view of the ruins, and seemed much concerned, and said if God would give him leave he would rebuild it much finer than before. . . .

Yesterday [14 June 1699] a violent fire happened in St. Saviour's Dock in Hornsey Down, Southwark, by carelessness as they were pitching a new vessel, and burnt till this morning, which consumed several ships and between two and three hundred houses, besides a great quantity of deals, &c.

F. SPORT, TRAGEDY AND CRIME

190. Sir John Reresby on his quarrels and duels, 1660–1683
(*Memoirs*, pp. 33–34, 41–42, 46, 137–138, 188–189, 316–318, 325–326)

10 September 1660. I came into Yorkshire, and after some short stay at my own house at Thrybergh went for York by the way of Selby, where a quarrel happening between my company and some others about first going into the boat, I was struck over the head with a cudgel, which provoked me to wound one or two with my sword. This gave so great an alarm to the country people there met together upon the occasion of the market that I was encompassed, and two gentlemen with me and our servants, and after a long defence pulled off my horse, and had certainly been knocked on the head had I not been rescued by my Moor, who got hold of the man's arm that had me down, as he was going to give the blow. Being got up again, I defended myself till I got into the house of an honest man, that gave us protection till the rabble was appeased.

From York I went to Malton, a famous fair for horses, where with other gentlemen I was invited to dinner at Sir Thomas Northcliffe's, who had several handsome daughters, especially one who was to be speedily married to a young gentleman with whom I had a quarrel about his mistress which had near spoiled the match. We should have fought the next day, but considering better of it he submitted (though it was he that had received the affront, for I threw a glass of wine in his face), and so we were reconciled. . . .

2 June 1662. This summer I came into Yorkshire, and was at Thrybergh . . . till July, that I went to Scarborough Spa. There was many persons of quality that went that summer for their health or their diversion. There was amongst others a lord that had a fine woman to his wife, a relation of mine. The lord after a short stay was for going away with his lady, that told me she had a mind to stay a little longer. I endeavoured to persuade his lordship to it, but could not prevail; but finding he had a friend with him who had much power to persuade him, I went and told him that except my lord stayed some few days longer I should look upon him as the reason of his going, and should expect reparation from him for that neglect put upon by my lord's refusing to do what I desired. He seemed very much unconcerned at what I said, and declared he would give me what satisfaction I would desire the next morning, it being then late. I answered I would not trust him except he lay with me all night, which he did; but the next morning he was of another mind, and went and prevailed with my lord and his company to stay some time longer, which put an end to the dispute. . . .

12 July 1663. Sir Henry Belasyse sent to invite me to dinner to the Bear at the bridge foot, where one Mack de Mar, an Irish gentleman, was to give him a venison pasty. After dinner he provoked me to give him some language, which he so far resented that he demanded satisfaction, either by my denying that I meant any injury to him by the saying of the words, and asking his pardon, or by fighting with him.

I denied the first, and so being challenged was obliged to fight him that afternoon in Hyde Park, which I did, an Irish gentleman that he met by the way being his second, and Sir Henry Belasyse mine. At the first pass I hurt him slightly on the sword-hand, and at the same time he closing with me we both fell to the ground, he having hold of my sword and I of his. Sir Henry and his man were fighting at the same time close by, and Sir Henry had got the better, wounded the other in the belly and disarmed him, and was coming in to us as we were both risen and I had got his sword out of his hand, which I took home with me, but sent it to him the next day. The second to Mack de Mar was in danger of death by his wound for some weeks, which made us abscond. . . . But at last it pleased God he recovered. . . .

19 March 1678. This day in the afternoon I had a quarrel at the King's Playhouse upon this occasion. As I sat in the pit a gentleman whose name I afterwards heard to be Mr. Symons came and placed himself next to me, and not content to rest there, after a while desired me to give him my seat, or to exchange with him (pretending he was to speak to one of his acquaintance on the other side). I had no mind to quit my seat, which was better to see than his. Besides, he having been drinking, his manner of asking was not altogether so grateful, insomuch as I denied it. Hereupon he said I was uncivil, and I told him he was a rascal; upon which words we were both prepared to strike one another, had not a gentleman that sat near us (one Sir Jonathan Trelawny) put his hand between us to prevent it.

After a while (when I saw nobody observed us) I whispered him in the ear to follow me out, telling him I would stay for him at the out door. But before I got thither, one (that observed my speaking to him and going out upon it) acquainted the captain of the guard, who was accidentally at the play, with what had passed, and that we should certainly fight if not prevented, who sent one after me and another to him to secure us by a guard, till being the next day brought before the duke of Monmouth (who acted as General), he made us friends, who had not been long enemies, for I had never seen the gentleman to my knowledge before in my life, nor scarce after but once in the street that he desired to give me a bottle of wine, and told me he was very sorry that he had the misfortune to have a dispute with one of whom he heard so good a character. . . .

22 September 1679. Was the day named to poll at Pontefract. My friends that went in with me stayed for me at Ringstone Hill a little longer than ordinary.

That day Sir John Jackson of Hickleton . . . came to me at Pontefract (there having been some coolness between us before) and told me I had affronted him in bringing in his tenants with me to vote for Sir John Kaye, when he designed to bring them in himself. I answered that I wrote to all (or sent to them) that I thought qualified to vote to come in, without regarding who was their landlords; but if he took that ill in his own particular I was a man to give him what satisfaction he required. But I found him not much inclined to fight, for after several words he told me that he neither desired to court my friendship nor enmity. Then I told him we were very equal in that particular, for I thought his friendship was very little to be valued or enmity to be feared; and so we parted. . . .

23 October 1683. I went to my command at York, where these accidents did

happen – that one Mr. Rogers, ensign to Major Sterling's company, having had some dispute with my porter, that gave him some ill language, he had complained to me of him by letter, but in a strain or phrase not so respectful as I expected, which I returned an answer of with some sharpness. At our meeting he began to expostulate the matter, till I told him he was insolent. He replied that he was a gentleman, and could take that language from the governor, but from nobody else. I told him I would take no protection from that character, and if he thought himself injured I divested myself of it from that minute to give him what satisfaction he desired. After this the gentleman was more moderate, and I made him so sensible of the provocation he had first given by his letter to me that he was very submissive, and willing to sit down with my answer and reply.

The Sunday following, being in the Minster, I found the cushion which used to be in my seat removed into the next, where Sir John Brookes was to sit (a person that I had thought fit, with other deputy lieutenants, to disarm in our late search for arms). This gentleman rising at the psalms, I took up the cushion and replaced it in my seat. Service being ended, Sir John asked me if I had the same commission to take his cushion that I had to take his arms. I said I took it as my own, as I should always do when I saw it misplaced ; and if he took his being disarmed ill from me he made choice of an ill place to quarrel in, and that he durst not say those things in any other.

The next day I expected to hear from him, he seeming very much disturbed with this treatment; but not sending to me for reparation, the next morning I sent the captain that then commanded a company in York to tell him that I had stayed some time at home, thinking to hear from him, and believed the reason why I did not to be the character I bore in that city, and did therefore now send to him to tell him that if he had any resentment either for my taking his cushion or arms, I was ready to give him satisfaction as a private person. He returned me this answer, that he was most concerned at my taking away the cushion, because it did prevent his giving it to me, which he intended; but that for satisfaction he thought what had passed between us did not oblige him to ask it in his circumstances, and was willing to be quiet. So that the substance of this matter was this, that he foolishly owned himself under such circumstances as to own himself affronted, but not to see himself righted. I could have been very well content that no occasion of such disputes had offered themselves, but when they do I have found that the best way to prevent them for the future is not to seem too backward in seeking reparation. . . .

18 December 1683. Dining in the city with six gentlemen of quality, coming away with two of them after dinner, they quarrelled in a coffee-house, where we stayed to drink coffee, and though I did what I could to reconcile them went presently out and drew in the street, and made a pass one at the other, but missing one another, closed. By this time I got in to them and broke one of their swords, and so they were parted. The one of them, which was Major Orby, eldest son of Sir Thomas Orby of Lincolnshire (the other's name was Bellingham, of the north, the chief of that family), not thinking this full satisfaction, notwithstanding all my endeavours to make them friends, challenged Bellingham a second time; and taking coach, and I with them, bought new swords by the way, and came towards Hyde Park to fight. As we came

by the way I offered to be second, since they would fight, to either of them, and the other should look out for another to be his. Mr. Orby chose me, and bid Bellingham seek his friend. Bellingham said he never would make use of any second, but . . . would confide in my honour to see fair play done between them; which at the last I accepted at both their entreaties, and by the mercy of heaven missing one another's bodies as they passed one against another the second time, and closing together, I came in to part them, and Mr. Orby's footman doing the same with me, we held their swords so as no mischief was done, only Mr. Orby had a slight prick in the thigh, and Mr. Bellingham had a raze on the forehead, and myself a slight hurt as I came in to part them. After this we went all to supper, and parted good friends.

191. John Evelyn's condemnation of gambling and brutal sports, 1662–1670
(Diary, ed. 1879, II, pp. 140–141, 223, 245)

6 January 1662. This evening, according to custom, his Majesty opened the revels of that night by throwing the dice himself in the privy chamber, where was a table set on purpose, and lost his £100. The year before he won £1,500. The ladies also played very deep. I came away when the duke of Ormonde had won about £1,000, and left them still at passage, cards, &c. At other tables, both there and at the groom-porter's, observing the wicked folly and monstrous excess of passion amongst some losers, sorry am I that such a wretched custom as play to that excess should be countenanced in a court which ought to be an example of virtue to the rest of the kingdom. . . .

17 August 1667. There was now a very gallant horse to be baited to death with dogs; but he fought them all, so as the fiercest of them could not fasten on him, till they ran him through with their swords. This wicked and barbarous sport deserved to have been punished in the cruel contrivers to get money, under pretence that the horse had killed a man, which was false. I would not be persuaded to be a spectator. . . .

16 June 1670. I went with some friends to the bear-garden, where was cock-fighting, dog-fighting, bear- and bull-baiting, it being a famous day for all these butcherly sports or rather barbarous cruelties. The bulls did exceedingly well, but the Irish wolf-dog exceeded, which was a tall greyhound, a stately creature indeed, who beat a cruel mastiff. One of the bulls tossed a dog full into a lady's lap, as she sat in one of the boxes at a considerable height from the arena. Two poor dogs were killed, and so all ended with the ape on horseback, and I most heartily weary of the rude and dirty pastime, which I had not seen, I think, in twenty years before.

192. Count Lorenzo Magalotti on cock-fighting, 1669
(Travels of Cosmo, Grand Duke of Tuscany, pp. 312–314)

His Highness went out in his carriage to see the theatre appropriated to cock-fighting, a common amusement of the English, who even in the public streets take a delight in seeing such battles. And their partiality towards these animals is carried to such a height that considerable bets are made on the victory of the one or the other. To render the cocks fit for fighting they select the best of the breed, cut off their crests and spurs, keeping them in separate coops or walks, and mix with their usual food pepper, cloves and other aromatics, and the yolks of eggs, to heat them and render them more vigorous in battle. And when they want to bring them to the trial, they convey them in a bag, put on artificial spurs of silver or steel, very long and sharp, and let them out at the place appointed for the sport.

As soon as the cocks are put down they walk round the field of battle with great animation, each watching for an opportunity to attack his rival with advantage. The first who is attacked places himself in a posture of defence, now spreading himself out, now falling in his turn on the assailant; and in the progress of the contest they are inflamed to such a pitch of rage that it is almost incredible to such as have never witnessed it with what fury each annoys his adversary, striking one another on the head with their beaks, and tearing one another with the spurs, till at length he that feels himself superior, and confident of victory, mounts on the back of his opponent, and never quits him till he has left him dead, and then by a natural instinct crows in applause of his own victory.

This amusement was not new to his Highness, for he had seen it on board ship, on his voyage from Spain to England, the two young volunteers who were on board frequently diverting themselves with making two cocks fight, which they had previously trained for the purpose.

193. Newsletter account of Thomas Blood's theft of the crown and globe, 1671
(British Museum, Additional MSS. 36916, f. 223)

13 May 1671

About a month since an ancient man in parson's habit brings a young gentlewoman, supposed his daughter, to see the crown and other regalia in the Tower, which are usually showed for money by Mr. Edwards, who hath the keeping of them. Whilst he was showing them, the young woman falls into a swoon, at which the old man seemed much concerned; but by the assistance of Mr. Edwards, his wife and daughter, she was quickly recovered. For this the old man was very thankful then in words, and promised to be more.

Accordingly in few days he brings his wife and daughter to give them further thanks, and would needs fasten a dozen of gloves upon Mr. Edwards's daughter. This begat some acquaintance. About a week after, as a further acknowledgment, they invited Mr. Edwards, his wife and daughter, abroad to a treat, where they very handsomely entertained them. There the old man proposed a young gentleman who had a good estate a fit match for Edwards's daughter. This was kindly received by him, who to requite their kindnesses treated the old man, his wife and daughter, at the Tower on Monday last. Before parting, the old man begged the favour of Mr. Edwards to let three of his friends, who were to go out of town early the next morning, see the crown, &c., before they went. Mr. Edwards promised they should as soon as the Tower was open.

Accordingly he and three more came at 6 o'clock, having left their horses with a fourth person on Tower wharf, to Mr. Edwards, who freely showed them. Upon which they presently seized him, and bound, gagged and wounded him, and took away the globe and crown, which for conveniency of carriage they bent, and leaving Mr. Edwards in that condition walked out of the Tower towards their horses without being discovered, and had got away clear had they but locked or shut the door after them. For before they were out of the Tower they met Mr. Edwards's son-in-law, who was that morning come from Dunkirk and going to see his father, whom not finding in his lodgings, being told where he was, went immediately to that room, where he found him in that condition. Upon sight of him he pointed to the place where the crown used to be, which the young man missing immediately ran forth and cried treason, the crown was stole.

The noise reached the thieves' ears just as they were going over the drawbridge, which made them hasten to their horses, but before they could all mount were overtaken, and two of them, whereof the old man was one, who had the crown and globe, were taken. The other three escaped, but one of them, falling from his horse at Whitechapel and dropping a pistol, and being wounded by a shot from a sentinel as he got on horseback, was there seized on. The other two are got clear away. Those three that were taken were carried up to Whitehall. They were examined by the king, to whom the old man talked very boldly such things that I dare not write. They are all sent to the Tower and put into the dungeon.

The old man is Captain Blood, a very stout man, formerly a papist and captain in the old king's army under Sir Lewis Dyve. Afterwards he was under General Monck in Ireland, where he had an estate of 300*l.* a year; but being discontented engaged in that plot about eight years since for surprise of the Castle of Dublin, for which some were executed, and he flying was outlawed for treason, and his estate being forfeited was given the Lord Ossory. He got into England, where the next prank he played was the rescuing of one Captain Mason from a party of horse who were carrying him down to York to be tried about the northern plot, for which several were executed seven years since. He and three more carried him off without ever being taken.

The last exploit he made before this was the attempt on the duke of Ormonde, which he hath confessed, and that they knew where he had 25,000*l.* in a goldsmith's hands, and that they resolved to have kept him till they had got 10,000*l.* of it, and then he should have had his liberty. But failing in that, necessity, he saith, put him upon this bold attempt, which he did not doubt of succeeding in, and had, if they had but shut the door. One of those taken is his son, who went by the name of Hunt and was in the proclamation about the duke of Ormonde. The other is one Perrot, a dyer. They will all be hanged at least, as they justly deserve. This from all relations is the truest account I can learn of this extraordinary attempt.

194. Sir John Reresby on the murder of Thomas Thynne, 1682
(*Memoirs*, pp. 249–257)

12 February 1682. There happened the most barbarous murder that had happened in England for some time. Mr. Thynne, a gentleman of 9,000*l.* a year (lately married to my Lady Ogle, who repenting of the match had fled from him into Holland before

they were bedded), was set upon by three ruffians and shot to death as he was coming along the street in his coach. He being one deeply engaged in the duke of Monmouth's interest, it was much feared what construction might be made of it by that party, the authors escaping and not known. I was at court that evening when the king, hearing the news, seemed much concerned at it, not only for the horror of the action itself, to which his good-nature was very averse, but also apprehending the ill constructions that the anti-court party might make of it.

At eleven o'clock the same night, as I was going into bed, Mr. Thynne's gentleman came to me to grant a hue and cry, and soon after the duke of Monmouth's page, to desire me to come to him at Mr. Thynne's lodging, sending his coach to fetch me, which I made use of to go to him. I found him surrounded with several gentlemen and lords, friends to Mr. Thynne, and Mr. Thynne mortally wounded by five bullets, which had entered his belly and side, shot from a blunderbuss. I granted immediately several warrants of search for several persons suspected to be privy to the design and that might give some intelligence of the parties that had acted that murder. At the last, by intelligence from a chairman that had the same afternoon conveyed one of the ruffians from his lodging in Westminster to take horse at the Black Bull, and by a whore that used to visit that gentleman, the constables found out both his lodging in Westminster, and there took his man, a Swede by his nation, who, being brought before me, at last confessed that he served a gentleman, a German captain, that had told him that he had a quarrel with Mr. Thynne, and had often appointed him to watch his coach as he passed by; and that particularly that day, so soon as the captain did know that the coach was gone by, he had booted himself, and with two others, a Swedish lieutenant and a Polander, gone, as he supposed, in quest of Mr. Thynne on horseback.

13 February. By this servant I further understood where possibly the captain and his two friends might be found, and after searched several houses with the duke of Monmouth, Lord Mordaunt, &c., as he directed us, till at six o'clock in the morning, having been in chase almost the whole night, I personally took the captain at the house of a Swedish doctor in Leicester Fields, going first into the room, followed by my Lord Mordaunt, where I found him in bed and his sword at some distance from him upon the table, which I first seized and afterwards his person, committing him to two constables. . . .

Several persons suspected for accessories and the two accomplices, viz., the Swedish lieutenant and the Polander, whose names were Stern and Borosky (and the captain's name was Vratz), were soon after taken by constables with my warrant and brought to my house, where before I could finish all the examinations, the king sent for me to attend him in Council, which was called on purpose for that occasion, with the papers and prisoners. His Majesty ordered me to inform him of my proceedings in that matter, both as to the way of the prisoners' apprehending and their examinations, and then examined them himself, giving me order at the rising of the Council to put what had been said there into writing and form in order to the trial. . . .

15 February. The Council meeting again, amongst other things to examine the governor to young Count Königsmarck (a young gentleman resident in Monsieur

Faubert's academy in London), supposed to be privy to the murder, the king sent for me to attend the Council, where he confessing that the eldest Count Königsmarck (who had been in England some months before, and had made addresses to my Lady Ogle before she had married Mr. Thynne) had ten days before the murder come *incognito* into England, and lain disguised till it was committed, gave great cause of suspicion that the said count was in the bottom of it. Whereupon his Majesty commanded me to go search his lodging, which I performed with two constables, but found he was gone the day after the deed was done betimes in the morning, of which I presently returned to give the king an account. . . .

Upon the whole matter we discovered, partly by the confession of the ruffians and the information of others, that Captain Vratz had been eight years a companion and a particular friend to Count Königsmarck (one of the greatest men in the kingdom of Sweden, his uncle being at that time governor of Pomerania, and near being married to that king's aunt); that whilst he was here in England some months before, and had made addresses to the Lady Ogle (the only daughter and heiress to the earl of Northumberland, married after to the now murdered Mr. Thynne), the said count had resented something as done towards him as an affront from the said Mr. Thynne; and that the said captain, out of friendship to the count (but as he then pretended not with his privity), was resolved to be revenged of him, to which intent he, with the assistance of the said Stern and Borosky, had committed this so barbarous act, by obliging the last to discharge a blunderbuss upon him in his coach, the other being present. . . .

20 February. It was much suspected all this while that Count Königsmarck was not got over sea, and on the 20th[1] he was found by the duke of Monmouth's servant disguised at Gravesend alone, coming out of a sculler, intending the next day to go aboard a Swedish ship. The king, having notice, called an extraordinary Council to examine him that afternoon, at which I was present. He appeared before the king with all the assurance imaginable, was a fine gentleman of his person; his hair was the longest for a man's I ever saw, for it came below his waist, and his parts were very quick. His examination before the king and Council was very superficial, but he was after that appointed the same day to be examined, by order of the king in Council, by the Lord Chief Justice, Mr. Bridgeman, the Attorney-General and myself, which was accordingly done; but he confessed nothing as to his being either privy or concerned in the murder, laying his . . . going away in a disguise after the fact was done upon the advice of some friends, who told him that it would reflect upon him were it known he was in England, when a person that was his friend was under so notorious a suspicion for committing so black a crime. . . .

26 February. A gentleman that kept the French academy in London, one Monsieur Faubert, came and desired me to direct him if there was any method to be followed for the saving of Count Königsmarck's life, insinuating at the same time that as he was a gentleman of a vast estate he was sensible he could not lay it out to greater advantage than to support his innocence, and to secure him against the danger of the law in a strange country. I told him that if he was innocent the law would acquit him,

[1] Really the 19th.

though he was a foreigner, as well as if he were a native; but that he ought to be careful how he made any offers of that kind, it being rather the way to make a man of honour his enemy than to gain him for his friend. . . .

27 February. The bills against the three murderers of Mr. Thynne had been found against them as principals, and against the count as accessory at the sessions at Hicks his Hall, where the sessions had begun the 20th of February and ended the 28th, all the rest of the persons apprehended or bound over for that offence being reserved as witnesses till the trial. On the 28th they were tried at the Old Bailey, where, after a trial that lasted from nine in the morning till five in the afternoon, and a very strict prosecution by the relations of Mr. Thynne, the three were brought in principals of the said murder, and received sentence of death accordingly; and the count was acquitted as not accessory by the same jury. . . .

10 March. The captain and other two that were guilty of Mr. Thynne's murder were hanged in the same street where it was committed. The captain died without any expression of fear, or laying any guilt upon Count Königsmarck. Seeing me in my coach as he passed by in the cart to execution, he bowed to me with a steady look, as he did to those he knew amongst the spectators before he was turned off. In fine his whole carriage, from his first being apprehended till the last, relished more of gallantry than religion.

195. Letter from Lady Wentworth to Lord Raby on a determined suicide, 1709
(Wentworth Papers, ed. J. J. Cartwright, p. 81)

March 29, 1709

. . . Poor Mr. Tilson's brother last Saturday in the morning bought a pair of pistols and half a dozen pistol bullets and powder. He charged each pistol with a brace of bullets, set himself in a chair in his chamber, and shot both these pistols into his head, which split his skull in pieces. He left a paper upon his table by him, "Let none be surprised at my death; my time was come, and I have freed myself from a melancholy world." He buried his wife two years ago, and has three children. He was in a very plentiful condition. It is in print, and there they commend him for a very good man, but say it was for a young gentlewoman in Westminster he was in love with. Your Mr. Tilson is very melancholy. I hope he will not do so.

G. CONTEMPORARY STATISTICS

196. Excise farms, 1665–1673[1]

(Historical Manuscripts Commission, *Tenth Report*, VI, p. 178;
Calendar of Treasury Books, I, pp. 638–641; III, p. 833; IV, p. 156)

County	1665	1671 Old Excise	1671 Additional Excise	1671 Total	1673
London, Middlesex and Surrey	£140,000	£140,000	£54,000	£194,000	£200,000
Bedford	1,700	2,652½	467½	3,120	3,300
Berkshire	2,800	4,400	800	5,200	5,600
Buckingham	2,400				4,500
Essex	8,600				14,000
Kent	15,000	60,835	12,195	73,030	25,000
Norfolk	13,800				21,000
Suffolk	7,600				12,000
Cambridge	4,380	6,637½	1,207½	7,845	8,200
Hertford	4,600	7,475	1,325	8,800	9,200
Somerset	4,600	7,150	1,350	8,500	9,000
Yorkshire	16,000	25,805	8,395	34,200	30,000
Sussex	3,800				
Cheshire	2,800	4,025	775	4,800	
Cornwall	2,100	3,637½	662½	4,300	
Cumberland and Westmorland	2,000	2,837½	562½	3,400	
Derby	2,400	4,325	750	5,075	
Devon	9,500	11,500	2,875	14,375	
Dorset	2,700				
Hampshire	3,200	9,950	2,450	12,400	
Wiltshire	3,300				
Durham, Northumberland and Berwick	4,700	6,462½	1,292½	7,755	
Gloucester (with Bristol)	8,000	11,800	2,200	14,000	
Hereford	1,700	2,032½	467½	2,500	188,200
Huntingdon	1,400	1,637½	362½	2,000	
Lancashire	4,400	6,662½	1,237½	7,900	
Leicester and Rutland	3,800	4,800	1,000	5,800	
Lincoln	7,200	9,300	1,900	11,200	
Northampton	3,200	4,287½	912½	5,200	
Nottingham	3,100	3,875	825	4,700	
Oxford	4,200	6,425	1,175	7,600	
Shropshire	2,800	3,725	775	4,500	
Stafford	2,900	3,700	800	4,500	
Warwick	3,000	4,150	850	5,000	
Worcester	3,000	3,875	825	4,700	
North Wales	2,200	2,550	550	3,100	
South Wales	3,500	5,225	975	6,200	
	312,380	371,737½	103,962½	475,700	530,000

[1] For the farm of 1662 see No. 108.

513

197. Sir William Petty's scheme for a census, 1686

(Petty Papers, ed. Marquis of Lansdowne, I, pp. 258–260)

Fiant

Our royal will and pleasure is that you forthwith prepare a *fiant* in due form of law, for letters patents to be passed unto our trusty and well-beloved A.B., containing our grant unto him, his sufficient deputy and deputies, of the full powers and authorities hereafter mentioned, that is to say:

1. To take the number of all our subjects inhabiting in every city, town, county, barony, hundred, parish, village and hamlet in all or any of our dominions throughout the whole world, mentioning the sex, age, marriage and widowhood of each of them.

2. To take an accompt of all the births, burials, baptisms and marriages happening every year within any of the divisions above mentioned.

3. To return of what religion every of our said subjects (male and female of above sixteen years old) are, or do profess to be of, viz., Roman Catholics, Protestants of the Church of England, Jews, Socinians, Quakers, Anabaptists, Presbyterians, Independents, or neuters to any of the seven said sorts above mentioned.

4. Of what dignity or title any of the aforementioned persons are, viz., princes, dukes, marquises, earls, viscounts, barons, baronets, knights, esquires, gentlemen or yeomen, and of what degree in the university or Inns of Court.

5. What offices or employments, ecclesiastical, civil or military, any of them doth bear.

6. And of what quality they are, as freeholders, tenants, freemen of corporations, foreign merchants, sellers by wholesale or by retail, artisans, handicraftsmen, mariners, fishermen, husbandmen or labourers.

7. Mentioning who are in any prison, workhouse, college or free school; as also who are impotent, or live upon public alms, or are common beggars.

8. Who are absent at sea or in foreign parts, or sick in their beds.

9. Hereby requiring all archbishops, bishops, parsons, vicars, curates, churchwardens, parish clerks, and all mayors, bailiffs, justices of peace, constables, headboroughs, tithing-men and beadles, as also all lords and stewards of manors, sheriffs and their bailiffs, and all persons employed by us in collecting or managing our duty of Excise and Hearths, to be aiding and assisting unto the said A.B., &c., by their books, entries and papers concerning the premises; and from time to time to give unto the said A.B. or his deputies copies and extracts of all such books and papers as they have or ought to have concerning the same.

10. And empowering the said A.B., &c., to abstract, regulate and methodize all the several accompts above mentioned, and to make such observations and inferences thereupon as to him shall seem meet and useful for us and our subjects.

11. And the said accompt books, tables and observations to set forth, print and publish; in books and tables, general, special and particular; in great and small volume; every year, month or week, as to him (the said A.B., &c.) shall seem most convenient and useful for ourself or subjects, and with power to licence the same only by such printers or stationers as they shall appoint.

12. Strictly forbidding all persons whatsoever besides the said A.B., &c., to print or sell the same in great or small volume, or in any other method or form than what is set forth and made by the said A.B., &c.

13. Always provided that ourself or Privy Council shall and may forbid to be so published what they shall expressly declare to be prejudicial to our service.

14. Hereby allowing to the said A.B. the yearly stipend or salary of   for his pains and care in and about the premises, to continue to the said A.B., their heirs or assigns, for the space of   years next after the date hereof.

198. Gregory King's estimate of the numbers and incomes of different classes, 1688

("Natural and Political Observations and Conclusions upon the State and Condition of England", in G. Chalmers, *An Estimate of the Comparative Strength of Great Britain*, ed. 1804)

*The annual income and expense of the nation
as it stood anno 1688*

That the yearly income of the nation, anno 1688, was	£43,500,000
That the yearly expense of the nation was	41,700,000
That then the yearly increase of wealth was	1,800,000
That the yearly rent of the lands was about	10,000,000
Of the burgage, or housing, about	2,000,000
Of all other hereditaments about	1,000,000
In all	13,000,000
That the yearly produce of trade, arts and labours was about	30,500,000
In all	43,500,000
That the number of inhabited houses being about	1,300,000
the number of families about	1,360,000
and the number of people about	5,500,000

the people answer to 4¼ per house and 4 per family

That the yearly estates or income of the several families answer

in common to about	£32	0	0 per family
and about	7	18	0 per head
That the yearly expense of the nation is about	7	11	4 per head
And the yearly increase about	0	6	8 per head

That the whole value of the kingdom, in general, is about	£650,000,000

viz.,

The thirteen millions of yearly rents at about eighteen years purchase	234,000,000
The thirty millions and a half per annum by trade, arts, labours, &c., at near eleven years purchase, which, being the value of the five millions and a half of people at £60 per head, comes to	330,000,000

The stock of the kingdom in money, plate, jewels and household goods, about   28,000,000

The stock of the kingdom in shipping, forts, ammunition, stores, foreign or
home goods, wares and provisions for trade abroad or consumption at home,
and all instruments and materials relating thereto   33,000,000

The livestock of the kingdom in cattle, beasts, fowl, &c.   25,000,000

                                                                       ─────────────
                              In all   650,000,000

*A scheme of the income and expense of the several families of England
calculated for the year 1688[1]*

Number of families	Ranks, degrees, titles and qualifications	Heads per family	Number of persons	Yearly income per family	Total of the estates or income	Yearly income per head	Ex-pense per head	In-crease per head	Total increase per annum
				£	£	£	£	£	£
160	Temporal lords	40	6,400	2,800	448,000	70	60	10	64,000
26	Spiritual lords	20	520	1,300	33,800	65	55	10	5,200
800	Baronets	16	12,800	880	704,000	55	51	4	51,000
600	Knights	13	7,800	650	390,000	50	46	4	31,200
3,000	Esquires	10	30,000	450	1,200,000	45	42	3	90,000
12,000	Gentlemen	8	96,000	280	2,880,000	35	32½	2½	240,000
5,000	Persons in greater offices	8	40,000	240	1,200,000	30	27	3	120,000
5,000	Persons in lesser offices	6	30,000	120	600,000	20	18	2	60,000
2,000	Merchants and traders by sea	8	16,000	400	800,000	50	40	10	160,000
8,000	Merchants and traders by land	6	48,000	200	1,600,000	33	28	5	240,000
10,000	Persons in the law	7	70,000	140	1,400,000	20	17	3	210,000
2,000	Eminent clergymen	6	12,000	60	120,000	10	9	1	12,000
8,000	Lesser clergymen	5	40,000	45	360,000	9	8	1	40,000
40,000	Freeholders of the better sort	7	280,000	84	3,360,000	12	11	1	280,000
140,000	Freeholders of the lesser sort	5	700,000	50	7,000,000	10	9½	½	350,000
150,000	Farmers	5	750,000	44	6,600,000	8¾	8½	¼	187,000
16,000	Persons in sciences and liberal arts	5	80,000	60	960,000	12	11½	½	40,000
40,000	Shopkeepers and trades-men	4½	180,000	45	1,800,000	10	9½	½	90,000
60,000	Artisans and handicrafts	4	240,000	40	2,400,000	10	9½	½	120,000
5,000	Naval officers	4	20,000	80	400,000	20	18	2	40,000
4,000	Military officers	4	16,000	60	240,000	15	14	1	16,000
511,586		5¼	2,675,520	67	34,495,800	$12\frac{9}{10}$	12	$\frac{9}{10}$	2,447,100

[1] This calculation is given in slightly varying forms, and it must not be assumed that it is even strictly consistent in itself.

Number of families	Ranks, degrees, titles and qualifications	Heads per family	Number of persons	Yearly income per family	Total of the estates or income	Yearly income per head	Expense per head	Decrease per head	Total decrease per annum
				£	£	£	£	£	£
50,000	Common seamen	3	150,000	20	1,000,000	7	$7\frac{1}{2}$	$\frac{1}{2}$	75,000
364,000	Labouring people and out-servants	$3\frac{1}{2}$	1,275,000	15	5,460,000	$4\frac{1}{2}$	$4\frac{6}{10}$	$\frac{1}{10}$	127,500
400,000	Cottagers and paupers	$3\frac{1}{4}$	1,300,000	$6\frac{1}{2}$	2,000,000	2	$2\frac{1}{4}$	$\frac{1}{4}$	325,000
35,000	Common soldiers	2	70,000	14	490,000	7	$7\frac{1}{2}$	$\frac{1}{2}$	35,000
849,000		$3\frac{1}{4}$	2,795,000	$10\frac{1}{2}$	8,950,000	$3\frac{1}{4}$	$3\frac{9}{20}$	$\frac{1}{5}$	562,000
	Vagrants	—	30,000	—	60,000	2	3	1	60,000
849,000		$3\frac{1}{4}$	2,825,000	$10\frac{1}{2}$	9,010,000	$3\frac{3}{20}$	$3\frac{3}{8}$	$\frac{9}{40}$	622,000

So the general account is

Number of families	Ranks, degrees, titles and qualifications	Heads per family	Number of persons	Yearly income per family	Total of the estates or income	Yearly income per head	Expense per head	Decrease per head	Total decrease per annum
511,586	Increasing the wealth of the kingdom	$5\frac{1}{4}$	2,675,520	67	34,495,800	$12\frac{9}{10}$	12	$\frac{9}{10}$	2,447,100
849,000	Decreasing the wealth of the kingdom	$3\frac{1}{4}$	2,825,000	$10\frac{1}{2}$	9,010,000	$3\frac{3}{20}$	$3\frac{3}{8}$	$\frac{9}{40}$	622,000
1,360,586	Net totals	$4\frac{1}{20}$	5,500,520	32	43,505,800	$7\frac{9}{10}$	$7\frac{45}{80}$	$\frac{27}{80}$	1,825,100

199. Letter from Edmund Halley to John Houghton on the acreage of the several counties of England and Wales, 1690

(Private Correspondence of Samuel Pepys, ed. J. R. Tanner, 1, pp. 39–41)

SIR,

You engaged me not long since to give you an estimate of the quantity of land contained in the kingdom of England, which you conceive may be of use to you in your design of the improvements of husbandry and trade. The question is of that nature that I presume a million or two of acres will break no squares, and to nearer than that I believe the very best of our maps are not true.

The method I took for the doing it was by weighing in nice scales that part of the sheet-map of England copied from Mr. [John] Adams (which I esteem the best), that represents the land, and comparing the weight of the whole with that of a circle taken out of the middle of the map, whose diameter was $138\frac{2}{3}$ miles or two degrees (which is the greatest that the kingdom can afford, being so much between the Severn Sea in the west and the inlet by Lynn Regis in the east; so that the most distant place in England from saltwater is not above 70 miles; but how far the rivers may be navigable, and how far the inland counties may be benefited by them, is a question well worth inquiry and very much conducing to your design). I found that the land of the whole map, together with the isles of Wight, Anglesey and Man, weighed just four times as much as the said circle, and consequently that the acres in the whole kingdom were four times as many as in the circle, which are by computation 9,645,000,[1] whence the whole kingdom must be 38,660,000[1] acres; and this I believe to be no wide conjecture. But from it you are to deduct for the roads, rivers and unimprovable mountains according to judgment.

When my hand was in I thought it might tend to the same end, or be otherwise serviceable to you, to give you the acres of each county of England, which I have derived from the same method of weighing, having cut a six-sheet map in pieces for that purpose, in which each 40,000 acres weighed about a grain. In this I took care to avoid two inconveniences—the one that, the map consisting of several sheets of paper, they were found to be of different thickness or compactness, so as to make a sensible difference, which obliged me to examine the proportion between the weight and area in each sheet. The other was that the moisture of the air imbibed by the paper did very notably increase its weight, which made me very well dry the pieces before I weighed them, that so I might be assured there was no error upon that account; and in so doing I found that in a very few minutes of time their weight would sensibly increase by their re-imbibing the humidity out of the air. This method I conceive exact enough for the uses you design; and that I have not much erred will appear by the consent of this trial with the former. The acres of each county are as follows:

England

	1690	1950[2]
Kent	1,248,000	971,990
Sussex	1,140,000	908,985
Hampshire	1,162,000	933,296
Isle of Wight	150,500	94,146
Dorsetshire	772,000	622,843
Devonshire	1,920,000	1,660,948
Cornwall	960,000	868,167
Essex	1,240,000	962,696
Middlesex	247,000	223,541
Surrey	592,000	449,216
Berks	527,000	454,725
Bucks	441,000	479,360
Wilts	876,000	860,829
Gloucester	800,000	782,646
Somersetshire	1,075,000	1,031,666
Suffolk	995,000	940,157
Hertford	451,000	404,520
Oxford	534,000	470,808
Bedford	260,000	302,942
Worcester	540,000	439,953
Hereford	660,000	538,924

[1] These figures do not agree.   [2] This column is added for purposes of comparison.

	1690	1950
Norfolk	1,148,000	1,303,568
Cambridge	570,000	553,241
Huntingdon	240,000	233,985
Northampton	550,000	635,143
Warwick	670,000	560,702
Stafford	810,000	686,901
Shropshire	890,000	861,800
Lincoln	1,740,000	1,693,697
Nottingham	560,000	529,079
Leicester	560,000	524,197
Rutland	110,000	97,273
Derby	680,000	640,701
Cheshire	720,000	631,180
York	3,770,000	3,719,994
Lancaster	1,150,000	1,050,889
Durham	610,000	627,641
Westmorland	510,000	504,917
Cumberland	1,040,000	968,598
Northumberland	1,370,000	1,279,153

Wales

	1690	1950
Monmouth	340,000	345,001
Carmarthen	700,000	588,472
Glamorgan	540,000	469,112
Pembroke	420,000	393,003
Radnor	310,000	301,165
Brecknock	620,000	469,281
Cardigan	520,000	443,189
Montgomery	560,000	510,110
Merioneth	500,000	422,372
Flint	160,000	163,707
Denbigh	410,000	427,977
Carnarvon	370,000	364,108
Anglesey	200,000	176,695
	5,650,000	5,074,192
	39,938,500	36,579,209

Which is not the 3,000th part of the surface of the globe of the earth, and not above the 1,500th part of the habitable world. I am,

Your very humble servant,

E[dmund] H[alley]

200. John Houghton's examination of the incidence of the property tax, 1693

(*Somers Tracts*, ed. 1809–1815, x, pp. 596–597)

AN ACCOUNT OF THE ACRES AND HOUSES,
WITH THE PROPORTIONAL TAX, &C.,
OF EACH COUNTY IN ENGLAND AND WALES,
HUMBLY PRESENTED TO THE LORDS AND COMMONS, 1693

MY LORDS AND GENTLEMEN,

Of the proportional tax in decimals an arithmetician, in two or three hours, may proportion each county's share of any number of thousand pounds, whatsoever shall be laid; and if it should be laid wholly on acres or houses it would prove nearly as in the table. In which I remark that London, or the lord mayor's jurisdiction only, without the suburbs in Middlesex and Southwark, bears near the sixteenth part of the tax; that Middlesex, abstracted from London (the lord mayor's jurisdiction), bears near the two and twentieth and half part of the tax; and both together, abstracted from Southwark, bear the ninth and half part of the tax; that Cumberland bears but one penny the acre towards the tax, but Middlesex, including London, bears five shillings and elevenpence the acre; that Yorkshire has about the tenth and half part of the acres of the whole kingdom, the eleventh part of the houses (much about the same number with the bills of mortality), and bears about a twentieth part of the tax. It seems to me that the places overcharged have about 150 parliament men, those undercharged about 130 men, those that have no reason to complain about 220 men. Whether this table may show reason for alteration of the method of taxing I submit to proper judges. The matter of fact I here endeavour to demonstrate, and am,

My Lords and Gentlemen,
Your most obedient servant,
John Houghton, F.R.S.

Counties	Monthly Tax, 1691			Acres	Houses	Acres per House	Year's Tax per Acre		Year's Tax per House	
Bedford	1,793	15	6	260,000	12,170	21	I	8	35	6
Bucks	2,630	12	10	441,000	18,390	24	I	5¼	34	6
Berks	2,264	13	2	527,000	16,906	31	I	0½	32	3
Cambridge	2,040	0	0 ⎫	570,000	17,347	33	I	2	38	0
Ely	699	15	10 ⎬							
Chester	1,495	14	4 ⎫	720,000	24,054	30	0	6½	16	0
Chester City	106	16	8 ⎬							
Cornwall	3,081	16	6	960,000	25,374	38	0	9¼	29	2
Cumberland	336	12	2	1,040,000	14,825	70	0	I	5	6
Derby	1,724	16	8	680,000	21,155	32	0	7¼	19	6
Devon	6,459	18	4 ⎫	1,920,000	56,310	34	0	10	28	8
Exeter	232	14	8 ⎬							

Counties	Monthly Tax 1691			Acres	Houses	Acres per House	Year's Tax per Acre	Year's Tax per House
Dorset	2,689	0	10 }	772,000	21,944	35	0 10	29 8
Poole	21	19	4					
Durham	647	13	6	610,000	15,984	38	0 3	9 9
York	6,938	10	4	3,770,000	106,151	35	0 5¼	15 8
Essex	6,196	17	8	1,240,000	34,819	36	1 2½	43 0
Gloucester	3,617	0	6 }	800,000	26,764	30	1 1¼	33 0
Gloucester City	78	16	0					
Hereford	2,263	6	8	660,000	15,006	44	0 10	36 3
Hertford	2,691	12	6	451,000	16,569	27½	1 5¼	39 0
Huntingdon	1,267	8	4	240,000	8,217	29	1 3¼	37 0
Kent	6,653	17	4	1,248,000	39,242	32	1 3¼	41 0
Lancaster	2,013	7	0	1,150,000	40,202	28½	0 5	12 0
Leicester	2,169	8	6	560,000	18,702	30½	0 11	28 0
Lincoln	5,150	4	0	1,740,000	40,590	43	0 8½	30 6
London	8,583	2	8 }	247,000 {	30,997			66 8
Middlesex,								
Westminster	6,081	3	0		69,139	3½	5 11	21 0
Monmouth	780	0	0	340,000	6,490	52	0 6½	28 10
Northampton	2,827	16	4	550,000	24,808	22	1 3	27 6
Nottingham	1,746	16	0	560,000	17,554	32	0 9	24 8
Norfolk	6,741	4	0 }	1,148,000	47,180	24	1 6	36 2
Norwich	360	0	0					
Northumberland	745	11	4	1,370,000	22,741	60	0 1½	7 10
Oxford	2,271	1	4	534,000	19,007	28	0 12¼	28 8
Rutland	480	17	10	110,000	3,263	34	1 0½	35 4
Shropshire	2,407	8	4	890,000	23,284	38½	0 7¾	24 10
Stafford	1,705	3	4 }	810,000	23,747	34	0 6¼	17 6
Lichfield	26	0	0					
Somerset	5,543	1	4	1,075,000	44,686	24	1 4	32 0
Bristol	398	16	8		5,122			18 8
Southampton	4,378	17	4	1,312,500	26,851	49	0 9½	39 2
Suffolk	6,597	1	4	995,000	34,422	29	1 7	46 0
Surrey	3,194	0	4	592,000	34,218	17½	1 3½	22 6
Sussex	3,642	15	6	1,140,000	21,537	53	0 9¼	40 8
Warwick	2,384	17	6	670,000	21,973	30	1 10¼	26 0
Worcester	2,107	18	0 }	540,000	20,634	26	0 11¾	25 10
Worcester City	110	19	0					
Wilts	3,933	15	2	876,000	27,093	32	1 1	35 0
Westmorland	232	0	0	510,000	6,501	79	0 1½	8 6
Anglesey	251	7	4	200,000	1,840	109	0 3½	32 4
Brecknock	565	0	11	620,000	5,934	104	0 2⅓	22 10

Counties	Monthly Tax 1691			Acres	Houses	Acres per House	Year's Tax per Acre		Year's Tax per House	
Cardigan	211	11	7	520,000	3,163	164	0	1¼	16	0
Carmarthen	544	13	4	700,000	5,352	131	0	2¼	24	5
Carnarvon	293	4	4	370,000	2,765	134	0	2¼	25	5
Denbigh	447	1	2	410,000	6,398	64	0	3⅛	16	9
Flint	237	14	8	160,000	3,150	51	0	4¼	18	1
Glamorgan	757	15	8	540,000	9,644	56	0	4	18	10
Merioneth	201	12	2	500,000	2,590	193	0	1¼	18	8
Montgomery	552	4	4	560,000	5,660	99	0	3	23	5
Pembroke	653	0	0	420,000	4,329	97	0	4¾	36	2
Haverfordwest	30	6	10							
Radnor	348	13	4	310,000	3,158	98	0	3¼	26	6
Total	137,641	18	2	39,938,500	1,175,951					

201. Charles Davenant's figures of the produce of taxes, 1695

(*Political and Commercial Works*, ed. Sir Charles Whitworth, I, p. 39)

A TABLE OF THE PRODUCE OF EACH COUNTY IN POOR RATES, EXCISE AND POLL MONEY

	Estimate of the poor rate for one year c. 1680–1685	*Excise on beer and ale in the year 1689*			*First quarterly poll 1692*		
	l.	*l.*	*s.*	*d.*	*l.*	*s.*	*d.*
Bedfordshire	6,911	5,549	7	3	6,400	11	9¾
Berkshire	9,800	9,105	12	9½	10,353	3	5
Buckinghamshire	14,800	7,261	16	5½	9,550	6	2
Cambridgeshire	9,128	10,442	7	1	9,612	15	2
Cheshire	5,796	9,836	10	4½	8,791	10	0
Cornwall	9,257	10,595	12	3½	9,613	19	10
Cumberland	4,988	5,746	10	4	2,116	11	6
Derbyshire	7,953	11,960	12	4¼	7,883	4	6
Devon	34,764	34,525	7	11	28,821	9	3
Dorset	13,885	7,568	11	7½	9,737	3	10
Durham, Northumberland and Berwick	13,620	21,216	8	3	13,028	19	9
Essex	37,348	21,676	4	5	20,820	10	2
Gloucestershire	19,600	14,704	8	3	13,508	17	9
Herefordshire	8,687	6,256	5	9½	6,480	12	10

	Estimate of the poor rate for one year c. 1680–1685	Excise on beer and ale in the year 1689			First quarterly poll 1692		
	l.	l.	s.	d.	l.	s.	d.
Hertfordshire	10,760	13,264	2	11½	11,054	1	1½
Huntingdonshire	5,850	4,437	7	4½	4,238	16	4
Kent	29,875	24,647	15	10½	24,275	2	5
Lancashire	7,200	14,501	4	4½	12,732	15	2
Leicestershire	11,600	8,258	18	9½	10,002	8	7½
Lincolnshire	31,500	15,949	4	5½	19,248	1	10
Norfolk	46,200	26,899	11	6¼	24,521	18	8
Northamptonshire	21,516	9,845	17	8½	12,348	1	8
Nottinghamshire	11,760	5,837	10	4¼	7,085	9	8
Oxfordshire	7,950	11,804	9	6	10,728	13	4
Rutland	3,730	1,435	8	8	1,785	7	4
Salop	13,375	9,874	9	3	10,783	12	8
Somerset and Bristol	30,263	31,133	9	2	22,295	14	3½
Southamptonshire	13,173	11,160	18	7½	14,083	6	2
Staffordshire	7,150	10,927	7	0	8,725	3	2
Suffolk	25,750	19,635	9	8½	19,865	3	10
Surrey and Southwark	15,600	34,234	1	10½	20,444	12	10
Sussex	18,720	7,730	10	1½	12,924	16	11½
Warwickshire	9,800	11,639	3	10	10,441	17	5
Westmorland	1,890	2,322	16	1	1,737	7	0
Wiltshire	18,240	10,679	8	8½	13,771	2	3½
Worcestershire	10,640	12,793	10	1½	9,763	18	3
Yorkshire	26,150	52,226	19	8½	39,289	9	1
Wales, North and South	33,753	26,431	18	4	21,029	11	0
London, Middlesex and Westminster	56,380	140,358	13	2	97,622	5	11
Grand totals	665,362	694,476	2	5¾	597,518	13	0¼

Of the eleven Home Counties, viz., Surrey and Southwark, Hertford, Bedford, Cambridge, Kent, Essex, Norfolk, Suffolk, Berkshire, Buckingham and Oxford, the total is	214,122	184,520	19	5¼	167,626	18	11¼
Of the rest of England, excluding London, Middlesex and Westminster, the total is	394,860	369,596	9	10½	332,269	8	2

Part VI
TRADE AND PLANTATIONS

TRADE AND PLANTATIONS

Introduction

IN the economic sphere the effect of the Restoration was to hasten the process, already begun, which was destined to transform England from a country mainly agricultural to a country largely commercial in character. To the influence of the enterprising merchants and financiers who had been brought to the front by the civil wars and the general upheaval of the Commonwealth period was now added the influence of monarchs and members of the landed aristocracy who had experienced during their exile on the Continent the advantages derived by the Dutch from their widespread commercial activities. Opposition had still to be faced from those who disliked any innovation, and were ready to argue that any development of commerce was bound to involve a fall in the value of land; but the opposition was much less serious than in other circumstances it would have been.

With the development of commerce was inseparably connected the progress of colonization. Under the early Stuarts colonization had been largely in the hands of those opposed to the religious or political system established in England, and the great majority of the colonizers had been drawn from the considerable body of men who hoped to found in other lands a community more in harmony with their own ideas. Such countenance as these men had received from the government had indeed been due mainly to a belief that unquiet spirits of this type were better out of the country. But now the leading statesmen became also the chief promoters of colonization, and the occupants of the throne gave it their fullest support. One of the earliest acts of the restored monarch was to establish a committee of Council to collect information and offer advice regarding the plantations,[1] and this body was continued, in various forms[2] but almost without interruption, until the establishment under William III of what was to become the permanent Board of Trade.[3]

At the same time a complete code was worked out, in part based on Commonwealth models, regulating the commerce of the plantations and the mother-country in the supposed interests of them both.[4] It is true that the framers of the code were better acquainted with, and paid more attention to, the needs of the mother-country than those of the plantations; and their tendency towards selfishness became more apparent in the frequent amendments by which the system was kept in force until late in the eighteenth century. But the regulations were by no means entirely one-sided. It was fully recognized that the plantations should have a monopoly of the English tobacco market, to the ruin of the English producer and the serious disadvantage of the English consumer;[5] and every effort was made, though without much success, to secure for them a similar monopoly of the supply of naval stores.[6] The reform of the coinage[7] was primarily intended to promote internal trade in England; but it might have done something to improve the financial relations of plantations and mother-country if so many of the former had not been in the position of debtor states,

[1] No. 202.   [2] No. 205.   [3] No. 207.   [4] No. 203.
[5] No. 204.   [6] No. 208.   [7] No. 206.

condemned, apparently permanently, to import more than they produced, and therefore to be always short of specie.

An inevitable consequence of the stress laid upon trade was that the colonies most highly prized at home were those in tropical or sub-tropical rather than those in temperate regions. The former supplied goods which the mother-country could not produce for herself; the latter merely competed with her in her own markets. Thus the East Indian settlements always bulked largely in the eyes of English statesmen, though the criticism was often made that the goods they sent home were mainly luxuries which could well be dispensed with. Under the early Stuarts the East India Company had established a number of factories or trading stations on the mainland of India, the most important being at Surat and Madras. To these was now added a factory at Bombay, surrendered by the Portuguese in full sovereignty to Charles II,[1] handed over by him to the Company, and extensively developed as the principal English station on the west coast.[2] As yet, however, the Moghul rulers of India were strong enough to keep the peace among the various groups of Europeans competing for the trade of the peninsula, and the Company had little temptation to develop, as it did in the eighteenth century, into a political power. Its main interest, indeed, lay in the European wars, on the outcome of which its fortunes were bound largely to depend, and in the problems of the long sea voyage by which alone its communications with its factories could profitably be maintained.[3]

Second in importance only to the East Indies were the West Indies, where the older and healthier settlements, with which may be included the Bermudas,[4] were in process of being eclipsed by tropical colonies better fitted to supply the wants of the home country. Most promising of all was Cromwell's acquisition, Jamaica, the rapidly developing prosperity of which[5] was scarcely checked even by the disastrous earthquake of 1692.[6]

Necessary adjuncts, in contemporary opinion, of the West Indian settlements were the stations on the West African coast from which the slaves were shipped on whose labour the settlements depended. These stations it was the task of successive African Companies[7] to establish and maintain; but the triple burden of excluding interlopers, contending with powerful European rivals, and facing a thoroughly unhealthy climate, proved too much for all of them, and by the close of Anne's reign the prospects of the merchants were bleak in the extreme.[8] The slave trade as then conducted was by no means as iniquitous as it became in the eighteenth century, and there was much to be said for the contention that slaves transported to America were rescued from even worse conditions at home; but even at the best it was clearly an unsavoury and degrading business.[9]

As yet the North American colonies which were to develop into the United States of America[10] were regarded with doubt. They were too strong, too independent in their outlook, and too closely akin to the mother-country in the character of their produce. Beyond them to the north, however, lay Newfoundland, the fisheries of which were highly valued both in themselves and as a training ground for seamen, and the Hudson Bay territory, which produced furs greatly esteemed in the European market. Paradoxically enough the original object of the home government was to prevent any extensive settlement in Newfoundland in order that the fishing might be

---

[1] No. 336.   [2] No. 210.   [3] No. 209.   [4] No. 212.
[5] No. 211.   [6] No. 213.   [7] No. 214.   [8] No. 216.
[9] No. 215.   [10] See vol. XIII of this series.

reserved for vessels operating from England; but this idea had to be abandoned when it became apparent that any failure of the English to establish themselves on the spot would simply mean the surrender of the fisheries to the French.[1] The same danger from France dominated the whole development of the Hudson Bay region, where the English company after 1682 found the greatest difficulty in maintaining itself against its enemies.[2]

In addition to these and other centres of trade the dominions of the English monarch necessarily included a growing number of military or semi-military stations, the main function of which was to assist in keeping open the trade routes and maintaining the maritime supremacy on which the prosperity of the home country was based. At an early stage Dunkirk was surrendered to France,[3] and thereafter any attempt on the part of England to control the Channel from both sides had to be based on friendship either with the French or with the Dutch. Compensation, it was believed, was to be found in Tangier, acquired almost at the same time as part of the dowry of Charles's queen.[4] But Tangier proved to be a disappointment. It was unattractive as a settlement, difficult to defend against the neighbouring Moors, and expensive to keep up.[5] Its evacuation towards the close of Charles's reign meant the partial abandonment of the Mediterranean, and England thereafter concentrated more on the Cape route to the East, which the permanent occupation of St. Helena had done much to secure. But the wars with France led to a revival of her interest in the Mediterranean, and the occupation in the reign of Anne first of Gibraltar[6] and then of Minorca.[7] These were both seized in the name of the Archduke Charles, recognized by England and her allies as King Charles III of Spain; but from the very first English statesmen hoped to be able to retain them, and the failure of Charles to make good his claim to the Spanish throne eventually enabled them to do so in the treaty of Utrecht.[8]

[1] No. 218.
[2] No. 217.
[3] No. 332.
[4] No. 336.
[5] No. 219.
[6] No. 220.
[7] No. 221.
[8] No. 348.

BIBLIOGRAPHY

There is no general bibliography of economic history, but many special bibliographies, the most important of which are referred to below (p. 531). For the materials of commercial history G. N. Clark, *Guide to English Commercial Statistics, 1696–1782* (London, 1938), is particularly helpful.

Much has been done to make the original records available. The activities of the Privy Council in the colonial sphere are covered for the whole period in *Acts of the Privy Council of England, Colonial Series*, vols. I and II, edited with valuable introductions by W. L. Grant and James Munro (1908 and 1910). Other papers are dealt with in the *Calendar of State Papers Colonial*, which covers the whole period in 31 vols. (1880–1927), but is practically confined to America and the West Indies. From 1704 onwards the *Journal of the Commissioners of Trade and Plantations* forms a separate series, the first two volumes dealing with the years 1704–1709 and 1708–1715 (1920 and 1925). Other similar series are mentioned below in their appropriate place (p. 531). Material for developments at home, though plentiful, is too scattered to lend itself to any brief summary.

Of the standard economic histories, William Cunningham, *The Growth of English Industry and Commerce in Modern Times* (6th edition, 2 vols., Cambridge, 1919), is still valuable, but has been largely superseded by E. Lipson, *The Economic History of England*, vols. II and III, *The Age of Mercantilism* (4th edition, London, 1947). An admirable introduction to the industrial and commercial history of the period is William Robert Scott, *The Constitution and Finance of English, Scottish and Irish Joint-Stock Companies to 1720* (3 vols., Cambridge, 1910–1912), which examines in detail all types of joint-stock companies, whether operating at home or abroad. With it should be compared such studies of particular industries as Herbert Heaton, *The York-shire Woollen and Worsted Industries from the Earliest Times up to the Industrial Revolution* (Oxford, 1920); E. Lipson, *The History of the Woollen and Worsted Industries* (London, 1921); G. W. Daniels, *The Early English Cotton Industry* (Manchester, 1920); Alfred P. Wadsworth and Julia de L. Mann, *The Cotton Trade and Industrial Lancashire, 1600–1780* (Manchester, 1931); Henry Hamilton, *The English Copper and Brass Industries to 1800* (London, 1926); G. R. Lewis, *The Stannaries, a Study of the English Tin Miner* (Boston, 1908); J. U. Nef, *The Rise of the British Coal Industry, 1550–1700* (2 vols., London, 1932); R. E. Prothero, *English Farming Past and Present* (London, 1927); and J. E. Thorold Rogers, *History of Agriculture and Prices in England* (7 vols., Oxford, 1866–1902).

There are a number of studies of trade with particular countries, of which the most important are Curtis Nettels, "England and the Spanish American Trade, 1680–1715", in *Journal of Modern History*, III (1931), pp. 1–32, which should be read in conjunction with Jean McLachlan, "Documents illustrating Anglo-Spanish Trade between the Commercial Treaty of 1667 and the Commercial Treaty and the Asiento Contract of 1713", in *Cambridge Historical Journal*, IV (1932–1934), pp. 299–311; Annie B. Wallis Chapman, "The Commercial Relations of England and Portugal, 1487–1807", in *Transactions of the Royal Historical Society, Third Series*, I (1907), pp. 157–179; and D. G. E. Hall, "Anglo-French Trade Relations under Charles II", in *History*, VII (1922), pp. 17–30.

Standard works on the development of the British Empire, although they inevitably devote much of their attention to the thirteen North American colonies which are beyond the scope of this volume, cannot be entirely ignored. Among them are *The Cambridge History of the British Empire*, of which seven volumes have appeared (Cambridge, 1929–1940); James A. Williamson, *A Short History of British Expansion*, vol. I, *The Old Colonial Empire* (London, 1930); and Hugh Edward Egerton, *A Short History of British Colonial Policy* (6th edition, London, 1920).

The machinery of colonial government, briefly reviewed in the introductions to the *Acts of the Privy Council of England, Colonial Series*, is further elucidated in C. M. Andrews,

British Committees, Commissions and Councils of Trade and Plantations, 1622–1675 (Baltimore, 1908); O. M. Dickerson, *American Colonial Government, 1696–1765* (Cleveland, 1912); Winifred T. Root, "The Lords of Trade and Plantations, 1675–1696", in *American Historical Review,* XXIII (1917), pp. 20–41; Ralph Paul Bieber, *The Lords of Trade and Plantations, 1675–1696* (Allentown, 1919), and the same writer's "The British Plantation Councils of 1670–4", in *English Historical Review,* XL (1925), pp. 93–106. Lawrence A. Harper, *The English Navigation Laws, a Seventeenth-Century Experiment in Social Engineering* (New York, 1939), devotes most attention to the latter part of the century. Violet Barbour, "Dutch and English Merchant Shipping in the Seventeenth Century", in *Economic History Review,* II (1930), pp. 261–290, is concerned mainly with the actual mechanism of commerce. C. R. Fay, "Locke versus Lowndes", in *Cambridge Historical Journal,* IV (1933), pp. 143–155, throws an interesting light on the whole problem of the reform of the coinage, and the same writer's "Newton and the Gold Standard", *ibid.,* V (1935), pp. 109–117, is of value for the problem of the relations of gold and silver.

On individual settlements there is an extensive literature, of which only the briefest indication can be given. Shafaat Ahmad Khan, *Sources for the History of British India in the Seventeenth Century* (Bombay, 1926), is a valuable guide to the manuscripts in all the principal repositories, but is least satisfactory when dealing with the records in the India Office. These are admirably described in *A Guide to the India Office Records, 1600–1858,* by Sir William Foster (London, 1919), and calendared in three series – *The English Factories in India,* edited by Sir William Foster, vols. XI–XIII of which (Oxford, 1923–1927) cover the years 1661–1669; *The English Factories in India, New Series,* (1) *The Western Presidency, 1670–1677,* edited by Sir Charles Fawcett (Oxford, 1936); and *A Calendar of the Court Minutes of the East India Company,* edited by E. B. Sainsbury, vols. VII–XI of which (Oxford, 1922–1938) cover the years 1660–1679. William W. Hunter, *A History of British India,* vol. II, 1623–1708 (London, 1900), and Paul E. Roberts, *India,* in *The Historical Geography of the British Dominions,* edited by Charles P. Lucas (11 vols., Oxford, 1887–1925), are standard works.

The best guide to the local records of the West Indies is Richard Pares, "Public Records in British West India Islands", in *Bulletin of the Institute of Historical Research,* VII (1930), pp. 149–157; and to records in Britain, C. S. S. Higham, *The Colonial Entry Books, a Brief Guide to the Colonial Records in the Public Record Office before 1696* (London, 1921). There are two good bibliographies by Frank Cundall – *Bibliographia Jamaicensis* (Kingston, 1902, with supplement, 1908), and *Bibliography of the West Indies, excluding Jamaica* (Kingston, 1909, with supplements, 1915 and 1919).

Of the buccaneering with which the West Indian settlements were originally so closely connected there is a famous contemporary description in John Esquemeling, *Bucaniers of America, or a True Account of the most Remarkable Assaults committed of Late Years upon the Coasts of the West Indies by the Bucaniers of Jamaica and Tortuga, especially the Exploits of Sir Henry Morgan* (London, 1684, 1699 and many later editions); and good modern accounts in Clarence H. Haring, *The Buccaneers in the West Indies in the Seventeenth Century* (London, 1910), and Violet Barbour, "Privateers and Pirates of the West Indies", in *American Historical Review,* XVI (1911), pp. 529–566. Apart from the buccaneers the settlements had little in common, and the only general surveys of any value are Thomas Dalby, *An Historical Account of the Rise and Growth of the West India Colonies, and of the Great Advantages they are to England in Respect of Trade* (London, 1690), a mercantilist pamphlet reprinted in *Harleian Miscellany,* IX, pp. 403–445; Thomas Southey, *Chronological History of the West Indies* (3 vols., London, 1827), a purely factual compilation; and *Colonising Expeditions to the West Indies and Guiana, 1623–1667,* edited by Vincent T. Harlow for the Hakluyt Society (1925).

Recent work on the West Indies has mainly taken the form of monographs on individual colonies, of which the most important are C. S. S. Higham, *The Development of the Leeward Islands under the Restoration, 1660–1688* (Cambridge, 1921), and the same writer's "The General Assembly of the Leeward Islands", in *English Historical Review,* XLI (1926), pp. 190–209,

366–388; James A. Williamson, *English Colonies in Guiana and on the Amazon, 1604–1688* (Oxford, 1923), and the same writer's *The Caribbee Islands under the Proprietary Patents* (Oxford, 1926); Vincent T. Harlow, *A History of Barbados, 1625–1685* (Oxford, 1926), and the same writer's *Christopher Codrington, 1668–1710* (Oxford, 1928); and Henry C. Wilkinson, *The Adventurers of Bermuda, 1522–1784* (Oxford, 1933). On the constitutional side are L. M. Penson, *The Colonial Agents of the British West Indies, a Study in Colonial Administration, mainly in the Eighteenth Century* (London, 1924); and Agnes M. Whitson, *The Constitutional Development of Jamaica, 1660–1729* (Manchester, 1929).

The whole subject of the West African slave trade is illuminated by Elizabeth Donnan, *Documents illustrative of the History of the Slave Trade to America* (3 vols., Washington, 1930–1932), and by Arthur B. Keith, *West Africa* (Oxford, 1933), one of the few accounts of the settlements. On Newfoundland the principal authority is Daniel W. Prowse, *The History of Newfoundland, from the English, Colonial and Foreign Records* (London, 1896); but Ralph G. Lounsbury, *The British Fishery at Newfoundland, 1634–1763* (New Haven, 1934), should also be consulted. Beckles Willson, *The Great Company, being a History of the Honourable Company of Merchants-Adventurers trading to Hudson's Bay* (2 vols., London, 1900), is to be preferred to other works on the same subject. E. M. G. Routh, *Tangier, England's lost Atlantic Outpost, 1661–1684* (London, 1912), is an admirable account of the fortunes of that station, giving a full list of the authorities on it.

A. GENERAL ORGANIZATION

202. Order of Council constituting a committee for plantations, 1660

(Acts of the Privy Council, Colonial Series, I, p. 295)

Whitehall, 4 July 1660

Upon a petition presented to his Majesty by divers merchants and others interested in and trading to the English plantations in America, exposing the good behaviour and great merit of Colonel James Russell, late governor of the island of Nevis in the West Indies, and humbly beseeching his Majesty to grant his commission for continuance of him, the said Colonel Russell, in the government of the said island, his Majesty this day sitting in Council hath appointed the Lord Chamberlain, the earl of Southampton, the earl of Leicester, the Lord Viscount Say and Seal, the Lord Robartes, Mr. Denzil Holles, Mr. Secretary Nicholas, Mr. Secretary Morice, Mr. Arthur Annesley and Sir Anthony Ashley Cooper, or any three or more of them, to meet and sit as a committee every Monday and Thursday at three of the clock in the afternoon, to receive, hear, examine and deliberate upon any petitions, propositions, memorials or other addresses which shall be presented or brought in by any person or persons concerning the plantations, as well in the continent as islands of America, and from time to time make their report to this Board of their proceedings.

203. Navigation Act, 1660

(Statutes of the Realm, v, pp. 246–250)

AN ACT FOR THE ENCOURAGING AND INCREASING OF SHIPPING AND NAVIGATION

(12 Car. II, cap. 18)

For the increase of shipping and encouragement of the navigation of this nation, wherein under the good providence and protection of God the wealth, safety and strength of this kingdom is so much concerned, be it enacted . . . that from and after the first day of December one thousand six hundred and sixty . . . no goods or commodities whatsoever shall be imported into or exported out of any lands, islands, plantations or territories to his Majesty belonging or in his possession, or which may hereafter belong unto or be in the possession of his Majesty, his heirs and successors, in Asia, Africa or America, in any other ship or ships, vessel or vessels whatsoever, but in such ships or vessels as do truly and without fraud belong only to the people of England or Ireland, dominion of Wales or town of Berwick-upon-Tweed, or are of the built of and belonging to any of the said lands, islands, plantations or territories as the proprietors and right owners thereof, and whereof the master and three fourths of the mariners at least are English, under the penalty of the forfeiture and loss of all the goods and commodities which shall be imported into, or exported out of, any the aforesaid places in any other ship or vessel, as also of the ship or vessel with all its guns, furniture, tackle, ammunition and apparel, one third part thereof to his Majesty, his heirs and successors, one third part to the governor of such land, plantation, island or territory where such default shall be committed, in case the said ship or goods be there seized, or otherwise that third part also to his Majesty, his heirs and successors, and the other third part to him or them who shall seize, inform or sue for the same. . . . And all admirals and other commanders at sea of any the ships of war or other ship having commission from his Majesty, or from his heirs or successors, are hereby authorized and strictly required to seize and bring in as prize all such ships or vessels as shall have offended contrary hereunto, and deliver them to the Court of Admiralty, there to be proceeded against; and in case of condemnation one moiety of such forfeitures shall be to the use of such admirals or commanders and their companies, to be divided and proportioned amongst them according to the rules and orders of the sea in cases of ships taken prize, and the other moiety to the use of his Majesty, his heirs and successors.

II. And be it enacted, that no alien or person not born within the allegiance of our sovereign lord the king, his heirs and successors, or naturalized or made a free denizen, shall from and after the first day of February which shall be in the year of our Lord one thousand six hundred sixty-one[1] exercise the trade or occupation of a merchant or factor in any the said places, upon pain of the forfeiture and loss of all his goods and chattels, or which are in his possession, one third to his Majesty, his heirs and successors, one third to the governor of the plantation where such person shall so offend, and the other third to him or them that shall inform or sue for the same in any of his Majesty's courts in the plantation where such offence shall be committed. . . .

III. And it is further enacted . . . that no goods or commodities whatsoever of the growth, production or manufacture of Africa, Asia or America, or of any part thereof, . . . be imported into England, Ireland or Wales, islands of Guernsey or Jersey or town of Berwick-upon-Tweed, in any other ship or ships . . .[2] under the penalty of the forfeiture of all such goods and commodities, and of the ship or vessel in which they were imported. . . .

IV. And it is further enacted . . . that no goods or commodities that are of foreign growth, production or manufacture, and which are to be brought into England, Ireland, Wales, the islands of Guernsey and Jersey or town of Berwick-upon-Tweed in English-built shipping, or other shipping belonging to some of the aforesaid places, and navigated by English mariners as abovesaid, shall be shipped or brought from any other place or places, country or countries, but only from those of their said growth, production or manufacture, or from those ports where the said goods and commodities can only or are or usually have been first shipped for transportation, . . . under the penalty of the forfeiture of all such of the aforesaid goods as shall be imported from any other place or country contrary to the true intent and meaning hereof, as also of the ship in which they were imported. . . .

V. And it is further enacted . . . that any sort of ling, stockfish, pilchard or any other kind of dried or salted fish usually fished for and caught by the people of England, Ireland, Wales or town of Berwick-upon-Tweed, or any sort of codfish or

---

[1] 1661/2.   [2] As in section I.

herring, or any oil or blubber made or that shall be made of any kind of fish what-soever, or any whale fins or whale bones which shall be imported into England, Ireland, Wales or town of Berwick-upon-Tweed, not having been caught in vessels truly and properly belonging thereunto as proprietors and right owners thereof, and the said fish cured, saved or dried, and the oil and blubber aforesaid (which shall be accounted and pay as oil) not made by the people thereof, and shall be imported into England, Ireland or Wales or town of Berwick-upon-Tweed, shall pay double aliens' Custom.

VI. And be it further enacted . . . that from henceforth it shall not be lawful to any person or persons whatsoever to load or cause to be loaden and carried in any bottom or bottoms, ship or ships, vessel or vessels whatsoever, whereof any stranger or strangers born (unless such as shall be denizens or naturalized) be owners, part owners or master, and whereof three fourths of the mariners at least shall not be English, any fish, victual, wares, goods, commodities or things of what kind or nature soever the same shall be, from one port or creek of England, Ireland, Wales, islands of Guernsey or Jersey or town of Berwick-upon-Tweed to another port or creek of the same or of any of them, under penalty for every one that shall offend contrary to the true meaning of this branch of this present Act to forfeit all such goods as shall be loaden and carried in any such ship or vessel, together with the ship or vessel. . . .

VII. And it is further enacted . . . that where any ease, abatement or privilege is given in the book of rates[1] to goods or commodities imported or exported in English-built shipping, that is to say shipping built in England, Ireland, Wales, islands of Guernsey or Jersey or town of Berwick-upon-Tweed, or in any the lands, islands, dominions or territories to his Majesty in Africa, Asia or America belonging or in his possession, that it is always to be understood and provided that the master and three fourths of the mariners of the said ships at least be also English. . . .

VIII. And it is further enacted . . . that no goods or commodities of the growth, production or manufacture of Muscovy, or of any the countries, dominions or territories to the great duke or emperor of Muscovy or Russia belonging, as also that no sorts of masts, timber or boards, no foreign salt, pitch, tar, rosin, hemp or flax, raisins, figs, prunes, olive oils, no sort of corn or grain, sugar, potashes, wines, vinegar or spirits called aqua vitae or brandy wine, shall from and after the first day of April which shall be in the year of our Lord one thousand six hundred sixty-one be imported into England, Ireland, Wales or town of Berwick-upon-Tweed in any ship or ships, vessel or vessels whatsoever, but in such as do truly and without fraud belong to the people thereof or of some of them as the true owners and proprietors thereof, and whereof the master and three fourths of the mariners at least are English; and that no currants nor commodities of the growth, production or manufacture of any the countries, islands, dominions or territories to the Ottoman or Turkish Empire belong-ing shall from and after the first day of September which shall be in the year of our Lord one thousand six hundred sixty-one be imported into any the forementioned places in any ship or vessel but which is of English built and navigated as aforesaid and in no other, except only such foreign ships and vessels as are of the built of that

[1] No. 103.

country or place of which the said goods are the growth, production or manufacture respectively, or of such port where the said goods can only be, or most usually are, first shipped for transportation, and whereof the master and three fourths of the mariners at least are of the said country or place, under the penalty and forfeiture of ship and goods. . . .

XIV. Provided also, that it shall and may be lawful to and for any of the people of England, Ireland, Wales, islands of Guernsey or Jersey or town of Berwick-upon-Tweed, in vessels or ships to them belonging and whereof the master and three fourths of the mariners at least are English, to load and bring in from any of the ports of Spain or Portugal or western islands, commonly called Azores or Madeira or Canary Islands, all sorts of goods or commodities of the growth, production or manufacture of the plantations or dominions of either of them respectively.

XV. Provided that this Act or anything therein contained extend not to bullion, nor yet to any goods taken, or that shall be bona fide taken, by way of reprisal by any ship or ships belonging to England, Ireland or Wales, islands of Guernsey or Jersey or town of Berwick-upon-Tweed, and whereof the master and three fourths of the mariners at least are English, having commission from his Majesty, his heirs and successors.

XVI. Provided always, that this Act or anything therein contained shall not extend or be construed to extend to lay aliens' duties upon any corn of the growth of Scotland, or to any salt made in Scotland, nor to any fish caught, saved and cured by the people of Scotland and imported directly from Scotland in Scotch-built ships, and whereof the master and three fourths of the mariners are of his Majesty's subjects, nor to any seal oil of Russia imported from thence into England, Ireland, Wales or town of Berwick-upon-Tweed in shipping bona fide to some of the said places belonging, and whereof the master and three fourths of the mariners at least are English.

XVII. Provided also, and it is hereby enacted, that every ship or vessel belonging to any the subjects of the French king which from and after the twentieth day of October in the year of our Lord one thousand six hundred and sixty shall come into any port, creek, harbour or road of England, Ireland, Wales or town of Berwick-upon-Tweed, and shall there lade or unlade any goods or commodities, or take in or set on shore any passengers, shall pay to the collector of his Majesty's Customs in such port, creek, harbour or road for every ton of which the said ship or vessel is of burthen, to be computed by such officer of the Customs as shall be thereunto appointed, the sum of five shillings current money of England; . . . and that this duty shall continue to be collected, levied and paid for such time as a certain duty of fifty sols per ton lately imposed by the French king or any part thereof shall continue to be collected upon the shipping of England lading in France, and three months after and no longer.

XVIII. And it is further enacted . . . that from and after the first day of April which shall be in the year of our Lord one thousand six hundred sixty-one no sugars, tobacco, cotton-wool, indigos, ginger, fustic or other dyeing wood of the growth, production or manufacture of any English plantations in America, Asia or Africa, shall be shipped, carried, conveyed or transported from any of the said English plantations to any land, island, territory, dominion, port or place whatsoever other than to such other English plantations as do belong to his Majesty, his heirs and successors, or to the kingdom of England or Ireland or principality of Wales or town of Berwick-upon-Tweed, there to be laid on shore, under the penalty of the forfeiture of the said goods or the full value thereof, as also of the ship. . . .

XIX. And be it further enacted . . . that for every ship or vessel which from and after the five and twentieth day of December in the year of our Lord one thousand six hundred and sixty shall set sail out of or from England, Ireland, Wales or town of Berwick-upon-Tweed for any English plantation in America, Asia or Africa, sufficient bond shall be given with one surety to the chief officers of the custom-house of such port or place from whence the said ship shall set sail, to the value of one thousand pounds if the ship be of less burthen than one hundred tons, and of the sum of two thousand pounds if the ship shall be of greater burthen; that in case the said ship or vessel shall load any of the said commodities at any of the said English plantations, that the same commodities shall be by the said ship brought to some port of England, Ireland, Wales, or to the port or town of Berwick-upon-Tweed, and shall there unload and put on shore the same, the danger of the seas only excepted; and for all ships coming from any other port or place to any of the aforesaid plantations who by this Act are permitted to trade there, that the governor of such English plantation shall before the said ship or vessel be permitted to load on board any of the said commodities take bond in manner and to the value aforesaid for each respective ship or vessel, that such ship or vessel shall carry all the aforesaid goods that shall be laden on board in the said ship to some other of his Majesty's English plantations, or to England, Ireland, Wales or town of Berwick-upon-Tweed; and that every ship or vessel which shall load or take on board any of the aforesaid goods until such bond given to the said governor or certificate produced from the officers of any custom-house of England, Ireland, Wales, or of the town of Berwick, that such bond have been there duly given, shall be forfeited; . . . and the said governors and every of them shall twice in every year after the first day of January one thousand six hundred and sixty[1] return true copies of all such bonds by him so taken to the chief officers of the Custom in London.

204. Tobacco Act, 1660

(*Statutes of the Realm*, v, p. 297)

AN ACT FOR PROHIBITING THE PLANTING, SETTING OR SOWING
OF TOBACCO IN ENGLAND AND IRELAND

(*12 Car. II, cap. 34*)

Your Majesty's loyal and obedient subjects, the Lords and Commons in this present Parliament assembled, considering of how great concern and importance it is that the colonies and plantations of this kingdom in America be defended, protected, maintained and kept up, and that all due and possible encouragement be given

[1] 1660/1.

unto them, and that not only in regard great and considerable dominions and countries have been thereby gained and added to the imperial Crown of this realm, but for that the strength and welfare of this kingdom do very much depend upon them in regard of the employment of a very considerable part of its shipping and seamen, and of the vent of very great quantities of its native commodities and manufactures, as also of its supply with several considerable commodities which it was wont formerly to have only from foreigners and at far dearer rates; and forasmuch as tobacco is one of the main products of several of those plantations, and upon which their welfare and subsistence and the navigation of this kingdom and vent of its commodities thither do much depend; and in regard it is found by experience that the tobaccos planted in these parts are not so good and wholesome for the takers thereof, and that by the planting thereof your Majesty is deprived of a considerable part of your revenue arising by Customs upon imported tobacco, do most humbly pray that it may be enacted by your Majesty, and it is hereby enacted . . . that no person or persons whatsoever shall or do from and after the first day of January in the year of our Lord one thousand six hundred and sixty[1] set, plant, improve to grow, make or cure any tobacco either in seed, plant or otherwise in or upon any ground, earth, field or place within the kingdom of England, dominion of Wales, islands of Guernsey or Jersey or town of Berwick-upon-Tweed or in the kingdom of Ireland, under the penalty of the forfeiture of all such tobacco or the value thereof, and of the sum of forty shillings for every rod or pole of ground so planted, set or sown as aforesaid. . . .

II. And it is hereby further enacted, that all sheriffs, justices of the peace, mayors, bailiffs, constables and every of them, upon information or complaint made unto them or any of them by any the officers of the Customs, or by any other person or persons whatsoever, that there is any tobacco set, sown, planted or growing within their jurisdictions or precincts contrary to this Act, shall within ten days after such information or complaint cause to be burnt, plucked up, consumed or utterly destroyed all such tobacco so set, sown, planted or growing.

III. And it is hereby further enacted, that in case any person or persons shall resist or make forcible opposition against any person or persons in the due and thorough execution of this Act, that every such person or persons for every such offence shall forfeit the sum of five pounds. . . .

IV. Provided always, and it is hereby enacted, that this Act or anything therein contained shall extend to the hindering of the planting of tobacco in any physic garden of either university, or in any other private garden for physic or surgery, only so as the quantity so planted exceed not one half of one pole in any one place or garden.

205. Order reconstituting the committee for trade and plantations, 1675
(Acts of the Privy Council, Colonial Series, 1, pp. 619–620)

Whitehall, 12 March 1675

The Right Honourable the Lord Keeper of the Great Seal of England this day acquainted the Board by his Majesty's command, that his Majesty, having been pleased to dissolve and extinguish his late Council of Trade and Foreign Plantations,

---

[1] 1660/1.

whereby all matters under their cognizance are left loose and at large, had thought fit to commit what was under their inspection and management to the committee of this Board appointed for matters relating to trade and his foreign plantations, viz., the Lord Treasurer, Lord Privy Seal, duke of Lauderdale, duke of Ormonde, marquis of Worcester, earl of Ossory, Lord Chamberlain, earl of Bridgewater, earl of Essex, earl of Carlisle, earl of Craven, Viscount Fauconberg, Viscount Halifax, Lord Berkeley, Lord Holles, Mr. Vice-Chamberlain, Mr. Secretary Coventry, Mr. Secretary Williamson, Mr. Chancellor of the Exchequer, Mr. Chancellor of the Duchy and Mr. Speaker, and did particularly order, that the Lord Privy Seal, the earl of Bridgewater, earl of Carlisle, earl of Craven, Viscount Fauconberg, Viscount Halifax, Lord Berkeley, Mr. Vice-Chamberlain and Mr. Chancellor of the Exchequer should have the immediate care and intendancy of those affairs, in regard they had been formerly conversant and acquainted therewith, and therefore that any five of the last-named lords should be a quorum of the said committee, and that their lordships meet constantly at least once a week and make report to his Majesty in Council of their results and proceedings from time to time, and that they have power to send for all books, papers and other writings concerning any of his Majesty's said plantations, in whosesoever custody they shall be informed the same do remain; and his lordship further signified his Majesty's pleasure that Sir Robert Southwell do constantly attend the said committee.

206. Recoinage Act, 1696

(*Statutes of the Realm*, VII, pp. 1–4)

AN ACT FOR REMEDYING
THE ILL STATE OF THE COIN OF THE KINGDOM

(*7 & 8 Gul. III, cap. 1*)

Whereas the silver coins of this realm (as to a great part thereof) do appear to be exceedingly diminished by such persons who (notwithstanding several good laws formerly provided and many examples of justice thereupon) have practised the wicked and pernicious crime of clipping, until at length the course of the moneys within this kingdom is become difficult and very much perplexed, to the unspeakable wrong and prejudice of his Majesty and his good subjects in their affairs as well public as particular, and no sufficient remedy can be applied to the manifold evils arising from the clipping of the moneys without recoining the clipped pieces; now to the end a regular and effectual method may be observed and put in execution in and for the recoining of the said clipped moneys, whether the same be sterling silver or be silver of a coarser alloy than the standard, and to the end the loss upon the said moneys so to be recoined (to wit, the quantity of silver that is clipped away or deficient in the said moneys) may be better known and adjusted in order to the making satisfaction for the same by a public charge or contribution, be it enacted . . . that on or before the first day of February one thousand six hundred ninety-five[1] the present Commissioners of his Majesty's Treasury or any one or more of them now being, or the Lord

[1] 1695/6.

High Treasurer or any one or more of the Commissioners of the Treasury for the time being, shall with the assistance of the Chamberlains of the Exchequer, the Under-Treasurer, the Auditor of the Receipt, the Clerk of the Pells and the Deputy-Chamberlains there, or with the assistance of any three or more of them, and in the presence of any persons who have loans owing to them at the Exchequer and will voluntarily offer themselves to be present, cause all the clipped money, being sterling silver or being silver of a coarser alloy than the standard, and which shall be then actually remaining in the king's Receipt of the Exchequer upon the account of taxes, revenues, loans or otherwise, to be exactly numbered or told, and to be also carefully weighed, and the tale and weight thereof to be fairly entered in a book to be kept for that purpose within the said Receipt, whereunto all persons concerned shall have free access at all seasonable times without fee or charge; and in the same book there shall not only be expressed the general tale of all the said clipped moneys that shall be then found within the said Receipt, but also the particular remains thereof shall likewise be set down and inserted (to wit, how much thereof is for Customs, how much thereof for Excise, how much thereof for any aid, and so of all the rest); and shall thereupon immediately cause all such clipped money so found in the said Receipt to be there or in some convenient place within the precincts thereof melted down and cast into ingots, and so to be assayed and delivered by weight into his Majesty's mint or mints, where the officers shall receive the same by indenture, to be there immediately refined or otherwise reduced to sterling, and to be coined by the mill and press into the current money of this realm. . . .

II. And be it further enacted . . . that all the new money proceeding from the silver of the said clipped moneys (except the necessary charge of making the said new money, which charge shall not exceed fourteen pence upon every pound weight troy, and except the necessary charge of melting and refining) shall from time to time, as fast as such new money shall be coined or at least by weekly payments, be brought back into the Receipt of his Majesty's Exchequer, and be there placed to the respective accounts of the said particular revenues, taxes, loans or other branches to which the clipped moneys belonged, in such manner as that the new money shall be applied to every particular branch or fund in such or the like proportion as the clipped money taken from that particular branch or fund shall bear to the sum of the clipped money so as aforesaid to be taken from the whole, and shall be issued, paid out and disposed accordingly so far as the same will extend, and so as that in all cases where any of the said clipped moneys were appropriated by any former Act or Acts of Parliament for repayment of loans, or for satisfaction of interest money, or for payment of annuities or other uses, the new moneys coming instead thereof so far as the same will extend shall be appropriated, issued and applied to the same respective uses. . . .

III. And be it further enacted . . . that a true account shall be kept in the said Receipt of Exchequer expressing therein particularly every sum of the new moneys which shall be brought to that Receipt from the mint or mints for the proceed of the said clipped money appointed to be recoined as aforesaid, to the end the differences between the sums in tale of the said clipped money and the sums in tale of the said new moneys proceeding therefrom may be plainly known and manifested, and to the end the deficiencies which will thereby be occasioned in the produce of the said revenues, taxes, loans and other branches may be ascertained, in order to the making them good at the public charge, to which book all persons concerned at seasonable times shall also have free access without fee or charge.

IV. And be it further enacted . . . that the several receivers general and their several deputies and the particular receivers, collectors and other officers who have or shall have or be entrusted with the receipt or collection of his Majesty's revenues . . . shall . . . accept and take in payment for his Majesty's use, for or upon account of any of the said revenues, . . . such clipped moneys as aforesaid, being sterling silver or being silver moneys of a coarser alloy than the standard, from such person or persons, bodies politic or corporate, as shall tender the same in or for such payments respectively, at any time or times before the fourth day of May which shall be in the year of our Lord one thousand six hundred ninety-six, at the same rate or value as if such moneys were unclipped or undiminished. . . .

V. And be it further enacted . . . that the tellers in the Receipt of his Majesty's Exchequer respectively shall, at any time or times before the four and twentieth day of June one thousand six hundred ninety-six, not only receive and take to his Majesty's use at the Receipt of Exchequer the said clipped moneys which shall have been so received or collected by the said receivers general and their several deputies, or by the particular receivers, collectors or other officers, . . . but shall also at any time or times before the said four and twentieth day of June receive and take to his Majesty's use in such clipped money as aforesaid any loans which shall be authorized to be made or received there, or any other payments which shall be due to his Majesty. . . .

VI. And be it further enacted . . . that the said tellers in the Receipt of his Majesty's Exchequer shall take care to separate and keep apart all the said clipped moneys that shall hereafter be received by them for loans, taxes, revenues or any other cause whatsoever, so that it may be known which specifical parcels of money brought in shall appertain to every particular tax, fund or branch, and that the present Commissioners of the Treasury or any one or more of them, or the Lord Treasurer or any one or more of the Commissioners of the Treasury for the time being, shall once or oftener in every fourteen days, in the presence and with the assistance of such officers of the Exchequer as are above mentioned, and of such persons having loans due to them from the Exchequer as shall desire to be there present, cause all the said clipped moneys . . .[1]

VII. And be it further enacted . . . that a true account shall be kept in the said Receipt of the Exchequer expressing therein particularly every sum of the new moneys which shall so from time to time be brought to the said Receipt from the mint or mints. . . .[2]

IX. And in regard such of the coins of this realm formerly made with the hammer and not by the mill and press, and which do at this time remain whole and unclipped, will still be most liable and subject to that pernicious crime of clipping or rounding by wicked persons who regard their own unjust lucre more than the preservation of

[1] Provisions follow substantially as in sections I and II.   [2] As in section III.

their native country; for the better prevention thereof be it further enacted . . . that every person having such unclipped hammered moneys in his, her or their hands, custody or possession, do before the tenth day of February one thousand six hundred ninety-five,[1] or before they dispose of the same, cause such unclipped moneys to be struck through about the middle of every piece with a solid punch that shall make a hole without diminishing the silver; and that after the said tenth day of February no unclipped hammered moneys (that is to say, such pieces as have both rings or the greatest part of the letters appearing thereon) shall be current unless it be so struck through; and if any piece struck through shall appear afterwards to be clipped, no person shall tender or receive the same in payment under the penalty of forfeiting as much as the clipped moneys so. punched through shall amount to in tale, to be recovered to the use of the poor of the parish where such money shall be so tendered or received. . . .

207. Order establishing a Council of Trade, 1696

(*Manuscripts of the House of Lords*, 1695–1697, pp. 416–419)

William the Third, by the grace of God, king of England, Scotland, France and Ireland, Defender of the Faith, &c., to our Keeper of the Great Seal of England or Chancellor of England for the time being, our President of our Privy Council for the time being, our Keeper of our Privy Seal for the time being, our First Commissioner of our Treasury and our Treasurer of England for the time being, our First Commissioner of our Admiralty and our Admiral of England for the time being, and our Principal Secretaries of State for the time being, and the Chancellor of our Exchequer for the time being; to our right trusty and right well-beloved cousins and counsellors, John, earl of Bridgewater, and Ford, earl of Tankerville; to our trusty and well-beloved Sir Philip Meadows, knight, William Blathwayt, John Pollexfen, John Locke, Abraham Hill and John Methuen, esquires, Greeting.

Whereas we are extremely desirous that the trade of our kingdom of England, upon which the strength and riches thereof do in a great measure depend, should by all proper means be promoted and advanced; and whereas we are persuaded that nothing more will effectually contribute thereto than the appointing of knowing and fit persons to inspect and examine into the general trade of our said kingdom and the several parts thereof, and to inquire into the several matters and things hereinafter mentioned relating thereunto, with such powers and directions as are hereinafter specified and contained; know ye therefore that we, reposing especial trust and confidence in your discretions, abilities and integrities, have nominated, authorized and constituted, and do by these presents nominate, authorize and appoint the said Keeper of our Great Seal or Chancellor for the time being, . . .[2] to be our commissioners, during our royal pleasure, for promoting the trade of this our kingdom and for inspecting and improving our plantations in America and elsewhere. . . .

---

[1] 1695/6.   [2] Sixteen names in all, as in the first paragraph.

And we do by these presents authorize and empower you our said commissioners, or any three or more of you, to inquire, examine into, and take an account of, the state and condition of the general trade of England, and also of the several particular trades in all foreign parts, and how the same respectively are advanced or decayed and the causes or occasions thereof; and to inquire into and examine what trades are or may prove hurtful, or are or may be made beneficial, to our kingdom of England, and by what ways and means the profitable and advantageous trades may be more improved and extended, and such as are hurtful and prejudicial rectified or discouraged; and to inquire into the several obstructions of trade and the means of removing the same, and also in what manner and in what proper methods the trade of our said kingdom may be most effectually protected and secured in all the parts thereof; and to consider by what means the several useful and profitable manufactures already settled in our said kingdom may be further improved, and how and in what manner new and profitable manufactures may be introduced.

And we do further by these presents authorize and require you our said commissioners, or any three or more of you, to consider of some proper methods for setting on work and employing the poor of our said kingdom and making them useful to the public, and thereby easing our subjects of that burden, and by what ways and means such design may be made most effectual; and in general, by all such methods and ways as you in your discretions shall think best, to inform yourselves of all things relating to trade and the promoting and encouraging thereof, as also to consider of the best and most effectual means to regain, encourage and establish the fishery of this kingdom.

And our further will and pleasure is that you our said commissioners, or any five or more of you, do from time to time make representations touching the premises to us or to our Privy Council, as the nature of the business shall require, which said representations are to be in writing, and to be signed by five or more of you.

And we do hereby further empower and require you our said commissioners to take into your care all records, grants and papers remaining in the plantation office or thereto belonging; and likewise to inform yourselves of the present condition of our respective plantations, as well with regard to the administration of the government and justice in those places as in relation to the commerce thereof; and also to inquire into the limits, soil and product of our several plantations, and how the same may be improved, and of the best means for easing and securing our colonies there, and how the same may be rendered most useful and beneficial to our said kingdom of England.

And we do hereby further empower and require you our said commissioners, more particularly and in a principal manner, to inform yourselves what naval stores may be furnished from our plantations, and in what quantities, and by what methods our royal purpose of having our kingdom supplied with naval stores from thence may be made practicable and promoted; and also to inquire into and inform yourselves of the best and most proper methods of settling and improving in our plantations such other staples and manufactures as our subjects of England are now obliged to fetch and supply themselves withal from other princes and states, and also what staples and manufactures may be best encouraged there, and what trades are taken up and exercised there which are or may prove prejudicial to England by furnishing themselves or other our colonies with what hath been usually supplied from England; and to find out proper means of diverting them from such trades and whatsoever else may turn to the hurt of our kingdom of England; and to examine and look into the usual instructions given to the governors of our plantations, and to see if anything may be added, omitted or changed therein to advantage; to take an account yearly, by way of journal, of the administration of our governors there, and to draw out what is proper to be observed and represented unto us; and as often as occasion shall require to consider of proper persons to be governors, or deputy governors, or to be of our Council, or of our counsel at law, or secretaries, in our respective plantations, in order to present their names to us in Council.

And we do hereby further authorize and empower you our said commissioners to examine into and weigh such Acts of the assemblies of the plantations respectively as shall from time to time be sent or transmitted hither for our approbation; and to set down and represent as aforesaid the usefulness or mischief thereof to our Crown, or to our said kingdom of England, or to the plantations themselves, in case the same should be established for laws there; and also to consider what matters may be recommended as fit to be passed in the assemblies there; to hear complaints of oppressions and maladministrations in our plantations in order to represent as aforesaid what you in your discretions shall think proper; and also to require an account of all moneys given for public uses by the assemblies in our plantations, and how the same are and have been expended or laid out. . . .

And we do hereby further declare our royal will and pleasure to be that we do not hereby intend that our Chancellor of England or Keeper of our Great Seal for the time being, . . .[1] should be obliged to give constant attendance at the meeting of our said commissioners, but only so often and when the presence of them, or any of them, shall be necessary and requisite, and as their other public service will permit. . . .

Witness Thomas, archbishop of Canterbury, and the rest of the Guardians and Justices of the realm, at Westminster, the fifteenth day of May, in the eighth year of our reign.

208. Naval Stores Act, 1704

(*Statutes of the Realm*, VIII, pp. 354–356)

AN ACT FOR ENCOURAGING THE IMPORTATION OF NAVAL STORES FROM HER MAJESTY'S PLANTATIONS IN AMERICA

(*3 & 4 Annae, cap. 9*)

Whereas the royal navy and the navigation of England, wherein under God the wealth, safety and strength of this kingdom is so much concerned, depends on the due supply of stores necessary for the same, which, being now brought in mostly from foreign parts in foreign shipping at exorbitant and arbitrary rates, to the great

---

[1] The eight official members as set forth in the first paragraph.

prejudice and discouragement of the trade and navigation of this kingdom, may be provided in a more certain and beneficial manner from her Majesty's own dominions; and whereas her Majesty's colonies and plantations in America were at first settled, and are still maintained and protected, at a great expense of the treasure of this kingdom, with a design to render them as useful as may be to England, and the labour and industry of the people there profitable to themselves; and in regard the said colonies and plantations by the vast tracts of land therein lying near the sea and upon navigable rivers may commodiously afford great quantities of all sorts of naval stores, if due encouragement be given for carrying on so great and advantageous an undertaking, which will likewise tend not only to the further employment and increase of English shipping and seamen, but also to the enlarging in a great measure the trade and vent of the woollen and other manufactures and commodities of this kingdom and of other her Majesty's dominions in exchange for such naval stores, which are now purchased from foreign countries with money or bullion; and for enabling her Majesty's subjects in the said colonies and plantations to continue to make due and sufficient returns in the course of their trade, be it therefore enacted . . . that every person or persons that shall within the time appointed by this Act import or cause to be imported into this kingdom directly from any of her Majesty's English colonies or plantations in America, in any ship or ships that may lawfully trade to her Majesty's plantations, manned as by law is required, any of the naval stores hereafter mentioned, shall have and enjoy as a reward or premium for such importation after and according to the several rates for such naval stores as follows, viz.:

For good and merchantable tar per ton containing eight barrels, and each barrel to gauge thirty-one gallons and an half, four pounds.

For good and merchantable pitch per ton, each ton containing twenty gross hundreds (net pitch) to be brought in eight barrels, four pounds.

For good and merchantable rosin or turpentine per ton, each ton containing twenty gross hundreds (net rosin or turpentine) to be brought in eight barrels, three pounds.

For hemp, water-rotted bright and clean, per ton, each ton containing twenty gross hundreds, six pounds.

For all masts, yards and bowsprits per ton, allowing forty foot to each ton girt measure according to the customary way of measuring round bodies, one pound. . . .

III. And to the end a particular benefit may accrue hereby to her Majesty's royal navy, and for the better supply of the same with naval stores, be it further enacted, that upon the importing of any naval stores from her Majesty's said colonies and plantations for which a reward or premium is hereby granted, the pre-emption or refusal of such naval stores shall be offered and tendered to the commissioners of her Majesty's navy upon landing the same. . . .

IV. And for the better preservation of all timber fit for the uses aforesaid, be it further enacted and ordained by the authority aforesaid, that no person or persons within her Majesty's colonies of New Hampshire, the Massachusetts Bay, Rhode Island and Providence Plantation, the Narragansett country or King's Province and Connecticut in New England, and New York and New Jersey, do or shall presume

19

to cut, fell or destroy any pitch-pine tree or tar trees not being within any fence or actual inclosure under the growth of twelve inches diameter at three foot from the earth, on the penalty or forfeiture of five pounds for each offence. . . .

VII. Provided also, that the several directions and provisions in this Act shall commence and take effect from the first day of January which shall be in the year of our Lord one thousand seven hundred and five,[1] and shall continue and be in force from thenceforward for the space of nine years and no longer.

[1] 1705/6.

B. EAST INDIES

209. Edward Barlow's narrative of his first voyage to the east, 1670–1671

(Barlow's Journal, ed. B. Lubbock, I, pp. 178–203)

So continuing on shore at London three or four months, intending my next voyage to go for the East Indies, for I still had a mind to see strange countries, and staying for a ship which I had a mind to go in,[1] which was then building at Blackwall but was not quite built, at last she was finished and launched, and, being rigged, I shipped myself at the East India House to go in her, she being bound for Surat in East India. And taking in our goods, Christmas being past, we set sail from Blackwall and came down to Erith, and there came to anchor, intending to stay there to take in the rest of our goods and provisions. The goods which we took in were lead and copper and alum, and broad-cloths of red and green colour for the most part, and some other small commodities. . . .

Having our half-pay paid to us, we weighed our anchors with two ships more, the one called the *Loyal Subject* and the other the *Hannibal,* and set sail from Gravesend to the Downs; and that night we came down into Leigh Road, and the next day to the Buoy of the Nore. And the *Loyal Subject* went round about through the King's Channel and so into the Downs, for she being a large ship they would not venture her over the flats. And we two coming down to the Buoy of the Red Sands, the next day we had a fair wind and came over the flats, and the same day into the Downs; and the day after came the *Loyal Subject* to us. And there was another ship, which was called the *Berkeley Castle,* which was bound to Surat, a new ship; but she was in the river of Thames and not ready to come along with us. . . .

At last a fair wind came, and we weighed our anchors and set sail out of the Downs on the 7th day of March in the year 1670, having on board twenty-two pieces of ordnance and sixty men, our ship being reckoned in burden 250 tons. . . . Two days after, meeting with a cross wind, but it not blowing very hard, and being fine weather, we made a shift to turn to windward in the Channel; and being come as high as Plymouth, the wind came fair again, and so we directed our course west-south-west till we were got out of the Channel, and then south-west and more southerly as we came farther off. . . .

And about three weeks after our departure out of England we had the sight of one of the Madeira Islands called Porto Santo, bearing from us W.S.W., about nine leagues distant from us. . . . And steering south-south-east, about seven or eight days afterward we had the sight of one of the Cape Verde Islands called Bonavista, being from us S.W. about seven leagues distant; . . . and sailing by it we came in sight of another called San Diego, where we did intend to touch and water our ships, for we had a long run afterward before we could come where we might get any more water. And so, coming into the bay or road, we came to an anchor, and stayed there four

---

[1] Called the *Experiment.*

or five days, watering our ship and refreshing our men with fresh provisions. . . . It is the first place of touching for ships which are bound to the East Indies or other places to the southward. . . .

So having stayed about seven days, and having all things ready, we weighed our anchors and set sail from San Diego; and steering our course south-east and south-east by south, about ten days afterward we came into the latitude of the rains, where we met with many a wet coat and thunder-clap and hard gales of wind. . . . At last, being got within three degrees of the equinoctial line, we were got out of them. And steering our course southerly, in the beginning of May we crossed the equinoctial line, every man who had not been so far before paying his bottle of strong waters as a forfeit, it being merrily drunk out by all the rest that had been there before, an old custom amongst seamen. And not long afterward we had a score of fish which followed us for a fortnight, of bonitos and albacores and some dolphins, which were a great refreshment to us, we taking many of them. . . .

So steering our course and coming into hot weather and eating salt victuals made us many times very dry, and we could have been glad many times of a drink of water if we could have told where to have got it, for it was scarce with us, for we were put to three pints of water a day for a man as soon as we came from San Diego. . . . And so coming in the latitude of 24 or 26 degrees southward of the equinoctial line we had more favourable winds, and we steered our course more easterly. And not long after, we met with very bad weather, . . . and the nights being long and dark, we lost one another. . . . Not long afterward we had a more fair wind, and making what sail we could by ourselves, and looking every day well out to see whether we could see either of our company, about ten days after, we met with the *Loyal Subject* again, but the *Hannibal* we could not see.

So we keeping company together, not long after we had the sight of Cape of Good Hope. . . . The Hollanders have a fort and small town upon it, but the English seldom touch there. And coming into 36 degrees our course lay north-east; but cross winds holding us a long time, and having had a passage of eleven weeks from the island of San Diego to the said Cape, and being driven into 38 degrees southerly, and the wind continuing contrary and our water growing short, we were forced to go to a quart of water a day for a man. . . .

At last we had a fair wind, and we steered our course north-east; but it did not long continue with us, but we met with cross winds again. And three or four days after, we, judging ourselves not to be far from land, and the next day looking well out and standing towards it, we had the sight of the island of St. Lawrence, which is counted the greatest island in the world. . . . So steering our course easterly that night . . . we steered away for a small island called Johanna, intending there to touch and get water and refreshing for our men, for we had some sick of the disease called the scurvy, which happeneth in all ships after they come out of England and come into these changes of air and hot countries. And we had three men dead, and one that had a wife aboard, her husband dying the same night we came to anchor at the island.

So three days afterward we had the sight of the island of Johanna, . . . and that night we came to an anchor in the road. . . . And there we found the *Hannibal*, which we had lost in the bad weather; and she had arrived there three days before us. And she told us the *Berkeley Castle*, which was not ready to come out of England when we came out, nor did come out till ten days after, had been there fourteen days at the island, and was gone ten days before we came, the wind having favoured her so much and us so little that she got to Surat a month before us.

So the next day we put our sick men on shore, and our casks for water; and making a tent there, our cooper fitted them on shore, and the sick men lay in the tent, and having good refreshing recovered their health apace. And so fitting all things, and getting water on board, and four or five cows to carry along with us, not intending to stay longer than needs must, and so staying five or six days, and having all things ready to sail, we weighed our anchors and set sail from the island of Johanna. . . . The island lieth in a wholesome air, between the island of St. Lawrence and the mainland of Africa, in 12 degrees south.

So, being under sail and having a fair wind, we steered our course north-east, and north-east and by east, till we came to the equinoctial line again. And crossing it again we steered our course again easterly, and being in a trade wind we did not lack for a fair wind. And not long afterward, on the 7th day of September, we had the sight of the land of the coast of East India, not being far from the port of Bombay, where we were bound first, having been on our passage from the Downs in England just six months, having run in that time above sixteen thousand miles. And the day following, being the 8th of September, we arrived at Bombay. And coming to an anchor not far distant from the town, there we found the *Berkeley Castle*, having been there three weeks, and was then ready to go to Surat, which was forty leagues farther to the northward.

And we had some women on board, which came passengers out of England to come to their husbands, which lived at Bombay in the East India Company's service; and news was brought on board that some of them were dead, which presently caused a great sorrow amongst the female kind, having left all their friends and native country, and now having that bad fortune to hear of their husbands' death.

So putting out some goods and other things on shore, which we brought out of England for that place, being it belongs to the East India Company, and staying there three or four days, we weighed anchor again, and set sail for Surat or Swallow Road. . . . So in about seven days we came in sight of the sands which lie at the going in, so that we were forced to come to an anchor; but the day after, we got in, coming to an anchor in Swallow Road. Two days afterward we delivered our goods out, and as any of us came on shore we were presently met with the countrymen, which were called bunnias, it being their custom that time of year, when ships come up thither, to come down from Surat, being ten miles distant, and bring their goods down to Swallow Road; and there they have booths and tents built, which they live in all the time the ships tarry there.

And their custom is to come to every man, inquiring what trade he hath to sell, and to see which one of them you will choose to be your merchant to deal with you for what you have to sell or change for their commodities, their custom being to give to them which they trade with a small pish-cash or gift, both at his first coming and at his departing, being very cunning and subtle people in all their dealings. . . . They are all buyers and sellers, and many of them very rich; and they are apt to learn any language. Their children of six and seven years of age can speak English.

So preparing to sail, and getting on board our water, our men being come from Surat again, two days after, we and the *Hannibal* set sail from Swallow Hole, leaving the *Loyal Subject* behind us, for she was not ready to go along with us; and the *Berkeley Castle*, she was to stay and load to go to England the first ship, and to go all alone. And being under sail we directed our course southerly, and having a fair wind in nine days time we got as far as a place called Goa, having passed by a place called Rajapur, which belongeth to the aforesaid savagie. The English formerly had a factory there, and through the cruelty of the inhabitants, for little or no cause, were all most barbarously killed; and since that time we have had no dealings with them. The most commodity it yieldeth is pepper, and some brown and coarse calicos. But this city of Goa is a great place and very strong. It belongeth to the Portugals, and is the chief place that they have or have had in all East India. . . .

And two or three days afterward we came to a place called Karwar, where we were to touch for to deliver some moneys and some letters to the English factory there; but the *Hannibal* did not touch there, for she was bound to a place farther called Beliapatam. . . . This place of Karwar lieth upon the coast of Malabar, the inhabitants being all blacks and tawny Moors, being lusty and strong-proportioned men. The place yielded only pepper and ordinary brown calico, and betel-nuts and some cardamoms, and fruits, as oranges and plantains and bananas and coconuts and pineapples and other suchlike fruits. Here is an English factory for the East India Company. The air is very hot and not very healthful. They have some small ships and other small junks and vessels which they trade with, some going into Arabia and the Red Sea.

So being under sail we steered south-south-east; and two days after, we met with a Holland ship, and speaking with her, she came from Batavia upon the island of Java, and she was bound for Surat and Persia. And the next day we arrived at Beliapatam; and coming to an anchor in the bay we found there the *Hannibal*, which was loading of pepper. And the same day the merchant which lay there as factor came on board, and having some lead to deliver there we put it on shore; but there we were not to have our loading. . . .

Being under sail we steered southerly; and the day after, we had some hard gales of wind and rain, and not far distant from us we espied a spout break out of the sea, it being usual sometimes in these hot countries, when it bloweth hard, for a spout of water to be thrown up into the sky out of the sea with such force that it seemeth to us as though a small river of water were running up right out of the sea into the sky. But what the reason or cause is that doth it we know not.

So the next day we passed by Calicut, and came to a place not far distant from Calicut called Tanur; and there coming to an anchor, there came a country boat on board to see what we were, being sent by the English merchant that lay there as factor for the East India Company at Calicut, he being at that place then about buying of pepper. And coming near us, at first they were something fearful to come on board of us, taking us to be a Hollander, for there are few in all East India of the country people but are fearful of them and cannot abide nor love any of them, having been so abused, and their goods taken from them in many places by the Hollanders. So the next day came on board the factor for the Company, and he ordered us to go five leagues farther to the southward to a place called Ponnani to load pepper; but there was pepper for us where we were, but it was not ready, and we were to come thither again and take it in.

So that night we weighed our anchor and set sail, and by daylight we came to Ponnani, . . . and so half loading our ship there we prepared to come back to Tanur again, and having stayed four or five days we weighed our anchors. . . . And being under sail, the next day we came to Tanur. . . . And so, coming to an anchor again, the day following we had pepper sent on board, and in two or three days more we loaded our ship, taking in as much as conveniently we could, and preparing all things ready to sail back to Calicut, for we were to touch there. . . .

So being under sail, two days afterward we arrived at Calicut, and coming to anchor in six fathom water, and staying two days there, and having watered our ship there, and put on shore some little goods which we had to deliver there, and having all things ready to sail, the chief factor which was there came on board of us for to go to Beliapatam to be chief there, for he that was chief at Beliapatam we were to carry to Surat.

And so weighing our anchors, we set sail from Calicut in East India. . . . It formerly hath been a place of great strength and good trade, but now is become a few scattering houses, being destroyed by wars. . . . The factories that lie at this place for the East India Company serve for the two other places, Tanur and Ponnani. The Company sendeth yearly from Surat two or three coast ships to load pepper to carry to Surat, for the ships to carry for England amongst their other goods. . . . So being under sail, three days after, we came again to Beliapatam, and coming to an anchor we stayed there two days. And Master Grexby, the chief factor there, being come on board, and we having all things ready, we weighed our anchor and set sail again from Beliapatam, and directed our course northerly for Surat. And having an indifferent good wind, in three days we got as far as Karwar; and coming in sight of the road, and seeing the *Loyal Subject* at an anchor, we sent our boat on board to see whether she was ready to sail along with us. But being not ready, we sailed away, . . . and not long after we came as far as Bombay, and there we sent our boat on shore with two or three bunnias which had been down upon the coast with us, they intending to go from Bombay by land to Surat. . . .

In five or six days we arrived in Swallow Road, having been on our voyage two months. And coming to an anchor there, we found a French ship or two and a Holland ship riding before their factories. And the day following we began to unliver our pepper; and putting two parts of it out, we kept the rest on board, and took in other goods of several sorts, and so loaded our ship for England. Yet we kept our Christmas there before we were loaden. But the *Berkeley Castle* was loaden and went away a month before us. And I, having a small venture for myself and some of my friends and acquaintance, bought some small commodities, and taking care of my friends' goods more than I did of my own, and when I came home I had scarce thanks for all my care and trouble; but it was the first time, and it shall be the last, that I shall meddle with any in that matter. . . .

So having all things ready to sail, we weighed our anchors and set sail from Swallow Road, and steered our course for Bombay. And staying there two days to provide ourselves with water, and with hens and hogs, which we could not have at Surat, and having two or three men passengers which were to go for England come on board, and having all things clear and ready to sail, we weighed our anchors and set sail from Bombay, the place to which we first arrived. And the next day, being the 15th of January, we sailed out of sight of land, being all three together as we came out of England, our own ship and the *Loyal Subject* and the *Hannibal*.

And having an indifferent fair wind, we directed our course south-south-west till such time as we came off from the land forty or fifty leagues, and then we steered south, and south and by west. . . . At last it began to blow harder and to look black and rain, and it did look as though it would be bad weather. And one Sunday, at night, it blowed very hard all night, and the next day morning, being Monday the 27th February in the year 1671, and looking still as though it would be bad weather and more wind, we got down our topgallant yards and took in our top-sails, being come as far as an island called the Mauritius, and into 30 degrees south latitude, being then to the eastward of the Cape of Good Hope about five hundred leagues, where many ships meet with bad weather. . . .

Having cut down our mizzen mast, the ship by God's great mercy bearing up and the winds and waves something abating, we looked out for the other two ships, the *Loyal Subject* and the *Hannibal*, but we could not see any of them. And getting our main topmast down upon deck for to fish and mend it, by reason that we had cut into it before she bore up to cut it down, and hoisting our main yard, we set our main-sail and brought our ship to the wind, and took in our sprit-sail and foresail, and let her lie a-try under our main-sail. And pumping all the water out, having had five foot water in the hold, and it beginning to be more moderate weather, and we still looking out for the other ships, but we could have no sight of them.

And two days after, we had a fair wind, and getting our topmast up again we steered away our course for the Cape of Good Hope, west-south-west. . . . But our fair wind continued not long with us, for on the Monday following we met with a hard gale of wind, which continued with us three or four days; and likewise three Mondays, one after another, we had very foul weather. At last, having more favourable winds, we came into the latitude of 36 degrees, and judging that we were upon the soundings that lie off the Cape land, we sounded and found ninety fathoms; so we knew that we were not far from the Cape, but having cross winds we could not have the sight of it.

And not long after, we had a fair wind again, and being got to the northward of the Cape we steered our course north-west and by north, and north-west, for the island of St. Helena, for there we did intend to touch, and get some water and refresh our men. And having a continuing fair wind, which always is trade and bloweth one way, being good for all ships bound to the northward; and being got to the northward of the Cape you need not fear a foul wind till you come into 20 degrees northward of the equinoctial line.

And in three weeks sail from the Cape we arrived at St. Helena, and so coming to an anchor on the west side of the island against Chapel Valley, where the fort stands, having been in our passage from Bombay in East India twelve weeks. But we found no ships at the island, and a boat coming on board of us from the fort she told us that the *Berkeley Castle*, which came from Surat a month before us, had been there, and was gone seven days before we came, away along with another ship called the *Constantinople*, which came from Bantam. The *Berkeley Castle* had met with very bad weather in her passage. And the next day after we arrived came the *Loyal Subject* and the *Hannibal*, and two ships more that came from Bantam, and one which came from the Coast, which they had met withal in their way, all of them being laden with East India Company's goods.

When the two ships which were in our company saw us got there before them, they wondered, thinking at first that it was not our ship, for the *Hannibal*, having seen our mast which we cut by the board, and some other things which were washed overboard off the deck, judged that we were cast away; yet it pleased God other ways. . . . So we all staying at the island about ten or twelve days, and having watered our ships and also refreshed ourselves with such provisions as the island afforded, and having all things ready to sail, we weighed our anchors and set sail from the island of St. Helena. . . .

In former times it was inhabited by the Portugals; but being a place which produceth no commodities, and being out of the way of their trade, and their people not liking very well to work, as they must do that intend to live upon it, they left it, and since then our East India Company have taken it in possession, and have transported people thither to till it and keep it for them, sending out of England a stock of cattle with them, which have increased very much through our people's industry, for the island produceth nothing of itself, only some few oranges and plenty of fresh water, for it is all over very mountainous and rocky. Yet there are some valleys which are full of low scrubby wood and very good grass in some places, which keep the cattle very fat and in good case, they multiplying very much upon it. And there is very good soil in some places upon it, where the inhabitants plant plenty of potatoes and beans and Indian corn and coleworts, and some other herbs, with store of parsley growing in the valleys everywhere. And our English make very good butter of the cattle. There is some wild fowl upon it, as guinea-hens and partridges, and now it is plentiful in all manner of provisions, as excellent good beef and hogs and goats and hens; but bread corn they have none, for they cannot sow any by reason of the roughness of the ground. The island is but small, and very little even ground upon it; but there is plenty of fish about the island. They have planted now some banana and plantain trees, and here are very good yams, a thing much like a potato, but far bigger.

The East India Company have a fort here upon it, which is indifferent well fortified, the island being governed by a governor under the East India Company. Here their ships touch yearly as they come from the East Indies, seldom any missing the island; and sometimes Portugal ships stop there which come from Angola and are bound to Brazil, and also French ships that come from the East Indies, and sometimes other English ships, which go to buy negroes at Mozambique and the island of St. Lawrence, and sometimes from the coast of Guinea. But now the people that live upon it are free from the East India Company, and you must buy what you have of them, except beeves, which the Company hath of their own, which every ship hath some of when they touch there, without paying for it. The island lieth under a good and wholesome air; yet it is between the Line and Tropic, and very hot weather.

And being under sail we steered again north-west for the island of Ascension, for to stop there to take some turtle for to eat, they being very good for a refreshing of our men. And in eight days sail we arrived there, and coming to an anchor in Turtle Bay, all of us at night, we sent some men on shore out of every ship to lie all night on shore, and watch when the turtle came out of the sea to lay their eggs on shore, and when they came, to turn them upon their backs, and there let them lie till morning to fetch them on board, it being the turtle's use, four or five months in the summer-time, to come on shore upon that island to breed their young. . . . And the turtles, being thus caught, are carried on board and there kept alive, eating one of them every day, for one of them will serve forty or fifty men. One of them, shell and all together, will weigh three or four hundred pounds; and they will live on board without victuals or drink four or five and twenty days. . . .

So having stayed there about three days, having got, every ship of us, turtle enough to serve us about ten days, and having all things on board ready to sail, we weighed our anchors and set sail from the island of Ascension. . . . And being under sail, we steered our course still north-west, and north-west and by north, till we came to the equinoctial line, and then we held more northerly. . . . So coming into 40 degrees north, and into a westerly wind's way, we had a westerly wind, which continued with us till we came into 47 degrees, and then it proved little wind for three or four days. . . .

So not long after, having a fair wind and being a great way to the westward, we steered our course east, and east and by north, for the Soundings at the entering in of our Channel; and coming into the Soundings, we sounded and had sixty-five fathom water, and then we steered east-north-east, and north-east and by east. And two or three days afterward we had the sight of Old England again, it being the Lizard. And having a fair and fresh gale of wind, two days afterward we arrived in the Downs, having put our purser and two or three passengers on shore at Dover as we came by, they intending to go to London by land. And coming to an anchor in the Downs, having had a passage of five whole months and twenty-five days, and staying a little while for a pilot, at last came one on board, and weighing our anchor we set sail again to come up the river of Thames. And that tide we came up into Margate Road, and coming to an anchor we rode there that night.

And the next day we weighed our anchors again and came over the flats, and the day following to Gravesend. And in two days more we got up to Blackwall, and there we stayed and unlivered our goods out of the ship. . . . And having livered out all our goods, we hauled our ship into the dock to new-grave and fit her.

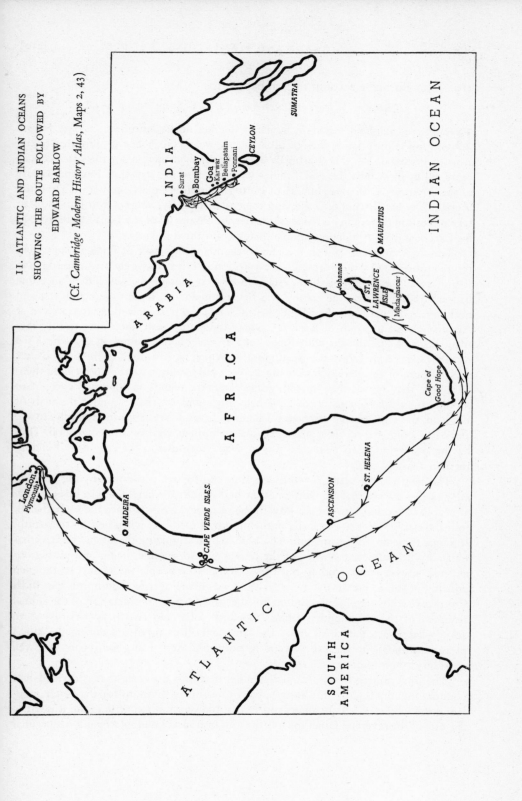

II. ATLANTIC AND INDIAN OCEANS

SHOWING THE ROUTE FOLLOWED BY

EDWARD BARLOW

(Cf. Cambridge Modern History Atlas, Maps 2, 43)

210. John Burnell's account of Bombay, 1710

(Bombay in the Days of Queen Anne, ed. S. T. Sheppard, pp. 1–26)

Bombay is an island seated in nineteen degrees north latitude. . . . The Moors continued proprietors thereof till about the year 1550, when it submitted to the arms of Portugal. . . . The Portugals having flourished therein for the space of 112 years, till in anno 1661 this and Tangier were given to the crown of England as part of the dowry of Catherine, Infanta of Portugal, upon her marriage with Charles the Second of Great Britain, &c., the king soon after sends five ships of war into India to take possession thereof in his name and under the command of my Lord Marlborough, his Excellency Sir Abraham Shipman being constituted governor.

The ships, arriving, laid their claim to the island in behalf of England, but were refused possession by the Portugals, they protesting it was above the royal prerogative to give away the divers hereditary estates there were therein, the which their ancestors had enjoyed ever since the colony was first planted. . . . Some time being past and nothing agreed upon, his Excellency sailed out of the port, and soon after arrived at Anjidiv (an island south of Karwar), where the colony sent out, being mostly raw men, began to fall down with fluxes, and to die off like rotten sheep. The Lord Marlborough, considering the great mortality which raged among the men, soon after set sail again for Bombay, where being arrived, and having with threats brought them to reason, they would then unanimously deliver the island, on condition every man should enjoy his own to his and his heirs male and by charter under the seals of England, the which being assented to, the island was delivered to the English crown, and Mr. Cooke, the survivor of Sir Abraham Shipman, was constituted general. Thus having possession, their next care was to secure the same to the crown by building thereon a stately castle. . . .

The centre of the island is wholly destitute of product, occasioned by the frequent salt-marshes the sea maketh there in every high water (the land being so low), which at neap tide retiring into the sea leaveth the ooze dry, from whence the sun exhaleth foul and sickly vapours, especially in the month of October, when he is in the zenith. It is then those unwholesome fumes do arise, which stagnizing the air and renders that mortality it is subject to, whereof the crown was so sensible, being at a prodigious expense in every year sending out new colonies to repeople the island; to retrench which, but still to preserve it as a royalty, it was made over to the English East India Company, who were become suitors for the same, that in consideration of the annual payment of twenty pounds sterling (to which some add two pepper-corns) as an acknowledgment, they shall enjoy the same and all its privileges during the king's pleasure, minding to keep the several fortifications thereof in good repair, and well garrisoned with soldiers.

The government of the island resembles that of a province that is divided into counties, hundreds, &c., this being subject to as many divisions for the better regulating the whole. . . . As to affairs concerning the preservation of the soul, it is left to the care of the reverend father in God, the lord bishop of London, seeing it is a peculiar to his diocese, being accounted as part of Stepney parish, as is most places in India under the English nation. . . .

Civil affairs relating to this island are lodged in a generalissimo whom the Company nominates and sendeth out (and not the king as formerly). He is likewise assisted with a council consisting of ten, he having two voices. Of this council the one half always reside in Surat, as doth the deputy-governor, being president of our factory there, though the first of the five council resident in Bombay represents his person because of his absence, and acts as deputy. . . . Under the metropolitan of Bombay are divers subordinate factories, as Surat, whose chief hath the title of president, and is always, or ought to be, deputy-governor of Bombay; next Isfahan, where the Company have an agent; then Gombroon or Bandar Abbas in Persia. On the Malabar Coast are Tellicherry, Calicut, Anjengo and Brinjaon; to all which the general sendeth governors, councils, factors, writers; and ships from England, as likewise of the country built, he dispatcheth to these distant places, and receiveth them from thence; and of all the three governments he is the greatest factor the Company have in India. . . .

The military of this island consists of five companies of Christians (that is Europeans, topasses and cofferes), three whereof mount and relieve alternate in Bombay Castle. . . . Besides these forces are eight companies of sepoys, seven of them containing eighty men each. . . . The militia are divided into two classes, Bombay and Mahim. They consist of Moors, Gentews, Mustees, Portuguese, all freemen of the island. They are usually called up once a month to their exercise, which they do with as much grace as a cow might make a curtsy. We had them up every night in our late troubles, which so fatigued our new campaigners that they agreed to raise two companies at their own charge to be excused from lying out of their beds at nights, which after I left the island I heard was accepted of. As to the amount of the whole soldiery of the island in constant service, it is about 1,200 men. . . .

The Castle of Bombay is a square of four bastions, whereof one hath two batteries of cannon. They are not equally proportioned, those towards land, termed the Tank and Plumtree Bastions, being larger than those towards the sea. It is founded on a point of rocks so close to the water that the sea constantly washeth the walls of one half of the Castle quite from the Flag Staff to the Tank Bastion. . . . Its ramparts are large and regular, having a broad terreplein, mounted with 112 pieces of cannon. It hath two large tanks that contain twenty months' water for a thousand men, and likewise a strong magazine, caserns for the small arms and lodgments for the soldiers, of which one company is constantly upon guard. . . .

The hospital stands on a point near the sea, and is a strange, old-fashioned, ill-contrived thing. It is seldom empty, occasioned from the unhealthiness of the place. It is enough to make a man die with the thoughts of going into it, for it stands hardly fifty yards off of a high grave. Then the concert of some hundreds of jackals every night shall awake him to his meditation, to think what a dainty morsel he is like to make them. Few enter it above the degrees of soldiers and sailors, especially of the former; so many have gone in ill and have come out so well that they never ailed anything after. Though a physician and doctor is allowed by the Company, and are yearly supplied with chests of fresh doses, yet I am too sensible that many of my fraternity going under their hands never lived to tell the excellency of their medicines.

Adjoining is seated the most famous European repository in the east, Mendham's Point, a name more terrible to a sick Bombayan than the Inquisition to a heretic; a cormorant paunch never satisfied with the daily supplies it receives, but is still gaping for more, though it hath swallowed more English flesh than the Bengal Tamarind Tree, Madras Guava Garden and the Green Hill at Bencoolen, yet still it hath room for those numbers twice told, and when those are digested it will be as ravenous as ever. . . .

C. WEST INDIES

211. Richard Blome's account of Jamaica and other West Indian settlements, 1672

(A Description of the Island of Jamaica, with the other Isles and Territories in America, ed. 1672, pp. 1–124)

The island of Jamaica . . . is in most parts (especially the north) of a rich and fat soil, being of a blackish earth, in many places mixed with a clay; and in some (as the south-west parts) it is of a more red and loose earth; but everywhere incomparable apt to produce, and liberally to answer the cultivator's cost and pains for what is planted, being always springing, and its trees and plants never disrobed of their summer livery, every month being to them as our May or April.

Here are many savannas, which are intermixed with the hills and woods, especially in the north and south parts, where are great store of wild cattle. . . . The air is here more temperate than in any of the Caribbee Isles, as seated more northerly, and of as mild a temperature (as to heat) as any place between the tropics, being always cooled with fresh breezes, that constantly blow easterly, and refreshed with frequent showers of rain, and such dews that fall in the night (much quickening the growth of what is planted) that it may truly be called temperate and healthful, and by reason of its continual verdure (as I have before noted) exceeding delightful. . . .

This isle hath and produceth many excellent commodities, and that in exceeding great plenty, as sugars so good that they outsell those of the Barbados 5s. per cent, there being at present about seventy sugar works, which may produce yearly 1,710,000 weight of sugar, those still increasing and divers others a-going up; cocoa, the principal and most beneficial commodity of the isle, . . . and that by reason of the aptness of the ground to produce and bear it above other places, here being at present above sixty cocoa walks, besides abundance of young walks which are a-growing up and still more a-planting, so that in time it will become the only noted place for that commodity in the world, which is so much made use of by us and other nations. . . .

Indigo this isle produceth very good, there being at present more than sixty indigo works, which may produce about 50,000 weight of indigo per annum, and do likewise much increase. Cotton here hath an especial fineness, and is by all preferred before that of the Caribbee Isles. Tobacco is here indifferent good, being esteemed better than that of the Barbados; but it is not much planted, only a sufficiency to serve themselves, the other commodities being more beneficial. Hides, of which great quantities have been yearly made, and are found to be very large and good. Great store of tortoises are taken on this coast, whose meat (being excellent) they eat; and their shells, so much esteemed here in England for several curious works, find good vent.

Here are great variety of woods for dyers, as fustic, redwood, a kind of logwood, &c., also cedar, mahogany, braziletto, lignum-vitae, ebony, granadilla, and many other excellent, sweet-smelling and curious woods fit for choice works, whose names are as yet not known, nor indeed their excellencies, but are exported in great quantities. Copper they are assured is in this isle, for they have seen the ore, wrought out of a mine here; and by the Spaniards' report the bells that hung in the great church of St. Iago were cast of the copper of this island. Silver may probably be here, as well as in Cuba and in the Main; and the English have been shown where the Spaniards had found a silver mine, behind the mountains west of Cagway. . . .

Ginger grows better in this isle than in many of the Caribbee Islands, of which here is sufficiency planted. . . . Pimento, or Jamaica pepper, a spice of the form of East India pepper, very aromatical and of a curious gusto, having the mixed taste of divers spices, grows here in great plenty, wild in the mountains. . . . These with some others are the commodities that this island produceth, which if well improved would soon become the best and richest plantation that ever the English were (or are like to be) masters of. . . .

It hath been experimentally found that there is no such antipathy betwixt the constitutions of the English and this clime for the occasioning sickness to be mortal or contagious more than in other parts, for if a good diet and moderate exercises are used, without excess of drinking, they may enjoy a competent measure of health. The diseases that strangers are most incident to are dropsies (occasioned often by ill diet, drunkenness and slothfulness); calentures (too frequently the product of surfeits); also fevers and agues, which although very troublesome yet are seldom mortal. . . .

This island abounds with good bays, roads and harbours, the principal amongst which are:

Port Royal, formerly called Cagway, situate on the extreme end of that long point of land which makes the harbour, which is exceedingly commodious for shipping, and secured by one of the strongest and most considerable castles that his Majesty hath in all America, in which are mounted about sixty pieces of ordnance, and is well guarded with soldiers. . . . The harbour is two or three leagues across in most places, and hath everywhere good anchorage, which is so deep that a ship of a thousand ton may lay her sides to the shore of the point and load and unload with planks afloat, which commodiousness doth make it to be the most frequented by men-of-war and merchants' ships of any in the island, and as much inhabited by the merchants, store-house-keepers, vintners and alehouse-keepers, being the only noted place of trade in the isle, and doth contain (since the English became masters of it) about 800 houses, being about twelve miles and a half in length, and the houses are as dear rented as if they stood in well-traded streets in London. Yet its situation is very unpleasant and uncommodious, having neither earth, wood or fresh water, but only made up of a hot, loose sand. . . .

Port Morant, in the eastern point, a very capacious and secure harbour, where ships do conveniently wood, water and ride safe from the winds; and about this place is a potent colony of the English seated.

Old Harbour, westwards from St. Jago, a good bay for ships to ride in.

Port Negril, in the extreme western point, very good and sufficiently convenient and secure to windward, in which men-of-war do often ply when they look for the Spanish ships. . . .

Port Antonio, seated on the north, a very safe, landlocked harbour; only the coming in is somewhat difficult, the channel being narrowed by a little island that lies off the mouth of the port. . . .

There are at present but three towns of considerable note in the island, to wit,

St. Jago, or St. Jago de la Vega, seated six miles within the land north-west, in a plain by a river, and about twelve miles from Port Royal already treated of, which makes another of the three towns. This town of St. Jago, when the Spaniards were masters of the isle, was a large city and of great account, containing about 2,000 houses, and for divine worship had two churches, two chapels and an abbey, which when the English first took the isle (under the conduct of General Venables) were destroyed to about four or five hundred houses, and its churches and chapels to a fewer number, and those that remained were sufficiently spoiled and harassed. But since the English have made a settlement this town is now of considerable account, where the governor resideth and where the chief courts of judicature are held, which makes it to be well resorted unto and inhabited, so that most of its ruinous houses are in a fair way of being repaired; . . . and the inhabitants live in great pleasure, where they have their havana, in which the better sort recreate themselves every evening in their coaches or on horseback, as the gentry do here in Hyde Park.

Passage, seated on the mouth of the river, six miles distant from St. Jago and as many from Port Royal, where there are about twenty houses, built for the conveniency of going to Port Royal. . . .

The island is divided into fourteen precincts, divisions or parishes, . . . many of which said precincts are well inhabited by the English, where they have very good plantations, especially all the southern part. . . . I cannot certainly affirm the number of the English in this isle, but according to the last survey taken and returned into England some years since by Sir Thomas Modyford, late governor, each precinct or parish contained as followeth:

Parishes	Families	Inhabitants
Port Royal	500	3,500
St. Catherine	658	6,270
St. John	83	996
St. Andrew	194	1,552
St. David	80	960
St. Thomas	59	590
Clarendon	143	1,430
	1,714	15,298

Note that the four parishes on the north side of the isle, . . . as also the leewardmost parish . . . together with the two not named . . was not as then so particularly surveyed, by reason of their distance and new settlements. Nevertheless they were found according to calculation to amount to about 2,000 inhabitants. But all these parts, as also those seven aforenamed, are now exceedingly increased, being supposed to be increased to double if not treble the number. And the great encouragement of gaining riches, with a pleasant life, doth invite every year abundance of people to inhabit here, quitting their concerns at Barbados and other our American plantations, so that in a short time without doubt it will become the most potent and richest plantation in the West Indies.

And besides the aforesaid number of inhabitants in the said fourteen precincts or parishes there are reckoned to belong to the island, of privateers, hunters, sloop and boatmen (which ply about the isle) at the least 3,000 lusty and stout fighting men, whose courage hath been sufficiently evidenced in their late exploit and attempt made against the Spaniards at Panama. . . .

Some considerations why his Majesty should keep, preserve and support this island

1. Jamaica is large and capacious, whose extent I have already noted; so that it is capable of receiving very great numbers of people.

2. It is seated in the heart of the Spaniards' American territories, so that the Spanish ships coming into the West Indies, and sailing from port to port, either make this isle or may be immediately met by the ships which ply on this coast, which renders it to be of great importance to us as well as to the Spaniards, for all the Plate Fleet which comes from Cartagena steer directly from San Domingo in Hispanoila, and from thence must pass by one of the ends of this isle to recover Havana, which is the common rendezvous of the Armada, before it returns home through the Gulf of Florida. . . .

3. Jamaica is found to precede all the English plantations in America in the very commodities that are proper to their several colonies, and produceth also of its own cocoa, hides, tortoise shells, wood for dyers, gums, drugs and other commodities already treated of; and for fruits, fowl and fish, infinite store, many of which are unknown unto them; likewise such abundance of horses and cows that none other of the English plantations can equalize them. And as this island is found thus advantageous in the furnishing us with such good commodities, so is it no less profitable in the taking off our manufactures and commodities, as well of the product of this kingdom as those from foreign parts. . . .

4. It appears to be a place of no small concernment, for it hath not only subsisted at the beginning but bettered its condition, being settled by an army (the worst kind of people to plant) that have had such grand discouragements from England as want of pay, provisions and recruits of men, yet amongst themselves talked of all encouragements to plant, the establishment of justice and government, besides the frequent attempts of the Spanish forces. And if it thus thrived under these and suchlike considerable obstructions it is more than probable it will in a short time become a great and profitable colony both to the king and kingdom, for when well planted it may bring in to his Majesty some hundred thousand pounds per annum, Barbados (which is so little compared to this) yielding about 10,000*l.* per annum, and employing about 150 or 200 sail of ships yearly.

5. This island being so large and so fertile, it is capable of the receiving those great numbers of people that are forced to desert the Caribbee Isles, their plantations being worn out and their woods wasted; as likewise those multitudes of vagrants and beggars that are so great a charge and shame to the kingdom, if transported thither, would by their labours live both honestly and plentifully, here being observed to be no beggars, nor such loose vagabond people.

6. This island, being well settled, will be capable of itself to carry on a war against the Spaniards in the West Indies (as occasion requireth), because of the conveniences of its ports and its strength of inhabitants and shipping, having already about twenty or thirty sail of privateers; and will in a short time be so numerous and potent that they will become so obnoxious to the Spaniards that probably they will rather admit of a trade into his ports (which would prove a grand advantage both to them and this kingdom) than suffer so disadvantageous a war. . . .

9. It cannot be imputed a disadvantage that Jamaica lieth so far off, for thereby are more ships employed, and by consequence more sailors, shipwrights, rope-makers and many other tradesmen maintained, whose dependence is thereon. . . .

10. And lastly, to conclude, the English have one more considerable advantage by this isle, and that is, the coast of Virginia being subject to gusts of wind, the ships loaden with goods and passengers have been often forced forth to sea, and so disabled that they could not ply to any of the outward Caribbee Islands, but have been constrained to bear up and put into the Spanish leeward ports; and likewise some of our merchants have been forced out of the Caribbee Isles by hurricanes (which are there common), and so disabled that they could not keep sea, but (as all vessels thus distressed) have put into some of the Spanish leeward ports, where they have always been made prizes. Now Jamaica, being so far leeward, is a convenient harbour for all vessels thus distressed, and did some few years since save three Virginia ships full of passengers and goods, and formerly others, as also some driven by hurricanes from the Windward Islands; all which, without the conveniency and assistance of this isle, had perished.

A Description of the Island of Barbados

Barbados, the most considerable colony the English hath amongst that fry of isles called the Caribbee Isles or the Antilles. . . . Although but of a small circuit (being accounted not above eight leagues in length and five in breadth where broadest, being of an oval form), yet is it a potent colony, being able as occasion requireth to arm 10,000 fighting men, which, with the strength that nature hath bestowed on it, it is able to bid defiance to the stoutest foe, having been several times (but in vain) assaulted by the Spaniards. . . .

The commodities that this isle produceth are sugars (which, though not so white as those of Brazil, yet better when refined, being of a fairer grain), indigo, cotton, wool, ginger, logwood, fustic and lignum-vitae. And these commodities, especially sugar, indigo, cotton and ginger, are here in such great abundance that about 200 sail of ships and vessels, both great and small, have yearly their loading, which, after imported in the several ports of England and Ireland, is again in great quantities exported to foreign parts to our great enrichment, and the rather for that they are not permitted to trade with any other nation but the English and such of his Majesty's subjects in New England, Virginia and Bermudas. And in exchange of those commodities they take such as are necessary for the use of man, as well for the back and belly as for their houses and plantations, with many of which they are supplied from New England, Virginia and the Bermudas, together with servants and slaves. . . .

This isle is very hot, especially for eight months, yet not so but that travel and labour is sufferable; but were it not for the cool breezes of wind, which riseth with the sun and bloweth fresher as the sun mounteth up, it would be insufferable. . . .

This island is severed into eleven precincts or parishes, in which are fourteen churches and chapels; and here are many places which may not inaptly be called towns, as being composed of a long and spacious street, which are beautified with fair houses. . . .

1. St. Michael's, formerly called Bridgetown or Indian Bridge, situate at the bottom of Carlisle Bay in the leeward or southern part of the isle, which bay is very capacious, deep and secure for ships, being large enough to entertain 500 vessels at one time. The town is long, containing several streets, and graced with abundance of well-built houses. It is very populous, being the residence of the governor or his deputy, the place of judicature, and the scale of trade, where most of the merchants and factors in the isle have their storehouses for the negotiation of their affairs; and from these storehouses or shops the inhabitants are supplied with such commodities as they have occasion of, in exchange of theirs, which are the product of the isle. . . . This town for its defence and security of the ships hath two strong forts opposite to each other, with a platform in the midst which also commands the road, all which are well fortified with great guns, &c. The principal of these forts is called Charles Fort, being seated on Nedham's Point.

2. Little Bristol, formerly Speight's Bay, situate about four leagues leeward from St. Michael's, hath a commodious road for ships, is a place well frequented and traded unto, and is strongly defended by two powerful forts.

3. St. James, formerly called the Hole, seated not far from Bristol, hath the accommodation of a good road for ships and is a place of a considerable trade; for its defence, besides a large platform, hath fortified breast-works; and in this town is kept, for the precinct, the monthly courts.

4. Charlestown, seated windward of St. Michael's about two leagues, and on Oistin Bay. It is secured by two strong forts, the one to windward and the other to leeward of the town and road, with a platform in the midst. This town hath the accommodation of weekly markets, and here is kept the monthly courts for the precinct. . . .

The inhabitants of this isle may be ranged under three heads or sorts, to wit, masters (which are English, Scotch and Irish, with some few Dutch, French and Jews), Christian servants and negro slaves. And these three sorts are exceeding numerous, for according to a calculation not long since made the masters and servants did amount to about 50,000, and the negroes to about double the number.

The masters for the most part live at the height of pleasure. The servants, at the expiration of five years, become freemen of the island, and employ their times according to their abilities and capacities, either to get a small plantation, or to work at day-labour in other plantations, or else to exercise their trades, if so capacitated. The negro slaves are never out of their bondage, and the children they get are likewise perpetual slaves. They have but mean allowance of diet, clothes and lodging, and though held to such hard labour, and so ill treated, yet are they well contented with their conditions; and if their master is but anything kind they think nothing too much to be done for them; and therefore it is great pity to wrong such poor creatures.

The chiefest stock of a planter consists in his servants and slaves, but especially the slaves, who are more numerous. And these they buy on shipboard, as men buy horses in a fair, and according as they are handsome, lusty, well-shapen and young, either the men or women, they give more or less, the general rates for the Christian servants being about 10l.; but if one that hath a good trade, as a carpenter, joiner, smith or the like, then far more. Likewise a female that is young and handsome is higher valued. The general rule for the better sort of negro men is 20l. or 25l. sterling, and for women about 15l. For the increase of stock of negroes they generally take as many men as women. . . .

This island is very strong, as well by nature as art, being sheltered with rocks and shoals; and where nature hath not thus defended it, it is fortified by trenches and ramparts, with palisades, curtains and counterscarps. Besides, round about the isle, regarding the sea, is standing wood. Here are also for its further defence three forts, one for a magazine for the ammunition and powder to lie in, and the other two for places of retreats as occasion serveth. They have also for their further security a standing militia, consisting of two regiments of horse and five of foot, which are stout and well-disciplined men, and always to be ready on beat of drum. . . .

A Description of the Isles of Bermudas
or the Somers Isles

East of Virginia and Carolina, which is a part of Florida, lieth the isles of Bermudas, so called from Juan Bermudez, a Spaniard, by whom they were first discovered. They are also called the Somers Isles, from the shipwreck that one George Somers, an Englishman, there suffered. . . . Of these isles the greatest, called St. George's, is five or six leagues long, and almost throughout not above a quarter, a third, or half a league broad. The others are much less. . . .

The earth is exceeding fertile, yielding two crops yearly. Their maize they gather in July and December. . . . Their chief commodities are oranges, cochineal and tobacco, with some pearl and ambergris; and with these they drive some small trade. . . . They have no fresh water for their occasions but that of wells and pits, which ebbs and flows with the sea, there being neither fountain nor stream in these isles. . . . The sky is almost always serene, and when darkened with clouds it commonly thunders and lightneth. And the air is very temperate, and so exceeding healthful that it is rare to hear that anyone dieth of any distemper but only old age; insomuch that many have removed from England hither, only for the enjoyment of a long and healthful life. . . .

The English first settled themselves on these isles about the year 1612, and have now established a powerful colony, there being at present about four or five thousand inhabitants, who have strongly fortified the approaches, which with the rocks in the sea renders them impregnable.

212. Andrew Marvell on the Bermudas

(*Complete Works*, ed. A. B. Grosart, I, p. 82)

Where the remote Bermudas ride
   In th' ocean's bosom unespied,
From a small boat, that rowed along,
The list'ning winds received this song.
   What should we do but sing his praise
That led us through the wat'ry maze,
Unto an isle so long unknown,
And yet far kinder than our own?
Where he the huge sea-monsters wracks.
That lift the deep upon their backs.
He lands us on a grassy stage,
Safe from the storms and prelate's rage.
He gave us this eternal spring,
Which here enamels everything;
And sends the fowls to us in care
On daily visits through the air.
He hangs in shades the orange bright,
Like golden lamps in a green night;
And does in the pom'granates close
Jewels more rich than Ormus shows.
He makes the figs our mouths to meet,
And throws the melons at our feet;
But apples plants of such a price
No tree could ever bear them twice.
With cedars, chosen by his hand
From Lebanon, he stores the land,
And makes the hollow seas that roar
Proclaim the ambergris on shore.
He cast (of which we rather boast)
The gospel's pearl upon our coast,
And in these rocks for us did frame
A temple where to sound his name.
Oh let our voice his praise exalt,
Till it arrive at heaven's vault,

Which thence (perhaps) rebounding may
Echo beyond the Mexic Bay.
    Thus sang they, in the English boat,
An holy and a cheerful note;
And all the way, to guide their chime,
With falling oars they kept the time.

213. Anonymous account of the earthquake in Jamaica, 1692

(Historical Manuscripts Commission, *Kenyon MSS.*, pp. 266–269)

A FULL ACCOUNT
OF THE LATE DREADFUL EARTHQUAKE
AT PORT ROYAL IN JAMAICA,
WRITTEN IN TWO LETTERS FROM THE MINISTER OF THAT PLACE
FROM ABOARD THE *GRANADA* IN PORT ROYAL HARBOUR

22 June 1692

I doubt not but you will, both from gazettes and letters, hear of the great calamity that hath befallen this island by a terrible earthquake on the 7th instant, which has thrown down almost all the houses, churches, sugar-works, mills and bridges through the whole country. It tore the rocks and mountains, and destroyed some whole plantations and threw them into the sea; but Port Royal had much the greatest share in this terrible judgment of God. I will therefore be more particular in giving you account of its proceedings in that place, that you may know what my danger was and how unexpected my preservation.

On Wednesday the 4th of June[1] I had been at church reading prayers, which I did every day since I was rector of Port Royal, to keep up some show of religion amongst a most ungodly and debauched people, and was gone to a place hard by the church where the merchants used to meet; and there the president of the council was, who acts in chief till we have a new governor, who came into my company and engaged me to take a glass of wormwood wine with him as a whet before dinner. He being my very great friend I stayed with him, upon which he lighted a pipe of tobacco, which he was very long a-taking; and not being willing to leave him before it was out, this detained me from going to dinner to one Captain Rudens, where I was to dine, whose house upon the first concussion sunk first into the earth and then into the sea, with his wife and family and some that were come to dine with him. Had I been there I had been lost.

But to return to the president and his pipe of tobacco. Before that was out I found the ground rolling and moving under my feet, upon which I said to him, Lord, sir, what is this? He replied very composedly, being a very grave man, It is an earthquake; be not afraid, it will soon be over. But it increased, and we heard the church and tower fall, upon which we ran to save ourselves. I quickly lost him and made towards Morgan's Fort, which being a wide open place I thought to be there securest from the

[1] The 4th of June was a Saturday. The earthquake occurred on Tuesday the 7th.

falling houses; but as I made towards it I saw the earth open and swallow up a multitude of people, and the sea mounting in over the fortification.

I then laid aside all thoughts of escaping, and resolved to make towards my own lodging and there to meet death in as good a posture as I could. From the place where I was, I was forced to cross and run through two or three very narrow streets. The houses and walls fell on each side of me, some bricks came rolling over my shoes, but none hurt me. When I came to my lodging I found there all things in the same order I left them, not a picture (of which there were several fair ones in my chamber) being out of its place. I went to my balcony to view the street in which our house stood, and saw never a house down there, nor the ground so much as cracked.

The people, seeing me there, cried out to me to come and pray with them. When I came into the street every one laid hold on my clothes and embraced me, that with their fear and kindness I was almost stifled. I persuaded them at last to kneel down and make a large ring, which they did. I prayed with them near an hour, when I was almost spent with the heat of the sun and the exercise. They then brought me a chair, the earth working all the while with new motions and tremblings, like the rollings of the sea, insomuch that when I was at prayer I could hardly keep myself upon my knees. By that time I had been half an hour longer with them, in setting before them their sins and heinous provocations, and in seriously exhorting them to repentance, there came some merchants to me in the place, who desired me to go aboard some ship in the harbour and refresh myself, telling me they had gotten a boat to carry me off. So, coming to the sea, which had entirely swallowed up the wharf, with all these goodly brick houses upon it (most of them as fine as those in Cheapside), and two entire streets beyond that, I, upon the tops of some houses which were levelled with the surface of the water, got first into a carol, then into a long-boat, which put me aboard a ship called the *Siam Merchant*, where I found the president safe, who was overjoyed to see me. There I continued that night, but could not sleep for the returns of the earthquake almost every hour, which made all the guns in the ship to jar and rattle.

The next day I went from ship to ship to visit those that were bruised and a-dying, and to pray with them, and likewise to do the last office at the sinking several corpses that came floating from the Point, which indeed hath been my sorrowful employment ever since I came aboard this ship with design to come for England. We having nothing but shakings of the earth and thunder and lightning and foul weather ever since, and the people being so desperately wicked, makes me afraid to stay in the place; for that very day the terrible earthquake was, as soon as night came on a company of lewd rogues, whom they call privateers, fell on breaking open warehouses and houses deserted, to rob and rifle their neighbours, whilst the earth trembled under them and some of the houses fell on them in the act, and those audacious whores that remain still in the place are as impudent and drunken as ever.

I have been twice on shore to pray with the bruised and dying people, and to christen children, where I found too many drunk a-swearing. I did not spare them, nor the magistrates neither, who have suffered wickedness to grow to so great a height. I have, I bless God, to the best of my skill and power discharged my duty in this place, which you will hear from most persons that came from hence. I have preached so seasonably to them in the church; I set before them what would be the issue of their impenitence and wickedness, that they have since confessed that it was more like a prophecy than a sermon. I had, I confess, an impulse upon me to do it, and many times I have preached in this pulpit things that I never premeditated at home, and could not, methought, do otherwise.

The day when all this befell, it was very clear, afforded not the suspicion of the least evil; but in the space of three minutes, about half an hour after eleven in the morning, Port Royal, the fairest town of all the English plantations, best emporium and mart of that part of the world, exceeding in its riches, plentiful in all good things, was shaken and shattered to pieces, sunk into and covered for the greatest part by the sea, and will in a short time be wholly eaten up by it, for few of these houses that yet stand are left whole, and every day we hear them fall, and the sea daily encroaches upon it. We guess that by the falling of the houses and opening of the earth there are lost 1,500 persons, and many of good note. I came, I told you, on board this ship in order to come home, but the people are so importunate with me to stay I know not what to say to them. I must undergo great hardship if I continue here, the country being all broken to pieces and dissettled.

Ever since that fatal day, the most terrible that ever I saw in my life, I have lived on board a ship, for the shakings of the earth return every now and then. Yesterday we had a very great one, but it seems less terrible on shipboard than on shore. Yet I have ventured to Port Royal no less than three times since its desolation, among the shattered houses, to bury the dead and pray with the sick and christen the children. Sunday last I preached to them in a hut, the houses that remain being so shaken that I durst not venture to preach in them. The people are overjoyed to see me among them, and wept bitterly when I preached unto them. I hope by this terrible judgment God will make them reform their lives, for there was not a more ungodly people upon the face of the whole earth.

It is a sad sight to see all this harbour, one of the fairest and goodliest I ever saw, covered with dead bodies of people of all conditions floating up and down without burial, for our great burial place, called the Palisadoes, was destroyed by the earthquake, and the sea washed the carcases of those that were buried out of their graves. Their tombs were dashed in pieces by the earthquake, of which there were hundreds in that place.

We have had accounts from several parts of these islands of the mischief done by the earthquake. From St. Ann's we [hear] of above 1,000 acres of woodland changed into the sea, and carried with it whole plantations; but no place suffered like [Port Royal]. Some were swallowed up to the neck, and the earth shut upon them and squeezed them to death, and in that manner several are found buried with their heads above ground; only some heads the dogs have eaten, others are covered with the dust by the people that live to avoid the stench.

Thus I have told you a long and sad story, and God knows what worse may happen. Yet the people tell me they hear noises and bellowings on mountains, and some think it is by fire. If so I fear it will be more destructive than the earthquake. I am afraid to stay, and yet I know not how in such a case as this to quit my station.

D. WEST AFRICA

214. Charter of the African Company, 1672

(Public Record Office, Treasury Papers, T.70/1505)

Charles the Second, by the grace of God king of England, Scotland, France and Ireland, Defender of the Faith, &c., to all to whom these presents shall come, Greeting.

Whereas all and singular the regions, countries, dominions and territories, continents, coasts and places, now or at any time heretofore called or known by the name or names of Guinea, Benin, Angola and South Barbary or by any of them, . . . and all and singular ports and havens, rivers, creeks, islands and places in the parts of Africa to them or any of them belonging, and the sole and only trade and traffic thereof, are the undoubted right of us, our heirs and successors, and are and have been enjoyed by us and by our predecessors for many years past as in right of this our crown of England.

And whereas the trade of the said regions, countries and places is of great advantage to our subjects of this kingdom, and for the improvement thereof divers attempts have been made and several charters granted by our royal progenitors to several persons, with such powers and authorities as were then conceived proper for the carrying on of the said trade, but all the said endeavours proved ineffectual until we by letters patents under our great seal of England bearing date the tenth day of January in the fourteenth year of our reign[1] did give and grant unto our royal consort Queen Catherine, Mary the queen our mother (since deceased), our dearest brother James, duke of York, and others therein named the propriety and government of all the said regions . . . in trust for the Company of Royal Adventurers of England trading into Africa, and for the better managing of the trade and traffic thereof did create and make them and such as they should think fit to receive into their society one body politic and corporate by the name of the Company of the Royal Adventurers of England trading into Africa, granting them and their successors the sole trade of the said regions, . . . and several other liberties and privileges as by the said letters patents may appear, whereby the said trade is very much advanced and improved.

Nevertheless by accidents in the late wars and other casualties the said Company have sustained great losses, by means whereof their stock hath been so impaired that, besides the great debts they were liable unto, there remained not sufficient to manage the said trade, whereupon all persons refused to advance any more money upon that account, lest it should be subject to the payment of those debts and not be employed in the said trade.

And it being found also by experience that the powers and privileges in our said letters patents granted were not sufficient for those purposes for which they were designed.

[1] 1663.

570

Thereupon the said Company, to enable them to pay and satisfy their just debts so far as the value of what remains unto them will extend unto, have treated with the persons hereafter named, who upon that occasion have made subscriptions towards a new stock, and have for valuable considerations undertaken to assure unto them all the said regions . . . by us granted as aforesaid, and all the right and privilege in the trade thereof, and for that end to become humble suitors to us that we would be graciously pleased to accept a surrender of all their right and interest either in law or equity in the said regions, . . . and of all their whole right and privilege of trade unto those parts, and that we would be pleased to make the said persons hereafter named a new society or corporation, to whom the said regions . . . and the sole trade thereof may be granted, with such powers and privileges as shall be most convenient for the advancement and carrying on the said trade. And the said Company have accordingly besought us on that behalf, and have under their common seal surrendered the said propriety and sole privileges unto us for the purposes aforesaid.

Now know ye that . . . we have accepted of the said surrender, and of our more especial grace, certain knowledge and mere motion we have given and granted, and for us, our heirs and successors do hereby give and grant unto our dearest brother James, duke of York, Anthony, earl of Shaftesbury, . . .[1] their executors and assigns, all and singular the regions . . . lying and being within the limits and bounds hereafter mentioned, that is to say, beginning at the port of Sallee in South Barbary inclusive and extending from thence to the Cape of Good Hope inclusive, with all the islands near adjoining to those coasts and comprehended within the limits aforesaid, which regions . . . and islands have been heretofore called or known by the name of South Barbary, Guinea, Benin or Angola, . . . and all and singular ports, harbours, creeks, islands, lakes and places in the parts of Africa to them or any of them belonging, or being under the obedience of any king, state or potentate of any region, dominion or country within the limits aforesaid, to have and to hold all and singular the said regions, . . . and all and singular other the premises within the limits aforesaid, to the said James, duke of York, Anthony, earl of Shaftesbury, . . .[1] their executors and assigns, from the making of these our letters patents for and during the term and unto the full end and term of one thousand years, yielding and rendering therefor unto us, our heirs and successors, two elephants whensoever we, our heirs and successors or any of them, shall arrive, land or come into the dominions. . . before mentioned or any of them.

Nevertheless our will and pleasure is, and we do hereby declare the true intent and meaning of these presents to be, that this our present grant and demise of the regions . . . aforesaid, and all the benefit, commodity, profit and advantage made and to be made and gotten out of the same or by reason of the term aforesaid, shall be and shall be interpreted to be in trust and for the sole use, benefit and behoof of the Royal African Company of England hereafter mentioned and their successors, and after, in and by these presents incorporated or mentioned to be incorporated; and therefore for the setting forward and furtherance of the trade intended in the parts aforesaid, and

[1] Twenty-four names in all.

the encouragement of the undertakers in the discovering the golden mines and setting of plantations, being an enterprise so laudable and conducing to so worthy an end as the increase of traffic and merchandise wherein this nation hath been famous, of our further and more ample grace and favour, certain knowledge and mere motion, we do will, ordain, constitute, appoint, give and grant unto our said dearest brother James, duke of York, his Highness Prince Rupert, Anthony, earl of Shaftesbury, . . .[1] that they and all such others as they shall from time to time think fit and convenient to receive into their company and society to be traders and adventurers with them to the said countries shall be one body politic and corporate of themselves, in deed and in name, by the name of the Royal African Company of England. . . .

And for the better ordering and governing of the said Company we have given and granted, and by these presents for us, our heirs and successors do give and grant, unto the said Royal African Company of England and their successors that there shall from time to time be a governor, sub-governor and deputy-governor and twenty-four assistants members of the said Company, which said governor, sub-governor and deputy-governor and assistants, or any seven or the major part of them (of which the governor, sub-governor or deputy-governor to be one) and their successors we will shall be and be called the Court of Assistants of the Royal African Company of England. . . .

And further, . . . we do hereby, for us, our heirs and successors, grant unto the said Royal African Company of England and their successors that it shall and may be lawful to and for the said Company and their successors and none others, from time to time to set to sea such and so many ships, pinnaces and barques as shall be thought fitting by the said Court of Assistants for the time being, of which the governor, sub-governor or deputy-governor to be one, prepared and furnished with ordnance, artillery and ammunition or any other habiliments in warlike manner fit and necessary for their defence, and shall for ever hereafter have, use and enjoy all mines of gold and silver (subject to the proviso and limitation in that behalf hereinafter contained) which are or shall be found in all or any the places above mentioned, and the whole, entire and only trade, liberty, use and privilege of trade and traffic into and from the said parts of Africa above mentioned. . . .

And our further will and pleasure is, and we do also hereby further charge, prohibit and forbid all and every the factors and masters of ships, mariners and members of the said Company and their successors, that they or any of them do not, directly or indirectly, presume to trade, adventure or traffic for themselves or any of them in or from the regions . . . aforesaid or any of them, unless it be with licenses and consent of the said Company first had and obtained in writing under their common seal as aforesaid; and for the further effecting of our pleasure herein we do hereby, for us, our heirs and successors, give and grant full power and authority unto the said Royal African Company of England and their successors for the time being, that they, by themselves, their factors, deputies and assigns, shall and may, from time to time and at all times hereafter, enter into any ship, vessel, house, shop, cellar or workhouse, and attach, arrest, take and seize all and all manner of ships, vessels,

---

[1] The previous 24 names are repeated, with 179 others.

negroes, slaves, goods, wares and merchandises whatsoever which shall be brought from or carried to the places beforementioned or any of them, contrary to our will and pleasure before in these presents expressed. . . .

And we do . . . give and grant unto the said Royal African Company of England, that the governor, sub-governor, deputy-governor and assistants of the said Company for the time being, or any seven of them, . . . shall and may have the ordering, rule and government of all such forts, factories and plantations as now are or shall be at any time hereafter settled by or under the said Company within the parts of Africa aforementioned, and also full power to make and declare peace and war with any of the heathen nations that are or shall be natives of any countries within the said territories in the said parts of Africa as there shall be occasion. . . .

Provided also, and our further will and true intent and meaning is, that we, our heirs and successors, shall and may have, take and receive two third parts of all the gold mines which shall be found, seized, possessed or wrought in the parts and places aforesaid, we, our heirs and successors, paying and bearing two third parts of all the charges incident to the discovering, buying, keeping, defending, maintaining, working and transporting of the said gold. . . .

Witness ourself at Westminster, the seven and twentieth day of September, in the four and twentieth year of our reign.

215. A Frenchman's account of the slave trade, 1682

(John Barbot's "Description of Guinea", in *Voyages and Travels*,
ed. A. and J. Churchill, 1732, v, pp. 270–272)

[The slaves in Guinea] are for the most part people taken in war, but sometimes sold into bondage by their own relations. . . . Others are sometimes stolen away out of their own countries by robbers, or spirited by kidnappers, who often carry away many children of both sexes as they find them about the country, being set to watch the cornfields of their relations. . . . Some also through extreme want in hard times, also insolvent debtors and such as are condemned to fines they are not able to pay, sell themselves willingly for slaves to others of their country people, and there are of both sexes and all ages; but the much greater number of slaves, as has been said, are taken in war, either in battle or by making excursions into the enemies' country.

The trade of slaves is in a more peculiar manner the business of kings, rich men and prime merchants, exclusive of the inferior sort of Blacks. These slaves are severely and barbarously treated by their masters, who subsist them poorly and beat them in-humanly, as may be seen by the scabs and wounds on the bodies of many of them when sold to us. They scarce allow them the least rag to cover their nakedness, which they also take off from them when sold to Europeans; and they always go bareheaded. The wives and children of slaves are also slaves to the master under whom they are married; and when dead they never bury them, but cast out the bodies into some by-place, to be devoured by birds or beasts of prey.

This barbarous usage of those unfortunate wretches makes it appear that the fate of such as are bought, and transported from the coast to America or other parts of the world by Europeans, is less deplorable than that of those who end their days in their native country; for aboard ships all possible care is taken to preserve and subsist them for the interest of the owners, and when sold in America the same motive ought to prevail with their masters to use them well, that they may live the longer and do them more service: not to mention the inestimable advantage they may reap of becoming Christians and saving their souls, if they make a true use of their condition. . . .

The Gold Coast, in times of war between the inland nations and those nearer the sea, will furnish great numbers of slaves of all sexes and ages, sometimes at one place and sometimes at another, as has been already observed, according to the nature of the war and the situation of the countries between which it is waged. I remember to this purpose that in the year 1681 an English interloper at Commendo got three hundred good slaves almost for nothing besides the trouble of receiving them at the beach in his boats, as the Commendo men brought them from the field of battle, having obtained a victory over a neighbouring nation and taken a great number of prisoners.

At other times slaves are so scarce there that in 1682 I could get but eight from one end of the coast to the other, not only because we were a great number of trading ships on the coast at the same time but by reason the natives were everywhere at peace. At another time I had two hundred slaves at Acra only, in a fortnight or three weeks time; and the upper coast men, understanding I had those slaves aboard, came down to redeem them, giving me two for one of such as I understood were their near relations, who had been stolen away by inland Blacks, brought down to Acra, and sold to us.

I also remember that I once, among my several runs along that coast, happened to have aboard a whole family, man, wife, three young boys and a girl, bought one after another at several places; and cannot but observe here what mighty satisfaction those poor creatures expressed to be so come together again, though in bondage. For several days successively they could not forbear shedding tears of joy, and continually embracing and caressing one another, which moving me to compassion, I ordered they should be better treated aboard than commonly we can afford to do it where there are four or five hundred in a ship; and at Martinique I sold them all together to a considerable planter at a cheaper rate than I might have expected had they been disposed of severally, being informed of that gentleman's good-nature, and having taken his word that he would use that family as well as their circumstances would permit, and settle them in some part by themselves.

I . . . shall conclude this chapter . . . with an odd remark, which is, that many of those slaves we transport from Guinea to America are prepossessed with the opinion that they are carried like sheep to the slaughter, and that the Europeans are fond of their flesh; which notion so far prevails with some as to make them fall into a deep melancholy and despair, and to refuse all sustenance, though never so much compelled and even beaten to oblige them to take some nourishment; notwithstanding all which they will starve to death, whereof I have had several instances in my own slaves both aboard and at Guadaloupe.

216. Thomas Phillips's journal of the voyage of the *Hannibal* to Africa and Barbados, 1693–1694

(*Voyages and Travels*, ed. A. and J. Churchill, VI, pp. 173–174, 204–205)

After my return to England I was for some time destitute of employment, until my ever honoured patron and benefactor, Sir Jeffrey Jeffreys, knight, out of his extraordinary generosity and good-will to me, understanding that the ship *Hannibal*, of four hundred and fifty tons and thirty-six guns, was to be sold, gave me orders to buy her. Having done this, he was pleased to deposit the money for her presently out of his own pocket; and after, by his interest, to bring in his worthy brother, John Jeffreys, esquire, Samuel Stanyer, esquire, then sub-governor of the African Company, and some other eminent merchants, to be part-owners with me; and then to recommend me and the ship to the Royal African Company of England, from whom upon his account I found acceptance.

Being entered into their service on a trading voyage to Guinea for elephants' teeth, gold and negro slaves, and having the needful cargoes on board wherewith to purchase them, as well as supplies of merchandise, stores, &c., for the Company's castles and factories, my business being completed at London, I took boat for Gravesend the fifth of September [1693], in the evening, and got on board about eleven at night, with money to pay my men their river-pay and one month's pay advance-money as per agreement. . . . .

Until the fifth of October, in the morning, we had fair weather, smooth sea and a small gale of wind at S.S.W., which towards evening veered about to the S.E. and E., and invited us and the rest of the outward-bound ships in the Downs to go to sea, of which those for Guinea were the *East-India Merchant*, of thirty guns, Captain Thomas Shirley commander; the *Hannibal*, of thirty-six guns, Thomas Phillips, for the Gold Coast; the *Mediterranean*, of twenty-four guns, Captain Daniel, for Angola; the *Jeffrey*, of twelve guns, Captain Somes, for the Bight; the *Fortune*, of twelve guns, Captain Hereford, for Angola; and the *Eagle* packet boat, Captain Perry, for Gambo and the Coast. We having agreed among ourselves that Captain Thomas Shirley, who had been long acquainted with the Guinea trade, should give sailing orders, shape the course and carry the light, we came on board to unmoor our ships, and about eight were under sail. . . .

27 February [1694]. The castle of Cape Coast is the chief of all those our African Company have upon this coast, and where their agents or chief factors always reside, to which all the other factories are subordinate. This castle has a handsome prospect from the sea, and is a very regular and well-contrived fortification, and as strong as it can be well made considering its situation, being encompassed with a strong and high brick wall, through which you enter by a well-secured and large gate facing the town, and come into a fine, spacious square, wherein four or five hundred men may very conveniently be drawn up and exercised. It has four flankers, which have a covered communication with each other and are mounted with good guns; and over the tank is a noble battery of fifteen whole culverin and demi-cannon, lying low and pointing upon the road, where they would do good execution upon any ships that should

pretend to attack the castle, if there were a sufficient number of men to ply them briskly that understood the sport.

Under this battery is a curious tank or cistern, which will contain 400 tons of water, being with great labour cut in a long square out of a rock and terraced over, having a convenient pair of stairs to descend into it to fetch the water. This tank is filled every rain time, and not only supplies the castle with water all the year (which no enemy can cut off from them or poison), but frequently the Company's agents permit their ships to fill much of their water there. . . . Of these tanks every castle upon the Coast has one, but very small, and in proportion to the number of soldiers they are allowed to man them. . . .

We landed out of the *Hannibal* at this place thirty soldiers for the Company, in as good health as we received them aboard in England. But in two months time that we lay here to complete our business they were near half dead, and scarce enough of the survivors able to carry their fellows to the grave. . . .

E. NORTH AMERICA

217. John Oldmixon's account of the Hudson's Bay Company
(*British Empire in America*, ed. 1741, I, pp. 544–566)

The civil wars in England put discoveries out of men's heads; the bold had other work cut out for them; and we hear of no more such adventures till the year 1667,[1] when Zachariah Gillam in the *Nonsuch* ketch passed through Hudson Strait, and then into Baffin Bay to 75 degrees, and thence southward into 51 degrees, where in a river, afterwards called Prince Rupert's river, he had a friendly correspondence with the natives, built a fort, named it Charles Fort, and returned with success. . . .

When Gillam returned the adventurers concerned in fitting them out applied themselves to King Charles II for a patent, who granted one to them and their successors for the bay called Hudson Bay and the strait called Hudson Strait. The patent bears date the 2nd of May in the 22nd year of that king's reign, A.D. 1670. The first proprietors or company, called the Hudson's Bay Company, were Prince Rupert, Sir James Hayes, Mr. William Young, Mr. Gerard Weymans, Mr. Richard Cradock, Mr. John Letton, Christopher Wren, esq., Mr. Nicholas Hayward. . . .

Before we proceed any farther in the history it will not be improper to give an account of the country, climate, product, trade and inhabitants. The mouth of the strait, which is in about 61 degrees north latitude, is 6 leagues over. At the mouth is an island called Resolution. Charles Island, Salisbury Island and Nottingham are in the strait, and Mansel Island in the mouth of the bay. Hudson Strait, which leads to the bay, is about 120 leagues in length, the land on both sides inhabited by savages of whom we have little or no knowledge. The south coast is known by the name of the Terra Labrador, the north by as many names as men of several nations have been there and pretended to the discovery of it. On the west side of the bay the English made a settlement, built a fort at Port Nelson; and all that country goes by the name of New South Wales. The bay here is called Button's, and Hudson Bay, which is broadest in this place, may be near 130 leagues broad.

On the other shore, or the coast of Labrador, lie several islands, called the Sleeper Islands and the Baker's Dozen. The bottom of the bay, by which we understand all that part of it from Cape Henrietta Maria in New South Wales to Redonda below Prince Rupert's river, is about 80 leagues long and much of one breadth all the way, being between 40 and 50 leagues over. . . . The two opposite shores are called the East Main and West Main. The former is Labrador and the latter New South Wales. The continent at the bottom of the bay is by the French pretended to be part of New France, and indeed to cross the country from St. Margaret's river, which runs into the river of Canada, to Rupert's river, at the bottom of Hudson Bay, is not above 150 miles.

At Rupert's river the English built their first fort, which they called Charles Fort. They never had any towns or plantations here, and probably never will. They live

[1] Really 1668.

within their forts in little houses or huts, wherein the builders consider nothing but to defend them from the cold and rains, though they are not so much disturbed by the latter as by the former. . . .

The commodities for trade here are guns, powder, shot, cloth, hatchets, kettles, tobacco, &c., which the English exchange with the Indians for furs, beavers, marten, fox, moose and other peltry; and the curious, who have any taste of commerce, will not think it a digression to insert a standard of trade which the Hudson's Bay Company fixed several years ago. . . .[1]

The standard how the Company's goods must be bartered in the southern part of the bay

Guns	One with another, 10 good skins (that is winter beaver); 12 skins for the biggest sort, 10 for the mean, and 8 for the smallest.
Powder	A beaver for half a pound.
Shot	A beaver for four pounds.
Hatchets	A beaver for a great and little hatchet.
Knives	A beaver for six great knives or eight jack-knives.
Beads	A beaver for half a pound of beads.
Laced coats	Six beavers for one good laced coat.
Plain coats	Five beaver skins for one red plain coat.
Coats	For women, laced, two yards, 6 beavers.
Coats	For women, plain, 5 beavers.
Tobacco	A beaver for one pound.
Powder-horns	A beaver for one large powder-horn and two small ones.
Kettles	A beaver for one pound of kettle.
Looking glasses and combs	Two skins.

It is plain by this standard the company got prodigiously, and had they traded much their actions might have been now[1] 300 per cent, as they were once; but their returns were small, and their charges great. Ten thousand beavers in all their factories was one of the best years of trade they ever had, besides other peltry. . . .

The company intended to plant a colony at Charlton Island, and ordered Mr. Sergeant to build a fort there and always keep some men upon it. Warehouses were also built to receive the furs that were brought thither from the factories, and conveniences were made for the reception of such as were obliged to winter there. The company always enjoined their governors to endeavour to save the great charge they were at in sending constant supplies of provisions, by planting corn and other grain there. But alas! though the climate by its distance from the sun should be as warm as ours, yet for reasons which the naturalists will easily give us it is so cold and frosty that it kills almost all sorts of roots in the ground which are sown there; and those plantations, so often recommended by the company, were chimerical and impracticable. . . .

[1] The account was first published in 1708.

The trade to this bay has decreased ever since the use of beavers has fallen off in England. Peltry is not now the commodity it was, and this company, of consequence, does not make the figure they did thirteen or fourteen years ago. In the present war[1] they lost Port Nelson to the French, and have either given up or deserted all their settlements except Fort Albany, where Mr. Knight managed their affairs till the year 1706. . . .

218. Representation of the Board of Trade to the Privy Council on the affairs of Newfoundland, 1702

(*Acts of the Privy Council, Colonial Series*, II, pp. 397–401)

Approved, 26 March 1702

The season of the year approaching for the usual convoys to be sent to Newfoundland, we humbly take leave to lay before your Majesty such account of the state of that place as we conceive necessary for the further security and advantage thereof.

The importance of that trade and fishery being very great to this kingdom, and several provisions having been made by a late Act of Parliament for the better regulating the same, we did in pursuance thereof prepare particular heads of inquiry and directions, which were accordingly given by the Lords Commissioners of the Admiralty to Captain Graydon, commander-in-chief of the squadron sent thither the last year, unto which we received answers; and humbly offer to your Majesty that it does appear to us:

That the inhabitants in general have not a due regard to the several regulations for the more advantageous management of the fishery, it being found that northward of St. John's as far as Carbonear, and to the southward as far as Ferryland, the trees are rinded and the woods destroyed as much as before the late Act.

That the admirals and masters of ships do not exactly observe the rules prescribed by Act of Parliament.

That the vessels from Newfoundland supply the people of Newfoundland with provisions.

That European commodities are carried directly from France, Spain and Portugal to Newfoundland in English ships, contrary to law, and sold or trucked with the traders from New England for tobacco, sugar and other of the enumerated commodities, and carried to foreign parts; so that at the latter end of the year the masters are wholly taken up in the management of that illegal trade, which might in some measure be prevented had the officer or officers commanding your Majesty's ships power like that of a Custom House officer to seize such goods.

That the New England traders seldom depart the country till the men-of-war are first sailed, and then they carry with them numbers of handicraftsmen, seamen and fishermen, whom they entice thither in expectation of great wages.

That the masters of ships are very negligent in bringing their men home, whereby they save the charge of their passage; and those men so left are enticed and carried to New England.

---

[1] War of the Spanish Succession.

Against which irregularities we humbly conceive it necessary that the commander of the convoy now going thither be directed to take care, as far as in him lies, that upon his arrival there the best remedies be applied for the prevention of those mischiefs; and that upon his report some further clauses be proposed at the next sessions of Parliament for the more effectual regulating that trade.

As for the state of the fortifications in St. John's harbour, which is the principal place of defence, we have already humbly represented that stone and other materials are wanting for completing the same, for the transporting of which we have disposed some merchants to be assistant with their ships at easy charge; and we humbly offer that your Majesty would be pleased to give the necessary directions therein to the master general of your Majesty's ordnance.

And whereas there is wanting a boom and other materials for floating and fixing a chain, which has been sent thither some time since for the security of that harbour; and the officers of your Majesty's ordnance having alleged that the charge thereof ought to be borne by the Navy Board, and that Board (on the other side) having insisted that the care of this service appertains to the Board of Ordnance; we humbly offer that your Majesty be pleased to interpose your directions that this necessary service be performed. . . .

And whereas your Majesty has there one company of foot consisting of 80 men beside officers, for whom all necessaries are yearly sent by every convoy, we humbly lay before your Majesty hereunto annexed the several accounts of what appears to us to be wanting for the support of the said company in subsistence, clothing and provisions, for the providing of which the most speedy orders are requisite.

In relation to the said company we further humbly report that we have received from Captain Powell, their commander, several letters of complaints against the agent employed in transacting for them here, as if he had not duly remitted the subsistence money allowed them according to their establishment, to which having required the said agent to give answer, he has stated and laid before us such accounts of his transactions as seem to us to be without exception. But in order to the more perfect examination of those matters we humbly offer that copies of all papers relating thereunto be given to the commander of this year's convoy, and that he be directed to report his opinion thereupon, and redress as far as in him lies what he shall find amiss.

We likewise humbly represent to your Majesty that the commander of the Newfoundland convoy may have the like commission to command in chief the soldiers in pay there as has been given the former years.

And whereas we have also received from the lord bishop of London a great complaint of the ill and scandalous usage that Mr. Jackson, the minister of St. John's in Newfoundland, hath received from Captain Powell and Samuel Francis, his first lieutenant, and of their profligate lives, which is of very ill example to the soldiers and inhabitants of that place, we cannot but represent to your Majesty that one or both of them be removed from their employments there, and succeeded by such as may behave themselves as they ought to do.

And whereas Mr. John Thurston has been employed for three years past in the business of Newfoundland relating to the soldiers there, which has been a matter of great trouble and some expense, for which he has as yet had no reward, we do think he may deserve the sum of one hundred pounds in consideration of his said services and expenses, and that an allowance of forty pounds per annum be allowed him for the future during the said agency, the company there no ways contributing thereunto.

An account of small clothing to be sent the company at Newfoundland, this year 1702

	l. s. d.	l. s. d.
88 pair of strong shoes for soldiers and non-commission officers, being one pair for each man at 4s. 6d. per pair		19 16 0
80 pair of stockings for soldiers at 18d. a pair	6 0 0	
5 pair of do. for corporals and drummers at 20d.	8 4	
3 pair of do. for sergeants at 3s.	9 0	
		6 17 4
160 shirts for soldiers (being 2 for each man) at 3s. 6d.	28 0 0	
10 do. for 5 corporals and drummers at do.	1 15 0	
6 do. for sergeants at 5s.	1 10 0	
		31 5 0
160 neckcloths for soldiers at 12d.	8 0 0	
10 do. for corporals and drummers at 1s. 6d.	15 0	
6 do. for sergeants at 4s.	1 4 0	
		9 19 0
		67 17 4
Freight, with charge of packing, &c.		5 0 0
		72 17 4

An account of provisions to be sent, this year 1702, for the company at Newfoundland

Biscuit	24,752 pounds
Malt	93 quarters 4 bushels
Beef	2,358 pieces
Pork	3,536 pieces
Pease	110 bushels 4 gallons
Oat-meal	165 bushels 6 gallons
Butter	1,326 pounds
Cheshire cheese	1,772 pounds
Flour	3,536 pounds
Suet	589 pounds
Hops	$2\frac{1}{2}$ hundredweight

An account of money wanting for the company at Newfoundland

One year's subsistence for a captain at 3s. per diem; a first lieutenant at 2s. 6d.; a second lieutenant at 2s.; 3 sergeants at 4d. each; 5 corporals and drummers at 3d. each; and 80 private soldiers each at 2d.; in all 1l. 3s. 1d. per diem	415	4	7
One year's contingent money ending 1st September 1702	50	0	0
Several small necessaries for the company	72	17	4
A year's subsistence for a surgeon's mate, which is represented to us as absolutely necessary in addition to the establishment, at 2s. a day beside provision	36	10	0
A chest of medicines	25	0	0
Left unsatisfied of the clothing provided the last year	79	10	7
One year's contingent money in arrear	50	0	0
	729	2	6

F. MEDITERRANEAN OUTPOSTS

219. Establishment for Tangier, 1682

(*Calendar of Treasury Books*, VII, pp. 1009–1011)

	l.	s.	d.
The governor	1,500	0	0
The minister at 10s. a day	182	10	0
The physician at 15s. a day	273	15	0
The town mayor at 10s. a day, without any manner of perquisites or other advantages	182	10	0
Judge advocate at 8s. a day	146	0	0
Chirurgeon at 4s. a day	73	0	0
Chirurgeon's mate at 2s. 6d. a day	45	12	0
Quartermaster provost marshal and his servants at 5s. a day	91	5	0
Commissaries of the musters at 6s.	109	10	0
Storekeeper for the garrison at 3s. 4d.	60	16	8
Engineer at 6s. a day	109	10	0
Storekeeper of the ammunition and stores, for himself and assistants at 6s. 8d. a day	121	13	4
Master carpenter	54	0	0
Fire master at 5s.	91	5	0
Master gunner at 3s.	54	15	0
Gunsmith at 2s. 6d.	45	12	0
Sixteen gunners at 1s. per day each besides victuals	292	0	0
The above seven items to depend on the Master of the Ordnance			
Two regiments of foot, each consisting of 16 companies, and each company of a captain at 8s. a day, a lieutenant at 4s., an ensign at 3s., 2 sergeants at 1s. each besides victuals, 3 corporals and 1 drummer at 6d. each besides victuals, 50 privates at 3d. each besides victuals, or 574l. 17s. 6d. per company per annum, which for 32 companies is	18,396	0	0
For the field and staff officers of the said two regiments, viz., two colonels at 12s. a day each, two lieutenant-colonels at 7s. a day each, two majors at 5s. a day each, or 438l. per annum for each regiment	876	0	0
Four troops of horse, each to consist of a captain at 14s. a day, lieutenant at 10s., cornet at 9s., quartermaster at 6s., two corporals at 3s. each, trumpeter at 2s. 2d. besides victuals, farrier at 2s. besides victuals, 25 private horsemen at 2s. each besides victuals; or 1,809l. 15s. 10d. per troop	7,239	3	4
For the hospital, besides the value of the sick soldiers' victuals added to the hospital towards maintenance	700	0	0

For coals and candles	500	0	0
For boatmen, boats, intelligence, messages, presents and other contingencies at Tangier	400	0	0

The total of the above, viz., 31,544*l*. 17*s*. 4*d*., by paying 4*s*. 9*d*. with every 4*s*. 6*d*., will be defrayed by	29,884	12	$2\frac{10}{19}$
To the victuallers for victualling 1,916 men at 2*s*. 6*d*. a week each, viz., 1,600 foot, 64 sergeants, 96 corporals, 32 drummers, 100 troopers, 4 trumpeters, 4 farriers and 16 gunners	12,454	0	0
	42,338	12	$2\frac{10}{19}$

Memorandum, that the 3*d*. a day in money made payable by this establishment to each foot soldier of the garrison of Tangier shall be from time to time paid to the colonels of each regiment, out of which they are to furnish the said soldiers with clothes, shirts, shoes, stockings and other necessaries, the same to be always bought in Ireland and nowhere else, and that at as easy rates as may be, and to pay the remainder, if any, in money to the said soldiers.

Memorandum, that 8*d*. a day out of the 2*s*. a day hereby payable to each trooper of said garrison shall from time to time be paid to such surveyor as the king shall appoint, to be by him laid out for providing such stores and quantities of horse meat as are now allowed to each horseman at Tangier, and the remaining 16*d*. a day shall be paid to the respective captains of horse, out of which they are to furnish the said troopers with clothes, boots, belts and other necessaries to be bought in Ireland, etc., *ut supra*.

The Lord Lieutenant of Ireland is to appoint some fit persons to supervise the buying of the said clothes and necessaries, to see that they are good in kind and at the cheapest rates.

220. Stephen Martin-Leake's account, based on Sir John Leake's papers, of the capture of Gibraltar, 1704

(*Life of Sir John Leake*, ed. G. Callender, I, pp. 152–156)

The 16th [July 1704] the admiral[1] having received the king of Spain's[2] proposals for attempting Cadiz, a council of war was called thereupon the next day, the fleet being then about seven leagues to the eastward of Tetuan, and the attempt upon Cadiz was determined impracticable without an army to co-operate with the fleet. This design being laid aside, they then took into consideration what other service might be practicable, and they came to a resolution to land the marines, both English and Dutch, under the command of the prince of Hesse in the bay of Gibraltar, to cut off that town from any communication with the main, and at the same time to bombard and cannonade the place, and endeavour to reduce it to the obedience of the king of Spain.

---

[1] Sir George Rooke.   [2] Charles III.

This enterprise upon Gibraltar had been thought on some time before by Vice-Admiral Leake as the most advantageous conquest that could be made for the benefit of trade, as well as the fleet, during the war with France and Spain, and therefore it had been proposed by him to the admiral and the prince of Hesse, who both approved of it. But being restrained by their orders to act no otherwise than with the approbation of the kings of Spain and Portugal, who were bent upon the attempt of Barcelona and Cadiz, though they would contribute no land-forces to the effecting of either, the admirals could not act as they thought most beneficial to the common cause. But no sooner was the expedition to Cadiz judged impracticable, and they were at liberty, than the attempt against Gibraltar immediately took place, as the most agreeable and beneficial service they could go upon.

The fortress of Gibraltar is a small but very strong city and castle in the province of Andalusia, seated at the foot of a rocky mountain, which makes a peninsula, and is joined to the rest of Spain only by a small isthmus of land. By its situation it commands the trade and is the key of the Mediterranean Sea, being at the opening of the strait's mouth opposite the Apes' Hill in Barbary at about seven leagues distance, which two hills were the famous Herculean Pillars, of which there have been so many uncertain traditions. The bay wherein the town lies is also a very commodious harbour for the largest ships, there being likewise two moles projecting into the bay from the walls of the town, making a secure retreat for smaller vessels. Thus [is the place] happily situated for the protection of trade and annoyance of an enemy, but more especially useful in the war with France and Spain when we had no port in the Mediterranean.

According to the resolutions of the flag officers the fleet on the 20th pushed over from the Barbary shore, and the next day at three in the afternoon the marines, to the number of 1,800, were landed by the prince of Hesse-Darmstadt's direction on the neck of land to the northward of the town, to cut off all communication with the country. And a summons was sent to the governor to surrender the place for the service of his Catholic Majesty, to which he returned answer that the garrison had taken an oath of fidelity to their natural lord King Philip V, and that as faithful and loyal subjects they would sacrifice their lives in the defence of the city. Hereupon, the 22nd in the morning, twelve third-rates, four fourth, with six of the Dutch and three bombs, were ordered in to bombard and cannonade the place; but the wind blowing contrary they could not take their posts till the day was spent. However the bombs made a beginning, and hove in seventeen shells. In the meantime, to amuse the enemy, some boats were sent in, who burnt a French privateer of 12 guns at the Old Mole.

The next day, by five in the morning, the signal was given to begin the cannonade, and likewise for the bombs to play, which was done with great fury till eleven, when they fired more leisurely, plying only their lower tier. By this time the enemy being beaten from their guns, especially at the South Mole head, all the boats manned and armed were sent under the command of Captain Whitaker to endeavour to possess themselves of that post. Accordingly they landed, but were no sooner on shore than the enemy sprang a mine, which blew up the fortifications upon the Mole, with the loss of 2 lieutenants and 40 seamen blown to pieces and 60 others wounded. Notwithstanding which they kept possession of the platform, and advancing took a redoubt, or detached small bastion, half way between the Mole and the town, and possessed themselves of many of the enemy's cannon. It being Sunday, the women were at their devotions at a little chapel out of the town, and by this means were cut off from the city; and this made their husbands in the place more importunate with the governor to capitulate.

Upon this success the prince of Hesse sent a message to the governor, peremptorily [summoning him] to surrender the town at the north gate, where the marines were; and considering he had but a small garrison, not able to stand an assault, he desired to capitulate, and had honourable articles granted him. The prince immediately marched in and took possession of the town, where he found about 100 guns mounted, but the garrison no more than 150 men. It was certainly a most gross neglect of Spain to have no better garrison there, unless it be that depending upon the natural strength of the place they thought it sufficient. . . . This important conquest was made with the loss only of 2 lieutenants, 1 master and 60 common seamen killed, and 1 captain, 7 lieutenants, 1 boatswain and about 216 common seamen wounded.

221. Letter from General Stanhope to Lord Sunderland on the capture and importance of Minorca, 1708

(*Byng Papers*, ed. B. Tunstall, II, pp. 299–303)

Port Mahon

MY LORD,   30 September 1708

I acquainted your lordship in my last that I landed here the 19th instant with 2,600 men, 1,200 of them English including the marines, about 600 Portuguese, and the rest Spaniards. We found great difficulties in landing and transporting our heavy artillery and stores through a country very rocky, and where there are very few beasts of burden. But with continual labour we did in twelve days get up all our artillery, which consisted of 42 pieces of cannon and 15 mortars, to the place near which we proposed to make use of it, and by the 28th at break of day got nine pieces of cannon in battery against two towers which supported a line the enemies had made from sea to sea. In a few hours we beat them down, and made some breaches in the line, which I designed to attack the next day. But Brigadier Wade being posted with two battalions at some distance from me on the right, some of his grenadiers without orders advanced to the line, and found a way to get into it. To support them he marched with what men he could readily get together to sustain them, and got in. So soon as we heard the fire I took the ordinary guard of the battery and advanced to the line next to me, and such was the consternation of the enemy that they nowhere stood us, but abandoned two other towers which we could not have taken without cannon.

We lodged ourselves the same evening at the foot of the glacis of the main castle, and traced our main battery to beat it. But the morning following they beat a parley, and at five of the clock in the afternoon the capitulation was signed, which I have not time to get translated, but is as they would have it. This morning I have taken possession of one gate and all their outworks, and find them to be above a thousand men under arms, which are to be transported in our ships, some to France and some to

Spain. We have not had fifty men killed or wounded in this siege. I only have had the misfortune to lose my brother, who had been very instrumental in engaging the seamen in this enterprise, and unfortunately would have too great a share in the execution of it. But since he died in doing service to her Majesty and his country I shall think his life well bestowed, as I would my own.

I hope the want of ports will no longer be an objection to wintering a squadron here, her Majesty being now mistress of the two best ports in the Mediterranean, this and Fornelles in the same island, which though not so much known is by many seamen preferred to this. And having mentioned it to your lordship, I must do justice to Captain Butler and Captain Fairborne, who with their two ships went in and battered the fort till they forced the garrison to yield themselves prisoners of war. A detachment of foot I sent has likewise taken prisoners of war 100 soldiers who were in Civadella, the capital of this island, which is now entirely ours.

A great part of our success in reducing the island is owing to the zeal and affection the people have for us, which is beyond expression; and whoever shall take care to keep up this disposition, which is easily to be done, need not fear to lose any of the three above-mentioned fortresses. This consideration makes me offer it as my humble opinion that England ought never to part with this island, which will give the law to the Mediterranean both in time of war and peace. For this reason I will leave an English garrison here, and hope I have so disposed it as not to give any jealousy or uneasiness to the king of Spain, for, troops being mightily wanted in Catalonia, I shall make rather a merit to myself by carrying back thither all that I brought out, and borrow marines of the ships to leave here.

As for a governor, I have with me Colonel Petit, an engineer, who for his eminent services in both sieges of Barcelona, the good success of which may chiefly be imputed to him, had got from the king a commission of brigadier and frequent promises of some further reward. Him therefore I leave here as governor, and will be answerable for his behaviour. I give him two commissions, the one as empowered by the queen, which he is not to make show of but upon necessity, and the other as a general of the king's, for I know not whether I have informed your lordship that I have a commission from the king of Spain of lieutenant-general, which has enabled me to perform this service and many others which I could not have done without it; and I hope I shall have her Majesty's approbation for having accepted of it. . . .

I shall stay here a few days to settle this garrison and give directions for adding to the fortifications what may be necessary. We have found in it above 100 cannon, 3,000 barrels of powder, and all things necessary to make a good defence except resolution in the garrison, 500 of which are French marines. I am ever, with all imaginable respect, My Lord,

Your lordship's most humble and obedient servant,

JAMES STANHOPE

Part VII
SCOTLAND

SCOTLAND

Introduction

TO the great majority of Scotsmen the chief attraction of the Restoration was the prospect it offered of the recovery of their national independence. Any advantages in the way of better administration or freedom of trade which they had derived from the Cromwellian union with England were more than balanced in their eyes by the heavy taxation which the system involved, and by the fact that it was foreign in origin, republican in its political principles, and a support for what Scotsmen almost without exception regarded as religious anarchy. The majority of Englishmen, on the other hand, felt that they had little to gain by retaining their hold over Scotland, which was neither a danger to be guarded against nor a source of profit to be exploited. With surprisingly little opposition, in consequence, the principle was accepted that the English officials and English garrisons in Scotland should be withdrawn, and that the network of fortresses established at Leith, Ayr, Perth and Inverness should be demolished.[1]

Once agreement on this crucial point had been reached the Restoration in Scotland had in large measure been effected, for the Scots had never repudiated Charles II, but had merely been prevented by a foreign army of occupation from obeying him. Charles issued no declaration of Breda to his subjects north of the Tweed, for the simple reason that he had no need to purchase, with promises of good behaviour, a throne which he already occupied. He had been proclaimed at Edinburgh, with the full support of the nation, on 5 February 1649, and the proclamation of his title by the English Parliament,[2] which was received with such demonstrations of joy in the Scottish capital on 14 May 1660,[3] amounted, so far as Scotland was concerned, to little more than an intimation that his authority was again effective. He had been crowned at Scone on 1 January 1651, and this ceremony it was never considered necessary or desirable to repeat. With the return of the Scottish records removed by Cromwell the recognition of Scottish independence appeared virtually complete, though the operation was carried out so carelessly that a considerable proportion of the records were lost in the course of their transit by sea.[4]

Unfortunately the independence so joyfully hailed in Scotland was soon shown to be largely illusory. Even had Charles wished to do so, he would have found it difficult to adopt in Scotland a policy disapproved by his advisers in England; but his dislike of Scottish principles in Church and State was strong enough to preclude any such desire on his part, and he readily followed English advice in forcing upon Scotland a much more reactionary conception of the Restoration than England itself would have endured. Without seeking the advice and consent of any Scottish Parliament, which a statute of 1641 had declared imperative, he appointed his own Privy Council, the immediately effective section of which was to sit in London and consisted largely of Englishmen. With more reason, and at the petition of Scottish representatives who journeyed south to greet him, he provided an actual executive body north of the Tweed by reviving the Committee of Estates appointed by the Parliament of 1651 at

[1] No. 224. [2] No. 2. [3] No. 222. [4] No. 223.

591

which he had himself been present;[1] but this was merely a temporary expedient, and the real settlement of Scotland was left to the Parliament which he summoned to meet at Edinburgh on 1 January 1661.

In Scotland, unlike England, it was thus the king who restored Parliament, not Parliament that recalled the king; and the result was soon apparent in their relations with each other. The real interest of Scotsmen lay less in constitutional than in ecclesiastical affairs, and in that sphere Charles had prepared the way with a reassuring letter, intended to be read in all presbyteries, in which he undertook to preserve the government of the Church as settled by law.[2] As he had probably planned and foreseen, however, one of the first measures passed by the extravagantly loyal Parliament produced by the Restoration was the Act Rescissory, which at one blow annulled the proceedings of every Parliament since 1633, even when the king had himself approved of these proceedings at the time.[3] In virtue of this Act the Church "settled by law" became the Church established by James VI, and in accordance with instructions received from Charles the Privy Council hastened to give effect to the original royal assurance by an order providing for the restoration of the episcopal system which the majority of the nation had condemned.[4] Something like a third of the clergy abandoned their livings rather than submit.

In secular affairs the work of restoration was carried even further. Not merely was the absolute monarchy of James VI re-established by a series of statutes declaring the king entitled to all the prerogatives of which he had recently been deprived, but a regular revenue unprecedented in Scottish history was granted for the support of the government,[5] a test was imposed on all officials by which they were required to repudiate the Covenants and other measures of the period of troubles,[6] and authority was given for the raising of a militia which practically provided the king with an army of his own.[7] Parliament was again reduced to the undignified position it had occupied under the early Stuarts. The newly created bishops, all royal nominees, were readmitted to it,[8] and on their unfailing support was based the ingeniously contrived committee of Lords of the Articles, by means of which the activities of Parliament could largely be directed by the king.[9]

Had Scotland been left to itself the considerable majority who disapproved of these proceedings could soon have reduced the pretensions of the minority, drawn mainly from the nobility, gentry and clergy, who supported them. But so long as the minority had the ear of the absentee king, and could rely on the resources of England, opposition was vain, and the sole question was whether the minority, by persecution, by conciliation or by a mixture of both, could induce the majority to submit. Persecution was tried in Acts re-establishing the lay patronage to which Scottish reformers so strongly objected,[10] imposing penalties on both clergymen and laymen who failed to conform,[11] and restricting the movements of the ejected clergy somewhat in the manner of the later English Five Mile Act.[12] But the only result was a great increase of field conventicles,[13] which were the more alarming to the government inasmuch as members of the congregations were beginning to attend in arms. Indulgence was then attempted,[14] eliciting an unexpected remonstrance from the established clergy of the diocese of Glasgow, which had to be met by a reiteration of the royal supremacy in ecclesiastical affairs.[15] Finally the expedient was adopted of making land-owners and

[1] No. 225.	[2] No. 226.	[3] No. 227.	[4] No. 228.	[5] No. 258.
[6] No. 229.	[7] No. 230.	[8] No. 260.	[9] No. 261.	[10] No. 232.
[11] No. 233.	[12] Nos. 138, 234.	[13] No. 235.	[14] No. 236.	[15] No. 231.

masters responsible for the behaviour of their tenants and servants,[1] and quartering a disorderly rabble of Highlanders and militia on the recalcitrant inhabitants of the south-west, where opposition to the ecclesiastical settlement was strongest. Charles warmly approved of these last measures;[2] but they produced as little effect as further attempts at indulgence extending to the closing months of James's reign.[3]

The surprising thing is that these measures gave rise to so little active resistance. But the Scots were as disinclined as the English for any renewal of civil disturbances; the Presbyterian majority were much divided in opinion as to the attitude to be adopted to the government's attempts at conciliation; and the wiser heads among them were well aware that the extremists on the government side were hoping for a show of opposition as providing an excuse for further persecution. As a result the Pentland Rising, which was in any case premature, received remarkably little support,[4] and the later and more promising insurrection in the west was a dismal failure. Beginning with a striking success at Drumclog,[5] it developed with sufficient rapidity to give serious alarm to the government; but its leaders could not agree on a common policy even in the field, and it was eventually crushed with ease at Bothwell Bridge.[6] Thereafter the majority of the malcontents sank back into a state of dull apathy, relieved only by the exploits of a few enthusiasts, whose declarations against the government bore witness at least to their courage and to the strength of their convictions,[7] and whom no cruelties or disasters to their leaders could daunt.

It is thus doubtful whether the Scots by themselves could have offered any effective opposition to James VII. Shortly before the close of Charles II's reign the Scottish Parliament had submissively enacted that no difference of religion could justify subjects in refusing recognition to the lawful heir to the throne,[8] and had imposed a more complicated test than ever before on all office-holders.[9] Immediately after the accession of James the earl of Argyll had endeavoured to unite all the elements of opposition to that monarch in a rebellion, but with conspicuous lack of success.[10] On England, in consequence, fell the task of repaying to Scotland the debt it had incurred in 1640. Just as the Scots had enabled the English to make effective opposition to Charles I, so the English now enabled the Scots to free themselves from the tyranny of James VII. Immediately upon news of James's flight to France reaching Edinburgh his government in Scotland began to go to pieces. Without a blow having been struck on his behalf he was declared by Parliament to have forfeited the throne,[11] and a Claim of Right was drawn up reciting his many breaches of the law as a warning to his successors, William and Mary.[12]

Meanwhile the clergy imposed upon the people by the governments of Charles II had been expelled from their livings, in some cases with unnecessary violence, while the survivors of those extruded under Charles had in many cases made their way back. This process was now authorized and regularized by Parliament,[13] while at the same time the supremacy of State over Church, which had made possible the original change, was repudiated.[14] Lay patronage was once more abolished,[15] and the whole Presbyterian system, in spite of strong expressions of disapproval in England, was re-established.[16]

With the Revolution ended one of the darkest periods in the history of Scotland, and yet a period during which the country had been not unprosperous. Unlike

[1] No. 237.   [2] No. 238.   [3] No. 239.   [4] No. 240.
[5] No. 241.   [6] No. 242.   [7] No. 243.   [8] No. 245.
[9] No. 246.   [10] No. 244.   [11] No. 247.   [12] No. 248.
[13] No. 250.   [14] No. 249.   [15] No. 252.   [16] No. 251.

England and Ireland, it had suffered little during the civil wars, and since 1651 had enjoyed the blessing of almost constant peace coupled with strong though brutal government. The few unprejudiced Englishmen who visited the country during the reigns of William and Anne were impressed by the modest comfort which they saw, and by evidence of a culture which, while it failed to reach the highest level attained in England, was much more widely spread.[1] With the accession of William and Mary it seemed not unreasonable to suppose that further progress was at hand.

Unfortunately the development of Scotland was hampered by two serious obstacles–on the one hand the disorderly and backward condition of the Highlands, which constituted a permanent threat to the more peaceful Lowlands, and on the other a lack of the capital necessary for any considerable enterprises by way of improvement. William's well-meant efforts to deal with the former evil met with some success; but the massacre of Glencoe[2] did much to destroy any impression he had made, and the problem of the Highlands had eventually to be left to the Hanoverians to solve. The latter evil was inseparably connected with the character of the relations between Scotland and England. Ever since the crowns of the two countries had been united Scotland had in effect found itself debarred from developing foreign trade or colonies of its own, and yet excluded from sharing in the benefit of the trade or colonies of England. Under the more favourable conditions which seemed to be provided by the accession of William a great national effort was made at profitable expansion abroad; but the Darien Company[3] proved to be a dismal failure, owing partly to English hostility, and partly to mismanagement due to inexperience. Scotland might develop its system of education,[4] establish a national bank, and improve commercial facilities at home; but any expansion abroad was subject to a permission from England which had not the slightest chance of being granted if English interests were in any way threatened.

Yet the Scots were very unwilling to contemplate a closer connexion with England. Attempts at union made by James I and Charles II had shown that it could be obtained, if at all, only on unfavourable terms. Moreover, they were much influenced by a natural desire to retain their national institutions. Chief of these was their Church, which they were well aware the English desired to remodel to suit their own ideas. But they had also a growing affection for their Parliament, which, freed by the Revolution from the despotic control of their kings, was now enjoying an Indian summer of power and prosperity. In Scotland there was no such hostility to parliamentary reform as in England, and Acts were passed making the single Scottish chamber in some ways more truly representative than its English counterparts.[5] The committee of Lords of the Articles was abolished,[6] and the revenue improved.[7] The Scottish Parliament had always been more colourful than the English House of Commons,[8] and with increased power now came also a new sense of dignity.

Thus the form first assumed by Scottish dissatisfaction with existing relations with England was a movement for complete independence. Towards that end the control of foreign affairs was transferred from the Crown to Parliament,[9] and the provision made in England for the succession on the death of Anne was deliberately rejected.[10] But the whole Scottish position was undermined by the lack of a suitable candidate for the throne. The titular James VIII, son of James VII, although regarded with much

[1] Nos. 253, 257. [2] No. 254. [3] No. 255. [4] No. 256.
[5] Nos. 259, 265; map 15; appendix IV. [6] No. 264.
[7] Nos. 262, 266. [8] No. 263. [9] No. 268. [10] No. 269.

more favour in Scotland than in England, was not in the least likely to secure general support. The only Protestant line descending from James VI had been adopted by the English Parliament. To find a candidate of their own the Scottish Parliament had to go back as far as James II, from whose daughter Mary the duke of Hamilton was descended.[1] In consequence when the English were induced by the dangers threatening them on the Continent to seek better relations with the Scots they were met half-way, and after a good deal of bargaining, and with a good deal of reluctance on both sides, agreement was reached in the treaty of union.[2]

That treaty was in itself a most statesmanlike measure. It is true that the representation it granted to Scotland in the united Parliament was inadequate, for it was determined mainly by the relative wealth of the two countries as indicated by taxation,[3] and Scotland, being a feudal country, where many of the functions of government were still in private hands, had never had any need of taxation on a level comparable to that of England. But it is doubtful whether greater representation would have made any appreciable difference to Scotland, and on other points the treaty was reasonable and even generous.

The real source of trouble was that the more irresponsible elements in English political life could see no reason why the promises embodied in the treaty should be kept. Although intended to be a permanent settlement, and considered at the very least to be incapable of any unilateral modification, the treaty had hardly been accepted when the immense English majority in the united Parliament was employed to alter it. The point which impressed Scotsmen as most scandalous of all was the reintroduction of lay patronage in their national Church;[4] but scarcely less discreditable were the abolition of the Scottish Privy Council, the extension to Scotland of the English law of treason,[5] the denial of membership of the House of Lords to Scottish peers who were given British titles,[6] and the threatened imposition on Scotland of a malt tax from which it had been promised exemption so long as the war should last. So keenly were these breaches of faith felt that a motion for dissolving the union was made in the House of Lords, and pressed so strongly that it was defeated only by the use of proxies.[7] Not until well on in the eighteenth century were the relations of Scotland and England to become even reasonably stable.

[1] Table 6.   [2] No. 270.   [3] No. 266.   [4] No. 272.   [5] No. 271.   [6] No. 80.   [7] No. 273.

BIBLIOGRAPHY

There is no really satisfactory bibliography of Scottish history; but the relevant sections of the general bibliographies are valuable, and Henry W. Meikle, *A Brief Bibliography of Scottish History*, compiled for the Historical Association (London, 1937), is useful as an introductory guide. W. H. Marwick, "A Bibliography of Scottish Economic History", in *Economic History Review*, III (1931), pp. 117–137, is of service for general as well as for purely economic history. Much wider in scope than its title and purpose would suggest is *An Introductory Survey of the Sources and Literature of Scots Law*, by various authors, edited by Hector McKechnie for the Stair Society (Edinburgh, 1936). Two compilations are by Charles Sanford Terry are indispensable—*An Index to the Papers relating to Scotland described or calendared in the Historical Manuscripts Commission's Reports, 1870–1908* (Glasgow, 1908), and *A Catalogue of the Publications of Scottish Historical and Kindred Clubs and Societies, and of the Volumes relative to Scottish History issued by his Majesty's Stationery Office, 1780–1908* (Glasgow, 1909). Both of these have been continued by Cyril Matheson in *A Catalogue of the Publications of . . . Clubs and Societies, and of the Papers . . . issued by H.M. Stationery Office, including the Reports of the Royal Commission on Historical Manuscripts, 1908–1927* (Aberdeen, 1928).

The standard guide to the Scottish records is Matthew Livingstone, *Guide to the Public Records of Scotland deposited in H.M. General Register House, Edinburgh* (1905), and the most serviceable account of the vicissitudes through which they have passed is Henry M. Paton, *The Scottish Records, their History and Value* (Edinburgh, 1933). The considerable sections of the national archives which suffered destruction at the hands of the English all belonged to the years before 1660, and for the later Stuarts the records are thus reasonably complete. Not only so, but they have to a large extent been printed, those of Parliament in *The Acts of the Parliaments of Scotland*, vols. VI–XII (1820–1875), a series much wider in its scope than its English equivalent, inasmuch as it includes both statutes and parliamentary proceedings; those of the Privy Council as far as 1689 in *The Register of the Privy Council of Scotland, Third Series* (14 vols., 1909–1933); and those of the major Crown grants as far as 1668 in *The Register of the Great Seal of Scotland*, vol. XI (1914). As the later Stuart monarchs were normally resident in England much information about Scottish affairs is also to be found scattered throughout the more important English series such as the *Calendar of State Papers Domestic*.

Among collections of correspondence the most valuable are *The Lauderdale Papers*, edited by Osmund Airy for the Camden Society (3 vols., 1884–1885), with which should be associated the same writer's "Letters addressed to the Earl of Lauderdale" in *The Camden Miscellany*, VIII (1883), pp. 1–43; *Letters illustrative of Public Affairs in Scotland addressed by Contemporary Statesmen to George, Earl of Aberdeen, 1681–4*, edited by J. Dunn for the Spalding Club (1851); *Leven and Melville Papers, 1689–1691*, edited by William Leslie Melville for the Bannatyne Club (1843); *State Papers and Letters addressed to William Carstares relating to Public Affairs in Great Britain, but more particularly in Scotland, during the Reigns of King William and Queen Anne*, edited by Joseph McCormick (Edinburgh, 1774); *A Selection from the Papers of the Earls of Marchmont illustrative of Events from 1685 to 1750*, edited by Sir G. H. Rose, vol. III (London, 1831), which should be studied in conjunction with the first and second "Report on the Marchmont Muniments at Marchmont House" in Historical Manuscripts Commission, *Fourteenth Report*, Appendix III, pp. 56–173 (1894); *Correspondence of George Baillie of Jerviswood, 1702–8*, edited by Lord Minto for the Bannatyne Club (1842); and the vast mass of Seafield papers calendared in *Seafield Correspondence from 1685 to 1708*, edited by James Grant for the Scottish History Society (1912), *Letters relating to Scotland in the Reign of Queen Anne by James Ogilvy, first Earl of Seafield, and others*, edited by P. Hume Brown for the same body (1915), and "Report upon the Correspondence of Lord Chancellor Seafield with Sidney, Earl of Godolphin, and Others", in Historical Manuscripts Commission, *Fourteenth Report*, Appendix III, pp. 191–238.

Other important collections among the publications of the Historical Manuscripts Commission are *The Manuscripts of the Duke of Hamilton*, edited by William Fraser (1887), which contains much of value for the years to 1707; *Report on the Manuscripts of the Duke of Buccleuch and Queensberry at Drumlanrig Castle* (2 vols., 1897 and 1903), the documents in which concern mainly the years 1682–1685; *The Manuscripts of the Duke of Athole and of the Earl of Home*, edited by William Fraser (1891); *The Manuscripts of J. J. Hope Johnstone* (1897), and *Report on the Manuscripts of the Earl of Mar and Kellie*, by Henry Paton (2 vols., 1904 and 1930), which deal mainly with the concluding years of the period. The *Report on the Laing Manuscripts preserved in the University of Edinburgh*, by Henry Paton (2 vols., 1914 and 1925), is of value for the whole period.

Outstanding among contemporary memoirs and histories is Burnet's *History of My Own Time*, already referred to (p. 42), for Burnet was himself a Scotsman, and even after 1674, when he became permanently resident in England or on the Continent, retained his Scottish connexions and his interest in his native land. The writings of Sir John Lauder of Fountainhall are also of great value, but have been published in very scattered fashion, his *Historical Observes of Memorable Occurrents in Church and State from October 1680 to April 1686*, edited by A. Urquhart and D. Laing for the Bannatyne Club (1840), his *Historical Notices of Scottish Affairs, 1661–1688*, edited by David Laing for the same body (2 vols., 1848), his *Journals, with his Observations on Public Affairs, 1665–1676*, edited by Donald Crawford for the Scottish History Society (1900), and *Chronological Notes of Scottish Affairs from 1680 till 1701, being chiefly taken from the Diary of Lord Fountainhall*, edited by Sir Walter Scott (Edinburgh, 1822).

Apart from these the best contemporary accounts are, for the period before the Revolution, John Nicoll, *A Diary of Public Transactions and other Occurrences, chiefly in Scotland, from January 1650 to June 1667*, edited by David Laing for the Bannatyne Club (1836); James Turner, *Memoirs of His Own Life and Times*, edited by Thomas Thomson for the same body (1829); Sir George Mackenzie, *Memoirs of the Affairs of Scotland from the Restoration of King Charles II*, edited by Thomas Thomson (Edinburgh, 1821), which surveys the events of the years 1660–1677 very much from the government's point of view; and the *Diary of John Erskine of Carnock, 1683–1687*, edited by Walter Macleod for the Scottish History Society (1893), which throws considerable light on Argyll's rebellion: for the Revolution, Colin, earl of Balcarres, *Memoirs Touching the Revolution in Scotland, 1688–1690*, edited by Lord Lindsay for the Bannatyne Club (1841); and Hugh Mackay, *Memoirs of the War carried on in Scotland and Ireland, 1688–1691*, edited by John Mackay for the same body (1833): for the reign of William, *Memoirs of the Life of Sir John Clerk of Penicuik*, edited by John M. Grey for the Scottish History Society (1892): and for the reign of Anne, *The Lockhart Papers, containing Memoirs and Commentaries upon the Affairs of Scotland from 1702 to 1715*, by George Lockhart (2 vols., London, 1817), the Jacobite tone of which evoked strong criticism in John Oldmixon, *Memoirs of North Britain* (London, 1715).

Of special importance for ecclesiastical affairs, which bulk so largely during the whole period, is Robert Wodrow, *The History of the Sufferings of the Church of Scotland from the Restoration to the Revolution*, edited by Robert Burns (4 vols., Glasgow, 1828–1840), biased in favour of the Presbyterians, but based on contemporary documents, which it prints.

The Darien tragedy has its own "Bibliography of Printed Documents and Books relating to the Scottish Company commonly called the Darien Company", compiled by John Scott, in *Papers of the Edinburgh Bibliographical Society, 1901–1904* (1906), pp. 19–70; but this is not sufficiently up to date to include such publications as *Papers relating to the Ships and Voyages of the Company of Scotland Trading to Africa and the Indies, 1696–1707*, edited by George P. Insh for the Scottish History Society (1924); and Francis Russell Hart, *The Disaster of Darien* (London, 1929), which includes many documents drawn from Spanish sources. The chief collection of documents dealing with the massacre of Glencoe is *Papers illustrative of the Political Condition of the Highlands of Scotland, 1689–1696*, edited by J. Gordon for the Maitland Club (1845). Daniel Defoe, *The History of the Union of Great Britain* (Edinburgh, 1709), is of the first importance for the event with which it deals, for at the time of the union Defoe was living in Edinburgh as an agent of the English government.

There is a useful series of extracts dealing with the Jacobite attempt of 1708 in *The Jacobites and the Union*, edited by Charles Sanford Terry (Cambridge, 1922), with which should be compared *The Chevalier de St. George and the Jacobite Movements in His Favour, 1701–1720*, by the same editor (London, 1901). An interesting volume, illustrating one of the by-ways of Scottish history, is *The Old Scots Navy from 1689 to 1710*, edited by James Grant for the Navy Records Society (1914).

Valuable account books, all published by the Scottish History Society, are *Diary and Account Book of William Cunningham of Craigends, 1673–1680*, edited by James Dodds (1887); *The Account Book of Sir John Foulis of Ravelston, 1671–1707*, edited by A. W. Cornelius Hallen (1894); and *The Household Book of Lady Grisell Baillie, 1692–1733*, edited by R. Scott-Moncrieff (1911). With them, as illustrating economic life and progress, should be associated *Records of a Scottish Cloth Manufactory at New Mills, Haddingtonshire, 1681–1703*, edited by William Robert Scott for the Scottish History Society (1905).

Scotsmen in the seventeenth century were little addicted to writing descriptions of their native land, and for such accounts reliance has to be placed on foreign visitors, either French or English, who were usually so ignorant of their subject, or so violently prejudiced against everything Scottish, that what they have to say is of little value. A number of accounts have been gathered together in *Early Travellers in Scotland*, edited by P. Hume Brown (Edinburgh, 1891), and *Tours in Scotland, 1677 and 1681, by Thomas Kirk and Ralph Thoresby*, by the same editor (Edinburgh, 1892). The best English description of the country is Thomas Morer, *A Short Account of Scotland* (London, 1702). Morer was an Oxford graduate, and served for some months as chaplain to Sir John Lanier's regiment in Scotland during 1689. Martin Martin, *A Description of the Western Islands of Scotland, circa 1695* (Glasgow, 1884), is a painstaking account of all the islands, including even Bute and Arran.

The best general account of Scottish affairs is P. Hume Brown, *History of Scotland*, vols. II and III (Cambridge, 1902 and 1909); but other general histories by Andrew Lang (4 vols., Edinburgh, 1900–1907), John Hill Burton (8 vols., Edinburgh, 1873), and Malcolm Laing (4 vols., London, 1819), are on a somewhat larger scale and should not be neglected. There is no history specially devoted to the later Stuarts. A useful short sketch of the period is P. Hume Brown, "Scotland from the Restoration to the Union of the Parliaments, 1660–1707", in *The Cambridge Modern History*, V (1908), pp. 278–300, and a good introduction on a larger scale William Law Mathieson, *Politics and Religion, a Study in Scottish History from the Reformation to the Revolution*, vol. II (Glasgow, 1902), followed by the same writer's *Scotland and the Union, 1695–1747* (Glasgow, 1905).

Macaulay's narrative of events in Scotland, written before all but a few of these works had been published, is inevitably out of date; but it should still be read, in conjunction with the critical essays in John Paget, *The New Examen* (Manchester, 1934). It contains no survey of the state of Scotland comparable to its survey of the state of England, and for this recourse must be had to Hume Brown's *History of Scotland*, III, chap. II, and G. M. Trevelyan's *England under Queen Anne*, II, chaps. X and XI. More elaborate accounts of the social and economic condition of Scotland are to be found in James Mackinnon, *The Social and Industrial History of Scotland from the Earliest Times to the Union* (London, 1920), a comprehensive but not very inspiring volume.

Scottish trade was largely with England and the Netherlands. The best general account of it is in W. R. Scott's *Joint-Stock Companies*, already referred to (p. 530); and the most satisfactory accounts of particular aspects of it are Theodora Keith, *Commercial Relations of England and Scotland, 1603–1707* (Cambridge, 1910); M. P. Rooseboom, *The Scottish Staple in the Netherlands* (The Hague, 1910); and J. Davidson and A. Gray, *The Scottish Staple at Veere* (London, 1909). George Pratt Insh, *Scottish Colonial Schemes, 1620–86* (Glasgow, 1922), is an admirable discussion of the efforts of Scotsmen to found their own colonies, as is Theodora Keith, "Scottish Trade with the Plantations before 1707", in *Scottish Historical Review*, VI (1909), pp. 32–48, of their attempts to establish profitable relations with the English colonies. William Robert Scott, "The Fiscal Policy of Scotland before the Union", *ibid.*, I (1904), pp. 173–190, is the best introduction to the financial side of commerce, and the same writer's "Scottish Industrial Undertakings before the Union", *ibid.*, I (1904), pp. 407–415; II (1905), pp. 53–60, 287–297, 406–411; III (1906), pp. 71–76, is the best account of the rise of industry. The standard work on the Darien venture is George Pratt Insh, *The Company of Scotland Trading to Africa and the Indies* (London, 1932), and a good account of one of the unhappy incidents that followed upon its failure, Sir Richard Carnac Temple, *New Light on the Mysterious Tragedy of the "Worcester", 1704–5* (London, 1930). Banking is dealt with in A. W. Kerr, *History of Banking in Scotland* (London, 1926), and Charles A. Malcolm, *The Bank of Scotland, 1695–1945* (Edinburgh, 1949).

Contrasting views of Scottish ecclesiastical history are to be found in Thomas Stephen, *History of the Church of Scotland from the Reformation to the Present Time* (4 vols., London, 1843–1845); John Cunningham, *The Church History of Scotland from the Commencement of the Christian Era to the Present Century* (2 vols., Edinburgh, 1882); G. Grub, *An Ecclesiastical History of Scotland from the Introduction of Christianity to the Present Time* (4 vols., Edinburgh, 1861); and J. King Hewison, *The Covenanters, a History of the Church in Scotland from the Reformation to the Revolution* (2 vols., Glasgow, 1913). There are some admirable studies in George D. Henderson, *Religious Life in Seventeenth-Century Scotland* (Cambridge, 1937).

The only comprehensive and authoritative account of the Scottish Parliament is Robert S. Rait, *The Parliaments of Scotland* (Glasgow, 1924); but this has not entirely superseded Charles Sanford Terry, *The Scottish Parliament, its Constitution and Procedure, 1603–1707* (Glasgow, 1905). Useful for the reign of William III are Kennedy Stewart, "Scottish Parliament, 1690–1702", in *Juridical Review*, XXXIX (1927), pp. 10–37, 169–190, 291–312, 408–433; and Edith E. B. Thomson, *The Parliament of Scotland, 1690–1702* (Oxford, 1929). With these should be read Theodora Pagan, *The Convention of Royal Burghs* (Glasgow, 1926); and J. D. Mackie and G. S. Pryde, *The Estate of the Burgesses in the Scots Parliament and its Relation to the Convention of Royal Burghs* (St. Andrews, 1923).

The story of the union between England and Scotland is the subject of an extensive literature. The best short sketch is *The Treaty of Union of Scotland and England, 1707*, edited with an introduction by George S. Pryde (Edinburgh, 1950). James Mackinnon, *The Union of England and Scotland, a Study of International History* (London, 1896), and P. Hume Brown, *The Legislative Union of England and Scotland* (Oxford, 1914), are standard works. *The Union of 1707*, by various authors, with an introduction by P. Hume Brown (Glasgow, 1907), is an anniversary survey. Albert V. Dicey and Robert S. Rait, *Thoughts on the Union between England and Scotland* (London, 1920), has the supreme merit of being the joint production of a great English lawyer and a great Scottish historian.

A. END OF THE ENGLISH OCCUPATION

222. John Nicoll's account

(Diary of Public Transactions, pp. 283–367)

This proclamation [of Charles II as king], being solemnly acted at London the 8 of May 1660, was thereafter proclaimed at the Mercat Cross of Edinburgh upon Monday thereafter, being the 14 of the same month, with all solemnities requisite, by ringing of bells, setting out of bonfires, sounding of trumpets, roaring of cannons, tucking of drums, dancing about the fires, and using all other tokens of joy for the advancement and preference of their native king to his crown and native inheritance. Whereat also there was much wine spent, the spouts of the Cross running and venting out abundance of wine placed there for that end, and the magistrates and council of the town being present, drinking the king's health and breaking numbers of glasses.

There was also given orders by the governor of the Castle of Edinburgh to the cannoneers for discharging of three volleys from the Castle the day foresaid in the afternoon. These orders being given by the governor to Mr. Brown, chief cannoneer, he did convene all his under-cannoneers and show them what orders he had received from the governor for giving these three volleys in gladness that the two Houses of Parliament had proclaimed King Charles the Second to be king of the three kingdoms. One of the under-cannoneers said to the chief cannoneer that he would not obey these orders to shoot any cannon for that effect, and further said, The devil blow him in the air that loosed a cannon for that purpose; and further said, if he loosed any cannon that day some man should repent it. Mr. Brown, chief cannoneer, hearing these words, . . . advised the governor, and desired him to place this man toward the West Kirk, where there was least danger. And this man having gotten orders to shoot the first cannon lying foranent the West Kirk, after the first shot he went and charged again for the second volley, having put in a ladleful of powder and being standing before the mouth of the cannon, being some fire in the cannon left in the former shot, the cannon gives fire presently and shoots his belly from him, and blew him quite over the Castle wall, to the sight of many people that were present; and was presently buried in the West Kirkyard. . . .

The kingdom of Scotland having taken to their consideration the great things and wonderful that the Lord God had done for them, in restoring unto them their native sovereign lord and king after so long banishment, and that in a wonderful way, worthy of admiration, they resolved upon several days of thanksgiving to be set apart for his Majesty's restoration and for his mercies to this poor land, who had opened a door of hope to his people for settling these three kingdoms in religion and justice. And first this day of thanksgiving began at Edinburgh, and through all the kirks and parts of Lothian, upon Tuesday the nineteenth day of June 1660, where there were sermons made through all the kirks, and whereat all the magistrates of Edinburgh and the Common Council were present, all of them in their best robes, the great mace and sword of honour carried before them to the sermon, and through the whole streets as they went, all that day.

And after the sermon ended, the magistrates and council of Edinburgh, with a great number of the citizens, went to the Mercat Cross of Edinburgh, where a great long board was covered with all sorts of sweetmeats, and there drank the king's health, and his brother, the spouts of the Cross running all that time with abundance of claret wine. There were three hundred dozen of glasses all broken and cassen through the streets, with sweetmeats in abundance. Major-General Morgan, commander-in-chief of all the forces in Scotland, and the governor of the Castle of Edinburgh, being both Englishmen, with some of the special officers of the army, were all present. There was a guard also of the most able burgesses of the town, who did guard the Cross, table and streets during this feast, all of them well apparelled and with partisans in their hands, to the number of four or five hundred persons or thereby, in very good equipage and order.

And in the meantime, while they were thus feasting at the Cross, the whole bells in Edinburgh and Canongate did ring, the drums did beat, trumpets sounded, the whole troops on horseback and soldiers on foot . . . gave their several volleys. . . . Further at night there was bonfires put out through the whole streets of Edinburgh, and fireworks both there and at the Castle of Edinburgh and within the Citadel of Leith that night in abundance, till after 12 hours and more. . . . And in the end of this solemnity the effigies of that notable tyrant and traitor Oliver being set up upon a pole, and the devil upon another, upon the Castle Hill of Edinburgh, it was ordered by firework, engine and train, the devil did chase that traitor, and pursued him still, till he blew him in the air. . . .

It is observed that Protector Oliver, being then general of the English army, came into Scotland and won Dunbar fight in September 1650, and all that army were ordered to remove from Scotland in September 1660. . . .

Upon the fifth day of November 1660 there was great solemnity used in all the special burghs of Scotland, by outsetting of bonfires, ringing of bells, sounding of trumpets, firing and discharging of cannons, in commemoration of that great day of delivery of his Majesty's dearest grandsire and his royal race from the fearful plot of gunpowder treason attempted against them by some English traitors in the year 1605; which day, being these many years past neglected, and durst not be practised, yea not spoken of because of the English usurper's power for the time, was now, after his Majesty's restoration, revived and solemnly kept by the Scots as before their bondage. . . .

Likewise at this time these three ancient honours of the kingdom of Scotland, viz., the crown, the sceptre and the sword, being miraculously preserved by the Earl Marshal and his brothers, were brought in by them to Edinburgh, to be made use of at the down-sitting of the approaching Parliament; the earl and his two brothers being eminent both in their services and sufferings for the royal interest; and when the two elder were prisoners in England, by the particular care and industry of the younger the same sacred honours, so much hunted after by enemies, were miraculously preserved. . . .

There were sundry orders given out for removing of the English soldiers who were yet remaining in the Scottish garrisons; but in respect of the frequent divisions both in Church and State, and fearing further distractions among ourselves in Scotland, these English soldiers were suffered to stay for a time. Yet notwithstanding, in the month of November 1661, new orders were sent down from his Majesty that all the English garrisons should remove from Scotland, and all the citadels through this whole land should be slighted and cassen down. And in respect the downlesing thereof would be chargeable, the town of Edinburgh took upon them to demolish the Citadel of Leith, built by the English. . . .

The king's Majesty having now resolved to send ten thousand men to Portugal, all the citadels wherein the English soldiers were quartered were now emptied, and all of them removed and shipped at Leith for Portugal upon the fifteenth, sixteenth and seventeenth days of May 1662, so that Scotland was freed of these English soldiers after many years residence in this kingdom, and there was none in arms in all Scotland, either native or stranger, except the life-guard for his Majesty's use and welfare of his subjects.

223. Gilbert Burnet on the return of the Scottish records, 1660
(History of My Own Time, ed. Airy, 1, pp. 200–202)

While these things were doing, Primrose got an order from the king to put up all the public registers of Scotland, which Cromwell had brought up and lodged in the Tower of London, as a pawn upon that kingdom, and in imitation of what King Edward I was said to have done when he subdued that nation. They were put up in fifty hogsheads, and a ship was ready to carry them down. But it was suggested to Clarendon that the original Covenant signed by the king, and some other declarations under his hand, were among them; and he apprehending that at some time or other an ill use might have been made of these, he would not suffer them to be shipped till they were visited; nor would he take Primrose's promise of searching for these carefully and sending them up to him.

So he ordered a search to be made. None of the papers he looked for were found. But so much time was lost that the summer was spent. So they were sent down in winter, and by some easterly gusts the ship was cast away near Berwick. So we lost all our records, and we have nothing now but some fragments in private hands to rely on, having made at that time so great a shipwreck of all our authentic writings. This heightened the displeasure the nation had at the designs then on foot.

224. Order of the Scottish Privy Council for the dismantling of the fortress of Inverness, 1661
(Register of the Privy Council of Scotland, Third Series, 1, pp. 6–7

13 July 1661

The Lords of Secret Council give order and warrant to Alexander, earl of Moray, to cause demolish and slight the walls, strengths and fortifications of the Citadel of Inverness, and to cause to fill up the ditches thereof, except so much of the same as are built upon the sea-coast, which shall be found necessary to preserve the houses built therein from the storm and tempest of the sea, and to preserve the whole stones thereof, and to take care that the houses and fabric thereof in doors, windows, locks and other appurtenances be kept entire and not embezzled while farther order; and give warrant to the said earl to require and charge the inhabitants of the next adjacent shire and parishes to repair to the said Citadel for performing that service, and if need be ordains letters of horning to be directed *simpliciter* against them for that effect in case of their disobedience, charging them thereto under the pain of rebellion; and appoint the said earl to report his diligence to his Majesty's Secret Council anent the performance of the premises with all conveniency.

B. RECONSTRUCTION IN CHURCH AND STATE

225. Petition of Scottish representatives in London to Charles II, 1660

(Lauderdale Papers, ed. O. Airy, 1, pp. 32–33)

May it please your sacred Majesty,

We, the noblemen, gentlemen and burgesses of your Majesty's ancient kingdom of Scotland, met at London by your Majesty's authority, do in obedience to your Majesty's command humbly offer, that until the meeting of the Parliament your kingdom of Scotland be governed by your Majesty and the Committee of Estates nominated in your last Parliament, 1651, which Committee your Majesty may be pleased to authorize to meet at such a day as your Majesty shall think fit.

And as we humbly conceive that the sole power of calling and holding of Parliaments, and the way and manner thereof, doth reside in your Majesty, so it is our humble opinion that at this time your Majesty emit a proclamation calling all the nobility, and appointing some gentlemen in each shire for convening such as by law have voice in the election of commissioners, and also the burghs to meet and choose commissioners for the Parliament, at such a time and place as your Majesty shall be pleased to appoint.

And it is our humble petition to your Majesty that all the English forces may be removed out of Scotland before the sitting of the Parliament; and (if your Majesty shall find it necessary for the good of your service) that your Majesty employ such of your Scottish subjects as you shall think fit for securing of the garrisons and the peace of the kingdom.

226. Letter from Charles II to the presbytery of Edinburgh, 1660

(Robert Wodrow, History of the Sufferings of the Church of Scotland, 1, pp. 80–81)

CHARLES R.

Trusty and well beloved, we greet you well.

By the letter you sent to us with this bearer, Mr. James Sharp, and by the account he gave of the state of our Church there, we have received full information of your sense of our sufferings, and of your constant affection and loyalty to our person and authority. And therefore we will detain him here no longer (of whose good services we are very sensible), nor will we delay to let you know by him our gracious acceptance of your address, and how well we are satisfied with your carriages and with the generality of the ministers of Scotland in this time of trial, whilst some under specious pretences swerved from that duty and allegiance they owed to us. And because such who by the countenance of usurpers have disturbed the peace of that our Church may also labour to create jealousies in the minds of well-meaning people, we have thought fit by this to assure you that by the grace of God we resolve to discountenance profanity, and all contemners and opposers of the ordinances of the gospel. We do also resolve to protect and preserve the government of the Church of Scotland, as it is settled by law, without violation; and to countenance in the due exercise of their functions all such ministers who shall behave themselves dutifully and peaceably as becomes men of their calling. We will also take care that the authority and acts of the general assembly at St. Andrews and Dundee, 1651, be owned and stand in force until we shall call another general assembly (which we purpose to do as soon as our affairs will permit), and we do intend to send for Mr. Robert Douglas and some other ministers that we may speak with them in what may further concern the affairs of that Church.

And as we are very well satisfied with your resolution not to meddle without your sphere, so we do expect that Church judicatories in Scotland and ministers there will keep within the compass of their station, meddling only with matters ecclesiastic, and promoting our authority and interest with our subjects against all opposers; and that they will take special notice of such who, by preaching or private conventicles or any other way, transgress the limits of their calling, by endeavouring to corrupt the people or sow seeds of disaffection to us or our government. This you shall make known to the several presbyteries within that our kingdom. . . .

And so we bid you heartily farewell.

Given at our court at Whitehall,

the 10th of August 1660,

and of our reign the twelfth year.

227. Act Rescissory, 1661

(Acts of the Parliaments of Scotland, VII, pp. 86–87)

ACT RESCINDING AND ANNULLING THE PRETENDED PARLIAMENTS IN THE YEARS 1640, 1641, &C.

The Estates of Parliament considering that the peace and happiness of this kingdom, and of his Majesty's good subjects therein, doth depend upon the safety of his Majesty's person and the maintenance of his royal authority, power and greatness; and that all the miseries, confusions and disorders which this kingdom hath groaned under these twenty-three years have issued from, and been the necessary and natural products of, these neglects, contempts and invasions which in and from the beginning of these troubles were upon the specious (but false) pretexts of reformation (the common cloak of all rebellions) offered unto the sacred person and royal authority of the king's Majesty and his royal father of blessed memory: and notwithstanding that by the sacred right inherent to the imperial crown (which his Majesty holds immediately from God Almighty alone), and by the ancient constitution and fundamental laws of the kingdom, the power of convocating and keeping assemblies of the subjects; the power of calling, holding, proroguing and dissolving of Parliaments and making of laws; the power of entering into bonds, covenants, leagues and treaties; the power of raising armies, keeping of strengths and forts, are essential parts and inseparable privileges of the royal authority and prerogative of the kings of this kingdom; yet such hath been the madness and delusion of these times that even religion itself, which holds the right of kings to be sacred and inviolable, hath been pretended unto for warrant of all these injurious violations and encroachments, so publicly done and owned, upon and against his Majesty's just power, authority and government. . . .

And although the late king's Majesty, out of his mere grace and respects to this his native kingdom and the peace and quiet of his people, and for preventing the consequences which such a bad example and practice might occasion to the disturbance of the peace of his other kingdoms, was pleased in the year 1641 to come into this country, and by his own presence at their pretended Parliaments and otherways to comply with and give way to many things nearly concerning the undoubted interest and prerogative of the crown, expecting that such unparalleled condescensions should have made his subjects ashamed of their former miscarriages, and the very thoughts thereof to be hateful to them and their posterity for ever, yet such was the prevalency of the spirit of rebellion that raged in many for the time that not content of that peace and happiness which even above their desires was secured unto them, nor of those many grants of honour and profit by which his Majesty endeavoured to endear the most desperate of them to their duty and obedience, they then, when his Majesty had not left unto them any pretence or shadow of any new desire to be proposed, either concerning themselves or the kingdom, did most unworthily engage to subvert his Majesty's government and the public peace of the kingdom of England; for which purpose having joined in a league with some there, they for the better prosecution of the same did assume unto themselves the royal power, kept and held Parliaments at their pleasure, by the pretended authority of which they laid new exactions upon the people (which in one month did far exceed whatever by the king's authority had been raised in a whole year), levied armies, sent out edicts requiring obedience unto their unlawful demands, and with all manner of violence pursued such as out of duty to his Majesty's authority opposed them by fines, confinements, imprisonment, banishment, death and forfeiture of their posterity, and with their army thus raised invaded his Majesty's kingdom of England, and joined with such as were in arms against his Majesty there. . . .

And forasmuch as now it hath pleased Almighty God, by the power of his own right hand, so miraculously to restore the king's Majesty to the government of his kingdoms and to the exercise of his royal power and sovereignty over the same, the Estates of Parliament do conceive themselves obliged, in discharge of their duty and conscience to God and the king's Majesty, to employ all their power and interest for vindicating his Majesty's authority from all these violent invasions that have been made upon it. . . . And considering that, besides the unlawfulness of the public actings during these troubles, most of the acts in all and every of the meetings of these pretended Parliaments do highly encroach upon and are destructive of that sovereign power, authority, prerogative and right of government which by the law of God and the ancient laws and constitutions of this kingdom doth reside in and belong to the king's Majesty, and do reflect much upon the honour, loyalty and reputation of this kingdom, or are expired, and serve only as testimonies of disloyalty and reproach upon the kingdom, and are unfit to be any longer upon record, therefore the king's Majesty and Estates of Parliament do hereby rescind and annul the pretended Parliaments kept in the years 1640, 1641, 1644, 1645, 1646, 1647 and 1648, and all acts and deeds passed and done in them, and declare the same to be henceforth void and null.

And his Majesty, being unwilling to take any advantage of the failings of his subjects during those unhappy times, . . . doth therefore by advice and consent of his Estates of Parliament grant his full assurance and indemnity to all persons that acted in, or by virtue of, the said pretended Parliaments and other meetings flowing from the same, to be unquestioned in their lives or fortunes for any deed or deeds done by them in their said usurpation, or by virtue of any pretended authority derived therefrom, excepting always such as shall be excepted in a general Act of Indemnity to be passed by his Majesty in this Parliament. And it is hereby declared that all acts, rights and securities passed in any of the pretended meetings abovewritten, or by virtue thereof, in favour of any particular persons for their civil and private interests, shall stand good and valid unto them, until the same be taken into further consideration and be determined in this or the next session of Parliament.

228. Order of Council for the restoration of episcopacy, 1661
(*Register of the Privy Council of Scotland, Third Series*, I, pp. 30–32)

6 September 1661

The Lords of his Majesty's Privy Council, having considered his Majesty's letter of the date at Whitehall, the fourteenth day of August last, bearing that whereas his Majesty by his letter to the presbytery of Edinburgh in the month of August, one thousand six hundred and sixty years,[1] declared his royal purpose to maintain the government of the Church of Scotland settled by law; and the Estates of Parliament of this kingdom having since that time not only rescinded all the Acts since the troubles began relating to that government, but also declared all those Parliaments null and void, leaving to his Majesty the settling of Church government; therefore in compliance with that Act Rescissory,[2] and in pursuance of his Majesty's proclamation of the tenth of June last, and in contemplation of the inconveniences that accompanied and issued from the Church government as it hath been exercised these twenty-three years past, and of the unsuitableness thereof to his Majesty's monarchical estate, . . . his Majesty, having respect to the glory of God and the good and interest of the Protestant religion, and being zealous of the order, unity, peace and stability of the Church within this kingdom, and of its better harmony with the government of the Churches of England and Ireland, hath been pleased, after mature deliberation, to declare unto his Council his firm resolution to interpose his royal authority for restoring of this Church to its right government by bishops as it was by law before the late troubles, during the reigns of his Majesty's royal father and grandfather of blessed memory, and as it now stands settled by law, and that the rents belonging to the several bishoprics and deaneries be restored and made useful to the Church, according to justice and the standing law, have therefore, in obedience of and conform to his Majesty's royal pleasure aforesaid, ordained and by these presents ordain the Lyon King at Arms and his brethren heralds, pursuivants and messengers-at-arms, to pass to the Mercat Cross

[1] No. 226. [2] No. 227.

of Edinburgh and other royal burghs of the kingdom, and there by open proclamation to make publication of his Majesty's royal pleasure for restoring the Church of this kingdom to its right government by bishops, and in his Majesty's name to require all his good subjects to compose themselves to a cheerful acquiescence and obedience to the same; . . . and to inhibit and discharge the assembling of ministers in their several synodical meetings until his Majesty's further pleasure therein be known. . . .

229. Test Act, 1662
(*Acts of the Parliaments of Scotland*, VII, pp. 405-406)
ACT CONCERNING THE DECLARATION TO BE SIGNED
BY ALL PERSONS IN PUBLIC TRUST

Forasmuch as it hath pleased Almighty God in his Majesty's restitution to his royal government to restore this kingdom to its ancient liberties and peace; . . . and the Estates of Parliament finding themselves obliged . . . to use all means for the due preservation of that peace and happiness they now enjoy under his royal government, and to prevent and suppress everything that may tend to the renewing or favouring of these courses by which the late rebellion hath been fomented and carried on, and conceiving that the employing of persons of sound principles and entire loyalty in all offices of trust and places of public administration will conduce much to these ends : therefore, and for quieting the spirits of his Majesty's good subjects and begetting a confidence in them of their security for the future, his Majesty hath thought fit, with advice and consent of his Estates of Parliament, to statute, ordain and enact . . . that all such persons as shall hereafter be called or admitted to any public trust or office under his Majesty's government within this kingdom, that is to say to be officers of state, members of Parliament, Privy Councillors, Lords of Session, commissioners in Exchequer, members of the College of Justice, sheriffs, stewards or commissaries, their deputes and clerks, magistrates and council of burghs, justices of peace and their clerks, or any other public charge, office and trust within this kingdom, shall, at and before their admission to the exercise of such places or offices, publicly in face of the respective courts they relate to, subscribe the declaration underwritten. . . .

I, A.B., do sincerely affirm and declare that I judge it unlawful to subjects upon pretence of reformation, or other pretence whatsoever, to enter into leagues and covenants, or to take up arms against the king or those commissionated by him; and that all these gatherings, convocations, petitions, protestations and erecting and keeping of council tables that were used in the beginning and for carrying on of the late troubles were unlawful and seditious; and particularly that those oaths, whereof the one was commonly called the National Covenant (as it was sworn and explained in the year 1638 and thereafter), and the other entitled a Solemn League and Covenant, were and are in themselves unlawful oaths, and were taken by and imposed upon the subjects of this kingdom against the fundamental laws and liberties of the same; and that there lieth no obligation upon me or any of the subjects from the said oaths or either of them to endeavour any change or alteration of the government either in Church or State as it is now established by the laws of the kingdom.

21

230. Act for raising a militia, 1663

(Acts of the Parliaments of Scotland, VII, pp. 480–481)

A HUMBLE TENDER TO HIS SACRED MAJESTY ·
OF THE DUTY AND LOYALTY OF HIS ANCIENT KINGDOM OF SCOTLAND

Forasmuch as the Estates of Parliament, upon consideration of the great blessings this kingdom enjoyeth under the protection of his Majesty's authority and the administrations of his royal government, being thereby not only delivered from their former troubles and all the evils which attend such usurpations, but being fully restored to and possessed of all the liberties and privileges of a free people, have by their several addresses to his sacred Majesty made offer of their lives and fortunes and all that is dearest to them for the advancement of his royal honour, authority and greatness, . . . therefore the Estates of Parliament, . . . as they do cheerfully recognize his Majesty's royal prerogative and undoubted right of the sole power of the raising, arming and commanding of his subjects, so in a further acknowledgment of their duty they do make humble and hearty offer to his Majesty of twenty thousand footmen and two thousand horsemen sufficiently armed and furnished with forty days' provision, to be raised from the several shires of the kingdom according to the proportions following, viz.,[1]

Shire	Foot	Horse
Roxburgh and Selkirk	1,333	148
Berwick	800	74
Edinburgh	800	74
Haddington	800	74
Peebles	266	29
Linlithgow	333	42
Edinburgh, Leith and Canongate	800	—
Dumfries	800	88
Wigtown	800	88
Ayr and Renfrew	1,333	176
Lanark	1,000	148
Stirling and Clackmannan	666	88
Fife and Kinross	1,600	176
Perth	1,600	176
Forfar	1,000	103
Kincardine, including [Earl] Marshal's part of Aberdeen	800	74
Aberdeen and Banff	1,066	176
Elgin, Nairn and this side of Ness	1,000	88
Inverness (earl of Seaforth and Lord Lovat's division)	666	88
Sutherland, Caithness and the rest of Inverness	1,066	88
Argyll, Dumbarton and Bute	800	—
Orkney	666	—

[1] The tabular method here adopted of indicating the quotas is not that of the original Act.

Which forces are to be in readiness, as they shall be called for by his Majesty, to march to any part of his dominions of Scotland, England or Ireland for suppressing of any foreign invasion, intestine trouble or insurrection, or for any other service wherein his Majesty's honour, authority or greatness may be concerned. . . .

231. Assertory Act, 1669

(Acts of the Parliaments of Scotland, VII, p. 554)

ACT ASSERTING HIS MAJESTY'S SUPREMACY OVER ALL PERSONS
AND IN ALL CAUSES ECCLESIASTICAL

The Estates of Parliament, having seriously considered how necessary it is for the good and peace of the Church and State that his Majesty's power and authority in relation to matters and persons ecclesiastical be more clearly asserted by an Act of Parliament, have therefore thought fit it be enacted, asserted and declared . . . that his Majesty hath the supreme authority and supremacy over all persons and in all causes ecclesiastical within this kingdom; and that by virtue thereof the ordering and disposal of the external government and policy of the Church doth properly belong to his Majesty and his successors as an inherent right to the crown; and that his Majesty and his successors may settle, enact and emit such constitutions, Acts and orders concerning the administration of the external government of the Church and the persons employed in the same, and concerning all ecclesiastical meetings and matters to be proposed and determined therein, as they in their royal wisdom shall think fit; which Acts, orders and constitutions, being recorded in the books of Council and duly published, are to be observed and obeyed by all his Majesty's subjects, any law, Act or custom to the contrary notwithstanding. . . .

C. PERSECUTION AND INDULGENCE

232. Act re-establishing lay patronage, 1662

(Acts of the Parliaments of Scotland, VII, p. 376)

ACT CONCERNING SUCH BENEFICES AND STIPENDS
AS HAVE BEEN POSSESSED
WITHOUT PRESENTATIONS FROM THE LAWFUL PATRONS

The king's most excellent Majesty being desirous that all his good subjects may be sensible of the happy effects and fruits of the royal government by a free, peaceable and safe enjoyment of their due interests and properties under his protection, and that in his restitution they may find themselves restored to these rights which by law were secured unto them, and by the violence and injustice of these late troubles and confusions have been wrested from them; and considering that, notwithstanding the right of patronages be duly settled and established by the ancient and fundamental laws and constitutions of this kingdom, yet divers ministers in this Church have and do possess benefices and stipends in their respective cures without any right or presentation to the same from the patrons; . . . therefore his Majesty, with advice and consent of his Estates of Parliament, doth statute and ordain, that all these ministers who entered to the cure of any parish in burgh or land within this kingdom in or since the year 1649 (at and before which time the patrons were most injuriously dispossessed of their patronages) have no right unto, nor shall receive, uplift nor possess the rents of any benefice, modified stipend, manse or glebe for this present crop 1662 nor any year following, but their places, benefices and kirks are *ipso jure* vacant.

Yet his Majesty, to evidence his willingness to pass by and cover the miscarriages of his people, doth with advice foresaid declare, that this Act shall not be prejudicial to any of these ministers in what they have possessed or is due to them since their admission; and that every such minister who shall obtain a presentation from the lawful patron, and have collation from the bishop of the diocese where he liveth, betwixt and the twentieth of September next to come,[1] shall from thenceforth have right to and enjoy his Church benefice, manse and glebe as fully and freely as if he had been lawfully presented and admitted thereto at his first entry, or as any other minister within the kingdom doth or may do. And for that end it is hereby ordained, that the respective patrons shall give presentations to all the present incumbents who in due time shall make application to them for the same. . . .

[1] 20 September 1662.

233. Act enforcing the ecclesiastical settlement, 1663[1]

(*Acts of the Parliaments of Scotland*, VII, pp. 455–456)

ACT AGAINST SEPARATION AND DISOBEDIENCE
TO ECCLESIASTICAL AUTHORITY

Forasmuch as the king's Majesty . . . hath, . . . with advice and consent of his Estates of Parliament, by several Acts passed in the second session of this Parliament, restored the Church to its ancient and right government by archbishops and bishops,[2] . . . and hath also statute and ordained, that all these ministers who entered to the cure of any parish without right or presentations from the lawful patrons in and since the year 1649, and should not betwixt and the twentieth of September last obtain presentations from their several patrons and collation from the bishop of the diocese where they lived, should have no right to the uplifting the rents of any benefice or stipend for the year 1662, but that their places, benefices and kirks should be *ipso jure* vacant,[3] and that whatever ministers should without a lawful excuse, to be admitted by the ordinary, absent themselves from the diocesan assembly, or who should not concur in all the acts of the Church discipline, as they should be thereunto required by the archbishop or bishop of the diocese, should be for the first fault suspended from their office and benefice till the next diocesan meeting, and if they amend not should be deprived, and the church and benefice to be provided as in other cases of vacancies; and the king's Majesty, having resolved to conserve and maintain the Church in the present state and government thereof by archbishops and bishops and others bearing office therein, and not to endure nor give any way nor connivance to any variation therein in the least, doth therefore, with advice and consent of his Estates convened in this third session of his Parliament, ratify and approve the aforementioned Acts and all other Acts and laws made in the two former sessions of Parliament in order to the settling of episcopal dignity, jurisdiction and authority within this kingdom. . . .

And in pursuance of his Majesty's royal resolution herein, his Majesty, with advice aforesaid, doth recommend to the lords of his Majesty's Privy Council to take speedy and effectual course that these Acts receive ready and due obedience from all his Majesty's subjects, and for that end that they call before them all such ministers who, having entered in or since the year 1649 and have not as yet obtained presentations and collations as aforesaid, yet dared to preach in contempt of the law, and to punish them as seditious persons and contemners of the royal authority; as also that they be careful that such ministers who keep not the diocesan meetings, and concur not with the bishops in the acts of Church discipline, being for the same suspended or deprived as said is, be accordingly after deprivation removed from their benefices, glebes and manses, . . . and if they shall thereafter presume to exercise their ministry that they be punished as seditious persons and such as contemn the authority of Church and State.

And as his Majesty doth expect from all his good and dutiful subjects a due acknowledgment and hearty compliance with his Majesty's government, ecclesiastical and civil, as it is now established by law within this kingdom, and that in order

---

[1] Generally known as the "Bishops' Drag-net".
[2] No. 228   [3] No. 232.

thereunto they will give their cheerful concurrence, countenance and assistance to such ministers as by public authority are or shall be admitted in their several parishes, and attend all the ordinary meetings of divine worship in the same, so his Majesty doth declare that he will and doth account a withdrawing from and not keeping and joining in these meetings to be seditious and of dangerous example and consequence. And therefore, and for preventing the same for the future, his Majesty with advice and consent of his Estates in Parliament doth hereby statute, ordain and declare that all and every such person or persons who shall hereafter ordinarily and wilfully withdraw and absent themselves from the ordinary meetings of divine worship in their own parish church on the Lord's Day (whether upon the account of popery or other disaffection to the present government of the Church) shall thereby incur the pains and penalties underwritten, viz., each nobleman, gentleman and heritor, the loss of a fourth part of each year's rent in which they shall be accused and convicted; and every yeoman, tenant or farmer, the loss of such a proportion of their free movables (after the payment of their rents due to their master and landlord) as his Majesty's Council shall think fit, not exceeding a fourth part thereof; and every burgess to lose the liberty of merchandising, trading and all other liberties within burgh and fourth part of their movables.

And his Majesty with advice aforesaid doth hereby authorize and require the lords of his Majesty's Privy Council to be careful to see this Act put to due execution; and for that end to call before them all such persons as after admonition of the minister in presence of two sufficient witnesses, and by him so attested, shall be given up to the Council as transgressors of this Act in withdrawing from their parish churches as aforesaid; and the same after hearing of the parties being duly found, to decern and inflict the censures and penalties abovementioned and such other corporal punishment as they shall think fit. . . .

234. Order of Council against ejected ministers, 1663
(Register of the Privy Council of Scotland, Third Series, I, pp. 403-404)

13 August 1663

Forasmuch as it doth appear that divers ministers, who by the law have no right to preach or remain in those parishes which did belong to their cure, do notwithstanding presume to assemble his Majesty's subjects in churches and elsewhere, to preach, administer the sacraments, and to keep conventicles and disorderly meetings; and do go about to corrupt and dissuade the people from that affection, duty, obedience and gratitude they owe to his Majesty's government, the laws and authority established, under which the kingdom does enjoy this great tranquillity and the blessings thereof; as likewise that many subjects do countenance and join in these unlawful meetings, contrary to the Acts of Parliament prohibiting the same: therefore the lords of his Majesty's Privy Council, . . . in pursuance of what is recommended by his Majesty and the Estates of Parliament in the late Act of the tenth of July, entituled, *Act against separation and disobedience to ecclesiastical authority*,[1] do hereby command and

[1] No. 233.

charge all ministers who are or shall be found to preach seditiously against the govern-ment of the Church and State, who entered in or since the year 1649 and have not since obtained presentations from their lawful patrons and collations and admissions from the ordinary, and have notwithstanding continued to preach or exercise any duty proper to the function of the ministry either at these parish kirks where they were incumbents or at any other place, house or family, to remove themselves, their families, and goods belonging to them, within twenty days after publication hereof, out of these respective parishes where they were incumbents, and not to reside within twenty miles of Edinburgh or any cathedral church, or three miles within any royal burgh of this kingdom, with certification that if they fail to remove themselves, as said is, and to give exact obedience hereunto (unless they have the permission of the lords of Privy Council or of the bishop of the diocese), they are to incur the penalties of the laws against movers of sedition; . . . and do hereby inhibit and discharge all heritors or householders in burgh or land to give any presence or countenance to any or more of these ministers, removed by this Act, to preach or exercise any duty proper to the function of the ministry, with certification if they after publication hereof shall presume so to do they are to be proceeded against according to law.

And being likewise informed that divers ministers who were entered by lawful presentations before the year 1649, and do still continue in the exercise of their ministry, do yet forbear to attend ecclesiastical meetings appointed by authority, and to exercise discipline in their parishes, without giving any account of their administrations, to the great detriment of the order and peace of the Church, therefore they command and charge all these ministers to keep the diocesan synods and other ecclesiastical meetings appointed by authority, with certification that, if after publica-tion hereof they fail so to do, and disobey the Acts of Parliament and Council made thereanent, they are to be proceeded against as contemners of his Majesty's authority. . . .

235. Letter from the earl of Rothes to the earl of Lauderdale on field conventicles, 1665

(*Lauderdale Papers*, ed. O. Airy, 1, pp. 233–234)

24 November [1665]

As to the dispositions of the people in the country I dare not say they are well inclined, but must acknowledge I think they are worse than I did imagine. Had they any opportunity I dare not answer but I judge it more than probable they would undertake, though it were desperate enough. But as they are I do assure you I have not the least apprehension of any further trouble from them than their keeping conventicles and private meetings, which is too much, and has of late been too frequent, though the secret conveyance renders it most difficult to discover till they be over, and then they do immediately disperse to all corners of the country.

Their meeting-places are most commonly at the side of a moss or at the side of a river, and they have their spies at a distance on all hands, who give warning if any party appear, which makes them run, were the party never so small. But the truth is the cause of most of this trouble we receive in this kind is occasioned by some outed ministers against whom both Council and commission have proceeded against; and they have put themselves in disguise, so as when they preach they are in grey clothes and long periwigs, and it is alleged some of them preach in masks. And these rogues stir up the women so as they are worse than devils. Yea, I dare say if it were not for the women we should have little trouble with conventicles or such kind of stuff. But there are such a foolish generation of people in this country who are so influenced with their fanatic wives as I think will bring ruin upon them.

Now to prevent all these troubles I have dispersed parties through the country. One of horse I have sent to that renowned place, Mauchline Tower, to quarter in the town of Mauchline and in the Newmilns which is near to it. Another party, but of foot, I have sent to Irvine, there being no accommodation for horse in that place. And one I am to send to Galloway, both of horse and foot, which I will make as considerable as I can; but I delay it till I speak with the bishop, who will be here this night. And another party of horse I send to Jedburgh, for in Teviotdale there are many persons as disaffected as in the west, and presently there has been a great disorder in the parish of Ancrum, they refusing to let the minister come into the pulpit. But the persons are seized, and will be severely punished.

Now those parties I have so dispersed I hope will not only prevent these disorderly meetings, but will either catch those roguish ministers, or fear of them will chase them out of the country. . . .

236. First letter of indulgence, 1669
(Register of the Privy Council of Scotland, Third Series, III, pp. 38–40)

CHARLES R.

Right trusty and right well-beloved cousins and counsellors, right trusty and well-beloved counsellors and trusty and well-beloved counsellors, we greet you well.

Whereas by the act of Council and proclamation at Glasgow in the year 1662 a considerable number of ministers were at once turned out, and so debarred from preaching of the gospel and exercise of the ministry, we are graciously pleased to authorize you, our Privy Council, to appoint so many of the outed ministers as have lived peaceably and orderly in the places where they have resided to return to preach and exercise other functions of the ministry in the parish churches where they formerly served (provided they be vacant), and to allow patrons to present to other vacant churches such others of them as you shall approve of; and that such of these ministers as shall take collation from the bishop of the diocese, and keep presbyteries and synods, may be warranted to lift their stipends as other ministers of the kingdom; but for such as are not or shall not be collated by the bishops, that they have no warrant to meddle with the local stipend, but only to possess the manse and glebe; and that you appoint a collector for those and all other vacant stipends, who shall issue the same, and pay a yearly maintenance to the said not collated ministers, as you shall see fit to appoint.

That all who are restored or allowed to exercise the ministry be, in our name and by our authority, enjoined to constitute and keep kirk-sessions, and to keep presbyteries and synods, as was done by all ministers before the year 1638, and that such of them as shall not obey our commands in keeping presbyteries be confined within the bounds of the parishes where they preach, until they give assurance to keep presbyteries for the future.

That all who shall be allowed to preach be strictly enjoined not to admit any of their neighbour or other parishes into their communions, nor baptize their children, nor marry any of them without the allowance of the minister of the parish to which they belong, unless it be vacant for the time; and if it be found, upon complaint made by any presbytery to you our Privy Council, that the people of the neighbouring or other parishes resort to their preachings, and desert their own parish churches, that according to the degree of the offence and disorder you silence the minister who countenances the same for shorter or longer time, and upon a second complaint verified silence again for a longer time, or altogether turn out, as you see cause; and upon complaint made and verified of any seditious discourse or expressions in the pulpit or elsewhere uttered by any of these ministers, you are immediately to turn them out, and further punish them according to law and the degree of the offence.

That such of the outed ministers who live peaceably and orderly, and are not re-entered or presented as aforesaid, have allowed to them four hundred merks Scots yearly out of the vacant church for their maintenance till they be provided of churches, and that even such who shall give assurance to live so for the future be allowed the same yearly maintenance.

And seeing we have by these orders taken away all pretences for conventicles, and provided for the wants of such as are and will be peaceable, if any shall be found hereafter to preach without authority or keep conventicles, our express pleasure is that you proceed with all severity against the preachers and hearers as seditious persons and contemners of our authority. So, leaving the management of these orders to your prudence, and recommending them to your care, we bid you farewell.

Given at our court at Whitehall,
the seventh day of June 1669,
and of our reign the 21st year.

237. Proclamation requiring land-owners to become sureties for the behaviour of their tenants, 1677

(*Register of the Privy Council of Scotland, Third Series*, v, pp. 206–209)

Forasmuch as notwithstanding of the many good laws and Acts made in our Parliaments and Privy Council for securing the Protestant religion, the order and unity of the Church and the tranquillity and peace of the kingdom, many do obstinately continue through ignorant prejudice or disaffection to withdraw from the public worship and to frequent house and field conventicles, which we have so often declared to be the nurseries of schism and rendezvouses of rebellion, tending to debauch our subjects from that reverence due to religion and that obedience they owe to our authority; and considering that these offenders take encouragement from their supposing a remissness in the due and vigorous execution of our good and wholesome laws and Acts provided against them; therefore we, with advice of the lords of our Privy Council, in pursuance of our late proclamation dated the 18th day of June, 1674 years, commanding all heritors, landlords and life-renters to require their rentallers and tenants to subscribe the bond thereto subjoined; and of the seventh Act of the second session of our second Parliament, whereby all our subjects were discharged to separate or withdraw from the established meetings of divine worship, declaring that every person who should absent themselves without a reasonable cause, to be allowed or disallowed by the judges and magistrates therein mentioned, should, if they had any land in heritage, life-rent or proper wadset, pay the fifth part of his or her valued yearly rent, every tenant six pounds, every cottar or servant forty shillings; as also of the sixth Act of the same Parliament all our subjects were prohibited to cause baptize their children by any save their own parish minister, or such as are authorized by the established government of the Church, &c., declaring that the parent offender should pay the fourth part of his valued rent if an heritor, life-renter or proper wadsetter, fifty pound if a tenant, twenty pound if a cottar, half a year's fee if a servant; as also of the thirty-fourth Act of the first session of our first Parliament, discharging all our subjects to procure themselves to be married by Jesuits, priests, deposed or suspended ministers, or any others not authorized by law, each nobleman under the penalty of one thousand pounds, each baron one thousand merks, each gentleman and burgess five hundred pounds, and each other person of one hundred merks Scots; and in pursuance of the other laws and Acts thereanent provided, do, with advice foresaid, hereby require and command all masters of families to cause their chamberlains, grieves, domestic servants and others entertained by them give due and exact obedience to the foresaid Acts, and in case of their disobedience to remove them out of their service, under the pains and penalties contained in the said Acts.

Likewise we strictly require and command all heritors, life-renters, wadsetters and landlords to require their rentallers and tenants to subscribe the bond hereunto subjoined, authorizing them hereby to raise letters to charge them for that effect upon six days, and to denounce and registrate them to our horn if they be tenants who have tacks, and if they be movable tenants that they shall upon their disobedience recover decreets of removal and ejection against them. And we do hereby discharge the said heritors, life-renters, landlords, &c., to set their lands hereafter to any person by word or write without inserting the foresaid surety in their tacks, and taking bonds apart, in case there be no written tacks, that their said tacksmen, rentallers and others, their hinds, cottars and others who shall live under them in the said lands shall give obedience in manner foresaid, and in case of their disobedience that their rights, tacks and possessions shall be void and null *ipso facto* without any declarator to pass thereupon.

It is likewise hereby declared that, if any cottars or servants for whom the rentallers or tenants stand bound shall be found guilty by transgressing the foresaid laws and Acts, the respective masters shall have their relief of the said contraveners. And it is further declared that all masters of families, landlords and heritors who shall not give punctual obedience, they shall be liable in the same pains and penalties due by the contraveners, without prejudice always of proceeding against the contraveners and inflicting upon them the pains contained in the said Acts of Parliament.

And seeing the single and life-rent escheat of such as live within regalities belong to the respective lords thereof, we, noways intending to prejudge the civil rights of our subjects, do allow them to have the benefit thereof according to law, but, with advice foresaid, do strictly charge and command them to use exact diligence against the contraveners of the foresaid laws within their respective jurisdictions, with certification that if they prosecute them not without collusion within thirty days after their delinquence we will call them before our Council and punish them for the neglect of their duty. . . .

Given under our signet at Edinburgh,
the second day of August 1677,
and of our reign the twenty-ninth year.

238. Letter from the earl of Arran to the duke of Lauderdale on the king's view of the Highland Host, 1678

(*Lauderdale Papers*, ed. O. Airy, III, pp. 99–102)

May it please your Grace,

This morning I waited upon his Majesty in his bedchamber, where there was the bishops of Winchester and Chichester and a great many others. As soon as his Majesty saw me he called me to him, and said aloud that at last he had got the paper from Earl Cassillis, and that he had given it to my Lord Maynard to send it to the duke of Lauderdale, to be considered and answered in the Council of Scotland; that for his part he thought it a very silly paper, and that he could make a shift to answer it himself; although he was no lawyer yet he knew Scotland pretty well.

Then he said that it was a strange thing that he had been tormented for several weeks with horrible complaints of the cruelty and outrages done in the west of Scotland, yet he had done them fair play, for he had caused send down to Scotland as many complaints as he could get; and that he had now received a full account of the whole proceedings in the west, and that it was from persons he would trust; that he found all to be false as hell, and that there was nothing done there but what was done by law, and that things were not pushed so far as the law allowed; that as he was a Christian he did not see what else could be done to prevent open rebellion; that he approved of what was done, and that he thought himself obliged in duty not to fall in a snare a second time; that he was now resolved to be beforehand with the fanatics; that he was sure they made use of religion as a pretence only; that he understood their designs, and to show religion was not their business he had granted them indulgence, and allowed them their own ministers, but that would not serve turn, for they withdrew, and railed more at these ministers than they did against the bishops; that now matters were come to that height that there was a necessity to use severity, for that now they kept field conventicles of three or four thousand men, most armed.

Then his Majesty said to the bishop of Winchester that a special friend of his (I mean of the king's) had complained of the severity of quartering, which he answered by telling him of a severer course in England, that is that the hundred of Twickenham had paid alone, in one year, three thousand pound sterling for robberies committed in Hounslow Heath, which they had not committed nor could not prevent, and that he thought that indeed very hard and severe. But, said his Majesty, that person told me it was so, but yet it was by law. Then, said the king, I answered that the quartering in Scotland was as much by law, and in cases of less consequence, for my cash-keeper can send men upon free quarter to compel people to pay my revenue.

The bishop of Winchester said he thought it would be much for his Majesty's service to cause print a relation of all the late proceedings of the Council of Scotland; that it would disabuse people much, and do his servants in Scotland justice and right. The king said he would certainly do it, but he expected some fuller accounts from Scotland, and then he would do it. Then his Majesty said to me there was one very pretty passage, that there was a certain person of Scotland that had complained how the proceedings of the Council had ruined his estate, that the bond made all his tenants run away; but the jest is he hath no tenants, but a miserable annuity. I said I knew another Scotsman now in England, that had gotten an estate in Scotland from his Majesty for his service against the rebels in sixty-six, and that this estate did belong to a fanatic; that now this gentleman had changed his opinion, and would not answer or give bond for his tenants.

His Majesty said he knew Scotland as well as anybody; that he had been in it in the worst of times; that he was sure it was so far from being unjust and severe to make gentlemen answer for their tenants that he knew it was the easiest thing in the world for them to do it; that there was no nation or kingdom in the world where the tenants had so great a dependence upon the gentlemen as in Scotland, and he was glad it was so, and that therefore they must be answerable for their tenants; that all they were to do was to punish them according to law when they went to conventicles, either by delivering them into the hands of justice or turning them out of their land; and that if everybody did so they would certainly be peaceable, when nobody could receive them. And I am sure, said the king, the commons in Scotland can do nothing without a head; but there are some people that, because they are not in themselves, and have a prejudice at some who serve me in Scotland, and therefore they must fall upon me and stir up these people to rebellion; but they are fools, and know not their own interest, for it is a foolish thing for Scotsmen to complain or make work here, or to endeavour a rebellion in Scotland, for if it should begin there, and afterwards come into England, and that England should turn commonwealth, Scotland would be a province next summer after. He said he thought they would not like that well. I said it was not very pleasant the last time they tried it, and that those persons had as good estates and as much to lose as anybody. . . .

239. James VII's indulgence, 1687

(Robert Wodrow, *History of the Sufferings of the Church of Scotland*, IV, pp. 426–427)

James VII, by the grace of God king of Scotland, England, France and Ireland, Defender of the Faith, &c., to all and sundry our good subjects whom these presents do or may concern, greeting.

Whereas by our royal proclamation of the date the 12th day of February 1686/7 we were graciously pleased, for the causes and on the terms therein mentioned, to grant our royal toleration to the professors of the Christian religion therein named, with and under certain restrictions and limitations, all which are in the said proclamation more at length expressed, we now, taking into our royal consideration the sinistrous interpretations which either have or may be made of some restrictions therein mentioned, have thought fit by this our royal proclamation further to declare that we will protect our archbishops and bishops, and all our subjects of the Protestant religion, in the free exercise of their Protestant religion as it is by law established, and in the quiet and full enjoyment of all their possessions, without any molestation or disturbance whatsoever. And we do likewise by our sovereign authority, prerogative royal and absolute power, suspend, stop and disable all penal and sanguinary laws made against any for nonconformity to the religion established by law in that our ancient kingdom, or for exercising their respective worships, religions, rites and ceremonies, all which laws are hereby stopped, suspended and disabled to all intents and purposes.

And to the end that by the liberty thereby granted the peace and security of our government in the practice thereof may not be endangered, we have thought fit, and do hereby straitly charge and command all our loving subjects, that as we do give them leave to meet and serve God after their own way and manner, be it in private houses, chapels or places purposely hired or built for that use, so that they take care that nothing be preached or taught among them which may any ways tend to alienate the hearts of our people from us or our government, and that their meetings be peaceably, openly and publicly held, and all persons freely admitted to them, and that they do signify and make known to some one or more of the next privy councillors, sheriffs, stewards, bailies, justices of the peace or magistrates of burghs royal, what place or places they set apart for these uses, with the names of the preachers.

And that all our subjects may enjoy such their religious assemblies with greater assurance and protection, we have thought fit, and do hereby command, that no disturbance of any kind be made or given unto them, under pain of our royal displeasure and to be further proceeded against with the utmost severity; provided always that their meetings be in houses or places provided for the purpose, and not in the open fields, for which now after this our royal grace and favour shown (which surpasses the hopes and equals the very wishes of the most zealously concerned) there is not the least shadow of excuse left; which meetings in fields we do hereby strictly prohibit and forbid, against all which we do leave our laws and Acts of Parliament in full force and vigour, notwithstanding the premises; and do further command all our judges, magistrates and officers of our forces to prosecute such as shall be guilty of the said field conventicles or assemblies with the utmost rigour, as they would avoid our highest displeasure, for we are confident none will, after these liberties and freedoms we have given to all without reserve to serve God in their own way, presume to meet in these assemblies except such as make a pretence of religion to cover their treasonable designs against our royal person and the peace of our government. . . .

  Given at our court at Windsor,
  the twenty-eighth day of June one thousand six hundred and eighty-seven,
  and of our reign the third year.

D. INSURRECTION

240. Letter from Major-General Drummond to the earl of Rothes on the Pentland Rising, 1666

(*Scottish Historical Review*, III, pp. 451–452)

Pentland, November 29th, 1666

May it please your Grace,

. . . Upon Sunday the 18th instant our march began from all our several quarters, and upon Tuesday the 20th we met at Glasgow. We spent Wednesday in preparations for what we wanted, whereof bandoleers was a chief defect, and in consultations with my Lord Glasgow and the other noblemen who commanded. Thursday the 22nd the horse watched Kilmarnock, and the foot upon Friday at much ado. There we understood that the rebels were convened at Mauchline with all their force and a resolution to fight us. They had been in Ayr and taken about 200 arms of all sorts out of the tollbooth, which had been formerly gathered out of the country when it was disarmed. All the gentlemen's houses they searched for horses and arms, and I believe found divers ready to their hands, which must be judged as taken by force. Saturday the 24th we came to Mauchline. The rebels were gone to Cumnock, and from thence to the Muirkirk of Kyle and to Douglas. We judged (and not amiss) that they designed for Clydesdale, Hamilton and Glasgow, and there upon Sunday took a nearer way to stop that course, and marched through Avondale to Strathaven, where we had notice that they were at Lesmahagow, but four miles from us.

That Sunday, they knowing of us, as they used to have quick intelligence of our motions in a country of their own friends disaffected to us, they passed the river Clyde to Lanark, their foot in two boats which immediately they sank, and forded with their horses not without danger, the river being great. Upon Monday the 26th our fore-party had a view of them on the riverside over against us, as if they meant to forbid our passage; but when our body of horse began to appear they marched off, and kept a lusty rearguard with more order than could have been hoped from them. We passed the ford instantly, deep and strong, which made us very doubtful whether it was wadeable by the foot, and followed them four miles on their rear, but in regard of the distance from our foot and approach of the night could not with any reason engage with them. We got over the foot that night with much danger, but not one lost.

Tuesday we followed the rebels' track for eight miles through a black moss, and marking their way to make for Huhthgour[1] we were afraid of Edinburgh, and bent our course to Torphichen hither. The rebels had marched on Monday from Lanark to Bathgate Huhthgour[1] and were at Colinton, two miles from Edinburgh, on Tuesday the 27th by mid-day to our admiration. Whatever their design or invitation was for so desperate a march, they found their plot prevented. We judged rightly they would get off to Biggar, and betook us to fall in their way, going over the Pentland Hills at Currie. Our foreparty of about a hundred horse discovered them on their march towards Linton the Biggar way near a place called Glencorse Kirk, and

[1] Possibly Newbridge (*Scottish Historical Review*, IV, pp. 114–116).

with great boldness set upon them, and endured the danger to face all their strength, horse and foot, until our cavalry far behind came up; and that spent near two hours. So had God blinded these fools to neglect their advantage, our party being in a ground whence they could not come off. Some sharp charges passed in this time, which the rebels gave and received with desperate resolution to our prejudice.

At last our horse comes on and gave breathing to that weary party, but our foot was yet four miles from us. We found it convenient to draw from that ground, very advantageous for their foot, which they after much consideration began to employ against us; but we prevented them, and got off a little to a better ground, where they made a fashion to annoy us without any gain. So soon as our foot came up we put ourselves in order and embattled in a fair plain upon their noses. They upon the hill above did the like, but gave us no disturbance, though well they might.

By this time the sun was set; we must make haste, and advanced a party of horse and foot from our right hand to assault their left wing of horse, which instantly came down and met them. And there the work began. We fought obstinately a long time with swords, until they mixed like chess-men in a bag. We advanced our right wing and they their left to give relief. There again it was disputed toughly. Then came a strong party of foot from their body, and forced our right wing back to the foot in some disorder; but this was instantly rectified. Their right wing of horse came from their ground foolishly and crosses their foot, apprehending their left wing to be in distress (wherein they were mistaken), and so gave our left wing their slack, which opportunity we had hold on and there went their cavalry in disorder. Our whole body then advanced and beat in their horse upon their foot. Then confusion and flight followed. We pursued in the dark, killed all the foot, and but for the night and steep hills had wholly destroyed them.

Some prisoners there are fit for examples. I know not how many, but I conjecture not above 140, for there was sound payment. Our loss I cannot tell, but it is greater than many of their skins were worth. Their number was about fifteen or sixteen hundred, and would without doubt have increased if God had not confounded their imaginations and rebellious dispositions. Upon Monday the rebels swore the Covenant at Lanark, and all to die in defence of it. Most of these who led their troops were cashiered preachers. . . .

241. Letter from John Graham of Claverhouse to the earl of Linlithgow on the battle of Drumclog, 1679
(Mark Napier, *Life and Times of John Graham of Claverhouse*, II, pp. 221–223)

Glasgow, June the 1st, 1679

MY LORD,

Upon Saturday's night, when my Lord Ross came into this place, I marched out; and because of the insolency that had been done two nights before at Rutherglen I went thither, and inquired for the names. So soon as I got them I sent out parties to seize on them, and found not only three of those rogues but also an intercommuned minister called King. We had them at Strathaven about six in the morning yesterday;

and, resolving to convey them to this, I thought that we might make a little tour, to see if we could fall upon a conventicle; which we did, little to our advantage.

For when we came in sight of them we found them drawn up in battle upon a most advantageous ground, to which there was no coming but through mosses and lakes. They were not preaching, and had got away all their women and children. They consisted of four battalions of foot, and all well armed with fusils and pitchforks, and three squadrons of horse. We sent, both, parties to skirmish, they of foot and we of dragoons. They ran for it, and sent down a battalion of foot against them. We sent threescore of dragoons, who made them run again shamefully. But in the end (they perceiving that we had the better of them in skirmish) they resolved a general engagement, and immediately advanced with their foot, the horse following.

They came through the loch, and the greatest body of all made up against my troop. We kept our fire till they were within ten pace of us. They received our fire and advanced to shock. The first they gave us brought down the cornet, Mr. Crawford, and Captain Blyth. Besides that with a pitchfork they made such an opening in my sorrel horse's belly that his guts hung out half an ell; and yet he carried me off a mile, which so discouraged our men that they sustained not the shock, but fell into disorder. Their horse took the occasion of this, and pursued us so hotly that we got no time to rally. I saved the standards, but lost on the place about eight or ten men besides wounded. But the dragoons lost many more. They are not come easily off on the other side, for I saw several of them fall before we came to the shock. . . .

242. Privy Council's account, sent to the duke of Lauderdale, of the battle of Bothwell Bridge, 1679

(*Lauderdale Papers*, ed. O. Airy, III, pp. 171–173)

May it please your Grace,

We send the flying packet with great joy, that your Grace may give his Majesty the good and happy news of a total and absolute victory obtained this day over the rebels by his Majesty's forces in this kingdom under the conduct of his grace the duke of Buccleuch, which happened in this manner.

This morning by seven o'clock our army was drawn up at Bothwell Bridge, which the enemy, lying on the other side thereof, had barricaded. Here a supplication is brought to the Lord General by one of the rebels, giving him notice that they would lay down their arms upon no other terms than those expressed in their large declaration. His grace told the bearer these were destructive to the king's authority and fundamental constitution of this kingdom, and that they were to expect no other articles from him but to lay down arms and render themselves to his mercy. This they refused to do, and immediately the guns began to play upon them, which did somewhat disorder them. Then a party attacked the bridge, and after some short dispute carried it. The rebels, being beaten from it, retreated a little, and stayed at some distance till most of his Majesty's forces were got over that pass. Soon after, by some more play with the guns and another assault, their horse began to run and scatter upon all corners, leaving their flying foot to the mercy of our army, who pursued them with all diligence and zeal, and have killed some hundreds of them and taken many hundreds prisoners. Many of their foot fled into the wood of Hamilton, which is surrounded by his Majesty's forces, and a detached party under Lieutenant-Colonel Douglas is sent in after them, which will give a good account of them. Our army is still in pursuit of the rebels when Lundin came away about ten o'clock, who having been sent from us to wait on the general had the good fortune to be an actor as well as witness in this engagement, so that his Majesty may be assured that this is a total rout and discomfiture of these insolent rebels.

The Lord General hath behaved himself with exceeding great conduct and magnanimity, and all the officers, gentlemen and soldiers have carried themselves with great cheerfulness and resolution against the enemies of our religion, king and country; and above all, the mercy of God hath been most signal and wonderful to us, even to a miracle, insomuch that though the rebels were near seven thousand yet are they totally routed without any loss to his Majesty's forces save of two or three common soldiers.

22 June 1679.

243. Sanquhar Declaration, 1680

(Robert Wodrow, *History of the Sufferings of the Church of Scotland*, III, pp. 212–213)

It is not amongst the smallest of the Lord's mercies to this poor land that there have been always some who have given their testimony against every course of defection (that many are guilty of), which is a token for good, that he doth not as yet intend to cast us off altogether, but that he will leave a remnant in whom he will be glorious, if they through his grace keep themselves clean still, and walk in his way and method, as it has been walked in and owned by him in our predecessors of truly worthy memory, in their carrying on of our noble work of reformation in the several steps thereof, from popery, prelacy and likewise Erastian supremacy, so much usurped by him who (it is true so far as we know) is descended from the race of our kings, yet he hath so far deborded from what he ought to have been, by his perjury and usurpation in Church matters and tyranny in matters civil, as is known by the whole land, that we have just reason to account it one of the Lord's great controversies against us that we have not disowned him and the men of his practices (whether inferior magistrates or any other), as enemies to our Lord and his crown, and the true Protestant and Presbyterian interest in these lands, our Lord's espoused bride and Church.

Therefore, although we be for government and governors such as the word of God and our Covenant allows, yet we for ourselves and all that will adhere to us, as the representative of the true Presbyterian kirk and covenanted nation of Scotland, considering the great hazard of lying under such a sin any longer, do by these presents disown Charles Stuart, that has been reigning (or rather tyrannizing, as we may say) on the throne of Britain these years bygone, as having any right, title to or interest in the said crown of Scotland for government, as forfeited several years since by his perjury and breach of covenant both to God and his kirk, and usurpation of his crown and royal prerogatives therein, and many other breaches in matters ecclesiastic, and by his tyranny and breach of the very *leges regnandi* in matters civil; for which reason we declare that several years since he should have been denuded of being king, ruler or magistrate, or of having any power to act or to be obeyed as such.

As also, we being under the standard of our Lord Jesus Christ, Captain of Salvation, do declare a war with such a tyrant and usurper, and all the men of his practices, as enemies to our Lord Jesus Christ and his cause and covenants, and against all such as have strengthened him, sided with or any wise acknowledged him in his tyranny, civil or ecclesiastic, yea, against all such as shall strengthen, side with or any wise acknowledge any other in the like usurpation and tyranny, far more against such as would betray or deliver up our free reformed mother-kirk unto the bondage of Antichrist, the Pope of Rome. And by this we homologate that testimony given at Rutherglen the 29th of May 1679, and all the faithful testimonies of these who have gone before, as also of these who have suffered of late.

And we do disclaim that declaration published at Hamilton, June 1679, chiefly because it takes in the king's interest, which we are several years since loosed from because of the foresaid reasons and others which may after this (if the Lord will) be published. As also we disown, and by this resent the reception of, the duke of York, that professed papist, as repugnant to our principles and vows to the most high God, and as that which is the great, though not alone just, reproach of our kirk and nation. We also by this protest against his succeeding to the crown, and whatever has been done, or any are essaying to do, in this land (given to the Lord) in prejudice to our work of reformation.

And to conclude, we hope after this none will blame us for, or offend at, our rewarding these that are against us, as they have done to us, as the Lord gives opportunity. This is not to exclude any that have declined, if they be willing to give satisfaction according to the degree of their offence.

Given at Sanquhar, June 22nd, 1680.

244. Gilbert Burnet's account of Argyll's rebellion, 1685

(Supplement to Burnet's History of My Own Time, pp. 155–160)

Argyll had lived near two years secretly in Friesland; but he came often over into Amsterdam, and met there with the rest of the Scotch exiles, the chief of whom were Sir John Cochrane and Sir Patrick Hume. They all knew how odious the king's person, as well as his religion, was in Scotland; and they reckoned that those who had felt his severity so much when he was only a subject would very probably apprehend it much more now that he was a king. Argyll believed that if he had but money to buy a stock of arms and ammunition he might venture into Scotland without taking any precaution for the preparing people to it. He thought his own interest would bring all his Highlanders together, and he fancied the western and southern counties were under such apprehensions, both for religion and liberty, that they wanted nothing but arms and a head. And a rich widow in Amsterdam, who was a zealous lover both of presbytery and of a commonwealth, hearing that it was believed ten thousand pound sterling might compass this great design, laid down the money.

Argyll now fancied Scotland was his own, and was very insolent in all his discourses with the other gentlemen, who really thought his brain turned. Hume knew the state of the southern and western counties much better than he did, for many had that opinion of Argyll that if at any time the king had offered him his estate again he would have made his own peace and have betrayed all his friends; but they had trusted themselves to Hume, so that he was sure of above 4,000 persons, and they had engaged above the half of the garrison that was in the castle of Edinburgh; so that here would have been a formidable rebellion if Argyll could have managed it.

He went about the business of buying arms and his vessel to carry them over with so much dexterity that this passed as if it had been for the service of the Venetians. But when he and the rest came to reason about the methods of carrying on their business they differed in every point. Hume was for the shortest passage and for landing in the south, but Argyll thought the fastnesses of his own country made that it would be properest, since he reckoned the country would gather to him safer there; and in short he rather dictated to the rest than advised with them. Hume thought often to have left him, and would never trust him with the secrets of those who he knew were waiting for a fit opportunity; nor would he trust it to Cochrane. Monmouth, hearing of all this, came to them, and though he did not like the business, and thought it was too early, yet he studied to make them all friends, and showed great temper in his way of managing them. He had such inclinations to have set himself at the head of them, that if Argyll had offered it to him he seemed ready to have accepted of the command. But Argyll was strangely blown up, and, as it appeared afterwards, he seemed guilty of the folly of fancying that he could make himself king of Scotland. He had provided all things with so much secrecy that the king had not the least suspicion of him till he heard he had set sail. . . .

Argyll had a very prosperous voyage, and some few English went with him, in particular Mr. Ayloffe and one Mr. Rumbold, that dwelt in Rye House, where it was pretended the plot was laid for murdering the late and the present king. He sent out a boat at Orkney to get intelligence and to take prisoners, but went away in such haste as to leave his men to be made prisoners. The winds were very favourable, and turned as his occasions required, so that in a very few days after he sailed from Holland he arrived in Argyllshire. . . . At his landing he was much surprised to find that almost all of the gentry of the country had been called to Edinburgh, for the king sent the advertisement that he had received from Holland with all haste to Scotland, upon which the Privy Council had sent for all the most considerable gentlemen of his country. He had not behaved himself in his prosperity like a man that thought he might at some time or another need the affections of his people, and he felt that now, for though he always reckoned that he was sure he could raise 5,000 men in his country yet he could not bring together five and twenty hundred men to come to him.

If with these he had immediately gone over to the western counties of Ayr and Renfrew he might have given the government much trouble, but he lingered too long, hoping still to have brought more of his Highlanders together. He reckoned

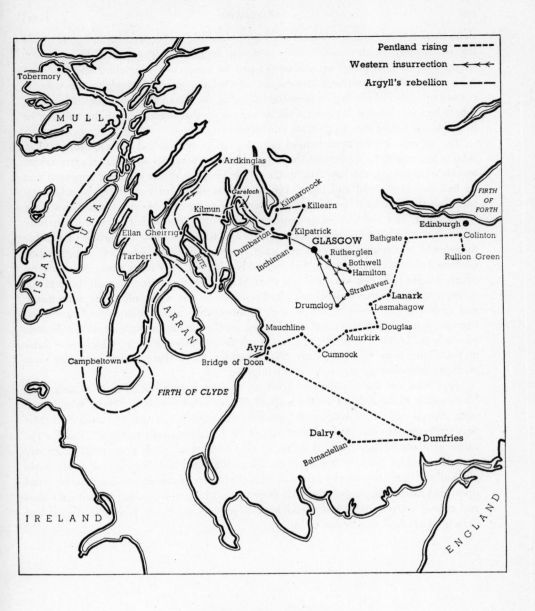

Pentland rising ------
Western insurrection ←←←
Argyll's rebellion — — —

Tobermory
MULL
ISLAY
JURA
Ellan Gheirrig
Tarbert
Campbeltown
ARRAN
BUTE
Ardkinglas
Gareloch
Kilmun
Kilmaronock
Killearn
Dumbarton
Kilpatrick
Inchinnan
GLASGOW
Rutherglen
Bothwell
Hamilton
Strathaven
Drumclog
Mauchline
Ayr
Bridge of Doon
Cumnock
Muirkirk
Douglas
Lesmahagow
Lanark
Bathgate
Edinburgh
Colinton
Rullion Green
FIRTH OF FORTH
FIRTH OF CLYDE
Dalry
Balmaclellan
Dumfries
IRELAND
ENGLAND

12. SOUTHERN SCOTLAND
ILLUSTRATING INSURRECTIONARY MOVEMENTS OF 1665–1685

these were sure to him, and would obey him blindfold; whereas if he had gone out of his own country with a small force those who might have come in to his assistance might also have disputed his authority, and he could not bear contradiction. And when at last he should have crossed the arm of the sea, and come to the western counties, instead of landing in them he landed in the isle of Bute, a poor little island, where he spent twelve days more, till he had eat up that island, pretending still that he hoped to be joined by more of his Highlanders.

He had also left his arms behind him in a castle, with a body of men to guard it, who were routed by a party of the king's and ran away. So all his arms were taken, and then his design was lost. And in the whole progress of the matter it appeared that he had lost both head and heart. His men were now got out of the island, but a rebellion that begins to go backward is quickly at an end. He put himself in a poor man's habit, and had almost got out of their hands; but at last he was shamefully taken. Yet a body of his men stuck together and fought, so that though in that feeble opposition which the king's troops gave them some were wounded, others taken (amongst these were Cochrane, Ayloffe and Rumbold), Sir Patrick Hume with several others fought out their way and got clear of their enemies. But now all those in the western and southern counties who had resolved to rise were still in the same mind, and upon the first news of the duke of Monmouth's success there would have been a second and much more considerable rising. So they lay in the way where the packets passed from London to Edinburgh, and took two or three of them, which gave those at the Council at Edinburgh no small disorder, since there passed so many days without their hearing any news from England. . . .

And thus was the rebellion in Scotland dissipated with the effusion of very little blood either in the field or on the scaffold. The greatest number of those who joined with Argyll were Highlanders, whose following their lord was so suitable to their way of living that the government thought it fit to be gentle to them. And for the other gentlemen, they had got away, so that none were taken that could make any great discoveries. And the truth was the Council fancied that Argyll must needs know all. And so when they saw by him that he had no correspondence with any in Scotland upon that matter they concluded that there was nothing in it; so that many men's lives and estates were saved who would have been very probably ruined if Argyll had drawn all Hume's secrets out of him.

E. REVOLUTION AND SETTLEMENT

245. Act of Succession, 1681

(*Acts of the Parliaments of Scotland*, VIII, pp. 238–239)

ACT ACKNOWLEDGING AND ASSERTING
THE RIGHT OF SUCCESSION TO THE IMPERIAL CROWN OF SCOTLAND

The Estates of Parliament, considering that the kings of this realm, deriving their royal power from God Almighty alone, do succeed lineally thereto according to the known degrees of proximity in blood, which cannot be interrupted, suspended or diverted by any Act or statute whatsoever, and that none can attempt to alter or divert the said succession without involving the subjects of this kingdom in perjury and rebellion, and without exposing them to all the fatal and dreadful consequences of a civil war, do therefore, from a hearty and sincere sense of their duty, recognize, acknowledge and declare that the right to the imperial crown of this realm is by the inherent right and nature of the monarchy, as well as by the fundamental and unalterable laws of this realm, transmitted and devolved by a lineal succession according to the proximity of blood; and that upon the death of the king or queen who actually reigns the subjects of this kingdom are bound by law, duty and allegiance to obey the next immediate and lawful heir, either male or female, upon whom the right and administration of the government is immediately devolved; and that no difference in religion, nor no law nor Act of Parliament made or to be made, can alter or divert the right of succession and lineal descent of the crown to the nearest and lawful heirs according to the degrees aforesaid, nor can stop or hinder them in the full, free and actual administration of the government according to the laws of the kingdom.

Likewise our sovereign lord, with advice and consent of his said Estates of Parliament, do declare it is high treason in any of the subjects of this kingdom by writing, speaking or any other manner of way to endeavour the alteration, suspension or diversion of the said right of succession, or the debarring the next lawful successor from the immediate, actual, full and free administration of the government, conform to the laws of the kingdom; and that all such attempts or designs shall infer against them the pain of treason.

246. Test Act, 1681

(*Acts of the Parliaments of Scotland*, VIII, pp. 243–245)

ACT ANENT RELIGION AND THE TEST

Our sovereign lord, with his Estates of Parliament, considering that albeit by many wholesome laws made by his royal grandfather and father of glorious memory, and by himself in this and his other Parliaments since his happy restoration, the Protestant religion is carefully asserted, established and secured against popery and fanaticism, yet the restless adversaries of our religion do not cease to propagate their errors, and to seduce his Majesty's subjects from their duty to God and loyalty to his vicegerent, and to overturn the established religion by introducing their superstitions and delusions into this Church and kingdom; and knowing that nothing can more increase the numbers and confidence of papists and schismatical dissenters from the established Church than the supine neglect of putting in execution the good laws provided against them, together with their hopes to insinuate themselves into offices and places of trust and public employment; therefore his Majesty, from his princely and pious zeal to maintain and preserve the true Protestant religion contained in the confession of faith recorded in the first Parliament of King James the Sixth, which is founded on and agreeable to the written word of God, doth, with advice and consent of his Estates of Parliament, require and command all his officers, judges and magistrates to put the laws made against popery and papists, priests, Jesuits and all persons of any other order in the popish Church, especially against sayers and hearers of mass, venders and dispersers of forbidden books, and resetters of popish priests and excommunicate papists, as also against all fanatic separatists from this national Church, against preachers at house or field conventicles and the resetters and harbourers of preachers who are intercommuned, against disorderly baptisms and marriages and irregular ordinations and all other schismatical disorders, to full and vigorous execution according to the tenor of the respective Acts of Parliament thereanent provided.

And that his Majesty's princely care to have these laws put in execution against those enemies of the Protestant religion may the more clearly appear, he doth, with advice and consent foresaid, statute and ordain that the ministers of each parish give up in October yearly to their respective ordinaries true and exact lists of all papists and schismatical withdrawers from the public worship in their respective parishes, which lists are to be subscribed by them; and that the bishops give in a double of the said lists subscribed by them to the respective sheriffs, stewards, bailies of royalty and regality and magistrates of burghs, to the effect the said judges may proceed against them according to law; as also the sheriffs and other magistrates foresaid are hereby ordained to give to his Majesty's Privy Council in December yearly an account of their proceedings against those papists and fanatical separatists, as they will be answerable at their highest peril. And that the diligences done by the sheriffs, bailies of regalities and other magistrates foresaid may be the better inquired into by the Council, the bishops of the respective dioceses are to send exact doubles of the lists of the papists and fanatics to the Clerks of Privy Council, whereby the diligences of the sheriffs and other judges foresaid may be controlled and examined.

And to cut off all hopes from papists and fanatics of their being employed in offices and places of public trust, it is hereby statute and ordained that the following oath shall be taken by all persons in offices and places of public trust, civil, ecclesiastical and military, especially by all members of Parliament and all electors of members of Parliament, . . .[1] and if any shall presume to exercise any of the said offices or

---

[1] A very comprehensive list follows of those required to take the oath, including even collectors of the revenue and private soldiers.

employments, or any public office or trust within this kingdom (the king's lawful brothers and sons only excepted), until they take the oath foresaid and subscribe it, to be recorded in the registers of the respective courts, they shall be declared incapable of all public trust thereafter, and be further punished with the loss of their movables and life-rent escheat, the one half whereof to be given to the informer, and the other half to belong to his Majesty; and his Majesty with advice foresaid recommends to his Privy Council to see this Act put to due and vigorous execution.

Follows the tenor of the oath to be taken by all persons in public trust.

I, A.B., solemnly swear in presence of the Eternal God, whom I invocate as judge and witness of my sincere intention of this my oath, that I own and sincerely profess the true Protestant religion contained in the confession of faith recorded in the first Parliament of King James the Sixth, and that I believe the same to be founded on and agreeable to the written word of God. And I promise and swear that I shall adhere thereto during all the days of my lifetime, and shall endeavour to educate my children therein, and shall never consent to any change nor alteration contrary thereto; and that I disown and renounce all such principles, doctrines or practices, whether popish or fanatical, which are contrary unto and inconsistent with the said Protestant religion and confession of faith.

And for testification of my obedience to my most gracious sovereign Charles the Second, I do affirm and swear by this my solemn oath that the king's Majesty is the only supreme governor of this realm, over all persons and in all causes, as well ecclesiastical as civil; and that no foreign prince, person, pope, prelate, state or potentate hath or ought to have any jurisdiction, power, superiority, pre-eminency or authority, ecclesiastical or civil, within this realm. And therefore I do utterly renounce and forsake all foreign jurisdictions, powers, superiorities and authorities, and do promise that from henceforth I shall bear faith and true allegiance to the king's Majesty, his heirs and lawful successors, and to my power shall assist and defend all rights, jurisdictions, prerogatives, privileges, pre-eminencies and authorities belonging to the king's Majesty, his heirs and lawful successors.

And I further affirm and swear by this my solemn oath that I judge it unlawful for subjects, upon pretence of reformation or any other pretence whatsoever, to enter into covenants or leagues, or to convocate, convene or assemble in any councils, conventions or assemblies, to treat, consult or determine in any matter of state, civil or ecclesiastic, without his Majesty's special command or express licence had thereto, or to take up arms against the king or those commissionated by him, and that I shall never so rise in arms or enter into such covenant or assemblies; and that there lies no obligation on me from the National Covenant, or the Solemn League and Covenant (so commonly called), or any other manner of way whatsoever, to endeavour any change or alteration in the government, either in Church or State, as it is now established by the laws of this kingdom. And I promise and swear that I shall with my utmost power defend, assist and maintain his Majesty's jurisdiction foresaid against all deadly; and I shall never decline his Majesty's power and jurisdiction, as I shall answer to God.

And finally I affirm and swear that this my solemn oath is given in the plain, genuine sense and meaning of the words, without any equivocation, mental reservation or any manner of evasion whatsoever; and that I shall not accept or use any dispensation from any creature whatsoever. So help me God.

247. Lord Balcarres on the settlement of the Crown, 1689

(*Memoirs touching the Revolution in Scotland, presented to King James*, ed. 1841, pp. 35–36)

A few days thereafter the Committee of Estates prepared all was intended for the great meeting, who were in difficulties as to the manner of declaring the crown vacant. Some were for abdication, as had been done in England; but that could not pass, as the most violent could not pretend you had abdicated Scotland. Others were for making use of an old obsolete word, 'fore-letting', used for a bird's forsaking her nest; but Sir John Dalrymple ended the controversy by giving such reasons against both that they went into his motion, which was to have it declared that by doing acts contrary to law you had forfeited your right to the crown—not that they intended to forfeit your Majesty as a criminal, but that you of yourself had forfeited, which would render the whole clear, and likewise remove any right the prince of Wales might afterwards pretend to. Next day it was voted unanimously, none dissenting except the archbishop of Glasgow, Lord Boyne, Sir George Mackenzie, Lord Advocate, and Mr. Ogilvie, son to the earl of Findlater.

After the crown was declared vacant they immediately proposed the filling it; and the duke of Hamilton, although president and not obliged to vote, yet to show a good example, as he said himself, proposed to make an humble offer of the crown to the prince and princess of Orange, now king and queen of England. This last vote passed more unanimously than the other declaring the throne vacant. The duke of Queensberry and the marquis of Atholl, having withdrawn at the first vote, came to the second, and told the House that they were not fully convinced of their own right of declaring the crown vacant, but since the Estates had done it they thought none deserved so well to fill it as the prince and princess of Orange. The vote being over, they all went to the market-cross of Edinburgh and proclaimed them king and queen of Scotland. . . .

After this they dispatched the Lord Lorne, Sir James Montgomery and Sir John Dalrymple with the offer of the crown, upon condition of having their grievances redressed and the Claim of Right[1] assented to, which they pretended were naturally and legally the rights of the people, inherent to them, though never established by any former law or Act of Parliament. Until the return of these three members, and that they were informed if the prince of Orange would accept of the crown, their present, they resolved upon an adjournment for some days; and, that they might be in the greater security, a full power was given to the duke of Hamilton to imprison whoever he suspected to be acting against the common interest until their next meeting.

[1] No. 248.

248. Claim of Right, 1689

(Acts of the Parliaments of Scotland, IX, pp. 38–40)

THE DECLARATION OF THE ESTATES OF THE KINGDOM OF SCOTLAND,
CONTAINING THE CLAIM OF RIGHT AND THE OFFER OF THE CROWN
TO THE KING AND QUEEN OF ENGLAND

Whereas King James the Seventh, being a professed papist, did assume the regal power and acted as king without ever taking the oath required by law, whereby the king at his access to the government is obliged to swear to maintain the Protestant religion and to rule the people according to the laudable laws; and did by the advice of wicked and evil counsellors invade the fundamental constitution of this kingdom, and altered it from a legal, limited monarchy to an arbitrary, despotic power; and in a public proclamation asserted an absolute power to cass, annul and disable all the laws, particularly arraigning the laws establishing the Protestant religion; and did exercise that power to the subversion of the Protestant religion, and to the violation of the laws and liberties of the kingdom;

By erecting public schools and societies of the Jesuits, and not only allowing mass to be publicly said but also inverting Protestant chapels and churches to public mass-houses, contrary to the express laws against saying and hearing of mass;

By allowing popish books to be printed and dispersed, by a gift to a popish printer, designing him printer to his Majesty's household, college and chapel, contrary to the laws;

By taking the children of Protestant noblemen and gentlemen, sending and keeping them abroad to be bred papists, making great funds and dotations to popish schools and colleges abroad, bestowing pensions upon priests, and perverting Protestants from their religion by offers of places, preferments and pensions;

By disarming Protestants, while at the same time he employed papists in the places of greatest trust, civil and military, such as Chancellor, Secretaries, Privy Councillors and Lords of Session, thrusting out Protestants to make room for papists, and entrusting the forts and magazines of the kingdom in their hands;

By imposing oaths contrary to law;

By giving gifts and grants for exacting money, without consent of Parliament or Convention of Estates;

By levying or keeping on foot a standing army in time of peace without consent of Parliament, which army did exact locality, free and dry quarters;

By employing the officers of the army as judges through the kingdom, and imposing them where there were heritable offices and jurisdictions, by whom many of the lieges were put to death summarily, without legal trial, jury or record;

By imposing exorbitant fines, to the value of the party's estates, exacting extravagant bail, and disposing fines and forfeitures before any process or conviction;

By imprisoning persons without expressing the reason, and delaying to put them to trial;

By causing pursue and forfeit several persons upon stretches of old and obsolete laws, upon frivolous and weak pretences, upon lame and defective probations, as particularly the late earl of Argyll, to the scandal and reproach of the justice of the nation;

By subverting the right of the royal burghs, the third estate of Parliament, imposing upon them not only magistrates but also the whole town council and clerks, contrary to their liberties and express charters, without the pretence either of sentence, surrender or consent, so that, the commissioners to Parliaments being chosen by the magistrates and council, the king might in effect as well nominate that entire estate of Parliament, and many of the said magistrates put in by him were avowed papists, and the burghs were forced to pay money for the letters imposing these illegal magistrates and councils upon them;

By sending letters to the chief courts of justice, not only ordaining the judges to stop and desist *sine die* to determine causes, but also ordering and commanding them how to proceed in cases depending before them, contrary to the express laws, and by changing the nature of the judges' gifts *ad vitam aut culpam*, and giving them commissions *ad beneplacitum*, to dispose them to compliance with arbitrary courses, and turning them out of their offices when they did not comply;

By granting personal protections for civil debts contrary to law;

All which are utterly and directly contrary to the known laws, statutes and freedoms of this realm;

Therefore the Estates of the kingdom of Scotland find and declare that King James the Seventh, being a professed papist, did assume the regal power and acted as king without ever taking the oath required by law, and hath by the advice of evil and wicked counsellors invaded the fundamental constitution of the kingdom, and altered it from a legal, limited monarchy to an arbitrary, despotic power, and hath exercised the same to the subversion of the Protestant religion and the violation of the laws and liberties of the kingdom, inverting all the ends of government, whereby he hath forfeited the right to the crown, and the throne is become vacant.

And whereas his Royal Highness William, then prince of Orange, now king of England, whom it hath pleased Almighty God to make the glorious instrument of delivering these kingdoms from popery and arbitrary power, did, by the advice of several lords and gentlemen of this nation at London for the time, call the Estates of this kingdom to meet the fourteenth of March last, in order to such an establishment as that their religion, laws and liberties might not be again in danger of being subverted; and the said Estates, being now assembled in a full and free representative of this nation, taking to their most serious consideration the best means for attaining the ends aforesaid, do in the first place, as their ancestors in the like cases have usually done for the vindicating and asserting their ancient rights and liberties, declare

That by the law of this kingdom no papist can be king or queen of this realm, nor bear any office whatsoever therein; nor can any Protestant successor exercise the regal power until he or she swear the coronation oath;

That all proclamations asserting an absolute power to cass, annul and disable laws, the erecting schools and colleges for Jesuits, the inverting Protestant chapels and churches to public mass-houses, and the allowing mass to be said, are contrary to law;

That the allowing popish books to be printed and dispersed is contrary to law;

That the taking the children of noblemen, gentlemen and others, sending and keeping them abroad to be bred papists, the making funds and dotations to popish schools and colleges, the bestowing pensions on priests and the perverting Protestants from their religion by offers of places, preferments and pensions, are contrary to law;

That the disarming of Protestants and employing papists in the places of greatest trust, both civil and military, the thrusting out Protestants to make room for papists and the entrusting papists with the forts and magazines of the kingdom, are contrary to law;

That the imposing oaths without authority of Parliament is contrary to law;

That the giving gifts or grants for raising of money without the consent of Parliament or Convention of Estates is contrary to law;

That the employing the officers of the army as judges through the kingdom, or imposing them where there were heritable offices and jurisdictions, and the putting the lieges to death summarily and without legal trial, jury or record, are contrary to law;

That the imposing of extraordinary fines, the exacting of exorbitant bail, and the disposing of fines and forfeitures before sentence, are contrary to law;

That the imprisoning persons without expressing the reason thereof, and delaying to put them to trial, is contrary to law;

That the causing pursue and forfeit persons upon stretches of old and obsolete laws, upon frivolous and weak pretences, upon lame and defective probation, as particularly the late earl of Argyll, are contrary to law;

That the nominating and imposing the magistrates, councils and clerks upon burghs, contrary to their liberties and express charters, is contrary to law;

That the sending letters to the courts of justice ordaining the judges to stop or desist from determining causes, or ordaining them how to proceed in causes depending before them, and the changing the nature of the judges' gifts *ad vitam aut culpam* into commissions *durante beneplacito*, are contrary to law;

That the granting personal protections for civil debts is contrary to law;

That the forcing the lieges to depone against themselves in capital crimes, however the punishment be restricted, is contrary to law;

That the using torture without evidence, or in ordinary crimes, is contrary to law;

That the sending of an army in a hostile manner upon any part of the kingdom in a peaceable time, and exacting of locality and any manner of free quarters, is contrary to law;

That the charging of the lieges with lawburrows, at the king's instance, and the imposing of bonds, without the authority of Parliament, and the suspending advocates from their employment for not compearing when such bonds were offered, were contrary to law;

That the putting of garrisons in private men's houses in time of peace without their consent or the authority of Parliament is contrary to law;

That the opinions of the Lords of Session in the two cases following were contrary to law, viz., 1, that the concealing the demand of a supply for a forfeited person, although not given, is treason; 2, that persons refusing to discover what are their private thoughts and judgments in relation to points of treason or other men's actions are guilty of treason;

That the fining husbands for their wives' withdrawing from the Church was contrary to law;

That prelacy and the superiority of any office in the Church above presbyters is and hath been a great and insupportable grievance and trouble to this nation, and contrary to the inclinations of the generality of the people ever since the Reformation (they having reformed from popery by presbyters), and therefore ought to be abolished;

That it is the right and privilege of the subjects to protest for remede of law to the king and Parliament against sentences pronounced by the Lords of Session, providing the same do not stop execution of these sentences;

That it is the right of the subjects to petition the king, and that all imprisonments and prosecutions for such petitioning are contrary to law;

That for redress of all grievances, and for the amending, strengthening and preserving of the laws, Parliaments ought to be frequently called and allowed to sit, and the freedom of speech and debate secured to the members.

And they do claim, demand and insist upon all and sundry the premises as their undoubted right and liberties, and that no declarations, doings or proceedings to the prejudice of the people in any of the said premises ought in any ways to be drawn hereafter in consequence or example, but that all forfeitures, fines, loss of offices, imprisonments, banishments, pursuits, persecutions, tortures and rigorous executions be considered, and the parties laesed be redressed; to which demand of their rights and redressing of their grievances they are particularly encouraged by his Majesty the king of England his declaration for the kingdom of Scotland of the   day of October last, as being the only means for obtaining a full redress and remedy therein.

Having therefore an entire confidence that his said Majesty the king of England will perfect the deliverance so far advanced by him, and will still preserve them from the violation of their rights which they have here asserted, and from all other attempts upon their religion, laws and liberties, the said Estates of the kingdom of Scotland do resolve that William and Mary, king and queen of England, France and Ireland, be, and be declared, king and queen of Scotland, to hold the crown and royal dignity of the said kingdom of Scotland to them, the said king and queen, during their lives and the longest liver of them, and that the sole and full exercise of the regal power be only in and exercised by him, the said king, in the names of the said king and queen during their joint lives; and after their decease the said crown and royal dignity of the said kingdom to be to the heirs of the body of the said queen, which failing to the Princess Anne of Denmark and the heirs of her body, which also failing to the heirs of the body of the said William, king of England; and they do pray the said king and queen of England to accept the same accordingly, and that the oath hereafter mentioned be taken by all Protestants of whom the oath of allegiance and any other oaths and declarations might be required by law, instead of them, and that the said oath of allegiance and other oaths and declarations may be abrogated.

I, A.B., do sincerely promise and swear that I will be faithful and bear true allegiance to their Majesties King William and Queen Mary. So help me God.

249. Act repealing Assertory Act, 1690

(*Acts of the Parliaments of Scotland*, IX, p. 111)

ACT RESCINDING THE FIRST ACT
OF THE SECOND PARLIAMENT, 1669

Our sovereign lord and lady the king and queen's Majesties taking into their consideration that by the second article of the grievances presented to their Majesties by the Estates of this kingdom it is declared that the first Act of the second Parliament of King Charles the Second, entitled, *Act asserting his Majesty's supremacy over all persons and in all causes ecclesiastical*,[1] is inconsistent with the establishment of the Church government now desired, and ought to be abrogated, therefore their Majesties, with advice and consent of the Estates of Parliament, do hereby abrogate, rescind and annul the foresaid Act, and declare the same in the whole heads, articles and clauses thereof to be of no force or effect in all time coming.

250. Act restoring Presbyterian clergy, 1690

(*Acts of the Parliaments of Scotland*, IX, p. 111)

ACT RESTORING THE PRESBYTERIAN MINISTERS
WHO WERE THRUST FROM THEIR CHURCHES SINCE THE 1ST OF JANUARY 1661

Forasmuch as by an Act of this present Parliament relative to and in prosecution of the Claim of Right[2] prelacy and the superiority of church officers above presbyters is abolished, and that many ministers of the Presbyterian persuasion since the first of January 1661 have been deprived of their churches or banished for not conforming to prelacy and not complying with the courses of the time, therefore their Majesties with advice and consent of the Estates of Parliament ordain and appoint, that all these Presbyterian ministers yet alive who were thrust from their charges since the first day of January 1661, or banished for not conforming to prelacy and not complying with the courses of the time, have forthwith free access to their churches, that they may presently exercise the ministry in these parishes without any new call thereto, and allows them to brook and enjoy the benefices and stipends thereunto belonging, and that for the whole crop 1689; and immediately to enter to the churches and manses where the churches are vacant, and where they are not vacant then their entry thereto is declared to be the half of the benefice and stipend due and payable at Michaelmas last for the half-year immediately preceding betwixt Whitsunday and Michaelmas, declaring that the present incumbent shall have right to the other half of the stipend and benefice payable for the Whitsunday last by-past.

And to the effect that these ministers may meet with no stop or hindrance in

---

[1] No. 231.   [2] No. 248.

entering immediately to their charges, the present incumbents in such churches are hereby appointed, upon intimation hereof, to desist from their ministry in these parishes, and to remove themselves from the manses and glebes thereunto belonging betwixt and Whitsunday next to come, that the Presbyterian ministers formerly put out may enter peaceably thereto; and appoints the Privy Council to see this Act put to execution.

251. Act re-establishing Presbyterianism, 1690

(Acts of the Parliaments of Scotland, IX, pp. 133–134)

ACT RATIFYING THE CONFESSION OF FAITH
AND SETTLING PRESBYTERIAN CHURCH GOVERNMENT

Our sovereign lord and lady the king and queen's Majesties and three Estates of Parliament conceiving it to be their bound duty, after the great deliverance that God hath lately wrought for this Church and kingdom, in the first place to settle and secure therein the true Protestant religion according to the truth of God's word as it hath of a long time been professed within this land, as also the government of Christ's Church within this nation agreeable to the word of God and most conducive to the advancement of true piety and godliness and the establishment of peace and tranquillity within this realm, . . . therefore their Majesties, with advice and consent of the said three Estates, do hereby revive, ratify and perpetually confirm all laws, statutes and Acts of Parliament made against popery and papists, and for the maintenance and preservation of the true reformed Protestant religion, and for the true Church of Christ within this kingdom, in so far as they confirm the same or are made in favour thereof.

Likewise they by these presents ratify and establish the confession of faith now read in their presence, and voted and approven by them as the public and avowed confession of this Church, containing the sum and substance of the doctrine of the reformed churches, which confession of faith is subjoined to this present Act. As also they do establish, ratify and confirm the Presbyterian Church government and discipline, that is to say, the government of the Church by kirk sessions, presbyteries, provincial synods and general assemblies, ratified and established by the 114 Act, James VI, Parl. 12, anno 1592, entitled, *Ratification of the liberty of the true kirk*, &c., and thereafter received by the general consent of this nation to be the only government of Christ's Church within this kingdom, reviving, renewing and confirming the foresaid Act of Parliament in the whole heads thereof, except that part of it relating to patronages, which is hereafter to be taken into consideration,[1] and rescinding, annulling and making void the Acts of Parliament following, viz., *Act anent restitution of bishops*, James VI, Parl. 18, cap. 2; *Act ratifying the Acts of the Assembly 1610*, James VI, Parl. 21, cap. 1; *Act anent the election of archbishops and bishops*, James VI, Parl. 22, cap. 1; Act entitled, *Ratification of the five articles of the General Assembly at Perth*, James VI, Parl. 23, cap. 1; Act entitled, *For the restitution and re-establishment of the ancient government of the Church by archbishops and bishops*, Charles II, Parl. 1, sess. 2, Act 1; *Act anent*

[1] No. 252.

the constitution of a national synod, Charles II, Parl. 1, sess. 3, Act 5; *Act against such as refuse to depone against delinquents*, Charles II, Parl. 2, sess. 2, Act 2; Act entitled, *Act acknowledging and asserting the right of succession to the imperial crown of Scotland*, Charles II, Parl. 3, Act 2;[1] Act entitled, *Act anent religion and the test*, Charles II, Parl. 3, Act 6,[2] with all other Acts, laws, statutes, ordinances and proclamations, and that in so far allenerly as the said Acts and others generally and particularly above mentioned are contrary or prejudicial to, inconsistent with or derogatory from the Protestant religion and Presbyterian government now established, and allowing and declaring that the Church government be established in the hands of, and exercised by, these Presbyterian ministers who were outed since the first of January 1661 for nonconformity to prelacy, or not complying with the courses of the time, and are now restored by the late Act of Parliament,[3] and such ministers and elders only as they have admitted or received, or shall hereafter admit or receive, and also that all the said Presbyterian ministers have and shall have right to the maintenance, rights and other privileges by law provided to the ministers of Christ's Church within this kingdom, as they are or shall be legally admitted to particular churches.

Likewise, in pursuance of the premises, their Majesties do hereby appoint the first meeting of the General Assembly of this Church as above established to be at Edinburgh the third Thursday of October next to come in this instant year 1690. And because many conform ministers either have deserted or were removed from preaching in their churches preceding the 13 of April 1689, and others were deprived for not giving obedience to the Act of the Estates made the said 13 day of April 1689, entitled, *Proclamation against the owning of the late King James, and appointing public prayers for King William and Queen Mary*, therefore their Majesties, with advice and consent foresaid, do hereby declare all the churches, either deserted or from which the conform ministers were removed or deprived as said is, to be vacant; and that the Presbyterian ministers exercising their ministry within any of these parishes, or (where the last incumbent is dead) by the desire or consent of the parish, shall continue their possession and have right to the benefices and stipends according to their entry in the year 1689, and in time coming, until the Church as now established take further course therewith.

And to the effect the disorders that have happened in this Church may be redressed, their Majesties, with advice and consent foresaid, do hereby allow the general meeting and representatives of the foresaid Presbyterian ministers and elders in whose hands the exercise of the Church government is established, either by themselves or by such ministers and elders as shall be appointed and authorized visitors by them, according to the custom and practice of Presbyterian government throughout the whole kingdom and several parts thereof, to try and purge out all insufficient, negligent, scandalous and erroneous ministers by due course of ecclesiastical processes and censures, and likewise for redressing all other Church disorders. And further it is hereby provided that whatsoever minister, being convened before the said general meeting and representatives of the Presbyterian ministers and elders, or the visitors to be appointed by them, shall either prove contumacious in not compearing or be found guilty, and

---

[1] No. 245.   [2] No. 246.   [3] No. 250.

22

shall be therefore censured, whether by suspension or deposition, they shall *ipso facto* be suspended from or deprived of their stipends and benefices, and ordains this Act to be printed and published.

252. Act abolishing lay patronage, 1690
(*Acts of the Parliaments of Scotland*, IX, pp. 196–197)
ACT CONCERNING PATRONAGES

Our sovereign lord and lady the king and queen's Majesties, considering that the power of presenting ministers to vacant churches of late exercised by patrons hath been greatly abused, and is inconvenient to be continued in this realm, do therefore, with the advice and consent of the Estates of Parliament, hereby discharge, cass, annul and make void the aforesaid power heretofore exercised by any patron of presenting ministers to any kirk now vacant, or that shall hereafter happen to vaike within this kingdom. . . .

And to the effect the calling and entering ministers in all time coming may be orderly and regularly performed, their Majesties, with consent of the Estates of Parliament, do statute and declare that in case of the vacancy of any particular church, and for supplying the same with a minister, the heritors of the said parish (being Protestants) and the elders are to name and propose the person to the whole congregation, to be either approven or disapproven by them; and if they disapprove, that the disapprovers give in their reasons to the effect the affair may be cognosced upon by the presbytery of the bounds, at whose judgment and by whose determination the calling and entry of a particular minister is to be ordered and concluded; and it is hereby enacted, that if application be not made by the eldership and heritors of the parish to the presbytery for the call and choice of a minister within the space of six months after the vacancy, that then the presbytery may proceed to provide the said parish, and plant a minister in the church *tanquam jure devoluto*. . . .

And in lieu and recompense of the said right of presentation hereby taken away their Majesties, with advice and consent foresaid, statute and ordain the heritors and life-renters of each parish, and the town councils for the burgh, to pay to the said patrons betwixt and Martinmas next the sum of six hundred merks, proportionally effeiring to their valued rents in the said parish, viz., two parts by the heritors and a third part by the life-renters, deducing always the patron's own part effeiring to his proportion as an heritor, and that upon the said patron his granting a sufficient and formal renunciation of the said right of presentation in favour of the said heritors, town council for the burgh, and kirk session. . . .

F. LAND AND PEOPLE

253. Thomas Morer on Scotland in 1689

(A Short Account of Scotland, ed. 1702)

Scotland is distinguished into Highlands and Lowlands. . . . The Highlanders are not without considerable quantities of corn, yet have not enough to satisfy their numbers, and therefore yearly come down with their cattle, of which they have greater plenty, and so traffic with the Lowlanders for such proportions of oats and barley as their families or necessities call for. They are in great subjection to their lords, who have almost an absolute power over them; so that whenever they summoned them they immediately got together and attended them whithersoever they went, though to the loss of their lives and the little fortune they had. But of late years the scene is changed; and though at this day there are divers instances to be seen of that power of their lords, yet their present case is much better, and the yoke easier than it was before. Nor are they more obedient to their lords than affectionate to their clans and the heads of their tribes or families, whom they usually have so great a regard to that they will not, as far as lies in them, suffer them to sink under any misfortune; but in case of a small estate they make an honourable contribution on their behalf, as a common duty or concern to support the credit of their Houses. . . .

The quarrels and animosities between their great ones made it always necessary in elder times to be very well armed, and the custom continues to this day, so that you shall seldom see them, though only taking the air, without sword and dirk, which is a short dagger. In war they had formerly bows and such kind of arrows as, once entered the body, could not be drawn out without tearing away the flesh with them; but now they carry muskets and other firearms. And when they are on the defensive part they depend much on the targes or targets, which are shields of that form the Latins call by the name of *clipeus*, round and equidistant from the centre, and are made of the toughest wood they can get, lined within and covered without with skins, fenced with brass nails, and made so serviceable that no ordinary bullet, much less a sword, can penetrate to injure them or their masters, who have such an artificial way of twisting themselves within the compass of these shields that it is almost a vain attempt for their enemy to seek to annoy them. And indeed they fight with too much odds when they come so near us, because they not only have the protection of their bucklers but are withal very expert at their swords, which consist of the best blades now in being, and were therefore much sought after by our officers and soldiers, who were very well furnished with them before we left the Highlands.

Once or twice a year great numbers of them get together and make a descent into the Lowlands, where they plunder the inhabitants and so return back and disperse themselves. And this they are apt to do in the profoundest peace, it being not only natural to them to delight in rapine, but they do it on a kind of principle and in conformity to the prejudice they continually have to the Lowlanders, whom they generally take for so many enemies.

The Lowlands are so called by way of comparison and as they relate to the Highlands I just spoke of. Not but that the mountains here are both numerous and lofty, and we pass not many miles without climbing some of them, so that this tract of ground, independently taken, might be very well named the hill country. Yet considering its neighbourhood to the northern provinces, whose mountains are more contiguous and of greater number, it may in some measure justify the distinction, though I should choose rather to make the difference between them on the account of the language, garb, humour and spirit of the people than the strict etymology of the word or situation of the country. . . .

The Lowlanders have plenty of most sorts of grain, especially oats and barley; and as for cattle, though they have large herds and lags of their own, yet their plenty of this kind depends much on the yearly descent of the Highlanders, who come hither with considerable droves to exchange for corn, when their own is spent at home. Their habit is mostly English, saving that the meaner sort of men wear bonnets instead of hats and plaids instead of cloaks; and those plaids the women also use in their ordinary dress when they go abroad either to market or church. They cover head and body with them, and are so contrived as to be at once both a scarf and hood. The quality go thus attired when they would be disguised, and is a morning dress good enough when some hasty business calls them forth, or when the weather disheartens them to trick themselves better.

Their language is generally English, but have many words derived from the French, and some peculiar to themselves. They are great critics in pronunciation, and often upbraid us for not giving every word its due sound, as when we call 'enough' enou, or enuff, without making it a guttural, but neglecting the 'gh' as if not written; wherein, however, they are as faulty themselves, as I showed them by divers examples in their daily discourse. . . .

This is all occurs at present concerning the Lowlands, as before distinguished. What I add more treats of the Scotch in common. . . .

The houses of their quality are high and strong, and appear more like castles than houses, made of thick stone walls, with iron bars before their windows, suited to the necessity of those times they were built in, living then in a state of war and constant animosities between their families. Yet now they begin to have better buildings, and to be very modish both in the fabric and furniture of their dwellings, though still their avenues are very indifferent, and they want their gardens, which are the beauty and pride of our English seats.

The vulgar houses, and what are seen in the villages, are low and feeble. Their walls are made of a few stones jumbled together without mortar to cement them, on which they set up pieces of wood meeting at the top, ridge-fashion, but so ordered that there is neither sightliness nor strength, and it does not cost much more time to erect such a cottage than to pull it down. They cover these houses with turf of an inch thick and in the shape of larger tiles, which they fasten with wooden pins and renew as often as there is occasion; and that is very frequently done. It is rare to find chimneys in these places, a small vent in the roof sufficing to convey the smoke away; so that considering the humility of those roofs and the gross nature of the fuel we may easily guess what a smother it makes and what little comfort there is in sitting at one of their fires. However, in their towns and cities the case is otherwise, but of them when I come to particular places. It was matter of wonder at first that so great a corn country as Scotland is should not be able to afford them straw enough to thatch the houses. But calling to mind their want of hay, which makes them employ the straw in feeding their horses as well as foddering their other cattle, I was quickly satisfied as to this point. . . .

Orchards they have few, and their apples, pears and plums are not of the best kind. Their cherries are tolerably good, and they have one sort of pear, large and well-tasted but seldom had. Wall-fruit is very rare, but for gooseberries, currants, strawberries and the like, they have of each, but growing in gentlemen's gardens; and yet from thence we sometimes meet with them in the markets of their boroughs.

They have excellent pit-coal, so bituminous and pitchy that it burns like a candle and is both pleasant and useful. But this is chiefly for their gentry and boroughs. The common people deal in peat and turf, cut and dried in the summer, and would be no bad fuel but that at first kindling it makes a very thick and offensive smother. . . .

The water is good, and they have several considerable rivers, the chief whereof which fell within my knowledge and are navigable were the Forth, the Tay and the Clyde. The first runs from Leith to Stirling, and farther upwards with tide; the next from Dundee to Perth; and the last from the Irish Sea to Glasgow–three very serviceable currents, and would contribute much to enrich the bordering places if they had sufficient shipping. This makes the trade of this kingdom inconsiderable, having, as was said, very few ships and those of light burden. With these they fetch their wines from France, and some other commodities had from thence and Ireland; but other merchandise comes at second-hand from the citizens of London and Bristol. . . .

They have many bridges for the ease and safety of travellers, very strong and well built, sometimes consisting but of one mighty arch, whose height and breadth deserves admiration. Stage coaches they have none, yet there are a few hackneys at Edinburgh, which they may hire into the country upon urgent occasions. The truth is the roads will hardly allow them those conveniencies, which is the reason that their gentry, men and women, choose rather to use their horses. However, their great men often travel with coach and six, but with so much caution that besides their other attendance they have a lusty running footman on each side the coach to manage and keep it up in rough places. . . . They have no horse posts besides those that ply betwixt Berwick and Edinburgh, and from thence to Portpatrick for the sake of the Irish packets; and, if I forget not, every town the post passes through contributes to the charges. But from Edinburgh to Perth, and so to other places, they use foot posts and carriers, which though a slow way of communicating our concerns to one another yet is such as they acquiesce in till they have a better.

The revenue of Scotland is low. Some computed it at 30,000*l.* per annum sterling in the reign of King James VI, but after the Restoration the Parliament granted King Charles II an addition, afterwards continued, besides what is raised on emergent occasions, which never amounts to a very great sum, though sometimes heavy enough considering the country. . . . As to the forces, their main dependence is on the militia and the tenures of the nobles and gentry, who are obliged to find the king so many men in time of service, and who thinking the burden too heavy to continue them long they seldom exceed forty days before they are disbanded. Yet of late years some small number of horse, foot and dragoons are kept standing, as appears in the establishments of King Charles II, 1678 and 1681. . . .

The government of Scotland is monarchical, and has been so (they say) for above two thousand years. . . . The authority of their princes was heretofore very much eclipsed by the power of their nobles, but upon the union with England the prerogative began to receive some lustre, and was at length screwed to such a pitch as to be obeyed without reserve. . . . The kings of Scotland, as of England, govern by Parliaments made out of the three estates, Lords Spiritual, Lords Temporal and Commons, which are called by the royal writ to treat of arduous matters, yet are not left to their own heads concerning the points to be debated at their sessions, but are bounded and guided by a certain number of their fellow-peers commissioned by the king, according to the usage and constitution of that kingdom. And these are commonly known by the name of the Lords of the Articles, being in number thirty-two. . . . But I should rather say this was, than that it is, the constitution of Scotland at this time, for it was one of the grievances presented to, and allowed by, King William, so that now they are, I think, left to an absolute liberty to propose what they will. . . .

They have fourteen bishops in Scotland, two whereof, viz., St. Andrews and Glasgow, have archiepiscopal dignity. They are all peers of the land, and sit in Parliament. Their revenues are not great, yet valuable considering the country. One thousand pounds sterling per year for an archbishop, and five or six hundred for a bishop, is thought a competency where provision is very cheap and a good table kept with little charges. Their not having courts or cathedrals lessens their figure; but though this want likens them the more to the Presbyterian party yet the enmity holds on, and the very name of episcopacy is (to be sure their revenues are) popish enough to pull them down.

The number of parishes in Scotland are about 900; but the ministers exceed that number, because in their larger towns every church hath two preachers for the ease of each other. The ministers are regular, and whilst episcopacy kept its standing the prelates and they wore gowns and cassocks, which, as they are garments of distinction, so they warn the wearers to walk more carefully and do nothing unbecoming their profession. They have a greater equality in their benefices than the clergy of England, few exceeding 100l. sterling, and as few below 20l., so that as the first stipend will hardly allow them to live great, the other is not so mean in that cheap kingdom but they may live without scandal. . . .

Edinburgh is in Lothian. . . . It is now the royal city, having the king's palace, the Courts of Justice and the Parliament House, which was before the reign of King James V held indifferently at Perth, Stirling or Forfar. It is seated on an hill, and consists chiefly of one fair street from west to east, about a mile long from the Castle to Holyrood House. But then we include Canongate, though a distinct corporation, and in strictness is rather the suburbs of Edinburgh than any part of the city itself, like

London and Westminster, and has the name of Canongate from a society of canons who formerly dwelt in it. The street is wide and well paved, and the Scotchman is apt to say that it is such another as Cheapside. It swells in the middle, the kennels being made on each side, so that it is commonly very clean and is thereupon their parade. . . .

Their old houses are cased with boards, and have oval windows (without casements or glass) which they open or shut as it stands with their conveniency. Their new houses are made of stone, with good windows modishly framed and glazed, and so lofty that five or six stories is an ordinary height, and one row of buildings there is near the Parliament Close with no less than fourteen. The reason of it is their scantness of room, which not allowing them large foundations, they are forced to make it up in the superstructure, to entertain comers, who are very desirous to be in or as near as they can to the city. Most of the houses, as they are parted into divers tenements, so they have as many landlords as stories; and therefore have no dependence on one another otherwise than as they stand on the same foundation, so that in this respect they may be compared to our students' apartments at the Inns of Court, which are bought and sold without regard to the chambers above or below them. Their stairs are unsightly and inconvenient, for being built out of the street for the service of every story they are sometimes so steep, narrow and fenceless that it requires care to go up and down for fear of falling. But in their new houses the contrivance is better, and the staircase being made within the yard or foundation of the building the ascent and descent is more decent and easy, and rids the street of an encumbrance which cannot be avoided in the other houses. . . .

The pride of Edinburgh is the Parliament Yard, or Close, as they call it, in the midst whereof is the effigy of King Charles II on horseback, a well-proportioned figure of stone, and natural enough. The yard is square and well paved, beautified with good buildings round about it; and the only fault is that it is no bigger, the height of the houses bearing no correspondence to the dimensions of the area.

Its western boundary is the Parliament House, a large room and high roofed. Over the entrance is the Scotch arms, with Mercy and Truth on each side, like two supporters . . . Within the room, on the south of it, is an high throne, and on each side several benches, one above another, the uppermost whereof is level with the throne and the lowest reaches the pit, well furnished with forms for the conveniency and ease of the members. Opposite to the throne, and without the area, is a pulpit, for sermons in sessions of Parliament upon special occasions. Behind the pulpit is a large partition, where strangers stand and hear the sermon, and sometimes the delator of the House; which to my thoughts were not managed with gravity enough, but was next door to wrangling.

East of this House but south of the square is the Privy Council Chamber, and not far from it the Royal Exchange, made up of a double row of shops, very small and meanly furnished. There is also another exchange inferior to this, but both above stairs and without any piece of magnificence to distinguish them from the other buildings. In the first floors level with the yard are three or four booksellers and as many goldsmiths, whose shops are sufficiently stocked to let us see their occupations and trades.

The northern boundary is the wall of the High Church, which with a few shops joining to it (leaving room for coaches to pass to the Parliament House) concludes the figure of this Close. . . .

On the west of the High Street, and a musket-shot distance from the houses, stands the Castle. . . . The Castle is certainly a strong building, both from art and nature, well stored with ordnance and other conveniencies to bear a siege, provided it be well manned, as it was not when the duke of Gordon delivered it up. . . . South of the Castle, and not far distant from it, we have the beautiful front of a large hospital, built by one Heriot, a goldsmith, for the education of 40 boys, who, if they take learning and go to the College, have an exhibition each of 7*l*. sterling or thereabouts; if put to trades, about 200 marks, or about 11*l*. sterling, for the encouragement of their masters.

South of the Cowgate and on a rising stands the College, consisting of one small quadrangle and some other lodgings without uniformity or order, built at several times and by divers benefactors, who thought probably to be better distinguished by this variety of forms and situations in those buildings. In the midst hereof is the library, a large and convenient room made about sixty years ago for that purpose. The roof is covered with lead, and is neatly kept within; well furnished with books, and those put in very good order, and cloistered with doors made of wire which none can open but the keeper, and which is thought a better way than our multitudes of chains encumbering a library, and are equally troublesome and chargeable to us. It has (as all other public libraries) many benefactors, whose books are distinguished by their several apartments, and the donors' names set over them in golden letters. . . .

The cap wherewith they graduate their scholars is round and made of velvet, like the physicians' cap with us. This they put on the head of the promoted party, and thereby signify his being called to be Master. . . . The College was built about 1581, and passes for an University, but is not really so. Yet a petition was made to King James VI to that purpose, who thereupon promised it should be done, but was not, though the instruments are ready for the royal allowance, and, as the Principal told me, wants only peace and quietness to perfect the design. The first cause of building this College was the legacy of one Mr. Clement Little, a commissary, who bequeathed his valuable study to Edinburgh and the Kirk of God, 1580; whereupon the citizens were obliged to build a convenient place for them, and accordingly did so the year following, after which additions were made from time to time till the whole came to the bulk we now see it in. Among the rest is a chapel used by the French Protestants in and about the city, and a spacious garden for the professors in common to walk and divert themselves in the evening. . . .

They have but one term in the year, beginning October the 10th and ending July the 12th, which is the time of their Act or Commencement; so that their vacation being short, and the term continued so many months (all which while the professors are very diligent) they make some amends for the years wanting in our account to make up the stated terms for receiving degrees. And so much for the College of Edinburgh, which, as an university, has the lord provost of the city for its Chancellor, and the Principal his Vice-Chancellor to govern it and dispatch business.

The east end of the great street of Edinburgh brings you to the royal palace, formerly an abbey but converted into this use by King James V, yet still retains its old name and is sometimes called the Abbey, and Holyrood House. It is a noble structure, built of stone, well carved and beautified, in the fashion of a square, with a piazza or gallery under it, from whence by several staircases they ascend to such apartments as their respect or business engage them. The gallery above is very fine, extended to a considerable length and set out with the pictures of their 112 kings, and hath also a billiard table for the diversion of the house. The lodgings are stately enough, and not meanly furnished. The house is guarded from surprise by a large court, where the soldiers draw up when they relieve one another. . . .

Here is no cathedral, and though there be a chapter when there is a bishop yet the prebendaries are little more than nominal, the stipends being deducted out of the bishop's revenue, which being not great in itself very ill affords those defalcations; and though the prebendaries demand not above 8 or 10l. yearly each of them, yet are seldom paid, and thereupon sometimes murmur. But the reason of that neglect I take to be this, that because these prebends are not given by the king or bishops, but are appendages to the neighbouring benefices and follow the presentation to such living, therefore the bishop thinks he is not bound to take that notice of them as he might otherwise do were they creatures of his own. . . .

A mile from Edinburgh is Leith, a mart town, at the mouth of the Forth, having a fine pier stretching itself a great way into the sea, and serves for the safety of the vessels and the pleasure of those who walk on it. It may be called the warehouse of Edinburgh, to supply the merchants and other citizens. It was formerly a great check to Edinburgh when King James VI was there, and often threatened them to remove his palace and courts of judicature thither to keep the citizens in better obedience. It is a thriving town, having a double advantage, the sea-trade and the citizens' recreation, to enrich it, for thither they flock by foot or in coaches to divert themselves, having no playhouse, music meetings or spring garden to tempt them to those superfluous expenses.

The second city of Scotland is Perth, or St. John's Town, because St. John is its tutelar saint or guardian. It stands on the bank of the river Tay, and not being above twenty miles from the sea is every day saluted with the tide, which brings up vessels thither. There are two long, spacious streets, besides others of less moment for inter-course, which being well paved are at all times tolerably clean. The houses are not stately, but after the Scotch way make a good appearance. . . . The trade of the town depends chiefly on linen, which the Highlanders bring thither and which they export to the value of 40,000l. sterling per annum. It was in former days the seat of divers Parliaments, is a county town governed by a lord provost and bailiffs, has the style of royal borough, with the honours and privileges of the most eminent places of Scotland; and the inhabitants speak very big whenever they have occasion to mention the city, as we see in the instrument of burgess-ship given us, and which is a civility and honour they confer on strangers. . . .

While we stayed at Perth our curiosity led us to visit Scone, being a walk of pleasure or short mile thither. It was formerly a monastery, though now made a lay mansion belonging to my Lord Stormont, and has a few houses about it to the bulk of a country village, but hardly fit to be called a town. The honour of the place is a little chapel, where the kings of Scotland are usually crowned, and where King Charles II took the Covenant when he was in that kingdom. . . .

From Perth we marched northerly to Forfar, a place of no great noise, saving that it is a country town, a royal borough, and anciently the seat of several Parliaments; governed by a provost and bailiffs, and had once the king's palace, though now we scarce see the ruins of it. While we quartered here we took the air so far as Dundee, a very pretty town seated at the bottom of an hill almost at the mouth of the river Tay, which runs up to Perth. It is furnished with two or three small piers for the conveniency of shipping, and the buildings are such as speak the substance and riches of the place. It is a royal borough, and considerable for its trade, wherein it has supplanted St. Andrews on the other side the river and about seven miles from it. Here we were handsomely treated at the charges of the Corporation, who complimented us with burgess-ships. . . .

Returning back to Perth, we received orders to march to Glasgow, and in our way thither we passed through Dunblane, a bishop's see, but a very ordinary town, without anything worthy remembrance but Bishop Leighton's new library; a large church much abused by the wild Cameronians; and the late bishop's kindness, whose name is Douglas, a very reverend and hospitable gentleman, and entertained me courteously.

About four miles farther was Stirling, a fine town and in two instances a copy of Edinburgh, as standing on a considerable rising and having a strong castle to defend it, built on a steep rock and by a great river, over which is a long stone bridge and a strong gate. It is a town of good trade, having the benefit of the Forth to bring up vessels to it. It is a royal borough, was formerly the king's palace and seat of Parliaments, is well built, and continues still in much reputation and honour. . . . Twelve miles hence, and the midway between Stirling and Edinburgh, is the town of Linlithgow, a royal borough with a large building called the Castle, and was formerly the residence of several princes. It is still owned for the king's house, but used by my Lord Livingstone, and consists of a stately quadrangle, in the midst of which is a fine fountain. . . .

It is from Linlithgow to Glasgow 24 miles, and we go through Falkirk and Kilsyth, two boroughs of royalties. . . . Glasgow is a place of great extent and good situation, and has the reputation of the finest town in Scotland, not excepting Edinburgh, though the royal city. The two main streets are made crosswise, well paved and bounded with stately buildings, especially about the centre, where they are mostly new, with piazzas under them. It is a metropolitan see, and at the upper end of the great street stands the archbishop's palace, formerly without doubt a very magnificent structure, but now in ruins and has no more left in repair than what was the ancient prison and is at this time a mean dwelling. A little higher is the church, a great fabric with a lofty steeple, built by St. Mungo, who lies buried between four pillars in that part of the church they call the barony, for it is divided into three parts, the upper, the lower, and the barony, which is assigned the country people thereabouts for their use, and the town has nothing to do with it. This cathedral, with one large church more in the heart of the city where the magistrates attend, are all the places of public worship at Glasgow, the nest of fanaticism and the most factious town in all that kingdom. The yard belonging to the cathedral is the common burial-place, and the fence or wall consists of continued monuments or stones erected for the memory of the dead, a pretty device and useful.

From hence to the river the city reaches a mile in length, the half of which is upon a declension. This river is a great current, called the Clyde, and conduces much to the riches of the inhabitants, and makes it the most considerable town of that nation. Here are several hospitals or houses of charity; and many spires, more for ornament than use; and a tolbooth or common hall, very magnificent (as most of them are in the towns of Scotland) for public entertainments or city business.

Here is an university, but it consists only of one college, as at Edinburgh; erected by Archbishop Turnbull, with the consent of King James II and by the bull of Pope Nicholas V about 1451, who endowed it with the privileges of the University of Bologna. What those privileges were is uncertain, the bull and other evidences being conveyed away by Archbishop Beaton at the time of the Reformation; so that being altogether left in the dark and no little distraction, there being no face of an university for several years, it pleased King James VI by a charter of erection to found it *de novo* and give it the privileges of an university, endowing it with such a revenue as he thought convenient (without respect had to any former foundation), but short of what it had before, as appears by some records they afterwards recovered and by the directions of which they govern themselves as far as is agreeable with the present state and good of the society.

The college is composed of a neat quadrangle with some other buildings, well digested and uniform enough. The front or entrance is stately and well carved, and is in the main street. Behind is a garden, very large and which they are surrounding with an high wall. It has a small chapel, several schools and a common hall. The library is well digested, and the books so ordered, not as at Edinburgh where they are marshalled and distinguished according to the benefactors, but as the sciences direct them; and the superscriptions serve only to show what books they are and not who gave them. The college has (besides students and servants) a Chancellor, Rector, Dean of the Faculty, Principal and four Regents, according to King James VI's foundation and the charter of King Charles I (1630), confirmed by Parliament (1633), saving that there is added to the preceding number one Professor of Divinity. . . .

There are no students belonging to the college such as we call foundation-men or scholars; and as for the rest who meet in term-time they are indifferently habited with red gowns and long sleeves, though of several years and classes. These youths for the first five days in the week are taught, examined, and dispute in their proper schools; but on Saturday they meet all in the common hall, and from 10 to 12 in the morning exercise themselves on those theses or subjects the regents propose to debate upon. . . .

Glasgow is as factious as it is rich; yet the most considerable persons for quality are well disposed to the church. But the disaffected make up that defect with number, and sometimes call the hillmen or field conventiclers to assist them. Over the river Clyde is a very fine bridge with a great number of arches, and on the other side is a little town, which is the suburbs of Glasgow and is as Southwark to London. . . .

We went from Glasgow to Ayr, a country town and royal borough situate near the Clyde, the same river that runs up to Glasgow, from whence it is distant 24 miles. Here are seen the ruins of a citadel built by Oliver Cromwell about the year 1652, and was demolished after the Restoration. In this town King William and Queen Mary were first proclaimed and owned for their sovereign. The town is pretty enough, and had formerly a very great trade, but is much impaired of late years by the losses they have sustained, so that now they give way to the success of Glasgow, and choose rather to freight other men's ships than be at the hazard to build any of their own. There is a small river runs by the town side into the Clyde, with a good bridge upheld by four arches. . . .

It is from hence to Loch Ryan 34 miles and ill way; but at length we shipped ourselves and horses, and the next morning, the admiral firing a gun, the fleet immediately prepared for sailing. And in seven hours time, by the help of a strong north-east wind, we got to the lough of Carrickfergus, and the next morning, being October 17, 1689, we landed safely at Belfast in the kingdom of Ireland.

254. Letter from Major Robert Duncanson to Captain Robert Campbell of Glenlyon authorizing the massacre of Glencoe, 1692

(Papers illustrative of the Highlands of Scotland, 1689–1696, ed. J. Gordon, p. 72)

You are hereby ordered to fall upon the rebels, the Macdonalds of Glencoe, and put all to the sword under seventy. You are to have a special care that the old fox and his sons do upon no account escape your hands. You are to secure all the avenues, that no man escape. This you are to put in execution at five of the clock precisely; and by that time, or very shortly after it, I will strive to be at you with a stronger party. If I do not come to you at five, you are not to tarry for me, but to fall on. This is by the king's special command, for the good and safety of the country, that these miscreants be cut off root and branch. See that this be put in execution without feud or favour, else you may expect to be dealt with as one not true to king nor government, nor a man fit to carry commission in the king's service.

Expecting you will not fail in the fulfilling hereof, as you love yourself, I subscribe these with my hand at Ballachulish, February 12, 1692.

ROBERT DUNCANSON

255. Charter of the Darien Company, 1695

(Acts of the Parliaments of Scotland, IX, pp. 377–381)

ACT FOR A COMPANY TRADING TO AFRICA AND THE INDIES

Our sovereign lord taking into his consideration that by an Act passed in this present Parliament, entitled, *Act for encouraging of foreign trade*, his Majesty for the improvement thereof did, with advice and consent of the Estates of Parliament, statute

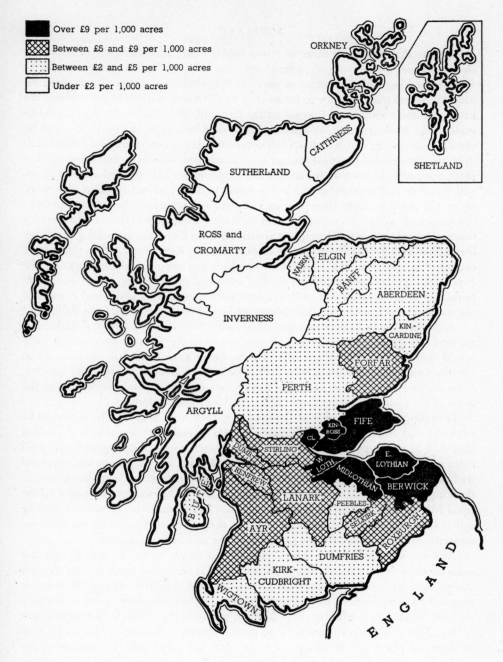

ORKNEY

SHETLAND

CAITHNESS

SUTHERLAND

ROSS and
CROMARTY

ELGIN

NAIRN

BANFF

ABERDEEN

KIN-
CARDINE

INVERNESS

FORFAR

PERTH

ARGYLL

FIFE

KIN-
ROSS

CL.

STIRLING

DUMB.

BUTE

RENFREW

W.
LOTH.

MIDLOTHIAN

E.
LOTHIAN

BERWICK

LANARK

PEEBLES

AYR

SELKIRK

ROXBURGH

DUMFRIES

KIRK-
CUDBRIGHT

WIGTOWN

E N G L A N D

13. SCOTLAND

SHOWING DISTRIBUTION OF WEALTH AS INDICATED BY THE APPORTIONMENT OF
THE CESS OF 1696

and declare that merchants more or fewer may contract and enter into such societies and companies for carrying on of trade as to any subject of goods or merchandise to whatsoever kingdoms, countries or parts of the world, not being in war with his Majesty, where trade is in use to be, or may be followed, and particularly, beside the kingdoms and countries of Europe, to the East and West Indies, the Straits, and to trade in the Mediterranean, or upon the coast of Africa, or in the northern parts, or elsewhere as above; which societies and companies, being contracted and entered into upon the terms and in the usual manner as such companies are set up and in use in other parts, consistent always with the laws of this kingdom, his Majesty with consent aforesaid did allow and approve, giving and granting to them and each of them all powers, rights and privileges as to their persons, rules and orders that by the laws are given to companies allowed to be erected for manufactories; ... and his Majesty understanding that several persons, as well foreigners as natives of this kingdom, are willing to engage themselves with great sums of money in an American, African and Indian trade, to be exercised in and from this kingdom, if enabled and encouraged thereunto by the concessions, powers and privileges needful and usual in such cases: therefore, and in pursuance of the foresaid Act of Parliament, his Majesty, with advice and consent of the said Estates of Parliament, doth hereby make and constitute John, Lord Belhaven,[1] ... with such others as shall join with them within the space of twelve months after the first day of August next,[2] and all others whom the foresaid persons and these joined with them, or the major part of them being assembled, shall admit and join into their joint stock and trade, who shall all be reputed as if herein originally inserted, to be one body incorporate, and a free incorporation with perpetual succession, by the name of the Company of Scotland trading to Africa and the Indies.

Providing always, ... that of the fund or capital stock that shall be agreed to be advanced and employed by the foresaid undertakers and their co-partners the half at least shall be appointed and allotted for Scottish men within this kingdom who shall enter and subscribe to the said company before the first day of August one thousand six hundred and ninety-six years. And if it shall happen that Scotsmen living within this kingdom shall not betwixt and the foresaid term subscribe for and make up the equal half of the said fund or capital stock, then and in that case allenarly it shall be and is hereby allowed to Scotsmen residing abroad, or to foreigners, to come in, subscribe and be assumed for the superplus of the said half, and no otherwise. ...

And the said company is hereby empowered to equip, fit, set out, freight and navigate their own or hired ships in such manner as they shall think fit, and that for the space of ten years from the date hereof, ... and that from any of the ports or places of this kingdom, or from any other ports or places in amity or not in hostility with his Majesty, in warlike or other manner, to any lands, islands, countries or places in Asia, Africa or America, and there to plant colonies, build cities, towns or forts, in or upon the places not inhabited, or in or upon any other place by consent of the natives or inhabitants thereof and not possessed by any European sovereign, potentate, prince or state, and to provide and furnish the foresaid places, cities, towns or forts

---

[1] Twenty names in all are given, half of them those of London merchants, and half those of Scottish merchants and men of affairs.   [2] 1 August 1695.

with magazines, ordnances, arms, weapons, ammunition and stores of war, and by force of arms to defend their trade and navigation, colonies, cities, towns, forts and plantations and other effects whatsoever, as also to make reprisals, and to seek and take reparation of damage done by sea or by land, and to make and conclude treaties of peace and commerce with the sovereigns, princes, estates, rulers, governors or proprietors of the foresaid lands, islands, countries or places in Asia, Africa or America; providing always, . . . that all ships employed by them shall return to this kingdom with their effects, under the pain of confiscation, forfeiture and seizure of the ship and goods in case of breaking of bulk before their return, excepting the case of necessity, for preserving the ship, the company and loading allenarly.

And his Majesty, with consent aforesaid, doth further statute and ordain, that none of the lieges of this kingdom shall or may trade or navigate to any lands, islands, countries or places in Asia or Africa in any time hereafter, or in America for and during the space of thirty-one years, to be counted from the passing of this present Act, without licence and permission in writing from the said company, . . . excepting always and without prejudice to any of the subjects of this kingdom to trade and navigate during the said space to any part of America where the colonies, plantations or possessions of the said company shall not be settled. . . .

And further it is hereby statute that all ships, vessels, merchandise, goods and other effects whatsoever belonging to the said company shall be free of all manner of restraints or prohibitions, and of all Customs, taxes, cesses, supplies or other duties imposed or to be imposed by Act of Parliament or otherwise for and during the space of twenty-one years, excepting always the whole duties of tobacco and sugar that are not of the growth of the plantations of the said company. . . .

256. Education Act, 1696
(*Acts of the Parliaments of Scotland*, x, pp. 63–64)
ACT FOR SETTLING OF SCHOOLS

Our sovereign lord considering how prejudicial the want of schools in many places have been, and how beneficial the establishing and settling thereof in every parish will be, to this Church and kingdom, therefore his Majesty, with the advice and consent of the Estates of Parliament, statutes and ordains that there be a school settled and established and a schoolmaster appointed in every parish not already provided by advice of the heritors and minister of the parish; and for that effect that the heritors in every parish meet and provide a commodious house for a school, and settle and modify a salary to a schoolmaster, which shall not be under one hundred merks nor above two hundred merks, to be paid yearly at two terms, Whitsunday and Martinmas, by equal portions, and that they stent and lay on the said salary conform to every heritor's valued rent within the parish; . . . and if the heritors or major part of them shall not convene, or being convened shall not agree among themselves, then and in that case the Presbytery shall apply to the commissioners of the supply of the shire, who, or any five of them, shall have power to establish a school, and settle and modify a salary for a schoolmaster not being under one hundred merks nor above two hundred merks yearly as said is, and to stent and lay on the same upon the heritors conform to their valued rent, which shall be as valid and effectual as if it had been done by the heritors themselves. . . .

257. Edmund Calamy on Scotland in 1709
(An Historical Account of My Own Life, ed. J. T. Rutt, II, pp. 144–223)

This year (1709) I took a journey into North Britain, and travelled upwards of twelve hundred miles. . . . I had been oft earnestly invited into North Britain by my good friend Mr. Carstares and many others, and had promised to attempt it some time or other, and this time seemed as convenient as any; for the union having been so lately compassed, a friendly correspondence between the brethren there and us in South Britain was thought very desirable. I was also willing to know the state of their universities, because my eldest son, bred at the Grammar School in Westminster, was in a little time to be sent to one place or other in order to academical education. . . .

We set forward in April, on Monday morning, reached York Friday evening, and continued there till Monday morning following. Dr. Coulton, the worthy pastor of a congregation there, treated us with abundant respect and civility. . . . Thence towards Newcastle, a close and smoky place, remarkable for traffic and the riches and plenty usually attending. We stayed here but one night, yet saw the Town House, Exchange and Custom House. Next morning we went forwards for Scotland. Mr. Bennet, minister of the chief congregation in that town, bore us company. We passed through Morpeth and Alnwick in our way to Berwick, and there had some free conversation with Mr. Horsley and Dr. Harle, the dissenting ministers. . . .

Next day we went for Dunbar, where we had a sight of that neck of land (not a mile and a half from sea to sea) in which Cromwell and his army were shut up, as in a pound, in 1650, when he was in so much danger and afterwards gained so great a victory over the Scottish army. Leaving my company behind in bed I the next morning (Saturday), with Mr. Lowe and my servant, rode to Edinburgh to get lodgings before the rest arrived. We got there by ten o'clock, and were soon provided, and by three o'clock the rest arrived. We had presently a great number of visitors, ministers, gentlemen and citizens vying with each other who should show us most civility.

Monday, I went into the Assembly, conducted by Mr. Carstares, the earl of Glasgow sitting as the queen's Commissioner and Mr. Currey, of Haddington, Moderator. I was placed upon a bench at the foot of the throne, at the right hand of the Moderator, and had liberty to attend from day to day and hear all that passed, making my remarks and observations. To get the better insight into their affairs I not only went into the Committee of Overtures and the Committee of Bills, but had a meeting every evening over a glass of wine which had in it one out of each of their synods, who by kindly giving me an account of what had passed in their respective synods with regard to the several matters laid before their General Assembly gave me a clear and distinct view of their proceedings. . . .

The close of the Assembly was to me peculiarly agreeable. Soon as all the business was gone through, Lord Glasgow, the High Commissioner, made an handsome speech, returning them thanks in her Majesty's name and in his own for their unanimity and dispatch, the zeal they had on all occasions shown for the government and the many expressions of their respect for him; at the same time, in a very obliging manner, taking particular notice of the Moderator and his prudent conduct. Then he appointed another General Assembly to meet about that time twelvemonth.

Afterwards the Moderator, in the name of the whole Assembly, returned thanks to the Lord Commissioner for all the expressions of his kind regard; and to all the members for their harmony among themselves, concern for the public and respect for him, who hoped they would overlook and forgive the unwilling failures and infirmities he had been chargeable with in that difficult station to which they had chosen him. Then, without the least word as to any inherent power of the Church to fix the time (which had formerly occasioned such warm debates), he proposed the same day as had been mentioned by the Commissioner for the next General Assembly. Then they, with one consent, sang the hundred and thirty-third psalm throughout. I must freely own I never heard that psalm sung by any company with more life and vigour, or with more appearance of joy and warm devotion; upon which they broke up and parted, full of the utmost content and satisfaction, blessing God and applauding the government. . . .

I took opportunities, as they offered, of seeing what was most curious in Edinburgh. The principal street I must own to be the finest (of a single street) that I ever saw. The houses are commonly seven stories high; and in the Parliament Close several are fourteen stories, all built of stone. For its bigness, this city is reckoned as populous as any in Europe. At the end of it stands the royal palace of Holyrood House, a handsome building. . . . I saw there, among other things, the long gallery in which are the pictures of the kings of Scotland, down from Fergus I. I saw also the Castle, which stands on so high, hard and steep a rock at the other end of the city. It is, undoubtedly, a place of great natural strength, but seemed when I saw it to be ill provided with ammunition; and as far as I could perceive very few of the guns were fit for service, a thing freely complained of afterwards when the Pretender made his descent upon North Britain. In this Castle, since the union of the two kingdoms, they keep the crown, sceptre and sword of state, in an iron chest with several locks and keys. They are not to be seen unless they that keep the several keys are all present at the same time, which, I was informed upon the spot, had never been known since the union. I saw also Heriot's Hospital, which is well endowed, carefully managed, and justly esteemed a noble charity; and the Anatomy Hall, very commodious for the purpose. . . .

The college is a good building, with three courts. There is a high tower over the great gate, which looks to the city. The public schools are large and convenient. There are also accommodations in the college for a number of students to lodge, though they are seldom made use of but by those in meaner circumstances. There are also handsome dwellings for the professors and Principal, with good gardens. At another time I spent an afternoon in the Advocates' Library, which is large and well furnished. There is also a large collection of medals and coins, made by Mr. Sutherland, some of which are very nice and curious.

One passage as to their Parliament House I must not forget. Walking one afternoon in the close adjoining, a man stepped to me with a key in his hand, asking if I was disposed to take a view of their Parliament House. I presently made answer that I fully intended to have a sight of it before I left Edinburgh, but that was not a convenient time, because I was expecting a gentleman whom I had appointed to meet me there. He replied that he would leave a youth upon the spot, with orders to let any gentleman he should observe walking there know how I was employed, and that I should be with him presently. He added it would be a pleasure to him to gratify a stranger (as he perceived me to be) with the sight.

He carried me through the several apartments, telling me that this was for such a purpose and that for another; in such a place the officers of the crown used to sit; there such and such persons commonly sat. As he was talking he mixed sighs with his words. I asked him the occasion, and he made me this reply, that it forced sighs from him to think that all this was now no more. I told him it was to be hoped the union would compensate for anything formerly among them that would now be wanting.

Upon coming out I was about to give the honest man somewhat for his pains. He seemed to resent it, that I should offer anything of that nature, telling me that he had not so mercenary a spirit as to have attempted to put me upon a thing of that kind if he had expected anything in return, and that it was a pleasure to him to be able in such a way to pay his respects to a stranger. I have often thought that a stranger might walk long enough with us where there was anything to be seen, in London or Westminster, before he would meet with like treatment.

The first Lord's Day after I reached Edinburgh I was an hearer in the New Church. There were many noblemen present, the magistrates of the city and members of the Assembly. The auditory was much crowded, as was the case also in Glasgow and Aberdeen. . . . It was their usual way to expound some portion of Scripture during about half an hour, which they called lecturing. After a short prayer a sermon followed of the same length. They usually take as much pains in studying for lecturing as for sermons, and some a great deal more. The second Lord's Day I was desired by Mr. Carstares to give them a sermon in the New Church. Though it was hard upon me to forbear the use of notes in the pulpit, yet I could not refuse to comply with the motion. . . .

Soon after, I was invited to dinner by Sir Patrick Johnston, one of the Commissioners for the Union and afterwards terribly insulted by the mob on that account. He was lord provost, and entertained us very handsomely. I was, according to their usual compliment, made a free burgess and guild brother of Edinburgh, and presented with my burgess ticket without any charge. This they reckon one of the greatest compliments they can pass upon strangers. . . .

A few days after, Principal Carstares, calling on me in the morning, told me that at a meeting of the masters of their college (of which, by the way, I had not the least notice) it had been determined not to let me go from among them without conferring a token of their respect in an academical way. I told him I was very thankful (as I had good reason) for the many civilities already received, for which I was at a loss how to make them a suitable return. He said they had agreed to present me with a diploma for a doctorate, and begged my acceptance of it. My reply was that if they would make me a Master of Arts I should not at all demur upon accepting it, but as for anything farther I begged their excuse and desired it might be waived, and that for this reason among others, that it would look like affectation and a piece of singularity for me to take the title of Doctor when so many of my superiors went without it.

To which he replied that he found the very same thing as he mentioned was designed by other academies in their parts when I came to visit them; that they would express their respect in that way; that they of Edinburgh were desirous to be first; that I should hardly escape it in other places; that they should think I affronted them if I refused their intended civility; and that the method they had determined to take would effectually prevent any charge of affectation or singularity, for at the time they paid this respect to me they would also send a diploma for a Doctor's degree to Mr. Daniel Williams and Mr. Joshua Oldfield. As matters then stood I was apprehensive that my refusing the offer would have been thought a piece of rudeness, and thereupon I submitted. . . .

Though it was my design, from first going into North Britain, to make my chief and longest stay at Edinburgh, yet being there I was for seeing other places also. . . . Therefore after taking leave of my friends at Edinburgh, with hearty thanks for all their civilities, and a cold treat given the Principal and Masters of the College one evening (which was all that I could prevail with them to accept), I left that city to go to Aberdeen. . . .

We went directly to Lord Hopetoun's, a noble seat upon the Firth of Forth, new-built after the modern form with apartments sufficient for several noble families. . . . From thence we took water at Queensferry, crossed the firth and landed at Kinghorn, whence we went to Kirkcaldy and Dysart, at which we lodged. . . . From thence, the next morning, we went for St. Andrews, another of the Scottish universities. . . . We visited the three colleges in this city, St. Salvator's, St. Mary's and St. Leonard's. The masters were from home, except my old acquaintance, Principal Haddow, one of my fellow-students at Utrecht. Their colleges are much decayed. The great church appears by its ruins to have been an exceeding large and very noble structure; some say the largest in Christendom, being seven feet longer and two broader than St. Peter's at Rome. . . .

The next morning we crossed the Tay in a ferry-boat, and left the beautiful town of Dundee a little on our left hand. After landing we went for Forfar, where we found the Presbyterians, though of the church legally established, far from beloved. . . We went from thence to Montrose, by the sea-side, and there lodged. That seems to be a pretty town, and to stand well for trade. The next day we carried provisions with us, being to pass through a poor country, and came at night to Aberdeen. There are two towns of that name, Old Aberdeen and New, a mile distant from each other. One stands upon the Don and the other upon the Dee. We went first to the New Town. . . . We afterwards met with the utmost civility during the whole of our stay, and found this one of the politest towns in North Britain.

Salmon, with us so dear, is here extremely cheap. Being so informed I was for making trial, and accordingly bought in the common market as good a salmon for twelve pence as one need desire to see. I told our landlady the price of it, as thinking I had enough in conscience for my money. She told me I was imposed on, and that if she had gone to market they would not have had the face to have asked her above two groats for the very same fish, and very probably might have taken six pence.

The next day we saw the Marischal College, where Principal Anderson and Professor Smith (both afterwards ejected at the visitation of the College, for being in the interest of the Pretender) were exceedingly civil. The latter presented me with several things he had printed. We were much pleased with the pictures of men of letters in their long gallery, and afterwards took a view of the town, and were everywhere treated with abundance of respect. . . .

The day following we were invited to Old Aberdeen, where stands King's College, which has produced a number of learned men; but we found the building greatly decayed. . . . Before I left my inn in the morning I was given to understand that the masters of the College intended that afternoon to confer a degree upon me in form and with solemnity in their chapel. That I might not be deficient in due respect I bespoke a supper to be ready that evening for the entertainment of the masters and all the servants of the College, leaving it entirely to the landlady to provide what she thought proper and handsome and that would be agreeable upon such an occasion, reckoning there would be near half a hundred persons present. When we returned after dinner from the river to the College we were carried into the chapel, where Dr. Middleton, who was then Principal (and had been dean of that diocese in the episcopal times), in a most respectful manner officiated in conferring on me the degree of D.D. Professor Cumin (who bore me company from Edinburgh) at the same time took the degree of Doctor of Laws. After viewing the library, which is not very large, but lately improved by Dr. Fraser, who has lived so long and is so well known in England, having a place many years in Chelsea College, we adjourned to our inn, where there was an handsome supper provided, with which the gentlemen seemed well pleased.

The next morning, after thanks returned for all civilities received, we returned to New Aberdeen, which is a well-built town and has a pretty trade, both for salmon and the finest knit worsted stockings anywhere to be met with. I heard of some of five guineas a pair, the beauty of which is best seen through glasses. Those of two guineas a pair were very common. We there waited upon the provost, at his desire, and received burgess tickets which were got ready for us, were treated very civilly, and at length left the town. . . .

Some were pressing for our going yet farther north into the shire of Moray, which, they say, is the finest country in all North Britain, having large woods of fir trees and plenty of provisions of all sorts. And it was moved that we should go to Elgin, where may be seen the ruins of a cathedral that for magnificence and fine architecture was scarce exceeded by any in Europe; and to Inverness, the people of which town are said to be very polite, and to express themselves in better language than they commonly do at Edinburgh. But we were generally inclined by this time to look homeward, the rather because our horses were hard put to it. Though we could get as many oats as we desired, there was no hay to be had upon any terms; and our beasts could not, like those of that country, take up with straw. . . . We therefore determined to return, and went back again to Montrose, and so by Brechin and Auchterhouse to Perth. . . .

I would very willingly have spent a Lord's Day at Perth, and have taken that opportunity of being at one of their communions; but as things now stood with me it would have broken all my measures. Therefore we set out the next morning for Stirling, . . . a very handsome town, and manifestly one of the keys of the country because of its commanding a passage over the Forth. Here is a stately stone bridge, of four large arches, with an iron gate in the middle. Ships come up to the bridge at a full tide, but the haven lies a little below it. The Castle is strong both by art and nature. . . . We were very civilly treated both by the minister and the provost, and presented with burgess tickets.

After a day's stay we went for Glasgow, another of the universities of North Britain and as pleasant a place as any I have seen in our king's dominions. This city is well built. The four principal streets cross one another, and divide it into four equal parts, each adorned with public buildings. The College is a good building, and so is the Tollbooth or town-house. It has a lofty tower, with melodious bells which chime every two hours. The chief church is very large, and of the Gothic sort. The church-yard has as many odd epitaphs in it as one shall commonly meet with. The College library has a good collection of books and some manuscripts. Among the rest there is a second volume of Calderwood's *History of the Church of Scotland*. In it are also preserved several stones with Latin inscriptions taken out of the old Roman wall in the neighbourhood and kept in very good order. This city is generally reckoned to have gained most by the union. Its traffic is much advanced, and its wealth increased, by reason of its standing so well for the West India and plantation trade.

Spending a Lord's Day here I, being desired, preached in the new church to as fine an auditory as I have seen. The church is built in the Roman form, like the Theatre at Oxford, without pillars, so that everyone may see the pulpit and all hear commodiously without any occasion for the minister's straining his voice. On the left hand of the pulpit were divers of the nobility that lived in or near the city; on the right hand the masters and scholars of the University, with their beadles in their formalities. Right before sat the magistrates, in great state and order. The rest of the pews, both above and below, were filled with citizens and strangers. . . .

Principal Stirling was (as before intimated) my very good friend, and seemed from my first appearing there to study to express his respect in all ways possible in his own house and in all company. He introduced me to several persons of distinction, brought me to great freedom with the masters, and at last would oblige me a third time to receive a Doctor's degree, which he did in such a way as that I could not have demurred upon accepting it without manifest rudeness, and gave me my diploma in a silver box. They were also pleased to send a diploma for a Doctor's degree at the same time in a silver box to Mr. Daniel Williams of London, by Mr. George Smith, who, having pursued his studies for some years in that university, was now about leaving it and returning home with us.

After so many civilities shown, the gentlemen of the College, instead of receiving a treat from me in token of my gratitude, would needs invite me to an entertainment, and a noble one it was. I never drank better French claret than upon that occasion. All that I was able to prevail for was that, spending a few hours with me in the evening before I left them, they would eat a cold fowl and ham and tongues with me to relish a glass of wine the better. I had also many civilities from the magistrates, and, among others, was presented with a burgess ticket.

The masters of the College were so complaisant as, most of them, to accompany me out of town as far as Hamilton. In our way we went over Bothwell Bridge, where the duke of Monmouth routed them that appeared in arms in King Charles's time. When we came to Hamilton, Principal Stirling sent his servant to the palace to wait on the old duchess, with his humble duty to her grace and to let her know that such persons were there and desired her grace's leave to see the palace at a time convenient. The servant brought back word that her grace expected the Principal and me to come and dine with her; and if the rest would come after dinner they should have liberty of seeing what was to be seen. . . .

Taking leave of the duchess we went to our inn, where returning abundant thanks to the Principal and the masters we that were now going for South Britain mounted our horses and went forward towards that which they commonly call the western road, which is by the way of Carlisle. We got that afternoon to Douglas. . . . From thence we went the next morning to Drumlanrig, belonging to the duke of Queensberry. The house is plain, but the gardens are fine, considering how far they lie towards the north. . . . From thence we went to Dumfries, a large town, good buildings in it, and a considerable trade. . . . The next day, through a pretty difficult way, in which we were often forced to be making inquiry, we made a shift to get to Carlisle, after having spent about five weeks in North Britain.

As we everywhere met with great civility, which we have reason thankfully to own, so was it our common sense and apprehension that those of North Britain, speaking generally, are much more civil to strangers than we in the south. Nor could we help making other remarks, as the course of our conversation lay. If they have not among them in North Britain many scholars of the first rank, they yet have many of a middle size, who have a competent share of knowledge and are well furnished for their proper offices in their several stations. They improve considerably by being sent abroad, and have opportunities given them to see the world, for which they have prudently provided by the support of a number that are students of divinity, to whom this course is mighty advantageous.

As for the children of their families of distinction, they are commonly sent abroad for education very young, by which they are many ways exposed; and it is to be feared that this in time may prove to have bad consequences. Were but care taken to encourage some learned foreigners to come amongst them, and to have suitable masters to teach to ride the great horse and other exercises proper for persons of quality; and were the children of their nobility and gentry kept and trained up in their own colleges at home, not going abroad till they came towards manhood, they would then see the world more to advantage, and be more likely to be useful at home afterwards than going abroad so early as is now common.

They have too many small bursaries in their colleges, which are temptations to the

MORER ———
CALAMY ‹———

Aberdeen

Brechin   Montrose
Forfar
Auchterhouse
Broughty Ferry
Perth   Dundee   St. Andrews
Kinross
Dunblane   Dysart
Stirling   Kirkcaldy   Dunbar
Kinghorn
GLASGOW   S. Queensferry   Edinburgh   Berwick
Bothwell   Linlithgow
Hamilton   Kilsyth   Falkirk   Alnwick
Ayr   Douglas   Morpeth
Newcastle
Drumlanrig
LOCH RYAN   Dumfries
Carlisle
BELFAST   Cockermouth
Whitehaven   York
Kendal
Burton
Lancaster
Preston
Wigan   Manchester

14. SCOTLAND AND NORTHERN ENGLAND

SHOWING THE ROUTES FOLLOWED BY THOMAS MORER AND EDMUND CALAMY inhabitants to breed up for the ministry more than they are able to support and provide for when they have gone through the course of their education. . . . As for the settled ministers of the Church of Scotland, though they are not so plentifully or profusely provided for as many of the established church in England yet are there none but what have a competency, whereupon to live easily and conveniently and above contempt. . . .

Carlisle . . . is a small city, but very pleasantly situated. Not finding anything to be seen here very curious we only stayed to refresh ourselves and went forward; but instead of taking the direct road for London, which goes through Penrith, we turned off to the right and went to Cockermouth and Whitehaven. . . . Whitehaven is a seaport with a custom-house, and a considerable trading town that, in a degree like Liverpool, has much increased in traffic and wealth since the Revolution and the war that followed. There we spent a Lord's Day, and on the Monday morning went for Kendal, a considerable town in Westmorland. . . . In our way . . . we went just by Windermere, so famous for the fish called chars, which come potted to London and are reckoned so very delicious. Kendal is a large populous town, noted for a woollen manufacture. We went from thence to Burton and so to Lancaster, a pretty town with a castle (made use of as a prison) standing very pleasantly. From thence we went to Preston, a very pretty town with abundance of gentry in it, commonly called Proud Preston; but I must own we there met with a great deal of civility. . . . From Preston we went to Wigan, and so to Manchester, where we spent the last Lord's Day in our journey. . . . This exceeds all the towns of that county in buildings, populousness, trade and wealth, and has a college in it, with a warden and four fellows.

Thence we came by Holmes Chapel, Newcastle-under-Lyme, Lichfield and Coventry, Daventry, Towcester, Stony Stratford and Dunstable (where some friends came to meet us, as more did the next day at Barnet) to London, after we had been about nine weeks absent, and had a great deal of reason to be very thankful that after riding over so much ground as we had done in so little time, and passing through so many changes, we should by a kind providence be brought back again in health and safety.

G. PARLIAMENT AND PUBLIC FINANCE

258. Grant of additional revenue, 1661

(*Acts of the Parliaments of Scotland*, VII, pp. 88–95)

ACT FOR RAISING THE ANNUITY OF 40,000*l.* STERLING
GRANTED TO HIS MAJESTY

The Estates of Parliament, in pursuance of their Act of the date the 22 day of this instant,[1] whereby they have made offer to his Majesty of the sum of forty thousand pounds sterling yearly during all the days of his Majesty's lifetime, towards the entertainment of any such forces as his Majesty shall think fit to raise and keep up within this kingdom, or otherwise towards the defraying of the necessary charge of his government according to his royal pleasure, appoints and ordains the said sum of forty thousand pounds sterling, being four hundred fourscore thousand pounds Scots money, to be raised, levied, collected and paid in manner underwritten, viz., ninety-six thousand pounds Scots thereof to be raised yearly of the inland salt and foreign commodities aftermentioned, to wit, threescore twelve pounds Scots upon each ton of Spanish wine, Rhenish wine, canary, malvoisie, and all other wines of the like kind; forty-eight pounds money aforesaid upon each ton of French wine; and twelve pennies money aforesaid upon each pint of vinegar;[2] . . . twelve pennies money aforesaid upon each pound of tobacco imported by the natives of this kingdom from the tobacco plantations, and three shillings upon each pound imported thence by foreigners; . . . twelve shillings upon each ell of cloth imported into this kingdom above six pounds the ell, and six shillings upon each ell of imported cloth at or below six pounds the ell; . . . twenty shillings upon each horse, eighteen shillings upon each cow, and two shillings money aforesaid upon each sheep imported into this kingdom, to be paid by the importer thereof; . . . and the remainder of the aforesaid four hundred fourscore thousand pounds Scots money, being three hundred eighty-four thousand pounds, to be raised out of the beer, ale, aqua-vitae and strong waters at the rate of two merks Scots upon each boll of malt brewed and sold within this kingdom; three shillings money aforesaid upon each pint of aqua-vitae or strong waters not made of malt brewed and sold within this kingdom; six shillings upon each pint of foreign aqua-vitae or strong waters; and twelve shillings upon each barrel of imported beer. And what this imposition shall be short of the quota of Excise imposed upon the several shires and burghs by the list underwritten, the same to be supplied by the said shires and burghs in lieu of the malt brewed in their own houses in manner after-mentioned.

As it is hereby declared that the said several shires and burghs shall be and are by these presents liable in the payment of the respective monthly proportions underwritten, viz.,

[1] 22 March. [2] Only a selection of the duties is here given.

	1661[1]	1663[2]
Shire of Edinburgh	2,664 0 0	2,140 0 0
Town of Edinburgh (with Canongate and Leith)	3,732 0 0	2,932 0 0
Haddington	1,695 0 0	1,291 0 0
Berwick	610 16 0	610 16 0
Roxburgh	784 16 0	772 16 0
Selkirk	153 10 0	147 10 0
Peebles	137 10 0	137 10 0
Lanark	968 8 0	968 8 0
Glasgow	1,744 4 0	1,076 4 0
Dumfries	576 0 0	656 0 0
Wigtown	204 12 0	271 12 0
Kirkcudbright	348 0 0	461 0 0
Ayr	1,675 16 0	1,639 16 0
Dumbarton	194 0 0	254 0 0
Bute	57 0 0	57 0 0
Renfrew	457 4 0	457 4 0
Stirling	920 8 0	960 8 0
Linlithgow	799 4 0	799 4 0
Perth	2,374 16 0	2,374 16 0
Kincardine	363 12 0	363 12 0
Aberdeen	2,518 19 0	2,418 19 0
Banff	387 3 0	447 3 0
Inverness	694 8 0	794 8 0
Elgin and Nairn	536 4 0	596 4 0
Cromarty	30 0 0	24 0 0
Argyll	193 16 0	443 16 0
Fife and Kinross	4,088 8 0	3,608 8 0
Forfar	1,084 4 0	1,024 4 0
Dundee	1,162 4 0	718 4 0
Sutherland	72 12 0	72 12 0
Caithness	133 4 0	153 4 0
Orkney and Shetland	193 16 0	243 16 0
Clackmannan	242 2 0	206 2 0
Ross	204 0 0	204 0 0

And if the Excise imposed upon the inland salt and foreign commodities shall exceed the aforesaid sum of ninety-six thousand pounds appointed by this Act to be raised of the same, then the surplus to be employed and made use of by such as shall be entrusted by his Majesty with that affair for the relief of such shires and burghs as they shall find to be overburdened or disproportioned by the foresaid list. . . .

[1] The tabular form of statement is not that adopted in the Act.
[2] For purposes of comparison this second column gives revised figures laid down two years later (*Acts of the Parliaments of Scotland*, VII, p. 469).

259. Act concerning shire elections, 1661

(Acts of the Parliaments of Scotland, VII, pp. 235–236)

ACT CONCERNING THE ELECTION AND CHARGES
OF THE COMMISSIONERS FROM THE SHIRES TO THE PARLIAMENT

The king's Majesty, considering that divers debates have formerly occurred concerning the persons who ought and should have vote in the election of commissioners from the several shires of this kingdom to Parliament, and who are capable to be commissioners to Parliaments, and that it is necessary for the good of his service that the same be cleared for the future, do therefore, with advice and consent of his Estates of Parliament, statute, enact and declare, that beside all heritors who hold a forty-shilling land of the king's Majesty *in capite*, that also all heritors, liferenters and wadsetters holding of the king, and others who held their lands formerly of the bishops or abbots and now hold of the king, and whose yearly rent doth amount to ten chalder of victual or one thousand pound, all feu duties being deducted, shall be and are capable to vote in the election of commissioners of Parliaments, and to be elected commissioners to Parliaments, excepting always from this Act all noblemen and their vassals.

And it being just that those who shall be chosen and accordingly attend his Majesty's and the kingdom's service in Parliaments have an allowance for their charges, his Majesty doth therefore with advice foresaid modify and appoint five pound Scots of daily allowance to every commissioner from any shire, including the first and last days of the Parliament, together with eight days for their coming and as much for their return from the farthest shires of Caithness and Sutherland, and proportionably at nearer distances; and that the whole freeholders, heritors and liferenters holding of the king and prince shall, according to the proportion of their lands and rents lying within the shire, be liable and obliged in payment of the said allowance, excepting noblemen and their vassals. . . .

And because at this time some commissioners of shires have been put to extraordinary expenses in providing of foot mantles for the riding of the Parliament, it is hereby statute that the commissioners shall be relieved of the prices thereof, to be given in under their hands, and that the prices of the foot mantles be raised in the same way and by the same execution with the daily allowance foresaid, the commissioners always at the rising of each Parliament making the foot mantles forthcoming to the shire to be disposed as they shall think fit.

260. Act restoring bishops to Parliament, 1662

(Acts of the Parliaments of Scotland, VII, pp. 370–371)

ACT FOR CALLING IN THE BISHOPS
TO THE PARLIAMENT

Forasmuch as the king's Majesty hath been graciously pleased to restore the Church to its ancient and right government by archbishops and bishops, dean and chapter, yet seeing by the troubles and confusions these twenty-four years past that government has been suppressed, so as their election and establishment at this time could not be in the form prescribed by the Act of Parliament by dean and chapter, his Majesty has, with advice and consent of his Estates in Parliament, thought fit to dispense with the present manner of election, and declares the same to be sufficient and good and as valid as if the same had been done by dean and chapter; and therefore his Majesty with advice foresaid ratifies and approves the same.

And considering that the clergy did always in the right constitution of Parliaments represent the first State, and that now, archbishops and bishops being restored, it is fit the Parliament be returned to its ancient constitution, and that the clergy have their place and vote in Parliament as formerly, therefore his Majesty with advice foresaid gives commission to the earls of Kellie and Wemyss, the Lord Torphichen, the lairds of Cromarty, Blackbarronie and Prestoun, the commissioners for Edinburgh, Ayr and St. Andrews, to go and in his Majesty's name invite the archbishops and bishops to come and take their place, and vote in Parliament as in former times before these troubles.

261. Constitution of the Lords of the Articles, 1663
(*Acts of the Parliaments of Scotland*, VII, p. 449)

The which day [18 June 1663] the earl of Rothes, his Majesty's Commissioner, represented to the Estates of Parliament that it was his Majesty's express pleasure that in the constitution of Parliaments and choosing of Lords of the Articles at this session and in all time coming the same form and order should be kept which had been used before these late troubles, especially in the Parliament holden in the year one thousand six hundred and thirty-three. And the manner of the election of the Lords of the Articles at that time being now seen and considered by the Estates of Parliament, they did with all humble duty acquiesce in his Majesty's gracious pleasure thus signified unto them.

And in prosecution thereof the clergy retired to the Exchequer Chamber, and the nobility to the inner house of the Session, the barons and burgesses keeping their places in the Parliament House. The clergy made choice of eight noblemen to be on the Articles, viz.,[1] . . . and the nobility made choice of eight bishops, viz.,[1] . . . . Which being done, the clergy and nobility met together in the inner Exchequer House, and having shown their elections to other, the persons elected, at the least so many of them as were present, stayed together in that room (whilst all others removed), and they jointly made choice of eight barons and eight commissioners of burghs, viz.,[2] . . . and then represented the whole elections to his Majesty's Commissioner, who, being satisfied thereof, did then with the clergy and nobility return to the Parliament House, where, the list of the eight bishops, eight noblemen, eight barons and eight burgesses being read, it was approven, and his Majesty's Commissioner did add to the list the officers of estate, and appointed the Lord Chancellor to be president in the meetings of the Lords of the Articles, who are to proceed in discharge of their trust in preparing of laws, Acts, overtures and ordering all things remitted to them by the Parliament, and in doing everything else which by the law or practice of the kingdom belonged or were proper to be done by the Lords of the Articles at any time by-gone.

[1] The eight names follow.   [2] The sixteen names follow.

262. Act imposing Cess, 1667

(Acts of the Parliaments of Scotland, VII, pp. 540–547)

ACT OF THE CONVENTION OF ESTATES OF THE KINGDOM OF SCOTLAND
FOR A NEW AND VOLUNTARY OFFER TO HIS MAJESTY
OF SEVENTY-TWO THOUSAND POUNDS MONTHLY FOR THE SPACE OF TWELVE MONTHS

The Estates of the kingdom of Scotland, . . . taking to their consideration the great happiness this kingdom doth enjoy under his Majesty's royal and wise government, . . . and withal understanding that his Majesty is still engaged in a just and necessary war against so many powerful enemies, who will probably endeavour the invading of his Majesty's dominions, do conceive themselves obliged in conscience, honour and duty to provide all suitable remedies for defence of the kingdom against all foreign invasion and other enemies whatsoever. And therefore the Convention of Estates . . . do humbly beseech his Majesty may be graciously pleased to accept the unanimous, willing and cheerful offer of a new supply of threescore and twelve thousand pounds monthly for the space of twelve months to commence from the first day of this current month of January; and the Estates do declare that this supply is over and above the former supplies of four hundred and fourscore thousand pounds granted by the late Parliament to his Majesty yearly during his lifetime, and the other supply of an hundred and thirty-three thousand pounds granted by the late Convention yearly for the space of five years, and which new supply of threescore twelve thousand pounds monthly is ordered to be raised and paid by the several shires and burghs of this kingdom according to the valuations in the year of God one thousand six hundred and sixty, and at the proportions underwritten respective, that is to say,

Shires[1]	1667			1707[2]		
	l.	*s.*	*d.*	*l.*	*s.*	*d.*
Edinburgh	3,183	8	0	264	13	4
Haddington	2,782	7	0	231	6	4½
Berwick	2,813	1	0	233	17	6¼
Roxburgh	3,686	17	6	306	10	6½
Selkirk	904	9	0	75	3	10½
Peebles	1,042	8	0	86	13	3
Lanark	3,091	12	0	257	0	8½
Dumfries	2,712	17	0	225	10	10
Wigtown	1,004	15	0	83	10	8
Kirkcudbright	1,674	11	0	139	4	4
Ayr	3,870	5	0	321	15	6
Dumbarton	764	10	0	63	11	2
Bute	308	8	3	25	10	10¼
Renfrew	1,353	7	0	112	10	3
Stirling	1,754	4	6	145	17	0

[1] The tabular form of statement is not that adopted in the Act.
[2] For purposes of comparison the figures of the land tax after the Union [No. 118] are given, in sterling.

Shires

	1667			1707		
	l.	*s.*	*d.*	*l.*	*s.*	*d.*
Linlithgow	1,169	18	0	97	5	3
Perth	5,038	14	0	418	18	4
Kincardine	984	1	0	81	16	2
Aberdeen	4,077	19	0	339	8	$1\frac{1}{4}$
Inverness	1,213	1	6	100	17	0
Ross	1,377	17	6	114	11	$2\frac{1}{4}$
Nairn	277	16	0	23	1	$10\frac{1}{2}$
Cromarty	68	5	0	5	13	$5\frac{3}{4}$
Argyll	1,947	10	9	161	18	$5\frac{1}{2}$
Fife and Kinross	5,172	0	0	430	0	3
Forfar	3,273	15	0	272	3	9
Banff	1,150	4	0	95	12	$7\frac{1}{4}$
Sutherland	336	0	0	27	18	$8\frac{3}{4}$
Caithness	599	5	0	49	16	$5\frac{1}{2}$
Elgin	1,059	5	0	88	1	$3\frac{1}{4}$
Orkney and Shetland	1,088	10	0	90	10	0
Clackmannan	352	7	3	29	5	$11\frac{1}{4}$

Cities and burghs

	1667	1678[1]	1696[1]	1707[1]		
Edinburgh	4,320	4,000	3,880	332	11	$4\frac{3}{4}$
Perth	480	462	360	38	8	3
Dundee	840	732	560	60	17	$2\frac{1}{4}$
Aberdeen	800	840	726	66	16	$11\frac{1}{4}$
Stirling	132	216	172	17	19	2
Linlithgow	216	204	156	16	19	$2\frac{1}{2}$
St. Andrews	326	278	72	14	16	0
Glasgow	780	1,440	1,800	119	15	$0\frac{1}{2}$
Ayr	168	208	128	17	5	10
Haddington	216	216	192	17	19	2
Dysart	168	96	30	7	19	$7\frac{1}{2}$
Kirkcaldy	288	276	288	22	18	11
Montrose	240	228	240	18	19	$1\frac{1}{2}$
Cupar	132	120	108	9	19	$6\frac{1}{2}$
Anstruther Easter	96	24	18	1	19	$10\frac{3}{4}$
Dumfries	200	200	230	16	12	$6\frac{3}{4}$

[1] While the apportionment of the Cess among the shires, which was controlled by Parliament, remained practically the same throughout the later Stuart period, the apportionment of their share among the royal burghs, which was controlled by the Convention of Royal Burghs, varied considerably according to real or supposed changes in the prosperity of the burghs. The three additional columns indicate the apportionment made of the tax at three dates after 1667. The figures in the last column, coming after the Union, are sterling, not Scots money [see No. 118]. The order in which the burghs are ranked is that of their traditional precedence.

Cities and burghs

	1667	1678	1696	1707		
				l.	s.	d.
Inverness	264	216	180	17	19	2
Burntisland	132	198	72	19	15	9
Inverkeithing	60	48	30	3	19	9½
Kinghorn	54	54	42	4	9	9½
Brechin	72	66	54	5	7	9
Irvine	120	108	60	8	19	7
Jedburgh	108	108	102	8	19	7
Kirkcudbright	96	96	36	7	19	7½
Wigtown	84	84	36	6	19	8
Pittenweem	80	80	30	6	13	0¼
Dunfermline	102	80	90	7	19	7½
Anstruther Wester	36	30	6	2	9	10
Selkirk	80	80	72	6	13	0¼
Dumbarton	72	60	30	4	19	6½
Renfrew	48	48	36	3	19	9½
Dunbar	132	72	60	5	19	8¼
Lanark	72	72	60	5	19	8¼
Arbroath	54	54	54	4	9	9½
Elgin	80	120	138	9	19	6½
Peebles	60	72	66	5	19	8¼
Crail	132	108	36	8	19	7
Tain	60	42	30	3	9	9¾
Culross	54	48	24	3	19	9½
Banff	40	48	42	3	19	9½
Whithorn	24	12	8	0	19	11¼
Forfar	24	24	24	1	19	10¾
Rothesay	36	36	30	2	19	10
Nairn	24	18	9	1	9	11
Forres	36	30	24	2	9	10
Rutherglen	24	18	12	1	9	11
North Berwick	24	6	6	0	9	11¾
Cullen	18	12	8	0	19	11¼
Lauder	42	36	30	2	19	10
Kintore	12	12	9	0	19	11¼
Kilrenny	18	12	8	0	19	11¼
Annan	12	12	12	0	19	11¼
Lochmaben	12	12	18	0	19	11¼
Sanquhar	12	12	6	0	19	11¼
New Galloway	6	6	6	0	9	11¾
Dingwall	12	12	8	0	19	11¼
Dornoch	18	18	18	1	9	11¾

Cities and burghs

	1667	1678	1696	1707
				l. s. d.
Queensferry	54	60	54	4 19 9
Fortrose	30	30	18	2 9 10½
Cromarty	30	30		2 9 10½
Inveraray			24	
Inverurie	18	18	12	1 9 11¾
Wick	20	20	20	1 13 3
Inverbervie		6	6	0 9 11¾
Kirkwall	·		72	4 19 9
Stranraer			12	

And to the effect this supply so cheerfully offered to his Majesty by his good subjects may be equally and justly laid on, proportioned and raised upon all persons liable, and who have any real rent in lands, teinds or otherwise within the said shires and burghs belonging to them, and that no person may have just reason to complain that they pay more nor their just proportion, the king's Majesty, with advice of his Estates, doth hereby nominate and appoint the Lords of his Majesty's Privy Council, and the senators of the College of Justice within the several respective shires where any part of their lands and estates doth lie, and also the persons underwritten within the several shires, to be commissioners. . . .

263. Thomas Middleton on the Riding of the Parliament, 1677
(J. Spottiswoode, *History of the Church of Scotland*, ed. 1677, App., pp. 33–34)

When the day comes in which the Parliament is to be held, the regalia, the crown, sceptre and sword of state, which are kept in the castle of Edinburgh, are brought down in state to the king's palace, and are to be carried by three of the ancientest earls that are upon the place, bareheaded, before the king or his Commissioner. In the great court before the king's palace all the members of Parliament do mount on horseback with footcloths, &c. The burgesses ride first; the commissioners of the shires next; then the lords, viscounts and earls, in their robes, the last of whom do carry the regalia, the Lyon Herald, with some heralds and pursuivants, riding before the Honours. Last of all, when the king is present in person, rides the Lord Chancellor, bearing the great seal; but this is not done before a Commissioner. After these rides the king or his Commissioner, with the High Constable . . . on his right hand, with a white baton in his hand, and the Great Marshal . . . on his left hand, with a silver baton in his hand. If the king be present in person the marquises and dukes ride after the earls, but if his Commissioner only be there they follow him at some distance.

At the outward gate of the Parliament House they all alight off their horses, and the High Constable receives and conducts the king to the inner gate, where he is received by the Earl Marshal and led into the House where the Parliament is held. The throne is raised six steps high with a state over it, and there the king, or his Commissioner in his absence, sits. And in the first step under him, on a bench, sits the Lord Chancellor, with other officers of state on both hands of him. In the next step under these sit the Lords of Session or judges, also the eldest sons of peers. On the right hand of the throne is the bishops' bench, that rises up three steps and rows of benches. . . . On the left hand of the throne there is another great bench of three steps and rows of benches, on which sit the nobility according to their precedency. In the middle of the floor there are two tables. On the one of them the regalia are laid, and in two great chairs by them sit the Constable and the Marshal. At the other table sits the Lord Clerk of Registers with his deputy-clerks, who are the clerks of the Parliament. There are also forms placed on the floor. Those on the right side are for the commissioners of the shires, and those on the left hand are for the commissioners of the burghs.

264. Act abolishing the Lords of the Articles, 1690

(Acts of the Parliaments of Scotland, IX, p. 113)

ACT CONCERNING THE ELECTION OF COMMITTEES OF PARLIAMENT

Forasmuch as the meeting of the Estates of this kingdom did by their vote of the 13th of April 1689 represent, amongst other grievances, that the committee of Parliament called the Articles is a great grievance to the nation, and that there ought to be no committees of Parliament but such as are freely chosen by the Estates to prepare motions and overtures that are first made in the House, therefore our sovereign lord and lady the king and queen's Majesties, with advice and consent of the Estates of Parliament, do hereby discharge and abrogate in all time coming the foresaid committee of Parliament called the Articles, and further cass and annul and rescind the 1st Act, 3rd session, Parliament first, Charles II,[1] anent the way and manner of election of the Lords of the Articles, with all other Acts, laws and constitutions establishing the said committee or Lords of Articles.

Likewise their Majesties, with advice and consent foresaid, do hereby enact and declare that this present and all succeeding Parliaments and three Estates thereof may choose and appoint committees of what numbers they please, there being always an equal number of each Estate to be chosen, viz., the noblemen by the Estate of noblemen, the barons by the Estate of barons, and the burghs by the Estate of burghs, for preparing all motions and overtures first made in the House; and they may alter and change the said committees at their pleasure, without prejudice always to the Estates of Parliament to treat, vote and conclude upon matters proponed or brought before them in plain Parliament without committees as they shall think fit, and also providing that in all committees to be hereafter appointed some of the officers of state may be present by their Majesties' or their Commissioner's appointment as to them shall seem necessary, and that to the effect and with power to the said officers of state present in the said committees freely to propose and debate allenarly, but not to vote, declaring, as it is hereby declared, that no officers of state shall be otherwise admitted in any

[1] No. 261.

committee of Parliament but as it is here allowed, without prejudice always to the Estate of the noblemen to choose such of their own bench as are officers of state to be members of the committees if they think fit.

265. Act concerning shire elections, 1690

(*Acts of the Parliaments of Scotland*, IX, p. 152)

ACT FOR AN ADDITIONAL REPRESENTATION IN PARLIAMENT
OF THE GREATER SHIRES OF THIS KINGDOM

Forasmuch as the meeting of the Estates of this kingdom did represent, amongst other grievances, that the manner and measure of the lieges their representation in Parliament is to be considered and redressed in the first Parliament, and that by an Act, James I, Parliament 7, cap. 101, the barons and freeholders may out of each shire send two or more commissioners, according to its largeness, to represent them in Parliament, and which Act is ratified in all its heads in the 11th Parliament, James VI, cap. 114; . . . therefore their Majesties, with advice and consent of the Estates of Parliament, statute and ordain that in all Parliaments, meetings, and Conventions of Estates to be holden henceforth and hereafter, the barons and freeholders of the shires after-mentioned shall add to their former representation the number of commissioners after-expressed, viz., the shire of Edinburgh, two; the shire of Haddington, two; the shire of Berwick, two; the shire of Roxburgh, two; the shire of Lanark, two; the shire of Dumfries, two; the stewartry of Kirkcudbright, one; the shire of Ayr, two; the shire of Stirling, one; the shire of Perth, two; the shire of Aberdeen, two; the shire of Argyll, one; the shire of Fife, two; the shire of Forfar, two; and the shire of Renfrew, one.

And it is hereby declared that this Act shall take effect in the next session of this Parliament, and in all Parliaments and Conventions of Estates thereafter.

266. Revenue under Anne, 1705

(*Acts of the Parliaments of Scotland*, XI, App., p. 196)

A STATE OF THE PUBLIC REVENUE OF SCOTLAND
AS IT NOW IS AND MAY AMOUNT TO

The Excise on ale and beer is 2s. sterling per Scotch gallon and now farmed for 33,500l. sterling, and if exacted in the same manner as in England may amount to	£50,000
The Customs have been let at 34,000l., and are now in time of war let for 28,500l., with a condition in the lease that upon a peace the Lords of the Treasury may let a new lease, and may amount to	50,000
The Crown rents about	5,500
The casualty of superiorities and compositions at the Exchequer *communibus annis* about	3,000

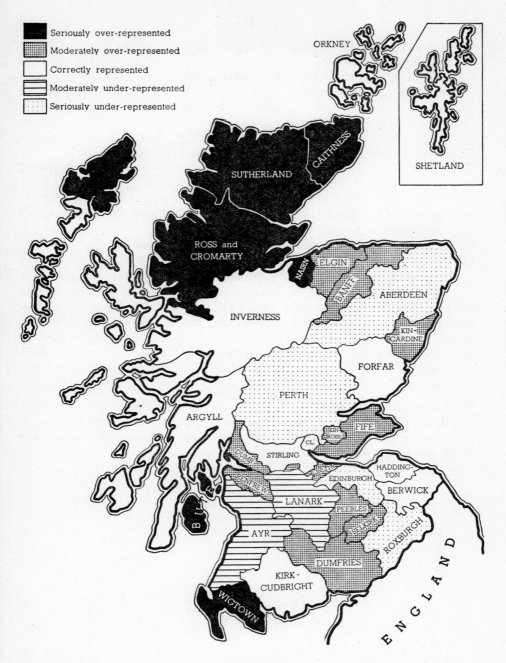

15. SCOTLAND

SHOWING INEQUALITIES IN PARLIAMENTARY REPRESENTATION

(See Appendix IV)

The Post Office, farmed at 1,194*l.*, but if collected may amount to	£2,000
The impositions for coinage	1,500
Land tax is now 36,000*l.*, and to make it equal with the 4*s.* per pound in England it is proposed to be	48,000
	160,000

The debts due to the army, civil list, and other charges of the government, about	160,000

267. Speech of the Lord High Commissioner on bringing the last session of Parliament to an end, 1707

(Acts of the Parliaments of Scotland, XI, p. 491)

MY LORDS AND GENTLEMEN,

The public business of this session being now over, it is full time to put an end to it.

I am persuaded that we and our posterity will reap the benefit of the union of the two kingdoms, and I doubt not that, as this Parliament has had the honour to conclude it, you will in your several stations recommend to the people of this nation a grateful sense of her Majesty's goodness and great care for the welfare of her subjects in bringing this important affair to perfection, and that you will promote an universal desire in this kingdom to become one in hearts and affections, as we are inseparably joined in interest, with our neighbour nation.

MY LORDS AND GENTLEMEN,

I have a very deep sense of the assistance and respect I have met with from you in this session of Parliament, and I shall omit no occasion of showing, to the utmost of my power, the grateful remembrance I have of it.

H. UNION WITH ENGLAND

268. Act restricting royal control of foreign policy, 1703

(Acts of the Parliaments of Scotland, XI, p. 107)

ACT ANENT PEACE AND WAR

Our sovereign lady, with advice and consent of the Estates of Parliament, statutes, enacts and declares, that after her Majesty's decease, and failing heirs of her body, no person being king or queen of Scotland and England shall have the sole power of making war with any prince, potentate or state whatsoever without consent of Parliament, and that no declaration of war without consent aforesaid shall be binding on the subjects of this kingdom, declaring always that this shall no ways be understood to impede the sovereign of this kingdom to call forth, command and employ the subjects thereof to suppress any insurrection within the kingdom or repel any invasion from abroad according to former laws, and also declaring that everything which relates to treaties of peace, alliance and commerce is left to the wisdom of the sovereign with consent of the Estates of Parliament who shall declare the war; and her Majesty, with consent aforesaid, repels, casses and annuls all former Acts of Parliament in so far as they are contrary hereunto or inconsistent herewith.

269. Act of Security, 1704

(Acts of the Parliaments of Scotland, XI, pp. 136–137)

ACT FOR THE SECURITY OF THE KINGDOM

Our sovereign lady the queen's Majesty, with advice and consent of the Estates of Parliament, doth hereby statute and ordain, that in the event of her Majesty's death, or of the death of any of her Majesty's heirs or successors, kings or queens of this realm, this present Parliament or any other Parliament that shall be then in being shall not be dissolved by the said death, but shall and is hereby required and ordained if assembled to sit and act in manner aftermentioned notwithstanding of the said death; and if the said Parliament be under adjournment the time of the said death, it shall notwithstanding meet precisely at Edinburgh the twentieth day after the said death, excluding the day thereof, whether the day of the said adjournment be sooner or later. And it is further statute and ordained, that in case there shall be no Parliament in being at the time of the death aforesaid, then the Estates or members of the last preceding Parliament, without regard to any Parliament that may be indicted but never met nor constituted, shall meet at Edinburgh on the twentieth day after the said death, the day thereof excluded. . . .

And the said Estates of Parliament, appointed in case of the death aforesaid to continue or meet as above, are hereby authorized and empowered to act and administrate the government in manner aftermentioned, that is, that upon the death of her Majesty, leaving heirs of her own body or, failing thereof, lawful successors designed or appointed by her Majesty and the Estates of Parliament, or upon the death of any succeeding king or queen, leaving lawful heirs and successors as said is, the said Estates of Parliament are authorized and empowered, after having read to the said heir or successor the Claim of Right,[1] and desired them to accept the government in the terms thereof, to require of and administrate to the said heir or lawful successors, by themselves or such as they shall commissionate, the coronation oath, and that with all convenient speed, not exceeding thirty days after the meeting of the said Estates, if the said heir or successor be within the isle of Britain, or, if without the same, not exceeding three months after the said meeting, in order to their exercising the regal power, conform to the declaration of the Estates containing the Claim of Right; and also in case of the said heir or successor their being under age, which as to the exercise of the government is hereby declared to be until their attaining to seventeen years complete, to provide for, order and settle, within the space of sixty days after the said meeting, a regency for the kingdom until the said heir or successor take the coronation oath, and do actually enter to the exercise of the government, the regent or regents to be so appointed always having the Claim of Right read to him or them as above, and he or they taking at his or their entry the coronation oath, and to continue for such space as the said Estates shall appoint. . . .

And further, upon the said death of her Majesty without heirs of her body or a successor lawfully designed and appointed as above, or in the case of any other king or queen thereafter succeeding and deceasing without lawful heir or successor, the aforesaid Estates of Parliament convened or meeting are hereby authorized and empowered to nominate and declare the successor to the imperial crown of this realm, and to settle the succession thereof upon the heirs of the said successor's body, the said successor and the heirs of the successor's body being always of the royal line of Scotland and of the true Protestant religion; providing always that the same be not successor to the crown of England, unless that in this present session of Parliament, or any other session of this or any ensuing Parliament during her Majesty's reign, there be such conditions of government settled and enacted as may secure the honour and sovereignty of this crown and kingdom, the freedom, frequency and power of Parliaments, the religion, liberty and trade of the nation from English or any foreign influence. . . .

And it is hereby expressly provided and declared, that it shall be high treason for any person or persons to administrate the coronation oath, or be witnesses to the administration thereof, but by the appointment of the Estates of Parliament in manner above mentioned, or to own or acknowledge any person as king or queen of this realm, in the event of her Majesty's decease leaving heirs of her own body, until they have sworn the coronation oath and accepted the crown in the terms of the Claim of Right, and in the event of her Majesty's decease without heirs of her body, until they swear the coronation oath and accept on the terms of the Claim of Right and of such other conditions of government as shall be settled in this or any ensuing Parliament, or added in the said meeting of Estates, and be thereupon declared and admitted as above, which crime shall be irremissible without consent of Parliament.

[1] No. 248.

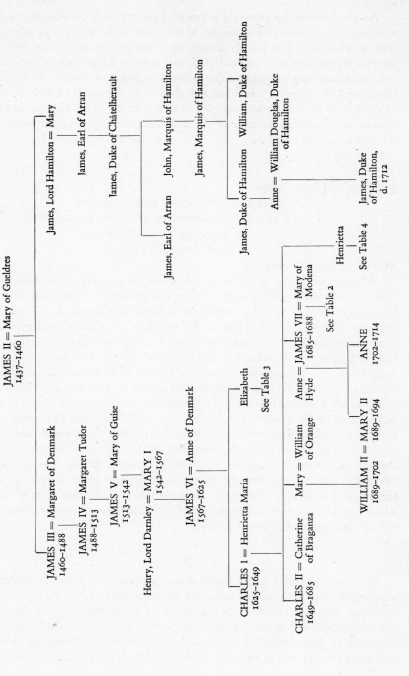

TABLE 6

The Scottish Succession

JAMES II = Mary of Gueldres
1437-1460

JAMES III = Margaret of Denmark   James, Lord Hamilton = Mary
1460-1488

JAMES IV = Margaret Tudor   James, Earl of Arran
1488-1513

JAMES V = Mary of Guise   James, Duke of Châtelherault
1513-1542

Henry, Lord Darnley = MARY I   James, Earl of Arran   John, Marquis of Hamilton
                      1542-1567

JAMES VI = Anne of Denmark   James, Marquis of Hamilton
1567-1625

CHARLES I = Henrietta Maria   Elizabeth   James, Duke of Hamilton   William, Duke of Hamilton
1625-1649   See Table 3

                                                Anne = William Douglas, Duke
                                                       of Hamilton

CHARLES II = Catherine   Mary = William   Anne = JAMES VII = Mary of   Henrietta
1649-1685   of Braganza   of Orange Hyde   1685-1688   Modena
                                                               See Table 2   See Table 4

                          WILLIAM II = MARY II   ANNE   James, Duke
                          1689-1702   1689-1694   1702-1714   of Hamilton,
                                                                              d. 1712

And because in the aforesaid interval of twenty days betwixt the said death and meeting of the Estates of Parliament, in case there be no Parliament assembled for the time, it is necessary that the administration of the government be provided for in that interim, therefore it is hereby declared, that in case of the death of her Majesty, or of any succeeding king or queen of this realm, then and in all or either of the events above mentioned the aforesaid administration shall be in the hands of such of the members of the Estates of Parliament, and such members of the Privy Council last in being, as shall be at Edinburgh the time of the said death, or shall come to Edinburgh before the said twentieth day. . . .

270. Act of Union, 1707

(*Statutes of the Realm,* VIII, pp. 566–577)

AN ACT FOR AN UNION OF THE TWO KINGDOMS
OF ENGLAND AND SCOTLAND

(*6 Annae, cap. 11*)

MOST GRACIOUS SOVEREIGN,

Whereas articles of union were agreed on the twenty-second day of July in the fifth year of your Majesty's reign,[1] by the commissioners nominated on behalf of the kingdom of England under your Majesty's great seal of England, . . . and the commissioners nominated on the behalf of the kingdom of Scotland under your Majesty's great seal of Scotland; . . . and whereas an Act hath passed in the Parliament of Scotland at Edinburgh the sixteenth day of January in the fifth year of your Majesty's reign,[2] wherein it is mentioned that the Estates of Parliament, considering the said articles of union of the two kingdoms, had agreed to and approved of the said articles of union with some additions and explanations, and that your Majesty, with advice and consent of the Estates of Parliament, for establishing the Protestant religion and Presbyterian Church government within the kingdom of Scotland, had passed in the same session of Parliament an Act intituled, *Act for securing of the Protestant religion and Presbyterian Church government*, which by the tenor thereof was appointed to be inserted in any Act ratifying the treaty, and expressly declared to be a fundamental and essential condition of the said treaty or union in all times coming, the tenor of which articles as ratified and approved of with additions and explanations by the said Act of Parliament of Scotland follows.

Article I

That the two kingdoms of England and Scotland shall upon the first day of May which shall be in the year one thousand seven hundred and seven, and for ever after, be united into one kingdom by the name of Great Britain; and that the ensigns armorial of the said united kingdom be such as her Majesty shall appoint, and the crosses of St. George and St. Andrew be conjoined in such manner as her Majesty shall think fit, and used in all flags, banners, standards and ensigns both at sea and land.

[1] 22 July 1706.　　　　　　　　　　　　[2] 16 January 1707.

Article II

That the succession to the monarchy of the united kingdom of Great Britain and of the dominions thereto belonging, after her most sacred Majesty and in default of issue of her Majesty, be, remain and continue to the most excellent Princess Sophia, electress and duchess dowager of Hanover, and the heirs of her body being Protestants. . . .[1]

Article III

That the united kingdom of Great Britain be represented by one and the same Parliament, to be styled the Parliament of Great Britain.

Article IV

That all the subjects of the united kingdom of Great Britain shall from and after the union have full freedom and intercourse of trade and navigation to and from any port or place within the said united kingdom and the dominions and plantations thereunto belonging, and that there be a communication of all other rights, privileges and advantages which do or may belong to the subjects of either kingdom, except where it is otherwise expressly agreed in these articles.

Article V

That all ships or vessels belonging to her Majesty's subjects of Scotland at the time of ratifying the treaty of union of the two kingdoms in the Parliament of Scotland, though foreign built, be deemed and pass as ships of the built of Great Britain. . . .

Article VI

That all parts of the united kingdom for ever, from and after the union, shall have the same allowances, encouragements and drawbacks, and be under the same prohibitions, restrictions and regulations of trade, and liable to the same Customs and duties on import and export; and that the allowances, encouragements and drawbacks, prohibitions, restrictions and regulations of trade, and the Customs and duties on import and export settled in England when the union commences shall from and after the union take place throughout the whole united kingdom, excepting and reserving the duties upon export and import of such particular commodities from which any persons the subjects of either kingdom are specially liberated and exempted by their private rights, which after the union are to remain safe and entire to them in all respects as before the same; and that from and after the union no Scots cattle carried into England shall be liable to any other duties either on the public or private accompts than those duties to which the cattle of England are or shall be liable within the said kingdom; and seeing by the laws of England there are rewards granted upon the exportation of certain kinds of grain, wherein oats grinded or ungrinded are not expressed, that from and after the union, when oats shall be sold at fifteen shillings sterling per quarter or under, there shall be paid two shillings and sixpence sterling for

[1] In accordance with the provisions already made for the succession to the throne of England by the Bill of Rights [No. 40] and the Act of Settlement [No. 43].

every quarter of the oatmeal exported in the terms of the law whereby and so long as rewards are granted for exportation of other grains, and that the beer of Scotland have the same rewards as barley; and in respect the importations of victual into Scotland from any place beyond sea would prove a discouragement to tillage, therefore that the prohibition as now in force by the law of Scotland against importation of victuals from Ireland or any other place beyond sea into Scotland do after the union remain in the same force as now it is, until more proper and effectual ways be provided by the Parliament of Great Britain for discouraging the importation of the said victuals from beyond sea.

Article VII

That all parts of the united kingdom be for ever from and after the union liable to the same Excises upon all excisable liquors, . . . and that the Excise settled in England . . . when the union commences take place throughout the whole united kingdom.

Article VIII

That from and after the union all foreign salt which shall be imported into Scotland shall be charged at the importation there with the same duties as the like salt is now charged with being imported into England, and to be levied and secured in the same manner; but in regard the duties of great quantities of foreign salt imported may be very heavy upon the merchants importers, that therefore all foreign salt imported into Scotland shall be cellared and locked up under the custody of the merchants importers and the officers employed for levying the duties upon salt, and that the merchant may have what quantity thereof his occasion may require, not under a wey or forty bushels at a time, giving security for the duty of what quantity he receives payable in six months. But Scotland shall for the space of seven years from the said union be exempted from paying in Scotland for salt made there the duty or Excise now payable for salt made in England, but from the expiration of the said seven years shall be subject and liable to the same duties for salt made in Scotland as shall be then payable for salt made in England. . . .

Article IX

That whensoever the sum of one million nine hundred ninety-seven thousand seven hundred and sixty-three pounds eight shillings and fourpence halfpenny shall be enacted by the Parliament of Great Britain to be raised in that part of the united kingdom now called England, on land and other things usually charged in Acts of Parliament there for granting an aid to the crown by a land tax, that part of the united kingdom now called Scotland shall be charged by the same Act with a further sum of forty-eight thousand pounds free of all charges as the quota of Scotland to such tax, and so proportionably for any greater or lesser sum raised in England by any tax on land and other things usually charged together with the land, and that such quota for Scotland in the cases aforesaid be raised and collected in the same manner as the Cess now is in Scotland, but subject to such regulations in the manner of collecting as shall be made by the Parliament of Great Britain.

Article X

That during the continuance of the respective duties on stamped paper, vellum and parchment by the several Acts now in force in England, Scotland shall not be charged with the same respective duties.

Article XI

That during the continuance of the duties payable in England on windows and lights, which determine on the first day of August one thousand seven hundred and ten, Scotland shall not be charged with the same duties.

Article XII

That during the continuance of the duties payable in England on coals, culm and cinders, which determine the thirtieth day of September one thousand seven hundred and ten, Scotland shall not be charged therewith for coals, culm and cinders consumed there, but shall be charged with the same duties as in England for all coals, culm and cinders not consumed in Scotland.

Article XIII

That during the continuance of the duty payable in England upon malt, which determines the twenty-fourth day of June one thousand seven hundred and seven, Scotland shall not be charged with that duty.

Article XIV

That the kingdom of Scotland be not charged with any other duties laid on by the Parliament of England before the union except these consented to in this treaty, in regard it is agreed that all necessary provision shall be made by the Parliament of Scotland for the public charge and service of that kingdom for the year one thousand seven hundred and seven; provided nevertheless that if the Parliament of England shall think fit to lay any further impositions by way of Customs, or such Excises with which by virtue of this treaty Scotland is to be charged equally with England, in such case Scotland shall be liable to the same Customs and Excises, and have an equivalent to be settled by the Parliament of Great Britain; with this further provision, that any malt to be made and consumed in that part of the united kingdom now called Scotland shall not be charged with any imposition on malt during this present war....

Article XV

That whereas by the terms of this treaty the subjects of Scotland, for preserving an equality of trade throughout the united kingdom, will be liable to several Customs and Excises now payable in England which will be applicable towards payment of the debts of England contracted before the union, it is agreed that Scotland shall have an equivalent for what the subjects thereof shall be so charged towards payment of the said debts of England, in all particulars whatsoever in manner following, viz., that before the union of the said kingdoms the sum of three hundred ninety-eight thousand

and eighty-five pounds ten shillings be granted to her Majesty by the Parliament of England for the uses after mentioned, being the equivalent to be answered to Scotland for such parts of the said Customs and Excises upon all excisable liquors with which that kingdom is to be charged upon the union as will be applicable to the payment of the said debts of England, according to the proportions which the present Customs in Scotland, being thirty thousand pounds per annum, do bear to the Customs in England, computed at one million three hundred forty-one thousand five hundred and fifty-nine pounds per annum, and which the present Excises on excisable liquors in Scotland, being thirty-three thousand and five hundred pounds per annum, do bear to the Excises on excisable liquors in England, computed at nine hundred forty-seven thousand six hundred and two pounds per annum, which sum of three hundred ninety-eight thousand eighty-five pounds ten shillings shall be due and payable from the time of the union. And in regard that after the union, Scotland becoming liable to the same Customs and duties payable on import and export and to the same Excises on all excisable liquors as in England, as well upon that accompt as upon the accompt of the increase of trade and people (which will be the happy consequence of the union) the said revenues will much improve beyond the before-mentioned annual values thereof, of which no present estimate can be made, yet nevertheless for the reasons aforesaid there ought to be a proportionable equivalent answered to Scotland, it is agreed that after the union there shall be an accompt kept of the said duties arising in Scotland, to the end it may appear what ought to be answered in Scotland as an equivalent for such proportion of the said increase as shall be applicable to the payment of the debts of England. And for the further and more effectual answering the several ends hereafter mentioned, it is agreed that from and after the union the whole increase of the revenues of Customs and duties on import and export and Excises upon excisable liquors in Scotland over and above the annual produce of the said respective duties as above stated shall go and be applied for the term of seven years to the uses hereafter mentioned, and that upon the said accompt there shall be answered to Scotland annually from the end of seven years after the union an equivalent in proportion to such part of the said increase as shall be applicable to the debts of England, and generally that an equivalent shall be answered to Scotland for such parts of the English duties as Scotland may hereafter become liable to pay by reason of the union, other than such for which appropriations have been made by Parliament in England of the Customs or other duties on export and import, Excises on all excisable liquors, in respect of which debts equivalents are herein before provided. And as for the uses to which the said sum of three hundred ninety-eight thousand eighty-five pounds ten shillings to be granted as aforesaid, and all other moneys which are to be answered or allowed to Scotland as aforesaid, are to be applied, it is agreed that in the first place out of the aforesaid sum what consideration shall be found necessary to be had for any losses which private persons may sustain by reducing the coin of Scotland to the standard and value of the coin of England may be made good; in the next place that the capital stock or fund of the African and Indian Company of Scotland advanced, together with interest for the said capital stock after the rate of five per cent per annum, from the respective times of the payment thereof, shall be paid, upon payment of which capital stock and interest it is agreed the said Company be dissolved and cease; . . . and as to the overplus of the said sum of three hundred ninety-eight thousand eighty-five pounds ten shillings, . . . and also the whole increase of the said revenues of Customs, duties and Excises above the present value which shall arise in Scotland during the said term of seven years, together with the equivalent which shall become due upon the improvement thereof in Scotland after the said term, and also as to all other sums which according to the agreements aforesaid may become payable to Scotland by way of equivalent for what that kingdom shall hereafter become liable towards payment of the debts of England, it is agreed that the same be applied in manner following, viz., that all the public debts of the kingdom of Scotland as shall be adjusted by this present Parliament shall be paid, and that two thousand pounds per annum for the space of seven years shall be applied towards encouraging and promoting the manufacture of coarse wool within those shires which produce the wool, and that the first two thousand pounds sterling be paid at Martinmas next, and so yearly at Martinmas during the space aforesaid, and afterwards the same shall be wholly applied towards the encouraging and promoting the fisheries, and such other manufactures and improvements in Scotland as may most conduce to the general good of the united kingdom; and it is agreed that her Majesty be empowered to appoint commissioners who shall be accomptable to the Parliament of Great Britain for disposing the said sum of three hundred ninety-eight thousand and eighty-five pounds ten shillings, and all other moneys which shall arise to Scotland upon the agreements aforesaid, to the purposes before mentioned. . . .

Article XVI

That from and after the union the coin shall be of the same standard and value throughout the united kingdom as now in England. . . .

Article XVII

That from and after the union the same weights and measures shall be used throughout the united kingdom as are now established in England. . . .

Article XVIII

That the laws concerning regulation of trade, Customs, and such Excises to which Scotland is by virtue of this treaty to be liable, be the same in Scotland from and after the union as in England, and that all other laws in use within the kingdom of Scotland do after the union and notwithstanding thereof remain in the same force as before (except such as are contrary to or inconsistent with this treaty), but alterable by the Parliament of Great Britain, with this difference betwixt the laws concerning public right, policy and civil government, and those which concern private right, that the laws which concern public right, policy and civil government may be made the same throughout the whole united kingdom, but that no alteration be made in laws which concern private right except for evident utility of the subjects within Scotland.

Article XIX

That the Court of Session or College of Justice do after the union and notwithstanding thereof remain in all time coming within Scotland as it is now constituted by the laws of that kingdom, and with the same authority and privileges as before the union, subject nevertheless to such regulations for the better administration of justice as shall be made by the Parliament of Great Britain, and that hereafter none shall be named by her Majesty or her royal successors to be ordinary Lords of Session but such who have served in the College of Justice as advocates or principal Clerks of Session for the space of five years, or as writers to the signet for the space of ten years, with this provision, that no writer to the signet be capable to be admitted a Lord of the Session unless he undergo a private and public trial on the civil law before the faculty of advocates and be found by them qualified for the said office two years before he be named to be a Lord of the Session, yet so as the qualifications made or to be made for capacitating persons to be named ordinary Lords of Session may be altered by the Parliament of Great Britain. And that the Court of Justiciary do also after the union and notwithstanding thereof remain in all time coming within Scotland as it is now constituted by the laws of that kingdom, and with the same authority and privileges as before the union, subject nevertheless to such regulations as shall be made by the Parliament of Great Britain and without prejudice of other rights of justiciary. And that all Admiralty jurisdictions be under the Lord High Admiral or Commissioners for the Admiralty of Great Britain for the time being; and that the Court of Admiralty now established in Scotland be continued, and that all reviews, reductions or suspensions of the sentences in maritime cases competent to the jurisdiction of that court remain in the same manner after the union as now in Scotland, until the Parliament of Great Britain shall make such regulations and alterations as shall be judged expedient for the whole united kingdom, so as there be always continued in Scotland a Court of Admiralty such as in England for determination of all maritime cases relating to private rights in Scotland competent to the jurisdiction of the Admiralty Court, subject nevertheless to such regulations and alterations as shall be thought proper to be made by the Parliament of Great Britain. And that the heritable rights of Admiralty and Vice-Admiralties in Scotland be reserved to the respective proprietors as rights of property, subject nevertheless as to the manner of exercising such heritable rights to such regulations and alterations as shall be thought proper to be made by the Parliament of Great Britain. And that all other courts now in being within the kingdom of Scotland do remain, but subject to alterations by the Parliament of Great Britain; and that all inferior courts within the said limits do remain subordinate as they are now to the supreme courts of justice within the same in all time coming. And that no causes in Scotland be cognoscible by the Courts of Chancery, Queen's Bench, Common Pleas or any other court in Westminster Hall; and that the said courts or any other of the like nature after the union shall have no power to cognosce, review or alter the acts or sentences of the judicatures within Scotland, or stop the execution of the same. And that there be a Court of Exchequer in Scotland after the union for deciding questions concerning the revenues of Customs and Excises there, having the same power and authority in such cases as the Court of Exchequer has in England; and that the said Court of Exchequer in Scotland have power of passing signatures, gifts, tutories, and in other things as the Court of Exchequer at present in Scotland hath; and that the Court of Exchequer that now is in Scotland do remain until a new Court of Exchequer be settled by the Parliament of Great Britain in Scotland after the union. And that after the union the Queen's Majesty and her royal successors may continue a Privy Council in Scotland for preserving of public peace and order until the Parliament of Great Britain shall think fit to alter it or establish any other effectual method for that end.

Article XX

That all heritable offices, superiorities, heritable jurisdictions, offices for life and jurisdictions for life be reserved to the owners thereof as rights of property, in the same manner as they are now enjoyed by the laws of Scotland, notwithstanding this treaty.

Article XXI

That the rights and privileges of the royal burghs in Scotland as they now are do remain entire after the union and notwithstanding thereof.

Article XXII

That by virtue of this treaty, of the peers of Scotland at the time of the union sixteen shall be the number to sit and vote in the House of Lords, and forty-five the number of the representatives of Scotland in the House of Commons of the Parliament of Great Britain; and that when her Majesty, her heirs or successors shall declare her or their pleasure for holding the first or any subsequent Parliament of Great Britain, until the Parliament of Great Britain shall make further provision therein, a writ do issue under the great seal of the united kingdom, directed to the Privy Council of Scotland, commanding them to cause sixteen peers who are to sit in the House of Lords to be summoned to Parliament, and forty-five members to be elected to sit in the House of Commons of the Parliament of Great Britain according to the agreement in this treaty, in such manner as by an Act of this present session of the Parliament of Scotland is or shall be settled, which Act is hereby declared to be as valid as if it were a part of and engrossed in this treaty; and that the names of the persons so summoned and elected shall be returned by the Privy Council of Scotland into the court from whence the said writ did issue; and that if her Majesty, on or before the first day of May next, on which day the union is to take place, shall declare under the great seal of England that it is expedient that the Lords of Parliament of England and Commons of the present Parliament of England should be the members of the respective Houses of the first Parliament of Great Britain for and on the part of England, then the said Lords of Parliament of England and Commons of the present Parliament of England shall be the members of the respective Houses of the first Parliament of Great Britain for and on the part of England; and her Majesty may by her royal proclamation under the great seal of Great Britain appoint the said first Parliament of Great Britain to meet at such time and place as her Majesty shall think fit, which time shall not be less than fifty days after the date of such proclamation; and the time and place of the meeting of such Parliament being so appointed, a writ shall be immediately issued under the great seal of Great Britain directed to the Privy Council of Scotland for the summoning the sixteen peers and for electing forty-five members by whom Scotland is to be represented in the Parliament of Great Britain; and the Lords of Parliament of England and the sixteen peers of Scotland, such sixteen peers being summoned and returned in the manner agreed in this treaty, and the members of the House of Commons of the said Parliament of England and the forty-five members for Scotland, such forty-five members being elected and returned in the manner agreed in this treaty, shall assemble and meet respectively in the respective Houses of the Parliament of Great Britain at such time and place as shall be so appointed by her Majesty, and shall be the two Houses of the first Parliament of Great Britain, and that Parliament may continue for such time only as the present Parliament of England might have continued if the union of the two kingdoms had not been made, unless sooner dissolved by her Majesty. And that every one of the Lords of Parliament of Great Britain and every member of the House of Commons of the Parliament of Great Britain in the first and all succeeding Parliaments of Great Britain, until the Parliament of Great Britain shall otherwise direct, shall take the respective oaths appointed to be taken instead of the oaths of allegiance and supremacy by an Act of Parliament made in England in the first year of the reign of the late King William and Queen Mary intituled, *An Act for the abrogating of the oaths of supremacy and allegiance and appointing other oaths,*[1] and make, subscribe and audibly repeat the declaration mentioned in an Act of Parliament made in England in the thirtieth year of the reign of King Charles the Second intituled, *An Act for the more effectual preserving the king's person and government by disabling papists from sitting in either House of Parliament,*[2] and shall take and subscribe the oath mentioned in an Act of Parliament made in England in the first year of her Majesty's reign intituled, *An Act to declare the alterations in the oath appointed to be taken by the Act intituled, An Act for the further security of his Majesty's person and the succession of the crown in the Protestant line, and for extinguishing the hopes of the pretended prince of Wales and all other pretenders and their open and secret abetters, and for declaring the Association to be determined,*[3] at such time and in such manner as the members of both Houses of Parliament of England are by the said respective Acts directed to take, make and subscribe the same, upon the penalties and disabilities in the said respective Acts contained. And it is declared and agreed that these words, "This realm", "The crown of this realm", and "The queen of this realm", mentioned in the oaths and declaration contained in the aforesaid Acts, which were intended to signify the crown and realm of England, shall be understood of the crown and realm of Great Britain, and that in that sense the said oaths and declaration be taken and subscribed by the members of both Houses of the Parliament of Great Britain.

Article XXIII

That the aforesaid sixteen peers of Scotland mentioned in the last preceding article to sit in the House of Lords of the Parliament of Great Britain shall have all privileges

[1] 1 Gul. & Mar., cap. 8. [2] No. 144. [3] 1 Annae, cap. 16.

of Parliament which the peers of England now have, and which they or any peers of Great Britain shall have after the union, and particularly the right of sitting upon the trials of peers; . . . and that in case any trials of peers shall hereafter happen when there is no Parliament in being, the sixteen peers of Scotland who sat at the last preceding Parliament shall be summoned in the same manner, and have the same powers and privileges at such trials, as any other peers of Great Britain; and that all peers of Scotland and their successors to their honours and dignities shall from and after the union be peers of Great Britain, and have rank and precedency next and immediately after the peers of the like orders and degrees in England at the time of the union, and before all peers of Great Britain of the like orders and degrees who may be created after the union, and shall be tried as peers of Great Britain, and shall enjoy all privileges of peers as fully as the peers of England do now, or as they or any other peers of Great Britain may hereafter enjoy the same, except the right and privilege of sitting in the House of Lords and the privileges depending thereon, and particularly the right of sitting upon the trials of peers.

Article XXIV

That from and after the union there be one great seal for the united kingdom of Great Britain, which shall be different from the great seal now used in either kingdom, and that the quartering the arms and the rank and precedency of the Lyon King of Arms of the kingdom of Scotland as may best suit the union be left to her Majesty; . . . and that a seal in Scotland after the union be always kept and made use of in all things relating to private rights or grants which have usually passed the great seal of Scotland, and which only concern offices, grants, commissions and private rights within that kingdom; . . . and that the crown, sceptre and sword of state, the records of Parliament and all other records, rolls and registers whatsoever, both public and private, general and particular and warrants thereof, continue to be kept as they are within that part of the united kingdom now called Scotland, and that they shall so remain in all time coming notwithstanding the union.

Article XXV

That all laws and statutes in either kingdom, so far as they are contrary to or inconsistent with the terms of these articles or any of them, shall from and after the union cease and become void, and shall be so declared to be by the respective Parliaments of the said kingdoms.

As by the said articles of union, ratified and approved by the said Act of Parliament of Scotland, relation being thereunto had, may appear.

II. And the tenor of the aforesaid *Act for securing the Protestant religion and Presbyterian church government* within the kingdom of Scotland is as follows.

Our sovereign lady and the Estates of Parliament considering that by the late Act of Parliament for a treaty with England for an union of both kingdoms it is provided that the commissioners for that treaty should not treat of or concerning any alteration of the worship, discipline and government of the Church of this kingdom as now by law established, which treaty being now reported to the Parliament, and it being reasonable and necessary that the true Protestant religion as presently professed within this kingdom, with the worship, discipline and government of this Church, should be effectually and unalterably secured, therefore her Majesty, with advice and consent of the said Estates of Parliament, doth hereby establish and confirm the said true Protestant religion and the worship, discipline and government of this Church to continue without any alteration to the people of this land in all succeeding generations; and more especially her Majesty, with advice and consent aforesaid, ratifies, approves and for ever confirms the fifth Act of the first Parliament of King William and Queen Mary intituled, *Act ratifying the Confession of Faith and settling Presbyterian Church government*,[1] with all other Acts of Parliament relating thereto, in prosecution of the declaration of the Estates of this kingdom containing the Claim of Right[2] bearing date the eleventh of April one thousand six hundred and eighty-nine; and her Majesty, with advice and consent aforesaid, expressly provides and declares that the foresaid true Protestant religion contained in the above-mentioned Confession of Faith, with the form and purity of worship presently in use within this Church, and its Presbyterian Church government and discipline, that is to say the government of the Church by kirk sessions, presbyteries, provincial synods and general assemblies, all established by the foresaid Acts of Parliament pursuant to the Claim of Right, shall remain and continue unalterable, and that the said Presbyterian government shall be the only government of the Church within the kingdom of Scotland.

And further, for the greater security of the foresaid Protestant religion and of the worship, discipline and government of this Church as above established, her Majesty, with advice and consent foresaid, statutes and ordains that the Universities and Colleges of St. Andrews, Glasgow, Aberdeen and Edinburgh as now established by law shall continue within this kingdom for ever, and that in all time coming no professors, principals, regents, masters or others bearing office in any university, college or school within this kingdom be capable or be admitted or allowed to continue in the exercise of their said functions but such as shall own and acknowledge the civil government in manner prescribed or to be prescribed by the Acts of Parliament, as also that before or at their admissions they do and shall acknowledge and profess and shall subscribe to the foresaid Confession of Faith as the confession of their faith, and that they will practise and conform themselves to the worship presently in use in this Church, and submit themselves to the government and discipline thereof, and never endeavour, directly or indirectly, the prejudice or subversion of the same, and that before the respective presbyteries of their bounds, by whatsoever gift, presentation or provision they may be thereto provided.

And further, her Majesty with advice aforesaid expressly declares and statutes that none of the subjects of this kingdom shall be liable to, but all and every one of them for ever free of, any oath, test or subscription within this kingdom contrary to or inconsistent with the foresaid true Protestant religion and Presbyterian Church government, worship and discipline as above established, and that the same within the bounds of this Church and kingdom shall never be imposed upon or required of them in any sort; and lastly that after the decease of her present Majesty (whom God

[1] No. 251.   [2] No. 248.

long preserve) the sovereign succeeding to her in the royal government of the kingdom of Great Britain shall in all time coming, at his or her accession to the crown, swear and subscribe that they shall inviolably maintain and preserve the foresaid settlement of the true Protestant religion, with the government, worship, discipline, right and privileges of this Church as above established by the laws of this kingdom in prosecution of the Claim of Right.

And it is hereby statute and ordained that this Act of Parliament, with the establishment therein contained, shall be held and observed in all time coming as a fundamental and essential condition of any treaty or union to be concluded betwixt the two kingdoms, without any alteration thereof or derogation thereto in any sort for ever; as also that this Act of Parliament and settlement therein contained shall be insert and repeated in any Act of Parliament that shall pass for agreeing and concluding the foresaid treaty or union betwixt the two kingdoms, and that the same shall be therein expressly declared to be a fundamental and essential condition of the said treaty or union in all time coming, which articles of union and Act immediately above written her Majesty, with advice and consent aforesaid, statutes, enacts and ordains to be and continue in all time coming the sure and perpetual foundation of a complete and entire union of the two kingdoms of Scotland and England, under the express condition and provision that this approbation and ratification of the foresaid articles and Act shall be no ways binding on this kingdom until the said articles and Act be ratified, approved and confirmed by her Majesty with and by the authority of the Parliament of England as they are now agreed to, approved and confirmed by her Majesty with and by the authority of the Parliament of Scotland, declaring nevertheless that the Parliament of England may provide for the security of the Church of England as they think expedient, to take place within the bounds of the said kingdom of England, and not derogating from the security above provided for establishing of the Church of Scotland within the bounds of this kingdom; as also the said Parliament of England may extend the additions and other provisions contained in the articles of union as above insert in favour of the subjects of Scotland to and in favour of the subjects of England, which shall not suspend or derogate from the force and effect of this present ratification, but shall be understood as herein included without the necessity of any new ratification in the Parliament of Scotland.

And lastly her Majesty enacts and declares that all laws and statutes in this kingdom, so far as they are contrary to or inconsistent with the terms of these articles as above mentioned, shall from and after the union cease and become void.

III. And whereas an Act hath passed in this present session of Parliament intituled, *An Act for securing the Church of England as by law established*,[1] the tenor whereof follows.

Whereas by an Act made in the session of Parliament held in the third and fourth year of her Majesty's reign, whereby her Majesty was empowered to appoint commissioners under the great seal of England to treat with commissioners to be authorized by the Parliament of Scotland concerning an union of the kingdoms of England and Scotland, it is provided and enacted that the commissioners to be named in pursuance of the said Act should not treat of or concerning any alteration of the liturgy, rites,

[1] 6 Annae, cap. 8.

ceremonies, discipline or government of the Church as by law established within this realm, . . . and whereas it is reasonable and necessary that the true Protestant religion professed and established by law in the Church of England and the doctrine, worship discipline and government thereof should be effectually and unalterably secured, be it enacted . . . that an Act made in the thirteenth year of the reign of Queen Elizabeth of famous memory intituled, *An Act for the ministers of the Church to be of sound religion,*[1] and also another Act made in the thirteenth year of the reign of the late King Charles the Second intituled, *An Act for the uniformity of the public prayers and administration of sacraments and other rites and ceremonies, and for establishing the form of making, ordaining and consecrating bishops, priests and deacons in the Church of England*[2] (other than such clauses in the said Acts or either of them as have been repealed or altered by any subsequent Act or Acts of Parliament), and all and singular other Acts of Parliament now in force for the establishment and preservation of the Church of England and the doctrine, worship, discipline and government thereof shall remain and be in full force for ever.

And be it further enacted . . . that after the demise of her Majesty (whom God long preserve) the sovereign next succeeding to her Majesty in the royal government of the kingdom of Great Britain, and so for ever hereafter every king or queen succeeding and coming to the royal government of the kingdom of Great Britain, at his or her coronation shall in the presence of all persons who shall be attending, assisting or otherwise then and there present, take and subscribe an oath to maintain and preserve inviolably the said settlement of the Church of England and the doctrine, worship, discipline and government thereof as by law established within the kingdoms of England and Ireland, the dominion of Wales and town of Berwick-upon-Tweed and the territories thereunto belonging.

And be it further enacted . . . that this Act and all and every the matters and things therein contained be and shall for ever be holden and adjudged to be a fundamental and essential part of any treaty of union to be concluded between the said two kingdoms, and also that this Act shall be inserted in express terms in any Act of Parliament which shall be made for settling and ratifying any such treaty of union, and shall be therein declared to be an essential and fundamental part thereof.

IV. May it therefore please your most excellent Majesty that it may be enacted, and be it enacted, . . . that all and every the said articles of union, as ratified and approved by the said Act of Parliament of Scotland as aforesaid and herein before particularly mentioned and inserted, and also the said Act of Parliament of Scotland for establishing the Protestant religion and Presbyterian Church government within that kingdom intituled, *Act for securing the Protestant religion and Presbyterian Church government,* and every clause, matter and thing in the said articles and Act contained shall be, and the said articles and Act are hereby, for ever ratified, approved and confirmed.

V. And it is hereby further enacted, . . . that the said Act passed in this present session of Parliament intituled, *An Act for securing the Church of England as by law established,* and all and every the matters and things therein contained, and also the

---

[1] 13 Eliz., cap. 12.   [2] No. 137.

said Act of Parliament of Scotland intituled, *Act for securing the Protestant religion and Presbyterian Church government*, with the establishment in the said Act contained, be and shall for ever be held and adjudged to be and observed as fundamental and essential conditions of the said union, and shall in all times coming be taken to be, and are hereby declared to be, essential and fundamental parts of the said articles and union, and the said articles of union so as aforesaid ratified, approved and confirmed by Act of Parliament of Scotland and by this present Act, and the said Act passed in this present session of Parliament intituled, *An Act for securing the Church of England as by law established*, and also the said Act passed in the Parliament of Scotland intituled, *Act for securing the Protestant religion and Presbyterian Church government*, are hereby enacted and ordained to be and continue in all times coming the complete and entire union of the two kingdoms of England and Scotland.

VI. And whereas since the passing the said Act in the Parliament of Scotland for ratifying the said articles of union one other Act intituled, *Act settling the manner of electing the sixteen peers and forty-five members to represent Scotland in the Parliament of Great Britain*, hath likewise passed in the said Parliament of Scotland at Edinburgh the fifth day of February one thousand seven hundred and seven, the tenor whereof follows.

Our sovereign lady considering that by the twenty-second article of the treaty of union . . . it is provided that . . . of the peers of Scotland at the time of the union sixteen shall be the number to sit and vote in the House of Lords, and forty-five the number of the representatives of Scotland in the House of Commons of the Parliament of Great Britain, . . . therefore her Majesty, with advice and consent of the Estates of Parliament, statutes, enacts and ordains that the said sixteen peers who shall have right to sit in the House of Peers in the Parliament of Great Britain on the part of Scotland by virtue of this treaty shall be named by the said peers of Scotland whom they represent, their heirs or successors to their dignities and honours, out of their own number, and that by open election and plurality of voices of the peers present and of the proxies for such as shall be absent, . . . declaring also that such peers as are absent . . . may send to all such meetings lists of the peers whom they judge fittest, validly signed by the said absent peers, which shall be reckoned in the same manner as if the parties had been present and given in the said list; and in case of the death or legal incapacity of any of the said sixteen peers, that the aforesaid peers of Scotland shall nominate another of their own number in place of the said peer or peers in manner before and after mentioned. And that of the said forty-five representatives of Scotland in the House of Commons in the Parliament of Great Britain thirty shall be chosen by the shires or stewartries and fifteen by the royal burghs as follows, viz., one for every shire and stewartry excepting the shires of Bute and Caithness, which shall choose one by turns, Bute having the first election; the shires of Nairn and Cromarty, which shall also choose by turns, Nairn having the first election; and in like manner the shires of Clackmannan and Kinross shall choose by turns, Clackmannan having the first election. . . . And that the said fifteen representatives for the royal burghs be chosen as follows, viz., that the town of Edinburgh shall have right to elect and send one member to the Parliament of Great Britain, and that each of the other burghs shall elect a commissioner in the same manner as they are now in use to elect commissioners to the Parliament of Scotland, which commissioners and burghs (Edinburgh excepted) being divided in fourteen classes or districts shall meet at such time and burghs within their respective districts as her Majesty, her heirs or successors shall appoint, and elect one for each district, viz., the burghs of Kirkwall, Wick, Dornoch, Dingwall and Tain, one; the burghs of Fortrose, Inverness, Nairn and Forres, one; the burghs of Elgin, Cullen, Banff, Inverurie and Kintore, one; the burghs of Aberdeen, Inverbervie, Montrose, Aberbrothock and Brechin, one; the burghs of Forfar, Perth, Dundee, Cupar and St. Andrews, one; the burghs of Crail, Kilrenny, Anstruther Easter, Anstruther Wester and Pittenweem, one; the burghs of Dysart, Kirkcaldy, Kinghorn and Burntisland, one; the burghs of Inverkeithing, Dunfermline, Queensferry, Culross and Stirling, one; the burghs of Glasgow, Renfrew, Rutherglen and Dumbarton, one; the burghs of Haddington, Dunbar, North Berwick, Lauder and Jedburgh, one; the burghs of Selkirk, Peebles, Linlithgow and Lanark, one; the burghs of Dumfries, Sanquhar, Annan, Lochmaben and Kirkcudbright, one; the burghs of Wigtown, New Galloway, Stranraer and Whithorn, one; and the burghs of Ayr, Irvine, Rothesay, Campbeltown and Inveraray, one. And it is hereby declared and ordained that where the votes of the commissioners for the said burghs met to choose representatives from their several districts to the Parliament of Great Britain shall be equal, in that case the president of the meeting shall have a casting or decisive vote, and that by and according to his vote as a commissioner from the burgh from which he is sent, the commissioner from the eldest burgh presiding in the first meeting, and the commissioners from the other burghs in their respective districts presiding afterwards by turns in the order as the said burghs are now called in the rolls of the Parliament of Scotland. . . . It is always hereby expressly provided and declared that none shall be capable to elect or be elected for any of the said estates but such as are twenty-one years of age complete and Protestant, excluding all papists or such who being suspect of popery and required refuse to swear and subscribe the formula contained in the third Act made in the eighth and ninth sessions of King William's Parliament intituled, *Act for preventing the growth of popery*; and also declaring that none shall be capable to elect or be elected to represent a shire or burgh in the Parliament of Great Britain for this part of the united kingdom except such as are now capable by the laws of this kingdom to elect or be elected as commissioners for shires or burghs to the Parliament of Scotland. . . . And whereas by the said twenty-second article it is agreed that if her Majesty shall on or before the first day of May next declare that it is expedient the Lords and Commons of the present Parliament of England should be the members of the respective Houses of the first Parliament of Great Britain for and on the part of England, they shall accordingly be the members of the said respective Houses for and on the part of England, her Majesty, with advice and consent aforesaid, in that case only doth hereby statute and ordain that the sixteen peers and forty-five commissioners for shires and burghs who shall be chosen by the peers, barons and burghs respectively in this present session of Parliament and out of the members thereof, in the same manner as committees of Parliament are usually now chosen, shall be the members of the respective Houses of the said first Parliament of Great Britain for and on the part of Scotland. . . .

VII. As by the said Act passed in Scotland for settling the manner of electing the sixteen peers and forty-five members to represent Scotland in the Parliament of Great Britain may appear, be it therefore further enacted . . . that the said last-mentioned Act passed in Scotland for settling the manner of electing the sixteen peers and forty-five members to represent Scotland in the Parliament of Great Britain as aforesaid shall be, and the same is hereby declared to be, as valid as if the same had been part of and engrossed in the said articles of union, ratified and approved by the said Act of Parliament of Scotland and by this Act as aforesaid.

271. Treason Act, 1708

(Statutes of the Realm, IX, pp. 93–95)

AN ACT FOR IMPROVING THE UNION OF THE TWO KINGDOMS

(7 Annae, cap. 21)

Whereas nothing can more conduce to the improving the union of the two kingdoms which by her Majesty's great wisdom and goodness hath been happily effected than that the laws of both parts of Great Britain should agree as near as may be, especially those laws which relate to high treason and the proceedings thereupon, . . . to the end therefore that the said union may be more effectually improved, be it enacted, . . . that from and after the first day of July in the year of our Lord one thousand seven hundred and nine such crimes and offences which are high treason or misprision of high treason within England shall be construed, adjudged and taken to be high treason and misprision of high treason within Scotland, and that from thenceforth no crimes or offences shall be high treason or misprision of high treason within Scotland but those that are high treason or misprision of high treason in England.

II. And that from and after the said first day of July in the said year of our Lord one thousand seven hundred and nine the queen's Majesty, her heirs and successors, may issue out commissions of oyer and terminer in Scotland under the seal of Great Britain to such persons as her Majesty, her heirs and successors shall think fit, and that three of the Lords of the Justiciary be in the said commission of oyer and terminer, whereof one to be of the quorum, to inquire of, hear and determine such high treasons and misprision of high treason in such manner as is used in England. . . .

IV. And be it further enacted . . . that from and after the said first day of July one thousand seven hundred and nine the justice court and other courts having power to judge in cases of high treason and misprision of high treason in Scotland shall have full power and authority, and are hereby required, to inquire by the oaths of twelve or more good and lawful men of the county, shire or stewartry where the respective courts shall sit of all high treasons and misprisions of high treason committed within the said counties, shires or stewartries, and thereupon to proceed, hear and determine the said offences whereof any person shall be indicted before them in such manner as the Court of Queen's Bench or justices of oyer and terminer in England may do by the laws of England. . . .

V. And that from and after the said first day of July in the said year of our Lord one thousand seven hundred and nine all persons convicted or attainted of high treason or misprision of high treason in Scotland shall be subject and liable to the same corruption of blood, pains, penalties and forfeitures as persons convicted or attainted of high treason or misprision of high treason in England. . . .

VIII. And that from and after the said first day of July in the said year of our Lord one thousand seven hundred and nine no person accused of any capital offence or other crime in Scotland shall suffer or be subject or liable to any torture, provided that this Act shall not extend to take away that judgment which is given in England against persons indicted of felony who shall refuse to plead or decline trial. . . .

XIII. Provided always, and be it further enacted . . . that after the decease of the person who pretended to be prince of Wales during the life of the late King James, and since pretends to be king of Great Britain, and at the end of the term of three years after the immediate succession to the crown upon the demise of her present Majesty shall take effect, as the same is and stands limited by an Act made in the first year of the reign of their late Majesties King William and Queen Mary intituled, *An Act for declaring the rights and liberties of the subject and settling the succession of the crown*,[1] and by one other Act made in the twelfth year of the reign of his late Majesty King William the Third intituled, *An Act for the further limitation of the Crown and better securing the rights and liberties of the subject*,[2] no attainder for treason shall extend to the disheriting of any heir nor to the prejudice of the right or title of any person or persons other than the right or title of the offender or offenders during his, her or their natural lives only. . . .

XIV. And be it further enacted . . . that from and after the decease of the person who pretended to be prince of Wales[3]. . . . when any person is indicted for high treason or misprision of treason, a list of the witnesses that shall be produced on the trial for proving the said indictment, and of the jury, mentioning the names, profession and place of abode of the said witnesses and jurors, be also given at the same time that the copy of the indictment is delivered to the party indicted, and that copies of all indictments for the offences aforesaid with such lists shall be delivered to the party indicted ten days before the trial and in presence of two or more credible witnesses, any law or statute to the contrary notwithstanding.

272. Act restoring lay patronage in Scotland, 1712

(*Statutes of the Realm*, IX, pp. 680–681)

AN ACT TO RESTORE THE PATRONS TO THEIR ANCIENT RIGHTS
OF PRESENTING MINISTERS TO THE CHURCHES VACANT
IN THAT PART OF GREAT BRITAIN CALLED SCOTLAND

(*10 Annae, cap. 21*)

Whereas by the ancient laws and constitution of that part of Great Britain called Scotland the presenting of ministers to vacant churches did of right belong to the patrons, until by the twenty-third Act of the second session of the first Parliament of the late King William and Queen Mary held in the year one thousand six hundred

[1] No. 40.   [2] No. 43.   [3] As in the preceding section.

and ninety, intituled, *Act concerning patronages*,[1] the presentation was taken from the patrons and given to the heritors and elders of the respective parishes, and in place of the right of presentation the heritors and life-renters of every parish were to pay to the respective patrons a small and inconsiderable sum of money for which the patrons were to renounce their right of presentation in all times thereafter, and whereas by the fifteenth Act of the fifth session and by the thirteenth Act of the sixth session of the first Parliament of the said King William, the one intituled, *An Act for encouraging of preachers at vacant churches be north Forth*, and the other intituled, *Act in favour of preachers be north Forth*, there are several burthens imposed upon vacant stipends to the prejudice of the patrons' right of disposing thereof, and whereas that way of calling ministers has proved inconvenient, and has not only occasioned great heats and divisions among those who by the aforesaid Act were entitled and authorized to call ministers but likewise has been a great hardship upon the patrons whose predecessors had founded and endowed those churches, and who have not received payment or satisfaction for their right of patronage from the aforesaid heritors or life-renters of the respective parishes, nor have granted renunciations of their said rights on that account; be it therefore enacted, . . . that the aforesaid Act made in the year one thousand six hundred and ninety intituled, *Act concerning patronages*, in so far as the same relates to the presentation of ministers by heritors and others therein mentioned, be and is hereby repealed and made void, and that the aforesaid fifteenth Act of the fifth session and thirteenth Act of the sixth session of the first Parliament of King William be and are hereby likewise repealed and made void, and that in all time coming the right of all and every patron or patrons to the presentation of ministers to churches and benefices, and the disposing of the vacant stipends for pious uses within the parish, be restored, settled and confirmed to them, . . . and that from and after the first day of May one thousand seven hundred and twelve it shall and may be lawful for her Majesty, her heirs and successors, and for every other person or persons who have right to any patronage or patronages of any church or churches whatsoever in that part of Great Britain called Scotland (and who have not made and subscribed a formal renunciation thereof under their hands) to present a qualified minister or ministers to any church or churches whereof they are patrons which shall at any time after the said first day of May happen to be vacant, and the presbytery of the respective bounds shall and is hereby obliged to receive and admit in the same manner such qualified person or persons, minister or ministers, as shall be presented by the respective patrons as the persons or ministers presented before the making of this Act ought to have been admitted. . . .

273. Letters from Lord Berkeley of Stratton and Peter Wentworth to the earl of Strafford on the attempt to dissolve the union, 1713

(*Wentworth Papers*, ed. J. J. Cartwright, pp. 331, 336–337)

2 May 1713. Yesterday was taken up with a long debate concerning the Scotch. My Lord Seafield, after a long speech of the hardships his nation had endured, concluded with a motion for leave to bring in a bill to dissolve the union, preserving the

---

[1] No. 252.

succession. All his countrymen joined with him, and most of the Whigs, but were beat by a majority only of four, and that by proxies, for the present lords made an equality. What hath provoked the Scotch is the malt tax, after the assurances given them in the articles of the union that it should not be taxed during the war; and before it is well ended it is imposed upon them, though to pay the debts of the war. Lord Peterborough was very pleasant in comparing the union to a marriage, and owned we had been a little rough to our spouse. Though this matter is over in Parliament it is to be feared it will not be so in Scotland, where they will never pay this tax, and the officers who are to gather it will be in some danger, as well as the justices of the peace if they take their part.

26 May 1713. Since you seem to like my accounts of what is done in Parliament I shall give a relation of what I have heard of the malt tax, since now it is like to make so much noise. The Court did manage themselves so nicely that they carried it in the committee, but by the Speaker's voice, that the Scotch should be excused the duty upon malt. When they reported it to the House they disagreed with their committee by 25, notwithstanding there were speeches that told them it was a breach of the union, for there it was expressly stipulated that during the war they should have no additional taxes laid upon them, and if it was levied it must be by a standing army. The answer to this was that when the peace was they had agreed to be taxed in all things alike to the English, which the Scotch allow. But here is the breach, they say, that what they were to pay towards the war was mentioned in the articles of union, and no more than that burden were they to bear to support the war; and now by making them come in this year to an equal proportion with us in this malt tax, which is appropriated to defray some of the expenses of the war, they are made to pay towards the war. The reason that weighed with a great many country gentlemen, that do not depend upon the Court for bringing them in, is that they may be easied of this tax next year, which they are apprehensive will be asked of them again, being what is levied with the most ease. If the Scotch are with them they know they will join with the country gentlemen to take it off.

When the Scotch found there was no way of getting themselves off, they joined with the Whigs now to throw out the bill; but they could not succeed in that. So last night all the members of both Houses had a meeting, and agreed upon an address to the queen, full of respect to her, but in short it is to desire that leave may be given to bring in a bill to dissolve the union. There was not one man, either Lords or Commons, dissented from it. The duke of Argyll and Lord Mar, Mr. Lockhart and Mr. Cockburn, presented it to the queen today. I am told their answer was that she was surprised that in a matter of so great a consequence they should take so hasty and rash a resolve.

Part VIII
IRELAND

IRELAND

Introduction

BY the native Irish, as by the Scots, the Restoration was welcomed as holding out some prospect of one particular thing, in their case the return of the land to its original owners. For nearly a century Ireland had been colonized or 'planted' as ruthlessly as North America, by much the same type of men, and, owing to its proximity to England, with much greater efficiency. During the twenty years preceding the Restoration this process had reached its climax. A formidable Irish rebellion had been crushed; the native Irish landowners and many even of the earlier English settlers had been dispossessed; and roughly three-quarters of the land of Ireland had been parcelled out to meet the claims of the English 'adventurers' who had financed the reconquest and the soldiers of the English Commonwealth who had effected it. These with few exceptions were the bitter opponents of the House of Stuart, whereas the native Irish, with some stretching of the truth, could claim that once the initial rebellion was over they had shown themselves its supporters. The return of the Stuarts, otherwise regarded with little favour by the Irish, might therefore be expected to mean the restoration of their land.

So far did this reasoning commend itself to Charles that he showed himself willing at least to do what he conveniently could for the Irish. Almost as a matter of course the Cromwellian union with England was dissolved, the early Stuart system of government revived, and the Irish Parliament re-established, though subject, as before, to the legislative supervision of the English Privy Council. A number of principles were laid down in a declaration of 30 November 1660,[1] in accordance with which it was hoped to meet the most justifiable of the Irish claims to land. But it soon became apparent that nothing serious could be done without a considerable expropriation of the new landowners in Ireland, and that any such expropriation might well prove fatal to the Stuart cause in England. The fact that the new owners were largely Puritans was a matter for regret to those now in authority in the latter country; but any Englishman was to be preferred to an Irishman, and any weakening of the English element in Ireland was to be deprecated as likely to endanger the control of England itself over Ireland. Moreover the Irish land settlement had now been in existence for some considerable time, and had become complicated by subsequent sales and leases, which could not be cancelled without grave injustice to those concerned; while investigation soon revealed that as a result of the numerous expropriations effected during the previous twenty years the total claims to Irish land were far beyond the capacity of all the land in Ireland to satisfy. The most the restored monarch could countenance, in consequence, was a modest compromise, involving the surrender of a proportion of their land by the new owners in order to meet some of the most valid claims of the old owners. To this effect was given by two Acts of the Irish Parliament, the Act of Settlement of 1662[2] and the Act for the Explanation of the Act of Settlement of 1665, which were to remain the basis of the land situation in Ireland until the nineteenth century.

Thus the Restoration was a disappointment to the native Irish, and a source of

---

[1] No. 274, p. 711. [2] No. 274.

much bitter feeling directed both against the English in general and against the House of Stuart in particular. Nevertheless the reign of Charles II was a period of considerable prosperity for Ireland, little marked by open expressions of dissatisfaction. In part this was due to the failure of many of the smaller men among the adventurers and soldiers to take up or retain their proportion of Irish land, for their wealthier associates who bought their claims, being dependent on Irish labour for the cultivation of their estates, were unwilling that the Irish should be too harshly treated. In part also it was due to the energy and capacity of the whole body of new settlers, who devoted themselves with the utmost resolution to introducing better methods of agriculture and repairing the ravages of twenty years of civil war and disorder in their adopted country. Having little faith in the permanence of their interest in the land they turned largely to pasture farming, and in a surprisingly short time built up a highly profitable export trade in cattle and sheep, which were sent mainly to the English market. It is true that this immediately roused the jealousy of English agricultural interests, with the result that an Act was passed by the English Parliament prohibiting the importation into England of any livestock from Ireland,[1] and that the original English Navigation Act,[2] which had placed Ireland substantially on the same footing as England, was amended so as to exclude Ireland from its benefits, and in particular from direct trade with the colonies. But this involved only temporary hardship, for the Irish thereupon took to slaughtering their cattle, and built up a trade in beef, tallow and hides instead; while at the same time they devoted much more attention to sheep rearing, developed a most profitable export trade in wool,[3] and when restrictions on this were in turn enforced[4] established an even more profitable woollen manufacture of their own.

The main reason for the tranquillity and prosperity of the country, however, lay in the character of the chief governors appointed by Charles II.[5] With scarcely an exception these were men who had the general welfare at heart, and while determined to maintain the Protestant ascendancy were opposed to persecution or further exploitation of the Catholics, and to excessive subordination of Ireland as a whole to England. Especially was this true of the duke of Ormonde, whose two periods of office as Lord Lieutenant covered more than half of Charles's reign. Under his moderate rule Protestant nonconformists and Roman Catholics alike were much better off than their co-religionists in England. Visitors to Ireland were favourably impressed by the signs of progress they saw,[6] although some allowance must be made for the fact that their visits were practically confined to the eastern districts where wealth was greatest and conditions best.[7] The revenue rapidly increased,[8] and the financial position of the government would have been a strong one had the military establishment not been out of all proportion to the size of the country and a considerable part of the revenue diverted to purely English uses.[9] Even at the crisis of the Popish Plot scare Ireland was little affected and remained substantially undisturbed.

A very different situation arose when James ascended the throne. James had no more real sympathy with the native Irish than the average Englishman of his day; but his devotion to the Catholic faith made him a little readier to do something for them, and inspired him with the hope that he might enlist their support for his scheme of bringing England back to the Catholic fold. With that object in view he placed Richard Talbot, earl of Tyrconnel, at the head of the Irish administration, and

---

[1] No. 279.   [2] No. 203.   [3] No. 280.
[4] No. 282.   [5] App. II.   [6] No. 277.
[7] No. 278.   [8] Nos. 283–286.   [9] No. 284.

encouraged him not merely to promote Catholics to official posts but also to remodel the army on an Irish Catholic basis. Tyrconnel and his supporters, however, had no intention of allowing Ireland to be used to further any schemes in England, and as soon as the outbreak of revolution in that country gave them their opportunity proceeded to enlist James's unwilling assistance for their own scheme of an independent Ireland. In the Patriot Parliament of 1689, held by James after he had fled from London and reappeared with French support in Dublin, measures were passed formally recognizing him as king,[1] declaring Ireland to be independent of the English Parliament and of the English law courts,[2] repealing the Acts of Settlement and Explanation and restoring the land to the heirs of the original owners,[3] providing for the encouragement of Irish trade and navigation,[4] and attainting more than 2,000 individuals who had adhered to the prince of Orange.[5]

Meanwhile the Protestants of Ireland had fled the country, or had drawn together for mutual defence in the north and appealed to the new government in England for assistance. The result was a bitterly contested civil war, in the course of which Ireland became for a time the battle-ground of Europe. So equally matched were the forces of Louis XIV and his opponents on the Continent that the outcome of the struggle which had just begun there seemed to depend on the part to be played by England; that itself depended on whether William or James could establish himself firmly on the English throne; and that in turn was likely to be determined by the course of the Irish war. Troops of all nationalities, in consequence, were poured into Ireland. The siege and relief of Londonderry,[6] Schomberg's indecisive campaign in Ulster,[7] William's success at the Boyne and Ginkel's at Aughrim,[8] engaged the attention of all western Europe. The treaty of Limerick,[9] which ended the war, was much more than an Irish settlement, and in that lies one of the main reasons for its moderation, for William was anxious not to alienate his Catholic allies on the Continent, and deliberately made the terms as generous as possible.

Unfortunately, while William was laudably anxious that full effect should be given to the treaty, and did in fact secure the punctual observance of the military provisions, which were entirely within his province as commander-in-chief, he proved unable to enlist the support either of the English or of the Irish Parliament for the civil provisions. The first step in breach of the agreement was taken within a few weeks by the English Parliament, which passed an Act requiring all Irish officials and members of Parliament to take the oaths of allegiance and supremacy and subscribe a declaration against transubstantiation.[10] This was a gross infringement upon the independence of all Ireland; but it was acquiesced in by the Irish Protestants because it so greatly strengthened their position. Having the Irish Parliament now entirely under their control they proceeded to make their own attack on the privileges guaranteed to the Catholics by the treaty, and in the sessions of 1695 and 1697 laid the foundations of the penal code against them which was to be one of the features of the eighteenth century. Not until the latter year was the treaty even nominally confirmed by Act of Parliament, and then only in so far as it consisted with the safety and welfare of his Majesty's subjects in Ireland.[11]

Thus the condition of Ireland was decidedly worse under William than it had been under Charles. During the revolutionary war the country had been more thoroughly

[1] No. 287. [2] No. 288. [3] No. 275. [4] No. 281.
[5] No. 289. [6] No. 290. [7] No. 291. [8] No. 292.
[9] Nos. 293, 294. [10] No. 296. [11] No. 295.

devastated than ever, and the constructive work of the earlier reign had been largely undone.[1] Not only so, but the process of recovery was gravely impeded by renewed uncertainty about the ownership of the land, for the new owners had first fled or been deprived by the Patriot Parliament, and then the old owners had in turn been dispossessed on the assumption that the legislation of that Parliament was invalid, while most of the supporters of James in the civil war, whether old owners or new, were held to have forfeited their estates by high treason. Of these forfeited estates William undertook not to make any grants pending a decision by the English Parliament; but in actual fact he made very extensive grants, many of them to foreigners and personal favourites, producing such a wave of indignation in England that in 1700 Parliament passed an Act resuming all such grants since William's accession, and vesting the estates in trustees, who were to sell them, to Protestants only, for the benefit of the nation.[2] Not until the reign of Anne was it even reasonably clear to whom much of the land in Ireland was to belong.

Trade also was injured by the wars with France, and industry restricted by the jealousy of rival interests in England. Throughout the greater part of William's reign Ireland continued to benefit from its recently established woollen industry; but in 1699 the English Parliament was induced by the prosperity of that industry to pass an Act prohibiting the export of Irish woollen goods except to England, where the import duties were prohibitive,[3] and surplus Irish woollens had thereafter to depend on smuggling for a market. As compensation for the destruction of the woollen industry much was done to encourage the growth of a linen industry, for which Ireland was considered to be specially suited, but it may be doubted whether the gain came within measurable distance of balancing the loss.

One cause of unrest, it is true, had been temporarily relegated to the background, for the native Irish had been too thoroughly crushed to be capable of further effort, and as the penal laws were steadily added to under Anne[4] their degradation steadily increased. But although the problem of Ireland was thus reduced to the relations of the English and Scottish settlers with each other and with the government at home that problem was troublesome enough. Inevitably it centred in the Irish Parliament, which like the Scottish Parliament reached its final form in the reign of William. Modelled on the English Parliament, it consisted of a House of Lords, in which the 4 archbishops of the established Church, 18 bishops and approximately 100 lay peers were entitled to sit, and a House of Commons, in which the 32 counties, 117 boroughs, and the University of Dublin, were each represented by two members.[5] But it had neither the independence, the traditional prestige, nor the actual authority of the English Parliament. As there was no Irish equivalent of the English Triennial Act, and as the considerable Irish revenue, including quit-rents, Customs, Excise and Hearth Tax, was the hereditary possession of the kings, there was no very good reason why the Irish Parliament should be summoned at all; and in actual fact only one such Parliament was summoned by Charles, two by William and two by Anne. Moreover even when it met its legislation was subject to the approval of the English Privy Council and capable of being overridden by the English Parliament.

Thus the Irish Parliament had good reason for raising difficulties with the English government, but little prospect of achieving any result if it did so. In 1692 William's first Parliament endeavoured to assert an exclusive right to originate money bills, only to receive a formal rebuke from the Lord Lieutenant, Lord Sidney.[6] In 1698 William

[1] No. 278.   [2] No. 276.   [3] No. 282.   [4] No. 301.   [5] App. IV.   [6] No. 297.

Molyneux, one of the representatives of the University of Dublin in William's second Parliament, published a pamphlet asserting the legislative independence of the Irish Parliament, only to have it condemned by the English House of Commons.[1] Early in Anne's reign, inspired no doubt by events in Scotland, the Irish House of Commons revived a project which had long been entertained by speculative thinkers,[2] and petitioned for a parliamentary union with England;[3] but it was not very serious about the matter, the English, apprehending no such danger from Ireland as they apprehended from Scotland, were indifferent, and the proposal came to nothing. Thereafter Ireland sank back into comparative quietude, until roused from its lethargy by the troubles leading up to the American Revolution.

[1] No. 298.   [2] No. 299.   [3] No. 300.

BIBLIOGRAPHY

Robert H. Murray, *Ireland 1603–1714* (London, 1920), in the "Helps for Students of History" series, is a useful, though unpretentious, bibliographical guide. Constantia Maxwell, *A Short Bibliography of Irish History* (London, 1921), published under the direction of the Historical Association, is a general compilation, now somewhat out of date, with special sections on the early and later Stuarts, the dividing line being 1689. P. L. Prendeville, "A Select Bibliography of Irish Economic History, Part Two, The Seventeenth and Eighteenth Centuries", in *Economic History Review*, III (1932), pp. 402–416, is valuable for political history as well. Recent publications are indicated in the articles on "Writings on Irish History" which appear periodically in *Irish Historical Studies*.

The records and Record Office at Dublin were destroyed during the troubles of 1922, with a loss to historical scholarship which can be estimated from Herbert Wood, *A Guide to the Records Deposited in the Public Record Office of Ireland* (Dublin, 1919), and from the same writer's "The Public Records of Ireland before and after 1922", in *Transactions of the Royal Historical Society, Fourth Series*, XIII (1930), pp. 17–49. Before the catastrophe, however, much had been published, to which the *Guide* serves as a useful book of reference; and much is being done by the Irish Manuscripts Commission to repair the loss. Irish statutes are printed in *The Statutes at Large passed in the Parliaments held in Ireland*, vols. II–IV (Dublin, 1765), and in Thomas Davis, *The Patriot Parliament of 1689*, edited by Sir Charles Gavan Duffy (London, 1893). Parliamentary proceedings are contained in *The Journals of the House of Lords of the Kingdom of Ireland*, vols. I and II (Dublin, 1779–1780); *Collection of the Protests of the Lords of Ireland from 1634 to 1771* (Dublin, 1772); and *The Journals of the House of Commons of the Kingdom of Ireland*, vols. I–III (Dublin, 1753). The *Calendar of State Papers relating to Ireland, 1660–1670*, edited by Robert Pentland Mahaffy (4 vols., 1905–1911), deals with the Irish papers in the Public Record Office for these years, after which such papers are included in the general *Calendar of State Papers Domestic*.

The correspondence of successive Lords Lieutenants of Ireland is to be found in the *Calendar of the Manuscripts of the Marquess of Ormonde*, already referred to (p. 40); in *Essex Papers*, edited by Osmund Airy for the Camden Society (1890), *Letters written by Arthur Capel, Earl of Essex, in the year 1675* (London, 1770), and *Selections from the Correspondence of Arthur Capel, Earl of Essex, 1675–1677*, edited by Clement Edwards Pike for the Royal Historical Society (1913); and in *The Correspondence of Henry Hyde, Earl of Clarendon, and Laurence Hyde, Earl of Rochester*, already mentioned (p. 43).

The *Calendar of the Orrery Papers*, edited by Edward MacLysaght for the Irish Manuscripts Commission (Dublin, 1941), deals with a very varied collection of documents, most of them belonging to the period 1660–1689. Much interesting information about intrigues in the reign of James II is contained in Thomas Sheridan's "Historical Account", printed in *Calendar of the Stuart Papers preserved at Windsor Castle*, edited by F. H. Blackburne Daniell for the Historical Manuscripts Commission, VI (1916), pp. 1–75. Material for the period of the Revolution is particularly full. George Walker, *True Account of the Siege of Londonderry* (London, 1689), has been corrected and supplemented on some material points by Stephen Martin-Leake's *Life of Sir John Leake*, edited by Geoffrey A. R. Callender for the Navy Records Society (2 vols., 1920). On the Protestant side the chief spokesman is William King, whose *State of the Protestants of Ireland under the late King James's Government* (London, 1691) is a determined vindication of the Revolution. On the Catholic or Jacobite side are *The Journal of John Stevens, 1689–1691*, edited by Robert H. Murray (Oxford, 1912); and the narrative known to Macaulay and others as "A Light to the Blind", which has been partly printed in Historical Manuscripts Commission, *Tenth Report*, App. V (1885), pp. 107–200, and edited by John T. Gilbert under the title *A Jacobite Narrative of the War in Ireland, 1688–1691* (Dublin, 1892). The views of a military expert are set forth in the "Autobiography of Dr. George Clarke", printed in *Report on the Manuscripts of*

F. W. Leyborne-Popham, edited by Sophia C. Lomas for the Historical Manuscripts Commission (1899), pp. 259–289; and those of an acute foreign observer in *Négociations de M. le Comte d'Avaux en Irlande, 1689–90* (Dublin, 1934).

There is an admirable introductory sketch of "Ireland from the Restoration to the Act of Resumption, 1660–1700", by Robert Dunlop, in *The Cambridge Modern History*, v (1908), pp. 301–323, continued in the same writer's "Ireland in the Eighteenth Century", *ibid.*, VI (1909), pp. 479–505. Macaulay's account of Irish affairs, in chaps. VI, XII, XVI and XVII of his *History*, is valuable, though far from complete. The early chapters both of James Anthony Froude, *The English in Ireland in the Eighteenth Century* (3 vols., London, 1872–1874), and of William Edward Hartpole Lecky, *A History of Ireland in the Eighteenth Century* (5 vols., London, 1896–1898), have much to say about the later years of the seventeenth century, valuable in the one case for the extensive use made of original authorities, and in the other for the unusual objectivity of outlook displayed. Most works on Irish history are prejudiced, and many are frankly partisan. Richard Bagwell, *Ireland under the Stuarts, vol. iii, 1660–1690* (London, 1916), presents the moderate Protestant point of view, and is joined in this by Robert H. Murray, *Revolutionary Ireland and its Settlement* (London, 1911), which brings out the importance of Ireland as a factor in European affairs. John P. Prendergast, *Ireland from the Restoration to the Revolution, 1660 to 1690* (London, 1887), is not yet entirely out of date.

Other works on Irish history are concerned with particular periods or particular aspects of the subject. The best account of the early years of Charles II's reign is to be found in Carte's *Life of James, Duke of Ormond*, referred to later (p. 895). Clement E. Pike, "The Intrigue to deprive the Earl of Essex of the Lord Lieutenancy of Ireland", in *Transactions of the Royal Historical Society, Third Series*, v (1911), pp. 89–103, and the same writer's "The Origin of the Regium Donum", *ibid.*, III (1909), pp. 255–269, deal with obscure episodes in the reign of Charles II. J. S. Reid, *History of the Presbyterian Church in Ireland, comprising the Civil History of the Province of Ulster from the Accession of James the First*, edited by W. D. Killen (3 vols., Belfast, 1867), is still the best survey of its subject. Scholarly studies of associated problems are J. C. Beckett, *Protestant Dissent in Ireland, 1687–1780* (London, 1948), and the same writer's "The Government and the Church of Ireland under William III and Anne", in *Irish Historical Studies*, II (1941), pp. 280–302, and "William King's Administration of the Diocese of Derry, 1691–1703", *ibid.*, IV (1944), pp. 164–180. J. G. S. Macneill, *Constitutional and Parliamentary History of Ireland till the Union* (London, 1917), is the chief authority on constitutional development, and Grace Lawless Lee, *The Huguenot Settlements in Ireland* (London, 1936), the chief authority on foreign immigration.

On military operations Demetrius Charles Boulger, *The Battle of the Boyne, together with an Account based on French and other unpublished Records of the War in Ireland, 1688–1691* (London, 1911), is useful, though hardly impartial. It should be supplemented by Mary F. Sandars, *Lauzun, Courtier and Adventurer: the Life of a Friend of Louis XIV* (2 vols., London, 1908).

Of the land settlement and kindred matters the best account is to be found in Lord Edmond Fitzmaurice, *The Life of Sir William Petty, 1623–1687* (London, 1895). Social history is surveyed in Edward MacLysaght, *Irish Life in the Seventeenth Century* (Oxford, 1950). Economic history in the widest sense is dealt with, not very critically, in Alice E. Murray, *The History of the Commercial and Financial Relations between England and Ireland from the Period of the Restoration* (London, 1903), and George O'Brien, *The Economic History of Ireland in the Seventeenth Century* (Dublin, 1919). More valuable within its restricted limits is Conrad Gill, *The Rise of the Irish Linen Industry* (Oxford, 1925), which gives most of the credit for the development of the industry to the Huguenot refugees of the later part of the seventeenth century.

A. THE LAND

274. (Irish) Act of Settlement, 1662

(Irish *Statutes at Large*, II, pp. 239–263)

AN ACT FOR THE BETTER EXECUTION
OF HIS MAJESTY'S GRACIOUS DECLARATION
FOR THE SETTLEMENT OF HIS KINGDOM OF IRELAND
AND SATISFACTION OF THE SEVERAL INTERESTS OF ADVENTURERS,
SOLDIERS AND OTHER HIS SUBJECTS THERE

Whereas an unnatural insurrection did break forth against your Majesty's royal father of ever blessed memory, his crown and dignity, in this your Majesty's kingdom of Ireland, upon the 23 of October in the year of our Lord God 1641, . . . which afterwards . . . settled into and became a formed and almost national rebellion of the Irish papists, . . . to the destruction of the English and Protestants inhabiting in Ireland, the which Irish papists, being represented in a general assembly chosen by themselves, and acting by a council called by them the Supreme Council of the Confederate Roman Catholics of Ireland, did first assume, usurp and exercise the power of life and death, make peace and war, . . . and afterwards acted under a foreign authority, by all the said ways disowning and rejecting your royal father and your Majesty's undoubted right to this kingdom ; . . . and whereas several of your Majesty's subjects, by whom as instruments the said rebels were totally subdued, did in the time of your Majesty's absence beyond the seas . . . inquire into the authors, contrivers and abetters of the said rebellion and war, and . . . did dispossess such of the said popish Irish rebels of their lands, tenements and hereditaments, as they found guilty of, and to have been engaged in, the said rebellion or war aforementioned, and did withal distribute and set out the said lands to be possessed by sundry persons, their agents and tenants, who by advancing of their moneys and goods, or by hazarding of their lives, had contributed unto the said conquest ; . . . and whereas several of your Majesty's Protestant subjects, as soon as with much difficulty and hazard they had gotten the power of this kingdom into their hands, did according to their bounden duty, with all humility and cheerfulness, invite your Majesty into this your kingdom, with a faithful engagement to serve your Majesty with their lives and estates, and afterwards, when your sacred Majesty, their sovereign lord and king, by your gracious letters from Breda bearing date the 4/14 day of April in the twelfth year of your Majesty's reign, intimated your royal intentions of returning to the exercise of your regal authority, they, with others of your Majesty's Protestant subjects, did readily and dutifully yield up themselves and the said subdued people with this your kingdom of Ireland unto your Majesty's absolute obedience and disposition, who thereupon, after many months consideration and the public hearing of all parties, . . . did at length in your princely wisdom, grace and justice set forth a declaration bearing date the 30 day of November in the twelfth year of your Majesty's reign, with several explanations

and instructions relating thereunto, expressing your royal pleasure concerning the
people and territories of this your Majesty's said kingdom, . . . be it enacted . . . that
all honours, manors, castles, houses, places, lands, tenements and hereditaments, right,
title, service, chiefry, use, trust, condition, fee, rent-charge, chattels real, mortgage,
right of redemption of any mortgages, recognizance, judgments, forfeitures, extent,
right of action, right of entry, statute or any other estate of what nature or kind soever,
in all and every the counties, baronies, cities, towns corporate and walled towns in this
kingdom, which at any time from and after the said 23 day of October in the year of
our Lord 1641 were seized or sequestered into the hands or to the use of his late
Majesty King Charles the First, or of your most gracious Majesty that now is, or
otherwise disposed of, distributed, set out or set apart by reason of or upon account
of the said rebellion or war, or which were allotted, assigned, given, granted, ordered,
disposed, distributed, demised, set out or set apart to or for any person or persons, use
or uses, for adventures, arrears, reprisals or otherwise, or whereof his late Majesty, or
your Majesty that now is, or any adventurer, soldier, reprisable person or others
respectively had and received the rent, issue or profits, by reason or upon account of
the said rebellion or war, or whereof the adventurers, officers or soldiers now or
formerly of the English army in this kingdom, or transplanted or transplantable
persons or any of them, or their or any of their heir, heirs or assigns, or any other
person or persons whatsoever, upon account of the said rebellion or war, were in
seisin, possession or occupation by themselves, their tenants, agents or assigns, on the
seventh day of May 1659, or which were assigned, given, granted, laid out, set apart
or reserved for or towards the satisfaction of any the said adventurers, soldiers or other
persons for or in consideration of any money or provisions advanced, lent or furnished, or for arrears of pay, or in compensation of any service or reputed services, or
other account whatsoever, or reserved or mentioned to be reserved for or in order to
a reprisal or reprisals for such encumbrances as then were, now are, or shall be adjudged
due to any person or persons out of the said lands, tenements or hereditaments, or for
any other use, intent or purpose whatsoever, or whereof any *custodiam,* lease for year or
years or other disposition or grant whatsoever hath been made, or unto which your
royal father or your Majesty that now is are any ways entitled by reason of, or upon
account of, the said rebellion or war, or which are wrongfully detained or concealed
by any person or persons whatever; as also all chantries, and all manors, lands,
tenements, rents, tithes, pensions, portions and other hereditaments or things whatsoever belonging to them or any of them, which were in the seisin, possession or
occupation, and out of which any rent, duty, tenure or other service was reserved, of
any person or persons who by the qualifications in this Act shall not be adjudged
innocent persons; as also all lands, tenements and hereditaments belonging to any
ecclesiastical person or persons in his or their politic capacity, and that have formerly
by them or any of them been let in fee farm, the right whereof, or title thereunto, or
interest therein, was in any person or persons, his or their heirs or assigns, who by the
qualifications in this Act expressed shall not be adjudged innocent persons; as also all
leases that have been made by any ecclesiastical persons of any lands, tenements or
hereditaments belonging unto them in their politic capacity, to any person or persons,

their executors, administrators or assigns, who by the qualifications in this Act expressed shall not be adjudged innocent persons; as also all impropriations or appropriate tithes belonging to any person or persons, his or their heirs, executors, administrators or assigns, who by the qualifications in this present Act expressed shall not be adjudged innocent, are and shall be, and are hereby declared, deemed and adjudged, as from the said 23 day of October 1641, forfeited, and to have been forfeited, to your Majesty, your heirs and successors, without any office or inquisition thereof found, or hereafter to be found. . . .

IV. Provided likewise that this Act or anything therein contained shall not vest, nor be understood or construed to vest, in your Majesty, your heirs or successors, or otherwise be prejudicial unto or take away, any estate, right, title. . .[1] from any Protestant or Protestants, their heirs, executors, administrators or assigns, who did not join with the said rebels before the 15th day of September 1643, . . . nor to the vesting any of the lands, tenements, hereditaments or chattels real, right, title. . .[2] of any innocent papist, or their innocent heirs, executors, administrators or assigns.

V. And be it further enacted, . . . that all and every such person or persons, his and their executors, administrators and assigns, to whom any lands, tenements or hereditaments belonging unto such Protestant or innocent papist have been assigned or distributed, set out or enjoyed, shall forthwith, and before any other reprisals whatsoever to be set out, be reprized, anything in this Act to the contrary notwithstanding. . . .

VII. And whereas your sacred Majesty hath by your said gracious declaration and instructions declared your royal pleasure and intentions how the said honours, manors, castles, houses, lands, tenements and hereditaments, and all other the estates and interests hereby forfeited unto and vested in your Majesty, your heirs and successors, should be disposed of, and also by commission under your great seal of this your kingdom, bearing date the 30th day of April in the 13th year of your Majesty's reign, appointed certain commissioners for putting in execution all the matters and things in the said declaration and instructions contained, be it enacted . . . that all the said honours, manors, lands, castles, houses, tenements, hereditaments, and all other the estates and interests hereby vested and settled in your Majesty, your heirs and successors (except before excepted or provided for as aforesaid), shall be and remain in your sacred Majesty, your heirs and successors, to the intent to be settled, confirmed, restored or disposed to and for such use and uses, and in such manner, as in and by the said declaration and instructions hereafter following, and by this present Act and the true intent and meaning thereof, is declared, limited, meant, intended or appointed.

His Majesty's gracious declaration
for the settlement of his kingdom of Ireland and satisfaction
of the several interests of adventurers, soldiers
and other his subjects there

Charles the Second, by the grace of God, king of England, Scotland, France and Ireland, Defender of the Faith, &c., to all our loving subjects of our kingdom of

---

[1] As in section i.   [2] As above.

Ireland of what degree or quality soever, greeting. It having pleased Almighty God, out of his great mercy and compassion towards us and all our subjects, to restore us in so wonderful a manner to each other, . . . we think it agreeable to the just sense we have, and ought to have, of the good affection of all our good subjects who have contributed so much in bringing this unspeakable blessing upon us and themselves, that we acknowledge that our good subjects in our kingdom of Ireland have borne a very good part in procuring this happiness. . . . However, it was not easy for us to make any public declaration with reference to that our kingdom, there being many difficulties in the providing for and complying with the several interests and pretences there. . . . We well knew the Acts of Parliament which had formerly passed for the security of the adventurers in that kingdom, and had heard of the proceedings which had been thereupon, by which very many officers, soldiers and others, as well of this as that our kingdom, were in possession of a great part of the lands of that our kingdom, and of whose interests we resolve to be very careful.

II. We well remember the cessation and the peace which our royal father of blessed memory had been forced during the late troubles to make with the Irish subjects of that our kingdom, and by which he was compelled to give them a full pardon for what they had before done amiss, upon their return to their duty and their promise of giving his Majesty a vigorous assistance, and that from that time divers persons of honour and quality had not (that we know or have heard of) swerved from their allegiance towards him or us. We could not forget the peace that ourself was afterwards necessitated to make with our said subjects, in the time when they who wickedly usurped the authority in this kingdom had erected that odious court for the taking away of the life of our dear father; and then nobody can wonder that we were desirous, though upon difficult conditions, to get such an united power of our own subjects as might have been able, with God's blessing, to have prevented that infamous and horrible parricide.

III. And therefore we could not but hold ourself obliged to perform what we owe by that peace to those who had honestly and faithfully performed what they had promised to us, though we and they were miserably disappointed of the effect of those promises by an unhappy part of them which foolishly forfeited all the grace which they might have expected from us.

IV. And in the last place, we did and must always remember the great affection a considerable part of that nation expressed to us during the time of our being beyond the seas, when with all cheerfulness and obedience they received and submitted to our orders, and betook themselves to that service which we directed as most convenient and behoveful at that time to us. . . . And yet all these important considerations and obligations appeared so many contradictions to the present interest of our good subjects in that our kingdom, who had at this time likewise merited very much from us, and for whose security and advantage we held ourself obliged to provide as well as for their indemnity. . . .

VI. And therefore in the first place, in order to a settlement of that interest claimed by the adventurers, . . . we do hereby declare that all the lands, tenements and hereditaments of which all or any of the adventurers were possessed the seventh day of May one thousand six hundred fifty-nine, having been allotted or set out to them or enjoyed by them as adventurers in satisfaction of and for their adventures, shall be confirmed and made good to them, their heirs and assigns for ever, with allowance or correction of the admeasurement, according to the tenor and directions of the respective Acts of Parliament of 17 and 18 Caroli, as to the English or plantation measure, except as is hereafter excepted; and that the deficient adventurer, either in part or in whole, shall be satisfied out of the moiety of the counties of Limerick, Tipperary and Waterford in the province of Munster, the King's County, the Queen's County and the counties of Eastmeath and Westmeath in the province of Leinster, and the counties of Down, Antrim and Armagh in the province of Ulster, not yet set out to the said adventurers, as also the forfeited lands in the county of Louth (except the barony of Atherdee in the said county) and said province of Leinster, such adventurers claiming and making their deficiencies appear before the first day of May next. . . .

VII. And whereas the officers and soldiers now of our army in Ireland, and that have been formerly of the army in Ireland, have had also lands set out to them respectively in satisfaction of their arrears of pay for their service in that our kingdom, and are accordingly possessed of the same by former pretended orders and powers then in being, and although the incompetency of such powers may justly render such possessions and estates liable to question, to our very great advantage, . . . yet in regard of our letter to General Monck from Breda in the twelfth year of our reign, and of our several declarations and proclamations concerning the army, and of the full assurance of the forwardness and readiness of the said army and loving subjects in Ireland to contribute, as in duty bound, all that in them lay for our restoration, we are pleased of our special grace and favour to declare, and do hereby declare, that all officers and soldiers, their heirs and assigns, who have been and are of the said army in Ireland, and to whom lands have been given out in satisfaction of their arrears for their service in that our kingdom, and have by the general convention of Ireland or by any other public act declared submission and obedience to us, according to our said declaration of the 4/14 of April last, dated at Breda, shall enjoy their respective estates conferred on them for their arrears for service in the kingdom of Ireland, according to their respective possessions on the seventh day of May one thousand six hundred fifty-nine, in full satisfaction of all such arrears for which lands were set out to them respectively as aforesaid, so that they and every of them, having received an equal proportion with others in the like case, are and shall be for ever barred from demanding or receiving any further satisfaction therefor, although they had allowance but for thirteen shillings in the pound or thereabouts. . . .

IX. Being sensible that several officers who were engaged in our service in Ireland, and eminently acted and suffered therein, have by the partiality and injustice of the powers then in being received no satisfaction for the same, we are therefore further pleased graciously to declare that all commissioned officers, their heirs or assigns, who were in regiments, troops or companies raised in Ireland, or transported out of England, and served our royal father or ourself in the wars in Ireland, at any time before the fifth of June 1649, other than those who have received lands or money for their pay due unto them since the fifth of June 1649, shall be satisfied their respective personal arrears out of the particulars following, viz., out of the forfeited lands, tenements and hereditaments undisposed of to adventurers or soldiers in the counties of Wicklow, Longford, Leitrim and Donegal, out of all the forfeited lands, tenements and hereditaments undisposed of in the province of Connaught and county of Clare lying within one mile of the river Shannon (or of the sea), commonly called the Mile Line, out of all the houses and tenements forfeited in Ireland in the several walled towns and corporations, and lands thereunto belonging, not already set out to the adventurers or soldiers, . . . out of the benefit arising from the redemption of mortgages, statutes-staples and judgments, where the lands are not already disposed of to adventurers or soldiers, . . . out of one year's rent and profits of the lands set out to the officers and soldiers for their arrears in the year 1653, and likewise of the army now in being, according as those respective said estates yielded in the year 1659, as also out of one year and a half's rent and profits arising out of the lands for the arrears of those officers and soldiers who were ordered or received satisfaction for their said arrears in the years 1655, 1656 and 1657, according as the estates yielded in the year 1659.

X. And it is further declared, that all commissioned officers before one thousand six hundred forty-nine, who have had no satisfaction in lands or otherwise set out to them for services since one thousand six hundred forty-nine, shall be immediately, out of the whole security that is above assigned for satisfaction of arrears before one thousand six hundred forty-nine, satisfied twelve shillings six pence in the pound of what is due to them; and then the remaining part of all the said respective securities to be equally divided amongst all and every the said commissioned officers who have any arrears due for services in Ireland before one thousand six hundred forty-nine; all which rents abovesaid shall be paid in such way and manner as shall be by us appointed. . . .

XI. That such Protestants whose estates have been given out for satisfaction of adventurers or soldiers, or otherwise disposed of to any other persons, shall be forthwith restored to their former estates, and a reprisal of equal value, worth and purchase forthwith assigned to such adventurers or soldiers as shall be removed out of their said estates.

XII. Provided no person or persons shall have benefit hereof, who were in the rebellion before the fifteenth of September one thousand six hundred forty and three, and have taken out decrees for lands in the province of Connaught or county of Clare in recompense of their former estates. . . .

XVI. And whereas we understand that by the late usurped powers, during the distempers of these times, several Irish proprietors of the popish religion have been dispossessed of their estates merely for being papists, and have sued out decrees, and are possessed of lands in the province of Connaught and county of Clare in compensation of their former estates, which being an act of their own we might without any injustice deny to relieve them in, yet so willing we are that any interest entitling itself to equitable mercy might not be disappointed that we declare that all innocent papists, being such as shall prove themselves to have been faithful and loyal unto, and never acted against, our royal father or ourself since the two and twentieth day of October one thousand six hundred forty-one, though they have sued out decrees and are possessed of lands in the province of Connaught or county of Clare in lieu of their former estates, shall notwithstanding be restored to their said estates by the second of May one thousand six hundred sixty-one. . . .

XVII. Provided also that whatsoever adventurer or soldier that shall be removed from his present possession to make room for any such papist shall forthwith have a reprise of equal value, worth and purchase in other forfeited lands.

XVIII. Provided always that whereas the corporations of Ireland are now planted with English, who have considerably improved at their own charges and brought trade and manufacture into that our kingdom, and by their settlement there do not a little contribute to the peace and settlement of that country, the disturbing or removal of which English would in many respects be very prejudicial, that all such of the popish religion, of any corporations in Ireland, who have been for public security dispossessed of their estates within any corporation, shall be forthwith reprised in forfeited lands, tenements and hereditaments near the said corporations, to the full value, worth and purchase of such estate as he was dispossessed of within such corporation. . . .

XXII. And as we cannot but with extraordinary sadness of heart remember, and even at present behold, the desolate and distracted condition that our kingdom of Ireland hath been and is reduced unto by the unnatural insurrection begun in the year one thousand six hundred forty-one, and consequently abhor and detest the contrivers and obstinate promoters of the same against us, our crown and dignity, so we cannot, upon the considerations formerly expressed in this our declaration, deny all just and reasonable provision that may stand with the present juncture of our affairs unto such of the Irish nation who not only gave early evidences of their repentance for their crimes but also persevered in their loyalty to us and our commands, and that as near as we can, our justice and our mercy in accommodating this interest might not jostle each other, we are in a different manner to consider of such of them as are justly entitled to the benefit of those articles of peace formerly mentioned, and such who did not submit unto the same, or after a submission made a departure from the same, which two latter sorts have justly forfeited that favour which otherwise they might have received. We are also further to consider of those who embraced the said articles, and submitted to the said peace without any apostacy, in a different notion, as of those who remained in that our kingdom, who sued out decrees and received lands in satisfaction of their ancient estates, and those who, being transported into foreign parts, through many difficulties united, rendezvoused and served under our obedience. So that upon these considerations we think fit to declare, and accordingly do declare, that as to those who embraced the said articles and submitted to the said peace and constantly adhered thereunto, and remaining at home sued out decrees and obtained possession of lands in the province of Connaught or county of Clare, that they are to stand bound by them, and not to be relieved against their own act, who contented themselves to enjoy a part of satisfaction for their own rather than to attend our restitution or submit themselves to our command in foreign parts as others did; and yet if the conditions of those seem hard, they can no more reasonably expect that we should further relieve them than our friends in England and Ireland can expect that we should pay back to them all the moneys they were compelled in the evil times to pay for their compositions, which they would have avoided had it been in their power. . . .

XXIV. And as to those who continued with us, or served faithfully under our ensigns beyond the seas, we think fit, and accordingly declare, that they shall be restored to their former estates, if they by themselves or agents authorized by them have not prosecuted and obtained decrees and lands in the province of Connaught or county of Clare in compensation of their former estates, a reprise being first assigned and legally set out of the remaining forfeited lands undisposed of, to such adventurer or soldier, or other person before named, of equal value, worth and purchase to the estate out of which such adventurer or soldier or other person aforesaid shall be so removed. . . .

XXVIII. And though some, not sensible of the great perplexities we have laboured under to reconcile these jarring interests, may infer that where we judge persons fitting to be restored to their estates yet the limitation of a previous reprisal may eclipse much of our grace, to this we say . . . how hard it would be that the English, . . . after so many thousands of families, who have sold their interests in England, have transported and settled themselves in Ireland and have made great improvements in buildings and otherwise, should in the interval of those accommodations (reprisal not being first provided for) be dispossessed of their houses, and their stocks (the sole subsistence of them and their families) exposed to certainty of loss (though greater inconveniences we pretermit), may easily be judged. . . . And lest any ambiguity or controversy might arise for precedency in restitution to their former rights, we do declare that first all innocent Protestants and those persons termed innocent papists (who never took out any decree, or had lands assigned to them in Connaught or Clare) be first restored; in the next place that those innocent Protestants and papists who took out decrees, and had lands allotted to them in pursuance thereof in Connaught or Clare, shall be restored, and that such transplanted persons as shall be dispossessed of their decreed estates in Connaught or Clare, by virtue of this our declaration, shall be reprised out of other forfeited lands of equal value, worth and purchase in the said province of Connaught or county of Clare or elsewhere before they be dispossessed of their said estates; and that then such of the Irish papists who constantly served under our ensigns abroad, having right to the articles of peace, are to be restored. . . .

Clause XI of the Instructions. Whereas by our said declaration several innocent Protestants and papists are to be restored to their estates, and a reprise of equal value, worth and purchase is to be assigned to such adventurers and soldiers and other persons as do possess the same, in the doing thereof you are to observe these following directions, viz., not to restore any as an innocent papist that at or before the cessation which was made upon 15 September 1643 were of the rebels' party; nor any who being of full age and sound memory enjoyed their estates, real or personal, in the rebel quarters; . . . nor such as entered into the Roman Catholic confederacy at any time before the articles of peace concluded 1648; nor such as at any time adhered to the nuncio's or clergy's party, or papal power, in opposition to the king's authority; nor such as have been excommunicated for adhering to the king's authority, and afterwards owned their offences for so doing and were relaxed thereupon from their excommunication; nor such who derived their titles to their estates from any who died guilty of any the aforementioned crimes; nor such as pleaded the articles of peace for their estates; nor such as being in the quarters which were under the authority of our royal father or ourself held correspondence with or gave intelligence to such as were then in opposition against our said royal father or ourself in Ireland; nor such as before any of the peaces in 1646 or 1648 sat in any of the confederate Roman Catholic assemblies or councils, or acted upon any commissions or powers derived from them or any of them; nor such as empowered agents or commissioners to treat with any foreign papal power beyond the seas for bringing into Ireland foreign forces, or were persons which acted in such negotiations; nor such persons as have been wood-kerns or tories, before the marquis of Clanrickarde's leaving the government of that kingdom.

    Given at our court at Whitehall,
    the 30 day of November 1660,
    in the twelfth year of our reign.

275. (Irish) Act repealing the Act of Settlement, 1689
(*Dublin Magazine*, February 1843, pp. 78–90)

AN ACT FOR REPEALING THE ACTS OF SETTLEMENT AND EXPLANATION, RESOLUTION OF DOUBTS, AND ALL GRANTS, PATENTS AND CERTIFICATES PURSUANT TO THEM OR ANY OF THEM

Whereas the Roman Catholic subjects of this kingdom have for several years, to the apparent hazard of their lives and estates, under the royal authority defended this kingdom, until at last they were overpowered by the usurper, Oliver Cromwell, in which quarrel many of them lost their lives, and divers of them (rather than take any conditions from the said usurper) did transport themselves into foreign parts, where they faithfully served under his late Majesty and his present Majesty, until his late Majesty was restored to the crown; and whereas the said usurper hath seized and sequestered all the lands, tenements and hereditaments of the said Roman Catholics within this kingdom, upon the account of their religion and loyalty, and disposed of the same among his officers and soldiers and others his adherents; and though his Majesty's said Roman Catholic subjects, not only upon the account of the peace made by his late Majesty in the year 1648, but also for their eminent loyalty and firm adherence to the royal cause, might have justly expected to partake of his late Majesty's favour and bounty upon his happy restoration, . . . yet such were the contrivances set on foot to destroy his Majesty's said Catholic subjects of this realm that two Acts of Parliament passed here, the one entituled, *An Act for the better execution of his Majesty's gracious declaration for the settlement of his kingdom of Ireland, and satisfaction of the several interests of adventurers, soldiers and other his subjects there*;[1] the other Act

----

[1] No. 274.

entituled, *An Act for explaining of some doubts arising upon an Act entituled, An Act for the better execution of his Majesty's gracious declaration for the settlement of his kingdom of Ireland, and satisfaction of the several interests of adventurers, soldiers and other his subjects there, and for making some alterations of and additions unto the said Act for the more speedy and effectual settlement of the kingdom,* by which many of the said Catholic subjects were ousted of their ancient inheritances without being so much as heard, and the same were distributed among Cromwell's soldiers and others, who in justice could not have the least pretension to the same, contrary to the said peace made in the year 1648, and contrary to justice and natural equity; and whereas it is now high time to put an end to the unspeakable sufferings of the said Roman Catholics, natives of this realm (who have eminently manifested their loyalty to his Majesty against the usurper, the prince of Orange), and to remove the unparalleled grievances brought upon them under colour of the said two statutes, . . . be it therefore enacted . . . that the said two several Acts hereinbefore mentioned, commonly called the Acts of Settlement and Explanation, and the Acts of State, or Act of Council, commonly called the Resolution of Doubts, by the Lord Lieutenant and Council upon the Acts of Settlement and Explanation thereof, . . . and all and every grant, patent and certificate passed by virtue of . . . the said Acts and resolutions, . . . be and are hereby absolutely repealed, annulled and made void. . . .

II. And be it further enacted, that all manner of persons who were any way entituled to any lands, tenements or hereditaments, or whose ancestors were any way seized, possessed of or entituled to any lands, tenements or hereditaments, in use, possession, reversion or remainder in this kingdom of Ireland, on the 22nd day of October 1641, their heirs or assigns, and every person lawfully claiming by, from or under them and his and their feoffees and trustees, to and for their use or uses, or in trust for them or any of them, and who were barred, excluded, hindered or prejudiced by the said Acts, resolutions, grants, patents and certificates, shall and may have and take such and the like remedy by action or otherwise for revesting or recovering the same as they, or any or either of them, now might, could or ought to have had or taken, in case the said Acts, resolutions, or any grant, patent or certificate had never been made or passed. . . .

III. And be it further enacted . . . that all attainders and outlawries for treason or any other offence, and also all treasons and other offences whatsoever upon account or pretence of the rebellion mentioned or expressed to have begun or arisen in this kingdom on the 23rd day of October 1641, and also all penalties, pains, forfeitures, bars and disabilities accrued or supposed to be accrued thereby, . . . be and are hereby made void, released and discharged to all intents and purposes whatsoever. . . .

V. And to the end that every person or persons . . . may with all convenient speed be put into and be established in his and their rights, titles and possessions, be it further enacted . . . that such three or more persons as by your Majesty, your heirs or successors, by commission under the great seal of Ireland, shall be to that purpose appointed from time to time, shall be commissioners to hear and determine the claims and title by English Bill of such person or persons, their heirs, executors, administrators and assigns, who are or ought to be restorable or entituled unto any lands, tenements or hereditaments by reason of the repealing or making void of the said several Acts and resolutions of doubts, grants, letters patents, certificates or any other matter or thing hereinbefore mentioned to be made void, repealed, released or discharged. . . .

276. Act of Resumption, 1700

(*Statutes of the Realm*, VII, pp. 545–581)

AN ACT FOR GRANTING AN AID TO HIS MAJESTY
BY SALE OF THE FORFEITED AND OTHER ESTATES AND INTERESTS
IN IRELAND, AND BY A LAND TAX IN ENGLAND,
FOR THE SEVERAL PURPOSES THEREIN MENTIONED

(*11 Gul. III, cap. 2*)

Whereas soon after your Majesty and your late royal consort of ever blessed memory were graciously pleased to accept the crown and royal dignity of this kingdom and the dominions thereunto belonging, many of your Majesties' subjects, contrary to their duty and allegiance traitorously adhering to your Majesties' enemies, levied and maintained within your realm of Ireland a desperate and bloody war and rebellion against your Majesties, who by the blessing of God upon your Majesties' royal conduct and courage, and the assistance and very great expense of your Majesties' English subjects, were reduced unto their due obedience to the crown of England; and whereas it is highly reasonable that the estates of such rebels and traitors should be applied in ease of your Majesty's faithful subjects of this kingdom to the use of the public, we, your Majesty's most dutiful and loyal subjects the Commons in Parliament assembled, most humbly beseech your Majesty that it may be enacted, and be it enacted . . . that all and every the honours, manors, baronies, castles, messuages, lands, tenements, rents, reversions, services, remainders, possessions, royalties, franchises, jurisdictions, privileges and appurtenances thereunto belonging or in any wise appertaining, rights of entry, rights of action, titles, conditions, uses, trusts, powers and authorities, leases for life, lives or years, pensions, annuities, rent-charges and hereditaments, whether freehold, copyhold, or of what nature or kind soever they be within the said realm of Ireland, whereof any person or persons who stand convicted or attainted of the said high treason or rebellion, or other treason committed in foreign parts, since the thirteenth day of February one thousand six hundred eighty-eight,[1] or who shall be convicted or attainted of any such treason as aforesaid by or before the last day of Trinity Term which shall be in the year of our Lord one thousand seven hundred and one, or who stand convicted or attainted of high treason by reason of being found by inquisition to have died or been slain in actual rebellion since the said thirteenth day of February one thousand six hundred eighty and eight,[1] was or were seized or possessed, or interested in or entituled unto, on the thirteenth day of February one thousand six hundred eighty-eight,[1] or at any time since, in their own right or to their own use, or whereof any other person or persons was or were seized or possessed or interested in to the use of or in trust for them or any of them on the said thirteenth day of February, or at any time since, or whereof the late King James the Second or

[1] 1688/9.

any in trust for him or to his use was seized or possessed or interested in at the time of his accession to the crown of England; and all judgments, statutes, recognizances, extents, mortgages and securities for money, right of redemption of mortgages or other securities, debts of record and other debts, specialties, obligations, goods and chattels of what nature or kind soever, which any of the said persons so convicted or attainted, or to be convicted or attainted, were possessed of or interested in in their own right, or any other in trust for them or any of them stood possessed of or interested in, on the said thirteenth day of February one thousand six hundred eighty-eight[1] or at any time since, shall be and are hereby vested and settled and adjudged, declared and taken to be in the actual and real possession and seisin of Sir Cyril Wyche, knight, Francis Annesley, esquire, James Hamilton, esquire, John Baggs, esquire, John Trenchard, esquire, John Isham, esquire, Henry Langford, esquire, James Hooper, esquire, John Cary, gentleman, Sir Henry Sheeres, knight, Thomas Harrison, esquire, William Fellowes, esquire, and Thomas Rawlins, esquire (trustees nominated and appointed for putting in execution the powers and authorities hereinafter enacted, relating to the said forfeited and other estates and interests in Ireland), and their heirs, executors, administrators and assigns respectively, from the second day of November one thousand six hundred ninety and nine, . . . to the end the same may be bargained, sold, disposed of and applied by the said trustees and the survivors of them to and for such uses, intents and purposes as are hereinafter expressed, mentioned and declared. . . .

II. And for the avoiding all grants, alienations and dispositions at any time since the said thirteenth day of February one thousand six hundred eighty-eight[1] made or granted of the said forfeited or forfeitable estates or interests, or of any other the premises or any part or parcel thereof, or of all or any the quit-rents, crown rents, composition rents or chiefries belonging to the Crown of Ireland, be it enacted that all and every grant, demise, surrender, release custodiam, lease, confirmation or other alienation or disposition whatsoever, at any time since the said thirteenth day of February one thousand six hundred eighty-eight[1] made or granted, or mentioned to be made or granted, under the great seal of England or Ireland, or seal of the Exchequer in Ireland, or by any Act or Acts of Parliament in Ireland or otherwise, of any of the said forfeited or forfeitable estates or interests, or of the estate of the said late King James or any part thereof, or of any the quit-rents, crown rents, composition rents or chiefries belonging to the Crown of Ireland, shall be and are hereby declared to be null and void to all intents and purposes whatsoever.

III. Provided nevertheless, that nothing herein contained shall be construed or taken to make any such grantees, their heirs, executors, administrators or assigns, accountable for the rents, issues and profits of any such honours, manors, baronies, castles, messuages, lands, tenements, rents and hereditaments by them or any of them had, received or taken by or before the said second day of November one thousand six hundred ninety and nine. . . .

XXII. And that all and every the honours, baronies, manors, castles, messuages, lands, tenements, rents, reversions, remainders, estates, interests and hereditaments, of what nature soever, hereinbefore vested in the said trustees, may be disposed of in

---

[1] 1688/9.

the most beneficial manner for the public, and the produce or value thereof applied to the uses, intents and purposes hereinafter appointed, be it further enacted that . . . the said trustees, or any seven or more of them, shall, and are hereby enabled and required, at any time or times before the five and twentieth day of March one thousand seven hundred and two, to sell all and singular the estates and interests vested in them as aforesaid, and every or any part or parcel thereof, . . . as soon as conveniently may be after the tenth day of November one thousand seven hundred. . . .

LXIII. And we your Majesty's said most dutiful and loyal subjects the Commons of England in Parliament assembled, taking into consideration the great expense which is necessary for maintaining as well your Majesty's navy as your guards and garrisons, and being desirous to raise a supply for that purpose, as also towards discharging the debt which is due to seamen and for other necessary occasions, have cheerfully and unanimously given and granted unto your Majesty the rates and assessments hereafter mentioned; and we do humbly beseech your Majesty that it may be enacted, and be it enacted, . . . that the sum of nine hundred eighty-nine thousand nine hundred sixty-five pounds nineteen shillings and sixpence halfpenny shall be raised, levied and paid unto his Majesty within the space of one year, from the fifteenth day of February one thousand six hundred ninety-nine,[1] and shall be assessed and taxed in the several counties, cities, boroughs, towns and places within the kingdom of England, dominion of Wales and town of Berwick-upon-Tweed, according to the proportions and in the manner following. . . .

[1] 1699/1700.

B. SOCIAL CONDITIONS

277. By Albert Jouvin de Rochefort, 1668

(*Antiquarian Repertory*, ed. 1807–1809, IV, pp. 586–599)

Chester lies at the mouth of the river Dee, where it enlarges itself into the form of a gulf, in which by the assistance of the tide vessels may come up to the town. On this account it may be reckoned among the good sea-ports, since it is the ordinary passage of the packet-boat, messengers and merchandise, going from England to Ireland. . . . The first thing I did on my arrival at Chester was to learn when the packet-boat would sail for Dublin. It had set off some days before, but I found a trading vessel laden with divers merchandises, in which I took my passage for Ireland. . . .

I embarked, then, in this vessel, which set sail at four in the afternoon, the weather bad and rainy; on account whereof, after we got out of the gulf and the mouth of this river, within sight of the town of Flint and its strong castle, we chose not to expose ourselves much to the sea, when the wind was so furious and so contrary that it split all our sails and obliged us to put out all our anchors, one of which broke as the storm augmented. . . . This lasted all the night, but the dawn of day brought us a stark calm, attended with rain, which ceased when the wind became fair, although this did not last long, for as we could not, for want of depth of water, pass the straits that lie between the land and the isle of Anglesey we turned round about to go to the village of Holyhead, distant from Chester more than sixty miles, to embark the merchandise and passengers who come to this place as a rendezvous from England to go to Dublin. . . . We anchored in this port, during which time we went to walk in the village and about the island, which seemed fruitful in corn. We saw the post arrive, who gave his packet to the captain of our ship. . . .

This did not prevent our embarking with a very favourable wind, which carried us that day to Dublin, a distance of fifty miles. Dublin is the capital city of the kingdom of Ireland, situated on the river Liffey, where the tide rises near two fathoms, by which large barks are brought up to a quay in the middle of the town, and loaded vessels remain at anchor at its mouth, under cover of some high mountains which run out into the sea in form of a promontory. We landed at the little village of Ringsend, which is on the borders of that little gulf, from whence we entered into a great suburb, where stands the college of the university, which I visited after having found an inn at the Mitre, in the little part of the town separated by the river which runs through it.

On the morrow, being accompanied by a French merchant who lived there, I went to see this grand college. I was introduced to the Principal, who was a man of great wit and learning. He showed me a fine library, in which were many very scarce books. Among others he lent me that of Camdenus Britannicus, who has written the history and description of England, enriched with maps of every county and the plans of all the cities. This man was curious to hear me speak of the city of Paris and of the French customs, and seemed astonished that out of mere curiosity I should come to see Ireland, which is a country so retired and almost unknown to foreign travellers. . . .

I returned him thanks in leaving him to see the palace of the viceroy, Monsieur the duke of Ormonde, uncle to the king, who has a fine court and a suite altogether royal; among them are several French gentlemen. This Castle is at one of the ends of the town, and within its ancient walls, which at present do not contain one third of its extent. The Castle is strong, enclosed by thick walls and by many round towers that command the whole town. On them are mounted a good number of cannon. The court is small, but the lodgings, although very ancient, are very handsome, and worthy of being the dwelling of the viceroy.

The principal gate is in a great street called Castle Street, that runs from one end to the other of the town. In the middle of it is an open space in which the principal streets of Dublin meet. That of High Street is fine. In it is the town-hall, with a fine clock, which is before Christ Church. This great church seems to me to have been some abbey. The cloisters are converted into shops of tradesmen, and the abbey-house serves for the court in which pleadings are held. This same street passes by the open place called Fishamble Street, which is the fish market, that terminates at one of the ancient city gates between two great towers, where are the town prisons. Beyond this is a great suburb, which is at present both the best and largest part of Dublin. A little river runs through the largest street, called Thomas Street, wherein dwell several workmen of different trades for the conveniency of this rivulet of which they make use, and that waters and cleanses all the suburb, the houses of which are fine and straight.

I went to see the metropolitan church of St. Patrick, tutelar of all Ireland. It has been much damaged by thunder, and principally its high tower. There is an open spot used for the market-place, like that called the Haymarket. Here is a large covered market-house. So that Dublin with its suburbs is one of the greatest and best peopled towns in Europe, and the residence of all the nobility of the kingdom of Ireland. There is a stone bridge, which joins that small part of the town called Oxmantown to the greater. On that side which lies by the water is a great quay, where are the finest palaces in Dublin. I was there shown the ancient abbey of St. Mary, formerly, after that of Armagh, the richest in the whole island; at present only the ruins of it are remaining. I lodged in this suburb, from whence I often went to walk in the great meadows by the side of the river, contemplating the country and the situation of this famous town, which seemed to me to be near high mountains on one side and on the other adjoining to a fine country, with this advantage that it is in the middle of the island of Ireland, so that the produce of the country may be conveniently brought thither from every part, as well as what comes by sea from foreign countries with which by the means of its port it may traffic.

One may go to the town of Kilkenny, which lies fifty miles from Dublin, to see the fine castle of Monsieur the duke of Ormonde, rich on every side with marble, and ornamented with many things so curious that those who have seen it say that it surpasses many palaces of Italy. It is only ten leagues from Waterford, which is one of the good sea-ports of this kingdom, as are those of Wexford, Cork, Kinsale, Limerick and Galway, from whence sail every year many vessels loaded with leather, butter, cheese, tallow, salt meat and fish, as also with a kind of cloth manufactured in the country, which is very cheap, and is carried to Spain, Italy and often to the American islands, from whence a return is made of divers merchandises of those countries, as I have observed in several sea-ports of this kingdom, which is the richest of all Europe in things necessary for human life, but the poorest in money. This causes provisions to be so cheap that butter and cheese are commonly sold at a penny the pound; a pound of beef at the butchery for eight deniers; veal and mutton, a penny; a large salmon just out of the sea, three pence; a large fresh cod, two pence; a pair of soles, or quaviver, above a foot broad, a penny; an hundred herrings, three pence; so that one is served with flesh and fish in the best manner for twelve pence a day. In fine, this is the land of plenty. And, moreover, on the road, if you drink two pennyworth of beer at a public-house, they will give you of bread, meat, butter, cheese, fish, as much as you choose; and for all this you only pay your two pence for the beer, it being the custom of the kingdom, as I have experienced wherever I have been.

This island . . . has several large towns, great castles and good sea-ports. They have suffered much in the last civil wars on account of religion, when they were almost all ruined, the inhabitants punished and the rest banished from the kingdom for having resisted the will of their king, and persisted in following the Catholic religion, which was rooted in the hearts of many. These have been forbidden upon pain of death to return, for fear that the religion might in time revive and little by little increase in the kingdom. In truth the Irish are naturally inclined to the Catholic religion. There are even in Dublin more than twenty houses where mass is secretly said, and above a thousand places and subterraneous vaults and retired spots in the woods where the peasants assemble to hear mass celebrated by some priests they secretly maintain. I consider it as a fact that one third of the Irish are Catholics, wherefore if any Catholic prince was to attempt the conquest of Ireland I believe he would be readily seconded by the inhabitants. On this account perhaps it is that there are garrisons in all the maritime places, and the entries and ports are always guarded. . . .

I left Dublin in my way to Scotland, and on my route passed through an agreeable country, having a view of the sea-coast and the towns of Santry and Swords, where is a ruined castle. On the way we saw several of these small castles, all ruined in the last wars. I found afterwards some meadows, and many herds of oxen, cows and calves, which are not naturally large, the climate of this country being too cold; but when transported into a warmer country they become large and robust. From thence the road lies by Ardeath and a castle near Bardelet. In the inland parts of Ireland they speak a particular language, but in the greatest part of the towns and villages on the sea-coast only English is spoken. At length I arrived at Drogheda.

Drogheda is one of the biggest and most populous towns in the kingdom, occasioned by her traffic on the sea, as well on account of the goodness and safety of its port as of its being placed in a country full of all kinds of provisions, and situated on the river Boyne, bordered by two hills, whereof it occupies the greatest part, which makes it a very strong place, with a castle in the highest part of the town on the side by which I entered, where it appeared almost in ruins; but the walls of the town are still entire and defensible. Here is always a garrison, as in the most important place of the kingdom. Passing over a bridge which joins this part of the town to the larger, you come to a great quay, bordered by vessels, which come hither from all parts of Europe. The tide here rises near a fathom and a half, and the river would be deep enough and capable of bearing large vessels if the entrance had not been greatly damaged and almost stopped up by the sands which it brings with it from the mountains wherein it rises. From this bridge you come to a fine and broad street, which forms a square in its centre, which serves for a parade. Here is the town-house, towards which tend most of the best streets in the town.

I was there on a Sunday, and was told that if I was desirous of hearing mass one would be said at two miles distance from the town. It would be astonishing to relate the numbers of Catholics that I saw arrive from across the woods and mountains to assemble at this mass, which was said in a little hamlet and in a chamber poorly fitted up. Here I saw, before mass, above fifty persons confess, and afterwards communicate with a devotion truly Catholic, and sufficient to draw these blind religionists to the true faith. . . .

Thence I returned to lodge at Drogheda. I left it on the next morning, and came into an open country, by a road almost all paved, to Dunleer and Castlebellingham, on a river, from whence you approach the sea-side, which you must follow, and afterwards pass over a river near Dundalk. Dundalk is a small town, consisting almost of one great street, situated near the bank of a small river which at high water has sufficient depth to bring vessels nearly up to the town, if the sands did not choke the entry. Near it are to be seen a chain of high mountains, which run out into the sea, where they form a promontory, seen in front on leaving the town after passing this river, over which there is no bridge. I never saw finer fish and so great a variety as in the market of this little place. It must be owned that the coasts of Ireland and Scotland are the most abundant in fish of any in Europe. Water-fowl are frequently here taken in such quantities, and sold so cheap, as to take away the pleasure of sporting for them. For my part, I will say that I could never have believed it, however it might have been affirmed to me, if I had not seen them in flocks on the sea-shore, and sometimes the air for leagues together darkened by these fowl. There are, besides, in the interior parts of the country, several large lakes and pools full of fish. . . .

It is a peculiarity in this island that there are no venomous animals, not even frogs, toads, lizards, spiders nor any other kind, which is a mark of the purity and goodness of its air. Some persons have tried the experiment whether any creatures of this sort brought from other places would live here, but it is a certainty that they die as soon as they arrive in the country. And farther it is said that the touch of a native of Ireland proves mortal to any of these animals in any foreign country whatsoever, and that a circle being made about any venomous creature with a stick which grew in this island the animal will instantly die. Let not then the island of Malta boast of being the only island in the world which neither nourishes nor suffers any venomous animals. . . .

After having passed the little river at the end of Dundalk you must ascend the high mountains which enclose the small town of Carlingford. These I left on my right, and on the left hand Armagh, distant about twenty miles from thence. It was formerly the capital town of this kingdom, and in Catholic times had an archbishopric, one of the four which are in this island, over nine and twenty bishoprics. At present it is only a village, remarkable for the fine antiquities of an abbey and its handsome church, equal in size to the largest in all England. The way by these mountains is through a desert strewed with flint and other stones, from whence one sees on the left hand some valleys filled with cattle, where I passed a river, and farther on came down over a large wooden bridge and arrived at Newry. A great gulf is formed here that brings vessels up to the town, which is situated on an eminence, extending to the river's side.

Here I feasted on fish, which made me halt here for the space of two days, during which time I diverted myself with walking and visiting the environs. From hence I set out for the mountains by a desert road, covered with flint stones, to Loughbrick-land. Continuing still by the mountains I came to a river, from whence I arrived at Dromore, upon a river. They pretended to me that it was a good town, and had formerly a bishopric, but there is no appearance of it. I remember I ate of a salad made according to the mode of the country, of I know not what herbs. I think there were sorrel and beets chopt together. It represented the form of a fish, the whole without oil or salt and only a little vinegar made of beer, and a quantity of sugar strewed over it that it resembled Mount Etna covered with snow, so that it is impossible to be eaten by anyone not accustomed to it. I made my host laugh heartily in the presence of a gentleman, a lord of the town, on asking for oil to season this salad according to the French fashion, and after having dressed it I persuaded the gentleman to taste it, who was pleased to hear me speak of the state and customs of France.

He had studied at Dublin, and told me he was extremely desirous of seeing France, and that before he died he would certainly make that voyage. He begged me to stay only eight days in his house, promising that I should pass my time in all sorts of pleasures and diversions, both of walking and the chase; that he rarely saw any strangers or Frenchmen pass through those parts; and he was still more astonished when I informed him that I came only out of curiosity, after having visited the most southern parts of Europe. He showed me many curiosities in his cabinet, as well as all the apartments of his castle, which were well furnished and hung with tapestry. He knew not how sufficiently to entertain and make me welcome in order to induce me to remain with him some days; but as I had resolved to prosecute my journey I was obliged to thank and take leave of him.

He conducted me a mile on the way, after which I got to Hillsborough, where there is a large castle, one of the finest in Ireland, situated on a river which runs out of a large pool, where I passed over a great causey, which finished where the mountains begin near Lisnagarvey, whose large castle and its garden are filled with wonders, like many others in the same town, which is on an eminence, the foot whereof is washed by the river. After this the country is but ill-cultivated and corn dear. Few windmills are to be seen in Ireland. They eat here, as well as in some parts of Scotland, cakes called kets, which they bake on thin iron plates over a fire. Being sufficiently baked on one side they turn them on the other, till they become as dry as a biscuit. They are made without leaven, and sometimes so ill-baked that a person who is not used to them cannot eat them. Nevertheless throughout all the inns on the road no

16. IRELAND AND THE WEST COAST OF BRITAIN
SHOWING THE ROUTE FOLLOWED BY ALBERT JOUVIN DE ROCHEFORT

other sort of bread is eaten. However, they do not spare to cover them with butter and thick cheese, here very cheap, costing only a penny per pound. The common people live chiefly on this, especially in places distant from the rivers and lakes.

Afterwards I arrived at Belfast, situate on a river at the bottom of a gulf where barks and vessels anchor on account of the security and goodness of the port; wherefore several merchants live here who trade to Scotland and England, whither they transport the superfluities of this country. Here is a very fine castle and two or three large and straight streets, as in a new-built town. One may often procure a passage here for Scotland; but as I could not meet with one I went to Carrickfergus, which is at the entry of this gulf and within eight miles of Belfast.

Carrickfergus is a strong town and one of the most ancient in the kingdom. It is situated, as it were, at one of the ends of the island, at the entry of a gulf environed by mountains, whereby it is sheltered from the wind, having besides a port, enclosed by a great mole built with flints, composing a large quay in the form of a semicircle, by the side of which there are always a number of vessels. The entrance is defended by a huge castle on the sea-shore, elevated upon a rock that renders it difficult to be scaled. There are garrisons in both the town and castle, as there are in all the strong places in Ireland. I was not disappointed in procuring a passage for Scotland, but the wind being contrary obliged me to wait eight days, during which time I walked about all the environs of the town, and upon the sea-shore, which are very agreeable. I was well entertained here, both on fish and flesh, for a shilling a day, exclusive of my horse, which I had sent back to Dublin, where I hired him to this place. . . .

The wind at length became favourable for leaving Carrickfergus, from whence we kept the Irish coast for some time until it was stark calm. This gave occasion to our sailors to observe that it was a presage of our having presently a brisk gale; and in effect, early in the morning so violent a wind arose that though it was abaft it obliged us to take in all our sails and run into the great gulf of Dumbarton, at the entry of which there is the great rock Ailsa. The storm increased so much that the sea often covered our vessel and passed over it, threatening to bury us in its waves. This gulf is skirted by high mountains and bare rocks, whence we saw on the right hand Irvine.

Towards the approach of night the wind began to abate, owing to some clouds portending rain and a change of wind, which came on with a fury and in so tempestuous a manner that resistance was impossible, and in the little gulf of Greenock our sailors were obliged to put out all the anchors they had, trusting to the mercy of God, in whom was placed all our hope. We arrived there after the storm was over, which both wetted and greatly fatigued our sailors, happy to get off so well. This town is the passage of the Scotch post and packet-boat to Ireland. Its port is good, sheltered by the mountains which surround it and by a great mole, by the side of which are ranged the barks and other vessels for the conveniency of loading and unloading more easily. We made good cheer together as companions of fortune, after which I left this town and coasted the gulf of Dumbarton.

278. By John Stevens, 1690

(Journal of John Stevens, ed. R. H. Murray, pp. 138–140)

Wednesday the 9th of July. Orders were given to all officers to endeavour to gather the remains of their regiments, and to ours in particular to march four miles to the westward of Limerick to a village called Carrig O'Gunnel and the adjacent places, there to quarter till the rest of our dispersion came up and we received fresh orders. . . .

We had here plenty of meat and barley bread baked in cakes over or before the fire, and abundance of milk and butter, but no sort of drink. Yet there this is counted the best of quarters, the people generally being the greatest lovers of milk I ever saw, which they eat and drink above twenty several sorts of ways, and what is strangest, for the most part love it best when sourest. They keep it in sour vessels and from time to time till it grows thick, and sometimes to that perfection it will perfume a whole house; but generally speaking they order it so that it is impossible to boil it without curdling four hours after it comes from the cow.

Oaten and barley bread is the common fare, and that in cakes, and ground by hand. None but the best sort or the inhabitants of great towns eat wheat, or bread baked in an oven, or ground in a mill. The meaner people content themselves with little bread, but instead thereof eat potatoes, which with sour milk is the chief part of their diet, their drink for the most part water, sometimes coloured with milk. Beer or ale they seldom taste, unless they sell something considerable in a market town.

They all smoke, women as well as men, and a pipe an inch long serves the whole family several years, and though never so black or foul is never suffered to be burnt. Seven or eight will gather to the smoking of a pipe, and each taking two or three whiffs gives it to his neighbour, commonly holding his mouth full of smoke till the pipe comes about to him again. They are also much given to taking of snuff.

Very little clothing serves them, and as for shoes and stockings much less. They wear brogues, being quite plain without so much as one lift of a heel, and are all sewed with thongs, and the leather not curried, so that in wearing it grows hard as a board, and therefore many always keep them wet; but the wiser that can afford it grease them often, and that makes them supple.

In the better sort of cabins there is commonly one flock bed, seldom more, feathers being too costly. This serves the man and his wife. The rest all lie on straw, some with one sheet and blanket, others only their clothes and blanket to cover them. The cabins have seldom any floor but the earth, or rarely so much as a loft. Some have windows, others none. They say it is of late years that chimneys are used, yet the house is never free from smoke. That they have no locks to their doors is not because there are not thieves but because there is nothing to steal.

Poverty with neatness seems somewhat the more tolerable, but here nastiness is in perfection, if perfection can be in vice; and the great cause of it, laziness, is most predominant. It is a great happiness that the country produces no venomous creature, but it were much happier in my opinion did it produce no vermin. Whether nastiness or the air be the cause of it I know not, but all the kingdom, especially the north, is infected with the perpetual plague of the itch.

In fine, unless it be the Scotch, no people have more encouragement to be soldiers than these, for they live not at home so well at best as they do at worst in the army both for diet and clothes, and yet none will sooner murmur and complain of hardship than they. It is not through prejudice I give this account, but of love to truth, for few strangers love them better or pity them more than I do. And therefore to do them justice, I cannot but say it is not to be admired they should be poor, having been so long under the heavy yoke of the Oliverian English party, whose study it was always to oppress and if possible to extirpate them.

Poverty is a source from whence all other worldly miseries proceed. It makes them ignorant, not having wherewithal to apply themselves to studies. It enervates the spirits and makes them dull and slothful, and so from race to race they grow more and more degenerate, wanting the improvements of a free and ingenuous education, and being still brought up in a sort of slavery and bondage. This may be easily evinced by such of their gentry who, having been abroad, become very accomplished men either in learning, warlike affairs or the more soft and winning arts of the court.

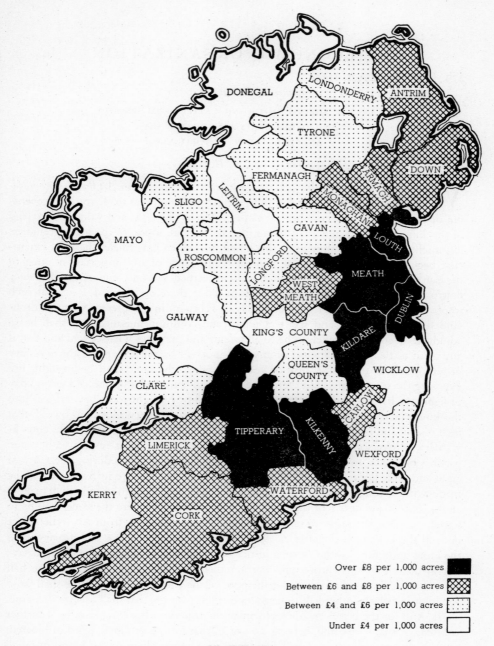

DONEGAL

LONDONDERRY

ANTRIM

TYRONE

DOWN

FERMANAGH

ARMAGH

MONAGHAN

SLIGO

LEITRIM

CAVAN

LOUTH

MAYO

ROSCOMMON

LONGFORD

WEST MEATH

MEATH

DUBLIN

GALWAY

KING'S COUNTY

KILDARE

WICKLOW

QUEEN'S COUNTY

CLARE

TIPPERARY

KILKENNY

CARLOW

WEXFORD

LIMERICK

WATERFORD

KERRY

CORK

Over £8 per 1,000 acres	■
Between £6 and £8 per 1,000 acres	
Between £4 and £6 per 1,000 acres	
Under £4 per 1,000 acres	□

17. IRELAND

SHOWING DISTRIBUTION OF WEALTH AS INDICATED BY THE APPORTIONMENT OF THE
ASSESSMENT OF £120,000 IN 1698

C. ECONOMIC ORGANIZATION

279. Irish Cattle Act, 1666

(*Statutes of the Realm*, v, p. 597)

AN ACT AGAINST IMPORTING CATTLE FROM IRELAND
AND OTHER PARTS BEYOND THE SEAS,
AND FISH TAKEN BY FOREIGNERS

(*18 & 19 Car. II, cap. 2*)

Whereas by an Act of this present Parliament entituled, *An Act for the encourage-ment of trade*,[1] amongst other things some provision was made for the prevent-ing of coming in of vast numbers of cattle, whereby the rents and values of the land of this kingdom were much fallen and like daily to fall more, to the great prejudice, detriment and impoverishment of this kingdom, which nevertheless hath by experi-ence been found to be ineffectual, and the continuance of any importation either of the lean or fat cattle, dead or alive, hereinafter specified, not only unnecessary but very destructive to the welfare of this kingdom, be it therefore enacted, . . . that such importation from and after the second day of February in this present year one thou-sand six hundred sixty and six[2] is a public and common nuisance, and shall be so adjudged, deemed and taken to be to all intents and purposes whatsoever; and that if any great cattle, sheep or swine, or any beef, pork or bacon (except for the necessary provision of the respective ships or vessels in which the same shall be brought, not exposing the same or any part thereof to sale) shall from and after the said second day of February by any wise whatsoever be imported or brought from beyond seas into this kingdom of England, dominion of Wales or town of Berwick-upon-Tweed, that then it shall and may be lawful for any constable, tithingman, headborough, church-wardens or overseers of the poor or any of them, within their respective liberties, parishes or places, to take and seize the same, and keep the same during the space of eight and forty hours in some public and convenient place where such seizure shall be made, within which time if the owner or owners, or any for them or him, shall make it appear unto some justice of the peace of the same county where the same shall be so seized, . . . that the same were not imported from Ireland or from any other place beyond the seas not hereinafter excepted after the said second day of February, then the same upon the warrant of such justice of peace shall be delivered without delay; but in default of such proof and warrant then the same to be forfeited, one half thereof to be disposed to the use of the poor of the parish where the same shall be so found or seized, the other half to be to his or their own use that shall so seize the same.

II. And for the better encouragement of the fishery of this kingdom, be it further enacted . . . that if any ling, herring, cod or pilchard, fresh or salted, dried or bloated, or any salmons, eels or congers, taken by any foreigners aliens to this kingdom, shall be imported, uttered, sold or exposed to sale in this kingdom, that then it shall and

---

[1] 15 Car. II, cap. 7.　　　　　　　　　[2] 1666/7.

732

may be lawful for any person or persons to take and seize the same, the one half thereof to be disposed of to the use of the poor of the parish where the same shall be so found or seized, the other half to his or their own use which shall so seize the same.

III. Provided always, that nothing in this Act shall be construed to hinder the importation of cattle from the Isle of Man in this kingdom of England, so as the number of the said cattle do not exceed six hundred head yearly, and that they be not of any other breed than of the breed of the Isle of Man, and that they be landed at the port of Chester or some of the members thereof and not elsewhere; this Act to continue until the end of seven years, and from thence to the end of the first session of the next Parliament.

280. Sir William Temple's survey, 1673

(*Works*, ed. 1740, I, pp. 109–121)

AN ESSAY

UPON THE ADVANCEMENT OF TRADE IN IRELAND,
WRITTEN TO THE EARL OF ESSEX, LORD LIEUTENANT OF THAT KINGDOM,
DUBLIN, 22 JULY 1673

The want of trade in Ireland proceeds from the want of people; and this is not grown from any ill qualities of the climate or air, but chiefly from the frequent revolutions of so many wars and rebellions, so great slaughters and calamities of mankind, as have at several intervals of time succeeded the first conquest of this kingdom in Henry the Second's time until the year 1653. Two very great plagues followed the two great wars, those of Queen Elizabeth's reign and the last, which helped to drain the current stream of generation in the country. The discredit which is grown upon the constitutions or settlements of this kingdom, by so frequent and unhappy revolutions that for many ages have invested it, has been the great discouragement to other nations to transplant themselves hither, and prevailed further than all the invitations which the cheapness and plenty of the country has made them; so that had it not been for the numbers of the British, which the necessity of the late wars at first drew over, and of such who either as adventurers or soldiers seated themselves here upon account of the satisfaction made to them in land, the country had by the last war and plague been left in a manner desolate.

Besides, the subordinacy of the government, changing hands so often, makes an unsteadiness in the pursuit of the public interests of the kingdom, gives way to the emulations of the different factions, and draws the favour or countenance of the government sometimes to one party or interest, sometimes to another. . . . This subordinacy in the government and emulation of parties, with the want sometimes of authority in the governor (by the weakness of his credit and support at Court), occasions the perpetual agencies or journeys into England of all persons that have any considerable pretences in Ireland and money to pursue them, which end many times in long abodes and frequent habituating of families there, though they have no money to support them but what is drawn out of Ireland. Besides the young gentlemen go of course for their breeding there. Some seek their health and others their entertainment in a better climate or scene. By these means the country loses the expense of many of the richest persons or families at home, and mighty sums of money must needs go over from hence into England, which the great stock of rich native commodities here can make the only amends for. . . .

Since my late arrival in Ireland I have found a very unusual, but I doubt very just, complaint concerning the scarcity of money, which occasioned many airy propositions for the remedy of it, and among the rest that of raising some or all of the coins here. This was chiefly grounded upon the experience made, as they say, about the duke of Ormonde's coming first over hither in 1663, when the plate pieces of eight were raised three pence in the piece, and a mighty plenty of money was observed to grow in Ireland for a year or two after. But this seems to me a very mistaken account, and to have depended wholly upon other circumstances little taken notice of, and not at all upon the raising of the money to which it is by some great men attributed. For first, there was about that time a general peace and serenity, which had newly succeeded a general trouble and cloud throughout all his Majesty's kingdoms. Then after two years' attendance in England upon the settlement of Ireland (there on the forge) by all persons and parties here that were considerably interested in it, the Parliament being called here, and the main settlement of Ireland wound up in England and put into the duke of Ormonde's hands to pass here into an Act, all persons came over in a shoal, either to attend their own concernments in the main, or more particularly to make their court to the Lord Lieutenant, upon whom his Majesty had at that time in a manner wholly devolved the care and disposition of all affairs in this kingdom. This made a sudden and mighty stop of that issue of money which had for two years run perpetually out of Ireland into England, and kept it all at home. Nor is the very expense of the duke of Ormonde's own great patrimonial estate, with that of several other families that came over at that time, of small consideration in the stock of this kingdom. Besides there was a great sum of money in ready coin brought over out of England at the same time towards the arrears of the army, which are all circumstances that must needs have made a mighty change in the course of ready money here. All the effect that I conceive was made by crying up the pieces of eight was to bring in much more of that species, instead of others current here (as indeed all the money brought from England was of that sort, and complained of in Parliament to be of a worse alloy), and to carry away much English money in exchange for plate pieces; by which a trade was driven very beneficial to the traders, but of mighty loss to the kingdom in the intrinsic value of their money.

The circumstances at this time seem to be just the reverse of what they were then –the nations engaged in a war the most fatal to trade of any that could arise; the settlement of Ireland shaken at the Court, and falling into new disquisitions (whether in truth, or in common opinion, is all a case). This draws continual agencies and journeys of people concerned into England to watch the motions of the main wheel there. Besides, the Lieutenants of Ireland since the duke of Ormonde's time have had little in their disposition here, and only executed the resolutions daily taken at Court, in particular as well as general affairs, which has drawn thither the attendance of all private pretenders. The great estates of this kingdom have been four or five years constantly spent in England. Money, instead of coming over hither for pay of the army, has, since the war began, been transmitted thither for pay of those forces that were called from hence. And lastly, this war has had a more particular and mortal influence upon the trade of this country than upon any other of his Majesty's kingdoms.

For by the Act against transportation of cattle into England the trade of this country, which ran wholly thither before, was turned very much into foreign parts. But by this war the last is stopped, and, the other not being opened, there is in a manner no vent for any commodity but of wool. This necessity has forced the kingdom to go on still with their foreign trade; but that has been with such mighty losses by the great number of Dutch privateers plying about the coasts, and the want of English frigates to secure them, that the stock of the kingdom must be extremely diminished. Yet by the continuance of the same expense and luxury in point of living money goes over into England to fetch what must supply it, though little commodities go either there or abroad to make any considerable balance. By all which it must happen that with another year's continuance of the war there will hardly be money left in this kingdom to turn the common markets, or pay any rents, or leave any circulation further than the receipts of the Customs and quit-rents, and the pays of the army, which in both kinds must be the last that fail.

In such a conjuncture the crying up of any species of money will but increase the want of it in general, for while there goes not out commodity to balance that which is brought in, and no degree of gains by exportation will make amends for the venture, what should money come in for unless it be to carry out other money as it did before, and leave the stock that remains equal indeed in denomination but lower in the intrinsic value than it was before? In short, while this war lasts, and our seas are ill guarded, all that can be done towards preserving the small remainder of money in this kingdom is first to introduce, as far as can be, a vein of parsimony throughout the country in all things that are not perfectly the native growths and manufactures; then, by severity and steadiness of the government (as far as will be permitted) to keep up in some credit the present peace and settlement; and lastly, to force men to a degree of industry, by suffering none to hope that they shall be able to live by rapine or fraud. . . .

This being premised as peculiar either to the government in general or to the present conjuncture, I shall proceed to such observations as occur concerning the ways of advancing the common and standing trade of this kingdom. The trade of a country arises from the native growths of the soil or seas, the manufactures, the commodiousness of ports, and the store of shipping which belong to it. The improvement, therefore, of trade in Ireland must be considered in the survey of all these particulars, the defects to which at present they are subject, and the increases they are capable of receiving, either from the course of time, the change of customs, or the conduct and application of the government.

The native commodities or common easy manufactures which make up the exportation of this kingdom, and consequently furnish both the stock of foreign commodities consumed in the country and that likewise of current money by which all trade is turned, are wool, butter, beef, cattle, fish, iron; and by the improvement of these, either in the quantity, the credit, or the further manufacture, the trade of Ireland seems chiefly to be advanced.

In this survey one thing must be taken notice of as peculiar to this country, which is that, as in the nature of its government, so in the very improvement of its trade and riches, it ought to be considered not only in its own proper interest but likewise in its relation to England, to which it is subordinate, and upon whose weal in the main that of this kingdom depends; and therefore a regard must be had of those points wherein the trade of Ireland comes to interfere with any main branches of the trade of England, in which cases the encouragement of such trade ought to be either declined or moderated, and so give way to the interest of trade in England, upon the health and vigour whereof the strength, riches and glory of his Majesty's crowns seem chiefly to depend. But on the other side some such branches of trade ought not wholly to be suppressed, but rather so far admitted as may serve the general consumption of this kingdom, lest by too great an importation of commodities, though out of England itself, the money of this kingdom happen to be drawn away in such a degree as not to leave a stock sufficient for turning the trade at home. The effect hereof would be general discontents among the people, complaints or at least ill impressions of the government, which in a country composed of three several nations, different to a great degree in language, customs and religion as well as interests (both of property and dependences), may prove not only dangerous to this kingdom but to England itself. . . .

The wool of Ireland seems not to be capable of any increase, nor to suffer under any defect, the country being generally full stocked with sheep, cleared of wolves, the soil little subject to other rots than of hunger. And all the considerable flocks being of English breed, and the staple of wool generally equal with that of Northampton or Leicestershire, the improvement of this commodity by manufactures in this kingdom would give so great a damp to the trade of England (of which clothes, stuffs and stockings make so mighty a part) that it seems not fit to be encouraged here, at least no further than to such a quantity of one or two summer-stuffs, Irish frieze, and cloth from six shillings to fourteen, as may supply in some measure the ordinary consumption of the kingdom. That which seems most necessary in this branch is the careful and severe execution of the statutes provided to forbid the exportation of wool to any other parts but to England, which is the more to be watched and feared, since thereby the present riches of this kingdom would be mightily increased, and great advantages might be made by the connivance of governors, whereas on the other side this would prove a most sensible decay, if not destruction, of manufactures both here and in England itself.

Yarn is a commodity very proper to this country, but made in no great quantities in any parts besides the north, nor anywhere into linen to any great degree, or of sorts fit for the better uses at home or exportation abroad, though of all others this ought most to be encouraged, and was therefore chiefly designed by the earl of Strafford. The soil produces flax kindly and well, and fine too, answerable to the care used in choice of seed and exercise of husbandry; and much land is fit for it here which is not so for corn. The manufacture of it, in gathering or beating, is of little toil or application, and so the fitter for the natives of the country. Besides, no women are apter to spin it well than the Irish, who, labouring little in any kind with their hands, have their fingers more supple and soft than other women of the poorer condition among us. And this may certainly be advanced and improved into a great manufacture of linen, so as to beat down the trade both of France and Holland, and draw much of the money which goes from England to those parts upon this occasion into the hands of his Majesty's subjects of Ireland, without crossing any interest of trade in England. For besides what has been said of flax and spinning, the soil and climate are proper for whitening, both by the frequency of brooks and also of winds in the country. . . .

Hide, tallow, butter, beef arise all from one sort of cattle, and are subject to the same general defects, and capable of the same common improvements. The three first are certain commodities, and yield the readiest money of any that are turned in this kingdom, because they never fail of a price abroad. Beef is a drug, finding no constant vent abroad, and therefore yielding no rate at home, for the consumption of the kingdom holds no proportion with the product that is usually made of cattle in it, so that in many parts at this time an ox may be bought in the country markets, and the hide and tallow sold at the next trading town for near as much as it cost. The defects of these commodities lie either in the age and feeding of the cattle that are killed, or in the manufacture and making them up for exportation abroad.

Until the transportation of cattle into England was forbidden by the late Act of Parliament, the quickest trade of ready money here was driven by the sale of young bullocks, which for four or five summer months of the year were carried over in very great numbers; and this made all the breeders in the kingdom turn their lands and stocks chiefly to that sort of cattle. Few cows were bred up for the dairy more than served the consumption within, and few oxen for draught, which was all performed by rascally small horses; so as the cattle generally sold either for slaughter within or exportation abroad were of two, three, or at best four years old, and those such as had never been either handled or wintered at hand-meat, but bred wholly upon the mountains in summer and upon the withered long grass of the lower lands in the winter. The effect hereof was very pernicious to this kingdom in what concerned all these commodities. The hides were small, thin and lank; the tallow much less in quantity, and of quicker consumption. Little butter was exported abroad, and that discredited by the housewifery of the Irish in making it up, most of what was sent coming from their hands who alone kept up the trade of dairies, because the breed of their cattle was not fit for the English markets. But above all, the trade of beef for foreign exportation was prejudiced and almost sunk; for the flesh being young and only grass-fed (and that on a sudden by the sweetness of the summer's pasture, after the cattle being almost starved in the winter) was thin, light and moist, and not of a substance to endure the salt, or be preserved by it for long voyages or a slow consumption. . . .

After the Act in England had wholly stopped the transportation of cattle the trade of this kingdom was forced to find out a new channel. A great deal of land was turned to sheep, because wool gave ready money for the English markets, and by stealth for those abroad. The breeders of English cattle turned much to dairy, or else by keeping their cattle to six and seven years old, and wintering them dry, made them fit for the beef trade abroad; and some of the merchants fell into care and exactness in barrelling them up. And hereby the improvements of this trade were grown so sensible in the course of a few years, that in the year 1669 some merchants in Holland assured me that they had received parcels of beef out of Ireland which sold current and very near the English, and of butter which sold beyond it; and that they had observed it spent as if it came from the richer soil of the two. It is most evident that if the Dutch War had not broken out so soon after the improvements of all these trades (forced at first by necessity, and growing afterwards habitual by use) a few years would have very much advanced the trade and riches of this kingdom, and made it a great gainer, instead of losing, by the Act against transportation of their cattle. But the war gave a sudden damp to this and all other trade, which is sunk to nothing by the continuance of it. . . .

Cattle for exportation are sheep, bullocks, horses; and of one or other of these kinds the country seems to be full stocked, no ground that I hear of being untenanted. The two first seem sufficiently improved in the kinds as well as the number, most of both being of the English breed; and though it were better for the country if the number of horses being lessened made room for that of increasing sheep and great cattle, yet it seems indifferent which of these two were most turned to, and that will be regulated by the liberty or restraint of carrying live cattle into England. When the passage is open, land will be turned most to great cattle; when shut, to sheep, as it is at present; though I am not of opinion it can last, because that Act seems to have been carried on rather by the interests of particular counties in England than by that of the whole, which in my opinion must be evidently a loser by it. For first, the freight of all cattle that were brought over, being in English vessels, was so much clear gain to England, and this was, one with another, near a third or at least a fourth part of the price. Then their coming over young and very cheap to the first market made them double the price by one year's feeding, which was the greatest improvement to be made of our dry pasture-land in England. The trade of hides and tallow, or else of leather, was mightily advanced in England, which will be beaten down in foreign markets by Ireland if they come to kill all their cattle at home. The young Irish cattle served for the common consumption in England, while their own large old fat cattle went into the barrel for the foreign trade, in which Irish beef had in a manner no part, though by the continuance of this restraint it will be forced upon improvement, and come to share with England in the beef trade abroad. Grounds were turned much in England from breeding either to feeding or dairy, and this advanced the trade of English butter, which will be extremely beaten down when Ireland turns to it too, and in the way of English housewifery, as it has done a great deal since the restraint upon cattle. And lastly, whereas Ireland had before very little trade but with England, and with the money for their cattle bought all the commodities there which they wanted, by this restraint they are forced to seek a foreign market; and where they sell they will be sure to buy too, and all the foreign merchandise which they had before from Bristol, Chester and London, they will have in time from Rouen, Amsterdam, Lisbon and the Straits. . . .

Horses in Ireland are a drug, but might be improved to a commodity, not only of greater use at home, but also fit for exportation into other countries. The soil is of a sweet and plentiful grass, which will raise a large breed; and the hills, especially near the sea-coasts, are hard and rough, and so fit to give them shape and breath and sound feet. The present defects in them are breeding without choice of stallions either in shape or size, and trusting so far to the gentleness of the climate as to winter them abroad, without ever handling colts till they are four years old. This both checks the growth of the common breeds and gives them an incurable shyness, which is the general vice of Irish horses and is hardly ever seen in Flanders, because the hardness of the winters in those parts forces the breeders there to house and handle their colts for at least six months every year. In the studs of persons of quality in Ireland, where care is taken and cost is not spared, we see horses bred of excellent shape and vigour and size, so as to reach great prices at home and encourage strangers to find the market here; among whom I met with one this summer that came over on that errand, and bought about twenty horses to carry over into the French army, from twenty to threescore pounds price at the first hand. . . .

The fishing of Ireland might prove a mine under water as rich as any under ground, if it were improved to those vast advantages it is capable of, and that we see it raised to in other countries. But this is impossible under so great a want of people and cheapness of all things necessary to life throughout the country, which are in all places invincible enemies of industry and improvements. . . .

Iron seems to me the manufacture that of all others ought the least to be encouraged in Ireland, or if it be which requires the most restriction to certain places and rules; for I do not remember to have heard that there is any ore in Ireland (at least I am sure the greatest part is fetched from England), so that all this country affords of its own growth towards this manufacture is but the wood, which has met but with too great consumptions already in most parts of this kingdom, and needs not this to destroy what is left. So that iron-works ought to be confined to certain places, where either the woods continue vast and make the country savage, or where they are not at all fit for timber or likely to grow to it, or where there is no conveyance for timber to places of vent so as to quit the cost of the carriage.

Having run through the commodities of Ireland, with their defects and improvements, I will only touch the other two points mentioned at first as the grounds likewise of trade in a country. Those are the commodiousness of ports and the store of shipping, in one of which this kingdom as much abounds as it fails in the other. The haven of Dublin is barred to that degree as very much to obstruct the trade of the city. The clearing or opening of it is a great work, and proper either for the city or the whole province of Leinster to undertake. But whether it be feasible, or at such charges as will quit cost, I will not judge, especially considering the many good havens that are scattered upon that whole eastern coast of Ireland. Besides this I know not what to propose upon this head, unless it be the making of two free ports, one in Kerry and the other upon the north-west coast, which may thereby grow to be magazines for the West India trade, and from thence those commodities may be dispersed unto all other parts of Europe after having paid the Customs which they ought to pay in England, where this must be concerted. . . .

281. (Irish) Navigation Act, 1689

(*Dublin Magazine*, January 1843, pp. 39–42)

AN ACT FOR THE ADVANCE AND IMPROVEMENT OF TRADE, AND FOR ENCOURAGEMENT AND INCREASE OF SHIPPING AND NAVIGATION

Whereas this kingdom of Ireland, for its good situation, commodious harbours and great quantity of goods, the growth, product and manufacture thereof, is and standeth very fit and convenient for trade and commerce with most nations, kingdoms and plantations; and several laws, statutes and ordinances having heretofore been made and enacted, and time to time prohibiting and disabling the king's subjects of this realm to export or carry out of this kingdom unto any other the king's islands, plantations or colonies, in Asia, Africa or America, several of the goods, wares, merchandises and commodities of this nation, or to import into this kingdom the goods or merchandises of the said plantations, colonies and islands, without landing and discharging in England, Wales or the town of Berwick-upon-Tweed, under great penalties and forfeitures, not only to the decay of the king's revenue but also to the very great prejudice and disadvantage of all the inhabitants in this kingdom; . . . and whereas the increase of shipping and the encouragement of navigation, under the good Providence of God and the careful protection of his sacred Majesty, are the best and fittest means and foundations whereon the wealth, safety and strength of this island and kingdom may be built and established: be it therefore enacted . . . that it shall and may be lawful, to and for his Majesty's subjects of this realm of Ireland, and to and for every other person and persons, of what nation soever, residing and inhabiting here, during the time of such residence, freely to trade into and from all and every his Majesty's plantations, colonies and islands, in Asia, Africa and America, and to export from this kingdom and carry unto all and every the said plantations, colonies and islands, and there sell, dispose of and barter, all sorts of goods, wares, merchandises and commodities, as well of the growth, product or manufacture of this kingdom as of any other part of Europe, commonly called European goods, and import and bring into this kingdom of Ireland all sorts of goods, wares, merchandises and commodities of the growth, product or manufacture of all or any the said islands, colonies and plantations without being obliged to land or unload in England, Wales or the town of Berwick-upon-Tweed; . . . provided always that the master or owner of all and every such ship or ships, vessel or vessels, so trading from this kingdom unto all or any the said islands, colonies or plantations, his or their agents or factors, shall and do before such ship or ships, vessel or vessels, sail from any part of this kingdom towards the said islands, colonies or plantations, perfect and enter into a bond . . . with condition to bring the goods, wares and merchandises which such ship or vessel shall take in at all or any the said plantations, colonies or islands into England, Ireland, Wales or the town of Berwick-upon-Tweed and to no other place, and there to abide and put the same on shore, the danger of the seas only excepted.

II. Be it likewise enacted . . . that all goods and merchandises whatsoever, which shall be carried, conveyed or exported out of this kingdom of Ireland to the said islands, colonies and plantations shall be liable and pay to the king's Majesty, his heirs and successors in the said islands, plantations and colonies the same or so much Customs, Excise or other duties as the like goods or merchandises, being exported out of England into all or any the said plantations, colonies or islands, and all goods or merchandises imported into this kingdom out of all or any the said islands, colonies and plantations (tobacco and sugar only excepted) shall pay in this kingdom, to the use of the king's Majesty, his heirs and successors, the same or like duties, Custom and Excise . . . as in the like Acts of Parliament made in this kingdom in the fourteenth and fifteenth years of the reign of the late King Charles the Second, the one entituled, *An Act for settling the subsidy of poundage and granting a subsidy of tonnage and other sums of money unto his royal Majesty, his heirs and successors, the same to be paid upon merchandise imported and exported into or out of the kingdom of Ireland, according to a book of rates hereunto annexed*; and the other entituled, *An Act for the settling of the Excise or new impost upon his Majesty, his heirs and successors, according to the book of rates therein inserted*, and as in the said book of rates, and as in the rules, orders and directions to the said Acts and books of rates annexed, are contained and specified.

III. And whereas the duties and Custom and Excise on tobacco of the king's Majesty's plantations, imported into this kingdom, amount to no more, according to the said two late Acts of Parliament in this kingdom and books of rates to them annexed, but to two pence per pound, which is too small a duty, be it therefore enacted . . . that all tobacco of the growth or product of all or any his Majesty's new plantations or islands, or any plantations belonging to his Most Christian Majesty, imported into this kingdom out of all or any the said plantations and islands, shall from and after the eighteenth day of July 1689 be charged and liable to pay unto his Majesty, his heirs and successors, the sum of five pence sterling for each pound, Custom and Excise, that is to say two pence for each pound Custom, and three pence for each pound Excise, and no more. . . .

V. And for the more encouragement of building good and serviceable ships, be it enacted . . . that any person or persons who shall within the space of ten years, to commence the 24th of June 1689, build or cause to be built within this kingdom of Ireland any ship or vessel above twenty-five ton and under one hundred ton burden, shall and may, for the first three voyages any such ship or vessel shall make out of this kingdom, . . . have, receive or be allowed to his and their own proper use one eighth part of the duties of Customs and Excise which shall be due or payable to the king, his heirs or successors, for and out of all the goods and commodities so imported ; . . . and likewise that any person or persons who shall within the said space of ten years, commencing as aforesaid, build or cause to be built in this kingdom any ship or vessel exceeding in burden one hundred ton shall, for the first four voyages such ship or vessel shall make out of this kingdom, . . . have and receive to his and their own proper use one eighth part of the duties of Custom and Excise which shall be due or payable. . . .

VI. And to the end that masters of ships, seamen, mariners, shipwrights, carpenters, rope-makers and block-makers may be encouraged and invited to come and dwell in this kingdom, and that thereby navigation may improve and increase, be it further enacted . . . that all and every masters of ships and shipwrights, ship-carpenters, sea-men, mariners, rope-makers and block-makers, who are at present residing within this kingdom, or who shall or do at any time from henceforth come and reside in this kingdom of Ireland, and shall pursue and follow his trade or calling, shall and may for the time and space of ten years after his or their so coming into this kingdom be freed, exempted and discharged of and from all sorts of taxes and cesses, watch, ward and quarterings of soldiers and officers in and throughout this kingdom, and shall likewise have and be allowed his and their freedom *gratis* in any town, city, seaport, corporation or borough where he or they shall please to reside and pursue his or their calling and trade.

VII. And be it further enacted . . . that in the respective cities and towns of Dublin, Belfast, Waterford, Cork, Limerick and Galway there shall be established, erected and settled, before the first day of December 1689, in each of the said towns and cities, and so continued for ever hereafter, a free school for teaching and instructing the mathematics and the art of navigation. . . .

282. Wool Act, 1699
(*Statutes of the Realm*, VII, pp. 524–528)
AN ACT TO PREVENT THE EXPORTATION OF WOOL
OUT OF THE KINGDOMS OF IRELAND AND ENGLAND INTO FOREIGN PARTS,
AND FOR THE ENCOURAGEMENT OF THE WOOLLEN MANUFACTURES
IN THE KINGDOM OF ENGLAND
(*10 Gul. III, cap. 16*)

Forasmuch as wool and the woollen manufactures of cloth, serge, baize, kerseys and other stuffs made or mixed with wool are the greatest and most profitable commodities of this kingdom, on which the value of lands and the trade of the nation do chiefly depend; and whereas great quantities of the like manufactures have of late been made and are daily increasing in the kingdom of Ireland and in the English plantations in America, and are exported from thence to foreign markets heretofore supplied from England, which will inevitably sink the value of lands and tend to the ruin of the trade and the woollen manufactures of this realm; for the prevention whereof, and for the encouragement of the woollen manufactures within this king-dom, be it enacted . . . that no person or persons whatsoever from and after the four and twentieth day of June in the year of our Lord one thousand six hundred ninety-nine shall directly or indirectly export, transport, ship off, carry or convey, or cause or procure to be exported, transported, shipped off, carried or conveyed, out of or from the said kingdom of Ireland into any foreign realm, states or dominions, or into any parts or places whatsoever other than the parts within the kingdom of England or the dominion of Wales, any the wool, wool fells, shortlings, mortlings, wool flocks, worsted, bay or woollen yarn, cloth, serge, baize, kerseys, says, friezes, druggets, cloth-serges, shalloons or any other drapery, stuffs or woollen manufactures whatso-ever made up or mixed with wool or wool flocks. . . .

II. And be it enacted . . . that all and every of the offender and offenders, offence and offences aforesaid, shall be subject and liable to the respective pains and penalties and forfeitures hereafter following, that is to say, the said wool, wool fells, . . .[1] so exported, transported, shipped off, or carried, conveyed or loaden contrary to the true intent and meaning of this Act shall be forfeited; and that every of the offender and offenders therein shall likewise forfeit the sum of five hundred pounds for every such offence; and all and every ship, vessel, barge, boat or other bottom whatsoever, wherein any of the said commodities are or shall be shipped or laid on board contrary to the true intent and meaning of this Act, shall be forfeited, with all her tackle, apparel and furniture to them and every of them belonging; and the masters and mariners thereof, or any porters, carriers, waggoners, boatmen or other persons whatsoever knowing such offence, and wittingly aiding and assisting therein, shall forfeit forty pounds, of which one moiety shall be to him or them that shall sue for the same, . . . and the other moiety thereof to the encouragement of setting up the linen manufactures in Ireland, to be disposed of by the Court of Exchequer there for that use only. . . .

III. And to prevent evading the penalties of this Act by pretension of prosecution or acquittals in Ireland, be it enacted . . . that no acquittal, nor any indictment, information or suit (unless the offender be thereupon convicted) in Ireland for any offence provided against in this Act shall be pleaded or allowed in bar or delay of any indictment, information, suit or prosecution within the kingdom of England. . .

X. And be it further enacted . . . that all such goods as aforesaid as shall from time to time be exported from the said kingdom of Ireland into the ports of this kingdom or dominion of Wales in manner as aforesaid shall be shipped off and entered at the ports of Dublin, Waterford, Youghal, Kinsale, Cork and Drogheda in the said kingdom of Ireland, and at or from no other port or place within the said kingdom, nor shall the same be imported into any parts of the kingdom of England or dominion of Wales other than the ports of Bideford, Barnstaple, Minehead, Bridgwater, Bristol, Milford Haven, Chester and Liverpool, anything in this Act to the contrary thereof in any wise notwithstanding. . . .

XIX. And for the more effectual encouragement of the woollen manufacture of this kingdom be it further enacted . . . that from and after the first day of December in the year of our Lord one thousand six hundred ninety-nine no wool, wool fells, . . .[2] being of the product or manufacture of any of the English plantations in America, shall be loaden or laid on board in any ship or vessel in any place or parts within any of the said English plantations upon any pretence whatsoever; as likewise that no such wool, wool fells, . . .[2] being of the product or manufacture of any of the English plantations in America as aforesaid, shall be loaded upon any horse, cart or other carriage to the intent and purpose to be exported, transported, carried or conveyed out of the said English plantations to any other of the said plantations, or to any other place whatsoever, upon the same and like pains, penalties and forfeitures to and upon all and every the offender and offenders herein, within all and every of the said English plantations respectively, as are prescribed and provided by this Act for the like offences committed within the kingdom of Ireland. . . .

---

[1] As in the preceding section. [2] As in section I.

D. PUBLIC FINANCE

283. Revenue, 1664–1665

(Calendar of State Papers, Ireland, 1663–1665, p. 555)

STATEMENT OF THE RECEIPTS OF THE REVENUE IN THE IRISH TREASURY
FOR THE YEAR ENDING 20 MARCH 1664[1]

	£	s.	d.
The old crown rents	9,361	10	0
New rents	467	5	6
Composition rents	351	13	6
New quit rents	38,042	5	1
Rents of impropriate rectories, &c.	109	11	3
The Excise and Customs	55,490	18	6
The Inland Excise	30,274	15	9
Fines for licence to sell beer and ale, &c.	3,379	0	0
Green wax, &c.	3,306	6	3
Goods of felons and fugitives	51	10	8
The profits of the Hamper Office	240	15	0
First Fruits and twentieth parts	493	2	6
Hearth Money	11,637	5	8
	153,205	19	8

284. Establishment to commence from 25 March 1676

(Calendar of State Papers Domestic, 1676–1677, pp. 39–40)

Civil Affairs	£	s.	d.
Court of Exchequer	3,646	14	2
Court of King's Bench	1,407	10	0
Court of Chancery	1,297	19	11
Court of Common Pleas	1,307	10	0
Officers attending the State	1,289	1	10
Incidents	2,187	0	0
Officers of the Customs	238	6	8
Creation Money	544	11	8
Perpetuities	489	15	6
Temporary payments	8,997	11	4
Concordatums	4,500	0	0
To uses to be appropriated by sign manual	20,000	0	0
	45,906	1	1

[1] 1664/5.

Military Affairs	£	s.	d.			
Lord Lieutenant and general officers	8,623	18	8			
Officers of the Ordnance	1,616	9	0			
Horse	51,870	12	0			
Foot	84,150	0	0			
				146,260	19	8
Pensions				10,400	2	3
In all				202,567	3	0

285. Revenue, 1682–1685

(William King, *State of the Protestants of Ireland*, p. 312)

A GENERAL ABSTRACT

OF THE GROSS PRODUCE OF HIS MAJESTY'S REVENUE IN IRELAND

IN THE THREE FIRST YEARS OF THE MANAGEMENT,

BEGINNING AT CHRISTMAS 1682, ENDING CHRISTMAS 1685

	1683	1684	1685
Customs Inwards and Imported Excise	£85,845	91,424	91,118
Customs Outwards	32,093	33,426	29,428
Seizures and Fines	965	615	460
Prizage	1,452	1,693	1,882
Inland Excise	68,344	77,580	79,169
Ale Licenses	8,284	9,538	9,996
Wine, &c., Licenses	2,737	3,115	3,468
Quit, Crown and Custodiam Rents	68,699	68,385	68,922
Hearth Money	31,041	31,646	32,954
Casual Revenue	820	1,746	1,565
Totals	£300,280	319,168	318,962

	1683	1684	1685
Arrears of each of the above years remaining uncollected at Christmas 1685	7,659	9,799	34,971

Net cash paid into the Treasury in the three years above mentioned, over and besides the charges of management and salaries to the officers of the revenue in the said time £712,973

Cash remaining in the collectors' hands at Christmas 1685, ready to be paid in 55,655

The solvent part of the above-mentioned arrears, which was actually levied and paid into the Treasury before Christmas 1688 30,000

Total cash £798,628

Which, at a medium for three years, amounts for each year to the sum of £266,209

286. Charge and discharge, 1683

(Clarendon Correspondence, ed. S. W. Singer, 1, p. 651)

AN ABSTRACT OF THE ACCOUNT OF THE REVENUE OF IRELAND FOR THE
YEAR ENDING THE 25TH DECEMBER 1683

Is debtor	£	s.	d.	Is creditor	£	s.	d.
To Customs and Impost	118,497	12	8	By money paid to the Receiver General	236,979	1	9
To Prizage and Butlerage	1,452	0	0	By warrants of the Lord Deputy for wine to Privy Councillors, and other free warrants	732	2	3
To French tonnage	371	5	0				
To Inland Excise	68,379	18	$1\frac{1}{8}$				
To ale licences	9,101	8	$3\frac{1}{2}$				
To wine and strong water licences	1,921	11	$5\frac{5}{8}$	By cash in collectors' hands unassigned	9,545	5	$3\frac{5}{8}$
To Hearth Money	31,041	0	0				
To quit rents, &c.	68,535	10	$0\frac{1}{4}$				
To casual revenue	1,614	17	10	Total of cash aforesaid	247,256	9	$3\frac{5}{8}$
				By arrears not collected at Christmas	23,221	12	$1\frac{7}{8}$
				Total of cash and arrears	270,478	1	$5\frac{1}{2}$
				By salaries	24,633	5	$9\frac{1}{2}$
				By incidencies of management, and extraordinary expenses of lawsuits, and prosecution of several debtors to the king	4,135	6	$1\frac{3}{4}$
				By repayment to merchants, victualling and portage bills, &c.	1,668	10	0
	300,915	3	$4\frac{3}{4}$		300,915	3	$4\frac{3}{4}$

E. CATHOLIC ASCENDANCY UNDER JAMES II

287. (Irish) Act of Recognition, 1689

(*Manuscripts of the House of Lords, 1689–1690, pp. 156–159*)

AN ACT OF RECOGNITION OF THE JUST AND MOST UNDOUBTED RIGHTS OF HIS MAJESTY'S IMPERIAL CROWN

Most Gracious Sovereign. We, your Majesty's most dutiful and loyal subjects, the Lords Spiritual and Temporal and Commons in this present Parliament assembled, most joyfully acknowledging the transcendent mercy of Almighty God in giving your sacred Majesty a safe and happy arrival to this your kingdom of Ireland, in a glorious and peaceable manner in despite of the conspiracies and machinations of execrable traitors and power of foreign enemies, cannot without horror consider the detestable defections and treasons of many of our fellow subjects, as well in this realm as in your Majesty's other kingdoms, who, being desperately wicked and hardened in impiety, by unspeakable treachery lately assisted the prince of Orange, against the laws of God and man, unnaturally to invade your kingdom of England, and there, by odious arts and devices strengthening themselves in power and faction, by seducing from their allegiance great numbers of your Majesty's subjects of that kingdom, first forced your Majesty to withdraw your sacred person from your palace of Whitehall, and soon after your return, to the great joy of many thousands of your loyal subjects in those parts of England, put your Majesty under a guard of foreigners, compelling you to go to Rochester, where you remained in restraint until it pleased God, of his infinite mercy to your Majesty and these kingdoms, to give you a happy deliverance out of the hands of your enemies by escaping into France, from whence your Majesty, to the inexpressible joy of all your loyal subjects, happily came into this kingdom; and the said prince of Orange having, by the detestable assistance of such traitors and enemies, first plotted and contrived the ruin and destruction of this excellent monarchy and of all the rights and liberties of your subjects, found it necessary, in order to the carrying on of his pernicious designs by aid of the said traitors and foreign enemies, to throw down all the bulwarks and fences of law, and to subvert the very being and constitutions of Parliaments, that so at last he and they might make their way open to the unnatural and perfidious usurpation afterward by him and them accomplished; who first professing, by several deceitful declarations, that his intent was not to deprive your Majesty of your Imperial Crown, but to preserve the Protestant religion and rights of your subjects, by him speciously but most falsely pretended to be subverted, under the abusive and unknown name and authority of a Convention of Lords and Commons meeting at Westminster, against the laws of your Majesty's kingdoms, by force and fraud and an unparalleled example of impudence and injustice, they took upon them to declare your royal throne vacant, and (as if it were their right to dispose of the same) offered your Imperial Crown to the said prince of Orange, in such horrid manner and odious circumstances as is but too well known to the world, which execrable fact nothing can equal but the barbarous murder of your royal father of ever blessed and glorious memory, by a party of wretched men from whom these late traitors have borrowed and revived their desperate antimonarchic principles; and because by this abominable action a most insupportable shame and infamy may be imputed to millions of your Majesty's subjects no wise guilty of this treason, we, therefore, your Majesty's said dutiful and loyal subjects, the Lords Spiritual and Temporal and Commons in Parliament assembled, being touched with a true sense of our duty, do hereby renounce, abominate and protest against that impious fact, the late usurpation of the said prince of Orange and the most unparalleled treason and perfidiousness of such of your Majesty's subjects as have by their defections in any sort promoted the same, and all proceedings tending thereunto, and do beseech your Majesty that it may be declared that the said horrid usurpation and all acts tending to and promoting of the same are against the law of God, nature and nations, and have fixed an indelible infamy on the perjured heads of such as have been guilty thereof, all or most of these offenders having sworn that it was not lawful to take up arms against your Majesty on any pretence whatsoever.

And the said perfidious criminals being conscious of their guilt and breach of faith to God and their natural sovereign, after they had manifestly violated the before-recited oath, and also broke the oaths of allegiance and supremacy, have by their own usurped authority taken upon them to abrogate the said oaths, and invented new and impious assurances of fidelity to the usurper. We, therefore, your Majesty's most loyal and most dutiful subjects aforesaid, out of our bounden duty to God and your Majesty, and for the vindication of ourselves from any crime that may be imputed to us by reason of the said treasonable transactions, . . . do hereby acknowledge, with one full voice of tongue and heart, that your Majesty is our lawful and undoubted liege, sovereign lord and king. . . . And we do hereby further declare that your Majesty's right to your said Imperial Crown is originally, by nature and descent of blood, from God alone, by whom kings reign, and not from your people, nor by virtue or pretext of any contract made with them, or any Act of your estates on that behalf, an assertion which we abominate, detest and condemn as false and traitorous, taken up formerly and since revived by the most odious parricides that every lived; and do hereby further publish and declare that by the undoubted fundamental laws of this kingdom and of England neither the peers of this realm, nor the Commons, nor both together, in Parliament nor out of Parliament, nor the people collectively or representatively, nor any other persons whatsoever, ever had, have or ought to have any coercive power over the persons of the kings of this realm; and that our allegiance to your Majesty, our natural liege lord and sovereign, is indissoluble, and cannot be renounced by us or our posterities, which allegiance of us your subjects is due to your Majesty in your natural person, from which the royal power cannot be separated.

And we do further recognize and declare that within all your Majesty's realms and dominions the sole and supreme power, government, command and disposition of the militia, and of all forces by sea and land, and of all forts and places of strength, is, and by the laws of this realm and of England ever was, the undoubted right of your Majesty and your royal predecessors, kings and queens of these realms; and that both or either of the Houses of Parliament, or the people collectively or representatively, or a convention or assembly of Lords Spiritual, Temporal, and Commons, or any of them, on any account whatsoever, cannot nor ought to pretend to the same, nor can or lawfully may raise or levy any war, offensive or defensive, against your Majesty, your heirs and lawful successors.

And . . . we do hereby further recognize, publish and declare that, as it is against the law of nature to hinder or deprive your Majesty's subjects of your royal protection, so it is directly against the same law, and the laws and statutes of this realm thereon grounded, to hinder or deprive your Majesty from the service of your subjects in peace or war (being inseparably annexed to and inherent in your royal person), of what persuasion in religion soever they be, when your Majesty shall have occasion to use the same, whereof your Majesty is the only judge; and that it is utterly unlawful for your Majesty's subjects of this or any of your kingdoms, on any pretence whatsoever, actually to resist your Majesty, or our lawful hereditary king for the time being, by violence or force of arms, or to withdraw their allegiance from your Majesty, your heirs and lawful successors, but that the decision in all cases of a misused authority by our lawful hereditary king (if any such should happen) must be left to the sole judgment of God, the King of Kings and only ruler of princes. . . .

288. (Irish) Declaratory Act, 1689

(*Dublin Magazine*, January 1843, pp. 30–32)

AN ACT DECLARING THAT THE PARLIAMENT OF ENGLAND CANNOT BIND IRELAND, AGAINST WRITS OF ERROR AND APPEALS TO BE BROUGHT FOR REMOVING JUDGMENTS, DECREES AND SENTENCES GIVEN IN IRELAND INTO ENGLAND

Whereas his Majesty's realm of Ireland is, and hath been always, a distinct kingdom from that of his Majesty's realm of England, always governed by his Majesty and his predecessors according to the ancient customs, laws and statutes thereof; and as the people of this kingdom did never send members to any Parliament ever held in England, but had their laws continually made and established by their own Parliaments, . . . be it therefore enacted . . . that no Act of Parliament passed or to be passed in the Parliament of England, though Ireland should be therein mentioned, can be or shall be any way binding in Ireland, excepting such Acts passed or to be passed in England as are or shall be made into law by the Parliament of Ireland.

II. And whereas several writs of error were formerly sued out and returnable into the King's Bench in England, in order to reverse judgments given in his Majesty's Court of King's Bench in Ireland; and whereas most of the said writs of error have been brought for delay, and thereby many of his Majesty's subjects of this realm were greatly hindered from recovering their just rights, and put to vast charges in attending such suits in England; for the prevention whereof, be it hereby enacted . . . that no writ of error shall be hereafter brought out of England in order to remove any record, or transcript of record, out of his Majesty's Court of King's Bench in Ireland, or out of any other court of record here, into England, in order to reverse any such judgments. . . .

VII. And whereas of late times several persons have brought appeals before the House of Lords in England, in order to reverse decrees granted in the High Court of Chancery. in Ireland, which tend to the great trouble, charge and vexation of such of his Majesty's subjects as have obtained such decrees, and is an apparent new encroachment upon the fundamental constitutions of this realm, and also appeal before delegates in England, be it further enacted . . . that no person or persons whatsoever do hereafter presume to sue out any such appeals, or to tender or produce any such appeal to the Lord Chancellor or Lord Keeper of Ireland, or to any of the officers of the said Court of Chancery, and that such appeals shall be void. . . .

289. (Irish) Act of Attainder, 1689
(William King, *State of the Protestants of Ireland*, pp. 241–298)

AN ACT FOR THE ATTAINDER OF DIVERS REBELS,
AND FOR PRESERVING THE INTEREST OF LOYAL SUBJECTS

Humbly beseech your Majesty the Commons in this present Parliament assembled, that whereas a most horrid invasion was made by your unnatural enemy the prince of Orange, invited thereunto and assisted by many of your Majesty's rebellious and traitorous subjects of your Majesty's dominions, and such their inviting and assisting made manifest by their perfidious deserting your Majesty's service, in which by your many princely obligations, besides their natural duties, they were bounden; and having likewise, to obtain their wicked ends, raised and levied open rebellion and war in several places in this kingdom . . . to quell which your sacred Majesty's late deputy in this kingdom, Richard, then earl and now duke of Tyrconnel, before your Majesty's happy arrival in this kingdom, and your sacred Majesty since your arrival here, have been necessitated to raise an army, to your Majesty's great charge and expense; and though the said rebels and traitors, after their having the impudence to declare for the prince and princess of Orange against your sacred Majesty, were with all mildness and humanity called in to their allegiance by proclamations, and promises of pardon for their past offences and protection for the future; . . . that it may be enacted, and be it enacted, . . . that the persons hereafter named, being persons who have notoriously joined in the said rebellion and invasion, and some of which are upon indictments condemned, some executed for high treason, and the rest run away or absconded, or are now in the actual service of the prince of Orange against your Majesty, and others killed in open rebellion, viz., Francis Marsh, lord archbishop of Dublin; James Butler, duke of Ormonde; . . . .[1] shall be deemed, taken and reputed, and are hereby declared and adjudged, traitors, convicted and attainted of high treason, and shall suffer such pains of death, penalties and forfeitures respectively as in cases of high treason are accustomed. Provided that in case it happen that any of the persons hereby attainted, or to be attainted, do now abide or dwell in this kingdom,

[1] Some 1,340 names are given, of persons in all classes of society.

and are amenable to the law, that then and in such case, if such person and persons do by the tenth day of August one thousand six hundred eighty-nine, without compulsion, of his own accord come in and deliver himself to the Lord Chief Justice of your Majesty's Court of King's Bench in Ireland, or to any other of the judges of the said Court or of any other of your Majesty's four courts in Dublin, or to any judge of assize in their circuits, to be charged with any treason to be charged or imputed to him or them, that then and in such case such person and persons (if after acquitted by the laws of this land, or discharged by proclamation) shall be freed, discharged and acquitted from all pains, punishments and forfeitures by this Act incurred, laid or imposed, anything in this Act to the contrary in any wise notwithstanding.

And whereas the several persons hereafter named, viz., John Vesey, lord archbishop of Tuam; Arthur Chichester, earl of Donegal; . . . .[1] have absented themselves from this kingdom, and have gone into England or some other places beyond the seas, since the fifth day of November last or in some short time before, and did not return, although called home by your Majesty's gracious proclamation; which absenting and not returning cannot be construed otherwise than to a wicked and traitorous purpose; . . . be it therefore enacted . . . that in case the said person and persons do not by the first day of September one thousand six hundred eighty and nine, of his own or their own accord, without compulsion, return into this kingdom, and tender him and themselves to the Chief Justice of his Majesty's Court of King's Bench, or to some other judge of the said Court, or judge of assize in the circuit, or any of the lords of your Majesty's most honourable Privy Council, to be charged with any crimes to him or them to be imputed, that then . . . such person and persons so absent and not returning as aforesaid . . . shall, from and after the first day of September one thousand six hundred eighty-nine, be deemed, reputed and taken as traitors convict and attainted of high treason, and shall suffer such pains of death and other forfeitures and penalties as in cases of high treason are accustomed. . . .

And whereas the several persons hereafter named, viz., Robert Ridgeway, earl of Londonderry; Arthur Loftus, Viscount Loftus of Ely; . . .[2] have before the said fifth day of November last absented themselves from this kingdom, and live in England, Scotland or the Isle of Man, and there now abide, and by their not coming or returning into this kingdom upon your Majesty's proclamation, to assist in defence of this realm according to their allegiance, must be presumed to adhere to the said prince of Orange, in case they return not within the time by this Act prescribed, . . . be it therefore enacted . . . that in case the said person and persons last mentioned do not by the first day of October one thousand six hundred eighty-nine, of his and their own accord, without compulsion, return into this kingdom. . . .[3]

Provided always that in case your Majesty shall happen to go into the kingdom of England or Scotland before the first day of October one thousand six hundred eighty-nine, then if the said Sir William Meredith, . . .[4] whose dwelling and residence always hath been in England, shall give your Majesty such testimony of their loyalty and fidelity as that your Majesty will be pleased, on or before the said first day of October

---

[1] Some 840 names are given.   [2] Some 200 names are given.   [3] As in the preceding paragraph.
[4] Some 60 names are given, of individuals included in the previous list.

one thousand six hundred eighty-nine, to certify under your privy signet or sign manual unto your chief governor or governors of this kingdom, that your Majesty is satisfied or assured of the loyalty and fidelity of the persons last before named, or of any of them, that then if such certificate shall on or before the first day of November one thousand six hundred eighty-nine be produced to your chief governor or governors of this kingdom, and enrolled in your Majesty's High Court of Chancery, the same shall be a sufficient discharge and acquittal to such of the persons last before named, and every of them respectively, whose loyalty and fidelity your Majesty will be pleased to certify in manner as aforesaid.

And be it further enacted that in the meantime, and until such return and acquittal, all the lands, tenements and hereditaments within this kingdom belonging to all and every absentee and absentees, or other person, to be attainted as aforesaid, shall be and are hereby vested in your Majesty, your heirs and successors, as from the first day of August last past.

And whereas several persons hereafter named, viz., Lionel, earl of Orrery, . . .[1] are, and for some time past have been, absent out of this kingdom, and by reason of sickness, nonage, infirmities or other disabilities, may for some time further be obliged so to stay out of this kingdom or be disabled to return thereunto; nevertheless it being much to the weakening and impoverishing of this realm that any of the rents or profits of the lands, tenements or hereditaments therein should be sent into, or spent in, any other place beyond the seas, but that the same should be kept and employed within the realm for the better support and defence thereof, be it therefore enacted . . . that all the lands, tenements and hereditaments, use, trust, possession, reversion, remainder, and all and every other estate, title and interest whatsoever belonging or appertaining to all and every of the persons hereinbefore last mentioned, within this kingdom, be and are hereby vested in your Majesty, your heirs and successors, to the use of your Majesty, your heirs and successors. . . .

Provided always, that if your sacred Majesty at any time before the first day of November next, by letters patents under the broad seal of England, if residing there, or by letters patents under the great seal of Ireland, during your Majesty's abode here, shall grant your gracious pardon or pardons to any one or more of the persons hereinbefore mentioned or intended to be attainted, who shall return to their duty and loyalty; that then and in such case such person and persons so pardoned shall be and is hereby excepted out of this present Act . . .

---

[1] Some 90 names are given, mainly of women.

F. WARS OF THE REVOLUTION

290. Letter from George Holmes to William Fleming on the siege of Londonderry, 1689

(Historical Manuscripts Commission, *Twelfth Report*, App. VII, pp. 264–265)

Strabane, 16 November 1689

I must confess that I have been very negligent in writing to you to give you an account that I am yet in the land of the living; but to give you a brief account of my travels this twelve months, I was one of the first (that did wear a red coat) that revolted from King James and helped to set up a flag of defiance against him and popery in the city of Londonderry, that now lies in a ruinous condition, yet defies all the king and queen's enemies.

After some little routs in the country, on the 12th of April last the Irish army appeared before our city, but at that distance that one of our cannons had enough to do to reach them; but in short time they approached nearer to our walls. In the first place we burned all our suburbs and hewed down all our brave orchards, making all about us as plain as a bowling-green. About the 18th of April King James came within a mile of our walls, but had no better entertainment than bullets of 14, 16 and 22 pounds weight. He sent us a letter under his own hand, sealed with his own seal, to desire us to surrender, and we should have our own conditions. The messenger was a lord with a trumpet, and out of grand civility we sent three messengers, all gentlemen; but two of them ran away from us, and the other came again. In short we would not yield.

Then we proceeded, and chose captains and completed regiments, made two governors. We had 116 companies in the city. All our officers fled away, so we made officers of those that did deserve to be officers. I was made captain. And then we began to sally out, and the first sally that we made we slew their French general and several of their men with the loss of nine or ten of our men, which was the greatest loss that ever we lost in the field. Every day afterward we sallied out and daily killed our enemies, which put us in great heart; but it being so soon of the year, and we having no forage for our horses, we was forced to let them out, and the enemy got many. The rest of them died for hunger.

About the 20th of May the enemy gave us a general onset on all sides, but was so defeated that we were not troubled with them again for a week. Their own account told us that that day they lost 500 men, but I assure you we saw 150 stripped, beside all that they carried away on their backs, which was a trick they had still when they ran, to take a dead man on their back; it was good harness. To be short, we took no prisoners except nine great officers, and they were so wounded that most of them died. We have three or four left yet.

Ten days after that battle they came again very boldly, but in half an hour's time returned with greater loss than before. They began to run their approaches near us on one side. They came within 100 yards of us, and one night they attempted so near that one of them knocked at our gate and called for faggots to burn it with. This being in the dead of the night and our men being gone off their posts we were in some danger. The drums beat alarm, and we got a party together and sallied out at another gate, fell upon them and put them to the rout and recovered our own ground again, came so near them that we might have taken them alive, but we gave them old quarter. This night our great guns did execution with case-shot off the walls; that's musket bullets.

At this time they played abundance of bombs (the weight of many of them was near three hundredweight), which killed many people. One bomb slew seventeen persons. I was in the next room one night at my supper (which was but mean), and seven men were thrown out of the third room next to that we were in, all killed, and some of them in pieces. Into this city they played 596 bombs, which destroyed many of our people and demolished many of our houses. Cannon bullets flew as fast as you could count them, and as soon as we took up their bullets we sent them back again post paid. Thus men, horses and all went to destruction.

But at last our provision grew scant and our allowance small. One pound of oatmeal and one pound of tallow served a man a week; sometimes salt hides. It was as bad as Samaria, only we had no pigeon's dung.[1] I saw 2s. a quarter given for a little dog, horse blood at 4d. per pint; all the starch was eaten, the graves of tallow, horse flesh was a rarity, and still we resolved to hold out.

Four days before we got relief from England we saw a great drove of cows very near us, and we were very weak, but we resolved to sally out, and in order thereto we played our great guns off the walls and sallied out on our enemy. I led the forlorn hope, which was about 100 men of the best we had, with which I ran full tilt into their trenches; and before our body came up we had slain 80 men, put many to the rout. We got arms enough and some beef, but durst not stay long, not above half an hour. This vexed our enemies much; they said we took them asleep. I praise God I had still my health, and has yet.

After the ships came in with provision to us our enemies thought it was in vain to stay any longer, so on Lammas day they left us the wide fields to walk in. In the siege we had not above 60 men killed, except with the bombs killed. But I believe there died 15,000 men, women and children, many of which died for meat. But we had a great fever amongst us, and all the children died, almost whole families not one left alive. This is a true account of the siege of Londonderry. I would have given you a larger account, but I know you have had it before. This is but a trouble, only the nights is long and it will serve you to read.

I know my sister and several of my friends will think I am dead. Pray tell them I am well. I was shot in the skirt of my coat, and both the hinder skirts of it taken off with a cannon bullet, and I was not hurt, I praise God. I was in the head of my company, and the pike that was in my hand was cut in two with a cannon bullet, and I not hurt. Musket bullets has light about me like crabs off a tree, and still God protected me. I had a good character given of me to Major-General Kirke for my service, for which he made me major to a regiment. My quarters is in this town, ten

---

[1] See 2 Kings VI. 25.

miles from the city of Derry; but I am for the most in Derry myself. My wife I have neither seen nor heard from since Christmas last, at which time I parted with her at Dublin. She went to her father's house near Waterford. I hope shortly to hear from her. . . .

291. Anonymous account of Schomberg's campaign, 1689–1690

(*A Jacobite Narrative of the War in Ireland*, ed. J. T. Gilbert, pp. 87–94)

Marshal de Schomberg from Hoylake, near Liverpool, landed with ten thousand men on the thirteenth of August at Bangor in the province of Ulster, and having refreshed his troops, and being considerably reinforced by the Protestant rebels of that country to near twenty thousand men in all, he resolved to march straight by the seaside into the province of Leinster and up to the city of Dublin. But first he would halt at the town of Carrickfergus, which he invested on the twentieth of August. The castle of this place is strong; the governor of it was Colonel MacCarthy Mor. Schomberg summoned him to yield; but he would not, till on the twenty-seventh he was forced to surrender for want of powder, on condition that he and his garrison, being his own regiment of foot and that of Colonel Owen MacCarthy, should march away to the next Irish quarters with arms and baggage, a strange neglect in time of war, when the stores were full of ammunition.

After taking Carrickfergus Marshal Schomberg marched forwards and came to Newry, in the county of Down, on the sixth of September, which he found burned a little before by the duke of Berwick. On the seventh he arrived at Dundalk, in the county of Louth, a small maritime town. Here he pitched his camp in a low ground and intrenched, having heard that the king was not far off and was resolved to meet and fight him. On the eighth the marshal received from the north the regiments of Major-General Kirke, of Sir John Hanmer, and Brigadier Stuart.

The king, hearing that Marshal de Schomberg was come as far as Dundalk, gave orders to his army to decamp from Drogheda and march down to the enemy. A part of the royal forces marched first to Ardee, and thence in a day or two to the Bridge of Fane, upon a small river within three miles of Dundalk. Hither the king came on the fifteenth of September with the rest of his army, and encamped. His Majesty found the army to be twenty-six thousand strong. Both armies lay quiet for a few days without coming to any action of moment. At last the king resolved to try his fortune; whereupon he drew out his army on the twenty-first of September, and marched in order of battle near unto the enemy, in hopes he would quit his trenches and accept of the challenge. But the marshal durst not, as finding the royal troops too numerous for his; and the king would not attack him in his trenches, fearing the victory would prove too dear, though General de Rosen, upon good grounds, was altogether for it, since they could not get the enemy to fight otherwise. . . .

At this the king drew back to the town of Ardee, where the army lay encamped, to observe the motions of the enemy, until about the fourth of November; at which time his Majesty, seeing no hopes of a battle upon the square, nor the enemy inclined to go off till the Irish army had first decamped, resolved to remain in the field no longer to the prejudice of his troops, the bad weather being at hand. And so he ordered his army to go into winter quarters, while he himself returned to Dublin.

Marshal Schomberg, perceiving his enemy gone off the field, immediately rose, which was on the eighth, ninth and tenth of November, after being encamped in an unwholesome place about nine weeks, and afflicted awhile with rainy weather, whereby it came to pass that eight thousand of his army died, part in the camp, part in the marching to winter quarters, and part in their quarters and hospitals. The marshal, decamping, marched to the north, where he quartered his men. Newry, in possession of the rebels, was the line near the sea between both parties that winter, as Cavan, Belturbet and Charlemont, in the hands of the loyalists, were the line within the land, so that there remained to the king three provinces of the kingdom, Leinster, Munster and Connaught, and part of the fourth, Ulster. . . .

There happened no winter action of any note between the Catholic and Protestant troops on the frontiers of Ulster, except two or three. On the twenty-fourth of November Captain Christopher Plunkett of Lagore, in the lord of Louth's regiment, was sent with his company of grenadiers by Major-General Boisseleau from Dundalk to take the above-mentioned Newry, an open town then garrisoned by a few of Schomberg's army. He marched in the night-time, and by the dawn of the day he made himself master thereof by the slaughter of a few of the enemies; and as he was going to plunder the place, which was furnished with good store of money, and had horses and black cattle, the captain received an order from the major-general to retire immediately to his quarters. What reason there was for this order we have not been informed, otherwise than that the first design was only but to show to the rebels that the king's frontier garrison was watchful and bold. . . .

There happened a small fight at Cavan, on the frontiers of Ulster, between the loyalists and the rebels. Marshal Schomberg, designing to straiten the Irish quarters on the borders of the north, ordered Brigadier Wolseley to take a party of Enniskilleners and of English soldiers and march to Cavan, the head of that county, and fix there. The king, being informed thereof, sent from Dublin his commands to Brigadier Nugent to march to the said Cavan with eight hundred men from the counties of Westmeath and Longford; and at the same time his Majesty enjoined the duke of Berwick to march from the county of Dublin with the like quota to the same place, in order to hinder the enemy from gaining ground. Both the royal corps for the most part arrived at the open town of Cavan on the tenth of February. They were all foot, except a troop or two of horse. Brigadier Wolseley came to the place on the eleventh, in the morning, with seven hundred foot and three hundred horse and dragoons.

The duke of Berwick, commander-in-chief, being alarmed and not well prepared, drew, however, his men out of the town to an open ground, by which he gave an advantage to the enemy, who was come to attack him, for the enemy seeing that posture, he placed his foot within the hedges and ditches of the avenues of the town, and so took the defensive. The king's forces, being divided into two wings, assaulted the rebels within their fences. The charge being given and maintained smartly, a party of Irish horse broke another of the enemy's. But the left wing of the royalists was so overpowered by fighting at such an inequality that they were forced to retire into a fort that was near them. The right, fighting at the like disadvantage, retreated also thither, by which the rebels gained the field. Of the royal party there were about two hundred killed, amongst whom was Brigadier Nugent, much regretted for his bravery. . . . Brigadier Wolseley returned to his own quarters, having first burned the town of Cavan, not being able to keep it, because the castle was in the possession of the Irish.

The month of April being come in the year 1690, Marshal Schomberg, like a vigilant general, draws out of winter quarters his army into the field, in order to take the king's fortress called Charlemont, in the county of Armagh, before the landing of the prince of Orange and his forces, to the end his Highness might find the whole province of Ulster entirely under his obedience at his arrival. The marshal then sat down before Charlemont, about the twenty-second of April, which held out three weeks, until the garrison had nothing to eat; upon which the governor, Sir Thady O'Regan, delivered it upon honourable terms, the fourteenth of May, that the garrison, being eight hundred men, should march away with their arms and baggage.

292. Dr. George Clarke's account of the Boyne, Aughrim and Limerick, 1690–1691

("Autobiography" in Historical Manuscripts Commission, *Leyborne-Popham MSS.*, pp. 271–281)

I waited upon his Majesty all along the way to Chester and Gayton-in-Wirral, where he lay some few nights till the wind seemed to turn, and then the king went on board at Hoylake and in two or three days landed at Belfast. The old duke of Schomberg was quartered there and received his Majesty. In the time the king stayed at Belfast, among others the Presbyterian ministers presented a long address and claimed the king's protection and favour upon three accounts: 1st, for their numbers, as being the most numerous of all the Protestants of the north; 2nd, their services, especially at Londonderry; and 3rd, because his Majesty and his ancestors were all of their persuasion, or to that effect. I remember when they read the second article, Mr. Walker, who had been governor of Londonderry, and with whom I was talking, could not contain himself, but contradicted what they said with a good deal of warmth, though not loud enough for the king to hear.

I cannot omit in this place to take notice of the little regard the king showed to that very great man, the old duke of Schomberg. All the countenance and confidence was in the Dutch general officers, Count Solms, Monsieur Scravenmoer, &c., insomuch that the duke, who commanded next under his Majesty, was not so much as advised with about the march of the army, as he complained to me himself while we were at Belfast, and said if the king had supposed that he had not been entirely negligent in informing himself of the country that winter he would have thought fit to have asked his opinion which was the most proper way for it to advance, and if he had he should have told his Majesty the difficulties he might probably meet with in going by Newry, and that the better way was by Armagh and the Fewes, &c., but that he had never till then heard so much of what was intended as I had told him, for which he thanked me.

Indeed I think that the duke resented these slights and ill-usage so much that he was not unwilling to expose himself more than was really proper, in hopes of putting an end to his uneasiness in the manner he did. And I am the more confirmed in this thought by some discourse I had with him two or three days before the battle of the Boyne, and what passed between his grace and a friend of mine the very evening that preceded his death. His grace was killed immediately after the head of the line passed the river, and poor Mr. Walker of Londonderry with him. The king had immediate notice of it by some of the duke's aides-de-camp, but did not seem to be concerned. . . .

The day before the battle, as the army marched up to the Boyne and drew up upon a rise that sloped towards the river as fast as they came to their ground, the king, after eating a little at Count Schomberg's, rode along the line with intent to view the river he intended to pass and the enemy on the other side of it. He had not rode half a quarter of a mile before the Irish fired two field-pieces, which we saw them place upon a rising ground almost over against us (I mean the place where the king had dined and we were dining, on the side of the Boyne). The company that followed the king rode up the rising ground from the river in some disorder, as we perceived, upon the firing these two pieces, which were immediately after pointed against the horse guards, who upon that were ordered to dismount that they might be the less exposed to the shot that flew pretty thick and had done mischief among the horses. Upon the movement made by the company that attended the king the enemy gave a great shout; but we who were at the head of the guards did not know that any of the shot had taken place, and indeed when we were told a little after that the king was wounded on the shoulder with a cannon ball, but not dangerously, I could not bring myself to believe that he was alive, and thought it was only given out in that manner to prevent the confusion which the telling his true condition would have occasioned. But to my great satisfaction I saw him soon after riding towards that place where he received his hurt, and so all along the line; but nobody except the Marshal Schomberg was allowed to ride with him, that he might not be again exposed to their shot from his quality being discovered by the number of his attendants. . . .

Next morning, about eight or nine o'clock, our cannon began to fire upon two houses with yards walled about, that stood on each side the road on the other side the Boyne just over against the ford where the guards were to pass. The enemy had posted some foot in those houses, whose fire was silenced by our cannon; but as the guards were got almost through the water they rose up from behind the walls and gave one fire upon them and ran away. Part of the troops marched directly on between these two houses up the hill, and there the duke of Schomberg and Mr. Walker were killed, and news was brought of it to the king, who had not passed the river, but was looking upon the action, and in great concern for his Blue Guards, who had marched to the left between the two houses and the river, and were forming as fast as they could to receive a body of Irish horse that was coming towards them upon a full trot. The king was in a good deal of apprehension for them, there not being hedge nor ditch before them nor any of our horse to support them, and I was so near his Majesty as to hear him say softly to himself, "My poor guards, my poor guards, my poor guards", as the enemy were coming down upon them. But when he saw them stand their ground and fire by platoons, so that the horse were forced to run away in great disorder, he breathed out, as people use to do after holding their breath upon a fright or suspense, and said he had seen his guards do that which he had never seen foot do in his life.

He then immediately called for his horse and went over the river, near the place where the guards had passed before, and that part of the army which was with the king got over there and lower towards Drogheda. The other part, commanded by Count Meinhard, afterwards duke of Schomberg, went over at Slane, where there was little opposition and in neither place much to do after the troops were passed, the Irish returning before them to Duleek, about two miles off. There some cornets of horse made a little stand by the advantage of a small river and a stone bridge, so that the cannon were sent for, and in the meantime we could see their foot making the best of their way without any manner of order towards Dublin. I think, too, that their horse quitted Duleek before the cannon came. Our horse and dragoons pursued them till dusk of the evening, but they got through a defile before we could come up with them and made another stand, so that our dragoons drew up in a line to face them, and stayed for the cannon that were coming up. By this time it was just dark, and the king went back to Duleek, where the foot were ordered to halt, and his Majesty lay that night in the prince of Denmark's coach, for the baggage was not come up. We shifted as well as we could without tents or servants, and slept very heartily upon the ground. In the night the enemy's horse that faced our dragoons marched away, and we heard no more of them.

We were told that King James went off with a good body of horse soon after the action began, for the general officers had addressed to him the night before in a council of war not to expose his person. He came to Dublin that evening, and went to the Castle to Lady Tyrconnel, and about four o'clock next morning set out for Duncannon and got thither by night. There he went aboard a ship that he found in the harbour and sailed for France, but was driven back either to Cork or Kinsale, and hearing that there were seventeen or nineteen French frigates in the other of these harbours he sent to them to convoy him, which they did, and by that means were prevented from scouring St. George's Channel, intercepting provisions and cutting off all correspondence with England, which were the services for which they were designed, so that if it had not been for this accident our army would have had great difficulty to subsist, the French being masters at sea by their success at Beachy fight, which happened about the time of that at the Boyne, and Ireland not in a condition to have supplied us with corn.

A day or two after the battle of the Boyne the army marched and encamped at Finglas by Dublin, and from thence the king sent some of the general officers and myself to see what could be done to secure our provision ships, which were come from Carlingford to that harbour, for his Majesty had received an account of those seventeen or nineteen frigates before-mentioned that were designed to destroy them, and did not know that King James had taken them with him to France to secure him in his passage thither. The necessary orders were given to have gabards, &c., ready to be sunk in the entrance of the harbour if there should be occasion, and so we returned to the camp. . . .

From Finglas the army marched southwards, and came at last to Carrick, where the king stayed till he received an account from Major-General Kirke, who commanded before Waterford, that the place had capitulated and the garrison was to march out next day. Upon that his Majesty went thither and returned at night to Carrick, and next day went for Dublin in order to go to England, where he thought his presence necessary to quiet the apprehension the nation were under upon the French threatening to land, for they hovered about the coast some time after the advantage they had over our fleet off of Beachy. But by that time his Majesty got to Dublin the fright was over, and he did not pursue his voyage, but took a resolution of returning to the army. . . .

After the king left Carrick the army, under command of Count Solms, advanced to Golden Bridge, and there his Majesty joined it again from Dublin and marched it to Limerick. In his march he received an account that the French regiments had left the place and were gone to Galway, which was very true, and they continued at Galway all the time the army lay before Limerick, and as soon as the siege was raised set sail for Brest, and the earl of Tyrconnel and Monsieur Lauzun with them. Indeed the French did little or no service in Ireland, not having struck a stroke that I know of while they were there, for they retired from the Boyne very early in the day, and marched by the way of Limerick to Galway, from whence they embarked for France, as is before mentioned. The ill-success at Limerick is well known to be owing to the want of ammunition occasioned by Sarsfield's falling upon the artillery, &c., at Cullen, as it was coming up to the siege, so that after a fruitless attack of a breach, which we had not powder or shot to make larger, the king left the army and embarked at Duncannon for England, leaving Count Solms at the head of the troops. . . .

I cannot recollect at this distance of time where we were when we first heard of Lord Marlborough being before Cork, but I remember we marched to Cashel, and there Count Solms left the army under command of Monsieur Ginkel, afterwards earl of Athlone, and went for England, and as soon as Lord Marlborough's arrival was known Monsieur Scravenmoer was detached with some troops to him at Cork, and I think we did not get to winter quarters at Kilkenny till we had news of the surrender of the place, or very little before. . . .

We passed the winter of 1690 at Kilkenny and Dublin in making preparations for next summer's campaign, and endeavouring to prevent the occasion for one by trying to persuade the Irish to submit, for which purpose we had several correspondences with them; but lest they should not be successful Monsieur Ginkel was as active as the season would let him, and by himself and those who commanded under him made several expeditions in the winter, both in the north and south of the kingdom. Particularly he marched himself to Ross Castle, which he took, and then returned to Kilkenny and sent the detachment that had been with him into quarters. . . .

Before the campaign opened the king sent for Sir John Lanier and Major-General Kirke away from Ireland, and so he did for Lieutenant-General Douglas some time after, for the latter and the two first could never agree. . . . In their room the king sent over Lieutenant-General Mackay, Major-General Talmash and Monsieur Ruvigny, a major-general, afterwards earl of Galway. I think they came to us when the army was before Ballymore. At least Monsieur Ruvigny was there.

Ballymore was soon taken, and the army advanced to Athlone, where it met with great difficulties, for after the taking of the town on this side the water they were to pass the river over a ford that was guarded by the works of the town that is on the other, and all the Irish army was encamped at so small a distance behind that they might send what numbers of men they thought fit to oppose us. Indeed it was apprehended that they had laid open the walls on the back of the town, and that instead of a garrison we should have had their army to have encountered when we got over the water, if that was possible to be done, which was much doubted. This attempt was looked upon to be so hazardous that Monsieur Ginkel ordered a guinea to be given to each of the eight hundred grenadiers who were picked out for the service, and many of them had horse armour for their security.

The first day they were drawn out the Irish army had notice from a deserter who swam the river at some distance from the town, and marched down in such numbers that it was thought fit to defer the execution of the design, which the enemy took to be so difficult that they believed it entirely laid aside. But next day it was resumed with success, and our men got over the river before the Irish were aware; and by that time Major-General Maxwell, who commanded that day in the place, was got from his house to the bridge he was surrounded and taken prisoner, as he told me himself. In this action Major-General Mackay commanded the detachment that passed the river, and though from his great caution he was against the thing in the council of war, yet no man exposed himself more freely when the resolution was taken. Major-General Talmash was a volunteer, and carried over the water upon men's shoulders after the grenadiers had possessed themselves of the works.

When the Irish army saw Athlone was taken they marched to Aughrim, about ten miles on the road to Galway, and took a very strong camp with two bogs before it, and a *tougher* or causeway between the bogs, over which those must pass who would attack them in the centre. There four of our regiments of foot were put into great disorder; but some of the horse got over and made a stand, while the most of the rest of the horse, being drawn to the left, attacked the enemy's right and made them give way, and together with those who were got over the bog in the centre pursued them as long as it was light. Their cannon and most of their baggage were taken, and a great part of their tents left standing. In the beginning of this action St. Ruth, the French general who commanded, was killed by a cannon shot, and to his death the Irish attribute the success the English had that day. Indeed, considering the strength of the post and the inequality of the numbers (for the Irish were thirty thousand, as Lord Bellew, who was brought prisoner to Monsieur Scravenmoer about four in the morning, when he and I were at breakfast in the field, told us, and the English army did not amount to eighteen thousand), it must be looked upon as a very great action. . . . I remember before the engagement that our apprehensions were more from the Irish horse than foot, but the contrary appeared in the battle.

After some short stay the army advanced to Galway, which surrendered before any trenches were opened upon articles, and then we marched over Banagher Bridge and so to Limerick, where there was so strong a garrison that we durst not break ground and make approaches to attack it, for they had at least as many foot in the place as we had before it; but it being too soon to go into winter quarters we battered and bombed it, and lay there in expectation of what might happen. The town was open to their horse on the Connaught side for a good while after we were encamped before it; but at last our horse got over the Shannon and between the town and their horse, which put them upon capitulating. And they did it at a time when we could not have stayed there any longer, and had actually drawn off several of our cannon and mortars and sent them on board the artillery ships which lay in the Shannon.

When they beat the chamade the first thing they desired to know was whether they might be allowed to go and serve where they had a mind, which was consented to, and next day, as I remember, they sent out their demands in writing; but those being very large it was thought better to send them a draft of the terms we would grant them than to retrench and alter theirs. Accordingly articles were drawn up, and the Irish deputed six persons to treat with us upon them. When we met, the first question Sir Toby Butler asked us was what we meant by the title, viz., Articles granted by Lieutenant-General Ginkel, Commander-in-Chief, &c., to all persons in the city of Limerick and in the Irish army that is in the counties of Clare, Kerry, Cork and Mayo, and other garrisons that are in their possession.

I answered that we meant to capitulate with and grant terms to those who were in a condition to oppose us. Sir Toby replied that if we meant to go no further there must be an end of the treaty, and Sarsfield added that he would lay his bones in those old walls rather than not take care of those who stuck by them all along. So the second article was explained to extend to all such as are under their protection in the said counties, which I mention the more particularly because those words, though first agreed to, were omitted by mistake in transcribing that copy of the articles which was signed, and the mistake not found out till next day, when Monsieur Ginkel's son was actually gone towards England with the original or a copy to be laid before their Majesties. This occasioned a great deal of trouble, for when we came into England Monsieur Ginkel, Major-General Talmash and I either gave certificates or depositions of what passed and that which was left out by mistake was granted the Irish under the broad seal of England, and as I take it by Act of Parliament in Ireland, for I sent over the very original draft of the articles from whence the signed copy was made to Lord Chancellor Porter, in order to satisfy the Parliament there, where many were averse from doing the Irish that piece of justice, and aspersed Lord Coningsby, who was one of the Justices that signed the articles, as if by his means the broad seal had been obtained to give the Irish a favour that was never intended them at the time of the treaty, whereas in reality it was the first thing insisted upon by them and agreed to by us, and further I have reason to believe that if it had not been for that lord, the general's son had been sent for back, and the words that were left out been inserted.

After we had gone over all the articles in a cursory manner the further consideration and finishing the agreement was referred till the Lords Justices Porter and Coningsby came from Dublin to the camp, which they were desired to do, for the properties and civil rights of the Irish being to be settled by these articles it was thought proper that they should be signed by the civil governors as well as the military, which they were on the 3rd of October 1691, about ten o'clock at night, and a gate of

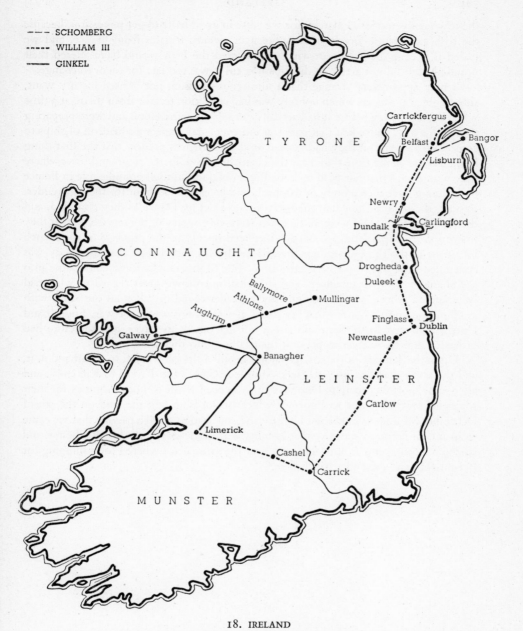

18. IRELAND

ILLUSTRATING THE CAMPAIGNS OF MARSHAL SCHOMBERG, WILLIAM III, AND
GENERAL GINKEL

(Cf. *Cambridge Modern History Atlas*, Map 47)

the town delivered immediately, for we were in great haste to get possession, because the Irish expected a squadron of eighteen or twenty frigates from France, and we feared if it came before the town was delivered the Irish would have altered their minds; but it did not arrive in the Shannon till it was too late for them to change.

It may appear very strange that a numerous garrison, not pressed by any want, should give up a town which nobody was in a condition to take from them, at a time when those who lay before it had actually drawn off their cannon and were preparing to march away, and when that garrison did every day expect a squadron of ships to come to their relief, if they had needed any. But when we reflect that the first thing insisted upon at the time they beat the chamade was a liberty to go and serve where they would, and that Sarsfield reckoned upon making himself considerable in France by bringing over such a body of troops, it will be easy to account for their surrender. Besides, the Irish did not find themselves so assisted by France as they expected, and the French officers who were in the town were very weary of the service, so that they first proposed capitulating, as Sarsfield averred openly in the presence of the French intendant at the time of signing the articles. It was very happy that the treaty was concluded as it was, for a very little time after Monsieur Chateaurenault came into the Shannon with his squadron, and if he had not shown great regard to what had been agreed ashore would undoubtedly have destroyed or taken all our ships with ammunition and provisions that lay there, as well as seven men-of-war, English and Dutch, that were with them and could not get out of the river, and therefore had orders to sink themselves to prevent their falling into their hands.

Upon the delivery of the town Major-General Talmash was left to command in it, and the army marched into quarters. Monsieur Ginkel and I went to Kilkenny, and after some short stay there to Dublin, from whence I wrote to Lord Romney for their Majesties' leave to come to England, which his lordship sent me, and on the 5th of December Monsieur Ginkel and I left Ireland, and had so good a passage that we came to an anchor before it was dark that evening within a league of the bar of Chester, and landed next morning at Hoylake, very near the same place where I took shipping for Ireland about a year and a half before.

G. PEACE SETTLEMENT

293. Treaty of Limerick, 1691

(*Harleian Miscellany*, ed. 1808–1811, x, pp. 141–149)

ARTICLES, CIVIL AND MILITARY, AGREED UPON THE THIRD DAY OF OCTOBER 1691 . . . IN THE BEHALF OF THE IRISH INHABITANTS IN THE CITY AND COUNTY OF LIMERICK, THE COUNTIES OF CLARE, KERRY, CORK, SLIGO AND MAYO

(i) The Civil Articles

In consideration of the surrender of the city of Limerick and other agreements made between . . . Lieutenant-General Ginkel, the governor of the city of Limerick and the general of the Irish army, bearing date with these presents, for the surrender of the said city and submission of the said army, it is agreed that:

I. The Roman Catholics of this kingdom shall enjoy such privileges in their exercise of their religion as are consistent with the laws of Ireland, or as they did enjoy in the reign of King Charles the Second; and their Majesties, as soon as their affairs will permit them to summon a Parliament in this kingdom, will endeavour to procure the said Roman Catholics such farther security in that particular as may preserve them from any disturbance upon the account of their said religion.

II. All the inhabitants or residents of Limerick, or any other garrison now in possession of the Irish, and all officers and soldiers now in arms under any commission of King James or those authorized to grant the same in the several counties of Limerick, Clare, Kerry, Cork and Mayo, or in any of them, and all the commissioned officers in their Majesties' quarters that belong to the Irish regiments now in being that are treated with, and who are not prisoners of war or have taken protection, and who shall return and submit to their Majesties' obedience, their and every of their heirs, shall hold, possess and enjoy all and every their estates of freehold and inheritance, and all the right, title and interest, privileges and immunities which they, and every or any of them, held, enjoyed, or were rightfully and lawfully entitled to in the reign of King Charles the Second, or at any time since, by the laws and statutes that were in force in the said reign of King Charles the Second, and shall be put in possession by order of the government of such of them as are in the king's hands, or the hands of their tenants, without being put to any suit or trouble therein; and all such estates shall be freed and discharged from all arrears of crown-rents, quit-rents, and other public charges incurred and become due since Michaelmas 1688 to the day of the date hereof. All persons comprehended in this article shall have, hold and enjoy all their goods and chattels, real and personal, to them or any of them belonging or remaining either in their own hands, or the hands of any person or persons whatsoever in trust for or for the use of them or any of them. And all and every the said persons of what trade, profession or calling soever they be, shall and may use, exercise and practise their several and respective professions, trades and callings as freely as they did use, exercise and enjoy the same in the reign of King Charles the Second; provided that nothing in this article contained be construed to extend to or restore any forfeiting person, now out of the kingdom, except what are hereafter comprised; provided also that no person whatsoever shall have and enjoy the benefit of this article, that shall neglect or refuse to take the oath of allegiance, made by Act of Parliament in England in the first year of the reign of their present Majesties, when thereunto required.

III. All merchants or reputed merchants of the city of Limerick, or of any other garrison now possessed by the Irish, or of any town or place in the counties of Clare or Kerry, who are absent beyond the seas, that have not borne arms since their Majesties' declaration in February 1688/9, shall have the benefit of the second article in the same manner as if they were present, provided such merchants and reputed merchants do repair into this kingdom within the space of eight months from the date hereof. . . .

V. That all and singular the said persons comprised in the second and third articles shall have a general pardon of all attainders, outlawries, treasons, misprisions of treason, premunires, felonies, trespasses and other crimes and misdemeanors whatsoever by them or any of them committed since the beginning of the reign of King James the Second; and if any of them are attainted by Parliament, the Lords Justices and the General will use their best endeavours to get the same repealed by the Parliament, and the outlawries to be reversed gratis, all but the writing-clerks' fees.

VI. Whereas the present wars have drawn great violences on both parties, and that, if leave were given for bringing all sorts of private actions, the animosities would probably continue that have been so long on foot, and the public disturbance last; for the quieting and settling therefore of the kingdom, and avoiding those inconveniences which would be the necessary consequence of the contrary, no person or persons whatsoever comprised in the foregoing articles shall be sued, molested or impleaded, at the suit of any party or parties whatsoever, for any trespass by them committed, or for any arms, horses, money, goods and chattels, merchandise or provision whatsoever by them seized or taken during the time of the war. And no person or persons whatsoever in the second or third articles comprised shall be sued, impleaded or made accountable for the rents or mean rates of any lands, tenements or houses by him or them received or enjoyed in this kingdom since the beginning of this present war to the day of the date hereof, nor for any waste or trespass by him or them committed in any such lands, tenements or houses; and it is also agreed that this article shall be mutual and reciprocal on both sides.

VII. Every nobleman and gentleman comprised in the said second and third articles shall have liberty to ride with a sword and case of pistols if they think fit, and keep a gun in their houses for the defence of the same or for fowling. . . .

IX. The oath to be administered to such Roman Catholics as submit to their Majesties' government shall be the oath abovesaid and no other. . . .

XII. Lastly, the Lords Justices and General do undertake that their Majesties will ratify these articles within the space of eight months or sooner, and use their utmost endeavours that the same shall be ratified and confirmed in Parliament. . . .

(ii) The Military Articles

I. That all persons without any exceptions, of what quality or condition soever, that are willing to leave the kingdom of Ireland, shall have free leave to go beyond the seas, to any country (England and Scotland excepted) where they think fit, with their families, household-stuff, plate and jewels.

II. That all the general officers, colonels and generally all other officers of horse, dragoons and foot-guards, troops, dragoons, soldiers of all kinds, that are in any garrison, place or post now in the hands of the Irish, or encamped in the counties of Cork, Clare or Kerry, as also those called rapparees or volunteers, that are willing to go beyond seas as aforesaid, shall have free liberty to embark themselves wheresoever the ships are that are appointed to transport them, and to come in whole bodies, as they are now composed, or in parties, companies or otherwise, without having any impediment, directly or indirectly.

III. That all persons above-mentioned that are willing to leave Ireland and go into France have leave to declare it at the places and times hereafter mentioned, viz., the troops in Limerick, on Tuesday next at Limerick; the horse at their camp, on Wednesday; and the other forces that are dispersed in the counties of Clare, Kerry and Cork, the 18th day of this instant, and on no other, before Monsieur Tumeron, the French intendant, and Colonel Withers; and after such declaration so made the troops that will go into France must remain under the command and discipline of their officers that are to conduct them thither; and deserters of each side shall be given up and punished accordingly.

IV. That all English and Scotch officers that serve now in Ireland shall be included in this capitulation, as well for the security of their estates and goods in England, Scotland and Ireland, if they are willing to remain here, as for passing freely into France or any other country to serve.

V. That all the general French officers, the intendant, the engineers, the commissaries at war and of the artillery, the treasurer and other French officers, strangers and others whatsoever, that are in Sligo, Ross, Clare or in the army, or that do trade or commerce or are otherwise employed in any kind of station or condition, shall have leave to pass into France or any other country, and shall have leave to ship themselves, with all their horses, equipage, plate, papers and all other effects whatsoever. . . .

VII. That to facilitate the transporting of the troops the General will furnish fifty ships, and each ship burden two hundred tons, for which the persons to be transported shall not be obliged to pay, and twenty more, if there shall be occasion, without their paying for them; and if any of the said ships shall be of lesser burden, he will furnish more in number to countervail, and also give two men of war to embark the principal officers and serve for a convoy to the vessels of burden.

VIII. That a commissary shall be immediately sent to Cork to visit the transport ships and see what condition they are in for sailing, and that as soon as they are ready the troops to be transported shall march with all convenient speed the nearest way in order to be embarked there; and if there shall be any more men to be transported than can be carried off in the said fifty ships, the rest shall quit the English town of Limerick and march to such quarters as shall be appointed for them, convenient for their transportation, where they shall remain till the other twenty ships are ready, which are to be in a month's time, and may embark in any French ship that may come in the meantime.

IX. That the said ships shall be furnished with forage for horses, and all necessary provisions to subsist the officers, troops, dragoons and soldiers, and all other persons that are shipped to be transported into France, which provisions shall be paid for as soon as all is disembarked at Brest or Nantes on the coast of Brittany, or any other port in France they can make.

X. And to secure the return of the said ships (the danger of the seas excepted) and the payment for the said provisions, sufficient hostages shall be given.

XI. That the garrisons of Clare Castle, Ross, and all other foot that are in garrisons in the counties of Clare, Cork and Kerry shall have the advantage of this capitulation, and such part of the garrisons as design to go beyond the seas shall march out with their arms, baggage, drums beating, ball in mouth, match lighted at both ends, colours flying, with all their provisions and half the ammunition that is in the said garrison's town, with the horse that march to be transported, or, if then there is not shipping enough for the body of foot that is to be transported next after the horse, General Ginkel will order that they be furnished with carriages for that purpose and what provision they shall want for their march, they paying for the said provisions, or else that they may take it out of their own magazines.

XII. That all the troops of horse and dragoons that are in the counties of Cork, Kerry and Clare shall have the benefit of this capitulation, and that such as will pass into France shall have quarters given them in the counties of Clare and Kerry, apart from the troops commanded by General Ginkel, until they can be shipped; and within their quarters they shall pay for all things, excepting forage and pasture for their horses, which shall be furnished gratis.

XIII. Those of the garrison of Sligo that are joined to the Irish army shall have the benefit of this capitulation, and orders shall be sent to them that are to convey them up to bring them hither to Limerick the shortest way.

XIV. The Irish may have liberty to transport nine hundred horse, including horses for the officers, which shall be transported gratis; and as for the troops that stay behind, they shall dispose of themselves as they shall think fit, giving up their arms and horses to such persons as the General shall appoint. . . .

XVII. That all prisoners of war that were in Ireland the twenty-eighth of September shall be set at liberty on both sides; and the General promises to use his endeavours that the prisoners that are in England and Flanders shall be set at liberty also. . . .

XX. That all those of the said troops, officers and others, of what character soever, that would pass into France, shall not be stopped on the account of debt or any other pretence. . . .

XXIII. In consideration of the present capitulation the two towns of Limerick shall be delivered and put into the hands of the General, or any other person he shall appoint, at the time and days hereafter specified, viz., the Irish town, except the magazines and hospital, on the day of signing the present articles; and as for the English town, it shall remain, together with the island and the free passage of Thomond Bridge, in the hands of those of the Irish army that are in the garrison, or that shall hereafter come from the counties of Cork, Clare, Kerry, Sligo and other places above-mentioned, until there be convenience found for their transportation. . . .

XXV. That it shall be lawful for the said garrison to march out all at once, or at different times, as they can be embarked, with arms, baggage, drums beating, match lighted at both ends, bullet in mouth, colours flying, six brass guns, such as the besieged will choose, two mortar-pieces, and half the ammunition that is now in the magazines of the said place. . . .

XXVI. All the magazines of provisions shall remain in the hands of those that are now employed to take care of the same, for the subsistence of those of the Irish army that will pass into France; and that, if there shall not be sufficient in the stores for the support of the said troops, while they stay in this kingdom and are crossing the seas, that upon giving account of their number the General will furnish them with sufficient provisions at the king's rates; and that there shall be a free market at Limerick and other quarters where the said troops shall be; and in case any provisions shall remain in the magazines of Limerick when the town shall be given up it shall be valued, and the price deducted out of what is to be paid for the provisions to be furnished to the troops on shipboard.

XXVII. That there shall be a cessation of arms at land, and also at sea with respect to the ships, whether English, Dutch or French, designed for the transportation of the said troops, until they be returned to their respective harbours; and that on both sides they shall be furnished sufficiently with passports, both the ships and men; and if any sea commander or captain of a ship, or any officer, troop, dragoon, soldier or other person, shall act contrary to this cessation, the persons so acting shall be punished on either side, and satisfaction shall be made for the wrong done; and officers shall be sent to the mouth of the river of Limerick to give notice to the commanders of the English and French fleets of the present conjuncture, that they may observe the cessation of arms accordingly. . . .

294. Ratification of the treaty of Limerick, 1692

(*A Jacobite Narrative of the War in Ireland*, ed. J. T. Gilbert, pp. 313–314)

William and Mary, by the Grace of God, &c., to all to whom these presents shall come, greeting.

Whereas certain articles bearing date the third day of October last past, made and agreed on between our Justices of our kingdom of Ireland and our General of our forces there on the one part, and several officers there commanding within the city of Limerick in our said kingdom on the other part, whereby our said Justices and General did undertake that we should ratify those articles within the space of eight months or sooner, and use our utmost endeavours that the same should be ratified and confirmed in Parliament; . . . and whereas the said city of Limerick hath been since, in pursuance of the said articles, surrendered unto us; now know ye that we, having considered of

26

the said articles, are graciously pleased hereby to declare that we do for us, our heirs and successors, as far as in us lies, ratify and confirm the same, and every clause, matter and thing therein contained. And as to such parts thereof for which an Act of Parliament shall be found to be necessary, we shall recommend the same to be made good by Parliament, and shall give our royal assent to any bill or bills that shall be passed by our two Houses of Parliament to that purpose.

And whereas it appears unto us that it was agreed between the parties to the said articles that after the words "Limerick, Clare, Kerry, Cork, Mayo or any of them" in the second of the said articles, the words following, viz., "and all such as are under their protection in the said counties", should be inserted and be part of the said articles, which words having been casually omitted by the writer, the omission was not discovered till after the said articles were signed, but was taken notice of before the second town was surrendered; and that our said Justices and General, or one of them, did promise that the said clause should be made good, it being within the intention of the capitulation and inserted in the foul draught thereof, our further will and pleasure is, and we do hereby ratify and confirm the said omitted words, viz., "and all such as are under their protection in the said counties", hereby for us, our heirs and successors, ordaining and declaring that all and every person and persons therein concerned shall and may have, receive and enjoy the benefit thereof, in such and the same manner as if the said words had been inserted in their proper place in the said second article, any omission, defect or mistake in the said second article in any wise notwithstanding. Provided always, and our will and pleasure is, that these our letters patents shall be enrolled in our Court of Chancery in our said kingdom of Ireland within the space of one year next ensuing.

In witness, &c., witness ourselves at Westminster, the twenty-fourth day of February, in the fourth year of our reign.

295. (Irish) Act confirming the treaty of Limerick, 1697
(Irish *Statutes at Large*, III, pp. 343–348)

AN ACT FOR THE CONFIRMATION OF ARTICLES
MADE AT THE SURRENDER OF THE CITY OF LIMERICK

Whereas divers doubts have arisen on the articles made at the treaty for the late surrender of the city of Limerick, the third day of October one thousand six hundred ninety-one, and concerning the true intent and meaning of several parts thereof; and whereas your Majesty hath been graciously pleased to recommend to your Parliament that the said articles, or so much of them as may consist with the safety and welfare of your Majesty's subjects of this kingdom, may be confirmed by authority of this present Parliament, we, the Lords Spiritual and Temporal and the Commons in this present Parliament assembled, having due regard to your Majesty's honour, for declaring the true sense and meaning of the said articles and taking away all occasions of doubt for the time to come, do most humbly beseech your Majesty that it may be enacted, and be it enacted . . . that the second article in the aforesaid

articles mentioned be, and is hereby, confirmed and ratified in the sense and intend-
ment following, and no otherwise, that is to say, that all the inhabitants or residents
of Limerick, or any other garrison in the possession of the Irish at the time of making
the said articles, and all officers and soldiers then in arms under any commission of the
late King James or those authorized by him to grant the same in the several counties
of Limerick, Clare, Kerry, Cork and Mayo, and all the commissioned officers in the
quarters of his Majesty that belonged to the Irish regiments then in being, that were
treated with, and who were not prisoners of war, nor had at any time before that
time enjoyed the benefit of protections for the safety of themselves, or their goods
and families, which said officers have in pursuance of the said articles returned to their
obedience and submitted to his Majesty and to her late Majesty Queen Mary; such
inhabitants or residents of Limerick or any other garrison as aforesaid, such officers
and soldiers respectively as aforesaid, and their and every of their heirs, shall hold,
possess and enjoy all and every their estates of freehold and inheritance, and all the
rights, titles and interests, privileges and immunities to the said estates of freehold and
inheritance belonging, which they and every or any of them held, enjoyed or were
rightfully and lawfully intituled to in the reign of King Charles the Second, or at any
time since, by the laws and statutes that were in force in the said reign of King Charles
the Second; and such possession as was given the said inhabitants, officers and soldiers,
in whose behalf the said articles were as aforesaid made, of lands then in his Majesty's
hands, or in the hands of his tenants, by order of the then government under his
Majesty, is, as to the possession only and no more, confirmed and ratified by the
authority of this Act against his Majesty, his heirs and successors; and all such estates
of freehold and inheritance shall be freed and discharged, and by the authority of this
present Act are declared and enacted to be and stand freed and discharged of and from
all arrears of crown-rents, quit-rents and other public charges incurred or become due
from and after the feast of St. Michael the Archangel,[1] in the year of our Lord one
thousand six hundred eighty-eight, to the day of the date of the said articles. . . .

X. And whereas some questions or doubts have arisen for and concerning the time
of the beginning of the rebellion or war in this kingdom, be it enacted by the authority
aforesaid that the said rebellion or war is hereby declared to have begun upon the
tenth day of April one thousand six hundred eighty-nine, the same being the day
limited to the said rebels and traitors by his Majesty and her late Majesty's declaration,
in February one thousand six hundred eighty-eight,[2] for the said rebels and traitors
laying down of their arms, and accepting of their said Majesties' grace and mercy on
the terms in the said declaration proposed. . . .

[1] 29 September.   [2] 1688/9.

H. PARLIAMENT AND THE PENAL LAWS

296. Act excluding papists from public trust in Ireland, 1691

(Statutes of the Realm, VI, pp. 254–257)

AN ACT FOR THE ABROGATING THE OATH OF SUPREMACY IN IRELAND AND APPOINTING OTHER OATHS

(3 Gul. & Mar., cap. 2)

Whereas by a statute made in Ireland in the second year of the reign of our late sovereign lady Queen Elizabeth entituled, *An Act restoring to the Crown the ancient jurisdiction over the estate ecclesiastical and spiritual, and abolishing all foreign power repugnant to the same,*[1] the persons therein mentioned are thereby obliged to take the oath in the said Act expressed, be it enacted . . . that from henceforth no person whatsoever residing in Ireland shall be obliged to take the said oath by force or virtue of the said recited statute or any other statute whatsoever, but that the said statute and every other statute for so much only as concerns the said oath shall be and are hereby repealed, utterly abrogated and made void.

II. And be it further enacted, that the oaths appointed, intended or required by this Act to be taken, from and after the first day of January next in the year of our Lord one thousand six hundred ninety-one,[2] be taken by the persons herein and hereafter mentioned, and by every such other person and persons as were appointed and required by the said recited Act or any other statute whatsoever made in Ireland to take the said abrogated oath, before such person or persons and in such court as hereafter in this Act is expressed, that is to say, all and every archbishop and bishop of the realm of Ireland that now is, and all and every person of or above the degree of a baron of Parliament there, and all and every other person and persons inhabitants of or residing within the said realm of Ireland now having any promotion, office or employment ecclesiastical, civil or military, or receiving any pay, salary, fee or wages by reason of any patent or grant of their Majesties or any of their predecessors, or being master, governor, head or fellow of the college or university of Dublin, or master of any hospital or school, or barrister-at-law, clerk in chancery, attorney or professor of law, physic or other science that shall inhabit, be or reside within the city of Dublin or within thirty miles of the same, on the first day of Hilary term next, or at any time during the said term, in their Majesties' high court of Chancery in that kingdom, or in the Court of King's Bench there, in public and open court between the hours of nine of the clock and twelve in the forenoon, and all the said persons which inhabit at greater distance from the said city, at the general quarter-sessions to be holden for that county, barony or place in Ireland aforesaid where he or they shall be or reside, in open court between the said hours of nine and twelve in the forenoon at any time before the five and twentieth day of July next; and shall likewise make and subscribe and audibly repeat the declaration herein and hereafter mentioned and expressed. . . .

[1] Irish Act of Supremacy.　　　　　　　　　　[2] 1691/2.

IV. And forasmuch as great disquiet and many dangerous attempts have been made to deprive their Majesties and their royal predecessors of the said realm of Ireland by the liberty which the popish recusants there have had and taken to sit and vote in Parliament, be it enacted . . . that from and after the last day of January next no person that now is or shall be hereafter a peer of that realm or member of the House of Peers there shall vote or make his proxy in the said House of Peers, or sit there during any debate in the said House, nor any person that after the said last day of January shall be a member of the House of Commons shall be capable to vote in the said House, or sit there during any debate in the same after their Speaker is chosen, until he first take the oaths herein and hereafter mentioned and expressed, and make, subscribe and audibly repeat this declaration following:

I, A.B., do solemnly and sincerely in the presence of God profess, testify and declare that I do believe that in the sacrament of the Lord's Supper there is not any transubstantiation of the elements of bread and wine into the body and blood of Christ at or after the consecration thereof by any person whatsoever, and that the invocation or adoration of the Virgin Mary or any other saint and the sacrifice of the mass as they are now used in the Church of Rome are superstitious and idolatrous. And I do solemnly in the presence of God profess, testify and declare that I do make this declaration and every part thereof in the plain and ordinary sense of the words read unto me as they are commonly understood by Protestants, without any evasion, equivocation or mental reservation whatsoever, and without any dispensation already granted me for this purpose by the Pope or any other authority or person whatsoever, or without any hope of any such dispensation from any person or authority whatsoever, or without believing that I am or can be acquitted before God or man, or absolved of this declaration or any part thereof, although the Pope or any other person or persons or power whatsoever should dispense with or annul the same or declare that it was null and void from the beginning.

Which said oaths and declaration shall be in the next and every succeeding Parliament to be held in Ireland solemnly and publicly made and subscribed betwixt the hours of nine in the morning and four in the afternoon by every such peer and member of the House of Peers there at the table in the middle of the said House before he take his place in the said House of Peers, and whilst a full House of Peers is there present and their Speaker in his place, and by every such member of the House of Commons at the table in the middle of the said House, and whilst a full House of Commons is there duly sitting with their Speaker in his chair. . . .

V. And be it further enacted . . that if any person that now is or hereafter shall be a peer of Ireland or member of the House of Peers or member of the House of Commons there, or that shall become a barrister-at-law, attorney, clerk, or officer in Chancery or any other court, and all and every deputy or deputies in any office whatsoever, shall presume to offend contrary to this Act, that then every such peer and member and such other person and persons so offending shall be thenceforth disabled to hold or execute any office or place of profit or trust, ecclesiastical, civil or military, in any of their Majesties' realms of Ireland or England or dominion of Wales or town of Berwick-upon-Tweed, or in any of their Majesties' islands or foreign plantations to the said realms belonging, and shall be disabled from thenceforth to sit or vote in either House of Parliament of the said realm of Ireland, or make a proxy in the House of Peers there, or to sue or use any action, bill, plaint or information in course of law, or to prosecute any suit in any court of equity, or to be guardian of any child, or executor or administrator of any person, or capable of any legacy or deed of gift, and shall forfeit for every wilful offence against this Act the sum of five hundred pounds, to be recovered and received by him, her or them that will sue for the same. . . .

VI. And be it further enacted, that the oaths that are intended and required to be taken by this Act are the oaths in these express words hereafter following:

I, A.B., do sincerely promise and swear that I will be faithful and bear true allegiance to their Majesties King William and Queen Mary. So help me God, &c.

I, A.B., do swear that I do from my heart abhor, detest and abjure as impious and heretical that damnable doctrine and position that princes excommunicated or deprived by the Pope or any authority of the See of Rome may be deposed or murdered by their subjects or any other whatsoever; and I do declare that no foreign prince, person, prelate, state or potentate hath or ought to have any jurisdiction, power, superiority, pre-eminence or authority, ecclesiastical or spiritual, within this realm. So help me God, &c. . . .

IX. Provided always, that this Act or anything herein contained shall not extend to hinder or disable any person or persons who on the third of October one thousand six hundred ninety-one were inhabiting or residing in Limerick or any other garrison then in the possession of the Irish, or any officers or soldiers then in arms by virtue of any commission of the late King James or those authorized by him to grant the same in the several counties of Limerick, Clare, Kerry, Cork and Mayo or any of them, or any commissioned officers then in their Majesties' quarters that did belong to the Irish regiments then in being, or were then treated with, or who were not prisoners of war and who had not then taken protection, and have since returned and submitted to their Majesties' obedience, from using, exercising and practising his or their profession or calling of barrister-at-law, clerk in chancery or attorney or practiser of law or physic, but they may freely use, exercise and practise the same as they did in the reign of the late King Charles the Second, anything herein contained to the contrary notwithstanding. . . .

XI. And be it further enacted . . . that it shall and may be lawful for two or more justices of the peace, whereof one shall be of the quorum, within any county, city or town corporate in the said kingdom of Ireland, and they are hereby required, to direct their warrant or warrants to any constable, tithingman, headborough or other officer, to summon any person of the age of eighteen years or upwards to appear before such justices at such time and place as shall be mentioned in such warrant, to take the oath before mentioned to be faithful and bear true allegiance to their Majesties; and if such person being so summoned shall not appear at the time and place, having no lawful let or impediment, or appearing shall refuse to take the said oath being tendered to him or her by the said justices, the said justices shall commit such person making default or refusing to take the said oath to the common gaol or house of correction, there to remain without bail or mainprize for the space of three months, unless such offender shall pay down to the justices or any of them such sum of money not exceeding forty shillings as they the said justices shall require such offender to pay, which money shall be paid to the churchwardens or overseers of the poor of such parish or place where such offender did last inhabit. And at some time after the end of three months after such default or refusal two or more of such justices as aforesaid shall have power, and are hereby required, to direct their warrant in manner as aforesaid to summon such offender to appear before them to take the said oath; and if such offender shall be summoned and make default at the time and place appointed, not having any lawful let or impediment, or appearing shall refuse to take the said oath being tendered to him or her, the said justices shall commit such offender to the common gaol or house of correction, there to remain for the space of six months without bail or mainprize, unless such offender shall pay down to the said justices or any of them such sum of money not exceeding ten pounds nor under five pounds as the said justices shall require, which said money shall be disposed of to the relief of the poor of such parish or place in manner as aforesaid, and unless such offender shall become bound with two sufficient sureties with condition to appear at the next assizes or general gaol delivery to be holden for such county where such offender shall inhabit or reside, and in the meantime to be of good behaviour; at which assizes or gaol delivery the said oath shall be tendered to such offender by the justices of assize or general gaol delivery in their open assizes or sessions, and if upon such tender such offender shall refuse to take the said oath he shall incur the danger and penalty of praemunire mentioned in the Statute of Praemunire in the sixteenth year of the reign of King Richard the Second, except women covert, who upon refusal of the said oath shall be by the said justices of assize in their open assize or general gaol delivery committed only to the common gaol, there to remain without bail or mainprize till they will take the said oath.

XII. Provided nevertheless, that whereas there are certain dissenters in Ireland, commonly called Quakers, who scruple the taking any oath, it shall be sufficient for every such dissenter, he or she producing a certificate under the hands and seals of six or more sufficient men of the congregation to which he or she belongs owning him or her for one of them, to make and subscribe the following declaration:

I, A.B., do sincerely promise and solemnly declare before God and the world that I will be true and faithful to King William and Queen Mary, and I do solemnly profess and declare that I do from my heart abhor, detest and renounce as impious and heretical that damnable doctrine and position that princes excommunicated or deprived by the Pope or any authority of the See of Rome may be deposed or murdered by their subjects or any other whatsoever; and I do declare that no foreign prince, person, prelate, state or potentate hath or ought to have any power, jurisdiction, superiority, pre-eminence or authority, ecclesiastical or spiritual, within this realm.

And every such dissenter so subscribing shall be and is hereby exempted from the penalties mentioned in this Act.

XIII. Provided nevertheless, that no such person called Quaker shall by such declaration and subscription be capable to take, have or hold any office, employment,

place, pay, salary, fee, grant, wages, or any other place of profit or trust whereunto
any person taking the said oaths and making and subscribing the declaration in the
courts aforesaid shall or may be entituled, anything herein contained to the contrary
notwithstanding. . . .

297. Protest of Lord Sidney against the claim of the Irish House of Commons to control taxation, 1692

(Journals of the House of Lords of Ireland, I, pp. 477-478)

Whereas at a Parliament holden at Drogheda in the tenth year of the reign of
King Henry VII an Act was made for and concerning the order, manner and
form of Parliaments to be holden and kept in this realm of Ireland, and by another
Act made at a Parliament holden at Dublin in the third and fourth year of King Philip
and Queen Mary it was ordained, enacted and established that no Parliament should
be summoned or holden within this realm of Ireland until such time as the Lieutenant,
Lord Deputy, Lord Justice or Lords Justices, chief governor or governors or any of
them, and the council of this realm for the time being, should have certified the king
and queen's Majesties, their heirs and successors, under the great seal of this realm of
Ireland, the considerations, causes and articles of such Act, provisions and ordinances
as by them should be thought meet and necessary to be enacted and passed here by
Parliament; . . . and whereas in this present session of Parliament a bill entitled, *An
Act for granting unto their Majesties an additional duty on beer, ale and other liquors*, which
had been certified by us, the Lord Lieutenant of this kingdom, and the council unto
the king and queen's Majesty, under the great seal of this kingdom, and by their
Majesties approved of and returned under the great seal of England, and by us sent
to the House of Commons to be considered of in this present Parliament, the said
Commons, having the said bill lying upon their table on the 27th day of the month
of October last, did come to a vote thereupon and resolve, that it is the sole and
undoubted right of the said Commons to prepare heads of bills for raising money;
and further on the 28th day of the same October, a motion being made in the said
House and the question put, that a bill then on the table, which had likewise been
regularly transmitted in the same form, entitled, *An Act for granting to their Majesties
certain duties for one year*, might be read, it passed in the negative, and the said House of
Commons resolved that the said bill be rejected by that House, and further resolved
that it be entered in the journals of that House that the reason why the said bill was
rejected is that the same had not its rise in that House; all which resolutions and
proceedings appear in the journals of the House of Commons, printed by their order
and authority, by which votes and resolutions the said House of Commons do exclude
their Majesties and the crown of England from the right of transmitting any bills for
granting of money or other aids to their Majesties and their successors; which recited
votes, resolutions and proceedings of the House of Commons, being contrary to the
said recited Acts of Parliament and the continued usage and practice ever since the
making thereof, and a great invasion upon their Majesties' prerogative and the rights
of the crown of England, we, the Lord Lieutenant, as well to assert the rights of their

Majesties, and the rights of the crown of England (whereof we are and ever will be most tender), in transmitting such bills under the great seal of England to be considered of in Parliament, as to discharge the trust reposed in us, and prevent the inconveniences which may hereafter happen in case these votes and resolutions of the House of Commons should be made public, or remain in their journals, without any contradiction or animadversion, have thought it necessary this day, in full Parliament, to protest; and we do accordingly protest against the aforesaid votes and resolutions made by the House of Commons and entered in their journals, and do assert, protest and declare, that it is their Majesties' prerogative, and the undoubted right of the crown of England, observing the forms in the said several Acts prescribed, to transmit bills under the great seal of England for granting of aids to their Majesties, their heirs and successors, which said bills, so transmitted, ought to be read and considered of by the House of Commons in this kingdom, and therefore the said recited votes and proceedings of the House of Commons are contrary to the Acts of Parliament above mentioned, and the constant practice and usage in all Parliaments since the making thereof, and also highly derogatory to their Majesties' royal authority and the rights of the crown of England.

298. Address of the English House of Commons against any claim of independence for Ireland, 1698

(*Journals of the House of Commons*, XII, p. 337)

30 June 1698

MOST GRACIOUS SOVEREIGN,

We, your Majesty's most dutiful and loyal subjects, the Commons in Parliament assembled, conceive ourselves in duty bound to represent to your Majesty the dangerous attempts that have been of late made by some of your subjects of Ireland to shake off their subjection to, and dependence on, this kingdom, which has manifestly appeared to us, not only by the bold and pernicious assertions in a book, published and dedicated to your most excellent Majesty, entituled, *The Case of Ireland's being bound by Acts of Parliament in England stated*, which book we examined and considered, upon its being brought to us, by your Majesty's leave, but more fully and authentically by the votes and proceedings of the House of Commons in Ireland in their late sessions, and by a bill sent hither, under the great seal of Ireland, entituled, *An Act for the better security of his Majesty's royal person and government*, whereby they would have an Act passed in the Parliament of England, expressly binding Ireland, to be re-enacted there, and alterations therein made, some of which amount to a repeal of what is required by the said Act made in England, and in other of the said alterations pretending to give authority to and oblige the courts of justice and great seal here in England.

This we cannot but look on as an occasion and encouragement to the forming and publishing the dangerous positions contained in the said book. The consequences of such positions and proceedings will be so fatal to this kingdom, and even Ireland itself, that they need not be enlarged on or aggravated. Therefore we, your dutiful subjects, rest satisfied that your Majesty by your royal prudence will prevent their being drawn into example. And we with all duty and humility assure your Majesty of our ready concurrence and assistance, in a parliamentary way, to preserve and maintain the dependence and subordination of Ireland to the imperial crown of this realm. And we humbly beseech your Majesty that you would be graciously pleased to give effectual orders to prevent anything of the like nature for the future, and the pernicious consequences of what is past, by punishing and discountenancing those that have been guilty thereof.

And we beseech your Majesty to take all necessary care that the laws which direct and restrain the Parliament of Ireland in their actings be not evaded but strictly observed, and that your Majesty would be pleased to discourage all things which may in any degree tend to lessen the dependence of Ireland upon England.

299. Sir William Petty's scheme for a union between England and Ireland

(*Petty Papers*, ed. Marquis of Lansdowne, I, pp. 13–14)

OF UNITING ENGLAND AND IRELAND
BY A COMMON PARLIAMENT

Forasmuch as an Act of Parliament in England (wherein Ireland is named) bindeth Ireland, so as the Act made 17 Car. I,[1] made in England, sitting the Parliament of Ireland, did dispose of lands, tenements and hereditaments there; and whereas the last judicature for all matters in Ireland is the House of Peers in England, it concerns Ireland, being now no longer a conquered nation, but restored to all civil and military powers there, to be represented in the Parliament of England, in due proportion of members, both Lords and Commons.

Now Ireland by many computations is found in real effects to be one twelfth part of England; and consequently, if England have 480 in its House of Commons, that 40 more (being one twelfth of the said 480) should be added to them out of Ireland. And it is found that one twelfth part of the peers of England are peers of Ireland also. Wherefore the said addition of 40 Commons (and 2 bishops) would make the very best Parliament, a safe representative of Ireland also.

That there are about 9,600 parishes in England, whereof one quarter part (2,400) are big enough to be cut into halves, so as to make 12,000 parochial divisions. Wherefore let all men of twenty-one years old in every such division meet, by himself or proxy, on a certain day or time to choose an elector, viz., 12,000 in all. Let 480 places be appointed, at which 25 out of the said electors or proxies may meet to choose a member of Parliament.

Whereas in Ireland there are 240,000 families, let the men of twenty-one years old of 200 families meet to choose an elector, viz., 1,200 in all. Let the next day the said electors meet in 40 appointed places, viz., 30 at each, to choose a member to be sent to the House of Commons in England.

This Parliament to meet annually, or triennially, according to law or custom.

[1] Act of Subscription, 16 Car. I, cap. 33.

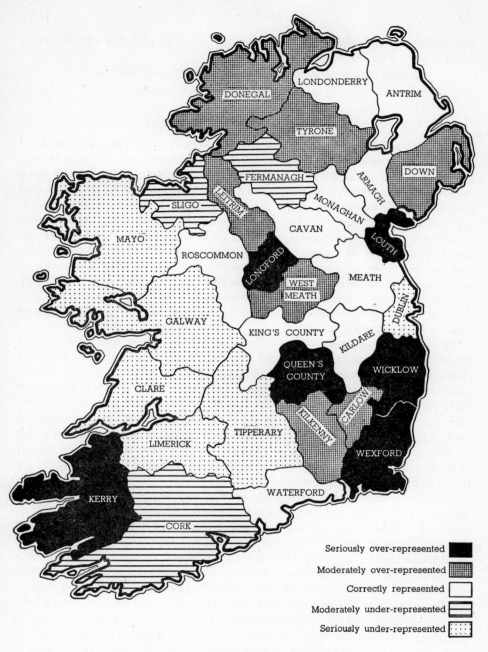

Seriously over-represented ■
Moderately over-represented ▦
Correctly represented □
Moderately under-represented ▤
Seriously under-represented ⬚

19. IRELAND
SHOWING INEQUALITIES IN PARLIAMENTARY REPRESENTATION
(*See Appendix IV*)

300. Petition of the Irish House of Commons in favour of union with England, 1703

(Journals of the House of Commons of the Kingdom of Ireland, III, pp. 65–67)

TO THE QUEEN'S MOST EXCELLENT MAJESTY,
THE HUMBLE REPRESENTATION OF THE KNIGHTS,
CITIZENS AND BURGESSES OF IRELAND IN PARLIAMENT ASSEMBLED

Forasmuch as it hath pleased your most sacred Majesty to give us, your most loyal and obedient subjects of Ireland, an opportunity of representing to your Majesty in Parliament the distressed condition of this your kingdom, . . . we should think ourselves wanting to that great trust reposed in us by our country . . . if we neglected to make use of so proper an occasion of laying before your Majesty, with all submission, this our humble representation, wherein is contained a true state of our deplorable condition in several weighty instances (which we have chosen out of many others too long to be enumerated), together with our most humble opinion by what means we may best be relieved; . . . protesting and declaring that no groundless discontent is in any measure the inducement or motive of this application to your Majesty, but a deep sense of the present evil state of this your kingdom, . . . together with a just consideration that your Majesty is the only one under God from whom we can or ought to look for both protection and relief.

We further assure your Majesty that it is the unanimous resolution of your Majesty's Protestant subjects of Ireland to uphold and maintain all your Majesty's rights, titles and prerogatives to the imperial crown of this your realm, and the succession of the Protestant line (as the same stands limited by two Acts of Parliament lately passed in England) even to the last drop of our blood. And as we have hitherto been remarkable for our steady loyalty and firm adherence to the Crown of England (as well upon the account of our services and sufferings as for the great supplies which we have given from time to time since the late happy revolution toward the support of the government in this kingdom), so we resolve to continue to do the like for the future to the utmost of our ability. . . .

Whereas your Majesty's royal predecessors of blessed memory have always had the glory to be kings and queens of a free people, distinguished from the rest of Europe by that eminent privilege of being governed by their own laws, and of enjoying liberty under the dominion of a sovereign prince according to the most equal and just model of government that was ever framed, yet so it is that the constitution of this your kingdom of Ireland hath been of late greatly shaken, the lives, liberties and estates of the subjects thereof being called in question and tried in a manner wholly unknown to our ancestors. And when we consider that the charges which the subjects of this kingdom have been unnecessarily put to by the late trustees, in defending such their just rights and titles as have, after many and expensive delays, been allowed by the said trustees, hath exceeded in value the present current cash of this kingdom, we have but too great reason to believe that this hath been principally occasioned through false and malicious reports and misrepresentations made of the Protestants of this kingdom by designing and ill-meaning men, in order to create misunderstandings between England and Ireland and to procure beneficial employments to themselves. . . .

We cannot without the greatest grief of heart reflect upon the vast decay and loss of our trade, and this your Majesty's kingdom's being almost exhausted of its coin. We are hindered from earning our livelihoods, and from maintaining our own manufactures, and our poor are thereby become very numerous, especially the industrious Protestants, who in a country wherein the number and power of the papists is very formidable ought (as we humbly conceive) to be encouraged. Very many Protestant families have been constrained to remove out of this kingdom, as well into Scotland as into the dominions of foreign princes and states. Our foreign trade and its returns are under such restrictions and discouragements as to be now become in a manner unprofitable, although this kingdom hath of late by its blood and treasure contributed to secure the plantation trade to the people of England.

The want of holding frequent Parliaments in your Majesty's kingdom of Ireland has been a great encouragement to evil-minded men, who intend nothing but their own gain, though accompanied with the ruin and oppression of your Majesty's good subjects. Many civil officers are arrived at such a pitch of corruption, through hopes of impunity, as is almost insupportable, thereby getting vast estates in a short time in a poor country; and others in considerable civil employments do dwell and reside for the most part out of the kingdom, thereby neglecting the personal attendance on their duties, whilst in the meantime their offices (which in effect are made mere sinecures) are but indifferently executed, to the great detriment of your Majesty's good subjects and the great failure of justice. So that we, your Majesty's dutiful subjects, are fully convinced that nothing but frequent Parliaments, with a permission for them to sit and do the business of the nation, can prevent or reform so great and notorious abuses.

This our most humble representation we, your Majesty's most loyal and distressed subjects of Ireland, your Commons assembled in Parliament, do . . . offer to your princely consideration, not doubting your Majesty's care and protection of us, when the true state of this kingdom is laid before your Majesty. . . . We cannot despair of your Majesty's goodness being extended towards us in such prudent and gracious methods as may afford us relief according to the exigency of our condition, and by restoring us to a full enjoyment of our constitution, or by promoting a more firm and strict union with your Majesty's subjects of England, which will be to the advantage of that kingdom, nothing being a more certain truth than that whatever riches the people of Ireland can acquire must at last necessarily centre in the seat of the government. . . .

301. (Irish) Act to prevent the growth of popery, 1704

(Irish *Statutes at Large*, IV, pp. 12–31)

AN ACT TO PREVENT THE FURTHER GROWTH OF POPERY

Whereas divers emissaries of the Church of Rome, popish priests and other persons of that persuasion, taking advantage of the weakness and ignorance of some of her Majesty's subjects, or the extreme sickness and decay of their reason and senses, in the absence of friends and spiritual guides, do daily endeavour to persuade and pervert them from the Protestant religion, to the great dishonour of Almighty God, the weakening of the true religion, by his blessing so happily established in this realm, to the disquieting the peace and settlement, and discomfort of many particular families thereof; and in further manifestation of their hatred and aversion to the said true religion many of the said persons so professing the popish religion in this kingdom have refused to make provision for their own children, for no other reason but their being of the Protestant religion; and also have, by cunning devices and contrivances, found out ways to avoid and elude the intents of an Act of Parliament made in the ninth year of the reign of the late King William the Third for preventing Protestants intermarrying with papists, and of several other laws made for the security of the Protestant religion; and whereas many persons so professing the popish religion have it in their power to raise division among Protestants by voting in elections for members of Parliament, and also have it in their power to use other ways and means tending to the destruction of the Protestant interest in this kingdom, for remedy of which great mischiefs, and to prevent the like evil practices for the future, be it enacted . . . that if any person or persons, from and after the twenty-fourth day of March in this present year of our Lord one thousand seven hundred and three,[1] shall seduce, persuade or pervert any person or persons professing, or that shall profess, the Protestant religion to renounce, forsake or abjure the same and to profess the popish religion, or reconcile him or them to the Church of Rome, then and in such case every such person and persons so seducing, as also every such Protestant and Protestants who shall be so seduced, perverted and reconciled to popery, shall for the said offences, being thereof lawfully convicted, incur the danger and penalty of premunire mentioned in the Statute of Premunire made in England in the sixteenth year of the reign of King Richard the Second; and if any person or persons, being a papist or professing the popish religion, shall from and after the said twenty-fourth day of March send, or cause or willingly suffer to be sent or conveyed, any child under the age of one and twenty years, except sailors, ship-boys, or the apprentice or factor of some merchant in trade of merchandise, into France or any other parts beyond the seas, out of her Majesty's dominions, without the special license of her Majesty, her heirs or successors, or of her or their chief governor or governors of this kingdom and four or more of her or their Privy Council of this realm under their hands in that behalf first had and obtained, he, she and they so sending or conveying, or causing to be sent or conveyed, away such child, shall incur the pains, penalties and forfeitures mentioned in an Act made in the seventh year of his late Majesty King William, entitled, *An Act to restrain foreign education.* . . .

III. And to the end that no child or children of popish parent or parents, who have professed or embraced, or who shall profess or embrace, the Protestant religion, or are or shall be desirous or willing to be instructed and educated therein, may in the lifetime of such popish parent or parents, for fear of being cast off or disinherited by them, or for want of fitting maintenance or future provision, be compelled and necessitated to embrace the popish religion, or be deterred or withheld from owning

[1] 1703/4.

and professing the Protestant religion, be it further enacted . . . that from and after the said twenty-fourth day of March one thousand seven hundred and three,[1] upon complaint in the High Court of Chancery by bill founded on this Act against such popish parent, it shall and may be lawful for the said court to make such order for the maintenance of every such Protestant child, not maintained by such popish parent, suitable to the degree and ability of such parent and to the age of such child, and also for the portion of every such Protestant child, to be paid at the decease of such popish parent, as that court shall adjudge fit, suitable to the degree and ability of such parent; and in case the eldest son and heir of such popish parent shall be a Protestant, that then from the time of the enrolment in the High Court of Chancery of a certificate of the bishop of the diocese in which he shall inhabit, testifying his being a Protestant and conforming himself to the Church of Ireland as by law established, such popish parent shall become, and shall be, only tenant for life of all the real estate whereof such popish parent shall be then seized in fee tail or fee simple, and the reversion in fee shall be vested in such eldest son being a Protestant. . . .

IV. And that care may be taken for the education of children in the communion of the Church of Ireland as by law established, be it enacted . . . that no person of the popish religion shall or may be guardian unto, or have the tuition or custody of, any orphan child or children under the age of twenty-one years; but that the same, where the person having or entitled to the guardianship of such orphan child or children is or shall be a papist, shall be disposed of by the High Court of Chancery to some near relation of such orphan child or children, being a Protestant and conforming himself to the Church of Ireland as by law established, to whom the estate cannot descend, in case there shall be any such Protestant relation fit to have the education of such child; otherwise to some other Protestant conforming himself as aforesaid. . . .

VI. And be it further enacted . . . that every papist or person professing the popish religion shall from and after the said twenty-fourth day of March be disabled, and is hereby made incapable, to buy and purchase, either in his or their own name, or in the name of any other person or persons to his or her use, or in trust for him or her, any manors, lands, tenements or hereditaments, or any rents or profits out of the same, or any leases or terms thereof other than any term of years not exceeding thirty-one years, whereon a rent not less than two thirds of the improved yearly value, at the time of the making such lease of the tenements leased, shall be reserved and made payable during such term. . . .

X. And be it further enacted . . . that all lands, tenements and hereditaments, whereof a papist now is or hereafter shall be seized in fee simple, or fee tail, shall from henceforth, so long as any papist shall be seized of or intituled to the same in fee simple or fee tail, be of the nature of gavelkind; and if not sold, aliened or disposed of by such papist in his lifetime for good and valuable consideration of money really and *bona fide* paid for such estate, shall from such papist descend to and be inherited by all and every the sons of such papist any way inheritable to such estate, share and share alike. . . .

[1] 1703/4.

Part IX
ARMED FORCES

ARMED FORCES
Introduction

AT the moment of the Restoration the armed forces of England consisted of the militia, which existed in theory rather than in fact; the feudal levy, which scarcely existed even in theory, but might be revived if the Commonwealth abolition of the feudal system was not confirmed; a powerful standing army; and an equally powerful standing navy. Almost immediately, however, it became obvious that the feudal levy would not be revived, and that the choice for purposes which were consistently represented as being defensive lay between the militia, the army and the navy. Of these the militia was regarded with great favour, partly because it was the people themselves in arms, partly because it was inefficient and therefore as harmless to friend as to foe; the navy was regarded with modified favour, for though it involved a heavy burden of taxation its successes had been won abroad, not at home; the army was regarded with great disfavour, partly as being extremely expensive and partly as the instrument by which the nation had been enslaved for eleven years.

One of the most troublesome causes of dispute between Charles I and Parliament had been the command of the armed forces, for the king was as unwilling to let this out of his hands as Parliament was to see it remain in them. The Convention of 1660 inclined to solve the problem by getting rid of the armed forces altogether, and endeavoured with more enthusiasm than discretion to disband the entire army and much of the navy.[1] But the Cavalier Parliament which succeeded it could hardly, in view of the antecedents of many of its members, reject the royal claim to command the forces, while it was restrained from pushing disbandment too far by a dangerous insurrection which broke out shortly before it met, and demonstrated the need for some force to maintain law and order.[2] One of the earliest Acts it passed, in consequence, vested the supreme command of the forces in the Crown,[3] and although, by combining the enunciation of this principle with provisions for the reorganization of the militia, it clearly indicated its views as to the type of forces that were desirable, it did not exclude the possibility that forces of another kind might have to be established. Thereafter militia, army and navy existed with varying fortunes side by side.

(a) Militia

The organization of the militia was completed by two further statutes,[4] which based the duty of supplying horsemen and foot-soldiers on a property qualification,[5] and established in all essentials the system which was to remain in force until 1757. In reality, however, the reconstituted body was of little value as a military weapon, and served mainly as a butt for satirists.[6] Privates and troopers were unwilling to attend the musters, and when they came inclined to treat the occasion as a holiday. Officers were more interested in the social importance they derived from their commissions than in their military duties. Rulers, especially James II, deliberately neglected the militia in order that the standing army might appear more necessary. Although

---

[1] No. 307.
[4] No. 303.

[2] No. 308.
[5] No. 304.

[3] No. 302.
[6] No. 305.

frequently called out, it saw little service except in the south-west of England during Monmouth's rebellion, when much of it proved untrustworthy and all of it ineffective.[1]

(b) Army

The attitude of Parliament to the standing army was typically English. In view of the possessions which England held abroad, the fortresses that required garrisons at home, and the need for maintaining order in a distracted community, even the Commons could hardly deny that something of the nature of a standing army was necessary; but they could at least show their disapproval of such a force by refusing to make any provision for it, either in the shape of money, or of quarters, or of disciplinary regulations. The result was to reduce to a minimum the chance that the army would do any good, and increase to a maximum the likelihood that it would do serious harm. Disorders in the army in Ireland, which had to deal with a subject population, were perhaps inevitable;[2] but disorders in the army even in England were also deplorably frequent,[3] and only confirmed Parliament in its refusal to accord it the proper recognition which was itself one of the main causes of these disorders. Had it not been for the danger of dismissal from the service, discipline could hardly have been maintained at all; but rates of pay on the whole were good, and officers especially hesitated to face the prospect of being cashiered.

Nevertheless the distrust of a standing army inherited from the Commonwealth period was a most valuable tradition. It produced a strong undercurrent of opposition to the attempts frequently made by Charles II to increase the modest force retained at the time of the general disbandment.[4] It inspired real hostility to the much larger force raised by James II,[5] which was regarded with special suspicion, inasmuch as there seemed to be no justification for it in the internal condition of the country, and it was officered to a large extent by Catholics. Finally, when the outbreak of war with France under William III demonstrated the need for a really considerable standing force, and a dangerous mutiny in a discontented regiment convinced the most hesitating of the desirability of a proper disciplinary code, it led to the Act authorizing the code being passed only for short intervals at a time.[6] It is true that the original code was the barest minimum, doing little more than provide severe penalties for mutiny and desertion; but the temporary character of the enactment enabled Parliament to secure control, it could be and was expanded when necessary, and meanwhile the situation was saved by the fact that the forces, when abroad and therefore no danger to the liberties of England, could be subjected to much more elaborate articles of war imposed by the sovereign on his own authority.

The serious mistake came after the treaty of Ryswick, when Parliament, alarmed both by the size of the army which had been engaged in the war and by the fact that it contained a high proportion of foreigners, insisted that it must be reduced to the size customary under Charles II, and must contain none but the king's natural-born British subjects.[7] As a result England entered on the War of the Spanish Succession very inadequately prepared, and was always in difficulties for men. Before the war was half over, in fact, recourse had to be had to the expedient, as yet unusual, of compulsory enlistment of the less desirable elements in the population.[8]

A natural consequence of civilian suspicion and disregard of the army was that its

---

[1] No. 306.	[2] No. 309.	[3] No. 310.	[4] No. 308.
[5] No. 14.	[6] No. 311.	[7] No. 312.	[8] No. 313.

reputation, both at home and abroad, rapidly declined from the high level it had reached under the Commonwealth. Immediately after the Restoration a force dispatched to the assistance of Portugal, composed largely of veterans from Cromwell's campaigns, fully maintained the old traditions;[1] but thereafter a quarter of a century followed during which calls on the army were infrequent and its performance undistinguished. Even the wars of William III did little to improve matters. The campaigns in Ireland[2] were waged against an ill-equipped enemy and to a considerable extent by foreign troops. Such battles as Steinkirk[3] and Landen reflected much credit on the English soldiery but little on English generalship or organizing capacity. Not until the reign of Anne, when Marlborough's genius at last secured free play, did the British army gain a truly international reputation. The four most famous victories with which Marlborough's name is associated—Blenheim,[4] Ramillies,[5] Oudenarde[6] and Malplaquet[7]—established its fame on a level which it had not attained since the fifteenth century. Even the Spanish campaigns, so full of successes[8] as well as of failures,[9] reflected credit at least on the British section of the very mixed forces with which they were conducted; and in amphibious operations, such as the capture of Gibraltar[10] and of Minorca,[11] the land forces played a distinguished part.

(c) Navy

So far as the navy was concerned the trouble that arose was almost entirely financial. The English people were proud of their navy and of its successes since the time of the Armada. They fully realized that it was necessary for the defence of their growing commerce against the Dutch and of their territory against the French. At the very beginning of Charles's reign they signified their acceptance of the principle of a standing navy by giving parliamentary sanction to a permanent disciplinary code for it.[12] But they could never forget that the navy was responsible for the largest single item in the expenditure of the government, and that the Customs duties had originally been granted in medieval times to defray the cost of defence by sea, so that special grants for the upkeep of the navy should not be necessary.

As a result the navy was always insufficiently supplied. Pay was not merely inadequate but constantly in arrears,[13] and while conditions of service were reasonably satisfactory for officers they were certainly not so for men. Before the eyes of all ratings was dangled the prospect of prize-money, which could on occasion mean a small fortune for a ship's complement; but prize-money was by no means an exclusive perquisite of the royal navy, there was little chance of any being forthcoming in time of peace, and even in time of war the share that fell to the lot of the ordinary seaman was miserably small.[14] Any other service at sea, in consequence, was preferred to that in the navy, and while merchant vessels and privateers had little difficulty in securing full complements ships of war frequently could not put to sea for lack of men. To man the navy at all, in fact, it was constantly necessary to have recourse to special proclamations summoning seamen to enlist,[15] and to the practice of impressment, both of which were apt to prove ineffective, for the proclamations were ignored, and the whole population conspired in assisting seamen to evade the press.[16]

It is not surprising, therefore, that the success of the navy was not as great as might

[1] No. 314. [2] Nos. 291, 292. [3] No. 315. [4] No. 316.
[5] No. 317. [6] No. 319. [7] No. 320. [8] No. 321.
[9] Nos. 318, 322. [10] No. 220. [11] No. 221. [12] No. 323.
[13] No. 324. [14] No. 327. [15] No. 325. [16] No. 326.

have been anticipated. Although England was a much more populous country than the United Netherlands, and had much larger ultimate resources, the Anglo-Dutch wars were singularly indecisive. The resounding English success off Lowestoft in the first war was balanced by the triumphant Dutch attack on the Thames.[1] The battles of the second war were typical evenly waged struggles. In the French wars the English and Dutch fleets combined were at first unequal to their opponents, and suffered a serious defeat at Beachy Head. Not until the French were compelled to devote a greater proportion of their resources to the struggle on land were the allies able to establish their ascendancy at La Hogue,[2] and even after that their control of the sea was precarious. During the War of the Spanish Succession, however, the French were much too heavily involved on land to give adequate attention to affairs at sea, and the Anglo-Dutch success at Vigo, followed by the capture of Gibraltar,[3] the rather indecisive battle of Malaga,[4] and the seizure of Minorca[5] established English naval power on a basis that could not be shaken.

[1] No. 328.   [2] No. 329.   [3] No. 220.
[4] No. 330.   [5] No. 221.

BIBLIOGRAPHY

Not only have military and naval history been grievously neglected in Britain, but little effort has been made to effect any co-ordination between them, with the result that any bibliography of works on the services inevitably falls into two sections.

(i) *Military*

There is no satisfactory guide to the literature of military history, and no considerable collection of material for it. The best contemporary manual is *Abridgment of the English Military Discipline, printed by his Majesty's Special Command for the Use of his Majesty's Forces* (London, 1686). Available information regarding the identity of commissioned officers is set forth in Charles Dalton, *English Army Lists and Commission Registers, 1661–1714* (6 vols., London, 1892–1904). Military dispatches were rare so long as campaigns were short and unimportant, and while King William was his own commander-in-chief; but Marlborough made a practice of sending home regular dispatches, which have been collected in *The Letters and Dispatches of John Churchill, first Duke of Marlborough, from 1702 to 1712*, edited by Sir George Murray (5 vols., London, 1845).

The ablest statement of the case for popular opposition to the army is to be found in John Trenchard and Walter Moyle, *An Argument showing that a Standing Army is Inconsistent with a Free Government and absolutely Destructive to the Constitution of the English Monarchy* (London, 1697), and John Trenchard, *A Short History of Standing Armies in England* (London, 1698). The best of the many pamphlets on the other side is John Somers, *A Letter balancing the Necessity of keeping a Land Force in Times of Peace with the Dangers that may follow it* (London, 1697). There is a careful examination of the reasons advanced by these and other writers in E. Arnold Miller, "Some Arguments used by English Pamphleteers, 1697–1700, concerning a Standing Army", in *Journal of Modern History*, XVIII (1946), pp. 306–313.

On the constitutional side the standard modern work, though badly needing revision, is C. M. Clode, *The Military Forces of the Crown, their Administration and Government* (2 vols., London, 1869). More important on the operational side is J. W. Fortescue, *A History of the British Army*, which, however, devotes only part of vol. 1 (London, 1899) to the later Stuart period. Sir S. D. Scott, *The British Army, its Origin, Progress and Equipment* (3 vols., London, 1868–1880), comes to an end in 1689, and Clifford Walton, *History of the British Standing Army, 1660–1700* (London, 1894), continues only a few years longer; but the remainder of the Stuart period is dealt with in Frank Taylor, *The Wars of Marlborough, 1702–1709* (2 vols., Oxford, 1921), and in the various biographies of Marlborough referred to later (p. 895). A valuable study of one of the less important theatres of war is Arthur Parnell, *The War of the Succession in Spain during the Reign of Queen Anne, 1702–1711* (London, 1888), which draws much on original sources but is somewhat prejudiced in its conclusions.

(ii) *Naval*

The most comprehensive guide to the literature of naval history is G. E. Manwaring, *A Bibliography of British Naval History* (London, 1930), which includes both printed and manuscript sources; but a shorter yet serviceable introduction is provided by *A Bibliography of Naval History*, compiled for the Historical Association by G. A. R. Callender, Part I (London, 1924). Many naval papers are printed or summarized in the *Calendar of State Papers Domestic*, and in Historical Manuscripts Commission, *Dartmouth MSS.*, vols. I and III, and *Portland MSS.*, vol. VIII, mentioned above (p. 40).

No one did more for the navy than Samuel Pepys, and the fortunate circumstance that his *Diary* has captured the imagination of generations of readers has secured for his solid administrative work a degree of attention which it might not otherwise have received. Even on purely naval matters the *Diary* is a valuable source of information; but much more important are

Pepys's manuscripts, which form the subject of *A Descriptive Catalogue of the Naval Manuscripts in the Pepysian Library at Magdalene College, Cambridge*, edited, with a long and extremely valuable introduction, by J. R. Tanner for the Navy Records Society (4 vols.; 1903-1923). With this should be associated *Samuel Pepys's Naval Minutes*, also edited by J. R. Tanner for the Navy Records Society (1926), a series of very miscellaneous notes made by Pepys in preparation for a projected history of the navy; *The Tangier Papers of Samuel Pepys*, edited by Edwin Chappell for the same body (1935), which is at least as important for the navy as for Tangier; *Private Correspondence and Miscellaneous Papers of Samuel Pepys, 1679-1703*, edited by J. R. Tanner (2 vols., London, 1926); and *Further Correspondence of Samuel Pepys, 1662-1679*, also edited by J. R. Tanner (London, 1929).

Quite apart from the Pepysian manuscripts an enormous amount of material for the history of the navy has been made available by the Navy Records Society, the most important among whose other publications on the later Stuart period are *Fighting Instructions, 1530-1816*, edited by Julian S. Corbett (1905); *The Life of Sir John Leake, Rear-Admiral of Great Britain*, by Stephen Martin-Leake, edited by Geoffrey Callender (2 vols., 1930), giving an account of a distinguished commander of the reigns of William and Anne; *Journal of Sir George Rooke, 1700-1702*, edited by Oscar Browning (1897); *The Byng Papers, selected from the Letters and Papers of Admiral Sir George Byng, first Viscount Torrington, and of his Son, Admiral John Byng*, edited by Brian Tunstall (3 vols., 1930-1932), of special value for the War of the Spanish Succession; *The Sergison Papers*, edited by R. D. Merriman (1950), mainly concerned with administration; and three series produced under the editorship of R. C. Anderson—*The Journal of Edward Montagu, first Earl of Sandwich, 1659-1665* (1929), which is of some importance for diplomatic as well as for naval history; *The Journals of Sir Thomas Allin, 1660-1678* (2 vols., 1939-1940); and *Journals and Narratives of the Third Dutch War* (1946), a rather miscellaneous collection of more or less associated accounts.

Among contemporary writers the most important is Josiah Burchett, clerk to Pepys and then for nearly fifty years Secretary to the Admiralty, whose *Memoirs of Transactions at Sea during the War with France, 1688-1697* (London, 1703), and *A Complete History of the most Remarkable Transactions at Sea, from the earliest Accounts of Time to the Conclusion of the Last War with France* (London, 1720), are invaluable for the naval aspect of the wars of William and Anne. A good sketch of naval operations between 1678 and 1705 is contained in the anonymous *Memoirs relating to the Lord Torrington*, edited by John Knox Laughton for the Camden Society (1889). *The Diary of Henry Teonge, 1675-1679*, edited by G. E. Manwaring (London, 1927), gives a lively picture of life at sea, suggesting that the naval chaplain at least had a fairly easy and not unpleasant time.

The standard modern work on the subject is *The Royal Navy*, by W. Laird Clowes and others, vol. VI (London, 1897); but this is both unsatisfactory and out of date, with the result that reliance has to be placed on a number of admirable studies covering more restricted fields. Of these the most important is Julian S. Corbett, *England in the Mediterranean, a Study of the Rise and Influence of British Power within the Straits, 1603-1713* (2 vols., London, 1904), in which the author deals with what he considers the really significant development in naval affairs during that period. It should be read in conjunction with John Ehrman, "William III and the Emergence of a Mediterranean Naval Policy, 1692-4", in *Cambridge Historical Journal*, IX (1949), pp. 269-292. A. T. Mahan, *The Influence of Sea Power upon History, 1660-1783* (London, 1890), is concerned mainly with naval strategy, on the study of which it had a remarkable effect. Arthur W. Tedder, *The Navy of the Restoration from the Death of Cromwell to the Treaty of Breda* (Cambridge, 1916), deals with the operations of the first Dutch War of Charles II's reign. Edward B. Powley, *The English Navy in the Revolution of 1688* (Cambridge, 1928), should be studied in conjunction with the naval correspondence in the *Dartmouth MSS.* referred to earlier (p. 791). J. H. Owen, *War at Sea under Queen Anne, 1702-1708* (Cambridge, 1938), is a valuable corrective to the many accounts which concentrate almost exclusively on the war on land. A useful companion volume is Ruth M. Bourne, *Queen Anne's Navy in the West Indies* (New Haven, 1939), which also throws much light on colonial affairs.

A. THE MILITIA

302. First Militia Act, 1661

(Statutes of the Realm, v, pp. 308–309)

AN ACT DECLARING THE SOLE RIGHT OF THE MILITIA TO BE IN THE KING,
AND FOR THE PRESENT ORDERING AND DISPOSING THE SAME

(13 Car. II, stat. I, cap. 6)

Forasmuch as within all his Majesty's realms and dominions the sole supreme government, command and disposition of the militia, and of all forces by sea and land, and of all forts and places of strength, is, and by the laws of England ever was, the undoubted right of his Majesty and his royal predecessors, kings and queens of England; and that both or either of the Houses of Parliament cannot, nor ought to, pretend to the same, nor can, nor lawfully may, raise or levy any war, offensive or defensive, against his Majesty, his heirs or lawful successors; and yet the contrary thereof hath of late years been practised almost to the ruin and destruction of this kingdom, and during the late usurped governments many evil and rebellious principles have been distilled into the minds of the people of this kingdom, which unless prevented may break forth to the disturbance of the peace and quiet thereof; and whereas an Act is under consideration for exercising the militia with most safety and ease to the king and his people, which Act cannot as yet be perfected; be it therefore enacted . . . that the militia and land forces of this kingdom, and of the dominion of Wales and town of Berwick-upon-Tweed, now under the power of lieutenants or their deputies, shall be exercised, ordered and managed until the five and twentieth day of March next ensuing[1] in such manner as the same now is actually exercised, ordered and managed, according to such commissions and instructions as they formerly have or from time to time shall receive from his Majesty. . . .

V. Provided that no person whatsoever shall be capable of acting as lieutenant or deputy lieutenant or other officer or soldier by virtue of this Act who hath not already taken the oaths of allegiance and supremacy since the return of his Majesty into England, until he shall take the same according to the laws and statutes of this kingdom. . . .

303. Second Militia Act, 1662

(Statutes of the Realm, v, pp. 358–364)

AN ACT FOR ORDERING THE FORCES IN THE SEVERAL COUNTIES
OF THIS KINGDOM

(14 Car. II, cap. 3)

Forasmuch as within all his Majesty's realms and dominions . . . peace and quiet thereof;[2] be it therefore declared and enacted . . . that the king's most excellent Majesty, his heirs and successors, shall and may, from time to time as occasion shall

[1] 25 March 1662.　　　　[2] To this point the wording is the same as in the preceding Act.

require, issue forth several commissions of lieutenancy to such persons as his Majesty, his heirs and successors, shall think fit to be his Majesty's lieutenants for the several and respective counties, cities and places of England and dominion of Wales and town of Berwick-upon-Tweed, which lieutenants shall have full power and authority to call together all such persons at such times, and to arm and array them in such manner, as is hereafter expressed and declared, and to form them into companies, troops and regiments, and in case of insurrection, rebellion or invasion them to lead, conduct and employ, or cause to be led, conducted and employed, as well within the said several counties, cities and places for which they shall be commissionated respectively, as also into any other the counties and places aforesaid, for suppressing of all such insurrections and rebellions and repelling of invasions as may happen to be, according as they shall from time to time receive directions from his Majesty, his heirs and successors; and that the said respective lieutenants shall have full power and authority from time to time to constitute, appoint and give commissions to such persons as they shall think fit to be colonels, majors, captains and other commission officers of the said persons so to be armed, arrayed and weaponed, and to present to his Majesty, his heirs and successors, the names of such person and persons as they shall think fit to be deputy lieutenants, and upon his Majesty's approbation of them shall give them deputations accordingly; always understood that his Majesty, his heirs and successors, have power and authority to direct and order otherwise, and accordingly at his and their pleasure may appoint and commissionate or displace such officers, anything in this Act to the contrary notwithstanding. . . .

II. And for the providing horse and arms and furniture thereunto belonging for the arming and weaponing the persons aforesaid, and also for the defraying and paying the necessary charges thereunto belonging in manner as hereafter followeth, be it further enacted, that the said respective lieutenants . . . and their deputies . . . have hereby full power and authority to charge any person with horse, horseman and arms, or with foot-soldier and arms, in the same county, shire, city, borough or town corporate where his, her or their estates lie, having respect unto and not exceeding the limitations and proportions hereafter mentioned, that is to say: no person shall be charged with finding a horse, horseman and arms unless such person or persons have a revenue of five hundred pounds by the year in possession, or have an estate of six thousand pounds in goods or money besides the furniture of his or their houses, and so proportionably for a greater estate in lands in possession or goods as the respective lieutenants and their deputies as aforesaid in their discretions shall see cause and think reasonable; and they are not to charge any person with finding a foot-soldier and arms that hath not a yearly revenue of fifty pounds in possession, or a personal estate of six hundred pounds in goods or moneys (other than the stock upon the ground), and after the aforesaid rate proportionably for a greater or lesser revenue or estate. . . .

III. Provided that . . . it shall be lawful to and for the respective lieutenants and deputies . . . to impose the finding and providing of horse, horseman and arms as aforesaid by joining two or three or more persons together in the charge, as to their judgment shall appear most conducible to the service of this kingdom. . . .

V. Be it further enacted, that the said lieutenants and deputies . . . shall require and direct all persons so charged as aforesaid with horse, horseman and arms to allow two shillings by the day to the troopers that serve with their horse and arms for the maintenance of the man and horse, and twelve pence a day for the foot-soldiers (if they serve not in their own persons), for so many days as they shall be absent from their dwellings and callings by occasion of muster or exercise. . . .

VII. And be it enacted, . . . that the said lieutenants or deputies, or the chief officers upon the place, shall and may imprison mutineers and such soldiers as do not their duties as soldiers at the day of their musters and training, and shall and may inflict for punishment for every such offence any pecuniary mulct not exceeding five shillings, or the penalty of imprisonment without bail or mainprize not exceeding twenty days. . . .

XVII. Provided also that no person being a peer of this realm shall be capable of acting or serving as lieutenant or deputy lieutenant by virtue of this Act unless he or they shall first before six of the Lords of his Majesty's Privy Council for the time being, or such other persons as shall be authorized by his Majesty to administer the same, take the oaths of allegiance and supremacy, and also this oath following, I, A.B., do declare and believe that it is not lawful upon any pretence whatsoever to take arms against the king, and that I do abhor that traitorous position that arms may be taken by his authority against his person or against those that are commissioned by him in pursuance of such military commissions: so help me God. . . .

XVIII. And that no person being under the degree of a peer of this realm shall be capable of acting as lieutenant, deputy lieutenant, officer or soldier by virtue of this Act unless he or they shall first take the oaths of allegiance and supremacy, and this oath following. . . .[1]

XXIV. Provided always, and it is hereby further enacted and declared, that no person charged with the finding of horse or foot or with contributing thereunto as aforesaid shall be compellable to serve in his or their proper person, but may, according to such proportion as they are or shall respectively be charged by this Act, find one or more fit or sufficient man or men, qualified according to this Act. . . .

304. Assessment for the North Riding, 1663

(Historical Manuscripts Commission, *Various Collections*, II, pp. 118–119)

A LIST OF THE YEARLY VALUE OF THE ESTATES

OF THE PEERS IN THE NORTH RIDING OF THE COUNTY OF YORK,

TOGETHER WITH THE NUMBER OF HORSES ASSESSED UPON EACH OF THEM

Duke of Buckingham, value per annum, 2,300*l.* four horses
Marquis of Newcastle,   650*l.*   one horse
Earl of Northumberland,   800*l.*   one horse
Earl of Mulgrave,   840*l.*   one horse
Earl Rivers   1,400*l.*   two horses
Lady Monmouth   400*l.*   half a horse

[1] As above.

Earl of Carlisle	1,050*l*.	two horses
Earl of Elgin	2,900*l*.	five horses
Viscount Fauconberg	2,400*l*.	four horses
Lord Darcy	1,600*l*.	three horses
Lord Wharton	600*l*.	one horse
Lord Cornwallis	800*l*.	one horse

305. John Dryden on the militia

(Cymon and Iphigenia, ll. 399–408)

The country rings around with loud alarms,
And raw in fields the rude militia swarms; ·
Mouths without hands; maintained at vast expense,
In peace a charge, in war a weak defence;
Stout once a month they march, a blustering band,
And ever, but in times of need, at hand.
This was the morn when, issuing on the guard,
Drawn up in rank and file they stood prepared
Of seeming arms to make a short essay,
Then hasten to be drunk, the business of the day.

306. Adam Wheeler's account of the operations of the Wiltshire militia against the duke of Monmouth, 1685

(Camden Miscellany, XII, pp. 159–166)

ITER BELLICOSUM

OR

A PERFECT RELATION OF THE HEROIC
MARCH OF HIS MAJESTY'S TRULY LOYAL SUBJECT
AND MAGNANIMOUS SOLDIER, COLONEL JOHN WYNDHAM, ESQ.,
WITH HIS REGIMENT OF FOOT
INTO THE WESTERN PARTS OF ENGLAND FOR
THE SUPPRESSING OF JAMES SCOTT AND HIS
ACCOMPLICES IN THEIR REBELLIOUS
INSURRECTION, TOGETHER WITH SOME REMARKABLE OCCURRENCES
HAPPENING IN THAT EXPEDITION,
FAITHFULLY SET DOWN BY ADAM WHEELER,
ONE OF THE DRUMS OF HIS HONOUR'S OWN COMPANY

1685, June 16. Being Wednesday,[1] I was summoned by a command from his Honour to appear in the market-place of New Sarum in the county of Wilts, by eight of the clock in the morning, in his regiment, completely armed according to my place as a drum; where the regiment, being drawn together, was discharged till the next morning. When again met, being the seventeenth day, they were discharged

---

[1] Really 17 June. Wheeler's dates in the earlier part of his narrative are all one day wrong.

until Friday the eighteenth of June; and the nineteenth, being Saturday, the regiment was exactly completed by his Honour, and accommodated fit for war according to military discipline, and that day by his command, about six of the clock in the evening, the drums beating and the colours displayed, leaving the city we directed our march to Wilton, being about two miles distant, and quartered there that night, where his Honour ordered his carriage and ammunition to be brought to him.

June 20. The next day, being Sunday, on which day in the afternoon, leaving the town of Wilton, we continued our march to Market Lavington.

June 21. Early the next morning his Honour marched to the Devizes, and there refreshed his regiment for the weary and hard afternoon's march they sustained the day before. In the afternoon, by beat of drum, the regiment marched as far as Chippenham; and June the 22, being Tuesday, they marched from Chippenham to the city of Bath, where they quartered that night.

June 23. The regiment, leaving the city of Bath, went as far as Bradford. That night being very dark, there was an alarm, by reason of which the regiment could not unite into a body till they came to Trowbridge, which was June 24. . . . Here the whole regiment lay.

June 25. The Right Honourable the lord lieutenant earl of Pembroke gave command for some of the regiment and some of the militia horse to go with him to Frome, where he forced the rebels to lay down their arms, and brought away with him the constable of that town to Trowbridge, who proclaimed the duke of Monmouth king, and several cruel and new invented murthering weapons as scythes and the like. . . .

June 26. We continued our march from Trowbridge to Kingsdown, where divers other regiments met. Here his Honour's regiment was by his grace the duke of Grafton and the Right Honourable the earl of Feversham set in battalia, as if presently to engage the enemy. Thence we marched to Bath.

June 27. From Bath the regiment was led by his Honour Colonel Wyndham to Trowbridge, where they made no stay, but marched forwards into Bratton Lane, and there by an alarm of the enemy's being near caused the regiment to encamp in that land's end, and the blue regiment also; and the yellow Hampshire regiment encamped in a ground near the said Lane.

June 28. The regiment marched into Bratton Fields, and was there drawn up, and after some small stay moved to Westbury, and thence directed its march near to Frome, where his Honour's tent was erected, and we encamped there in a certain ground near the town.

June 29. Dislodging from thence, we marched directly into Frome, where the king's Majesty's gracious pardon was proclaimed to all such as had taken up arms against him, if in eight days they would come in and accept thereof, some persons only excepted who were therein mentioned.

July 1. Being Wednesday,[1] his Honour's regiment took their march to Shepton Mallet. Here, not far from the town, a ground was shown which lay within prospect, where Monmouth and his army was drawn up and exercised.

[1] This date and those that follow are correct.

July 2. Being Thursday, we marched from Shepton Mallet to Glastonbury, and from thence we removed and went towards Somerton, in which march we had the sight of King's Sedgemoor, being about one mile distant from us. And here we received a command to return and march back to Charlton.

July 4. From whence we marched to King's Sedgemoor, marching eight miles in the moor so far as Middlezoy, where being alarmed;

July 6. The Right Honourable the earl of Pembroke, lord lieutenant, in great haste came riding to the house where his Honour Colonel Wyndham was quartered, it being between twelve and one of the clock in the morning, calling out, "Colonel Wyndham, Colonel Wyndham, the enemy is engaged", and asking for his drums. The colonel's answer was that he was ready; and so forthwith prepared himself. There being then no drum in the house but Adam Wheeler, who opened the door and answered his lordship that he was ready to obey his command, so his lordship immediately commanded him to beat an alarm, which he presently performed, although some of the regiment did endeavour to have the credit of that piece of service ascribed to themselves; one saying, "It was I that did first beat the alarm"; another in like manner saying the same; so that Wheeler may justly complain, as the poet Virgil did concerning his *Sic vos non vobis*, and somewhat after the same manner as he spoke superscribe, *Hos ego versiculos feci tulit alter honores.*

When the alarm was beaten by Adam Wheeler in Middlezoy according to the lord lieutenant's command, the regiment marched through Weston into Weston Moor with as much expedition as possible could be, where they were drawn up three deep in order to engage if occasion required. The aforesaid sixth of July the fight began very early in the morning, which battle was over within the space of two hours, and the enemy received a total rout. Here Adam Wheeler (being then at his post) was one of those of the right wing of his Honour Colonel Wyndham's regiment, who after the enemy began to run desired leave of his Honour to get such pillage in the field as they could find. But his Honour's answer and command was that upon pain of death not a man of his regiment should move from his post, saying that if the enemy should rally together again, and the regiment be in disorder, every man of them might lose his life.

The battle being over, the Right Honourable the earl of Feversham, general of his Majesty's army, came to the head of Colonel Wyndham's regiment and gave him many thanks for his readiness, saying his Majesty should not hear of it by letter but by word of mouth, and that he would certify the king himself of it.

An account of the prisoners that were brought along by the right wing of his Honour Colonel Wyndham's regiment to Weston Church, as they were tied together, Adam Wheeler writing them down on his drumhead as they passed by:

The first number was fifty and five, most of them tied together.

The second number was thirty and two, tied in like manner.

The third was two wounded in their legs, crawling upon the ground on their hands and knees to Weston Church.

The fourth was thirty-seven in number, many of them tied and pinnacled together.

The fifth was one alone, being naked, only his drawers on.

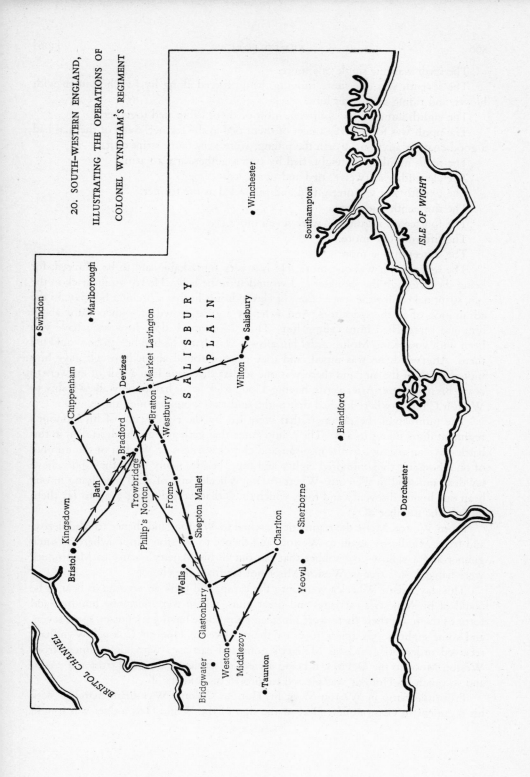

20. SOUTH-WESTERN ENGLAND,
ILLUSTRATING THE OPERATIONS OF
COLONEL WYNDHAM'S REGIMENT

The sixth was one single one more.

The seventh was one more running, being forced along by two horsemen with blows, and riding close after him.

The eighth number was fourteen, most of them being tied together.

The ninth was forty-seven, most of them tied as the former. Such of them as had a good coat, or anything worth the pilling, were very fairly stript of it.

The tenth number was eight, tied by two together, arm to arm.

The eleventh was twelve, tied and pinnacled.

The twelfth was seventeen, tied and pinnacled as the former.

The thirteenth one more.

The fourteenth in number were seven more.

The fifteenth one more.

The sixteenth one more.

The seventeenth was one more. He was very remarkable and to be admired, for being shot through the shoulder and wounded in the belly. He lay on his back in the sun, stript naked, for the space of ten or eleven hours in that scorching hot day, to the admiration of all the spectators. And as he lay a great crowd of soldiers came about him and reproached him, calling him, Thou Monmouth dog, how long have you been with your King Monmouth? His answer was that if he had breath he would tell them. Afterwards he was pitied, and they opened round about him and gave him more liberty of the air; and there was one soldier that gave him a pair of drawers to cover his nakedness. Afterwards, having a long stick in his hands, he walked feebly to Weston Church, where he died that night, and two wounded men more.

The number of the prisoners that were led by the right wing of his Honour's regiment did amount to 228.[1] The countrymen that gathered up the dead slain in this battle gave an account to the minister and churchwardens of Weston of the number of one thousand three hundred eighty and four, besides many more they did believe lay dead unfound in the corn. Where Adam Wheeler saw of dead men lying in one heap one hundred seventy and four, which those that were digging a pit to lay them in gave the number of.

From Weston Moor the regiment marched to Weston, and thence to Middlezoy, and from Middlezoy again to Weston, and thence to Weston Moor, where a Dutch gunner and a yellow-coat soldier that ran out of his Majesty's army to Monmouth were hanged on a tree in Weston Moor not far from the church.

This day Adam Wheeler went into the camp, and took an account as near as he could of his Majesty's carriages and great guns, where were near one hundred and forty of them. Of these there were nineteen guns, some having six horses, some seven, and some eight horses apiece to draw them. Here his Honour Colonel Wyndham received orders to guard his Majesty's guns and carriages with his regiment from Weston Moor to the Devizes, it being a piece of service of no small trust and credit, and so much his Honour was pleased to inform his soldiers of. . . .

From the camp in Weston Moor his Honour Colonel Wyndham marched with his regiment to Glastonbury. Here at the sign of the White Hart a duel was fought

[1] Really 238.

between Captain Love and Major Talbot. The major fell, and Captain Love fled for it. Here also were six men of the prisoners that were taken hanged on the sign-post of that inn, who after as they hung were stripped naked, and so left hanging there all night. Here also at this town of Glastonbury there was an alarm, whereupon the regiment was commanded to the Abbey cloister. His Honour's regiment marched from Glastonbury (where those six men were left hanging on the sign-post) to Wells. Thence they marched to Embetch, and so to Philip's Norton.

July 8. The regiment left Philip's Norton, and marched to the Devizes (guarding his Majesty's carriages and guns), where his Honour was discharged of that trust; and here his Honour discharged the regiment likewise till the next summons by beat of drum. . . .

B. THE ARMY

(a) ORIGIN, DISCIPLINE AND RECRUITMENT

307. Disbanding Act, 1660

(*Statutes of the Realm*, v, pp. 238–241)

AN ACT FOR THE SPEEDY DISBANDING OF THE ARMY
AND GARRISONS OF THIS KINGDOM
(*12 Car. II, cap. 15*)

Whereas the people of this kingdom lie under a great burthen and charge in the maintenance and payment of the present army; now to the end the same may be disbanded and the country eased, and the officers and soldiers who were in the army on the five and twentieth day of April one thousand six hundred sixty, appearing by the musters taken the seventh of May following (being under God instrumental in the just and happy restitution of his Majesty to the exercise of his government, and the people to their laws and liberties), may be satisfied their just arrears, be it enacted . . . that the said army and all the respective regiments, troops and companies, officers and soldiers, whether in field or garrison, within this kingdom of England, dominion of Wales and town of Berwick-upon-Tweed, together with all the English forces now in Scotland, except such as are in the following rules excepted, be with all convenient speed disbanded and discharged.

II. And it is further enacted, that his Royal Highness the duke of York, the duke of Albemarle, the Lord Great Chamberlain, the Lord Steward, the earl of Leicester and the Lord Robartes, Sir Richard Browne, Sir William Doyley, John Birch, William Prynne, Edward King and Robert Scawen, esquires, or any three or more of them, whereof one of the commissioners named by the House of Lords and one of the commissioners named by the House of Commons to be two, shall be and are hereby constituted and appointed commissioners for that purpose, and shall act therein according to the rules, orders and instructions hereafter expressed, or such other directions and rules as shall hereafter be made on that behalf by the Lords and Commons in Parliament assembled. . . .

Rules, orders and instructions for disbanding the army

1. The commissioners hereby appointed for disbanding the army and respective forces shall proceed therein in manner following, that is to say. The name of the officer in chief of each regiment and garrison within this kingdom (except such as are hereafter excepted) shall be written in a paper, which paper shall be close rolled and sealed up, and put into a glass and left with the Speaker of the House of Commons sitting the Parliament, or with the Lord Chancellor in the interval of Parliament; and when the aforesaid commissioners shall be ready to disband any the forces, they shall when the House of Commons is sitting, or in the interval when his Majesty's Council is sitting, draw forth a certain number of names not exceeding three, and having there

publicly read the names proceed forthwith to disband them, and so from time to time until the whole be disbanded, yet so as four companies in Hull, four companies in Berwick and two companies in Carlisle, of such as are now in the said garrisons respectively or such as shall be thereunto appointed by the king's Majesty, be last disbanded.

2. All general officers of the army who were in service the five and twentieth of April one thousand six hundred and sixty, appearing by their commissions, and all other officers and soldiers who were in service the five and twentieth of April one thousand six hundred and sixty, and are found upon the muster rolls taken the seventh of May then next following, and have not been since discharged for refusing to take the oaths of allegiance and supremacy, shall have and receive upon their disbanding their just arrears from the fourteenth of March one thousand six hundred fifty-eight,[1] defalcating for quarters by them owing for such time for which arrears shall be to them due and payable before the said five and twentieth of April or since.

3. That the regiments of their Royal Highnesses the dukes of York and Gloucester, and Lord General's regiments of horse and foot, shall be last disbanded, except the four companies in Hull, the four companies in Berwick and the two companies in Carlisle aforesaid.

4. That all garrisons within this kingdom, or dominion of Wales and town of Berwick-upon-Tweed and the islands of Guernsey or Jersey, shall be with all convenient speed, in respect of their fortifications and walls and numbers of men, put into the same condition they were in, in the year one thousand six hundred thirty-seven, and the soldiers in them disbanded and discharged, except such of them, or any other, as his Majesty shall think fit otherwise to dispose and provide for at his own charge.

5. That if his Majesty shall think fit to continue in Scotland three regiments of foot and one troop of horse of the English forces now there they are not to be paid and maintained at the charge of this kingdom. . . .

12. That if any officer or soldier hereby appointed to be disbanded shall refuse to give obedience thereunto, or dissuade others from disbanding, he or they shall be forthwith secured by the Lord General, and forfeit their whole arrears, and be proceeded against as mutineers. . . .

20. That the chief officer of his Majesty's navy do with all convenient speed deliver in unto the commissioners appointed for disbanding the army a list of the names of the twenty-five ships now in the river which are intended to be discharged, with a particular account of the moneys due to every ship and the names of the officers and seamen to whom it is due, to the end that so soon as any competent sum of money shall be received that is hereby appointed for that service the said ships may be paid off and discharged accordingly. . . .

[1] 1658/9.

308. William Dicconson's account, based on James II's papers, of the origin of the army, 1661

(*Life of James the Second*, ed. J. S. Clarke, 1, pp. 388–391)

Soon after this, in the beginning of January 1661, one Venner, a fifth-monarchy man and a holder forth amongst them, after having preached to his congregation and fasted all the day with them, being full of the spirit of rebellion, marched out of their meeting-house with thirty in his company all armed, between eleven and twelve at night, and ran about the streets crying, "Live King Jesus", and that all should follow him that were for King Jesus, and those that did not should keep their houses. Some of the constables, hearing this, went to suppress them; but though three or four of the watches joined together they durst not venture upon them; so that Venner marched through the town without any opposition, and, none of his party being mad enough to come and join with him, he and his company betook themselves to the woods near Highgate.

At this time it happened that his Majesty was at Portsmouth, having gone thither with the queen his mother and his sister Princess Henrietta, to see them embark there for France; but the duke, being somewhat indisposed, stayed behind at Whitehall. The general, who was at the Cockpit, had soon the alarm, and came and waked the duke to give him an account of it, whereupon they sent out some of the few horse which were yet left not paid off, and the general's own troop commanded by Sir Philip Howard, to look after them; but Venner keeping the woods, and the horse not knowing the country, did not light on them.

After two or three days lurking Venner and his men, leaving the woods before day, marched into London, and came through Aldgate about seven in the morning, crying as before, "Live King Jesus", and that such as were for him should join them. There they found no resistance, and so passing by Leadenhall, and driving before them such loose men of the militia as offered to appear upon the noise, they passed on by the old Exchange, and advanced as far as Wood Street, where a party of about twenty horse commanded by one Corbet came up to them; but the street was so narrow that the horse could not break in upon them. By this time the train-bands were up, and came so thick upon them, who had only two men that joined them in all their march through the city, that they were forced to get into a house where they defended themselves.

Whilst this passed in the city, news of it was brought to the duke and the general at Whitehall by a messenger, who told them that when he came away Venner and his company were come up as far as Leadenhall, beating all before them. Whereupon the duke and the general immediately took horse, there being no more left on the guard; but as they went on so many of the nobility and gentry with their attendants came and joined them that when they were got as far as St. Paul's they were no less in number than fifteen hundred horse.

There they met the lord mayor, Sir Richard Browne, who told them that Venner and all his party were either taken or killed; that the militia which besieged them, and had been ordered to drive them out of the house which they so obstinately defended, could not do it without firing it, which for good reasons they durst not do; till at last one Lambert, a seaman (who afterwards for his good service was made commander of the duke's yacht, and in the end of the year 1665 was slain on board the *Anne*, a third-rate), persuaded some of them to follow him and get up on the top of the house, which they did, and forced their entry that way.

These desperate men were almost all killed or wounded before they could be mastered, and one only of them asked for quarter; at which a comrade of his, that lay wounded in the room, endeavoured with his sword to kill him, reviling him for being so mean as to ask quarter. Venner had no less than nineteen wounds on him, and it was with great difficulty that the surgeons kept him alive till he could be condemned and hanged, as he and the rest of his fanatic crew that were left alive soon were, except two who were made use of as witnesses against the rest.

And so ended this mad attempt of a furious zeal, which seemed in a manner designed by providence to convince the king and his ministers of the necessity of providing better for the safety of his person and the security of the government than hitherto they had done, by letting them see what dangerous spirits lay still scattered about in the body of the kingdom. . . . For this reason it was that the duke proposed to the Council, which was called in the time of the insurrection, that they should write to his Majesty, and desire him to stop the disbanding of the general's troop of horse guards, and the regiment of foot, which were to have been paid off that day, and that he would rather think of raising more men for the security of his person and government; which advice his Majesty followed, and immediately gave order for the raising a new regiment of guards, of twelve companies, to be commanded by Colonel John Russell, and a regiment of horse of eight troops, of which the earl of Oxford was to be colonel, and also a troop of horse guards to be commanded by the Lord Gerard. He likewise sent for the duke's troop of guards, which were then at Dunkirk. . . .

309. Petition of John Andrewes to the Lord Lieutenant of Ireland, 1667
(Historical Manuscripts Commission, *Tenth Report*, v, p. 33)

That your petitioner, being a soldier belonging to Captain Broughton's foot company in the Royal Regiment under your grace's command, about a year last past and upwards being commanded out amongst others towards Kilkenny; and that upon his march, coming into his quarters, being fallen sick suddenly and very faint and disconsolate, did desire his landlord that he would cause a chicken or pullet to be made ready for him for his refreshment, and that your petitioner would give any reasonable satisfaction for the same to be done accordingly. Whereupon your petitioner walked forth into the back side of the said house, where he found great store of poultry of all sorts, so that he immediately destroyed one of them for his refreshment as aforesaid. That suddenly, before he could return back, there came a stranger unknown to your petitioner, and fell violently upon him with opprobrious words, and struck at him, and abused your petitioner in a high degree; so that your petitioner, being a soldier, could not abrook the same, but was suddenly forced in his own defence to draw his weapon to defend himself. Whereupon his adversary ran violently upon the point of your petitioner's weapon and wounded himself to death, so that your petitioner thereupon was apprehended and tried for his life, and so convicted before Judge Povey, who, taking into consideration the condition of the thing, and understanding that the party so slain was long before excommunicated and outlawed, the said judge was graciously pleased to give your petitioner a reprieve for his life.

Ever since, a year past and upwards, your petitioner hath lain in prison in the county gaol near Maryborough, in a sad, miserable and deplorable condition, being there like to perish unless your grace's favour be unto him extended for enlargement. May it therefore please your grace to take the premises into your noble, pious and serious consideration, and to grant him an order for his enlargement out of prison, being ready to starve, and that he may be banished out of this kingdom in such manner and form as your grace shall think fit.

310. Sir John Reresby's account of the garrison at York, 1682–1688
(*Memoirs*, pp. 264–493)

10 May 1682. That day I took the oaths as governor of York and justice of the peace within the liberty of St. Peter's in York. I was in all these commissions at that time, viz., as governor of York, governor of Bridlington, captain of a troop of horse in the west riding of the county of York, justice of the peace for that riding, for Middlesex, for Westminster, and the liberty of St. Peter's within the city of York, as also deputy lieutenant for the said west riding. . . .

27 June. I went to Clifford's Tower to take possession of it. . . . I went afterwards to wait on my lord mayor, and to show him my commission. I told him I understood that in my Lord Frescheville's time the civil power had something intrenched upon the military, which I should not suffer for the time to come; that if the soldiers committed capital crimes, as treason or felony, I was willing (notice being first given to me) to deliver them up to justice; but for less crimes, as batteries, quarrels or smaller misdemeanours, I expected complaint to be made to me, and to have the punishment of them myself; which his lordship confessed to be reasonable, though not long before he had bound the officer that was deputy-governor to the peace. . . .

2 December. Captain Bristow's company mutinied upon the main guard, upon the occasion of some arrears due to them from the captain, as to which I must confess the captain was not to blame, the said arrears not being in his hands, but in his that commanded that company before. Complaint being made to me that one of them had drawn his sword upon the sergeant for endeavouring to quell them, I sent for the soldier, who denied to obey orders, and the corporal (that commanded the guard) to seize him, all the rest of the company taking their parts and saying if one suffered they would all fare alike. Having notice of this, I rose from dinner and went immediately with the ensign and my own servants to the guard, where finding them together I seized the mutineer by the throat, took away his arms (with the corporal and two more of the ringleaders), committed them all four to the dungeon for that

night and the next day, and then cashiered the chief of them. The rest (submitting themselves and begging pardon by petition, I was willing to pardon) returned to their duty. In such cases the remedy must be speedy and resolute. . . .

12 June 1684. I received an account by express from Doncaster of a quarrel that had happened there between the mayor of that corporation and my company of foot quartering there in their march to York, upon the occasion of the beating of a drum by the leave or license of the mayor, and without the leave of the officer commanding in chief, or indeed without his knowledge, who went upon the presumption that no drum ought to beat where the king's drum is without the officer's knowledge. However, the mayor to justify his power took the part of the drummer, licensed by himself, and the officer sending a sergeant and three soldiers to take away the drum was encountered by the rabble headed by the mayor, and being overpowered in number they were seized and their arms taken away; and afterwards the rest of the soldiers were fallen upon in their quarters, and some of them having wounded a justice of the peace in the fray were committed to prison. . . .

21 January 1686. I received notice from my lieutenant at York that the day the countess of Strafford's body came there to be buried (being attended with several gentlemen of the country and a guard out of my company) the rabble, to tear off the escutcheons from the hearse, had made an assault upon them; that the soldiers, endeavouring to beat them off, were driven and pursued into the Minster, where the choir, being hung with black cloth and escutcheons, was plundered of them, several of the soldiers hurt as well as those of the rabble, so that a greater riot hath not been known in that place; that he (meaning my lieutenant) had complained to my lord mayor of some of the leaders of this fray, and that he refused to punish them as he ought. At the same time I had a letter from my lord mayor, who complained of the lieutenant and the soldiers, and denied but that he was ready and active to inflict such punishment upon the offenders as the law allowed in that case. . . .

27 August. I went to York. The 29th there marched into that garrison four companies of Colonel Oglethorpe's regiment, and the 2nd of September five of the earl of Huntingdon's regiment. My own company was come from Hull some days before, so that there was ten complete companies well officered. The officers by commission were some fifteen, amongst which were my Lord Hunsdon, lieutenant-colonel to Colonel Oglethorpe; Captain Cornwallis, brother to the Lord Cornwallis; Major Morgan, major to my Lord Huntingdon, with several others of good quality. All these gentlemen understood their duty and the discipline of war so well that they paid me all fit obedience and respect as governor; and I was careful not to be un-reasonable or too imposing, but I demeaned myself with civility, and was so careful in giving of orders suitable to the directions received from above, or consisting with the rules of war, that we agreed very well. This good understanding was not only amongst ourselves but also between the city and the garrison. . . .

The garrison I formed at that time into this method. The ten companies consisted of 500, besides officers, and the daily guards of 80 men, by detachment of 8 out of every company, of 4 sergeants, 6 corporals and 1 commissioned officer. These met at the place of parade in the Minster yard between nine and ten every morning. At ten o'clock they marched off to relieve the several guards, which guards were in all six, viz., the main guard, consisting of 32 private sentinels, 1 drummer, 1 commissioned officer, 1 sergeant, 1 corporal. The other guards were kept at the several gates, which were five. At Bootham Bar there was 8 soldiers, 1 sergeant, 1 corporal, 1 drummer. . . . At Micklegate Bar there was 12 soldiers, 1 sergeant and 1 corporal. . . . The rest were distributed to Walmgate, Castlegate, and Monk Bar. The tattoo was beaten every night by five drums at ten o'clock, at which hour every soldier was to go to his quarters, or be punished if found after that hour in the streets by the patrol that went the round of the streets to see that good order was kept.

No soldier was suffered (nor indeed citizen) to go out of the gates in the daytime with firearms, dogs, or engines for the destruction of game, except gentlemen or officers, or such as had leave in writing from myself. I did not suffer any quarters to be given without my allowance, and where I found the magistrates did oppress I relieved as I thought fit. . . . I punished such soldiers very severely against whom any complaint was made out to be just, which being done at the first prevented many disorders. There was one that was accused of a felony. I presently turned him over to be punished by the civil magistrate. I called but one council of war whilst I stayed there, and returned the 27th of September to Thrybergh. . . .

There happened a dispute between me and my own lieutenant, one Mr. Butler, who, being . . . not very easy in his fortune, and extravagant in his expenses, had sold some of my soldiers whilst he was at Hull with the company; that is he had taken money to set them at large, and entertained others in their room without my knowledge or consent. When I told him of this he justified himself in it, said that other lieutenants had done the same thing. I told him that was no rule to me, that it was me only that was to answer to the king for my company, which was impossible if he modelled it at his pleasure, and enlarged old disciplined men for money and took novices and inexperienced in their stead, and therefore expected that he begged my pardon and owned his error. This he denied to do, so that I sent to confine him and resolved to suspend him the next day, and the rather because he pretended to have some letters from me by which he was able to make out something to my prejudice. But the next morning he came and offered me to submit himself, which I would not accept till he brought me those letters and gave them into my hands, with great promises of repentance and of better carriage.

12 November. I went to York, where I found some disorders since I left that garrison. I had several complaints from the citizens against officers and soldiers for taking money for quarters, and giving ease to such as feed them the best. For this crime a Scotchman of my Lord Huntingdon's regiment was punished at a council of war, to lie at the marshal's for three days, to ride the wooden horse every day at the relief of the guard with a paper upon his breast expressing his crime. I confined two commissioned officers, one for lying out of the garrison without acquainting me with it, the other for quarrelling with and misusing a citizen, and afterwards committing him by his own authority to the guard with a file of musketeers. I committed another to the dungeon for beating a constable, and punished several for leaving the guard without leave and neglect of their duty. . . . Every day some disorder or other was

committed, though none passed unpunished either by judgment of a council of war or my own appointment, to the satisfaction of the city. . . .

5 December. I committed three soldiers to the guard, and then sent them to my lord mayor, two of them for suspicion of robbing a man of a gun and a pair of stockings in the highway, another for cutting cloth out of some tenters. Two more were concerned in the last felony, but they ran away before they could be caught, and so committed one felony by deserting to escape the punishment of another. I caused a hue and cry to be sent after them.

5 February 1687. I committed two prisoners to the main guard, there to remain till the next day, that one was to ride the wooden horse, and the other to be tied neck and heels at the relief of the guard. The captain of the guard, one Lieutenant Fry, took upon him without any order from me to change my order, and sent them both to the marshal's. I sent for the captain, and inquiring of him by what authority he had done this, he justified himself, which put me into that heat that I presently confined him for thirty hours, and had represented that and some other misdemeanours by him formerly committed to the king and his colonel, had he not presently submitted himself, both by words and in writing, and obtained of all the officers of the garrison to come and to intercede for him, he being very sensible that had I complained it would probably have cost him his commission. . . .

7 February. That afternoon as I was going to visit the main guard, seeing a great crowd and disorder in the streets, I found it was occasioned by six soldiers, three of each regiment, who had quarrelled and fought, two of them being fresh killed upon the place, and a third desperately wounded. I took all the speedy care to get the last man dressed by a surgeon, and to pursue the murderers that had escaped. One of them we soon took. For the other two I doubled the guards, and caused search to be made for them that night, but ineffectually.

8 February. Being Shrove Tuesday, a day that the youth and apprentices of York do claim to themselves a more than usual liberty, having some years committed great disorders on that day, I continued the guards doubled. At night I had some notice that Doningfield, the person that wounded him that was not yet dead, was in such a house. I sent a file of musketeers to take him, but he being locked in a chamber denied to render himself, so that I was forced to send more men, and was going myself as I had news he was taken. I sent him to my lord mayor, who took his examination and committed him. He denied that he had wounded the party, or that he had a sword, but it was proved that he got his comrade's sword and made use of it in that fray.

11 February. As I was going for Thrybergh I had letters from the Secretary that I should receive orders (as it happened the next post) for Colonel Oglethorpe's battalion to march to Carlisle and other garrisons northwards, and my Lord Huntingdon's to Chester the week following, and my company only to remain at York. I presently called the officers, and gave such necessary orders herein as the shortness of time and the care of the soldiers' paying their quarters and parting well with the town required. Afterwards I went to my lord mayor to give him so timely notice that he might see right to be done to the town; and so, recommending it to the

officers that all things might be done at their departure that might conduce to the king's service and their own credits (of which I said I should give the king a suitable account), I pursued my journey. . . .

7 March. I removed with my family to York, the assizes having begun there upon the 5th, attended but by one judge, Serjeant Powell. The two soldiers that had been of the number which had killed the three of my Lord Huntingdon's company were tried; but no malice appearing the jury brought it in manslaughter, and they were burnt in the hand. The jury would not find it felony against the soldier that deserted, so he was acquitted. . . .

19 August. I had notice from my first lieutenant that my company was on their march towards York as far as Doncaster, all the men returning safe but three since the time they went from thence. One was discharged, another deserted, and the third, quarrelling upon the road with some reapers of corn, was cut into brains with a scythe or reaping-hook by one of them after he had killed one and wounded several of them, so that he died upon the place before the rest of the company overtook him. . . .

21 August. I went to meet Colonel Cornwall's regiment in their march to York at Doncaster, where I gave necessary orders against they came to York as to their deportment there, and wrote to my lord mayor to accommodate them with quarters and other conveniences in the meantime. . . .

30 August. Lieutenant-Colonel Purcell and the rest of the officers of Colonel Cornwall's regiment came to visit me, being sixteen in number.

31 August. I called a council of war, wherein I acquainted them with the customs and orders to be observed in that garrison, and what I expected as to their demeanour there both from soldiers and officers. I had fair assurances, but a few days after there happened a drunken quarrel between a gentleman of quality of the town and a captain of that regiment, which I had much ado to reconcile, blows having passed. But at last I did it effectually, and with much entreaty from all the officers did not complain of the captain to the king, fearing it might cost him his commission, he having killed a gentleman not long before in a like fray. . . .

4 September. I heard that some soldiers had exacted money from their landlords. I called a council of war, wherein I found the officers not inclining to punish them, pretending they had done it in other garrisons. I told them that they were not to teach us there the rules of other garrisons, but to learn those of this, which I knew to be grounded upon the king's orders, and with much ado a severe sentence did pass the council to be inflicted upon the offenders or some of them. . . . Some soldiers in my company committed a robbery, and three others mutinied upon the guard and broke the leg of the sergeant that commanded. I gave the king an account of it. This was after I left the town, for my first lieutenant was but a bad officer and infirm, my second was absent from the garrison. . . .

30 December. I had the king's order that the soldiers that mutinied of my company should be tried by a council of war so soon as Colonel Cornwall's regiment returned to York, which was ordered then to return from Hull to that garrison. The regiment returned to their quarters in York the 29th of January. I sent orders in writing to

Colonel Purcell, lieutenant-colonel of the regiment, that the guards should be the same and all other things in the same manner as when they left that garrison, which the lieutenant-colonel wrote back word should be complied with in every particular.

A court-martial sitting at York upon the three mutineers according to his Majesty's order, the sentence was so very severe that I acquainted the king with it, not presuming to mitigate it without his leave, the court having sat by his own appointment. But the king would not have it moderated in the least. . . .

1 March 1688. I had notice by the deputy recorder of York by an express that the lieutenant-colonel commanding in my absence had dealt very severely and illegally with the citizens, and that the occasion of it was a little tumult raised on Shrove Tuesday in this manner. That day being one of great liberty for boys and apprentices to play and throw at cocks, some of them playing near a house in the Minster yard disturbed the company in it. The master comes out, strikes one of the boys, and knocks down another. They, getting some of their companions together, throw stones at the man, and accidentally break the window of a popish chapel that was in his house. He, being a Roman Catholic, presently makes his religion the cause of the quarrel, sends to the lieutenant-colonel for two files of musketeers, who presently sends them, being of his own persuasion and very ready to espouse the dispute upon that foot. At the coming of the soldiers the boys disperse, some of them are taken, and some citizens (being by as spectators but not concerned in the matter) to the number of fifteen. The soldiers carry them to the main guard, tie them neck and heels, and make them ride the wooden horse, not carrying them at all to the lord mayor (which ought to have been done, being citizens) to be punished according to law. And an ensign, one Ord, struck a citizen in the presence of my lord mayor. The lieutenant-colonel's account was little different as to the fact, but altered as to the occasion, for he said that some priests had informed him the night before that they heard the rabble intended to pull down that house and the chapel, which made him act more severely; but I truly believe the uproar was merely accidental. I gave the king a particular account of the thing as it appeared most likely from the recorder; the lieutenant-colonel gave another himself. . . .

7 March. I received notice from Colonel Oglethorpe that this unruly regiment of Colonel Cornwall's would be sent to Berwick, and five companies of his regiment would come to relieve them at York very speedily. I call it unruly because I had great complaints of their disorders. This piece of a letter was sent me by a friend: We have had sad work with the soldiers; they are so insolent that they neither spare age nor sex, insomuch that a man cannot be safe in his own house, and if abroad after nine o'clock he cannot without a fee avoid having the guard room for his lodging, with several other insupportable injuries. . . .

9 March. The Secretary of War wrote to me thus, that the king utterly disapproved of the military punishment inflicted upon the citizens, for when they committed faults they ought to be turned over to the civil magistrate to be dealt with according to law; and as for the officer that struck the citizen, the king commanded me to inquire more particularly into the fact, and to return his name that he might have his due punishment. So little was the king pleased with this insolent proceeding. . . .

17 April. Five companies that were come of my Lord Montgomery's regiment into York the 4th instant marched out, and the eight remaining companies of Colonel Oglethorpe's marched in, so that the whole garrison then consisted of that entire regiment, being thirteen companies. The officers were all civil gentlemen, but the soldiers had committed some disorders. One had wounded his landlord, another had beaten a citizen and caused a great disturbance in the street, another had been very insolent to his officer. I called a council of war, where their respective punishments were appointed. . . .

311. Mutiny Act, 1689

(Statutes of the Realm, VI, pp. 55–56)

AN ACT FOR PUNISHING OFFICERS OR SOLDIERS WHO SHALL MUTINY
OR DESERT THEIR MAJESTIES' SERVICE
(1 Gul. & Mar., cap. 5)

Whereas the raising or keeping a standing army within this kingdom in time of peace, unless it be with consent of Parliament, is against law; and whereas it is judged necessary by their Majesties and this present Parliament that during this time of danger several of the forces which are now on foot should be continued and others raised for the safety of the kingdom, for the common defence of the Protestant religion and for the reducing of Ireland; and whereas no man may be forejudged of life or limb, or subjected to any kind of punishment by martial law, or in any other manner than by the judgment of his peers and according to the known and established laws of this realm; yet nevertheless it being requisite for retaining such forces as are or shall be raised during this exigence of affairs in their duty an exact discipline be observed, and that soldiers who shall mutiny or stir up sedition or shall desert their Majesties' service be brought to a more exemplary and speedy punishment than the usual forms of law will allow.

II. Be it therefore enacted . . . that from and after the twelfth day of April in the year of our Lord one thousand six hundred eighty-nine every person being in their Majesties' service in the army, and being mustered and in pay as an officer or soldier, who shall at any time before the tenth day of November in the year of our Lord one thousand six hundred eighty-nine excite, cause or join in any mutiny or sedition in the army, or shall desert their Majesties' service in the army, shall suffer death or such other punishment as by a court-martial shall be inflicted.

III. And it is hereby further enacted and declared, that their Majesties, or the general of their army for the time being, may by virtue of this Act have full power and authority to grant commissions to any lieutenants-general or other officers not under the degree of colonels from time to time to call and assemble court-martials for punishing such offences as aforesaid.

IV. And it is hereby further enacted and declared, that no court-martial which shall have power to inflict any punishment by virtue of this Act for the offences aforesaid shall consist of fewer than thirteen, whereof none to be under the degree of captains.

V. Provided always, that no field officer be tried by other than field officers, and that such court-martial shall have power and authority to administer an oath to any witness in order to the examination or trial of the offences aforesaid.

VI. Provided always, that nothing in this Act contained shall extend or be construed to exempt any officer or soldier whatsoever from the ordinary process of law.

VII. Provided always, that this Act or anything therein contained shall not extend or be any ways construed to extend to or concern any the militia forces of this kingdom.

VIII. Provided also, that this Act shall continue and be in force until the said tenth day of November in the said year of our Lord one thousand six hundred eighty-nine, and no longer.

IX. Provided always and be it enacted, that in all trials of offenders by courts-martial to be held by virtue of this Act, where the offence may be punished by death, every officer present at such trial, before any proceedings be had thereupon, shall take an oath upon the Evangelists before the court (and the Judge Advocate or his deputy shall, and are hereby respectively authorized to, administer the same) in these words, that is to say:

You shall well and truly try and determine according to your evidence the matter now before you between our sovereign lord and lady the king and queen's Majesties and the prisoner to be tried. So help you God.

X. And no sentence of death shall be given against any offender in such case by any court-martial unless nine of thirteen officers present shall concur therein. And if there be a greater number of officers present then the judgment shall pass by the concurrence of the greater part of them so sworn and not otherwise; and no proceedings, trial or sentence of death shall be had or given against any offender but between the hours of eight in the morning and one in the afternoon.

312. Disbanding Act, 1699

(*Statutes of the Realm*, VII, pp. 452–453)

AN ACT

FOR GRANTING AN AID TO HIS MAJESTY FOR DISBANDING THE ARMY AND OTHER NECESSARY OCCASIONS

(*10 Gul. III, cap. 1*)

Be it enacted . . . that the army, and all the respective regiments, troops, companies, officers and soldiers of the said army, within the kingdom of England, dominion of Wales and town of Berwick-upon-Tweed, shall, on or before the six and twentieth day of March one thousand six hundred ninety-nine, be disbanded, except such regiments, troops and companies, consisting only of his Majesty's natural-born subjects, not exceeding seven thousand persons, commission and non-commission officers included, as before the first day of March one thousand six hundred ninety-eight[1] shall

[1] 1698/9.

be particularly expressed in and by his Majesty's royal proclamation under the great seal of England. . . .

IV. And be it further enacted, that . . . the army, regiments, troops, companies, officers and soldiers within the . . . kingdom of Ireland shall on or before the first day of May one thousand six hundred ninety-nine be disbanded, except such regiments, troops and companies, consisting only of his Majesty's natural-born subjects, not exceeding twelve thousand persons, commission and non-commission officers included, as before the tenth day of April one thousand six hundred ninety-nine shall be particularly expressed in and by his Majesty's royal proclamation under the great seal of Ireland. . . .

VI. And be it further enacted and declared, that all such forces within the said kingdom of Ireland not hereby directed to be disbanded, which shall be maintained within that kingdom, shall be maintained at the sole charge of the said kingdom of Ireland.

VII. And be it further enacted, that all and every commission officer and officers who shall exercise any power or authority over the soldiers in their respective regiments, troops or companies after such officer or officers shall be disbanded . . . shall incur and sustain the pains, penalties and forfeitures limited, ordained and provided in and by the Statute of Provision and Premunire made in the sixteenth year of King Richard the Second; . . . and none of the said soldiers or non-commissioned officers disbanded as aforesaid shall after the space of two days after such disbanding continue together above ten in a company. . . .

313. Proclamation imposing compulsory service, 1708
(*London Gazette*, 23–26 February 1707/8)

A PROCLAMATION
FOR THE BETTER RECRUITING HER MAJESTY'S
LAND-FORCES AND THE MARINES

ANNE R.

Whereas by an Act made in this present session of our Parliament of Great Britain for the better recruiting our land-forces and marines it is amongst other things enacted, that it shall and may be lawful for any two or more justices of the peace of every county, riding, liberty and place within our kingdom of Great Britain, who have no military offices or employments other than in the militia, and the mayor or other head-officer or officers of every city or town corporate within this our realm, together with one or more justice or justices of the peace of the same city or town corporate respectively where such justices are, or in default of such justice or justices then with one or more justice or justices of the peace of the county wherein such city or town is, who shall be so qualified as aforesaid, from time to time between the last day of this instant February and the first day of March which shall be in the year of our Lord one thousand seven hundred and eight,[1] within their several and respective limits and

---
[1] 1708/9.

jurisdictions, to raise and levy such able-bodied men as have not any lawful calling or employment, or do not follow or exercise the same, or do not make use of any lawful means for their support and maintenance, and have not any vote in the election of any member or members to serve in Parliament for any borough or other place within our kingdom of Great Britain, to serve as soldiers for the purposes aforesaid; and shall require and command all and every the high constables, head-boroughs and tithing-men within their respective jurisdictions to be aiding and assisting to them in putting the said Act in execution, and for that purpose shall issue out their warrants . . . requiring and commanding such . . . parish officers to make . . . search . . . for all such persons as they can find who are within the description of the said Act, and to bring such persons before such justices and magistrates as aforesaid; . . . and if the said justices and magistrates so authorized to put the said Act in execution shall find the persons so brought before them to be such persons as are intended by the said Act to be entertained as soldiers in our service, that they cause such persons to be delivered over by the said . . . parish officers unto such officer or officers belonging to our forces as shall be appointed to raise and receive such men; . . . and the respective officers who shall receive such new-raised men are by the said Act required to pay to every person so raised twenty shillings, and also to the constable or other officer employed in the raising of them the like sum of twenty shillings a man, and to cause the fourteenth and twenty-third articles of war against mutiny and desertion to be read to such new-raised men in the presence of such justices or magistrates. . . .

And for encouragement of fit and able persons voluntarily to enter themselves in our service, every officer who shall be appointed to raise such recruits is by the said Act required forthwith to pay to every person who shall so voluntarily enter himself in our service at any time before the first day of May one thousand seven hundred and eight the sum of four pounds, and at any time between the last day of April one thousand seven hundred and eight and the first day of March following the sum of forty shillings. . . .

Now for the better expediting of this so necessary a service, and that all justices and magistrates, and all high constables, petty constables, tithing-men and other parish officers and persons whom it may concern may be the more speedily informed of their several duties in relation to the premises, of the encouragements given by the said Act and the penalties thereby imposed for the neglect thereof, we have thought fit, by and with the advice of our Privy Council, to issue this our royal proclamation; and we do hereby strictly require and charge all our justices of the peace, mayors and other officers who shall be authorized to put the said Act in execution, that they use their utmost diligence in the due execution of the said Act. . . .

And that there may not be wanting persons authorized to receive such recruits as shall from time to time be raised in any part of our said kingdom, we have given directions that a competent number of officers of our forces, or other trusty persons, shall be appointed to be ready at all times to attend the meetings of such justices and other magistrates as shall in any place assemble to put the before-mentioned Act in execution. And we do hereby strictly charge and command all our loving subjects that they do in no wise hinder and obstruct any person or persons in the due execution of the said Act, as they will answer the contrary at their perils of being prosecuted for such offences according to the utmost severity of law.

  Given at our court at Kensington,
  this twenty-third day of February,
  in the sixth year of our reign.

(b) ENGAGEMENTS ON LAND

314. Colonel James Apsley's relation of the battle of Amegial, 1663
(Historical Manuscripts Commission, *Heathcote MSS.*, pp. 103–105)

Next morning, being the eighth of this present June,[1] we understood by divers parties that the baggage of the enemy was marched towards Estremoz, and that the army of Don John was drawn up in *batalia* upon the plain to cover and hide that march. Upon that advice we made very great haste to possess ourselves of the mountains which were a little league from Estremoz. The enemy did the same with his foot, and planted them cannon shot from us on the top of two mountains, of which one of them was possessed by the right wing, the other by the left wing of their foot. At the bottom of the mountains the horse were drawn up upon the plain in the way they were to march in two lines. By this order of *batalia* their baggage lay under a good covert, and they had leisure enough to draw off by the sides of the two hills. About evening, his excellency the earl of Schomberg having observed the left wing of the enemy's army to be without horse, the foot keeping the tops of the mountains which they possessed on that side, after many irresolutions of the Portuguese generals his excellency the earl of Schomberg persuaded them at last to attack the enemy's horse which were in the plains with all our horse, strengthened with a good quantity of foot, and that our foot, who were in two lines as the enemy's were, should attack the enemy's foot on the tops of the two mountains and in the valley between them.

  In this manner we gave the onset an hour before sunset, and the English foot with much pains climbed up the highest mountain, which was possessed by the right wing of the enemy's army, and guarded with five pieces of cannon. The English marched on, shouting as if victorious, but discharged no shot till they came within push of pike of the enemy; and then they poured in their shot so thick upon them that made them quit their ground and fly towards the left wing, leaving their cannon behind them, which were afterwards turned upon them, much to their prejudice. Notwithstanding the rich baggages and coaches and wealthy plunder which were on the top of the hill–the English seeing the field not cleared–there was not one man of them stirred out of his rank, but kept close serried together to prevent any second onset, which immediately followed, for they were assaulted front, flank and rear by divers of the enemy's troops of horse, but having their fire ready at all hands they quickly quitted themselves of those troops. This was performed rather with an absolute resolution than any conduct or order, for after soldiers had serried themselves close no officer's voice could be heard, but each soldier would give the word of command either as they saw or feared their enemy; but all this while a man could not but joy to see so

---

[1] 29 May/8 June 1663.

vivid a courage and so firm a resolution as was in every common soldier to die by one another. The Portuguese generals, having not been accustomed to see so close an approach before firing, did give the English for lost, and did believe they all had intended to have joined with the Castilians; but when they saw their thick firing, and the good success the English obtained thereupon, they called us comrades and good Christians.

Our horse in the plains had not so good success, for the English horse were too forward in charging, and were not at all seconded by the reserves of Portuguese, which was the loss of Colonel Dongan, Captain Paulinge, and many other gallant Englishmen. Our cavalry, though not seconded by their reserves, rallied and charged three or four times, and at their last repulse they were able to charge no more. The two English regiments of foot joined together and marched down in the valley for the relief of their horse, where they were met by his excellency the earl of Schomberg, drawn up by a wood side. His excellency caused them to face to the left, and marched them through the wood. The enemy's horse, which remained firm, had no sooner espied the foot but they cried, "There comes the English redcoats, who give no quarter," and so they betook themselves to flight just at the entrance of the night, and left us absolute masters of the field.

That night we kept guard within the wood; but the next morning we perceived the field was clear, and that it was an absolute victory on our party. The enemy had an inestimable damage, having lost his cannon and train of artillery, and generally all the baggage of his army. There were fourteen coaches taken of several princes, dukes and earls. It is such a loss that the Castilians cannot repair in a short time. The foot were all entirely routed, a good part of them being fallen into the hands of the peasants, who used no kindness towards them. Most part of their colonels and chief officers were either killed or taken, as also the general officers of the horse. But that which is most remarkable is that after so great a victory the enemy were too many for us.

We lost out of the two English regiments not above forty in each regiment, and no officers killed but Captain Atkinson and Captain Goudinge, both of Colonel Apsley's regiment; and we had not above forty or fifty in both regiments who were wounded. The loss of the horse was greater, for besides the loss of Colonel Dongan and Captain Paulinge, who died in the field, and Cornet Meakinge and Cornet Wharton, who were mortally wounded, they had above an hundred killed and wounded in those five troops.

315. Anonymous account of the battle of Steinkirk, 1692
(London Gazette, 28 July–1 August 1692)

> From his Majesty's camp at Lambeque,
> 25 July, O.S. [1692]

On Friday last we passed the river Senne, and encamped in this place. The same day the French army decamped from Soignies, and marched to Enghien, six English miles from us. On Saturday the Hanover troops, with the regiments of Galway and Langston, joined our army. His Majesty, who had so long sought an opportunity to attack the enemy, resolved to do it now, upon the information of some persons who were thought to understand the nature of the ground. Accordingly the army marched yesterday morning very early, the heavy baggage being ordered to repass the Senne at Hal. There were several defiles to pass, and the ways to be made, which took us up some hours in our march. The enemy were encamped on a rising ground, with their left towards Enghien and a wood lying before them encompassed with a thick hedge, so that there was no coming to them but by the sides of that wood; and the way lay through hedges and ditches which the French had possessed themselves of. Whilst the army was advancing there was firing on both sides with cannon, which lasted about three hours.

Between one and two in the afternoon the fight began on our left wing with ten battalions of foot, whereof four were English, the rest Dutch and Danes, commanded by the duke of Würtemberg, who fell upon the enemy with so much vigour that they beat them from hedge to hedge, and drove them beyond one of their batteries of seven pieces of cannon, which we were possessed of above half an hour. But the enemy coming down upon our men in greater numbers, and the foot that was to have supported them not being able to advance so fast by reason of the difficulties of the ways through which they were to pass, we could not maintain that post. The fight lasted with great heat for four hours, and considerable numbers were killed on both sides, not less of the French than of ours, we having likewise taken some of their officers prisoners and killed several others of note. But there appearing so many difficulties, or rather an impossibility as their camp was situated to get to the flank of the enemy as was designed and so to come to a general engagement, and they being reinforced by Monsieur Boufflers' troops that joined them the same day, it was thought advisable to desist from the enterprise, and about 6 o'clock orders were given for our army to return to their camp, which was done in great order and without any loss. And though the French made a show of falling on our rear yet they never attempted it. We left behind us two little field pieces; and two wagons with powder breaking by the way our men set fire to them.

There cannot yet be any certain list made of such as are killed or wounded. The Lord Mountjoy, Lieutenant-General Mackay, Sir Robert Douglas and Lieutenant-Colonel Hawley of Lord Fitzhardinge's dragoons are killed, and several other officers of note are missing; but whether they are killed or taken is not yet known. Our whole loss by the best computation docs not exceed 2,000 men killed and 1,000 wounded. The horse was not engaged, though they suffered a little by the enemies' cannon and small shot, as they were ordered to sustain and bring off the foot that attacked the enemy. The bravery of our men was extraordinary, and admired by all, ten battalions of ours having engaged above thirty of the French at one time, and Sir Robert Douglas at the head of one battalion of his own regiment having driven four battalions of the enemy from their cannon.

The part the king had in all the danger has been no less than is usual to his Majesty on the like occasions, having very much exposed himself both in the action and in the retreat, and more especially to the cannon, which destroyed many of our men very near his Majesty's person. The difficulties of coming at the enemy were the greatest

our men had to struggle with, and the cause we had not the success we might otherwise have expected, for nothing else could withstand their courage, seeing we beat
them from some of their most advantageous posts with so unequal a number; which
the French themselves seem sensible of by placing, as they do, their greatest security
in the fastnesses of their camps.

316. Letter, written on the battle-field of Blenheim, from the duke to the duchess of Marlborough, 1704

(W. Coxe, *Memoirs of the Duke of Marlborough*, I, p. 306)

August 13,[1] 1704

I have not time to say more but to beg you will give my duty to the queen, and let
her know her army has had a glorious victory. M. Tallard and two other generals
are in my coach, and I am following the rest. The bearer, my aide-de-camp Colonel
Parke, will give her an account of what has passed. I shall do it in a day or two by
another more at large.

MARLBOROUGH

317. Letter from the earl of Orkney describing the battle of Ramillies, 1706

(*English Historical Review*, XIX, pp. 315–316)

Camp at Beauvechain, 24th May 1706, 7 o'clock

You will be extremely glad to hear we have fought a very great battle yesterday[2]
and beat the French, and I in very good health, but am hardly able to hold up my
head, I am so weary and faint, for it is forty-eight hours I have not eaten nor drunk,
but once or twice a glass of wine and bit of bread. I really cannot tell you any
particulars yet of this battle, nor well what loss we have, nor what they have.

We could hardly fail of meeting, since we marched with a firm resolution to
attack them, and I find they did the same out of their line to attack us. However, they
seeing us coming up to them, they took up a very good post at the head of the Geete,
and possessed themselves of several villages on their front, and a marshy ground with
a little brook before them,[3] so that when we came to attack it was impossible for us
to extend our line, so were drawn up in several lines, one behind another, and indeed
even in confusion enough, which I own gave me at first a very ill prospect of things.
But since it was so we made our effort at a village in the centre, which they call
Ramillies; and that post was attacked very furiously by chiefly stranger troops, except
Churchill's and Mordaunt's regiments, who have suffered greatly. This post was at
last forced and taken, and our army pierced into others by that village, where our
horse and theirs had some sharp activity. My Lord Marlborough was rid over, but
got other squadrons, which he led up again. Major Bringfield, holding his stirrup to
give him another horse, was shot with a cannon bullet which went through my lord's
legs. In truth there was no scarcity of them.

Where I was with most of the English foot there was a morass and brook before
us, which they said was impossible to pass over; but however we tried, and after some
difficulty got over with ten or twelve battalions. And Mr. Lumley brought over some

[1] 2/13 August.   [2] 12/23 May.   [3] The Little Geete.

squadrons of horse with very great difficulty; and I endeavoured to possess myself of a village,[1] which the French brought down a good part of their line to take possession of; and they were on one side of the village and I on the other, but they always retired as we advanced. As I was going to take possession I had ten aides-de-camp to me to come off, for the horse could not sustain me. We had a great deal of fire at this, both musketry and cannon; and indeed I think I never had more shot about my ears. And I confess it vexed me to retire. However we did it very well and in good order; and whenever the French pressed upon us, with the battalion of guards and my own I was always able to make them stand and retire. Cadogan came and told me it was impossible I could be sustained by the horse if we went on then, and since my lord could not attack everywhere he would make the grand attack in the centre, and try to pierce there, which, I bless God, succeeded.

I do not know myself what prisoners we have. I am told several major-generals and others of less note. Lord John Hay's dragoons and others got in upon the Regiment du Roi, which they beat entirely. There is at least seven or eight hundred of them prisoners, and everywhere you see colours and standards, and I hear there is at least forty pieces of cannon and a great deal of their baggage; for whenever they saw that village forced they immediately retired with such expedition that one could hardly think it possible. We pursued them till dark night, but their horse it was impossible to get at. Their foot Mr. Lumley with several English squadrons came nigh, but without foot it was impossible to attack them. He sent to me that, if I could come up with the foot, he did not doubt but we would take eight or nine battalions of them that were in a body together. I marched, I am sure, as fast as it was possible for men to march, and ordered them to lose no time, and that I would ride up to Mr. Lumley myself. I own it vexed me to see a great body of them going off, and not many horse with them; but for my heart I could not get up our foot in time, and they dispersed and got into strong ground where it was impossible to follow them.

We are just now met with the left of the army, for all night we knew nothing of one another, and Mr. Lumley and I had resolved to march straight to the Dyle to their lines. But here we are endeavouring to make a camp and form in some order, for we look like a beaten army. I really fancy we shall march to-morrow to the Dyle to see if it be possible to force their lines now in the consternation they are in. That is the place certainly they will make head again, for their lines are strong. I am sure whenever we can get at them with any kind of reason these troops will never stand us. They were 74 battalions, 128 squadrons, of the best troops in France, with orders to attack us; we 73 battalions, 123 squadrons. So there was a pretty near equality if there had been any in the ground. We had two young gentlemen prisoners with us all night, both men of great quality, a nephew of Marshal Luxemburg and Marshal Tallard's only son. . . .

The battle began yesterday at twelve, and ended chiefly about five at night, when we pierced and got the better. Though this be of great consequence it is nothing like Höchstädt, because of the numbers taken in the village. Maybe they have lost five or six thousand men, but truly it is hard to guess.

[1] Autre Eglise.

318. Anonymous account of the battle of Almanza, 1707

(N. Tindal's Continuation of Rapin's *History of England*, ed. 1743–1747, IV, pp. 8–9)

News being brought that the enemy were near the town of Almanza, a great council of war was held, in which it was unanimously agreed to go the next day and give them battle. Accordingly, about three in the morning we began to march in four columns, till we had passed the hilly country, which was computed at six long miles; and then, coming into better ground, the army formed, and marched the other three miles in order of battle. About twelve we saw from some rising grounds the town of Almanza, and soon after the enemy drawn up and ready to receive us.

They began to fire very briskly with two or three batteries, and we returned their fire with one. Lord Galway, having seen the disposition of the right and of the centre, came to the left, which he commanded, as General Erle did the centre and the Marquis das Minas the right. He ordered the enemy's advanced guard to be attacked by a party of a hundred dragoons, who put them to flight. Being pursued beyond their second line, they left the army and took to the highroad with such haste upon a full gallop that they were soon got some miles from the field of battle; and meeting with the duke of Orleans, who was coming to take the command upon him, told him their army was beaten and all was lost. This put the duke upon going back till night, when he received other news.

Lord Galway viewed the right of the enemy, whose line was extended far beyond ours, having many more squadrons than we had in our left, and sent for Count Attalaia, who commanded in the second line, to bring up all the horse (which were eleven squadrons of Portuguese) and draw them up so on our left, as far as the centre, that they might prevent the enemy's flanking us. Then he commanded Carpenter's and Essex's squadrons to go and attack the battery over against our left, which did very much gall our horse.

This was instantly executed very gallantly, but with ill success. Here the battle began about two. The battery was placed upon a steep rising ground which covered everything behind it, so that when the two squadrons came up with it the guns were in a moment drawn away by the mules that continued fastened to them, and eight or ten squadrons of their best horse fell upon our two with incredible fury, and cut them all to pieces. Then they and the rest of their horse attacked our English and Dutch squadrons, who maintained a very obstinate and bloody fight near two hours, but were at last overpowered by their far superior number, and so cut off that not above four or five officers and ten or twelve private men were left in each squadron. The squadron of Guiscard's dragoons stood their ground the longest of any, and no wonder, for they had thirty-four officers in their front rank, most of them veterans who had served in all King William's wars.

They had charged three times, but when they saw their friends were gone the standard was ordered to be secured; after which they attacked three squadrons that faced them, having the Lords Galway and Tyrawley and Brigadier Carpenter at their head, of whom the commander begged, as they came separately to him, that they would be pleased to take the command of the squadron, which they all declined. So the brave old Colonel la Fabreque (whose name ought to be mentioned with honour for his courage and conduct), having these three great volunteers with him, fell upon the three squadrons with so much intrepidity that he routed them, and retired in good order from the field of battle with the three generals. Lord Galway received in this last bold attack a cut over his eye (having before lost his right hand, with which he might have parried the blow), and with such a long sword as wounded his aide-de-camp in the forehead at the same time.

The centre, that is the English and Dutch, were engaged all this while, and drove the enemy with great success before them. They had pushed the first line upon the second, so that, though our left was routed, we still had some hopes, in case the Portuguese horse in the right behaved well, to get the day. But our hopes were soon defeated, for as soon as the enemy marched up to them, and some battalions gave them a fire, they all galloped away, and the foot ran into some neighbouring woods upon our right, in which flight many of them fell, though none were killed in charging. The duke of Berwick, having nothing to fear from our right and left, ordered all his horse to come and sustain his foot, who had been very severely beaten by ours during three or four hours. The generals, to prevent their being surrounded, ordered all the battalions to form themselves into a hollow square, which so well answered the design that the enemy could gain no advantage of them, and by that means they retired from the field of battle with little or no loss, though still pursued till night parted them.

And if they could have continued their retreat a few miles farther the enemy would have had no great reason to boast of a victory, nor would the battle of Almanza have been so much talked of (to say no worse) as it has been in this nation. But the loss of twenty-three battalions, English and Dutch, was too great to be easily repaired at so great a distance. How these brave men, after having fought so gallantly for so many hours and made so glorious a retreat, could at last come to the resolution of surrendering to an enemy that was some miles from them and reckoned them quite out of his reach, is not so easy to be accounted for, unless their excuse be admitted, which was that the soldiers, after marching nine hours without any refreshment and fighting about six, could march no farther. They had spent all their ammunition, and had not so much as bread and water to refresh themselves with. They were all strangers to the country, and did not know of any place to retire to. Besides all this, they thought themselves in danger of being pursued and attacked the next morning by the enemy's whole army, against which they could not pretend to defend themselves, being abandoned by all the horse.

Upon these considerations, after a long consultation in which were very warm debates, they came to the resolution of surrendering themselves, as the French infantry had done at Blenheim, and of sending to the duke of Berwick to desire honourable terms, which were gladly and readily granted. . . . The duke of Berwick is said to have been astonished, and could hardly believe the officer who brought him this welcome message, which did complete his victory; for till then it might have been called a drawn battle, the number of the slain being reckoned very equal, our baggage safe, and only a Portuguese train of twenty field-pieces lost. . . . Two officers of dragoons, that were taken prisoners by the fall of their horses, assured the author of this account that when they were carried towards the town of Almanza they found it in our hands, and above a thousand prisoners in it, the enemy's foot being pushed far beyond it by ours. Almanza was in the centre of the field of battle, and the enemy's second line was on both sides of the town.

319. Letter from Francis Hare to George Naylor on the battle of Oudenarde, 1708

(Historical Manuscripts Commission, *Fourteenth Report*, IX, pp. 218–219)

Oudenarde, 12 July[1] 1708

This brings you news I did not dare to hope for when I wrote last, of a complete victory over the French. Upon our passing the Dendre at Lessines they drew off their troops that had invested this place and passed the Schelde yesterday morning at Gavre, which they continued to do until four in the afternoon, with intention to retire out of our way. But his grace has been too hard for them. We marched yesterday morning from Lessines to pass the Schelde at this place, and before the army Cadogan was sent with a strong detachment to make bridge and take post. Our army could not all pass before night, but with those that were over his grace resolved to attack the enemy as soon as he could, which he began to do about three in the afternoon; and though the ground was impracticable for anything but foot, and we had scarce a third part over, we attacked with that success that we continually gained upon them till night. They were posted in such difficult ground that they made a better defence than they used to do, to which it is to be presumed the presence of their princes likewise contributed something, and the advantage they had in numbers and situation cost us a good many men. But still we beat them from place to place until we could see no longer.

My Lord Marlborough and Prince Eugene continued all night on horseback, and as soon as it was day attacked again such of them as were not gone off in the night; and in a little time their whole army, or rather the remains of it, were entirely dispersed. Besides a great slaughter of them, we have made a prodigious number of prisoners. They have been coming by droves into this town for many hours, and among them are several officers of note. I do not hear we have lost any. I believe this day has entirely ruined the French foot. They are retiring towards Deynze and Ghent, and are pursued by a great body of horse, so that we expect a good account of them.

320. Colonel Blackader on the battle of Malplaquet, 1709

(*Life and Diary*, ed. A. Crichton, pp. 348–352)

29 August 1709. The enemy being now near we marched suddenly. In the afternoon they came in view, and our line of battle was formed and posted. They are in strong ground. They raised batteries and played upon us with their cannon. There was not a place in the whole line so much exposed as where our regiment and two or three more stood, and we had considerable loss. Many a cannon-ball came very near, but

[1] 1/12 July.

He gave His angels charge over me. *Thou art my shield and buckler*. This I trusted in, and repeated several times when I saw the cannon-balls coming straight towards me, as I thought; but the goodness of God let none of them touch me. This night was an unpleasant, uneasy night to our regiment, for they have wanted bread these five days and are faint. It was a cold, wet night, and we lay at our arms. I laid me down and slept sound, for God sustained me; and I am not afraid of ten thousands that set themselves against us round about.

30 August. Next morning we expected to have been saluted by break of day with their batteries, as last night; and we laid our account, if we stayed upon the same spot of ground, with having a third of our regiment killed and wounded, for the general would not allow us to draw back our men a little way behind a rising ground that covered us. But God in mercy prevented us, for the enemy had drawn off their cannon from that place and did not trouble us all the day. In the afternoon an extraordinary thing happened. The French officers and ours, as if it had been concerted between them, went out between the two camps, and conversed with one another, and called for their acquaintances, and talked together as friends, as if there had been a cessation of arms; but it was broken off by the generals on both sides. . . .

Early in the morning (the 31st) we attacked the enemy in their camp, a strong camp, and strongly intrenched by two days working. We fought, and by the mercy and goodness of God have obtained a great and glorious victory. The battle began about seven o'clock, and continued till near three in the afternoon. It was the most deliberate, solemn and well-ordered battle that ever I saw—a noble and fine disposition, and as nobly executed. Every man was at his post, and I never saw troops engage with more cheerfulness, boldness and resolution. . . . Providence ordered it so, that our regiment was no farther engaged than by being cannonaded, which was indeed the most severe that ever our regiment suffered, and by which we had considerable loss. But the soldiers endured it without shrinking, very patiently, and with great courage. . . . Our regiment, with some others, were honoured in particular to do some very good service, by marching up and manning a retrenchment which the enemy had left. And there we sustained our own horse, which were pushed by the French horse, and might have been of dangerous consequence had not the foot sustained them. . . . The French foot did not behave themselves well. They soon quitted their retrenchments; but the horse stood more stiffly to it. I did not expect to see a cowed army fight so well. I believe the loss may be about equal on both sides. It was as bloody a battle as has been fought either this war or the last. . . .

1 September. This morning I went to view the field of battle, to get a preaching from the dead, which might have been very edifying, for in all my life I have not seen the dead bodies lie so thick as they were in some places about the retrenchments, particularly at the battery where the Dutch Guards attacked. For a good way I could not go among them, lest my horse should tread on the carcasses that were lying, as it were, heaped on one another. I was also surprised to see how strong they had made their camp. They had a breast-work before them, round about like the rampart of a town, to fire over. The Dutch have suffered most in this battle of any. Their infantry is quite shattered, so that it is a dear victory. The potsherds of the earth are dashed

together, and God makes the nations a scourge to each other to work His holy ends by sweeping sinners off the face of the earth. It is a wonder to me the British escape so cheap, who are the most heaven-daring sinners in this army. But God's judgments are a great depth. He has many arrows in His quiver, and is not tied to our times and ways. We marched back at night to our camp which we left on the 29th.

321. Letter from General Stanhope to Robert Walpole on the battle of Almenara, 1710

(T. Somerville, *Great Britain during the Reign of Queen Anne*, pp. 636–638)

Camp at Almenara, 31 July 1710

DEAR SIR,

Three days after the date of my last to you, which went by Mr. Craggs, our succours joined us, upon which, a council being called, it was strenuously urged by the English, Dutch and Palatines to march immediately to Lerida, in order to force the enemies to a battle by cutting them off from that place; but the king and Marshal Starhemberg as strongly opposed, and showed themselves determined not to venture anything. Their pretence for not doing it was that the enemy's army might get to Lerida and pass the river before we could be up with them, which afterwards proved to be otherwise, since they did not get over the river by twelve hours so soon as was pretended they would.

Our next thought was to cross the Segre at Balaguer, and push to get over the Noguera; to which purpose I was detached with eight squadrons of dragoons and a thousand grenadiers, with which I marched at midnight, and took post at Alfarras, on the Aragon side of the Noguera, at six in the morning of the 27th.[1] The enemy had commanded ten squadrons of their horse, a thousand grenadiers and seven battalions of foot to prevent our taking post; but, notwithstanding they had much less way to march, the negligence of their commanding officer, the duke of Lerma, made them come late, for we did not discover them till nine in the morning, and when they did discover us, instead of attacking us, they possessed themselves of Almenara, a village on the Noguera about two miles from Alfarras, where we were.

About noon our left wing of horse passed the river, which I formed on a plain about cannon-shot from the river, between which plain and the river was a deep valley. By this time the enemy's horse came up apace and formed before me, about fifteen squadrons, which I was going to attack, when the marshal came up and prevented me, seeming still determined not to hazard anything. Both armies continued marching to get up, and about six all our infantry had passed the river and crossed the valley I mentioned, and got upon the high ground behind our horse. The marshal was pressed several times to attack the enemy's horse, which were before us, their foot marching at a great distance behind them in the valley where they could be of no use. About six the enemies, having got up all their horse, marched several squadrons down a little hill between us, upon which we all cried out shame, and I did earnestly press the king that we might have leave to dislodge them, which was at last complied with, but not till sunset.

[1] 16/27 July.

I therefore marched to them with the left wing, which consisted of twenty-two squadrons, which were formed in two lines, and a *corps de reserve* of four squadrons, the ground we were drawn up in not allowing us to make a greater front. So soon as we began to move, the enemies' squadrons which had come down the rising mentioned retired to their line. When we got up that rise with my first line, consisting but of ten squadrons, we found the enemy drawn up in two lines, the first of twenty-two squadrons and the second of twenty, with two battalions of foot betwixt their lines and a brigade of foot on their right. I was therefore forced, so soon as I came in presence, to make a halt to get up some squadrons from the second line, the ground where the enemies were being so much wider than that which I had marched from, besides that getting up the hill had put our line in some disorder. The enemies were so good as to give us the time we wanted.

We brought up six squadrons and put our line in good order, which consisted thus of sixteen in all, six English, four Dutch and six Palatines. Mr. Carpenter and I were on the left; Mr. Frankenburg, the Palatine general, and Major-General Pepper on the right. So soon as we were thus formed we attacked them, and by the grace of God broke their two lines, which consisted of forty-two squadrons. On the right were their *garde du corps* and other choice regiments, which did not do ill; but their left made no resistance.

I cannot sufficiently commend the behaviour of all the troops engaged, which never halted till we had driven their horse off the plain, beyond their infantry which was in the valley; and if we had had two hours daylight more you may be assured that not one foot soldier of their army could have escaped. The night gave them an opportunity to retire to Lerida, which they did in such confusion that they threw away their tents, lost good part of their baggage, some of their cannon, and have continued ever since encamped within and about the glacis of Lerida. The duke of Anjou and all his generals were in the action. . . .

This event will, I hope, sufficiently justify the earnestness with which I urged to come to a battle, since only sixteen squadrons of ours have defeated the enemy's cavalry, on which they principally relied. We can scarce expect to have such another occasion of ending the war as has been missed twice in three days, the first time in not marching to cut them off from Lerida, and the second time in not suffering us to attack some hours sooner, as we had pressed to do, and should have succeeded with less hazard, the enemies being much stronger when we attacked them than they had been when we first proposed it. . . .

322. Captain Cosby's account of the battles of Brihuega and Villa Viciosa, 1710

(A. Boyer, *History of the Life and Reign of Queen Anne*, pp. 466–467)

Before his Catholic Majesty left Ciempozuelos it was resolved in a council of war that the forces should retire into winter-quarters on the frontiers of Aragon, whereupon the several garrisons were drawn out of Toledo and the other posts, and the necessary dispositions made for the march of the whole army. The fatigues of a long campaign, the badness of the weather in a season so much advanced, and the want of tents and provisions made General Starhemberg judge it more convenient for the troops to march in several columns, with the commanders of each nation at the head of their own people; and accordingly they began their march on the 3rd of December, N.S. [1710], from Chinchon and Villarego.

By this disposition it was the post of the English, under the command of the Generals Stanhope, Carpenter, Wills, Pepper and Gore, to direct their course along the Tajuna; and in pursuance to the orders they had received they marched the 6th to Brihuega, a village of about one thousand houses, situated on the side of a mountain near the Tajuna. Here they halted the 7th, as did all the rest of the troops in their respective cantons. The same night General Stanhope, expecting Marshal Starhemberg's orders, commanded the forces to be in a readiness to march at an hour's warning.

The next day, about eleven o'clock, we discovered on the top of a hill that overlooks the town a body of two thousand horse and some foot; but having been followed in the two days' march before by several small parties of the enemy, whose design was to intercept such stragglers as fell into their hands, and not knowing anything of an army they had in those parts, where the whole country were our declared enemies and deprived us of all manner of intelligence, we conceived those troops that appeared on the hills consisted only of the small parties mentioned before, which were now joined in one body. However, General Stanhope gave orders to beat to arms, and immediately caused the troops to be assembled.

The enemy having marched their battalions and squadrons under the cover of the hills, and having possessed themselves of all the avenues to the town, they planted a battery of five pieces of cannon on the place where the two thousand horse were drawn up, and from thence played upon our people. When General Stanhope perceived himself invested in this manner he ordered Captain Cosby, his aide-de-camp, to go to Marshal Starhemberg, who then lay at Cifuentes, a town about four small leagues from Brihuega, and inform him of the circumstances he was in, particularly that he had but very little ammunition, which, however, he would manage in the best manner he could, and not fire a shot but where there was an absolute necessity; and that he would endeavour to maintain the place till his excellency had time to come to his relief or send him succours.

The aide-de-camp left the general at six in the evening, and being obliged to quit the direct road for fear of the enemy's parties he came not up to Marshal Starhemberg till eleven o'clock the same night. So soon as the marshal had notice of the danger the English were in he ordered all the troops that lay at Cifuentes and the adjacent villages to be assembled, and began his march the 9th a little before ten in the morning. Being arrived by five in the afternoon at a place half-way between Cifuentes and Brihuega he ordered nine pieces of cannon to be fired, as a signal to General Stanhope that he was marching to his relief, and there lay under arms all that night. Early the next morning, being the 10th, he disposed his army into a line, and so marched in good order till one o'clock, by which time he perceived the enemy forming themselves into order of battle, with their right wing at the village of Villa Viciosa and their left at a wood, on the plains of *los Campos de los Mancebos*; and having by this means all the advantage of the ground, the marshal found himself obliged to extend his left against some square walls, drawing the horse of his right in the rear of his first and second line, and covering his flank with four companies of grenadiers, two battalions and two squadrons.

In the meanwhile the cannon played on both sides, but ours with more success till about three o'clock, at which time the enemy attacked our right wing with much vigour, and made them give way at first; but they soon recovered and formed themselves into good order. At the same time our left was so closely pushed by a much superior number of horse that they were dispersed and pursued by the enemy, who meeting with our baggage, which lay in the rear of our second line, they left the pursuit and fell to plunder. Whilst this was doing, the second line of horse in their right had taken our left wing of foot in flank, front and rear, and after a very hot dispute had almost cut off eight battalions; after which, thinking themselves every way victorious, they also fell into pillage. This Marshal Starhemberg soon perceived, and made an advantage of it, for he instantly formed the foot of his right into hollow squares, and posting his cavalry on their flanks he charged their whole body of foot so vigorously that he entirely routed them, and our men pursued them for above half a league of ground together.

The success the enemy had in the beginning had so exasperated our soldiers that they did not trouble themselves to make many prisoners. However, some general officers were taken, who declared that they had made three breaches in the walls of Brihuega, and attacked General Stanhope five several times at each breach, and were as often repulsed with great slaughter; but renewing the attack at sunset they then obliged him and the troops under his command to surrender prisoners of war, which they had not done even then had they not spent all their ammunition.

Marshal Starhemberg pursued his victory till more than an hour after it was dark, and lay beyond the field of battle till eight the next morning, at which time he found the enemy had retired in great confusion by favour of the night, and that such of our baggage and artillery mules as their horse had not been able to destroy or carry off the peasants of the country had done for them; whereupon he was obliged to burn all the carriages, and nail up both our own cannon and those we had taken from the enemy; after which he pursued his march without any interruption towards the frontiers of Aragon. The enemy lost above six thousand men in the action; our loss does not amount to half the number. . . .

C. THE NAVY
(a) DISCIPLINE, PAY AND RECRUITMENT
323. Navy Discipline Act, 1661
(Statutes of the Realm, v, pp. 311–314)

AN ACT FOR THE ESTABLISHING ARTICLES AND ORDERS FOR THE
REGULATING AND BETTER GOVERNMENT OF HIS MAJESTY'S
NAVIES, SHIPS OF WAR AND FORCES BY SEA
(13 Car. II, stat. I, cap. 9)

For the regulating and better government of his Majesty's navies, ships of war and forces by sea, wherein under the good providence and protection of God the wealth, safety and strength of this kingdom is so much concerned, be it enacted . . . that all and every the articles and orders in this Act mentioned shall be duly and respectively put in execution, observed and obeyed in manner hereafter mentioned.

1. That all commanders, captains and other officers at sea shall cause the public worship of Almighty God according to the liturgy of the Church of England established by law to be solemnly, orderly and reverently performed in their respective ships, and that prayers and preachings by the respective chaplains in Holy Orders of the respective ships be performed diligently, and that the Lord's Day be observed according to law. . . .

3. If any officer, mariner, soldier or other person in the fleet shall give, hold or entertain intelligence to or with any king, prince or state being enemy to, or any persons in rebellion against, his Majesty, his heirs and successors, without direction or leave from the king's Majesty, the Lord High Admiral, vice-admiral or commander-in-chief of any squadron, every such person and persons so offending shall be punished with death. . . .

7. None in his Majesty's pay shall take out of any prize or ship or goods seized on for prize any money, plate, goods, lading or tackle before judgment thereof first passed in the Admiralty Court, . . . excepting that it shall be lawful for all captains, seamen, soldiers and others serving as aforesaid to take and to have to themselves as pillage without further or other account to be given for the same all such goods and merchandises (other than arms, ammunition, tackle, furniture or stores of such ship) as shall be found by them or any of them in any ship (they shall take in fight or prize) upon or above the gun deck of the said ship, and not otherwise. . . .

12. Every captain and all other officers, mariners and soldiers of every ship, frigate or vessel of war, that shall in time of any fight or engagement withdraw or keep back, or not come into the fight and engage and do his utmost to take, fire, kill and endamage the enemy, pirate or rebels, and assist and relieve all and every of his Majesty's ships, shall for such offence of cowardice or disaffection be tried, and suffer pains of death or other punishment, as the circumstances of the offence shall deserve and the court-martial shall judge fit.

13. The captains, officers and seamen of all ships appointed for convoy and guard

of merchants' ships or any other, shall diligently attend upon that charge without delay according to their instructions in that behalf; and whosoever shall be faulty therein, and shall not faithfully perform the same, and defend the ships and goods in their convoy without either diverting to other parts or occasions, or refusing or neglecting to fight in their defence if they be set upon or assailed, or running away cowardly and submitting those in their convoy to hazard and peril, or shall demand and exact any money or other reward from any merchant or master for conveying of any such ships or other vessels belonging to his Majesty's subjects, shall be condemned to make reparation of the damage to the merchants, owners and others as the Court of Admiralty shall adjudge, and also be punished criminally according to the quality of their offences, be it by pains of death or other punishment, according as shall be judged fit by the court-martial. . . .

19. No person in or belonging to the fleet shall utter any words of sedition or mutiny, nor make or endeavour to make any mutinous assemblies upon any pretence whatsoever, upon pain of death. . . .

21. None shall presume to quarrel with his superior officer, upon pain of severe punishment, nor to strike any such, upon pain of death or otherwise as a court-martial shall find the matter to deserve. . . .

34. And it is hereby further enacted, that the Lord High Admiral for the time being shall by virtue of this Act have full power and authority to grant commissions to inferior vice-admirals, or commander-in-chief of any squadron of ships, to call and assemble court-martials consisting of commanders and captains; and no court-martial where the pains of death shall be inflicted shall consist of less than five captains at least, the admiral's lieutenant to be as to this purpose esteemed as a captain; and in no case wherein sentence of death shall pass by virtue of the articles aforesaid or any of them (except in case of mutiny) there shall be execution of such sentence of death without the leave of the Lord High Admiral if the offence be committed within the Narrow Seas, but in case any of the offences aforesaid be committed in any voyage beyond the Narrow Seas, whereupon sentence of death shall be given in pursuance of the aforesaid articles or of any of them, then execution shall not be done but by order of the commander-in-chief of that fleet or squadron wherein sentence of death was passed. . . .

II. Provided also and be it further enacted, . . . that this Act or any thing or things therein contained shall not in any manner of wise extend to give unto the Lord Admiral of England for the time being, or to any his vice-admirals, judge or judges of the admiralty, his or their deputy or deputies, . . . any other power, right, jurisdiction, pre-eminence or authority than he or they or any of them lawfully have, hath or had or ought to have and enjoy before the making of this Act, other than for such of the offences specified in the several articles contained in this Act as hereafter shall be done upon the main sea, or in ships or vessels being and hovering in the main stream of great rivers only beneath the bridges of the same rivers nigh to the sea within the jurisdiction of the admiralty, and in none other places whatsoever, and committed only by such persons as shall be in actual service and pay in his Majesty's fleet or ships of war.

324. Petition for arrears of pay, 1667

(Calendar of State Papers Domestic, 1667, p. lx)

To the Right Honourable the Principal Officers and Commissioners of his Majesty's Navy,

The humble petition of the officers and seamen belonging to his Majesty's frigates the *Harp* and *Mary* yacht, on the coast of Ireland,

Humbly showeth,

That your poor petitioners having sent several petitions to your Honours, but receiving no answer, there being above fifty-two months' pay due to them, and having neither money nor credit nor wherewith to buy bread for their wives and children, who are now in a starving condition, being forced also to lie in the streets by reason their landlords will trust them no longer, and your petitioners going naked for want of clothes, which together are worse ten thousand times than to die by the hands of an enemy, for what can be more grievous than for men to see the starving of their wives and children,

Therefore the humble request of your poor petitioners is that your Honours will be pleased to take the miserable condition of themselves, their wives and children so into consideration as to order them their pay, that their families may not be altogether starved in the streets, and themselves go like heathens, having nothing to cover their nakedness.

And your poor petitioners shall ever pray, &c.

325. Proclamation summoning seamen to enlist, 1690

(London Gazette, 7–10 July 1690)

PROCLAMATION

REQUIRING ALL SEAMEN AND MARINERS TO RENDER THEMSELVES
TO THEIR MAJESTIES' SERVICE, 1690

MARIE R.

Whereas divers seamen and mariners have lately left their usual and ordinary places of abode, and have removed themselves into some private and obscure places, endeavouring thereby to avoid or escape from their Majesties' present service, their Majesties therefore, by the advice of their Privy Council, have upon the present extraordinary occasion thought fit to publish this their royal proclamation, and do hereby strictly charge and command all seamen and mariners remaining in any county of England or Wales, and not listed in their Majesties' service, that they forthwith render themselves unto the principal officers and commissioners of their Majesties' navy in London, or to the commissioners of the navy at Chatham, or to the commissioners of the navy at Portsmouth, or to Joseph Fownes, storekeeper and muster master for the navy at Harwich, or to John Addis, storekeeper and muster master for the navy at Plymouth, or to the bailiffs of Great Yarmouth, or to the mayor of Hull, or to the mayor of Newcastle, or to Robert Henley at Bristol, or to [Samuel] Atkinson at Hoylake and Liverpool, in order to their being received into pay and sent on board such of their Majesties' ships as shall be found most expedient for their Majesties' service. And if any of them shall hereafter be found out, or discovered to have neglected to obey this their Majesties' royal command, they shall be proceeded against with all severity.

And their Majesties do hereby require all mayors, bailiffs, sheriffs, justices of the peace, constables and other officers to whom it doth or may appertain, that they cause diligent search to be made within all and every of their precincts for the said seamen and mariners, and to seize and secure the persons of such of them as shall be there found, and also all loose and unknown persons whatsoever who may justly be suspected to be seamen or watermen, and to cause them to be sent to the principal officers and commissioners of their Majesties' navy in London, or to such other of the persons and places aforesaid to which they may most conveniently be sent, in order to their being employed in their Majesties' service. . . .

And their Majesties do hereby straitly charge and command, that no person or persons whatsoever do presume to conceal, or to further or favour the escape of, any seamen or mariners as aforesaid, upon pain that all and singular persons offending herein be forthwith committed to prison by the next justice of the peace or other magistrate, and with all severity prosecuted as persons conspiring against their Majesties and the safety of the kingdom. . . .

Given at our court at Whitehall,
the fifth day of July 1690,
in the second year of our reign.

326. Letter from Arthur Todd to John Roades illustrating the difficulties of pressmasters, 1694

(Historical Manuscripts Commission, *Various Collections*, VIII, pp. 75–76)

Hull, 13 May 1694

My trouble has increased mightily every day for want of places to secure my men, and my addresses to the magistrates here prevailed nothing; nor have I had any answer from above. And the people here consisting generally of seamen, neither I nor the pressmasters can be safe from flouts and curses; and not a house that I know of that would not receive a fugitive and shut the door on him, and wish they were all gone, and threatened in my hearing (the women) to bring a ladder to their chamber windows rather than they should not escape. I prevailed with the gaoler (the sheriff denying me) to take some of the seamen that I thought most dangerous a week ago, and, notwithstanding the strength of the place, from a turret higher than ours at Temple Newsam four men slipped away by a cord in a minute; but my great grief was that Brocklesbank, the king's pilot and my best seaman, was one of the number. If my spirits were not compounded with a little mirth I should be quite ruined.

Yesterday I took Mr. Wightman and went to the rest, which was nine, left behind, to inquire how this was done; and these nine, upon opening the door upon the top of a broad pair of stairs, forced one another forward upon us, and for a while we turned them with my cane and his stick. The main guard is next door, and the soldiers made a lane and encouraged the seamen to come down and break from us, and never a man would have turned them. I prayed any two musketeers to assist me, and I would give them a drink. They would not. So my wrath and Mr. Wightman's was kindled (for I should have been ashamed to let nine run away together), and we fell upon them with strokes, and drove them up by blows; but one stick in their hands would have beat us both down. And after we had struck them into the doors we sprung it to; and it was a half door with iron pricks, over which they threw at us all that was movable –a pail of water, pot lid, tubs–and our clothes wet fearfully. I could neither find mayor nor sheriff; and the governor chid his guard, and that was all.

Now a pressmaster dare scarce carry an impressed man through the streets. The men in hold threaten their lives, and call me such names as you never heard, and curse and damn all before them, and threatened if I gave not more allowance than the king's I should not see one of them next day. We capitulated after, and went among them with the gaoler, who was from home at our quarrel; and I promised if they would keep orderly and quietly, and attempt no escapes, I would give them 2d. per diem apiece to drink more than I gave the gaoler for them, and they promised fair; but I cannot trust them. I am forced to bear patiently all, and now several men begin to pity my condition. I am tormented every day, women crying, men complaining, all entreating, the mayor objecting I cannot impress here. I can neither eat nor drink nor sleep without complaints. One has children, another is a master, or the boat and lading in danger, or a protection will be produced. I am plagued of every side, and the worst was when I complained to the gaoler's wife that I feared remissness. She answers, Pray take them all away, I am weary of them. That cut my heart, for I might as well be desired to drive twenty foxes to market; for alas, I am constrained to bend, to beg and bow and pay; and yet no security. . . .

327. Proclamation regulating the distribution of prize and bounty money, 1708
(*London Gazette*, 27–31 May 1708)

A PROCLAMATION
APPOINTING THE DISTRIBUTION OF PRIZES TAKEN,
AND THE BOUNTY FOR TAKING SHIPS OF WAR AND PRIVATEERS
OF THE ENEMIES

ANNE R.

Whereas by an Act made and passed the last sessions of our last Parliament, in-tituled, *An Act for the better securing the trade of this kingdom by cruisers and convoys*,[1] it is enacted, for the better and more effectual encouragement of the sea-service, that from and after the six and twentieth day of March one thousand seven hundred and eight, if any ship or ships of war, privateer, merchant ship or other vessel shall be taken as prize by any of our ships of war, or by privateers, and adjudged as lawful prize in any of our courts of admiralty, the flag-officer or officers, commander or commanders, and other officers, seamen and others who shall be actually on board

[1] 6 Annae, cap. 65.

such ship or ships of war or privateers which shall so take such prize or prizes, shall after such condemnation have the sole interest and property in such prize or prizes so taken and adjudged, to their own use without further account to be given for the same, such prizes to be sold by such person or persons as shall be authorized and appointed so to do by the commander or commanders and other officers of such ship or ships as shall take such ship or ships, or the major part of them, under their hands and seals, and the whole produce thereof to be divided or distributed among the said officers, seamen and others according to their respective shares, in manner, form and proportion as by our most gracious proclamation, to be issued for that purpose, should be directed and appointed.

And whereas for the further encouragement of such officers, seamen and others who shall actually serve on board any such of our ships or privateers as shall take any ship or ships of war, privateer or privateers of the enemies, it is further enacted by the said Act that over and above the aforementioned encouragement there shall be paid by the treasurer of our navy . . . unto the officers, seamen and others that shall have been actually on board such of our ship or ships of war, or privateer or privateers, in such action where such ship of war or privateer shall have been so taken from the enemy, five pounds for every man who was living on board such ship or ships so taken at the beginning of the engagement between them. . . .

We have taken the premises into consideration, and do, pursuant to the said Acts of Parliament, with advice of our Privy Council, by this our royal proclamation order, direct and appoint that the net proceed of all prizes and bounty money for prisoners taken be divided into eight equal parts, whereof the captain or captains of any of our ships of war who shall be actually on board at the taking of any prize shall be allowed three eighth parts (but in case any prize shall be taken by any ship or ships of war under the command of a flag or flags the flag-officer or officers, being actually on board or directing and assisting in the capture, to have one eighth part of the said three eighths); to the marine captains, sea-lieutenants and master shall be allowed one eighth part, to be equally divided amongst them; the marine-lieutenants, boatswain, gunner, purser, carpenter, master's mate, chirurgeons and chaplain, one eighth part, to be equally divided amongst them; the midshipmen, carpenter's mates, boatswain's mates, gunner's mates, corporals, yeomen of the sheets, coxswain, quartermaster, quarter-master's mates, chirurgeon's mates, yeomen of the powder-room and sergeants of marines, one eighth part, to be equally divided amongst them; the trumpeters, quarter-gunners, carpenter's crew, steward, cook, armourer, steward's mate, cook's mate, gunsmith, cooper, swabber, ordinary trumpeter, barber, able seamen, ordinary seamen, volunteers by letter and marine-soldiers, two eighth parts, to be equally divided amongst them. . . .

And in regard privateers are set forth and manned at the charges of the particular owners thereof, who make agreements with their seamen what shares and proportion each man on board such privateer shall have of any prize which shall be taken . . . we do hereby ratify and confirm all and every such contracts and agreements which shall be entered into upon the putting forth any such privateer or letter of marque ship, and do hereby declare that every article and thing whatsoever which shall be contained in such contracts, stipulations and agreements shall be as firm, valid and effectual in law as if they had been set forth and mentioned in this our royal proclamation. . . .

Given at our court at Kensington,
the twentieth day of May,
in the seventh year of our reign.

(b) ENGAGEMENTS AT SEA

328. Dutch account of the attack on the Thames, 1667
(*Calendar of State Papers Domestic*, 1667, pp. xxi–xxiii)

SHORT AND RELIABLE ACCOUNT
OF ALL THAT HAS HAPPENED IN THE RIVER OF LONDON,
AND IN THE HAVEN OF CHATHAM, SHEPPEY, &C.,
9–13 JUNE 1667

The Dutch fleet set sail on 1st June 1667, under command of Lieutenant-Admiral de Ruyter. On the 4th a heavy storm arose from the south-south-west, by which some ships were forced to cut their cables; but on the 7th they again came safely to anchor before the river of London. On this the admiral put out a signal for all the principal officers to come on board, and hold a council of war how they might best sail up the river of London, with some of the lightest ships, to see whether they could there take some of the king's ships.

Thereupon on the 9th seventeen ships of war, four advice boats and four fire-ships sailed up the river Thames, under command of Lieutenant-Admiral van Ghent, with whom went de Witt as deputy of their High Mightinesses in the ship *Agatha*. The same evening they arrived between Queenborough and Gravesend; but there being nothing to be done there, on the 10th they came back to Queenborough, where de Ruyter had sent Star with some ships to support them. Having returned to the river of Rochester, conquering the island of Sheppey and Queenborough, a stronghold lying thereon, they thought good to attack the fort of Sheerness, which the English were beginning to make a little while before for defence of the passage to Rochester and Chatham. Our cannon so stormed the place that the enemy left it before Colonel Dolman, who had been sent for by some messengers, had arrived.

Our people found there an entire royal magazine, with very heavy anchors and cables and hundreds of masts. Our people took on board the ships as many of the cables, masts and round woods as they could, and they also acquired fifteen heavy pieces shooting balls of 18 lbs. The rest was destroyed or rendered useless, and the magazine burnt. The damage done to the English at this island was estimated at more than four tons of gold. It is a beautiful and fruitful island. Everyone was strictly forbidden, on pain of heavy punishment, to injure the inhabitants in life or goods.

On the 12th, the wind being east-north-east, they sailed before the tide about four miles up the river of Chatham under command of Thomas Tobias. There they made a severe attack. Before their coming the English had sunk there seven fire-ships, and closed the river with a thick and heavy iron chain, running on pulleys, which turned on wheels. Six of their ships, distributed in good order, lay before the chain. At the one end lay four, and at the other end two stout frigates which crossed the water. This notwithstanding, the Dutch, with more than mortal boldness, made an attack against all these dangers. Captain Brakel offered himself, and attacking with his frigate an English frigate called the *Jonathan* of 40 guns, took it, and burnt another English frigate by means of a fire-ship. Then the other four ships were left by their comrades; the crews in confusion sprang overboard; and our people took the ship *Royal Charles*, fitted to bear 100 pieces of cannon and with 32 guns on board. It was formerly commanded by the English Admiral Monck. Nothing more costly has been made in England, and it must have cost almost 100,000 dollars in the gilding alone. They also took the *Charles V*, which, with two others of the largest ships, the *Matthias* and *Castle of Honingen*, are burnt. The chain was burst into pieces, and all within it destroyed and annihilated, so that the English lose the admirals of the red and white flag, besides others of their largest ships, as the *Royal Charles*, the *Royal Oak*, the *Loyal London*, the *Royal James*, which they had sunk, the *Matthias*, the *Charles V*, the *Castle of Honingen*, and two stout frigates, the one named the *Friendship* or *Jonathan*, besides two other large ships and a good number of fire-ships, which they had sunk to stop the passage.

On land our people did not do much, for all was in commotion, and the English with 12,000 men came against them in arms. So the Dutch abandoned the places which they had taken, and came again with their ships into the river Thames. Vice-Admiral van Ghent was personally present throughout, and with other brave heroes of our fatherland manfully forwarded this great work. . . .

329. Admiral Russell's letter to the earl of Nottingham describing the battle of La Hogue, 1692

(*Harleian Miscellany*, ed. 1808–1811, XII, pp. 42–46)

Portsmouth, 2 June 1692

My Lord,

Since your lordship seems to think that an account, in general, of the fleet's good success is not so satisfactory as one setting forth the particulars, I here send it, with as much brevity as the matter will admit of. . . . Wednesday in the evening, being the eighteenth of May, standing over for Cape La Hogue, I ordered Captain Gillam in the *Chester* and the *Charles* galley to lie at such a distance to the westward of the fleet that they might discover any signals made from me.

Thursday the nineteenth, standing with a small gale S.S.W., the wind at W. and W. and by S., hazy weather, Cape Barfleur bearing then S.W. and by S. from me, distant about seven leagues, between three and four in the morning, we heard several guns to the westward, and in a short time I saw the two frigates making the signal of seeing the enemy, with their heads lying to the northward, which gave me reason to think the enemy lay with their heads that way; upon which I ordered the signal to be made for the fleet's drawing into a line of battle, after which I made the signal for the rear of the fleet to tack, that if the enemy stood to the northward we might the sooner come to engage. But soon after four o'clock the sun had a little cleared the weather, and I saw the French fleet standing to the southward, forming their line on the same tack that I was upon. I then ordered that signal for the rear to tack to be taken in, and at the same time bore away with my own ship so far to leeward as I judged each ship in the fleet might fetch my wake or grain; then brought to again, lying by with my fore-topsail to the mast, to give the ships in the fleet the better opportunity of placing themselves as they had been before directed.

By eight o'clock we had formed an indifferent line, stretching from the S.S.W. to the N.N.E., the Dutch in the van, the Red in the centre, and the Blue in the rear. By nine o'clock the enemy's vanguard had stretched almost as far to the southward as ours, their admiral and rear-admiral of the Blue, that were in the rear, closing the line, and their vice-admiral of the same division stretching to the rear of our fleet, but never coming within gunshot of them. About ten they bore down upon us, I still lying with my fore-topsail to the mast. I then observed Monsieur Tourville, the French admiral, put out his signal for battle. I gave order that mine should not be hoisted till the fleets began to engage, that he might have the fairer opportunity of coming as near me as he thought convenient; and at the same time I sent orders to Admiral Almonde that as soon as any of his squadron could weather the enemy's fleet they should tack and get to the westward of them, as also to the Blue to make sail and close the line, they being at some distance astern. But as soon as the fleet began to engage it fell calm, which prevented their so doing.

About half an hour after eleven Monsieur Tourville in the *Royal Sun* (being within three-quarters musket-shot) brought to, lying by me, at that distance, about an hour and a half, plying his guns very warmly, though I must observe to you that our men fired their guns faster. After which time I did not find his guns were fired with that vigour as before, and I could see him in great disorder, his rigging, sails and topsail-yards being shot; and nobody endeavouring to make them serviceable, and his boats towing of him to windward, gave me reason to think he was much galled. About two the wind shifted to the N.W. and by W., and some little time after that five fresh ships of the enemy's Blue squadron came and posted themselves, three ahead of Monsieur Tourville and two astern of him, and fired with great fury, which continued till after three. About four in the evening there came so thick a fog that we could not see a ship of the enemy's, which occasioned our leaving off firing for a little time; and then it cleared up, and we could see Monsieur Tourville towing away with his boats to the northward from us. Upon which I did the same, and ordered all my division to do the like; and about half an hour after five we had a small breeze of wind easterly. I then made the signal for the fleet to chase, sending notice to all the ships about me that the enemy were running.

About this time I heard several broadsides to the westward, and though I could not see the ships that fired I concluded them to be our Blue, that by the shift of wind had weathered the enemy. But it proved to be the rear-admiral of the Red, who had weathered Tourville's squadron and got between them and their admiral of the Blue, where they lay firing some time; and then Tourville anchored with some ships of his own division, as also the rear-admiral of the Red with some of his. This was the time that Captain Hastings in the *Sandwich* was killed, he driving through those ships by reason of his anchors not being clear. I could not see this part because of the great smoke and fog, but have received this information from Sir Clowdisley Shovell since. I sent to all the ships that I could think were near me to chase to the westward all night, telling them I designed to follow the enemy to Brest; and sometimes we could see a French ship, two or three, standing away with all the sail they could make to the westward. About eight I heard firing to the westward, which lasted about half an hour, it being some of our Blue fallen in with some of the ships of the enemy in the fog. It was foggy and very little wind all night.

Friday the twentieth it was so thick in the morning that I could see none of the enemy's ships, and but very few of our own. About eight it began to clear up. The Dutch, who were to the southward of me, made the signal of seeing the enemy; and as it cleared I saw about thirty-two or thirty-four sail, distant from us between two and three leagues, the wind at E.N.E. and they bearing from us W.S.W., our fleet chasing with all the sail they could make, having taken in the signal for the line of battle, that each ship might make the best of her way after the enemy. Between eleven and twelve the wind came to the S.W. The French plied to the westward with all the sail they could, and we after them. About four, the tide of ebb being done, the French anchored, as also we in forty-three fathom water, Cape Barfleur bearing S. and by W. About ten in the evening we weighed with the tide of ebb, the wind at S.W., and plied to the westward. About twelve my fore-topmast came by the board, having received several shot.

Saturday the twenty-first we continued still plying after the enemy till four in the morning. The tide of ebb being done I anchored in forty-six fathom water, Cape La Hogue bearing S. and by W., and the island of Alderney S.S.W. By my topmast's going away the Dutch squadron and the admiral of the Blue with several of his squadron had got a great way to windward of me. About seven in the morning several of the enemy's ships, being far advanced towards the Race, I perceived driving to the eastward with the tide of flood. Between eight and nine, when they were driven so far to the eastward that I could fetch them, I made the signal for the fleet to cut and follow the enemy, which they all did except the aforementioned weathermost ships, which rid fast to observe the motion of the rest of the enemy's ships that continued in the Race of Alderney. About eleven I saw three great ships fair under the shore tack and stand to the westward; but after making two or three short boards the biggest of them ran ashore, who presently cut his masts away. The other two, being to leeward of him, plied up to him. The reason, as I judge, of their doing this was that they could not weather our sternmost ships to the westward nor get out ahead of us to the eastward.

I observing that many of our ships hovered about those, I sent to Sir Ralph Delavall, vice-admiral of the Red, who was in the rear of our fleet, to keep such a number of ships and fire-ships with him as might be sufficient to destroy those of the enemy, and to order the others to follow me, I being then in pursuit of the rest of the enemy. An account of the performing that service I do not trouble your lordship with, he having given it you already. About four in the afternoon eighteen sail of the enemy's ships got to the eastward of Cape Barfleur, after which I observed they hauled in for La Hogue. The rear-admiral of the Red, vice-admiral of the Blue and some other ships were ahead of me. About ten at night I anchored in the bay of La Hogue, and lay till four the next morning, being Sunday the twenty-second; and then I weighed and stood in near the land of La Hogue. But when we found the flood came we anchored in good sandy ground. At two in the afternoon we weighed again, and plied close in with La Hogue, where we saw thirteen sail of the enemy's men-of-war hauled close in with the shore. The rear-admiral of the Red tells me that the night before he saw the other five, which made up the eighteen I first chased, stand to the eastward.

Monday the twenty-third I sent in Vice-Admiral Rooke, with several men-of-war and fire-ships, as also the boats of the fleet, to destroy those ships; but the enemy had gotten them so near the shore that not any of our men-of-war except the small frigates could do any service. But that night Vice-Admiral Rooke, with the boats, burnt six of them. Tuesday the twenty-fourth, about eight in the morning, he went in again with the boats and burnt the other seven, together with several transport ships and some vessels with ammunition. . . .

Wednesday the twenty-fifth I sailed from La Hogue, ordering the admiral of the Blue, with a squadron of English and Dutch ships under his command, to run along the enemy's coast as far as Havre de Grace, in hopes that some of the before-mentioned five ships that stood to the eastward might have been got thither; but he informs me that upon his appearing before that place he could perceive but one or two small vessels. The number of the enemy's ships did not exceed fifty men-of-war, by the best information, from fifty-six to one hundred and four guns; and though it must be confessed that our number was superior to theirs, which probably at first might startle them, yet by their coming down with that resolution I cannot think it had any great effect upon them. And this I may affirm for a truth, not with any intention to value our own action or to lessen the bravery of the enemy, that they were beaten by a number considerably less than theirs, the calmness and thickness of the weather giving very few of the Dutch or the Blue the opportunity of engaging, which I am sure they look upon as a great misfortune; and had the weather proved otherwise I do not see how it was possible for any of them to have escaped us. . . .

Vice-Admiral Rooke has given me a very good character of several men employed in the boats, and I have ordered him to give me a list of the names of such persons whose behaviour was remarkable, in order to their reward. I am, my Lord,

Your lordship's most faithful, humble servant,

E. RUSSELL

330. Sir Clowdisley Shovell's letter on the battle of Malaga, 1704

(N. Tindal's Continuation of Rapin's *History of England*, ed. 1743-1747, III, pp. 665-666)

This brings news of my health, and that we are on our way homeward. That which sends us home so soon is a very sharp engagement we have had with the French. Our number of ships that fought in the line of battle were pretty equal. I think they were 49, and we 53; but Sir George Rooke reserved some of the fifty-gun ships to observe if they attempted anything with their galleys, of which they had 24. Their ships did exceed in bigness. I judge they had 17 three-deck ships, and we had but 7.

The battle began on Sunday the 13th instant,[1] soon after ten in the morning, and in the centre and rear of the fleet it continued till night parted. But in the van of the fleet, where I commanded, and led by Sir John Leake, we having the weather-gage, gave me an opportunity of coming as near as I pleased, which was within pistol-shot, before I fired a gun, through which means, and God's assistance, the enemy declined us, and were upon the run in less than four hours, by which time we had little wind, and their galleys towed off their lame ships and others as they pleased, for the admiral of the White and Blue, with whom we fought, had 7 galleys tending upon him.

As soon as the enemy got out of the reach of our guns, and the battle continuing pretty hot astern, and some of our ships in the admiral's squadron towing out of the line, which I understood afterwards was for want of shot, I ordered all the ships of my division to slack all their sails, to close the line in the centre. This working had that good effect, that several of the enemies' ships astern, which had kept their line, having their top-sails and foresails set, shot up abreast of us, as the rear-admiral of the White and Blue and some of his division, and the vice-admiral of the White and some of his division. But they were so warmly received, before they got a-broadside, that with their boats ahead and their sprit-sails set they towed from us without giving us the opportunity of firing at them.

The ships that suffered most in my division were the *Lennox*, *Warspight*, *Tilbury* and *Swiftsure*. The rest escaped pretty well, and I the best of all, though I never took greater pains in all my life to be soundly beaten. For I set all my sails, and rowed with three boats ahead to get alongside with the admiral of the White and Blue; but he, outsailing me, shunned fighting, and lay alongside of the little ships. Notwithstanding, the engagement was very sharp, and I think the like between two fleets never has been in any time. There is hardly a ship that must not shift one mast, and some must shift all. A great many have suffered much, but none more than Sir George Rooke and Captain Jennings in the *St. George*. God send us well home. I believe we have not three spare topmasts nor three fishes in the fleet, and I judge there are ten jury-masts now up. After the fight we lay two days in sight of the enemy, preparing for a second engagement; but the enemy declined and stood from us in the night.

[1] 13/24 August 1704.

Part X
FOREIGN AFFAIRS

FOREIGN AFFAIRS

Introduction

WHILE in most spheres the Commonwealth Governments had pursued a distinctly revolutionary policy, in the sphere of foreign affairs they had been guided mainly by traditional ideas. To the advanced Protestants and enterprising merchants who formed the backbone of the Puritan community Spain had long been the religious and the United Netherlands the commercial enemy. The Commonwealth Governments, in consequence, had waged war with both these powers, and at the time of Charles's return to England the war with Spain was at least nominally still active.

That war had originally been conducted in alliance with France, and although France and Spain had come to terms with each other in the peace of the Pyrenees in 1659, it still embodied the pro-French attitude which had seemed natural to Englishmen in the days when France was willing to be "Catholic at home, Protestant abroad". Charles, therefore, whose personal inclinations were in the direction of a close association with France, was not running counter to any national sentiment when he viewed the war with some favour, and while putting an end to actual hostilities by a proclamation of 10 September 1660[1] sought to continue it in some underhand way.

The method adopted, at the suggestion of France, was to give assistance to the Portuguese, who were just struggling free from Spanish domination, and who, like the English, were suffering much from the commercial rivalry of the United Netherlands. In accordance with the practice of the sixteenth and seventeenth centuries a royal marriage was made the basis of an alliance. Charles, now that he was on the throne, had to seek a wife, and among the many possible brides suggested his choice fell upon Catherine of Braganza, sister of Alfonso VI, the reigning king of Portugal. The Portuguese undertook to provide a large dowry, and made extensive commercial concessions, including the surrender of Bombay and Tangier. The English guaranteed assistance, in certain eventualities, both against the Spaniards and against the Dutch. On 23 June 1661 the marriage treaty was formally signed,[2] and two years later English auxiliary forces took a decisive part in the battle of Amegial, which did much to secure Portuguese independence.[3]

Unfortunately for Charles, however, the national outlook was already imperceptibly changing. Since the peace of the Pyrenees Spain had ceased to be a serious danger to the other powers of Europe, and even in England this was slowly coming to be recognized. The fear and hatred with which Spain had hitherto been regarded began, in consequence, to be transferred to the rising power of France, and as early as the autumn of 1661 a struggle for ambassadorial precedence in the streets of London was seized upon by the mob as an opportunity for demonstrating beyond possibility of doubt that their sympathies lay with the Spaniards rather than with the French.[4] Thus when it was determined that the maintenance of Tangier as well as of Cromwell's

---

[1] No. 331. [2] No. 336. [3] No. 314. [4] No. 333.

843

conquest of Dunkirk was too heavy a burden for the national resources, and Charles entered into an agreement to sell Dunkirk to the French,[1] the step was extremely unpopular. Clarendon was held peculiarly responsible for it, and it was later made one of the charges in his impeachment.[2]

Nevertheless it was mainly in connexion with the first Dutch War of the reign that the reversal of the national attitude took place. That war was largely forced on Charles and his ministers, and was by no means unpopular. But the mismanagement apparent throughout its course, culminating in the failure to provide any adequate defence against the Dutch attack on the Thames,[3] caused much bitter feeling, which was directed not merely against the Dutch and the Government, but also against the French, who had come to the assistance of the Dutch during the war, as they were bound by treaty to do, and used the opportunity offered by the engagement of the two maritime powers with each other to overrun the Spanish Netherlands for themselves. Thus the treaty of Breda, which put an end to the war,[4] was regarded as a national humiliation; and yet the alliance between England and the United Netherlands which was concluded a few months later, and which Sweden also shortly joined, was viewed with the greatest favour, because its main object was to check the progress of the French.

It may be questioned whether this Triple Alliance[5] was ever as effective in restraining France as its supporters hoped and believed; but its general aim was so thoroughly in consonance with national aspirations that for many years it was regarded as the very embodiment of what English foreign policy ought to be. Thus in turning once more at this stage to France, Charles was very definitely running counter to national sentiment, and the situation was made even worse by the fact that a French alliance abroad was now to be associated with a Catholic policy at home. The Secret Treaty of Dover which Charles concluded with Louis XIV[6] provided not merely for a joint attack on the Dutch, and for French subsidies to assist the English king in meeting the cost, but also for an open profession of Catholicism by Charles, and French troops to support him in England if he required them.

Had this been generally known Charles's reign might well have come to an abrupt conclusion. As it was, the initial steps towards giving effect to the treaty involved nothing worse than a Declaration of Indulgence,[7] with which Charles thought it advisable to feel his way in the religious sphere, and the attack on the Dutch, for which it was still felt that there was considerable justification. What ruined his scheme was the fact that this attack was delivered in conjunction with Louis of France, and that while the English were on the whole unsuccessful, and singularly ill-supported by their allies, at sea, the French were strikingly successful on land. When lack of money at length compelled Charles to face Parliament, Shaftesbury made a great effort, in a speech which was long remembered against him,[8] to revive the earlier hostility to the Dutch, but without much success. Commercial rivalry was still strong; but however much some Englishmen would have liked to humble the Dutch, few were prepared to do so for the benefit of the French. Within a year Charles had found it necessary to abandon the war and come to terms in the treaty of Westminster.[9]

Thereafter for fifteen years English diplomacy abroad was almost entirely subordinate to the requirements of the situation at home, and the main feature of the situation

[1] No. 332.　　　　　[2] No. 71.　　　　　[3] No. 328.
[4] No. 343.　　　　　[5] No. 337.　　　　　[6] No. 338.
[7] No. 140.　　　　　[8] No. 334.　　　　　[9] No. 344.

at home was the need felt by Charles, and by James after him, for assistance in maintaining themselves against their own subjects. It is true that the earl of Danby in 1677 brought about the marriage of James's elder daughter Mary to her cousin William of Orange, concluded two new treaties with the Dutch, presented agreed terms of peace to France, and prepared for war to enforce the acceptance of these terms. But it is doubtful whether Charles ever had the slightest intention of actually going to war, or was aiming at anything more than raising his own price in the French diplomatic market. His real policy appears in a series of subsidy treaties which he concluded about the same time with France, culminating in the secret treaty of May 1678, by which he undertook to remain neutral if the Dutch and their allies did not accept French terms of peace within two months, and in return was to receive 6,000,000 livres from the French king.

With the Revolution a very different situation arose. Charles and James had become so thoroughly associated with France, and William of Orange so widely accepted as leader of the opposition to France, that the transference of the English crown from James to William almost automatically involved the transference of English support from France to the allies, and the engagement of England in actual war on their behalf. Danby's treaty of 1678 bound England to come to the assistance of the United Netherlands if attacked, as it already had been, by the French, and William was no sooner seated on the English throne than he recognized his obligations under the treaty, and dispatched a force to the Continent. The formal declaration of war came a few weeks later, and adhesion to the Grand Alliance which William had already built up to resist France[1] followed at the close of the year. The rising tide of indignation against Louis XIV had for some time been finding vent in a flood of pamphlets,[2] and the war of 1689 to 1697, or War of the English Succession as it is sometimes called, was a genuine national war, in the sense that it was fought to maintain the national choice of a king against a foreign power which sought to reverse it. Heavy war expenditure and the ineffectiveness of most of the operations caused much dissatisfaction; but the war itself was thoroughly approved until it was brought to a satisfactory end by the treaty of Ryswick.[3]

By that treaty William's title to the English throne was fully recognized; but the settlement of the English Succession question only made way for the much more important Spanish Succession question which had been hanging like a cloud over Europe for some time. Charles II of Spain was drawing near his end, and had no immediate heirs. If the French claimant to his vast dominions[4] were to inherit, not only would the dangerous power of France be immensely increased, but English and Dutch commercial interests in the Mediterranean and in the New World would be seriously threatened. William, accordingly, in the interests of peace, negotiated with France and the United Netherlands a partition treaty, which assigned the bulk of the Spanish dominions to the Bavarian claimant, with some compensation for the French and Austrian claimants, and then on the death of the Bavarian claimant negotiated a second Partition Treaty,[5] which assigned the Spanish dominions to the Austrian claimant, with compensation for his French rival.

These treaties, involving as they did serious entanglements on the Continent, were not popular in England, and the methods by which William negotiated them, without reference to his English ministers, were bitterly denounced. Thus when Charles II of

---

[1] No. 339.　　　[2] No. 335.　　　[3] No. 345.　　　[4] Table 7.　　　[5] No. 340.

Spain at length died, leaving his dominions by will to the French claimant, and Louis XIV decided to accept the will rather than to observe his undertakings in the Partition Treaty, it seemed at first that England might simply acquiesce. With ill-founded confidence in the strength of his position, however, Louis not only proceeded to treat the Spanish dominions almost as if they were already part of France, but on the death of James II of England broke another of his solemn promises by recognizing James's son as king of England. The revulsion of feeling which followed in England enabled William to bring his life's work to a fitting conclusion before he died. One of his last acts was to secure the formation of a new Grand Alliance against the French king,[1] one of Anne's first to confirm England's adhesion to that alliance and to issue a declaration of war against France.

That the contest which followed was primarily concerned with the succession in Spain was one of the main reasons for the conclusion of the Methuen Treaties,[2] by which England renewed her earlier alliance with Portugal, and secured the use of Lisbon as a base for her operations in the Mediterranean. But the main centre of hostilities was always the Low Countries, from which a way might be opened up to Paris itself, and there Marlborough was so successful that by 1709 Louis XIV was prepared to accept almost any terms of peace. Of the preliminary articles presented to him by the allies in that year, indeed, he accepted all but one, which provided that the whole settlement was to be void unless Philip V, the new French king of Spain, should hand over Spain itself to the Austrian claimant within two months of the conclusion of peace.[3] As no inducement was offered to Philip to make this surrender, and the Spaniards were resolved not to let him go, the article was virtually impossible of acceptance. Thus the war had to continue, in increasingly aimless fashion, for another four years, when war weariness and party revolutions in England at length brought it to an end by the treaty of Utrecht.[4]

[1] No. 341.   [2] No. 342.   [3] No. 346.   [4] Nos. 347, 348.

BIBLIOGRAPHY

A useful guide to some of the more easily accessible sources is provided by "Materials for English Diplomatic History, 1509–1783, calendared in the Reports of the Historical Manuscripts Commission, with References to Similar Materials in the British Museum", compiled by F. G. Davenport, in *Eighteenth Report of the Royal Commission on Historical Manuscripts* (1917), pp. 357–402. There is no bibliography devoted exclusively to foreign relations, and much of the published material is inevitably contained in foreign works which are not readily procurable.

With few exceptions the international agreements which mark the stages in the development of later Stuart policy are available in the form in which they were known to contemporaries. As the seventeenth century drew towards its close, the growing power of the House of Commons and the increasing popular interest in foreign affairs led to the publication, or submission to Parliament, of nearly all important treaties in official translations by the Government. These translations were then gathered together in a number of unofficial compilations, of which the most comprehensive are *A General Collection of Treaties, Declarations of War, Manifestoes and other Public Papers relating to Peace and War* (4 vols., London, 1732); Charles Jenkinson, *A Collection of all the Treaties of Peace, Alliance and Commerce between Great Britain and Other Powers, 1648–1783* (3 vols., London, 1785); and George Chalmers, *A Collection of Treaties between Great Britain and Other Powers* (2 vols., London, 1790). More modern translations of some of the treaties, and of parts of others, can be found in Frances G. Davenport, *European Treaties bearing on the History of the United States and its Dependencies*, vols. II and III, 1650–1697 and 1698–1715 (Washington, 1929 and 1934). Many of them can be found untranslated in Henri Vast, *Les grands Traités du Règne de Louis XIV* (3 parts, Paris, 1893–1899).

For the past thirty years the Royal Historical Society has been engaged in publishing a series of volumes of *British Diplomatic Instructions, 1689–1789*, modelled to some extent on the much more elaborate French *Recueil des Instructions données aux Ambassadeurs et Ministres de France, depuis les Traités de Westphalie jusqu'a la Révolution Française*. The volumes in the British series dealing with the later Stuart period are *Sweden, 1689–1727*, edited by James F. Chance (1922); *France, 1689–1721*, edited by L. G. Wickham Legg (1925); and *Denmark*, edited by James F. Chance (1926). Many volumes in the French series throw light on negotiations in which England was more or less deeply involved, but of special value are the two volumes on *Angleterre, 1648–90*, edited by J. J. Jusserand (Paris, 1929). A useful companion volume is *British Diplomatic Representatives, 1689–1789*, edited by D. B. Horn for the Royal Historical Society (1932). Similar lists of representatives with bibliographical notes are in *Notes on the Diplomatic Relations of England and France, 1603–1688*, edited by Sir C. H. Firth and Sophie C. Lomas (Oxford, 1906).

Selections from the papers of many of the leading ambassadors and Secretaries of State have been published, Arlington's in *The Right Honourable the Earl of Arlington's Letters to Sir W. Temple, Bart., and to the several Ambassadors to Spain*, edited by Thomas Bebington (2 vols., London, 1701); Temple's in his *Works*, already referred to (p. 43); Montagu's in the *Report on the Manuscripts of the Duke of Buccleuch and Queensberry preserved at Montagu House, Whitehall*, vol. I, edited by R. E. G. Kirk for the Historical Manuscripts Commission (1899), pp. 418–525; Jenkins's in William Wynne, *The Life of Sir Leoline Jenkins* (2 vols., London, 1724); Chudleigh's in *The Dispatches of Thomas Plott (1681–1682) and Thomas Chudleigh (1682–1685), English Envoys at The Hague*, edited by Frederick Arnold Middlebush (The Hague, 1926); Etheredge's, while emissary at Ratisbon during the years 1685–1688, in *The Letterbook of Sir George Etheredge*, edited by Sybil Rosenfeld (Oxford, 1928); Lord Preston's in "The Manuscripts of Sir Frederick Graham, Bart., at Netherby Hall", in *Seventh Report of the Royal Commission on Historical Manuscripts* (1879), pp. 261–428; Nottingham's in *Report on the Manuscripts of the late Allan George Finch*, vol. II, edited by Sophia C. Lomas for the Historical Manuscripts Commission

847

(1922); Trumbull's in *Report on the Manuscripts of the Marquess of Downshire*, vol. I, edited by E. K. Purnell for the Historical Manuscripts Commission (2 parts, 1924); Lexington's, while minister at Vienna during the years 1694–1698, in *The Lexington Papers*, edited by H. Manners Sutton (London, 1851); Shrewsbury's in *Private and Original Correspondence of Charles Talbot, Duke of Shrewsbury*, edited by William Coxe (London, 1821), and *Report on the Manuscripts of the Duke of Buccleuch and Queensberry preserved at Montagu House, Whitehall*, vol. II, edited by R. E. G. Kirk for the Historical Manuscripts Commission (2 parts, 1903); Vernon's in *Letters illustrative of the Reign of William III from 1696 to 1708 addressed to the Duke of Shrewsbury by James Vernon, Secretary of State*, edited by G. P. R. James (3 vols., London, 1841), many errors in which are indicated in Dorothy H. Somerville, "The Dates in the Vernon Correspondence", in *English Historical Review*, XLVIII (1933), pp. 624–630; Alexander Stanhope's in *Spain under Charles the Second*, edited by Lord Mahon (London, 1844); Matthew Prior's in *Calendar of the Manuscripts of the Marquis of Bath*, vol. III, edited by J. M. Rigg for the Historical Manuscripts Commission (1908); Hill's in *The Diplomatic Correspondence of Richard Hill, Envoy to the Duke of Savoy, from July 1703 to May 1706*, edited by William Blackley (2 vols., London, 1845); and Bolingbroke's in *Letters and Correspondence of Lord Viscount Bolingbroke during the Time he was Secretary of State to Queen Anne*, edited by Gilbert Parke (4 vols., London, 1798).

Much information about the marriage of Charles II and his early relations with Portugal and Spain may be found in *The Memoirs of Ann Lady Fanshawe*, edited by Herbert C. Fanshawe (London, 1907), which should be supplemented from the correspondence of Sir Richard Fanshawe in *The Manuscripts of J. M. Heathcote*, edited by Sophia C. Lomas for the Historical Manuscripts Commission (1899), and from *Original Letters and Negotiations of Sir Richard Fanshaw, the Earl of Sandwich, the Earl of Sunderland and Sir William Godolphin, wherein Divers Matters between the three Crowns of England, Spain and Portugal from 1663 to 1678 are set in a clearer Light than is anywhere else extant* (2 vols., London, 1724).

The correspondence of William III, largely concerned with foreign affairs, is printed in *Archives de la Maison d'Orange-Nassau*, second series, 1584–1688, edited by G. Groen van Prinsterer, vol. V (Leyden, 1862), and third series, 1689–1702, edited by F. J. L. Krämer (3 vols., Leyden, 1907–1909); and in *Correspondentie van Willem III en van Hans Willem Bentinck, eersten Graaf van Portland*, edited by N. Japikse, Part I (2 vols., The Hague, 1927–1928), and Part II (3 vols., The Hague, 1932–1937). There is much valuable information also in the dispatches of foreign envoys to their governments at home, which have already been mentioned (pp. 39–40).

Macaulay was too insular in his outlook to be altogether successful in dealing with foreign affairs, and his account requires to be corrected and supplemented from Ranke's *History of England*. The best short survey is to be found in Clark's *Later Stuarts*. Apart from the relevant sections of such general histories there is no good account of foreign policy. Sir John R. Seeley, *The Growth of British Policy* (2 vols., Cambridge, 1895), covers the period 1558–1714, but although stimulating and still valuable is little more than a brilliant essay. Sir A. W. Ward's introduction to *The Cambridge History of British Foreign Policy, 1783–1919*, edited by Sir A. W. Ward and G. P. Gooch, vol. I (1922), devotes less than forty pages to the later Stuarts.

There are, however, many excellent studies of particular periods or aspects of foreign policy. Keith Feiling, *British Foreign Policy, 1660–1672* (London, 1930), is concerned mainly with the developments leading to the Secret Treaty of Dover, a subject on which much light is also thrown by Cyril Hughes Hartmann, *Charles II and Madame* (London, 1934). Clyde Leclare Grose, "The Anglo-Dutch Alliance of 1678", in *English Historical Review*, XXXIX (1924), pp. 349–372, 526–551, deals with the very complicated situation which arose towards the end of Danby's period of power; and Ruth Clark, *Sir William Trumbull in Paris, 1685–1686* (Cambridge, 1938), with English diplomacy in connexion with the revocation of the Edict of Nantes. G. F. Abbott, *Under the Turk in Constantinople, a Record of Sir John Finch's Embassy, 1674–1681* (London, 1920), investigates the whole problem of Levantine relations. G. N. Clark, *The Dutch Alliance and the War against French Trade, 1688–1697* (Manchester, 1923), with which should be read the same writer's "War Trade and Trade War, 1701–1713" in *Economic History Review*, I,

(1927–1928), pp. 262–280, and "Neutral Commerce in the War of the Spanish Succession and the Treaty of Utrecht", in *British Year-Book of International Law, 1928*, pp. 69–83, is concerned mainly with the use of sea-power against commerce. Roderick Geikie and Isabel A. Montgomery, *The Dutch Barrier, 1705–1719* (Cambridge, 1930), discusses one of the problems of the peace settlement in which the English people were specially interested. Jean O. McLachlan, *Trade and Peace with Old Spain* (Cambridge, 1940), stresses the importance of England's trade with Spain as distinct from the Spanish colonies.

Other studies are Clyde L. Grose, "The Anglo-Portuguese Marriage of 1662", in *Hispanic American Historical Review*, X (1930), pp. 313–352, and the same writer's "England and Dunkirk", in *American Historical Review*, XXXIX (1934), pp. 1–27; Carl Brinkmann, "Charles II and the Bishop of Münster in the Anglo-Dutch War of 1665–6", in *English Historical Review*, XXI (1906), pp. 686–698, and the same writer's "England and the Hanse under Charles II", *ibid.*, XXIII (1908), pp. 683–708, and "The Relations between England and Germany, 1660–88", *ibid.*, XXIV (1909), pp. 247–277, 448–469; H. L. Schoolcraft, "England and Denmark, 1660–7", *ibid.*, XXV (1910), pp. 457–479; Margery Lane, "Relations between England and the Northern Powers, 1689–97, Part I, Denmark", in *Transactions of the Royal Historical Society, Third Series*, V (1911), pp. 157–191; L. A. Robertson, "The Relations of William III with the Swiss Protestants, 1689–1697", *ibid., Fourth Series*, XII (1929), pp. 137–162; June Milne, "The Diplomacy of Dr. John Robinson at the Court of Charles XII of Sweden, 1697–1709", *ibid.*, XXX (1948), pp. 75–93; J. F. Chance, "England and Sweden in the Time of William III and Anne", in *English Historical Review*, XVI (1901), pp. 676–711; and Edgar Prestage, *The Diplomatic Relations of Portugal with France, England and Holland from 1640 to 1668* (Watford, 1925).

Clyde L. Grose, "Louis XIV's Financial Relations with Charles II and the English Parliament", in *Journal of Modern History*, I (1929), pp. 177–204, discusses the extent to which foreign policy in the reign of Charles was determined by French bribery; and Robert H. George, "The Financial Relations of Louis XIV and James II", *ibid.*, III (1931), pp. 392–413, deals with substantially the same problem under Charles's successor. The importance of the English succession question in international affairs is well brought out in F. W. Head, *The Fallen Stuarts* (Cambridge, 1901).

The machinery of diplomacy has only recently attracted serious attention, and much still remains to be done. Violet Barbour, "Consular Service in the Reign of Charles II", in *American Historical Review*, XXXIII (1928), pp. 553–578; G. N. Clark, "Dutch Missions to England in 1689", in *English Historical Review*, XXXV (1920), pp. 529–557; and Margery Lane, "The Diplomatic Service under William III", in *Transactions of the Royal Historical Society, Fourth Series*, X (1927), pp. 87–109, deal with some of the problems involved. Particularly valuable within the limited sphere which it surveys is E. R. Adair, *The Exterritoriality of Ambassadors in the Sixteenth and Seventeenth Centuries* (London, 1929), with which should be associated the same writer's "The Law of Nations and the Common Law of England, a Study of 7 Anne, cap. 12", in *Cambridge Historical Journal*, II (1928), pp. 290–297.

A. PRELIMINARY SETTLEMENT

331. Proclamation of peace with Spain, 1660

CHARLES R.

Forasmuch as our dear brother the king of Spain, upon notice of our happy establishment upon our throne, hath sent orders into several his dominions commanding an entire cessation from all hostility between ours and his subjects, and hath further proposed that a certain day might be agreed upon for the publication thereof, we, by and with the advice of our Privy Council, having also thought it meet and expedient to renew our ancient amity and good intelligence betwixt our realms, countries, dominions and subjects, do by this our proclamation signify and make known to all our loving subjects that there is as full and entire a peace and amity betwixt us and our said dear brother the king of Spain as there was by the last treaty made betwixt our dear father of blessed memory and our said brother, and that all acts of hostility and war, both by sea and land, are ceased and shall cease; and that the said cessation hath taken beginning and commencement from the time of our arrival in this our kingdom of England, which was upon the twenty-fifth day of May last past.

And further we do hereby signify and declare that all prisoners, ships, goods, merchandise or whatsoever else taken upon one another, either by any of our subjects or the subjects of our said dear brother, since the said time of our arrival in England, be and shall be, upon due proof thereof, redelivered and restored. And lastly we do hereby straitly charge and command all our loving subjects, of what degree soever they be, to take notice of our will and pleasure signified by this our proclamation, and to observe, perform and accomplish all that hereunto belongeth, as it is to be published on the side of our said dear brother the king of Spain the date of these presents.

Given at our court at Whitehall,
the 10/20 day of September, ·
in the twelfth year of our reign, 1660.

332. Treaty for the sale of Dunkirk, 1662

(Collection of Treaties, ed. 1732, I, pp. 121–127)

The king of Great Britain, being desirous more and more to increase the friendship already contracted with his most Christian Majesty, has thought himself obliged to give ear to the proposals made to him on his part, to treat upon reasonable conditions concerning the town and citadel of Dunkirk, . . . and after several conferences . . . . the following articles have been agreed on. . . .

I. In the first place it is concluded and agreed that the town of Dunkirk, together with its citadel, redoubts, old and new fortifications, and in general everything that makes up the body of the place, . . . the whole in the condition now it is, shall be put into the hands of his most Christian Majesty, or such commissioners as he shall appoint and furnish with a full power for that end, within fifteen days to reckon from the date of his most Christian Majesty's ratification of this treaty, or sooner if it can be done. . . .

VI. That the said bargain and sale is made in consideration of the sum of five millions of livres, according to the computation and value of French money and the present currency thereof, viz., a silver crown at sixty sous; of which sum two millions of livres shall be paid down in the said place, at the same time that it shall be put into the hands of his most Christian Majesty or his commissioners, . . . and the other three millions remaining shall be paid in the two years following, viz., fifteen hundred thousand livres each year at four payments every three months, the three first to be of four hundred thousand livres each, and the last of three hundred thousand; . . . which payments in the said two years shall be made in the town of Dunkirk to those who shall be empowered to receive it by the king of Great Britain. . . .

VIII. And forasmuch as his most Christian Majesty hath desired that the said king of Great Britain would warrant the sale of the said town of Dunkirk, it is covenanted and agreed that the said king of Great Britain doth warrant the said place of Dunkirk, with all its circumstances and dependencies, for the space of two years only, to the most Christian king; and to that end does oblige himself that in case the king of Spain, from whom it was taken by the right of arms, should happen during that time (or any other aggressor) to dispute the matter with his most Christian Majesty, and by open force lay siege to the same, the king of Great Britain in that case does oblige himself and promise that he will, during the space of two years only as aforesaid and no longer, defend it in conjunction with his most Christian Majesty, and engages to furnish as numerous a fleet of ships as shall be adjudged sufficient for preserving a free passage to it to the seaward, by which those succours that are adjudged necessary may be thrown in. . . .

Done at London, October 27, 1662.

B. NATIONAL OUTLOOK

333. Samuel Pepys's account of the struggle for ambassadorial precedence in London, 1661

(Diary, 30 September 1661)

This morning up by moonshine, at 5 o'clock, . . . and heard of a fray between the two ambassadors of Spain and France, and that this day, being the day of the entrance of an ambassador from Sweden, they intended to fight for the precedence. Our king, I heard, ordered that no Englishman should meddle in the business, but let them do what they would; and to that end all the soldiers in the town were in arms all the day long, and some of the train-bands in the city. . . .

At Whitehall alight, and saw the soldiers and people running up and down the streets. So I went to the Spanish ambassador's and the French, and there saw great preparations on both sides; but the French made the most noise and vaunted most. The other made no stir almost at all, so that I was afraid the other would have had too great a conquest over them. Then to the Wardrobe, and dined there; and then abroad, and in Cheapside hear that the Spanish hath got the best of it, and killed three of the French coach-horses and several men, and is gone through the city next to our king's coach; at which it is strange to see how all the city did rejoice. And indeed we do naturally all love the Spanish and hate the French. But I, as I am in all things curious, presently got to the water-side, and there took oars to Westminster Palace, thinking to have seen them come in thither with all the coaches; but they being come and returned, I ran after them with my boy after me through all the dirt and the streets full of people, till at last, at the Mews, I saw the Spanish coach go, with fifty drawn swords at least to guard it, and our soldiers shouting for joy. And so I followed the coach, and then met it at York House, where the ambassador lies; and there it went in with great state.

So then I went to the French house, where I observe still that there is no men in the world of a more insolent spirit where they do well, nor before they begin a matter, and more abject if they do miscarry, than these people are; for they all look like dead men, and not a word among them, but shake their heads. The truth is, the Spaniards were not only observed to fight most desperately, but also they did outwit them; first in lining their own harness with chains of iron that they could not be cut; then in setting their coach in the most advantageous place, and to appoint men to guard every one of their horses, and others for to guard the coach and others the coachmen; and above all in setting upon the French horses and killing them, for by that means the French were not able to stir.

There were several men slain of the French, and one or two of the Spaniards, and one Englishman by a bullet. Which is very observable, the French were at least four to one in number, and had near a hundred case of pistols among them, and the Spaniards had not one gun among them, which is for their honour for ever, and the others' disgrace.

334. Speech of Lord Chancellor Shaftesbury denouncing the Dutch, 1673

(Journals of the House of Commons, IX, pp. 246–248)

5 February 1673

MY LORDS, AND YOU, THE KNIGHTS, CITIZENS AND BURGESSES OF THE HOUSE OF
COMMONS,

The king hath spoken so fully, so excellently well, and so like himself, that you are not to expect much from me. . . . His Majesty hath told you that he is now engaged in an important, very expensive, and indeed a war absolutely necessary and unavoidable. He hath referred you to his declaration, where you will find the personal indignities, by pictures and medals and other public affronts, his Majesty hath received from the States; their breach of treaties both in the Surinam and East India business; and at last they came to that height of insolence as to deny the honour and right of the flag, though an undoubted jewel of this crown, never to be parted with, and by them particularly owned in the late treaty of Breda,[1] and never contested in any age. And whilst the king first long expected, and then solemnly demanded, satisfaction, they disputed his title to it in all the courts of Christendom, and made great offers to the French king if he would stand by them against us. But the most Christian king too well remembered what they did at Münster, contrary to so many treaties and solemn engagements, and how dangerous a neighbour they were to all crowned heads.

The king and his ministers had here a hard time, and lay every day under new obloquies. Sometime they were represented as selling all to France for money to make this war. Portsmouth, Plymouth and Hull were to be given into the French hands for caution. The next day news came that France and Holland were agreed. Then the obloquy was turned from treachery to folly. The ministers were now fools that some days before were villains. . . . But both kings, knowing their interests, resolved to join against them who were the common enemy to all monarchies, and I may say especially to ours, their only competitor for trade and power at sea, and who only stand in their way to an universal empire as great as Rome. This the States understood so well, and had swallowed so deep, that under all their present distress and danger they are so intoxicated with that vast ambition that they slight a treaty and refuse a cessation.

All this you and the whole nation saw before the last war; but it could not then be so well timed, or our alliances so well made. But you judged aright, that at any rate *delenda est Carthago*; that government is to be brought down. And therefore the king may well say to you, it is your war. He took his measures from you, and they were just and right ones; and he expects a suitable assistance to so necessary and expensive an action, which he has hitherto maintained at his own charges. . . . And his Majesty commands me to tell you that unless it be a certain sum and speedily raised it can never answer the occasion. . . .

---

[1] No. 343.

335. Anonymous pamphlet denouncing the French, 1686

(Harleian Miscellany, ed. 1808–1811, IX, pp. 164–175)

THE DESIGNS OF FRANCE
AGAINST ENGLAND AND HOLLAND DISCOVERED

Henry the Eighth, king of England, did in his time cause a medal to be stamped, with a hand stretched out of a cloud holding a balance in equipoise, whereof both the scales represented Spain and France, with this motto, *Cui adhaereo praeest*, i.e., My alliance weighs it down. It seems that prince well knew his own might, whereas now England may be compared to an ox, who, being insensible of his own strength, quietly submits himself to the yoke. Evident it is that England has many advantages beyond other kingdoms, but especially this, that being an island it can easily secure itself against any foreign force. They that intend an invasion against it must be obliged to cross the seas, and struggle with the winds and waves and all the hazards and dangers of that unstable element, besides a very potent fleet which alone is sufficient to deter their hardiest enemy from any such design. Now this being so, it is manifest that the king of England (having peace and a strict alliance with Holland) can overbalance the party he designs against.

This is a truth France is so fully convinced of that, notwithstanding the great antipathy there is between both nations, he has hitherto spared nothing, and is still turning every stone, to take off England from its true interest and to engage it on his side, or at least to oblige it to stand neuter, and to be an idle, unconcerned spectator of the horrid tragedy the French king acts upon the theatre of Europe, because he well knows that England is better able to prevent it, and spoil his sport, than any other state or kingdom whatsoever, and rescue Europe from the universal slavery he prepares for it. Would the king of England only be pleased to open his eyes, fast closed with the enchanted slumbers of the French Delilah, to take a view of his own strength and true interest, he should soon find himself making another figure amongst the princes of Europe than of late years he hath done, and with ease mount that high degree of power and glory of being the professed umpire of the universe, the sovereign mediator and decider of controversies and the giver of peace to all Europe, which France in a vain bravado pretends to, when indeed he is the sole troubler of it.

To arrive at this transcendent pitch of grandeur and authority two things only (which the king of England may do when he pleases) are requisite. The first is that his Majesty do comport himself so as to engage the love of his people, and keep a right understanding between him and his Parliament; and the second that he enter into a strict alliance with Holland, living in sincere amity, perfect union and good correspondence with them, in order to their common defence and security. The former of these is very easy, and the king will do it as soon as he shall resolve to desire nothing of his Parliament but what is agreeable with the laws of the realm, which by his coronation oath he is obliged to observe and maintain; and the latter will be found to be of absolute necessity as soon as the king of England shall please to stop his ears to the false suggestions of France, and stifle those jealousies and resentments which his emissaries daily buzz into his head, there being nothing to fear for England from the States, whose desire is not to enlarge their dominions (as France does) by invading those of their neighbours, but only to keep what God has given them, and to maintain their subjects in the liberty they now enjoy. . . .

That there can be nothing so evidently destructive of the French designs as this union between England and Holland is very apparent. England can, when it pleases, overturn the projects of France against the Spanish Netherlands. Neither could that king ever have taken Luxemburg if the late king of England had had the least inclination to oppose him in that attempt; but the French king so well knew how to take him by the blind side that he did not perceive the mischief till the city was taken. It was a capital error for England to part with Dunkirk, a place that opened a passage for them to France and the Low Countries; but it would make the matter much worse if all those countries should be fain to submit to the tyranny of Louis the Great, and he by this means should join Newport and Ostend to Dunkirk, for then would Flushing follow by consequence, and that king be put into a condition to dispute the sovereignty of the sea with his British Majesty, and destroy the navigation and commerce of this flourishing kingdom. Having got thus far he would proceed to an entire conquest of the United Provinces, which point being once gained by him England would have but little reason to flatter itself with the hopes of a better lot. . . .

C. TREATIES OF ALLIANCE

336. Marriage Treaty with Portugal, 1661

(G. Chalmers, *Collection of Treaties*, II, pp. 286–296)

It being upon mature deliberation mutually and fully agreed between their Majesties, Charles by the Grace of God, king of Great Britain, France and Ireland, Defender of the Faith, &c., and Alfonso by the same Grace of God, king of Portugal and Algarve, &c., that the king of Great Britain shall, with all possible speed as such an affair can be transacted in, marry and take to wife the most excellent Princess Dona Catherina Infanta of Portugal, for a more firm and durable peace and alliance between the two crowns, and for the good of both nations, which are henceforward to take each other's interest to heart no less than their own, it is mutually consented and agreed as followeth:

I. That all treaties made between Great Britain and Portugal since 1641 until this very time shall be ratified and confirmed in all points and to all intents. . . .

II. The king of Portugal, by and with the advice of his Council, doth give, transfer, grant and by these presents confirm unto the king of Great Britain, his heirs and successors for ever, the city and castle of Tangier, with all its rights, territories, profits and appurtenances whatsoever. . . .

V. The king of Portugal doth promise and oblige himself by these presents to give unto the king of Great Britain, for a portion or dowry with the said Lady Infanta his sister, two millions, i.e. 2,000,000, of crowns Portuguese, and that one moiety thereof shall be really put on board the said fleet before the Infanta herself embarks, . . . and for the other moiety of the said portion, amounting to one million, i.e. 1,000,000, of crowns Portuguese, the king of Portugal doth oblige himself to pay the same within the space of one year after the arrival of the Infanta in England, by two payments, the one within six months next following, the other within the year. . . .

XI. That for the better improvement of the English interest and trade in the East Indies, and that the king of Great Britain may be better enabled to assist, defend and protect the subjects of the king of Portugal in those parts from the power and invasion of the States of the United Provinces, the king of Portugal, with the advice and consent of his Council, doth give, transfer, and by these presents grant and confirm unto the king of Great Britain, his heirs and successors for ever, the port and island of Bombay in the East Indies, with all the rights, profits, territories and appurtenances whatsoever thereunto belonging. . . .

XII. That the subjects of the king of Great Britain may enjoy the more full benefit of trade and commerce in all the dominions of the king of Portugal, it is agreed that their merchants or factors (above what hath been granted by former treaties) may, by virtue of this treaty, reside in all places they shall choose, and particularly that they shall live, and enjoy all privileges and immunities in order to trade which the Portuguese themselves enjoy, in the cities and towns of Goa, Cochin and Diu, provided that the subjects of his Majesty of Great Britain who are to reside in any of the said places shall not exceed the number of four families in any one place.

XIII. The like privileges, liberties and immunities the king of Great Britain's subjects shall enjoy in the towns of Bahia de todos os Santos, Pernambuco and Rio de Janeiro in the territory of Brazil, and in all other of the king of Portugal's dominions in the West Indies. . . .

XV. In consideration of all which grants and privileges . . . the king of Great Britain doth profess and declare, with the consent and advice of his Council, that he will take the interest of Portugal and all its dominions to heart, defending the same with his utmost power by sea and land even as England itself, and that he will transport thither at his proper costs and charges two regiments of horse, each regiment consisting of 500, and two regiments of foot, each consisting of 1,000, all which shall be armed at the charge of the king of Great Britain, but after they are landed in Portugal shall be paid by the king of Portugal; and in case the said regiments come to be diminished, by fight or otherwise, the king of Great Britain shall be obliged to fill up the number at his own charge; and that he shall cause the said regiments to be transported as soon as the Lady Infanta shall arrive in England, if it be so desired by the king of Portugal.

XVI. The king of Great Britain doth also promise, with the advice and consent of his Council, that when and as often as Portugal shall be invaded he will send thither (being thereunto desired by the king of Portugal) ten good ships of war; but when and as often as it shall be infested by pirates, three or four ships, all sufficiently manned and victualled for eight months from the time of their setting sail from England, to obey the orders of the king of Portugal. . . . But if the king of Portugal shall be pressed in any extraordinary manner by the power of the enemies, all the king of Great Britain's ships which shall at any time be in the Mediterranean Sea or at Tangier shall have instructions in such cases to obey any orders they shall receive from the king of Portugal, and shall betake themselves to his succour and relief. . . .

XVIII. The king of Great Britain doth profess and promise, with the advice and consent of his Council, that he will never make a peace with Castile which may be the least impediment to him, directly or indirectly, in his giving full and entire assistance to Portugal in order to its necessary defence; and that he will never deliver Dunkirk or Jamaica unto the king of Castile, nor ever forbear to do any act that is necessary for the relief of Portugal, though by so doing he shall be engaged in a war with the king of Castile. . . .

A Secret Article

It is by this secret article concluded and accorded that his Majesty of Great Britain, in regard of the great advantages and increase of dominion he hath purchased by the above-mentioned treaty of marriage, shall promise and oblige himself, as by this present article he doth, to defend and protect all conquests or colonies belonging to the crown of Portugal against all his enemies, as well future as present. Moreover his Majesty of Great Britain doth oblige himself to mediate a good peace between the king of Portugal and the States of the United Provinces and all companies or societies of merchants subject unto them, upon conditions convenient and becoming the mutual interest of England and Portugal; and in case such a peace ensue not, then his Majesty of Great Britain shall be obliged to defend with men and ships the said dominions and conquests of the king of Portugal. In case also that any towns, forts, castles or any other places shall be taken by the Dutch after the first of May this present year 1661, then his Majesty of Great Britain doth promise and engage to oblige the Dutch to a full and perfect restitution thereof. . . .

337. Triple Alliance, 1668
(*Works of Sir William Temple*, ed. 1740, II, pp. 69–80)

Whereas by the late treaty concluded at Breda between the king of Great Britain and the States General of the United Netherlands[1] both nations have been restored, through the blessing of God, to that ancient friendship and good correspondence which was between them; . . . and particularly by the eleventh article of the said treaty it was ordained that the said king and the said States General shall be obliged as friends, allies and confederates mutually to defend the rights and immunities of each other's subjects against all such as shall endeavour to disturb the peace of either state by sea or by land; . . . for the better ascertaining the mutual assistance that the parties are to give each other . . . we whose names are underwritten, in virtue of the orders and full powers granted to us, . . . do covenant and agree that the said king of Great Britain and the said States General of the United Netherlands shall be mutually obliged, united and confederated together . . . in a perpetual league defensive, in the manner and under the conditions following:

I. That if any prince, state or other person whatever, without exception, shall under any pretext invade or attempt to invade the territories, countries or any places that lie within the dominions of the said king of Great Britain, or shall exercise any acts of hostility by sea or by land against the said king or his subjects, the said States General shall be obliged . . . to send 40 ships of war, well furnished with all things necessary, to assist the said king to oppose, suppress and repel all such insults and acts of hostility, and to procure him due reparation for any damages sustained: that is to say 14 of the said ships shall carry from 60 to 80 great guns and 400 men, a just allowance and computation being made as well with respect to those ships that carry a greater as those that carry a lesser number of men; 14 other ships shall carry from 40 to 60 guns and, one with another, 300 men at the least, allowance to be made as before; and none of the rest to carry less than 36 guns and 150 men. Besides which they shall assist him with 6,000 foot soldiers and 400 horse, or shall pay a sum of money with due regard to the just value of such an assistance, either for the whole or a part at the choice of the said king. All these aids shall be furnished within six weeks after they shall be demanded, and the said king shall reimburse the whole charge to the said States within three years after the conclusion of the war.

II. That if any prince, state or other person whatever, without exception, shall under any pretext invade or attempt to invade the United Provinces, or any places situated within the jurisdiction of the said States General or garrisoned by their

---

[1] No. 343.

soldiers, or shall exercise any act of hostility by land or by sea against the said States General or their subjects, the said king shall be obliged. . . .[1]

III. The said ships of war and the said auxiliary forces of horse and foot, together with the commanders of the ships and forces and all the subaltern officers of both that shall be sent to the assistance of the party injured and attacked, shall be obliged to submit to his pleasure, and be obedient to the orders of him or them who shall be appointed to command the armies in chief either by sea or land.

IV. Now, that an exact computation may be made of the charges that are to be reimbursed within the space of three years after the conclusion of the war, . . . it is thought expedient that the 14 ships carrying from 60 to 80 pieces of cannon should be valued at the sum of 18,666 pounds sterling, or of English money; the other 14, which carry from 40 to 60 guns, at 14,000 pounds sterling; and the remaining 12 at 6,000 pounds of the same money; 6,000 foot at 7,500 pounds sterling, and 400 horse at 1,040 pounds for one month; the money to be paid by the said king of Great Britain at London and by the said States General at Amsterdam according as the course of the exchange shall be at the time when payment is to be made. . . .

The treaty for the pacification of France and Spain

. . . The most serene king of Great Britain and the High and Mighty States of the United Netherlands having with much labour and earnest entreaty induced the most Christian king to profess solemnly to the said States General that he would immediately lay down his arms, if the Spaniards would either consent to yield up to him in due form and manner by a treaty of peace all those places and forts, together with the chastellanies and their dependencies, which he possessed himself of in the expedition of the last year, or will be persuaded to transfer and make over to him all the right that remains to them in the duchy of Luxemburg (or else in the county of Burgundy), together with Cambrai and the Cambresis, Douai, Aire, St. Omer, Winoxbergen, Furnes and Lincken, with their bailiwicks, chastellanies and other dependencies; and in case they accept the alternative last mentioned the most Christian king will restore to the king of Spain all such places and territories as the French have possessed by their arms since they entered Flanders; provided the High and Mighty States General shall on their part promise, and render themselves guarantees to the most Christian king, that they will by their reasons and other effectual means induce the Spaniards to agree to these conditions; the said king of Great Britain and the said States General jointly conclude and judge that they can do no better service in this conjuncture and state of affairs . . . than by their joint counsels and utmost endeavours to exhort, and as much as in them lies oblige, the said two crowns to make peace upon the terms and conditions before mentioned. To which end we whose names are hereunto subscribed, having received full power to that effect, have by virtue of those injunctions concluded and agreed the following articles.

I. That the king of Great Britain and the States General of the United Netherlands shall . . . use their utmost endeavours and industry with the most Christian king to persuade him to promise and engage in the best form, and by a solemn treaty, to the

[1] Exactly the same obligation is imposed upon the king as by the previous article upon the States General.

king of Great Britain and to the States General of the United Netherlands, that he will conclude a peace and alliance with the king of Spain, . . . if the king of Spain shall be induced or persuaded by the king of Great Britain and the confederated states to yield to the most Christian king either the places he possessed himself of the last year in the Low Countries, or to give him an equivalent by delivering up the places above mentioned, or others in lieu of them, as shall be mutually agreed between the parties concerned.

II. That the most Christian king be induced to consent that the present cessation of arms in the Low Countries may be prolonged to the end of the month of May, to the end that the king of Great Britain and the confederated states may in the meantime employ themselves with all diligence, care and industry to procure the consent of the king or queen of Spain and their Council to the aforesaid terms and conditions.

III. But that the most Christian king may have no just occasion to refuse to prolong the cessation of arms, the king of Great Britain and the confederated states shall oblige themselves by the same treaty to take effectual care that the Spaniards shall yield to France all that was taken the last year by the French, or give them an equivalent, as shall be agreed with the consent of both parties.

IV. That the most Christian king shall be induced and persuaded to give entire credit to, and put full confidence in, the aforesaid promise, that his arms may not for the future disturb the quiet of the Low Countries; so that if it should happen, contrary to all hope and expectation, that the king of Great Britain and the confederated states shall not be able by their exhortations and earnest solicitations to persuade the Spaniards to give their consent to the conditions above mentioned before the end of the next ensuing May, and that it become necessary to use more effectual means to that purpose, nevertheless the French shall not move or introduce their arms within or upon the limits of the Low Countries, but the king of Great Britain and the confederated states shall engage, and take upon themselves such necessary provision, as may effectually oblige the Spaniards to accept the foresaid conditions of peace. . . .

V. That when the peace is made between the two crowns, not only the king of Great Britain and the confederated states, but likewise the Emperor and all the neighbouring kings and princes, who shall think themselves concerned that the quiet of Christendom remain unshaken, and the Low Countries be restored to the enjoyment of their former tranquillity, shall be guarantees and conservators of the same; to which end the number of forces and other means to be used against either of the parties that shall violate or infringe the said peace shall be determined and agreed, that the injury may cease and the party offended receive satisfaction. . . .

Separate articles
which shall be of the same force and authority as if they
had been inserted in the treaty concluded this day between the king of Great Britain
and the States General of the United Netherlands

I. If in the procuring of a peace between France and Spain any difficulty should arise about the point of the renunciation, it is to be so contrived that either no mention at all is to be made of it in the treaty, or at least the form is to be conceived and set down in such words as nothing may accrue to either of the two crowns on account of the said renunciation, nor any prejudice be created to either of them in point of right; but if either the king of Spain or the most Christian king refuse their consent to this expedient, then the king of Great Britain and the confederated states shall proceed against the refuser, as is agreed by the third and fourth article of the treaty and in the last of these articles respectively, with this condition, however, that in case such refusal proceed from the king of Spain the most Christian king shall oblige himself not to make war in the Low Countries, according to the tenor of the fourth article.

II. That the king of Great Britain and the States General of the United Netherlands, to the end that all parties may be satisfied, shall oblige themselves to use their utmost endeavours that a peace may at the same time be established between the kings of Spain and Portugal, but with this condition, that the most Christian king shall also oblige himself, in case this negotiation cannot be so soon accomplished, that such a delay shall no way hinder on his part the peace between him and Spain, except only that it shall be free for the said most Christian king to give succour and aid to the king of Portugal, his ally, either by way of attack, that he may draw the enemy from other parts, or by any other means which he shall judge to be most convenient and advantageous. And if the Spaniards can be brought to consent to a peace under the said condition, and the same be concluded accordingly, then the most Christian king shall be obliged wholly to abstain from the Low Countries, as possessed of peace and not involved in the disputes of either party. . . . But if, beyond and contrary to expectation, Spain should refuse to make peace with the king of Portugal, and also with the most Christian king, under that exception of leaving him free to assist his confederate, as has been already said, in this unexpected case the king of Great Britain and the confederated states shall be bound to employ themselves effectually to procure the consent of the Spaniards; yet with this provision, that the most Christian king do also oblige himself not to make war in the Low Countries, as in the former case is already said.

III. But if, beyond all expectation, the most Christian king should . . . refuse to promise that he will sign the treaty of peace as soon as the Spaniards shall consent to give up all those places which have been acquired by him in his last expedition, or such an equivalent as shall be agreed by mutual consent; or in case he shall not accomplish his promise, or shall disallow or reject the cautions and provisions that are expressed in the said treaty, which are so necessary to obviate the fears and jealousies that are most justly conceived of the most Christian king's intentions to make a farther progress with his victorious arms into the said Low Countries; . . . then England and the United Netherlands shall be bound and obliged to join themselves to the king of Spain and with all their united force and power to make war against France, not only to compel him to make peace upon the conditions aforesaid, but, if God should bless the arms taken up to this end and favour them with success, and if it shall be thought expedient to the parties concerned, to continue the war till things shall be restored to that condition in which they were at the time when the peace was made upon the borders of both kingdoms in the Pyrenean mountains. . . .

The Swedish Act

Whereas the king of Great Britain and the States of the United Provinces of the Netherlands have earnestly desired that the king of Sweden might be associated with them as one principal party in that league which is this day concluded and signed by their commissioners and plenipotentiaries; . . . and whereas the king of Sweden himself . . . has acquainted the king of Great Britain and the States of the United Netherlands with his good and sincere intentions and desire to associate and join himself to them in the business above mentioned, . . . for these reasons it is thought expedient for the common good that the present instrument between the ministers, deputies and plenipotentiaries of the said kings of Sweden and Great Britain and those of the said States of the United Netherlands be put down in writing, whereby on the one hand the king of Sweden should be obliged . . . to embrace the said league, to use the same endeavours, and to proceed equally and in like manner as the said king of Great Britain and the said States of the United Netherlands think fit to do in order to promote and carry on so useful a work; and on the other hand the said king of Sweden will be assured that a place is reserved for him, empty and entire, to enter as one principal party into this league, as by these presents he is desired in the most friendly manner, both by the king of Great Britain and by the States of the United Netherlands, who on their part will most readily employ themselves and all kind of good offices towards the Emperor and king of Spain to the end that all such differences as the said king of Sweden may have with them be composed and determined according to the rules of equity and justice. And forasmuch as concerns the aid which is required from the said king, the States General of the United Netherlands will not be wanting to send with expedition such necessary instructions to their ambassadors in the Court of England, that between them and such commissioners as the said king of Great Britain shall appoint to that purpose, and the extraordinary ambassador of the king of Sweden, who is now ready to begin his journey thither, together with other ministers residing there on the part of divers princes and states who are concerned and interested in this affair, such measures may be taken to settle all things which shall be requisite and necessary that the said league may acquire the substance as well as the form of a triple agreement, to which the respective parties shall make it their business to invite their friends and allies, if any of them should desire to be admitted.

Done at the Hague, 13/23 of January, 1668.

338. Secret Treaty of Dover, 1670
(J. Lingard, *History of England*, ed. 1874, IX, pp. 251–254)

1. It is agreed, determined and concluded that there shall be for ever a good, secure and firm peace, union, true fellowship, confederacy, friendship, alliance and good correspondence between the said lord king of Great Britain, his heirs and successors of the one part, and the said most Christian king of the other, and between all and every of their kingdoms, states and territories, as also between their subjects and vassals, that they have or possess at present, or may have, hold and possess hereafter, as well by sea and fresh waters as by land. And as evidence that this peace shall

remain inviolable, beyond the capacity of anything in the world to disturb it, there follow articles of so great confidence, and also so advantageous to the said lord kings, that one will hardly find in any age more important provisions determined and concluded.

2. The lord king of Great Britain, being convinced of the truth of the Catholic religion, and resolved to declare it and reconcile himself with the Church of Rome as soon as the welfare of his kingdom will permit, has every reason to hope and expect from the affection and loyalty of his subjects that none of them, even of those upon whom God may not yet have conferred his divine grace so abundantly as to incline them by that august example to turn to the true faith, will ever fail in the obedience that all peoples owe to their sovereigns, even of a different religion. Nevertheless, as there are sometimes mischievous and unquiet spirits who seek to disturb the public peace, especially when they can conceal their wicked designs under the plausible excuse of religion, his Majesty of Great Britain, who has nothing more at heart (after the quiet of his own conscience) than to confirm the peace which the mildness of his government has gained for his subjects, has concluded that the best means to prevent any alteration in it would be to make himself assured in case of need of the assistance of his most Christian Majesty, who, wishing in this case to give to the lord king of Great Britain an unquestionable proof of the reality of his friendship, and to contribute to the success of so glorious a design, and one of such service not merely to his Majesty of Great Britain but also to the whole Catholic religion, has promised and promises to give for that purpose to the said lord king of Great Britain the sum of two million livres tournois, of which half shall be paid three months after the exchange of the ratifications of the present treaty in specie to the order of the said lord king of Great Britain at Calais, Dieppe or Havre de Grace, or remitted by letters of exchange to London at the risk, peril and expense of the said most Christian king, and the other half in the same manner three months later. In addition the said most Christian king binds himself to assist his Majesty of Great Britain in case of need with troops to the number of 6,000 foot-soldiers, and even to raise and maintain them at his own expense, so far as the said lord king of Great Britain finds need of them for the execution of his design; and the said troops shall be transported by ships of the king of Great Britain to such places and ports as he shall consider most convenient for the good of his service, and from the day of their embarkation shall be paid, as agreed, by his most Christian Majesty, and shall obey the orders of the said lord king of Great Britain. And the time of the said declaration of Catholicism is left entirely to the choice of the said lord king of Great Britain.

3. It has also been agreed between the most Christian king and his Majesty of Great Britain that the said most Christian king shall never break or infringe the peace which he has made with Spain, and shall not contravene in any manner what he has promised by the treaty of Aix-la-Chapelle; and consequently it will be possible for the king of Great Britain to maintain the said treaty conformably to the conditions of the Triple Alliance and the engagements that depend upon it.

4. It is also agreed and accepted that if there should hereafter fall to the most Christian king any new titles and rights to the Spanish monarchy, the said lord king

of Great Britain shall assist his most Christian Majesty with all his forces both by sea and land to facilitate the acquisition of the said rights, the whole according to the particular conditions on which the said lord kings propose to agree, as well for the junction of their forces after the maturing of the said titles and rights shall have occurred as for the advantages which the said lord king can reasonably desire. And the said lord kings reciprocally bind themselves from the present moment not to make any treaty on one side or the other because of the said new rights and titles with any prince or potentate whatsoever except by mutual consent and agreement.

5. The said lord kings having each in his own right many more subjects than they would have any need of to justify to the world the resolution they have taken to humble the pride of the States General of the United Provinces of the Low Countries, and to reduce the power of a nation which has so often rendered itself odious by extreme ingratitude to its own founders and the creators of its republic, and which even has the insolence to aim now at setting itself up as sovereign arbiter and judge of all other potentates, it is agreed, decided and concluded that their Majesties will declare and wage war jointly with all their forces by land and sea on the said States General of the United Provinces of the Low Countries, and that neither of the said lord kings will make any treaty of peace, or truce, or suspension of arms with them without the knowledge and consent of the other, as also that all commerce between the subjects of the said lord kings and those of the said States shall be forbidden, and that the vessels and goods of those who carry on trade in defiance of this prohibition may be seized by the subjects of the other lord king, and shall be deemed lawful prize. And all previous treaties made between the said States and either of the said lord kings or their predecessors shall be void, except that of the Triple Alliance made for the maintenance of the treaty of Aix-la-Chapelle. And if after the declaration of war any prisoners are taken from among subjects of either of the said lord kings who shall be enrolled in the service of the said States, or shall at the time be found in it, they shall be put to death by authority of the said lord king whose subjects shall have taken them.

6. And for the purpose of waging and conducting the war as successfully as the said lord kings, in virtue of the justice of their common cause, expect, it is also agreed that his most Christian Majesty will undertake all the expense necessary for setting on foot, maintaining and supporting the operations of the armies required for delivering a powerful attack by land on the strongholds and territory of the said States, the said lord king of Great Britain binding himself only to contribute to the army of the said most Christian king, and to maintain there at his own expense, a body of 6,000 infantry, whose commanding officer shall hold the rank of general, and obey his most Christian Majesty and the supreme commander of the army in which the said body of troops shall serve as auxiliaries. That body shall be composed of six regiments of ten companies each, with a hundred men to each company, and the said troops shall be transported and landed at such ports and harbours, and at such times, as shall be agreed upon hereafter between the said lord kings, in such manner, nevertheless, that they may arrive on the coast of Picardy, or such other place as shall be arranged, one month at latest after the fleets shall unite in the neighbourhood of Portsmouth, as is appointed below.

7. As to what concerns the war at sea, the said lord king of Great Britain shall undertake that burden, and shall fit out at least fifty great ships and ten fire-ships, to which the said most Christian king shall bind himself to add a squadron of thirty good French vessels, of which the smallest shall carry forty pieces of cannon, and a sufficient number of fire-ships, even up to ten if necessary, according to the proportion which there ought to be in the fleet. This auxiliary squadron of French vessels shall continue to serve throughout the period of the said war at the charge and expense of his most Christian Majesty, and in the event of loss of men and vessels they shall be replaced as soon as possible by his most Christian Majesty; and the said squadron shall be commanded by a French vice-admiral or lieutenant-general, who shall obey the orders of his Royal Highness the duke of York in virtue of the powers which the said lord kings shall give to the said lord duke, each for the vessels which belong to him. And if the said lord duke shall attack and engage the Dutch vessels, and do all which he considers most proper for the good of the common cause, he shall enjoy also the honour of the flag, salutes, and all the other authorities, prerogatives and pre-eminences which admirals are accustomed to enjoy; and on the other side also the said French vice-admiral or lieutenant-general shall have for himself precedence in the councils, and for his ship and vice-admiral's flag precedence in sailing, over the English vice-admiral and ship of the same rank. In addition the captains, commanders, officers, sailors and soldiers of each nation shall behave as friends among themselves according to the agreement to be made hereafter, so that no incident may arise which may alter the good union. And in order that the said lord king of Great Britain may more easily support the expense of the war, his most Christian Majesty binds himself to pay to the said king each year that the said war shall last the sum of three millions of livres tournois in the aforesaid manner, of which the first payment, which shall be of 750,000 livres tournois, shall be made three months before the declaration of the war, the second of like sum at the time of the said declaration, and the remainder, amounting to 1,500,000 livres tournois six months after the said declaration. And in the years following, the first payment, which shall be of 750,000 livres tournois, shall be made on the 1st of February, the second of like sum on the 1st of May, and the third, amounting to 1,500,000 livres tournois, on the 15th of October; which sums shall be paid in specie to the order of the king of Great Britain at Calais, Dieppe or Havre de Grace, or else remitted by letters of exchange to London at the risk, peril and expense of the said most Christian king. It is also agreed and determined that the said lord king of Great Britain shall not be bound to declare this war until the auxiliary French squadron of the said thirty vessels and ten fire-ships shall have effected a junction with the English fleet in the neighbourhood of Portsmouth. And of all the conquests which shall be made from the States General his Majesty of Great Britain shall be content with the following places, viz., the island of Walcheren, Sluys, with the island of Cadsand; and the method of attack and the manner of continuing the war shall be regulated by a settlement which shall be agreed upon hereafter. And inasmuch as the dissolution of the government of the States General might involve some prejudice to the prince of Orange, nephew of the king of Great Britain, and also that some fortresses, towns and governments which belong to him are included in

the proposed division of the country, it has been determined and concluded that the said lord kings shall do all they can to secure that the said prince may find his advantage in the continuation and end of the war, as shall hereafter be provided in separate articles.

8. It has also been agreed that before the declaration of war the said lord kings shall do their utmost, jointly or severally as the occasion shall require, to persuade the kings of Sweden and Denmark, or one of them, to enter into this war against the States General, or at least to oblige them to remain neutral; and an attempt will likewise be made to secure the participation of the electors of Cologne and Branden-burg, the House of Brunswick, the duke of Neuburg and the bishop of Münster. The said lord kings shall also do their utmost to persuade even the Emperor and the crown of Spain not to oppose the conquest of the said country.

9. It is likewise agreed and accepted that after the said lord king of Great Britain shall have made the declaration specified in the second article of this treaty, which it is hoped by the grace of God will be followed with good success, it will be entirely within the power and discretion of the said most Christian king to determine the time when the said lord kings shall make war with their united forces against the States General, his Majesty of Great Britain promising to make his declaration of war conjointly at the time that his most Christian Majesty shall judge the most proper for that purpose, the said lord king of Great Britain being assured that his most Christian Majesty in naming the said time will have regard to the interests of the two crowns, which after the conclusion of this treaty will be common to both and inseparable.

10. If in any previous treaty made by one or other of the said lord kings with any prince or state whatever there should be found conditions inconsistent with those specified in this alliance, the said conditions shall be void, and those which are included in the present treaty shall remain in full force and vigour.

And for the better union of the minds and interests of the subjects of the said lord kings, it has been agreed that the treaty of commerce at present being made shall be concluded as soon as possible.

339. Grand Alliance, 1689

(C. Jenkinson, *Collection of Treaties*, I, pp. 286–292)

William the Third, by the Grace of God, king of Great Britain, France and Ireland, Defender of the Faith, &c., to all and every one to whom these presents shall come, greeting. Whereas a certain treaty of friendship and stricter alliance between the most serene, most potent and most invincible prince and lord, Leopold, by the Grace of God, elect Roman Emperor, . . . and the High and Mighty Lords the States General of the United Provinces, was made and concluded at Vienna, the 12th day of May last past,[1] . . . the tenor of which treaty is as follows:

I. There shall be and remain for ever a constant, perpetual and inviolable friend-ship and good correspondence between his Imperial Majesty and the States General. . . .

[1] 2/12 May 1689.

II. And whereas the French king has lately, without any lawful cause or pretext, attacked as well his Imperial Majesty as the States General by a most grievous and most unjust war, there shall be during the same not only a defensive but also an offensive alliance between the contracting parties, by virtue whereof they shall both of them act in a hostile manner with all their forces by sea and land against the said French king, and such of his allies as upon exhortation to be used for that purpose shall refuse to separate themselves from him. . . .

III. It shall not be lawful for either party to withdraw from this war with France, or to enter separately upon any convention, treaty of peace or cessation of arms with France and its adherents, upon any pretext whatsoever, without the consent and concurrence of the other party.

IV. There shall by no means any peace be concluded before the peace of Westphalia and those of Osnabrück, Münster and the Pyrenees have, by the help of God, and by common force, been vindicated, and that all things, both in Church and State, are restored to their former condition according to the tenor of the same. . . .

VI. After the present war, by common consent, shall be ended and a peace concluded, there shall remain between his sacred Imperial Majesty, his heirs and successors, and the States General of the United Provinces a perpetual defensive alliance against the often-mentioned crown of France and its adherents, by virtue whereof both parties shall use their utmost endeavours that the peace to be made may remain firm and perpetual.

VII. But if it should happen that the crown of France should again attack one or both of the confederate parties, . . . they shall be obliged faithfully to assist each other with all their forces and in the same manner as now, . . . and not to desist till all things are brought again into their former state, according to the conditions of the aforesaid peace, and that satisfaction be given to the party offended. . . .

IX. If there are any controversies between the contracting parties on occasion of the limits of their dominions, or that any such should arise hereafter, they shall be accommodated and composed in a friendly manner, either by a commission or ministers deputed by both sides, without making use of any manner of force; and in the meantime nothing shall be innovated therein.

X. There shall be invited into the society of this present treaty, by his Imperial Majesty the crown of Spain, and by the States General the crown of England; and there shall be likewise admitted into the same all the allies and confederates of either party who shall think fit to enter into the same. . . .

And whereas the States General have, by their ambassadors extraordinary, invited us by virtue of the tenth article to enter into the alliance of the aforesaid treaty, . . . know ye . . . that we, having perused and maturely considered the said treaty, have accepted, approved and ratified, as we do by these presents, for us, our heirs and successors, accept, approve and ratify the same. . . .

Given at our court at Hampton Court the 9th day of December, in the year of our Lord, as above, 1689, and of our reign the first.

WILLIAM R.

Separate Articles

France having openly declared, in several places and courts, that notwithstanding the most solemn renunciation they still pretend by force of arms to assert for the Dauphin the succession of the Spanish monarchy, in case his Catholic Majesty should die without lawful issue, and publicly aiming to make the said Dauphin king of the Romans, the States General of the United Provinces, maturely considering what a blow either of these pretensions would give to their state, and what prejudice it would bring to the public affairs and quiet, do promise by these separate articles, which are as valid as if they had been inserted word for word in the principal treaty, first, that in case the present king of Spain should die without lawful issue (which God forbid) they will with all their forces assist his sacred Imperial Majesty, or his heirs, in taking the succession of the Spanish monarchy, lawfully belonging to that house, together with its kingdoms, provinces, dominions and rights. . . .

They will likewise use all friendly offices and endeavours with the princes electors of the Empire, their confederates, that the most serene Joseph, king of Hungary, his Imperial Majesty's eldest son, may be speedily chosen king of the Romans; and if France should by threats or arms hinder, oppose or any way disturb this election they will, in opposition thereto, assist his sacred Imperial Majesty with their utmost force.

The crown of England shall be likewise invited to enter into the agreement of these articles, made at Vienna the 12th of May 1689.

340. Second Partition Treaty, 1700
(Manuscripts of the House of Lords, N.S., IV, pp. 252–258)

Be it known unto all who shall see these presents that the most serene and most potent prince Louis XIV, by the grace of God most Christian king of France and Navarre, and the most serene and most potent prince William III, also by the grace of God king of Great Britain, and the Lords States General of the United Provinces of the Netherlands, having no greater desire than . . . to prevent by taking timely measures those events which might raise new wars in Europe, have to this end given their full powers to[1]. . . . who by virtue of the said powers have agreed to the following articles.

I. The peace re-established by the treaty of Ryswick[2] between his most Christian Majesty, his Britannic Majesty and the Lords States General of the United Provinces of the Netherlands, . . . shall be firm and constant. . . .

III. And as the two kings and the Lords States General desire above all things the conservation of the public peace, . . . by accommodating the disputes and differences which might arise upon the subject of the [Spanish] succession, or by the umbrage of too many states reunited under one and the same prince, they have thought good to take beforehand necessary measures to prevent the evils which the sorrowful event of the Catholic king's death without children might produce.

IV. Therefore it is agreed that if the case before mentioned should happen, the

---

[1] Names of plenipotentiaries follow.   [2] No. 345.

Table 7

The Spanish Succession

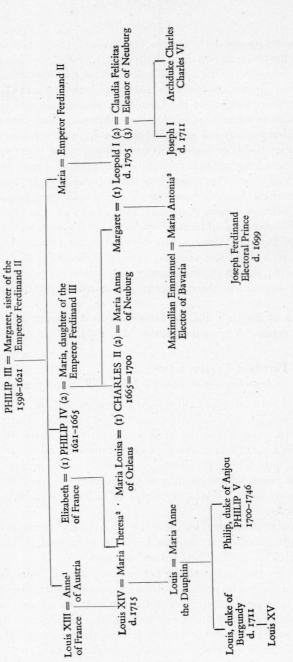

PHILIP III = Margaret, sister of the
1598–1621   Emperor Ferdinand II

Louis XIII = Anne[1]   Elizabeth = (1) PHILIP IV (2) = Maria, daughter of the   Maria = Emperor Ferdinand II
of France   of Austria   of France   1621–1665   Emperor Ferdinand III

Louis XIV = Maria Theresa[2] · Maria Louisa = (1) CHARLES II (2) = Maria Anna   Margaret = (1) Leopold I (2) = Claudia Felicitas
d. 1715   of Orleans   1665=1700   of Neuburg   d. 1705   (3) = Eleanor of Neuburg

Louis = Maria Anne   Maximilian Emmanuel = Maria Antonia[3]   Joseph I   Archduke Charles
the Dauphin   Elector of Bavaria   d. 1711   Charles VI

Philip, duke of Anjou   Joseph Ferdinand
PHILIP V   Electoral Prince
1700–1746   d. 1699

Louis, duke of
Burgundy
d. 1711

Louis XV

[1] Anne, on her marriage, formally renounced all claim to the Spanish inheritance.
[2] Maria Theresa, on her marriage, made a similar renunciation, but on conditions regarding the payment of her dowry which were not fulfilled.
[3] Maria Antonia, at the instance of her own father, made a purely private, and therefore invalid, renunciation.

most Christian king, as well in his own name as in that of his Royal Highness the Dauphin, his children, males or females, heirs and successors, born and to be born, as also his Royal Highness the Dauphin for himself, his children, males or females, born and to be born, shall hold themselves satisfied . . . that his Royal Highness the Dauphin shall have for his share in full property and possession, and in extinction of all his pretensions to the succession of Spain, to be enjoyed by him, his heirs, successors, descendants, males or females, born and to be born, for ever, . . . the kingdoms of Naples and Sicily in the same manner the Spaniards possess them at present; the places depending on the monarchy of Spain, situated on the coast of Tuscany or adjacent isles, comprehended under the name of Santo Stefano, Port' Ercole, Orbetello, Telamone, Portolongone, Piombino, in the same manner also as the Spaniards possess them at present; the town and marquisate of Finale, in the like manner as the Spaniards possess them; the province of Guipuzcoa, particularly the towns of Fuenterrabia and San Sebastian situated in that province, and especially the port of passage which is therein comprehended, with this restriction only, that if there be any places depending upon the said province which shall be found situated beyond the Pyrenees or the other mountains of Navarre, Alava or Biscay on the side of Spain they shall remain to Spain; and if there be any places in like manner depending upon the provinces subjected to Spain which are on this side the Pyrenees or other mountains of Navarre, Alava or of Biscay, on the side of the province of Guipuzcoa, they shall remain to France; and the passages of the said mountains and the said mountains which are betwixt the said province of Guipuzcoa, Navarre, Alava and Biscay, to whomsoever they belong, shall be divided between France and Spain, in such sort as there shall remain as much of the said mountains and passes to France on her side as shall remain to Spain on hers. . . . Further the dominions of the duke of Lorraine, that is to say the duchies of Lorraine and Bar, as Charles IV of that name possessed them and as they were restored by the treaty of Ryswick, shall be yielded and conveyed to his Royal Highness the Dauphin, his children, heirs and successors, males or females, born or to be born, in property and full possession, in lieu of the duchy of Milan, which shall be yielded and exchanged to the said duke of Lorraine, his children, males or females, heirs, descendants, successors, born and to be born, in property and full possession, who will not refuse so advantageous an offer, it being well understood that the county of Bitche belongs to his Highness the prince of Vaudemont, who shall enter into the possession of the lands which he heretofore enjoyed, which have been or ought to have been restored according to the treaty of Ryswick. . . .

VI. The said crown of Spain and the other kingdoms, islands, states, lands and places which the Catholic king at this time possesses, as well without as within Europe, shall be given and assigned to the most serene Archduke Charles, second son to the Emperor (except what has been declared in the fourth article to compose the share of his Royal Highness the Dauphin, and the duchy of Milan according to the said fourth article), in all property and full possession as his share, and extinguishing all his pretensions to the said succession of Spain, to enjoy the same, himself, his heirs and successors, born and to be born, for ever. . . .

VII. Immediately after the exchange of ratifications of this present treaty it shall be communicated to the Emperor, who shall be invited to enter thereunto; but if after three months' time from the day of the said communication and the said invitation, or the day that his Catholic Majesty should die, if it should happen before the expiration of the said three months, his Imperial Majesty and the king of the Romans should refuse to enter therein, and to agree to the share assigned to the most serene archduke, the two kings or their successors and the Lords States General shall agree upon a prince to whom that share shall be given. And in case, notwithstanding the present convention, the said most serene archduke would take possession either of the part which might fall to him, before he has accepted the present treaty, or of that part which might be assigned to his Royal Highness the Dauphin, or to him who shall have the duchy of Milan in exchange as above said, the said two kings and the Lords States General by virtue of this convention shall hinder it with all their forces. . . .

IX. If the most serene archduke should die without children, either before or after the death of the Catholic king, the share which is above assigned to him by the sixth article of this treaty shall come to such male or female child of the Emperor, the king of the Romans excepted, or to such child, male or female, of the king of the Romans, as his Imperial Majesty shall think fit to appoint, and in case his said Imperial Majesty should die without having made the said appointment it may be done by the king of the Romans, but on condition that the said share shall never be united nor belong to the person of him who shall be Emperor or king of the Romans, or is become one or the other, be it by succession, will, contract of marriage, donation, exchange, cession, appeal, revolt or otherwise; and in like manner the said share of the most serene archduke shall never come or belong to the person of a prince who shall be king or dauphin of France, or is become one or the other, be it by succession, will, contract of marriage, donation, exchange, cession, appeal, revolt or otherwise. . . .

XII. All kings, princes and states that will enter into the present treaty shall be admitted into the same, and it shall be lawful to the two kings and to the Lords States General and to each of them in particular to require and invite all those they shall think fit to enter into this present treaty, and to be in like manner guarantees of the execution thereof and of the validity of the renunciations herein contained.

XIII. And for the further securing the peace of Europe the said kings, princes and states shall not only be invited to be guarantees of the execution of the present treaty and of the validity of the said renunciations, as above, but if any one of the princes in favour of whom the partitions are made would in time to come break the order established by this treaty, begin new enterprises contrary to the same, and so aggrandize himself to the prejudice one of the other under any pretence whatsoever, the same guarantee of this treaty shall be understood in such case to extend so as that the kings, princes and states who promise the same shall be obliged to employ their forces to oppose the said enterprises and maintain all things in the condition agreed on by the said articles. . . .

Done and signed at London, 21st February, O.S., 1699/ 3rd March, N.S., 1700, by us, plenipotentiaries of France and England, and at the Hague, the 25th of the said month of March, 1700, by us, plenipotentiaries of France and of the Lords States General. . . .

341. Grand Alliance, 1701

(C. Jenkinson, *Collection of Treaties*, 1, pp. 326–331)

Whereas Charles the Second, king of Spain, of most glorious memory, being not long since dead without issue, his sacred Imperial Majesty has claimed the succession in the kingdoms and provinces of the deceased king as lawfully belonging to his august family; but the most Christian king, aiming at the same succession for his grandson the duke of Anjou, and pretending a right did accrue to him by a certain will of the deceased king, has usurped the possession of the entire inheritance, or Spanish monarchy, for the aforesaid duke of Anjou, and invaded by his arms the provinces of the Spanish Low Countries and the duchy of Milan, has a fleet ready fitted in the port of Cadiz, has sent several ships of war to the Spanish West Indies, and by this and many other ways the kingdoms of France and Spain are so closely united and cemented that they may seem henceforward not to be otherwise considered than as one and the same kingdom; so that it sufficiently appears, unless timely care be taken, that his Imperial Majesty will be destitute of all hopes of ever receiving satisfaction in his pretension, the sacred Roman Empire will lose its rights in the fiefs belonging to it in Italy and the Spanish Netherlands, the free intercourse of navigation and commerce which the English and Dutch have in the Mediterranean, the Indies and other places will be utterly destroyed, and the United Provinces will be deprived of the security which they enjoyed by the provinces of the Spanish Netherlands lying between them and the French, which is commonly called a barrier; lastly that the French and Spaniards, being thus united, will within a short time become so formidable to all that they may easily assume to themselves the dominion over all Europe: . . . these reasons inducing, his sacred Imperial Majesty, his sacred royal Majesty of Great Britain, and the High and Mighty Lords the States General of the United Provinces . . . have thought a strict conjunction and alliance between themselves necessary for repelling the greatness of the common danger, and to this end have agreed to the following articles of alliance:

I. There shall be and continue between his sacred Imperial Majesty, his sacred royal Majesty of Great Britain and the Lords the States General of the United Provinces a constant, perpetual and inviolable friendship and correspondence. . . .

II. His sacred Imperial Majesty, his sacred royal Majesty of Great Britain and the States General, desiring nothing more earnestly than the peace and general quiet of all Europe, have adjudged that nothing can be more effectual for the establishment thereof than the procuring an equitable and reasonable satisfaction to his Imperial Majesty for his pretension to the Spanish succession, and that the king of Great Britain and the States General may obtain a particular and sufficient security for their kingdoms, provinces and dominions, and for the navigation and commerce of their subjects. . . .

V. The confederates, in order to the procuring the satisfaction and security aforesaid, shall, amongst other things, use their utmost endeavours to recover the provinces of the Spanish Low Countries, that they may be a fence and rampart, commonly called a barrier, separating and distancing France from the United Provinces; . . . as likewise the duchy of Milan, with its dependencies, as a fief of the Empire and contributing to the security of his Imperial Majesty's hereditary countries; besides the kingdoms of Naples and Sicily and the lands and islands upon the coasts of Tuscany in the Mediterranean, that belong to the Spanish dominions and may serve to the same purpose, and will also be of advantage to the navigation and commerce of the subjects of the king of Great Britain and of the United Provinces.

VI. It shall be lawful for his royal Majesty of Great Britain and the Lords the States General, by common advice and for the benefit and enlargement of the navigation and commerce of their subjects, to seize by their forces what lands and cities they can, belonging to the Spanish dominions in the Indies; and whatsoever they shall so take shall be their own. . . .

VIII. It shall not be permitted to either party, when the war is once begun, to treat of peace with the enemy, unless jointly and with the common advices of the other parties; and no peace shall be made unless an equitable and reasonable satisfaction for his Imperial Majesty, and the particular security of the kingdoms, provinces, dominions, navigation and commerce for his Majesty of Great Britain and the States General, be first obtained; and unless care be taken by fitting security that the kingdoms of France and Spain shall never come and be united under the same government, nor that one and the same person shall be king of both kingdoms; and particularly that the French shall never get into the possession of the Spanish Indies, neither shall they be permitted to sail thither on the account of traffic, directly or indirectly, on any pretence whatsoever; and lastly, unless full liberty be granted unto the subjects of the king of Great Britain and the States General to exercise and enjoy all the same privileges, rights, immunities and franchises, of commerce by sea and land, in Spain, the Mediterranean and all lands and places which the king of Spain last deceased did possess at the time of his death, as well in Europe as elsewhere, which they used and enjoyed . . . before the death of the late king of Spain. . . .

XII. But if an agreement can now be made concerning the satisfaction and security so often mentioned, or if after a war entered into by necessity peace shall be again restored, there shall after such an agreement or peace concluded be, and always continue, between the contracting parties a defensive alliance for the maintenance of the said agreement or peace.

XIII. All kings, princes and states that please to have a concern for the general peace shall be admitted into the society of this alliance. . . .

At the Hague, the 7th day of September[1] 1701.

[1] 27 August/7 September.

342. Methuen Treaties, 1703

(Journals of the House of Commons, XIV, pp. 222–226)

(i) TREATY OF A DEFENSIVE ALLIANCE,
CONCLUDED BETWEEN THE QUEEN AND THE STATES GENERAL ON ONE SIDE
AND THE KING OF PORTUGAL ON THE OTHER,
AT LISBON, MAY THE 16TH,[1] 1703

I. The treaties formerly concluded between the aforesaid potentates are approved, confirmed and ratified, that they may be exactly and fully observed, except in such matters as shall be otherwise taken care of and provided for by this treaty. . . .

II. If it shall at any time happen that the kings of Spain and France, as well the present as future, or either of them, have a mind or be suspected to intend to make war against the kingdom of Portugal in its continent or transmarine provinces (whatever kings they be) her sacred royal Majesty of Great Britain and the States General shall use their endeavours in a friendly manner to persuade the said kings, or either of them, that he or they will keep the treaties of peace with Portugal and not make war upon that kingdom.

III. But in case these offices shall avail nothing, but prove ineffectual, so that the said kings, or either of them, shall wage war against Portugal, the aforesaid potentates of Britain and Holland shall make war with all their might against the aforesaid king or kings that shall invade Portugal, and towards carrying on the war that shall be waged in the continent of that kingdom shall furnish twelve thousand soldiers, whom they shall be obliged to arm, and pay them what shall be needful, as well in quarters as out of them; and the confederates shall have that number complete by sending recruits as often as there shall be occasion.

IV. And in this case also the aforesaid potentates of Britain and Holland shall be obliged to have and maintain, upon the coast of Portugal and in the ports of that kingdom, a competent number of ships of war, to defend their coasts and ports, their commerce and merchant ships from any hostile insult. . . .

V. But if the aforesaid kings of Spain and France, or either of them, shall make war upon the transmarine provinces or dominions of Portugal, or if his sacred royal Majesty of Portugal shall know that they do design it, the aforesaid potentates of Britain and Holland shall furnish his sacred royal Majesty of Portugal with such a number of ships of war as shall be of equal force and strength with the enemy's fleet, and even superior, so that they may not only be able to resist them but also to hinder that war and irruption as long as the war shall last and there shall be occasion; but if the enemy shall possess themselves of any town or seize any place in the aforesaid transmarine provinces and dominions, which they may fortify, these succours shall continue until the full recovery of such town or place, or towns and places in case there shall be more taken.

VI. All these auxiliary ships shall be subject to the command of his sacred royal Majesty of Portugal, that they may do those things which shall be commanded by

[1] 5/16 May.

his said Majesty; but if they shall proceed to the transmarine provinces and dominions of Portugal they shall also do those things that shall be enjoined them by the viceroys and governors there in the name of his sacred royal Majesty. . . .

XI. If it should at any time happen that the kings of Spain and France, or either of them, should go about to make war against the kingdom of Great Britain or the United Provinces, his sacred royal Majesty of Portugal shall use his endeavours in a friendly manner to persuade the said kings, or either of them, to keep the treaties of peace with the foresaid kingdom of Great Britain and the United Provinces.

XII. But in case these offices should avail nothing, and prove ineffectual, so that the foresaid kings, or either of them, shall make war against the kingdom of Great Britain or the United Provinces, his sacred royal Majesty of Portugal shall in like manner be obliged to make war with all his might against the foresaid kings, or either of them; and in that case also the two potentates of Great Britain and the States General shall supply him with the same aids of soldiers and ships as are agreed by the precedent heads or articles in case that the kings of France and Spain, or either of them, shall make war against Portugal, and with all those things in the same manner as is there expressed.

XIII. As well in the first as second case of making war his sacred royal Majesty of Portugal shall be obliged to have ten ships of war for the defence of himself and his confederates; nevertheless in such manner that if the Spaniards and French together, or Spaniards only, make war against the confederates, in such case the ten ships of war of his sacred royal Majesty of Portugal shall not be obliged to stir from the coast of Portugal, where they will be of great use to divert the forces of the enemy; but if war is made only by the French it shall be lawful for the ships of Portugal to assist the confederates in conjunction with their fleets.

XIV. Neither peace nor truce shall be made but by the mutual consent of the confederates; and this league shall be perpetual, not determined by any limits of time. . . .

(ii) TREATY OF AN OFFENSIVE ALLIANCE,
CONCLUDED BETWEEN THE EMPEROR, THE QUEEN AND THE
STATES GENERAL ON ONE SIDE AND THE KING OF PORTUGAL ON THE OTHER,
AT LISBON, MAY THE 16TH,[1] 1703

I. The three confederate potentates above mentioned shall contribute their endeavours unanimously that the most serene Archduke Charles, second son of his imperial Majesty, be put into the possession of all Spain, as the Catholic king, Charles the Second, did possess it, with this, however, that his sacred royal Majesty of Portugal be not bound to make an offensive war except in Spain itself.

II. For the making this offensive war in Spain his sacred royal Majesty of Portugal shall not be bound to have and maintain at his own charge above twelve thousand foot and three thousand horse, which he is to bring into the field.

III. Besides, his sacred royal Majesty of Portugal shall raise thirteen thousand

[1] 5/16 May.

Portuguese soldiers, that in the whole the forces of Portugal may be twenty-eight thousand men, whereof five thousand shall be horse and twenty-three thousand foot.

IV. Of these thirteen thousand soldiers, viz., eleven thousand foot, two thousand horse, those eleven thousand foot shall be armed with proper arms, which for that purpose the confederates are to furnish, and over and above, as an addition, two thousand arms for those soldiers.

V. The confederates shall be bound to give to his sacred royal Majesty of Portugal ten hundred thousand silver Philips, Spanish money, or, as commonly called, a million of pattacoons each year while the war lasts for the charge of the said thirteen thousand soldiers, as well for their pay as for all other expenses whereof they shall stand in need, as well in quarters as in the field. . . .

VIII. Besides the said ten hundred thousand silver Philips, Spanish money, or million of pattacoons, which the confederates are to give every year for the payment of the thirteen thousand Portuguese soldiers, as above said, they shall be bound further to give to his sacred royal Majesty of Portugal five hundred thousand silver Philips, or five hundred thousand pattacoons, for his preparations of the army and what else is necessary this first year; and they shall deliver this sum of money at the time of the ratification of this treaty.

IX. The confederates shall furnish, and shall always have ready every year during the war, twelve thousand foreign veteran soldiers, viz., ten thousand foot, one thousand horse and one thousand dragoons; which twelve thousand soldiers they shall not only recruit from time to time at their own expense as it shall be necessary, but they shall also arm and pay them with their own money what shall be needful for them. . . .

XVII. The maritime potentates shall be bound to have and maintain, on the maritime coast of Portugal and in the havens thereof, a competent number of ships of war, for defending safely the coast and havens and also the trade and fleets of merchant ships against any hostile force, so as that it being found, or even understood, that the havens themselves and the said fleets may be invaded by a greater hostile force, the said confederates shall be bound, before the case of that invasion happens, to send into Portugal that number of ships of war which may be equal and even superior to the ships and forces of the enemies who shall design to invade the havens and fleets aforesaid. . . .

XVIII. But if any potentates shall make war in the transmarine provinces or dominions of Portugal, or if his sacred royal Majesty of Portugal shall know that the enemy does design it, the confederates shall furnish. . . .[1]

XIX. All the auxiliary ships shall be subject to the commands of his sacred royal Majesty of Portugal, that they do. . . .[2]

XXI. Neither peace nor truce shall be made but by mutual consent of all the confederates, and they shall not be made at any time while the most Christian king's grandson, the Dauphin's second son, or any other prince of the House of France remains in Spain, nor yet unless that the crown of Portugal do entirely possess and reign over all lands, kingdoms, islands, states, dominions, castles, towns, villages

[1] As in Article V of the Defensive Treaty.   [2] As in Article VI of the Defensive Treaty.

and their territories and appurtenances which it now possesses, as well in as out of Spain. . . .

XXIV. The most serene Archduke Charles shall come hither into Portugal, and shall land in it with all the succours which the confederates are to send, as is covenanted in this treaty; and his sacred royal Majesty of Portugal shall not be bound to make war till the most serene archduke be landed in Portugal and the succours, both of men and ships, are arrived there. . .

D. TREATIES OF PEACE

343. Treaty of Breda, 1667

(G. Chalmers, *Collection of Treaties*, I, pp. 133–149)

I. First, that from this day there be a true, firm and inviolable peace, sincere friendship, a nearer and straiter alliance and union between the most serene king of Great Britain and the High and Mighty States General of the United Provinces of the Netherlands. . . .

III. . . . That both the parties and either of them shall keep and possess hereafter, with plenary right of sovereignty, propriety and possession, all such lands, islands, cities, forts, places and colonies (how many soever) as during this war, or in any former times before this war, they have, by force of arms or any other way whatsoever, gotten and detained from the other party, and that altogether after the same manner as they had gotten and did possess them the 10/20 day of May last past, none of the same places being excepted.

IV. Moreover, that all ships, with their furniture and merchandise, and all movables which during this war or at any time heretofore have come into the power of either of the forementioned parties or their subjects, be and remain to the present possessors without any compensation or restitution. . . .

VI. But if after the 10/20 day of May expressed in the precedent third article, or after the peace is made or this treaty signed, either party shall intercept and get from the other any lands, islands, cities, forts, colonies or other places whatsoever, all and every of them, without any distinction of place or time, shall be restored bona fide in the same state and condition wherein they shall be found to be at the time whensoever it shall be known in those places that the peace is made. . . .

XI. That the said king of Great Britain and the said States General remain friends, confederate, united and allied, for the defence and preservation of the rights, liberties and immunities of either ally and their subjects against all whomsoever who shall endeavour to disturb the peace of either's state by sea or land, or such as, living within either's dominions, shall be declared public enemies to either. . . .

XIX. That the ships and vessels of the said United Provinces, as well men-of-war as others, meeting any men-of-war of the said king of Great Britain's in the British seas, shall strike the flag and lower the top-sail in such manner as the same hath been formerly observed in any times whatsoever. . . .

XXII. That in case the said king of Great Britain or the said States General do make any treaty of amity or alliance with any other kings, republics, princes or states, they shall therein comprehend each other and their dominions, if they desire to be therein comprehended, and shall give to the other notice of all such treaties, or friendship and alliance. . . .

XXVIII. That the men-of-war or convoys of either nation, meeting or overtaking at sea any merchant ship or ships belonging to the subjects or inhabitants of the other, holding the same course or going the same way, shall be bound, as long as they keep one course together, to protect and defend them against all and every one who would set upon them. . . .

XXXI. That if any injury be done or practised by either nation, or the subjects or inhabitants of the same, against the subjects or inhabitants of the other, or against any of the articles of this present treaty, or against common right, yet nevertheless no letters of reprisal, marque or countermarque shall be granted by either side till justice hath been first demanded according to the ordinary course of law. . . .

Done at Breda,
the 21/31 day of July 1667.

344. Treaty of Westminster, 1674
(G. Chalmers, *Collection of Treaties*, I, pp. 172–177)

I. It is concluded and agreed that from this day there shall be a firm and inviolable peace, union and friendship betwixt his Majesty the king of Great Britain and the High and Mighty Lords, the States General of the United Provinces, and betwixt all their subjects, whether within Europe or without, in all regions and places whatsoever.

II. That this good union betwixt the abovesaid king and the said States General may the sooner take its effect, it is by them agreed and concluded that immediately upon the publication of this treaty of peace all actions of hostility shall on both sides be immediately forbid. . . .

III. But in respect the distances of places are so different that the orders and commands of the respective sovereigns cannot at the same time reach all their subjects, it hath been thought fit to appoint these following limits for the committing any acts of hostility or force upon each other, viz., that after the expiration of twelve days next following the publication of this treaty no hostility shall be acted from the Soundings to the Naze in Norway; nor after the term of six weeks betwixt the Soundings and Tangier; nor after the term of ten weeks betwixt the said Tangier and the Equator, neither in the Ocean, Mediterranean or elsewhere; nor after the term of eight months in any part of the world. . . .

IV. That the aforesaid States General of the United Provinces, in due acknowledgment on their part of the king of Great Britain's right to have his flag respected in the seas hereafter mentioned, shall and do declare and agree that whatever ships or vessels belonging to the said United Provinces, whether vessels of war or others, or whether single or in fleets, shall meet in any of the seas from Cape Finisterre to the middle point of the land Van Staten in Norway with any ships or vessels belonging to his Majesty of Great Britain, whether those ships be single or in greater number, if they carry his Majesty of Great Britain's flag or jack, the aforesaid Dutch vessels or ships shall strike their flag and lower their top-sail in the same manner and with as much respect as hath at any time or in any place been formerly practised towards any ships of his Majesty of Great Britain or his predecessors by any ships of the States General or their predecessors.

V. Whereas the colony of Surinam and the articles made upon the surrender thereof in 1667 betwixt William Byam, then governor thereof for his Majesty of

Great Britain, and Abraham Quirini, commander for the States General, have in the execution of them administered much occasion of dispute, and contributed much to the late misunderstanding betwixt his Majesty and the said States General; to remove all grounds of future mistakes the said States General do by these presents agree and covenant with the said king of Great Britain that not only the fore-named articles shall be executed without any manner of tergiversation or equivocation, but that likewise it shall be free for his Majesty to depute one or more persons thither, to see the condition of his subjects there and to adjust with them a time for their departure; and that it shall be lawful for his Majesty to send one, two or three ships at one time, and thereon to embark and carry away the said subjects, their goods and slaves. . . .

VI. It is agreed and concluded that whatever country, island, town, haven, castle or fortress hath been or shall be taken by either party from the other since the beginning of the late unhappy war, whether in Europe or elsewhere, and before the expiration of the times above limited for hostility, shall be restored to the former owner in the same condition it shall be in at the time of the publishing this peace. . . .

VII. That the treaty of Breda made in the year 1667,[1] as all other former treaties confirmed by the said treaty, be renewed, and remain in their full force and vigour, so far forth as they contradict nothing in this present treaty. . . .

X. That whereas the most serene queen regent of Spain hath given assurance to his Majesty of Great Britain that the said States General should, upon the making of the peace, pay unto his said Majesty the king of Great Britain the sum of 800,000 patacoons, the said States General do promise and covenant to pay the said 800,000 patacoons in this following manner, viz., a fourth part as soon as the ratification of this treaty shall be mutually exhibited, and the rest the three ensuing years, by equal portions. . . .

Done at Westminster,
the 9/19 day of February 1673/4.

345. Treaty of Ryswick, 1697
(Manuscripts of the House of Lords, N.S., IV, pp. 232–238)

I. There shall be a universal perpetual peace and a true and sincere friendship between the most serene and mighty prince Louis XIV, the most Christian king, and the most serene and mighty prince William III, king of Great Britain, their heirs and successors, and between the kingdoms, states and subjects of both. . . .

IV. And as the intention of the most Christian king has always been that the peace should be firm and solid, his Majesty engages and promises for himself and for his successors, kings of France, not to trouble or disturb any way whatsoever the king of Great Britain in the possession of his kingdoms, countries, states, lands or governments which his said Britannic Majesty now enjoys, giving for this purpose his royal word not to assist directly or indirectly any of the enemies of the said king of Great Britain, nor to countenance in any manner whatsoever the conspiracies, plots or

[1] No. 343.

rebellions which may be carried on in England, and consequently, without any exception or reserve, not to aid with arms, ammunition, provisions, ships or any other thing by sea or by land any person whatsoever who shall pretend to molest the said king of Great Britain in the peaceable possession of the said kingdoms, countries, states, lands or governments under what pretence soever it may be. And in like manner the king of Great Britain on his side promises and engages for himself and his successors, kings of Great Britain, inviolably and mutually, without any exception or reserve, to do the same in respect to the most Christian king, his kingdoms, countries, states and dominions. . . .

VII. The said most Christian king shall cause to be restored to the king of Great Britain all the countries, islands, fortresses and colonies in what part of the world soever situated which the English did possess before the declaration of this present war. And in like manner the said king of Great Britain shall restore to the said most Christian king all the countries, islands, fortresses and colonies in what part of the world soever situated which the French did possess before the declaration of this present war. And this restitution shall be made on both sides within the space of six months, and sooner if it can be done. . . .

VIII. It is agreed that commissioners shall be appointed on both sides to examine and determine the mutual rights and pretensions which each of the said kings may have to the places situated in Hudson's Bay, which the French took in the time of the last peace, and which were retaken by the English since the present war and are by virtue of the preceding article to be restored to his most Christian Majesty; as likewise that the capitulation granted by the English to the commander of Fort Bourbon, at the time of its being last taken on the 5th of September[1] 1696, shall be performed according to its form and tenor, . . . and the disputes which may remain on account of the performance of the said capitulation . . . shall be adjudged and determined by the said commissioners, who in like manner shall have power to treat concerning the settling of the limits and confines of the countries yielded and restored on either side by the foregoing article, and of the exchanges which may be found fitting to be made for the common convenience as well of his most Christian as of his Britannic Majesty. . . .

XIII. For what concerns the principality of Orange and other lands and lordships appertaining to the king of Great Britain, the separate article of the treaty of Nimeguen, concluded the 10th of August[2] 1678 between his most Christian Majesty and the States General of the United Provinces, shall be fully executed according to its form and tenor, and in pursuance thereof all innovations and alterations there which shall be found to have been since made contrary to the said treaty, of what kind soever they may be, shall have reparation made without any exception. . . .

XIV. The treaty of peace between the most Christian king and the late elector of Brandenburg, made at St. Germain en Laye the 29th of June[3] 1679, shall be reestablished between his most Christian Majesty and his present Electoral Highness of Brandenburg, in all its points and articles.

XV. Whereas it much concerns the public tranquillity that the peace concluded

---

[1] 26 August/5 September.   [2] 31 July/10 August.   [3] 19/29 June.

between his most Christian Majesty and his Royal Highness the duke of Savoy, the 9th of August[1] 1696, should be exactly observed, it has been agreed to confirm the same by this present treaty. . . .

Made at Ryswick in Holland, 20th September[2] 1697.

346. Preliminary articles for a settlement, 1709

(Manuscripts of the House of Lords, N.S., IX, pp. 269, 275)

Article 4

And inasmuch as the duke of Anjou is at present in possession of a great part of the kingdoms of Spain, of the coasts of Tuscany, of the Indies and of a part of the Low Countries, it has been mutually agreed that to ensure the execution of the said articles, and of the treaties of peace which are to be made, the said treaties shall be completed within the space of two months, counting from the first of June next, if possible, during which time his most Christian Majesty shall so manage it that the kingdom of Sicily shall be restored to his Catholic Majesty Charles III, and the said duke shall depart from the limits of the kingdom of Spain, in full security and liberty, with his spouse, the princes his children, their belongings, and in general all people who wish to follow them, so that if the said interval comes to an end without the said duke of Anjou consenting to the execution of the present convention, the most Christian king and the princes and states concerned in this agreement shall take in concert suitable measures to secure the full execution thereof, that all Europe, by the conclusion of the said treaties of peace, may immediately enjoy perfect tranquillity. . . . .

Article 37

And in case the most Christian king performs all that has been stipulated above, and the whole monarchy of Spain is surrendered and given up to the said King Charles III as is appointed by these articles within the stipulated time, it is agreed that the cessation of arms between the armies of the parties at war shall continue until the conclusion and ratification of the treaties of peace which are to be made. . . .

347. Assiento, 1713

(C. Jenkinson, Collection of Treaties, I, pp. 375–399)

THE KING.

Whereas the Assiento agreed on with the Royal Guinea Company, settled in France, for the introducing of negro slaves into the Indies, is determined, and the queen of Great Britain being desirous of coming into this commerce, and in her name the English company, as is stipulated in the preliminaries of the peace, and that this Assiento should continue for the time and space of thirty years, Don Manuel Menasses

[1] 30 July/9 August.   [2] 10/20 September.

Gilligan, deputed by her Majesty of Great Britain, did in pursuance thereof put into my hands a draft made for that purpose, containing forty-two articles, for the regulating this contract, . . . and, . . . it being my intention to conclude and finish this Assiento with all possible condescension and complacency towards the queen of Great Britain, I have thought fit, by my royal decree of the 12th of this present month,[1] to admit and approve of the said forty-two articles contained in the aforementioned draft, in the manner hereafter specified, with the enlargement which over and above I have of my own free will resolved to grant to the said company by my said decree; all which is in the manner following:

I. First then, to procure by this means a mutual and reciprocal advantage to the sovereigns and subjects of both crowns, her British Majesty does offer and undertake for the persons whom she shall name and appoint that they shall oblige and charge themselves with the bringing into the West Indies of America, belonging to his Catholic Majesty, in the space of the said thirty years, to commence on the 1st day of May 1713,[2] and determine on the like day which will be in the year 1743, viz., 144,000 negroes, *Piezas de India*, of both sexes and of all ages, at the rate of 4,800 negroes, *Piezas de India*, in each of the said thirty years, with this condition, that the persons who shall go to the West Indies to take care of the concerns of the Assiento shall avoid giving any offence, for in such case they shall be prosecuted and punished in the same manner as they would have been in Spain, if the like misdemeanours had been committed there.

II. That for each negro, *Pieza de India*, of the regular standard of seven quarters, not being old or defective, according to what has been practised and established hitherto in the Indies, the Assientists shall pay 33 pieces of eight and one third of a piece of eight, in which sum shall be accounted to be, and shall be comprehended, all and all manner of duties . . . that now are or hereafter shall be imposed, belonging to his Catholic Majesty, so that nothing more shall be demanded. . . .

III. That the said Assientists shall advance to his Catholic Majesty, to supply the urgent occasions of the crown, two hundred thousand pieces of eight in two even payments of one hundred thousand pieces of eight each, the first to be made two months after his Majesty shall have approved and signed this Assiento, and the second at the end of two other months next after the first payment; which sum so advanced is not to be reimbursed before the end of the first twenty years of this Assiento, and then it may be deducted by equal portions in the ten last remaining years, after the rate of twenty thousand pieces of eight yearly, out of the produce of the duty upon negroes which they are to pay in those years. . . .

XVIII. That from the 1st day of May of this present year 1713 till they shall have taken possession of this Assiento, nor after their taking such possession, it shall not be lawful for the French Guinea Company or any other person whatsoever to introduce any negro slaves into India, and if they do his Catholic Majesty will declare, as by this present article he does declare, them to be confiscated and forfeited, in favour and for the benefit of these Assientists, to whom they shall remain, they being obliged to pay the duties for the negroes thus imported contrary to this article. . . .

[1] 1/12 March 1713.   [2] 20 April/1 May 1713.

Additional Article

Besides the foregoing articles stipulated on behalf of the English company, his Catholic Majesty, considering the losses which former Assientists have sustained, and upon this express condition, that the said company shall not carry on nor attempt any unlawful trade, directly nor indirectly, under any pretence whatsoever; and to manifest to her Britannic Majesty how much he desires to pleasure her, and to confirm more and more a strict and good correspondence, has been pleased, by his royal decree of the 12th of March in this present year, to allow to the company of this Assiento a ship of five hundred tons yearly during the thirty years of its continuance, to trade therewith to the Indies, in which his Catholic Majesty is to partake a fourth part of the gain, as in the Assiento; besides which fourth his Catholic Majesty is to receive five per cent out of the net gain of the other three parts which belong to England, upon this express condition, that they may not sell the goods and merchandises which each of those ships shall carry but only at the time of the fair; and if any of these ships shall arrive in the Indies before the flotas and galleons, the factors of the Assiento shall be obliged to land the goods and merchandise with which they shall be laden, and put them into warehouses that shall be locked with two keys, one of which to remain with the royal officers and the other with the factors of the company, to the end the said goods and merchandise may be sold during the continuance of the said fair only; and they are to be free of all duties in the Indies. . . .

Given at Madrid, the twenty-sixth day of March one thousand seven hundred and thirteen.[1]

348. Treaty of Utrecht, 1713
(G. Chalmers, *Collection of Treaties*, I, pp. 340–386)

I. That there be an universal perpetual peace and a true and sincere friendship between the most serene and most potent Princess Anne, queen of Great Britain, and the most serene and most potent Prince Louis the XIVth, the most Christian king, and their heirs and successors, as also the kingdoms, states and subjects of both, as well without as within Europe. . . .

IV. Furthermore, for adding a greater strength to the peace which is restored, and to the faithful friendship which is never to be violated, and for cutting off all occasions of distrust which might at any time arise from the established right and order of the hereditary succession to the crown of Great Britain, and the limitation thereof by the laws of Great Britain (made and enacted in the reigns of the late King William the Third of glorious memory and of the present queen) to the issue of the abovesaid queen, and in default thereof to the most serene Princess Sophia, dowager of Brunswick-Hanover, and her heirs in the Protestant line of Hanover; that therefore the said succession may remain safe and secure, the most Christian king sincerely and solemnly acknowledges the abovesaid limitation of the succession to the kingdom of Great Britain, and on the faith and word of a king, on the pledge of his own and his successors' honour, he does declare and engage that he accepts and approves the same,

[1] 15/26 March 1713.

and that his heirs and successors do and shall accept and approve the same for ever. And under the same obligation of the word and honour of a king the most Christian king promises that no one besides the queen herself, and her successors according to the series of the said limitation, shall ever by him or by his heirs or successors be acknowledged or reputed to be king or queen of Great Britain. And for adding more ample credit to the said acknowledgment and promises, the most Christian king does engage that whereas the person who, in the lifetime of the late King James the Second, did take upon him the title of prince of Wales, and since his decease that of king of Great Britain, is lately gone of his own accord out of the kingdom of France to reside in some other place, he the aforesaid most Christian king, his heirs and successors, will take all possible care that he shall not at any time hereafter, or under any pretence whatsoever, return into the kingdom of France or any the dominions thereof.

V. Moreover the most Christian king promises, as well in his own name as in that of his heirs and successors, that they will at no time whatever disturb or give any molestation to the queen of Great Britain, her heirs and successors, descended from the aforesaid Protestant line, who possess the crown of Great Britain and the dominions belonging thereunto. Neither will the aforesaid most Christian king, or any one of his heirs, give at any time any aid, succour, favour or counsel, directly or indirectly, by land or by sea, in money, arms, ammunition, warlike provision, ships, soldiers, seamen or any other way, to any person or persons, whosoever they be, who for any cause or under any pretext whatsoever should hereafter endeavour to oppose the said succession, either by open war or by fomenting seditions and forming conspiracies against such prince or princes who are in possession of the throne of Great Britain by virtue of the Acts of Parliament afore-mentioned, or against that prince or princess to whom the succession to the crown of Great Britain shall be open according to the said Acts of Parliament.

VI. Whereas the most destructive flame of war, which is to be extinguished by this peace, arose chiefly from thence, that the security and liberties of Europe could by no means bear the union of the kingdoms of France and Spain under one and the same king; and whereas it has at length been brought to pass . . . that this evil should in all times to come be obviated, by means of renunciations drawn in the most effectual form and executed in the most solemn manner, the tenor whereof is as follows :[1]

Now whereas it is provided and settled by the preceding renunciation (which is always to have the force of a pragmatic, fundamental and inviolable law) that at no time whatever either the Catholic king himself, or anyone of his lineage, shall seek to obtain the crown of France or ascend the throne thereof; and by reciprocal renunciations on the part of France, and by settlements of the hereditary succession there tending to the same purpose, the crowns of France and Spain are so divided and separated from each other that . . . they can never be joined in one; wherefore the most serene queen of Great Britain and the most serene the most Christian king engage to each other solemnly and on their royal words that nothing ever shall be done by them

---

[1] The renunciations are inserted at this point.

or their heirs and successors, or allowed to be done by others, whereby the aforesaid renunciations and the other transactions aforementioned may not have their full effect. . . . Moreover the most Christian king consents and engages that he will not, for the interest of his subjects, hereafter endeavour to obtain, or accept of, any other usage of navigation and trade to Spain and the Spanish Indies than what was practised there in the reign of the late King Charles the Second of Spain, or than what shall likewise be fully given and granted at the same time to other nations and people concerned in trade. . . .

IX. The most Christian king shall take care that all the fortifications of the city of Dunkirk be razed, that the harbour be filled up, and that the sluices or moles which serve to cleanse the harbour be levelled, and that at the said king's own expense; . . . on this express condition also, that the said fortifications, harbour, moles or sluices be never repaired again. . . .

X. The said most Christian king shall restore to the kingdom and queen of Great Britain, to be possessed in full right for ever, the bay and straits of Hudson, together with all lands, seas, sea-coasts, rivers and places situate in the said bay and straits and which belong thereunto, no tracts of land or of sea being excepted, which are at present possessed by the subjects of France. . . . It is, however, provided that it may be entirely free for the company of Quebec and all other the subjects of the most Christian king whatsoever to go by land or by sea whithersoever they please out of the lands of the said bay, together with all their goods, merchandises, arms and effects of what nature or condition soever. . . . But it is agreed on both sides to determine within a year, by commissaries to be forthwith named by each party, the limits which are to be fixed between the said bay of Hudson and the places appertaining to the French, which limits both the British and French subjects shall be wholly forbid to pass over, or thereby to go to each other by sea or by land. The same commissaries shall also have orders to describe and settle in like manner the boundaries between the other British and French colonies in those parts.

XI. The above-mentioned most Christian king shall take care that satisfaction be given, according to the rule of justice and equity, to the English company trading to the bay of Hudson for all damages and spoil done to their colonies, ships, persons and goods by the hostile incursions and depredations of the French in time of peace, an estimate being made thereof by commissaries to be named at the requisition of each party. The same commissaries shall moreover inquire as well into the complaints of the British subjects concerning ships taken by the French in time of peace, as also concerning the damages sustained last year in the island called Montserrat and others; as into those things of which the French subjects complain relating to the capitulation in the island of Nevis and castle of Gambia; also to French ships, if perchance any such have been taken by British subjects in time of peace; and in like manner into all disputes of this kind which shall be found to have arisen between both nations and which are not yet ended; and due justice shall be done on both sides without delay.

XII. The most Christian king shall take care to have delivered to the queen of Great Britain, on the same day that the ratifications of this treaty shall be exchanged, solemn and authentic letters or instruments, by virtue whereof it shall appear that the

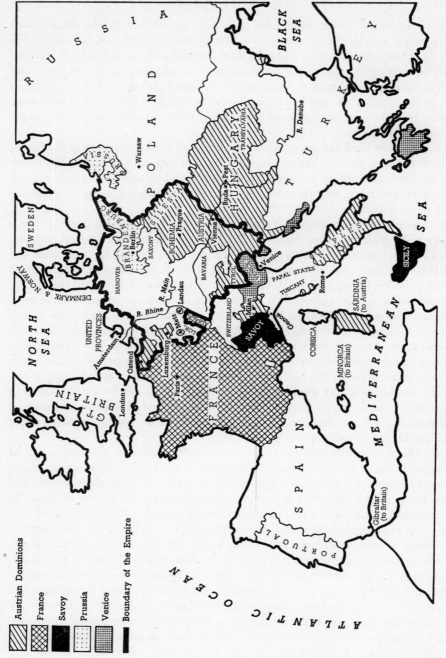

21. WESTERN EUROPE AFTER THE TREATY OF UTRECHT

island of St. Christopher is to be possessed alone hereafter by British subjects, likewise all Nova Scotia or Acadie, with its ancient boundaries, as also the city of Port Royal, now called Annapolis Royal, and all other things in those parts which depend on the said lands and islands, together with the dominion, propriety and possession of the said islands, lands and places, . . . and that in such ample manner and form that the subjects of the most Christian king shall hereafter be excluded from all kind of fishing in the said seas, bays and other places on the coasts of Nova Scotia, that is to say on those which lie towards the east within thirty leagues, beginning from the island commonly called Sable, inclusively, and thence stretching along towards the south-west.

XIII. The island called Newfoundland, with the adjacent islands, shall from this time forward belong of right wholly to Britain; and to that end the town and fortress of Placentia, and whatever other places in the said island are in the possession of the French, shall be yielded and given up within seven months from the exchange of the ratifications of this treaty, or sooner if possible, by the most Christian king to those who have a commission from the queen of Great Britain for that purpose. . . . Moreover it shall not be lawful for the subjects of France to fortify any place in the said island of Newfoundland, or to erect any buildings there, besides stages made of boards and huts necessary and usual for drying of fish, or to resort to the said island beyond the time necessary for fishing and drying of fish. But it shall be allowed to the subjects of France to catch fish, and to dry them on land in that part only (and in no other besides that) of the said island of Newfoundland which stretches from the place called Cape Bonavista to the northern point of the said island, and from thence running down by the western side reaches as far as the place called Point Rich. But the island called Cape Breton, as also all others both in the mouth of the river of St. Lawrence and in the gulf of the same name, shall hereafter belong of right to the French, and the most Christian king shall have all manner of liberty to fortify any place or places there. . . .

XX. Just and reasonable satisfaction shall be given to all and singular the allies of the queen of Great Britain in those matters which they have a right to demand from France. . . .

XXX. In witness whereof we the under-written ambassadors extraordinary and plenipotentiaries of the queen of Great Britain, and of the most Christian king, have put our seals to these present instruments, subscribed with our own hands at Utrecht, the 31/11 day of March/April, in the year 1713.

Part XI

SOVEREIGNS, POLITICIANS, AND SOME OTHER MEN

SOVEREIGNS, POLITICIANS, AND SOME OTHER MEN

Introduction

BEYOND any other period in the history of Great Britain the seventeenth century was an age of striking personalities. The innumerable controversies which marked its course almost inevitably produced, not necessarily great or good men, but at least men of strong views, varied outlook, and marked individuality. To observers at the time, however, this wealth of personal character seemed not so much the result as the cause of the great developments of the century. The more general causes of events, on which it is now the custom to lay, if anything, undue stress, were but dimly appreciated before the era of the Industrial Revolution, and all developments in the seventeenth century tended to be explained by reference to the principal actors in them.

From this arose the practice of character-sketching which is so marked a feature of the literature of the period. Historians, diarists and memoir-writers, on first mentioning any important individual, or on recording his death, made it their custom to add an estimate of his personal qualities. Essayists constructed elaborate character-sketches as independent compositions. Writers of satires, epigrams, epitaphs and squibs of all kinds became more active and more personal than ever. Much of this literature was ephemeral, and much has no doubt perished; but a vast mass still remains. From it a veritable gallery of verbal portraits can be constructed, throwing light no less upon the authors of the portraits than upon the individuals portrayed.

Not unnaturally the men and women with the most complex, enigmatic and attractive characters received chief attention. Among rulers and pretenders Charles II[1] and the duke of Monmouth[2] were the subject of many more and much better character-sketches than James II,[3] William III,[4] or Anne.[5] Among statesmen Buckingham[6] attracted the attention of writers rather than Clarendon;[7] Shaftesbury[8] and Halifax[9] rather than Danby.[10] So widespread was the fashion of character-sketching, however, that few men of any eminence entirely evaded the attention of the sketchers, and few writers failed to contribute in some measure towards the sketches.

[1] Nos. 349–351.　　[2] Nos. 354–356.　　[3] Nos. 352, 353.
[4] Nos. 357, 358.　　[5] Nos. 361, 362.　　[6] Nos. 367–370.
[7] Nos. 364–366.　　[8] Nos. 373, 374.　　[9] Nos. 376, 377.
[10] No. 378.

BIBLIOGRAPHY

Singularly little attention has been paid to this practice of characterization. David Nichol Smith, *Characters from the Histories and Memoirs of the Seventeenth Century* (Oxford, 1918), gives an excellent survey of the subject, followed by a judicious selection of characters. But the survey is short, the characters not very numerous, and the whole devoted primarily to the first half of the century. The characters of the second half of the century have to be sought in Clarendon's *Life*; Burnet's *History of My Own Time*; *Memoirs of the Secret Services of John Macky* (London, 1733); Dryden's *Absalom and Achitophel*, and innumerable other contemporary writings, the most important of which have been noted in earlier bibliographies.

Few of these contemporary writings are biographical in character, for so long as the vogue of the character-sketch persisted the development of formal biography was held in check. Among modern writers, however, the biography has been regarded with considerable favour, and much of the best recent work on the later seventeenth century has assumed biographical form. Specially important is *The Dictionary of National Biography* (66 vols., 1885–1901; 22 vols., 1908–1909), an invaluable work of reference, which, however, should be consulted in conjunction with the corrections periodically published in the *Bulletin of the Institute of Historical Research*. Similar compilations confined to a more specialized field are *The Complete Peerage of England, Scotland, Ireland, Great Britain and the United Kingdom*, by G. E. Cokayne, the eleven volumes already published in the latest edition of which (London, 1910–1949) have reached the letter S; *Collins's Peerage of England*, augmented and continued by Sir Egerton Brydges (9 vols., London, 1812); the *Complete Baronetage*, edited by G. E. Cokayne (6 vols., Exeter, 1900–1909); *Alumni Oxonienses, 1500–1714*, edited by Joseph Foster (4 vols., Oxford, 1891–1892); and *Alumni Cantabrigienses*, edited by John and John A. Venn, Part I, to 1751 (4 vols., Cambridge, 1922–1927).

Stuart sovereigns have scarcely received the attention they deserve from historians. Osmund Airy, *Charles II* (London, 1901), and Arthur Bryant, *King Charles II* (London, 1931), are brilliant and entertaining sketches; but the definitive life of Charles remains to be written. F. C. Turner, *James II* (London, 1948), is a much more solid and substantial production, and a reasonably adequate biography of the same monarch is F. M. G. Higham, *King James the Second* (London, 1934). Of James's successor, however, the only modern accounts in English are H. D. Traill, *William the Third* (London, 1888), and G. J. Renier, *William of Orange* (London, 1932), both of which are much too slight to be worthy of their subject, and the former of which is in addition badly out of date. Nellie M. Waterson, *Mary II, Queen of England, 1689–1694* (Durham, N. C., 1928), is an adequate study, which refrains from exaggerating Mary's importance; while a useful companion volume, in which Mary's not very numerous letters, memoirs and meditations are collected and printed in English, is Marjorie Bowen, *The Third Mary Stuart* (London, 1929). But Anne has been almost entirely neglected, Herbert Paul, *Queen Anne* (London, 1906), being little more than a sketch, and M. R. Hopkinson, *Anne of England* (London, 1934), a popular rather than a scholarly work.

Nor have the consorts and children of the reigning sovereigns fared much better. Martin Haile, *Queen Mary of Modena* (London, 1905), and the same writer's *James Francis Edward, the Old Chevalier* (London, 1907), are based on much research in foreign archives. George Roberts, *The Life, Progresses and Rebellion of James, Duke of Monmouth* (2 vols., London, 1844), is sound, though out of date, and can be supplemented from Allan Fea, *King Monmouth* (London, 1902). Sir Almeric Fitzroy, *Henry, Duke of Grafton, 1663–1690* (London, 1921), is at least as good an account as its subject merits. But Lillias C. Davidson, *Catherine of Braganza* (London, 1908); Janet Mackay, *Catherine of Braganza* (London, 1937); and J. R. Henslowe, *Anne Hyde, Duchess of York* (London, 1915), are intended mainly for popular consumption, and add little to the sum of historical knowledge. As might have been expected, Charles II's favourite sister has received special attention, and is the subject of two competent studies, Julia Cartwright, *Madame, a Life of Henrietta, Duchess of Orleans* (London, 1894), and Cyril Hughes Hartmann, *Charles II and Madame* (London, 1934); but of the many biographies inspired by the career of Charles's famous cousin, important after the Restoration no less than during the Civil War, few are of much value, and the best is still Eva Scott, *Rupert, Prince Palatine* (Westminster, 1899).

Really scholarly work, in fact, has been reserved mainly for the biographies of statesmen and politicians. Outstanding among these is H. C. Foxcroft, *The Life and Letters of Sir George Savile, first Marquis of Halifax* (2 vols., London, 1898), a veritable quarry for all engaged in research on the later Stuart period, but less suited to the general reader than the same author's *A Character of the Trimmer* (Cambridge, 1946), which presents the building without the scaffolding. Andrew Browning, *Thomas Osborne, Earl of Danby and Duke of Leeds, 1632–1712* (3 vols., Glasgow, 1944–1951), deals with Halifax's chief rival on a similar scale, devoting special attention to finance and party organization. Winston S. Churchill, *Marlborough, his Life and Times* (4 vols., London, 1933–1938), is disfigured by much special pleading, principally in its early stages, but is a truly monumental work, based upon masses of new material, and of the first importance for military history. Earlier lives of Marlborough, which have not been entirely superseded, are Thomas Lediard, *Life of John, Duke of Marlborough* (3 vols., London, 1736); William Coxe, *Memoirs of the Duke of Marlborough* (3 vols., London, 1818–1819); Viscount Wolseley, *The Life of John Churchill, Duke of Marlborough, to the Accession of Queen Anne* (2 vols., London, 1894); Stuart J. Reid, *John and Sarah, Duke and Duchess of Marlborough, 1660–1744* (London, 1914); and C. T. Atkinson, *Marlborough and the Rise of the British Army* (New York, 1921).

T. H. Lister, *Life and Administration of Edward, first Earl of Clarendon* (3 vols., London, 1837–1838), is still the best life of the architect of the Restoration, valuable both in itself and for the large collection of letters and papers printed in it; but it is now somewhat out of date, and should be read in conjunction with Sir Henry Craik, *The Life of Edward, Earl of Clarendon, Lord High Chancellor of England* (2 vols., London, 1911), which makes use of new material, and with C. H. Firth, *Edward Hyde, Earl of Clarendon, as Statesman, Historian, and Chancellor of the University* (Oxford, 1909), a commemorative lecture, reprinted in Firth's *Essays*, pp. 103–128. Similarly Thomas Carte, *The Life of James, Duke of Ormond* (6 vols., Oxford, 1851), is the most elaborate account of one of Clarendon's chief friends and supporters, but should be read in conjunction with Lady Burghclere, *The Life of James, first Duke of Ormonde, 1610–1688* (2 vols., London, 1912), which concentrates on the man rather than on his background; and W. D. Christie, *A Life of Anthony Ashley Cooper, first Earl of Shaftesbury, 1621–1683* (2 vols., London, 1871), is still the standard work on that most enigmatic statesman, but should be read in conjunction with Louise Fargo Brown, *The first Earl of Shaftesbury* (New York, 1933), which incorporates new information, especially in the related spheres of colonization and commerce. Walter Sichel, *Bolingbroke and his Times* (2 vols., London, 1901–1902), is the best complete account of an almost equally puzzling personality. It also should be read in conjunction with H. N. Fieldhouse, "Bolingbroke's Share in the Jacobite Intrigue of 1710–14", in *English Historical Review*, LII (1937), pp. 443–459, and the same writer's "Bolingbroke and the Idea of Non-Party Government", in *History*, XXIII (1938), pp. 41–56.

Apart from Shaftesbury the politicians of the so-called Cabal have been somewhat neglected. Violet Barbour, *Henry Bennet, Earl of Arlington* (Washington, 1914), is a scholarly work, but scarcely as full as its subject deserves. Cyril Hughes Hartmann, *Clifford of the Cabal, 1630–1673* (London, 1937), makes good use of Clifford's own papers, but these have not proved as enlightening as might have been hoped. Winifred, Lady Burghclere, *George Villiers, second Duke of Buckingham, 1628–1687* (London, 1903), and Hester W. Chapman, *Great Villiers* (London, 1949), leave much unexplained. W. C. Mackenzie, *The Life and Times of John Maitland, Duke of Lauderdale, 1616–1682* (London, 1923), is not at its best when dealing with English affairs. More serious is the neglect of the Junto of William III's reign. Teresa Merz, *The Junto* (Newcastle-upon-Tyne, 1907), gives an inadequate sketch, based mainly on secondary material, of each member of that body; but there is no satisfactory biography of any one of them. An intimate associate of theirs, however, is fully dealt with in T. C. Nicholson and A. S. Turberville, *Charles Talbot, Duke of Shrewsbury* (Cambridge, 1930). Marion E. Grew, *William Bentinck and William III; the Life of Bentinck, Earl of Portland* (London, 1924), is based on the Welbeck Correspondence and other original authorities, and is the best available account of the favourite adviser of William III.

Thomas Peregrine Courtenay, *Memoirs of the Life, Works and Correspondence of Sir William Temple* (2 vols., London, 1836), should be read in conjunction with the famous article which it inspired in *Critical and Historical Essays by Lord Macaulay*, edited by F. C. Montague (3 vols., London, 1903), II, pp. 241–327. Murray L. R. Beaven, *Sir William Temple* (Oxford, 1908), is an able sketch, but quite inadequate to meet the need for a modern life of Temple. Dorothea Townshend, *George Digby, second Earl of Bristol* (London, 1924), is a sober account of one of the more erratic figures in the Restoration period, and Lord John Russell, *Life of William Lord Russell* (4th edition, London, 1853), a painstaking study of one of the least erratic. Ruth Clark, *Anthony Hamilton, his Life and Works and his Family* (London, 1921), deals with the author of the *Memoirs of Count Grammont*, and J. G. Muddiman, *The King's Journalist, 1659–1689* (London, 1923), with the first editor of the *London Gazette* and his associates. Andrew Lang, *Sir George Mackenzie, his Life and Times, 1636–1691* (London, 1909), endeavours to present an impartial estimate of one of the best hated men in Scottish history. Alexander Robertson, *The Life of Sir Robert Moray, 1608–1673* (London, 1922), is a scholarly account of one who was himself an eminent scholar; and W. C. Mackenzie, *Andrew Fletcher of Saltoun, his Life and Times* (Edinburgh, 1935), a less satisfactory study of one of the stoutest opponents of the union between England and Scotland.

Three volumes of a full-scale biography of *Samuel Pepys*, by Arthur Bryant (Cambridge, 1933–1938), had appeared before the outbreak of the second World War. These have now been reprinted (London, 1947–1949), and are to be continued in one or more volumes which will bring the work to an end. Meanwhile the best complete account of Pepys's life is to be found in J. R. Tanner, *Mr. Pepys, an Introduction to the Diary together with a Sketch of his Later Life* (London, 1925), and the same writer's "Pepys and the Popish Plot", in *English Historical Review*, VII (1892), pp. 281–290, and "Samuel Pepys and the Trinity House", *ibid.*, XLIV (1929), pp. 573–587. Pepys's earliest patron is the subject of F. R. Harris, *The Life of Edward Mountagu, first Earl of Sandwich, 1625–1672* (2 vols., London, 1912). Useful accounts of other officials are John Beresford, *The Godfather of Downing Street, Sir George Downing, 1623–1684* (London, 1925); George Kitchin, *Sir Roger L'Estrange* (London, 1913); Gertrude Ann Jacobsen, *William Blathwayt* (New Haven, 1932); C. W. Firebrace, *Honest Harry, being a Biography of Sir Henry Firebrace, 1619–1691* (London, 1932); Florence E. Dyer, *The Life of Admiral Sir John Narbrough* (London, 1931); and L. G. Wickham Legg, *Matthew Prior, a Study of his Public Career and Correspondence* (Cambridge, 1921).

As might have been expected in the case of an age of ecclesiastical controversy, much attention has been paid to the leading clergymen of the period. Clarke and Foxcroft's *Life of Burnet* has already been mentioned (pp. 42–43). Vernon Staley, *The Life and Times of Gilbert Sheldon* (London, 1913), is an adequate account of the ecclesiastic whose task it was to perform much the same work of reconstruction in the Church as Clarendon performed in the State. George D'Oyly, *The Life of William Sancroft, Archbishop of Canterbury* (2 vols., London, 1821), is a similarly adequate account of his successor. E. H. Plumptre, *The Life of Thomas Ken, Bishop of Bath and Wells* (2 vols., London, 1890), throws light on the early history of the Nonjurors. Edward Carpenter, *Thomas Tenison, Archbishop of Canterbury, his Life and Times* (London, 1948), and the same writer's *Thomas Sherlock, 1678–1761* (London, 1936); A. Tindal Hart, *The Life and Times of John Sharp, Archbishop of York* (London, 1949); and C. E. Whiting, *Nathaniel Lord Crewe, Bishop of Durham, 1674–1721, and his Diocese* (London, 1940), are based on a vast amount of research into unpublished sources. Of the leading nonconformist divines the most notable biographies are Frederick J. Powicke, *A Life of the Reverend Richard Baxter, 1615–1691* (2 vols., London, 1924–1927), and Thomas Hodgkin, *George Fox* (London, 1896). The best life of

Bunyan is John Brown, *John Bunyan, 1628–1688, his Life, Times and Work,* revised edition by Frank Mott Harrison (London, 1928).

Of the more disreputable characters of later Stuart times there are many biographies, but few of real historical value. Wilbur Cortez Abbott, *Colonel Thomas Blood, Crown-Stealer, 1618–1680* (New Haven, 1911), is a scholarly study of the most puzzling among them, which has been reprinted in the same writer's *Conflicts with Oblivion* (New Haven, 1924), pp. 103–160. James Ferguson, *Robert Ferguson the Plotter* (Edinburgh, 1887), is a sober narrative, based largely on Ferguson's own letters and on other original documents, which it prints. Maurice Ashley, *John Wildman, Plotter and Postmaster* (London, 1947), is the product of much research. Jane Lane, *Titus Oates* (London, 1949), is the only full-scale biography of the arch-impostor.

The ladies of the court have been similarly favoured by the biographers, and with equally unsatisfactory results. The best of the many accounts are G. S. Steinman, *A Memoir of Barbara, Duchess of Cleveland* (Oxford, 1871, with Addenda, 1874 and 1878), and the same writer's *Some Particulars contributed towards a Memoir of Mrs. Myddelton, the great Beauty of the Time of Charles II* (Oxford, 1864, with Addenda, 1880); Philip W. Sergeant, *My Lady Castlemaine, being a Life of Barbara Villiers, Countess of Castlemaine, afterwards Duchess of Cleveland* (London, 1912); Peter Cunningham, *The Story of Nell Gwyn and the Sayings of Charles II,* edited by Henry B. Wheatley (London, 1903); H. Forneron, *Louise de Kéroualle, Duchesse de Portsmouth, 1649–1734* (Paris, 1886), and Jean M. P. J. Lemoine and André Lichtenberger, "Louise de Kéroualle, Duchesse de Portsmouth", in *Revue des Deux Mondes,* 5 ser., XIV (1903), pp. 114–146; Cyril Hughes Hartmann, *La Belle Stuart, Memoirs of Court and Society in the Times of Frances Teresa Stuart, Duchess of Richmond and Lennox* (London, 1924), and the same writer's *The Vagabond Duchess, the Life of Hortense Mancini, Duchesse Mazarin* (London, 1926). More general in character are Allan Fea, *James II and his Wives* (London, 1908), and Edwin and Marion Sharpe Grew, *The Court of William III* (London, 1910).

A. RULERS AND PRETENDERS

(a) CHARLES II

349. By James Welwood
(Memoirs of the most Material Transactions in England, pp. 148–152)

Thus reigned and thus died King Charles the Second, a prince endowed with all the qualities that might justly have rendered him the delight of mankind, and entitled him to the character of one of the greatest geniuses that ever sat upon a throne, if he had not sullied those excellent parts with the soft pleasures of ease, and had not entertained a fatal friendship that was incompatible with the interest of England. His religion was deism, or rather that which is called so; and if in his exile or at his death he went into that of Rome, the first was to be imputed to a complaisance for the company he was then obliged to keep, and the last to a lazy diffidence in all other religions, upon a review of his past life and the near approach of an uncertain state. His person was tall and well-made, his constitution vigorous and healthy; and it is hard to determine whether he took more pains to preserve it by diet and exercise or to impair it by excess in his pleasures. In health he was a great pretender to physic and encourager of quacks, by whom he was often cheated of considerable sums of money for their pretended secrets; but whenever he was indisposed he consulted his physicians and depended on their skill only.

His face was composed of harsh features, difficult to be traced with the pencil; yet in the main it was agreeable, and he had a noble majestic mien. In contradiction to all the common received rules of physiognomy he was merciful, good-natured, and in the last twenty-four years of his life fortunate, if to succeed in most of his designs may be called so. Never prince loved ceremony less, or despised the pageantry of a crown more; yet he was master of something in his person and aspect that commanded both love and veneration at once.

He was a great votary to love, and yet the easiest and most unconcerned rival. He was for the most part not very nice in the choice of his mistresses, and seldom possessed of their first favours; yet would sacrifice all to please them, and upon every caprice of theirs denied himself the use of his reason and acted contrary to his interest. He was a respectful, civil husband, a fond father, a kind brother, an easy enemy, but none of the firmest or most grateful friends; bountiful by starts, one day lavish to his servants, the next leaving them to starve; glad to win a little money at play and impatient to lose but the thousandth part of what within an hour after he would throw away in gross. He seemed to have had nothing of jealousy in his nature, neither in matters of love nor power. He bore patiently rivals in the one and competitors in the other; otherwise he would not have contributed to a foreign greatness at sea nor given his brother so uncontrolled a share in the government.

Though his understanding was quick and lively, with a vast compass of thought, yet he would submit his judgment in greatest matters to others of much inferior parts;

899

and as he had an extraordinary share of wit himself, so he loved it in others, even when pointed against his own faults and mismanagements. He had read but little, yet he had a good taste of learning and would reason nicely upon most sciences. The mechanics were one of his peculiar talents, especially the art of building and working of ships, which nobody understood better, nor if he had lived would have carried it farther. He had a strong laconic way of expression, and a genteel, easy and polite way of writing; and when he had a mind to lay aside the king, which he often did in select companies of his own, there were a thousand irresistible charms in his conversation. He loved money only to spend it, and would privately accept of a small sum paid to himself in lieu of a far greater to be paid into the Exchequer.

He loved not business and sought every occasion to avoid it, which was one reason that he passed so much of his time with his mistresses; yet when necessity called him none of his Council could reason more closely upon matters of state, and he would often by fits outdo his ministers in application and diligence. No age produced a greater master in the art of dissimulation, and yet no man was less upon his guard, or sooner deceived in the sincerity of others. If he had any one fixed maxim of government it was to play one party against another, to be thereby the more master of both; and no prince understood better how to shift hands upon every change of the scene. To sum up his character, he was dexterous in all the arts of insinuation, and had acquired so great an ascendant over the affections of his people, in spite of all the unhappy measures he had taken, that it may in some sense be said he died opportunely for England, since if he had lived it is probable we might in compliance with him have complimented ourselves out of all the remains of liberty, if he had had but a mind to be master of them, which it is but charity to believe he had not, at least immediately before his death.

350. By John Evelyn
(*Diary*, ed. 1879, II, pp. 444–445)

Thus died King Charles II, of a vigorous and robust constitution, and in all appearance promising a long life. He was a prince of many virtues, and many great imperfections; debonair, easy of access, not bloody nor cruel; his countenance fierce, his voice great, proper of person, every motion became him; a lover of the sea, and skilful in shipping; not affecting other studies, yet he had a laboratory, and knew of many empirical medicines, and the easier mechanical mathematics. He loved planting and building, and brought in a politer way of living, which passed to luxury and intolerable expense. He had a particular talent in telling a story, and facetious passages, of which he had innumerable. This made some buffoons and vicious wretches too presumptuous and familiar, not worthy the favour they abused. He took delight in having a number of little spaniels follow him and lie in his bedchamber, where he often suffered the bitches to puppy and give suck, which rendered it very offensive, and indeed made the whole court nasty and stinking.

He would doubtless have been an excellent prince had he been less addicted to women, who made him uneasy and always in want to supply their unmeasurable profusion, to the detriment of many indigent persons who had signally served both him and his father. He frequently and easily changed favourites, to his great prejudice. As to other public transactions and unhappy miscarriages, it is not here I intend to number them; but certainly never had king more glorious opportunities to have made himself, his people and all Europe happy, and prevented innumerable mischiefs, had not his too easy nature resigned him to be managed by crafty men, and some abandoned and profane wretches who corrupted his otherwise sufficient parts, disciplined as he had been by many afflictions during his banishment, which gave him much experience and knowledge of men and things; but those wicked creatures took him off from all application becoming so great a king.

351. Anonymous
(*Complete Works of Andrew Marvell*, ed. A. B. Grosart, I, p. 343)

> Of a tall stature and of sable hue,
> Much like the son of Kish, that lofty Jew,
> Twelve years complete he suffered in exile,
> And kept his father's asses all the while.

(b) JAMES II

352. By Gilbert Burnet
(*History of My Own Time*, ed. 1833, IV, pp. 539-540)

King James died on the 6th day of September [1701]. He was a prince that seemed made for greater things than will be found in the course of his life, more particularly of his reign. He was esteemed in the former parts of his life a man of great courage, as he was quite through it a man of great application to business. He had no vivacity of thought, invention or expression; but he had a good judgment where his religion or his education gave him not a bias, which it did very often. He was bred with strange notions of the obedience due to princes, and came to take up as strange ones of the submission due to priests. He was naturally a man of truth, fidelity and justice; but his religion was so infused in him, and he was so managed in it by his priests, that the principles which nature had laid in him had little power over him when the concerns of his church stood in the way.

He was a gentle master, and was very easy to all who came near him; yet he was not so apt to pardon as one ought to be that is the vicegerent of that God who is slow to anger and ready to forgive. He had no personal vices but of one sort: he was still wandering from one amour to another. Yet he had a real sense of sin, and was ashamed of it; but priests know how to engage princes more entirely into their interests by making them compound for their sins by a great zeal for holy church, as they call it.

In a word, if it had not been for his popery he would have been, if not a great, yet a good prince. By what I once knew of him, and by what I saw him afterwards carried to, I grew more confirmed in the very bad opinion which I was always apt to have of the intrigues of the popish clergy and of the confessors of kings. He was undone by them, and was their martyr, so that they ought to bear the chief load of all the errors of his inglorious reign and of its fatal catastrophe.

353. By Arthur Onslow
(Burnet's History of My Own Time, ed. 1833, IV, pp. 541–542)

King James was certainly far a better man than his brother, although of a far inferior understanding. *His* designs were in general of a public nature; most pernicious indeed to this country, but the restoration of popery here was a great object in the eyes of most of his own faith everywhere, and was a great and meritorious attempt with them. He fell a sacrifice to it, and was undoubtedly very conscientious in it. Whereas King Charles, in *his* government, had himself neither conscience, religion, honour or justice; and he does not seem to have had even the feelings of them. He had no one truly public aim, as such, in the whole course of his reign. All he meant and sought, for which he tumbled and tossed from side to side, from one minister to another, and for what he was continually cheating his people, was to enjoy a lazy, thoughtless ease, in the constant debauchery of amours, and in the pleasures of wit and laughter, with the most worthless, vicious and abandoned set of men that even that age afforded, and who often made him the subject of their jokes and mirth, sometimes to his face. He was corrupted in France, and had all the pleasantry and vices of his grandfather, Henry the Fourth, but not one of his virtues, and which had made Henry great. Charles made the times here to be profligate; and instead of ministers spoiling him he spoiled most of his ministers, and did not love those whom he could not spoil.

(c) JAMES SCOTT, DUKE OF MONMOUTH

354. By James Welwood
(Memoirs of the most Material Transactions in England, pp. 172–175)

Monmouth seemed to be born for a better fate, for the first part of his life was all sunshine, though the rest was clouded. He was brave, generous, affable and extremely handsome, constant in his friendships, just to his word and an utter enemy to all sort of cruelty. He was easy in his nature and fond of popular applause, which led him insensibly into all his misfortunes; but whatever might be the hidden designs of some working heads he embarked with his own were noble, and chiefly aimed at the good of his country, though he was mistaken in the means to attain it. Ambitious he was, but not to the degree of aspiring to the crown, till after his landing in the west, and even then he was rather passive than active in assuming the title of king. It was importunity alone that prevailed with him to make that step, and he was inflexible till it was told him that the only way to provide against the ruin of those that should come in to his assistance, in case he failed in the attempt, was to declare himself king, that they might be sheltered by the statute made in the reign of Henry VII in favour of those that should obey a king *de facto*. . . .

In his latter years he used to complain of the little care had been taken of his education, and in his disgrace endeavoured to make up that want by applying himself to study, in which he made in a short time no inconsiderable progress. He took the occasion of his afflictions to inform his mind, and recollect and amend the errors of youth, which it was not strange he should be tainted with, being bred up in all the pleasures of a luxurious court. . . .

The duke of Monmouth, when he was brought prisoner to King James's presence, made the humblest submissions for his life, and it is a mystery what could move King James to see him, when he had no mind to pardon him. But the manner of his death three days after did more than acquit him of any meanness of spirit in desiring to live, since he died with the greatest constancy and tranquillity of mind, and such as became a Christian, a philosopher, and a soldier.

355. By Anthony Hamilton
(*Memoirs of Count Grammont*, ed. 1846, pp. 294-295)

His figure and the exterior graces of his person were such that nature, perhaps, never formed anything more complete. His face was extremely handsome; and yet it was a manly face, neither inanimate nor effeminate, each feature having its beauty and peculiar delicacy. He had a wonderful genius for every sort of exercise, an engaging aspect and an air of grandeur. In a word, he possessed every personal advantage. But then he was greatly deficient in mental accomplishments. He had no sentiments but such as others inspired him with, and those who first insinuated themselves into his friendship took care to inspire him with none but such as were pernicious. The astonishing beauty of his outward form caused universal admiration. Those who before were looked upon as handsome were now entirely forgotten at Court, and all the gay and beautiful of the fair sex were at his devotion. He was particularly beloved by the king, but the universal terror of husbands and lovers. This, however, did not long continue, for nature not having endowed him with qualifications to secure the possession of the heart the fair sex soon perceived the defect.

356. By John Dryden
(*Absalom and Achitophel*, ll. 17-30)

Of all this numerous progeny was none
So beautiful, so brave, as *Absalon*. . . .
Early in foreign fields he won renown
With kings and states allied to Israel's crown.
In peace the thoughts of war he could remove,
And seemed as he were only born for love.
Whate'er he did was done with so much ease,
In him alone 'twas natural to please;
His motions all accompanied with grace,
And Paradise was opened in his face.

(d) WILLIAM III

357. By Gilbert Burnet[1]

(*Supplement to Burnet's History of My Own Time*, pp. 190–193)

The prince has showed by his conduct and action that notwithstanding all the defects of his education, and his total want of literature, nature is capable of producing great matters, even when she is not at all assisted by art. He has a great application to affairs, and turns them much in his thoughts; and indeed perhaps too much, for his slowness in coming to a resolution is much complained of. But if he is slow in taking up a resolution he is as firm in adhering to it. He has a vast memory, and a true judgment, for he sees presently the critical point of any matter that is proposed to him. He is the closest man in the world, so that it is not possible so much as to guess at his intentions till he declares them. He is extreme calm both in council and actions, and hears very gently things that are said to him, even when he is not pleased with them. But he has the haughtiness of a great mind not to forget too soon injuries done him; but he has never been observed to affect revenges, only he does not easily return to confidences with those that have offended him.

His courage is indeed greater than it ought to be; and though it was very fit for one that had the ambition of arriving at the reputation of his ancestors to hazard his person sometimes, that so it might appear that he was a soldier as well as a general, yet his great carelessness of all personal danger both in time of peace and war has been censured as excessive, for to see him go about with a footman or two when so much depends on his life has been called rather a tempting of providence than a trusting to it. This some have ascribed to his belief of predestination, as if that pushed him on headlong in this confidence that all things will be as God will have them. But though he is firmly persuaded of predestination, yet he said to me he never reflected upon it in any of his counsels before things fall out; but he owned to me, when things fall out, the belief that God would have them so quieted his mind much, and has helped him to bear many misfortunes and disappointments very easily. This is his peculiar carriage and the nature of his courage that it does not sink with misfortunes, for when things have miscarried in his hands he has been observed to have the same calm equality that he had upon happier occasions.

He understands the government of Holland exactly, and if he does stick in some things too close to his rights as he is stadtholder, yet he has often assured me that he has never gone beyond them. He has great virtues. He is temperate and sober. If he has been guilty of any of the disorders that are too common to princes, yet he has not practised them as some to whom he is nearly related have done, but has endeavoured to cover them; though let princes be as secret as they will in such matters, they are always known. But a sincerity and a round plainness is of all his virtues that upon which he values himself most, and that justly, for he is very eminent in it even for a private man; and this is so extraordinary a virtue in a prince that it is the more singular in him, since he has very little of it round about him.

He seems to have a real sense of religion, and looks like a man that is in earnest

[1] Written about 1687.

when he is worshipping God. He is a hearty enemy to popery, and in particular to the cruelty of it, for he is a great enemy to persecution on the account of religion. He thinks the Church of England ought to be maintained, but softened a little both with relation to the nonconformists at home and to the foreign churches beyond sea. He has a coldness in his way that damps a modest man extremely, for he hears things with a dry silence that shows too much of distrust of those to whom he speaks. He seems to have made it a maxim to be slow in everything of resolution he takes, and this he carries too far, that he makes those to whom he intends to show favours wait on so long that the grace of giving them is much lost by the slowness; and he does not seem enough to consider the sourness of spirit under which men languish that are perplexed with uncertainty and want.

He has a true notion of government and liberty, and does not think that subjects were made to be slaves; but after the laws and foundations of government are over-turned by those who ought to maintain them he thinks the people may assert their freedom. He is a close manager of his affairs, and though he spends much in building yet he is not thought so free-hearted and generous as a great prince ought to be. His martial inclination will naturally carry him, when he comes to the crown of England, to bear down the greatness of France. And if he but hits the nature of the English nation right at first he will be able to give laws to all Europe. . . . But if the prince does not in many things change his way he will hardly gain the hearts of the nation. His coldness will look like contempt, and that the English cannot bear; and they are too impatient to digest that slowness that is almost become natural to him in the most inconsiderable things, and his silent way will pass for superciliousness. But that which is more important, he will be both the king of England and stadtholder. The Dutch will perhaps think a king of England too great to be their stadtholder, and the English will hardly be brought to trust a prince that has an army of 30,000 men at his command so near them.

358. By James Fitzjames, duke of Berwick

(*Memoirs*, I, pp. 156–157)

Whatever reason I may have not to be fond of the memory of this prince, I cannot deny him the character of a great man, and even of a great king had he not been an usurper. He had the art even from his youth to render himself almost absolute in his republic, notwithstanding the credit and authority of the de Wit's He had a very extensive understanding, was an able politician, and was never dis-couraged in his pursuits whatever obstacles he might meet with. He was very rigid but not naturally cruel, very enterprising but no general. He was suspected of not having much courage; yet it must be acknowledged that at least he had courage as far as to the drawing of his sword. His ambition was evident in all his intrigues to dethrone a prince who was his uncle and his father-in-law, in which he could not have succeeded but by numbers of ways as contrary to the duties of an honest man as they are repugnant to Christianity.

(e) MARY II

359. By Gilbert Burnet[1]
(Supplement to Burnet's History of My Own Time, pp. 194–196)

The princess was born with all the advantages of nature, dignity and sweetness mixing almost equally in everything that she did or said. She has a vivacity of thought, a liveliness of apprehension and a correctness of judgment that surprise all that see her. She has all the cheerfulness in her that becomes her age, but tempered with such an exactness of decency that those who had observed her deportment long, with a sort of malicious criticalness, wishing to find somewhat to censure, have protested they could never find it. In her devotions there is a solemn gravity that edifies all that see her. There is no sort of affectation in it; but yet there is an exactness both in her secret and chapel devotions and at sacrament that shows that she does not think the sublimity of her rank exempts her from the strictest duty of Christianity.

She has accomplished herself by reading a great variety of books, both in divinity, history and poetry, and she forgets very little of whatsoever she reads. She has a modesty and humility in her that wants a name, and that gentleness with which she charms all people is of so peculiar a composition that at the same time she seems to invite them to a familiarity she inspires them with respects. She is much animated against popery, and seems to have a true notion of government, that the chief end of power ought to be the doing of good. She is certainly in all respects the best wife that ever was, the most united to the prince in friendship, confidence and affection; and if she governs as well as she obeys her reign will be the happiest that ever was.

In short, considering her age, her education, and the company that has been always about her (who have never been able to exalt her), she seems to be a person raised and prepared by God Almighty to make the nations happy. Of which she herself thinks so little that one having presumed to ask her if she knew her own mind so far as to apprehend how she could bear the king's having a son she answered, she did not care to talk of these things lest it might seem an affectation, but she believed she should be very little troubled at it, for in all these things the will of God was to be considered; and if it were not for the doing good to others she said for her own particular it would be perhaps better for her to live and die what she was. She is hearty to the Church of England, but will never be drawn in to like the superstition and fierceness of some of our divines, for she thinks we have aggravated too much the matters of conformity.

All that I can possibly set against this character is that she is the most reserved person alive, unto whose thoughts no creature can enter further than as she discovers them; and that her goodness is too general, without carrying her into the particularities of friendship with any person. Her closeness is the strangest thing that ever was seen in one of her age and sex, and gives some colour to fear there may be something under all this secrecy. Her engaging into no friendships may be justly enough resolved in this, that she has not yet had any ladies about her that were capable of it. Otherwise

---

[1] Written about 1687.

it looks like a mind too much recollected within itself, when it does not flow out into some vigorous friendship.

I am sensible I have not set faults or defects enough in opposition to all the princess's virtues; but I protest I have taken all the pains I could to seek for them, for I know the good I say of her would be the better believed if I had mixed more ill things with it; but it will appear almost incredible that one of her birth and way of breeding should have come into a strange country when she was but a little past fifteen, and that during her ten years' stay in it she has never said nor done the least thing that has given any offence to any one person whatsoever, and that neither the difference in religion, nor the sorriness of the ministers or of some of the sects here, nor the factions that are against the prince, have produced the least censure of any of her actions. When one talked once to her of this, she said it was a particular blessing of God to her, for she was confident there were many others that had fallen under much censure, that had as little deserved it.

360. By Gilbert Burnet[1]
(*Supplement to Burnet's History of My Own Time*, p. 405)

I never admired any person so entirely as I did her. In the course of above eight years' very particular knowledge of her I never saw any one thing that I could have wished to be otherwise than it was in her. The more I knew her, I still saw the more reason to admire both her understanding, her piety and her virtue, without discovering the least defect or fault in her. The purity and the sublimity of her mind was the perfectest thing I ever saw. I never felt myself sink so much under anything that had happened to me as by her death. It is a daily load upon my thoughts, and gives me great apprehensions of very heavy judgments hanging over us, for I am afraid that in losing her we have lost both our strength and our glory.

(f) ANNE

361. By Sarah, duchess of Marlborough
(*Private Correspondence*, II, pp. 119-125)

Queen Anne had a person and appearance not at all ungraceful, till she grew exceeding gross and corpulent. There was something of majesty in her look, but mixed with a sullen and constant frown, that plainly betrayed a gloominess of soul and a cloudiness of disposition within. She seemed to inherit a good deal of her father's moroseness, which naturally produced in her the same sort of stubborn positiveness in many cases, both ordinary and extraordinary, as well as the same sort of bigotry in religion.

Her memory was exceeding great, almost to a wonder, and had these two peculiarities very remarkable in it, that she could, whenever she pleased, forget what others would have thought themselves obliged by truth and honour to remember, and remember all such things as others would think it an happiness to forget. Indeed she

---

[1] Written in 1695.

chose to retain in it very little besides ceremonies and customs of courts and such like insignificant trifles, so that her conversation, which otherwise might have been enlivened by so great a memory, was only made the more empty and trifling by its chiefly turning upon fashions and rules of precedence, or observations upon the weather or some such poor topics, without any variety or entertainment. Upon which account it was a sort of unhappiness to her that she naturally loved to have a great crowd come to her, for when they were come to Court she never cared to have them come in to her, nor to go out herself to them, having little to say to them but that it was either hot or cold, and little to inquire of them but how long they had been in town, or the like weighty matters. She never discovered any readiness of parts, either in asking questions or in giving answers. In matters of ordinary moment her discourse had nothing of brightness or wit; and in weightier matters she never spoke but in a hurry, and had a certain knack of sticking to what had been dictated to her, to a degree often very disagreeable, and without the least sign of understanding or judgment. . . .

Her civility and good manners in conversation (to which the education of great persons naturally leads) were general enough, till in her latter days her new friends untaught her these accomplishments; and then her whole deportment was visibly changed to that degree that when some things disagreeable to her own honour or passion have been laid before her she would descend to the lowest and most shocking forms of contradiction, and what in any of a meaner station would have been esteemed the height of unpoliteness. Her friendships were flames of extravagant passion, ending in indifference or aversion. Her love to the prince seemed in the eye of the world to be prodigiously great; and great as was the passion of her grief her stomach was greater, for that very day he died she ate three very large and hearty meals, so that one would think that as other persons' grief takes away their appetites, her appetite took away her grief. Nor was it less remarkable, where there was so great an appearance of love, the peculiar pleasure she took before his funeral in settling the order of it, and naming the persons that were to attend, and placing them according to their rank and to the rules of precedence, which was the entertainment she gave herself every day till that solemnity was over. I know that in some libels she has been reproached as one who indulged herself in drinking strong liquors; but I believe this was utterly groundless, and that she never went beyond such a quantity of strong wines as her physicians judged to be necessary for her.

Her religion was chiefly implicit faith and subjection, accompanied with the form and course of a sort of piety. She had a zeal for the Church as for an infallible guide, and a devotion for churchmen to such a degree as if she thought this sufficient to sanctify every other part of her conduct. And the churchmen repaid her civility in compliments and adorations, for I have often blushed both for her and for her preachers when I have heard it almost constantly, with the most fulsome flattery, affirmed to her face, and to her satisfaction, that all we enjoyed was granted by Almighty God as the reward of her piety and religion. And indeed, if religion consist in such zeal and such devotion, or in punctual and formal preparations for the Communion, or the like (as she had learnt, without doubt, from such tutors as she had been blessed with), then it cannot be denied that she had as much religion as well could be lodged in one breast. But if religion be justice, truth, sincerity, honour, gratitude or the like, then one cannot tell what to say; but let her practice speak for herself, her broken vows, her violated alliances, her behaviour to her old friends at home, her conduct to her good allies abroad, and the returns she made to her native country for an immense treasure of money and blood spent for the vindication of her title and the security of her life. . . .

She loved fawning and adoration, and hated plain dealing, even in the most important cases. She had a soul that nothing could so effectually move as flattery or fear. A sudden surprise, in an unguarded moment, would make the truth sometimes discover itself in her look or in some unlucky word; but if she had time and warning enough to learn her lesson, all the arguments and reason in the world could extort nothing from her that she had not a mind to acknowledge. In such cases she seemed to have the insensibility of a rock, and would resolutely dissemble or disown anything in the world, and by repeating one single answer in the same words could tire out the patience and elude all such inquiries as were disagreeable to herself.

She had no native generosity of temper, nor was often known of herself to do a handsome action either as a reward or as a piece of friendship. The diligence and faithfulness of a servant signified but little with her, where she had no passion for the person. Nor did she hardly ever think either of rewarding any because they were deserving, or of raising any because they were miserable, till such things were urged upon her by those whom she loved. And even to such as she professed to love her presents were very few and generally very insignificant, as fruit, or venison, or the like, unless in cases where she was directed by precedents in the former reigns. In a word, she had little zeal for the happiness of others, but a selfishness that was great enough to make every other consideration yield to it. She was headstrong and positive in matters of the utmost importance, and at last preferred her own humour and passion before the safety and happiness of her own people and of all Europe, which she had either not sense enough to see or not goodness enough to regard. Whether her memory will be celebrated by posterity with blessings or curses, time will show.

362. By Abel Boyer

(History of the Life and Reign of Queen Anne, pp. 715–716)

Thus died Anne Stuart, queen of Great Britain, a princess of as many virtues as ever adorned a private life, and as few frailties as ever blemished a diadem. Her person was middle-sized and well made, but after she bore children corpulent; her hair dark brown, her complexion sanguine and ruddy; her features strong but regular; and the only blemish in her face was owing to the defluxion she had in her infancy in her eyes, which left a contraction in the upper lids, that gave a cloudy air to her countenance. She had an excellent ear, which qualified her for a true dancer, and gave her a great relish for music, insomuch that she was accounted one of the best performers on the guitar, an instrument formerly much in vogue. She had also a good taste of poetry, painting and all the liberal arts. What was most remarkable in her personal accomplishments was a clear, harmonious voice, particularly conspicuous in her graceful delivery of her speeches to her Parliaments.

Good-nature, the characteristic of the Stuarts, predominated in her temper, which was a compound of benevolence, generosity, indolence and timidity, not without a due sensibility of any slight which she thought was offered either to her person or dignity. To these may be referred all the actions of her private and public life. These were the sources both of her virtues and of her uneasinesses. Her greatest blessing on earth was the entire union of affections and inclinations between her and her royal consort, which made them a perfect pattern of conjugal love. She was a fond and tender mother, an easy and indulgent mistress, and a most gracious sovereign; but she had more than once reason to repent her giving up her heart and trusting her secrets without any reserve to her favourites.

She retained to the last the principles of true religion which she had early imbibed, being devout without affectation, and charitable without ostentation. She had a great reverence for clergymen eminent for learning and good morals, and no less benefi-cence towards the poorer sort of them, of which she left a monument that will perpetuate her name and bounty to all succeeding generations. She kept her family in excellent decorum and regularity, being an exact economist without descending to trifling particulars, and never launching into any extraordinary expense without consulting her treasurer.

If she was not equal to the weight of a crown and the management of arduous affairs, yet it must be owned that the wisdom of her counsels and the success of her arms were in some measure owing to her just discernment in her first choice of her prime minister and general. And if she was afterwards prevailed with to part with them, it cannot be denied that the abuse of her confidence and authority was the main occasion of it, and gave a handle to some men to make her frailties and resentments subservient to their own revenge and ambitious designs. After all, as the first warlike nine years of her reign eclipse the most glorious of any of her predecessors, so will they shine to the remotest posterity; and whatever censures may pass on the latter part of her administration, impartial men will not reflect on the peace she made before it is mended by more advantageous treaties. Till then her reign will justify the reflection against the Salic Law, that monarchies are sometimes best administered when women fill the throne, because then men govern; whereas when men wear the sceptre it is generally swayed by women.

(g) JAMES FRANCIS EDWARD STUART

363. By Charles Leslie

(A letter from Mr. Lesly to a Member of Parliament in London, London, 1714)

And first for the person of the Chevalier, which you desire to know. He is tall, straight and clean-limbed, slender, yet his bones pretty large. He has a very graceful mien, walks fast; and his gait has great resemblance to his uncle, King Charles II, and the lines of his face grow daily more and more like him. He uses exercise more for health than diversion; he walks abroad, shoots or hunts every day, but is not what they call a keen sportsman. Being asked what he most delighted in, he said it would be to hear wise men discourse upon useful subjects.

He is always cheerful but seldom merry, thoughtful but not dejected, and bears his misfortunes with a visible magnanimity of spirit. He frequents the public devotions, but there is no sort of bigotry about him. He has a great application to business, spends much time in his closet, and writes much, which no man does better and more succinctly. I have often admired his criticalness in the choice of words. He apprehends readily, and gives the direct answer. He is very affable, and has something strangely engaging in his voice and deportment, that none who ever conversed with him but are charmed with his good sense and sweetness of temper. Nor can any take it ill even when he grants not their request, for he always gives such a reason as must satisfy. Yet he can show displeasure, but without anger. . . .

. He has informed himself of past miscarriages, and knows well the difference betwixt the office of a king and a missionary. He will concern himself with no man's religion, but is resolved to defend that which is legally established and whose principles are true to monarchy and safe for government, for whose satisfaction and for his own restoration he thinks himself obliged to do everything that is consistent with conscience and honour. . . . I would not have said so much were it not to do him justice, and expose the vile clamours of his enemies that he has no regard to Protestants, which is known to be notoriously false to all who have the honour to attend him. He has given all the demonstrations possible to the contrary except parting with his conscience and honour, which some would have him do that they might object it against him, and represent him as unworthy to reign for so doing. . . .

B. STATESMEN AND POLITICIANS

(a) EDWARD HYDE, EARL OF CLARENDON, AND HIS FAMILY

364. By Gilbert Burnet

(Supplement to Burnet's History of My Own Time, pp. 53–56)

The great man with the king was Chancellor Hyde, afterwards made earl of Clarendon. He had been in the beginning of the Long Parliament very high against the judges upon the account of the ship-money, and became then a considerable man. He spake well. His style had no flaw in it, but had a just mixture of wit and sense; only he spoke too copiously. He had a great pleasantness in his spirit, which carried him sometimes too far into raillery, in which he sometimes showed more wit than discretion. He went over to the Court party when the war was like to break out, and was much in the late king's councils and confidence during the war. . . . He was a man that knew England well, and was lawyer good enough to be an able Chancellor, and was certainly a very incorrupt man. In all the king's foreign negotiations he meddled too much, for I have been told that he had not a right notion of foreign matters; but he could not be gained to serve the interests of other princes. Mr. Fouquet sent him over a present of 10,000 pounds after the king's restoration, and assured him he would renew that every year; but though both the king and the duke advised him to take it he very worthily refused it. He took too much upon him and meddled in everything, which was his greatest error.

He fell under the hatred of most of the cavaliers upon two accounts. The one was the Act of Indemnity, which cut off all their hopes of repairing themselves of the estates of those that had been in the rebellion. But he said it was the offer of the indemnity that brought in the king, and it was the observing of it that must keep him in. So he would never let that be touched; and many that had been deeply engaged in the late times, having expiated it by their zeal of bringing home the king, were promoted by his means, such as Manchester, Anglesey, Orrery, Ashley, Holles and several others. The other thing was that, there being an infinite number of pretenders to employments and rewards for their services and sufferings, so that the king could only satisfy some few of them, he upon that, to stand between the king and the displeasure which those disappointments had given, spoke slightly of many of them, and took it upon him that their petitions were not granted. And some of them having procured several warrants from the Secretaries for the same thing (the Secretaries considering nothing but their fees), he who knew on whom the king intended that the grant should fall took all upon him, so that those who were disappointed laid the blame chiefly if not wholly upon him. He was apt to talk very imperiously and unmercifully, so that his manner of dealing with people was as provoking as the hard things themselves were; but upon the whole matter he was a true Englishman and a sincere Protestant, and what has passed at Court since his disgrace has sufficiently vindicated him from all ill designs.

365. By Gilbert Burnet

(History of My Own Time, ed. Airy, I, pp. 462-464)

I will end this relation of Lord Clarendon's fall with an account of his two sons. The eldest, now the earl of Clarendon, is a man naturally sincere, except in the payment of his debts, in which he has a particular art, upon his breaking his promises, which he does very often, to have a plausible excuse and a new promise ever ready at hand, in which he has run longer than one could think possible. He is a friendly and good-natured man. He keeps an exact journal of all that passes, and is punctual to tediousness in all that he relates. He was very early engaged in great secrets, for his father, appre-hending of what fatal consequence it would have been to the king's affairs if his correspondence had been discovered by unfaithful secretaries, engaged him when very young to write all his letters to England in cipher; so that he was generally half the day writing in cipher, or deciphering, and was so discreet, as well as faithful, that nothing was ever discovered by him. He continued to be still the person whom his father trusted most, and was the most beloved of all the family, for he was humble and obliging, but was peevish and splenetic. His judgment was not to be much depended on, for he was much carried by vulgar prejudices and false notions. He was much in the queen's favour, and was her chamberlain long. His father's being so violently prosecuted on the account of her marriage made that she thought herself bound to protect him in a particular manner. He was so provoked at the ill usage his father met with that he struck in violently with the party that opposed the Court, and the king spoke always of him with great sharpness and much scorn.

His brother, now earl of Rochester, is a man of far greater parts. He has a very good pen, but speaks not gracefully. He was thought the smoothest man in the Court; and during all the dispute concerning his father he made his court so dexterously that no resentments appeared on that head. When he came into business, and rose to high posts, he grew both violent and insolent, but was thought by many an incorrupt man. He has high notions of government, and thinks it must be maintained with great severity. He delivers up his own notions to his party, that he may lead them; and on all occasions he is wilful and imperious. He passes for a sincere man, and seems to have too much heat to be false. This natural heat is inflamed by frequent excesses in drinking.

366. Anonymous

(Historical Manuscripts Commission, Egmont MSS., II, p. 18)

Here lies Tom Hyde.
It's pity that he died.
We had rather
It had been his father.
If it had been his sister,
We had not missed her.
If the whole generation,
It had been better for the nation.

(b) GEORGE VILLIERS, DUKE OF BUCKINGHAM

367. By Gilbert Burnet

(History of My Own Time, ed. Airy, I, pp. 182–183)

The first of these was a man of a noble presence. He had a great liveliness of wit, and a peculiar faculty of turning all things into ridicule with bold figures and natural descriptions. He had no sort of literature; only he was drawn into chemistry, and for some years he thought he was very near finding the philosopher's stone, which had the fate that attends on all such men as he was, when they are drawn in, to lay out for it. He had no principles either of religion, virtue or friendship. Pleasure, frolic and extravagant diversions was all that he laid to heart. He was true to nothing, for he was not true to himself. He had no steadiness nor conduct; he could keep no secret, nor execute any design without spoiling it. He could never fix his thoughts, nor govern his estate, though then the greatest in England. He was bred about the king, and for many years he had a great ascendant over him; but he spake of him to all persons with that contempt that at last he drew a lasting disgrace upon himself; and he also ruined both body and mind, fortune and reputation equally.

The madness of vice appeared in his person in very eminent instances, since at last he became contemptible and poor, sickly and sunk in his parts as well as in all other respects, so that his conversation was as much avoided as ever it had been courted. He found the king, when he came from his travels in the year '45, newly come to Paris, sent over by his father when his affairs declined; and finding him enough inclined to receive ill impressions he, who was then got into all the impieties and vices of the age, set himself to corrupt the king, in which he was too successful, being seconded in that wicked design by the Lord Percy.

368. By John Sheffield, duke of Buckingham

(An Essay on Satire, ll. 84–95)

And first behold the merriest man alive
Against his careless genius vainly strive;
Quit his dear ease some deep design to lay,
Appoint the hour, and then forget the day.
Yet he will laugh, ev'n at his friends, and be
Just as good company as Nokes, or Lee;
But when he would the Court or nation rule,
He turns himself the best to ridicule.
When serious, few for great affairs more fit;
But shew him mirth, and bait that mirth with wit,
That shadow of a jest shall be enjoyed,
Though he left all mankind to be destroyed.

369. By John Dryden

(Absalom and Achitophel, ll. 543–568)

Some of their chiefs were princes of the land;
 In the first rank of these did *Zimri* stand,
A man so various that he seemed to be
Not one, but all mankind's epitome.
Stiff in opinions, always in the wrong,
Was everything by starts and nothing long;
But in the course of one revolving moon
Was chymist, fiddler, statesman, and buffoon;
Then all for women, painting, rhyming, drinking,
Besides ten thousand freaks that died in thinking.
Blest madman, who could every hour employ
With something new to wish or to enjoy!
Railing and praising were his usual themes,
And both, to show his judgment, in extremes;
So over-violent, or over-civil,
That every man with him was God or Devil.
In squandring wealth was his peculiar art;
Nothing went unrewarded but desert.
Beggared by fools, whom still he found too late,
He had his jest, and they had his estate.
He laughed himself from Court; then sought relief
By forming parties, but could ne'er be chief,
For, spite of him, the weight of business fell
On *Absalom* and wise *Achitophel*.
Thus wicked but in will, of means bereft,
He left not faction, but of that was left.

370. By Alexander Pope

(Moral Essays, III, p. 309)

In the worst inn's worst room, with mat half-hung,
 The floors of plaster, and the walls of dung,
On once a flock-bed, but repaired with straw,
With tape-tied curtains never meant to draw,
The George and Garter dangling from that bed
Where tawdry yellow strove with dirty red,
Great Villiers lies. Alas! how changed for him
That life of pleasure and that soul of whim!
Gallant and gay in Cleveden's proud alcove,
The bower of wanton Shrewsbury and love;
Or just as gay, at council, in a ring
Of mimicked statesmen and their merry king.

No wit to flatter left of all his store!
No fool to laugh at, which he valued more.
There victor of his health, of fortune, friends,
And fame, this lord of useless thousands ends.

(c) HENRY BENNET, EARL OF ARLINGTON
371. By John Sheffield, duke of Buckingham
(*Works*, ed. 1729, II, pp. 84–88)

Henry Bennet, a younger son of a private gentleman, had followed the royal family into exile, at whose restoration he was made first Privy Purse, then Secretary of State, earl of Arlington, Knight of the Garter, and at last Lord Chamberlain to King Charles the Second, and to his brother King James the Second afterwards. He was for some years a kind of favourite minister (I mean conversant in his master's pleasures, as well as intrusted with his business), notwithstanding the constant enmity both of the duke of York and Chancellor Clarendon, whose superior power, especially in state affairs, was yet unable to shake King Charles's inclination to this gentleman, who therefore, at the other's banishment, remained if not sole minister at least the principal one for some time.

He met with one thing very peculiar in his fortune, which I have scarce known happen to any man else. With all his advancement (which is wont to create malice, but seldom contempt) he was believed in England by most people a man of much less abilities than he really had. For this unusual sort of mistake I can only imagine two causes. First, his over-cautious avoiding to speak in Parliament, as having been more conversant in affairs abroad, though nobody performed it better when obliged to give account of some treaties to the House of Lords or to defend himself in the House of Commons, by which last he once brought himself off with great dexterity. The other reason of it I fancy to have come from the duke of Buckingham, who, being his rival in Court after the fall of Clarendon, and having an extraordinary talent of turning anything into ridicule, exercised it sufficiently on this lord, both with the king and everybody else, which had its effect at last even to his being left out of his master's business but not his favour, which in some measure continued still, and long after this his supplanter was totally discarded.

Having been educated in order to be a divine, he was a better scholar than commonly courtiers are, and so well versed in the classic poets that I never knew any man apply them so properly on any subject whatsoever, and without any pedantic affectation. Yet he could never shake off a little air of formality that an embassy into Spain had infected him with; but it only hung about his mien, without the least tincture of it either in his words or behaviour. He once had the honour to procure a Triple League of great advantage to the defence of Europe against France; but he being one of those who for several years afterwards assisted in carrying on a quite contrary interest, it too plainly shows that, though none in this whole reign knew foreign affairs so well, yet after all he was rather a subtle courtier than an able statesman, too much regarding every inclination of his master and too little considering his true interest and that of the nation.

To end handsomely with him, he was of a generous temper, not only living splendidly but obliging his friends willingly and warmly. On which occasion I remember that, visiting him one day when newly a friend of his had turned ungratefully against him, he asked me what effect I thought it would have upon him. I, thinking he meant as to his fortune, was about to answer gravely, when he smilingly protested it should neither cool him in his present friendships nor hinder his assisting the next deserving person who came in his way, because that was the greatest satisfaction of his life, and he would not part with it upon any discouragement whatsoever. The truth of this he told me I should always find, and indeed I did so to the very end of his life, which therefore required this small piece of gratitude.

(d) JOHN MAITLAND, DUKE OF LAUDERDALE

372. By Gilbert Burnet

(*History of My Own Time*, ed. Airy, I, pp. 184–185)

The earl of Lauderdale, afterwards made duke, had been for many years a zealous Covenanter; but in the year '47 he turned to the king's interests, and had continued a prisoner from Worcester fight, where he was taken. . . . He made a very ill appearance. He was very big. His hair was red, hanging oddly about him. His tongue was too big for his mouth, which made him bedew all that he talked to, and his whole manner was rough and boisterous, and very unfit for a court. He was very learned, not only in Latin, in which he was a master, but in Greek and Hebrew. He had read a great deal in divinity, and almost all the historians, ancient and modern; so that he had great materials. He had with these an extraordinary memory, and a copious but unpolished expression. He was a man, as the duke of Buckingham called him to me, of a blundering understanding, not always clear, but often clouded, as his looks were always.

He was haughty beyond expression; abject to those he saw he must stoop to, but imperious and insolent and brutal to all others. He had a violence of passion that carried him often to fits like madness, in which he had no temper. If he took a thing wrong, it was a vain thing to study to convince him. That would rather provoke him to swear he would never be of another mind. He was to be let alone, and then perhaps he would have forgot what he had said, and come about of his own accord. He was the coldest friend and the violentest enemy I ever knew. I felt it too much not to know it. He at first seemed to despise wealth; but he delivered himself up afterwards to luxury and sensuality, and by that means he ran into a vast expense, and stuck at nothing that was necessary to support that. In his long imprisonment he had great impressions of religion on his mind; but he wore these out so entirely that scarce any trace of them was left.

His great experience in affairs, his ready compliance with everything that he thought would please the king, and his bold offering at the most desperate counsels, gained him such an interest in the king that no attempt against him, nor complaint of him, could ever shake it, till a decay of strength and understanding forced him to let go his hold. He was in his principles much against popery and arbitrary government; and yet, by a fatal train of passions and interests, he made way for the former and had almost established the latter. And whereas some by a smooth deportment make the first beginnings of tyranny less unacceptable and discernible, he by the fury of his behaviour heightened the severity of his ministry, which was liker the cruelty of an inquisition than the legality of justice, not to say mercy. With all this he was at first a Presbyterian, and retained his aversion to King Charles I and his party to his death.

(e) ANTHONY ASHLEY COOPER, EARL OF SHAFTESBURY

373. By Gilbert Burnet

(History of My Own Time, ed. Airy, I, pp. 172–174)

He had a wonderful faculty in speaking to a popular assembly, and could mix both the facetious and the serious way of arguing very agreeably. He had a particular talent of making others trust to his judgment and depend on it; and he brought over so many to a submission to his opinion that I never knew any man equal to him in the art of governing parties, and of making himself the head of them. He was, as to religion, a deist at best. He had the dotage of astrology in him to a high degree. He told me that a Dutch doctor had from the stars foretold him the whole series of his life; but that which was before him when he told me this proved false, if he told true, for he said he was yet to be a greater man than he had been. He fancied that after death our souls lived in stars. He had a general knowledge of the slighter parts of learning, but understood little to bottom; so he triumphed in a rambling way of talking, but argued slightly when he was held close to any point.

He had a wonderful faculty at opposing and running things down, but had not the like force in building up. He had such an extravagant vanity in setting himself out that it was very disagreeable. He pretended that Cromwell offered to make him king. He was indeed of great use to him in withstanding the enthusiasts of that time. He was one of those who pressed him most to accept of the kingship, because, as he said afterwards, he was sure it would ruin him. His strength lay in the knowledge of England, and of all the considerable men in it. He understood well the size of their understanding and their tempers; and he knew how to apply himself to them so dexterously that, though by his changing sides so often it was very visible how little he was to be depended on, yet he was to the last much trusted by all the discontented party.

He had no sort of virtue, for he was both a lewd and corrupt man, and had no regard either to truth or justice. He was not ashamed to reckon up the many turns he had made; and he valued himself on the doing it at the properest season and in the best manner, and was not out of countenance in owning his unsteadiness and deceitfulness. This he did with so much vanity and so little discretion that he lost many by it, and his reputation was at last run so low that he could not have held much longer, had he not died in good time either for his family or for his party. The former would have been ruined if he had not saved it by betraying his party.

374. By John Dryden

(Absalom and Achitophel, ll. 150–227)

Of these the false *Achitophel* was first;
   A name to all succeeding ages cursed;
For close designs and crooked counsels fit;
Sagacious, bold, and turbulent of wit; ·
Restless, unfixed in principles and place,
In power unpleased, impatient of disgrace;
A fiery soul, which, working out its way,
Fretted the pigmy body to decay,
And o'er-informed the tenement of clay.
A daring pilot in extremity,
Pleased with the danger when the waves went high,
He sought the storms; but for a calm unfit,
Would steer too nigh the sands to boast his wit. . . .
In friendship false, implacable in hate,
Resolved to ruin or to rule the state,
To compass this the triple bond he broke,
The pillars of the public safety shook,
And fitted Israel for a foreign yoke;
Then seized with fear, yet still affecting fame,
Usurped a patriot's all-atoning name. . . .
Yet fame deserved no enemy can grudge;
The statesman we abhor, but praise the judge.
In Israel's courts ne'er sat an Abethdin
With more discerning eyes, or hands more clean,
Unbribed, unsought, the wretched to redress;
Swift of despatch, and easy of access. . . .
But wild ambition loves to slide, not stand,
And fortune's ice prefers to virtue's land.
Achitophel, grown weary to possess
A lawful fame, and lazy happiness,
Disdained the golden fruit to gather free,
And lent the crowd his arm to shake the tree.
Now, manifest of crimes contrived long since,
He stood at bold defiance with his prince,
Held up the buckler of the people's cause ·
Against the Crown, and skulked behind the laws.
The wished occasion of the Plot he takes,
Some circumstances finds, but more he makes;
By buzzing emissaries fills the ears
Of listening crowds with jealousies and fears
Of arbitrary counsels brought to light,
And proves the king himself a Jebusite.

Weak arguments, which yet he knew full well
Were strong with people easy to rebel. . . .
Achitophel still wants a chief, and none
Was found so fit as warlike *Absalon*.
Not that he wished his greatness to create,
For politicians neither love nor hate;
But, for he knew his title not allowed
Would keep him still depending on the crowd,
That kingly power, thus ebbing out, might be
Drawn to the dregs of a democracy.

(f) SIR WILLIAM TEMPLE

375. By his sister, Martha, Lady Giffard

(*Works of Sir William Temple*, ed. 1740, I, pp. xiii–xiv)

Sir William Temple's person is best known by his pictures and prints. He was rather tall than low; his shape, when young, very exact; his hair a dark brown and curled naturally, and whilst that was esteemed a beauty nobody had it in greater perfection; his eyes grey, but lively; and his body lean, but extreme active, so that none acquitted themselves better at all sorts of exercise.

He had an extraordinary spirit and life in his humour, with so agreeable turns of wit and fancy in his conversation that nobody was welcomer in all sorts of company, and some have observed that he never had a mind to make anybody kind to him without compassing his design. He was an exact observer of truth, thinking none that had failed once ought ever to be trusted again; of nice points of honour; of great humanity and good-nature, taking pleasure in making others easy and happy; his passions naturally warm and quick, but tempered by reason and thought; his humour gay, but very unequal from cruel fits of spleen and melancholy, being subject to great damps from sudden changes of weather, but chiefly from the crosses and surprising turns in his business, and disappointments he met with so often in his endeavours to contribute to the honour and service of his country, which he thought himself two or three times so near compassing that he could not think with patience of what had hindered it, or of those that he thought had been the occasion of his disappointments. He never seemed busy in his greatest employments, was a great lover of liberty, and therefore hated the servitude of courts, said he could never serve for wages nor be busy (as one is so often there) to no purpose, and never was willing to enter upon any employment but that of a public minister.

He had been a passionate lover, was a kind husband, a fond and indulgent father, a good master and the best friend in the world; and knowing himself to be so was impatient of the least suspicion or jealousy from those he loved. He was ever kind to the memory of those he had once liked and esteemed, wounded to the heart by grief upon the many losses of his children and friends, till recovered by reason and philosophy, and that perfect resignation to Almighty God which he thought so absolute a part of our duty upon those sad occasions, often saying, His holy name be praised, His will be done.

He was not without strong aversions, so as to be uneasy at the first sight of some he disliked and impatient of their conversation; apt to be warm in disputes and expostulations, which made him hate the one and avoid the other, which he used to say might sometimes do well between lovers but never between friends. He turned his conversation to what was more easy and pleasant, especially at table, where he said ill-humour ought never to come, and his agreeable talk at it, if it had been set down, would have been very entertaining to the reader as well as to so many that had heard it. He had a very familiar way of conversing with all sorts of people, from the greatest princes to the meanest servants and even children, whose imperfect language and natural and innocent talk he was fond of, and made entertainment out of everything that could afford it. When that he liked best failed, the next served turn.

He lived healthful till forty-two, then began to be troubled with rheums upon his teeth and eyes, which he attributed to the air of Holland, and which ended, when he was forty-seven, in the gout, upon which he grew very melancholy, being then ambassador at the Hague. He said a man was never good for anything after it, and though he continued in business near three years longer it was always with design of winding himself out as fast as he could and making good his own rules, that nobody should make love after forty, nor be in business after fifty. And though from this time he had frequent returns of ill health he never cared to consult physicians, saying he hoped to die without them, and trusted wholly to the care and advice of his friends, which he often expressed himself so happy in as to want nothing but health, which since riches could not help him to he despised them. . . .

His religion was that of the Church of England, in which he was born and bred, and how loose soever Bishop Burnet in his history of his own time represents his principles (from that commonplace of hearsay that runs through the whole, for he was not acquainted with Sir William), yet there is no ground for such uncharitable reflections given in his writings, in which his excellent letter to the countess of Essex is a convincing proof both of his piety and eloquence, and to that picture, drawn by himself in his *Works*,[1] I refer those that care either to know or to imitate him.

(g) GEORGE SAVILE, MARQUIS OF HALIFAX

376. By Gilbert Burnet

(History of My Own Time, ed. Airy, I, pp. 483–485)

I name Sir George Savile last, because he deserves a more copious character. He rose afterwards to be viscount, earl and marquis of Halifax. He was a man of a great and ready wit, full of life and very pleasant, much turned to satire. He let his wit run much on matters of religion, so that he passed for a bold and determined atheist, though he often protested to me he was not one, and said he believed there was not one in the world. He confessed he could not swallow down everything that divines imposed on the world. He was a Christian in submission, and he believed as much as

[1] Ed. 1740, I, p. 128.

he could, and he hoped God would not lay it to his charge if he could not digest iron, as an ostrich did, nor take into his belief things that must burst him. If he had any scruples they were not sought for nor cherished by him, for he never read an atheistical book. These were his excuses, but I could not quite believe him. Yet in a fit of sickness I knew him very much touched with a sense of religion. I was then oft with him. He seemed full of good purposes, but they went off with his sickness. He was always talking of morality and friendship.

He was punctual in all payments and just in all his private dealings, but with relation to the public he went backwards and forwards, and changed sides so often that in conclusion no side trusted him. He seemed full of commonwealth notions, yet he went in to the worst part of King Charles's reign. He was out of measure vain and ambitious. The liveliness of his imagination was always too hard for his judgment. A severe jest was preferred by him to all arguments whatsoever. And he was endless in consultations; for when after much discourse a point was settled, if he could find a new jest to make even that which was suggested by himself seem ridiculous he could not hold, but would study to raise the credit of his wit though it made others call his judgment in question.

When he talked to me as a philosopher of his contempt of the world, I asked him what he meant to be getting so many new titles, which I called the hanging himself about with bells and tinsel. He had no other excuse for it but this, that since the world were such fools as to value those matters a man must be a fool for company. He considered them but as rattles; yet rattles please children, so these might be of use to his family. His heart was much set on raising his family; but though he made a vast estate for them he buried two of his sons himself, and almost all his grandchildren.

377. By John Dryden
(Absalom and Achitophel, ll. 882–887)

Jotham of piercing wit and pregnant thought,
  Endued by nature, and by learning taught
To move assemblies, who but only tried
The worse awhile, then chose the better side;
Nor chose alone, but turned the balance too;
So much the weight of one brave man can do.

(h) THOMAS OSBORNE, EARL OF DANBY AND DUKE OF LEEDS

378. By John Sheffield, duke of Buckingham
(An Essay on Satire, ll. 74–79)

Ernly and Anglesey, with all the race
  Of formal blockheads, shall have here no place,
At Council set, as foils, on Danby's score,
To make that great false jewel shine the more;
Who all the while is thought exceeding wise,
Only for taking pains, and telling lies.

(*i*) RICHARD TALBOT, EARL OF TYRCONNEL

379. By James Fitzjames, duke of Berwick
(Memoirs, I, pp. 94–95)

Richard Talbot, duke of Tyrconnel, was a native of Ireland, of a good family. His stature was above the ordinary size. He had great experience of the world, having been early introduced into the best company and possessed of an honourable employment in the household of the duke of York, who, upon his succession to the crown, raised him to the dignity of an earl, and, well knowing his zeal and attachment, made him soon after viceroy of Ireland. He was a man of very good sense, very obliging, but immoderately vain, and full of cunning. Though he had acquired great possessions it could not be said that he had employed improper means, for he never appeared to have a passion for money. He had not a military genius, but much courage. After the prince of Orange's invasion his firmness preserved Ireland, and he nobly refused all the offers that were made to induce him to submit. From the time of the battle of the Boyne he sank prodigiously, being become as irresolute in his mind as unwieldy in his person.

380. By Thomas Sheridan
(Historical Manuscripts Commission, Stuart Papers, VI, pp. 46–47)

To give his true character in few words, he was a tall, proper, handsome man, but publicly known to be most insolent in prosperity and most abject in adversity; a cunning, dissembling courtier, of mean judgment and small understanding, uncertain and unsteady in his resolutions, turning with every wind to bring about his ambitious ends and purposes; on which he was so intent that to compass them he would stick at nothing, and so false that a most impudent notorious lie was called at Whitehall and St. James's one of Dick Talbot's ordinary truths.

(*j*) ROBERT SPENCER, EARL OF SUNDERLAND

381. By Gilbert Burnet
(History of My Own Time, ed. Airy, II, p. 23)

Lord Sunderland was a man of a clear and ready apprehension and quick decision in business. He had too much heat both of imagination and passion, and was apt to speak very freely both of persons and things. His own notions were always good; but he was a man of great expense, and in order to the supporting himself he went into the prevailing counsels at Court, so that he changed sides often with little regard either to religion or to the interest of his country. He raised many enemies to himself by the contempt with which he treated those who differed from him. He had indeed the superior genius to all the men of business that I have yet known. And he had the dexterity of insinuating himself so entirely into the greatest degree of confidence with three succeeding princes, who set up on very different interests, that he came by this to lose his reputation so much that even those who esteemed his parts depended little on his firmness.

382. Anonymous

(Lampoon entitled *Faction Displayed*)

A Proteus, ever acting in disguise;
A finished statesman, intricately wise;
A second Machiavel, who soared above
The little ties of gratitude and love.

(k) EDWARD SEYMOUR

383. By Gilbert Burnet

(*History of My Own Time*, ed. Airy, II, pp. 79–80)

The ablest man of his party was Seymour, that was the first Speaker of that House that was not bred to the law. He was a man of great birth, being the elder branch of the Seymour family, and was a graceful man, bold and quick, but was the most immoral and impious man of the age. He had a sort of pride so peculiar to himself that I never saw anything like it. He had neither shame nor decency with it. And in all private as well as in public dealings he was the unjustest and blackest man that has lived in our time. He was violent against the Court till he forced himself into good posts.

He was the most assuming Speaker that ever sat in the chair. He knew the House and every man in it so well that by looking about he could tell the fate of any question. So if anything was put when the Court party were not well gathered together he would have held the House from doing anything, by a wilful mistaking or mis-stating the question, so that he gave time to those who were appointed for that mercenary work to go about and gather in all their party. And he would discern when they had got the majority, and then he would very fairly state the question, when he saw he was sure to carry it.

384. By John Dryden

(*Absalom and Achitophel*, ll. 898–913)

Indulge one labour more, my weary Muse,
For *Amiel*. Who can *Amiel's* praise refuse?
Of ancient race by birth, but nobler yet
In his own worth, and without title great,
The Sanhedrin long time as chief he ruled,
Their reason guided and their passion cooled.
So dexterous was he in the Crown's defence,
So formed to speak a loyal nation's sense,
That, as their band was Israel's tribes in small,
So fit was he to represent them all.
Now rasher charioteers the seat ascend,
Whose loose careers his steady skill commend.

> They, like the unequal ruler of the day,
> Misguide the seasons and mistake the way,
> While he, withdrawn, at their mad labour smiles,
> And safe enjoys the sabbath of his toils.

(*l*) SIDNEY GODOLPHIN, EARL OF GODOLPHIN

385. By Abel Boyer
(*History of the Life and Reign of Queen Anne*, p. 17)

As to his person, the Lord Godolphin was of a middle stature, well set, and of a strong constitution; his face of a brown complexion, somewhat disfigured with the small-pox, but enlivened with a quick, piercing eye; and the natural severity of his countenance was now and then sweetened with a smile. He had a prying, contemplative genius, a slow but unerring apprehension, an exquisite judgment, few words always to the purpose, was temperate in his diet and of a very amorous temper. His superior wisdom and spirit made him despise the low arts of vainglorious courtiers, for he never kept suitors unprofitably in suspense nor promised anything that he was not resolved to perform; but as he accounted dissimulation the worst of lying his denials were softened by the frankness and condescension with which he informed those he could not gratify.

His great abilities and consummate experience qualified him for a prime minister, and his exact knowledge of all the branches of the revenue particularly fitted him for the management of the Treasury. He was thrifty, without the least tincture of avarice or greediness of riches, being as good an economist of the public wealth as he was of his private fortune. He had, besides, a very clear conception of the whole policy of the government both in Church and State, which by the unskilfulness of some men had of late jostled each other too much. He perfectly knew the temper, genius and disposition of the English nation; and though his stern gravity was somewhat shocking and ungracious, yet his steady and impartial justice recommended him to the esteem of almost everybody, so that no man, in so many different public stations and so great a variety of business, ever had more friends or fewer enemies.

(*m*) ANDREW FLETCHER

386. By George Lockhart
(*The Lockhart Papers*, ed. 1817, I, pp. 75–77)

He was blessed with a soul that hated and despised whatever was mean and unbecoming a gentleman, and was so steadfast to what he thought right that no hazard nor advantage, no, not the universal empire nor the gold of America, could tempt him to yield or desert it. And I may affirm that in all his life he never once pursued a measure with the prospect of any by-end to himself, nor further than he judged it for the common benefit and advantage of his country. He was master of the

English, Latin, Greek, French and Italian languages, and well versed in history, the civil law and all kinds of learning; and as he was universally accomplished, he employed his talents for the good of mankind.

He was a strict and nice observer of all the points of honour, and his word sacred; as brave as his sword, and had some experience in the art of war, having in his younger years been some time a volunteer in both the land and sea service. In his travels he had studied, and came to understand, the respective interests of the several princes and states of Europe. In his private conversation affable to his friends (but could not endure to converse with those he thought enemies to their country), and free of all manner of vice. He had a penetrating, clear and lively apprehension, but so extremely wedded to his own opinions that there were few (and those too must be his beloved friends and of whom he had a good opinion) he could endure to reason against him; and did for the most part so closely and unalterably adhere to what he advanced (which was frequently very singular) that he would break with his party before he would alter the least jot of his scheme and maxims. And therefore it was impossible for any set of men, that did not give up themselves to be absolutely directed by him, to please him so as to carry him along in all points. And thence it came to pass that he often in Parliament acted a part by himself, though in the main he stuck close to the country party, and was their Cicero.

He was no doubt an enemy to all monarchical governments, at least thought they wanted to be much reformed; but I do very well believe his aversion to the English and the union was so great, in revenge to them he would have sided with the royal family. But as that was a subject not fit to be entered upon with him, this is only a conjecture from some innuendoes I have heard him make. But so far is certain, he liked, commended and conversed with high-flying Tories more than any other set of men, acknowledging them to be the best countrymen, and of most honour, integrity and ingenuity. To sum up all, he was a learned, gallant, honest, and every other way well-accomplished gentleman; and if ever a man proposes to serve and merit well of his country, let him place his courage, zeal and constancy as a pattern before him, and think himself sufficiently applauded and rewarded by obtaining the character of being like Andrew Fletcher of Saltoun.

(n) JOHN SOMERS, LORD SOMERS

387. By Jonathan Swift

(*Works*, ed. 1814, V, pp. 171–172)

I have hardly known any man with talents more proper to acquire and preserve the favour of a prince; never offending in word or gesture; in the highest degree courteous and complaisant, wherein he set an excellent example to his colleagues, which they did not think fit to follow. But this extreme civility is universal and undistinguished; and in private conversation, where he observes it as inviolably as if he were in the greatest assembly, it is sometimes censured as formal. Two reasons are assigned for this behaviour: first, from the consciousness of his humble origin he keeps all familiarity at the utmost distance, which otherwise might be apt to intrude; the second, that being sensible how subject he is to violent passions, he avoids all incitements to them, by teaching those he converses with, from his own example, to keep a great way within the bounds of decency and respect. And it is indeed true that no man is more apt to take fire upon the least appearance of provocation, which temper he strives to subdue, with the utmost violence upon himself; so that his breast has been seen to heave, and his eyes to sparkle with rage, in those very moments when his words and the cadence of his voice were in the humblest and softest manner.

Perhaps that force upon his nature may cause that insatiable love of revenge which his detractors lay to his charge, who consequently reckon dissimulation among his chief perfections. Avarice he has none, and his ambition is gratified by being the uncontested head of his party. With an excellent understanding, adorned by all the polite parts of learning, he has very little taste for conversation, to which he prefers the pleasure of reading and thinking; and in the intervals of his time amuses himself with an illiterate chaplain, an humble companion, or a favourite servant.

These are some few distinguishing marks in the character of that person who now presides over the discontented party, although he be not answerable for all their mistakes; and if his precepts had been more strictly followed perhaps their power would not have been so easily shaken. I have been assured, and heard him profess, that he was against engaging in that foolish prosecution of Dr. Sacheverell, as what he saw was likely to end in their ruin; that he blamed the rough demeanour of some persons to the queen as a great failure in prudence; and that, when it appeared her Majesty was firmly resolved upon a treaty of peace, he advised his friends not to oppose it in its progress but find fault with it after it was made, which would be a copy of the like usage themselves had met with after the treaty of Ryswick, and the safest, as well as the most probable, way of disgracing the promoters and advisers.

I have been the larger in representing to the reader some idea of this extraordinary genius because, whatever attempt has hitherto been made, with any appearance of conduct or probability of success, to restore the dominion of that party, was infallibly contrived by him; and I prophesy the same for the future, as long as his age and infirmities will leave him capable of business.

(o) ROBERT HARLEY, EARL OF OXFORD

388. By Sarah, duchess of Marlborough
(An Account of the Conduct of the Duchess of Marlborough, pp. 261–262)

He was a cunning and a dark man, of too small abilities to do much good, but of all the qualities requisite to do mischief and to bring on the ruin and destruction of a nation. This mischievous darkness of his soul was written in his countenance, and plainly legible in a very odd look, disagreeable to everybody at first sight, which, being joined with a constant awkward motion or rather agitation of his head and body, betrayed a turbulent dishonesty within, even in the midst of all those familiar airs, jocular bowing and smiling, which he always affected to cover what could not be covered. He had long accustomed himself so much to dissemble his real intentions, and to use the ambiguous and obscure way of speaking, that he could hardly ever be understood when he designed it, or be believed when he never so much desired it. His natural temper led him to so expensive and profuse a way of living that he had brought himself into great necessities, though he had long enjoyed the advantages of very great and profitable posts.

One principal and very expensive piece of his art, in which he seems to have excelled all that went before him, was to have in pay a great number of spies of all sorts, to let him into what was passing in all considerable families. It was remarkable that when he came most into favour with the queen he was perhaps the only man in whose ruin the two contending parties would have united, as one in whom there was no foundation to repose any confidence; and that when he came to have the greatest power with the queen he had lost all credit everywhere else.

C. SOLDIERS, CLERGYMEN, AND CIVIL OFFICIALS

(a) GEORGE MONCK, DUKE OF ALBEMARLE

389. By Thomas Skinner

(Life of General Monk, pp. 377–384)

They who daily possess the benefit of this great man's prudence and loyalty, and never had the happiness of seeing him, will expect here some character of his person, which was indeed rather comely than elegant. His stature was of the middle size, but contrived for strength and action. In his countenance there appeared something very great and august, yet without pride. His aspect was so truly martial that they who knew him not might have taken him for a general, and collected the ideas of an hero from the lines of his face. His eyesight served him to the last upon nearer objects, though at remoter distances it was somewhat defective, which imperfection was in some measure recompensed to him with a very extraordinary quickness of hearing, wherein he did so very far excel that it was dangerous to whisper a secret in the same room with him.

His constitution also was framed to a singular steadiness of temperament, which enabled him to live with a very little sleep, and without any of those emotions in his blood which most other men find from the want of it. Upon the same account he was capable of enduring long and frequent fasting, when imposed upon him either by religion, necessity or business, without any observable prejudice to his health or any other inconvenience. In his palate he was not curious, or at all studious how to gratify it. When he was young he had the small-pox, yet entertained them most part of the time on horseback, and marched every day with his regiment without any of those fatal effects which naturally follow from the least impression of the cold air.

But when we come to describe the virtues and endowments of his mind we enter upon a more copious and extensive subject. His courage and fortitude were beyond any hyperbolical strains of his friends, and were never yet questioned by his greatest enemies. They were not, like the uncertain and occasional impetuosity of the late usurper Cromwell, taken up by fits, but a steady and well-advised greatness of spirit, separate from rashness, and conducted by an extraordinary prudence and foresight; so that in those many engagements where he had commanded he was always attended with a smooth, uninterrupted success, which has rarely been constant to old generals. And in that single surprisal upon him by the Dutch fleet he fought them so stoutly with a very unequal force, and afterwards secured his retreat with so much resolution and bravery, that his enemies were obliged to acknowledge there was something in his greatness of mind and conduct that was more than human. . . .

If his virtues had been only military he and his armour might in peaceful times have rusted together. But as he had the sufficiency of a great general in war, so he had equal prudence and industry in civil business; and when there was no more occasion for his sword he became a most useful and necessary minister of state, wherein if some few have exceeded him in dispatch, yet none in sureness and fidelity. By his prudence he baffled all his enemies, and unravelled all the labyrinths of their crooked subtlety. By the same virtue he preserved to himself the continued affection and kindness of his Majesty, which shone upon him to the evening of his life without the interruption of the least cloud. By the like quality he kept up his estimation with his equals and the ministers of state, against whom he had never given in to any intriguing schemes. And as a reward of his prudence and integrity he had those advantages which have seldom been known to centre in the same person, of being equally the favourite of the king, the Court and the people.

390. By Samuel Pepys
(*Diary*, 23 October 1667)

I know not how, the blockhead Albemarle hath strange luck to be loved, though he be (and every man must know it) the heaviest man in the world, but stout and honest to his country.

(b) HUGH MACKAY

391. By Gilbert Burnet
(*History of My Own Time*, ed. 1833, IV, p. 176)

Here[1] Mackay was killed, being ordered to a post that he saw could not be maintained. He sent his opinion about it, but the former orders were confirmed; so he went on, saying only, The will of the Lord be done. He was a man of such strict principles that he would not have served in a war that he did not think lawful. He took great care of his soldiers' morals, and forced them to be both sober and just in their quarters. He spent all the time that he was master of in secret prayers, and in the reading of the Scriptures. The king often observed that when he had full leisure for his devotions he acted with a peculiar exaltation of courage. He had one very singular quality: in councils of war he delivered his opinion freely, and maintained it with due zeal; but how positive soever he was in it, if the council of war overruled it, even though he was not convinced by it, yet to all others he justified it, and executed his part with the same zeal as if his own opinion had prevailed.

(c) PATRICK SARSFIELD

392. By James Fitzjames, duke of Berwick
(*Memoirs*, I, pp. 95–97)

Patrick Sarsfield was by birth a gentleman, and succeeded by the death of his elder brother to an estate of about two thousand pounds a year. He was a man of an amazing stature, utterly void of sense, very good-natured and very brave. He had served as ensign in France, in the regiment of Monmouth, and had also been lieutenant of the life-guards in England. When the king went over to Ireland he gave him a

[1] At the battle of Steinkirk.

regiment of cavalry, and made him brigadier. The affair of the convoy, . . . in which he was victorious, elated him so much that he thought himself the greatest general in the world. Henry Luttrell contributed as much as possible to turn his head, by incessantly praising him in all companies, not out of any real esteem he had for him, but to make him popular and by that means render him subservient to his own designs. In effect the Irish in general conceived so high an opinion of him that the king to gratify them created him earl of Lucan, and in the next promotion made him major-general. After the capitulation of Limerick he went over to France, where the king gave him a troop of life-guards, and the most Christian king made him major-general. He was killed in 1693 at the battle of Neerwinden.

(d) SAMUEL PEPYS

393. By John Evelyn

(*Diary*, 26 May 1703)

This day died Mr. Samuel Pepys, a very worthy, industrious and curious person, none in England exceeding him in knowledge of the navy, in which he had passed through all the most considerable offices, Clerk of the Acts and Secretary of the Admiralty, all which he performed with great integrity. . . . He was universally beloved, hospitable, generous, learned in many things, skilled in music, a very great cherisher of learned men of whom he had the conversation. His library and collection of other curiosities were of the most considerable, the models of ships especially. Besides what he published of an account of the navy, as he found and left it, he had for divers years under his hand the history of the navy, or *Navalia* as he called it; but how far advanced, and what will follow of his, is left, I suppose, to his sister's son Mr. Jackson, a young gentleman whom Mr. Pepys had educated in all sorts of useful learning, sending him to travel abroad, from whence he returned with extraordinary accomplishments and worthy to be heir. Mr. Pepys had been for near forty years so much my particular friend that Mr. Jackson sent me complete mourning, desiring me to be one to hold up the pall at his magnificent obsequies, but my indisposition hindered me from doing him this last office.

(e) JOHN EVELYN

394. By Samuel Pepys

(*Diary*, 5 November 1665)

So I by water to Deptford, and there made a visit to Mr. Evelyn, who, among other things, showed me most excellent painting in little; in distemper, Indian ink, water-colours; graving; and, above all, the whole secret of mezzotint and the manner of it, which is very pretty, and good things done with it. He read to me very much also of his discourse he hath been many years and now is about, about gardenage, which will be a most noble and pleasant piece. He read me part of a play or two of his making, very good, but not as he conceits them, I think, to be. He showed me his *hortus hiemalis*, leaves laid up in a book of several plants kept dry, which preserve colour, however, and look very finely, better than any herbal. In fine, a most excellent person he is, and must be allowed a little for a little conceitedness; but he may well be so, being a man so much above others. He read me, though with too much gusto, some little poems of his own, that were not transcendent.

(f) SLINGSBY BETHEL

395. By Gilbert Burnet
(History of My Own Time, ed. 1833, II, pp. 248-249)

Bethel and Cornish were chosen sheriffs for the ensuing year.[1] Bethel was a man of knowledge, and had writ a very judicious book of the interests of princes. But as he was a known republican in principle, so he was a sullen and wilful man, and turned from the ordinary way of a sheriff's living into the extreme of sordidness, which was very unacceptable to the body of the citizens, and proved a great prejudice to the party. Cornish, the other sheriff, was a plain, warm, honest man, and lived very nobly all his year. The Court was very jealous of this, and understood it to be done on design to pack juries, so that the party should be always safe whatever they might engage in. It was said that the king would not have common justice done him hereafter against any of them, how guilty soever. The setting up Bethel gave a great colour to this jealousy, for it was said he had expressed his approving the late king's death in very indecent terms. These two persons had never before received the sacrament in the Church, being Independents; but they did it now to qualify themselves for this office, which gave great advantages against the whole party. It was said that the serving an end was a good resolver of all cases of conscience, and purged all scruples.

396. By John Dryden
(Absalom and Achitophel, ll. 583-629)

But he, though bad, is followed by a worse,
The wretch who Heaven's anointed dared to curse;
Shimei, whose youth did early promise bring
Of zeal to God and hatred to his king,
Did wisely from expensive sins refrain,
And never broke the Sabbath but for gain;
Nor ever was he known an oath to vent,
Or curse, unless against the government.
Thus heaping wealth by the most ready way
Among the Jews, which was to cheat and pray,
The city, to reward his pious hate
Against his master, chose him magistrate.
His hand a vare of justice did uphold;
His neck was loaded with a chain of gold.
During his office treason was no crime;
The sons of Belial had a glorious time;

[1] 1680-1681.

For *Shimei*, though not prodigal of pelf,
Yet loved his wicked neighbour as himself.
When two or three were gathered to declaim
Against the monarch of Jerusalem,
Shimei was always in the midst of them;
And if they cursed the king when he was by,
Would rather curse than break good company.
If any durst his factious friends accuse,
He packed a jury of dissenting Jews,
Whose fellow-feeling in the godly cause
Would free the suffering saint from human laws;
For laws are only made to punish those
Who serve the king, and to protect his foes.
If any leisure time he had from power
(Because 'tis sin to misemploy an hour),
His business was by writing to persuade
That kings were useless and a clog to trade;
And, that his noble style he might refine,
No Rechabite more shunned the fumes of wine.
Chaste were his cellars, and his shrieval board
The grossness of a city feast abhorred;
His cooks with long disuse their trade forgot;
Cool was his kitchen, though his brains were hot.
Such frugal virtue malice may accuse,
But sure 'twas necessary to the Jews;
For towns, once burnt, such magistrates require
As dare not tempt God's providence by fire.
With spiritual food he fed his servants well,
But free from flesh that made the Jews rebel;
And Moses' laws he held in more account,
For forty days of fasting in the mount.

(g) TITUS OATES

397. By Roger North

(Examen, p. 225)

He was a low man, of an ill-cut, very short neck, and his visage and features were most particular. His mouth was the centre of his face, and a compass there would sweep his nose, forehead and chin within the perimeter. *Cave quos ipse Deus notavit.* In a word, he was a most consummate cheat, blasphemer, vicious, perjured, impudent and saucy, foul-mouthed wretch, and were it not for the truth of history, and the great emotions in the public he was the cause of, not fit (so little deserving) to be remembered; and concerning whom the unhappiness is that truth cannot be wrote without a semblance of malice, since it is hard to think any mortal (at least one that partook of so much public countenance, not to say encouragement, as he had) could be really so bad as he was. And what is worse, that age cannot have its true character without a true character of him, who was the permitted instrument of those otherwise unaccountable turns, or in our author's language crises of politics, as depended on him.

398. By John Dryden

(Absalom and Achitophel, ll. 632–659)

Yet, *Corah*, thou shalt from oblivion pass;
  Erect thyself, thou monumental brass,
High as the serpent of thy metal made,
While nations stand secure beneath thy shade.
What though his birth were base, yet comets rise
From earthy vapours ere they shine in skies.
Prodigious actions may as well be done
By weaver's issue as by prince's son.
The arch-attester for the public good
By that one deed ennobles all his blood.
Who ever asked the witnesses' high race
Whose oath with martyrdom did Stephen grace?
Ours was a Levite, and as times went then
His tribe were God Almighty's gentlemen.
Sunk were his eyes, his voice was harsh and loud,
Sure signs he neither choleric was nor proud.
His long chin proved his wit, his saint-like grace
A church vermilion and a Moses' face.
His memory, miraculously great,
Could plots exceeding man's belief repeat,
Which therefore cannot be accounted lies,
For human wit could never such devise.
Some future truths are mingled in his book,
But where the witness failed the prophet spoke.
Some things like visionary flights appear;
The spirit caught him up, the Lord knows where,
And gave him his Rabbinical degree
Unknown to foreign university.

(h) GILBERT BURNET, BISHOP OF SALISBURY

399. Attributed to the marquis of Halifax

(Burnet's History of His Own Time, ed. 1833, VI, pp. 335–337)

Dr. Burnet is, like all men who are above the ordinary level, seldom spoke of in a mean. He must either be railed at or admired. He has a swiftness of imagination that no other man comes up to, and as our nature hardly allows us to have enough of anything without having too much he cannot at all times so hold in his thoughts but that at some time they may run away with him, as it is hard for a vessel that is brimful, when in motion, not to run over; and therefore the variety of matter that he ever carries about him may throw out more than an unkind critic would allow of. His first thoughts may sometimes require more digestion, not from a defect in his judgment, but from the abundance of his fancy, which furnishes too fast for him. His friends love him too well to see small faults, or, if they do, think that his greater talents give him a privilege of straying from the strict rules of caution, and exempt him from the ordinary rules of censure. He produces so fast that what is well in his writings calls for admiration, and what is incorrect deserves an excuse. He may in some things require grains of allowance which those only can deny him who are unknown or unjust to him.

He is not quicker in discerning other men's faults than he is in forgiving them, so ready, or rather glad, to acknowledge his own that from blemishes they become ornaments. All the repeated provocations of his indecent adversaries have had no other effect than the setting his good-nature in so much a better light, since his anger never yet went farther than to pity them. That heat which in most other men raises sharpness and satire, in him glows into warmth for his friends and compassion for those in want and misery. As dull men have quick eyes in discerning the smaller faults of those that nature has made superior to them, they do not miss one blot he makes; and being beholden only to their barrenness for their discretion they fall upon the errors which arise out of his abundance, and by a mistake into which their malice betrays them they think that by finding a mote in his eye they hide the beams that are in their own. His quickness makes writing so easy a thing to him that his spirits are neither wasted nor soured by it; the soil is not forced, everything grows and brings forth without pangs, which distinguishes as much what he does from that which smells of the lamp as a good palate will discern between fruit which comes from a rich mould and that which tastes of the uncleanly pains that have been bestowed upon it.

He makes many enemies, by setting an ill-natured example of living which they are not inclined to follow. His indifference for preferment, his contempt not only of splendour but of all unnecessary plenty, his degrading himself into the lowest and most painful duties of his calling, are such unprelatical qualities that, let him be never so orthodox in other things, in these he must be a dissenter. Virtues of such a stamp are so many heresies in the opinion of those divines who have softened the primitive injunctions so as to make them suit better with the present frailty of mankind. No wonder then if they are angry, since it is in their own defence, or that from a principal of self-preservation they should endeavour to suppress a man whose parts are a shame and whose life is a scandal to them.

400. By John Dryden

(The Hind and the Panther, ll. 2435–2464)

A portly prince, and goodly to the sight,
  He seemed a son of Anak for his height,
Like those whom stature did to crowns prefer,
Black-browed and bluff, like Homer's Jupiter;

Broad-backed and brawny, built for love's delight,
A prophet formed to make a female proselyte.
A theologue more by need than genial bent;
By breeding sharp, by nature confident,
Interest in all his actions was discerned;
More learned than honest, more a wit than learned;
Or forced by fear or by his profit led,
Or both conjoined, his native clime he fled;
But brought the virtues of his heaven along,
A fair behaviour and a fluent tongue.
And yet with all his arts he could not thrive,
The most unlucky parasite alive. . . .
But he, uncalled, his patron to control,
Divulged the secret whispers of his soul;
Stood forth the accusing Satan of his crimes,
And offered to the Moloch of the times.
Prompt to assail, and careless of defence,
Invulnerable in his impudence,
He dares the world, and eager of a name,
He thrusts about and justles into fame.
Frontless and satire-proof, he scours the streets,
And runs an Indian muck at all he meets;
So fond of loud report, that not to miss
Of being known (his last and utmost bliss)
He rather would be known for what he is.

401. Attributed to Jonathan Swift

(Historical Manuscripts Commission, *Sixth Report*, p. 468)

Here Sarum lies, who was as wise
  And learn'd as Tom Aquinas;
Lawn sleeves he wore, yet was no more
A Christian than Socinus.
Oaths pro and con he swallowed down,
Loved gold like any layman;
He preached and prayed, and yet betrayed
God's holy church and mammon.
If such a soul to heaven stole,
And passed the devil's clutches,
I do presume there may be room
For Marlbro' and his duchess.

(i) HENRY SACHEVERELL

402. By Sarah, duchess of Marlborough
(*Private Correspondence*, II, pp. 142–143)

Of the man himself no more need be said than that he had not one good quality that any man of sense ever valued him for. He once professed himself a great Whig; but King William dying he thought best to change with the torrent. It must be owned that a person more fitted for a tool could not have been picked out of the whole nation, for he had not learning enough to write or speak true English (as all his own compositions witness), but an heap of bombast, ill-connected words at command, which do excellently well with such as he was to move. He had so little sense as even to design and effect that popularity which now became his portion, and which a wise and good man knows not how to bear with. He had a haughty insolent air, which his friends found occasion often to complain of; but it made his presence more graceful in public.

His person was framed well for the purpose, and he dressed well. A good assurance, clean gloves, white handkerchief well managed, with other suitable accomplishments, moved the hearts of many at his appearance, and the solemnity of a trial added much to a pity and concern which had nothing in reason or justice to support them. The weaker part of the ladies were more like mad or bewitched than like persons in their senses.

(j) JOHN CHURCHILL, DUKE OF MARLBOROUGH

403. By Abel Boyer
(*History of the Life and Reign of Queen Anne*, pp. 16–17)

To give posterity a more particular idea of that great man, who is to make so shining a figure in this history, the earl of Marlborough was by nature designed for a favourite, by fortune and personal merit raised to be a general, and by his own observation and long experience of court intrigues made a statesman. His person was lofty and well made, his features manly yet beautiful, his look gracious and open, his mien great, his parts quick, his memory faithful and exact, his penetration deep, his judgment solid, his courage undaunted. He was consummate in all the arts of a courtier, supple, affable, sedate; reserved, both with friends and enemies; sober, averse to luxury; and though in a voluptuous court he indulged himself in some liberties of life, yet he still preserved a good reputation with all men. He was ambitious, but free from haughtiness and ostentation. His ascent was so gradual, and so long foreseen, that it appeared rather a growth than a flight; and therefore was the less envied, as it seemed the more merited.

As a soldier he ever was a man of nice honour, punctual, vigilant, indefatigable. Before he was advanced to the degree of a general he had a courage of the most keen temper, not without some appetite of danger; and in the most perilous encounters he had about him an extraordinary cheerfulness. When raised to the command of an army he exposed his person as far as necessity required, with the same unconcernment as he did before; and in a day of battle gave his orders with all the clearness and composedness imaginable, leading on his troops without the least hurry or perturbation, and rallying those that were disordered without sharp or sour reproofs, which rather damp than animate the soldier's courage. He was an excellent discerner and pursuer of advantage upon his enemy, but preserved humanity even amidst the horrors of the field, endeavouring to restrain the slaughter which usually attends victory, in which he took no greater delight than to spare the lives of the conquered. He was a strict observer of his word and promise; and he gained the affections of the soldiers by his good-nature, and of the officers by his affability.

As a statesman he managed variety of business, either single or in concert with the prime minister, with great dexterity, ease and sufficiency. In council he never was supercilious or assuming, but could bear contradiction without passion and by cool argumentation bring others over to his own opinion. No man had ever fewer idle words, and though he was not master of oratory yet in debates of importance he always expressed himself very pertinently; and by his temper and reservedness in discourse he still maintained his reputation of a wise man. He had a particular talent of insinuating himself, and gaining upon the minds of those he dealt with, so that no general ever commanded troops of different nations with more ease, nor was any politician more successful in the most weighty and arduous negotiations, which will appear the more surprising because liberality was not the brightest virtue that entered the composition of this excellent character.

To sum up, King William said of this great man that he had the coolest head and the warmest heart he ever knew, which from so good a judge might seem the greatest eulogy, were it not that, in another respect, what was most true of the earl of Marlborough could not be said of any other general, either ancient or modern, that he never sat before a town which he did not take, nor ever fought a battle which he did not win.

404. By Joseph Addison

(The Campaign, ll. 273–292)

But O, my muse, what numbers wilt thou find
To sing the furious troops in battle joined!
Methinks I hear the drum's tumultuous sound
The victor's shouts and dying groans confound;
The dreadful burst of cannon rend the skies,
And all the thunder of the battle rise.
'Twas then great Marlbro's mighty soul was proved,
That, in the shock of charging hosts unmoved,
Amidst confusion, horror, and despair,
Examined all the dreadful scenes of war;
In peaceful thought the field of death surveyed,
To fainting squadrons sent the timely aid,
Inspired repulsed battalions to engage,
And taught the doubtful battle where to rage.

So when an angel, by divine command,
With rising tempests shakes a guilty land,
Such as of late o'er pale Britannia passed,
Calm and serene he drives the furious blast,
And, pleased th' Almighty's orders to perform,
Rides in the whirlwind, and directs the storm.

Appendices

Appendix I

RECKONINGS OF TIME

THE problems presented by the dating of events under the later Stuarts are due, partly to the lack of a uniform method of reckoning time within the British Isles themselves, and partly to divergences between the commoner British practices and those of many continental countries. On one point alone was complete uniformity observed. The week was everywhere the same, seven days in length, and with the day of rest enjoined by the Church the same day throughout Christendom.

Over the reckoning of the days of the month, on the other hand, there was a serious divergence, due to the fact that two different calendars were extensively in use. In England, Scotland and Ireland, as well as in all the Orthodox and some of the Protestant countries of Europe, the calendar observed was still the old or Julian calendar, instituted by Julius Caesar in 45 B.C., while all Catholic and a few Protestant countries had adopted the more accurate reformed or Gregorian calendar introduced by Pope Gregory XIII in 1582. The sole difference between the two calendars lay in the provision made for leap-year, which according to the Julian calendar came every fourth year, and according to the Gregorian calendar every fourth year with the exception of most of the even centuries. But the divergence thus produced amounted by the seventeenth century to ten days, and in the eighteenth century was to become eleven days, what an Englishman or Scotsman would call 3 August being 13 August in France before 1700, and 14 August thereafter. To prevent confusion the practice was sometimes adopted at the time, and has frequently been followed since, of distinguishing dates as Old Style (O.S.) and New Style (N.S.), or of writing them in the form 3/13 August; but in the text of this volume, as is indicated on page xi, the system used in England at the time, that is the Old Style, has been followed throughout.

As regards the year an even more troublesome situation existed, for on this point there was no uniform practice within the British Isles themselves. Events were dated by reference to two quite different years, on the one hand the calendar year, and on the other the year of the king's reign; and within each of these systems in turn there was an unfortunate absence of uniformity.

(1) *Calendar Years*

In England and Ireland the official calendar year began, not on 1 January, but on Lady Day or the feast of the Annunciation on 25 March.[1] In Scotland, on the other hand, and generally on the Continent, the year for all purposes began on 1 January, and this method of reckoning was coming into increasing favour even in England among private individuals. Thus what an English or Irish official would call 4 February 1677 was in Scotland 4 February 1678, and in France 14 February 1678; and in dealing with an English document it is often difficult, unless the year is given in the form 1677/8, to determine with certainty to what year dates in January, February or March really belong. In this volume, as is indicated on page xi, it has been assumed throughout that the year begins on 1 January, and it is on the basis of that assumption that the following calendars for the period have been compiled:

Year	Calendar	Date of Easter
1660	B1	April 22
1661	A3	April 14
1662	A4	March 30
1663	A5	April 19

[1] The official financial year in Britain still begins on Lady Day, which with the reform of the calendar in 1752 fell eleven days later, on 5 April instead of 25 March.

943

Year	Calendar	Date of Easter
1664	B6	April 10
1665	A1	March 26
1666	A2	April 15
1667	A3	April 7
1668	B4	March 22
1669	A6	April 11
1670	A7	April 3
1671	A1	April 23
1672	B2	April 7
1673	A4	March 30
1674	A5	April 19
1675	A6	April 4
1676	B7	March 26
1677	A2	April 15
1678	A3	March 31
1679	A4	April 20
1680	B5	April 11
1681	A7	April 3
1682	A1	April 16
1683	A2	April 8
1684	B3	March 30
1685	A5	April 19
1686	A6	April 4
1687	A7	March 27
1688	B1	April 15
1689	A3	March 31
1690	A4	April 20
1691	A5	April 12
1692	B6	March 27
1693	A1	April 16
1694	A2	April 8
1695	A3	March 24
1696	B4	April 12
1697	A6	April 4
1698	A7	April 24
1699	A1	April 9
1700	B2	March 31
1701	A4	April 20
1702	A5	April 5
1703	A6	March 28
1704	B7	April 16
1705	A2	April 8
1706	A3	March 24
1707	A4	April 13
1708	B5	April 4
1709	A7	April 24
1710	A1	April 9
1711	A2	April 1
1712	B3	April 20
1713	A5	April 5
1714	A6	March 28

(A) Normal Years

A1

1665, 1671, 1682, 1693, 1699, 1710

```
        JANUARY              FEBRUARY               MARCH
1   8 15 22 29           5 12 19 26           5 12 19 26
2   9 16 23 30           6 13 20 27           6 13 20 27
3  10 17 24 31           7 14 21 28           7 14 21 28
4  11 18 25 ..       1   8 15 22 ..       1   8 15 22 29
5  12 19 26 ..       2   9 16 23 ..       2   9 16 23 30
6  13 20 27 ..       3  10 17 24 ..       3  10 17 24 31
7  14 21 28 ..       4  11 18 25 ..       4  11 18 25 ..

         APRIL                 MAY                  JUNE
2   9 16 23 30           7 14 21 28           4 11 18 25
3  10 17 24 ..       1   8 15 22 29           5 12 19 26
4  11 18 25 ..       2   9 16 23 30           6 13 20 27
5  12 19 26 ..       3  10 17 24 31           7 14 21 28
6  13 20 27 ..       4  11 18 25 ..       1   8 15 22 29
7  14 21 28 ..       5  12 19 26 ..       2   9 16 23 30
1   8 15 22 29       6  13 20 27 ..       3  10 17 24 ..

          JULY               AUGUST              SEPTEMBER
2   9 16 23 30           6 13 20 27           3 10 17 24
3  10 17 24 31           7 14 21 28           4 11 18 25
4  11 18 25 ..       1   8 15 22 29           5 12 19 26
5  12 19 26 ..       2   9 16 23 30           6 13 20 27
6  13 20 27 ..       3  10 17 24 31           7 14 21 28
7  14 21 28 ..       4  11 18 25 ..       1   8 15 22 29
1   8 15 22 29       5  12 19 26 ..       2   9 16 23 30

        OCTOBER              NOVEMBER              DECEMBER
1   8 15 22 29           5 12 19 26           3 10 17 24 31
2   9 16 23 30           6 13 20 27           4 11 18 25 ..
3  10 17 24 31           7 14 21 28           5 12 19 26 ..
4  11 18 25 ..       1   8 15 22 29           6 13 20 27 ..
5  12 19 26 ..       2   9 16 23 30           7 14 21 28 ..
6  13 20 27 ..       3  10 17 24 ..       1   8 15 22 29
7  14 21 28 ..       4  11 18 25 ..       2   9 16 23 30 ..
```

A2

1666, 1677, 1683, 1694, 1705, 1711

```
            JANUARY              FEBRUARY               MARCH
S     7 14 21 28           4 11 18 25           4 11 18 25
M   1   8 15 22 29           5 12 19 26           5 12 19 26
Tu  2   9 16 23 30           6 13 20 27           6 13 20 27
W   3  10 17 24 31           7 14 21 28           7 14 21 28
Th  4  11 18 25 ..       1   8 15 22 ..       1   8 15 22 29
F   5  12 19 26 ..       2   9 16 23 ..       2   9 16 23 30
S   6  13 20 27 ..       3  10 17 24 ..       3  10 17 24 31

             APRIL                 MAY                  JUNE
S   1   8 15 22 29           6 13 20 27           3 10 17 24
M   2   9 16 23 30           7 14 21 28           4 11 18 25
Tu  3  10 17 24 ..       1   8 15 22 29           5 12 19 26
W   4  11 18 25 ..       2   9 16 23 30           6 13 20 27
Th  5  12 19 26 ..       3  10 17 24 31           7 14 21 28
F   6  13 20 27 ..       4  11 18 25 ..       1   8 15 22 29
S   7  14 21 28 ..       5  12 19 26 ..       2   9 16 23 30

              JULY               AUGUST              SEPTEMBER
S   1   8 15 22 29           5 12 19 26           2 9 16 23 30
M   2   9 16 23 30           6 13 20 27           3 10 17 24 ..
Tu  3  10 17 24 31           7 14 21 28           4 11 18 25 ..
W   4  11 18 25 ..       1   8 15 22 29           5 12 19 26 ..
Th  5  12 19 26 ..       2   9 16 23 30           6 13 20 27 ..
F   6  13 20 27 ..       3  10 17 24 31           7 14 21 28 ..
S   7  14 21 28 ..       4  11 18 25 ..       1   8 15 22 29

            OCTOBER              NOVEMBER              DECEMBER
S     7 14 21 28           4 11 18 25           2 9 16 23 30
M   1   8 15 22 29           5 12 19 26           3 10 17 24 ..
Tu  2   9 16 23 30           6 13 20 27           4 11 18 25 ..
W   3  10 17 24 31           7 14 21 28           5 12 19 26 ..
Th  4  11 18 25 ..       1   8 15 22 29           6 13 20 27 ..
F   5  12 19 26 ..       2   9 16 23 30           7 14 21 28 ..
S   6  13 20 27 ..       3  10 17 24 ..       1   8 15 22 29
```

A3

1661, 1667, 1678, 1689, 1695, 1706

```
        JANUARY              FEBRUARY               MARCH
6 13 20 27               3 10 17 24           3 10 17 24 31
7 14 21 28               4 11 18 25           4 11 18 25 ..
1   8 15 22 29           5 12 19 26           5 12 19 26 ..
2   9 16 23 30           6 13 20 27           6 13 20 27 ..
3  10 17 24 31           7 14 21 28           7 14 21 28 ..
4  11 18 25 ..       1   8 15 22 ..       1   8 15 22 29
5  12 19 26 ..       2   9 16 23 ..       2   9 16 23 30 ..

         APRIL                 MAY                  JUNE
7 14 21 28               5 12 19 26           2 9 16 23 30
1   8 15 22 29           6 13 20 27           3 10 17 24 ..
2   9 16 23 30           7 14 21 28           4 11 18 25 ..
3  10 17 24 ..       1   8 15 22 29           5 12 19 26 ..
4  11 18 25 ..       2   9 16 23 30           6 13 20 27 ..
5  12 19 26 ..       3  10 17 24 31           7 14 21 28 ..
6  13 20 27 ..       4  11 18 25 ..       1   8 15 22 29

          JULY               AUGUST              SEPTEMBER
7 14 21 28               4 11 18 25           1   8 15 22 29
1   8 15 22 29           5 12 19 26           2   9 16 23 30
2   9 16 23 30           6 13 20 27           3  10 17 24 ..
3  10 17 24 31           7 14 21 28           4  11 18 25 ..
4  11 18 25 ..       1   8 15 22 29           5  12 19 26 ..
5  12 19 26 ..       2   9 16 23 30           6  13 20 27 ..
6  13 20 27 ..       3  10 17 24 31           7  14 21 28 ..

        OCTOBER              NOVEMBER              DECEMBER
6 13 20 27               3 10 17 24           1   8 15 22 29
7 14 21 28               4 11 18 25           2   9 16 23 30
1   8 15 22 29           5 12 19 26           3  10 17 24 31
2   9 16 23 30           6 13 20 27           4  11 18 25 ..
3  10 17 24 31           7 14 21 28           5  12 19 26 ..
4  11 18 25 ..       1   8 15 22 29           6  13 20 27 ..
5  12 19 26 ..       2   9 16 23 30           7  14 21 28 ..
```

A4

1662, 1673, 1679, 1690, 1701, 1707

```
            JANUARY              FEBRUARY               MARCH
S     5 12 19 26           2 9 16 23           2 9 16 23 30
M     6 13 20 27           3 10 17 24 ..       3 10 17 24 31
Tu    7 14 21 28           4 11 18 25 ..       4 11 18 25 ..
W   1   8 15 22 29           5 12 19 26 ..       5 12 19 26 ..
Th  2   9 16 23 30           6 13 20 27 ..       6 13 20 27 ..
F   3  10 17 24 31           7 14 21 28 ..       7 14 21 28 ..
S   4  11 18 25 ..       1   8 15 22 ..       1   8 15 22 29

             APRIL                 MAY                  JUNE
S     6 13 20 27           4 11 18 25           1   8 15 22 29
M     7 14 21 28           5 12 19 26           2   9 16 23 30
Tu  1   8 15 22 29           6 13 20 27           3  10 17 24 ..
W   2   9 16 23 30           7 14 21 28           4  11 18 25 ..
Th  3  10 17 24 ..       1   8 15 22 29           5  12 19 26 ..
F   4  11 18 25 ..       2   9 16 23 30           6  13 20 27 ..
S   5  12 19 26 ..       3  10 17 24 31           7  14 21 28 ..

              JULY               AUGUST              SEPTEMBER
S     6 13 20 27           3 10 17 24 31           7 14 21 28
M     7 14 21 28           4 11 18 25 ..       1   8 15 22 29
Tu  1   8 15 22 29           5 12 19 26 ..       2   9 16 23 30
W   2   9 16 23 30           6 13 20 27 ..       3  10 17 24 ..
Th  3  10 17 24 31           7 14 21 28 ..       4  11 18 25 ..
F   4  11 18 25 ..       1   8 15 22 29           5  12 19 26 ..
S   5  12 19 26 ..       2   9 16 23 30           6  13 20 27 ..

            OCTOBER              NOVEMBER              DECEMBER
S     5 12 19 26           2 9 16 23 30           7 14 21 28
M     6 13 20 27           3 10 17 24 ..       1   8 15 22 29
Tu    7 14 21 28           4 11 18 25 ..       2   9 16 23 30
W   1   8 15 22 29           5 12 19 26 ..       3  10 17 24 31
Th  2   9 16 23 30           6 13 20 27 ..       4  11 18 25 ..
F   3  10 17 24 31           7 14 21 28 ..       5  12 19 26 ..
S   4  11 18 25 ..       1   8 15 22 29           6  13 20 27 ..
```

A5

1663, 1674, 1685, 1691, 1702, 1713

	JANUARY	FEBRUARY	MARCH
S	4 11 18 25	1 8 15 22	1 8 15 22 29
M	5 12 19 26	2 9 16 23	2 9 16 23 30
Tu	6 13 20 27	3 10 17 24	3 10 17 24 31
W	7 14 21 28	4 11 18 25	4 11 18 25 ..
Th	1 8 15 22 29	5 12 19 26	5 12 19 26 ..
F	2 9 16 23 30	6 13 20 27	6 13 20 27 ..
S	3 10 17 24 31	7 14 21 28	7 14 21 28 ..

	APRIL	MAY	JUNE
S	5 12 19 26	3 10 17 24 31	7 14 21 28
M	6 13 20 27	4 11 18 25 ..	1 8 15 22 29
Tu	7 14 21 28	5 12 19 26 ..	2 9 16 23 30
W	1 8 15 22 29	6 13 20 27 ..	3 10 17 24 ..
Th	2 9 16 23 30	7 14 21 28 ..	4 11 18 25 ..
F	3 10 17 24 ..	1 8 15 22 29 ..	5 12 19 26 ..
S	4 11 18 25 ..	2 9 16 23 30 ..	6 13 20 27 ..

	JULY	AUGUST	SEPTEMBER
S	5 12 19 26	2 9 16 23 30	6 13 20 27
M	6 13 20 27	3 10 17 24 31	7 14 21 28
Tu	7 14 21 28	4 11 18 25 ..	1 8 15 22 29
W	1 8 15 22 29	5 12 19 26 ..	2 9 16 23 30
Th	2 9 16 23 30	6 13 20 27 ..	3 10 17 24 ..
F	3 10 17 24 31	7 14 21 28 ..	4 11 18 25 ..
S	4 11 18 25 ..	1 8 15 22 29 ..	5 12 19 26 ..

	OCTOBER	NOVEMBER	DECEMBER
S	4 11 18 25	1 8 15 22 29	6 13 20 27
M	5 12 19 26	2 9 16 23 30	7 14 21 28
Tu	6 13 20 27	3 10 17 24 ..	1 8 15 22 29
W	7 14 21 28	4 11 18 25 ..	2 9 16 23 30
Th	1 8 15 22 29	5 12 19 26 ..	3 10 17 24 31
F	2 9 16 23 30	6 13 20 27 ..	4 11 18 25 ..
S	3 10 17 24 31	7 14 21 28 ..	5 12 19 26 ..

A6

1669, 1675, 1686, 1697, 1703, 1714

	JANUARY	FEBRUARY	MARCH
S	3 10 17 24 31	7 14 21 28	7 14 21 28
M	4 11 18 25 ..	1 8 15 22 ..	1 8 15 22 29
Tu	5 12 19 26 ..	2 9 16 23 ..	2 9 16 23 30
W	6 13 20 27 ..	3 10 17 24 ..	3 10 17 24 31
Th	7 14 21 28 ..	4 11 18 25 ..	4 11 18 25 ..
F	1 8 15 22 29 ..	5 12 19 26 ..	5 12 19 26 ..
S	2 9 16 23 30 ..	6 13 20 27 ..	6 13 20 27 ..

	APRIL	MAY	JUNE
S	4 11 18 25	2 9 16 23 30	6 13 20 27
M	5 12 19 26	3 10 17 24 31	7 14 21 28
Tu	6 13 20 27	4 11 18 25 ..	1 8 15 22 29
W	7 14 21 28	5 12 19 26 ..	2 9 16 23 30
Th	1 8 15 22 29	6 13 20 27 ..	3 10 17 24 ..
F	2 9 16 23 30	7 14 21 28 ..	4 11 18 25 ..
S	3 10 17 24 ..	1 8 15 22 29 ..	5 12 19 26 ..

	JULY	AUGUST	SEPTEMBER
S	4 11 18 25	1 8 15 22 29	5 12 19 26
M	5 12 19 26	2 9 16 23 30	6 13 20 27
Tu	6 13 20 27	3 10 17 24 31	7 14 21 28
W	7 14 21 28	4 11 18 25 ..	1 8 15 22 29
Th	1 8 15 22 29	5 12 19 26 ..	2 9 16 23 30
F	2 9 16 23 30	6 13 20 27 ..	3 10 17 24 ..
S	3 10 17 24 31	7 14 21 28 ..	4 11 18 25 ..

	OCTOBER	NOVEMBER	DECEMBER
S	3 10 17 24 31	7 14 21 28	5 12 19 26
M	4 11 18 25 ..	1 8 15 22 29	6 13 20 27
Tu	5 12 19 26 ..	2 9 16 23 30	7 14 21 28
W	6 13 20 27 ..	3 10 17 24 ..	1 8 15 22 29
Th	7 14 21 28 ..	4 11 18 25 ..	2 9 16 23 30
F	1 8 15 22 29 ..	5 12 19 26 ..	3 10 17 24 31
S	2 9 16 23 30 ..	6 13 20 27 ..	4 11 18 25 ..

A7

1670, 1681, 1687, 1698, 1709

	JANUARY	FEBRUARY	MARCH
S	2 9 16 23 30	6 13 20 27	6 13 20 27
M	3 10 17 24 31	7 14 21 28	7 14 21 28
Tu	4 11 18 25 ..	1 8 15 22 ..	1 8 15 22 29
W	5 12 19 26 ..	2 9 16 23 ..	2 9 16 23 30
Th	6 13 20 27 ..	3 10 17 24 ..	3 10 17 24 31
F	7 14 21 28 ..	4 11 18 25 ..	4 11 18 25 ..
S	1 8 15 22 29	5 12 19 26 ..	5 12 19 26 ..

	APRIL	MAY	JUNE
S	3 10 17 24	1 8 15 22 29	5 12 19 26
M	4 11 18 25	2 9 16 23 30	6 13 20 27
Tu	5 12 19 26	3 10 17 24 31	7 14 21 28
W	6 13 20 27	4 11 18 25 ..	1 8 15 22 29
Th	7 14 21 28	5 12 19 26 ..	2 9 16 23 30
F	1 8 15 22 29	6 13 20 27 ..	3 10 17 24 ..
S	2 9 16 23 30	7 14 21 28 ..	4 11 18 25 ..

	JULY	AUGUST	SEPTEMBER
S	3 10 17 24 31	7 14 21 28	4 11 18 25
M	4 11 18 25 ..	1 8 15 22 29	5 12 19 26
Tu	5 12 19 26 ..	2 9 16 23 30	6 13 20 27
W	6 13 20 27 ..	3 10 17 24 31	7 14 21 28
Th	7 14 21 28 ..	4 11 18 25 ..	1 8 15 22 29
F	1 8 15 22 29 ..	5 12 19 26 ..	2 9 16 23 30
S	2 9 16 23 30 ..	6 13 20 27 ..	3 10 17 24 ..

	OCTOBER	NOVEMBER	DECEMBER
S	2 9 16 23 30	6 13 20 27	4 11 18 25
M	3 10 17 24 31	7 14 21 28	5 12 19 26
Tu	4 11 18 25 ..	1 8 15 22 29	6 13 20 27
W	5 12 19 26 ..	2 9 16 23 30	7 14 21 28
Th	6 13 20 27 ..	3 10 17 24 ..	1 8 15 22 29
F	7 14 21 28 ..	4 11 18 25 ..	2 9 16 23 30
S	1 8 15 22 29	5 12 19 26 ..	3 10 17 24 31

(B) *Leap Years*

B1

1660, 1688

JANUARY	FEBRUARY	MARCH
1 8 15 22 29	5 12 19 26	4 11 18 25
2 9 16 23 30	6 13 20 27	5 12 19 26
3 10 17 24 31	6 13 20 27	6 13 20 27
4 11 18 25 ..	1 8 15 22 29	7 14 21 28
5 12 19 26 ..	2 9 16 23 ..	1 8 15 22 29
6 13 20 27 ..	3 10 17 24 ..	2 9 16 23 30
7 14 21 28 ..	4 11 18 25 ..	3 10 17 24 31

APRIL	MAY	JUNE
1 8 15 22 29	6 13 20 27	3 10 17 24
2 9 16 23 30	7 14 21 28	4 11 18 25
3 10 17 24 ..	1 8 15 22 29	5 12 19 26
4 11 18 25 ..	2 9 16 23 30	6 13 20 27
5 12 19 26 ..	3 10 17 24 31	7 14 21 28
6 13 20 27 ..	4 11 18 25 ..	1 8 15 22 29
7 14 21 28 ..	5 12 19 26 ..	2 9 16 23 30

JULY	AUGUST	SEPTEMBER
1 8 15 22 29	5 12 19 26	2 9 16 23 30
2 9 16 23 30	6 13 20 27	3 10 17 24 ..
3 10 17 24 31	7 14 21 28	4 11 18 25 ..
4 11 18 25 ..	1 8 15 22 29	5 12 19 26 ..
5 12 19 26 ..	2 9 16 23 30	6 13 20 27 ..
6 13 20 27 ..	3 10 17 24 31	7 14 21 28 ..
7 14 21 28 ..	4 11 18 25 ..	1 8 15 22 29

OCTOBER	NOVEMBER	DECEMBER
7 14 21 28	4 11 18 25	2 9 16 23 30
1 8 15 22 29	5 12 19 26	3 10 17 24 31
2 9 16 23 30	6 13 20 27	4 11 18 25 ..
3 10 17 24 31	7 14 21 28	5 12 19 26 ..
4 11 18 25 ..	1 8 15 22 29	6 13 20 27 ..
5 12 19 26 ..	2 9 16 23 30	7 14 21 28 ..
6 13 20 27 ..	3 10 17 24 ..	1 8 15 22 29

B2

1672, 1700

	JANUARY	FEBRUARY	MARCH
S	7 14 21 28	4 11 18 25	3 10 17 24 31
M	1 8 15 22 29	5 12 19 26	4 11 18 25 ..
Tu	2 9 16 23 30	6 13 20 27	5 12 19 26 ..
W	3 10 17 24 31	7 14 21 28	6 13 20 27 ..
Th	4 11 18 25 ..	1 8 15 22 29	7 14 21 28 ..
F	5 12 19 26 ..	2 9 16 23 ..	1 8 15 22 29 ..
S	6 13 20 27 ..	3 10 17 24 ..	2 9 16 23 30 ..

	APRIL	MAY	JUNE
S	7 14 21 28	5 12 19 26	2 9 16 23 30
M	1 8 15 22 29	6 13 20 27	3 10 17 24 ..
Tu	2 9 16 23 30	7 14 21 28	4 11 18 25 ..
W	3 10 17 24 ..	1 8 15 22 29	5 12 19 26 ..
Th	4 11 18 25 ..	2 9 16 23 30	6 13 20 27 ..
F	5 12 19 26 ..	3 10 17 24 31	7 14 21 28 ..
S	6 13 20 27 ..	4 11 18 25 ..	1 8 15 22 29 ..

	JULY	AUGUST	SEPTEMBER
S	7 14 21 28	4 11 18 25	1 8 15 22 29
M	1 8 15 22 29	5 12 19 26	2 9 16 23 30
Tu	2 9 16 23 30	6 13 20 27	3 10 17 24 ..
W	3 10 17 24 31	7 14 21 28	4 11 18 25 ..
Th	4 11 18 25 ..	1 8 15 22 29	5 12 19 26 ..
F	5 12 19 26 ..	2 9 16 23 30	6 13 20 27 ..
S	6 13 20 27 ..	3 10 17 24 31	7 14 21 28 ..

	OCTOBER	NOVEMBER	DECEMBER
S	6 13 20 27	3 10 17 24	1 8 15 22 29
M	7 14 21 28	4 11 18 25	2 9 16 23 30
Tu	1 8 15 22 29	5 12 19 26	3 10 17 24 31
W	2 9 16 23 30	6 13 20 27	4 11 18 25 ..
Th	3 10 17 24 31	7 14 21 28	5 12 19 26 ..
F	4 11 18 25 ..	1 8 15 22 29	6 13 20 27 ..
S	5 12 19 26 ..	2 9 16 23 30	7 14 21 28 ..

B3

1684, 1712

	JANUARY	FEBRUARY	MARCH
	6 13 20 27	3 10 17 24	2 9 16 23 30
	7 14 21 28	4 11 18 25	3 10 17 24 31
u	1 8 15 22 29	5 12 19 26	4 11 18 25 ..
h	2 9 16 23 30	6 13 20 27	5 12 19 26 ..
	3 10 17 24 31	7 14 21 28	6 13 20 27 ..
	4 11 18 25 ..	1 8 15 22 29	7 14 21 28 ..
	5 12 19 26 ..	2 9 16 23 ..	1 8 15 22 29 ..

	APRIL	MAY	JUNE
	6 13 20 27	4 11 18 25	1 8 15 22 29
	7 14 21 28	5 12 19 26	2 9 16 23 30
u	1 8 15 22 29	6 13 20 27	3 10 17 24 ..
h	2 9 16 23 30	7 14 21 28	4 11 18 25 ..
	3 10 17 24 ..	1 8 15 22 29	5 12 19 26 ..
	4 11 18 25 ..	2 9 16 23 30	6 13 20 27 ..
	5 12 19 26 ..	3 10 17 24 31	7 14 21 28 ..

	JULY	AUGUST	SEPTEMBER
	6 13 20 27	3 10 17 24 31	7 14 21 28
	7 14 21 28	4 11 18 25 ..	1 8 15 22 29
u	1 8 15 22 29	5 12 19 26 ..	2 9 16 23 30
h	2 9 16 23 30	6 13 20 27 ..	3 10 17 24 ..
	3 10 17 24 31	7 14 21 28 ..	4 11 18 25 ..
	4 11 18 25 ..	1 8 15 22 29 ..	5 12 19 26 ..
	5 12 19 26 ..	2 9 16 23 30 ..	6 13 20 27 ..

	OCTOBER	NOVEMBER	DECEMBER
	5 12 19 26	2 9 16 23 30	7 14 21 28
	6 13 20 27	3 10 17 24 ..	1 8 15 22 29
u	7 14 21 28	4 11 18 25 ..	2 9 16 23 30
h	1 8 15 22 29	5 12 19 26 ..	3 10 17 24 31
	2 9 16 23 30	6 13 20 27 ..	4 11 18 25 ..
	3 10 17 24 31	7 14 21 28 ..	5 12 19 26 ..
	4 11 18 25 ..	1 8 15 22 29 ..	6 13 20 27 ..

B4

1668, 1696

	JANUARY	FEBRUARY	MARCH
S	5 12 19 26	2 9 16 23	1 8 15 22 29
M	6 13 20 27	3 10 17 24	2 9 16 23 30
Tu	7 14 21 28	4 11 18 25	3 10 17 24 31
W	1 8 15 22 29	5 12 19 26	4 11 18 25 ..
Th	2 9 16 23 30	6 13 20 27	5 12 19 26 ..
F	3 10 17 24 31	7 14 21 28	6 13 20 27 ..
S	4 11 18 25 ..	1 8 15 22 29	7 14 21 28 ..

	APRIL	MAY	JUNE
S	5 12 19 26	3 10 17 24 31	7 14 21 28
M	6 13 20 27	4 11 18 25 ..	1 8 15 22 29
Tu	7 14 21 28	5 12 19 26 ..	2 9 16 23 30
W	1 8 15 22 29	6 13 20 27 ..	3 10 17 24 ..
Th	2 9 16 23 30	7 14 21 28 ..	4 11 18 25 ..
F	3 10 17 24 ..	1 8 15 22 29 ..	5 12 19 26 ..
S	4 11 18 25 ..	2 9 16 23 30 ..	6 13 20 27 ..

	JULY	AUGUST	SEPTEMBER
S	5 12 19 26	2 9 16 23 30	6 13 20 27
M	6 13 20 27	3 10 17 24 31	7 14 21 28
Tu	7 14 21 28	4 11 18 25 ..	1 8 15 22 29
W	1 8 15 22 29	5 12 19 26 ..	2 9 16 23 30
Th	2 9 16 23 30	6 13 20 27 ..	3 10 17 24 ..
F	3 10 17 24 31	7 14 21 28 ..	4 11 18 25 ..
S	4 11 18 25 ..	1 8 15 22 29 ..	5 12 19 26 ..

	OCTOBER	NOVEMBER	DECEMBER
S	4 11 18 25	1 8 15 22 29	6 13 20 27
M	5 12 19 26	2 9 16 23 30	7 14 21 28
Tu	6 13 20 27	3 10 17 24 ..	1 8 15 22 29
W	7 14 21 28	4 11 18 25 ..	2 9 16 23 30
Th	1 8 15 22 29	5 12 19 26 ..	3 10 17 24 31
F	2 9 16 23 30	6 13 20 27 ..	4 11 18 25 ..
S	3 10 17 24 31	7 14 21 28 ..	5 12 19 26 ..

B5

1680, 1708

	JANUARY	FEBRUARY	MARCH
S	4 11 18 25	1 8 15 22 29	7 14 21 28
M	5 12 19 26	2 9 16 23 ..	1 8 15 22 29
Tu	6 13 20 27	3 10 17 24 ..	2 9 16 23 30
W	7 14 21 28	4 11 18 25 ..	3 10 17 24 31
Th	1 8 15 22 29	5 12 19 26 ..	4 11 18 25 ..
F	2 9 16 23 30	6 13 20 27 ..	5 12 19 26 ..
S	3 10 17 24 31	7 14 21 28 ..	6 13 20 27 ..

	APRIL	MAY	JUNE
S	4 11 18 25	2 9 16 23 30	6 13 20 27
M	5 12 19 26	3 10 17 24 31	7 14 21 28
Tu	6 13 20 27	4 11 18 25 ..	1 8 15 22 29
W	7 14 21 28	5 12 19 26 ..	2 9 16 23 30
Th	1 8 15 22 29	6 13 20 27 ..	3 10 17 24 ..
F	2 9 16 23 30	7 14 21 28 ..	4 11 18 25 ..
S	3 10 17 24 ..	1 8 15 22 29 ..	5 12 19 26 ..

	JULY	AUGUST	SEPTEMBER
S	4 11 18 25	1 8 15 22 29	5 12 19 26
M	5 12 19 26	2 9 16 23 30	6 13 20 27
Tu	6 13 20 27	3 10 17 24 31	7 14 21 28
W	7 14 21 28	4 11 18 25 ..	1 8 15 22 29
Th	1 8 15 22 29	5 12 19 26 ..	2 9 16 23 30
F	2 9 16 23 30	6 13 20 27 ..	3 10 17 24 ..
S	3 10 17 24 31	7 14 21 28 ..	4 11 18 25 ..

	OCTOBER	NOVEMBER	DECEMBER
S	3 10 17 24 31	7 14 21 28	5 12 19 26
M	4 11 18 25 ..	1 8 15 22 29	6 13 20 27
Tu	5 12 19 26 ..	2 9 16 23 30	7 14 21 28
W	6 13 20 27 ..	3 10 17 24 ..	1 8 15 22 29
Th	7 14 21 28 ..	4 11 18 25 ..	2 9 16 23 30
F	1 8 15 22 29 ..	5 12 19 26 ..	3 10 17 24 31
S	2 9 16 23 30 ..	6 13 20 27 ..	4 11 18 25 ..

B6

1664, 1692

	JANUARY	FEBRUARY	MARCH
S	3 10 17 24 31	7 14 21 28	6 13 20 27
M	4 11 18 25 ..	1 8 15 22 29	7 14 21 28
Tu	5 12 19 26 ..	2 9 16 23 ..	1 8 15 22 29
W	6 13 20 27 ..	3 10 17 24 ..	2 9 16 23 30
Th	7 14 21 28 ..	4 11 18 25 ..	3 10 17 24 31
F	1 8 15 22 29 ..	5 12 19 26 ..	4 11 18 25 ..
S	2 9 16 23 30 ..	6 13 20 27 ..	5 12 19 26 ..

	APRIL	MAY	JUNE
S	3 10 17 24	1 8 15 22 29	5 12 19 26
M	4 11 18 25	2 9 16 23 30	6 13 20 27
Tu	5 12 19 26	3 10 17 24 31	7 14 21 28
W	6 13 20 27	4 11 18 25 ..	1 8 15 22 29
Th	7 14 21 28	5 12 19 26 ..	2 9 16 23 30
F	1 8 15 22 29	6 13 20 27 ..	3 10 17 24 ..
S	2 9 16 23 30	7 14 21 28 ..	4 11 18 25 ..

	JULY	AUGUST	SEPTEMBER
S	3 10 17 24 31	7 14 21 28	4 11 18 25
M	4 11 18 25 ..	1 8 15 22 29	5 12 19 26
Tu	5 12 19 26 ..	2 9 16 23 30	6 13 20 27
W	6 13 20 27 ..	3 10 17 24 31	7 14 21 28
Th	7 14 21 28 ..	4 11 18 25 ..	1 8 15 22 29
F	1 8 15 22 29 ..	5 12 19 26 ..	2 9 16 23 30
S	2 9 16 23 30 ..	6 13 20 27 ..	3 10 17 24 ..

	OCTOBER	NOVEMBER	DECEMBER
S	2 9 16 23 30	6 13 20 27	4 11 18 25
M	3 10 17 24 31	7 14 21 28	5 12 19 26
Tu	4 11 18 25 ..	1 8 15 22 29	6 13 20 27
W	5 12 19 26 ..	2 9 16 23 30	7 14 21 28
Th	6 13 20 27 ..	3 10 17 24 ..	1 8 15 22 29
F	7 14 21 28 ..	4 11 18 25 ..	2 9 16 23 30
S	1 8 15 22 29 ..	5 12 19 26 ..	3 10 17 24 31

B7

1676, 1704

	JANUARY	FEBRUARY	MARCH
S	2 9 16 23 30	6 13 20 27	5 12 19 26
M	3 10 17 24 31	7 14 21 28	6 13 20 27
Tu	4 11 18 25 ..	1 8 15 22 29	7 14 21 28
W	5 12 19 26 ..	2 9 16 23 ..	1 8 15 22 29
Th	6 13 20 27 ..	3 10 17 24 ..	2 9 16 23 30
F	7 14 21 28 ..	4 11 18 25 ..	3 10 17 24 31
S	1 8 15 22 29	5 12 19 26 ..	4 11 18 25 ..

	APRIL	MAY	JUNE
S	2 9 16 23 30	7 14 21 28	4 11 18 25
M	3 10 17 24 ..	1 8 15 22 29	5 12 19 26
Tu	4 11 18 25 ..	2 9 16 23 30	6 13 20 27
W	5 12 19 26 ..	3 10 17 24 31	7 14 21 28
Th	6 13 20 27 ..	4 11 18 25 ..	1 8 15 22 29
F	7 14 21 28 ..	5 12 19 26 ..	2 9 16 23 30
S	1 8 15 22 29	6 13 20 27 ..	3 10 17 24 ..

	JULY	AUGUST	SEPTEMBER
S	2 9 16 23 30	6 13 20 27	3 10 17 24
M	3 10 17 24 31	7 14 21 28	4 11 18 25
Tu	4 11 18 25 ..	1 8 15 22 29	5 12 19 26
W	5 12 19 26 ..	2 9 16 23 30	6 13 20 27
Th	6 13 20 27 ..	3 10 17 24 31	7 14 21 28
F	7 14 21 28 ..	4 11 18 25 ..	1 8 15 22 29
S	1 8 15 22 29	5 12 19 26 ..	2 9 16 23 30

	OCTOBER	NOVEMBER	DECEMBER
S	8 15 22 29	5 12 19 26	3 10 17 24 31
M	2 9 16 23 30	6 13 20 27	4 11 18 25 ..
Tu	3 10 17 24 31	7 14 21 28	5 12 19 26 ..
W	4 11 18 25 ..	1 8 15 22 29	6 13 20 27 ..
Th	5 12 19 26 ..	2 9 16 23 30	7 14 21 28 ..
F	6 13 20 27 ..	3 10 17 24 ..	1 8 15 22 29 ..
S	7 14 21 28 ..	4 11 18 25 ..	2 9 16 23 30 ..

(2) *Regnal Years*

In connexion with this method of reckoning time a considerable degree of uniformity had been secured at an early stage by the convenient assumption that each king's reign began on the death of his predecessor, a date which could not vary, as the day of the new king's coronation inevitably would, in different parts of his dominions. Nevertheless a certain amount of difficulty was still caused by minor discrepancies. Two of the later Stuart kings had different titles in Scotland from those they bore in England, and the joint rulers William and Mary, owing to the peculiar circumstances of their accession, began their reign in Scotland nearly two months after they had ascended the throne of England. Thus while the regnal years of the later Stuarts were the same for England and Ireland, they were not quite the same for England and Scotland, as is shown in the following translation of regnal years for both countries into calendar years:

England   Scotland

Charles II

Regnal year

12	29 May 1660 to 29 January 1661
13	30 January 1661 to 29 January 1662
14	30 January 1662 to 29 January 1663
15	30 January 1663 to 29 January 1664
16	30 January 1664 to 29 January 1665
17	30 January 1665 to 29 January 1666
18	30 January 1666 to 29 January 1667
19	30 January 1667 to 29 January 1668
20	30 January 1668 to 29 January 1669
21	30 January 1669 to 29 January 1670
22	30 January 1670 to 29 January 1671
23	30 January 1671 to 29 January 1672
24	30 January 1672 to 29 January 1673
25	30 January 1673 to 29 January 1674
26	30 January 1674 to 29 January 1675
27	30 January 1675 to 29 January 1676
28	30 January 1676 to 29 January 1677
29	30 January 1677 to 29 January 1678
30	30 January 1678 to 29 January 1679
31	30 January 1679 to 29 January 1680
32	30 January 1680 to 29 January 1681
33	30 January 1681 to 29 January 1682
34	30 January 1682 to 29 January 1683
35	30 January 1683 to 29 January 1684
36	30 January 1684 to 29 January 1685
37	30 January 1685 to 6 February 1685

James II   James VII

	England		Scotland
1	6 February 1685 to 5 February 1686	1	6 February 1685 to 5 February 1686
2	6 February 1686 to 5 February 1687	2	6 February 1686 to 5 February 1687
3	6 February 1687 to 5 February 1688	3	6 February 1687 to 5 February 1688
4	6 February 1688 to 11 December 1688	4	6 February 1688 to 11 December 1688

Interregnum

12 December 1688 to 12 February 1689   12 December 1688 to 10 April 1689

England

William III and Mary II

1	13 February 1689 to 12 February 1690
2	13 February 1690 to 12 February 1691
3	13 February 1691 to 12 February 1692
4	13 February 1692 to 12 February 1693
5	13 February 1693 to 12 February 1694
6	13 February 1694 to 27 December 1694

William III

6	28 December 1694 to 12 February 1695
7	13 February 1695 to 12 February 1696
8	13 February 1696 to 12 February 1697
9	13 February 1697 to 12 February 1698
10	13 February 1698 to 12 February 1699
11	13 February 1699 to 12 February 1700
12	13 February 1700 to 12 February 1701
13	13 February 1701 to 12 February 1702
14	13 February 1702 to 8 March 1702

Scotland

William II and Mary II

1	11 April 1689 to 10 April 1690
2	11 April 1690 to 10 April 1691
3	11 April 1691 to 10 April 1692
4	11 April 1692 to 10 April 1693
5	11 April 1693 to 10 April 1694
6	11 April 1694 to 27 December 1694

William II

6	28 December 1694 to 10 April 1695
7	11 April 1695 to 10 April 1696
8	11 April 1696 to 10 April 1697
9	11 April 1697 to 10 April 1698
10	11 April 1698 to 10 April 1699
11	11 April 1699 to 10 April 1700
12	11 April 1700 to 10 April 1701
13	11 April 1701 to 8 March 1702

Anne

1	8 March 1702 to 7 March 1703
2	8 March 1703 to 7 March 1704
3	8 March 1704 to 7 March 1705
4	8 March 1705 to 7 March 1706
5	8 March 1706 to 7 March 1707
6	8 March 1707 to 7 March 1708
7	8 March 1708 to 7 March 1709
8	8 March 1709 to 7 March 1710
9	8 March 1710 to 7 March 1711
10	8 March 1711 to 7 March 1712
11	8 March 1712 to 7 March 1713
12	8 March 1713 to 7 March 1714
13	8 March 1714 to 1 August 1714

Appendix II

PRINCIPAL OFFICIALS

Ｆ ROM 1660 to 1707 each of the three kingdoms, England, Scotland and Ireland, had its own independent body of officials, although some of the Irish officials were partially subordinated to the corresponding English officials, and appointments to Irish (and to a lesser degree Scottish) official posts were apt in practice to be determined by the interests of England. In 1707 the chief political (though not legal or ecclesiastical) offices in England and Scotland were merged, and a new body of British officials came into being. Irish officials, however, remained a separate body, and continued to enjoy a varying and precarious amount of independence until the nineteenth century.

(a) ENGLISH OFFICIALS
(1) Archbishops of Canterbury

1660	William Juxon	1691	John Tillotson
1663	Gilbert Sheldon	1695	Thomas Tenison
1678	William Sancroft		

(2) Archbishops of York

1660	Accepted Frewen	1688	Thomas Lamplugh
1664	Richard Sterne	1691	John Sharp
1683	John Dolben	1714	William Dawes

(3) Bishops of London

1660	Gilbert Sheldon	1675	Henry Compton
1663	Humphrey Henchman	1714	John Robinson

(4) Lord Chancellors and Keepers of the Great Seal

1660	Sir Edward Hyde, later earl of Clarendon
1667	Sir Orlando Bridgeman, Lord Keeper
1672	Anthony Ashley Cooper, earl of Shaftesbury
1673	Sir Heneage Finch, later earl of Nottingham, Lord Keeper to 1675
1682	Sir Francis North, later Lord Guilford, Lord Keeper
1685	George, Lord Jeffreys
1689	Commissioners
1693	Sir John Somers, later Lord Somers, Lord Keeper to 1697
1700	Sir Nathan Wright, Lord Keeper
1705	William Cowper, later Lord Cowper, Lord Keeper

(5) Lord Treasurers and First Lords of the Treasury

1660	Thomas Wriothesley, earl of Southampton
1667	George Monck, duke of Albemarle, First Lord
1670	Anthony, Lord Ashley, later earl of Shaftesbury, First Lord
1672	Thomas, Lord Clifford
1673	Sir Thomas Osborne, later earl of Danby
1679	Arthur Capel, earl of Essex, First Lord
	Laurence Hyde, later earl of Rochester, First Lord
1684	Sidney Godolphin, later Lord Godolphin, First Lord

1685 Laurence Hyde, earl of Rochester
1687 John, Lord Belasyse, First Lord
1689 Charles Mordaunt, earl of Monmouth, First Lord
1690 Sir John Lowther, First Lord
      Sidney, Lord Godolphin, First Lord
1697 Charles Montagu, First Lord
1699 Forde Grey, earl of Tankerville, First Lord
1700 Sidney, Lord Godolphin, First Lord
1701 Charles Howard, earl of Carlisle, First Lord
1702 Sidney, Lord Godolphin, later earl of Godolphin

(6) Principal Secretaries of State

1660	Sir Edward Nicholas	Sir William Morice
1662	Sir Henry Bennet, later earl of Arlington	
1668		Sir John Trevor
1672		Henry Coventry
1674	Sir Joseph Williamson	
1679	Robert Spencer, earl of Sunderland	
1680		Sir Leoline Jenkins
1681	Edward Conway, earl of Conway	
1683	Robert Spencer, earl of Sunderland	
1684		Sidney Godolphin, later Lord Godolphin
		Charles Middleton, earl of Middleton
1688	Richard Graham, Viscount Preston	
1689	Charles Talbot, earl of Shrewsbury	Daniel Finch, earl of Nottingham
1690	Henry Sidney, Viscount Sidney	
1693	Sir John Trenchard	
1694		Charles Talbot, earl of Shrewsbury, later duke of Shrewsbury
1695	Sir William Trumbull	
1697	James Vernon	
1699		Edward Villiers, earl of Jersey
1700		Sir Charles Hedges
1702		Charles Montagu, earl of Manchester
1702	Daniel Finch, earl of Nottingham	Sir Charles Hedges
1704	Robert Harley	
1706		Charles Spencer, earl of Sunderland

(7) Speakers of the House of Commons

1660	Sir Harbottle Grimston		1685	Sir John Trevor
1661	Sir Edward Turner		1689	Henry Powle
1673	Sir Job Charlton		1690	Sir John Trevor
	Edward Seymour		1695	Paul Foley
1678	Sir Robert Sawyer		1698	Sir Thomas Littleton
	Edward Seymour		1701	Robert Harley
1679	William Gregory		1705	John Smith
1680	William Williams			

(b) SCOTTISH OFFICIALS

(1) Archbishops of St. Andrews

1661	James Sharp	1684	Arthur Rose
1679	Alexander Burnet		

(2) Archbishops of Glasgow

1661	Andrew Fairfoul	1679	Arthur Rose
1664	Alexander Burnet	1684	Alexander Cairncross
1671	Robert Leighton	1687	John Paterson

(3) Lord High Commissioners to the General Assembly

1690   John, Lord Carmichael
1692   Robert Kerr, earl of Ancram
1694–9   John, Lord Carmichael
1700   James Ogilvy, Viscount Seafield
1701   William Johnston, earl of Annandale
1702   Patrick Hume, earl of Marchmont
1703   James Ogilvy, earl of Seafield
1704   William, Lord Ross
1705   William Johnston, marquis of Annandale
1706–10   David Boyle, earl of Glasgow
1711   William Johnston, marquis of Annandale
1712–14   John Murray, duke of Atholl

(4) Lord Chancellors

1661   William Cunningham, earl of Glencairn
1667   John Leslie, earl of Rothes, later duke of Rothes
1682   George Gordon, earl of Aberdeen
1684   James Drummond, earl of Perth
1689   Commissioners
1692   John Hay, earl of Tweeddale, later marquis of Tweeddale
1696   Patrick Hume, Lord Polwarth, later earl of Marchmont
1702   James Ogilvy, earl of Seafield
1704   John Hay, marquis of Tweeddale
1705   James Ogilvy, earl of Seafield

(5) Secretaries of State

1660   John Maitland, earl of Lauderdale, later duke of Lauderdale
1680   Alexander Stewart, earl of Moray

1682	Alexander Stewart, earl of Moray	Charles Middleton, earl of Middleton
1684		John Drummond, later Viscount and earl of Melfort
1689	George, Lord Melville, later earl of Melville	
1691	George Melville, earl of Melville	John Dalrymple, master of Stair
1692	James Johnston	
1696	Sir James Ogilvy, later earl of Seafield	John, Lord Murray, later earl of Tullibardine
1699		John, Lord Carmichael, later earl of Hyndford
1702	George Mackenzie, earl of Cromarty	James Douglas, duke of Queensberry
1704	James Ogilvy, earl of Seafield	John Ker, earl of Roxburgh
1705	William Johnston, marquis of Annandale John Erskine, earl of Mar	Hugh Campbell, earl of Loudoun

(6) Lord High Commissioners to Parliament

1660 John Middleton, earl of Middleton
1663 John Leslie, earl of Rothes, later duke of Rothes
1669 John Maitland, earl of Lauderdale,
         later duke of Lauderdale
1680 James, duke of York
1685 William Douglas, duke of Queensberry
1686 Alexander Stewart, earl of Moray
1689 William Douglas, duke of Hamilton
1690 George Melville, earl of Melville
1692 William Douglas, duke of Hamilton
1695 John Hay, marquis of Tweeddale
1696 John Murray, earl of Tullibardine
1698 Patrick Hume, earl of Marchmont
1700 James Douglas, duke of Queensberry
1704 John Hay, marquis of Tweeddale
1705 John Campbell, duke of Argyll
1706 James Douglas, duke of Queensberry

(c) BRITISH OFFICIALS

(1) Lord Chancellors and Keepers of the Great Seal

1707 William, Lord Cowper
1708 Commissioners
1710 Sir Simon Harcourt, later Lord Harcourt,
         Lord Keeper to 1713

(2) Lord Treasurers and First Lords of the Treasury

1707 Sidney Godolphin, earl of Godolphin
1710 John Poulett, earl Poulett, First Lord
1711 Robert Harley, earl of Oxford
1714 Charles Talbot, duke of Shrewsbury

(3) Principal Secretaries of State

	Southern	Northern	Scottish
1707	Charles Spencer, earl of Sunderland	Robert Harley	
1708		Henry Boyle	
1709			James Douglas, duke of Queensberry and duke of Dover
1710	William Legge, Lord Dartmouth, later earl of Dartmouth	Henry St. John, later Viscount Bolingbroke	
1713	Henry St. John, Viscount Bolingbroke	William Bromley	John Erskine, earl of Mar

(4) Speakers of the House of Commons

1707 John Smith   1710 William Bromley
1708 Sir Richard Onslow   1714 Sir Thomas Hanmer

(d) IRISH OFFICIALS

(1) Archbishops of Armagh

1661	John Bramhall
1663	James Margetson
1678	Michael Boyle

1703	Narcissus Marsh
1714	Thomas Lindsay

(2) Archbishops of Dublin

1661	James Margetson
1663	Michael Boyle
1679	John Parker

1682	Francis Marsh
1694	Narcissus Marsh
1703	William King

(3) Lords Lieutenants and Lord Deputies

1660	George Monck, duke of Albemarle
1661	Lords Justices
1662	James Butler, duke of Ormonde
1669	John, Lord Robartes
1670	John, Lord Berkeley of Stratton
1672	Arthur Capel, earl of Essex
1677	James Butler, duke of Ormonde
1685	Lords Justices
1686	Henry Hyde, earl of Clarendon
1687	Richard Talbot, earl of Tyrconnel, Lord Deputy
1689	James II present in person

1690	William III present in person
	Lords Justices
1692	Henry Sidney, Viscount Sidney
1693	Lords Justices
1695	Henry, Lord Capel, Lord Deputy
1696	Lords Justices
1701	Laurence Hyde, earl of Rochester
1703	James Butler, duke of Ormonde
1707	Thomas Herbert, earl of Pembroke
1709	Thomas Wharton, earl of Wharton
1711	James Butler, duke of Ormonde
1713	Charles Talbot, duke of Shrewsbury

(4) Lord Chancellors

1660	Sir Maurice Eustace
1665	Michael Boyle
1686	Sir Charles Porter
1687	Sir Alexander Fitton
1690	Commissioners
	Sir Charles Porter

1697	Commissioners
	John Methuen
1703	Sir Richard Cox
1707	Richard Freeman
1710	Commissioners
1711	Sir Constantine Phipps

ATTENDANCE OF LORDS AND COMMONERS AT EACH MEETING OF PARLIAMENT[1]

(Based on lists of those present in *Journals of the House of Lords* and figures of divisions in *Journals of the House of Commons*)

(1) *Parliament of England*

Number of meeting	Date		Average attendance of Lords			Attendance of Commoners	
			Temporal	Spiritual	Total	Average	Highest
1	1660	25 April–13 September	65	—	65	233	341
2	1660	6 November–29 December	65	—	65	194	340
3	1661	8 May–30 July	80	—	80	261	365
4	1661–2	20 November–19 May	63	18	81	159	234
5	1663	18 February–27 July	59	14	73	165	280
6	1664	16 March–17 May	72	18	90	196	250
7	1664–5	24 November–2 March	52	15	67	147	274
8	1665	9–31 October	23	9	32	127	155
9	1666–7	18 September–8 February	59	11	70	158	283
10	1667	10 October–19 December	67	18	85	161	322
11	1668	6 February–9 May	60	12	72	144	246
12	1669	19 October–11 December	65	12	77	219	326
13	1670	14 February–11 April	66	14	80	177	313
14	1670–1	24 October–22 April	56	11	67	151	286
15	1673	4 February–29 March	71	12	83	224	284
16	1674	7 January–24 February	74	15	89	253	330
17	1675	13 April–9 June	80	15	95	248	345
18	1675	13 October–22 November	67	15	82	260	331
19	1677	15 February–28 May	72	14	86	226	346
20	1678	28 January–13 May	67	14	81	251	355
21	1678	23 May–15 July	57	10	67	248	371
22	1678	21 October–30 December	63	11	74	264	320
23	1679	18 March–27 May	70	12	82	293	360
24	1680–1	21 October–10 January	68	11	79	230	314
25	1681	21–28 March	53	13	66	No divisions	
26	1685	19 May–2 July	70	18	88	292	413
27	1685	9–20 November	64	17	81	357	365
28	1689	22 January–12 February	81	14	95	346	373
29	1689	13 February–20 August	58	7	65	195	329
30	1689–90	23 October–27 January	59	9	68	271	372
31	1690	20 March–23 May	70	9	79	267	381
32	1690–1	2 October–5 January	54	7	61	257	381
33	1691–2	22 October–24 February	58	11	69	210	361
34	1692–3	4 November–14 March	60	15	75	206	375
35	1693–4	7 November–25 April	53	14	67	214	369
36	1694–5	12 November–3 May	54	12	66	190	325
37	1695–6	22 November–27 April	58	12	70	229	397

[1] The 'meetings' have been somewhat arbitrarily determined. Each continuous group of sittings has been taken as a 'meeting', whether corresponding to a session in the legal sense or not. Purely formal sittings of the Lords have been ignored.

Number of meeting		Date	Average attendance of Lords			Attendance of Commoners	
			Temporal	Spiritual	Total	Average	Highest
38	1696–7	20 October–16 April	71	12	83	237	370
39	1697–8	3 December–5 July	50	10	60	199	352
40	1698–9	6 December–4 May	62	10	72	242	377
41	1699–1700	16 November–11 April	50	12	62	238	414
42	1701	6 February–24 June	61	12	73	251	386
43	1701–2	30 December–25 May	54	9	63	189	434
44	1702–3	20 October–27 February	57	11	68	198	315
45	1703–4	9 November–3 April	56	9	65	198	363
46	1704–5	24 October–14 March	47	8	55	191	385
47	1705–6	25 October–19 March	49	10	59	266	453
48	1706–7	3 December–8 April	46	10	56	223	390

(2) Parliament of Great Britain

49	1707–8	23 October–1 April	59	9	68	213	405
50	1708–9	16 November–21 April	60	9	69	242	377
51	1709–10	15 November–5 April	64	8	72	261	393
52	1710–11	25 November–12 June	63	9	72	205	378
53	1711–12	7 December–21 June	71	10	81	220	435
54	1713	9 April–16 July	73	8	81	221	414
55	1714	16 February–9 July	76	11	87	221	397

REPRESENTATION IN PARLIAMENT

(a) ENGLAND

	Counties	Cities and Boroughs	Cinque Ports and Universities	Total	Assessments 1665–91[1]	Assessments 1692–1714[1]	Number of Houses[2]	Poll Tax of 1692[3]
		Actual			*In proportion to*			
Bedford	2	2	—	4	7	7	5	6
Berkshire	2	7	—	9	8	11	7	9
Buckingham	2	12	—	14	10	12	8	8
Cambridge	2	2	2	6	10	8	8	8
Cheshire	2	2	—	4	6	7	10	8
Cornwall	2	42	—	44	11	8	11	8
Cumberland	2	4	—	6	1	1	6	2
Derby	2	2	—	4	6	6	9	7
Devon	2	24	—	26	25	21	25	24
Dorset	2	18	—	20	10	9	10	8
Durham[4]	2	2	—	4	2	3	7	6
Essex	2	6	—	8	23	23	15	18
Gloucester[5]	2	6	—	8	14	12	12	12
Hereford	2	6	—	8	8	5	7	6
Hertford	2	4	—	6	10	11	7	10
Huntingdon	2	2	—	4	5	4	4	4
Kent	2	8	8	18	25	21	17	20
Lancashire	2	12	—	14	8	5	18	11
Leicester	2	2	—	4	8	9	8	9
Lincoln	2	10	—	12	19	19	18	17
Middlesex	2	6	—	8	55	84	44	82
Monmouth	2	1	—	3	3	3	3	3
Norfolk	2	10	—	12	26	22	21	21
Northampton	2	7	—	9	11	12	11	11
Northumberland	2	6	—	8	3	4	10	5
Nottingham	2	6[6]	—	8	7	7	8	6
Oxford	2	5	2	9	8	10	8	9
Rutland	2	—	—	2	2	1	1	2
Shropshire	2	10	—	12	9	8	10	8
Somerset[7]	2	16	—	18	22	19	22	19
Southampton	2	24	—	26	16	14	12	12
Stafford[8]	2	8	—	10	6	7	10	7
Suffolk	2	14	—	16	25	19	15	17
Surrey	2	12	—	14	12	17	15	18
Sussex	2	18	8	28	14	16	9	11
Warwick[9]	2	4	—	6	9	10	10	9

[1] No. 115. [2] No. 200. [3] *Calendar of Treasury Books*, IX, pp. 1837–1838.
[4] After 1675. [5] Excluding Bristol. [6] After 1673. [7] Including Bristol.
[8] Including Tamworth. [9] Excluding Tamworth.

	Actual				In proportion to			
	Counties	Cities and Boroughs	Cinque Ports and Universities	Total	Assessments 1665–91	1692–1714	Number of Houses	Poll Tax of 1692
Westmorland	2	2	—	4	1	1	3	1
Wiltshire	2	32	—	34	15	13	12	11
Worcester	2	7	—	9	8	9	9	8
York	2	28	—	30	26	24	46	34
Wales								
Anglesey	1	1	—	2			1	1
Brecon	1	1	—	2			3	1
Cardigan	1	1	—	2			1	1
Carmarthen	1	1	—	2			2	3
Carnarvon	1	1	—	2			1	1
Denbigh	1	1	—	2	19	11	3	1
Flint	1	1	—	2			1	1
Glamorgan	1	1	—	2			4	3
Merioneth	1	—	—	1			1	1
Montgomery	1	1	—	2			2	2
Pembroke	1	2	—	3			2	2
Radnor	1	1	—	2			1	1

(b) SCOTLAND

	Actual			In proportion to
	Shires	Burghs	Total	Cess of 1696
Aberdeen	4	3	7	11
Argyll	3	2	5	4
Ayr	4	2	6	9
Banff	2	2	4	3
Berwick	4	1	5	6
Bute	2	1	3	1
Caithness	2	1	3	1
Clackmannan	1	—	1	1
Cromarty	2	—	2	1
Dumbarton	2	1	3	2
Dumfries	4	4	8	6
Edinburgh	4	2	6	16
Elgin	2	2	4	3
Fife	4	13	17	14
Kinross	1	—	1	
Forfar	4	5	9	10
Haddington	4	3	7	7
Inverness	2	1	3	3
Kincardine	2	1	3	2
Kirkcudbright	3	2	5	4
Lanark	4	3	7	10
Linlithgow	2	2	4	3

| | Actual | | | In proportion to |
	Shires	Burghs	Total	Cess of 1696
Nairn	2	1	3	1
Orkney and Shetland	2	1	3	3
Peebles	2	1	3	2
Perth	4	2	6	12
Renfrew	3	1	4	3
Ross	2	3	5	2
Roxburgh	4	1	5	8
Selkirk	2	1	3	2
Stirling	3	1	4	4
Sutherland	2	1	3	1
Wigtown	2	3	5	2

(c) IRELAND

| | Actual | | | In proportion to |
	Counties	University	Towns	Total	Tax of 1698
Antrim	2	–	10	12	12
Armagh	2	–	4	6	6
Carlow	2	–	4	6	4
Cavan	2	–	4	6	6
Clare	2	–	2	4	9
Cork	2	–	24	26	32
Donegal	2	–	10	12	10
Down	2	–	12	14	10
Dublin	2	2	6	10	25
Fermanagh	2	–	2	4	5
Galway	2	–	6	8	14
Kerry	2	–	6	8	5
Kildare	2	–	8	10	9
Kilkenny	2	–	14	16	11
King's County	2	–	4	6	5
Leitrim	2	–	4	6	4
Limerick	2	–	6	8	12
Londonderry	2	–	6	8	8
Longford	2	–	8	10	3
Louth	2	–	10	12	6
Mayo	2	–	2	4	8
Meath	2	–	12	14	15
Monaghan	2	–	2	4	5
Queen's County	2	–	6	8	5
Roscommon	2	–	6	8	8
Sligo	2	–	2	4	6
Tipperary	2	–	6	8	22
Tyrone	2	–	8	10	8
Waterford	2	–	8	10	9
Westmeath	2	–	8	10	7
Wexford	2	–	16	18	7
Wicklow	2	–	8	10	4

INDEX TO TEXTS

The figures refer to the numbered documents, not to the pages. All documents the authorship of which is unknown or doubtful are indexed under their titles (if any), and are also grouped together under the heading 'Anonymous'. All Bills and Acts of Parliament are similarly grouped under the heading 'Statutes'.